AN OCEAN NAVIGATION EXERCISE

AN OCEAN NAVIGATION EXERCISE

Bermuda to the Azores

BY THOMAS M. STOUT

Centreville   Maryland

CORNELL MARITIME PRESS

To the memory of my brother, Robert Hayes Stout,
late Master of the Yacht *Dragon*

Library of Congress Cataloging-in-Publication Data

Stout, Thomas M., 1935-
    An ocean navigation exercise.

    Bibliography: p.
    Includes index.
    1. Navigation—Problems, exercises, etc.
I. Title.
VK559.5.S76   1985   623.89′076   85-47835
ISBN 0-87033-344-5

Manufactured in the United States of America

First edition

CONTENTS

PREFACE

This ocean navigation exercise employs you, the reader, as Master and Navigator of the M/V PEREGRINE. You will start your voyage in Bermuda, bound for the Azores. The track you will follow and the eventual destination -- well, that's for you to work out.

Just as on any ocean passage, each separate navigation problem leads into the next and depends on solutions to the previous. Except for a radio time signal receiver, a shallow-water depth sounder and a 36-mile radar, no electronic aids to navigation are available. You are on your own until you make landfall.

PEREGRINE is a power-driven vessel -- as evidenced by her steady speeds and infrequent changes of course. Other than these characteristics, and a moderate height of eye, she could well be a sailing vessel. She is about 100 feet long, having enough power to make a top speed of 13½ knots, but usually cruises at an economical speed of 8½ knots.

She is equipped with a good 7½-inch magnetic compass which you recently adjusted in Charleston, South Carolina, and swung to show not more than 2½ degrees residual deviation on any point. The azimuth circle is new and properly aligned. The chronometers are both reliable, showing a steady daily rate; radio time checks have never been a difficulty. Your sextants -- well, a good craftsman is known by the condition and quality of his tools.

The chart room is fully stocked with up-to-date charts and publications which you have kept properly corrected. For this exercise, necessary excerpts from appropriate publications appear in the Appendix where some are bisected. So, you may prefer to provide your own publications. Also, you may wish to save the bother of making your own position plotting sheets by purchasing some. They should include latitudes 32 through 39.

The publications which were used in developing these problems and in working their solutions are listed below. Of course, the 1968 Almanac data (all shown in the Appendix) are critical. Otherwise, alternate publications and methods of solution should provide perfectly adequate answers.

The Nautical Almanac for the Year 1968: U.S. Naval Observatory, 1966 / H.M. Stationery Office, 1966.

H.O. Pub. No. 9, American Practical Navigator, Bowditch, Volume II, 1981: Defense Mapping Agency.

H.O. Pub. No. 16, Pilot Chart of the North Atlantic Ocean, April: Defense Mapping Agency, 1973-1983.

H.O. Pub. No. 229, Vol. 3, Sight Reduction Tables for Marine Navigation, Latitudes 30° - 45°, Inclusive: U.S. Naval Oceanographic Office, 1970.

Merchant Ship Search and Rescue Manual, (MERSAR), third edition, 1980 (reprinted 1984): International Maritime Organization (IMO).

Position Plotting Sheets, DMA Stock Numbers WOXZP 5960, 5961, 5963 and 5965: Defense Mapping Agency, 1973-1974.

Star Finder and Identifier No. 2102-D: U.S. Naval Oceanographic Office, 1965.

North Atlantic Ocean Charts, DMA Stock Numbers 26AHA26341, 51AC051041 and 51AC051061: Defense Mapping Agency, 1980-1984.

AN OCEAN NAVIGATION EXERCISE

THE VOYAGE

On 12 April 1968 M/V PEREGRINE is berthed in St. George's Harbour, Bermuda. She is bound for Fayal, Azores. You plan a great circle track from a departure point three miles due East of St. David's Island Light to Ponta Comprida Light. (St. David's I. Lt. is at 32-22 N, 064-39 W; Ponta Comprida Lt. is at 38-36 N, 028-50W.)

What is the departure position?

DEPARTURE LATITUDE = _____ (1)

DEPARTURE LONGITUDE = _____ (2)

What is the great circle distance?

TOTAL DISTANCE = _____ (3)

If PEREGRINE leaves the departure position at 1800 Atlantic Standard (+4) Time and maintains an average speed of 8.5 knots, what is the ETA in Greenwich Mean Time for this great circle distance?

ETA (GMT) -- INCLUDING DATE = _____ (4)

Reckoning on a fuel consumption of 12 gallons per hour, with an additional 50% safety margin, how much fuel should PEREGRINE have for this passage?

GALLONS OF FUEL NEEDED = _____ (5)

What is the true initial great circle course?

TRUE COURSE = _____ (6)

With a local variation of 15 W, to the nearest half degree, what is the initial magnetic course from the departure position?

INITIAL MAGNETIC COURSE = _____ (7)

Late that afternoon (12 APR 68), PEREGRINE gets underway and takes departure at the position three miles East of St. David's I. Lt. at the planned time of 1800 (+4), with the log indicating a speed of 8.5 knots and a compass course equal to the initial magnetic course. At about 1845 (+4), you take an

3

amplitude observation of the setting sun, compass bearing 293.9.

What is the true azimuth of the sun?

    SUN'S TRUE AZIMUTH = _____ (8)

What is the compass error on this course?

    COMPASS ERROR = _____ (9)

With a local variation of 15 W, what is the deviation on this course?

    COMPASS DEVIATION = _____ (10)

At 1900 (+4), having logged 8.5 miles from departure, you change the compass course to allow for deviation. To the nearest half degree, what should this compass course be so as to steer the initial great circle course?

    COMPASS COURSE = _____ (11)

Figuring on an average variation of 15½ W, having remained on this course and having maintained a speed of 8.5 knots, what should be PEREGRINE's DR at 0500 (+4) the next morning (13 APR 68)?

    0500 DR LATITUDE = _____ (12)

    0500 DR LONGITUDE = _____ (13)

At morning star time on 13 APR 68, you take sights as are shown below. Your height of eye is 16 feet, your sextant index error is 3.7 minutes on the arc, the chronometer (keeping GMT) is 5 seconds fast.

Name:	DENEB	NUNKI	ALKAID
Hs:	61-41.8	30-38.2	36-04.4
CT:	09-11-38	09-14-20	09-16-51

What is the 0500 (+4) position?

4

0500 LATITUDE = _____ (14)

0500 LONGITUDE = _____ (15)

What is the direction and distance from the 0500 DR to the 0500 fix?

DIRECTION = _____ (16)

DISTANCE = _____ (17)

Over the eleven hours since departure, what was the average current?

CURRENT SET = _____ (18)

CURRENT DRIFT (SPEED) = _____ (19)

What is the new great circle course from the 0500 (+4) position to destination?

NEW TRUE COURSE = _____ (20)

Figuring the current and the logged speed (8.5 knots) to remain about the same, what is the true course to steer so as to make good the new great circle course?

NEW TRUE COURSE TO STEER = _____ (21)

At 0600 (+4), you change course. Figuring the deviation to remain the same and with a local variation of 16 W, what should be this compass course to the nearest half degree?

0600 COMPASS COURSE = _____ (22)

Later that morning (13 APR 68) at CT = 11-00-05, you observe the sun's azimuth with a compass bearing of 103.5. The chronometer (keeping GMT) remains 5 seconds fast.

What is the true azimuth of the sun?

SUN'S TRUE AZIMUTH = _____ (23)

What is the compass error on this course?

COMPASS ERROR = _____ (24)

With a local variation of 16 W, what is the deviation on this course?

COMPASS DEVIATION = _____ (25)

At 0800 (+4), having logged 25.5 miles since 0500 (+4), you change compass course. Figuring on an average local variation of 16½ W, what should this compass course be (to the nearest half degree) so as to steer the new true course?

0800 COMPASS COURSE = _____ (26)

Having planned ahead so as to get a sun line nearly parallel to PEREGRINE's track, you take a sight at CT = 15-28-32, CE = 5 seconds fast; sextant altitude of the lower limb = 64-11.8, IE = 3.7 minutes on the arc, HE = 16 feet.

Having continued to log a speed of 8.5 knots, at the 1128½ (+4) DR, how far to the right of the DR track does this line of position lie?

DISTANCE TO RIGHT (STBD) OF TRACK = _____ (27)

What was the course made good since 0500?

COURSE MADE GOOD = _____ (28)

Omitting a LAN observation, but planning ahead so as to get a sun line nearly perpendicular to PEREGRINE's track, you take a sight at CT = 18-53-22, CE = 5 seconds fast; sextant altitude of the lower limb = 44-30.6, IE = 3.7 minutes on the arc, HE = 16 feet.

What is the distance of this line of position from the 0500 (+4) star fix?

0500 - 1453½ DISTANCE = _____ (29)

What is PEREGRINE's speed made good since 0500 (+4)?

SPEED MADE GOOD = _____ (30)

Using this speed made good and the course made good as determined by your 1128½ (+4) sun line, you plot the 1500 (+4) estimated position.

What is this estimated position?

1500 ESTIMATED LATITUDE = _____ (31)

1500 ESTIMATED LONGITUDE = _____ (32)

By comparing this estimated position with your 1500 (+4) DR, you estimate the average set and drift of the current since 0500 (+4).

What was the average current?

ESTIMATED CURRENT SET = _____ (33)

ESTIMATED CURRENT DRIFT (SPEED) = _____ (34)

From the 1500 (+4) EP, what is the new great circle course to destination?

NEW TRUE COURSE = _____ (35)

Figuring the current and the logged speed (8.5 knots) to remain about the same, what is the true course to steer so as to make good the new great circle course?

NEW TRUE COURSE TO STEER = _____ (36)

At 1600 (+4), you change course. Having figured the deviation to remain the same and with a local variation of 17½ W, what should be this compass course to the nearest half degree?

1600 COMPASS COURSE = _____ (37)

Planning ahead to evening star time, you determine when to expect: sunset, the beginning of civil twilight and moonrise.

What are the (+4) zone times of these events?

TIME OF SUNSET = _____ (38)

TIME OF CIVIL TWILIGHT = _____ (39)

TIME OF MOONRISE = _____ (40)

Also, what is the calculated altitude and azimuth of JUPITER, to the nearest whole degree, at 1900 (+4)?

JUPITER'S CALCULATED ALTITUDE = _____ (41)

JUPITER'S CALCULATED AZIMUTH = _____ (42)

As so often happens after doing this sort of planning ahead, evening star time found PEREGRINE in a rain squall which obscured the sky. 0055
0100 (14)

However, at 2059 (+4), you did observe POLARIS with a sextant altitude of 33-17.3 and, at CT = 01-00-16, you take the sextant altitude of the lower limb of the moon as 16-38.7. CE = 4 seconds fast, IE = 3.7 minutes on the arc, HE = 16 feet.

What is the 2100 (+4) position?

2100 LATITUDE = _____ (43)

2100 LONGITUDE = _____ (44)

Continuing to log 8.5 knots, at 2200 (+4) you change course to allow for an average local variation of 18 W.

To the nearest half degree, what should be this compass course?

2200 COMPASS COURSE = _____ (45)

Figuring the logged speed to remain the same, what should be PEREGRINE's DR at 0500 (+4) the next morning?

0500 DR LATITUDE = _____ (46)

0500 DR LONGITUDE = _____ (47)

At dawn on 14 APR, you take star sights as are shown below. (When planning this fix, you selected stars which would yield an approximate rectangle rather than the traditional sort of pinwheel -- such as on the previous morning. This selection can resolve a variety of observation errors including dip, index error, abnormal refraction, personal observation bias and geoid height anomaly.)

Name:	ENIF	NUNKI	KOCHAB	ARCTURUS
Hs:	38-49.0	29-31.9	42-05.2	31-39.2
CT:	08-50-42	08-53-27	08-55-04	08-58-20

The height of eye is 16 feet, the index error is 3.7 minutes on the arc, the chronometer (keeping GMT) remains 4 seconds fast.

8

What is the 0500 (+4) position?

    0500 LATITUDE = _____ (48)

    0500 LONGITUDE = _____ (49)

What is the direction and distance from the 0500 (+4) DR to the 0500 (+4) fix?

    DIRECTION = _____ (50)

    DISTANCE = _____ (51)

Over the previous twenty-four hours, what was the average current?

    CURRENT SET = _____ (52)

    CURRENT DRIFT (SPEED) = _____ (53)

What is the new great circle course from the 0500 (+4) position to destination?

    NEW TRUE COURSE = _____ (54)

Figuring the current and the logged speed (8.5 knots) to remain about the same, what is the true course to steer so as to make good the new great circle course?

    NEW TRUE COURSE TO STEER = _____ (55)

At 0600 (+4), you change course. Figuring the deviation to remain the same and with a local variation of 18½ W, what should be this compass course to the nearest half degree?

    0600 COMPASS COURSE = _____ (56)

A little after sunrise you take an amplitude to find that the deviation on this course is 1.5 E. Later, at CT = 15-16-38, you take another observation so as to get a sun line parallel to the track. At the time of observation a squall obscures the horizon below the sun, as you take a back sight yielding a sextant altitude of 116-25.3 on the lower limb. (This actually appears in the horizon glass as an apparent upper limb.)

With index error, chronometer error, height of eye and logged speed (8.5 knots) unchanged, how far to the right of the 1116½ DR does this sun line lie?

9

DISTANCE TO RIGHT (STBD) OF TRACK = _____ (57)

What was the course made good since 0500 (+4)?

COURSE MADE GOOD = _____ (58)

Again you omit a LAN observation, and again you plan ahead so as to get a sun line nearly perpendicular to PEREGRINE's track.

At CT = 18-54-04, you take a sight. CE = 4 seconds fast; HE = 16 feet; IE = 3.7 minutes on the arc; sextant altitude of the sun's lower limb is 41-16.7.

What is the distance of this line of position from the 0500 (+4) star fix?

0500 - 1454 DISTANCE = _____ (59)

What was PEREGRINE's speed made good since 0500 (+4)?

SPEED MADE GOOD = _____ (60)

Using this speed made good and the course made good as determined by your 1116½ (+4) sun line, you plot the 1500 (+4) estimated position.

What is this estimated position?

1500 ESTIMATED LATITUDE = _____ (61)

1500 ESTIMATED LONGITUDE = _____ (62)

Since PEREGRINE is apparently on track, you maintain course from the 1500 (+4) EP until evening stars. However, for your DR, you figure on a local variation of 19 W after 1500 (+4).

At evening star time on 14 APR, PEREGRINE is still logging 8.5 knots under a sky broken by clouds. With patience you get three sure observations as follows.

Name:	POLARIS	DENEBOLA	MARS
Hs:	34-37.3	43-33.1	09-05.1
CT:	22-50-17	22-54-30	22-58-05

10

Also, at CT = 23-21-57, you take a good sight on an unknown star bearing due South with Hs = 12-14.9.

You figure your height of eye to be 16½ feet; CE = 3 seconds fast; IE = 3.7 minutes on the arc. The weather conditions have turned unusual, showing a temperature of 25° C and a barometer reading of 1000 millibars.

What is the name of the star observed at CT = 23-21-57?

STAR'S NAME = _____ (63)

What is the 1900 (+4) position?

1900 LATITUDE = _____ (64)

1900 LONGITUDE = _____ (65)

What is the direction and distance from the 1900 (+4) DR to the 1900 (+4) fix?

DIRECTION = _____ (66)

DISTANCE = _____ (67)

Over the fourteen hours since the 0500 (+4) fix, what was the average current?

CURRENT SET = _____ (68)

CURRENT DRIFT (SPEED) = _____ (69)

What is the new great circle course from the 1900 (+4) position to destination?

NEW TRUE COURSE = _____ (70)

Figuring the current and the logged speed of 8.5 knots to remain about the same, what is the true course to steer so as to make good the new great circle course?

NEW TRUE COURSE TO STEER = _____ (71)

At 2000 (+4), you change course. Figuring the deviation to remain the same and with a local variation of 19½ W, what should this compass course be to the nearest half degree?

2000 COMPASS COURSE = _____ (72)

Planning ahead to morning star time, you determine when to expect: the beginning of nautical twilight, the beginning of civil twilight and sunrise.

What are the (+4) zone times of these events?

    TIME OF NAUTICAL TWILIGHT = _____ (73)

    TIME OF CIVIL TWILIGHT = _____ (74)

    TIME OF SUNRISE = _____ (75)

Also, what will be the calculated altitude and azimuth of VENUS, to the nearest whole degree, at 0500 (+4)?

    CALCULATED ALTITUDE OF VENUS = _____ (76)

    CALCULATED AZIMUTH OF VENUS = _____ (77)

A little after 0200 (+4) the next morning (15 APR), a faint but distinct distress call is heard on Channel 16, VHF-FM, giving a position of 35-45 N, 056-25 W. The nature of distress is anxiously, but vaguely described in unaccented language as some sort of medical emergency.

This distress call is heard repeated, with the same position given. You are called to listen and decide a course of action. You hear no further communications on this or any other VHF channel. The distressed vessel, giving the name MERLIN, reported no course or speed. So, presuming that she is stopped, you determine the course to her position from the 0230 (+4) DR.

What is PEREGRINE's 0230 (+4) DR?

    0230 DR LATITUDE = _____ (78)

    0230 DR LONGITUDE = _____ (79)

Figuring on an average local variation of 19½ W for the run to MERLIN's reported position, no deviation on the new course, and discounting current, you work out the rhumb-line course to the distress scene. At 0230 (+4), you change to this course, increasing speed to 13.5 knots.

To the nearest half degree, what is the 0230 (+4) compass course?

    COMPASS COURSE = _____ (80)

12

Then you draft a message to Bermuda Radio requesting aircraft search and confirmation of the situation. In this message you include the reported distress position and nature, PEREGRINE's description, your SAR capabilities (including your lack of any VHF D/F), your 0230 (+4) DR, course and speed, and your ETA (+4) at MERLIN's reported position.

What is this (+4) ETA at a speed of 13.5 knots?

ETA AT DISTRESS SCENE = _____ (81)

After some protracted communications, Bermuda Radio reports that a fixed-wing aircraft departed McKinley Field at 0400 (+4) to rendezvous with PEREGRINE at 0600 (+4). Also you learn that a search of registers has turned up a 48-foot auxiliary ketch named MERLIN with the same radio call sign as the one heard in the distress message.

To provide a good reference position for a coordinated ship/aircraft search, you take a full round of sights at morning star time as are shown below.

Name:	ENIF	NUNKI	ALTAIR	KOCHAB	ALKAID	ARCTURUS
Hs:	36-04.0	27-42.0	56-13.5	43-56.5	38-49.0	32-46.0
CT:	08-21-56	08-24-13	08-26-20	08-29-02	08-34-15	08-36-41

The height of eye is 16½ feet, the index error is 3.7 minutes on the arc, the chronometer (keeping GMT) is 3 seconds fast.

Also, while you are working the sights, at about 0512 (+4) you take an amplitude observation of the rising sun, compass bearing 097.9.

What is the 0430 (+4, 15 APR) position?

0430 LATITUDE = _____ (82)

0430 LONGITUDE = _____ (83)

Working the amplitude observation taken earlier, with a local variation of 19½ W, what is the compass deviation on your present course?

COMPASS DEVIATION = _____ (84)

13

So as to get as good an indication of local current as is possible, you compare your 0430 (+4) DR to the 0430 (+4) fix.

What was the average current since the 1900 (+4) fix?

CURRENT SET = _____ (85)

CURRENT DRIFT (SPEED) = _____ (86)

Maintaining PEREGRINE's course and speed (13.5 knots) as well as a constant radar watch, at 0550 (+4) you pick up the aircraft approaching from the WSW. On Channel 6 you agree to a ship/aircraft coordinated search pattern (see Figure 18) with PEREGRINE's course and speed unchanged and the aircraft's speed reduced to 120 knots. This will yield, over a two-hour period, a 27-mile-square search pattern.

This pattern is begun at 0600 (+4) and will be continued until 0800 (+4) when, with the aircraft to leave the scene for refueling, you plan to head PEREGRINE for a new datum at 35-53.5 N, 055-58.5 W.

Figuring the local variation to remain the same (19½ W), no deviation on the new course, and discounting current, you determine the rhumb-line course to the new datum.

To the nearest half degree, what will be the 0800 (+4) course to the new datum?

COMPASS COURSE = _____ (87)

At 0800 (+4) the aircraft heads back to Bermuda and you head PEREGRINE on this new course at 13.5 knots. At 1012 (+4) you start her into an expanding square search pattern (see Figure 19). This pattern will have 18-minute track spacing at 13.5 knots, and an initial compass course of 161½. Course changes of ninety degrees to starboard will be made at (+4) times of 1030, 1048, 1124, and 1200.

At local apparent noon you observe meridian transit of the sun: CT = 15-43-45, CE = 3 seconds fast; sextant altitude of the lower limb = 63-53.4, IE = 3.7 minutes on the arc, HE = 16½ feet.

What is the local apparent noon position?

LAN LATITUDE = _____ (88)

LAN LONGITUDE = _____ (89)

At 1224 (+4) the aircraft returns to the scene and you agree to recommence the ship/aircraft coordinated search pattern at 1230 (+4) on your 161½ compass course.

At 1345 (+4) the aircraft reports sighting a small surface vessel and at 1348 (+4) reports circling over a ketch-rigged sailing vessel apparently dead in the water with sails down. Having the aircraft on radar, you immediately head PEREGRINE for it, maintaining a speed of 13.5 knots and steering a compass course of 065. At 1400 (+4) the radar shows both the aircraft and boat on the same compass bearing of 065 at a range of 7½ miles.

What is the position of the other vessel?

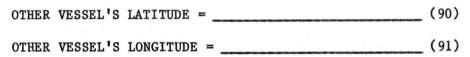

The aircraft reports having heard a very weak and unreadable signal on Channel 16 and then having seen one person come on deck and make a visual distress signal. Also, you are warned of various ropes streaming from the vessel.

At 1436 (+4) you stop PEREGRINE about 50 yards to leeward of the distressed vessel and inspect her while the dinghy is lowered. Her transom shows the name MERLIN and the port of registry reported by Bermuda Radio. There is no evident damage to hull or rig. Two small signal flags, "N" and "C" show as a hoist to her port main spreader.

With the aircraft still circling overhead as some insurance against foul play, you pull over to MERLIN, board and find two exhausted persons. The man is barely rousable; the woman manages to convey that the engine wouldn't start and the water tank leaked out after they had both suffered a bad bout of vomiting and diarrhea, apparently brought on by fish poisoning.

Word from PEREGRINE's loud hailer reminds you that the aircraft needs to head back to Bermuda. So you lower the hoist and return the "C" to the port main spreader. The aircraft, with a wing salute, heads for Bermuda at 1500.

When you have confirmed that there is no potable water or other drinkables and have checked the other liquid levels, you send the dinghy back to PEREGRINE with requests for another hand, fluids, the complete medicine chest, a charged battery, hook-up wires, and jumper cables. Meanwhile, you try to make the couple as comfortable as possible, haul the sheets on deck, square away the rest of the running rigging and sails, and get fenders out.

On return of the dinghy, you examine the couple thoroughly while the others get MERLIN's engine started up and briefly resume communications with the aircraft, giving a status report and promising a full report to Bermuda Radio as soon as possible. Soon you are able to start Lactated Ringer's solution into the man and find that the woman can tolerate small amounts of fluid by mouth. It is clear that both may need further examination and care beyond PEREGRINE's capabilities. Also, there is MERLIN to salvage.

With the aircraft now fading out of VHF range, you point out various options to the couple and work out a satisfactory plan. PEREGRINE will head back towards Bermuda with the couple, leaving two hands to power MERLIN in the same direction. (Bermuda is dead upwind from here.) You expect that a helicopter can rendezvous with PEREGRINE the next day to deliver two hands for the rest of MERLIN's passage and pick up the distressed couple.

MERLIN is brought alongside PEREGRINE, the couple transferred, MERLIN's fuel and water topped-off and her provisions replenished. With MERLIN's batteries charging nicely, a radio check shows continuing clear VHF communications as both vessels start back for Bermuda, leaving the distress scene at 1642, steering an initial compass course of 265.

Working PEREGRINE's speed up to the maximum consistent with head seas and relative comfort for the patients, by 1700 (+4) she seems to plug along well at 10.4 knots, having logged a distance of 2.6 miles from the distress scene. Radar checks on MERLIN show her distance astern at 1700 (+4) to be 0.75 mile and speed to be settling at 7.5 knots.

Figuring the current to be the same as that determined at 0430 (+4), what is the 1700 (+4) EP?

1700 EP LATITUDE = _____ (92)

1700 EP LONGITUDE = _____ (93)

What is the rhumb-line course to St. David I. Lt. from the 1700 (+4) EP?

NEW TRUE COURSE = _____ (94)

16

Figuring on an average local variation of 19½ W, no deviation, and discounting any current, to the nearest half degree, what compass course should you steer (and send to MERLIN) so as to make this true rhumb-line course to Bermuda?

NEW MAGNETIC/COMPASS COURSE = _____ (95)

At 1730 (+4) you change to this course, maintaining a speed of 10.4 knots.

Further communications with Bermuda Radio confirm that a helicopter can and will rendezvous with PEREGRINE (at a rhumb-line radius of) 300 miles from St. David's I. Lt. for the proposed transfer.

At a speed of 10.4 knots, what is the tentative rendezvous position and PEREGRINE's ETA there?

RENDEZVOUS LATITUDE = _____ (96)

RENDEZVOUS LONGITUDE = _____ (97)

(+4) ETA AT RENDEZVOUS = _____ (98)

Fortunately, the patients' conditions seems to be improving. Also, a sky becoming overcast precludes an evening star fix, so you have a look at the fuel budget.

Assuming a consumption of 12 gallons per hour at 0 to 8.5 knots, 16 gallons per hour at 10.4 knots, and 22 gallons per hour at 13.5 knots (along with a total of 65 gallons to be transferred to MERLIN), how many gallons of fuel should you expect PEREGRINE to have left at time of rendezvous tomorrow?

GALLONS OF FUEL REMAINING = _____ (99)

Figuring on proceeding at 1330 (+4) on the intended voyage to destination (which would be some 300 miles shorter than originally) at a speed of 8.5 knots and, with a further 43 minutes' delay in the rendezvous with MERLIN, what percent fuel safety margin would PEREGRINE have left in had on arrival at destination?

% FUEL SAFETY MARGIN REMAINING = _____ (100)

Not wanting to return to Bermuda, even 'though your salvage claim will pretty well cover any expenses, you re-work the fuel budget for a destination of Santa Cruz, Flores, at

39-27 N, 031-08 W, and the same 1330 (+4) departure from the rendezvous point.

What is this great-circle distance and what will be your ETA at Santa Cruz at a speed of 8.5 knots?

GREAT CIRCLE DISTANCE = _____ (101)

ETA (GMT)--INCLUDING DATE = _____ (102)

With this new destination and distance, and figuring the other variables to remain the same, what percent fuel safety margin would PEREGRINE have left in hand on arrival at Santa Cruz?

% FUEL SAFETY MARGIN REMAINING = _____ (103)

Just to make sure, at 1900 (+4) you get thorough tank soundings and determine that PEREGRINE has 2,600 gallons ± 5% fuel remaining. With this confirmation, a projected daylight arrival, and figuring on prevailing fair winds with no contrary current, you plan to continue on to the Azores after rendezvous without returning to St. George's for refueling.

You leave word for a midnight (+4) course change to 265½ to allow for an average local variation of 19 W. The logged speed remains 10.4 knots throughout an uneventful night and on into the morning of the 16th.

Dawn arrives with the sky remaining overcast, but later the sun breaks through to allow a sight of the lower limb, Hs = 64-06.2 at CT = 15-15-14; and then, with meridian transit observed at CT = 15-55-27, a local apparent noon sight of the lower limb, Hs = 65-48.8.

With CE = 2 seconds fast, IE = 3.7 minutes on the arc, HE = 16½ feet, what is the local apparent noon 1200 (+4) position as derived from the running fix position?

1200 LATITUDE = _____ (104)

1200 LONGITUDE = _____ (105)

By 1215 (+4) you have established radio communication with the helicopter and are able to send your 1200 (+4) position, course and speed. Then with a little time in hand, you calculate the set and drift of the current from 1143½ (+4) yesterday to the 1200 (+4) position, today.

18

Over the last 24.3 hours, what was the average current?

CURRENT SET = _____ (106)

CURRENT DRIFT (SPEED) = _____ (107)

At 1230 (+4) you pick up the helicopter approaching from the West. At 1236 (+4) you change course to 285 C and slow to an indicated speed of 4.5 knots. This is agreeable to the helicopter, so it sends down the two crew members for MERLIN, picking up the two patients (who are now both ambulatory) on each return lift. (The helicopter also has sent down four liters of Lactated Ringer's solution, a bunch of I.V. administration replacements and, with a quick third drop, your two life jackets.)

By 1248 (+4) the transfer is completed, and you head PEREGRINE away from Bermuda again, taking a compass course of 085, and increasing speed to 8.5 knots.

By DR, what was MERLIN's distance from PEREGRINE at 1248 (+4)?

MERLIN'S DISTANCE AWAY = _____ (108)

At 1554 (+4) you pick up a clear radar target fine on the starboard bow, range 7½ miles. Twenty minutes later you confirm that it is MERLIN, and at 1630 (+4) both vessels stop to transfer crew and to top-off MERLIN's fuel and water.

What is your best estimate of the 1630 (+4) position?

1630 EP LATITUDE = _____ (109)

1630 EP LONGITUDE = _____ (110)

Having given this position and best wishes to MERLIN, at 1724 (+4) you head PEREGRINE on a compass course of 086½ at a speed of 8.5 knots.

From the 1630 (+4) EP, what is the new great circle course to Santa Cruz, Flores?

NEW TRUE COURSE = _____ (111)

Figuring the current to remain about as it had been over the last day, with an average local variation of 19½ W and a deviation of 1.5 E, to the nearest half degree, what should

19

PEREGRINE's compass course be so as to make good the true great circle course?

COMPASS COURSE = _____ (112)

At 1800 (+4) you change to this compass course. Later, at evening star time, the sky is obscured by a light overcast which persists throughout the night and well past dawn the next morning (17 APR).

With this weather persisting -- the sun showing through the overcast but not showing a clear limb -- you change to another sextant having a telescope which can be reversed. This sextant (which has an index error of 2.3 minutes off the arc) allows you to make altitude observations on the sun's **center** with fair accuracy.

So, at CT = 15-06-15 and, later that afternoon at CT = 18-36-23, you take observations of the sun's **center**, Hs = 64-00 and Hs = 42-38, respectively. CE = 1 second fast; HE = 17 feet.

What was the 1106 (+4) DR?

1106 DR LATITUDE = _____ (113)

1106 DR LONGITUDE = _____ (114)

Using the DR, instead of the usually more convenient assumed position, you calculate the altitude intercept and azimuth for the CT = 15-06-15 observation.

What was the point on this line of position closest to PEREGRINE's 1106 (+4) DR?

1106 EP LATITUDE = _____ (115)

1106 EP LONGITUDE = _____ (116)

What was the course made good and distance travelled to this estimated position from yesterday's 1630 (+4) EP?

COURSE MADE GOOD = _____ (117)

DISTANCE TRAVELLED = _____ (118)

Using the 1106 (+4) EP instead of the usually more convenient assumed position, you calculate the altitude intercept and azimuth for the CT = 18-36-23 observation.

20

What distance does this calculation indicate that PEREGRINE travelled between 1106 (+4) and 1436½ (+4)?

1106 - 1436½ DISTANCE = _____ (119)

What speed has PEREGRINE made good since yesterday's 1630 (+4) EP?

SPEED MADE GOOD = _____ (120)

Using this course made good and speed made good, you determine the 1500 (+4) EP.

What is the 1500 (+4) EP?

1500 EP LATITUDE = _____ (121)

1500 EP LONGITUDE = _____ (122)

What is your best estimate of the average current since yesterday's noon position?

CURRENT SET = _____ (123)

CURRENT DRIFT (SPEED) = _____ (124)

What is the new great circle course from the 1500 (+4) EP to Santa Cruz?

NEW TRUE COURSE = _____ (125)

Figuring the current, the logged speed (8.5 knots) and the deviation to remain about the same, and the local variation to have increased to 20 W, to the nearest half degree, what compass course should you order at 1600 (+4)?

1600 COMPASS COURSE = _____ (126)

The overcast persists through evening star time. So, with a time-zone change coming up at about 0300 (+4), you leave word to set the clocks ahead at midnight (+4), and turn in for a sleep to be shortened by one hour.

Morning star time found PEREGRINE in a gale from the west under lowering skies and in a quartering sea. Indicated speed increased to an average of 9.0 knots from 0300 (+3) to 0600 (+3) and then settled at 9.1 knots after 0600 (+3).

21

Expecting to maintain this indicated speed, what should be PEREGRINE's DR at noon on 18 APR?

1200 DR LATITUDE = _____ (127)

1200 DR LONGITUDE = _____ (128)

Also, reckoning on the **average** current to have remained in the same direction but to have increased in speed by 10% since 1500 (+4) on the 17th, what should be PEREGRINE's estimated position at noon (+3)?

1200 EP LATITUDE = _____ (129)

1200 EP LONGITUDE = _____ (130)

What is the new great circle course to Santa Cruz, Flores from the 1200 (+3) EP?

NEW TRUE COURSE = _____ (131)

Figuring the current to remain the same (as used to determine the 1200 EP), the logged speed to persist at 9.1 knots until the gale abates, the deviation to remain about the same and the local variation to have increased to 20½ W, what compass course should you order at 1200 (+3)?

1200 COMPASS COURSE = _____ (132)

Having changed to this course at noon (+3), by 1500 (+3), the gale had abated and, by evening star time, there was enough clear sky and clear ('though lumpy) horizon for a good round of stars, as follows.

Name:	REGULUS	SIRIUS	ALIOTH	MIRFAK
Hs:	60-34.9	27-57.1	47-49.0	29-55.0
CT:	22-26-40	22-28-54	22-34-17	22-36-53

Also, at CT = 22-45-00, you took an azimuth of SIRIUS, compass bearing 240.5.

Having logged an average speed of 8.9 knots from noon to 1900 (+3) and then settling at a steady 8.7 knots, what was the 1930 (+3) DR?

22

1930 DR LATITUDE = _____ (133)

1930 DR LONGITUDE = _____ (134)

Figuring on a height of eye of 17 feet, no chronometer error and an index error of 3.7 minutes on the arc, what was the 1930 (+3) position?

1930 LATITUDE = _____ (135)

1930 LONGITUDE = _____ (136)

What was the average current since the noon (+4) position on 16 APR?

CURRENT SET = _____ (137)

CURRENT DRIFT (SPEED) = _____ (138)

From the 1930 (+3) position, what is the new great circle course to Santa Cruz?

NEW TRUE COURSE = _____ (139)

What was the deviation on the course you were holding at 1945 (+3)?

DEVIATION = _____ (140)

Figuring on this deviation, this current, an average indicated speed of 8.6 knots and the local variation remaining at 20½ W, to what compass course should you change at 2100 (+3)?

2100 COMPASS COURSE = _____ (141)

Having changed to this course at 2100, you plan ahead to morning star time.

What will be the (+3) zone times of: the beginning of nautical twilight, the beginning of civil twilight and sunrise?

TIME OF NAUTICAL TWILIGHT = _____ (142)

TIME OF CIVIL TWILIGHT = _____ (143)

TIME OF SUNRISE = _____ (144)

Morning star time yields the following observations.

Name: MARKAB   KAUS AUSTR.   POLARIS   ARCTURUS

Hs: 23-04.1   18-25.4   37-07.0   32-36.4

CT: 07-36-36   07-43-13   07-45-25   07-50-44

Also, with a clear sunrise, you take an amplitude observation of the rising sun at about 0537 (+3), compass bearing 095.8.

With the height of eye and index error remaining unchanged and a chronometer error of 1 second slow, what is the 0500 (+3) position?

     0500 LATITUDE = _____ (145)

     0500 LONGITUDE = _____ (146)

Having logged an average speed of 8.6 knots from 2100 (+3) until midnight and an actual distance of 42.50 miles from midnight until 0500 (+3), what was the average current since yesterday evening's star fix?

     CURRENT SET = _____ (147)

     CURRENT DRIFT (SPEED) = _____ (148)

Working the amplitude taken at 0537 (+3), what is the deviation on this course?

     DEVIATION = _____ (149)

What is the new great circle course from the 0500 (+3) position to destination?

     NEW TRUE COURSE = _____ (150)

To what compass course should you change at 0600 (+3)?

     0600 COMPASS COURSE = _____ (151)

At what (+3) zone time should you take a sun line which will be almost parallel to your new true course?

     ZONE TIME FOR SUN LINE = _____ (152)

Having determined by this observation that PEREGRINE is on track, you plan ahead to get a sun line perpendicular to the new true course.

24

At what (+3) zone time should you take this observation?

ZONE TIME FOR SUN LINE = _____ (153)

Having determined by this observation that PEREGRINE has made good a speed of 9.10 knots since 0500 (+3), what is the 1600 (+3) EP?

1600 EP LATITUDE = _____ (154)

1600 EP LONGITUDE = _____ (155)

At evening star time the sky is mostly obscured by fair weather cumulus, but you are able to get the following observations.

Name:	REGULUS	PROCYON	CAPELLA
Hs:	63-36.6	52-03.3	47-05.3
CT:	22-11-33	22-14-07	22-16-48

With a height of eye of 17 feet, index error of 3.7 minutes on the arc and the chronometer error remaining at one second slow, you reduce these observations and find a substantial discrepancy with the REGULUS line of position.

What is the 1900 (+3) position if JUPITER is substituted for REGULUS?

1900 LATITUDE = _____ (156)

1900 LONGITUDE = _____ (157)

Having logged 111.11 miles from 0600 (+3) to 1900 (+3), what was the average current between 0500 (+3) and 1900 (+3)?

CURRENT SET = _____ (158)

CURRENT DRIFT (SPEED) = _____ (159)

What was the speed made good between 0500 (+3) and 1900 (+3)?

SPEED MADE GOOD = _____ (160)

Figuring on maintaining this speed made good, what is the new great circle course to and ETA (GMT) at destination?

25

TRUE COURSE = _____ (161)

ETA (GMT)--INCLUDING DATE = _____ (162)

Having found (with earlier azimuth checks) that the deviation on this course had remained substantially unchanged, reckoning that the indicated speed will remain at 8.55 knots and that the average variation over the next 12 hours will have returned to 20 W, to what compass course should you change at 2030 (+3)?

2030 COMPASS COURSE = _____ (163)

After making this course change you get thorough tank soundings and find that there are 1,400 gallons ± 5% fuel remaining at 2100 (+3). This shows a consumption rate of 12.4 gallons per hour at the indicated speed of around 8.5 knots.

With a projected late night arrival at Flores, you look again at Fayal as a destination. Figuring on maintaining the latest speed made good, what would be the ETA at Ponta Comprida Lt.?

ETA (GMT)--INCLUDING DATE = _____ (164)

With all variables remaining unchanged to destination, what percent fuel safety margin would PEREGRINE have left in hand on arrival at Ponta Comprida Lt.?

% FUEL SAFETY MARGIN REMAINING = _____ (165)

These projected arrival times and fuel budget suggest Fayal as a better destination than Flores (where fueling would probably need to be done with the dinghy and jerry cans). However, since Flores is almost *en route* to Fayal, you decide to hold PEREGRINE on track for Flores -- at least for a couple of days.

To confirm your compass error you take an azimuth on VEGA, compass bearing 070.7 at CT = 00-48-13.

What is the deviation on this course?

COMPASS DEVIATION = _____ (166)

Morning star time yields the following observations.

Name:	MARKAB	DUBHE	ALTAIR	ARCTURUS
Hs:	25-20.1	24-36.0	56-15.8	31-06.0
CT:	07-26-11	07-28-22	07-34-00	07-36-49

With a height of eye of 17 feet, index error of 3.7 minutes on the arc and a chronometer error of 2 seconds slow, what is the 0430 (+3) position?

0430 LATITUDE = _____ (167)

0430 LONGITUDE = _____ (168)

Having logged an average speed of 8.55 knots since 1900 (+3), what was the average current between yesterday evening's and this morning's star fixes?

CURRENT SET = _____ (169)

CURRENT DRIFT (SPEED) = _____ (170)

What is the new great circle course from the 0430 (+3) position to Flores?

NEW TRUE COURSE = _____ (171)

Figuring the compass error to remain unchanged from last night's and the average indicated speed to remain at 8.55 knots, what compass course should you order at 0600 (+3)?

0600 COMPASS COURSE = _____ (172)

Later in the morning, then with meridian transit at local apparent noon and again in the afternoon of 20 APR you observe the sun's lower limb as follows.

CT:	14-28-28	14-48-22	18-36-00
Hs:	62-45.5	63-07.3	32-21.3

With HE = 17 feet, IE = 3.7 minutes on the arc and CE = 2 seconds slow, what was the course made good from 0430 (+3) to 1128½ (+3) and the speed made good from 0430 (+3) to 1536 (+3)?

COURSE MADE GOOD = _____ (173)

SPEED MADE GOOD = _____ (174)

Using this course and speed made good you advance your 1128½ (+3) LOP and retire your 1536 (+3) LOP to the time of local apparent noon.

How far away from the LAN position is this estimated position?

DISTANCE AWAY = _____ (175)

Using this verified course and speed made good you advance all four sun lines to 1700 (+3).

What will be the 1700 (+3) estimated position?

1700 EP LATITUDE = _____ (176)

1700 EP LONGITUDE = _____ (177)

What will be the new great circle course from the 1700 (+3) EP to Flores?

NEW TRUE COURSE = _____ (178)

What was the difference between the resultant course steered and the course made good between 0430 (+3) and 1128½ (+3)?

OFFSET DIFFERENCE = _____ (179)

Using this offset, with deviation unchanged and variation reduced to 19½ W, what compass course should you order at 1700 (+3)?

COMPASS COURSE = _____ (180)

Overcast, which precludes an evening star fix, persists on into the night. Figuring that morning stars might also be obscured, you determine the projected 0500 (+3) EP.

What is this estimated position?

PROJECTED 0500 EP LATITUDE = _____ (181)

PROJECTED 0500 EP LONGITUDE = _____ (182)

Using the same course offset as before, with deviation unchanged and variation reduced to 19 W, what compass course should be steered from 0500 (+3)?

28

COMPASS COURSE = _____ (183)

This course change was made at 0500 (+3) under still overcast skies. However, by 1100 (+3), the overcast had broken and you managed to take a LAN sight of the lower limb at CT = 14-29-46, Hs = 62-51.0.

With HE = 17 feet, IE = 3.7 minutes on the arc and CE = 3 seconds slow, what is the 1130 (+3) position?

1130 LATITUDE = _____ (184)

1130 LONGITUDE = _____ (185)

Having continued to log an average speed of 8.55 knots, what was the average current since yesterday's LAN sight?

CURRENT SET = _____ (186)

CURRENT DRIFT (SPEED) = _____ (187)

Your inspection of the Western Azores chart suggests redefinition of your destination as 39-20.0 N, 031-10.0 W for a landfall convenient to approaching Santa Cruz or, as appropriate, continuing on to Fayal.

For this destination, reckoning on the current just determined, a continuing indicated speed of 8.55 knots and compass error remaining unchanged, what compass course should you order at 1230 (+3)?

COMPASS COURSE = _____ (188)

Having held this course from 1230 (+3), at 1400 (+3) you set the clocks ahead one hour to 1500 (+2) and change compass course one-half degree to port so as to allow for a local variation of 18½ W.

Planning to take an azimuth at about 1745 (+2), what is the projected 1745 (+2) EP?

1745 EP LATITUDE = _____ (189)

1745 EP LONGITUDE = _____ (190)

Figuring all variables except compass error to have remained constant, what should be the true course to steer from the 1745 (+2) EP to 39-20.0 N, 031-10.0 W?

NEW TRUE COURSE TO STEER = _____ (191)

At CT = 19-45-00 you take an azimuth on the sun, compass bearing 291.7.

With chronometer error remaining at 3 seconds slow and local variation still at 18½ W, what is the deviation on this course?

COMPASS DEVIATION = _____ (192)

Figuring on an average variation of 18½ W, what compass course should you order at 1800 (+2)?

1800 COMPASS COURSE = _____ (193)

Having changed to this course at 1800 (+2), you take evening star sights as follows.

Name:	ALIOTH	SPICA	PROCYON	CAPELLA
CT:	21-45-54	21-47-36	21-50-25	21-53-11
Hs:	51-46.8	15-03.5	48-27.8	44-10.0

With a height of eye of 17 feet, an index error of 3.7 minutes on the arc and the chronometer error increased to 4 seconds slow, what is the 2000 (+2) position?

2000 LATITUDE = _____ (194)

2000 LONGITUDE = _____ (195)

What was the average current from 1130 (+3) to 2000 (+2)?

CURRENT SET = _____ (196)

CURRENT DRIFT (SPEED) = _____ (197)

What is the new rhumb line course from the 2000 (+2) position to 39-20.0 N, 031-10.0 W?

NEW TRUE COURSE = _____ (198)

Figuring on the most recent determination of current, a logged speed of 8.55 knots, an average variation of 18 W and the same deviation, what compass course should you order at 2100 (+2)?

30

2100 COMPASS COURSE = _____ (199)

Having changed to this compass course at 2100 (+2) and expecting to continue logging on average of 8.55 knots, what should be PEREGRINE's DR at 0500 (+2) on 22 APR?

0500 DR LATITUDE = _____ (200)

0500 DR LONGITUDE = _____ (201)

At morning star time you take the following observations.

Name:	MARKAB	KAUS AUSTR.	POLARIS	ARCTURUS
CT:	06-43-16	06-45-47	06-50-24	06-54-10
Hs:	25-35.6	16-31.7	38-54.1	30-45.3

With HE = 17 feet, IE = 3.7 minutes on the arc and CE = 4 seconds slow, what is the 0500 (+2) position?

0500 LATITUDE = _____ (202)

0500 LONGITUDE = _____ (203)

Having held course and speed through the night, what was the average current between 2000 (+2) and 0500 (+2)?

CURRENT SET = _____ (204)

CURRENT DRIFT (SPEED) = _____ (205)

What is the rhumb line course from the 0500 (+2) position to Ponta Comprida Lt. (at 38-36 N, 028-50 W)?

TRUE COURSE = _____ (206)

At what distance from Ponta das Lajes Lt. on Flores (at 39-22.5 N, 031-10.3 W) would this rhumb line lie?

DISTANCE OFF = _____ (207)

Since this distance off is well within radar range to a high, precipitous cliff, you decide to change course for Fayal at 0630 (+2).

Figuring on the most recent determination of current, a logged speed of 8.55 knots, an average variation of 17½ W and the same deviation, what should be the compass course ordered at 0630 (+2)?

0630 COMPASS COURSE = _____ (208)

Changing to this compass course at 0630 (+2), you soon take an azimuth on the sun, compass bearing 101.5 at CT = 08-36-18.

With CE = 4 seconds slow, what is the deviation on this compass course?

COMPASS DEVIATION = _____ (209)

Allowing for this deviation, what compass course should you order at 0700 (+2) so as to make good the previously determined rhumb line course to Fayal?

0700 COMPASS COURSE = _____ (210)

This slight course change was made at 0700 (+2), and PEREGRINE continued to log an average speed of 8.55 knots through the morning.

At CT = 14-11-13 you observe LAN with meridian passage of the lower limb, Hs = 63-05.4.

With HE = 17 feet, IE = 3.7 minutes on the arc and CE = 4 seconds slow, what is the LAN position?

1211½ LATITUDE = _____ (211)

1211½ LONGITUDE = _____ (212)

What was the average current from 0500 (+2) to 1211½ (+2)?

CURRENT SET = _____ (213)

CURRENT DRIFT (SPEED) = _____ (214)

What is the rhumb line course from the 1211½ (+2) position to Ponta Comprida Lt.?

TRUE COURSE = _____ (215)

Reckoning on the most recent determination of current, a logged speed of 8.55 knots, an average variation of 17 W and the same deviation, what compass course should you order at 1300 (+2)?

32

1300 COMPASS COURSE = _____ (216)

Having made this small course change at 1300 (+2), at about 1848 (+2) you take an amplitude observation, the sun bearing 303.5.

With a local variation of 17 W, what is the deviation on this course?

COMPASS DEVIATION = _____ (217)

At evening star time you make these observations.

Name:	JUPITER	ARCTURUS	SIRIUS	CAPELLA	POLARIS
CT:	21-20-57	21-26-13	21-29-37	21-34-07	21-43-21
Hs:	63-56.2	25-19.0	22-46.4	43-34.1	38-42.8

With chronometer error increased to 5 seconds slow and all other corrections unchanged, what is the 1930 (+2) position?

1930 LATITUDE = _____ (218)

1930 LONGITUDE = _____ (219)

Having held course since 1300 (+2) and having continued to log 8.55 knots, what was the average current between 1211½ (+2) and 1930 (+2)?

CURRENT SET = _____ (220)

CURRENT DRIFT (SPEED) = _____ (221)

An overtaking vessel on the starboard quarter (giving no evidence of intent to keep well clear) causes you to change compass course at 2024 (+2) to 080. at 2057 (+2) the other vessel has reached its closest point of approach and, at 2100 (+2), you bring PEREGRINE back on the course from the 1930 (+2) position to Ponta Comprida Lt..

Figuring on the latest determination of current, an average variation of 16½ W, the same deviation and logged speed as before, what should be this compass course?

2100 COMPASS COURSE = _____ (222)

Having changed to this course at 2100 (+2), about one hour later, having already picked up Flores on radar, you see the

33

loom of Ponta das Lajes Lt. on the port bow. Climbing to the top of the wheelhouse (HE = 25 feet), you observe the light rising at 2210 (+2), compass bearing 030.

With the light charted as 90 meters above mean sea level (at 39-22.5 N, 031-10.3 W), what is the 2210 (+2) position?

2210 LATITUDE = _____ (223)

2210 LONGITUDE = _____ (224)

What was the average current between 1930 (+2) and 2210 (+2)?

CURRENT SET = _____ (225)

CURRENT DRIFT (SPEED) = _____ (226)

Figuring on this latest determination of current and the same compass error and logged speed as before, what should be the compass course from the 2210 (+2) position to Ponta Comprida Lt.?

COMPASS COURSE = _____ (227)

At 2230 (+2) you change to this compass course.

By 0200 (+2) surface traffic requires a variety of course changes as follows.

Time Span	Cc	Time Span	Cc
0203-0227	145	0312-0321	160
0227-0239	120	0321-0336	120
0239-0251	160	0336-0351	140
0251-0312	120	0351-0400	120

By 0400 (+2) the traffic allows return to the 2230 (+2) compass course.

Having continued to log 8.55 knots, what is PEREGRINE's 0430 (+2) DR?

0430 DR LATITUDE = _____ (228)

0430 DR LONGITUDE = _____ (229)

Morning star observations yield the following.

34

Name:	MARKAB	POLARIS	NUNKI	ARCTURUS
CT:	06-36-21	06-43-43	06-45-10	06-48-30
Hs:	28-32.5	38-33.2	25-07.0	27-34.2

With all corrections unchanged from last evening's star fix, what is the 0430 (+2) position.

0430 LATITUDE = _____ (230)

0430 LONGITUDE = _____ (231)

What was the average current between 2210 (+2) and 0430 (+2)?

CURRENT SET = _____ (232)

CURRENT DRIFT (SPEED) = _____ (233)

Holding the 2210 (+2) compass course, but figuring on a local variation after 0430 (+2) of 16 W, what will be the 0600 (+2) estimated position?

0600 EP LATITUDE = _____ (234)

0600 EP LONGITUDE = _____ (235)

Figuring on the latest determination of current, no change in deviation, a local variation of 16 W and a continued logged speed of 8.55 knots, what compass course should be taken at 0600 (+2) to approach the arrival point for the port of Horta which you have chosen at 38-30.0 N, 028-45.0 W?

0600 COMPASS COURSE = _____ (236)

Having changed to this compass course at 0600 (+2), by 0630 (+2) the mountain peaks of Fayal and Pico are both showing clearly, fine on the port bow.

No further course or speed changes are made until 1148 (+2) when PEREGRINE arrives at the approaches to Horta at 38-30.5 N, 028-45.0 W.

By 1330 (+2) on 23 APR PEREGRINE is berthed and finished with engines.

THE CALCULATIONS

1-2.   This is a parallel sailing problem.

POSITION OF LIGHT: 32-22.0 N,   064-39.0 W

DISTANCE EAST = DEPARTURE = p = 3.0 miles E

DIFFERENCE OF LONGITUDE = DLo = p (sec L) = 3.0 (1.18394) E = 3.55 E

LONGITUDE OF DEPARTURE = (064-39.0 W) - 3.55 E = 064-35.45 W

POSITION OF DEPARTURE: 32-22.0 N,   064-35.4 W

3, 6.   This is a great circle sailing problem. It can be solved by calculation or, as shown below, by linear interpolation from sight reduction tables (inspection tables). The tables used in this book are H.O. Pub. No. 229.

As is suggested in such tables, interpolation is not always linear, and procedures for non-linear interpolation are provided. However, these procedures do not yield a better value for azimuth angle, and since the navigator is more interested in the initial great circle course, linear interpolation is most appropriate.

DLo = (064-35.45 W) - (028-50.0 W) = 35-45.45 E = t = 35.76 E

DESTINATION L   = 38-36.0 N = d = 38.60 N

DEPARTURE L   = 32-22.0 N = L = 32.37 N

values	t = 35.76 E	d = 38.60 N	L = 32.37 N
base	35/60-53.3/68.3	38/60-53.3/68.3	32/60-53.3/68.3
next	36/60-06.0/68.3	39/60-51.1/66.2	33/61-14.6/70.0
difference	-47.3/ZERO	-02.2/-2.1	+21.3/+1.7
multiplier	.76	.60	.37
product	-35.9/ZERO	-01.3/-1.3	+07.9/+0.6
	-01.3/-1.3	90-00.0	
	+07.9/+0.6	60-24.0	
increments	-29.3/-0.7	29-36.0 = z = 1,776.0 miles	
base	60-53.3/68.3	Z = N 67.6 E	
result	60-24.0/67.6	Zn = 067.6	

(The calculated values from trigonometric solution of the oblique spherical triangle are: z = 1,774.8 miles and Zn = 067.7.)

4-5.   This is a time and operations problem.

DEPARTURE ZONE DATE/TIME = 12 APR / 18 h 00 m

ZONE DESCRIPTION   =   +4

DEPARTURE GMT DATE/TIME = 12 APR / 22 h 00 m

PASSAGE DURATION   = 1776 miles / 8.5 knots = 208.94 hours

                         = 208 h $56\frac{1}{2}$ m = 8 d 16 h $56\frac{1}{2}$ m

DEPARTURE GMT DATE/TIME =   12 d 22 h 00 m

ARRIVAL GMT DATE/TIME   =   20 d 38 h $56\frac{1}{2}$ m

                         = 21 APR / 14 h $56\frac{1}{2}$ m

REGULAR FUEL CONSUMPTION = 12 gallons/hour

SAFETY MARGIN   = 1.5

SAFE FUEL CONSUMPTION   = 18 gallons/hour

PASSAGE DURATION   = 208.94 hours

FUEL NEEDED   = (18) (208.94) gallons

                         = 3,761 gallons (about $12\frac{1}{2}$ tons)

7.   This is a compass conversion problem.

TRUE COURSE   = Cn = 067.6

VARIATION   = V = 15.0 W

MAGNETIC COURSE = Cm = 082.6 To the nearest half degree,

                 Cm = $082\frac{1}{2}$

8-11.   This is an amplitude and compass conversion problem.

ZT	18-45	
ZD	+4	
GMT	22-45	
h d	N 08-57.7	
+.9	+0.7	
final d	N 08-58.4 = N 08.97	
DR L	32-25.0 N = 32.42 N	
values	d = 08.97 N	L = 32.42 N
base	9/10.6	32/10.6
next	8.5/10.0	34/10.9
difference	-0.6	+0.3
multiplier	.06	.21
product	-.036	+.063
		-.036
increment		+.027
base		10.6
result		W 10.6 N
plus 270°		270
azimuth		280.6
bearing		293.9
compass error		13.3 W
variation		15.0 W
deviation		1.7 E
TRUE COURSE	= Cn = 067.6	
COMPASS ERROR	= CE = 13.3 W	
COMPASS COURSE	= Cc = 080.9	
To the nearest half degree,	Cc = 081	

12-13.   This is either a plotting problem (see Figure 1) or a
traverse and mid-latitude sailing problem.

Time Span	Cc	V(W)	Dev	CE(W)	Cn	D(mi)	l (N+)	p (E+)
1800-1900	082½	15	1.7 E	13.3	069.2	8.50	3.02	7.95
1900-0500	081	15½	1.7 E	13.8	067.2	85.00	32.94	78.36
1800-0500							35.96	86.31

Lm = (32-22.0 N) + 35.96/2 = 32-40.0 N

DLo = p (sec Lm) = 86.31 (1.18790) E = 102.5 E = 001-42.5 E

1800 POSITION	32-22.0 N	064-35.4 W
l, DLo	35.9 N	001-42.5 E
0500 DR	32-57.9 N	062-52.9 W

14-15.   This is a star fix problem. The sight reductions are
shown below. The plot is shown in Figure 2.

FROM THE NAUTICAL ALMANAC, 13 APR 68:

Name	DENEB
CT	09-11-38
CE	0-05 fast
GMT	09-11-33
h GHA	336-36.7
SHA/d	49-55.0/N45-09.5
m,s GHA	2-53.7
final GHA	389-25.4
a λ	062-25.4 W
LHA	327
t	33 E
Hs	61-41.8
IE & dip	7.6
Ha	61-34.2
refr	0.5
Ho	61-33.7

FROM H.O. PUB. NO. 229, ASSUMING A LATITUDE OF 33 N:

H/d/Z	61-56.5/-15.2/ 55.0
corr'n	-02.4
Hc/Z	61-54.1/N 55.0 E
Ho	61-33.7
a	20.4 away
Zn	055.0
DR to 0500	-1.6 miles
0500 POSITION	32-53.6 N

NUNKI	ALKAID
09-14-20	09-16-51
0-05 fast	0-05 fast
09-14-15	09-16-46
336-36.7	336-36.7
76-40.5/S26-20.4	153-25.1/N49-28.1
3-34.3	4-12.2
416-51.5	494-14.0
062-51.5 W	063-14.0 W
354	071
6 E	71 W
30-38.2	36-04.4
7.6	7.6
30-30.6	35-56.8
1.7	1.3
30-28.9	35-55.5
30-43.5/-59.7/173.7	36-10.2/+10.6/ 50.2
-20.3	+05.0
30-23.2/N 173.7 E	36-15.2/N 50.2 W
30-28.9	35-55.5
5.7 towards	19.7 away
173.7	309.8
-2.0 miles	-2.4 miles

062-51.6 W

16-19.   This is either a plotting problem (see Figure 2) or a mid-latitude sailing problem.

        (It could, of course, be a Mercator sailing problem, but since the distance is quite small, the solution to the mid-latitude sailing problem should be quite satisfactory.)

0500 DR   32-57.9 N   062-52.9 W

0500 FIX   32-53.6 N   062-51.6 W

ℓ, DLo   4.3 S   1.3 E

Lm = (32-53.6 N) + 4.3/2 = 32-55.75 N

p = DLo (cos Lm) = 1.3 (0.83934) E = 1.09 E

C = arc tan p / ℓ = S 14.2 E

D = ℓ (sec C) = 4.3 (1.03169) = 4.44 miles

Cn = 180 – C = 180 – 14.2 = 165.8

CURRENT SPEED = 4.44 miles/11 hours = 0.404 knots

44

20.   This is a great circle sailing problem.

DLo = (062-51.6 W) - (028-50.0 W) = 34-01.6 E = t = 34.03 E
DESTINATION L   = 38-36.0 N = d = 38.60 N
DEPARTURE L   = 32-53.6 N = L = 32.89 N

values	t = 34.03 E	d = 38.60 N	L = 32.89 N
base	34/68.2	38/68.2	32/68.2
next	35/68.3	39/66.1	33/70.0
difference	+0.1	-2.1	+1.8
multiplier	.03	.60	.89
product	+0.00	-1.26	+1.60
			-1.26
increment			+0.34
base			68.2
result, Z =			N 68.5 E
Zn =			068.5

21-22.   This is a current vector and compass conversion
problem. It can be solved graphically or trigonometrically as
shown below.

SET   = 165.8

DRIFT   =   0.404 knots

COURSE TO MAKE GOOD (CMG) = 068.5

LOGGED SPEED   =   8.5 knots

COURSE TO STEER (CTS) = CMG - X

         where sin X = (DRIFT) sin (SET - CMG) / LOGGED SPEED

                 = (0.404) sin (165.8 - 068.5) / 8.5

                 = (0.404) sin (97.3) / 8.5

                 = 0.404 (0.99189) / 8.5

                 = 0.04714

         so, X = 2.70216 degrees

       and CTS = CMG - X

       so, CTS = (068.5 - 2.7)

           Cn = 065.8

            V =   16.0 W

           Cm = 081.8

          Dev =   1.7 E

           Cc = 080.1   To the nearest half degree,

           Cc = 080

46

23-26.   This is an azimuth (by inspection tables) and
compass conversion problem.

CT   11-00-05
CE   0-05 fast
GMT   11-00-00
GHA/d   344-52.5/N09-09.4 = N 09.16
DR λ   062-23.8 W
LHA   282-28.7
t   77-31.3 E   = 77.52 E
DR L   33-03.9 N   = 33.06 N
values   t = 77.52 E   d = 09.16 N   L = 33.06 N
base   77/89.4   09/89.4   33/89.4
next   78/88.9   10/88.5   34/89.7
difference   -0.5   -0.9   +0.3
multiplier   .52   .16   .06
product   -0.26   -0.14   +0.02
                   -0.14
                   +0.02   Z = N 89.0 E
increment   -0.38   Zn =   089.0
base   89.4   bearing =   103.5
result   89.0   CE =   14.5 W
                                               V =   16.0 W
                                             Dev =   1.5 E
                                              Cn =   065.8
                                               V =   16.5 W
                                              Cm =   082.3
                                             Dev =   1.5 E
                                              Cc =   080.8
                     To the nearest half degree, Cc =   081

                                                              47

27-28.   This is a sun sight problem. The sight reduction
is shown below. The plot is shown in Figure 3.

FROM THE NAUTICAL ALMANAC, 13 APR 68:

CT	15-28-32
CE	0-05 fast
GMT	15-28-27
h GHA/d	044-53.1/N09-13.0
m,s GHA/d	07-06.8/0.9=+0.4
final GHA/d	051-59.9/N09-13.4
a λ	061-59.9 W
LHA	350
t	10 E
Hs	64-11.8
IE & dip	7.6
Ha	64-04.2
main	15.5
Ho	64-19.7

FROM H.O. PUB. NO. 229, ASSUMING A LATITUDE OF   33 N:

H/d/Z	64-17.1/+56.4/156.7
corr'n	+12.6
Hc/Z	64-29.7/N 156.7 E
Ho	64-19.7
a	10.0 away
Zn	156.7

This puts the sun line 1.7 miles to starboard of the 1128½ DR,
and shows a course made good of 067.8 since the 0500 star fix.

29-32.   This is a sun sight problem. The sight reduction
is shown below. The plot is shown in Figure 3.

FROM THE NAUTICAL ALMANAC, 13 APR 68:

CT   18-53-22

CE   0-05 fast

GMT   18-53-17

h GHA/d   089-53.6/N09-15.8

m,s GHA/d   13-19.3/.9 + .8

final GHA/d   103-12.9/N09-16.6

a λ   061-12.9 W

LHA   042

t   42 W

Hs   44-30.6

IE & dip   7.6

Ha   44-23.0

main   15.0

Ho   44-38.0

FROM H.O. PUB. NO. 229, ASSUMING A LATITUDE OF   33 N:

H/d/Z   44-29.4/+36.7/112.1

corr'n   +10.1

Hc/Z   44-39.5/N 112.1 W

Ho   44-38.0

a   1.5 away

Zn   247.9

This puts the sun line 80.8 miles ahead of the 0500 star fix.
The speed made good since 0500 is (80.8/9.89) knots = 8.17
knots, yielding a 1500 EP of 33-24.3 N, 061-21.2 W.

33-34.   This is either a plotting problem (see Figure 3) or a traverse and mid-latitude sailing problem.

Time Span	Cc	V(W)	Dev	CE(W)	Cn	D(mi)	L (N+)	p (E+)
0500-0600	081	16	1.7 E	14.3	066.7	8.50	3.36	7.81
0600-0800	080	16	1.7 E	14.3	065.7	17.00	7.00	15.49
0800-1128½	081	16½	1.5 E	15.0	066.0	29.54	12.02	26.99
1128½-1500	081	17	1.5 E	15.5	065.5	29.96	12.42	27.26
0500-1500							34.80	77.55

Lm = (32-53.6 N) + 34.80/2 = 33-11.0 N

DLo = p (sec Lm) = 77.55 (1.19485) E = 92.7 E = 001-32.7 E

0500 FIX	32-53.6 N	062-51.6 W
L, DLo	34.8 N	001-32.7 E
1500 DR	33-28.4 N	061-18.9 W
1500 EP	33-24.3 N	061-21.2 W
L, DLo	4.1 S	2.3 W

Lm = (33-28.4 N) - 4.1/2 = 33-26.4 N

p = DLo (cos Lm) = 2.3 (0.83446) W = 1.92 W

C = arc tan p / L = S 25.1 W

D = L (sec C) = 4.1 (1.10414) = 4.53 miles

SET = Cn = 180 + C = 205.1

DRIFT (SPEED) = 4.53 miles/10 hours = 0.453 knots

35.   This is a great circle sailing problem.

DLo = (061-21.2 W) - (028-50.0 W) = 32-31.2 E = t = 32.52 E

DESTINATION L   = 38-36.0 N = d = 38.60 N

DEPARTURE L   = 33-24.3 N = L = 33.40 N

values	t = 32.52 E	d = 38.60 N	L = 33.40 N
base	32/70.0	38/70.0	33/70.0
next	33/70.0	39/67.7	34/71.9
difference	ZERO	-2.3	+1.9
multiplier	.52	.60	.40
product	ZERO	-1.38	+0.76
		+0.76	
increment		-0.6	
base		70.0	
result, Z =		N 69.4 E	
Zn =		069.4	

36-37.   This is a current vector and compass conversion problem. It can be solved graphically or trigonometrically as shown below.

SET   = 205.1
DRIFT   =   0.453 knots
COURSE TO MAKE GOOD (CMG) = 069.4
LOGGED SPEED   =   8.5 knots

COURSE TO STEER (CTS) = CMG − X

$\qquad$ where sin X = (DRIFT) sin (SET − CMG) / LOGGED SPEED

$\qquad\qquad\qquad$ = (0.453) sin (205.1 − 069.4) / 8.5

$\qquad\qquad\qquad$ = (0.453) sin (135.7) / 8.5

$\qquad\qquad\qquad$ = 0.453 (0.69842) / 8.5

$\qquad\qquad\qquad$ = 0.03722

$\qquad$ so, X = 2.13312 degrees

$\qquad$ and CTS = CMG − X

$\qquad$ so, CTS = (069.4 − 2.1)

$\qquad\qquad$ Cn = 067.3

$\qquad\qquad$ V =   17.5 W

$\qquad\qquad$ Cm = 084.8

$\qquad\qquad$ Dev =   1.5 E

$\qquad\qquad$ Cc = 083.3   To the nearest half degree,

$\qquad\qquad$ Cc = 083.5

38-40.   These are rising/setting problems.

ZT	EP λ (W)	LMT	EP L (N)
1830	060-49	1827	33-35
1845	060-47	1842	33-35
1900	060-45	1857	33-36
1915	060-43	1912	33-37

FROM THE NAUTICAL ALMANAC, 13 APR 68:

	L (N)	SUNSET	C. TWILIGHT	MOONRISE
	35	1831	1857	1910
	30	1826	1850	1903
difference	5	5	7	7
corr'n from Table I		+3	+3	+3
LMT		1829	1853	1906
corr'n from Table II				+13
LMT				1919
λ corr'n		+1	+1	+1
ZT (to nearest min.)		1830	1854	1920

41-42.   This is an inverted sight reduction problem.

FROM THE NAUTICAL ALMANAC, 13 APR 68:

ZT   19-00

ZD   +4

GMT   23-00

GHA/d   038-35.2/N14-00.6 = N 14.01

EP λ   060-45   W

LHA   337-50.2

t   22-09.8 E   =   22.16 E

FROM H.O. PUB. NO. 229, ASSUMING A LATITUDE OF 33-36 N:

values	t = 22.16 E	d = 14.01 N	L = 33.60 N
base	22/62-24.4/128.3	14/62.24.4/128.3	33/62-24.4/128.3
next	23/61-44.5/126.8	15/63-08.1/126.8	34/61-46.7/129.8
difference	-39.9/ -1.5	+43.7/ -1.5	-37.7/ +1.5
multiplier	.16	.01	.60
product	-06.4/ -0.2	+00.4/ZERO	-22.6/ +0.9
	-22.6		
	+00.4/ +0.9		
increments	-28.6/ +0.7		
base	62-24.4/128.3		
result	61-55.8/129.0		

To the nearest whole degree, H = 62, Zn = 129.0

43.   This is a latitude by Polaris problem.

FROM THE NATUICAL ALMANAC, 14 APR 68:

ZT	2059	Hs	33-17.3
ZD	+4	IE & dip	7.6
GMT	00-59	Ha	33-09.7
h GHA	202-13.6	refr	1.5
m,s GHA	14-47.4	Ho	33-08.2
final GHA	217-01.0	a_0	1-30.3
EP λ	060-26. W	a_1	0.4
LHA	156-35.	a_2	1.0
		sum	34-39.9
		minus 1°	-1
		L	33-39.9 N

44.   This is a moon sight problem. The sight reduction
is shown below. The plot is shown in Figure 4.

FROM THE NAUTICAL ALMANAC, 14 APR 68:

CT	01-00-16
CE	0-04 fast
GMT	01-00-12
h GHA/d	004-10.7/ S 14-59.2
v = 7.8	0-00.1
m,s GHA/d	00-02.9/+15.6=+0.1 HP = 61.1
final GHA/d	004-13.7/ S 14-59.3
a λ	060-13.7 W
LHA	304
t	56 E
Hs	16-38.7
IE & dip	7.6
Ha	16-31.1
main	62.7
add'l	9.2
Ho	17-43.0

FROM H.O. PUB. NO. 229, ASSUMING A LATITUDE OF   34 N:

H/d/Z	17-38.5/+41.6/122.8
corr'n	.5
Hc/Z	17-39.0/N 122.8 E
Ho	17-43.0
a	4.0 towards
Zn	122.8

This line of position intersects the latitude by Polaris
parallel at 060-23.4 W.

56

45.   This is a compass conversion problem.

TRUE COURSE   = Cn   = 067.3
VARIATION   = V   = 18.0 W
MAGNETIC COURSE   = Cm   = 085.3
DEVIATION   = Dev   =   1.5 E
COMPASS COURSE   = Cc   = 083.8
To the nearest half degree = 084

46-47.   This is a traverse and mid-latitude sailing
problem. Note that this DR is run from the 0500 star fix on 13
APR 68. If the DR is run from the 2100 position (a poor choice
-- low altitude moon shot and poor horizon), the 0500 DR would
be 34-06.0 N, 059-07.8 W.

Time Span	Cc	V(W)	Dev	CE(W)	Cn	D(mi)	$\angle$ (N+)	p (E+)
0500-0600	081	16	1.7 E	14.3	066.7	8.50	3.36	7.81
0600-0800	080	16	1.7 E	14.3	065.7	17.00	7.00	15.49
0800-1128½	081	16½	1.5 E	15.0	066.0	29.54	12.02	26.99
1128½-1600	081	17	1.5 E	15.5	065.5	38.46	15.94	34.99
1600-2100	083½	17½	1.5 E	16.0	067.5	42.50	16.26	39.26
2100-2200	083	17½	1.5 E	16.0	067.0	8.50	3.32	7.82
2200-0500	084	18	1.5 E	16.5	067.5	59.50	22.77	54.97
0500-0500							80.67	187.33

Lm = (32-53.6 N) + 80.67/2 = 33-33.0 N

DLo = p (sec Lm) = 187.33 (1.20011) E = 224.8 E = 3-44.8 E

0500 POSITION	32-53.6 N	062-51.6 W
$\angle$, DLo	1-20.7 N	3-44.8 E
0500 DR	34-14.3 N	059-06.8 W

57

48–49.   This is a star fix problem. As noted in the
narrative, the stars selected have azimuths in approximately
opposite directions. The sight reductions are shown below.
The plot is shown in Figure 5.

FROM THE NAUTICAL ALMANAC, 14 APR 68:

Name	ENIF	NUNKI
CT	08-50-42	08-53-27
CE	4 fast	4 fast
GMT	08-50-38	08-53-23
h GHA	322-33.3	322-33.3
SHA/d	34-20.9/N09-43.4	76-40.5/S26-20.4
m,s GHA	12-41.6	13-22.9
final GHA	369-35.8	412-36.7
a λ	058-35.8 W	058-36.7 W
LHA	311	354
t	49 E	6 E
Hs	38-49.0	29-31.9
IE & dip	7.6	7.6
Ha	38-41.4	29-24.3
refr	1.2	1.7
Ho	38-40.2	29-22.6

FROM H.O. PUB. NO. 229, ASSUMING A LATITUDE OF 34 N:

H/d/Z	39-15.1/-35.1/106.3	29-43.8/-59.7/173.8
corr'n	9.7	20.3
Hc/Z	39-05.4/N 106.3 E	29-23.5/N 173.8 E
Ho	38-40.2	29-22.6
a	25.2 away	0.9 away
Zn	106.3	173.8
DR to 0500	+1.4 miles	+0.9 miles
0500 POSITION	33-58.7 N	059-07.3 W

58

KOCHAB	ARCTURUS
08-55-04	08-58-20
4 fast	4 fast
08-55-00	08-58-16
322-33.3	322-33.3
137-16.8/N74-16.9	146-26.5/N19-20.6
13-47.3	14-36.4
113-37.4	123-36.2
058-37.4 W	058-36.2 W
055	065
55 W	65 W
42-05.2	31-39.2
7.6	7.6
41-57.6	31-31.6
1.1	1.6
41-56.5	31-30.0
41-57.5/-24.8/ 17.7	30-53.2/+28.7/ 86.9
7.0	9.9
41-50.5/N 17.7 W	31-03.1/N 86.9 W
41-56.5	31-30.0
6.0 towards	26.9 towards
342.3	273.1
+0.7 miles	+0.3 miles

50-53.   This is either a plotting problem (see Figure 5) or a mid-latitude sailing problem.

0500 DR   34-14.3 N   059-06.8 W

0500 FIX   33-58.7 N   059-07.3 W

$\mathcal{L}$, DLo   15.6 S   0.5 W

Lm = (34-14.3 N) - 15.6/2 = 34-06.5 N

p = DLo (cos Lm) = 0.5 (0.82798) W = 0.41 W

C = arc tan p / $\mathcal{L}$ = S 1.5 W

DRIFT (DISTANCE) = D = $\mathcal{L}$ (sec C) = 15.6 (1.00035) = 15.6 miles

CURRENT SET = Cn = 180 + C = 181.5

DRIFT (SPEED) = 15.6 miles/24 hours = 0.650 knots

54.   This is a great circle sailing problem.

DLo = (059-07.3 W) − (028-50.0 W) = 30-17.3 E = t = 30.29 E

DESTINATION L   = 38-36.0 N = d = 38.60 N

DEPARTURE L   = 33-58.7 N = L = 33.98 N

values	t = 30.29 E	d = 38.60 N	L = 33.98 N
base	30/69.8	38/69.8	33/69.8
next	31/69.9	39/67.5	34/71.9
difference	+0.1	−2.3	+2.1
multiplier	.29	.60	.98
product	+0.03	−1.38	+2.06
			+0.03
			−1.38
increment			+0.71
base			69.8
result, Z =			N 70.5 E
Zn =			070.5

55-56.   This is a current vector and compass conversion
problem. It can be solved graphically or trigonometrically as
shown below.

SET   = 181.5

DRIFT   =   0.650 knots

COURSE TO MAKE GOOD (CMG) = 070.5

LOGGED SPEED   =   8.5

COURSE TO STEER (CTS) = CMG - X

           where sin X = (DRIFT) sin (SET - CMG) / LOGGED SPEED

                       = (0.650) sin (181.5 - 070.5) / 8.5

                       = (0.650) sin (111.0) / 8.5

                       = 0.650 (0.93358) / 8.5

                       = 0.07139

             so, X = 4.09391 degrees

           and CTS = CMG - X

           so, CTS = (070.5 - 4.1) = 066.4

                               V =   18.5 W

                              Cm = 084.9

                             Dev =   1.5 E

                              Cc = 083.4

       To the nearest half degree, Cc = 083½

57-58.   This is a sun sight problem. The sight reduction
is shown below. The plot is shown in Figure 5. (To reduce
this back sight to the observed altitude, you must apply index
error and subtract dip -- as usual. Then you must find the
supplement of this angle so as to get the apparent altitude.
Finally, semi-diameter and refraction corrections are applied
in the usual way.)

FROM THE NAUTICAL ALMANAC, 14 APR 68:

CT	15-16-38
CE	4 fast
GMT	15-16-34
h GHA/d	044-56.9/N09-34.6
m,s GHA/d	4-08.5/0.9=+0.2
final GHA/d	049-05.4/N09-34.8
a λ	058-05.4 W
LHA	351
t	9 E
Hs	116-25.3
IE & dip	7.6
sum	116-17.7
from 180°	180
Ha	63-42.3
main	+15.5
Ho	63-57.8

FROM H.O. PUB. NO. 229, ASSUMING A LATITUDE OF   34 N:

H/d/Z	64-37.3/-57.1/158.9
corr'n	24.0
Hc/Z	64-13.3/N 158.9 E
Ho	63-57.8
a	15.5 away
Zn	158.9

This puts the sun line 3.7 miles to starboard of the 1116½ DR,
and shows a course made good of 070.7 since the 0500 star fix.

59-62.   This is a sun sight problem. The sight reduction
is shown below. The plot is shown in Figure 5.

FROM THE NAUTICAL ALMANAC, 14 APR 68:

CT	18-54-04
CE	0-04 fast
GMT	18-54-00
h GHA/d	089-57.3/N09-37.3
m,s GHA/d	13-30.0/0.9=+0.8
final GHA/d	103-27.3/N09-38.1
a λ	057-27.3 W
LHA	046
t	46 W
Hs	41-16.7
IE & dip	7.6
Ha	41-09.1
main	+14.9
Ho	41-24.0

FROM H.O. PUB. NO. 229, ASSUMING A LATITUDE OF   34 N:

H/d/Z	41-37.5/-35.9/108.6
corr'n	13.1
Hc/Z	41-24.4/N 108.6 W
Ho	41-24.0
a	0.4 away
Zn	251.4

This puts the sun line 79.3 miles ahead of the 0500 star fix.
The speed made good since 0500 is (79.3/9.9) knots = 8.0 knots,
yielding a 1500 EP of 34-25.2 N, 057-35.6 W.

63.   This is a star identification problem. Since the star is bearing due South, its declination and SHA can be determined without reference to sight reduction tables or other devices for its identification.

FROM THE NAUTICAL ALMANAC, 14 APR 68:

CT	23-21-57
CE	0-03 fast
GMT	23-21-54
h GHA	188-10.3
m,s GHA	05-29.4
T GHA	193-39.7
EP λ	056-55.7 W
LHA	136-44.0
from 360°	360
SHA	223-16.0 (approx)
Hs	12-14.9
IE & dip	7.6
H	12-07.3
atmospheric	+0.3
Ha	12-07.6
refr	4.4
Ho	12-03.2
from 90°	90
z	77-56.8
EP L	34-36.8 N
d	43-20.0 S (approx)

The SHA and d show this star to be SUHAIL.

64-65.　　This is a latitude by Polaris problem coupled with regular star and planet sight problems.　The sight reductions are shown below.　The plot is shown in Figure 5.

FROM THE NAUTICAL ALMANAC, 14 APR 68:

Name	POLARIS	DENEBOLA
CT	22-50-17	22-54-30
CE	0-03 fast	0-03 fast
GMT	22-50-14	22-54-27
h GHA/d	173-07.8	173-07.8
v/SHA/d		183-08.1/N14-44.9
m,s GHA	12-35.6	13-39.0
final GHA/d	185-43.4	369-54.9/N14-44.9
EP λ/a λ	057-01.4 W	056-54.9 W
LHA	128-42.	313
t		47 E
Hs	34-37.3	43-33.1
IE & dip	7.6	7.6
H	34-29.7	43-25.5
atmospheric	+0.1	+0.1
Ha	34-29.8	43-25.6
refr	1.4	1.0
Ho	34-28.4	43-24.6
a_0	1-06.9	FROM H.O. PUB. NO. 229,
a_1	0.4	H/d/Z　43-28.7/-33.5/103.2
a_2	0.9	corr'n　-08.4
sum	35-36.6	Hc/Z　43-20.3/N 103.2 E
minus 1°	-1	Ho　43-24.6
L	34-36.6 N	a　4.3 towards
		Zn　103.2
DR to 1900	+1.4 miles	+0.8 miles
EP to 1900	+1.3 miles	+0.7 miles
1900 POSITION		34-37.4 N

```
                    MARS                    SUHAIL
                    22-58-05                23-21-57
                        0-03 fast               0-03 fast
                    22-58-02                23-21-54
                    132-31.2/N15-53.2       188-10.3
                     0.7=+.7/0.6=+0.6       223-17.6/S43-18.4
                    14-30.5                  05-29.4
                    147-02.4/N15-53.8       416-57.3/S43-18.4
                    057-02.4 W              056-57.3 W
                    090                     360
                     90 W                    0
                    09-05.1                 12-14.9
                        7.6                     7.6
                    08-57.5                 12-07.3
                        +0.4                    +0.3
                    08-57.9                 12-07.6
                        5.9                     4.4
                    08-52.0                 12-03.2
ASSUMING A LATITUDE OF 35 N:
                    09-05.8/-33.4/ 76.8     12-00.0/-60.0/180
                       -03.5                   -18.4
                    09-02.3/N 76.8 W        11-41.6/N 180.0 X
                    08-52.0                 12-03.2
                        10.3 away               21.6 towards
                    283.2                   180.0
                       +0.3 miles              -3.1 miles
                       +0.2 miles              -2.9 miles
                    056-55.5 W
```

66-69.   This is either a plotting problem (see Figure 5) or a traverse and mid-latitude sailing problem.

Time Span	Cc	V(W)	Dev	CE(W)	Cn	D(mi)	ℓ (N+)	p (E+)
0500-0600	084	18	1.5 E	16.5	067.5	8.50	3.25	7.85
0600-1116½	083½	18½	1.5 E	17.0	066.5	44.80	17.86	41.08
1116½-1500	083½	18½	1.5 E	17.0	066.5	31.70	12.64	29.07
1500-1900	083½	19	1.5 E	17.5	066.0	34.00	13.83	31.06
0500-1900							47.58	109.06

Lm = (33-58.7 N) + 47.58/2 = 34-22.5 N

DLo = p (sec Lm) = 109.06 (1.21159) = 132.1 E = 2-12.1 E

0500 POSITION	33-58.7 N	059-07.3 W
ℓ, DLo	47.6 N	2-12.1 E
1900 DR	34-46.3 N	056-55.2 W
1900 FIX	34-37.4 N	056-55.5 W
ℓ, DLo	8.9 S	0.3 W

Lm = (34-37.4 N) + 8.9/2 = 34-41.8 N

p = DLo (cos Lm) = 0.3 (0.82218) W = 0.247 W

C = arc tan p / ℓ = S 1.6 W

D = ℓ (sec C) = 8.9 (1.00038) = 8.90 miles

Cn = 180 + C = 181.6

CURRENT SPEED = 8.90 miles/14 hours = 0.636 knots

70.   This is a great circle sailing problem.

DLo = (056-55.5 W) - (028-50.0 W) = 28-05.5 E = t = 28.09 E

DESTINATION L   = 38-36.0 N = d = 38.60 N

DEPARTURE L   = 34-37.4 N = L = 34.62 N

values	t = 28.09 E	d = 38.60 N	L = 34.62 N
base	28/71.8	38/71.8	34/71.8
next	29/71.9	39/69.3	35/74.1
difference	+0.1	-2.5	+2.3
multiplier	.09	.60	.62
product	+0.01	-1.50	+1.43
			+0.01
			-1.50
increment			-0.06
base			71.8
result, Z =			N 71.7 E
Zn =			071.7

71-72.   This is a current vector and compass conversion problem. It can be solved graphically or trigonometrically as shown below.

SET =   181.6
DRIFT =   0.636 knots
COURSE TO MAKE GOOD (CMG) = 071.7
LOGGED SPEED =   8.5 knots

COURSE TO STEER (CTS) = CMG - X

where sin X = (DRIFT) sin (SET - CMG) / LOGGED SPEED

= (0.636) sin (181.6 - 071.7) / 8.5

= (0.636) sin (109.9) / 8.5

= 0.636 (0.94029) / 8.5

= 0.07062

so, X = 4.03442 degrees

and CTS = CMG - X

so, CTS = (071.7 - 4.0) = 067.7

V =   19.5 W

Cm = 087.2

Dev =   1.5 E

Cc = 085.7

To the nearest half degree, Cc = 085½

70

73-75.   These are rising/setting problems dependent on DR which can be plotted (see Figure 6) or done by traverse and mid-latitude sailing.

Time Span	Cc	V(W)	Dev	CE(W)	Cn	D(mi)	∠ (N+)	p (E+)
1900-2000	083½	19	1.5 E	17.5	066.0	8.50	3.46	7.76
2000-2400	085½	19½	1.5 E	18.0	067.5	34.00	13.01	31.41
0000-0430	085½	19½	1.5 E	18.0	067.5	38.25	14.64	35.34
1900-0430							31.11	74.51

$$Lm = (34\text{-}37.4\ N) + 31.11/2 = 34\text{-}53.0\ N$$
$$DLo = p\ (sec\ Lm) = 74.51\ (1.21904)\ E = 90.8\ E = 01\text{-}30.8\ E$$

1900 POSITION	34-37.4 N	056-55.5 W
∠, DLo	31.1 N	01-30.8 E
0430 DR	35-08.5 N	055-24.7 W

FROM THE NAUTICAL ALMANAC, 15 APR 68:

L(N)	N. TWILIGHT	C. TWILIGHT	SUNRISE
40	0419	0453	0521
35	0430	0501	0527
5	11	8	6
corr'n from Table I	0	0	0
LMT	0430	0501	0527
λ corr'n	-18	-19	-19
ZT (to nearest min.)	0412	0442	0508

76-77.   This is an inverted sight reduction problem.

FROM THE NAUTICAL ALMANAC, 15 APR 68:

ZT   05-00

ZD   +4

GMT   09-00

GHA/d   330-40.3/N01-45.5 = N 01.76

DR λ   055-20.3 W

LHA   275-20.0

t   84-40.0 E   =   84.67 E

FROM H.O. PUB. NO. 229, ASSUMING A LATITUDE OF 35-10.2 N:

values	t = 84.67 E	d = 01.76 N	L = 35.17 N
base	84/05-29.2/92.6	01/05-29.2/92.6	35/05-29.2/92.6
next	85/04-40.1/92.1	02/06-03.7/91.8	36/05-26.4/92.7
difference	-49.1/-0.5	+34.5/-0.8	-02.8/+0.1
multiplier	.67	.76	.17
product	-32.9/-0.3	+26.2/-0.6	-00.5/ZERO
	-00.5/ZERO		
	-26.2/-0.6		
increments	-07.2/-0.9		
base	05-29.2/92.6		
result	05-22.0/91.7		

To the nearest whole degree, H = 05, Zn = 092

78-79.   This is either a plotting problem (see Figure 6) or a traverse and mid-latitude sailing problem.

Time Span	Cc	V(W)	Dev	CE(W)	Cn	D(mi)	$\mathcal{L}$ (N+)	p (E+)
1900-2000	083½	19	1.5 E	17.5	066.0	8.50	3.46	7.76
2000-0230	085½	19½	1.5 E	18.0	067.5	55.25	21.14	51.04
1900-0230							24.60	58.80

Lm = (34-37.4 N) + 24.60/2 = 34-49.7 N

DLo = p (sec Lm) = 58.80 (1.21822) E = 71.6 E = 1-11.6 E

1900 POSITION	34-37.4 N	056-55.5 W
$\mathcal{L}$, DLo	24.6 N	1-11.6 E
0230 DR	35-02.0 N	055-43.9 W

80-81.   This is either a plotting problem (see Figure 6) or a mid-latitude sailing problem, along with a compass conversion problem.

0230 DR	35-02.0 N	055-43.9 W
MERLIN's POSITION	35-45 N	056-25 W
$\mathcal{L}$, DLo	43.0 N	41.1 W

Lm = (35-02.0 N) + 43.0/2 = 35-23.5 N

p = DLo (cos Lm) = 41.1 (0.81521) W = 33.5 W

C = arc tan p / $\mathcal{L}$ = N 37.9 W

D = $\mathcal{L}$ (sec C) = 43.0 (1.26773) = 54.5 miles

T = D/T = 54.5 miles/13.5 knots = 4.04 h = 4h 02m

Cn = 360 - C = 322.1   0230 DR = 2h 30m

V =   19.5 W   ETA = 6h 32m

Cm = Cc =   341.6   To the nearest half degree,

Cc =   341½

82-83.   This is a star fix problem. The sight reductions are shown below. The plot is shown in Figure 6.

FROM THE NAUTICAL ALMANAC, 15 APR 68:

Name	ENIF	NUNKI	ALTAIR
CT	08-21-56	08-24-13	08-26-20
CE	0-03 fast	0-03 fast	0-03 fast
GMT	08-21-53	08-24-10	08-26-17
h GHA	323-32.5	323-32.5	323-32.5
SHA/d	34-20.8/N09-43.5	076-40.5/S26-20.4	062-41.6/N08-46.7
m,s GHA	5-29.1	6-03.5	6-35.3
final GHA	363-22.4	405-16.5	392-49.4
a λ	056-22.4 W	056-16.5 W	055-49.4 W
LHA	307	349	337
t	53 E	11 E	23 E
Hs	36-04.0	27-42.0	56-13.5
IE & dip	7.6	7.6	7.6
Ha	35-56.4	27-34.4	56-05.9
refr	1.3	1.9	0.7
Ho	35-55.1	27-32.5	56-05.2

FROM H.O. PUB. NO. 229, ASSUMING A LATITUDE OF 35 N:

	ENIF	NUNKI	ALTAIR
H/d/Z	35-48.6/-35.2/104.1	28-07.1/-59.1/168.8	56-33.7/-48.6/135.5
corr'n	-09.7	-20.1	-10.8
Hc/Z	35-38.9/N 104.1 E	27-47.0/N 168.8 E	56-22.9/N 135.5 E
Ho	35-55.1	27-32.5	56-05.2
a	16.2 towards	14.5 away	17.7 away
Zn	104.1	168.8	135.5
DR to 0430	+1.8 miles	+1.3 miles	+0.8 miles

0430 POSITION   35-19.1 N   055-58.6 W

74

KOCHAB	ALKAID	ARCTURUS
08-29-02	08-34-15	08-36-41
0-03 fast	0-03 fast	0-03 fast
08-28-59	08-34-12	08-36-38
323-32.5	323-32.5	323-32.5
137-16.8/N74-16.9	153-25.0/N49-28.2	146-26.5/N19-20.6
7-15.9	8-34.4	9-11.0
108-05.2	125-31.9	119-10.0
056-05.2 W	055-31.9 W	056-10.0 W
052	070	063
52 W	70 W	63 W
43-56.5	38-49.0	32-46.0
7.6	7.6	7.6
43-48.9	38-41.4	32-38.4
1.0	1.2	1.5
43-47.9	38-40.2	32-36.9

43-39.5/-27.4/ 17.5	38-04.5/+12.2/ 51.5	32-34.3/+29.8/ 88.6
-07.7	+05.7	+10.2
43-31.8/N 17.5 W	38-10.2/N 51.5 W	32-44.5/N 88.6 W
43-47.9	38-40.2	32-36.9
16.1 towards	30.0 towards	7.6 away
342.5	308.5	271.4
+0.2 miles	-0.9 miles	-1.5 miles

84.   This is an amplitude and compass conversion
problem.

ZT	0512	
ZD	+4	
GMT	09-12	
h d	N 09-50.7	
+.9	+0.2	
final d	N 09-50.9 = N 09.85	
DR L	35-26.2 N = 35.44 N	
values	d = 09.85 N	L = 35.44 N
base	10/12.4	36/12.4
next	9.5/11.8	34/12.1
difference	-0.6	-0.3
multiplier	.30	.28
product	-.180	-.084
		-.180
increment		-.264
base		12.4
result		E 12.1 N
from 90°		090
azimuth		077.9
bearing		097.9
compass error		20.0 W
variation		19.5 W
deviation		0.5 W

85-86.   This is either a plotting problem (see Figure 6) or a traverse and mid-latitude sailing problem.

Time Span	Cc	V(W)	Dev	CE(W)	Cn	D(mi)	$\angle$ (N+)	p (E+)
0230-0430	341½	19½	0.5 W	20.0	321.5	27.00	21.13	-16.81

Lm = (35-02.1 N) + 21.13/2 = 35-12.7 N

DLo = p (sec Lm) = 16.81 (1.22395) W = 20.6 W

0230 DR	35-02.1 N	055-43.9 W
$\angle$, DLo	21.1 N	20.6 W
0430 DR	35-23.2 N	056-04.5 W
0430 FIX	35-19.1 N	055-58.6 W
$\angle$, DLo	4.1 S	5.9 E

Lm = (35-18.8 N) + 4.1/2 = 35-20.85 N

p = DLo (cos Lm) = 5.9 (0.81566) E = 4.8 E

C = arc tan p / $\angle$ = S 49.6 E

D = $\angle$ (sec C) = 4.1 (1.54198) = 6.32 miles

SET = Cn = 180 - C = 130.4

DRIFT (SPEED) = 6.32 miles/9.5 hours = 0.665 knots

87.   This is either a plotting problem (see Figure 6) or a traverse and mid-latitude sailing problem.

Time Span	Cc	V(W)	Dev	CE(W)	Cn	D(mi)	l (N+)	p (E+)
0430-0800	341½	19½	0.5 W	20.0	321.5	47.25	36.98	-29.41

Lm = (35-19.1 N) + 36.98/2 = 35-37.6 N

DLo = p (sec Lm) = 29.41 (1.23027) W = 36.2 W

0430 FIX	35-19.1 N	055-58.6 W
l, DLo	37.0 N	36.2 W
0800 DR	35-56.1 N	056-34.8 W
NEW DATUM	35-53.5 N	055-58.5 W
l, DLo	2.6 S	36.3 E

Lm = (35-53.5 N) + 2.6/2 = 35-54.8 N

p = DLo (cos Lm) = 36.3 (0.80990) E = 29.4 E

C = arc tan p / l = S 84.9 E

D = l (sec C) = 2.6 (11.35166) = 29.51 miles

T = D/S = 29.51 miles/13.5 knots = 2h 11m

Cn = 180 - C = 095.1

            V = 19.5 W

     Cc = Cm = 114.6   To the nearest half degree,

            Cc = 114½

88-89.   This is a LAN sight problem.

FROM THE NAUTICAL ALMANAC, 15 APR 68:

CT	15-43-45
CE	0-03 fast
GMT	15-43-42
EqT/h d	ZERO/N09-56.1
GAT/m,s d	15-43-42/0.9=+0.7
12h/final d	12 h /N09-56.8
λ in time	3-43-42
λ in arc	055-55.5 W
Hs	63-53.4
IE & dip	7.6
Ha	63-45.8
main	+15.5
Ho	64-01.3
from 90°	90
z	25-58.7
d	N09-56.8
L	35-55.5 N

90-91.   This is either a plotting problem (see Figure 6) or a traverse and mid-latitude sailing problem.

Time Span	Cc	V(W)	Dev	CE(W)	Cn	D(mi)	∠ (N+)	p (E+)
1143½–1200	071½	19½	2.0 E	17.5	054.0	3.66	2.15	2.96
1200–1348	161½	19½	ZERO	19.5	142.0	24.30	-19.15	14.96
1348–1400	065	19½	2.0 E	17.5	047.5	2.70	1.82	1.99
RADAR					047.5	7.50	5.07	5.53
1143½–1436							-10.11	25.44

Lm = (35-55.5 N) - 10.11/2 = 35-50.4 N

DLo = p (sec Lm) = 25.44 (1.23357) E = 31.4 E

1143½ FIX   35-55.5 N   055-55.5 W

∠, DLo   10.1 S   31.4 E

VESSEL'S POSITION   35-45.4 N   055-24.1 W

92-93.   This is either a plotting problem (see Figure 6) or a traverse and mid-latitude sailing problem.

Time Span	Cc	V(W)	Dev	CE(W)	Cn	D(mi)	∠ (N+)	p (E+)
1436–1642	ESTIMATED DRIFT				130.4	1.40	-0.91	1.07
1642–1700	265	19½	ZERO	19.5	245.5	2.60	-1.08	-2.36
1436–1642							-1.99	-1.29

Lm = (35-45.4 N) - 1.99/2 = 35-44.4 N

DLo = p (sec Lm) = 1.29 (1.23202) W = 1.6 W

1436 DR   35-45.4 N   055-24.1 W

∠, DLo   2.0 S   1.6 W

1700 EP   35-43.4 N   055-25.7 W

94-98.   These are Mercator sailing problems along with a compass conversion problem.

	$\underline{L}$	$\underline{M}$	$\underline{\lambda}$
1700 EP	35-43.4 N	2,284.1	055-25.7 W
St. David's	32-22. N	2,042.1	064-39. W
$\mathcal{L}$, m, DLo	3-21.4 S	242.0 S	(9-13.3 W)
	201.4 S		553.3 W

$$C = \text{arc tan } DLo/m = \text{arc tan } 553.3/242.0 = S\ 66.4\ W$$
$$Cn = 180 + C = 180 + 66.4 = 246.4$$
$$V = 19.5\ W$$
$$Cm = 265.9$$

To the nearest half degree, $Cm = 266$

On $Cc = 266$, $D = \mathcal{L}$ (sec C) = 201.4 (2.50784) miles = 505.1 miles

Helicopter range = 300. miles

Distance from 1700 EP to rendezvous = 205.1 miles

Time to rendezvous = 205.1 miles/10.4 knots = 19.72 hours

ETA at rendezvous = 17.00 hours + 19.72 hours

= 1243 on 16 APR 68

$\mathcal{L}$ = D (cos C) = 205.1 (0.39875) S = 81.78 S = 1-21.8 S

rendezvous L = (35-43.4 N) - (1-21.8 S) = 34-21.6 N

rendezvous M = 2,184.6

1700 M = 2,284.1

m = 99.5 S

DLo = m (tan C) = 99.5 (2.29984) W = 228.8 W = 3-48.8 W

rendezvous λ = (055-25.7 W) + (3-48.8 W) = 059-14.5 W

99-100.   These are operations problems.

Date (APR 68)	Time Span	Hours	Speed (knots)	Fuel Consumption Rate(gph)	Amount(gal)
12	1600-1800	2.0	var	12	24.0
12	1800-2400	6.0	8.5	12	72.0
13	0000-2400	24.0	8.5	12	288.0
14	0000-2400	24.0	8.5	12	288.0
15	0000-0230	2.5	8.5	12	30.0
15	0230-1430	12.0	13.5	22	264.0
15	1430-1642	2.2	var	12	26.4
15	1642-2400	7.3	10.4	16	116.8
16	0000-1243	12.7	10.4	16	203.2
15-16	FUEL TO MERLIN				65.0
12-16	FUEL CONSUMED				1,377.4
12	FUEL AT START				3,761.
16	1243	FUEL REMAINING			2,383.6

original passage distance   1,776. miles
rendezvous distance from Bermuda   300. miles
remaining passage distance   1,476. miles
passage speed   8.5 knots
remaining passage duration
(including 1½ hours for both rendezvous)   175.1 hours
fuel consumption rate   12   gallons/hour
fuel required   2,101.2 gallons
projected fuel remaining at rendezvous   2,383.6 gallons
fuel balance on arrival at Fayal   282.4 gallons
% safety margin   11.8 %

82

101-103.   This is a great-circle sailing problem along with a time and operations problem.

DLo = (059-14.5 W) - (031-08.0 W) = 28-06.5 E = t = 28.11 E

DESTINATION L   = 39-27.0 N = d = 39.45 N

DEPARTURE L   = 34-21.6 N = L = 34.36 N

values	t = 28.11 E	d = 39.45 N	L = 34.36 N
base	28/67-02.4/69.3	39/67-02.4/69.3	34/67-02.4/69.3
next	29/66-15.9/69.4	40/66-57.2/66.7	35/67-22.6/71.5
difference	-46.5/+0.1	-05.2/-2.6	+20.2/+2.2
multiplier	.11	.45	.36
product	-05.1/ZERO	-02.3/-1.2	+07.3/+0.8
		-05.1/ZERO	90-00.0
		+07.3/+0.8	67-02.3
increments		-00.1/-0.4	22-57.7 = 1,377.7 mi.
base		67-02.4/69.3	Z = N 68.9 E
result		67-02.3/68.9	Zn = 068.9

DEPARTURE ZONE DATE/TIME   = 16 APR/13 h 30 m

ZONE DESCRIPTION   =   +4

DEPARTURE GMT DATE/TIME   = 16 APR/17 h 30 m

PASSAGE DURATION, STEAMING   = 1,377.7 miles/8.5 knots = 162.08 hours

                             = 162 h 05 m = 6 d 18 h 05 m

MERLIN RENDEZVOUS/TRANSFER   = 0.72 h   =   43 m

TOTAL PASSAGE DURATION   = 162.60 h   = 6 d 18 h 48 m

DEPARTURE GMT DATE/TIME   =   16 d 17 h 30 m

ARRIVAL GMT DATE/TIME   =   22 d 36 h 18 m

                             = 23 APR/12 h 18 m

TOTAL PASSAGE DURATION   = 162.60 h

CONSUMPTION RATE AT 8.5 KNOTS = 12 gallons/hour

FUEL REQUIRED FOR PASSAGE   = 1,951.2 gallons

FUEL AT START OF PASSAGE   = 2,383.6 gallons

PROJECTED FUEL REMAINING   =   432.4 gallons

% SAFETY MARGIN   = 18.1%

104-105.   This is a sun sight/running fix/LAN sight problem.
The sight reductions are shown below.   The plot is shown in
Figure 7.

FROM THE NAUTICAL ALMANAC, 16 APR 68:

CT	15-15-14	CT	15-55-27
CE	0-02 fast	CE	0-02 fast
GMT	15-15-12	GMT	15-55-25
h GHA/d	045-04.2/N 10-17.4	EqT/h d	00-15/N 10-17.4
m,s GHA/d	3-48.0/0.9= +0.2	GAT/m,s d	15-55-40/0.9= +0.8
final GHA/d	048-52.2/N 10-17.6	12h/final d 12h	/N 10-18.2
a λ	058-52.2 W	λ in time	3-55-40
LHA	350	λ in arc	058-55.0
t	10 E		
Hs	64-06.2	Hs	65-48.8
IE & dip	7.6	IE & dip	7.6
Ha	63-58.6	Ha	65-41.2
main	15.5	main	+15.5
Ho	64-14.1	Ho	65-56.7
FROM H.O. PUB. NO. 229,		from 90°	90-00.0
ASSUMING A LATITUDE OF 34 N:		z	24-03.3
H/d/Z	64-18.5/+56.5/156.8	d	N 10-18.2
corr'n	+16.6	L	34-21.5 N
Hc/Z	64-35.1/N 156.8 E		
Ho	64-14.1		
a	21.0 away		
Zn	156.8		

All of these lines of position, when advanced to 1200 (+4),
yield a position of 34-21.1 N, 058-55.8 W

106-107.   This is a traverse and mid-latitude sailing problem.

Time Span	Cc	V(W)	Dev	CE(W)	Cn	D(mi)	L (N+)	p (E+)
1143½-1200	071½	19½	2.0 E	17.5	054.0	3.66	2.15	2.96
1200-1348	161½	19½	ZERO	19.5	142.0	24.30	-19.15	14.96
1348-1400	065	19½	2.0 E	17.5	047.5	2.70	1.82	1.99
1400-1436	065	19½	2.0 E	17.5	047.5	7.50	5.07	5.53
1436-1642	STOPPED, DRIFTING							
1642-1730	265	19½	ZERO	19.5	245.5	7.80	-3.23	-7.10
1730-2400	266	19½	ZERO	19.5	246.5	67.60	-26.96	-61.99
0000-1200	265½	19	ZERO	19.0	246.5	124.80	-49.76	-114.45
1143½-1200							-90.06	-158.10
							(1-30.06S)	(158.10W)

Lm = (35-55.5 N) − 90.06/2 = 35-10.5 N

DLo = p (sec Lm) = 158.10 (1.22340) W = 193.4 W = 003-13.4 W

1143½ POSITION	35-55.5 N	055-55.5 W
L, DLo	01-30.1 S	003-13.4 W
1200 DR	34-25.4 N	059-08.9 W
1200 POSITION	34-21.1 N	058-55.8 W
L, DLo	4.3 S	13.1 E

Lm = (34-21.1 N) + 4.3/2 = 34-23.2 N

p = DLo (cos Lm) = 13.1 (0.82524) E = 10.8 E

C = arc tan p / L = S 68.3 E

D = L (sec C) = 4.3 (2.70570) = 11.63 miles

Cn = 180 − C = 180 − 68.3 = 111.7 = SET

CURRENT SPEED = 11.63 miles/24.3 hours = 0.479 knots

108.   This is a series of traverse and mid-latitude sailing problems.

Time Span	Cc	V(W)	Dev	CE(W)	Cn	D(mi)	ι (N+)	p (E+)
1200–1236	265½	19	ZERO	19.0	246.5	6.24	-2.49	-5.72
1236–1248	285	19	ZERO	19.0	266.0	0.90	-0.06	-0.90
1200–1248							-2.55	-6.62

Lm = (34-25.5 N) - 2.55/2 = 34-24.2 N

DLo = p (sec Lm) = 6.62 (1.21201) W = 8.02 W

PEREGRINE 1200 DR		34-25.5 N	059-08.9 W
ι, DLo		2.6 S	8.0 W
PEREGRINE 1248 DR		34-22.9 N	059-16.9 W

Time Span	Cn	D(mi)	ι (N+)	p (E+)
1642–1700	245.5	1.85	-0.77	-1.68
1700–2400	246.5	52.50	-20.93	-48.14
0000–1248	246.5	96.00	-38.28	-88.04
1642–1248			-59.98	-137.86

Lm = (35-45.4 N) - 59.98/2 = 35-15.4 N

DLo = p (sec Lm) = 137.86 (1.22463) W = 168.8 W = 002-48.8 W

MERLIN 1642 DR	35-45.4 N	055-24.1 W
ι, DLo	01-00.0 S	002-48.8 W
MERLIN 1248 DR	34-45.4 N	058-12.9 W
PEREGRINE 1248 DR	34-22.9 N	059-16.9 W
ι, DLo	22.5 S	1-04.0 W

Lm = (34-22.9 N) + 22.5/2 = 34-34.2 N

p = DLo (cos Lm) = 64.0 (0.82343) W = 52.7 W

C = arc tan p / ι = S 66.9 W

and its reciprocal yields Cn = 066.9

D = ι (sec C) = 22.5 (2.54883) = 57.35 miles

109-110.   This is either a plotting problem (see Figure 7) or a traverse and mid-latitude sailing problem.

Time Span	Cc	V(W)	Dev	CE(W)	Cn	D(mi)	L (N+)	p (E+)
1200-1248	VARIOUS (see previous traverse)						-2.55	-6.62
1248-1630	085	19	1.5 E	17.5	067.5	31.45	12.04	29.06
1200-1630							9.49	22.44

Lm = (34-21.1 N) + 9.49/2 = 34-25.9 N

DLo = p (sec Lm) = 22.44 (1.21241) E = 27.2 E

1200 POSITION	34-21.1 N	058-55.8 W
L, DLo	9.5 N	27.2 E
1630 DR	34-30.6 N	058-28.6 W

	Cn	D(mi)	L (N+)	p (E+)
CURRENT (111.7/0.479 kn)	111.7	2.16	-0.80	2.01

DLo = p (sec Lm) = 2.01 (1.21241) E = 2.44 E

1630 DR	34-30.6 N	058-28.6 W
CURRENT	.8 S	2.4 E
1630 EP	34-29.8 N	058-26.2 W

111.   This is a great circle sailing problem.

DLo = (058-26.2 W) - (031-08.0 W) = 27-18.2 E = t = 27.30 E

DESTINATION L   = 39-27.0 N = d = 39.45 N

DEPARTURE L   = 34-29.8 N = L = 34.50 N

values	t = 27.30 E	d = 39.45 N	L = 34.50 N
base	27/69.1	39/69.1	34/69.1
next	28/69.3	40/66.5	35/71.5
difference	+0.2	−2.6	+2.4
multiplier	.30	.45	.50
product	+0.06	−1.17	+1.20
			+0.06
			−1.17
increments			+0.09
base			69.1
result, Z=			N 69.2 E
Zn =			069.2

88

112.   This is a current vector and compass conversion problem. It can be solved graphically or trigonometrically as shown below.

SET   = 111.7

DRIFT   =   0.479 knots

COURSE TO MAKE GOOD (CMG) = 069.2

LOGGED SPEED   =   8.5 knots

COURSE TO STEER (CTS) = CMG − X

      where sin X = (DRIFT) sin (SET − CMG) / LOGGED SPEED

                 = (0.479) sin (111.7 − 069.2) / 8.5

                 = (0.479) sin (42.5) / 8.5

                 = 0.479 (0.67559) / 8.5

                 = 0.03807

        so, X = 2.18186 degrees

       and CTS = CMG − X

       so, CTS = (069.2 − 2.2)

           Cn = 067.0

            V =   19.5 W

          Cm = 086.5

        Dev =   1.5 E

          Cc = 085.0

113-114. This is a traverse and mid-latitude sailing problem.

Time Span	Cc	V(W)	Dev	CE(W)	Cn	D(mi)	∠ (N+)	p (E+)
1630–1724	STOPPED, DRIFTING							
1724–1800	086½	19	1.5 E	17.5	069.0	5.10	1.83	4.76
1800–2400	085	19½	1.5 E	18.0	067.0	51.00	19.93	46.94
0000–1106	085	19½	1.5 E	18.0	067.0	94.38	36.88	86.88
1630–1106							58.64	138.58

Lm = (34–30.6 N) + 58.64/2 = 34–59.9 N

DLo = p (sec Lm) = 138.58 (1.22075) E = 169.2 E = 002–49.2 E

1630 DR	34–30.6 N	058–28.6 W
∠, DLo	58.6 N	002–49.2 E
1106 DR	35–29.2 N	055–39.4 W

90

115-116.   This is a sun sight problem. The sight reduction
is shown below. The plot is shown in Figure 8.

FROM THE NAUTICAL ALMANAC, 17 APR 68:

CT	15-06-15
CE	0-01 fast
GMT	15-06-14
h GHA/d	045-07.7/N10-38.5
m,s GHA/d	1-34.0/0.9=+0.1
final GHA/d	046-41.7/N10-38.6=10.64N
DR λ	055-39.4 W
LHA	351-02.3
t	8-57.7E = 8.96E
Hs	64-00.
IE & dip	-1.7
Ha	63-58.3
refr	-0.5
Ho	63-57.8

FROM H.O. PUB. NO. 229, USING A LATITUDE OF 35-29.2 N = 35.49 N:

values	t = 8.96 E	d = 10.64 N	L = 35.49 N
base	8/63-57.4/161.8	10/63-57.4/161.8	35/63-57.4/161.8
next	9/63-41.1/159.7	11/64-55.2/161.2	36/63-00.3/162.4
difference	-16.3/ -2.1	+57.8/ -0.6	-57.1/ +0.6
multiplier	.96	.64	.49
product	-15.6/ -2.0	+37.0/ -0.4	-28.0/ +0.3
	-28.0/ +0.3		
	+37.0/ -0.4	Lm	= (35-29.2 N) - 6.57/2 = 35-25.9 N
increments	-06.6/ -1.9	DLo	= p (sec Lm) = 2.40 (1.22728) E
			= 2.94
base	63-57.4/161.8		
Hc/Z	63-50.8/N159.9E	1106 DR	35-29.2 N 055-39.4 W
Ho/Zn	63-57.8/159.9	∠, DLo	6.6 S 2.9 E
a	7.0 towards,	1106 EP	35-22.6 N 055-36.5 W

yielding: ∠ = -6.57 and p = 2.40

117-118.   This is a mid-latitude sailing problem.

1630 EP   34-29.8 N   058-26.2 W
1106 EP   35-22.6 N   055-36.5 W
L, DLo   52.8 N   2-49.7 E = 169.7 E
Lm = (34-29.8 N) + 52.8/2 = 34-56.2 N
p = DLo (cos Lm) = 169.7 (0.81978) E = 139.1 E
C = arc tan p / L = N 69.2 E, yielding Cn = 069.2
D = L (sec C) = 52.8 (2.81819) = 148.8 miles

92

119-120.   This is a sun sight problem. The sight reduction is shown below. The plot is shown in Figure 8.

FROM THE NAUTICAL ALMANAC, 17 APR 68:

CT	18-36-23		
CE	0-01 fast		
GMT	18-36-22		
h GHA/d	090-08.1/N10-41.1	Hs	42-38.
m,s GHA/d	9-05.5/0.9=+0.5	IE & dip	-1.7
final GHA/d	099-13.6/N10-41.6 = 10.69N	Ha	42-36.3
1106 λ	055-36.5 W	refr	-1.0
LHA	043-37.1	Ho	42-35.3
t	43-37.1 W = 43.62 W		

FROM H.O. PUB. NO. 229, USING THE 1106 LATITUDE = 35-22.6 N = 35.38 N:

values	t = 43.62 W	d = 10.69 N	L = 35.38 N
base	43/43-35.9/112.0	10/43-35.9/112.0	35/43-35.9/112.0
next	44/42-50.1/111.1	11/44-13.7/110.9	36/43-13.0/112.8
difference	-45.8/ -0.9	+37.8/ -1.1	-22.9/ +0.8
multiplier	.62	.69	.38
product	-28.4/ -0.6	+26.1/ -0.8	-08.7/ +0.3
	+26.1/ -0.8		
	-08.7/ +0.3		
increments	-11.0/ -1.1		
base	43-35.9/112.0		
Hc/Z	43-24.9/N 110.9 W		
Ho/Zn	42-35.3/249.1		
a	49.6 away		
1630-1106	148.8 miles	So, the speed made good equals	
1630-1436½	198.4 miles	198.4 miles/22.10 hours = 8.976 knots	

121-122.   This is either a plotting problem (see Figure 8)
or a mid-latitude sailing problem.

1106-1436½ DISTANCE = 49.6 miles

1436½-1500 DISTANCE = 8.976 knots (0.3958 hours) = 3.6 miles

1106-1500 DISTANCE = 53.2 miles

1106-1500 COURSE = 069.2

1106-1500 $\mathcal{L}$ = D (cos C) = 53.2 (0.35511) = 18.89 N

1106-1500 p = D (sin C) = 53.2 (0.93482) = 49.73 E

Lm = (35-22.6 N) + 18.89/2 = 35-32.0 N

DLo = p (sec Lm) = 49.73 (1.22884) E = 61.1 E = 001-01.1 E

1106 EP	35-22.6 N	055-36.5 W
$\mathcal{L}$, DLo	18.9 N	1-01.1 E
1500 EP	35-41.5 N	054-35.4 W

123–124.   This is a traverse and mid-latitude sailing problem.

Time Span	Cc	V(W)	Dev	CE(W)	Cn	D(mi)	∠ (N+)	p (E+)
1106–1500	085	19½	1.5 E	18.0	067.0	33.11	12.94	30.48

Lm = (35–29.2 N) + 12.94/2 = 35–35.7 N

DLo = p (sec Lm) = 30.48 (1.22978) E = 37.5 E

1106 DR		35–29.2 N	055–39.4 W
∠, DLo		12.9 N	37.5 E
1500 DR		35–42.1 N	055–01.9 W
1500 EP		35–41.5 N	054–35.4 W
∠, DLo		0.6 S	26.5 E

Lm = (35–42.1 N) – 0.6/2 = 35–41.8 N

p = DLo (cos Lm) = 26.5 (0.81212) E = 21.5 E

C = arc tan p / ∠ = S 88.4 E, yielding Cn = 091.6

D = ∠ (sec C) = 0.6 (35.88247) = 21.53 miles

CURRENT SPEED = 21.5 miles/27.0 hours = 0.797 knots

125.   This is a great circle sailing problem.

DLo = (054-35.4 W) - (031-08.0 W) = 023-27.4 E = t = 23.46 E

DESTINATION L   =   39-27.0 N = d = 39.45 N

DEPARTURE L   =   35-41.5 N = L = 35.69 N

values	t = 23.46 E	d = 39.45 N	L = 35.69 N
base	23/70.9	39/70.9	35/70.9
next	24/71.1	40/67.8	36/73.7
difference	+0.2	-3.1	+2.8
multiplier	.46	.45	.69
product	+0.09	-1.40	+1.93
	-1.40		
	+1.93		
increment	+0.62		
base	70.9		
result, Z =	71.5		
Zn =	071.5		

126.   This is a current vector and compass conversion problem. It can be solved graphically or trigonometrically as shown below.

SET   = 091.6

DRIFT   =   0.797 knots

COURSE TO MAKE GOOD (CMG) = 071.5

LOGGED SPEED   =   8.5 knots

COURSE TO STEER (CTS) = CMG − X

$\qquad$ where sin X = (DRIFT) sin (SET − CMG) / LOGGED SPEED

$\qquad\qquad$ = (0.797) sin (091.6 − 071.5) / 8.5

$\qquad\qquad$ = (0.797) sin (20.1) / 8.5

$\qquad\qquad$ = 0.797 (0.34366) / 8.5

$\qquad\qquad$ = 0.03222

$\qquad$ so, X = 1.84657 degrees

$\qquad$ and CTS = CMG − X

$\qquad$ so, CTS = (071.5 − 1.8) = 069.7

$\qquad\qquad\qquad$ V = 20.0 W

$\qquad\qquad\qquad$ Cm = 089.7

$\qquad\qquad\qquad$ Dev =   1.5 E

$\qquad\qquad\qquad$ Cc = 088.2

$\qquad$ To the nearest ½ degree, Cc = 088

127-128.   This is a traverse and mid-latitude sailing problem.

Time Span	Cc	V(W)	Dev	CE(W)	Cn	D(mi)	$\angle$ (N+)	p (E+)
1500-1600	085	20	1.5 E	18.5	066.5	8.50	3.39	7.80
1600-1200	088	20	1.5 E	18.5	069.5	166.60	58.34	156.05
1500-1200							61.73	163.85

Lm = (35-42.1 N) + 61.73/2 = 36-13.0 N

DLo = p (sec Lm) = 163.85 (1.23948) E = 203.1 E = 3-23.1 E

1500 DR	35-42.1 N	055-01.9 W
$\angle$, DLo	1-01.7 N	3-23.1 E
1200 DR	36-43.8 N	051-38.8 W

129-130.   This is a mid-latitude sailing problem.

1500-1200   CURRENT SET = 091.6 = C

1500-1200   CURRENT DRIFT (SPEED) = 1.1 (0.797) knots

1500-1200   CURRENT DRIFT (DISTANCE) = (20 hours) 1.1 (0.797) knots

$$D = 17.534 \text{ miles}$$

$\angle$ = D (cos C) = 17.5 (-0.02792) = 0.49 S

p = D (sin C) = 17.5 (0.99961) = 17.49 E

Lm = (36-43.8 N) - 0.49/2 = 36-43.6 N

DLo = p (sec Lm) = 17.49 (1.24766) E = 21.8 E

1200 DR	36-43.8 N	051-38.8 W
$\angle$, DLo	0.5 S	21.8 E
1200 EP	36-43.3 N	051-17.0 W

131.   This is a great circle sailing problem.

DLo = (051-17.0 W) - (031-08.0 W) = 020-09.0 E = t = 20.15 E
DESTINATION L   = 39-27.0 N = d = 39.45 N
DEPARTURE L   = 36-43.3 N = L = 36.72 N
values   t = 20.15 E   d = 39.45 N   L = 36.72 N
base   20/73.3   39/73.3   36/73.3
next   21/73.5   40/69.7   37/76.6
difference   +0.2   -3.6   +3.3
multiplier   .15   .45   .72
product   +0.03   -1.62   +2.38
                     -1.62
                     +2.38
increment   +0.79
base   73.3
result, Z =   74.1
      Zn =   074.1

132.   This is a current vector and compass conversion problem. It can be solved graphically or trigonometrically as shown below.

SET   = 091.6
DRIFT   =   0.877 knots
COURSE TO MAKE GOOD (CMG) = 074.1
LOGGED SPEED   =   9.1 knots

COURSE TO STEER (CTS) = CMG − X
            where sin X = (DRIFT) sin (SET − CMG) / LOGGED SPEED
                  = (0.877) sin (091.6 − 074.1) / 9.1
                  = (0.877) sin (17.5) / 9.1
                  = 0.877 (0.30070) / 9.1
                  = 0.02898
          so, X = 1.66067 degrees
         and CTS = CMG − X
         so, CTS = (074.1 − 1.7) = 072.4
                                V =   20.5 W
                               Cm = 092.9
                              Dev =   1.5 E
                               Cc = 091.4
      To the nearest ½ degree, Cc = 091½

133-134.   This is either a plotting problem (see Figure 9) or a traverse and mid-latitude sailing problem.

Time Span	Cc	V(W)	Dev	CE(W)	Cn	D(mi)	$\angle$ (N+)	p (E+)
1200-1900	091½	20½	1.5 E	19.0	072.5	62.30	18.73	59.42
1900-1930	091½	20½	1.5 E	19.0	072.5	4.35	1.31	4.15
1200-1930							20.04	63.57

Lm = (36-43.8 N) + 20.04/2 = 36-53.8 N

DLo = p (sec Lm) = 63.57 (1.25044) E = 79.5 E = 1-19.5 E

1200 DR		36-43.8 N	051-38.8 W
$\angle$, DLo		20.0 N	1-19.5 E
1930 DR		37-03.8 N	050-19.3 W

135-136. This is a star fix problem. The sight reductions are shown below. The plot is shown in Figure 9.

FROM THE NAUTICAL ALMANAC, 18 APR 68:

Name	REGULUS	SIRIUS
CT	22-26-40	22-28-54
CE	ZERO	ZERO
GMT	22-26-40	22-28-54
h GHA	177-04.4	177-04.4
SHA/d	208-19.6/N12-07.4	259-04.0/S16-40.3
m,s GHA	6-41.1	7-14.7
final GHA	392-05.1	083-23.1
a λ	050-05.1 W	050-23.1 W
LHA	342	033
t	18 E	33 W
Hs	60-34.9	27-57.1
IE & dip	7.7	7.7
Ha	60-27.2	27-49.4
refr	0.6	1.8
Ho	60-26.6	27-47.6

FROM H.O. PUB. NO. 229, ASSUMING A LATITUDE OF 37 N:

H/d/Z	60-14.1/+51.9/142.5	27-41.0/+52.4/144.0
corr'n	+06.4	+17.2
Hc/Z	60-20.5/N 142.5 E	27-58.2/N 144.0 W
Ho	60-26.6	27-47.6
a	6.1 towards	10.6 away
Zn	142.5	216.0
DR to 1930	+0.5 mile	+0.2 mile
1930 POSITION	36-58.8 N	049-56.2 W

```
ALIOTH                      MIRFAK
22-34-17                    22-36-53
     ZERO                        ZERO
22-34-17                    22-36-53
117-04.4                    117-04.4
166-49.7/N56-07.9           309-30.0/N49-45.1
 8-35.7                      9-14.8
352-29.8                    135-49.2
050-29.8 W                  049-49.2 W
302                         086
 58 E                        86 W

47-49.0                     29-55.0
  7.7                          7.7
47-41.3                     29-47.3
  0.9                          1.7
47-40.4                     29-45.6


47-21.4/-01.8/044.4         29-47.4/-23.6/047.6
 -00.2                       -05.9
47-21.2/N 044.4 E           29-41.5/N 047.6 W
47-40.4                     29-45.6
  19.2 towards                4.1 towards
 044.4                       312.4
 -0.6 mile                   -1.0 mile
```

137-138.   This is either a plotting problem (see Figure 9) or a mid-latitude sailing problem.

1930 DR   37-03.8 N   050-19.3 W

1930 FIX   36-58.8 N   049-56.2 W

ℓ, DLo   5.0 S   23.1 E

Lm = (37-03.8 N) - 5.0/2 = 37-01.3 N

p = DLo (cos Lm) = 23.1 (0.79841) E = 18.4 E

C = arc tan p / ℓ = S 74.8 E

D = ℓ (sec C) = 5.0 (3.82179) = 19.11 miles

SET = Cn = 180 - C = 105.2

DRIFT (SPEED) = 19.11 miles/54.5 hours = 0.351 knots

139.   This is a great circle sailing problem.

DLo = (049-56.2 W) - (031-08.0 W) = 18-48.2 E = t = 18.80 E

DESTINATION L   = 39-27.0 N = d = 39.45 N

DEPARTURE L   = 36-58.8 N = L = 36.98 N

values	t = 18.80 E	d = 39.45 N	L = 36.98 N
base	18/72.7	39/72.7	36/72.7
next	19/73.0	40/68.8	37/76.5
difference	+0.3	-3.9	+3.8
multiplier	.80	.45	.98
product	+0.24	-1.76	+3.72
	-1.76		
	+3.72		
increments	+2.20		
base	72.7		
result, Z =	N 74.9 E		
Zn =	074.9		

140.   This is an azimuth (by inspection tables) and
compass conversion problem.

CT	22-45-00		
CE	ZERO		
GMT	22-45-00		
h GHA	177-04.0		
SHA/d	259-04.0/S 16-40.3 = S 16.67		
m,s GHA	11-16.8		
final GHA	087-24.8		
DR λ	049-53.7 W		
LHA	037-31.1		
t	37-31.1 W	=	37.52 W
DR L	36-59.6 N	=	36.99 N
values	t = 37.52 W	d = 16.67 S	L = 36.99 N
base	37/139.4	16/139.4	36/139.4
next	38/138.5	17/140.0	37/139.7
difference	-0.9	+0.6	+0.3
multiplier	.52	.67	.99
product	-0.47	+0.40	+0.30
	+0.40		
	+0.30		Z = N 139.6 W
increment	+0.23		Zn = 220.4
base	139.4		bearing = 240.5
result	139.6		CE = 20.1 W
			V = 20.5 W
			Dev = 0.4 E

141.　　　　This is a current vector and compass conversion problem.　It can be solved graphically or trigonometrically as shown below.

SET   = 105.2

DRIFT   =   0.351 knots

COURSE TO MAKE GOOD (CMG) = 074.9

LOGGED SPEED   =   8.6 knots

COURSE TO STEER (CTS) = CMG − X

　　　　　where sin X = (DRIFT) sin (SET − CMG) / LOGGED SPEED

　　　　　　　　　　= (0.351) sin (105.2 − 074.9) / 8.6

　　　　　　　　　　= (0.351) sin (30.3) / 8.6

　　　　　　　　　　= 0.351 (0.50453) / 8.6

　　　　　　　　　　= 0.02059

　　　　　so, X = 1.17990 degrees

　　　　and CTS = CMG − X

　　　　so, CTS = (074.9 − 1.2) = 073.7

　　　　　　　　　　　　　V =   20.5 W

　　　　　　　　　　　　　Cm = 094.2

　　　　　　　　　　　　Dev =   0.4 E

　　　　　　　　　　　　　Cc = 093.8

　　　　To the nearest ½ degree, Cc = 094

142-144.   This is a traverse and mid-latitude sailing problem coupled with rising/setting problems.

Time Span	Cc	V(W)	Dev	CE(W)	Cn	D(mi)	l (N+)	p (E+)
1930-2100	091½	20½	0.4 E	20.1	071.4	13.05	4.16	12.37
2100-2400	094	20½	0.4 E	20.1	073.9	25.80	7.15	24.79
0000-0500	094	20½	0.4 E	20.1	073.9	43.00	11.92	41.31
1930-0500							23.23	78.47

Lm = (36-58.8 N) + 23.23/2 = 37-10.4 N

DLo = p (sec Lm) = 78.47 (1.25500) E = 98.48 E = 001-38.5 E

1930 POSITION	36-58.8 N	049-56.2 W
l, DLo	23.2 N	001-38.5 E
0500 DR (projected)	37-22.0 N	048-17.7 W

FROM THE NAUTICAL ALMANAC, 19 APR 68:

	L (N)	N. TWILIGHT	C. TWILIGHT	SUNRISE
	40	0414	0448	0516
	35	0426	0457	0523
difference	5	12	09	07
corr'n from Table I		-4	-4	-2
LMT		0422	0453	0521
λ corr'n		+13	+13	+13
ZT		0435	0506	0534

145-146. This is a latitude by Polaris problem along with a regular star sight problem. The sight reductions are shown below. The plot is shown in Figure 10.

FROM THE NAUTICAL ALMANAC, 19 APR 68:

Name	POLARIS	MARKAB
CT	07-45-25	07-36-36
CE	1 slow	1 slow
GMT	07-45-26	07-36-37
h GHA	312-26.6	312-26.6
SHA/d		014-12.7/N15-01.8
m,s GHA	11-23.4	9-10.8
final GHA	323-50.0	335-50.1
DR λ/a λ	048-21.7 W	047-50.1 W
LHA	275-28.3	288
t		72 E

	POLARIS	MARKAB
Hs	37-07.0	23-04.1
IE & dip	7.7	7.7
Ha	36-59.3	22-56.4
refr	1.3	2.3
Ho	36-58.0	22-54.1
a_0	1-21.3	FROM H.O. PUB. NO. 229,
a_1	.5	H/d/Z 23-12.8/+33.6/88.3
a_2	.4	corr'n +1.0
sum	38-20.2	Hc/Z 23-13.8/N 88.3 E
minus 1°	-1	Ho 22-54.1
L	37-20.2 N	a 19.7 away
		Zn 088.3

	POLARIS	MARKAB
DR to 0500	+2.1 miles	+3.6 miles
0500 POSITION		37-21.3 N

```
KAUS AUSTR.                      ARCTURUS
07-43-13                         07-50-44
         1 slow                          1 slow
07-43-14                         07-50-45
312-26.6                         312-26.6
084-28.9/S34-24.2                146-26.5/N19-20.7
 10-50.3                          12-43.3
407-45.8                         471-36.4
047-45.8 W                       048-36.4 W
000                              063
  0                               63 W


18-25.4                          32-36.4
   7.7                              7.7
18-17.7                          32-28.7
   2.9                              1.5
18-14.8                          32-27.2
ASSUMING A LATITUDE OF 37 N:
   19-00.0/-60.00/180.0          32-35.9/+31.9/89.9
     -24.2                          +11.0
   18-35.8/N 180.0               32-46.9/N 89.9 W
   18-14.8                       32-27.2
     21.0 away                     19.7 away
    180.0                         270.1
     +2.4 miles                    +1.3 miles


048-10.5 W
```

147-148.   This is either a plotting problem (see Figure 10) or a traverse and mid-latitude sailing problem.

Time Span	Cc	V(W)	Dev	CE(W)	Cn	D(mi)	ℓ (N+)	p (E+)
1930-2100	091½	20½	0.4 E	20.1	071.4	13.05	4.16	12.37
2100-0500	094	20½	0.4 E	20.1	073.9	68.30	18.94	65.62
1930-0500							23.10	77.99

Lm = (36-58.8 N) + 23.10/2 = 37-10.4 N

DLo = p (sec Lm) = 77.99 (1.25500) E = 97.88 E = 001-37.9 E

1930 FIX	36-58.8 N	049-56.2 W
ℓ, DLo	23.1 N	001-37.9 E
0500 DR	37-21.9 N	048-18.3 W
0500 FIX	37-21.3 N	048-10.5 W
ℓ, DLo	0.6 S	7.8 E

Lm = (37-21.9 N) - 0.6/2 = 37-21.6 N

p = DLo (cos Lm) = 7.8 (0.79484) E = 6.20 E

C = arc tan p / ℓ = S 84.5 E

D = ℓ sec C = 0.6 (10.38118) = 6.23 miles

Cn = 180 - C = 095.5

CURRENT SPEED = 6.23 miles/9.5 hours = 0.656 knots

149.　　　　　This is an amplitude and compass conversion
problem.

ZT	05-37	
ZD	+3	
GMT	08-37	
h d	N 11-14.1	
+.9	+0.6	
final d	N 11-14.7 = N 11.24	
DR L	37-22.7 N = 37.38 N	
values	d = 11.24 N	L = 37.38 N
base	11/14.0	38/14.0
next	11.5/14.7	36/13.6
difference	+0.7	-0.4
multiplier	.48	.31
product	+0.336	-0.124
	-0.124	
increment	+0.212	
base	14.0	
result	E 14.2 N	
from 90°	090	
azimuth	075.8	
bearing	095.8	
compass error	20.0 W	
variation	20.5 W	
deviation	.5 E	

150.   This is a great circle sailing problem.

DLo = (048-10.5 W) - (031-08.0 W) = 17-02.5 E = t = 17.04 E

DESTINATION L   = 39-27.0 N = d = 39.45 N

DEPARTURE L   = 37-21.3 N = L = 37.36 N

values	t = 17.04 E	d = 39.45 N	L = 37.36 N
base	17/76.3	39/76.3	37/76.3
next	18/76.5	40/72.1	38/80.4
difference	+0.2	−4.2	+4.1
multiplier	.04	.45	.36
product	+0.01	−1.89	+1.48
	−1.89		
	+1.48		
increment	−0.40		
base	76.3		
result, Z =	N 75.9 E		
Zn =	075.9		

112

151.   This is a current vector and compass conversion problem. It can be solved graphically or trigonometrically as shown below.

SET   = 095.5

DRIFT   =   0.656 knots

COURSE TO MAKE GOOD (CMG) = 075.9

LOGGED SPEED   =   8.5 knots

COURSE TO STEER (CTS) = CMG − X

        where sin X = (DRIFT) sin (SET − CMG) / LOGGED SPEED

                = (0.656) sin (095.5 − 075.9) / 8.5

                = (0.656) sin (19.6) / 8.5

                = 0.656 (0.33545) / 8.5

                = 0.02589

        so, X = 1.48349 degrees

       and CTS = CMG − X

       so, CTS = (075.9 − 1.5) = 074.4

                        V =   20.5 W

                   Cm = 094.9

                Dev =   .5 E

                 Cc = 094.4

    To the nearest half degree, Cc = 094½

152-153.   These are inverted sun sight problems.

	parallel	perpendicular
great circle course	075.9	075.9
plus 90°/plus 180°	90	180
required Zn	165.9	255.9
required Z	N 165.9 E	N 104.1 W
L	38 N	38 N
d	N 11	N 11
closest t/Z	7 E/165.1	54 W/104.5*
a λ	047 W	046 W
t	7 E	54 W
final GHA	040	100
GMT/h GHA	14/030-14.2	18/090-14.7
increment	9-45.8	9-45.3
m,s GMT	39-03	39-01
final GMT	14-39-03	18-39-01
ZD	+3	+3
ZT	11-39	15-39

*or 55 W/103.7

154-155.   This is a traverse and mid-latitude sailing
problem.

Time Span	CMG	S(kn)	D(mi)	l (N+)	p(E+)
0500-0600	075.4	9.10	9.10	2.29	8.81
0600-1600	075.9	9.10	91.00	22.17	88.26
0500-1600				24.46	97.07

Lm = (37-21.3 N) + 24.46/2 = 37-33.5 N

DLo = p (sec Lm) = 97.07 (1.26146) E = 122.4 E = 002-02.4 E

0500 FIX	37-21.3 N	048-10.5 W
l, DLo	24.5 N	002-02.4 E
1600 EP	37-45.8 N	046-08.1 W

156-157. This is a star fix problem which needs to be reworked as a star and planet fix. The sight reductions are shown below. The plot is shown in Figure 11.

FROM THE NAUTICAL ALMANAC, 19 APR 68:

Name	REGULUS	PROCYON
CT	22-11-33	22-14-07
CE	0-01 slow	0-01 slow
GMT	22-11-34	22-14-08
h GHA/d	178-03.5	178-03.5
v/SHA/d	208-19.6/N12-07.4	245-35.5/N05-18.5
m,s GHA	2-53.7	3-32.6
final GHA/d	389-16.8/N12-07.4	067-11.6/N05-18.5
a λ	045-16.8 W	045-11.6 W
LHA	344	022
t	16 E	22 W
Hs	63-36.6	52-03.3
IE & dip	7.7	7.7
Ha	63-28.9	51-55.6
refr	0.5	0.8
Ho	63-28.4	51-54.8

FROM H.O. PUB. NO. 229, ASSUMING A LATITUDE OF 38 N:

H/d/Z	60-20.1/+53.7/147.0	51-23.9/+52.7/143.3
corr'n	+06.7	+16.2
Hc/Z	60-26.8/N 147.0 E	51-40.1/N 143.3 W
Ho	63-28.4	51-54.8
a	181.6 towards	14.7 towards
Zn	147.0	216.7
EP to 1900	-1.8 miles	-2.1 miles
1900 POSITION	37-52.7 N	045-33.7 W

```
CAPELLA                          JUPITER
22-16-48                         22-11-33
      0-01 slow                        0-01 slow
22-16-49                         22-11-34
178-03.5                         029-33.2/N14-01.7
281-25.3/N45-58.3          + 2.5 = .5/0.0 = .0
  4-12.9                          2-53.3
103-41.7/N45-58.3                032-27.0/N14-01.7
045-41.7 W                       045-27.0 W
058                              347
 58 W                             13 E


47-05.3
  7.7
46-57.6
  0.9
46-56.7                          63-28.4


47-08.0/-10.7/60.0               63-22.4/+55.0/150.9
 -00.3                            +01.5
47-07.7/N 60.0 W                 63-23.9/N 150.9 E
46-56.7                          63-28.4
  11.0 away                        4.5 towards
300.0                            150.9
 -2.6 miles                       -1.8 miles
```

158–159.   This is a traverse and mid–latitude sailing
problem.

Time Span	Cc	V(W)	Dev	CE(W)	Cn	D(mi)	l (N+)	p (E+)
0500–0600	094	20½	0.5 E	20.0	074.0	8.50	2.34	8.17
0600–1900	094½	20½	0.5 E	20.0	074.5	111.11	29.69	107.07
0500–1900							32.03	115.24

Lm   = (37–21.3 N) + 32.03/2 = 37–37.3 N

DLo = p (sec Lm) = 115.24 (1.26253) E = 145.49 E = 002–25.5 E

0500 POSITION	37–21.3 N	048–10.5 W
l, DLo	32.0 N	002–25.5 E
1900 DR	37–53.3 N	045–45.0 W
1900 FIX	37–52.7 N	045–33.7 W
l, DLo	0.6 S	11.3 E

Lm = (37–53.3 N) – 0.6/2 = 37–53.0 N

p = DLo (cos Lm) = 11.3 (0.78926) E = 8.92 E

C = arc tan p / l = S 86.2 E

D = l (sec C) = 0.6 (14.89805) = 8.94 miles

Cn = 180 – C = 093.8

CURRENT SPEED = 8.94 miles/14 hours = 0.638 knots

160.   This is a mid-latitude sailing problem.

0500 POSITION   37-21.3 N   048-10.5 W
1900 POSITION   37-52.7 N   045-33.7 W
$\angle$, DLo   31.4 N   2-36.8 E = 156.8 E
Lm = (37-21.3 N) + 31.4/2 = 37-37.0 N
p = DLo (cos Lm) = 156.8 (0.79211) E = 124.2 E
C = arc tan p / $\angle$ = 75.8
D = $\angle$ (sec C) = 31.4 (4.07996) = 128.1 miles
S = D/T = 128.1 miles/14 hours = 9.15 knots

161-162.   This is a great circle sailing problem.

DLo = (045-33.7 W) - (031-08.0 W) = 14-25.7 E = t = 14.43 E

DESTINATION L   = 39-27.0 N = d = 39.45 N

DEPARTURE L   = 37-52.7 N = L = 37.88 N

values	t = 14.43 E	d = 39.45 N	L = 37.88 N
base	14/78-48.0/75.5	39/78-48.0/75.5	37/78-48.0/75.5
next	15/78-01.6/75.8	40/78-39.2/70.4	38/79-00.5/80.4
difference	-46.4/+0.3	-08.8/-5.1	+22.5/+4.9
multiplier	.43	.45	.88
product	-20.0/+0.1	-04.0/-2.3	+19.8/+4.3
	-04.0/-2.3		
	+19.8/+4.3	90-00.0	
increments	-04.2/+2.1	78-43.8	
base	78-48.0/75.5	11-16.2 = z =	676.2 miles
result	78-43.8/77.6	Z =	N 77.6 E
		Zn =	077.6

DEPARTURE ZONE TIME   = 19 APR 1900

ZONE DESCRIPTION   =   +3

DEPARTURE GMT DATE/TIME = 19 APR 2200

PASSAGE DURATION   = 676.2 miles/9.15 knots = 73.90 hours

                        = 3 d 01 h 54 m

DEPARTURE GMT DATE/TIME = 19 d 22 h 00 m

ARRIVAL GMT DATE/TIME   = 22 d 22 h 54 m

                        = 22 APR/22 h 54 m

163.   This is a current vector and compass conversion
problem. It can be solved graphically or trigonometrically as
shown below.

SET   = 093.8

DRIFT   =   0.638 knots

COURSE TO MAKE GOOD (CMG) = 077.6

LOGGED SPEED   =   8.55 knots

COURSE TO STEER (CTS) = CMG – X

           where sin X = (DRIFT) sin (SET – CMG) / LOGGED SPEED

                     = (0.638) sin (093.8 – 077.6) / 8.55

                     = (0.638) sin (16.2) / 8.55

                     = 0.638 (0.27899) / 8.55

                     = 0.02082

        so, X = 1.19288 degrees

      and CTS = CMG – X

      so, CTS = 077.6 – 1.2 = 076.4

                    V =   20.0 W

                  Cm = 096.4

                Dev =   .5 E

                  Cc = 095.9

    To the nearest half degree, Cc = 096

164-165.   This is a great circle sailing problem along with a time and operations problem.

DLo = (045-33.7 W) - (028-50.0 W) = 16-43.7 E = t = 16.73 E

DESTINATION L   = 38-36.0 N = d = 38.60 N

DEPARTURE L   = 37-52.7 N = L = 37.88 N

values	t = 16.73 E	d = 38.60 N	L = 37.88 N
base	16/77-17.0/80.6	38/77-17.0/80.6	37/77-17.0/80.6
next	17/76-29.7/80.6	39/77-15.1/76.1	38/77-24.4/85.1
difference	-47.3/ZERO	-01.9/-4.5	+07.4/+4.5
multiplier	.73	.60	.88
product	-34.5/ZERO	-01.1/-2.7	+06.5/+4.0
	-01.1/-2.7		
	+06.5/+4.0	90-00.0	
increments	-29.1/+1.3	76-47.9	
base	77-17.0/80.6	13-12.1 = z =	792.1 miles
result	76-47.9/81.9	Z =	N 81.9 E
		Zn =	081.9

PASSAGE DURATION   = 792.1 miles/9.15 knots = 86.57 hours

                        = 3 d 14 h 34 m

DEPARTURE GMT DATE/TIME = 19 d 22 h 00 m

ARRIVAL GMT DATE/TIME   = 23 d 12 h 34 m

FUEL AT DEPARTURE = 1,400 gal + 2(12.4) gal = 1,424.8 gal

FUEL CONSUMED = 86.57 hours (12.4 gal/hr) = 1,073.5 gal

PROJECTED FULE REMAINING ON ARRIVAL = 351.3 gal

% FUEL SAFETY MARGIN = 351.3 (100)/1424.8 = 24.6%

(This represents more than one day's steaming time at 8.55 knots.)

166.   This is an azimuth (by inspection tables) and
compass conversion problem.

CT	00-48-13		
CE	01 slow		
GMT	00-48-14		
h/GHA	208-08.5		
SHA/d	81-02.0/N 38-44.8 = 38.75 N		
m,s GHA	12-05.5		
final GHA	301-16.0		
EP λ	45-02.0 W		
LHA	256-14.0		
t	103-46.0 E	= 103.77 E	
EP L	37-58.2 N	= 37.97 N	
values	t = 103.77 E	d = 38.75 N	L = 37.97 N
base	103/52.1	38/52.1	37/52.1
next	104/51.6	39/51.2	38/52.3
difference	-0.5	-0.9	+0.2
multiplier	.77	.75	.97
product	-0.38	-0.68	+0.19
	-0.68		
	+0.19		Z = N 51.2 E
increment	-0.87		Zn = 051.2
base	52.1		bearing = 070.7
result	51.2		CE = 19.5 W
			V = 20.0 W
			Dev = 0.5 E

167-168.   This is a star fix problem. The sight reductions
are shown below. The plot is shown in Figure 12.

FROM THE NAUTICAL ALMANAC, 20 APR 68:

Name	MARKAB	DUBHE
CT	07-26-11	07-28-22
CE	02 slow	02 slow
GMT	07-26-13	07-28-24
h GHA	313-25.7	313-25.7
SHA/d	14-12.7/N15-01.8	194-32.6/N61-55.6
m,s GHA	6-34.3	7-07.2
final GHA	334-12.7	515-05.5
a λ	044-12.7 W	044-05.5 W
LHA	290	111
t	70 E	111 W
Hs	25-20.1	24-36.0
IE & dip	7.7	7.7
Ha	25-12.4	24-28.3
refr	2.1	2.1
Ho	25-10.3	24-26.2

FROM H.O. PUB. NO. 229, ASSUMING A LATITUDE OF 38 N:

H/d/Z	24-48.9/+34.5/90.0	24-16.1/-35.3/28.7
corr'n	+01.0	-02.6
Hc/Z	24-49.9/N 90.0 E	24-13.5/N 28.7 W
Ho	24-10.3	24-26.2
a	20.4 towards	12.7 towards
Zn	090.0	331.3
DR to 0430	+0.5 mile	+0.2 mile
0430 POSITION		

ALTAIR	ARCTURUS
07-34-00	07-36-49
02 slow	02 slow
07-34-02	07-36-51
313-25.7	313-25.7
62-41.5/N08-46.7	146-26.5/N19-20.7
8-31.9	9-14.3
384-39.1	469-06.5
043-39.1 W	044-06.5 W
341	065
19 E	65 W
56-15.8	31-06.0
7.7	7.7
56-08.1	30-58.3
0.7	1.6
56-07.4	30-56.7
56-19.6/-53.0/144.6	31-01.1/+33.0/89.3
-11.8	+11.4
56-07.8/N 144.6 E	31-12.5/N 89.3 W
56-07.4	30-56.7
0.4 away	15.8 away
144.6	270.7
-0.3 mile	-1.0 mile
38-12.1 N	043-45.4 W

169-170.   This is a traverse and mid-latitude sailing (and then a parallel sailing) problem.

Time Span	Cc	V(W)	Dev	CE(W)	Cn	D(mi)	l (N+)	p (E+)
1900-2030	094½	20½	0.5 E	20.0	074.5	12.82	3.42	12.35
2030-2400	096	20	0.5 E	19.5	076.5	29.92	6.98	29.09
2400-0430	096	20	0.5 E	19.5	076.5	38.48	8.98	37.42
1900-0430							19.38	78.86

Lm = (37-52.7 N) + 19.38/2 = 38-02.4 N

DLo = p (sec Lm) = 78.86 (1.26971) E = 100.1 E = 001-40.1 E

1900 POSITION	37-52.7 N	045-33.7 W
l, DLo	19.4 N	1-40.1 E
0430 DR	38-12.1 N	043-53.6 W
0430 FIX	38-12.1 N	043-45.4 W
l, DLo	0.0	8.2 E

Lm = 38-12.1 N

p = DLo (cos Lm) = 8.2 (0.78584) E = 6.44 E

C = N 90.0 E

D = p = 6.44 miles

Cn = 000 + C = 090.0

CURRENT SPEED = 6.44 miles/9.5 hours = 0.678 knots

171.   This is a great circle sailing problem.

DLo = (043-45.4 W) - (031-08.0 W) = 12-37.4 E = t = 12.62 E
DESTINATION L   = 39-27.0 N = d = 39.45 N
DEPARTURE L   = 38-12.1 N = L = 38.20 N

	values t = 12.62 E	d = 39.45 N	L = 38.20 N
base	12/80.2	39/80.2	38/80.2
next	13/80.4	40/74.2	39/86.2
difference	+0.2	-6.0	+6.0
multiplier	.62	.45	.20
product	+.1	-2.7	+1.2
	-2.7		
	+1.2		
increment	-1.4		
base	80.2		
result, Z =	N 78.8 E		
Zn =	078.8		

172.   This is a current vector and compass conversion problem. It can be solved graphically or trigonometrically as shown below.

SET = 090.0

DRIFT = 0.678 knots

COURSE TO MAKE GOOD (CMG) = 078.8

LOGGED SPEED = 8.55 knots

COURSE TO STEER (CTS) = CMG − X

where $\sin X$ = (DRIFT) sin (SET − CMG) / LOGGED SPEED

= (0.678) sin (090.0 − 078.8) / 8.55

= (0.678) sin (11.2) / 8.55

= 0.678 (0.19423) / 8.55

= 0.01540

so, X = 0.88253 degrees

and CTS = CMG − X

                so, CTS = 078.8 − 0.9 = 077.9
                            V =   20.0 W
                           Cm = 097.9
                          Dev =   0.5 E
                           Cc = 097.4
To the nearest half degree, Cc = 097½

173-177. These are regular sun sight problems along with a LAN
sight problem. The sight reductions are shown below.
The plot is shown in Figure 13.

FROM THE NAUTICAL ALMANAC, 20 APR 68:

CT	14-28-28	18-36-00
CE	02 slow	02 slow
GMT	14-28-30	18-36-02
h GHA/d	030-17.4/N11-39.9	090-17.9/N11-43.3
m,s GHA/d	7-07.5/.9 = 0.4	9-00.5/.9 = 0.5
final GHA/d	037-24.9/N11-40.3	099-18.4/N11-43.8
a λ	042-24.9 W	042-18.4 W
LHA	355	057
t	5 E	57 W
Hs	62-45.5	32-21.3
IE & dip	7.7	7.7
Ha	62-37.8	32-13.6
main	15.5	14.5
Ho	62-53.3	32-28.1

FROM H.O. PUB. NO. 229, ASSUMING A LATITUDE OF 38 N:

H/d/Z	63-37.2/-59.2/168.9	33-13.0/-36.6/101.3
corr'n	-19.4	-09.9
Hc/Z	63-17.8/N 168.9 E	33-03.1/N 101.3 W
Ho	62-53.3	32-28.1
a	24.5 away	35.0 away
Zn	168.9	258.7

```
                  14-48-22
                          02 slow
                  14-48-24
EqT/h d                01-08/N11-39.9
GAT/m,s d              14-49-32/.9 = 0.7
12 h/final d           12-00-00/N11-40.6
λ in time              02-49-32
λ in arc              042-23.0 W


                  63-07.3
                      7.7
                  62-59.6
                     15.5
                  63-15.1

from 90°           90-00.0
z                  26-44.9
d                  11-40.6
L                  35-25.5 N
```

These lines of position show a course made good of 078.8
and a speed made good of 8.96 knots, yielding a 1148½
(+3) EP about 0.6 mile from the LAN position
and a 1700 (+3) EP of 38-34.5 N, 041-25.1 W.

178.   This is a great circle sailing problem.

DLo = (041-25.1 W) - (031-08.0 W) = 10-17.1 E = t = 10.28 E

DESTINATION L   = 39-27.0 N = d = 39.45 N

DEPARTURE L   = 38-34.5 N = L = 38.58 N

values	t = 10.28 E	d = 39.45 N	L = 38.58 N
base	10/79.6	39/79.6	38/79.6
next	11/80.0	40/72.5	39/86.8
difference	+0.4	-7.1	+7.2
multiplier	.28	.45	.58
product	+0.1	-3.2	+4.2
	-3.2		
	+4.2		
increments	+1.1		
base	79.6		
result, Z =	N 80.7 E		
Zn =	080.7		

179-180.　　　This is a traverse and mid-latitude sailing problem along with a compass conversion problem.

Time Span	Cc	V(W)	Dev	CE(W)	Cn	D(mi)	L (N+)	p (E+)
0430-0600	096	20	0.5 E	19.5	076.5	12.82	2.99	12.46
0600-1128½	097½	20	0.5 E	19.5	078.0	46.81	9.73	45.79
0430-1128½							12.72	58.25

$C = $ arc tan p / $L = $ arc tan (12.72/58.25) = N 77.7 E

So, the resultant course steered from 0430 (+3) to

1128½ (+3) was:　　　　Cn = 077.7

and the course made good = 078.8

therefore the offset　　　=　1.1 degrees

NEW TRUE COURSE TO MAKE GOOD　　= 080.7

OFFSET　　　　　　　　　　　　=　1.1

NEW TRUE COURSE TO STEER　　　= 079.6

V =　19.5 W

Cm = 099.1

Dev =　0.5 E

Cc = 098.6

To the nearest half degree, Cc = 098½

181-182.   This is a traverse and mid-latitude sailing problem.

Time Span	CMG	SMG(kn)	D(mi)	L (N+)	p(E+)
1700-0500	080.6	8.96	107.52	17.56	106.08

Lm = (38-34.5 N) + 17.56/2 = 38-43.3 N

DLo = p (sec Lm) = 106.08 (1.28173) E = 136.0 E = 002-16.0 E

1700 EP	38-34.5 N	041-25.1 W
L, DLo	17.6 N	2-16.0 E
0500 EP	38-52.1 N	039-09.1 W

134

183.   This is a great circle sailing and compass conversion problem.

DLo = (039-09.1 W) - (031-08.0 W) = 8-01.1 E = t = 8.02 E

DESTINATION L   = 39-27.0 N = d = 39.45 N

DEPARTURE L   = 38-52.1 N = L = 38.87 N

values	$t = 8.02$ E	$d = 39.45$ N	$L = 38.87$ N
base	8/78.4	39/78.4	38/78.4
next	9/79.1	40/69.7	39/87.5
difference	+0.7	-8.7	+9.1
multiplier	.02	.45	.87
product	+0.0	-3.9	+7.9
	-3.9		
	+7.9		

increment	+4.0	
base	78.4	
result, Z =	N 82.4 E	
Zn =	082.4	
OFFSET =	1.1	
CTS =	081.3	
V =	19.0 W	
Cm =	100.3	
Dev =	0.5 E	
Cc =	099.8	To the nearest half degree,
Cc =	100	

184-185.   This is a LAN sight problem.

CT	14-29-46
CE	03 slow
GMT	14-29-49
EqT/h d	01-21/N12-00.3
GAT/m,s d	14-31-10/.8 = .4
12 h/final d	12-00-00/N12-00.7
λ in time	2-31-10
λ in arc	037-47.5 W
Hs	62-51.0
IE & dip	7.7
Ha	62-43.3
main	15.5
Ho	62-58.8
from 90°	90
z	27-01.2
d	12-00.7 N
L	39-01.9 N

186-187.   This is a traverse and mid-latitude sailing
problem.

Time Span	Cc	V(W)	Dev	CE(W)	Cn	D(mi)	$\angle$ (N+)	p (E+)
1148½–1700	097½	20	0.5 E	19.5	078.0	44.39	9.23	43.42
1700–0500	098½	19½	0.5 E	19.0	079.5	102.60	18.70	100.88
0500–1130	100	19	0.5 E	18.5	081.5	55.58	8.22	54.97
1148½–1130							36.15	199.27

Lm = (38–25.5 N) + 36.15/2 = 38–43.6 N

DLo = p (sec Lm) = 199.27 (1.28182) E = 255.4 E = 004–15.4 E

1148½ POSITION	38–25.5 N	042–23.0 W
$\angle$, DLo	36.2 N	4–15.4 E
1130 DR	39–01.7 N	038–07.6 W
1130 LAN	39–01.9 N	037–47.5 W
$\angle$, DLo	0.2 N	20.1 E

Lm = (39–01.7 N) + 0.2/2 = 39–01.8 N

p = DLo (cos Lm) = 20.1 (0.77682) E = 15.6 E

C = arc tan p / $\angle$ = N 89.3 E, yielding Cn = 089.3

D = $\angle$ (sec C) = 0.2 (78.07646) = 15.615 miles

S = D/T = 15.615 mi/23.692 hr = 0.659 knots

188.   This is a great circle sailing problem along with a current vector and compass conversion problem.

DLo = (037-47.5 W) - (031-10.0 W) = 6-37.5 E = t = 6.62 E

DESTINATION L   = 39-20.0 N = d = 39.33 N

DEPARTURE L   = 39-01.9 N = L = 39.03 N

values	t = 6.62 E	d = 39.33 N	L = 39.03 N
base	6/88.1	39/88.1	39/88.1
next	7/87.8	40/75.9	40/100.3
difference	−0.3	−12.2	+12.2
multiplier	.62	.33	.03
product	−0.2	−4.0	+0.4
	−4.0		
	+0.4	SET	= 089.3
increment	−3.8	DRIFT	= 0.659 knots
base	88.1	LOGGED SPEED	= 8.55 knots

result, Z   = N 84.3 E

       Zn = CMG = 084.3

COURSE TO STEER (CTS) = CMG − X

        where sin X = (DRIFT) sin (SET − CMG) / LOGGED SPEED

                  = (0.659) sin (5.0) / 8.55

                  = 0.659 (0.08716) / 8.55

                  = 0.00672

             so, X = 0.38489 degrees

              CTS = CMG − X = 084.3 − 0.4 = 083.9

                                      CE = 18.5 W

                                      Cc = 102.4

        To the nearest half degree, Cc = 102½

138

189-190.   This is a current vector problem along with a traverse and mid-latitude sailing problem.

SMG = sin (SET − CTS) (logged speed) / sin (SET − CMG)

   = sin (089.3 − 084.0) (8.55 kn) / sin (089.3 − 084.4)

   = sin (5.3) (8.55 kn) / sin (4.9)

   = (0.09237) 8.55 kn / (0.08542)

   = 9.246 knots

Time Span	CMG	SMG(kn)	D(mi)	∠ (N+)	p(E+)
1130−1230	081.9	9.25	9.25	1.30	9.16
1230−1745	084.4	9.25	39.31	3.84	39.12
1130−1745				5.14	48.28

Lm = (39−01.9 N) + 5.14/2 = 39−04.5 N

DLo = p (sec Lm) = 48.28 (1.28813) E = 62.2 E = 001−02.2 E

1130 POSITION	39−01.9 N	037−47.5 W
∠, DLo	5.1 N	1−02.2 E
1745 EP	39−07.0 N	036−45.3 W

191.　　　　This is a great circle sailing and current vector
problem.

DLo = (036-45.3 W) - (031-10.0 W) =　5-35.3 E = t =　5.59 E

DESTINATION L　　　　　　　　　　　= 39-20.0 N = d = 39.33 N

DEPARTURE L　　　　　　　　　　　= 39-07.0 N = L = 39.12 N

values	t = 5.59 E	d = 39.33 N	L = 39.12 N
base	5/88.4	39/88.4	39/88.4
next	6/88.1	40/73.9	40/102.9
difference	-0.3	-14.5	+14.5
multiplier	.59	.33	.12
product	-0.2	-4.8	+1.7
	-4.8		
	+1.7		
increment	-3.3		
base	88.4		

result, Z　　　= N 85.1 E

　　　Zn = CMG =　085.1

　　　　　CTS = CMG - X

　　　where X (as previously determined) = 0.4 degrees

　　so, CTS = 085.1 - 0.4 degrees

　　　　　= 084.7

140

192-193.   This is an azimuth (by inspection tables) and compass conversion problem.

CT	19-45-00
CE	0-03 slow
GMT	19-45-03
h GHA/d	105-21.1/N12-04.5
m,s GHA/d	11-15.8/.8 0.6
final GHA/d	116-36.9/N12-05.1 = 12.08N
EP λ	036-45.3 W
LHA	079-51.6
t	79-51.6 W = 79.86 W
EP L	39-07.0 N = 39.12 N

values	t = 79.86 W	d = 12.08 N	L = 39.12 N
base	79/87.4	12/87.4	39/87.4
next	80/86.8	13/86.5	40/87.7
difference	−0.6	−0.9	+0.3
multiplier	.86	.08	.12
product	−0.52	−0.07	+0.04
	−0.07		
	+0.04		Zn = 273.2
increment	−0.55		bearing = 291.7
base	87.4		CE = 18.5 W
result, Z =	N 86.8 W		V = 18.5 W
	Zn = (360−Z) = 273.2		Dev = ZERO
			CTS = 084.7
			V = 18.0 W
			Cm = 102.7
			Dev = ZERO
			Cc = 102.7

To the nearest half degree, Cc = 102½

194-195. This is a regular star fix problem. The sight reductions are shown below. The plot is shown in Figure 14.

FROM THE NAUTICAL ALMANAC, 21 APR 68:

Name	ALIOTH	SPICA
CT	21-45-54	21-47-36
CE	4 slow	4 slow
GMT	21-45-58	21-47-40
h GHA	164-59.3	164-59.3
SHA/d	166-49.8/N56-07.9	159-07.0/S10-59.9
m,s GHA	11-31.4	11-57.0
final GHA	343-20.5	336-03.3
a λ	036-20.5 W	036-03.3 W
LHA	307	300
t	53 E	60 E
Hs	51-46.8	15-03.5
IE & dip	7.7	7.7
Ha	51-39.1	14-55.8
refr	0.8	3.6
Ho	51-38.3	14-52.2

FROM H.O. PUB. NO. 229, ASSUMING A LATITUDE OF 39 N:

H/d/Z	51-33.6/-4.1/45.9	15-09.0/+43.1/118.3
corr'n	-00.5	ZERO
Hc/Z	51-33.1/N 45.9 E	15-09.0/N 118.3 E
Ho	51-38.3	14-52.2
a	5.2 towards	16.8 away
Zn	045.9	118.3
DR to 2000	2.0 miles	1.8 miles
2000 POSITION	39-09.1 N	036-19.2 W

```
PROCYON                    CAPELLA
21-50-25                   21-53-11
         4 slow                     4 slow
21-50-29                   21-53-15
164-59.3                   164-59.3
245-35.5/N5-18.5           281-25.3/N45-58.3
 12-39.3                    13-20.9
423-14.1                   459-45.5
036-14.1 W                 036-45.5 W
027                        063
 27 W                       63 W

 48-27.8                    44-10.0
    7.7                        7.7
 48-20.1                    44-02.3
    0.9                        1.0
 48-19.2                    44-01.3


48-07.8/+50.7/137.3        44-15.0/-14.8/59.8
  +15.6                       -00.4
48-23.4/N 137.3 W          44-14.6/N 59.8 W
48-19.2                    44-01.3
    4.2 away                   13.3 away
222.7                      300.2
    0.2 mile                    0.1 mile
```

196-197.   This is either a plotting problem (see Figure 14) or a traverse and mid-latitude sailing problem.

Time Span	Cc	V(W)	Dev	CE(W)	Cn	D(mi)	l (N+)	p (E+)
1130-1230	100	19	0.5 E	18.5	081.5	8.55	1.26	8.46
1230-1400	102½	19	0.5 E	18.5	084.0	12.82	1.34	12.75
1400-1500	TIME ZONE CHANGE, NO PROGRESS							
1500-1800	102	18½	0.5 E	18.0	084.0	25.65	2.68	25.51
1800-2000	102½	18½	ZERO	18.5	084.0	17.10	1.79	17.01
1130-2000	(only 7½ hours)						7.07	63.73

$Lm = (39-01.9 \text{ N}) + 7.1/2 = 39-05.4 \text{ N}$

$DLo = p (\sec Lm) = 63.73 (1.28840) \text{ E} = 82.1 \text{ E} = 001-22.1 \text{ E}$

1130 POSITION	39-01.9 N	037-47.5 W
l, DLo	7.1 N	1-22.1 E
2000 DR	39-09.0 N	036-25.4 W
2000 FIX	39-09.1 N	036-19.2 W
l, DLo	0.1 N	6.2 E

$Lm = (39-09.0 \text{ N}) + 0.1/2 = 39-09.0 \text{ N}$

$p = DLo (\cos Lm) = 6.2 (0.77550) \text{ E} = 4.81 \text{ E}$

$C = \arctan p / l = \text{N } 88.8 \text{ E}$, yielding $Cn = 088.8$

$D = l (\sec C) = 0.1 (48.09343) = 4.809$ miles

$S = D/T = 4.809/7.5 = 0.641$ knots

144

198.   This is a mercator sailing problem.

2000 FIX   39-09.1 N   2,542.1   036-19.2 W
DESTINATION   39-20.0 N   2,556.1   031-10.0 W
m   14.0 N   (5-09.2 E)
DLo   309.2 E
C = arc tan DLo/m = N 87.4 E
     yielding Cn = 087.4 = CMG

199.   This is a current vector and compass conversion
problem.

SET   = 088.8

DRIFT   =   0.641 knots

COURSE TO MAKE GOOD (CMG) = 087.4

LOGGED SPEED   =   8.55 knots

COURSE TO STEER (CTS) = CMG – X

        where sin X = (DRIFT) sin (SET – CMG) / LOGGED SPEED

                = (0.641) sin (088.8 – 087.4) / 8.55

                = (0.641) sin (1.4) / 8.55

                = 0.641 (0.02443) / 8.55

                = 0.00183

        so, X = 0.10495 degrees

      and CTS = CMG – X

      so, CTS = 087.4 – 0.1 = 087.3

                    V =   18.0

                  Cm = 105.3

              Dev = ZERO

                Cc = 105.3

To the nearest half degree, Cc = 105½

200–201.   This is a traverse and mid-latitude sailing
problem.

Time Span	Cc	V(W)	Dev	CE(W)	Cn	D(mi)	L (N+)	p (E+)
2000–2100	102½	18½	ZERO	18.5	084.0	8.55	0.89	8.50
2100–0500	105½	18	ZERO	18.0	087.5	68.40	2.98	68.33
2000–0500							3.87	76.83

Lm = (39–09.1 N) + 3.87/2 = 39–11.0 N

DLo = p (sec Lm) = 76.83 (1.29011) E = 99.1 E = 001–39.1 E

2000 POSITION	39–09.1 N	036–19.2 W
L, DLo	3.9 N	1–39.1 E
0500 DR	39–13.0 N	034–40.1 W

202-203. This is a regular star fix problem along with a latitude by Polaris problem. The sight reductions are shown below. The plot is shown in Figure 15.

FROM THE NAUTICAL ALMANAC, 22 APR 68:

Name	POLARIS		MARKAB
CT	06-50-24		06-43-16
CE	4 slow		4 slow
GMT	06-50-28		06-43-20
h GHA	300-21.5		300-21.5
SHA/d			14-12.6/N15-01.8
m,s GHA	12-39.1		10-51.8
final GHA	313-00.6		325-25.9
DR λ/a λ	034-40.1 W		034-25.9 W
LHA	278-20.5		291
t			69 E
Hs	38-54.1		25-35.6
IE & dip	7.7		7.7
Ha	38-46.4		25-27.9
refr	1.2		2.0
Ho	38-45.2		25-25.9
a_0	1-27.0		FROM H.O. PUB. NO. 229,
a_1	0.5	H/d/Z	25-35.3/+35.3/91.1
a_2	0.4	corr'n	+01.0
sum	40-13.1	Hc/Z	25-36.3/N 91.1 E
minus 1°	-1	Ho	25-25.9
L	39-13.1 N	a	10.4 away
		Zn	091.1
DR to 0500	1.4 miles		2.4 miles

0500 POSITION   39-13.8 N

148

```
KAUS AUSTR.                    ARCTURUS
06-45-47                       06-54-10
          4 slow                       4 slow
06-45-51                       06-54-14
300-21.5                       300-21.5
  84-28.9/S34-24.2             146-26.5/N19-20.7
  11-29.6                       13-35.7
396-20.0                       460-23.7
034-20.0 W                     034-23.7 W
002                            066
   2 W                           66 W
 16-31.7                        30-45.3
     7.7                            7.7
 16-24.0                        30-37.6
     3.3                            1.6
 16-20.7                        30-36.0
```

ASSUMING A LATITUDE OF 39 N:

```
     16-58.6/-60.0/178.3        30-14.9/+34.0/89.3
        -24.2                      +11.8
     16-34.4/N 178.3 W          30-26.7/N 89.3 W
     16-20.7                    30-36.0
        13.7 away                  9.3 towards
        181.7                    270.7
           2.0 miles               0.8 miles
```

```
034-34.8 W
```

204-205.   This is either a plotting problem (see Figure 15)
or a mid-latitude sailing problem.

0500 DR   39-13.0 N   034-40.1 W

0500 FIX   39-13.8 N   034-34.8 W

L, DLo   0.8 N   5.3 E

Lm = (39-13.0 N) + 0.8/2 = 39-13.4 N

p = DLo (cos Lm) = 5.3 (0.77469) E = 4.1 E

C = arc tan p / L = N 79.0 W, yielding Cn = 079.0

D = L (sec C) = 0.8 (5.1942) = 4.183 miles

S = D/T = 4.183/9.0   = 0.465 knots

206-207.   These are mercator sailing problems along with a plane trigonometry problem.

0500 POSITION	39-13.8 N	2,548.1	034-34.8 W
DESTINATION	38-36. N	2,499.8	028-50. W
m		48.3 S	(5-44.8 E)
DLo			344.8 E

C = arc tan DLo/m = S 82.0 E, yielding Cn = 098.0

PTA. DAS LAJES LT.	39-22.5 N	2,559.4	031-10.3 W
PTA. COMPRIDA LT.	38-36. N	2,499.8	028-50. W
l, m	46.5 S	59.6 S	(2-20.3 E)
DLo			140.3 E

C = arc tan DLo/m = S 67.0 E, yielding Cn = 113.0

D = l (sec C) = 46.5 (2.55762) = 118.9 miles

DIST. OFF PTA. DAS LAJES LT. = D (sin X)

where D = the distance between the two lights = 118.9 miles

and X = the difference between the two courses above = (113.0 - 98.0)

so, DIST. OFF = (118.9) sin (113.0 - 98.0) miles

= 30.8 miles

208.   This is a current vector and compass conversion
problem.

SET   = 079.0
DRIFT   =   0.465 knots
COURSE TO MAKE GOOD (CMG) = 098.0
LOGGED SPEED   =   8.55 knots

COURSE TO STEER (CTS) = CMG + X
         where sin X = (DRIFT) sin (CMG − SET) / LOGGED SPEED
                    = (0.465) sin (098.0 − 079.0) / 8.55
                    = (0.465) sin (19.0) / 8.55
                    = 0.465 (0.32557) / 8.55
                    = 0.01771
          so, X = 1.01455 degrees
         and CTS = CMG + X
         so, CTS = 098.0 + 1.0 = 099.0
                          V =   17.5 W
                         Cm = 116.5
                        Dev = ZERO
                         Cc = 116.5

209-210.   This is an azimuth (by inspection tables) and compass conversion problem.

CT	08-36-18		
CE	4 slow		
GMT	08-36-22		
h GHA/d	300-22.7/N12-15.4		
m,s GHA/d	9-05.5/.8 = .5		
final GHA/d	309-28.2/N12-15.9 = 12.26 N		
DR λ	034-17.1 W		
LHA	275-11.1 = 275.18		
t,d,L	t = 84.82 E	d = 12.26 N	L = 39.24 N
base	84/84.3	12/84.3	39/84.3
next	85/83.7	13/83.5	40/84.5
difference	-0.6	-0.8	+0.2
multiplier	.82	.26	.24
product	-0.49	-0.21	+0.05
	-0.21		
	+0.05		
increment	-0.65		
base	84.3		
result, Z =	N 83.6 E		
Zn =	083.6		
bearing =	101.5		
CE =	17.9 W		
V =	17.5 W		
Dev =	0.4 W		
CTS =	099.0		
CE =	17.9 W		
Cc =	116.9	To the nearest half	
degree, Cc =	117		

211-212.   This is a LAN sight problem.

CT	14-11-13
CE	4 slow
GMT	14-11-17
EqT/h d	1-33/N 12-20.5
GAT/m,s d	14-12-50/+.8 = .2
12 h/final d	12-00-00/N 12-20.7
λ in time	02-12-50
λ in arc	033-12.5 W
Hs	63-05.4
IE & dip	7.7
Ha	62-57.7
main	15.5
Ho	63-13.2
from 90°	90-00.0
z	26-46.8
d	12-20.7 N
L	39-07.5 N

213-214.   This is either a plotting problem (see Figure 15) or a traverse and mid-latitude sailing problem.

Time Span	Cc	V(W)	Dev	CE(W)	Cn	D(mi)	∠ (N+)	p (E+)
0500-0630	105½	18	ZERO	18	087.5	12.82	0.56	12.81
0630-0700	116½	17½	0.4 W	17.9	098.6	4.28	-0.64	4.23
0700-1211½	117	17½	0.4 W	17.9	099.1	44.39	-7.02	43.83
0500-1211½							-7.10	60.87

Lm = (39-13.8 N) - 7.10/2 = 39-10.2 N

DLo = p (sec Lm) = 60.87 (1.28986) E = 78.5 E = 001-18.5 E

0500 POSITION	39-13.8 N	034-34.8 W
∠, DLo	7.1 S	1-18.5 E
1211½ DR	39-06.7 N	033-16.3 W
1211½ POSITION	39-07.5 N	033-12.5 W
∠, DLo	0.8 N	3.8 E

Lm = (39-06.7 N) + 0.8/2 = 39-07.1 N

p = DLo (cos Lm) = 3.8 (0.77584) E = 2.95 E

C = arc tan p / ∠ = N 74.8 E, yielding Cn = 074.8

D = ∠ (sec C) = 0.8 (3.81853) = 3.05 miles

S = D/T = 3.05 mi/7.19 hr = 0.424 knots

215.   This is a mercator sailing problem.

1211½ FIX	39-07.5 N	2,540.0	033-12.5 W
DESTINATION	38-36. N	2,499.8	028-50. W
m		40.2 S	(4-22.5 E)
DLo			262.5 E

C = arc tan DLo/m = S 81.3 E

     yielding Cn = 098.7   = CMG

216. This is a current vector and compass conversion problem.

SET	= 074.8
DRIFT	= 0.424 knots
COURSE TO MAKE GOOD (CMG)	= 098.7
LOGGED SPEED	= 8.55 knots
COURSE TO STEER (CTS)	= CMG + X

     where sin X = (DRIFT) sin (CMG - SET) / LOGGED SPEED

          = (0.424) sin (098.7 - 074.8) / 8.55

          = (0.424) sin (23.9) / 8.55

          = 0.424 (0.40514) / 8.55

          = 0.02009

     so, X = 1.15122 degrees

     and CTS = CMG + X

          = 098.7 + 1.2 = 099.9

               V = 17.0 W

             Cm = 116.9

           Dev = 0.4 W

             Cc = 117.3

To the nearest half degree, Cc = 117½

217.   This is an amplitude and compass conversion
problem.

ZT	18–48	
ZD	+2	
GMT	20–48	
h d	N 12–25.5	
+.8	.6	
final d	N 12–26.1 = 12.44 N	
EP L	38–57.2 N = 38.95 N	
values	L = 38.95 N	d = 12.44 N
base	38/15.3	12/15.3
next	40/15.7	12.5/15.9
difference	+0.4	+0.6
multiplier	0.95/2	0.44/0.5
product	+0.19	+0.53
	+0.53	
increment	+0.72	
base	15.3	
result	16.0	
plus 270°	270	
azimuth	286.0	
bearing	303.5	
compass error	17.5 W	
variation	17.0 W	
deviation	0.5 W	

218-219. This is a latitude by Polaris problem along with regular star and planet sight problems. The sight reductions are shown below. The plot is shown in Figure 16.

FROM THE NAUTICAL ALMANAC, 22 APR 68:

Name	POLARIS	JUPITER
CT	21-43-21	21-20-57
CE	5 slow	5 slow
GMT	21-43-26	21-21-02
h GHA/d	165-58.5	017-28.6/N14-01.4
v/SHA/d		+2.5=0.9/ ZERO
m,s GHA	10-53.3	5-15.5
final GHA/d	176-51.8	022-45.0/N14-01.4
DR λ/a λ	031-50.9 W	031-45.0 W
LHA	145-00.9	351
t		9 E

	POLARIS	JUPITER
Hs	38-42.8	63-56.2
IE & dip	7.7	7.7
Ha	38-35.1	63-48.5
refr	1.2	0.5
Ho	38-33.9	63-48.0
a_0	1-21.2	FROM H.O. PUB. NO. 229,
a_1	0.5	H/d/Z 63-46.2/+57.6/159.9
a_2	1.0	corr'n +01.4
sum	39-56.6	Hc/Z 63-47.6/N 159.9 E
minus 1°	-1	Ho 63-48.0
L	38-56.6 N	a 0.4 towards
		Zn 159.9
DR to 1930	-1.9 miles	+1.3 miles

| 1930 POSITION | | 38-57.5 N |

158

ARCTURUS	SIRIUS	CAPELLA
21-26-13	21-29-37	21-34-07
5 slow	5 slow	5 slow
21-26-18	21-29-42	21-34-12
165-58.5	165-58.5	165-58.5
146-26.5/N19-20.7	259-04.0/S16-40.3	281-25.3/N45-58.3
6-35.6	7-26.7	8-34.4
319-00.6/N19-20.7	072-29.2/S16-40.3	095-58.2/N45-58.3
032-00.6 W	031-29.2 W	031-58.2 W
287	041	064
73 E	41 W	64 W
25-19.0	22-46.4	43-34.1
7.7	7.7	7.7
25-11.3	22-38.7	43-26.4
2.1	2.3	1.0
25-09.2	22-36.4	43-25.4

ASSUMING A LATITUDE OF 39 N:

24-49.0/+34.3/ 85.0	22-08.5/+50.2/137.4	43-34.7/-15.5/ 59.5
+11.9	+16.5	-00.4
25-00.9/N 85.0 E	22-25.0/N 137.4 W	43-34.3/N 59.5 W
25-09.2	22-36.4	43-25.4
8.3 towards	11.4 towards	8.9 away
085.0	222.6	300.5
+0.5 miles	ZERO	-0.6 miles

031-48.2 W

220-221.   This is either a plotting problem (see Figure 16) or a traverse and mid-latitude sailing problem.

Time Span	Cc	V(W)	Dev	CE(W)	Cn	D(mi)	$\mathcal{L}$ (N+)	p (E+)
1211½-1300	117	17½	0.4 W	17.9	099.1	6.91	-1.09	6.82
1300-1930	117½	17	0.5 W	17.5	100.0	55.58	-9.65	54.74
1211½-1930							-10.74	61.56

Lm = (39-07.5 N) - 10.74/2 = 39-02.1 N

DLo = p (sec Lm) = 61.56 (1.28740) E = 79.2 E = 001-19.2 E

1211½ POSITION	39-07.5 N	033-12.5 W
$\mathcal{L}$, DLo	10.7 S	1-19.2 E
1930 DR	38-56.8 N	031-53.3 W
1930 FIX	38-57.5 N	031-48.2 W
$\mathcal{L}$, DLo	0.7 N	5.1 E

Lm = (38-56.8 N) + 0.7/2 = 38-57.2 N

p = DLo (cos Lm) = 5.1 (0.77766) E = 4.0 E

C = arc tan p / $\mathcal{L}$ = N 80.0 E, yielding Cn = 080.0

D = $\mathcal{L}$ (sec C) = 0.7 (5.75337) = 4.03 miles

S = D/T = 4.03 mi/7.31 hr = 0.551 knots

222.   This is a mercator sailing problem along with a
current vector and compass conversion problem.

1930 POSITION	38-57.5 N	2,527.2	031-48.2 W
DESTINATION	38-36. N	2,499.8	028-50. W
m		27.4 S	(2-58.2 E)
DLo			178.2 E

C = arc tan DLo/m = S 81.2 E

    yielding, Cn = 098.8 = CMG

SET   = 080.0

DRIFT   =   0.551 knots

COURSE TO MAKE GOOD (CMG) = 098.8

LOGGED SPEED   =   8.55 knots

COURSE TO STEER (CTS) = CMG + X

        where sin X = (DRIFT) sin (CMG − SET) / LOGGED SPEED

                = (0.551) sin (098.8 − 080.0) / 8.55

                = (0.551) sin (18.8) / 8.55

                = 0.551 (0.32226) / 8.55

                = 0.02077

        so, X = 1.19002 degrees

        and CTS = CMG + X

        so, CTS = 098.8 + 1.2 = 100.0

                      V =   16.5 W

                    Cm = 116.5

                 Dev =   0.5 W

                   Cc = 117.0

223-224.   This is a compass conversion and mid-latitude sailing problem.

COMPASS BEARING = 030

COMPASS ERROR   = 17 W

TRUE BEARING   = 013

PLUS 180°   = 180

Cn   = 193

C   = S 13 W

FROM H.O. PUB. NO. 9, TABLE 8:

90-METER LIGHT DISTANCE TO HORIZON = 20.1 miles

25-FOOT HE DISTANCE TO HORIZON   = 5.9 miles

TOTAL DISTANCE = D   = 26.0 miles

l = D (cos C) = 26.0 (0.94370) = 25.33 S

p = D (sin C) = 26.0 (0.22495) = 5.85 W

Lm = (39-22.5 N) - 25.33/2 = 39-09.8 N

DLo = p (sec Lm) = 5.85 (1.28974) W = 7.5 W

LIGHT'S POSITON	39-22.5 N	031-10.3 W
l, DLo	25.3 S	7.5 W
2210 POSITION	38-57.2 N	031-17.8 W

225–226.   This is either a plotting problem (see Figure 16) or a traverse and mid-latitude sailing problem.

Time Span	Cc	V(W)	Dev	CE(W)	Cn	D(mi)	$\angle$ (N+)	p (E+)
1930–2024	117½	17	0.5 W	17.5	100.0	7.70	−1.34	7.58
2024–2100	080	16½	1.5 E	15.0	065.0	5.13	2.17	4.65
2100–2210	117	16½	0.5 W	17.0	100.0	9.97	−1.73	9.82
1930–2210							−0.90	22.05

Lm = (38–57.5 N) − 0.90/2 = 38–57.0 N

DLo = p (sec Lm) = 22.05 (1.28585) E = 28.4 E

1930 POSITION	38–57.5 N	031–48.2 W
$\angle$, DLo	0.9 S	28.4 E
2210 DR	38–56.6 N	031–19.8 W
2210 POSITION	38–57.2 N	031–17.8 W
$\angle$, DLo	0.6 N	2.0 E

Lm = (38–56.6 N) + 0.6/2 = 38–56.9 N

p = DLo (cos Lm) = 2.0 (0.77771) E = 1.56 E

C = arc tan p / $\angle$ = N 68.9 E, yielding Cn = 068.9

D = $\angle$ (sec C) = 0.6 (2.77856) = 1.67 miles

S = D/T = 1.67 mi/2.67 hr = 0.625 knots

227.   This is a mercator sailing problem along with a current vector and compass conversion problem.

2210 POSITION	38–57.2 N	2,526.9	031–17.8 W
DESTINATION	38–36. N	2,499.8	028–50. W
m		27.1 S	(2–27.8 E)
DLo			147.8 E

C = arc tan DLo/m = S 79.6 E

     yielding Cn = 100.4 = CMG

SET   = 068.9

DRIFT   =   0.625 knots

COURSE TO MAKE GOOD (CMG) = 100.4

LOGGED SPEED   =   8.55 knots

COURSE TO STEER (CTS) = CMG + X

        where sin X = (DRIFT) sin (CMG – SET) / LOGGED SPEED

                = (0.625) sin (100.4 – 068.9) / 8.55

                = (0.625) sin (31.5) / 8.55

                = 0.625 (0.52250) / 8.55

                = 0.03819

       so, X = 2.18891 degrees

     and CTS = CMG + X

    so, CTS = 100.4 + 2.2 = 102.6

                   CE = 17.0 W

                   Cc = 119.6

   To the nearest half degree, Cc = 119½

228-229. This is a traverse and mid-latitude sailing problem. Where courses do not approximate those on which deviation has been determined recently, the deviation is considered as zero.

Time Span	Cc	V(W)	Dev	CE(W)	Cn	D(mi)	l (N+)	p (E+)
2210-2230	117	16½	0.5 W	17.0	100.0	2.85	-0.49	2.81
2230-0203	119½	16½	0.5 W	17.0	102.5	30.35	-6.57	29.63
0203-0227	145	16½	ZERO	16.5	128.5	3.42	-2.13	2.68
0227-0239	120	16½	0.5 W	17.0	103.0	1.71	-0.38	1.67
0239-0251	160	16½	ZERO	16.5	143.5	1.71	-1.37	1.02
0251-0312	120	16½	0.5 W	17.0	103.0	2.99	-0.67	2.91
0312-0321	160	16½	ZERO	16.5	143.5	1.28	-1.03	0.76
0321-0336	120	16½	0.5 W	17.0	103.0	2.14	-0.48	2.08
0336-0351	140	16½	ZERO	16.5	123.5	2.14	-1.18	1.78
0351-0400	120	16½	0.5 W	17.0	103.0	1.28	-0.29	1.25
0400-0430	119½	16½	0.5 W	17.0	102.5	4.28	-0.93	4.18
2210-0430							15.52	50.77

Lm = (38-57.2 N) - 15.52/2 = 38-49.4 N

DLo = p (sec Lm) = 50.77 (1.28356) E = 65.2 E = 001-05.2 E

2210 FIX   38-57.2 N   031-17.8 W

l, DLo   15.5 S   1-05.2 E

0430 DR   38-41.7 N   030-12.6 W

230-231. This is a latitude by Polaris problem along with
regular star sight problems. The sight reductions
are shown below. The plot is shown in Figure 17.

FROM THE NAUTICAL ALMANAC, 23 APR 68:

Name	POLARIS		MARKAB
CT	06-43-43		06-36-21
CE	5 slow		5 slow
GMT	06-43-48		06-36-26
h GHA	301-20.7		301-20.7
SHA/d			14-26.6/N 15-01.8
m,s GHA	10-58.8		9-08.0
final GHA	312-19.5		324-41.3
DR λ/a λ	030-10.1 W		029-41.3 W
LHA	282-09.4		295
t			65 E
Hs	38-33.2		28-32.5
IE & dip	7.7		7.7
Ha	38-25.5		28-24.8
refr	1.2		1.8
Ho	38-24.3		28-23.0

a_0	1-15.7	FROM H.O. PUB. NO. 229,	
a_1	0.5	H/d/Z	28-41.6/+35.6/93.6
a_2	0.4	corr'n	+01.0
sum	39-40.9	Hc/Z	28-42.6/N 93.6 E
minus 1°	-1	Ho	28-23.0
L	38-40.9 N	a	19.6 away
		Zn	093.6
DR to 0430	-2.0 miles		-0.9 miles
0430 POSITION			38-42.2 N

166

```
            NUNKI                    ARCTURUS
            06-45-10                 06-48-30
                   5 slow                   5 slow
            06-45-15                 06-48-35
            301-20.7                 301-20.7
              76-40.5/S 26-20.4      146-26.5/N 19-20.7
             11-20.6                  12-10.7
            389-21.8                 099-57.9
            030-21.8 W               029-57.9 W
            359                      070
               1 E                    70 W

             25-07.0                  27-34.2
                7.7                      7.7
             24-59.3                  27-26.5
                2.1                      1.9
             24-57.2                  27-24.6
ASSUMING A LATITUDE OF 39 N:
            24-59.6/-60.0/179.0      27-08.6/+34.1/86.8
             -20.4                     +11.8
            24-39.2/N 179.0 E        27-20.4/N 86.8 W
            24-57.2                  27-24.6
              18.0 towards             4.2 towards
             179.0                    273.2
              -2.2 miles              -2.6 miles


            030-08.6 W
```

232-233.   This is either a plotting problem (see Figure 17) or a traverse and mid-latitude sailing problem.

0430 DR	38-41.7 N	030-12.6 W
0430 FIX	38-42.2 N	030-08.6 W
$\angle$, DLo	.5 N	4.0 E

Lm = (38-41.7 N) + 0.5/2 = 38-42.0 N

p = DLo (cos Lm) = 4.0 (0.78043) E = 3.12172 E

C = arc tan p / $\angle$ = N 80.9 E, yielding Cn = 080.9 = SET

D = $\angle$ (sec C) = 0.5 (6.32302) = 3.16151 miles

S = D/T = 3.16 mi/6.333 hr = 0.499 knots = DRIFT

234-236.   This is a traverse and mid-latitude sailing problem along with a current vector and compass conversion problem.

Time Span	Cc	V(W)	Dev	CE(W)	Cn	D(mi)	$\angle$ (N+)	p (E+)
0430-0600	119½	16	0.5 W	16.5	103.0	12.82	-2.88	12.49
CURRENT					080.9	0.75	0.12	0.74
SUM							-2.76	13.23

Lm = (38-42.2 N) - 2.76/2 = 38-40.8 N

DLo = p (sec Lm) = 13.23 (1.28099) E = 16.9 E

0430 POSITION	38-42.2 N	030-08.6 W
$\angle$, DLo	2.8 S	16.9 E
0600 EP	38-39.4 N	029-51.7 W
DESTINATION	38-30.0 N	028-45.0 W
$\angle$, DLo	9.4 S	1-06.7 E = 66.7 E

Lm = (38-30.0 N) + 9.4/2 = 38-34.7 N

p = DLo (cos Lm) = 66.7 (0.78176) E = 52.1 E

C = arc tan p / $\angle$ = S 79.8 E, yielding Cn = 100.2 = CMG

SET = 080.9; DRIFT = 0.499; LOGGED SPEED = 8.55

COURSE TO STEER (CTS) = CMG + X

where sin X = (DRIFT) sin (CMG - SET) / LOGGED SPEED

$\qquad$ = (0.499) sin (19.3) / 8.55

$\qquad$ = 0.01929

$\quad$ so, X = 1.10528 degrees

$\quad$ and CTS = CMG + X = 100.2 + 1.1 = 101.3

$$V = 16.0 \ W$$

$$Cm = 117.3$$

$$Dev = 0.5 \ W$$

$$Cc = 117.8$$

To the nearest half degree, Cc = 118

THE PLOTS

PLOT 1

POSITION PLOTTING SHEET

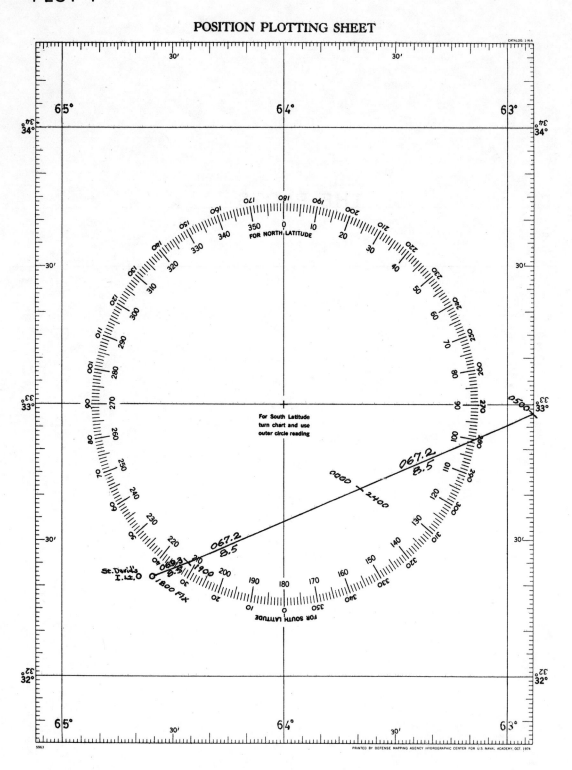

PLOT 2

POSITION PLOTTING SHEET

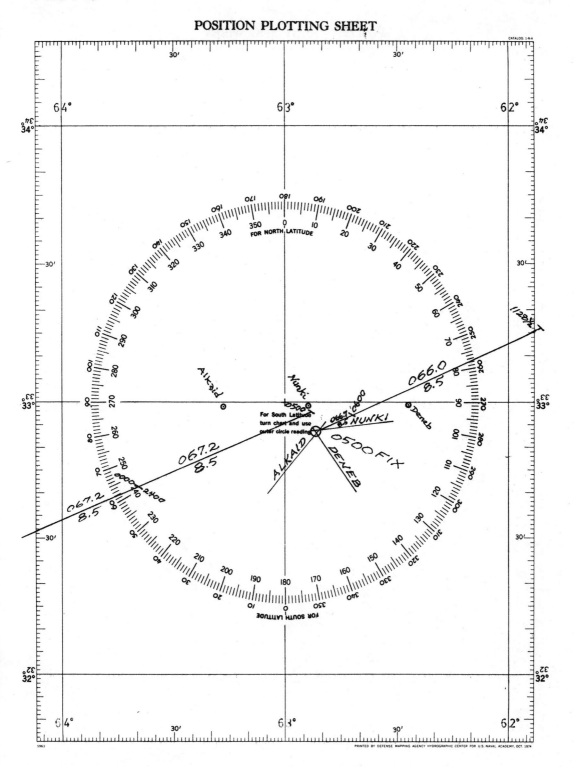

PLOT 3

POSITION PLOTTING SHEET

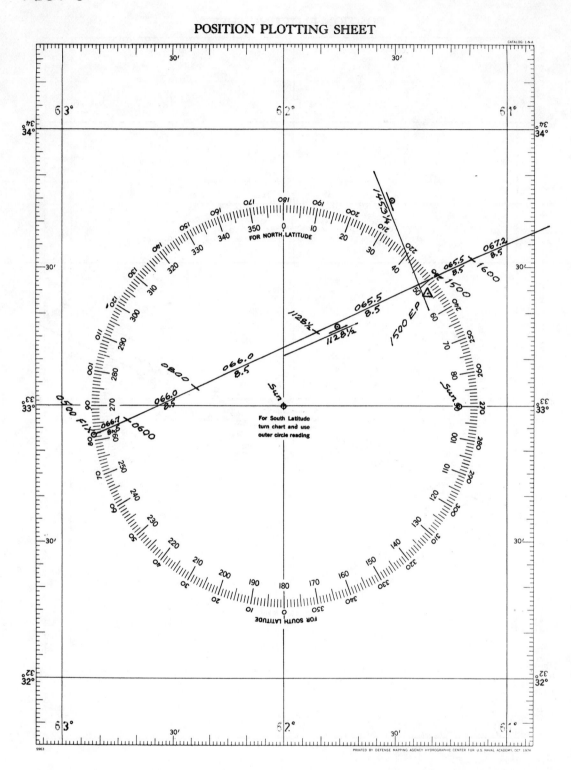

PLOT 4

POSITION PLOTTING SHEET

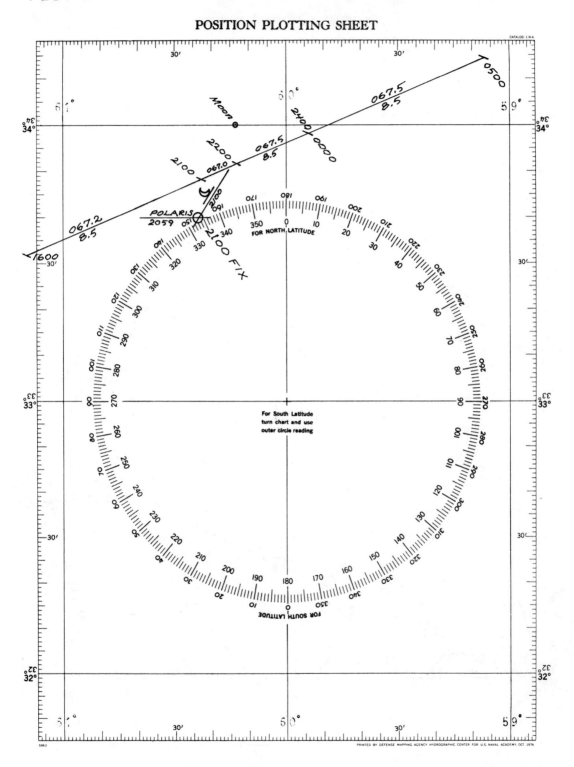

POSITION PLOTTING SHEET

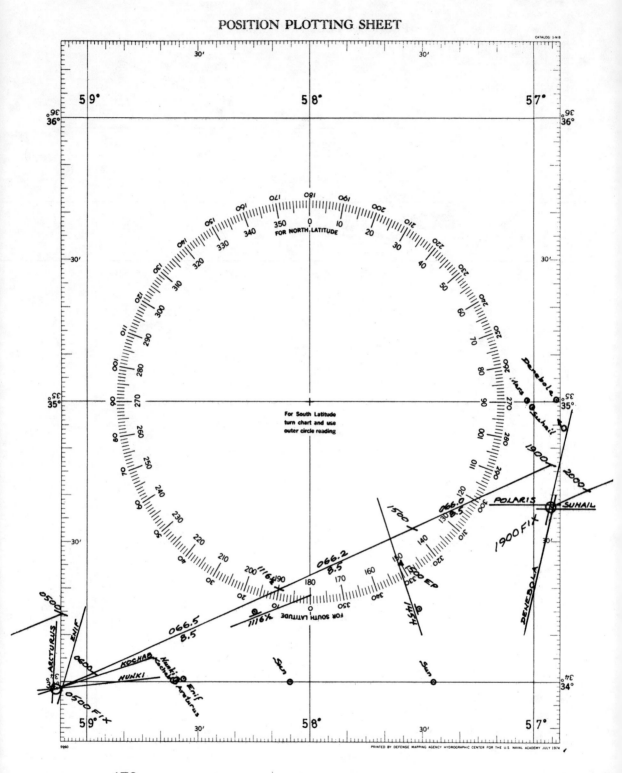

PLOT 6

POSITION PLOTTING SHEET

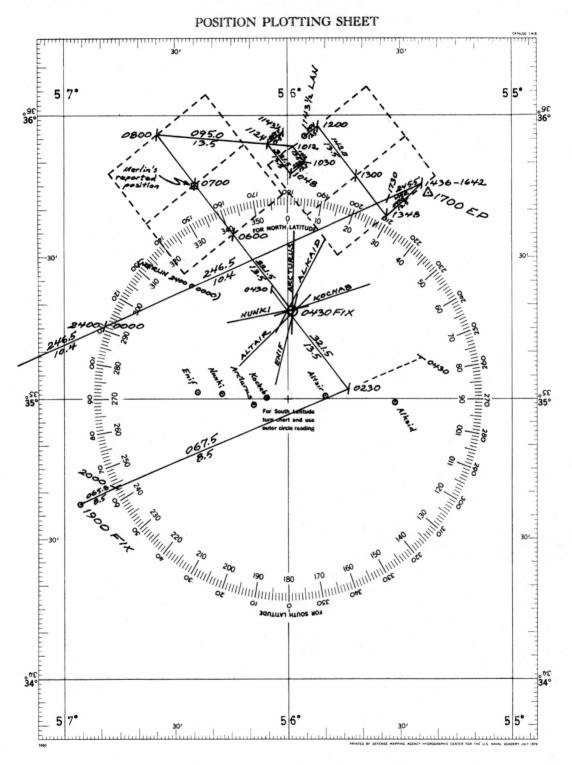

PLOT 7

POSITION PLOTTING SHEET

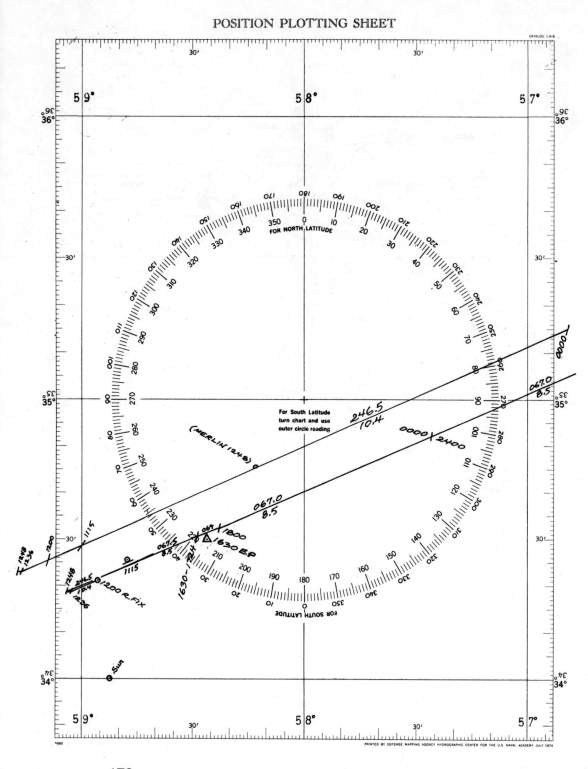

PLOT 8

POSITION PLOTTING SHEET

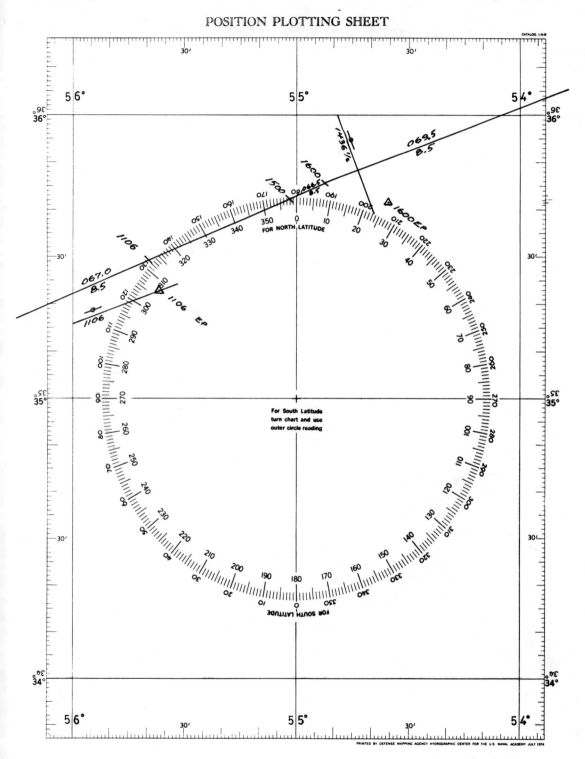

PLOT 9

POSITION PLOTTING SHEET

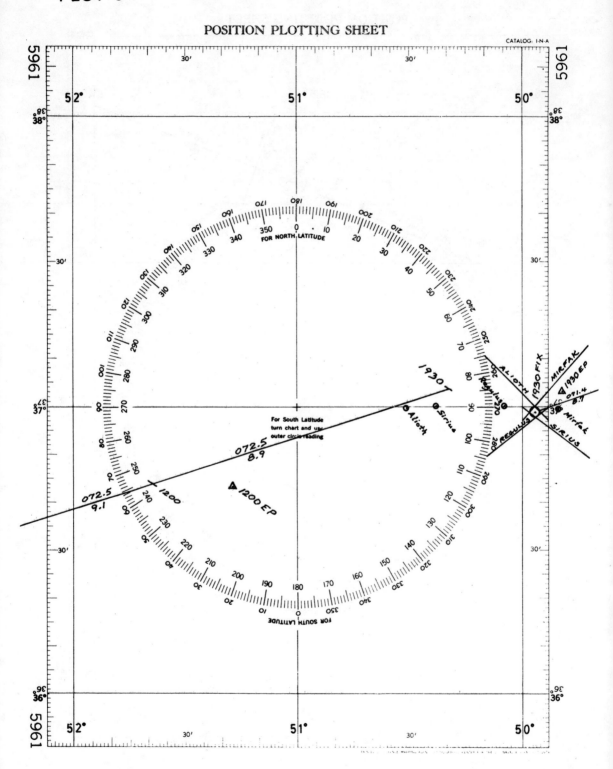

PLOT 10

POSITION PLOTTING SHEET

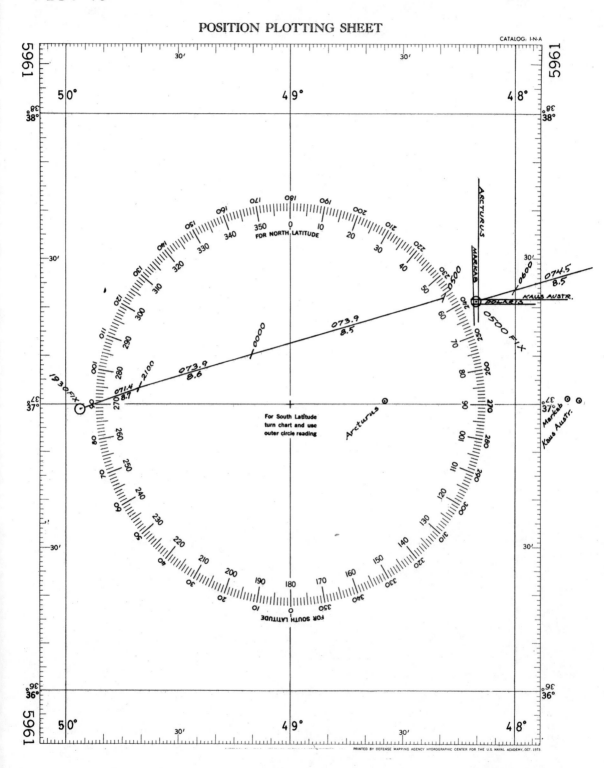

POSITION PLOTTING SHEET

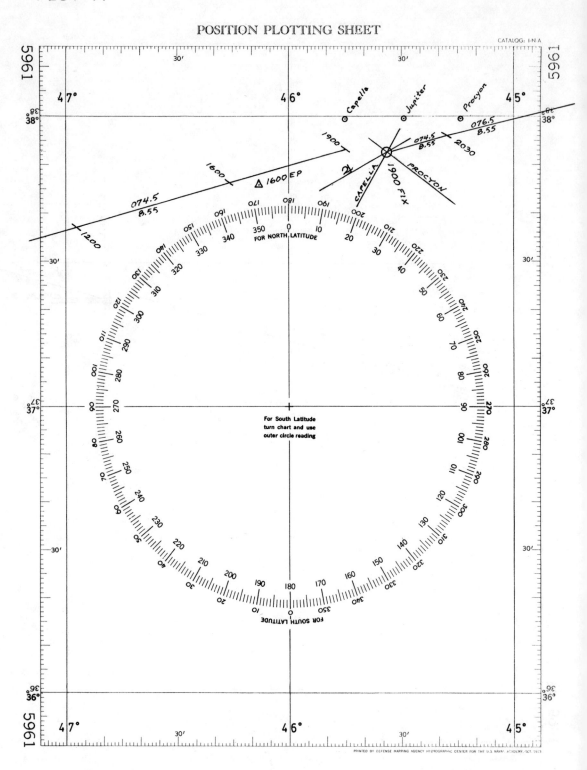

PLOT 12

POSITION PLOTTING SHEET

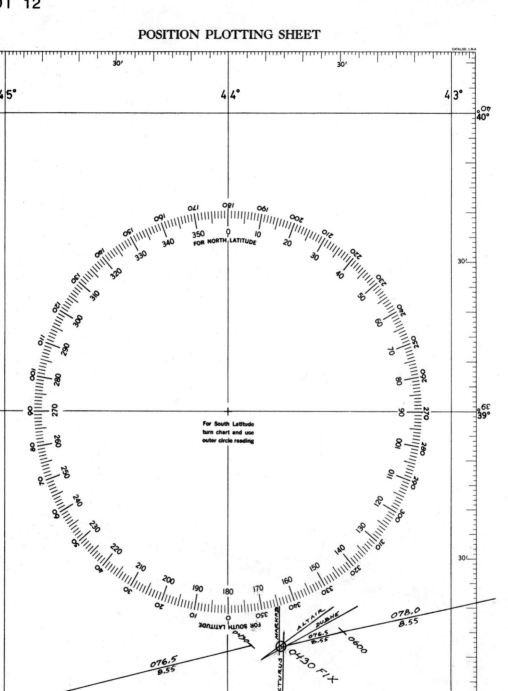

PLOT 13

POSITION PLOTTING SHEET

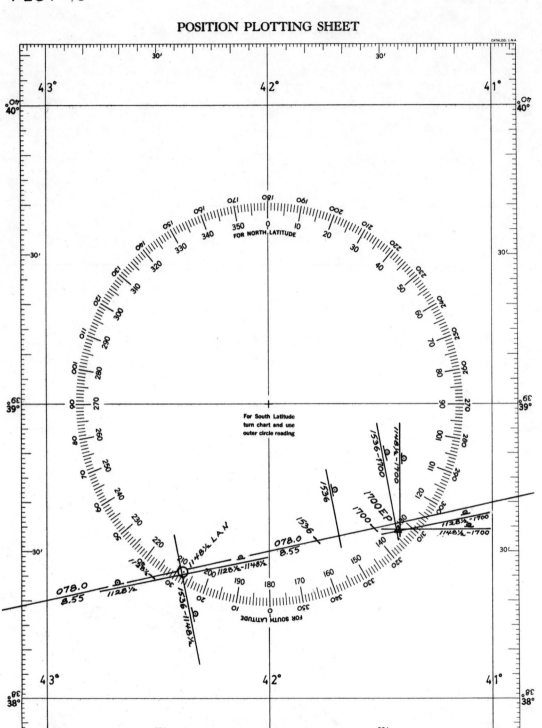

PLOT 14

POSITION PLOTTING SHEET

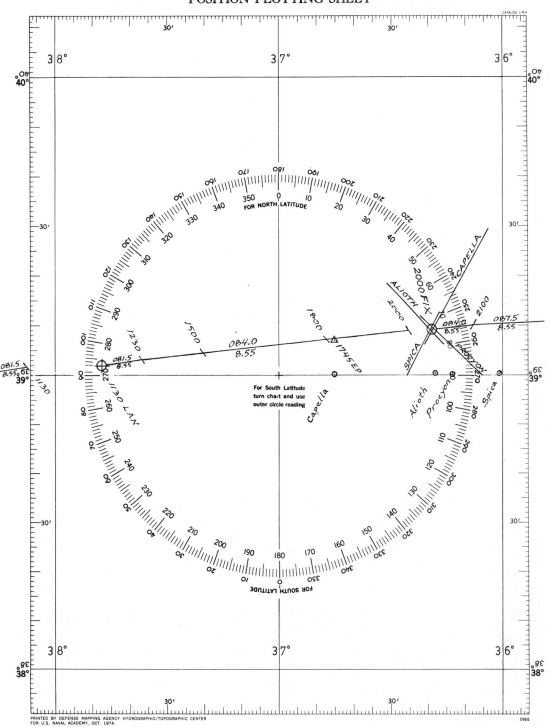

POSITION PLOTTING SHEET

PLOT 16

POSITION PLOTTING SHEET

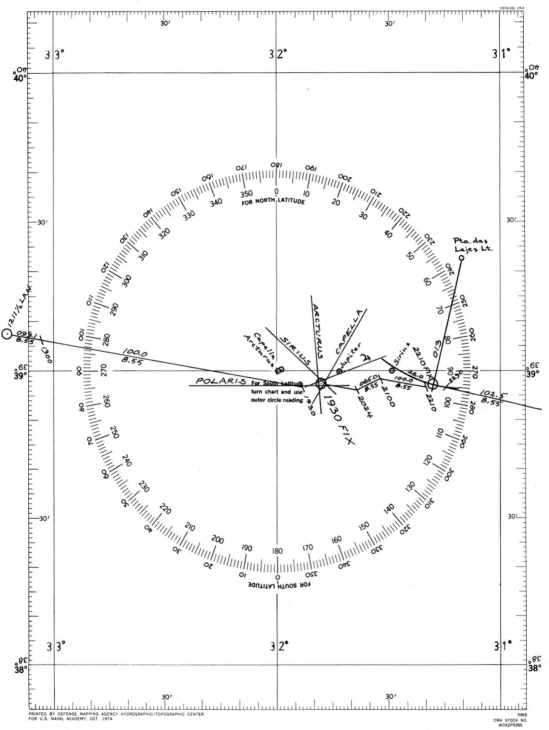

PLOT 17

POSITION PLOTTING SHEET

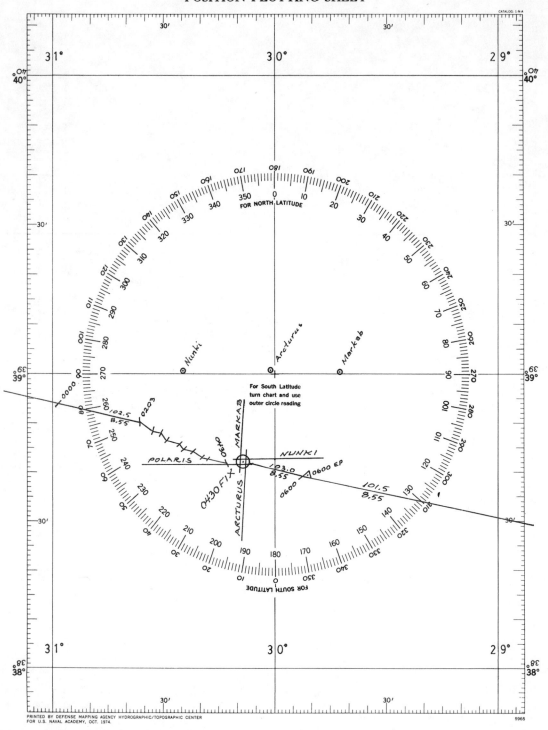

PRINTED BY DEFENSE MAPPING AGENCY HYDROGRAPHIC/TOPOGRAPHIC CENTER
FOR U.S. NAVAL ACADEMY, OCT. 1974.

APPENDIX

PATTERN 6

Ship/Aircraft Co-ordinated Search Pattern

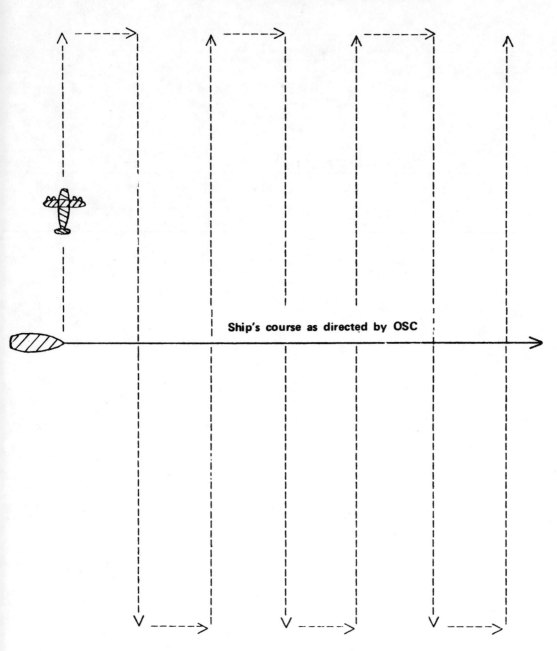

Ship's course as directed by OSC

Source: *Merchant Ship Search and Rescue Manual (MERSAR), third edition.* International Maritime Organization (IMO). 1984. p. 45.

190

PATTERN 1

Expanding Square Search Pattern—1 Ship

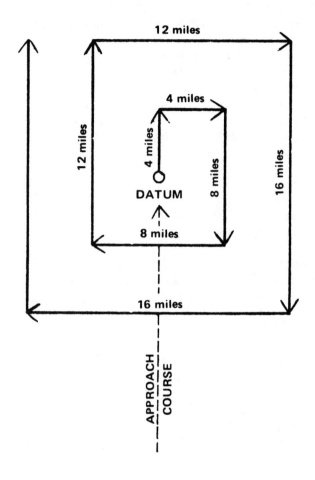

Source: *Merchant Ship Search and Rescue Manual (MERSAR), third edition.* International Maritime Organization (IMO). 1984. p. 39.

191

List of Abbreviations Used in This Work

a	altitude intercept
add'l	additional
arc	inverse (of a trigonometric function)
APR	April
C	Celsius or centigrade; course angle
C.	civil (as in civil twilight)
Cc	compass course
CE	compass error; chronometer error
Cm	magnetic course
CMG	course made good or course to make good
Cn	true course
corr'n	correction
CT	chronometer time
CTS	course to steer
D	distance
d	declination; day or days
Dev	deviation
D/F	direction finder (radio)
DLo	difference of longitude
DR	dead reckoning or dead reckoning position
E	East
EP	estimated position
EqT	equation of time
ETA	estimated time of arrival
FM	frequency modulation
gal	gallon, gallons
GAT	Greenwich apparent time
GHA	Greenwich hour angle
GMT	Greenwich mean time
gph	gallons per hour
H	altitude
h	hour or hours
Ha	apparent altitude
Hc	calculated altitude
HE	height of eye
Ho	observed altitude
HP	horizontal parallax
Hs	sextant altitude
I.	Island
IE	index error
I.V.	intravenous
kn	knot or knots
L	latitude
l	difference of latitude
LAN	local apparent noon

LHA	local hour angle
Lm	middle latitude
LMT	local mean time
LOP	line of position
Lt.	light or lighthouse
M	meridional parts
m	difference of meridional parts; minute or minutes
mi	mile or miles
min.	minute or minutes
M/V	motor vessel
N	North
N.	nautical (as in nautical twilight)
p	departure
refr	refraction
S	South; speed
s	second, seconds
sec	secant
SHA	sidereal hour angle
sin	sine
St.	Saint
STBD	starboard
T	time
t	meridian angle
V	variation
v	proportional hour-angle correction for planets
var	various
VHF	very high frequency
W	West
WSW	West Southwest
Z	azimuth angle
z	zenith distance
ZD	zone description
Zn	true azimuth
ZT	zone time
λ	longitude
♈	Aries

PEREGRINE's Traverse Board, April 1968

Date	Time Span	Cc	V(W)	Dev	CE(W)	Cn	D(mi)	∠ (N+)	p (E+)
12	1800-1900	082½	15	1.7 E	13.3	069.2	8.50	3.02	7.95
	1900-2400	081	15½	1.7 E	13.8	067.2	42.50	16.47	39.18
13	0000-0500	081	15½	1.7 E	13.8	067.2	42.50	16.47	39.18
	0500-0600	081	16	1.7 E	14.3	066.7	8.50	3.36	7.81
	0600-0800	080	16	1.7 E	14.3	065.7	17.00	7.00	15.49
	0800-1128½	081	16½	1.5 E	15.0	066.0	29.54	12.02	26.99
	1128½-1500	081	17	1.5 E	15.5	065.5	29.96	12.42	27.26
	1500-1600	081	17	1.5 E	15.5	065.5	8.50	3.52	7.73
	1600-2100	083½	17½	1.5 E	16.0	067.5	42.50	16.26	39.26
	2100-2200	083	17½	1.5 E	16.0	067.0	8.50	3.32	7.82
	2200-2400	084	18	1.5 E	16.5	067.5	17.00	6.50	15.70
14	0000-0500	084	18	1.5 E	16.5	067.5	42.50	16.26	39.26
	0500-0600	084	18	1.5 E	16.5	067.5	8.50	3.25	7.85
	0600-1116½	083½	18½	1.5 E	17.0	066.5	44.80	17.86	41.08
	1116½-1500	083½	18½	1.5 E	17.0	066.5	31.70	12.64	29.07
	1500-1900	083½	19	1.5 E	17.5	066.0	34.00	13.83	31.06
	1900-2000	083½	19	1.5 E	17.5	066.0	8.50	3.46	7.76
	2000-2400	085½	19½	1.5 E	18.0	067.5	34.00	13.01	31.41
15	0000-0230	085½	19½	1.5 E	18.0	067.5	21.25	8.13	19.63
	0230-0430	341½	19½	0.5 W	20.0	321.5	27.00	21.13	-16.81
	0430-0800	341½	19½	0.5 W	20.0	321.5	47.25	36.98	-29.41
	0800-1012	114½	19½	ZERO	19.5	095.0	29.70	-2.59	29.59
	1012-1030	161½	19½	ZERO	19.5	142.0	4.05	-3.19	2.49
	1030-1048	251½	19½	ZERO	19.5	232.0	4.05	-2.49	-3.19
	1048-1124	341½	19½	0.5 W	20.0	321.5	8.10	6.34	-5.04

Date	Time Span	Cc	V(W)	Dev	CE(W)	Cn	D(mi)	$\angle$ (N+)	p (E+)
15	1124–1143½	071½	19½	2.0 E	17.5	054.0	4.44	2.61	3.59
	1143½–1200	071½	19½	2.0 E	17.5	054.0	3.66	2.15	2.96
	1200–1348	161½	19½	ZERO	19.5	142.0	24.30	−19.15	14.96
	1348–1400	065	19½	2.0 E	17.5	047.5	2.70	1.82	1.99
	1400–1436	065	19½	2.0 E	17.5	047.5	7.50	5.07	5.53
	1436–1642	STOPPED, DRIFTING							
	1642–1730	265	19½	ZERO	19.5	245.5	7.80	−3.23	−7.10
	1730–2400	266	19½	ZERO	19.5	246.5	67.60	−26.96	−61.99
16	0000–1200	265½	19	ZERO	19.0	246.5	124.80	−49.76	−114.45
	1200–1236	265½	19	ZERO	19.0	246.5	6.24	−2.49	−5.72
	1236–1248	285	19	ZERO	19.0	266.0	0.90	−0.06	−0.90
	1248–1630	085	19	1.5 E	17.5	067.5	31.45	12.04	29.06
	1630–1724	STOPPED, DRIFTING							
	1724–1800	086½	19	1.5 E	17.5	069.0	5.10	1.83	4.76
	1800–2400	085	19½	1.5 E	18.0	067.0	51.00	19.93	46.94
17	0000–1106	085	19½	1.5 E	18.0	067.0	94.38	36.88	86.88
	1106–1500	085	19½	1.5 E	18.0	067.0	33.11	12.94	30.48
	1500–1600	085	20	1.5 E	18.5	066.5	8.50	3.39	7.80
	1600–2400	088	20	1.5 E	18.5	069.5	68.00	23.81	63.69
18	0000–0100	TIME ZONE CHANGE, NO PROGRESS							
	0100–0300	088	20	1.5 E	18.5	069.5	17.00	5.95	15.92
	0300–0600	088	20	1.5 E	18.5	069.5	27.00	9.46	25.29
	0600–1200	088	20	1.5 E	18.5	069.5	54.60	19.12	51.14
	1200–1900	091½	20½	1.5 E	19.0	072.5	62.30	18.73	59.42
	1900–1930	091½	20½	1.5 E	19.0	072.5	4.35	1.31	4.15
	1930–2100	091½	20½	0.4 E	20.1	071.4	13.05	4.16	12.37
	2100–2400	094	20½	0.4 E	20.1	073.9	25.80	7.15	24.79

Date	Time Span	Cc	V(W)	Dev	CE(W)	Cn	D(mi)	∠(N+)	p (E+)
19	0000-0500	094	20½	0.4 E	20.1	073.9	42.50	11.78	40.83
	0500-0600	094	20½	0.5 E	20.0	074.0	8.50	2.34	8.17
	0600-1900	094½	20½	0.5 E	20.0	074.5	111.11	29.69	107.07
	1900-2030	094½	20½	0.5 E	20.0	074.5	12.82	3.42	12.35
	2030-2400	096	20	0.5 E	19.5	076.5	29.92	6.98	29.09
20	0000-0430	096	20	0.5 E	19.5	076.5	38.48	8.98	37.42
	0430-0600	096	20	0.5 E	19.5	076.5	12.82	2.99	12.46
	0600-1128½	097½	20	0.5 E	19.5	078.0	46.81	9.73	45.79
	1128½-1148½	097½	20	0.5 E	19.5	078.0	2.85	0.59	2.79
	1148½-1536	097½	20	0.5 E	19.5	078.0	32.42	6.74	31.71
	1536-1700	097½	20	0.5 E	19.5	078.0	11.97	2.49	11.71
	1700-2400	098½	19½	0.5 E	19.0	079.5	59.85	10.91	58.85
21	0000-0500	098½	19½	0.5 E	19.0	079.5	42.75	7.79	42.03
	0500-1130	100	19	0.5 E	18.5	081.5	55.58	8.22	54.97
	1130-1230	100	19	0.5 E	18.5	081.5	8.55	1.26	8.46
	1230-1400	102½	19	0.5 E	18.5	084.0	12.82	1.34	12.75
	1400-1500	TIME ZONE CHANGE, NO PROGRESS							
	1500-1800	102	18½	0.5 E	18.0	084.0	25.65	2.68	25.51
	1800-2000	102½	18½	ZERO	18.5	084.0	17.10	1.79	17.01
	2000-2100	102½	18½	ZERO	18.5	084.0	8.55	0.89	8.50
	2100-2400	105½	18	ZERO	18.0	087.5	25.65	1.12	25.62
22	0000-0500	105½	18	ZERO	18.0	087.5	42.75	1.86	42.71
	0500-0630	105½	18	ZERO	18.0	087.5	12.82	0.56	12.81
	0630-0700	116½	17½	0.4 W	17.9	098.6	4.28	-0.64	4.23
	0700-1211½	117	17½	0.4 W	17.9	099.1	44.39	-7.02	43.83
	1211½-1300	117	17½	0.4 W	17.9	099.1	6.91	-1.09	6.82
	1300-1930	117½	17	0.5 W	17.5	100.0	55.58	-9.65	54.74

PEREGRINE's Traverse Board, April 1968 (cont'd)

Date	Time Span	Cc	V(W)	Dev	CE(W)	Cn	D(mi)	$\angle$ (N+)	p (E+)
22	1930–2024	117½	17	0.5 W	17.5	100.0	7.70	−1.34	7.58
	2024–2100	080	16½	1.5 E	15.0	065.0	5.13	2.17	4.65
	2100–2210	117	16½	0.5 W	17.0	100.0	9.97	−1.73	9.82
	2210–2230	117	16½	0.5 W	17.0	100.0	2.85	−0.49	2.81
	2230–2400	119½	16½	0.5 W	17.0	102.5	12.82	−2.77	12.52
23	0000–0203	119½	16½	0.5 W	17.0	102.5	17.53	−3.79	17.11
	0203–0227	145	16½	ZERO	16.5	128.5	3.42	−2.13	2.68
	0227–0239	120	16½	0.5 W	17.0	103.0	1.71	−0.38	1.67
	0239–0251	160	16½	ZERO	16.5	143.5	1.71	−1.37	1.02
	0251–0312	120	16½	0.5 W	17.0	103.0	2.99	−0.67	2.91
	0312–0321	160	16½	ZERO	16.5	143.5	1.28	−1.03	0.76
	0321–0336	120	16½	0.5 W	17.0	103.0	2.14	−0.48	2.08
	0336–0351	140	16½	ZERO	16.5	123.5	2.14	−1.18	1.78
	0351–0400	120	16½	0.5 W	17.0	103.0	1.28	−0.29	1.25
	0400–0430	119½	16½	0.5 W	17.0	102.5	4.28	−0.93	4.18
	0430–0600	119½	16	0.5 W	16.5	103.0	12.82	−2.88	12.49
	0600–1148	118	16	0.5 W	16.5	101.5	49.59	−9.89	48.59

TABLE 5
Meridional Parts

Lat.	30°	31°	32°	33°	34°	35°	36°	37°	38°	39°	Lat.
0	1876. 9	1946. 2	2016. 2	2087. 0	2158. 6	2231. 1	2304. 5	2378. 8	2454. 1	2530. 4	0
1	78. 0	47. 3	17. 4	88. 2	59. 8	32. 3	05. 7	80. 0	55. 3	31. 7	1
2	79. 2	48. 5	18. 5	89. 4	61. 0	33. 5	06. 9	81. 3	56. 6	33. 0	2
3	80. 3	49. 6	19. 7	90. 5	62. 2	34. 7	08. 1	82. 5	57. 9	34. 3	3
4	81. 5	50. 8	20. 9	91. 7	63. 4	35. 9	09. 4	83. 8	59. 1	35. 6	4
5	1882. 6	1952. 0	2022. 1	2092. 9	2164. 6	2237. 2	2310. 6	2385. 0	2460. 4	2536. 8	5
6	83. 8	53. 1	23. 2	94. 1	65. 8	38. 4	11. 8	85. 3	61. 7	38. 1	6
7	84. 9	54. 3	24. 4	95. 3	67. 0	39. 6	13. 1	87. 5	62. 9	39. 4	7
8	86. 1	55. 4	25. 6	96. 5	68. 2	40. 8	14. 3	88. 8	64. 2	40. 7	8
9	87. 2	56. 6	26. 8	97. 7	69. 4	42. 0	15. 5	90. 0	65. 5	42. 0	9
10	1888. 4	1957. 8	2027. 9	2098. 9	2170. 6	2243. 2	2316. 8	2391. 3	2466. 7	2543. 3	10
11	89. 5	58. 9	29. 1	2100. 1	71. 8	44. 5	18. 0	92. 5	68. 0	44. 5	11
12	90. 7	60. 1	30. 3	01. 2	73. 0	45. 7	19. 2	93. 8	69. 3	45. 8	12
13	91. 8	61. 3	31. 5	02. 4	74. 2	46. 9	20. 5	95. 0	70. 5	47. 1	13
14	93. 0	62. 4	32. 6	03. 6	75. 4	48. 1	21. 7	96. 3	71. 8	48. 4	14
15	1894. 1	1963. 6	2033. 8	2104. 8	2176. 6	2249. 3	2322. 9	2397. 5	2473. 1	2549. 7	15
16	95. 3	64. 8	35. 0	06. 0	77. 8	50. 6	24. 2	2398. 8	74. 3	51. 0	16
17	96. 4	65. 9	36. 2	07. 2	79. 0	51. 8	25. 4	2400. 0	75. 6	52. 3	17
18	97. 6	67. 1	37. 3	08. 4	80. 3	53. 0	26. 6	01. 3	76. 9	53. 6	18
19	98. 7	68. 2	38. 5	09. 6	81. 5	54. 2	27. 9	02. 5	78. 1	54. 8	19
20	1899. 9	1969. 4	2039. 7	2110. 8	2182. 7	2255. 4	2329. 1	2403. 8	2479. 4	2556. 1	20
21	1901. 0	70. 6	40. 9	12. 0	83. 9	56. 7	30. 4	05. 0	80. 7	57. 4	21
22	02. 2	71. 7	42. 1	13. 1	85. 1	57. 9	31. 6	06. 3	82. 0	58. 7	22
23	03. 3	72. 9	43. 2	14. 3	86. 3	59. 1	32. 8	07. 5	83. 2	60. 0	23
24	04. 5	74. 1	44. 4	15. 5	87. 5	60. 3	34. 1	08. 8	84. 5	61. 3	24
25	1905. 6	1975. 2	2045. 6	2116. 7	2188. 7	2261. 5	2335. 3	2410. 0	2485. 8	2562. 6	25
26	06. 8	76. 4	46. 8	17. 9	89. 9	62. 8	36. 5	11. 3	87. 0	63. 9	26
27	08. 0	77. 6	47. 9	19. 1	91. 1	64. 0	37. 8	12. 5	88. 3	65. 1	27
28	09. 1	78. 7	49. 1	20. 3	92. 3	65. 2	39. 0	13. 8	89. 6	66. 4	28
29	10. 3	79. 9	50. 3	21. 5	93. 5	66. 4	40. 3	15. 0	90. 9	67. 7	29
30	1911. 4	1981. 1	2051. 5	2122. 7	2194. 7	2267. 6	2341. 5	2416. 3	2492. 1	2569. 0	30
31	12. 6	82. 2	52. 7	23. 9	95. 9	68. 9	42. 7	17. 6	93. 4	70. 3	31
32	13. 7	83. 4	53. 8	25. 1	97. 1	70. 1	44. 0	18. 8	94. 7	71. 6	32
33	14. 9	84. 6	55. 0	26. 3	98. 4	71. 3	45. 2	20. 1	95. 9	72. 9	33
34	16. 0	85. 7	56. 2	27. 5	2199. 6	72. 5	46. 4	21. 3	97. 2	74. 2	34
35	1917. 2	1986. 9	2057. 4	2128. 7	2200. 8	2273. 8	2347. 7	2422. 6	2498. 5	2575. 5	35
36	18. 4	88. 1	58. 6	29. 9	02. 0	75. 0	48. 9	23. 8	2499. 8	76. 8	36
37	19. 5	89. 2	59. 7	31. 1	03. 2	76. 2	50. 2	25. 1	2501. 0	78. 1	37
38	20. 7	90. 4	60. 9	32. 2	04. 4	77. 4	51. 4	26. 3	02. 3	79. 4	38
39	21. 8	91. 6	62. 1	33. 4	05. 6	78. 7	52. 6	27. 6	03. 6	80. 6	39
40	1923. 0	1992. 8	2063. 3	2134. 6	2206. 8	2279. 9	2353. 9	2428. 9	2504. 9	2581. 9	40
41	24. 1	93. 9	64. 5	35. 8	08. 0	81. 1	55. 1	30. 1	06. 1	83. 2	41
42	25. 3	95. 1	65. 7	37. 0	09. 2	82. 3	56. 4	31. 4	07. 4	84. 5	42
43	26. 4	96. 3	66. 8	38. 2	10. 5	83. 6	57. 6	32. 6	08. 7	85. 8	43
44	27. 6	97. 4	68. 0	39. 4	11. 7	84. 8	58. 9	33. 9	10. 0	87. 1	44
45	1928. 8	1998. 6	2069. 2	2140. 6	2212. 9	2286. 0	2360. 1	2435. 2	2511. 2	2588. 4	45
46	29. 9	1999. 8	70. 4	41. 8	14. 1	87. 2	61. 3	36. 4	12. 5	89. 7	46
47	31. 1	2000. 9	71. 6	43. 0	15. 3	88. 5	62. 6	37. 7	13. 8	91. 0	47
48	32. 2	02. 1	72. 8	44. 2	16. 5	89. 7	63. 8	38. 9	15. 1	92. 3	48
49	33. 4	03. 3	73. 9	45. 4	17. 7	90. 9	65. 1	40. 2	16. 4	93. 6	49
50	1934. 6	2004. 5	2075. 1	2146. 6	2218. 9	2292. 2	2366. 3	2441. 5	2517. 6	2594. 9	50
51	35. 7	05. 6	76. 3	47. 8	20. 1	93. 4	67. 6	42. 7	18. 9	96. 2	51
52	36. 9	06. 8	77. 5	49. 0	21. 4	94. 6	68. 8	44. 0	20. 2	97. 5	52
53	38. 0	08. 0	78. 7	50. 2	22. 6	95. 8	70. 0	45. 2	21. 5	2598. 8	53
54	39. 2	09. 1	79. 9	51. 4	23. 8	97. 1	71. 2	46. 5	22. 8	2600. 1	54
55	1940. 4	2010. 3	2081. 1	2152. 6	2225. 0	2298. 3	2372. 5	2447. 8	2524. 0	2601. 4	55
56	41. 5	11. 5	82. 2	53. 8	26. 2	2299. 5	73. 8	49. 0	25. 3	02. 7	56
57	42. 7	12. 7	83. 4	55. 0	27. 4	2300. 8	75. 0	50. 3	26. 6	04. 0	57
58	43. 8	13. 8	84. 6	56. 2	28. 6	02. 0	76. 3	51. 6	27. 9	05. 3	58
59	45. 0	15. 0	85. 8	57. 4	29. 9	03. 2	77. 5	52. 8	29. 2	06. 6	59
60	1946. 2	2016. 2	2087. 0	2158. 6	2231. 1	2304. 5	2378. 8	2454. 1	2530. 4	2607. 9	60
Lat.	30°	31°	32°	33°	34°	35°	36°	37°	38°	39°	Lat.

TABLE 8
Distance of the Horizon

Height Feet	Nautical miles	Statute miles	Height meters	Height Feet	Nautical miles	Statute miles	Height meters
1	1.2	1.3	.30	120	12.8	14.7	36.58
2	1.7	1.9	.61	125	13.1	15.1	38.10
3	2.0	2.3	.91	130	13.3	15.4	39.62
4	2.3	2.7	1.22	135	13.6	15.6	41.15
5	2.6	3.0	1.52	140	13.8	15.9	42.67
6	2.9	3.3	1.83	145	14.1	16.2	44.20
7	3.1	3.6	2.13	150	14.3	16.5	45.72
8	3.3	3.8	2.44	160	14.8	17.0	48.77
9	3.5	4.0	2.74	170	15.3	17.6	51.82
10	3.7	4.3	3.05	180	15.7	18.1	54.86
11	3.9	4.5	3.35	190	16.1	18.6	57.91
12	4.1	4.7	3.66	200	16.5	19.0	60.96
13	4.2	4.9	3.96	210	17.0	19.5	64.01
14	4.4	5.0	4.27	220	17.4	20.0	67.06
15	4.5	5.2	4.57	230	17.7	20.4	70.10
16	4.7	5.4	4.88	240	18.1	20.9	73.15
17	4.8	5.6	5.18	250	18.5	21.3	76.20
18	5.0	5.7	5.49	260	18.9	21.7	79.25
19	5.1	5.9	5.79	270	19.2	22.1	82.30
20	5.2	6.0	6.10	280	19.6	22.5	85.34
21	5.4	6.2	6.40	290	19.9	22.9	88.39
22	5.5	6.3	6.71	300	20.3	23.3	91.44
23	5.6	6.5	7.01	310	20.6	23.7	94.49
24	5.7	6.6	7.32	320	20.9	24.1	97.54
25	5.9	6.7	7.62	330	21.3	24.5	100.58
26	6.0	6.9	7.92	340	21.6	24.8	103.63
27	6.1	7.0	8.23	350	21.9	25.2	106.68
28	6.2	7.1	8.53	360	22.2	25.5	109.73
29	6.3	7.3	8.84	370	22.5	25.9	112.78
30	6.4	7.4	9.14	380	22.8	26.2	115.82
31	6.5	7.5	9.45	390	23.1	26.6	118.87
32	6.6	7.6	9.75	400	23.4	26.9	121.92
33	6.7	7.7	10.06	410	23.7	27.3	124.97
34	6.8	7.9	10.36	420	24.0	27.6	128.02
35	6.9	8.0	10.67	430	24.3	27.9	131.06
36	7.0	8.1	10.97	440	24.5	28.2	134.11
37	7.1	8.2	11.28	450	24.8	28.6	137.16
38	7.2	8.3	11.58	460	25.1	28.9	140.21
39	7.3	8.4	11.89	470	25.4	29.2	143.26
40	7.4	8.5	12.19	480	25.6	29.5	146.30
41	7.5	8.6	12.50	490	25.9	29.8	149.35
42	7.6	8.7	12.80	500	26.2	30.1	152.40
43	7.7	8.8	13.11	510	26.4	30.4	155.45
44	7.8	8.9	13.41	520	26.7	30.7	158.50
45	7.8	9.0	13.72	530	26.9	31.0	161.54
46	7.9	9.1	14.02	540	27.2	31.3	164.59
47	8.0	9.2	14.33	550	27.4	31.6	167.64
48	8.1	9.3	14.63	560	27.7	31.9	170.69
49	8.2	9.4	14.94	570	27.9	32.1	173.74
50	8.3	9.5	15.24	580	28.2	32.4	176.78
55	8.7	10.0	16.76	590	28.4	32.7	179.83
60	9.1	10.4	18.29	600	28.7	33.0	182.88
65	9.4	10.9	19.81	620	29.1	33.5	188.98
70	9.8	11.3	21.34	640	29.5	34.1	195.07
75	10.1	11.7	22.86	660	30.1	34.6	201.17
80	10.5	12.0	24.38	680	30.5	35.1	207.26
85	10.8	12.4	25.91	700	31.0	35.6	213.36
90	11.1	12.8	27.43	720	31.4	36.1	219.46
95	11.4	13.1	28.96	740	31.8	36.6	225.55
100	11.7	13.5	30.48	760	32.3	37.1	231.65
105	12.0	13.8	32.00	780	32.7	37.6	237.74
110	12.3	14.1	33.53	800	33.1	38.1	243.84
115	12.5	14.4	35.05	820	33.5	38.6	249.94

TABLE 27
Amplitudes

Latitude	6°0	6°5	7°0	7°5	8°0	8°5	9°0	9°5	10°0	10°5	11°0	11°5	12°0	Latitude
0	6.0	6.5	7.0	7.5	8.0	8.5	9.0	9.5	10.0	10.5	11.0	11.5	12.0	0
10	6.1	6.6	7.1	7.6	8.1	8.6	9.1	9.6	10.2	10.7	11.2	11.7	12.2	10
15	6.2	6.7	7.2	7.8	8.3	8.8	9.3	9.8	10.4	10.9	11.4	11.9	12.4	15
20	6.4	6.9	7.5	8.0	8.5	9.0	9.6	10.1	10.6	11.2	11.7	12.2	12.8	20
25	6.6	7.2	7.7	8.3	8.8	9.4	9.9	10.5	11.0	11.6	12.2	12.7	13.3	25
30	6.9	7.5	8.1	8.7	9.2	9.8	10.4	11.0	11.6	12.1	12.7	13.3	13.9	30
32	7.1	7.7	8.3	8.9	9.4	10.0	10.6	11.2	11.8	12.4	13.0	13.6	14.2	32
34	7.2	7.8	8.5	9.1	9.7	10.3	10.9	11.5	12.1	12.7	13.3	13.9	14.5	34
36	7.4	8.0	8.7	9.3	9.9	10.5	11.1	11.8	12.4	13.0	13.6	14.3	14.9	36
38	7.6	8.3	8.9	9.5	10.2	10.8	11.5	12.1	12.7	13.4	14.0	14.7	15.3	38
40	7.8	8.5	9.2	9.8	10.5	11.1	11.8	12.4	13.1	13.8	14.4	15.1	15.7	40
42	8.1	8.8	9.4	10.1	10.8	11.5	12.1	12.8	13.5	14.2	14.9	15.6	16.2	42
44	8.4	9.1	9.8	10.5	11.2	11.9	12.6	13.3	14.0	14.7	15.4	16.1	16.8	44
46	8.7	9.4	10.1	10.8	11.6	12.3	13.0	13.7	14.5	15.2	15.9	16.7	17.4	46
48	9.0	9.7	10.5	11.2	12.0	12.8	13.5	14.3	15.0	15.8	16.6	17.3	18.1	48
50	9.4	10.1	10.9	11.7	12.5	13.3	14.1	14.9	15.7	16.5	17.3	18.1	18.9	50
51	9.6	10.4	11.2	12.0	12.8	13.6	14.4	15.2	16.0	16.8	17.7	18.5	19.3	51
52	9.8	10.6	11.4	12.2	13.1	13.9	14.7	15.6	16.4	17.2	18.1	18.9	19.7	52
53	10.0	10.8	11.7	12.5	13.4	14.2	15.1	15.9	16.8	17.6	18.5	19.3	20.2	53
54	10.2	11.1	12.0	12.8	13.7	14.6	15.4	16.3	17.2	18.1	18.9	19.8	20.7	54
55	10.5	11.4	12.3	13.2	14.0	14.9	15.8	16.7	17.6	18.5	19.4	20.3	21.3	55
56	10.8	11.7	12.6	13.5	14.4	15.3	16.2	17.2	18.1	19.0	20.0	20.9	21.8	56
57	11.1	12.0	12.9	13.9	14.8	15.7	16.7	17.6	18.6	19.6	20.5	21.5	22.4	57
58	11.4	12.3	13.3	14.3	15.2	16.2	17.2	18.1	19.1	20.1	21.1	22.1	23.1	58
59	11.7	12.7	13.7	14.7	15.7	16.7	17.7	18.7	19.7	20.7	21.7	22.8	23.8	59
60	12.1	13.1	14.1	15.1	16.2	17.2	18.2	19.3	20.3	21.4	22.4	23.5	24.6	60
61	12.5	13.5	14.6	15.6	16.7	17.8	18.8	19.9	21.0	22.1	23.2	24.3	25.4	61
62	12.9	14.0	15.0	16.1	17.2	18.4	19.5	20.6	21.7	22.8	24.0	25.1	26.3	62
63	13.3	14.4	15.6	16.7	17.9	19.0	20.2	21.3	22.5	23.7	24.9	26.0	27.3	63
64	13.8	15.0	16.2	17.3	18.5	19.7	20.9	22.1	23.3	24.6	25.8	27.1	28.3	64
65.0	14.3	15.5	16.8	18.0	19.2	20.5	21.7	23.0	24.3	25.5	26.8	28.1	29.5	65.0
65.5	14.6	15.8	17.1	18.3	19.6	20.9	22.2	23.5	24.8	26.1	27.4	28.7	30.1	65.5
66.0	14.9	16.2	17.4	18.7	20.0	21.3	22.6	23.9	25.3	26.6	28.0	29.4	30.7	66.0
66.5	15.2	16.5	17.8	19.1	20.4	21.8	23.1	24.5	25.8	27.2	28.6	30.0	31.4	66.5
67.0	15.5	16.8	18.2	19.5	20.9	22.2	23.6	25.0	26.4	27.8	29.2	30.7	32.1	67.0
67.5	15.9	17.2	18.6	19.9	21.3	22.7	24.1	25.5	27.0	28.4	29.9	31.4	32.9	67.5
68.0	16.2	17.6	19.0	20.4	21.8	23.2	24.7	26.1	27.6	29.1	30.6	32.2	33.7	68.0
68.5	16.6	18.0	19.4	20.9	22.3	23.8	25.3	26.8	28.3	29.8	31.4	33.0	34.6	68.5
69.0	17.0	18.4	19.9	21.4	22.9	24.4	25.9	27.4	29.0	30.6	32.2	33.8	35.5	69.0
69.5	17.4	18.9	20.4	21.9	23.4	25.0	26.5	28.1	29.7	31.4	33.0	34.7	36.4	69.5
70.0	17.8	19.3	20.9	22.4	24.0	25.6	27.2	28.9	30.5	32.2	33.9	35.7	37.4	70.0
70.5	18.2	19.8	21.4	23.0	24.6	26.3	27.9	29.6	31.3	33.1	34.9	36.7	38.5	70.5
71.0	18.7	20.3	22.0	23.6	25.3	27.0	28.7	30.5	32.2	34.0	35.9	37.8	39.7	71.0
71.5	19.2	20.9	22.6	24.3	26.0	27.8	29.5	31.3	33.2	35.1	37.0	38.9	40.9	71.5
72.0	19.8	21.5	23.2	25.0	26.8	28.6	30.4	32.3	34.2	36.1	38.1	40.2	42.3	72.0
72.5	20.3	22.1	23.9	25.7	27.6	29.4	31.3	33.3	35.3	37.3	39.4	41.5	43.7	72.5
73.0	20.9	22.8	24.6	26.5	28.4	30.4	32.3	34.4	36.4	38.6	40.7	43.0	45.3	73.0
73.5	21.6	23.5	25.4	27.4	29.3	31.4	33.4	35.5	37.7	39.9	42.2	44.6	47.1	73.5
74.0	22.3	24.2	26.2	28.3	30.3	32.4	34.6	36.8	39.0	41.4	43.8	46.3	49.0	74.0
74.5	23.0	25.1	27.1	29.3	31.4	33.6	35.8	38.1	40.5	43.0	45.6	48.2	51.1	74.5
75.0	23.8	25.9	28.1	30.3	32.5	34.8	37.2	39.6	42.1	44.8	47.5	50.4	53.4	75.0
75.5	24.7	26.9	29.1	31.4	33.8	36.2	38.7	41.2	43.9	46.7	49.6	52.8	56.1	75.5
76.0	25.6	27.9	30.2	32.7	35.1	37.7	40.3	43.0	45.9	48.9	52.1	55.5	59.3	76.0
76.5	26.6	29.0	31.5	34.0	36.6	39.3	42.1	45.0	48.1	51.3	54.8	58.7	63.0	76.5
77.0	27.7	30.2	32.8	35.5	38.2	41.1	44.1	47.2	50.5	54.1	58.0	62.4	67.6	77.0

200

TABLE 27
Amplitudes

Latitude	12°0	12°5	13°0	13°5	14°0	14°5	15°0	15°5	16°0	16°5	17°0	17°5	18°0	Latitude
°	°	°	°	°	°	°	°	°	°	°	°	°	°	°
0	12. 0	12. 5	13. 0	13. 5	14. 0	14. 5	15. 0	15. 5	16. 0	16. 5	17. 0	17. 5	18. 0	0
10	12. 2	12. 7	13. 2	13. 7	14. 2	14. 7	15. 2	15. 7	16. 3	16. 8	17. 3	17. 8	18. 3	10
15	12. 4	12. 9	13. 5	14. 0	14. 5	15. 0	15. 5	16. 1	16. 6	17. 1	17. 6	18. 1	18. 7	15
20	12. 8	13. 3	13. 9	14. 4	14. 9	15. 5	16. 0	16. 5	17. 1	17. 6	18. 1	18. 7	19. 2	20
25	13. 3	13. 8	14. 4	14. 9	15. 5	16. 0	16. 6	17. 1	17. 7	18. 3	18. 8	19. 4	19. 9	25
30	13. 9	14. 5	15. 1	15. 6	16. 2	16. 8	17. 4	18. 0	18. 6	19. 1	19. 7	20. 3	20. 9	30
32	14. 2	14. 8	15. 4	16. 0	16. 6	17. 2	17. 8	18. 4	19. 0	19. 6	20. 2	20. 8	21. 4	32
34	14. 5	15. 1	15. 7	16. 4	17. 0	17. 6	18. 2	18. 8	19. 4	20. 0	20. 7	21. 3	21. 9	34
36	14. 9	15. 5	16. 1	16. 8	17. 4	18. 0	18. 7	19. 3	19. 9	20. 6	21. 2	21. 8	22. 5	36
38	15. 3	15. 9	16. 6	17. 2	17. 9	18. 5	19. 2	19. 8	20. 5	21. 1	21. 8	22. 4	23. 1	38
40	15. 7	16. 4	17. 1	17. 7	18. 4	19. 1	19. 7	20. 4	21. 1	21. 8	22. 4	23. 1	23. 8	40
41	16. 0	16. 7	17. 3	18. 0	18. 7	19. 4	20. 1	20. 8	21. 4	22. 1	22. 8	23. 5	24. 2	41
42	16. 2	16. 9	17. 6	18. 3	19. 0	19. 7	20. 4	21. 1	21. 8	22. 5	23. 2	23. 9	24. 6	42
43	16. 5	17. 2	17. 9	18. 6	19. 3	20. 0	20. 7	21. 4	22. 1	22. 9	23. 6	24. 3	25. 0	43
44	16. 8	17. 5	18. 2	18. 9	19. 7	20. 4	21. 1	21. 8	22. 5	23. 3	24. 0	24. 7	25. 4	44
45	17. 1	17. 8	18. 5	19. 3	20. 0	20. 7	21. 5	22. 2	22. 9	23. 7	24. 4	25. 2	25. 9	45
46	17. 4	18. 2	18. 9	19. 6	20. 4	21. 1	21. 9	22. 6	23. 4	24. 1	24. 9	25. 7	26. 4	46
47	17. 7	18. 5	19. 3	20. 0	20. 8	21. 5	22. 3	23. 1	23. 8	24. 6	25. 4	26. 2	26. 9	47
48	18. 1	18. 9	19. 6	20. 4	21. 2	22. 0	22. 8	23. 5	24. 3	25. 1	25. 9	26. 7	27. 5	48
49	18. 5	19. 3	20. 1	20. 8	21. 6	22. 4	23. 2	24. 0	24. 8	25. 7	26. 5	27. 3	28. 1	49
50	18. 9	19. 7	20. 5	21. 3	22. 1	22. 9	23. 7	24. 6	25. 4	26. 2	27. 1	27. 9	28. 7	50
51	19. 3	20. 1	20. 9	21. 8	22. 6	23. 4	24. 3	25. 1	26. 0	26. 8	27. 7	28. 5	29. 4	51
52	19. 7	20. 6	21. 4	22. 3	23. 1	24. 0	24. 9	25. 7	26. 6	27. 5	28. 3	29. 2	30. 1	52
53	20. 2	21. 1	21. 9	22. 8	23. 7	24. 6	25. 5	26. 4	27. 3	28. 2	29. 1	30. 0	30. 9	53
54	20. 7	21. 6	22. 5	23. 4	24. 3	25. 2	26. 1	27. 0	28. 0	28. 9	29. 8	30. 8	31. 7	54
55	21. 3	22. 2	23. 1	24. 0	24. 9	25. 9	26. 8	27. 8	28. 7	29. 7	30. 6	31. 6	32. 6	55
56	21. 8	22. 8	23. 7	24. 7	25. 6	26. 6	27. 6	28. 5	29. 5	30. 5	31. 5	32. 5	33. 5	56
57	22. 4	23. 4	24. 4	25. 4	26. 4	27. 4	28. 4	29. 4	30. 4	31. 4	32. 5	33. 5	34. 6	57
58	23. 1	24. 1	25. 1	26. 1	27. 2	28. 2	29. 2	30. 3	31. 3	32. 4	33. 5	34. 6	35. 7	58
59	23. 8	24. 8	25. 9	27. 0	28. 0	29. 1	30. 2	31. 3	32. 4	33. 5	34. 6	35. 7	36. 9	59
60	24. 6	25. 7	26. 7	27. 8	28. 9	30. 1	31. 2	32. 3	33. 5	34. 6	35. 8	37. 0	38. 2	60
61	25. 4	26. 5	27. 6	28. 8	29. 9	31. 1	32. 3	33. 5	34. 6	35. 9	37. 1	38. 3	39. 6	61
62	26. 3	27. 5	28. 6	29. 8	31. 0	32. 2	33. 5	34. 7	36. 0	37. 2	38. 5	39. 8	41. 2	62
63	27. 3	28. 5	29. 7	30. 9	32. 2	33. 5	34. 8	36. 1	37. 4	38. 7	40. 1	41. 5	42. 9	63
64	28. 3	29. 6	30. 9	32. 2	33. 5	34. 8	36. 2	37. 6	39. 0	40. 4	41. 8	43. 3	44. 8	64
65. 0	29. 5	30. 8	32. 2	33. 5	34. 9	36. 3	37. 8	39. 2	40. 7	42. 2	43. 8	45. 4	47. 0	65. 0
65. 5	30. 1	31. 5	32. 9	34. 3	35. 7	37. 1	38. 6	40. 1	41. 7	43. 2	44. 8	46. 5	48. 2	65. 5
66. 0	30. 7	32. 1	33. 6	35. 0	36. 5	38. 0	39. 5	41. 1	42. 7	44. 3	46. 0	47. 7	49. 4	66. 0
66. 5	31. 4	32. 9	34. 3	35. 8	37. 3	38. 9	40. 5	42. 1	43. 7	45. 4	47. 2	48. 9	50. 8	66. 5
67. 0	32. 1	33. 6	35. 1	36. 7	38. 3	39. 9	41. 5	43. 2	44. 9	46. 6	48. 4	50. 3	52. 3	67. 0
67. 5	32. 9	34. 4	36. 0	37. 6	39. 2	40. 9	42. 6	44. 3	46. 1	47. 9	49. 8	51. 8	53. 9	67. 5
68. 0	33. 7	35. 3	36. 9	38. 6	40. 2	41. 9	43. 7	45. 5	47. 4	49. 3	51. 3	53. 4	55. 6	68. 0
68. 5	34. 6	36. 2	37. 9	39. 6	41. 3	43. 1	44. 9	46. 8	48. 8	50. 8	52. 9	55. 1	57. 5	68. 5
69. 0	35. 5	37. 2	38. 9	40. 6	42. 5	44. 3	46. 2	48. 2	50. 3	52. 4	54. 7	57. 0	59. 6	69. 0
69. 5	36. 4	38. 2	40. 0	41. 8	43. 7	45. 6	47. 7	49. 7	51. 9	54. 2	56. 6	59. 2	61. 9	69. 5
70. 0	37. 4	39. 3	41. 1	43. 0	45. 0	47. 1	49. 2	51. 4	53. 7	56. 1	58. 7	61. 5	64. 6	70. 0
70. 5	38. 5	40. 4	42. 4	44. 4	46. 4	48. 6	50. 8	53. 2	55. 7	58. 3	61. 1	64. 3	67. 8	70. 5
71. 0	39. 7	41. 7	43. 7	45. 8	48. 0	50. 3	52. 7	55. 2	57. 8	60. 7	63. 9	67. 5	71. 7	71. 0
71. 5	40. 9	43. 0	45. 1	47. 4	49. 7	52. 1	54. 7	57. 4	60. 3	63. 5	67. 1	71. 4	76. 9	71. 5
72. 0	42. 3	44. 5	46. 7	49. 1	51. 5	54. 1	56. 9	59. 9	63. 1	66. 8	71. 1	76. 7	90. 0	72. 0
72. 5	43. 7	46. 0	48. 4	50. 9	53. 6	56. 4	59. 4	62. 7	66. 4	70. 8	76. 5	90. 0		72. 5
73. 0	45. 3	47. 8	50. 3	53. 0	55. 8	58. 9	62. 3	66. 1	70. 5	76. 3	90. 0			73. 0
73. 5	47. 1	49. 6	52. 4	55. 3	58. 4	61. 8	65. 7	70. 2	76. 0	90. 0				73. 5
74. 0	49. 0	51. 7	54. 7	57. 9	61. 4	65. 3	69. 9	75. 8	90. 0					74. 0
74. 5	51. 1	54. 1	57. 3	60. 9	64. 9	69. 5	75. 6	90. 0						74. 5

201

Dec.	30° Hc	d	Z	31° Hc	d	Z	32° Hc	d	Z	33° Hc	d	Z	34° Hc	d	Z	35° Hc	d	Z	36° Hc	d	Z	37° Hc	d	Z	Dec.
0	60 00.0	-60.0	180.0	59 00.0	-60.0	180.0	58 00.0	-60.0	180.0	57 00.0	-60.0	180.0	56 00.0	-60.0	180.0	55 00.0	-60.0	180.0	54 00.0	-60.0	180.0	53 00.0	-60.0	180.0	0
1	59 00.0	60.0	180.0	58 00.0	60.0	180.0	57 00.0	60.0	180.0	56 00.0	60.0	180.0	55 00.0	60.0	180.0	54 00.0	60.0	180.0	53 00.0	60.0	180.0	52 00.0	60.0	180.0	1
2	58 00.0	60.0	180.0	57 00.0	60.0	180.0	56 00.0	60.0	180.0	55 00.0	60.0	180.0	54 00.0	60.0	180.0	53 00.0	60.0	180.0	52 00.0	60.0	180.0	51 00.0	60.0	180.0	2
3	57 00.0	60.0	180.0	56 00.0	60.0	180.0	55 00.0	60.0	180.0	54 00.0	60.0	180.0	53 00.0	60.0	180.0	52 00.0	60.0	180.0	51 00.0	60.0	180.0	50 00.0	60.0	180.0	3
4	56 00.0	60.0	180.0	55 00.0	60.0	180.0	54 00.0	60.0	180.0	53 00.0	60.0	180.0	52 00.0	60.0	180.0	51 00.0	60.0	180.0	50 00.0	60.0	180.0	49 00.0	60.0	180.0	4
5	55 00.0	-60.0	180.0	54 00.0	-60.0	180.0	53 00.0	-60.0	180.0	52 00.0	-60.0	180.0	51 00.0	-60.0	180.0	50 00.0	-60.0	180.0	49 00.0	-60.0	180.0	48 00.0	-60.0	180.0	5
6	54 00.0	60.0	180.0	53 00.0	60.0	180.0	52 00.0	60.0	180.0	51 00.0	60.0	180.0	50 00.0	60.0	180.0	49 00.0	60.0	180.0	48 00.0	60.0	180.0	47 00.0	60.0	180.0	6
7	53 00.0	60.0	180.0	52 00.0	60.0	180.0	51 00.0	60.0	180.0	50 00.0	60.0	180.0	49 00.0	60.0	180.0	48 00.0	60.0	180.0	47 00.0	60.0	180.0	46 00.0	60.0	180.0	7
8	52 00.0	60.0	180.0	51 00.0	60.0	180.0	50 00.0	60.0	180.0	49 00.0	60.0	180.0	48 00.0	60.0	180.0	47 00.0	60.0	180.0	46 00.0	60.0	180.0	45 00.0	60.0	180.0	8
9	51 00.0	60.0	180.0	50 00.0	60.0	180.0	49 00.0	60.0	180.0	48 00.0	60.0	180.0	47 00.0	60.0	180.0	46 00.0	60.0	180.0	45 00.0	60.0	180.0	44 00.0	60.0	180.0	9
10	50 00.0	-60.0	180.0	49 00.0	-60.0	180.0	48 00.0	-60.0	180.0	47 00.0	-60.0	180.0	46 00.0	-60.0	180.0	45 00.0	-60.0	180.0	44 00.0	-60.0	180.0	43 00.0	-60.0	180.0	10
11	49 00.0	60.0	180.0	48 00.0	60.0	180.0	47 00.0	60.0	180.0	46 00.0	60.0	180.0	45 00.0	60.0	180.0	44 00.0	60.0	180.0	43 00.0	60.0	180.0	42 00.0	60.0	180.0	11
12	48 00.0	60.0	180.0	47 00.0	60.0	180.0	46 00.0	60.0	180.0	45 00.0	60.0	180.0	44 00.0	60.0	180.0	43 00.0	60.0	180.0	42 00.0	60.0	180.0	41 00.0	60.0	180.0	12
13	47 00.0	60.0	180.0	46 00.0	60.0	180.0	45 00.0	60.0	180.0	44 00.0	60.0	180.0	43 00.0	60.0	180.0	42 00.0	60.0	180.0	41 00.0	60.0	180.0	40 00.0	60.0	180.0	13
14	46 00.0	60.0	180.0	45 00.0	60.0	180.0	44 00.0	60.0	180.0	43 00.0	60.0	180.0	42 00.0	60.0	180.0	41 00.0	60.0	180.0	40 00.0	60.0	180.0	39 00.0	60.0	180.0	14
15	45 00.0	-60.0	180.0	44 00.0	-60.0	180.0	43 00.0	-60.0	180.0	42 00.0	-60.0	180.0	41 00.0	-60.0	180.0	40 00.0	-60.0	180.0	39 00.0	-60.0	180.0	38 00.0	-60.0	180.0	15
16	44 00.0	60.0	180.0	43 00.0	60.0	180.0	42 00.0	60.0	180.0	41 00.0	60.0	180.0	40 00.0	60.0	180.0	39 00.0	60.0	180.0	38 00.0	60.0	180.0	37 00.0	60.0	180.0	16
17	43 00.0	60.0	180.0	42 00.0	60.0	180.0	41 00.0	60.0	180.0	40 00.0	60.0	180.0	39 00.0	60.0	180.0	38 00.0	60.0	180.0	37 00.0	60.0	180.0	36 00.0	60.0	180.0	17
18	42 00.0	60.0	180.0	41 00.0	60.0	180.0	40 00.0	60.0	180.0	39 00.0	60.0	180.0	38 00.0	60.0	180.0	37 00.0	60.0	180.0	36 00.0	60.0	180.0	35 00.0	60.0	180.0	18
19	41 00.0	60.0	180.0	40 00.0	60.0	180.0	39 00.0	60.0	180.0	38 00.0	60.0	180.0	37 00.0	60.0	180.0	36 00.0	60.0	180.0	35 00.0	60.0	180.0	34 00.0	60.0	180.0	19
20	40 00.0	-60.0	180.0	39 00.0	-60.0	180.0	38 00.0	-60.0	180.0	37 00.0	-60.0	180.0	36 00.0	-60.0	180.0	35 00.0	-60.0	180.0	34 00.0	-60.0	180.0	33 00.0	-60.0	180.0	20
21	39 00.0	60.0	180.0	38 00.0	60.0	180.0	37 00.0	60.0	180.0	36 00.0	60.0	180.0	35 00.0	60.0	180.0	34 00.0	60.0	180.0	33 00.0	60.0	180.0	32 00.0	60.0	180.0	21
22	38 00.0	60.0	180.0	37 00.0	60.0	180.0	36 00.0	60.0	180.0	35 00.0	60.0	180.0	34 00.0	60.0	180.0	33 00.0	60.0	180.0	32 00.0	60.0	180.0	31 00.0	60.0	180.0	22
23	37 00.0	60.0	180.0	36 00.0	60.0	180.0	35 00.0	60.0	180.0	34 00.0	60.0	180.0	33 00.0	60.0	180.0	32 00.0	60.0	180.0	31 00.0	60.0	180.0	30 00.0	60.0	180.0	23
24	36 00.0	60.0	180.0	35 00.0	60.0	180.0	34 00.0	60.0	180.0	33 00.0	60.0	180.0	32 00.0	60.0	180.0	31 00.0	60.0	180.0	30 00.0	60.0	180.0	29 00.0	60.0	180.0	24
25	35 00.0	-60.0	180.0	34 00.0	-60.0	180.0	33 00.0	-60.0	180.0	32 00.0	-60.0	180.0	31 00.0	-60.0	180.0	30 00.0	-60.0	180.0	29 00.0	-60.0	180.0	28 00.0	-60.0	180.0	25
26	34 00.0	60.0	180.0	33 00.0	60.0	180.0	32 00.0	60.0	180.0	31 00.0	60.0	180.0	30 00.0	60.0	180.0	29 00.0	60.0	180.0	28 00.0	60.0	180.0	27 00.0	60.0	180.0	26
27	33 00.0	60.0	180.0	32 00.0	60.0	180.0	31 00.0	60.0	180.0	30 00.0	60.0	180.0	29 00.0	60.0	180.0	28 00.0	60.0	180.0	27 00.0	60.0	180.0	26 00.0	60.0	180.0	27
28	32 00.0	60.0	180.0	31 00.0	60.0	180.0	30 00.0	60.0	180.0	29 00.0	60.0	180.0	28 00.0	60.0	180.0	27 00.0	60.0	180.0	26 00.0	60.0	180.0	25 00.0	60.0	180.0	28
29	31 00.0	60.0	180.0	30 00.0	60.0	180.0	29 00.0	60.0	180.0	28 00.0	60.0	180.0	27 00.0	60.0	180.0	26 00.0	60.0	180.0	25 00.0	60.0	180.0	24 00.0	60.0	180.0	29
30	30 00.0	-60.0	180.0	29 00.0	-60.0	180.0	28 00.0	-60.0	180.0	27 00.0	-60.0	180.0	26 00.0	-60.0	180.0	25 00.0	-60.0	180.0	24 00.0	-60.0	180.0	23 00.0	-60.0	180.0	30
31	29 00.0	60.0	180.0	28 00.0	60.0	180.0	27 00.0	60.0	180.0	26 00.0	60.0	180.0	25 00.0	60.0	180.0	24 00.0	60.0	180.0	23 00.0	60.0	180.0	22 00.0	60.0	180.0	31
32	28 00.0	60.0	180.0	27 00.0	60.0	180.0	26 00.0	60.0	180.0	25 00.0	60.0	180.0	24 00.0	60.0	180.0	23 00.0	60.0	180.0	22 00.0	60.0	180.0	21 00.0	60.0	180.0	32
33	27 00.0	60.0	180.0	26 00.0	60.0	180.0	25 00.0	60.0	180.0	24 00.0	60.0	180.0	23 00.0	60.0	180.0	22 00.0	60.0	180.0	21 00.0	60.0	180.0	20 00.0	60.0	180.0	33
34	26 00.0	60.0	180.0	25 00.0	60.0	180.0	24 00.0	60.0	180.0	23 00.0	60.0	180.0	22 00.0	60.0	180.0	21 00.0	60.0	180.0	20 00.0	60.0	180.0	19 00.0	60.0	180.0	34
35	25 00.0	-60.0	180.0	24 00.0	-60.0	180.0	23 00.0	-60.0	180.0	22 00.0	-60.0	180.0	21 00.0	-60.0	180.0	20 00.0	-60.0	180.0	19 00.0	-60.0	180.0	18 00.0	-60.0	180.0	35
36	24 00.0	60.0	180.0	23 00.0	60.0	180.0	22 00.0	60.0	180.0	21 00.0	60.0	180.0	20 00.0	60.0	180.0	19 00.0	60.0	180.0	18 00.0	60.0	180.0	17 00.0	60.0	180.0	36
37	23 00.0	60.0	180.0	22 00.0	60.0	180.0	21 00.0	60.0	180.0	20 00.0	60.0	180.0	19 00.0	60.0	180.0	18 00.0	60.0	180.0	17 00.0	60.0	180.0	16 00.0	60.0	180.0	37
38	22 00.0	60.0	180.0	21 00.0	60.0	180.0	20 00.0	60.0	180.0	19 00.0	60.0	180.0	18 00.0	60.0	180.0	17 00.0	60.0	180.0	16 00.0	60.0	180.0	15 00.0	60.0	180.0	38
39	21 00.0	60.0	180.0	20 00.0	60.0	180.0	19 00.0	60.0	180.0	18 00.0	60.0	180.0	17 00.0	60.0	180.0	16 00.0	60.0	180.0	15 00.0	60.0	180.0	14 00.0	60.0	180.0	39
40	20 00.0	-60.0	180.0	19 00.0	-60.0	180.0	18 00.0	-60.0	180.0	17 00.0	-60.0	180.0	16 00.0	-60.0	180.0	15 00.0	-60.0	180.0	14 00.0	-60.0	180.0	13 00.0	-60.0	180.0	40
41	19 00.0	60.0	180.0	18 00.0	60.0	180.0	17 00.0	60.0	180.0	16 00.0	60.0	180.0	15 00.0	60.0	180.0	14 00.0	60.0	180.0	13 00.0	60.0	180.0	12 00.0	60.0	180.0	41
42	18 00.0	60.0	180.0	17 00.0	60.0	180.0	16 00.0	60.0	180.0	15 00.0	60.0	180.0	14 00.0	60.0	180.0	13 00.0	60.0	180.0	12 00.0	60.0	180.0	11 00.0	60.0	180.0	42
43	17 00.0	60.0	180.0	16 00.0	60.0	180.0	15 00.0	60.0	180.0	14 00.0	60.0	180.0	13 00.0	60.0	180.0	12 00.0	60.0	180.0	11 00.0	60.0	180.0	10 00.0	60.0	180.0	43
44	16 00.0	60.0	180.0	15 00.0	60.0	180.0	14 00.0	60.0	180.0	13 00.0	60.0	180.0	12 00.0	60.0	180.0	11 00.0	60.0	180.0	10 00.0	60.0	180.0	9 00.0	60.0	180.0	44

Dec.	30° Hc	d	Z	31° Hc	d	Z	32° Hc	d	Z	33° Hc	d	Z	34° Hc	d	Z	35° Hc	d	Z	36° Hc	d	Z	37° Hc	d	Z	Dec.
0	59 27.6	-59.0	168.1	58 28.9	-59.1	168.5	57 30.1	-59.2	168.8	56 31.2	-59.3	169.1	55 32.2	-59.3	169.4	54 33.3	-59.4	169.6	53 34.2	-59.4	169.9	52 35.1	-59.4	170.1	0
1	58 28.6	59.1	168.5	57 29.8	59.2	168.8	56 30.9	59.3	169.1	55 31.9	59.3	169.4	54 32.9	59.3	169.6	53 33.9	59.4	169.9	52 34.8	59.4	170.1	51 35.7	59.5	170.3	1
2	57 29.5	59.2	168.8	56 30.6	59.2	169.1	55 31.6	59.2	169.4	54 32.6	59.3	169.6	53 33.6	59.4	169.9	52 34.5	59.4	170.1	51 35.4	59.4	170.3	50 36.2	59.5	170.5	2
3	56 30.3	59.2	169.1	55 31.3	59.2	169.4	54 32.4	59.4	169.6	53 33.3	59.3	169.9	52 34.2	59.4	170.1	51 35.1	59.4	170.3	50 35.9	59.4	170.5	49 36.7	59.5	170.7	3
4	55 31.1	59.3	169.4	54 32.1	59.3	169.6	53 33.0	59.3	169.9	52 34.0	59.4	170.1	51 34.8	59.4	170.3	50 35.7	59.5	170.5	49 36.5	59.5	170.7	48 37.2	59.5	170.9	4
5	54 31.8	-59.2	169.7	53 32.8	-59.3	169.9	52 33.7	-59.4	170.1	51 34.6	-59.4	170.4	50 35.4	-59.5	170.6	49 36.2	-59.5	170.8	48 37.0	-59.5	170.9	47 37.7	-59.6	171.1	5
6	53 32.6	59.4	169.9	52 33.5	59.4	170.2	51 34.3	59.4	170.4	50 35.2	59.5	170.6	49 35.9	59.4	170.8	48 36.7	59.5	171.0	47 37.4	59.5	171.1	46 38.1	59.5	171.3	6
7	52 33.2	59.3	170.2	51 34.1	59.4	170.4	50 34.9	59.4	170.6	49 35.7	59.4	170.8	48 36.5	59.5	171.0	47 37.2	59.6	171.1	46 37.9	59.5	171.3	45 38.6	59.6	171.5	7
8	51 33.9	59.4	170.4	50 34.7	59.4	170.6	49 35.5	59.4	170.8	48 36.3	59.5	171.0	47 37.0	59.5	171.2	46 37.6	59.5	171.3	45 38.4	59.6	171.5	44 39.0	59.6	171.6	8
9	50 34.5	59.4	170.6	49 35.3	59.5	170.8	48 36.1	59.5	171.0	47 36.8	59.5	171.2	46 37.5	59.6	171.4	45 38.1	59.5	171.5	44 38.8	59.6	171.6	43 39.4	59.6	171.8	9
10	49 35.1	-59.4	170.9	48 35.9	-59.5	171.0	47 36.6	-59.5	171.2	46 37.3	-59.5	171.4	45 37.9	-59.5	171.5	44 38.6	-59.6	171.7	43 39.2	-59.6	171.8	42 39.8	-59.6	172.0	10
11	48 35.7	59.5	171.0	47 36.4	59.5	171.1	46 37.1	59.5	171.4	45 37.8	59.5	171.6	44 38.4	59.6	171.7	43 39.0	59.6	171.8	42 39.6	59.6	172.0	41 40.2	59.6	172.1	11
12	47 36.2	59.4	171.3	46 36.9	59.5	171.4	45 37.6	59.5	171.6	44 38.2	59.5	171.7	43 38.8	59.5	171.9	42 39.4	59.6	172.0	41 40.0	59.6	172.1	40 40.6	59.7	172.3	12
13	46 36.8	59.5	171.5	45 37.4	59.5	171.6	44 38.1	59.6	171.8	43 38.7	59.6	171.9	42 39.3	59.6	172.0	41 39.8	59.6	172.2	40 40.4	59.7	172.3	39 40.9	59.6	172.4	13
14	45 37.3	59.5	171.7	44 37.9	59.5	171.8	43 38.5	59.5	171.9	42 39.1	59.6	172.1	41 39.7	59.6	172.2	40 40.2	59.6	172.3	39 40.7	59.6	172.4	38 41.3	59.7	172.5	14
15	44 37.8	-59.5	171.8	43 38.4	-59.6	172.0	42 39.0	-59.6	172.1	41 39.5	-59.6	172.2	40 40.1	-59.6	172.4	39 40.6	-59.6	172.5	38 41.1	-59.6	172.6	37 41.6	-59.7	172.7	15
16	43 38.3	59.6	172.0	42 38.8	59.5	172.1	41 39.4	59.6	172.3	40 39.9	59.6	172.4	39 40.5	59.7	172.5	38 41.0	59.7	172.6	37 41.5	59.7	172.7	36 41.9	59.6	172.8	16
17	42 38.7	59.5	172.2	41 39.3	59.6	172.2	40 39.8	59.6	172.4	39 40.3	59.6	172.5	38 40.8	59.6	172.6	37 41.3	59.6	172.7	36 41.8	59.7	172.8	35 42.3	59.7	172.9	17
18	41 39.2	59.6	172.4	40 39.7	59.6	172.5	39 40.2	59.6	172.6	38 40.7	59.6	172.7	37 41.2	59.6	172.8	36 41.7	59.7	172.9	35 42.1	59.6	173.0	34 42.6	59.7	173.1	18
19	40 39.6	59.6	172.5	39 40.1	59.6	172.6	38 40.6	59.6	172.7	37 41.1	59.6	172.8	36 41.6	59.7	172.9	35 42.0	59.7	173.0	34 42.4	59.7	173.1	33 42.9	59.7	173.2	19
20	39 40.0	-59.5	172.7	38 40.5	-59.6	172.8	37 41.0	-59.6	172.9	36 41.5	-59.7	173.0	35 41.9	-59.6	173.1	34 42.3	-59.6	173.1	33 42.8	-59.7	173.2	32 43.2	-59.7	173.3	20
21	38 40.5	59.6	172.8	37 40.9	59.7	172.9	36 41.4	59.7	173.1	35 41.8	59.6	173.1	34 42.3	59.7	173.1	33 42.7	59.7	173.3	32 43.1	59.8	173.3	31 43.5	59.7	173.4	21
22	37 40.9	59.7	173.0	36 41.3	59.6	173.1	35 41.7	59.6	173.1	34 42.2	59.7	173.3	33 42.6	59.7	173.3	32 43.0	59.7	173.4	31 43.4	59.7	173.4	30 43.8	59.8	173.5	22
23	36 41.2	59.6	173.1	35 41.7	59.7	173.2	34 42.1	59.7	173.3	33 42.5	59.6	173.4	32 42.9	59.7	173.4	31 43.3	59.7	173.5	30 43.7	59.8	173.6	29 44.0	59.7	173.6	23
24	35 41.6	59.6	173.3	34 42.0	59.6	173.3	33 42.4	59.6	173.5	32 42.8	59.6	173.5	31 43.2	59.7	173.6	30 43.6	59.7	173.6	29 44.0	59.7	173.7	28 44.3	59.7	173.7	24
25	34 42.0	-59.7	173.4	33 42.4	-59.7	173.4	32 42.8	-59.7	173.5	31 43.1	-59.6	173.6	30 43.5	-59.7	173.7	29 43.9	-59.7	173.7	28 44.2	-59.7	173.8	27 44.6	-59.8	173.9	25
26	33 42.3	59.6	173.5	32 42.7	59.6	173.5	31 43.1	59.7	173.7	30 43.5	59.7	173.7	29 43.8	59.7	173.8	28 44.2	59.7	173.8	27 44.5	59.7	173.9	26 44.8	59.7	174.0	26
27	32 42.7	59.7	173.6	31 43.1	59.7	173.8	30 43.4	59.7	173.8	29 43.8	59.7	173.9	28 44.1	59.8	173.9	27 44.5	59.7	174.0	26 44.8	59.8	174.0	25 45.1	59.8	174.1	27
28	31 43.0	59.7	173.9	30 43.4	59.7	173.8	29 43.7	59.7	173.9	28 44.1	59.7	174.0	27 44.4	59.7	174.0	26 44.7	59.7	174.1	25 45.0	59.8	174.1	24 45.4	59.8	174.2	28
29	30 43.4	59.7	173.9	29 43.7	59.7	174.0	28 44.0	59.6	174.0	27 44.4	59.7	174.1	26 44.7	59.7	174.1	25 45.0	59.7	174.2	24 45.3	59.7	174.2	23 45.6	59.7	174.3	29
30	29 43.7	-59.7	174.1	28 44.0	-59.7	174.1	27 44.4	-59.7	174.1	26 44.7	-59.7	174.2	25 45.0	-59.8	174.2	24 45.3	-59.8	174.3	23 45.6	-59.8	174.3	22 45.9	-59.8	174.4	30
31	28 44.0	59.7	174.1	27 44.3	59.7	174.3	26 44.7	59.8	174.3	25 45.0	59.7	174.3	24 45.2	59.7	174.3	23 45.5	59.7	174.4	22 45.8	59.8	174.4	21 46.1	59.8	174.5	31
32	27 44.4	59.7	174.3	26 44.7	59.8	174.3	25 44.9	59.7	174.4	24 45.2	59.7	174.4	23 45.5	59.7	174.4	22 45.8	59.8	174.5	21 46.1	59.8	174.5	20 46.3	59.7	174.6	32
33	26 44.7	59.7	174.4	25 45.0	59.7	174.5	24 45.2	59.7	174.5	23 45.5	59.8	174.5	22 45.8	59.8	174.5	21 46.1	59.8	174.5	20 46.3	59.7	174.6	19 46.6	59.8	174.7	33
34	25 45.0	59.8	174.5	24 45.2	59.7	174.5	23 45.5	59.7	174.6	22 45.8	59.7	174.6	21 46.1	59.8	174.6	20 46.3	59.7	174.7	19 46.6	59.8	174.7	18 46.8	59.8	174.7	34
35	24 45.3	-59.7	174.6	23 45.5	-59.7	174.6	22 45.8	-59.7	174.7	21 46.1	-59.8	174.7	20 46.3	-59.8	174.7	19 46.6	-59.8	174.8	18 46.8	-59.8	174.8	17 47.1	-59.8	174.8	35
36	23 45.6	59.8	174.7	22 45.8	59.7	174.7	21 46.1	59.7	174.8	20 46.3	59.7	174.8	19 46.6	59.8	174.9	18 46.8	59.7	174.9	17 47.0	59.7	174.9	16 47.3	59.8	174.9	36
37	22 45.9	59.7	174.8	21 46.1	59.7	174.9	20 46.3	59.7	174.9	19 46.6	59.7	174.9	18 46.8	59.7	174.9	17 47.1	59.8	174.9	16 47.3	59.8	175.0	15 47.5	59.8	175.0	37
38	21 46.2	59.8	174.9	20 46.4	59.8	174.9	19 46.6	59.8	175.0	18 46.8	59.7	175.0	17 47.1	59.8	175.0	16 47.3	59.8	175.1	15 47.5	59.8	175.1	14 47.7	59.8	175.1	38
39	20 46.4	59.7	175.0	19 46.7	59.8	175.0	18 46.9	59.7	175.1	17 47.1	59.7	175.1	16 47.3	59.7	175.1	15 47.5	59.7	175.2	14 47.7	59.8	175.2	13 48.0	59.8	175.2	39
40	19 46.7	-59.7	175.1	18 46.9	-59.7	175.1	17 47.1	-59.7	175.2	16 47.4	-59.8	175.2	15 47.6	-59.8	175.2	14 47.8	-59.8	175.2	13 48.0	-59.8	175.3	12 48.2	-59.8	175.3	40
41	18 47.0	59.7	175.2	17 47.2	59.8	175.2	16 47.4	59.8	175.3	15 47.6	59.7	175.3	14 47.8	59.8	175.3	13 48.0	59.8	175.3	12 48.2	59.8	175.4	11 48.4	59.8	175.4	41
42	17 47.3	59.8	175.3	16 47.5	59.8	175.3	15 47.7	59.8	175.4	14 47.9	59.8	175.4	13 48.0	59.7	175.4	12 48.2	59.7	175.4	11 48.4	59.7	175.4	10 48.6	59.8	175.5	42
43	16 47.5	59.7	175.4	15 47.7	59.7	175.4	14 47.9	59.7	175.5	13 48.1	59.7	175.5	12 48.3	59.8	175.5	11 48.5	59.8	175.5	10 48.7	59.8	175.5	9 48.8	59.8	175.6	43
44	15 47.8	59.7	175.5	14 48.0	59.8	175.5	13 48.2	59.8	175.6	12 48.3	59.7	175.6	11 48.5	59.7	175.6	10 48.7	59.7	175.6	9 48.9	59.8	175.6	8 49.0	59.7	175.6	44

8°, 352° L.H.A.   LATITUDE SAME NAME AS DECLINATION

N. Lat. { L.H.A. greater than 180°......Zn=Z
         { L.H.A. less than 180°.........Zn=360°−Z

Dec.	30° Hc	30° d	30° Z	31° Hc	31° d	31° Z	32° Hc	32° d	32° Z	33° Hc	33° d	33° Z	34° Hc	34° d	34° Z	35° Hc	35° d	35° Z	36° Hc	36° d	36° Z	37° Hc	37° d	37° Z	Dec.
0	59 02.9	+58.1	164.3	58 05.0	+58.5	164.7	57 07.1	+58.5	165.1	56 09.1	+58.6	165.5	55 10.9	+58.7	165.9	54 12.7	+58.8	166.2	53 14.4	+58.9	166.6	52 16.0	+59.0	166.9	0
1	60 01.2	58.1	163.8	59 03.5	58.3	164.3	58 05.6	58.5	164.7	57 07.7	58.4	165.1	56 09.6	58.7	165.5	55 11.5	58.7	165.9	54 13.3	58.8	166.2	53 15.0	58.9	166.6	1
2	60 59.3	58.1	163.3	60 01.8	58.2	163.8	59 04.1	58.3	164.3	58 06.3	58.4	164.7	57 08.3	58.6	165.1	56 10.3	58.7	165.5	55 12.1	58.8	165.9	54 13.9	58.9	166.2	2
3	61 57.4	57.9	162.8	61 00.0	58.1	163.3	60 02.4	58.3	163.8	59 04.7	58.3	164.3	58 06.9	58.5	164.7	57 09.0	58.6	165.2	56 10.9	58.7	165.5	55 12.8	58.8	165.9	3
4	62 55.3	57.8	162.2	61 58.1	57.9	162.8	61 00.7	58.1	163.3	60 03.1	58.3	163.9	59 05.4	58.4	164.3	58 07.6	58.5	164.8	57 09.6	58.7	165.2	56 11.6	58.7	165.6	4
5	63 53.1	+57.6	161.6	62 56.0	+57.9	162.3	61 58.8	+58.0	162.8	61 01.4	+58.2	163.4	60 03.8	+58.4	163.9	59 06.1	+58.5	164.3	58 08.3	+58.6	164.8	57 10.3	+58.7	165.2	5
6	64 50.7	57.5	161.0	63 53.9	57.6	161.7	62 56.8	57.9	162.3	61 59.6	58.0	162.9	61 02.2	58.2	163.4	60 04.6	58.3	163.9	59 06.9	58.5	164.4	58 09.0	58.6	164.8	6
7	65 48.2	57.2	160.3	64 51.5	57.5	161.0	63 54.7	57.7	161.7	62 57.6	57.9	162.3	62 00.4	58.1	162.9	61 02.9	58.3	163.4	60 05.4	58.4	163.9	59 07.6	58.4	164.4	7
8	66 45.4	57.0	159.6	65 49.0	57.3	160.3	64 52.4	57.6	161.1	63 55.5	57.8	161.7	62 58.5	57.9	162.3	62 01.2	58.1	162.9	61 03.8	58.3	163.5	60 06.2	58.4	163.9	8
9	67 42.4	56.8	158.8	66 46.3	57.1	159.6	65 50.0	57.3	160.4	64 53.3	57.6	161.1	63 56.4	57.9	161.8	62 59.3	58.1	162.4	62 02.1	58.2	163.0	61 04.6	58.4	163.5	9
10	68 39.2	+56.4	157.9	67 43.4	+56.8	158.8	66 47.3	+57.1	159.7	65 50.9	+57.4	160.4	64 54.3	+57.6	161.1	63 57.4	+57.8	161.8	63 00.3	+58.0	162.4	62 03.0	+58.2	163.0	10
11	69 35.6	56.2	156.9	68 40.2	56.6	157.9	67 44.4	56.9	158.9	66 48.3	57.2	159.7	65 51.9	57.5	160.5	64 55.2	57.7	161.2	63 58.3	57.9	161.8	63 01.2	58.1	162.5	11
12	70 31.8	55.7	155.9	69 36.8	56.2	157.0	68 41.3	56.6	158.0	67 45.5	57.0	158.9	66 49.4	57.2	159.8	65 52.9	57.6	160.5	64 56.2	57.8	161.2	63 59.3	58.0	161.9	12
13	71 27.5	55.3	154.8	70 33.0	55.8	156.0	69 37.9	56.3	157.1	68 42.5	56.6	158.1	67 46.6	57.0	158.9	66 50.5	57.3	159.8	65 54.0	57.6	160.5	64 57.3	57.8	161.3	13
14	72 22.8	54.8	153.5	71 28.8	55.4	154.8	70 34.2	55.9	156.0	69 39.1	56.4	157.1	68 43.6	56.8	158.1	67 47.8	57.1	159.1	66 51.6	57.4	159.8	65 55.1	57.4	160.7	14
15	73 17.6	+54.1	152.1	72 24.2	+54.8	153.5	71 30.1	+55.5	154.9	70 35.5	+56.0	156.1	69 40.4	+56.4	157.2	68 44.9	+56.8	158.2	67 49.0	+57.1	159.1	66 52.7	+57.5	160.0	15
16	74 11.7	53.4	150.6	73 19.0	54.3	152.2	72 25.6	54.9	153.7	71 31.5	55.5	154.9	70 36.8	56.1	156.2	69 41.7	56.5	157.3	68 46.1	56.9	158.3	67 50.2	57.2	159.2	16
17	75 05.1	52.6	148.9	74 13.3	53.5	150.7	73 20.5	54.4	152.3	72 27.0	55.1	153.8	71 32.9	55.6	155.1	70 38.2	56.1	156.3	69 43.0	56.6	157.4	68 47.4	56.9	158.4	17
18	75 57.7	51.5	146.9	75 06.8	52.7	149.0	74 14.9	53.7	150.8	73 22.1	54.5	152.5	72 28.5	55.2	153.9	71 34.3	55.8	155.2	70 39.6	56.2	156.4	69 44.4	56.6	157.5	18
19	76 49.2	50.3	144.8	75 59.5	51.7	147.1	75 08.6	52.8	149.1	74 16.6	53.7	151.0	73 23.7	54.6	152.6	72 30.1	55.2	154.0	71 35.8	55.9	155.4	70 41.0	56.4	156.6	19
20	77 39.5	+48.7	142.3	76 51.2	+50.4	144.9	76 01.4	+51.8	147.2	75 10.3	+53.0	149.3	74 18.3	+53.9	151.1	73 25.3	+54.8	152.7	72 31.7	+55.3	154.2	71 37.4	+55.9	155.5	20
21	78 28.2	46.9	139.5	77 41.6	48.9	142.4	76 53.2	50.6	145.1	76 03.3	52.0	147.4	75 12.2	53.1	149.4	74 20.1	54.0	151.2	73 27.0	54.9	152.7	72 33.3	55.5	154.3	21
22	79 15.1	44.5*	136.2	78 30.5	47.1*	139.6	77 43.8	49.1	142.6	76 55.3	50.7	145.2	76 05.3	52.1	147.5	75 14.1	53.2	149.6	74 21.9	54.1	151.4	73 28.8	54.9	153.0	22
23	79 59.6	41.7*	132.5	79 17.6	44.7*	136.4	78 32.9	47.2*	139.8	77 46.0	49.3	142.6	76 57.4	50.9	145.4	76 07.3	52.3	147.7	75 16.0	53.4	149.8	74 23.7	54.3	151.6	23
24	80 41.3	38.1*	128.2	80 02.3	42.0*	132.7	79 20.1	45.0*	136.6	78 35.3	47.5*	139.8	77 48.3	49.5	143.0	76 59.6	51.1	145.6	76 09.4	52.5	147.9	75 18.0	53.6	149.9	24
25	81 19.4	+33.8*	123.3	80 44.3	+38.3*	128.4	80 05.1	+42.2*	132.9	79 22.8	+45.2*	136.8	78 37.8	+47.7*	140.2	77 50.7	+49.7	143.2	77 01.9	+51.2	145.8	76 11.6	+52.6	148.1	25
26	81 53.2	28.3*	117.6	81 22.6	34.0*	123.5	80 47.3	38.7*	128.6	80 08.0	42.4*	133.1	79 25.5	45.5*	137.0	78 40.4	47.9*	140.4	77 53.1	49.9	143.4	77 04.2	51.4	146.0	26
27	82 21.5	22.0*	111.2	81 56.6	28.7*	117.8	81 26.0	34.2*	123.7	80 50.4	39.0*	128.8	80 11.0	42.7*	133.3	79 28.3	45.7*	137.3	78 43.0	48.2*	140.7	77 55.6	50.1	143.6	27
28	82 43.5	14.5*	104.0	82 25.3	22.2*	111.1	82 00.2	28.9*	118.0	81 29.4	34.5*	123.9	80 53.7	39.2*	129.1	80 14.0	43.0*	133.6	79 31.2	45.9*	137.5	78 45.7	48.4*	140.9	28
29	82 58.0	+6.4*	96.2	82 47.5	14.7*	104.1	82 29.1	22.4*	111.4	82 03.9	29.2*	118.1	81 32.9	34.8*	124.1	80 57.0	39.4*	129.3	80 17.1	43.2*	133.8	79 34.1	46.2*	137.8	29
30	83 04.4	−2.2*	88.0	83 02.2	+6.4*	96.2	82 51.5	+15.0*	104.2	82 33.1	+22.6*	111.6	82 07.7	+29.4*	118.4	81 36.4	+35.2*	124.3	81 00.3	+39.8*	129.6	80 20.3	+43.5*	134.1	30
31	83 02.2	10.7*	79.7	83 08.6	−2.1*	87.9	83 06.5	6.5*	96.2	82 55.7	15.2*	104.2	82 37.1	23.0*	111.8	82 11.6	29.7*	118.6	81 40.1	35.4*	124.6	81 03.8	40.1*	129.8	31
32	82 51.5	18.4*	71.7	83 06.5	10.8*	79.6	83 13.0	−2.1*	87.8	83 10.9	+6.6*	96.3	83 00.1	15.3*	104.4	82 41.3	23.2*	112.0	82 15.5	30.0*	118.8	81 43.9	35.7*	124.9	32
33	82 33.1	25.4*	64.2	82 55.7	18.6*	71.5	83 10.9	10.9*	79.6	83 17.5	−2.1*	87.8	83 15.4	+6.8*	96.3	83 04.5	15.5*	104.6	82 45.6	23.5*	112.0	82 19.6	30.4*	119.1	33
34	82 07.7	31.3*	57.4	82 37.1	25.5*	63.9	83 00.1	18.8*	71.2	83 15.4	10.9*	79.3	83 22.2	−2.2*	87.8	83 20.0	+6.9*	96.3	83 09.1	15.7*	104.6	82 50.0	23.7*	112.4	34
35	81 36.4	−36.1*	51.4	82 11.6	−31.5*	57.1	82 41.3	−25.8*	63.6	83 04.5	−18.9*	71.0	83 20.0	−10.9*	79.1	83 26.9	−2.1*	87.7	83 24.8	+7.0*	96.4	83 13.7	+15.9*	104.8	35
36	81 00.3	40.0*	46.1	81 40.1	36.3*	51.0	82 15.5	31.6*	56.7	82 45.6	26.0*	63.3	83 09.1	19.1*	70.5	83 24.8	11.1*	79.0	83 31.8	−2.2*	87.6	83 29.6	7.0*	96.4	36
37	80 20.3	43.2*	41.5	81 03.8	40.3*	45.1	81 43.9	36.6*	50.2	82 19.6	31.9*	56.7	82 50.0	26.2*	63.0	83 13.7	19.3*	70.5	83 29.6	11.1*	78.8	83 36.6	−2.2*	87.6	37
38	79 37.1	45.8*	37.5	80 23.5	43.4*	41.1	81 07.3	40.5*	45.3	81 47.7	36.8*	50.2	82 23.8	32.2*	56.0	82 54.4	26.4*	62.6	83 18.5	19.5*	70.2	83 34.6	11.3*	78.6	38
39	78 51.3	47.9	34.0	79 40.1	46.0*	37.1	80 26.8	43.6*	40.7	81 10.9	40.7*	44.9	81 51.6	37.1*	49.8	82 28.0	32.4*	55.6	82 59.0	26.7*	62.3	83 23.3	19.6*	70.0	39
40	78 03.4	−49.6	31.0	78 54.1	−48.0	33.6	79 43.2	−46.2*	36.7	80 30.2	−43.9*	40.3	81 14.5	−40.9*	44.4	81 55.6	−37.3*	49.4	82 32.3	−32.7*	55.2	83 03.7	−27.0*	61.9	40
41	77 13.8	50.9	28.4	78 06.1	49.8	30.6	78 57.0	48.2	33.2	79 46.3	46.4*	36.3	80 33.6	44.1*	39.8	81 18.3	41.3*	44.0	81 59.6	37.6*	48.9	82 36.7	33.0*	54.8	41
42	76 22.9	52.1	26.1	77 16.3	51.0	28.0	78 08.8	49.9	30.2	78 59.9	48.4	32.8	79 49.5	46.6*	35.8	80 37.0	44.3*	39.4	81 22.0	41.4*	43.6	82 03.7	37.8*	48.5	42
43	75 30.8	53.0	24.2	76 25.3	52.4	25.7	77 18.9	51.2	27.6	78 11.5	50.0	29.8	79 02.9	48.5	32.4	79 52.7	46.8*	35.4	80 40.6	44.6*	38.9	81 25.9	41.8*	43.1	43
44	74 37.8	53.8	22.2	75 33.1	53.2	23.7	76 27.7	52.4	25.3	77 21.5	51.4	27.2	78 14.3	50.2	29.4	79 05.9	48.8	32.0	79 56.0	47.0*	34.9	80 44.1	44.8*	38.5	44

205

9°, 351° L.H.A. LATITUDE SAME NAME AS DECLINATION

N. Lat. { L.H.A. greater than 180° .... Zn=Z
{ L.H.A. less than 180° .... Zn=360°−Z

Dec.	30° Hc	d	Z	31° Hc	d	Z	32° Hc	d	Z	33° Hc	d	Z	34° Hc	d	Z	35° Hc	d	Z	36° Hc	d	Z	37° Hc	d	Z	Dec.
0	58 48.0	+57.8	162.4	57 50.7	+58.0	162.9	56 53.3	+58.2	163.4	55 55.7	+58.3	163.8	54 58.1	+58.4	164.2	54 00.3	+58.5	164.6	53 02.4	+58.6	164.9	52 04.4	+58.7	165.3	0
1	59 45.8	57.8	161.9	58 48.7	57.9	162.4	57 51.5	58.0	162.9	56 54.0	58.2	163.4	55 56.5	58.3	163.8	54 58.8	58.5	164.2	54 01.0	58.6	164.6	53 03.1	58.7	164.9	1
2	60 43.6	57.5	161.4	59 46.6	57.8	161.9	58 49.5	57.9	162.4	57 52.2	58.1	162.9	56 54.8	58.2	163.4	55 57.3	58.3	163.8	54 59.6	58.5	164.2	54 01.8	58.6	164.6	2
3	61 41.1	57.5	161.0	60 44.4	57.6	161.6	59 47.4	57.6	161.9	58 50.3	58.0	162.4	57 53.0	58.0	162.9	56 55.6	58.3	163.4	55 58.1	58.4	163.8	55 00.4	58.5	164.2	3
4	62 38.6	57.2	160.1	61 42.0	57.5	160.8	60 45.3	57.6	161.4	59 48.3	57.9	161.9	58 51.2	58.0	162.4	57 53.9	58.2	162.9	56 56.5	58.3	163.4	55 58.9	58.5	163.8	4
5	63 35.8	+57.0	159.5	62 39.5	+57.3	160.2	61 42.9	+57.6	160.8	60 46.2	+57.7	161.4	59 49.2	+57.9	161.9	58 52.1	+58.1	162.5	57 54.8	+58.2	162.9	56 57.4	+58.3	163.4	5
6	64 32.8	56.9	159.0	63 36.8	57.1	159.5	62 40.5	57.3	160.2	61 43.9	57.6	160.8	60 47.1	57.8	161.4	59 50.2	58.0	162.0	58 53.0	58.1	162.5	57 55.7	58.3	163.0	6
7	65 29.7	56.6	158.0	64 33.9	56.9	158.8	63 37.8	57.2	159.5	62 41.5	57.4	160.2	61 44.9	57.6	160.9	60 48.1	57.8	161.4	59 51.1	58.0	162.0	58 54.0	58.2	162.5	7
8	66 26.3	56.3	157.2	65 30.8	56.6	158.1	64 35.0	56.9	158.8	63 38.9	57.2	159.6	62 42.5	57.5	160.3	61 45.9	57.7	160.9	60 49.1	57.9	161.5	59 52.2	58.0	162.0	8
9	67 22.6	56.0	156.3	66 27.4	56.4	157.2	65 31.9	56.7	158.1	64 36.1	57.0	158.9	63 40.0	57.3	159.6	62 43.6	57.5	160.3	61 47.0	57.8	160.9	60 50.2	57.9	161.5	9
10	68 18.6	+55.6	155.4	67 23.8	+56.1	156.4	66 28.6	+56.5	157.3	65 33.1	+56.8	158.1	64 37.3	+57.1	158.9	63 41.1	+57.4	159.7	62 44.8	+57.5	160.3	61 48.1	+57.8	161.0	10
11	69 14.2	55.2	154.3	68 19.9	55.7	155.4	67 25.1	56.1	156.4	66 29.9	56.5	157.4	65 34.4	56.8	158.2	64 38.5	57.1	159.0	63 42.3	57.5	159.7	62 45.9	57.7	160.4	11
12	70 09.4	54.8	153.2	69 15.6	55.3	154.4	68 21.2	55.8	155.5	67 26.4	56.2	156.5	66 31.2	56.6	157.4	65 35.6	56.9	158.2	64 39.8	57.2	159.0	63 43.6	57.5	159.8	12
13	71 04.2	54.2	152.0	70 10.9	54.9	153.3	69 17.0	55.5	154.5	68 22.6	55.9	155.6	67 27.8	56.3	156.6	66 32.6	56.6	157.5	65 37.0	57.0	158.3	64 41.1	57.2	159.1	13
14	71 58.4	53.7	150.6	71 05.8	54.3	152.1	70 12.5	54.9	153.4	69 18.5	55.5	154.6	68 24.1	56.0	155.6	67 29.2	56.4	156.6	66 34.0	56.7	157.6	65 38.3	57.1	158.4	14
15	72 52.1	+52.9	149.2	72 00.1	+53.8	150.7	71 07.4	+54.5	152.1	70 14.1	+55.0	153.5	69 20.1	+55.6	154.6	68 25.6	+56.1	155.7	67 30.7	+56.5	156.6	66 35.4	+56.8	157.6	15
16	73 45.0	52.0	147.5	72 53.9	53.0	149.2	72 01.9	53.8	150.8	71 09.1	54.6	152.3	70 15.7	55.2	153.5	69 21.7	55.7	154.7	68 27.2	56.2	155.8	67 32.2	56.6	156.8	16
17	74 37.0	51.1	145.7	73 46.9	52.2	147.6	72 55.7	53.2	149.4	72 03.7	54.0	150.9	71 10.9	54.7	152.4	70 17.4	55.3	153.7	69 23.4	55.8	154.9	68 28.8	56.3	155.9	17
18	75 28.1	49.9	143.6	74 39.1	51.2	145.8	73 48.9	52.3	147.7	72 57.7	53.3	149.4	72 05.6	54.1	151.1	71 12.7	54.8	152.5	70 19.2	55.3	153.8	69 25.1	55.9	155.0	18
19	76 18.0	48.4	141.4	75 30.3	50.0	143.8	74 41.2	51.4	145.9	73 51.0	52.4	147.7	72 59.7	53.4	149.6	72 07.5	54.2	151.2	71 14.5	54.9	152.6	70 21.0	55.4	153.9	19
20	77 06.4	+46.8	138.8	76 20.3	+48.7	141.5	75 32.6	+50.2	143.9	74 43.4	+51.6	146.1	73 53.1	+52.6	148.0	73 01.7	+53.6	149.8	72 09.4	+54.4	151.3	71 16.4	+55.1	152.7	20
21	77 53.2	44.7	135.9	77 09.0	47.0	139.0	76 22.8	48.9	141.7	75 35.0	50.4	144.1	74 45.7	51.7	146.2	73 55.3	52.7	148.2	73 03.8	53.7	149.9	72 11.5	54.4	151.5	21
22	78 37.9	42.3	132.6	77 56.0	44.9	136.1	77 11.7	47.1	139.1	76 25.4	49.0	141.8	75 37.4	50.6	144.3	74 48.0	51.9	146.4	73 57.5	52.9	148.3	73 05.9	53.9	150.1	22
23	79 20.2	39.3	128.9	78 40.9	42.5	132.8	77 58.8	45.2	136.3	77 14.4	47.4	139.3	76 28.0	49.2	142.0	75 39.9	50.7	144.4	74 50.4	52.1	146.6	73 59.8	53.1	148.5	23
24	79 59.5	35.6	124.7	79 23.4	39.6	129.1	78 44.0	42.8	133.0	78 01.8	45.4	136.4	77 17.2	47.6	139.5	76 30.6	49.5	142.0	75 42.5	50.9	144.6	74 52.9	52.2	146.8	24
25	80 35.1	+31.4	119.9	80 03.0	+35.9	124.9	79 26.8	+39.8	129.3	78 47.2	+43.0	133.2	78 04.8	+45.7	136.7	77 20.1	+47.8	139.7	76 33.4	+49.6	142.4	75 45.1	+51.1	144.8	25
26	81 06.5	26.1	114.5	80 38.9	31.6	120.1	80 06.6	36.2	125.1	79 30.2	40.1	129.5	78 50.5	43.2	133.4	78 07.9	45.9	136.9	77 23.0	48.1	139.9	76 36.2	49.9	142.6	26
27	81 32.6	20.3	108.6	81 10.5	26.4	114.7	80 42.8	31.8	120.1	80 10.3	36.4	125.3	79 33.7	40.4	129.7	78 53.8	43.5	133.6	78 11.1	46.1	137.1	77 26.1	48.2	140.2	27
28	81 52.9	13.4	102.0	81 36.9	20.5	108.7	81 14.6	26.7	114.9	80 46.7	32.2	120.5	80 14.1	36.7	125.6	79 37.3	40.7	129.9	78 57.2	43.8	133.8	78 14.3	46.1	137.3	28
29	82 06.3	+6.2	95.0	81 57.4	13.6	102.1	81 41.3	20.7	108.8	81 18.9	27.0	115.0	80 50.8	32.5	120.7	80 18.0	37.0	125.7	79 41.0	40.9	130.2	79 00.7	44.1	134.1	29
30	82 12.5	−1.5	87.7	82 11.0	+6.3	95.0	82 02.0	+13.8	102.2	81 45.9	+20.9	109.0	81 23.3	+27.2	115.2	80 55.0	+32.8	120.9	80 21.9	+37.4	126.0	79 44.8	+41.2	130.4	30
31	82 11.0	9.0	80.4	82 17.3	−1.5	87.7	82 15.8	6.4	95.1	82 06.8	14.0	102.3	81 50.5	21.1	109.1	81 27.8	27.5	115.4	80 59.3	33.1	121.1	80 26.0	37.7	126.2	31
32	82 02.0	16.1	73.2	82 15.8	9.0	80.2	82 22.2	−1.4	87.6	82 20.8	6.5	95.1	82 11.7	14.2	102.4	81 55.3	21.4	109.3	81 32.4	27.8	115.6	81 03.7	33.4	121.4	32
33	81 45.9	22.6	66.3	82 06.8	16.3	73.0	82 20.8	9.0	80.1	82 27.3	−1.4	87.5	82 25.9	6.6	95.1	82 16.7	14.4	102.5	82 00.2	21.7	109.4	81 37.1	28.1	115.8	33
34	81 23.3	28.3	60.0	81 50.5	22.7	66.1	82 11.8	16.3	72.7	82 25.9	9.2	79.9	82 32.5	−1.4	87.5	82 31.1	6.7	95.1	82 21.9	14.6	102.6	82 05.2	22.0	109.6	34
35	80 55.0	−33.1	54.3	81 27.8	−28.5	59.7	81 55.3	−22.9	65.5	82 16.7	−16.5	72.5	82 31.1	−9.2	79.8	82 37.8	−1.3	87.4	82 36.5	+6.8	95.1	82 27.2	+14.8	102.7	35
36	80 21.9	37.1	49.1	80 59.3	33.3	53.9	81 32.4	28.7	59.3	82 00.2	23.1	65.5	82 21.9	16.7	72.3	82 36.5	9.3	79.6	82 43.3	−1.3	87.4	82 42.0	6.9	95.2	36
37	79 44.8	40.5	44.6	80 26.0	37.3	48.7	81 03.7	33.5	53.5	81 37.1	28.9	59.0	82 05.2	23.3	65.2	82 27.2	16.9	72.0	82 42.0	9.4	79.5	82 48.9	−1.3	87.3	37
38	79 04.3	43.3	40.6	79 48.7	40.7	44.2	80 30.2	37.6	48.3	81 08.2	33.8	53.1	81 41.9	29.1	58.6	82 10.3	23.5	65.1	82 32.6	17.0	71.8	82 47.6	9.5	79.3	38
39	78 21.0	45.5	37.0	79 08.0	43.5	40.2	79 52.6	40.9	43.8	80 34.4	37.8	47.9	81 12.8	34.0	52.7	81 46.8	29.4	58.2	82 15.6	23.8	64.5	82 38.1	17.2	71.5	39
40	77 35.5	−47.5	33.9	78 24.5	−45.8	36.6	79 11.7	−43.7	39.7	79 56.6	−41.1	43.3	80 38.8	−38.1	47.5	81 17.4	−34.2	52.3	81 51.8	−29.6	57.9	82 20.9	−24.0	64.2	40
41	76 48.0	49.0	31.1	77 38.7	47.6	33.5	78 28.0	46.0	36.2	79 15.5	43.9	39.3	80 00.7	41.4	42.9	80 43.2	38.4	47.1	81 22.2	34.6	51.9	81 56.9	29.9	57.5	41
42	75 59.0	50.4	28.7	76 51.1	49.2	30.7	77 42.0	47.8	33.1	78 31.6	46.2	35.8	79 19.3	44.1	38.9	80 04.8	41.6	42.4	80 47.6	38.5	46.6	81 27.0	34.6	51.4	42
43	75 08.6	51.4	26.5	76 01.9	50.5	28.3	76 54.2	49.3	30.3	77 45.4	48.0	33.1	78 35.2	46.4	35.3	79 23.2	44.4	38.4	80 09.1	42.0	42.0	80 52.2	38.9	46.1	43
44	74 17.2	52.4	24.6	75 11.4	51.6	26.1	76 04.9	50.7	27.9	76 57.4	49.5	29.9	77 48.8	48.2	32.2	78 38.8	46.5	34.9	79 27.1	44.6	37.9	80 13.3	42.2	41.5	44

LATITUDE SAME NAME AS DECLINATION

N. Lat. {L.H.A. greater than 180°......Zn=Z
L.H.A. less than 180°......Zn=360°−Z

Dec.	30° Hc	d	Z	31° Hc	d	Z	32° Hc	d	Z	33° Hc	d	Z	34° Hc	d	Z	35° Hc	d	Z	36° Hc	d	Z	37° Hc	d	Z	Dec.
0	58 31.5	+57.4	160.6	57 34.8	+57.6	161.1	56 38.0	+57.7	161.6	55 41.0	+57.9	162.1	54 43.8	+58.1	162.5	53 46.5	+58.2	162.9	52 49.1	+58.3	163.3	51 51.6	+58.4	163.7	0
1	59 28.9	57.2	160.0	58 32.4	57.4	160.6	57 35.7	57.7	161.1	56 38.9	57.8	161.6	55 41.9	57.9	162.1	54 44.7	58.1	162.5	53 47.4	58.3	162.9	52 50.0	58.4	163.3	1
2	60 26.1	57.1	159.4	59 29.8	57.3	160.0	58 33.4	57.4	160.6	57 36.7	57.7	161.1	56 39.8	57.9	161.6	55 42.8	58.0	162.1	54 45.7	58.1	162.5	53 48.4	58.3	162.9	2
3	61 23.2	56.8	158.8	60 27.1	57.1	159.4	59 30.8	57.4	160.0	58 34.4	57.5	160.6	57 37.7	57.7	161.1	56 40.8	57.9	161.6	55 43.8	58.1	162.1	54 46.7	58.2	162.5	3
4	62 20.0	56.7	158.1	61 24.2	57.0	158.8	60 28.2	57.2	159.4	59 31.9	57.4	160.0	58 35.4	57.6	160.6	57 38.7	57.8	161.1	56 41.9	57.9	161.6	55 44.9	58.1	162.1	4
5	63 16.7	+56.4	157.4	62 21.2	+56.7	158.1	61 25.4	+56.9	158.8	60 29.3	+57.2	159.4	59 33.0	+57.5	160.0	58 36.5	+57.7	160.6	57 39.8	+57.9	161.1	56 43.0	+58.0	161.6	5
6	64 13.1	56.2	156.6	63 17.9	56.5	157.4	62 22.3	56.8	158.1	61 26.5	57.1	158.8	60 30.5	57.3	159.5	59 34.2	57.5	160.0	58 37.7	57.7	160.6	57 41.0	57.9	161.2	6
7	65 09.3	55.9	155.8	64 14.4	56.2	156.6	63 19.1	56.6	157.4	62 23.6	56.8	158.2	61 27.8	57.1	158.9	60 31.7	57.3	159.5	59 35.4	57.5	160.1	58 38.9	57.7	160.7	7
8	66 05.2	55.5	154.9	65 10.6	56.0	155.8	64 15.7	56.3	156.7	63 20.4	56.7	157.5	62 24.9	56.9	158.2	61 29.0	57.2	158.9	60 32.9	57.5	159.5	59 36.6	57.7	160.1	8
9	67 00.7	55.2	153.9	66 06.6	55.6	154.9	65 12.0	56.1	155.9	64 17.1	56.4	156.7	63 21.8	56.7	157.5	62 26.2	57.0	158.2	61 30.4	57.2	158.9	60 34.3	57.5	159.6	9
10	67 55.9	+54.8	152.9	67 02.2	+55.3	154.0	66 08.1	+55.7	155.0	65 13.5	+56.1	155.9	64 18.5	+56.5	156.8	63 23.2	+56.8	157.6	62 27.6	+57.1	158.3	61 31.7	+57.4	159.0	10
11	68 50.7	54.3	151.8	67 57.5	54.9	153.0	67 03.8	55.3	154.1	66 09.6	55.8	155.1	65 15.0	56.2	156.0	64 20.0	56.6	156.8	63 24.7	56.8	157.6	62 29.1	57.1	158.3	11
12	69 45.0	53.7	150.6	68 52.4	54.4	151.9	67 59.1	55.0	153.1	67 05.4	55.5	154.1	66 11.2	55.9	155.1	65 16.6	56.2	156.0	64 21.5	56.6	156.9	63 26.2	56.9	157.7	12
13	70 38.7	53.2	149.3	69 46.8	53.8	150.7	68 54.1	54.5	152.0	68 00.9	55.0	153.2	67 07.1	55.5	154.2	66 12.8	56.0	155.2	65 18.2	56.3	156.1	64 23.1	56.7	157.0	13
14	71 31.9	52.4	147.9	70 40.6	53.3	149.4	69 48.6	54.0	150.8	68 55.9	54.7	152.0	68 02.6	55.2	153.2	67 08.8	55.7	154.3	66 14.5	56.1	155.3	65 19.8	56.5	156.2	14
15	72 24.3	+51.6	146.3	71 33.9	+52.6	148.0	70 42.6	+53.4	149.5	69 50.6	+54.1	150.9	68 57.8	+54.8	152.1	68 04.5	+55.3	153.3	67 10.6	+55.8	154.4	66 16.3	+56.2	155.4	15
16	73 15.9	50.7	144.6	72 26.5	51.7	146.4	71 36.0	52.7	148.1	70 44.7	53.5	149.6	69 52.6	54.2	151.0	68 59.8	54.8	152.2	68 06.4	55.4	153.4	67 12.5	55.8	154.5	16
17	74 06.6	49.5	142.7	73 18.2	50.9	144.7	72 28.7	51.9	146.5	71 38.2	52.8	148.2	70 46.8	53.6	149.7	69 54.6	54.4	151.1	69 01.8	54.9	152.4	68 08.3	55.5	153.5	17
18	74 56.1	48.3	140.5	74 09.1	49.7	142.8	73 20.6	51.0	144.8	72 31.0	51.9	146.7	71 40.4	53.0	148.3	70 49.0	53.8	149.9	69 56.7	54.5	151.2	69 03.8	55.1	152.5	18
19	75 44.4	46.7	138.2	74 58.8	48.4	140.7	74 11.6	49.9	142.9	73 23.1	51.2	145.0	72 33.4	52.3	146.8	71 42.8	53.1	148.4	70 51.2	53.9	150.0	69 58.9	54.6	151.3	19
20	76 31.1	+44.9	135.6	75 47.2	+46.9	138.3	75 01.5	+48.7	140.8	74 14.3	+50.1	143.1	73 25.7	+51.3	145.1	72 35.9	+52.4	146.9	71 45.1	+53.3	148.6	70 53.5	+54.1	150.1	20
21	77 16.0	42.7	132.7	76 34.1	45.1	135.7	75 50.2	47.1	138.5	75 04.4	48.8	141.0	74 17.0	50.3	143.2	73 28.3	51.5	145.3	72 38.4	52.6	147.1	71 47.6	53.4	148.7	21
22	77 58.7	40.2	129.4	77 19.2	43.0	132.8	76 37.3	45.3	135.9	75 53.2	47.3	138.7	75 07.3	49.0	141.2	74 19.8	50.4	143.4	73 31.0	51.6	145.4	72 41.0	52.7	147.3	22
23	78 38.9	37.1	125.7	78 02.2	40.4	129.5	77 22.6	43.2	133.0	76 40.5	45.6	136.1	75 56.3	47.5	138.9	75 10.2	49.3	141.4	74 22.6	50.7	143.6	73 33.7	51.9	145.6	23
24	79 16.0	33.5	121.6	78 42.6	37.4	125.9	78 05.8	40.7	129.7	77 26.1	43.4	133.2	76 43.8	45.8	136.3	75 59.5	47.7	139.1	75 13.3	49.4	141.5	74 25.6	50.8	143.8	24
25	79 49.5	+29.2	117.0	79 20.0	+33.7	121.8	78 46.5	+37.6	126.1	78 09.5	+41.0	129.9	77 29.6	+43.8	133.4	76 47.2	+46.1	136.5	76 02.7	+48.0	139.3	75 16.4	+49.7	141.7	25
26	80 18.7	24.4	112.0	79 53.7	29.6	117.2	79 24.1	34.1	121.9	78 50.5	37.9	126.2	78 13.4	41.2	130.1	77 33.3	44.0	133.6	76 50.7	46.3	136.7	76 06.1	48.2	139.5	26
27	80 43.1	18.8	106.4	80 23.3	24.6	112.1	79 58.2	29.8	117.3	79 28.4	34.3	122.1	78 54.6	38.2	126.5	78 17.3	41.5	130.3	77 37.0	44.3	133.8	76 54.3	46.6	136.9	27
28	81 01.9	12.6	100.4	80 47.9	19.0	106.5	80 28.0	24.9	112.2	80 02.7	30.1	117.5	79 32.8	34.6	122.3	78 58.8	38.5	126.7	78 21.3	41.8	130.6	77 40.9	44.5	134.1	28
29	81 14.5	+6.1	94.1	81 06.9	12.8	100.5	80 52.9	19.2	106.6	80 32.8	25.2	112.4	80 07.4	30.4	117.7	79 37.3	34.9	122.5	79 03.1	38.8	126.9	78 25.4	42.1	130.8	29
30	81 20.6	−0.9	87.5	81 19.7	+6.2	94.1	81 12.1	+13.0	100.5	80 58.0	+19.4	106.7	80 37.8	+25.4	112.5	80 12.2	+30.7	117.9	79 41.9	+35.2	122.8	79 07.5	+39.1	127.2	30
31	81 19.7	7.6	80.9	81 25.9	−0.8	87.4	81 25.1	6.3	94.1	81 17.4	13.2	100.6	81 03.2	19.7	106.8	80 42.9	25.7	112.7	80 17.1	31.0	118.1	79 46.6	35.5	123.0	31
32	81 12.1	14.1	74.3	81 25.1	7.7	80.7	81 31.4	−0.8	87.3	81 30.6	6.4	94.1	81 22.9	13.4	100.7	81 08.6	20.0	107.0	80 48.1	26.0	112.9	80 22.1	31.3	118.3	32
33	80 58.0	20.2	68.0	81 17.4	14.2	74.1	81 30.6	7.7	80.6	81 37.0	−0.7	87.3	81 36.3	6.5	94.1	81 28.6	13.5	100.7	81 14.1	20.2	107.1	80 53.4	26.4	113.1	33
34	80 37.8	25.6	62.2	81 03.2	20.3	67.8	81 22.9	14.3	73.9	81 36.3	7.7	80.6	81 42.8	−0.7	87.2	81 42.1	6.6	94.1	81 34.3	13.8	100.8	81 19.8	20.4	107.3	34
35	80 12.2	−30.3	56.7	80 42.9	−25.8	61.8	81 08.6	−20.5	67.5	81 28.6	−14.5	73.7	81 42.1	−7.8	80.3	81 48.7	−0.6	87.1	81 48.1	+6.7	94.1	81 40.2	+14.0	100.9	35
36	79 41.9	34.4	51.8	80 17.1	30.5	56.4	80 48.1	26.0	61.5	81 14.1	20.7	67.2	81 34.3	14.5	73.4	81 48.1	7.9	80.1	81 54.8	−0.6	87.1	81 54.2	6.8	94.1	36
37	79 07.5	37.9	47.3	79 46.6	34.7	51.4	80 22.1	30.7	56.0	80 53.4	26.1	61.2	81 19.8	20.9	66.9	81 40.2	14.7	73.2	81 54.2	7.9	79.9	82 01.0	−0.5	87.0	37
38	78 29.6	40.8	43.3	79 11.9	38.0	46.9	79 51.4	34.9	51.0	80 27.3	30.7	55.6	80 58.9	26.4	60.8	81 25.5	21.0	66.6	81 46.3	14.7	73.0	82 00.5	7.9	79.8	38
39	77 48.8	43.3	39.7	78 33.9	41.1	42.9	79 16.5	38.3	46.5	79 56.3	35.1	50.6	80 32.5	31.2	55.2	81 04.5	26.6	60.4	81 31.4	21.2	66.3	81 52.5	15.0	72.7	39
40	77 05.5	−45.3	36.5	77 52.8	−43.4	39.3	78 38.2	−41.2	42.5	79 21.2	−38.5	46.1	80 01.3	−35.3	50.1	80 37.9	−31.5	54.8	81 10.2	−26.9	60.1	81 36.5	−21.5	66.0	40
41	76 20.2	47.1	33.7	77 09.4	45.6	36.1	77 57.0	43.7	38.9	78 42.7	41.5	42.0	79 26.0	38.8	45.6	80 06.4	35.6	49.7	80 43.3	31.7	54.4	81 16.0	27.1	59.7	41
42	75 33.1	48.6	31.1	76 23.8	47.6	33.3	77 13.3	45.7	35.7	78 01.2	43.9	38.4	78 47.2	41.7	41.6	79 30.8	39.0	45.2	80 11.6	35.6	49.3	80 48.9	32.0	53.9	42
43	74 44.5	49.9	28.9	75 36.6	48.8	30.7	76 27.6	47.5	32.8	77 17.3	45.9	35.2	78 05.5	44.2	38.0	78 51.8	42.0	41.1	79 35.7	39.3	44.7	80 16.9	36.2	48.8	43
44	73 54.6	50.9	26.8	74 47.8	50.0	28.4	75 40.1	48.9	30.3	76 31.4	47.7	32.4	77 21.3	46.1	34.8	78 09.8	44.4	37.5	78 56.4	42.2	40.6	79 40.7	39.6	44.2	44

Dec.	30° Hc	d	Z	31° Hc	d	Z	32° Hc	d	Z	33° Hc	d	Z	34° Hc	d	Z	35° Hc	d	Z	36° Hc	d	Z	37° Hc	d	Z	Dec.
0	58 13.4	-57.0	158.8	57 17.4	-57.2	159.3	56 21.2	-57.5	159.9	55 24.8	-57.9	160.4	54 28.2	-57.8	160.8	53 31.4	-57.9	161.3	52 34.5	-58.1	161.7	51 37.5	-58.2	162.1	0
1	57 16.4	57.2	159.3	56 20.2	57.4	159.9	55 23.7	57.5	160.4	54 27.1	57.7	160.8	53 30.4	57.9	161.3	52 33.5	58.0	161.7	51 36.4	58.1	162.1	50 39.3	58.3	162.5	1
2	56 19.2	57.4	159.9	55 22.8	57.6	160.4	54 26.2	57.7	160.9	53 29.4	57.8	161.3	52 32.5	58.0	161.7	51 35.5	58.2	162.1	50 38.3	58.2	162.5	49 41.0	58.3	162.9	2
3	55 21.8	57.4	160.4	54 25.2	57.6	160.9	53 28.5	57.8	161.3	52 31.6	58.0	161.7	51 34.5	58.0	162.1	50 37.3	58.1	162.5	49 40.1	58.3	162.9	48 42.7	58.4	163.2	3
4	54 24.4	57.6	160.9	53 27.6	57.7	161.4	52 30.7	57.9	161.8	51 33.6	58.0	162.1	50 36.4	58.1	162.5	49 39.2	58.3	162.9	48 41.8	58.4	163.2	47 44.3	58.5	163.6	4
5	53 26.8	-57.7	161.4	52 29.9	-57.9	161.8	51 32.8	-58.0	162.2	50 35.6	-58.1	162.6	49 38.3	-58.2	162.9	48 40.9	-58.3	163.3	47 43.4	-58.4	163.6	46 45.8	-58.5	163.9	5
6	52 29.1	57.8	161.8	52 32.0	57.9	162.2	50 34.8	58.0	162.6	49 37.5	58.2	163.0	48 40.1	58.3	163.3	47 42.6	58.4	163.6	46 45.0	58.6	163.9	45 47.3	58.6	164.2	6
7	51 31.3	57.9	162.3	50 34.1	58.0	162.7	49 36.8	58.2	163.0	48 39.3	58.2	163.3	47 41.8	58.3	163.7	46 44.2	58.5	164.0	45 46.5	58.6	164.2	44 48.7	58.6	164.5	7
8	50 33.4	58.0	162.7	49 36.1	58.1	163.0	48 38.6	58.2	163.4	47 41.1	58.4	163.7	46 43.4	58.4	164.0	45 45.7	58.5	164.3	44 47.9	58.6	164.6	43 50.1	58.7	164.8	8
9	49 35.4	58.0	163.1	48 38.0	58.1	163.4	47 40.4	58.3	163.7	46 42.8	58.3	164.0	45 45.0	58.4	164.3	44 47.2	58.5	164.7	43 49.3	58.6	164.9	42 51.4	58.7	165.1	9
10	48 37.4	-58.2	163.5	47 39.8	-58.2	163.8	46 42.1	-58.3	164.1	45 44.4	-58.4	164.4	44 46.6	-58.5	164.7	43 48.7	-58.6	164.9	42 50.7	-58.7	165.1	41 52.7	-58.8	165.4	10
11	47 39.2	58.2	163.9	46 41.6	58.3	164.2	45 43.8	58.4	164.4	44 46.0	58.5	164.7	43 48.1	58.6	165.0	42 50.1	58.7	165.2	41 52.0	58.7	165.4	40 53.9	58.7	165.7	11
12	46 41.0	58.2	164.2	45 43.3	58.4	164.5	44 45.4	58.4	164.8	43 47.5	58.5	165.0	42 49.5	58.6	165.3	41 51.4	58.6	165.5	40 53.3	58.7	165.7	39 55.2	58.9	165.9	12
13	45 42.8	58.3	164.6	44 44.9	58.4	164.8	43 47.0	58.5	165.1	42 49.0	58.6	165.3	41 50.9	58.7	165.5	40 52.8	58.8	165.8	39 54.6	58.8	165.9	38 56.3	58.8	166.2	13
14	44 44.5	58.4	164.9	43 46.5	58.5	165.1	42 48.5	58.6	165.4	41 50.4	58.6	165.6	40 52.2	58.7	165.8	39 54.0	58.7	166.0	38 55.8	58.8	166.2	37 57.5	58.9	166.4	14
15	43 46.1	-58.5	165.2	42 48.0	-58.5	165.5	41 49.9	-58.6	165.7	40 51.8	-58.7	165.9	39 53.5	-58.7	166.1	38 55.3	-58.8	166.3	37 57.0	-58.9	166.5	36 58.6	-58.9	166.7	15
16	42 47.6	58.5	165.5	41 49.5	58.6	165.8	40 51.3	58.6	166.0	39 53.1	58.7	166.2	38 54.8	58.8	166.4	37 56.5	58.8	166.6	36 58.1	58.9	166.6	35 59.7	59.0	166.9	16
17	41 49.2	58.6	165.8	40 51.0	58.7	166.0	39 52.7	58.7	166.2	38 54.4	58.7	166.4	37 56.0	58.8	166.6	36 57.7	58.9	166.8	35 59.2	58.9	167.0	35 00.7	58.9	167.1	17
18	40 50.6	58.5	166.1	39 52.3	58.6	166.3	38 54.0	58.7	166.5	37 55.7	58.8	166.7	36 57.2	58.8	166.7	35 58.8	58.9	167.0	35 00.3	58.9	167.2	34 01.8	59.0	167.3	18
19	39 52.1	58.7	166.4	38 53.7	58.7	166.6	37 55.3	58.7	166.8	36 56.9	58.8	167.0	35 58.4	58.9	167.1	34 59.9	58.9	167.3	34 01.4	59.0	167.4	33 02.8	59.0	167.6	19
20	38 53.4	-58.6	166.7	37 55.0	-58.7	166.9	36 56.6	-58.8	167.0	35 58.1	-58.8	167.2	34 59.6	-58.9	167.4	34 01.0	-58.9	167.5	33 02.4	-59.0	167.6	32 03.8	-59.1	167.8	20
21	37 54.8	58.7	167.0	36 56.3	58.8	167.1	35 57.8	58.8	167.3	34 59.3	58.9	167.4	34 00.7	58.9	167.6	33 02.1	59.0	167.7	32 03.4	59.0	167.9	31 04.7	59.0	168.0	21
22	36 56.1	58.7	167.3	35 57.6	58.8	167.4	34 59.0	58.8	167.5	34 00.4	58.9	167.7	33 01.8	59.0	167.8	32 03.1	58.9	168.0	31 04.4	59.0	168.1	30 05.7	59.1	168.2	22
23	35 57.4	58.8	167.5	34 58.8	58.8	167.6	34 00.2	58.9	167.8	33 01.5	58.9	167.9	32 02.8	59.0	168.0	31 04.1	59.0	168.2	30 05.4	59.1	168.3	29 06.6	59.1	168.4	23
24	34 58.6	58.8	167.7	34 00.0	58.8	167.9	33 01.3	58.9	168.0	32 02.6	58.9	168.1	31 03.9	59.0	168.3	30 05.1	59.0	168.4	29 06.3	59.0	168.5	28 07.5	59.1	168.6	24
25	33 59.8	-58.8	168.0	33 01.2	-58.9	168.1	32 02.4	-58.9	168.2	31 03.7	-59.0	168.4	30 04.9	-59.0	168.4	29 06.1	-59.0	168.6	28 07.3	-59.1	168.7	27 08.4	-59.1	168.8	25
26	33 01.0	58.8	168.2	32 02.3	58.9	168.3	31 03.5	59.0	168.5	30 04.7	59.0	168.6	29 05.9	59.0	168.7	28 07.1	59.1	168.8	27 08.2	59.1	168.8	26 09.3	59.1	169.0	26
27	32 02.2	58.9	168.4	31 03.4	58.9	168.6	30 04.6	59.0	168.7	29 05.7	58.9	168.8	28 06.9	59.1	168.8	27 08.0	59.1	169.0	26 09.1	59.1	169.1	25 10.2	59.2	169.2	27
28	31 03.1	58.8	168.6	30 04.5	59.0	168.8	29 05.6	58.9	168.9	28 06.8	59.1	169.0	27 07.8	59.0	169.0	26 08.9	59.1	169.2	25 10.0	59.2	169.2	24 11.1	59.1	169.4	28
29	30 04.5	59.0	168.9	29 05.6	59.0	169.0	28 06.7	59.0	169.1	27 07.7	59.0	169.2	26 08.8	59.1	169.2	25 09.8	59.0	169.4	24 10.9	59.2	169.5	23 11.9	59.2	169.5	29
30	29 05.5	-58.9	169.1	28 06.6	-59.0	169.2	27 07.7	-59.0	169.3	26 08.7	-59.0	169.4	25 09.7	-59.1	169.4	24 10.7	-59.1	169.6	23 11.7	-59.1	169.6	22 12.7	-59.2	169.7	30
31	28 06.6	58.9	169.3	27 07.7	59.0	169.4	26 08.7	59.1	169.5	25 09.7	59.1	169.6	24 10.6	59.1	169.6	23 11.6	59.1	169.8	22 12.6	59.2	169.8	21 13.5	59.2	169.9	31
32	27 07.7	59.0	169.5	26 08.7	59.1	169.6	25 09.6	59.0	169.7	24 10.6	59.1	169.8	23 11.5	59.0	169.8	22 12.5	59.2	169.9	21 13.4	59.2	170.0	20 14.3	59.2	170.1	32
33	26 08.7	59.0	169.7	25 09.7	59.1	169.8	24 10.6	59.1	169.9	23 11.5	59.1	170.0	22 12.4	59.1	170.0	21 13.3	59.1	170.1	20 14.2	59.2	170.2	19 15.1	59.2	170.2	33
34	25 09.7	59.0	169.9	24 10.6	59.0	170.0	23 11.5	59.0	170.1	22 12.4	59.1	170.2	21 13.3	59.1	170.2	20 14.2	59.2	170.3	19 15.0	59.2	170.4	18 15.9	59.3	170.4	34
35	24 10.7	-59.0	170.1	23 11.6	-59.0	170.2	22 12.5	-59.1	170.3	21 13.3	-59.1	170.4	20 14.2	-59.2	170.3	19 15.0	-59.1	170.5	18 15.8	-59.2	170.5	17 16.6	-59.2	170.6	35
36	23 11.7	59.0	170.3	22 12.6	59.1	170.4	21 13.4	59.1	170.5	20 14.2	59.1	170.5	19 15.0	59.1	170.6	18 15.8	59.2	170.6	17 16.6	59.2	170.7	16 17.4	59.2	170.7	36
37	22 12.7	59.1	170.5	21 13.5	59.1	170.5	20 14.3	59.1	170.7	19 15.1	59.2	170.7	18 15.9	59.2	170.7	17 16.6	59.2	170.8	16 17.4	59.2	170.9	15 18.2	59.3	170.9	37
38	21 13.6	59.1	170.7	20 14.4	59.1	170.8	19 15.2	59.1	170.8	18 15.9	59.1	170.9	17 16.7	59.1	170.9	16 17.4	59.2	171.0	15 18.2	59.2	171.1	14 18.9	59.2	171.1	38
39	20 14.6	59.1	170.9	19 15.3	59.1	171.0	18 16.1	59.2	171.0	17 16.8	59.2	171.1	16 17.5	59.2	171.1	15 18.2	59.1	171.1	14 19.0	59.3	171.2	13 19.7	59.3	171.2	39
40	19 15.5	-59.1	171.1	18 16.2	-59.1	171.1	17 16.9	-59.1	171.2	16 17.6	-59.1	171.2	15 18.3	-59.1	171.3	14 19.0	-59.2	171.3	13 19.7	-59.2	171.4	12 20.4	-59.3	171.4	40
41	18 16.4	59.1	171.3	17 17.1	59.1	171.3	16 17.8	59.1	171.4	15 18.5	59.2	171.4	14 19.2	59.2	171.4	13 19.8	59.2	171.5	12 20.5	59.3	171.5	11 21.1	59.2	171.6	41
42	17 17.3	59.1	171.5	16 18.0	59.1	171.5	15 18.7	59.2	171.5	14 19.3	59.2	171.6	13 20.0	59.2	171.6	12 20.6	59.2	171.7	11 21.2	59.2	171.7	10 21.9	59.3	171.7	42
43	16 18.2	59.1	171.6	15 18.9	59.2	171.7	14 19.5	59.1	171.7	13 20.1	59.2	171.8	12 20.7	59.2	171.8	11 21.4	59.2	171.8	10 22.0	59.3	171.8	9 22.6	59.3	171.9	43
44	15 19.1	59.1	171.8	14 19.7	59.1	171.9	13 20.3	59.1	171.9	12 20.9	59.1	171.9	11 21.5	59.2	172.0	10 22.1	59.2	172.0	9 22.7	59.3	172.0	8 23.3	59.3	172.0	44

14°, 346° L.H.A. LATITUDE SAME NAME AS DECLINATION

N. Lat. { L.H.A. greater than 180°........Zn=Z
 L.H.A. less than 180°........Zn=360°−Z

Dec.	30° Hc	d	Z	31° Hc	d	Z	32° Hc	d	Z	33° Hc	d	Z	34° Hc	d	Z	35° Hc	d	Z	36° Hc	d	Z	37° Hc	d	Z	Dec.
0	57 10.3	+55.2	153.5	56 16.5	+55.5	154.2	55 22.3	+55.9	154.8	54 27.9	+56.1	155.4	53 33.2	+56.4	156.0	52 38.3	+56.6	156.5	51 43.2	+56.8	157.0	50 47.8	+57.1	157.5	0
1	58 05.5	+55.0	152.8	57 12.0	+55.3	153.5	56 18.2	+55.6	154.2	55 24.0	+56.0	154.8	54 29.6	+56.2	155.4	53 34.9	+56.5	156.0	52 40.0	+56.7	156.5	51 44.9	+56.9	157.0	1
2	59 00.5	+54.6	152.0	58 07.3	+55.1	152.8	57 13.8	+55.4	153.5	56 19.8	+55.7	154.1	55 25.8	+56.1	154.8	54 31.4	+56.3	155.4	53 36.7	+56.6	156.0	52 41.8	+56.8	156.5	2
3	59 55.1	+54.4	151.2	59 02.4	+54.7	152.0	58 09.2	+55.1	152.8	57 15.7	+55.5	153.5	56 21.9	+55.8	154.1	55 27.7	+56.1	154.8	54 33.3	+56.4	155.4	53 38.6	+56.7	155.9	3
4	60 49.5	+54.0	150.3	59 57.1	+54.5	151.2	59 04.3	+54.9	152.0	58 11.2	+55.2	152.8	57 17.7	+55.6	153.5	56 23.8	+56.0	154.1	55 29.7	+56.2	154.8	54 35.3	+56.5	155.4	4
5	61 43.5	+53.6	149.4	60 51.6	+54.1	150.3	59 59.2	+54.6	151.2	59 06.4	+55.0	152.0	58 13.3	+55.3	152.8	57 19.8	+55.6	153.5	56 25.9	+56.0	154.2	55 31.8	+56.3	154.8	5
6	62 37.1	+53.2	148.5	61 45.7	+53.7	149.4	60 53.8	+54.2	150.4	60 01.4	+54.7	151.2	59 08.6	+55.1	152.0	58 15.4	+55.5	152.8	57 21.9	+55.8	153.5	56 28.1	+56.1	154.2	6
7	63 30.3	+52.7	147.4	62 39.4	+53.4	148.5	61 48.0	+54.0	149.5	60 56.1	+54.3	150.4	60 03.7	+54.8	151.2	59 10.9	+55.2	152.1	58 17.7	+55.6	152.8	57 24.2	+55.9	153.5	7
8	64 23.0	+52.2	146.4	63 32.8	+52.8	147.5	62 42.0	+53.4	148.5	61 50.4	+54.0	149.5	60 58.5	+54.5	150.4	60 06.1	+54.9	151.3	59 13.3	+55.3	152.1	58 20.1	+55.6	152.8	8
9	65 15.2	+51.7	145.2	64 25.6	+52.4	146.4	63 35.3	+53.0	147.5	62 44.4	+53.6	148.6	61 53.0	+54.1	149.5	61 01.0	+54.6	150.5	60 08.6	+55.1	151.3	59 15.7	+55.5	152.1	9
10	66 06.9	+51.0	144.0	65 18.0	+51.8	145.2	64 28.3	+52.5	146.4	63 38.0	+53.2	147.6	62 47.1	+53.7	148.6	61 55.6	+54.2	149.6	61 03.6	+54.7	150.5	60 11.2	+55.1	151.4	10
11	66 57.9	+50.3	142.6	66 09.8	+51.2	144.0	65 20.8	+52.0	145.3	64 31.2	+52.6	146.5	63 40.8	+53.3	147.6	62 49.8	+53.9	148.7	61 58.3	+54.4	149.6	61 06.3	+54.8	150.6	11
12	67 48.2	+49.5	141.2	67 01.0	+50.4	142.7	66 12.8	+51.3	144.1	65 23.8	+52.1	145.4	64 34.1	+52.8	146.6	63 43.7	+53.4	147.6	62 52.7	+54.0	148.7	62 01.1	+54.5	149.7	12
13	68 37.7	+48.7	139.7	67 51.4	+49.7	141.3	67 04.1	+50.7	142.8	66 15.9	+51.5	144.2	65 26.9	+52.3	145.4	64 37.1	+53.0	146.6	63 46.7	+53.6	147.8	62 55.6	+54.2	148.8	13
14	69 26.4	+47.6	138.1	68 41.1	+48.9	139.8	67 54.8	+49.9	141.4	67 07.4	+50.9	142.9	66 19.2	+51.6	144.2	65 30.1	+52.4	145.5	64 40.3	+53.1	146.7	63 49.8	+53.7	147.8	14
15	70 14.0	+46.5	136.3	69 30.0	+47.8	138.1	68 44.7	+49.0	139.8	67 58.3	+50.0	141.5	67 10.8	+51.0	142.9	66 22.5	+51.9	144.3	65 33.4	+52.6	145.6	64 43.5	+53.3	146.8	15
16	71 00.5	+45.3	134.4	70 17.8	+46.7	136.4	69 33.7	+48.0	138.2	68 48.3	+49.2	140.0	68 01.8	+50.3	141.6	67 14.4	+51.1	143.1	66 26.0	+52.0	144.4	65 36.8	+52.7	145.7	16
17	71 45.8	+43.8	132.3	71 04.5	+45.5	134.5	70 21.7	+47.0	136.5	69 37.5	+48.3	138.4	68 52.1	+49.4	140.1	68 05.5	+50.5	141.7	67 18.0	+51.4	143.2	66 29.5	+52.2	144.5	17
18	72 29.6	+42.2	130.1	71 50.0	+44.1	132.4	71 08.7	+45.7	134.6	70 25.8	+47.2	136.6	69 41.5	+48.5	138.5	68 56.0	+49.6	140.2	68 09.4	+50.6	141.8	67 21.7	+51.6	143.3	18
19	73 11.8	+40.4	127.7	72 34.1	+42.4	130.2	71 54.4	+44.3	132.5	71 13.0	+45.9	134.7	70 30.0	+47.4	136.7	69 45.6	+48.7	138.6	69 00.0	+49.9	140.3	68 13.3	+50.9	141.9	19
20	73 52.2	+38.3	125.1	73 16.5	+40.7	127.8	72 38.7	+42.7	130.3	71 58.9	+44.6	132.7	71 17.4	+46.2	134.9	70 34.3	+47.7	136.9	69 49.9	+48.9	138.8	69 04.2	+50.0	140.5	20
21	74 30.5	+36.0	122.3	73 57.2	+38.6	125.2	73 21.4	+41.0	127.8	72 43.5	+43.0	130.5	72 03.6	+44.8	132.8	71 22.0	+46.4	135.0	70 38.8	+47.9	137.0	69 54.2	+49.1	138.9	21
22	75 06.5	+33.4	119.2	74 35.8	+36.3	122.2	74 02.4	+38.9	125.3	73 26.5	+41.2	128.1	72 48.4	+43.3	130.6	72 08.4	+45.1	133.0	71 26.7	+46.6	135.2	70 43.3	+48.2	137.2	22
23	75 39.9	+30.5	115.9	75 12.1	+33.7	119.3	74 41.3	+36.5	122.5	74 07.7	+39.2	125.5	73 31.7	+41.5	128.2	72 53.5	+43.5	130.8	72 13.3	+45.4	133.2	71 31.5	+46.9	135.4	23
24	76 10.4	+27.1	112.4	75 45.8	+30.7	116.0	75 17.8	+34.0	119.5	74 46.9	+36.8	122.7	74 13.2	+39.4	125.6	73 37.0	+41.8	128.4	72 58.7	+43.8	131.0	72 18.4	+45.6	133.3	24
25	76 37.5	+23.6	108.6	76 16.5	+27.5	112.5	75 51.8	+31.0	116.1	75 23.7	+34.3	119.5	74 52.6	+37.2	122.8	74 18.8	+39.8	125.8	73 42.5	+42.1	128.6	73 04.0	+44.1	131.2	25
26	77 01.1	+19.6	104.5	76 44.0	+23.8	108.7	76 22.8	+27.8	112.6	75 58.0	+31.3	116.3	75 29.8	+34.6	119.7	74 58.6	+37.5	123.0	74 24.6	+40.1	126.0	73 48.1	+42.4	128.8	26
27	77 20.7	+15.4	100.3	77 07.8	+19.9	104.6	76 50.6	+24.1	108.7	76 29.3	+28.1	112.7	76 04.4	+31.6	116.4	75 36.1	+34.9	119.9	75 04.7	+37.8	123.2	74 30.5	+40.4	126.2	27
28	77 36.1	+10.8	95.8	77 27.7	+15.5	100.3	77 14.7	+20.1	104.7	76 57.4	+24.4	108.8	76 36.0	+28.4	112.8	76 11.0	+31.9	116.6	75 42.5	+35.2	120.1	75 10.9	+38.1	123.4	28
29	77 46.9	+6.1	91.2	77 43.2	+11.0	95.8	77 34.8	+15.8	100.3	77 21.8	+20.4	104.7	77 04.4	+24.7	108.9	76 42.9	+28.7	113.0	76 17.7	+32.3	116.7	75 49.0	+35.6	120.3	29
30	77 53.0	+1.2	86.5	77 54.2	+6.3	91.1	77 50.6	+11.2	95.8	77 42.2	+16.0	100.4	77 29.1	+20.6	104.8	77 11.6	+25.0	109.1	76 50.0	+29.0	113.1	76 24.6	+32.6	116.9	30
31	77 54.2	−3.6	81.7	78 00.5	+1.3	86.4	78 01.8	+6.3	91.1	77 58.2	+11.3	95.8	77 49.7	+16.3	100.4	77 36.6	+20.9	104.9	77 19.0	+25.2	109.2	76 57.2	+29.3	113.3	31
32	77 50.6	−8.4	77.0	78 01.8	−3.6	81.6	78 08.1	+1.4	86.3	78 09.5	+6.5	91.0	78 06.0	+11.5	95.8	77 57.5	+16.5	100.5	77 44.2	+21.2	105.0	77 26.5	+25.6	109.3	32
33	77 42.2	−13.1	72.3	77 58.2	−8.5	76.8	78 09.5	−3.5	81.4	78 16.0	+1.5	86.2	78 17.5	+6.7	91.0	78 14.0	+11.7	95.8	78 05.4	+16.8	100.5	77 52.1	+21.5	105.1	33
34	77 29.1	−17.5	67.7	77 49.7	−13.1	72.3	78 06.0	−8.5	76.6	78 17.5	−3.5	81.3	78 24.2	+1.5	86.1	78 25.7	+6.8	91.0	78 22.2	+11.9	95.8	78 13.6	+17.0	100.6	34
35	77 11.6	−21.6	63.4	77 36.6	−17.6	67.0	77 57.5	−13.3	71.8	78 14.0	−8.6	76.3	78 25.7	−3.5	81.1	78 32.5	+1.6	86.0	78 34.1	+6.9	90.9	78 30.6	+12.1	95.8	35
36	76 50.0	−25.4	59.2	77 19.0	−21.8	63.0	77 44.2	−17.7	67.1	78 05.4	−13.3	71.5	78 22.2	−8.6	76.1	78 34.1	−3.5	80.9	78 41.0	+1.7	85.9	78 42.7	+7.1	90.9	36
37	76 24.6	−28.8	55.3	76 57.2	−25.5	58.9	77 26.5	−21.9	62.7	77 52.1	−17.8	66.8	78 13.6	−13.4	71.2	78 30.6	−8.6	75.9	78 42.7	−3.5	80.8	78 49.8	+1.7	85.8	37
38	75 55.8	−32.0	51.6	76 31.7	−29.5	55.0	77 04.6	−25.7	58.5	77 34.3	−21.9	62.3	78 00.2	−18.0	66.2	78 22.0	−13.6	71.0	78 39.2	−8.7	75.7	78 51.5	−3.5	80.6	38
39	75 23.8	−34.7	48.2	76 02.6	−32.1	51.2	76 38.9	−29.3	54.5	77 12.2	−26.0	58.1	77 42.2	−22.3	62.0	78 08.4	−18.1	66.2	78 30.5	−13.6	70.7	78 48.0	−8.8	75.5	39
40	74 49.1	−37.2	45.0	75 30.5	−34.9	47.8	76 09.6	−32.3	50.8	76 46.2	−29.4	54.1	77 19.9	−26.1	57.7	77 50.3	−22.5	61.6	78 16.9	−18.4	65.8	78 39.2	−13.7	70.4	40
41	74 11.9	−39.3	42.1	74 55.6	−37.4	44.6	75 37.3	−35.2	47.0	76 16.8	−32.6	50.3	76 53.8	−29.7	53.6	77 27.4	−26.4	57.2	77 58.5	−22.6	61.2	78 25.5	−18.6	65.5	41
42	73 32.6	−41.4	39.4	74 18.2	−39.6	41.6	75 02.1	−37.6	44.1	75 44.2	−35.4	46.9	76 24.1	−32.8	49.9	77 01.4	−29.9	53.2	77 35.9	−26.7	56.8	78 06.9	−22.9	60.8	42
43	72 51.2	−43.0	36.9	73 38.6	−41.5	38.9	74 24.5	−39.8	41.2	75 08.8	−37.8	43.6	75 51.3	−35.7	46.4	76 31.5	−33.1	49.4	77 09.2	−30.1	52.7	77 44.0	−26.8	56.4	43
44	72 08.2	−44.6	34.6	72 57.1	−43.3	36.4	73 44.7	−41.7	38.4	74 31.0	−40.1	40.7	75 15.6	−38.1	43.2	75 58.4	−35.9	45.9	76 39.1	−33.4	48.9	77 17.2	−30.5	52.3	44

LATITUDE SAME NAME AS DECLINATION

N. Lat. { L.H.A. greater than 180°......Zn=Z / L.H.A. less than 180°.......Zn=360°-Z }

Dec.	30° Hc	d	Z	31° Hc	d	Z	32° Hc	d	Z	33° Hc	d	Z	34° Hc	d	Z	35° Hc	d	Z	36° Hc	d	Z	37° Hc	d	Z	Dec.
0	56 46.4	+54.7	151.8	55 53.4	+55.0	152.5	55 00.0	+55.3	153.2	54 06.3	+55.6	153.8	53 12.3	+56.0	154.4	52 18.1	+56.2	155.0	51 23.6	+56.5	155.5	50 28.9	+56.7	156.0	0
1	57 41.1	54.3	151.0	56 48.4	54.7	151.8	55 55.3	55.1	152.5	55 01.9	55.5	153.2	54 08.3	55.8	153.8	53 14.3	56.0	154.4	52 20.1	56.2	154.9	51 25.6	56.5	155.5	1
2	58 35.4	54.0	150.2	57 43.1	54.4	151.0	56 50.4	54.8	151.8	55 57.4	55.1	152.5	55 04.0	55.5	153.1	54 10.3	55.7	153.8	53 16.3	56.2	154.4	52 22.1	56.4	154.9	2
3	59 29.4	53.9	149.4	58 37.5	54.1	150.2	57 45.2	54.6	151.0	56 52.5	54.9	151.8	55 59.5	55.3	152.5	55 06.0	55.5	153.1	54 12.5	55.9	153.8	53 18.5	56.2	154.4	3
4	60 23.0	53.3	148.5	59 31.6	53.8	149.4	58 39.8	54.2	150.2	57 47.5	54.6	151.0	56 54.8	55.0	151.8	56 01.5	55.4	152.5	55 08.4	55.7	153.1	54 14.7	56.0	153.8	4
5	61 16.3	+52.9	147.6	60 25.4	+53.4	148.5	59 34.0	+53.9	149.4	58 42.1	+54.4	150.2	57 49.8	+54.8	151.0	56 57.7	+55.1	151.8	56 04.1	+55.5	152.5	55 10.7	+55.9	153.2	5
6	62 09.2	52.4	146.6	61 18.8	53.0	147.6	60 27.9	53.5	148.5	59 36.5	54.0	149.4	58 44.6	54.5	150.2	57 52.3	54.8	151.1	56 59.6	55.3	151.8	56 06.6	55.6	152.5	6
7	63 01.6	51.9	145.5	62 11.8	52.6	146.6	61 21.4	53.2	147.6	60 30.5	53.7	148.5	59 39.1	54.1	149.4	58 47.2	54.6	150.3	57 54.9	55.1	151.1	57 02.2	55.4	151.8	7
8	63 53.5	51.3	144.4	63 04.4	52.0	145.5	62 14.6	52.7	146.6	61 24.2	53.3	147.6	60 33.2	53.8	148.6	59 41.8	54.3	149.4	58 49.9	54.7	150.3	57 57.6	55.1	151.1	8
9	64 44.8	50.8	143.2	63 56.4	51.5	144.4	63 07.3	52.2	145.6	62 17.5	52.8	146.6	61 27.0	53.5	147.7	60 36.1	53.9	148.6	59 44.6	54.4	149.5	58 52.7	54.8	150.4	9
10	65 35.6	+50.0	141.9	64 47.9	+50.9	143.2	63 59.5	+51.6	144.5	63 10.3	+52.4	145.6	62 20.5	+52.9	146.7	61 30.0	+53.6	147.7	60 39.0	+54.1	148.7	59 47.5	+54.6	149.6	10
11	66 25.6	49.3	140.6	65 38.8	50.2	142.0	64 51.1	51.1	143.3	64 02.7	51.8	144.5	63 13.4	52.6	145.7	62 23.6	53.1	146.8	61 33.1	53.7	147.8	60 42.1	54.2	148.7	11
12	67 14.9	48.5	139.1	66 29.0	49.5	140.6	65 42.2	50.4	142.0	64 54.5	51.2	143.3	64 06.0	52.0	144.6	63 16.7	52.7	145.7	62 26.8	53.3	146.8	61 36.3	53.8	147.8	12
13	68 03.4	47.5	137.6	67 18.5	48.7	139.2	66 32.6	49.7	140.7	65 45.7	50.6	142.1	64 58.0	51.4	143.4	64 09.4	52.1	144.7	63 20.1	52.8	145.8	62 30.1	53.5	146.9	13
14	68 50.9	46.5	135.9	68 07.2	47.7	137.7	67 22.3	48.8	139.3	66 36.3	49.9	140.8	65 49.4	50.7	142.2	65 01.5	51.6	143.5	64 12.9	52.4	144.7	63 23.6	53.0	145.9	14
15	69 37.4	+45.3	134.1	68 54.9	+46.7	136.0	68 11.1	+48.0	137.7	67 26.2	+49.0	139.3	66 40.1	+50.1	140.9	65 53.1	+51.0	142.3	65 05.3	+51.7	143.6	64 16.6	+52.5	144.8	15
16	70 22.7	44.0	132.2	69 41.6	45.6	134.2	68 59.1	46.9	136.0	68 15.2	48.2	137.7	67 30.2	49.3	139.4	66 44.1	50.3	141.0	65 57.0	51.2	142.4	65 09.1	51.9	143.7	16
17	71 06.7	42.5	130.1	70 27.2	44.2	132.3	69 46.0	45.8	134.3	69 03.4	47.1	136.2	68 19.5	48.3	137.9	67 34.4	49.4	139.6	66 48.2	50.4	141.1	66 01.0	51.4	142.5	17
18	71 49.2	40.9	127.9	71 11.4	42.8	130.2	70 31.8	44.5	132.4	69 50.5	45.8	134.3	69 07.8	47.4	136.3	68 23.8	48.6	138.0	67 38.6	49.7	139.7	66 52.4	50.7	141.2	18
19	72 30.1	39.0	125.5	71 54.2	41.1	128.0	71 16.3	43.0	130.2	70 36.3	44.8	132.5	69 55.2	46.3	134.5	69 12.4	47.6	136.4	68 28.3	48.9	138.0	67 43.1	49.9	139.8	19
20	73 09.1	+37.0	122.9	72 35.3	+39.3	125.6	71 59.3	+41.4	128.1	71 21.3	+43.3	130.5	70 41.5	+45.0	132.6	70 00.0	+46.6	134.7	69 17.2	+47.8	136.6	68 33.0	+49.0	138.3	20
21	73 46.1	34.6	120.2	73 14.6	37.3	123.1	72 40.7	39.6	125.8	72 04.6	41.7	128.3	71 26.5	43.5	130.6	70 46.6	45.2	132.8	70 05.0	46.8	134.8	69 22.0	48.1	136.7	21
22	74 20.7	32.1	117.2	73 51.9	34.9	120.3	73 20.3	37.5	123.2	72 46.3	39.9	125.9	72 10.0	42.0	128.4	71 31.8	43.9	130.8	70 51.8	45.5	132.9	70 10.1	47.0	135.0	22
23	74 52.8	29.2	114.0	74 26.8	32.4	117.3	73 57.8	35.3	120.4	73 26.2	37.8	123.3	72 52.0	40.2	126.0	72 15.7	42.2	128.6	71 37.3	44.1	130.9	70 57.1	45.8	133.1	23
24	75 22.0	26.1	110.6	74 59.2	29.5	114.1	74 33.1	32.4	117.4	74 04.0	35.5	120.5	73 32.2	38.1	123.5	72 57.9	40.5	126.2	72 21.4	42.6	128.7	71 42.9	44.4	131.1	24
25	75 48.1	+22.6	107.0	75 28.7	+26.3	110.7	75 05.7	+29.8	114.2	74 39.5	+33.0	117.5	74 10.3	+35.9	120.7	73 38.4	+38.5	123.6	73 04.0	+40.8	126.4	72 27.3	+42.9	128.9	25
26	76 10.7	18.8	103.2	75 55.0	22.9	107.1	75 35.5	26.5	110.8	75 12.5	30.1	114.3	74 46.2	33.3	117.7	74 16.9	36.1	120.8	73 44.8	38.7	123.8	73 10.2	41.1	126.5	26
27	76 29.5	14.8	99.2	76 17.9	19.1	103.2	76 02.0	23.1	107.1	75 42.6	26.9	110.9	75 19.5	30.4	114.5	74 53.0	33.6	117.8	74 23.5	36.5	121.0	73 51.3	39.1	124.0	27
28	76 44.3	10.6	95.0	76 37.0	15.0	99.2	76 25.3	19.4	103.3	76 09.5	23.5	107.2	75 49.9	27.2	111.0	75 26.6	30.8	114.6	75 00.0	34.0	118.0	74 30.4	36.8	121.2	28
29	76 54.9	6.2	90.6	76 52.0	10.8	94.9	76 44.7	15.2	99.2	76 33.0	19.6	103.3	76 17.1	23.7	107.3	75 57.4	27.5	111.1	75 34.0	31.0	114.7	75 07.2	34.3	118.2	29
30	77 01.1	+1.7	86.2	77 02.8	+6.3	90.6	76 59.9	+11.0	94.9	76 52.6	+15.5	99.2	76 40.8	+19.9	103.4	76 24.9	+24.0	107.4	76 05.0	+27.9	111.3	75 41.5	+31.4	114.9	30
31	77 02.8	-2.9	81.8	77 09.1	1.8	86.1	77 10.9	6.5	90.5	77 08.1	11.1	94.9	77 00.7	15.7	99.2	76 48.9	20.1	103.4	76 32.9	24.3	107.5	76 12.9	28.2	111.4	31
32	76 59.9	7.3	77.3	77 10.9	-2.8	81.6	77 17.4	1.8	86.0	77 19.2	6.6	90.4	77 16.4	11.4	94.9	77 09.0	16.0	99.2	76 57.2	20.4	103.5	76 41.1	24.6	107.6	32
33	76 52.6	11.8	72.9	77 08.1	7.4	77.1	77 19.2	-2.8	81.5	77 25.8	1.8	85.9	77 27.8	6.7	90.4	77 25.0	11.6	94.9	77 17.6	16.2	99.3	77 05.7	20.7	103.6	33
34	76 40.8	15.9	68.6	77 00.7	11.8	72.7	77 16.4	7.4	76.9	77 27.8	-2.8	81.3	77 34.5	2.1	85.8	77 36.6	6.9	90.3	77 33.8	11.8	94.9	77 26.4	16.5	99.4	34
35	76 24.9	-19.9	64.5	76 48.9	-16.0	68.4	77 09.0	-11.8	72.4	77 25.0	-7.4	76.7	77 36.6	-2.8	81.1	77 43.5	+2.1	85.7	77 45.6	+7.0	90.3	77 42.9	+11.9	94.9	35
36	76 05.0	23.5	60.5	76 32.9	20.0	64.2	76 57.2	16.1	68.1	77 17.6	11.9	72.2	77 33.8	7.4	76.7	77 45.6	-2.7	81.0	77 52.6	2.2	85.6	77 54.8	7.2	90.2	36
37	75 41.5	26.9	56.8	76 12.9	23.7	60.2	76 41.1	20.2	63.8	77 05.7	16.2	67.7	77 26.4	12.0	71.9	77 42.9	7.5	76.3	77 54.8	-2.7	80.8	78 02.0	2.2	85.5	37
38	75 14.6	30.0	53.2	75 49.2	27.1	56.4	76 20.9	23.8	59.8	76 49.5	20.3	63.5	77 14.4	16.4	67.4	77 35.4	12.1	71.6	77 52.1	7.5	76.0	78 04.2	-2.6	80.6	38
39	74 44.6	32.8	49.9	75 22.1	30.2	52.8	75 57.1	27.3	56.0	76 29.2	24.1	59.4	76 58.0	20.4	63.1	77 23.3	16.5	67.1	77 44.6	12.2	71.3	78 01.6	7.6	75.8	39
40	74 11.8	-35.3	46.7	74 51.9	-33.0	49.4	75 29.8	-30.4	52.3	76 05.1	-27.5	55.5	76 37.6	-24.3	59.0	77 06.8	-20.6	62.7	77 32.4	-16.7	66.8	77 54.0	-12.3	71.1	40
41	73 36.5	37.5	43.8	74 18.9	35.5	46.3	74 59.4	33.2	48.9	75 37.6	30.6	51.9	76 13.3	27.7	55.1	76 46.2	24.5	58.6	77 15.7	20.8	62.4	77 41.7	16.8	66.4	41
42	72 59.0	39.6	41.1	73 43.4	37.9	43.3	74 26.2	35.7	45.8	75 07.0	33.4	48.3	75 45.6	30.8	51.4	76 21.7	27.9	54.7	76 54.9	24.7	58.2	77 25.9	21.1	62.0	42
43	72 19.4	41.3	38.6	73 05.7	39.8	40.6	73 50.5	38.0	42.9	74 33.6	36.0	45.3	75 14.8	33.7	48.0	75 53.8	31.1	51.0	76 30.2	28.2	54.2	77 03.8	24.9	57.7	43
44	71 38.1	42.9	36.2	72 25.9	41.5	38.1	73 12.5	40.0	40.1	73 57.6	38.2	42.4	74 41.1	36.2	44.8	75 22.7	34.0	47.5	76 02.0	31.3	50.5	76 38.9	28.5	53.7	44

LATITUDE SAME NAME AS DECLINATION

N. Lat. $\begin{cases} \text{L.H.A. greater than } 180° \ldots\ldots Zn=Z \\ \text{L.H.A. less than } 180° \ldots\ldots Zn=360°-Z \end{cases}$

Dec.	30° Hc	d	Z	31° Hc	d	Z	32° Hc	d	Z	33° Hc	d	Z	34° Hc	d	Z	35° Hc	d	Z	36° Hc	d	Z	37° Hc	d	Z	Dec.
0	56 21.2	+54.0	150.2	55 29.0	+54.4	150.9	54 36.4	+54.8	151.6	53 43.5	+55.1	152.2	52 50.2	+55.5	152.9	51 56.7	+55.7	153.4	51 02.9	+56.0	154.0	50 08.9	+56.2	154.5	0
1	57 15.2	53.7	149.4	56 23.4	54.1	150.1	55 31.2	54.5	150.9	54 38.6	54.9	151.6	53 45.7	55.3	152.2	52 52.4	55.6	152.8	51 58.9	55.9	153.4	51 05.1	56.1	154.0	1
2	58 08.9	53.3	148.5	57 17.5	53.8	149.4	56 25.7	54.2	150.1	55 33.5	54.6	150.9	54 40.9	55.0	151.5	53 48.0	55.3	152.2	52 54.8	55.6	152.8	52 01.2	56.0	153.4	2
3	59 02.2	53.0	147.7	58 11.3	53.5	148.5	57 19.9	53.9	149.3	56 28.1	54.4	150.1	55 35.9	54.7	150.8	54 43.3	55.1	151.5	53 50.4	55.5	152.2	52 57.2	55.7	152.8	3
4	59 55.2	52.6	146.7	59 04.8	53.1	147.6	58 13.8	53.6	148.5	57 22.5	54.0	149.3	56 30.6	54.5	150.1	55 38.4	54.9	150.8	54 45.9	55.2	151.5	53 52.9	55.6	152.2	4
5	60 47.8	+52.1	145.8	59 57.9	+52.7	146.7	59 07.4	+53.3	147.7	58 16.5	+53.7	148.5	57 25.1	+54.2	149.3	56 33.3	+54.6	150.1	55 41.1	+55.0	150.9	54 48.5	+55.3	151.5	5
6	61 39.9	51.6	144.7	60 50.6	52.2	145.8	60 00.7	52.8	146.7	59 10.2	53.4	147.7	58 19.3	53.8	148.5	57 27.9	54.3	149.4	56 36.1	54.7	150.1	55 43.8	55.1	150.9	6
7	62 31.5	51.0	143.6	61 42.8	51.8	144.7	60 53.5	52.4	145.8	60 03.6	53.0	146.8	59 13.1	53.6	147.7	58 22.2	54.0	148.6	57 30.8	54.4	149.4	56 38.9	54.9	150.2	7
8	63 22.5	50.5	142.5	62 34.6	51.2	143.7	61 45.9	51.9	144.8	60 56.6	52.5	145.8	60 06.7	53.1	146.8	59 16.2	53.6	147.7	58 25.2	54.1	148.6	57 33.8	54.6	149.4	8
9	64 13.0	49.8	141.3	63 25.8	50.6	142.5	62 37.8	51.4	143.7	61 49.1	52.1	144.8	60 59.8	52.7	145.8	60 09.8	53.3	146.8	59 19.3	53.8	147.8	58 28.4	54.2	148.6	9
10	65 02.8	+49.1	140.0	64 16.4	+50.0	141.3	63 29.2	+50.8	142.5	62 41.2	+51.6	143.7	61 52.5	+52.2	144.8	61 03.1	+52.9	145.9	60 13.1	+53.5	146.9	59 22.6	+54.0	147.8	10
11	65 51.9	48.3	138.6	65 06.4	49.3	140.0	64 20.0	50.2	141.3	63 32.8	51.0	142.6	62 44.7	51.8	143.8	61 56.0	52.4	144.9	61 06.6	52.6	145.9	60 16.6	53.5	146.9	11
12	66 40.2	47.4	137.1	65 55.7	48.5	138.6	65 10.2	49.5	140.1	64 23.8	50.3	141.4	63 36.5	51.1	142.7	62 48.4	51.9	143.8	61 59.6	52.6	145.0	61 10.1	53.2	146.0	12
13	67 27.6	46.5	135.5	66 44.2	47.7	137.2	65 59.7	48.7	138.7	65 14.1	49.7	140.1	64 27.6	50.6	141.5	63 40.3	51.3	142.7	62 52.2	52.0	143.9	62 03.3	52.8	145.0	13
14	68 14.1	45.3	133.8	67 31.9	46.6	135.6	66 48.4	47.8	137.2	66 03.8	48.9	138.8	65 18.2	49.9	140.2	64 31.6	50.8	141.5	63 44.2	51.6	142.8	62 56.1	52.2	144.0	14
15	68 59.4	+44.2	132.0	68 18.5	+45.6	133.9	67 36.2	+46.9	135.7	66 52.7	+48.1	137.3	66 08.1	+49.1	138.8	65 22.4	+50.1	140.3	64 35.8	+50.9	141.6	63 48.3	+51.8	142.9	15
16	69 43.6	42.8	130.1	69 04.1	44.4	132.1	68 23.1	45.8	134.0	67 40.8	47.1	135.8	66 57.2	48.3	137.4	66 12.5	49.3	138.9	65 26.7	50.3	140.4	64 40.1	51.1	141.7	16
17	70 26.4	41.3	128.1	69 48.5	43.0	130.2	69 08.9	44.7	132.2	68 27.9	46.1	134.1	67 45.5	47.3	135.9	67 01.8	48.5	137.5	66 17.0	49.6	139.1	65 31.2	50.5	140.5	17
18	71 07.7	39.6	125.9	70 31.5	41.6	128.2	69 53.6	43.3	130.3	69 14.0	44.8	132.3	68 32.8	46.3	134.2	67 50.3	47.6	136.0	67 06.6	48.7	137.6	66 21.7	49.8	139.2	18
19	71 47.3	37.7	123.5	71 13.1	39.9	126.0	70 36.9	41.8	128.1	69 58.8	43.6	130.4	69 19.1	45.2	132.4	68 37.9	46.6	134.3	67 55.3	47.8	136.1	67 11.5	48.9	137.8	19
20	72 25.0	+35.7	121.0	71 53.0	+38.0	123.6	71 18.7	+40.2	126.1	70 42.4	+42.1	128.4	70 04.3	+43.8	130.5	69 24.5	+45.4	132.4	68 43.1	+46.9	134.5	68 00.4	+48.1	136.2	20
21	73 00.7	33.5	118.3	72 31.0	36.0	121.1	71 58.9	38.3	123.7	71 24.5	40.5	126.2	70 48.1	42.8	128.5	70 09.9	44.1	130.7	69 30.0	45.6	132.7	68 48.5	47.1	134.6	21
22	73 34.2	30.8	115.4	73 07.0	33.7	118.4	72 37.2	36.3	121.2	72 05.0	38.6	123.8	71 30.5	40.8	126.3	70 54.0	42.7	128.6	70 15.6	44.4	130.8	69 35.6	45.9	132.9	22
23	74 05.0	28.1	112.3	73 40.7	31.2	115.5	73 13.5	34.0	118.5	72 43.6	36.6	121.3	72 11.3	38.9	124.0	71 36.7	41.0	126.5	71 00.0	43.0	128.8	70 21.5	44.7	131.0	23
24	74 33.1	25.1	109.0	74 11.9	28.4	112.4	73 47.5	31.5	115.6	73 20.2	34.3	118.6	72 50.2	36.9	121.4	72 17.7	39.3	124.1	71 43.0	41.4	126.6	71 06.2	43.3	129.0	24
25	74 58.2	+21.7	105.6	74 40.3	+25.4	109.1	74 19.0	+28.7	112.5	73 54.5	+31.8	115.7	73 27.1	+34.7	118.7	72 57.0	+37.2	121.6	72 24.4	+39.5	124.3	71 49.5	+41.7	126.8	25
26	75 19.9	18.2	101.9	75 05.7	22.0	105.6	74 47.7	25.6	109.2	74 26.3	29.0	112.6	74 01.8	32.1	115.8	73 34.2	35.0	118.8	73 03.9	37.6	121.7	72 31.2	39.9	124.4	26
27	75 38.1	14.5	98.1	75 27.7	18.4	102.0	75 13.3	22.3	105.7	74 55.3	26.0	109.2	74 33.9	29.3	112.7	74 09.2	32.1	115.8	73 41.5	35.3	119.0	73 11.1	37.9	121.9	27
28	75 52.6	10.4	94.2	75 46.1	14.7	98.1	75 35.6	18.7	102.0	75 21.3	22.6	105.7	75 03.2	26.2	109.3	74 41.6	29.7	112.8	74 16.8	32.8	116.1	73 49.0	35.6	119.2	28
29	76 03.0	6.3	90.1	76 00.8	10.6	94.1	75 54.3	14.9	98.1	75 43.9	18.9	102.0	75 29.4	22.9	105.8	75 11.3	26.5	109.4	74 49.6	29.9	112.9	74 24.6	33.1	116.2	29
30	76 09.3	+2.2	86.0	76 11.4	+6.4	90.0	76 09.2	+10.8	94.1	76 02.8	+15.1	98.1	75 52.3	+19.2	102.1	75 37.8	+23.2	105.6	75 19.5	+26.9	109.6	74 57.7	+30.3	113.1	30
31	76 11.4	-2.2	81.8	76 17.8	2.2	85.9	76 20.0	6.6	90.0	76 17.9	11.0	94.1	76 11.5	15.3	98.1	76 01.0	19.5	102.1	75 46.4	23.5	106.0	75 28.0	27.2	109.7	31
32	76 09.2	6.4	77.6	76 20.0	-2.1	81.6	76 26.6	2.3	85.7	76 28.9	6.8	90.0	76 26.8	11.2	94.0	76 20.5	15.5	98.2	76 09.9	19.7	102.2	75 55.2	23.8	106.1	32
33	76 02.8	10.5	73.5	76 17.9	6.4	77.4	76 28.9	-2.1	81.5	76 35.7	2.3	85.7	76 38.0	6.9	89.8	76 36.0	11.4	94.0	76 29.6	15.8	98.2	76 19.0	20.0	102.3	33
34	75 52.3	14.5	69.4	76 11.5	10.5	73.2	76 26.8	6.3	77.2	76 38.0	-2.0	81.5	76 44.9	2.5	85.5	76 47.4	7.1	89.8	76 45.4	11.6	94.0	76 39.0	16.1	98.2	34
35	75 37.8	-18.3	65.5	76 01.0	-14.6	69.1	76 20.5	-10.6	73.0	76 36.0	-6.4	77.0	76 47.4	-2.0	81.1	76 54.5	+2.5	85.4	76 57.0	+7.2	89.7	76 55.1	+11.8	94.0	35
36	75 19.5	21.8	61.7	75 46.4	18.4	65.1	76 09.9	14.7	68.8	76 29.6	10.6	72.7	76 45.4	6.4	76.8	76 57.0	-1.9	81.0	77 04.2	2.7	85.3	77 06.9	7.3	89.6	36
37	74 57.7	25.1	58.0	75 28.0	21.9	61.3	75 55.2	18.5	64.8	76 19.0	14.8	68.5	76 39.0	10.7	72.4	76 55.1	6.4	76.6	77 06.9	-1.9	80.8	77 14.2	2.8	85.2	37
38	74 32.6	28.2	54.6	75 06.1	25.3	57.6	75 36.7	22.1	60.9	76 04.2	18.6	64.5	76 28.3	14.8	68.2	76 48.7	10.8	72.2	77 05.0	6.5	76.3	77 17.0	-1.9	80.6	38
39	74 04.4	30.9	51.3	74 40.8	28.4	54.1	75 14.6	25.5	57.2	75 45.6	22.3	60.6	76 13.5	18.8	64.1	76 37.9	15.0	67.9	76 58.5	10.8	71.9	77 15.1	6.5	76.1	39
40	73 33.5	-33.5	48.2	74 12.4	-31.1	50.9	74 49.1	-28.5	53.7	75 23.3	-25.7	56.8	75 54.7	-22.5	60.6	76 22.9	-19.0	63.7	76 47.7	-15.2	67.6	77 08.6	-11.0	71.6	40
41	73 00.0	35.7	45.4	73 41.3	33.7	47.8	74 20.6	31.4	50.4	74 57.6	28.7	53.3	75 32.2	25.9	56.4	76 03.9	22.6	59.8	76 32.5	19.1	63.4	76 57.6	15.2	67.2	41
42	72 24.3	37.8	42.7	73 07.6	35.9	44.9	73 49.2	33.8	47.3	74 28.9	31.6	50.0	75 06.3	28.9	52.8	75 41.3	26.1	56.0	76 13.4	22.9	59.3	76 42.4	19.4	63.0	42
43	71 46.5	39.8	40.1	72 31.7	38.0	42.2	73 15.4	36.2	44.4	73 57.3	34.4	46.8	74 37.4	31.8	49.5	75 15.2	29.2	52.4	75 50.5	26.3	55.5	76 23.0	23.1	58.9	43
44	71 06.8	41.3	37.8	71 53.7	39.9	39.6	72 39.2	38.3	41.7	73 23.2	36.4	43.9	74 05.6	34.4	46.3	74 46.0	32.1	49.0	75 24.2	29.5	51.9	75 59.9	26.5	55.0	44

LATITUDE SAME NAME AS DECLINATION

N. Lat. { L.H.A. greater than 180°......Zn=Z
          L.H.A. less than 180°.........Zn=360°-Z

Dec.	30° Hc	30° d	30° Z	31° Hc	31° d	31° Z	32° Hc	32° d	32° Z	33° Hc	33° d	33° Z	34° Hc	34° d	34° Z	35° Hc	35° d	35° Z	36° Hc	36° d	36° Z	37° Hc	37° d	37° Z	Dec.
0	55 54.8	+53.3	148.6	55 03.4	+53.8	149.3	54 11.6	+54.2	150.0	53 19.4	+54.6	150.7	52 26.9	+55.0	151.3	51 34.1	+55.3	151.9	50 41.1	+55.5	152.5	49 47.7	+55.9	153.1	0
1	56 48.1	53.0	147.7	55 57.2	53.5	148.5	55 05.8	53.9	149.3	54 14.0	54.4	150.0	53 21.9	54.7	150.7	52 29.4	55.1	151.3	51 36.6	55.4	151.9	50 43.6	55.6	152.5	1
2	57 41.1	52.7	146.9	56 50.7	53.1	147.7	55 59.7	53.6	148.5	55 08.4	54.0	149.3	54 16.6	54.5	150.0	53 24.5	54.8	150.6	52 32.0	55.2	151.3	51 39.2	55.5	151.9	2
3	58 33.8	52.2	146.0	57 43.8	52.8	146.8	56 53.3	53.3	147.7	56 02.4	53.8	148.5	55 11.1	54.1	149.3	54 19.3	54.3	149.9	53 27.2	54.9	150.6	52 34.7	55.3	151.3	3
4	59 26.0	51.9	145.0	58 36.6	52.4	145.9	57 46.6	53.0	146.8	56 56.2	53.4	147.7	56 05.2	53.8	148.5	55 13.9	54.3	149.2	54 22.1	54.7	150.0	53 30.0	55.1	150.6	4
5	60 17.9	+51.3	144.0	59 29.0	+52.0	145.0	58 39.6	+52.5	145.9	57 49.6	+53.1	146.8	56 59.1	+53.6	147.7	56 08.2	+54.0	148.5	55 16.8	+54.5	149.2	54 25.1	+54.8	150.0	5
6	61 09.2	50.8	142.9	60 21.0	51.5	144.0	59 32.1	52.1	145.0	58 42.7	52.7	146.0	57 52.7	53.2	146.8	57 02.2	53.7	147.7	56 11.3	54.2	148.5	55 19.9	54.6	149.3	6
7	62 00.0	50.2	141.8	61 12.5	50.9	142.9	60 24.2	51.7	144.0	59 35.4	52.2	145.0	58 45.9	52.9	146.0	57 55.9	53.4	146.9	57 05.5	53.8	147.7	56 14.5	54.3	148.5	7
8	62 50.2	49.6	140.6	62 03.4	50.4	141.8	61 15.9	51.1	142.9	60 27.6	51.9	144.0	59 38.8	52.4	145.0	58 49.3	53.0	146.0	57 59.3	53.5	146.9	57 08.8	54.0	147.7	8
9	63 39.8	48.9	139.4	62 53.8	49.8	140.7	62 07.0	50.6	141.9	61 19.5	51.3	143.0	60 31.2	52.0	144.1	59 42.3	52.6	145.1	58 52.8	53.2	146.0	58 02.8	53.7	146.9	9
10	64 28.7	+48.2	138.1	63 43.6	+49.1	139.4	62 57.6	+50.0	140.7	62 10.8	+50.8	141.9	61 23.2	+51.5	143.0	60 34.9	+52.2	144.1	59 46.0	+52.8	145.1	58 56.5	+53.5	146.1	10
11	65 16.9	47.3	136.7	64 32.7	48.4	138.1	63 47.6	49.3	139.5	63 01.6	50.1	140.7	62 14.7	50.9	142.0	61 27.1	51.6	143.1	60 38.8	52.3	144.2	59 49.8	52.9	145.2	11
12	66 04.2	46.4	135.2	65 21.1	47.5	136.7	64 36.9	48.6	138.2	63 51.7	49.5	139.5	63 05.6	50.4	140.8	62 18.7	51.2	142.0	61 31.1	51.8	143.2	60 42.7	52.5	144.2	12
13	66 50.6	45.4	133.6	66 08.6	46.6	135.2	65 25.5	47.7	136.8	64 41.2	48.8	138.2	63 56.0	49.7	139.6	63 09.9	50.5	140.9	62 22.9	51.4	142.1	61 35.2	52.1	143.2	13
14	67 36.0	44.2	131.9	66 55.2	45.7	133.6	66 13.2	46.9	135.3	65 30.0	48.0	136.8	64 45.7	49.0	138.3	64 00.4	50.0	139.7	63 14.3	50.7	140.9	62 27.3	51.5	142.2	14
15	68 20.2	+43.1	130.1	67 40.9	+44.5	132.0	67 00.1	+45.8	133.7	66 18.0	+47.1	135.4	65 34.7	+48.2	136.9	64 50.4	+49.2	138.4	64 05.0	+50.2	139.7	63 18.8	+51.0	141.0	15
16	69 03.3	41.6	128.2	68 25.4	43.2	130.2	67 45.9	44.8	132.0	67 05.1	46.1	133.8	66 22.9	47.3	135.5	65 39.6	48.4	137.0	64 55.2	49.4	138.5	64 09.8	50.3	139.8	16
17	69 44.9	40.1	126.1	69 08.6	42.0	128.2	68 30.7	43.5	130.2	67 51.2	45.0	132.1	67 10.2	46.4	133.9	66 28.0	47.6	135.6	65 44.6	48.6	137.1	65 00.1	49.7	138.6	17
18	70 25.0	38.5	123.9	69 50.6	40.4	126.2	69 14.2	42.2	128.3	68 36.2	43.8	130.3	67 56.6	45.2	132.2	67 15.6	46.6	134.0	66 33.2	47.9	135.7	65 49.8	48.9	137.2	18
19	71 03.5	36.6	121.6	70 31.0	38.7	124.0	69 56.4	40.7	126.2	69 20.0	42.4	128.4	68 41.8	44.1	130.5	68 02.2	45.5	132.3	67 21.1	46.8	134.1	66 38.7	48.0	135.8	19
20	71 40.1	+34.5	119.1	71 09.7	+36.9	121.7	70 37.1	+39.0	124.1	70 02.4	+41.0	126.4	69 25.9	+42.8	128.6	68 47.7	+44.3	130.6	68 07.9	+45.8	132.5	67 26.7	+47.1	134.3	20
21	72 14.6	32.3	116.5	71 46.6	34.8	119.2	71 16.1	37.2	121.8	70 43.4	39.3	124.2	70 08.7	41.2	126.5	69 32.0	43.1	128.7	68 53.7	44.6	130.7	68 13.8	46.1	132.6	21
22	72 46.9	29.8	113.7	72 21.4	32.6	116.6	71 53.3	35.1	119.3	71 22.7	37.5	121.9	70 49.9	39.6	124.3	70 15.1	41.5	126.7	69 38.3	43.4	128.8	68 59.9	44.9	130.9	22
23	73 16.7	27.1	110.7	72 54.0	30.1	113.8	72 28.4	32.9	116.7	72 00.2	35.5	119.4	71 29.5	37.8	122.0	70 56.6	40.0	124.5	70 21.7	41.8	126.8	69 44.8	43.6	129.0	23
24	73 43.8	24.2	107.6	73 24.1	27.4	110.8	73 01.3	30.4	113.8	72 35.7	33.2	116.8	72 07.3	35.8	119.5	71 36.6	38.1	122.2	71 03.5	40.3	124.6	70 28.4	42.2	127.0	24
25	74 08.0	+21.0	104.3	73 51.5	+24.5	107.6	73 31.7	+27.7	110.8	73 08.9	+30.7	113.9	72 43.1	+33.5	116.9	72 14.7	+36.1	119.7	71 43.8	+38.4	122.3	71 10.6	+40.6	124.8	25
26	74 29.0	17.6	100.8	74 16.0	21.3	104.3	73 59.4	24.8	107.7	73 39.6	28.0	110.9	73 16.6	31.1	114.0	72 50.8	33.8	117.0	72 22.2	36.5	119.8	71 51.2	38.8	122.5	26
27	74 46.6	14.1	97.2	74 37.3	17.8	100.8	74 24.2	21.6	104.3	74 07.6	25.1	107.7	73 47.7	28.3	111.0	73 24.6	31.4	114.2	72 58.7	34.2	117.1	72 30.0	36.7	120.0	27
28	75 00.7	10.3	93.5	74 55.1	14.3	97.2	74 45.8	18.1	100.8	74 32.7	21.8	104.4	74 16.0	25.4	107.8	73 56.0	28.7	111.1	73 32.9	31.7	114.3	73 06.7	34.6	117.3	28
29	75 11.0	6.5	89.6	75 09.4	10.5	93.4	75 03.9	14.5	97.2	74 54.5	18.4	100.8	74 41.4	22.1	104.4	74 24.7	25.7	107.9	74 04.6	29.0	111.2	73 41.3	32.0	114.4	29
30	75 17.5	+2.4	85.7	75 19.9	+6.7	89.5	75 18.4	+10.7	93.4	75 12.9	+14.8	97.1	75 03.5	+18.7	100.9	74 50.4	+22.4	104.5	74 33.6	+26.0	108.0	74 13.3	+29.4	111.4	30
31	75 19.9	-1.5	81.8	75 26.5	2.6	85.6	75 29.1	6.8	89.5	75 27.7	10.9	93.3	75 22.2	15.0	97.1	75 12.8	19.0	100.9	74 59.6	22.7	104.6	74 42.7	26.3	108.1	31
32	75 18.4	5.5	77.8	75 29.1	-1.4	81.6	75 35.9	2.7	85.5	75 38.6	6.9	89.4	75 37.2	11.1	93.3	75 31.8	15.2	97.1	75 22.3	19.2	101.0	75 09.0	23.1	104.7	32
33	75 12.9	9.4	73.9	75 27.6	5.4	77.6	75 38.6	-1.4	81.4	75 45.5	2.8	85.3	75 48.3	7.1	89.3	75 47.0	11.3	93.2	75 41.5	15.5	97.2	75 32.1	19.5	101.0	33
34	75 03.5	13.1	70.1	75 22.2	9.4	73.7	75 37.2	5.4	77.4	75 48.3	-1.3	81.3	75 55.4	2.9	85.2	75 58.3	7.2	89.2	75 57.0	11.5	93.2	75 51.6	15.7	97.2	34
35	74 50.4	-16.8	66.3	75 12.8	-13.2	69.8	75 31.8	-9.5	73.4	75 47.0	-5.5	77.2	75 58.3	-1.3	81.1	76 05.5	+3.0	85.1	76 08.5	+7.4	89.1	76 07.3	+11.7	93.2	35
36	74 33.6	20.3	62.7	74 59.6	16.9	66.0	75 22.3	13.3	69.5	75 41.5	9.4	73.2	75 57.0	5.4	77.0	76 08.5	-1.2	80.9	76 15.9	3.1	85.0	76 19.0	7.5	89.1	36
37	74 13.3	23.4	59.2	74 42.7	20.4	62.3	75 09.0	17.0	65.7	75 32.1	13.4	69.2	75 51.6	9.6	72.9	76 07.3	5.5	76.8	76 19.0	-1.2	80.8	76 26.5	+3.2	84.9	37
38	73 49.9	26.4	55.8	74 22.3	23.6	58.8	74 52.0	20.5	61.9	75 18.7	17.1	65.3	75 42.0	13.4	68.9	76 01.8	9.6	72.6	76 17.8	5.5	76.5	76 29.7	-1.2	80.6	38
39	73 23.5	29.2	52.5	73 58.7	26.6	55.4	74 31.5	23.7	58.6	75 01.6	20.7	61.6	75 28.6	17.3	65.0	75 52.2	13.5	68.6	76 12.3	9.6	72.3	76 28.5	5.7	76.3	39
40	72 54.3	-31.7	49.6	73 32.1	-29.3	52.2	74 07.8	-26.8	55.0	74 40.9	-23.9	58.0	75 11.3	-20.8	61.2	75 38.7	-17.4	64.6	76 02.7	-13.7	68.2	76 23.1	-9.8	72.1	40
41	72 22.6	34.0	46.8	73 02.8	31.9	49.2	73 41.0	29.6	51.8	74 17.0	27.0	54.5	74 50.5	24.1	57.5	75 21.3	21.0	60.8	75 49.0	17.6	64.2	76 13.3	13.8	67.9	41
42	71 48.6	36.1	44.1	72 30.9	34.2	46.3	73 11.4	32.1	48.7	73 50.0	29.8	51.3	74 26.4	27.2	54.1	75 00.3	24.4	57.1	75 31.4	21.2	60.4	75 59.5	17.7	63.8	42
43	71 12.5	38.0	41.6	71 56.7	36.4	43.6	72 39.3	34.4	45.8	73 20.2	32.3	48.2	73 59.2	30.0	50.8	74 35.9	27.4	53.6	75 10.2	24.5	56.7	75 41.8	21.4	59.7	43
44	70 34.5	39.8	39.2	71 20.3	38.2	41.1	72 04.9	36.6	43.1	72 47.9	34.7	45.3	73 29.2	32.6	47.7	74 08.5	30.3	50.3	74 45.7	27.7	53.1	75 20.4	24.8	56.2	44

LATITUDE SAME NAME AS DECLINATION

N. Lat. { L.H.A. greater than 180° ......Zn=Z
L.H.A. less than 180° ......Zn=360°−Z }

Dec.	30° (Hc, d, Z)	31° (Hc, d, Z)	32° (Hc, d, Z)	33° (Hc, d, Z)	34° (Hc, d, Z)	35° (Hc, d, Z)	36° (Hc, d, Z)	37° (Hc, d, Z)	Dec.
0	55 27.0 +52.8 147.0	54 36.5 +53.2 147.8	53 45.6 +53.6 148.5	52 54.2 +54.1 149.2	52 02.5 +54.4 149.8	51 10.5 +54.8 150.5	50 18.1 +55.1 151.1	49 25.5 +55.4 151.6	0
1	56 19.8 52.3 146.9	55 29.7 52.9 146.9	54 39.2 53.3 147.8	53 48.3 53.7 148.5	52 56.9 54.2 149.1	52 05.3 54.5 149.8	51 13.2 54.9 150.4	50 20.9 55.2 151.0	1
2	57 12.1 52.0 145.2	56 22.6 52.5 146.1	55 32.5 53.0 146.9	54 42.0 53.5 147.7	53 51.1 53.9 148.4	52 59.8 54.3 149.1	52 08.1 54.7 149.8	51 16.1 55.0 150.4	2
3	58 04.1 51.5 144.3	57 15.1 52.1 145.2	56 25.5 52.7 146.1	55 35.5 53.2 146.9	54 45.0 53.6 147.7	53 54.1 54.1 148.4	53 02.8 54.5 149.1	52 11.1 54.9 149.8	3
4	58 55.6 51.1 143.3	58 07.2 51.7 144.3	57 18.2 52.3 145.2	56 28.7 52.8 146.1	55 38.6 53.0 146.9	54 48.2 53.7 147.7	53 57.3 54.1 148.4	53 06.0 54.5 149.1	4
5	59 46.7 +50.5 142.3	58 58.9 +51.2 143.3	58 10.5 +51.8 144.3	57 21.5 +52.4 145.2	56 31.9 +53.0 146.1	55 41.9 +53.5 146.9	54 51.4 +53.9 147.7	54 00.5 +54.4 148.4	5
6	60 37.2 50.0 141.2	59 50.1 50.7 142.3	59 02.3 51.4 143.3	58 13.9 52.0 144.3	57 24.9 52.6 145.2	56 35.4 53.1 146.1	55 45.3 53.6 146.9	54 54.9 54.0 147.7	6
7	61 27.2 49.4 140.1	60 40.8 50.2 141.2	59 53.7 50.9 142.3	59 05.9 51.6 143.3	58 17.5 52.2 144.4	57 28.5 52.7 145.2	56 38.9 53.3 146.1	55 48.9 53.8 146.9	7
8	62 16.6 48.8 138.9	61 31.0 49.6 140.1	60 44.6 50.4 141.2	59 57.5 51.1 142.3	59 09.7 51.7 143.3	58 21.2 52.4 144.3	57 32.2 52.9 145.2	56 42.7 53.4 146.1	8
9	63 05.4 48.0 137.6	62 20.6 49.0 138.9	61 35.0 49.8 140.1	60 48.6 50.5 141.3	60 01.4 51.3 142.3	59 13.6 51.9 143.4	58 25.1 52.5 144.4	57 36.1 53.1 145.3	9
10	63 53.4 +47.2 136.3	63 09.6 +48.2 137.6	62 24.8 +49.1 138.9	61 39.1 +50.0 140.1	60 52.7 +50.7 141.3	60 05.5 +51.5 142.4	59 17.6 +52.1 143.4	58 29.2 +52.7 144.4	10
11	64 40.6 46.4 134.8	63 57.8 47.4 136.3	63 13.9 48.4 137.7	62 29.1 49.3 139.0	61 43.4 50.2 140.2	60 57.0 50.9 141.3	60 09.7 51.7 142.4	59 21.9 52.2 143.5	11
12	65 27.0 45.4 133.3	64 45.2 46.6 134.9	64 02.3 47.7 136.3	63 18.4 48.7 137.7	62 33.6 49.6 139.0	61 47.9 50.4 140.2	61 01.4 51.1 141.4	60 14.1 51.9 142.5	12
13	66 12.4 44.3 131.7	65 31.8 45.6 133.4	64 50.0 46.8 134.9	64 07.1 47.9 136.4	63 23.2 48.8 137.8	62 38.3 49.7 139.1	61 52.5 50.6 140.3	61 06.0 51.3 141.5	13
14	66 56.7 43.3 130.0	66 17.4 44.7 131.8	65 36.8 45.9 133.4	64 55.0 47.0 135.0	64 12.0 48.1 136.5	63 28.0 49.1 137.8	62 43.1 50.0 139.1	61 57.3 50.8 140.4	14
15	67 40.0 +41.9 128.2	67 02.1 +43.4 130.1	66 22.7 +44.9 131.8	65 42.0 +46.2 133.5	65 00.1 +47.3 135.1	64 17.1 +48.4 136.5	63 33.1 +49.3 137.9	62 48.1 +50.2 139.2	15
16	68 21.9 40.6 126.3	67 45.5 42.2 128.3	67 07.6 43.7 130.2	66 28.2 45.1 131.9	65 47.4 46.4 133.6	65 05.5 47.5 135.1	64 22.4 48.6 136.6	63 38.3 49.5 138.0	16
17	69 02.5 39.0 124.3	68 27.7 40.9 126.4	67 51.3 42.5 128.4	67 13.3 44.0 130.2	66 33.8 45.4 132.0	65 53.0 46.6 133.7	65 11.0 47.8 135.2	64 27.8 48.8 136.7	17
18	69 41.5 37.3 122.1	69 08.6 39.3 124.4	68 33.8 41.1 126.5	67 57.3 42.7 128.5	67 19.2 44.3 130.3	66 39.6 45.7 132.1	65 58.8 46.9 133.8	65 16.6 48.1 135.4	18
19	70 18.8 35.5 119.8	69 47.9 37.6 122.2	69 14.9 39.6 124.4	68 40.0 41.4 126.6	68 03.5 43.0 128.6	67 25.3 44.5 130.4	66 45.7 45.9 132.2	66 04.7 47.1 133.9	19
20	70 54.3 +33.5 117.4	70 25.5 +35.8 119.9	69 54.5 +37.9 122.3	69 21.4 +39.9 124.5	68 46.5 +41.7 126.7	68 09.8 +43.4 128.7	67 31.6 +44.8 130.6	66 51.8 +46.2 132.4	20
21	71 27.8 31.2 114.8	71 01.3 33.8 117.5	70 32.4 36.1 120.0	70 01.3 38.3 122.4	69 28.2 40.2 124.7	68 53.2 41.8 126.8	68 16.4 43.6 128.8	67 38.0 45.1 130.7	21
22	71 59.0 28.9 112.1	71 35.1 31.5 114.9	71 08.5 34.1 117.6	70 39.6 36.4 120.1	70 08.4 38.6 122.5	69 35.2 40.5 124.8	69 00.0 42.3 126.9	68 23.1 44.0 128.9	22
23	72 27.9 26.2 109.3	72 06.6 29.2 112.2	71 42.6 31.9 115.0	71 16.0 34.4 117.7	70 47.0 36.7 120.2	70 15.7 38.8 122.6	69 42.3 40.9 124.9	69 07.1 42.6 127.1	23
24	72 54.1 23.4 106.2	72 35.8 26.5 109.2	72 14.5 29.4 112.2	71 50.4 32.1 115.0	71 23.7 34.7 117.8	70 54.5 37.1 120.3	70 23.2 39.2 122.8	69 49.7 41.1 125.1	24
25	73 17.5 +20.4 103.1	73 02.3 +23.7 106.3	72 43.9 +26.9 109.4	72 22.5 +29.8 112.3	71 58.4 +32.5 115.2	71 31.6 +35.1 117.9	71 02.4 +37.3 120.5	70 30.8 +39.6 122.9	25
26	73 37.9 17.1 99.8	73 26.0 20.6 103.1	73 10.8 24.0 106.3	72 52.4 27.1 109.4	72 30.9 30.1 112.4	72 06.7 32.8 115.3	71 39.7 35.4 118.0	71 10.4 37.7 120.6	26
27	73 55.0 13.8 96.3	73 46.6 17.5 99.7	73 34.8 20.9 103.1	73 19.5 24.3 106.3	73 01.0 27.5 109.5	72 39.5 30.4 112.5	72 15.1 33.2 115.4	71 48.1 35.7 118.2	27
28	74 08.8 10.3 92.8	74 04.1 14.0 96.3	73 55.7 17.7 99.7	73 43.8 21.2 103.1	73 28.5 24.6 106.4	73 09.9 27.8 109.6	72 48.3 30.8 112.6	72 23.8 33.6 115.5	28
29	74 19.1 6.6 89.2	74 18.1 10.4 92.7	74 13.4 14.2 96.3	74 05.0 18.0 99.8	73 53.1 21.5 103.2	73 37.7 24.9 106.5	73 19.1 28.1 109.7	72 57.4 31.1 112.8	29
30	74 25.7 +2.8 85.5	74 28.5 +6.8 89.1	74 27.6 +10.7 92.7	74 23.0 +14.4 96.2	74 14.6 +18.2 99.8	74 02.6 +21.9 103.2	73 47.2 +25.3 106.6	73 28.5 +28.5 109.8	30
31	74 28.5 −0.9 81.7	74 35.3 +3.0 85.4	74 38.3 6.9 89.0	74 37.4 10.9 92.6	74 32.8 14.7 96.2	74 24.5 18.4 99.8	74 12.5 22.1 103.3	73 57.0 25.5 106.7	31
32	74 27.6 4.6 78.0	74 38.3 −0.9 81.6	74 45.2 3.1 85.2	74 48.3 7.0 88.9	74 47.5 11.1 92.6	74 42.9 15.0 96.2	74 34.6 18.7 99.8	74 22.5 22.4 103.3	32
33	74 23.0 8.4 74.3	74 37.4 4.6 77.8	74 48.3 0.8 81.4	74 55.3 3.3 85.1	74 58.6 7.2 88.8	74 57.9 11.2 92.5	74 53.3 15.2 96.2	74 44.9 19.1 99.9	33
34	74 14.6 12.0 70.6	74 32.8 8.3 74.1	74 47.5 4.6 77.6	74 58.6 −0.7 81.2	75 05.8 3.3 84.9	75 09.1 7.4 88.7	75 08.5 11.5 92.5	75 04.0 15.4 96.2	34
35	74 02.6 −15.4 67.0	74 24.5 −12.0 70.3	74 42.9 −8.3 73.8	74 57.9 −4.6 77.4	75 09.1 −0.6 81.0	75 16.5 +3.5 84.8	75 20.0 +7.5 88.6	75 19.4 +11.7 92.4	35
36	73 47.2 18.7 63.6	74 12.5 15.5 66.7	74 34.6 12.1 70.1	74 53.3 8.4 73.5	75 08.5 4.5 77.1	75 20.0 −0.6 80.9	75 27.5 3.6 84.7	75 31.1 7.7 88.5	36
37	73 28.5 21.9 60.2	73 57.0 18.9 63.2	74 22.5 15.6 66.4	74 44.9 12.1 69.8	75 04.0 8.5 73.3	75 19.4 4.5 76.9	75 31.1 −0.5 80.7	75 38.8 3.6 84.6	37
38	73 06.6 24.7 56.9	73 38.1 22.0 59.8	74 06.9 19.0 62.8	74 32.8 15.7 66.1	74 55.5 12.1 69.4	75 14.9 8.5 73.0	75 30.6 4.6 76.7	75 42.4 −0.4 80.5	38
39	72 41.9 27.6 53.8	73 16.1 24.9 56.5	73 47.9 22.1 59.4	74 17.1 19.1 62.5	74 43.4 15.9 65.7	75 06.4 12.3 69.1	75 26.0 8.5 72.7	75 42.0 4.6 76.5	39
40	72 14.3 −30.0 50.9	72 51.2 −27.7 53.4	73 25.8 −25.1 56.1	73 58.0 −22.3 59.0	74 27.5 −19.2 62.1	74 54.1 −15.9 65.3	75 17.5 −12.4 68.8	75 37.4 −8.5 72.4	40
41	71 44.3 32.3 48.1	72 23.5 30.2 50.4	73 00.7 27.9 53.0	73 35.7 25.3 55.7	74 08.3 22.5 58.6	74 38.2 19.4 61.7	75 05.1 16.1 65.0	75 28.9 12.5 68.5	41
42	71 12.0 34.5 45.4	71 53.3 32.6 47.6	72 32.8 30.4 50.1	73 10.4 28.1 52.5	73 45.8 25.5 55.2	74 18.8 22.7 58.1	74 49.0 19.6 61.3	75 16.4 16.3 64.6	42
43	70 37.5 36.4 42.9	71 20.7 34.6 45.0	72 02.4 32.8 47.1	72 42.3 30.6 49.5	73 20.3 28.3 52.0	73 56.1 25.8 54.8	74 29.4 22.9 57.7	75 00.1 19.8 60.8	43
44	70 01.1 38.1 40.6	70 46.1 36.6 42.4	71 29.6 34.8 44.5	72 11.7 33.0 46.6	72 52.0 30.9 49.0	73 30.3 28.5 51.5	74 06.5 25.9 54.3	74 40.3 23.1 57.2	44

LATITUDE SAME NAME AS DECLINATION

N. Lat. { L.H.A. greater than 180° ...... Zn=Z ; L.H.A. less than 180° ...... Zn=360°−Z }

Dec.	30° Hc	d	Z	31° Hc	d	Z	32° Hc	d	Z	33° Hc	d	Z	34° Hc	d	Z	35° Hc	d	Z	36° Hc	d	Z	37° Hc	d	Z	Dec.
0	54 58.1	+52.1	145.4	54 08.5	+52.6	146.2	53 18.4	+53.1	147.0	52 27.9	+53.5	147.7	51 37.0	+53.9	148.4	50 45.7	+54.3	149.0	49 54.1	+54.7	149.6	49 02.2	+55.0	150.2	0
1	55 50.2	51.7	144.6	55 01.1	52.2	145.4	54 11.5	52.7	146.2	53 21.4	53.2	146.9	52 30.9	53.6	147.7	51 40.0	54.0	148.3	50 48.8	54.4	149.0	49 57.2	54.7	149.6	1
2	56 41.9	51.3	143.7	55 53.3	51.8	144.5	55 04.2	52.4	145.3	54 14.6	52.9	146.2	53 24.5	53.4	146.9	52 34.0	53.8	147.6	51 43.2	54.2	148.3	50 51.9	54.6	149.0	2
3	57 33.2	50.8	142.7	56 45.2	51.4	143.6	55 56.6	52.0	144.5	55 07.5	52.5	145.3	54 17.9	53.0	146.1	53 27.8	53.5	146.9	52 37.4	53.9	147.6	51 46.5	54.3	148.3	3
4	58 24.0	50.3	141.7	57 36.6	51.0	142.7	56 48.6	51.6	143.6	56 00.0	52.2	144.5	55 10.9	52.7	145.3	54 21.3	53.2	146.1	53 31.3	53.6	146.9	52 40.8	54.1	147.6	4
5	59 14.3	+49.8	140.6	58 27.6	+50.5	141.7	57 40.2	+51.1	142.7	56 52.2	+51.8	143.6	56 03.6	+52.3	144.5	55 14.5	+52.9	145.3	54 24.9	+53.4	146.1	53 34.9	+53.8	146.9	5
6	60 04.1	49.2	139.5	59 18.1	50.0	140.6	58 31.3	50.7	141.7	57 44.0	51.3	142.7	56 55.9	52.0	143.6	56 07.4	52.5	144.5	55 18.3	53.0	145.3	54 28.7	53.5	146.1	6
7	60 53.3	48.6	138.4	60 08.1	49.3	139.5	59 22.0	50.2	140.6	58 35.3	50.9	141.7	57 47.9	51.5	142.7	56 59.9	52.1	143.6	56 11.3	52.7	144.5	55 22.2	53.2	145.3	7
8	61 41.9	47.9	137.2	60 57.4	48.8	138.4	60 12.2	49.6	139.5	59 26.2	50.3	140.7	58 39.4	51.1	141.7	57 52.0	51.7	142.7	57 04.0	52.3	143.5	56 15.4	52.8	144.5	8
9	62 29.8	47.1	135.9	61 46.2	48.1	137.2	61 01.8	49.0	138.4	60 16.5	49.8	139.6	59 30.5	50.5	140.7	58 43.7	51.2	141.7	57 56.3	51.9	142.5	57 08.2	52.5	143.7	9
10	63 16.9	+46.3	134.5	62 34.3	+47.4	135.9	61 50.8	+48.3	137.2	61 06.3	+49.2	138.4	60 21.0	+50.0	139.6	59 34.9	+50.8	140.7	58 48.2	+51.4	141.8	58 00.7	+52.1	142.8	10
11	64 03.2	45.4	133.1	63 21.7	46.5	134.5	62 39.1	47.6	135.9	61 55.5	48.5	137.3	61 11.0	49.4	138.5	60 25.7	50.2	139.6	59 39.6	50.9	140.8	58 52.8	51.6	141.8	11
12	64 48.6	44.5	131.6	64 08.2	45.7	133.1	63 26.7	46.7	134.6	62 44.0	47.8	136.0	62 00.4	48.8	137.3	61 15.9	49.6	138.5	60 30.5	50.5	139.7	59 44.4	51.2	140.8	12
13	65 33.1	43.3	130.0	64 53.9	44.7	131.6	64 13.4	45.9	133.2	63 31.8	47.0	134.6	62 49.2	48.0	136.0	62 05.5	49.0	137.3	61 21.0	49.8	138.6	60 35.6	50.6	139.8	13
14	66 16.4	42.2	128.3	65 38.6	43.6	130.0	64 59.3	45.0	131.7	64 18.8	46.2	133.2	63 37.2	47.2	134.7	62 54.5	48.3	136.1	62 10.8	49.2	137.4	61 26.2	50.0	138.6	14
15	66 58.6	+41.0	126.5	66 22.2	+42.5	128.3	65 44.3	+43.9	130.1	65 05.0	+45.2	131.7	64 24.5	+46.4	133.3	63 42.8	+47.5	134.8	63 00.0	+48.5	136.2	62 16.2	+49.5	137.5	15
16	67 39.6	39.5	124.6	67 04.7	41.2	126.5	66 28.2	42.7	128.4	65 50.2	44.2	130.1	65 10.9	45.4	131.8	64 30.3	46.6	133.4	63 48.5	47.8	134.8	63 05.7	48.7	136.2	16
17	68 19.1	38.0	122.6	67 45.9	39.8	124.6	67 10.9	41.5	126.6	66 34.4	43.0	128.5	65 56.3	44.5	130.2	65 16.9	45.8	131.9	64 36.3	46.9	133.5	63 54.4	48.0	134.9	17
18	68 57.1	36.3	120.4	68 25.7	38.3	122.6	67 52.4	40.1	124.6	67 17.4	41.8	126.7	66 40.8	43.3	128.5	66 02.7	44.7	130.2	65 23.2	46.0	132.0	64 42.4	47.2	133.6	18
19	69 33.4	34.4	118.2	69 04.0	36.6	120.5	68 32.5	38.6	122.7	67 59.2	40.4	124.8	67 24.1	42.0	126.8	66 47.4	43.6	128.6	66 09.2	45.0	130.4	65 29.6	46.3	132.1	19
20	70 07.8	+32.5	115.8	69 40.6	+34.7	118.3	69 11.1	+36.9	120.6	68 39.6	+38.9	122.8	68 06.1	+40.8	124.9	67 31.0	+42.1	126.9	66 54.2	+43.9	128.8	66 15.9	+45.3	130.5	20
21	70 40.3	30.3	113.3	70 15.3	32.8	115.9	69 48.0	35.1	118.5	69 18.5	37.2	120.7	68 46.9	39.2	122.9	68 13.1	41.3	125.0	67 38.1	42.7	126.9	67 01.2	44.2	128.9	21
22	71 10.6	28.0	110.7	70 48.1	30.7	113.4	70 23.1	33.1	116.0	69 55.7	35.4	118.4	69 26.1	37.5	120.8	68 54.4	39.5	123.0	68 20.8	41.3	125.1	67 45.4	43.0	127.1	22
23	71 38.6	25.4	107.9	71 18.8	28.2	110.7	70 56.2	30.9	113.5	70 31.1	33.4	116.0	70 03.6	35.7	118.5	69 33.9	37.9	120.9	69 02.1	39.8	123.1	68 28.4	41.6	125.2	23
24	72 04.0	22.8	105.0	71 47.0	25.8	107.9	71 27.1	28.6	110.8	71 04.5	31.3	113.5	70 39.3	33.8	116.1	70 11.8	36.0	118.6	69 41.9	38.2	121.0	69 10.0	40.2	123.3	24
25	72 26.8	+19.8	102.0	72 12.8	+23.0	105.0	71 55.7	+26.1	108.0	71 35.8	+28.9	110.8	71 13.1	+31.6	113.6	70 47.8	+34.1	116.2	70 20.1	+36.5	118.7	69 50.2	+38.5	121.1	25
26	72 46.6	16.8	98.8	72 35.8	20.1	102.0	72 21.8	23.3	105.0	72 04.7	26.4	108.0	71 44.7	29.2	110.9	71 21.9	32.0	113.7	70 56.6	34.4	116.3	70 28.7	36.8	118.9	26
27	73 03.4	13.5	95.5	72 55.9	17.0	98.8	72 45.1	20.4	102.0	72 31.1	23.6	105.1	72 13.9	26.7	108.1	71 53.9	29.5	111.0	71 30.0	32.3	113.8	71 05.5	34.8	116.5	27
28	73 16.9	10.2	92.2	73 12.9	13.8	95.5	73 05.5	17.3	98.8	72 54.7	20.7	102.0	72 40.6	23.9	105.1	72 23.4	27.1	108.2	72 03.3	29.9	111.1	71 40.3	32.6	113.9	28
29	73 27.1	6.8	88.7	73 26.7	10.4	92.1	73 22.8	14.0	95.4	73 15.4	17.5	98.8	73 04.5	21.0	102.0	72 50.5	24.2	105.2	72 33.2	27.3	108.2	72 12.9	30.3	111.2	29
30	73 33.9	+3.2	85.2	73 37.1	+6.9	88.6	73 36.8	+10.6	92.0	73 32.9	+14.3	95.4	73 25.5	+17.8	98.7	73 14.7	+21.3	102.0	73 00.5	+24.6	105.2	72 43.2	+27.7	108.3	30
31	73 37.1	-0.3	81.7	73 44.0	3.4	85.1	73 47.4	7.1	88.5	73 47.2	10.8	91.9	73 43.3	14.5	95.4	73 36.0	18.0	98.8	73 25.1	21.6	102.1	73 10.9	24.9	105.3	31
32	73 36.8	3.9	78.1	73 47.4	-0.2	81.5	73 54.5	3.5	84.9	73 58.0	7.2	88.4	73 57.8	11.0	91.9	73 54.0	14.8	95.3	73 46.7	18.3	98.8	73 35.8	21.8	102.1	32
33	73 32.9	7.4	74.6	73 47.2	3.9	77.9	73 58.0	-0.2	81.3	74 05.2	3.6	84.8	74 08.8	7.5	88.3	74 08.8	11.2	91.8	74 05.0	15.0	95.3	73 57.6	18.7	98.8	33
34	73 25.5	10.8	71.1	73 43.3	7.3	74.4	73 57.8	3.8	77.4	74 08.8	0.0	81.1	74 16.3	3.7	84.7	74 20.0	7.6	88.1	74 20.0	11.4	91.8	74 16.3	15.2	95.3	34
35	73 14.7	-14.2	67.7	73 36.0	10.9	70.8	73 54.0	7.3	74.1	74 08.8	3.8	77.5	74 20.0	0.0	81.0	74 27.6	+3.8	84.5	74 31.4	+7.8	88.1	74 31.5	+11.7	91.7	35
36	73 00.5	17.3	64.3	73 25.1	14.2	67.4	73 46.7	10.9	70.5	74 05.0	7.4	73.8	74 20.0	3.7	77.3	74 31.4	+0.1	80.8	74 39.2	+4.0	84.4	74 43.2	+7.9	88.0	36
37	72 43.2	20.4	61.1	73 10.9	17.4	64.0	73 35.8	14.3	67.0	73 57.6	10.9	70.2	74 16.3	7.4	73.6	74 31.5	3.7	77.0	74 43.2	+0.1	80.6	74 51.1	+4.0	84.2	37
38	72 22.8	23.2	57.9	72 53.5	20.5	60.7	73 21.5	17.6	63.6	73 46.7	14.4	66.7	74 08.9	11.0	69.9	74 27.8	7.4	73.3	74 43.3	3.7	76.8	74 55.2	+0.2	80.4	38
39	71 59.6	25.9	54.9	72 33.0	23.4	57.5	73 03.9	20.6	60.3	73 32.3	17.6	63.2	73 57.9	14.5	66.3	74 20.4	11.1	69.6	74 39.6	7.4	73.0	74 55.4	3.7	76.6	39
40	71 33.7	-28.4	52.0	72 09.6	26.1	54.5	72 43.3	23.5	57.1	73 14.7	20.8	59.9	73 43.4	17.8	62.9	74 09.3	14.5	66.0	74 32.2	11.2	69.3	74 51.7	7.5	72.7	40
41	71 05.3	30.7	49.3	71 43.5	28.6	51.5	72 19.8	26.1	54.0	72 53.9	23.7	56.7	73 25.6	20.9	59.5	73 54.8	18.0	62.5	74 21.0	14.7	65.5	74 44.2	11.2	69.0	41
42	70 34.6	32.9	46.7	71 14.9	30.9	48.8	71 53.5	28.8	51.1	72 30.2	26.5	53.6	73 04.7	23.9	56.2	73 36.8	21.1	59.0	74 06.3	18.1	62.1	74 33.0	14.9	65.3	42
43	70 01.7	34.8	44.2	70 44.0	33.1	46.2	71 24.7	31.1	48.3	72 03.7	29.0	50.6	72 40.8	26.7	53.1	73 15.7	24.1	55.8	73 48.2	21.3	58.6	74 18.1	18.3	61.6	43
44	69 26.9	36.6	41.8	70 10.9	35.0	43.7	70 53.6	33.3	45.7	71 34.7	31.3	47.8	72 14.1	29.2	50.1	72 51.6	26.9	52.6	73 26.9	24.3	55.3	73 59.8	21.5	58.2	44

LATITUDE SAME NAME AS DECLINATION

N. Lat. { L.H.A. greater than 180° ......Zn=Z ; L.H.A. less than 180° ....Zn=360°−Z }

Dec.	30° Hc	d	Z	31° Hc	d	Z	32° Hc	d	Z	33° Hc	d	Z	34° Hc	d	Z	35° Hc	d	Z	36° Hc	d	Z	37° Hc	d	Z	Dec.
0	54 28.1	+51.4	143.9	53 39.4	+51.9	144.8	52 50.1	+52.5	145.5	52 00.5	+52.9	146.2	51 10.4	+53.3	146.9	50 19.9	+53.8	147.6	49 29.1	+54.1	148.2	48 37.9	+54.5	148.8	0
1	55 19.5	51.1	143.1	54 31.3	51.6	143.9	53 42.6	52.1	144.7	52 53.4	52.6	145.5	52 03.7	53.1	146.2	51 13.7	53.5	146.9	50 23.2	54.0	147.6	49 32.4	54.3	148.2	1
2	56 10.6	50.5	142.1	55 22.9	51.2	143.0	54 34.7	51.8	143.9	53 46.0	52.3	144.7	52 56.8	52.8	145.4	52 07.2	53.3	146.2	51 17.2	53.6	146.9	50 26.7	54.1	147.5	2
3	57 01.1	50.1	141.1	56 14.1	50.8	142.1	55 26.5	51.3	143.0	54 38.3	51.9	143.9	53 49.6	52.5	144.6	53 00.5	52.9	145.4	52 10.8	53.4	146.1	51 20.8	53.8	146.9	3
4	57 51.2	49.6	140.1	57 04.9	50.2	141.1	56 17.8	51.0	142.1	55 30.2	51.6	143.0	54 42.1	52.1	143.8	53 53.4	52.6	144.6	53 04.2	53.1	145.4	52 14.6	53.6	146.1	4
5	58 40.8	+49.0	139.0	57 55.1	+49.8	140.1	57 08.8	+50.4	141.1	56 21.8	+51.1	142.0	55 34.2	+51.7	142.9	54 46.0	+52.3	143.8	53 57.3	+52.8	144.6	53 08.2	+53.3	145.4	5
6	59 29.8	48.4	137.9	58 44.9	49.2	139.0	57 59.2	50.0	140.1	57 12.9	50.6	141.1	56 25.9	51.3	142.0	55 38.3	51.9	142.9	54 50.1	52.5	143.8	54 01.5	52.9	144.6	6
7	60 18.2	47.8	136.7	59 34.1	48.7	137.9	58 49.2	49.4	139.0	58 03.5	50.2	140.1	57 17.2	50.8	141.1	56 30.2	51.5	142.0	55 42.6	52.1	142.9	54 54.4	52.6	143.8	7
8	61 06.0	47.0	135.5	60 22.7	48.0	136.7	59 38.6	48.9	137.9	58 53.7	49.6	139.0	58 08.0	50.4	140.1	57 21.7	51.0	141.1	56 34.7	51.6	142.1	55 47.0	52.3	143.0	8
9	61 53.0	46.3	134.2	61 10.7	47.3	135.5	60 27.5	48.1	136.8	59 43.3	49.1	137.9	58 58.4	49.8	139.1	58 12.7	50.6	140.1	57 26.3	51.3	141.1	56 39.3	51.9	142.1	9
10	62 39.3	+45.4	132.8	61 58.0	+46.5	134.2	61 15.6	+47.5	135.5	60 32.4	+48.4	136.8	59 48.2	+49.3	138.0	59 03.3	+50.0	139.1	58 17.6	+50.7	140.1	57 31.2	+51.4	141.2	10
11	63 24.7	44.5	131.4	62 44.5	45.7	132.9	62 03.1	46.8	134.2	61 20.8	47.7	135.5	60 37.5	48.6	136.8	59 53.3	49.5	138.0	59 08.3	50.3	139.1	58 22.6	51.0	140.2	11
12	64 09.2	43.6	129.9	63 30.2	44.7	131.4	62 49.9	45.9	132.9	62 08.5	47.0	134.3	61 26.1	48.0	135.6	60 42.8	48.9	136.9	59 58.6	49.7	138.0	59 13.6	50.5	139.2	12
13	64 52.8	42.4	128.3	64 14.9	43.8	129.9	63 35.8	45.0	131.5	62 55.5	46.2	132.9	62 14.1	47.2	134.3	61 31.7	48.2	135.6	60 48.3	49.1	136.9	60 04.1	49.9	138.1	13
14	65 35.2	41.2	126.6	64 58.7	42.7	128.3	64 20.8	44.1	130.0	63 41.7	45.2	131.5	63 01.3	46.4	133.0	62 19.9	47.4	134.4	61 37.4	48.5	135.7	60 54.0	49.3	137.0	14
15	66 16.4	+40.0	124.8	65 41.4	+41.5	126.6	65 04.9	+42.9	128.4	64 26.9	+44.4	130.0	63 47.7	+45.6	131.6	63 07.3	+46.7	133.0	62 25.9	+47.7	134.5	61 43.3	+48.7	135.8	15
16	66 56.4	38.5	122.9	66 22.9	40.2	124.9	65 47.8	41.8	126.7	65 11.3	43.2	128.4	64 33.3	44.5	130.1	63 54.0	45.8	131.6	63 13.6	46.9	133.1	62 32.0	48.0	134.5	16
17	67 34.9	37.0	120.9	67 03.1	38.9	123.0	66 29.6	40.6	124.9	65 54.5	42.1	126.7	65 17.9	43.5	128.5	64 39.8	44.9	130.2	64 00.5	46.1	131.7	63 20.0	47.2	133.2	17
18	68 11.9	35.4	118.9	67 42.0	37.3	121.0	67 10.2	39.1	123.0	66 36.6	40.8	125.0	66 01.4	42.4	126.8	65 24.7	43.8	128.6	64 46.6	45.2	130.2	64 07.2	46.4	131.8	18
19	68 47.3	33.5	116.7	68 19.3	35.6	118.9	67 49.3	37.6	121.1	67 17.4	39.5	123.1	66 43.8	41.1	125.1	66 08.5	42.7	126.9	65 31.8	44.1	128.7	64 53.6	45.4	130.3	19
20	69 20.8	+31.6	114.3	68 54.9	+33.9	116.7	68 26.9	+36.0	119.0	67 56.9	+37.9	121.1	67 24.9	+39.8	123.2	66 51.2	+41.5	125.3	66 15.9	+43.0	127.0	65 39.0	+44.4	128.8	20
21	69 52.4	29.4	111.9	69 28.8	31.9	114.4	69 02.9	34.1	116.8	68 34.8	36.3	119.0	68 04.7	38.2	121.2	67 32.7	40.0	123.3	66 58.9	41.7	125.3	66 23.4	43.3	127.1	21
22	70 21.8	27.2	109.3	70 00.7	29.7	111.9	69 37.0	32.3	114.4	69 11.1	34.5	116.8	68 42.9	36.7	119.1	68 12.7	38.6	121.3	67 40.6	40.4	123.4	67 06.7	42.1	125.4	22
23	70 49.0	24.7	106.6	70 30.4	27.5	109.4	70 09.3	30.1	112.0	69 45.6	32.5	114.5	69 19.6	34.8	116.9	68 51.3	37.0	119.2	68 21.0	39.0	121.4	67 48.8	40.8	123.5	23
24	71 13.7	22.1	103.8	70 57.9	25.1	106.7	70 39.4	27.8	109.4	70 18.1	30.4	112.0	69 54.4	32.9	114.6	69 28.3	35.1	117.0	69 00.0	37.3	119.3	68 29.6	39.2	121.5	24
25	71 35.8	+19.4	100.9	71 23.0	+22.4	103.8	71 07.2	+25.3	106.7	70 48.5	+28.2	109.4	70 27.3	+30.7	112.1	70 03.4	+33.3	114.7	69 37.3	+35.5	117.1	69 08.8	+37.7	119.4	25
26	71 55.2	16.4	97.9	71 45.4	19.7	100.9	71 32.5	22.7	103.9	71 16.7	25.6	106.7	70 58.0	28.5	109.5	70 36.7	31.1	112.2	70 12.8	33.5	114.8	69 46.5	35.8	117.2	26
27	72 11.6	13.4	94.8	72 05.0	16.7	97.9	71 55.2	19.9	100.9	71 42.3	23.1	103.9	71 26.5	26.0	106.8	71 07.8	28.8	109.7	70 46.3	31.5	112.3	70 22.3	33.9	114.8	27
28	72 25.0	10.2	91.6	72 21.7	13.6	94.7	72 15.1	17.0	97.8	72 05.4	20.2	100.9	71 52.5	23.3	103.9	71 36.6	26.3	106.8	71 17.8	29.1	109.7	70 56.2	31.8	112.4	28
29	72 35.2	6.9	88.3	72 35.3	10.4	91.5	72 32.1	13.8	94.7	72 25.6	17.2	97.8	72 15.8	20.6	100.9	72 02.9	23.6	103.9	71 46.9	26.7	106.9	71 28.0	29.5	109.8	29
30	72 42.1	+3.6	85.0	72 45.7	+7.1	88.2	72 45.9	+10.6	91.4	72 42.8	+14.1	94.6	72 36.3	+17.5	97.8	72 26.5	+20.8	100.9	72 13.6	+23.9	104.0	71 57.5	+27.0	107.0	30
31	72 45.7	0.2	81.6	72 52.8	3.7	84.8	72 56.5	7.3	88.1	72 56.9	10.8	91.3	72 53.8	14.3	94.6	72 47.3	17.8	97.8	72 37.5	21.1	101.0	72 24.5	24.3	104.1	31
32	72 45.9	-3.1	78.2	72 56.5	0.4	81.4	73 03.8	3.9	84.7	73 07.7	7.4	87.9	73 08.1	11.0	91.2	73 05.1	14.5	94.5	72 58.6	18.1	97.8	72 48.8	21.4	101.0	32
33	72 42.8	6.5	74.9	72 56.9	-3.1	78.0	73 07.7	0.4	81.2	73 15.1	4.0	84.5	73 19.1	7.6	87.8	73 19.6	11.3	91.1	73 16.7	14.8	94.5	73 10.2	18.4	97.8	33
34	72 36.3	9.8	71.5	72 53.8	6.5	74.6	73 08.1	-3.0	77.8	73 19.1	0.5	81.0	73 26.7	4.2	84.4	73 30.9	7.8	87.7	73 31.5	11.4	91.1	73 28.6	15.0	94.5	34
35	72 26.5	-12.9	68.2	72 47.3	-9.8	71.2	73 05.1	-6.5	74.3	73 19.6	-2.9	77.6	73 30.9	+0.6	80.9	73 38.7	+4.2	84.2	73 42.9	+8.0	87.6	73 43.6	+11.7	91.1	35
36	72 13.6	16.1	65.0	72 37.5	13.0	67.9	72 58.6	9.8	70.9	73 16.7	6.5	74.1	73 31.5	-2.9	77.3	73 42.9	0.7	80.7	73 50.9	4.4	84.1	73 55.3	8.1	87.5	36
37	71 57.5	18.9	61.9	72 24.5	16.1	64.7	72 48.8	13.0	67.6	73 10.2	9.8	70.6	73 28.6	6.5	73.8	73 43.6	-2.9	77.1	73 55.3	0.7	80.5	74 03.4	4.5	83.9	37
38	71 38.6	21.8	58.8	72 08.4	19.0	61.5	72 35.8	16.2	64.3	73 00.4	13.1	67.2	73 22.1	9.8	70.6	73 40.7	6.4	73.5	73 56.0	-2.8	76.9	74 07.9	0.9	80.3	38
39	71 16.8	24.4	55.9	71 49.4	21.9	58.4	72 19.6	19.2	61.1	72 47.3	16.3	63.9	73 12.2	13.2	67.2	73 34.3	10.0	70.0	73 53.2	6.5	73.3	74 08.8	-2.9	76.6	39
40	70 52.4	-26.8	53.1	71 27.5	-24.6	55.5	72 00.4	-22.1	58.0	72 31.0	-19.4	60.7	72 59.0	-16.4	63.5	73 24.3	-13.3	66.5	73 46.7	-10.0	69.7	74 05.9	-6.5	73.0	40
41	70 25.6	29.2	50.4	71 02.9	27.0	52.6	71 38.3	24.7	55.5	72 11.6	22.2	57.6	72 42.6	19.5	60.3	73 11.0	16.5	63.2	73 36.7	13.4	66.2	73 59.4	10.1	69.4	41
42	69 56.4	31.3	47.8	70 35.9	29.4	49.9	71 13.6	27.2	52.6	71 48.8	24.9	54.6	72 23.1	22.4	57.1	72 54.5	19.7	59.9	73 23.3	16.7	62.8	73 49.3	13.5	65.8	42
43	69 25.1	33.3	45.4	70 06.5	31.5	47.3	70 46.4	29.5	49.4	71 24.5	27.4	51.7	72 00.7	25.1	54.1	72 34.8	22.5	56.7	73 06.6	19.8	59.4	73 35.8	16.9	62.3	43
44	68 51.8	35.1	43.0	69 35.0	33.4	44.9	70 16.9	31.8	46.8	70 57.1	29.8	48.9	71 35.6	27.6	51.2	72 12.3	25.4	53.6	72 46.8	22.8	56.2	73 18.9	20.0	59.0	44

21°, 339° L.H.A.   LATITUDE SAME NAME AS DECLINATION

N. Lat. { L.H.A. greater than 180° ...... Zn=Z ; L.H.A. less than 180° ...... Zn=360°−Z }

Dec.	30° Hc	d	Z	31° Hc	d	Z	32° Hc	d	Z	33° Hc	d	Z	34° Hc	d	Z	35° Hc	d	Z	36° Hc	d	Z	37° Hc	d	Z	Dec.
0	53 57.0	+50.8	142.5	53 09.2	+51.3	143.3	52 20.8	+51.9	144.1	51 32.0	+52.4	144.8	50 42.7	+52.9	145.5	49 51.1	+53.2	146.2	49 03.0	+53.7	146.9	48 12.6	+54.1	147.5	0
1	54 47.8	50.3	141.6	54 00.5	50.9	142.4	53 12.7	51.5	143.3	52 24.4	52.0	144.0	51 35.6	52.5	144.8	50 46.3	53.0	145.5	49 56.7	53.4	146.2	49 06.7	53.8	146.8	1
2	55 38.1	49.9	140.6	54 51.4	50.6	141.5	54 04.2	51.1	142.4	53 16.4	51.7	143.2	52 28.1	52.2	144.0	51 39.3	52.7	144.7	50 50.1	53.2	145.5	50 00.5	53.6	146.1	2
3	56 28.0	49.4	139.6	55 42.0	50.0	140.6	54 55.3	50.7	141.5	54 08.1	51.3	142.4	53 20.3	51.9	143.2	52 32.0	52.4	144.0	51 43.3	52.9	144.7	50 54.1	53.3	145.4	3
4	57 17.4	48.8	138.6	56 32.0	49.6	139.6	55 46.0	50.2	140.5	54 59.4	50.9	141.5	54 12.2	51.5	142.4	53 24.4	52.1	143.2	52 36.2	52.5	143.9	51 47.4	53.1	144.7	4
5	58 06.2	+48.3	137.5	57 21.6	+49.1	138.6	56 36.3	+49.8	139.6	55 50.3	+50.4	140.5	55 03.7	+51.1	141.4	54 16.5	+51.7	142.3	53 28.7	+52.3	143.1	52 40.5	+52.7	143.9	5
6	58 54.5	47.5	136.4	58 10.7	48.4	137.5	57 26.1	49.2	138.5	56 40.7	50.0	139.5	55 54.8	50.6	140.5	55 08.2	51.2	141.4	54 21.0	51.8	142.3	53 33.2	52.4	143.1	6
7	59 42.1	47.0	135.2	58 59.1	47.8	136.3	58 15.3	48.7	137.5	57 30.7	49.5	138.5	56 45.4	50.1	139.5	55 59.4	50.9	140.5	55 12.8	51.5	141.4	54 25.6	52.1	142.3	7
8	60 29.1	46.2	133.9	59 47.0	47.2	135.2	59 04.0	48.1	136.3	58 20.2	48.9	137.5	57 35.6	49.7	138.5	56 50.3	50.4	139.6	56 04.3	51.1	140.5	55 17.7	51.7	141.4	8
9	61 15.3	45.4	132.6	60 34.2	46.4	133.9	59 52.1	47.4	135.2	59 09.1	48.3	136.3	58 25.3	49.1	137.5	57 40.7	49.9	138.5	56 55.4	50.6	139.6	56 09.4	51.2	140.5	9
10	62 00.7	+44.6	131.2	61 20.6	+45.7	132.6	60 39.5	+46.7	133.9	59 57.4	+47.7	135.2	59 14.4	+48.5	136.4	58 30.6	+49.3	137.5	57 46.0	+50.1	138.5	57 00.6	+50.8	139.6	10
11	62 45.3	43.6	129.8	62 06.3	44.8	131.2	61 26.2	45.9	132.6	60 45.1	46.9	133.0	60 02.9	47.9	135.2	59 19.9	48.8	136.4	58 36.1	49.5	137.6	57 51.4	50.4	138.6	11
12	63 28.9	42.6	128.3	62 51.1	43.9	129.8	62 12.1	45.1	131.1	61 32.0	46.3	132.7	60 50.8	47.2	134.0	60 08.7	48.1	135.2	59 25.6	49.0	136.5	58 41.8	49.8	137.6	12
13	64 11.5	41.5	126.7	63 35.0	42.9	128.3	62 57.2	44.2	129.8	62 18.3	45.3	131.2	61 38.0	46.3	132.7	60 56.8	47.5	134.0	60 14.6	48.4	135.3	59 31.6	49.3	136.5	13
14	64 53.0	40.3	125.0	64 17.9	41.8	126.7	63 41.4	43.1	128.3	63 03.5	44.4	129.9	62 24.4	45.7	131.3	61 44.3	46.7	132.7	61 03.0	47.7	134.1	60 20.8	48.6	135.3	14
15	65 33.3	+39.1	123.2	64 59.7	+40.6	125.0	64 24.5	+42.1	126.7	63 47.9	+43.5	128.4	63 10.1	+44.7	129.9	62 31.0	+45.8	131.4	61 50.7	+47.0	132.8	61 09.4	+48.0	134.1	15
16	66 12.4	37.6	121.4	65 40.3	39.3	123.3	65 06.6	40.9	125.1	64 31.4	42.4	126.8	63 54.8	43.7	128.4	63 16.8	45.0	130.0	62 37.7	46.1	131.5	61 57.4	47.2	132.9	16
17	66 50.0	36.1	119.4	66 19.6	37.9	121.4	65 47.5	39.6	123.3	65 13.8	41.2	125.1	64 38.5	42.7	126.9	64 01.8	44.0	128.5	63 23.8	45.3	130.1	62 44.6	46.4	131.6	17
18	67 26.1	34.4	117.4	66 57.5	36.4	119.4	66 27.1	38.3	121.4	65 55.0	39.9	123.4	65 21.2	41.5	125.2	64 45.8	43.0	126.9	64 09.1	44.3	128.6	63 31.0	45.6	130.2	18
19	68 00.5	32.7	115.2	67 33.9	34.8	117.4	67 05.4	36.7	119.5	66 34.9	38.5	121.5	66 02.7	40.2	123.4	65 28.8	41.8	125.2	64 53.4	43.3	127.0	64 16.6	44.6	128.7	19
20	68 33.2	+30.7	112.9	68 08.7	+33.0	115.2	67 42.1	+35.1	117.4	67 13.4	+37.1	119.6	66 42.9	+38.9	121.6	66 10.6	+40.6	123.5	65 36.7	+42.1	125.4	65 01.2	+43.6	127.1	20
21	69 03.9	28.7	110.6	68 41.7	31.0	113.0	68 17.2	33.3	115.3	67 50.5	35.4	117.5	67 21.8	37.4	119.6	66 51.2	39.2	121.7	66 18.8	40.9	123.6	65 44.8	42.5	125.5	21
22	69 32.6	26.4	108.1	69 12.7	29.0	110.6	68 50.5	31.3	113.0	68 25.9	33.6	115.3	67 59.2	35.7	117.6	67 30.4	37.7	119.7	66 59.7	39.6	121.8	66 27.3	41.2	123.7	22
23	69 59.0	24.1	105.5	69 41.7	26.8	108.1	69 21.8	29.4	110.6	68 59.5	31.8	113.0	68 34.9	34.0	115.4	68 08.1	36.1	117.7	67 39.3	38.0	119.8	67 08.5	39.9	121.9	23
24	70 23.1	21.6	102.8	70 08.5	24.4	105.5	69 51.2	27.1	108.1	69 31.3	29.6	110.7	69 08.9	32.1	113.1	68 44.2	34.3	115.5	68 17.3	36.4	117.8	67 48.4	38.4	119.9	24
25	70 44.7	+19.0	100.0	70 32.9	+21.9	102.8	70 18.3	+24.7	105.5	70 00.9	+27.4	108.1	69 41.0	+29.9	110.7	69 18.5	+32.4	113.2	68 53.7	+34.7	115.6	68 26.8	+36.8	117.9	25
26	71 03.7	16.1	97.1	70 54.8	19.2	99.9	70 43.0	22.2	102.8	70 28.3	25.1	105.5	70 10.9	27.8	108.2	69 50.9	30.4	110.8	69 28.4	32.8	113.3	69 03.6	35.0	115.7	26
27	71 19.8	13.2	94.1	71 14.0	16.4	97.0	71 05.2	19.5	99.9	70 53.4	22.5	102.8	70 38.7	25.4	105.5	70 21.3	28.1	108.2	70 01.2	30.7	110.9	69 38.6	33.1	113.4	27
28	71 33.0	10.2	91.0	71 30.4	13.5	94.0	71 24.7	16.6	97.0	71 15.9	19.8	99.9	71 04.1	22.8	102.8	70 49.4	25.7	105.6	70 31.9	28.4	108.3	70 11.7	31.1	110.9	28
29	71 43.2	7.1	87.9	71 43.9	10.4	90.9	71 41.3	13.7	93.9	71 35.7	16.9	96.9	71 26.9	20.1	99.9	71 15.1	23.1	102.8	71 00.3	26.1	105.6	70 42.8	28.8	108.3	29
30	71 50.3	+4.0	84.7	71 54.3	+7.3	87.8	71 55.0	+10.7	90.8	71 52.6	+13.9	93.9	71 47.0	+17.2	96.9	71 38.2	+20.4	99.9	71 26.4	+23.4	102.9	71 11.6	+26.3	105.7	30
31	71 54.3	1.1	81.5	72 01.6	4.1	84.5	72 05.7	7.5	87.6	72 06.5	10.9	90.7	72 04.2	14.2	93.8	71 58.6	17.5	96.9	71 49.8	20.7	99.9	71 37.9	23.8	102.9	31
32	71 55.0	-2.4	78.3	72 05.7	0.8	81.3	72 13.2	4.2	84.4	72 17.4	7.6	87.5	72 18.4	11.0	90.6	72 16.1	14.4	93.8	72 10.5	17.8	96.9	72 01.7	21.0	99.9	32
33	71 52.6	5.7	75.1	72 06.5	2.3	78.1	72 17.4	1.0	81.1	72 25.0	4.4	84.2	72 29.4	7.6	87.4	72 30.5	11.3	90.6	72 28.3	14.6	93.7	72 22.7	18.1	96.9	33
34	71 47.0	8.8	71.9	72 04.2	5.6	74.8	72 18.4	2.3	77.8	72 29.4	1.1	80.9	72 37.3	4.5	84.1	72 41.8	8.0	87.3	72 42.9	11.5	90.5	72 40.8	14.9	93.7	34
35	71 38.2	-11.8	68.7	71 58.6	8.8	71.6	72 16.1	5.6	74.5	72 30.5	2.2	77.6	72 41.8	+1.1	80.7	72 49.8	+4.6	83.9	72 54.4	+8.2	87.2	72 55.7	+11.7	90.4	35
36	71 26.4	14.8	65.6	71 49.8	11.9	68.4	72 10.5	8.8	71.3	72 28.3	5.6	74.3	72 42.9	2.2	77.4	72 54.4	1.3	80.5	73 02.6	4.8	83.8	73 07.4	8.4	87.1	36
37	71 11.6	17.7	62.6	71 37.9	14.8	65.3	72 01.7	11.9	68.1	72 22.7	8.8	71.0	72 40.8	5.6	74.0	72 55.7	2.1	77.1	73 07.4	1.4	80.4	73 15.8	4.9	83.6	37
38	70 53.9	20.3	59.7	71 23.1	17.8	62.2	71 49.8	14.9	64.9	72 13.9	12.0	67.7	72 35.2	8.8	70.7	72 53.6	5.6	73.7	73 08.8	2.1	76.9	73 20.7	1.4	80.2	38
39	70 33.6	23.0	56.8	71 05.3	20.4	59.2	71 34.9	17.9	61.8	72 01.9	15.0	64.5	72 26.4	12.0	67.4	72 48.0	8.8	70.4	73 06.7	5.6	73.5	73 22.1	2.0	76.7	39
40	70 10.6	-25.4	54.1	70 44.9	-23.1	56.4	71 17.0	-20.6	58.8	71 46.9	-17.9	61.4	72 14.4	-15.2	64.2	72 39.2	-12.1	67.0	73 01.1	-8.9	70.0	73 20.1	-5.6	73.2	40
41	69 45.2	27.6	51.4	70 21.8	25.6	53.6	70 56.4	23.2	55.9	71 29.0	20.8	58.4	71 59.2	18.1	61.0	72 27.1	15.3	63.8	72 52.2	12.2	66.7	73 14.5	9.0	69.7	41
42	69 17.6	29.8	48.9	69 56.2	27.8	50.9	70 33.2	25.7	53.1	71 08.2	23.4	55.5	71 41.1	20.9	57.9	72 11.8	18.2	60.6	72 40.0	15.4	63.4	73 05.5	12.3	66.3	42
43	68 47.8	31.8	46.4	69 28.4	30.0	48.4	70 07.5	28.1	50.4	70 44.8	25.9	52.6	71 20.2	23.6	55.0	71 53.6	21.1	57.5	72 24.6	18.4	60.1	72 53.2	15.5	63.0	43
44	68 16.0	33.6	44.1	68 58.4	32.0	45.9	69 39.4	30.2	47.9	70 18.9	28.3	49.9	70 56.6	26.1	52.1	71 32.5	23.8	54.5	72 06.2	21.3	57.0	72 37.7	18.6	59.7	44

LATITUDE SAME NAME AS DECLINATION

N. Lat {L.H.A. greater than 180°......Zn=Z / L.H.A. less than 180°.........Zn=360°−Z

Dec.	30° Hc	d	Z	31° Hc	d	Z	32° Hc	d	Z	33° Hc	d	Z	34° Hc	d	Z	35° Hc	d	Z	36° Hc	d	Z	37° Hc	d	Z	Dec.
0	53 24.8	+50.2	141.1	52 37.9	+50.7	141.9	51 50.4	+51.3	142.7	51 02.5	+51.8	143.4	50 14.1	+52.3	144.2	49 25.2	+52.8	144.8	48 36.0	+53.2	145.5	47 46.3	+53.7	146.1	0
1	54 15.0	49.6	140.1	53 28.6	50.3	141.0	52 41.7	50.9	141.8	51 54.3	51.5	142.6	51 06.4	52.0	143.4	50 18.0	52.5	144.1	49 29.2	52.9	144.8	48 40.0	53.3	145.5	1
2	55 04.6	49.2	139.2	54 18.9	49.9	140.1	53 32.6	50.5	140.9	52 45.8	51.0	141.8	51 58.4	51.6	142.6	51 10.5	52.1	143.3	50 22.1	52.7	144.1	49 33.3	53.1	144.8	2
3	55 53.8	48.7	138.1	55 08.8	49.4	139.1	54 23.1	50.1	140.0	53 36.8	50.7	140.9	52 50.0	51.3	141.7	52 02.6	51.9	142.5	51 14.8	52.3	143.3	50 26.4	52.9	144.0	3
4	56 42.5	48.1	137.1	55 58.2	48.9	138.1	55 13.2	49.6	139.1	54 27.5	50.3	140.0	53 41.3	50.9	140.9	52 54.5	51.4	141.7	52 07.1	52.0	142.5	51 19.3	52.5	143.3	4
5	57 30.6	+47.5	136.0	56 47.1	+48.3	137.1	56 02.8	+49.1	138.1	55 17.8	+49.8	139.0	54 32.2	+50.4	140.0	53 45.9	+51.1	140.9	52 59.1	+51.7	141.7	52 11.8	+52.2	142.5	5
6	58 18.1	46.9	134.8	57 35.4	47.7	136.0	56 51.9	48.5	137.0	56 07.6	49.3	138.1	55 22.6	50.0	139.0	54 37.0	50.7	140.0	53 50.8	51.3	140.8	53 04.0	51.8	141.7	6
7	59 05.0	46.2	133.6	58 23.1	47.1	134.8	57 40.4	48.0	135.9	56 56.9	48.8	137.0	56 12.6	49.6	138.0	55 27.7	50.2	139.0	54 42.1	50.9	140.0	53 55.8	51.5	140.8	7
8	59 51.2	45.4	132.4	59 10.2	46.4	133.6	58 28.4	47.3	134.8	57 45.7	48.2	135.9	57 02.2	49.0	137.0	56 17.9	49.8	138.0	55 32.9	50.5	139.0	54 47.3	51.1	140.0	8
9	60 36.6	44.6	131.1	59 56.6	45.7	132.4	59 15.7	46.7	133.6	58 33.9	47.5	134.8	57 51.2	48.4	135.9	57 07.7	49.2	137.0	56 23.4	50.0	138.1	55 38.4	50.7	139.0	9
10	61 21.2	+43.7	129.7	60 42.3	+44.9	131.1	60 02.4	+45.9	132.4	59 21.4	+46.9	133.6	58 39.6	+47.8	134.8	57 56.9	+48.6	136.0	57 13.4	+49.4	137.0	56 29.1	+50.2	138.1	10
11	62 04.9	42.8	128.2	61 27.2	44.0	129.7	60 48.3	45.1	131.1	60 08.3	46.2	132.4	59 27.4	47.2	133.6	58 45.5	48.1	134.8	58 02.8	48.9	136.0	57 19.3	49.7	137.1	11
12	62 47.7	41.7	126.7	62 11.2	43.0	128.3	61 33.4	44.3	129.7	60 54.5	45.4	131.1	60 14.6	46.4	132.4	59 33.6	47.4	133.7	58 51.7	48.3	134.9	58 09.0	49.1	136.0	12
13	63 29.4	40.7	125.1	62 54.2	42.0	126.7	62 17.7	43.3	128.3	61 39.9	44.5	129.7	61 01.0	45.7	131.1	60 21.0	46.7	132.5	59 40.0	47.7	133.7	58 58.1	48.6	134.9	13
14	64 10.1	39.4	123.5	63 36.2	41.0	125.2	63 01.0	42.3	126.8	62 24.4	43.7	128.3	61 46.7	44.8	129.8	61 07.7	45.9	131.2	60 27.7	47.0	132.5	59 46.7	47.9	133.8	14
15	64 49.5	+38.2	121.7	64 17.2	+39.7	123.5	63 43.3	+41.3	125.2	63 08.1	+42.6	126.8	62 31.5	+43.9	128.3	61 53.6	+45.1	129.8	61 14.7	+46.2	131.3	60 34.6	+47.2	132.6	15
16	65 27.7	36.7	119.9	64 56.9	38.5	121.7	64 24.6	40.0	123.5	63 50.7	41.5	125.2	63 15.4	42.9	126.9	62 38.7	44.2	128.4	62 00.9	45.3	129.9	61 21.8	46.5	131.3	16
17	66 04.4	35.2	118.0	65 35.4	37.0	119.9	65 04.6	38.8	121.8	64 32.2	40.4	123.6	63 58.3	41.8	125.3	63 22.9	43.2	126.9	62 46.2	44.6	128.5	62 08.3	45.7	130.0	17
18	66 39.6	33.6	115.9	66 12.4	35.6	118.0	65 43.4	37.3	119.9	65 12.6	39.0	121.8	64 40.1	40.7	123.6	64 06.1	42.2	125.3	63 30.7	43.6	127.0	62 54.0	44.8	128.5	18
19	67 13.2	31.9	113.8	66 48.0	33.9	116.0	66 20.7	35.9	118.0	65 51.6	37.7	120.0	65 20.8	39.4	121.9	64 48.3	41.0	123.7	64 14.3	42.4	125.4	63 38.8	43.8	127.1	19
20	67 45.1	+30.0	111.6	67 21.9	+32.2	113.8	66 56.6	+34.3	116.0	66 29.3	+36.3	118.1	66 00.2	+38.0	120.1	65 29.3	+39.7	122.0	64 56.7	+41.3	123.8	64 22.6	+42.8	125.5	20
21	68 15.1	27.9	109.3	67 54.1	30.3	111.6	67 30.9	32.5	113.9	67 05.6	34.5	116.0	66 38.2	36.6	118.1	66 09.0	38.4	120.1	65 38.0	40.1	122.1	65 05.4	41.6	123.9	21
22	68 43.0	25.8	106.9	68 24.4	28.3	109.3	68 03.4	30.6	111.7	67 40.1	32.9	113.9	67 14.8	34.9	116.1	66 47.4	36.9	118.2	66 18.1	38.7	120.2	65 47.0	40.5	122.1	22
23	69 08.8	23.6	104.4	68 52.7	26.1	106.9	68 34.0	28.6	109.3	68 13.0	30.6	111.7	67 49.7	33.2	114.0	67 24.3	35.3	116.2	66 56.8	37.3	118.4	66 27.5	39.0	120.3	23
24	69 32.4	21.1	101.8	69 18.8	23.8	104.4	69 02.6	26.5	106.9	68 44.0	28.9	109.4	68 22.9	31.3	111.7	67 59.6	33.5	114.0	67 34.1	35.6	118.4	67 06.5	37.6	118.4	24
25	69 53.5	+18.5	99.1	69 42.6	+21.5	101.7	69 29.1	+24.2	104.4	69 12.9	+26.8	106.9	68 54.2	+29.3	109.4	68 33.1	+31.7	111.8	68 09.7	+33.9	114.1	67 44.1	+36.0	116.4	25
26	70 12.0	15.9	96.3	70 04.1	18.8	99.0	69 53.3	21.7	101.7	69 39.7	24.5	104.4	69 23.5	27.1	106.9	69 04.8	29.6	109.4	68 43.6	32.0	111.9	68 20.1	34.3	114.2	26
27	70 27.9	13.2	93.4	70 22.9	16.2	96.2	70 15.0	19.1	99.0	70 04.2	22.0	101.7	69 50.6	24.9	104.4	69 34.4	27.5	107.0	69 15.6	30.0	109.5	68 54.4	32.4	112.0	27
28	70 41.1	10.2	90.5	70 39.1	13.3	93.3	70 34.1	16.5	96.2	70 26.2	19.5	99.0	70 15.5	22.3	101.7	70 01.9	25.1	104.4	69 45.6	27.8	107.0	69 26.8	30.3	109.6	28
29	70 51.3	7.3	87.5	70 52.4	10.5	90.4	70 50.6	13.6	93.2	70 45.7	16.7	96.1	70 37.8	19.7	98.9	70 27.0	22.7	101.7	69 57.1	25.5	104.5	69 57.1	28.2	107.1	29
30	70 58.6	+4.3	84.4	71 02.9	+7.5	87.3	71 04.2	+10.7	90.3	71 02.4	+13.8	93.2	70 57.5	+17.0	96.1	70 49.7	+20.0	98.9	70 38.9	+23.0	101.7	70 25.3	+25.8	104.5	30
31	71 02.9	+1.3	81.4	71 10.4	4.5	84.3	71 14.9	7.6	87.2	71 16.2	10.9	90.2	71 14.5	14.1	93.1	71 09.7	17.3	96.0	71 01.9	20.4	98.9	70 51.1	23.3	101.8	31
32	71 04.2	−1.8	78.3	71 14.9	+1.3	81.2	71 22.5	4.6	84.1	71 27.1	7.9	87.1	71 28.6	11.1	90.1	71 27.0	14.4	93.0	71 22.3	17.5	96.0	71 14.4	20.7	98.9	32
33	71 02.4	4.9	75.2	71 16.2	−1.7	78.1	71 27.1	+1.5	81.0	71 35.0	4.7	84.1	71 39.7	8.1	87.0	71 39.8	11.3	90.0	71 39.8	14.6	93.0	71 35.1	17.8	96.0	33
34	70 57.5	7.8	72.2	71 14.5	4.8	75.0	71 28.6	−1.7	77.8	71 39.7	+1.7	80.8	71 47.8	4.9	83.8	71 52.7	8.2	86.8	71 54.4	11.6	89.9	71 52.9	14.9	93.0	34
35	70 49.7	−10.8	69.1	71 09.7	−7.8	71.9	71 27.0	−4.7	74.7	71 41.4	−1.6	77.6	71 52.7	+1.7	80.6	72 00.9	+5.1	83.6	72 06.0	+8.4	86.7	72 07.8	+11.8	89.8	35
36	70 38.9	13.6	66.1	71 01.9	10.8	68.8	71 22.3	7.9	71.6	71 39.8	4.7	74.4	71 54.4	−1.5	77.4	72 06.0	+1.8	80.2	72 14.4	5.0	83.5	72 19.6	8.6	86.6	36
37	70 25.3	16.4	63.2	70 51.1	13.7	65.8	71 14.4	10.8	68.5	71 35.1	7.8	71.3	71 52.9	4.7	74.1	72 07.8	−1.4	77.1	72 19.6	+1.9	80.2	72 28.2	5.3	83.3	37
38	70 08.9	19.0	60.4	70 37.4	16.4	62.8	71 03.6	13.7	65.4	71 27.3	10.9	68.1	71 48.2	7.8	71.0	72 06.4	4.7	73.9	72 21.5	−1.4	76.9	72 33.5	+2.0	80.0	38
39	69 49.9	21.6	57.6	70 21.0	19.2	60.0	70 49.9	16.6	62.5	71 16.4	13.8	65.1	71 40.4	10.9	67.8	72 01.7	7.9	70.7	72 20.1	4.6	73.6	72 35.5	−1.3	76.7	39
40	69 28.3	−23.9	54.9	70 01.8	−21.7	57.2	70 33.3	−19.2	59.5	71 02.6	−16.6	62.1	71 29.5	−13.9	64.7	71 53.8	−10.9	67.5	72 15.5	−7.9	70.3	72 34.2	−4.7	73.3	40
41	69 04.4	26.2	52.3	69 40.1	24.1	54.5	70 14.1	21.9	56.7	70 45.9	19.4	59.1	71 15.6	16.8	61.6	71 42.9	14.0	64.3	72 07.6	11.1	67.1	72 29.5	7.9	70.0	41
42	68 38.2	28.4	49.8	69 16.0	26.3	51.8	69 52.2	24.2	54.0	70 26.5	21.9	56.3	70 58.8	19.5	58.7	71 28.9	16.9	61.2	71 56.5	14.1	63.9	72 21.6	11.2	66.7	42
43	68 09.8	30.3	47.4	68 49.7	28.5	49.3	69 28.0	26.6	51.4	70 04.6	24.5	53.5	70 39.3	22.2	55.8	71 12.0	19.8	58.2	71 42.4	17.1	60.8	72 10.4	14.2	63.5	43
44	67 39.5	32.2	45.1	68 21.2	30.6	46.9	69 01.4	28.7	48.8	69 40.1	26.7	50.9	70 17.1	24.6	53.0	70 52.2	22.3	55.3	71 25.3	19.9	57.8	71 56.2	17.2	60.3	44

LATITUDE SAME NAME AS DECLINATION

N. Lat. { L.H.A. greater than 180° ...... Zn=Z
{ L.H.A. less than 180° ...... Zn=360°−Z

	30°			31°			32°			33°			34°			35°			36°			37°			
Dec.	Hc	d	Z	Hc	d	Z	Hc	d	Z	Hc	d	Z	Hc	d	Z	Hc	d	Z	Hc	d	Z	Hc	d	Z	Dec.
0	52 51.7	+49.5	139.7	52 05.7	+50.1	140.5	51 19.1	+50.7	141.3	50 32.0	+51.3	142.1	49 44.5	+51.7	142.8	48 56.5	+52.2	143.5	48 08.0	+52.7	144.2	47 19.2	+53.1	144.8	0
1	53 41.2	49.0	138.7	52 55.8	49.6	139.6	52 09.8	50.3	140.4	51 23.3	50.8	141.2	50 36.2	51.5	142.0	49 48.7	52.0	142.7	49 00.7	52.5	143.4	48 12.3	52.9	144.1	1
2	54 30.2	48.5	137.7	53 45.4	49.3	138.7	53 00.1	49.9	139.5	52 14.1	50.5	140.4	51 27.7	51.0	141.2	50 40.7	51.6	142.0	49 53.2	52.1	142.7	49 05.2	52.6	143.4	2
3	55 18.7	47.9	136.7	54 34.7	48.7	137.7	53 50.0	49.4	138.6	53 04.6	50.1	139.5	52 18.7	50.7	140.3	51 32.3	51.2	141.1	50 45.3	51.8	141.9	49 57.8	52.3	142.7	3
4	56 06.6	47.4	135.6	55 23.4	48.2	136.7	54 39.4	48.9	137.6	53 54.7	49.6	138.6	53 09.4	50.3	139.5	52 23.5	50.9	140.3	51 37.1	51.5	141.1	50 50.1	52.0	141.9	4
5	56 54.0	+46.8	134.5	56 11.6	+47.6	135.6	55 28.3	+48.4	136.6	54 44.3	+49.2	137.6	53 59.7	+49.8	138.5	53 14.4	+50.5	139.4	52 28.6	+51.1	140.3	51 42.1	+51.7	141.1	5
6	57 40.8	46.1	133.4	56 59.2	47.0	134.5	56 16.7	47.9	135.6	55 33.5	48.6	136.6	54 49.5	49.4	137.6	54 04.9	50.1	138.5	53 19.7	50.7	139.4	52 33.8	51.3	140.3	6
7	58 26.9	45.4	132.2	57 46.2	46.3	133.3	57 04.6	47.2	134.5	56 22.1	48.1	135.6	55 38.9	48.9	136.6	54 55.0	49.5	137.6	54 10.4	50.3	138.5	53 25.1	50.9	139.4	7
8	59 12.3	44.7	130.9	58 32.5	45.7	132.1	57 51.8	46.6	133.3	57 10.2	47.5	134.5	56 27.8	48.3	135.5	55 44.6	49.1	136.6	55 00.7	49.8	137.6	54 16.0	50.9	138.5	8
9	59 57.0	43.8	129.6	59 18.2	44.9	130.9	58 38.4	45.9	132.1	57 57.7	46.9	133.3	57 16.1	47.8	134.5	56 33.7	48.6	135.5	55 50.5	49.3	136.6	55 06.5	50.1	137.6	9
10	60 40.8	+42.9	128.2	60 03.1	+44.1	129.6	59 24.3	+45.2	130.9	58 44.6	+46.1	132.1	58 03.9	+47.1	133.3	57 22.3	+47.9	134.5	56 39.8	+48.8	135.6	55 56.6	+49.6	136.6	10
11	61 23.7	41.9	126.8	60 47.2	43.2	128.2	60 09.5	44.3	129.6	59 30.7	45.5	130.9	58 51.0	46.4	132.1	58 10.2	47.4	133.3	57 28.6	48.3	134.5	56 46.2	49.0	135.6	11
12	62 05.6	41.0	125.3	61 30.4	42.2	126.8	60 53.8	43.5	128.2	60 16.2	44.6	129.6	59 37.4	45.7	130.9	58 57.6	46.7	132.2	58 16.9	47.6	133.4	57 35.2	48.5	134.5	12
13	62 46.6	39.8	123.7	62 12.6	41.2	125.3	61 37.3	42.5	126.8	61 00.8	43.7	128.2	60 23.1	44.9	129.6	59 44.3	46.0	130.9	59 04.5	47.0	132.2	58 23.7	47.9	133.4	13
14	63 26.4	38.6	122.0	62 53.8	40.1	123.7	62 19.8	41.6	125.3	61 44.5	42.9	126.8	61 08.0	44.1	128.3	60 30.3	45.2	129.6	59 51.5	46.2	131.0	59 11.6	47.3	132.2	14
15	64 05.0	+37.3	120.3	63 33.9	+38.9	122.0	63 01.4	+40.4	123.7	62 27.4	+41.8	125.3	61 52.1	+43.1	126.8	61 15.5	+44.3	128.3	60 37.7	+45.5	129.7	59 58.9	+46.5	131.0	15
16	64 42.3	35.9	118.5	64 12.8	37.7	120.3	63 41.8	39.2	122.0	63 09.2	40.7	123.7	62 35.2	42.1	125.3	61 59.8	43.4	126.9	61 23.2	44.6	128.3	60 45.4	45.8	129.8	16
17	65 18.2	34.4	116.6	64 50.5	36.2	118.5	64 21.0	38.0	120.3	63 49.9	39.6	122.1	63 17.3	41.0	123.8	62 43.2	42.5	125.4	62 07.8	43.8	126.9	61 31.2	44.9	128.4	17
18	65 52.6	32.9	114.6	65 26.7	34.8	116.6	64 59.0	36.5	118.5	64 29.5	38.2	120.4	63 58.3	39.9	122.1	63 25.7	41.3	123.8	62 51.6	42.7	125.5	62 16.1	44.1	127.0	18
19	66 25.5	31.1	112.5	66 01.5	33.1	114.6	65 35.5	35.1	116.6	65 07.7	37.0	118.5	64 38.2	38.6	120.4	64 07.0	40.3	122.2	63 34.3	41.7	123.9	63 00.2	43.0	125.5	19
20	66 56.6	+29.2	110.4	66 34.6	+31.5	112.5	66 10.6	+33.8	114.6	65 44.7	+35.4	116.7	65 16.8	+37.3	118.6	64 47.3	+38.9	120.5	64 16.0	+40.6	122.3	63 43.2	+42.1	124.0	20
21	67 25.8	27.4*	108.1	67 06.1	29.6	110.4	66 44.1	31.8	112.6	66 20.1	33.8	114.7	65 54.1	35.7	116.7	65 26.2	37.6	118.7	64 56.6	39.3	120.5	64 25.3	40.8	122.3	21
22	67 53.2	25.2*	105.8	67 35.7	27.6*	108.1	67 15.9	29.9	110.4	66 53.9	32.1	112.6	66 29.8	34.2	114.7	66 03.8	36.1	116.8	65 35.9	37.9	118.7	65 06.1	39.7	120.6	22
23	68 18.4	23.0*	103.3	68 03.3	25.6*	105.8	67 45.8	28.0*	108.1	67 26.0	30.3	110.4	67 04.0	32.5	112.6	66 39.9	34.5	114.8	66 13.8	36.5	116.8	65 45.8	38.3	118.8	23
24	68 41.4	20.7*	100.8	68 28.9	23.3*	103.3	68 13.8	25.9*	105.8	67 56.3	28.3*	108.1	67 36.5	30.6	110.4	67 14.4	32.9	112.7	66 50.3	34.9	114.8	66 24.1	36.8	116.9	24
25	69 02.1	+18.3*	98.2	68 52.2	+21.0*	100.8	68 39.7	+23.6*	103.3	68 24.6	+26.3*	105.8	68 07.1	+28.7*	108.2	67 47.3	+31.0	110.5	67 25.2	+33.1	112.7	67 00.9	+35.3	114.9	25
26	69 20.4	15.7*	95.5	69 13.2	18.5*	98.2	69 03.3	21.4*	100.7	68 50.9	23.9*	103.3	68 35.8	26.5*	105.8	68 18.3	29.0*	108.2	67 58.3	31.4	110.5	67 36.2	33.5	112.8	26
27	69 36.1	13.0*	92.8	69 31.7	16.0*	95.5	69 24.7	18.8*	98.1	69 14.8	21.7*	100.7	69 02.3	24.4*	103.3	68 47.3	26.9*	105.8	68 29.7	29.4*	108.3	68 09.7	31.7	110.6	27
28	69 49.1	10.3*	90.0	69 47.7	13.3*	92.7	69 43.5	16.2*	95.4	69 36.5	19.1*	98.1	69 26.7	21.9*	100.7	69 14.2	24.6*	103.3	68 59.1	27.2*	105.8	68 41.4	29.8*	108.3	28
29	69 59.4	7.5*	87.1	70 01.0	10.5*	89.8	69 59.7	13.6*	92.6	69 55.6	16.5*	95.3	69 48.6	19.4*	98.0	69 38.8	22.3*	100.7	69 26.3	25.0*	103.3	69 11.2	27.6*	105.9	29
30	70 06.9	+4.6*	84.2	70 11.5	+7.7*	87.0	70 13.3	+10.7*	89.7	70 12.1	+13.8*	92.5	70 08.0	+16.8*	95.3	70 01.1	+19.7*	98.0	69 51.3	+22.6*	100.7	69 38.8	+25.3*	103.4	30
31	70 11.5	1.8*	81.3	70 19.2	4.8*	84.0	70 24.0	7.9*	86.8	70 25.9	11.0*	89.6	70 24.8	14.1*	92.4	70 20.8	17.1*	95.2	70 13.9	20.0*	98.0	70 04.1	22.9*	100.7	31
32	70 13.3	−1.2*	78.3	70 24.0	1.1*	81.1	70 31.9	5.0*	83.8	70 36.9	8.1*	86.7	70 38.9	11.2*	89.5	70 37.9	14.3*	92.4	70 33.9	17.4*	95.2	70 27.0	20.4*	98.0	32
33	70 12.1	4.1*	75.3	70 25.9	−1.1*	78.1	70 36.9	2.0*	80.8	70 45.0	5.1*	83.8	70 50.1	8.3*	86.5	70 52.2	11.4*	89.4	70 51.3	14.6*	92.3	70 47.4	17.7*	95.2	33
34	70 08.0	6.9*	72.4	70 24.8	4.0*	75.1	70 38.9	−1.0*	77.8	70 50.1	2.1*	80.6	70 58.4	5.2*	83.5	71 03.6	8.5*	86.4	71 05.9	11.6*	89.3	71 05.1	14.8*	92.2	34
35	70 01.1	−9.8*	69.5	70 20.8	−6.9*	72.1	70 37.9	−4.0*	74.8	70 52.2	−0.9*	77.6	71 03.6	+2.3*	80.4	71 12.1	+5.4*	83.3	71 17.5	+8.7*	86.3	71 19.9	+11.9*	89.2	35
36	69 51.3	12.5*	66.6	70 13.9	9.8*	69.2	70 33.9	6.9*	71.8	70 51.3	3.9*	74.6	71 05.9	−0.7*	77.4	71 17.5	2.4*	80.2	71 26.2	5.6*	83.2	71 31.8	8.8*	86.2	36
37	69 38.8	15.2*	63.8	70 04.1	12.5*	66.3	70 27.0	9.7*	68.8	70 47.4	6.9*	71.5	71 05.1	3.9*	74.3	71 19.9	−0.8*	77.1	71 31.8	2.4*	80.0	71 40.6	5.7*	83.0	37
38	69 23.6	17.8*	61.0	69 51.6	15.3*	63.4	70 17.3	12.7*	65.9	70 40.5	9.8*	68.5	71 01.2	6.9*	71.2	71 19.1	3.8*	74.0	71 34.2	−0.7*	76.9	71 46.3	2.6*	79.8	38
39	69 05.8	20.2*	58.3	69 36.3	17.9*	60.6	70 04.6	15.3*	63.0	70 30.7	12.7*	65.5	70 54.3	9.8*	68.2	71 15.3	6.9*	70.9	71 33.5	3.8*	73.7	71 48.9	−0.6*	76.6	39
40	68 45.6	−22.6*	55.7	69 18.4	−20.3*	57.9	69 49.3	−18.0*	60.2	70 18.0	−15.4*	62.6	70 44.4	−12.7*	65.2	71 08.4	−9.9*	67.8	71 29.7	−6.9*	70.6	71 48.3	−3.8*	73.4	40
41	68 23.0	24.8*	53.2	68 58.1	22.7*	55.3	69 31.3	20.4*	57.4	70 02.6	18.1*	59.8	70 31.7	15.5*	62.2	70 58.5	12.8*	64.8	71 22.8	10.0*	67.5	71 44.5	7.0*	70.3	41
42	67 58.2	26.9*	50.7	68 35.4	25.0*	52.7	69 10.9	22.6*	54.8	69 44.5	20.6*	57.0	70 16.2	18.2*	59.3	70 45.7	15.7*	61.8	71 12.8	12.9*	64.4	71 37.5	10.0*	67.1	42
43	67 31.3	28.9	48.4	68 10.4	27.2*	50.2	68 48.0	25.2*	52.2	69 23.9	23.1*	54.3	69 58.0	20.8*	56.5	70 30.0	18.4*	58.9	70 59.9	15.8*	61.4	71 27.5	13.1*	64.0	43
44	67 02.4	30.8	46.1	67 43.3	29.1	47.9	68 22.8	27.2*	49.7	69 00.8	25.3*	51.7	69 37.2	23.3*	53.8	70 11.6	20.9*	56.0	70 44.1	18.5*	58.4	71 14.4	15.9*	60.9	44

24°, 336° L.H.A. LATITUDE SAME NAME AS DECLINATION

Dec.	30° Hc	d	Z	31° Hc	d	Z	32° Hc	d	Z	33° Hc	d	Z	34° Hc	d	Z	35° Hc	d	Z	36° Hc	d	Z	37° Hc	d	Z	Dec.
0	52 17.6	+48.8	138.3	51 32.5	+49.5	139.2	50 46.8	+50.1	140.0	50 00.6	+50.7	140.7	49 13.9	+51.3	141.5	48 26.8	+51.7	142.2	47 39.2	+52.2	142.9	46 51.1	+52.7	143.5	0
1	53 06.4	48.4	137.4	52 22.0	49.0	138.2	51 36.9	49.7	139.1	50 51.3	50.3	139.9	50 05.2	50.8	140.7	49 18.5	51.4	141.4	48 31.4	51.9	142.1	47 43.8	52.4	142.8	1
2	53 54.8	47.8	136.4	53 11.0	48.6	137.3	52 26.6	49.3	138.2	51 41.6	49.9	139.0	50 56.0	50.5	139.8	50 09.9	51.1	140.6	49 23.3	51.6	141.4	48 36.2	52.1	142.1	2
3	54 42.6	47.3	135.3	53 59.6	48.0	136.3	53 15.9	48.7	137.2	52 31.5	49.5	138.1	51 46.5	50.1	139.0	51 01.0	50.7	139.8	50 14.9	51.3	140.6	49 28.3	51.8	141.3	3
4	55 29.9	46.7	134.2	54 47.6	47.5	135.3	54 04.6	48.3	136.2	53 21.0	49.0	137.2	52 36.6	49.7	138.1	51 51.7	50.3	138.9	51 06.2	50.9	139.7	50 20.1	51.5	140.5	4
5	56 16.6	+46.0	133.1	55 35.1	+47.0	134.2	54 52.9	+47.8	135.2	54 10.0	+48.5	136.2	53 26.3	+49.2	137.1	52 42.0	+49.9	138.0	51 57.1	+50.5	138.9	51 11.6	+51.1	139.7	5
6	57 02.6	45.4	132.0	56 22.1	46.3	133.1	55 40.7	47.1	134.2	54 58.5	48.0	135.2	54 15.5	48.8	136.2	53 31.9	49.5	137.1	52 47.6	50.2	138.0	52 02.7	50.8	138.9	6
7	57 48.0	44.6	130.7	57 08.4	45.6	131.9	56 27.8	46.6	133.1	55 46.5	47.4	134.1	55 04.3	48.2	135.2	54 21.4	49.0	136.2	53 37.8	49.7	137.1	52 53.5	50.3	138.0	7
8	58 32.6	43.9	129.5	57 54.0	44.9	130.7	57 14.4	45.9	131.9	56 33.9	46.8	133.0	55 52.5	47.7	134.1	55 10.4	48.4	135.1	54 27.5	49.2	136.1	53 43.8	50.0	137.1	8
9	59 16.5	43.0	128.2	58 38.9	44.1	129.5	58 00.3	45.2	130.7	57 20.7	46.1	131.9	56 40.2	47.0	133.0	55 58.8	47.9	134.1	55 16.7	48.7	135.1	54 33.8	49.4	136.1	9
10	59 59.5	+42.2	126.8	59 23.0	+43.4	128.1	58 45.5	+44.4	129.4	58 06.8	+45.5	130.7	57 27.2	+46.5	131.9	56 46.7	+47.4	133.0	56 05.4	+48.2	134.1	55 23.2	+49.0	135.2	10
11	60 41.7	41.1	125.3	60 06.4	42.4	126.8	59 29.9	43.6	128.1	58 52.3	44.7	129.4	58 13.7	45.7	130.7	57 34.1	46.7	131.9	56 53.6	47.6	133.0	56 12.2	48.4	134.1	11
12	61 22.8	40.2	123.8	60 48.8	41.4	125.3	60 13.5	42.7	126.8	59 37.0	43.9	128.1	58 59.4	45.0	129.4	58 20.8	46.0	130.7	57 41.2	46.9	131.9	57 00.6	47.9	133.1	12
13	62 03.0	39.0	122.3	61 30.2	40.5	123.8	60 56.2	41.7	125.3	60 20.9	43.0	126.8	59 44.4	44.1	128.1	59 06.8	45.2	129.5	58 28.1	46.3	130.7	57 48.5	47.2	131.9	13
14	62 42.0	37.8	120.6	62 10.7	39.3	122.3	61 37.9	40.8	123.8	61 03.9	42.0	125.3	60 28.5	43.4	126.8	59 52.0	44.5	128.2	59 14.4	45.6	129.5	58 35.7	46.6	130.8	14
15	63 19.8	+36.5	118.9	62 50.0	+38.1	120.6	62 18.7	+39.6	122.3	61 45.9	+41.1	123.9	61 11.9	+42.3	125.4	60 36.5	+43.6	126.8	60 00.0	+44.7	128.2	59 22.3	+45.9	129.5	15
16	63 56.3	35.2	117.1	63 28.1	36.9	118.9	62 58.3	38.5	120.6	62 27.0	40.0	122.3	61 54.2	41.4	123.9	61 20.1	42.7	125.4	60 44.7	44.0	126.9	60 08.2	45.0	128.3	16
17	64 31.5	33.7	115.3	64 05.0	35.5	117.1	63 36.8	37.2	118.9	63 07.0	38.7	120.7	62 35.6	40.3	122.3	62 02.8	41.7	123.9	61 28.7	43.0	125.5	60 53.2	44.3	126.9	17
18	65 05.2	32.1	113.3	64 40.5	34.0	115.3	64 14.0	35.8	117.1	63 45.7	37.6	119.0	63 15.9	39.1	120.7	62 44.5	40.6	122.4	62 11.7	42.0	124.0	61 37.5	43.3	125.5	18
19	65 37.3	30.4	111.3	65 14.5	32.4	113.3	64 49.8	34.3	115.3	64 23.3	36.1	117.2	63 55.0	37.9	119.0	63 25.1	39.5	120.7	62 53.7	40.9	122.4	62 20.8	42.4	124.0	19
20	66 07.7	+28.6	109.2	65 46.9	+30.8	111.3	65 24.1	+32.8	113.3	64 59.4	+34.7	115.3	64 32.9	+36.5	117.2	64 04.6	+38.2	119.0	63 34.6	+39.8	120.8	63 03.2	+41.3	122.5	20
21	66 36.3	26.7	107.0	66 17.7	28.9	109.2	65 56.9	31.1	111.3	65 34.1	33.1	113.4	65 09.4	35.0	115.3	64 42.8	36.8	117.3	64 14.4	38.6	119.1	63 44.5	40.1	120.9	21
22	67 03.0	24.7	104.7	66 46.6	27.1	107.0	66 28.0	29.3	109.2	66 07.2	31.5	111.3	65 44.4	33.5	113.4	65 19.6	35.4	115.4	64 53.0	37.2	117.3	64 24.6	38.9	119.2	22
23	67 27.7	22.6	102.4	67 13.7	25.0	104.7	66 57.3	27.1	107.0	66 38.7	29.6	109.2	66 17.9	31.8	111.3	65 55.0	33.9	113.4	65 30.2	35.8	115.4	65 03.5	37.6	117.4	23
24	67 50.3	20.3	99.9	67 38.7	22.9	102.3	67 24.4	25.4	104.7	67 08.3	27.8	107.0	66 49.7	30.0	109.2	66 28.9	32.1	111.4	66 06.0	34.2	113.5	65 41.1	36.1	115.5	24
25	68 10.6	+18.0	97.4	68 01.6	+20.6	99.9	67 50.1	+23.2	102.3	67 36.1	+25.7	104.7	67 19.7	+28.1	107.0	67 01.0	+30.4	109.2	66 40.2	+32.5	111.4	66 17.2	+34.6	113.6	25
26	68 28.6	15.6	94.8	68 22.2	18.3	97.3	68 13.3	20.9	99.8	68 01.8	23.5	102.3	67 47.8	26.0	104.7	67 31.4	28.4	107.0	67 12.7	30.7	109.3	66 51.8	32.9	111.5	26
27	68 44.2	12.9	92.2	68 40.5	15.8	94.7	68 34.2	18.6	97.3	68 25.3	21.3	99.8	68 13.8	23.8	102.3	67 59.8	26.2	104.7	67 43.4	28.8	107.1	67 24.7	31.1	109.4	27
28	68 57.1	10.4	89.5	68 56.3	13.3	92.1	68 52.8	16.1	94.7	68 46.6	18.9	97.2	68 37.7	21.6	99.8	68 26.2	24.3	102.3	68 12.2	26.8	104.7	67 55.8	29.2	107.1	28
29	69 07.5	7.7	86.7	69 09.6	10.6	89.3	69 08.9	13.5	92.0	69 05.5	16.3	94.6	68 59.3	19.2	97.2	68 50.5	21.9	99.8	68 39.0	24.5	102.3	68 25.0	27.1	104.8	29
30	69 15.2	+5.0	83.9	69 20.2	+7.9	86.6	69 22.4	+10.8	89.2	69 21.8	+13.8	91.9	69 18.5	+16.6	94.5	69 12.4	+19.4	97.2	69 03.5	+22.3	99.7	68 52.1	+24.9	102.3	30
31	69 20.2	2.2	81.1	69 28.1	5.1	83.8	69 33.2	7.9	86.4	69 35.6	11.0	89.1	69 35.1	14.0	91.8	69 31.8	17.0	94.5	69 25.8	19.8	97.1	69 17.0	22.5	99.8	31
32	69 22.4	−0.6	78.3	69 33.2	2.4	80.9	69 41.3	5.4	83.6	69 46.7	8.3	86.3	69 49.1	11.3	89.0	69 48.8	14.3	91.7	69 45.6	17.2	94.4	69 39.5	20.1	97.1	32
33	69 21.8	3.3	75.4	69 35.6	−0.5	78.0	69 46.7	2.4	80.7	69 55.0	5.4	83.4	70 00.4	8.5	86.1	70 03.1	11.5	88.9	70 02.8	14.5	91.6	69 59.6	17.6	94.4	33
34	69 18.5	6.1	72.6	69 35.1	3.3	75.2	69 49.1	−0.3	77.8	70 00.4	2.7	80.5	70 08.9	5.7	83.2	70 14.6	8.7	86.0	70 17.3	11.8	88.8	70 17.2	14.8	91.6	34
35	69 12.4	−8.9	69.8	69 31.8	−6.0	72.3	69 48.8	−3.2	74.9	70 03.1	−0.3	77.6	70 14.6	+2.7	80.3	70 23.3	+5.8	83.0	70 29.1	+8.9	85.9	70 32.0	+12.0	88.7	35
36	69 03.5	11.4	67.0	69 25.8	8.8	69.5	69 45.6	6.1	72.0	70 02.8	3.2	74.6	70 17.3	−0.1	77.3	70 29.1	2.9	80.1	70 38.0	6.0	82.9	70 44.0	9.0	85.7	36
37	68 52.1	14.1	64.3	69 17.0	11.5	66.7	69 39.5	8.8	69.1	69 59.6	6.1	71.7	70 17.2	3.1	74.4	70 32.0	−0.1	77.1	70 44.0	2.9	79.9	70 53.0	6.2	82.7	37
38	68 38.0	16.6	61.6	69 05.5	14.1	63.9	69 30.7	11.5	66.3	69 53.6	8.8	68.8	70 14.1	6.0	71.4	70 31.9	3.1	74.1	70 46.9	0.0	76.8	70 59.2	3.1	79.7	38
39	68 21.4	18.9	59.0	68 51.4	16.7	61.2	69 19.2	14.2	63.5	69 44.8	11.6	65.9	70 08.1	8.9	68.5	70 28.8	6.0	71.1	70 46.9	−3.0	73.8	71 02.3	0.0	76.6	39
40	68 02.5	−21.3	56.4	68 34.7	−19.1	58.6	69 05.0	−16.7	60.8	69 33.2	−14.2	63.1	69 59.2	−11.6	65.6	70 22.8	−8.8	68.1	70 43.9	−5.9	70.8	71 02.3	−3.0	73.5	40
41	67 41.2	23.5	54.1	68 15.6	21.4	56.0	68 48.3	19.2	58.1	69 19.0	16.8	60.4	69 47.6	14.3	62.7	70 14.0	11.7	65.2	70 37.9	8.9	67.8	70 59.3	6.0	70.4	41
42	67 17.7	25.5	51.5	67 54.2	23.6	53.5	68 29.1	21.5	55.5	69 02.2	19.4	57.7	69 33.3	17.0	59.9	70 02.3	14.5	62.3	70 29.0	11.8	64.8	70 53.3	9.0	67.4	42
43	66 52.2	27.6	49.2	67 30.6	25.7	51.0	68 07.6	23.8	53.0	68 42.8	21.5	55.0	69 16.3	19.5	57.2	69 47.8	17.1	59.5	70 17.2	14.6	61.9	70 44.3	11.9	64.4	43
44	66 24.6	29.3	47.0	67 04.9	27.7	48.7	67 43.8	25.9	50.5	68 21.1	23.9	52.5	68 56.8	21.8	54.5	69 30.7	19.6	56.7	70 02.6	17.2	59.0	70 32.4	14.7	61.4	44

27°, 333° L.H.A. LATITUDE SAME NAME AS DECLINATION

N. Lat. { L.H.A. greater than 180°......Zn=Z
{ L.H.A. less than 180°......Zn=360°−Z

Dec.	30° Hc	30° d	30° Z	31° Hc	31° d	31° Z	32° Hc	32° d	32° Z	33° Hc	33° d	33° Z	34° Hc	34° d	34° Z	35° Hc	35° d	35° Z	36° Hc	36° d	36° Z	37° Hc	37° d	37° Z	Dec.
0	50 30.1	+46.9	134.5	49 47.7	+47.7	135.5	49 04.8	+48.3	136.1	48 21.2	+49.0	136.9	47 37.1	+49.6	137.7	46 52.5	+50.2	138.4	46 07.4	+50.8	139.1	45 21.9	+51.2	139.7	0
1	51 17.0	46.4	133.5	50 35.4	47.1	134.4	49 53.1	47.9	135.2	49 10.2	48.6	136.0	48 26.7	49.2	136.8	47 42.7	49.8	137.6	46 58.2	50.4	138.3	46 13.1	51.0	139.0	1
2	52 03.4	45.8	132.4	51 22.5	46.7	133.4	50 41.0	47.4	134.3	49 58.8	48.1	135.1	49 15.9	48.8	135.9	48 32.5	49.5	136.7	47 48.6	50.0	137.5	47 04.1	50.6	138.2	2
3	52 49.2	45.3	131.4	52 09.2	46.1	132.4	51 28.4	46.9	133.3	50 46.9	47.7	134.2	50 04.7	48.4	135.1	49 22.0	49.0	135.9	48 38.6	49.7	136.7	47 54.7	50.3	137.4	3
4	53 34.5	44.6	130.3	52 55.3	45.5	131.3	52 15.3	46.4	132.3	51 34.6	47.1	133.2	50 53.1	47.9	134.1	50 11.0	48.7	135.0	49 28.3	49.3	135.8	48 45.0	49.9	136.6	4
5	54 19.1	+44.0	129.2	53 40.8	+44.9	130.2	53 01.7	+45.8	131.2	52 21.7	+46.7	132.2	51 41.0	+47.5	133.2	50 59.7	+48.1	134.1	50 17.6	+48.9	134.9	49 34.9	+49.6	135.8	5
6	55 03.1	43.3	128.0	54 25.7	44.3	129.1	53 47.5	45.2	130.2	53 08.4	46.0	131.1	52 28.5	46.9	132.2	51 47.8	47.7	133.1	51 06.5	48.4	134.0	50 24.5	49.1	134.9	6
7	55 46.4	42.5	126.8	55 10.0	43.6	127.9	54 32.7	44.5	129.0	53 54.4	45.5	130.1	53 15.4	46.3	131.1	52 35.5	47.2	132.1	51 54.9	48.0	133.1	51 13.6	48.7	134.0	7
8	56 28.9	41.7	125.5	55 53.6	42.8	126.7	55 17.2	43.9	127.8	54 39.9	44.9	129.0	54 01.7	45.8	130.1	53 22.7	46.6	131.1	52 42.9	47.4	132.1	52 02.3	48.2	133.0	8
9	57 10.6	40.9	124.2	56 36.4	42.0	125.4	56 01.1	43.1	126.7	55 24.8	44.1	127.8	54 47.5	45.1	128.9	54 09.3	46.1	130.0	53 30.3	46.9	131.1	52 50.5	47.8	132.1	9
10	57 51.5	+40.0	122.8	57 18.4	+41.2	124.1	56 44.2	+42.3	125.4	56 08.9	+43.4	126.6	55 32.6	+44.5	127.8	54 55.4	+45.4	128.9	54 17.2	+46.1	130.0	53 38.3	+47.2	131.1	10
11	58 31.5	38.9	121.4	57 59.6	40.3	122.8	57 26.5	41.5	124.1	56 52.3	42.7	125.3	56 17.1	43.7	126.6	55 40.8	44.8	127.8	55 03.6	45.7	128.9	54 25.5	46.6	130.0	11
12	59 10.4	38.0	119.9	58 39.9	39.3	121.4	58 08.0	40.6	122.7	57 35.0	41.8	124.1	57 00.8	43.0	125.3	56 25.6	44.0	126.6	55 49.3	45.1	127.8	55 12.1	46.0	128.8	12
13	59 48.4	36.8	118.4	59 19.2	38.2	119.9	58 48.6	39.7	121.3	58 16.8	40.9	122.7	57 43.8	42.1	124.1	57 09.6	43.3	125.3	56 34.4	44.3	126.6	55 58.1	45.4	127.8	13
14	60 25.2	35.7	116.8	59 57.4	37.2	118.4	59 28.2	38.7	119.9	58 57.7	40.0	121.3	58 25.9	41.3	122.7	57 52.9	42.5	124.1	57 18.7	43.6	125.3	56 43.5	44.7	126.6	14
15	61 00.9	+34.5	115.2	60 34.6	+36.1	116.8	60 06.9	+37.5	118.3	59 37.7	+38.9	119.9	59 07.2	+40.3	121.3	58 35.4	+41.5	122.7	58 02.3	+42.8	124.1	57 28.2	+43.9	125.4	15
16	61 35.4	33.1	113.5	61 10.7	34.7	115.1	60 44.4	36.4	116.8	60 16.6	37.9	118.3	59 47.5	39.3	119.8	59 16.9	40.7	121.3	58 45.1	42.0	122.7	58 12.1	43.1	124.1	16
17	62 08.5	31.7	111.7	61 45.4	33.1	113.4	61 20.8	35.1	115.1	60 54.5	36.7	116.8	60 26.8	38.2	118.3	59 57.6	39.7	119.9	59 27.1	41.0	121.3	58 55.2	42.3	122.8	17
18	62 40.2	30.2	109.9	62 18.9	32.1	111.7	61 55.9	33.8	113.4	61 31.2	35.5	115.1	61 05.0	37.1	116.8	60 37.3	38.5	118.3	60 08.1	40.0	119.9	59 37.5	41.3	121.4	18
19	63 10.4	28.7	108.0	62 51.0	30.6	109.8	62 29.7	32.4	111.6	62 06.7	34.2	113.4	61 42.1	35.8	115.1	61 15.8	37.5	116.8	60 48.1	38.9	118.4	60 18.8	40.4	119.9	19
20	63 39.1	+27.0	106.0	63 21.6	+29.0	107.9	63 02.1	+31.0	109.8	62 40.9	+32.8	111.6	62 17.9	+34.6	113.4	61 53.3	+36.2	115.1	61 27.0	+37.8	116.8	60 59.2	+39.3	118.4	20
21	64 06.1	25.2	104.0	63 50.6	27.3	106.0	63 33.1	29.4	107.9	63 13.7	31.3	109.8	62 52.5	33.1	111.6	62 29.5	34.9	113.4	62 04.8	36.6	115.1	61 38.5	38.2	116.8	21
22	64 31.3	23.4	101.9	64 17.9	25.6	103.9	64 02.5	27.7	105.9	63 45.0	29.7	107.9	63 25.6	31.7	109.8	63 04.4	33.5	111.6	62 41.4	35.3	113.4	62 16.7	37.0	115.3	22
23	64 54.7	21.5	99.7	64 43.5	23.8	101.8	64 30.2	25.9	103.9	64 14.7	28.1	105.9	63 57.3	30.1	107.9	63 37.9	32.1	109.8	63 16.7	33.9	111.7	62 53.7	35.6	113.5	23
24	65 16.2	19.5*	97.5	65 07.3	21.8*	99.7	64 56.1	24.1	101.8	64 42.8	26.3	103.8	64 27.4	28.4	105.9	64 10.0	30.5	107.9	63 50.6	32.4	109.8	63 29.3	34.3	111.7	24
25	65 35.7	+17.4*	95.2	65 29.1	+19.8*	97.4	65 20.2	+22.1	99.6	65 09.1	+24.4	101.7	64 55.8	+26.7	103.8	64 40.5	+28.8	105.9	64 23.0	+30.9	107.9	64 03.6	+32.8	109.8	25
26	65 53.1	15.2*	92.9	65 48.9	17.7*	95.1	65 42.3	20.2*	97.3	65 33.5	22.5	99.5	65 22.5	24.8	101.7	65 09.3	27.0	103.8	64 53.9	29.2	105.9	64 36.4	31.3	107.9	26
27	66 08.3	13.0*	90.5	66 06.6	15.5*	92.8	66 02.5	18.0*	95.0	65 56.0	20.5*	97.3	65 47.3	22.8*	99.5	65 36.3	25.1	101.7	65 23.1	27.3	103.8	65 07.7	29.5	105.9	27
28	66 21.3	10.7*	88.1	66 22.1	13.2*	90.4	66 20.5	15.8*	92.7	66 16.5	18.3*	95.0	66 10.1	20.8*	97.2	66 01.4	23.2*	99.4	65 50.4	25.6	101.7	65 37.2	27.8	103.8	28
29	66 32.0	8.3*	85.6	66 35.3	11.0*	88.0	66 36.3	13.5*	90.3	66 34.8	16.1*	92.6	66 30.9	18.6*	94.9	66 24.6	21.1*	97.2	66 16.0	23.5*	99.4	66 05.0	25.9	101.6	29
30	66 40.3	+6.0*	83.2	66 46.3	+8.6*	85.5	66 49.8	+11.2*	87.8	66 50.9	+13.8*	90.1	66 49.5	+16.4*	92.5	66 45.7	+19.0*	94.8	66 39.5	+21.4*	97.1	66 30.9	+23.9*	99.4	30
31	66 46.3	3.5*	80.6	66 54.9	6.1*	83.0	67 01.0	8.8*	85.3	67 04.7	11.4*	87.6	67 05.9	14.1*	90.0	67 04.7	16.7*	92.4	67 00.9	19.3*	94.7	66 54.8	21.8*	97.1	31
32	66 49.8	1.1*	78.1	67 01.0	3.7*	80.4	67 09.8	6.3*	82.7	67 16.1	9.0*	85.1	67 20.0	11.7*	87.5	67 21.4	14.3*	89.9	67 20.2	17.0*	92.3	67 16.6	19.5*	94.7	32
33	66 50.9	−1.4*	75.6	67 04.7	1.2*	77.8	67 16.1	3.9*	80.2	67 25.1	6.6*	82.6	67 31.7	9.2*	84.9	67 35.7	11.9*	87.4	67 37.2	14.6*	89.8	67 36.1	17.3*	92.2	33
34	66 49.5	3.8*	73.0	67 05.9	−1.2*	75.3	67 20.0	1.4*	77.6	67 31.7	4.0*	80.0	67 40.9	6.7*	82.4	67 47.6	9.5*	84.8	67 51.8	12.2*	87.2	67 53.4	14.9*	89.7	34
35	66 45.7	−6.2*	70.5	67 04.7	−3.8*	72.7	67 21.4	−1.2*	75.0	67 35.7	+1.5*	77.3	67 47.6	+4.2*	79.7	67 57.1	+6.9*	82.2	68 04.0	+9.6*	84.6	68 08.3	+12.4*	87.1	35
36	66 39.5	8.6*	68.0	67 00.9	6.1*	70.2	67 20.2	3.6*	72.4	67 37.2	−1.1*	74.7	67 51.8	1.6*	77.1	68 04.0	4.3*	79.5	68 13.6	7.1*	82.0	68 20.7	9.9*	84.5	36
37	66 30.9	11.0*	65.5	66 54.8	8.6*	67.6	67 16.6	6.2*	69.8	67 36.1	3.6*	72.1	67 53.4	−0.9*	74.4	68 08.3	1.7*	76.8	68 20.7	4.5*	79.3	68 30.6	7.3*	81.8	37
38	66 19.9	13.2*	63.0	66 46.2	11.0*	65.1	67 10.4	8.6*	67.2	67 32.5	6.1*	69.5	67 52.5	3.6*	71.8	68 10.0	−0.8*	74.1	68 25.2	1.8*	76.6	68 37.9	4.6*	79.1	38
39	66 06.7	15.5*	60.6	66 35.2	13.3*	62.6	67 01.8	11.0*	64.7	67 26.4	8.5*	66.9	67 48.9	6.1*	69.1	68 09.2	3.5*	71.5	68 27.0	−0.8*	73.9	68 42.5	1.9*	76.3	39
40	65 51.2	−17.6*	58.2	66 21.9	−15.5*	60.2	66 50.8	−13.3*	62.2	67 17.9	−11.1*	64.3	67 42.8	−8.6*	66.5	68 05.7	−6.1*	68.8	68 26.2	−3.4*	71.1	68 44.4	−0.7*	73.6	40
41	65 33.6	19.8*	55.9	66 06.4	17.5*	57.8	66 37.5	15.6*	59.8	67 06.8	13.4*	61.8	67 34.2	11.1*	63.9	67 59.6	8.6*	66.1	68 22.8	6.1*	68.4	68 43.7	3.4*	70.8	41
42	65 13.8	21.7	53.6	65 48.7	19.9*	55.4	66 21.9	17.8*	57.3	66 53.4	15.7*	59.3	67 23.2	13.5*	61.3	67 51.0	11.2*	63.5	68 16.7	8.7*	65.7	68 40.3	6.1*	68.1	42
43	64 52.1	23.6	51.4	65 28.8	21.8	53.1	66 04.1	20.0*	54.9	66 37.7	17.9*	56.8	67 09.7	15.8*	58.8	67 39.8	13.5*	60.9	68 08.0	11.2*	63.1	68 34.2	8.8*	65.3	43
44	64 28.5	25.5	49.3	65 07.0	23.8	50.9	65 44.1	22.0	52.6	66 19.8	20.1*	54.4	66 53.9	18.1*	56.3	67 26.3	16.0*	58.3	67 56.8	13.6*	60.4	68 25.4	11.3*	62.6	44

LATITUDE SAME NAME AS DECLINATION

N. Lat. { L.H.A. greater than 180°......Zn=Z / L.H.A. less than 180°......Zn=360−Z }

Dec.	30° Hc	d	Z	31° Hc	d	Z	32° Hc	d	Z	33° Hc	d	Z	34° Hc	d	Z	35° Hc	d	Z	36° Hc	d	Z	37° Hc	d	Z	Dec.
0	49 52.6	+46.3	133.2	49 11.2	+47.0	134.1	48 29.1	+47.8	134.9	47 46.5	+48.4	135.7	47 03.2	+49.1	136.4	46 19.5	+49.7	137.2	45 35.2	+50.3	137.9	44 50.5	+50.8	138.5	0
1	50 38.9	45.8	132.2	49 58.2	46.6	133.1	49 16.9	47.2	134.0	48 34.9	48.0	134.8	47 52.3	48.7	135.6	47 09.2	49.3	136.5	46 25.5	49.9	137.1	45 41.3	50.5	137.8	1
2	51 24.7	45.2	131.2	50 44.8	46.0	132.1	50 04.1	46.9	133.0	49 22.9	47.5	133.9	48 41.0	48.2	134.7	47 58.5	48.9	135.5	47 15.4	49.5	136.3	46 31.8	50.1	137.0	2
3	52 09.9	44.6	130.2	51 30.8	45.5	131.1	50 51.0	46.3	132.0	50 10.4	47.1	132.9	49 29.2	47.8	133.8	48 47.4	48.5	134.6	48 04.9	49.2	135.4	47 21.9	49.8	136.2	3
4	52 54.5	44.0	129.1	52 16.3	44.9	130.1	51 37.3	45.7	131.0	50 57.5	46.6	132.0	50 17.0	47.4	132.9	49 35.9	48.1	133.7	48 54.1	48.8	134.6	48 11.7	49.4	135.4	4
5	53 38.5	+43.3	127.9	53 01.2	+44.3	129.0	52 23.0	+45.2	130.0	51 44.1	+46.0	131.0	51 04.4	+46.8	131.9	50 24.0	+47.6	132.8	49 42.9	+48.3	133.7	49 01.1	+49.0	134.5	5
6	54 21.8	42.6	126.7	53 45.5	43.6	127.8	53 08.2	44.6	128.9	52 30.1	45.5	129.9	51 51.2	46.4	130.9	51 11.6	47.1	131.8	50 31.2	47.9	132.7	49 50.1	48.6	133.6	6
7	55 04.4	41.9	125.5	54 29.1	42.9	126.7	53 52.8	43.9	127.8	53 15.6	44.9	128.8	52 37.6	45.7	129.9	51 58.7	46.6	130.8	51 19.1	47.4	131.8	50 38.7	48.2	132.7	7
8	55 46.3	41.0	124.3	55 12.0	42.2	125.5	54 36.7	43.2	126.6	54 00.5	44.2	127.7	53 23.3	45.2	128.8	52 45.3	46.1	129.8	52 06.5	46.9	130.8	51 26.9	47.7	131.8	8
9	56 27.3	40.2	123.0	55 54.2	41.3	124.2	55 19.9	42.5	125.4	54 44.7	43.5	126.6	54 08.5	44.5	127.7	53 31.4	45.4	128.7	52 53.4	46.3	129.8	52 14.6	47.2	130.8	9
10	57 07.5	+39.3	121.6	56 35.5	+40.5	122.9	56 02.4	+41.7	124.1	55 28.2	+42.8	125.3	54 53.0	+43.8	126.6	54 16.8	+44.8	127.6	53 39.7	+45.8	128.7	53 01.8	+46.6	129.8	10
11	57 46.8	38.3	120.2	57 16.0	39.7	121.5	56 44.1	40.8	122.8	56 11.0	42.0	124.1	55 36.8	43.1	125.5	55 01.6	44.2	126.5	54 25.5	45.1	127.6	53 48.4	46.1	128.7	11
12	58 25.1	37.3	118.7	57 55.7	38.6	120.1	57 24.9	40.0	121.5	56 53.0	41.2	122.8	56 19.9	42.3	124.3	55 45.8	43.4	125.3	55 10.6	44.5	126.5	54 34.5	45.4	127.6	12
13	59 02.4	36.2	117.2	58 34.3	37.6	118.7	58 04.9	39.0	120.1	57 34.2	40.2	121.5	57 02.2	41.6	123.1	56 29.2	42.7	124.1	55 55.1	43.7	125.3	55 19.9	44.8	126.5	13
14	59 38.6	35.1	115.7	59 11.9	36.6	117.2	58 43.9	37.9	118.6	58 14.4	39.4	120.1	57 43.8	40.6	121.9	57 11.9	41.8	122.8	56 38.8	43.0	124.1	56 04.7	44.1	125.3	14
15	60 13.7	+33.8	114.0	59 48.5	+35.4	115.6	59 21.8	+36.9	117.1	58 53.8	+38.3	118.6	58 24.4	+39.7	120.7	57 53.7	+41.0	121.4	57 21.8	+42.2	122.8	56 48.8	+43.3	124.1	15
16	60 47.5	32.5	112.4	60 23.9	34.2	114.0	59 58.7	35.8	115.6	59 32.1	37.3	117.1	59 04.1	38.6	119.3	58 34.7	40.0	120.0	58 04.0	41.3	121.4	57 32.1	42.5	122.8	16
17	61 20.0	31.2	110.6	60 58.1	32.8	112.3	60 34.5	34.5	113.9	60 09.4	36.1	115.6	59 42.7	37.7	118.0	59 14.7	39.0	118.6	58 45.3	40.4	120.1	58 14.6	41.7	121.5	17
18	61 51.2	29.7	108.8	61 30.9	31.5	110.6	61 09.0	33.3	112.3	60 45.5	34.9	113.9	60 20.4	36.4	116.6	59 53.7	38.0	117.1	59 25.7	39.4	118.6	58 56.3	40.7	120.1	18
19	62 20.9	28.1	107.0	62 02.4	30.1	108.8	61 42.3	31.8	110.5	61 20.4	33.6	112.3	60 56.8	35.3	115.1	60 31.7	36.9	115.5	60 05.1	38.3	117.1	59 37.0	39.8	118.6	19
20	62 49.0	+26.6	105.1	62 32.5	+28.5	106.9	62 14.1	+30.4	108.7	61 54.0	+32.2	110.5	61 32.1	+34.0	113.6	61 08.6	+35.6	113.9	60 43.4	+37.3	115.6	60 16.8	+38.7	117.1	20
21	63 15.6	24.8	103.1	63 01.0	26.9	105.0	62 44.5	28.9	106.9	62 26.2	30.8	108.7	62 06.1	32.6	112.0	61 44.2	34.4	112.2	61 20.7	36.0	113.9	60 55.5	37.6	115.6	21
22	63 40.4	23.1	101.0	63 27.9	25.2	103.0	63 13.4	27.3	104.9	62 57.0	29.2	106.8	62 38.7	31.1	110.4	62 18.6	32.9	110.5	61 56.7	34.7	112.3	61 33.1	36.4	114.0	22
23	64 03.5	21.2	98.9	63 53.1	23.4	101.0	63 40.7	25.5	102.9	63 26.2	27.6	104.9	63 09.8	29.6	108.7	62 51.5	31.6	108.7	62 31.4	33.4	110.5	62 09.5	35.1	112.3	23
24	64 24.7	19.2	96.8	64 16.5	21.5	98.9	64 06.2	23.8	100.9	63 53.8	25.9	102.9	63 39.4	28.0	106.8	63 23.1	30.0	106.8	63 04.8	31.9	108.7	62 44.6	33.8	110.5	24
25	64 43.9	+17.3	94.6	64 38.0	+19.6	96.7	64 30.0	+21.8	98.8	64 19.7	+24.2	100.8	64 07.4	+26.3	105.0	63 53.1	+28.3	104.8	63 36.7	+30.4	106.8	63 18.4	+32.3	108.7	25
26	65 01.2	15.2	92.3	64 57.6	17.6	94.5	64 51.8	20.0	96.6	64 43.9	22.2	98.7	64 33.7	24.5	103.0	64 21.4	26.7	102.8	64 07.1	28.7	104.8	63 50.7	30.8	106.8	26
27	65 16.4	13.0	90.0	65 15.2	15.5	92.2	65 11.8	17.8	94.4	65 06.1	20.2	96.5	64 58.2	22.5	100.9	64 48.1	24.8	100.8	64 35.8	27.0	102.8	64 21.5	29.1	104.8	27
28	65 29.4	10.8	87.7	65 30.7	13.3	89.9	65 29.6	15.8	92.1	65 26.3	18.2	94.3	65 20.7	20.6	98.8	65 12.9	22.9	98.6	65 02.8	25.2	100.7	64 50.6	27.4	102.8	28
29	65 40.2	8.6	85.3	65 44.0	11.0	87.5	65 45.4	13.6	89.7	65 44.5	16.1	92.0	65 41.3	18.5	96.5	65 35.8	20.9	96.4	65 28.0	23.3	98.5	65 18.0	25.5	100.7	29
30	65 48.8	+6.2	82.9	65 55.0	+8.8	85.1	65 59.0	+11.3	87.3	66 00.6	+13.8	89.6	65 59.8	+16.4	94.1	65 56.7	+18.8	94.1	65 51.3	+21.2	96.3	65 43.5	+23.7	98.5	30
31	65 55.0	4.0	80.5	66 03.8	6.5	82.7	66 10.3	9.0	84.9	66 14.4	11.6	87.2	66 16.2	14.1	91.8	66 15.5	16.7	91.7	66 12.5	19.2	94.0	66 07.2	21.6	96.3	31
32	65 59.0	1.6	78.0	66 10.3	4.1	80.2	66 19.3	6.7	82.5	66 26.0	9.3	84.7	66 30.3	11.8	89.3	66 32.2	14.4	89.3	66 31.7	16.9	91.6	66 28.8	19.4	93.9	32
33	66 00.6	0.8	75.6	66 14.4	1.8	77.8	66 26.0	4.3	80.0	66 35.3	6.7	82.3	66 42.1	9.5	87.0	66 46.6	12.1	86.7	66 48.6	14.7	89.2	66 48.2	17.3	91.6	33
34	65 59.8	3.1	73.1	66 16.2	0.7	75.3	66 30.3	1.9	77.5	66 42.1	4.5	79.8	66 51.6	7.1	84.4	66 58.7	9.7	84.4	67 03.3	12.4	86.7	67 05.5	15.0	89.1	34
35	65 56.7	5.4	70.6	66 15.5	3.0	72.8	66 32.2	0.5	75.0	66 46.6	2.0	77.2	66 58.7	4.6	79.5	67 08.4	+7.3	81.9	67 15.7	+9.9	84.2	67 20.5	+12.6	86.6	35
36	65 51.3	7.8	68.2	66 12.5	5.3	70.3	66 31.7	2.9	72.5	66 48.6	0.4	74.7	67 03.3	2.2	77.0	67 15.7	4.8	79.3	67 25.6	7.5	81.7	67 33.1	10.1	84.1	36
37	65 43.5	10.0	65.8	66 07.2	7.7	67.8	66 28.8	5.3	70.0	66 48.2	2.9	72.2	67 05.5	0.3	74.4	67 20.5	2.3	76.7	67 33.1	4.8	79.1	67 43.2	7.6	81.5	37
38	65 33.5	12.2	63.4	65 59.5	10.0	65.4	66 23.5	7.7	67.5	66 45.4	5.3	69.6	67 05.2	2.8	71.8	67 22.8	0.2	74.1	67 38.0	2.4	76.5	67 50.8	5.1	78.8	38
39	65 21.3	14.4	61.0	65 49.5	12.3	63.0	66 15.8	10.0	65.0	66 40.1	7.7	67.1	67 02.4	5.2	69.3	67 22.6	2.8	71.5	67 40.4	0.1	73.8	67 55.9	2.6	76.2	39
40	65 06.9	-16.5	58.7	65 37.2	-14.4	60.6	66 05.8	-12.3	62.6	66 32.5	-10.1	64.6	66 57.2	-7.7	66.7	67 19.8	-5.2	68.9	67 40.3	-2.7	71.2	67 58.5	0.1	73.5	40
41	64 50.4	18.6	56.4	65 22.8	16.6	58.3	65 53.5	14.5	60.2	66 22.4	12.3	62.1	66 49.5	10.1	64.2	67 14.6	7.7	66.3	67 37.6	5.2	68.6	67 58.4	2.6	70.9	41
42	64 31.8	20.5	54.2	65 06.2	18.7	56.0	65 39.0	16.7	57.8	66 10.1	14.6	59.7	66 39.4	12.4	61.7	67 06.9	10.1	63.8	67 32.4	7.7	66.0	67 55.8	5.2	68.2	42
43	64 11.3	22.4	52.1	64 47.5	20.6	53.7	65 22.3	18.8	55.5	65 55.5	16.8	57.3	66 27.0	14.6	59.2	66 56.8	12.5	61.3	67 24.7	10.2	63.4	67 51.0	7.8	65.6	43
44	63 48.9	24.2	49.9	64 26.9	22.5	51.5	65 03.5	20.7	53.2	65 38.7	18.9	55.0	66 12.4	16.9	56.8	66 44.3	14.8	58.8	67 14.5	12.5	60.8	67 42.8	10.2	62.9	44

LATITUDE SAME NAME AS DECLINATION

N. Lat. { L.H.A. greater than 180° ...... Zn=Z ; L.H.A. less than 180° ...... Zn=360°−Z }

Dec.	30° Hc	d	Z	31° Hc	d	Z	32° Hc	d	Z	33° Hc	d	Z	34° Hc	d	Z	35° Hc	d	Z	36° Hc	d	Z	37° Hc	d	Z	Dec.
0	49 14.4	+45.6	132.1	48 33.8	+46.5	132.9	47 52.7	+47.2	133.7	47 10.9	+47.9	134.5	46 28.6	+48.5	135.3	45 45.7	+49.2	136.0	45 02.3	+49.8	136.7	44 18.4	+50.3	137.4	0
1	50 00.0	45.2	131.1	49 20.3	46.0	131.9	48 39.9	46.7	132.8	47 58.8	47.4	133.6	47 17.1	48.2	134.4	46 34.9	48.7	135.2	45 52.1	49.4	135.9	45 08.7	50.0	136.6	1
2	50 45.2	44.6	130.0	50 06.3	45.4	130.9	49 26.6	46.2	131.8	48 46.2	47.0	132.7	48 05.3	47.7	133.5	47 23.6	48.4	134.3	46 41.5	49.0	135.1	45 58.7	49.7	135.8	2
3	51 29.8	44.0	129.0	50 51.7	44.9	129.9	50 12.8	45.7	130.8	49 33.2	46.5	131.7	48 53.0	47.2	132.6	48 12.0	48.0	133.4	47 30.5	48.6	134.2	46 48.4	49.3	135.0	3
4	52 13.8	43.4	127.9	51 36.6	44.3	128.9	50 58.5	45.2	129.8	50 19.7	46.0	130.7	49 40.2	46.8	131.6	49 00.0	47.5	132.5	48 19.1	48.3	133.3	47 37.7	48.9	134.1	4
5	52 57.2	+42.6	126.7	52 20.9	+43.6	127.8	51 43.7	+44.6	128.8	51 05.7	+45.5	129.7	50 27.0	+46.3	130.7	49 47.5	+47.1	131.6	49 07.4	+47.8	132.4	48 26.6	+48.5	133.3	5
6	53 39.8	42.0	125.5	53 04.5	43.0	126.6	52 28.3	43.9	127.7	51 51.2	44.9	128.7	51 13.3	45.7	129.7	50 34.6	46.6	130.6	49 55.2	47.3	131.5	49 15.1	48.1	132.4	6
7	54 21.8	41.2	124.3	53 47.5	42.3	125.5	53 12.2	43.3	126.5	52 36.1	44.2	127.6	51 59.0	45.2	128.6	51 21.2	46.0	129.6	50 42.5	46.9	130.6	50 03.2	47.6	131.5	7
8	55 03.0	40.4	123.1	54 29.8	41.5	124.2	53 55.5	42.6	125.4	53 20.3	43.6	126.5	52 44.2	44.6	127.5	52 07.2	45.5	128.6	51 29.4	46.3	129.6	50 50.8	47.2	130.5	8
9	55 43.4	39.6	121.8	55 11.3	40.7	123.0	54 38.1	41.9	124.1	54 03.9	42.9	125.3	53 28.8	43.9	126.4	52 52.7	44.9	127.5	52 15.7	45.8	128.5	51 38.0	46.6	129.5	9
10	56 23.0	+38.6	120.4	55 52.0	+39.9	121.7	55 20.0	+41.0	122.9	54 46.8	+42.2	124.1	54 12.7	+43.2	125.3	53 37.6	+44.2	126.4	53 01.5	+45.2	127.5	52 24.6	+46.1	128.5	10
11	57 01.6	37.7	119.0	56 31.9	39.0	120.3	56 01.0	40.3	121.6	55 29.0	41.4	122.9	54 55.9	42.5	124.1	54 21.8	43.6	125.2	53 46.7	44.6	126.4	53 10.7	45.5	127.4	11
12	57 39.3	36.7	117.6	57 10.9	38.0	119.0	56 41.3	39.3	120.3	56 10.4	40.6	121.6	55 38.4	41.7	122.8	55 05.4	42.8	124.0	54 31.3	43.8	125.2	53 56.2	44.9	126.3	12
13	58 16.0	35.6	116.1	57 48.9	37.1	117.5	57 20.6	38.4	118.9	56 51.0	39.6	120.2	56 20.1	40.9	121.6	55 48.2	42.0	122.8	55 15.1	43.2	124.0	54 41.1	44.2	125.2	13
14	58 51.6	34.4	114.5	58 26.0	35.9	116.0	57 59.0	37.3	117.5	57 30.6	38.8	118.9	57 01.0	40.1	120.2	56 30.2	41.3	121.5	55 58.3	42.4	122.8	55 25.3	43.5	124.0	14
15	59 26.0	+33.3	112.9	59 01.9	+34.8	114.5	58 36.3	+36.3	116.0	58 09.4	+37.7	117.4	57 41.1	+39.0	118.8	57 11.5	+40.4	120.2	56 40.7	+41.6	121.5	56 08.8	+42.7	122.8	15
16	59 59.3	31.9	111.3	59 36.7	33.6	112.9	59 12.6	35.2	114.5	58 47.1	36.6	115.9	58 20.1	38.1	117.4	57 51.9	39.4	118.8	57 22.3	40.7	120.2	56 51.5	42.0	121.5	16
17	60 31.2	30.6	109.6	60 10.3	32.3	111.2	59 47.8	33.9	112.8	59 23.7	35.6	114.4	58 58.2	37.1	115.9	58 31.3	38.5	117.4	58 03.0	39.8	118.8	57 33.5	41.1	120.2	17
18	61 01.8	29.2	107.8	60 42.6	31.0	109.5	60 21.7	32.6	111.2	59 59.3	34.3	112.8	59 35.3	35.9	114.4	59 09.8	37.4	115.9	58 42.8	38.9	117.4	58 14.6	40.1	118.8	18
19	61 31.0	27.7	106.0	61 13.6	29.6	107.8	60 54.4	31.4	109.5	60 33.6	33.1	111.1	60 11.2	34.7	112.8	59 47.2	36.2	114.4	59 21.7	37.7	115.9	58 54.7	39.2	117.4	19
20	61 58.7	+26.1	104.1	61 43.2	+28.0	105.9	61 25.8	+29.9	107.7	61 06.7	+31.7	109.4	60 45.9	+33.4	111.1	60 23.4	+35.1	112.8	59 59.4	+36.7	114.4	59 33.9	+38.2	115.9	20
21	62 24.8	24.5	102.2	62 11.2	26.5	104.1	61 55.7	28.4	105.9	61 38.4	30.3	107.7	61 19.3	32.1	109.4	60 58.5	33.9	111.1	60 36.1	35.5	112.8	60 12.1	37.0	114.4	21
22	62 49.3	22.8	100.2	62 37.7	24.8	102.1	62 24.1	26.9	104.0	62 08.7	28.8	105.8	61 51.4	30.7	107.6	61 32.4	32.4	109.4	61 11.6	34.2	111.1	60 49.1	35.9	112.8	22
23	63 12.1	20.9	98.2	63 02.5	23.1	100.1	62 51.0	25.2	102.1	62 37.5	27.2	104.0	62 22.1	29.2	105.8	62 04.8	31.1	107.6	61 45.8	32.9	109.4	61 25.0	34.6	111.1	23
24	63 33.0	19.1	96.1	63 25.6	21.3	98.1	63 16.2	23.4	100.0	63 04.7	25.6	102.0	62 51.3	27.5	103.9	62 35.9	29.5	105.8	62 18.7	31.4	107.6	61 59.6	33.3	109.4	24
25	63 52.1	+17.2*	93.9	63 46.9	+19.4	96.0	63 39.6	+21.7	98.0	63 30.3	+23.8	100.0	63 18.8	+26.0	101.9	63 05.4	+28.0	103.9	62 50.1	+29.9	105.8	62 32.9	+31.8	107.6	25
26	64 09.3	15.1*	91.8	64 06.3	17.5*	93.8	64 01.3	19.7	95.9	63 54.1	21.9	98.0	63 44.8	24.1	99.9	63 33.4	26.3	101.9	63 20.0	28.4	103.8	63 04.7	30.3	105.8	26
27	64 24.4	13.1*	89.5	64 23.8	15.4*	91.6	64 21.0	17.8*	93.7	64 16.0	20.1	95.9	64 08.9	22.4	97.8	63 59.7	24.5	99.9	63 48.4	26.7	101.9	63 35.0	28.8	103.8	27
28	64 37.5	10.9*	87.3	64 39.2	13.4*	89.4	64 38.8	15.7*	91.5	64 36.1	18.1*	93.6	64 31.3	20.4*	95.7	64 24.2	22.7	97.8	64 15.1	24.9	99.8	64 03.8	27.0	101.8	28
29	64 48.4	8.8*	85.0	64 52.6	11.2*	87.1	64 54.5	13.7*	89.2	64 54.2	16.1	91.4	64 51.7	18.4*	93.5	64 46.9	20.8*	95.6	64 40.0	23.0	97.7	64 30.8	25.3	99.8	29
30	64 57.2	+6.6*	82.6	65 03.8	+9.0*	84.8	65 08.2	+11.4*	86.9	65 10.3	+13.9*	89.1	65 10.1	+16.3*	91.2	65 07.7	+18.7*	93.4	65 03.0	+21.1	95.5	64 56.1	+23.4	97.7	30
31	65 03.8	4.4*	80.3	65 12.8	6.8*	82.4	65 19.6	9.3*	84.6	65 24.2	11.7*	86.7	65 26.4	14.2*	88.9	65 26.4	16.7*	91.1	65 24.1	19.1*	93.3	65 19.5	21.4*	95.5	31
32	65 08.2	2.1*	77.9	65 19.6	4.6*	80.0	65 28.9	7.0*	82.0	65 35.9	9.5*	84.4	65 40.6	12.0*	86.6	65 43.1	14.4*	88.8	65 43.2	16.9*	91.0	65 40.9	19.4*	93.2	32
33	65 10.3	-0.2*	75.5	65 24.2	2.2*	77.6	65 35.9	4.7*	79.8	65 45.4	7.2*	82.0	65 52.6	9.8*	84.2	65 57.5	12.3*	86.4	66 00.1	14.8*	88.7	66 00.3	17.3*	90.9	33
34	65 10.1	2.4*	73.2	65 26.4	0.0*	75.2	65 40.6	2.5*	77.4	65 52.6	4.9*	79.6	66 02.4	7.4*	81.8	66 09.8	10.0*	84.0	66 14.9	12.5*	86.3	66 17.6	15.0*	88.5	34
35	65 07.7	-4.7*	70.8	65 26.4	-2.3*	72.8	65 43.1	+0.1*	75.0	65 57.5	+2.6*	77.1	66 09.8	+5.1*	79.3	66 19.8	+7.6*	81.6	66 27.4	+10.2*	83.8	66 32.6	+12.8*	86.1	35
36	65 03.0	6.9*	68.4	65 24.1	4.5*	70.4	65 43.2	2.3*	72.6	66 00.1	0.2*	74.7	66 14.9	2.7*	76.9	66 27.4	5.2*	79.1	66 37.6	7.8*	81.4	66 45.4	10.4*	83.7	36
37	64 56.1	9.1*	66.1	65 19.5	6.8*	68.0	65 40.9	4.5*	70.1	66 00.3	2.1*	72.2	66 17.6	0.3*	74.4	66 32.6	2.9*	76.6	66 45.4	5.4*	78.9	66 55.8	8.0*	81.2	37
38	64 47.0	11.3*	63.7	65 12.7	9.1*	65.7	65 36.4	6.8*	67.7	65 58.2	4.5*	69.7	66 17.9	2.0*	71.9	66 35.5	0.4*	74.1	66 50.8	3.0*	76.3	67 03.8	5.6*	78.6	38
39	64 35.7	13.3*	61.4	65 03.6	11.3*	63.3	65 29.6	9.1*	65.3	65 53.7	6.8*	67.3	65 53.9 														39
40	64 22.4	-15.4*	59.2	64 52.3	-13.4*	61.0	65 20.5	-11.3*	62.9	65 46.9	-9.0*	64.9	66 11.5	-6.8*	66.9	66 34.0	-4.4*	69.0	66 54.3	-1.9*	71.2	67 12.5	+0.6*	73.5	40
41	64 07.0	17.5	56.9	64 38.9	15.5*	58.7	65 09.2	13.4*	60.6	65 37.9	11.4*	62.5	66 04.7	9.1*	64.5	66 29.6	6.8*	66.5	66 52.4	4.3*	68.7	67 13.1	-1.8*	70.9	41
42	63 49.5	19.3	54.8	64 23.4	17.5	56.5	64 55.8	15.6*	58.2	65 26.5	13.5*	60.1	65 55.6	11.4*	62.0	66 22.8	9.1*	64.1	66 48.1	6.8*	66.1	67 11.3	4.4*	68.3	42
43	63 30.2	21.2	52.6	64 05.9	19.4	54.3	64 40.2	17.6	56.0	65 13.0	15.6*	57.8	65 44.2	13.6*	59.6	66 13.7	11.5*	61.6	66 41.3	9.2*	63.6	67 06.9	6.8*	65.8	43
44	63 09.0	23.0	50.5	63 46.5	21.4	52.1	64 22.6	19.5	53.8	64 57.4	17.7*	55.5	65 30.6	15.7*	57.3	66 02.2	13.7*	59.2	66 32.1	11.5*	61.1	67 00.1	9.2	63.2	44

222

30°, 330° L.H.A.   LATITUDE SAME NAME AS DECLINATION

Dec.	30° Hc	d	Z	31° Hc	d	Z	32° Hc	d	Z	33° Hc	d	Z	34° Hc	d	Z	35° Hc	d	Z	36° Hc	d	Z	37° Hc	d	Z	Dec.
0	48 35.4	+45.1	130.9	47 55.8	+45.9	131.7	47 15.6	+46.6	132.5	46 34.7	+47.3	133.3	45 53.2	+48.0	134.1	45 11.2	+48.6	134.8	44 28.7	+49.2	135.5	43 45.6	+49.8	136.2	0
1	49 20.5	44.6	129.9	48 41.7	45.4	130.8	48 02.2	46.1	131.6	47 22.0	46.9	132.4	46 41.2	47.6	133.2	45 59.8	48.3	134.0	45 17.9	48.9	134.7	44 35.4	49.6	135.4	1
2	50 05.1	44.0	128.9	49 27.1	44.8	129.8	48 48.3	45.7	130.6	48 08.9	46.4	131.5	47 28.8	47.2	132.3	46 48.1	47.9	133.1	46 06.8	48.6	133.9	45 25.0	49.1	134.6	2
3	50 49.1	43.3	127.8	50 11.9	44.3	128.7	49 34.0	45.1	129.7	48 55.3	46.0	130.5	48 16.0	46.7	131.4	47 36.0	47.4	132.2	46 55.4	48.1	133.0	46 14.1	48.8	133.8	3
4	51 32.4	42.8	126.7	50 56.2	43.7	127.7	50 19.1	44.6	128.6	49 41.3	45.4	129.6	49 02.7	46.2	130.5	48 23.4	47.0	131.3	47 43.5	47.7	132.1	47 02.9	48.4	132.9	4
5	52 15.2	+42.1	125.5	51 39.9	+43.0	126.6	51 03.7	+44.0	127.6	50 26.7	+44.9	128.5	49 48.9	+45.8	129.5	49 10.4	+46.6	130.4	48 31.2	+47.3	131.2	47 51.3	+48.1	132.1	5
6	52 57.3	41.3	124.4	52 22.9	42.4	125.4	51 47.7	43.3	126.5	51 11.6	44.3	127.5	50 34.7	45.1	128.5	49 57.0	46.0	129.4	49 18.5	46.8	130.3	48 39.4	47.5	131.2	6
7	53 38.6	40.6	123.2	53 05.3	41.7	124.3	52 31.0	42.7	125.4	51 55.9	43.6	126.4	51 19.8	44.6	127.4	50 43.0	45.5	128.4	50 05.3	46.3	129.3	49 26.9	47.1	130.3	7
8	54 19.2	39.8	121.9	53 47.0	40.9	123.1	53 13.7	42.0	124.2	52 39.5	43.1	125.3	52 04.4	44.0	126.3	51 28.5	44.9	127.4	50 51.6	45.8	128.3	50 14.0	46.7	129.3	8
9	54 59.0	38.9	120.6	54 27.9	40.1	121.8	53 55.7	41.3	123.0	53 22.6	42.3	124.1	52 48.4	43.4	125.2	52 13.4	44.3	126.3	51 37.4	45.3	127.3	51 00.7	46.1	128.3	9
10	55 37.9	−38.1	119.3	55 08.0	+39.3	120.5	54 37.0	+40.4	121.7	54 04.9	+41.6	122.9	53 31.8	+42.6	124.1	52 57.7	+43.6	125.2	52 22.7	+44.6	126.2	51 46.8	+45.5	127.3	10
11	56 16.0	37.0	117.9	55 47.3	38.4	119.2	55 17.4	39.7	120.5	54 46.5	40.8	121.7	54 14.4	41.9	122.9	53 41.3	43.0	124.0	53 07.3	44.0	125.1	52 32.3	45.0	126.2	11
12	56 53.0	36.1	116.5	56 25.7	37.4	117.8	55 57.1	38.7	119.1	55 27.3	39.9	120.4	54 56.3	41.2	121.6	54 24.3	42.3	122.8	53 51.3	43.3	124.0	53 17.3	44.3	125.1	12
13	57 29.1	35.0	115.0	57 03.1	36.4	116.4	56 35.8	37.8	117.8	56 07.2	39.1	119.1	55 37.5	40.3	120.4	55 06.6	41.5	121.6	54 34.6	42.6	122.8	54 01.6	43.7	124.0	13
14	58 04.1	33.9	113.5	57 39.5	35.4	114.9	57 13.6	36.8	116.3	56 46.3	38.2	117.7	56 17.8	39.4	119.0	55 48.1	40.7	120.3	55 17.2	41.9	121.6	54 45.3	42.9	122.8	14
15	58 38.0	+32.7	111.9	58 14.9	+34.2	113.4	57 50.4	+35.7	114.9	57 24.5	+37.1	116.3	56 57.2	+38.6	117.7	56 28.8	+39.8	119.0	55 59.1	+41.0	120.3	55 28.2	+42.2	121.6	15
16	59 10.7	31.4	110.3	58 49.1	33.1	111.8	58 26.1	34.6	113.3	58 01.6	36.1	114.8	57 35.8	37.5	116.2	57 08.6	38.8	117.6	56 40.1	40.2	119.0	56 10.4	41.4	120.3	16
17	59 42.1	30.1	108.6	59 22.2	31.8	110.2	59 00.7	33.4	111.8	58 37.7	35.0	113.3	58 13.3	36.5	114.8	57 47.4	37.9	116.2	57 20.3	39.2	117.6	56 51.8	40.5	119.0	17
18	60 12.2	28.8	106.9	59 54.0	30.5	108.5	59 34.1	32.2	110.1	59 12.7	33.8	111.7	58 49.8	35.3	113.3	58 25.3	36.9	114.8	57 59.5	38.3	116.2	57 32.3	39.7	117.6	18
19	60 41.0	27.2	105.1	60 24.5	29.1	106.8	60 06.3	30.9	108.5	59 46.5	32.6	110.1	59 25.1	34.2	111.7	59 02.2	35.7	113.2	58 37.8	37.2	114.7	58 12.0	38.6	116.2	19
20	61 08.2	+25.8	103.3	60 53.6	+27.6	105.0	60 37.2	+29.5	106.7	60 19.1	+31.2	108.4	59 59.3	+32.9	110.1	59 37.9	+34.6	111.7	59 15.0	+36.2	113.2	58 50.6	+37.7	114.8	20
21	61 34.0	24.1	101.4	61 21.2	26.1	103.2	61 06.7	28.0	104.9	60 50.3	29.9	106.7	60 32.2	31.7	108.4	60 12.5	33.3	110.0	59 51.2	34.9	111.7	59 28.3	36.5	113.2	21
22	61 58.1	22.5	99.4	61 47.3	24.5	101.3	61 34.7	26.4	103.1	61 20.2	28.4	104.9	61 03.9	30.2	106.6	60 45.8	32.1	108.3	60 26.1	33.8	110.0	60 04.8	35.3	111.7	22
23	62 20.6	20.7	97.5	62 11.8	22.9	99.3	62 01.1	24.9	101.2	61 48.6	26.9	103.0	61 34.1	28.8	104.8	61 17.9	30.6	106.6	60 59.9	32.4	108.3	60 40.1	34.2	110.0	23
24	62 41.3	19.0	95.4	62 34.7	21.0	97.3	62 26.0	23.2	99.2	62 15.4	25.2	101.1	62 02.9	27.2	103.0	61 48.5	29.1	104.8	61 32.3	31.0	106.6	61 14.3	32.8	108.3	24
25	63 00.3	+17.0	93.3	62 55.7	+19.3	95.3	62 49.2	+21.4	97.2	62 40.6	+23.6	99.2	62 30.1	+25.6	101.1	62 17.6	+27.6	102.9	62 03.3	+29.5	104.8	61 47.1	+31.4	106.6	25
26	63 17.3	15.1	91.2	63 15.0	17.4	93.2	63 10.6	19.6	95.2	63 04.2	21.7	97.1	62 55.7	23.9	99.1	62 45.2	26.0	101.0	62 32.8	28.0	102.9	62 18.5	29.9	104.8	26
27	63 32.4	13.2	89.1	63 32.4	15.4	91.1	63 30.2	17.7	93.1	63 25.9	20.0	95.1	63 19.6	22.1	97.1	63 11.2	24.3	99.0	63 00.8	26.4	101.0	62 48.4	28.4	102.9	27
28	63 45.6	11.1	86.9	63 47.8	13.4	88.9	63 47.9	15.7	90.9	63 45.9	18.0	92.9	63 41.7	20.3	95.0	63 35.5	22.5	97.0	63 27.2	24.6	99.0	63 16.8	26.8	100.9	28
29	63 56.7	9.0	84.6	64 01.2	11.4	86.7	64 03.6	13.8	88.7	64 03.9	16.0	90.8	64 02.0	18.4	92.8	63 58.0	20.6	94.9	63 51.8	22.9	96.9	63 43.6	25.0	98.9	29
30	64 05.7	+6.9	82.4	64 12.6	+9.3	84.4	64 17.4	+11.6	86.5	64 19.9	+14.0	88.6	64 20.4	+16.3	90.6	64 18.6	+18.7	92.7	64 14.7	+20.9	94.8	64 08.6	+23.2	96.9	30
31	64 12.6	4.8	80.1	64 21.9	7.1	82.1	64 29.0	9.5	84.2	64 33.9	11.9	86.3	64 36.7	14.3	88.4	64 37.3	16.6	90.5	64 35.6	19.0	92.6	64 31.8	21.3	94.7	31
32	64 17.4	2.5	77.8	64 29.0	4.9	79.8	64 38.5	7.3	81.9	64 45.8	9.8	84.0	64 51.0	12.2	86.1	64 53.9	14.6	88.3	64 54.6	17.0	90.4	64 53.1	19.3	92.5	32
33	64 19.9	0.5	75.5	64 33.9	2.8	77.5	64 45.8	5.2	79.6	64 55.6	7.6	81.7	65 03.2	10.0	83.8	65 08.5	12.4	86.0	65 11.6	14.9	88.1	65 12.4	17.3	90.3	33
34	64 20.4	−1.8	73.2	64 36.7	0.6	75.2	64 51.0	2.9	77.3	65 03.2	5.3	79.4	65 13.2	7.7	81.5	65 20.9	10.3	83.6	65 26.5	12.6	85.8	65 29.7	15.2	88.0	34
35	64 18.6	−3.9	70.9	64 37.3	−1.7	72.9	64 53.9	+0.7	74.9	65 08.5	+3.1	77.0	65 20.9	+5.6	79.1	65 31.2	+7.9	81.3	65 39.1	+10.5	83.4	65 44.9	+12.9	85.7	35
36	64 14.7	6.1	68.6	64 35.6	3.8	70.5	64 54.6	−1.5	72.5	65 11.6	0.8	74.6	65 26.5	3.2	76.7	65 39.1	5.8	78.9	65 49.6	8.2	81.0	65 57.8	10.7	83.3	36
37	64 08.6	8.2	66.3	64 31.8	6.1	68.2	64 53.1	3.8	70.2	65 12.4	−1.4	72.2	65 29.7	1.0	74.2	65 44.9	3.3	76.4	65 57.8	5.9	78.6	66 08.5	8.4	80.8	37
38	64 00.4	10.4	64.0	64 25.7	8.1	65.9	64 49.3	6.0	67.8	65 11.0	3.7	69.8	65 30.7	−1.4	71.9	65 48.2	1.1	74.0	66 03.7	3.5	76.2	66 16.9	6.0	78.4	38
39	63 50.0	12.3	61.8	64 17.6	10.3	63.6	64 43.3	8.1	65.5	65 07.3	6.0	67.5	65 29.3	3.6	69.5	65 49.3	−1.3	71.6	66 07.2	1.2	73.7	66 22.9	3.7	75.9	39
40	63 37.7	−14.4	59.6	64 07.3	−12.4	61.3	64 35.2	−10.3	63.2	65 01.3	−8.1	65.1	65 25.7	−6.0	67.1	65 48.0	−3.6	69.1	66 08.4	−1.2	71.2	66 26.6	+1.3	73.4	40
41	63 23.3	16.3	57.4	63 54.9	14.5	59.1	64 24.9	12.5	60.9	64 53.2	10.4	62.8	65 19.7	8.1	64.7	65 44.4	5.9	66.7	66 07.2	3.6	68.8	66 27.9	−1.2	70.9	41
42	63 07.0	18.3	55.3	63 40.4	16.4	56.9	64 12.4	14.4	58.6	64 42.8	12.4	60.4	65 11.6	10.4	62.3	65 38.5	8.1	64.3	66 03.6	5.9	66.3	66 26.7	3.5	68.4	42
43	62 48.7	20.0	53.2	63 24.0	18.3	54.8	63 58.0	16.5	56.4	64 30.4	14.6	58.2	65 01.2	12.5	60.0	65 30.4	10.5	61.9	65 57.7	8.2	63.9	66 23.2	5.9	65.9	43
44	62 28.7	21.8	51.1	63 05.7	20.1	52.6	63 41.5	18.4	54.2	64 15.8	16.6	55.9	64 48.7	14.7	57.7	65 19.9	12.6	59.5	65 49.5	10.5	61.4	66 17.3	8.3	63.4	44

LATITUDE SAME NAME AS DECLINATION

N. Lat. { L.H.A. greater than 180° ...... Zn=Z
{ L.H.A. less than 180° ...... Zn=360°−Z

Dec.	30° Hc	d	Z	31° Hc	d	Z	32° Hc	d	Z	33° Hc	d	Z	34° Hc	d	Z	35° Hc	d	Z	36° Hc	d	Z	37° Hc	d	Z	Dec.
0	47 55.8	+44.5	129.8	47 17.1	+45.3	130.6	46 37.7	+46.1	131.4	45 57.7	+46.8	132.2	45 17.1	+47.5	132.9	44 36.0	+48.1	133.7	43 54.3	+48.8	134.4	43 12.1	+49.4	135.0	0
1	48 40.3	44.0	128.8	48 02.4	44.8	129.6	47 23.8	45.6	130.5	46 44.5	46.4	131.3	46 04.6	47.1	132.1	45 24.1	47.8	132.8	44 43.1	48.4	133.6	44 01.5	49.0	134.3	1
2	49 24.3	43.4	127.7	48 47.2	44.3	128.6	48 09.4	45.1	129.5	47 30.9	45.9	130.4	46 51.7	46.6	131.2	46 11.9	47.4	132.0	45 31.5	48.0	132.7	44 50.5	48.7	133.5	2
3	50 07.7	42.8	126.6	49 31.5	43.7	127.6	48 54.5	44.6	128.5	48 16.8	45.4	129.4	47 38.3	46.2	130.2	46 59.3	46.9	131.1	46 19.5	47.7	131.9	45 39.2	48.3	132.6	3
4	50 50.5	42.1	125.5	50 15.2	43.1	126.5	49 39.1	44.0	127.4	49 02.2	44.8	128.4	48 24.5	45.7	129.3	47 46.2	46.5	130.1	47 07.2	47.2	131.1	46 27.5	47.9	131.8	4
5	51 32.6	+41.5	124.4	50 58.3	+42.4	125.4	50 23.1	+43.4	126.4	49 47.0	+44.3	127.4	49 10.2	+45.2	128.3	48 32.7	+46.0	129.2	47 54.4	+46.8	130.1	47 15.4	+47.6	130.9	5
6	52 14.1	40.7	123.2	51 40.7	41.8	124.3	51 06.5	42.7	125.3	50 31.3	43.8	126.3	49 55.4	44.6	127.3	49 18.7	45.4	128.2	48 41.2	46.3	129.1	48 03.0	47.0	130.0	6
7	52 54.8	40.0	122.0	52 22.5	41.1	123.1	51 49.2	42.2	124.2	51 15.1	43.1	125.2	50 40.0	44.0	126.2	50 04.1	45.0	127.2	49 27.5	45.8	128.1	48 50.0	46.6	129.0	7
8	53 34.8	39.2	120.8	53 03.6	40.3	121.9	52 31.4	41.4	123.0	51 58.2	42.4	124.1	51 24.1	43.4	125.2	50 49.1	44.4	126.2	50 13.3	45.2	127.1	49 36.6	46.1	128.1	8
9	54 14.0	38.4	119.5	53 43.9	39.6	120.7	53 12.8	40.6	121.8	52 40.6	41.8	123.0	52 07.5	42.8	124.0	51 33.5	43.7	125.1	50 58.5	44.7	126.1	50 22.7	45.6	127.1	9
10	54 52.4	+37.4	118.2	54 23.5	+38.6	119.4	53 53.4	+39.9	120.6	53 22.4	+41.0	121.8	52 50.3	+42.1	122.9	52 17.2	+43.1	124.0	51 43.2	+44.1	125.0	51 08.3	+45.1	126.1	10
11	55 29.8	36.5	116.8	55 02.1	37.9	118.1	54 33.3	39.1	119.3	54 03.4	40.2	120.5	53 32.4	41.3	121.7	53 00.3	42.5	122.8	52 27.3	43.5	123.9	51 53.4	44.4	125.0	11
12	56 06.3	35.5	115.4	55 40.0	36.8	116.7	55 12.4	38.1	118.0	54 43.6	39.4	119.3	54 13.7	40.6	120.5	53 42.8	41.7	121.7	53 10.8	42.7	122.8	52 37.8	43.8	123.9	12
13	56 41.8	34.5	113.9	56 16.8	35.9	115.3	55 50.5	37.3	116.6	55 23.0	38.5	117.9	54 54.3	39.8	119.2	54 24.5	40.9	120.4	53 53.5	42.1	121.6	53 21.6	43.1	122.8	13
14	57 16.3	33.3	112.4	56 52.7	34.8	113.9	56 27.8	36.2	115.2	56 01.5	37.6	116.6	55 34.1	38.9	117.9	55 05.4	40.1	119.2	54 35.6	41.3	120.4	54 04.7	42.4	121.6	14
15	57 49.6	+32.2	110.9	57 27.5	+33.7	112.4	57 04.0	+35.2	113.8	56 39.1	+36.6	115.2	56 13.0	+37.9	116.5	55 45.5	+39.3	117.9	55 16.9	+40.5	119.1	54 47.1	+41.7	120.4	15
16	58 21.8	30.9	109.3	58 01.2	32.6	110.8	57 39.2	34.1	112.3	57 15.7	35.6	113.7	56 50.9	37.0	115.1	56 24.8	38.3	116.5	55 57.4	39.6	117.8	55 28.8	40.9	119.1	16
17	58 52.7	29.7	107.6	58 33.8	31.3	109.2	58 13.3	32.9	110.7	57 51.3	34.5	112.2	57 27.9	36.0	113.7	57 03.1	37.4	115.1	56 37.0	38.8	116.5	56 09.7	40.0	117.8	17
18	59 22.4	28.3	105.9	59 05.1	30.0	107.6	58 46.2	31.7	109.1	58 25.8	33.3	110.7	58 03.9	34.8	112.2	57 40.5	36.3	113.6	57 15.8	37.7	115.1	56 49.7	39.1	116.5	18
19	59 50.7	26.9	104.2	59 35.1	28.7	105.9	59 17.9	30.4	107.5	58 59.1	32.1	109.1	58 38.7	33.7	110.6	58 16.8	35.3	112.1	57 53.5	36.7	113.6	57 28.8	38.1	115.1	19
20	60 17.6	+25.4	102.4	60 03.8	+27.3	104.1	59 48.3	+29.1	105.8	59 31.2	+30.8	107.5	59 12.4	+32.5	109.0	58 52.1	+34.1	110.6	58 30.2	+35.7	112.1	58 06.9	+37.1	113.6	20
21	60 43.0	23.8	100.6	60 31.1	25.7	102.3	60 17.4	27.6	104.0	60 02.0	29.4	105.7	59 44.9	31.2	107.4	59 26.2	32.9	109.0	59 05.9	34.5	110.6	58 44.0	36.1	112.1	21
22	61 06.8	22.2	98.7	60 56.8	24.2	100.5	60 45.0	26.2	102.2	60 31.4	28.0	104.0	60 16.1	29.8	105.7	59 59.1	31.5	107.3	59 40.4	33.2	109.0	59 20.1	34.9	110.6	22
23	61 29.0	20.6	96.8	61 21.0	22.5	98.6	61 11.2	24.5	100.4	60 59.4	26.6	102.1	60 45.9	28.4	103.9	60 30.6	30.3	105.6	60 13.6	32.0	107.3	59 55.0	33.6	108.9	23
24	61 49.6	18.8	94.8	61 43.6	20.9	96.6	61 35.7	23.0	98.5	61 26.0	24.9	100.3	61 14.3	26.9	102.1	61 00.9	28.7	103.8	60 45.6	30.6	105.6	60 28.6	32.4	107.3	24
25	62 08.4	+17.0	92.8	62 04.5	+19.1	94.6	61 58.7	+21.2	96.5	61 50.9	+23.3	98.4	61 41.2	+25.3	100.2	61 29.6	+27.3	102.0	61 16.2	+29.2	103.8	61 01.0	+31.0	105.6	25
26	62 25.4	15.1	90.7	62 23.6	17.3	92.6	62 19.9	19.5	94.5	62 14.2	21.6	96.4	62 06.5	23.7	98.3	61 56.9	25.7	100.1	61 45.4	27.7	102.0	61 32.0	29.6	103.8	26
27	62 40.5	13.2	88.6	62 40.9	15.5	90.5	62 39.4	17.6	92.5	62 35.8	19.8	94.4	62 30.2	22.0	96.3	62 22.6	24.1	98.2	62 13.1	26.1	100.1	62 01.6	28.1	101.9	27
28	62 53.7	11.3	86.5	62 56.4	13.5	88.4	62 57.0	15.8	90.4	62 55.6	18.0	92.3	62 52.2	20.1	94.3	62 46.7	22.3	96.2	62 39.2	24.4	98.1	62 29.7	26.5	100.0	28
29	63 05.0	9.2	84.3	63 09.9	11.5	86.3	63 13.6	13.8	88.2	63 13.6	16.0	90.2	63 12.3	18.3	92.2	63 09.0	20.5	94.2	63 03.6	22.7	96.1	62 56.2	24.8	98.1	29
30	63 14.2	+7.2	82.1	63 21.4	+9.5	84.1	63 26.8	+11.8	86.0	63 29.6	+14.1	88.1	63 30.6	+16.4	90.1	63 29.5	+18.6	92.1	63 26.3	+21.0	94.1	63 21.0	+23.0	96.1	30
31	63 21.4	5.2	79.9	63 30.9	7.5	81.9	63 38.4	9.7	83.9	63 43.7	12.1	85.9	63 47.0	14.4	87.9	63 48.1	16.7	89.9	63 47.1	19.0	92.0	63 44.0	21.2	94.0	31
32	63 26.6	3.0	77.7	63 38.4	5.3	79.6	63 48.1	7.7	81.6	63 55.8	10.0	83.7	64 01.4	12.3	85.7	64 04.8	14.7	87.8	64 06.1	17.0	89.8	64 05.2	19.3	91.9	32
33	63 29.6	1.0	75.4	63 43.7	3.3	77.4	63 55.8	5.6	79.4	64 05.8	7.9	81.4	64 13.7	10.3	83.5	64 19.5	12.6	85.5	64 23.1	15.0	87.6	64 24.5	17.3	89.7	33
34	63 30.6	−1.1	73.2	63 47.0	1.1	75.1	64 01.4	3.4	77.1	64 13.7	5.8	79.1	64 24.0	8.1	81.2	64 32.1	10.5	83.3	64 38.1	12.8	85.4	64 41.8	15.3	87.5	34
35	63 29.5	−3.2	71.0	63 48.1	−1.0	72.9	64 04.8	+1.3	74.8	64 19.5	+3.6	76.8	64 32.1	+6.0	78.9	64 42.6	+8.3	81.0	64 50.9	+10.8	83.1	64 57.1	+13.1	85.2	35
36	63 26.3	5.3	68.7	63 47.1	3.1	70.6	64 06.1	−0.9	72.5	64 23.1	1.4	74.5	64 38.1	3.7	76.6	64 50.9	6.2	78.6	65 01.7	8.5	80.7	65 10.2	11.0	82.9	36
37	63 21.0	7.4	66.5	63 44.0	5.2	68.3	64 05.2	3.0	70.3	64 24.5	−0.8	72.2	64 41.8	1.6	74.2	64 57.1	3.9	76.3	65 10.2	6.4	78.4	65 21.2	8.8	80.5	37
38	63 13.6	9.4	64.3	63 38.8	7.4	66.1	64 02.2	5.2	68.0	64 23.7	2.9	69.9	64 43.4	−0.7	71.9	65 01.0	1.7	73.9	65 16.6	4.0	76.0	65 30.0	6.5	78.1	38
39	63 04.2	11.4	62.1	63 31.4	9.3	63.9	63 57.0	7.3	65.7	64 20.8	5.1	67.6	64 42.7	2.9	69.6	65 02.7	−0.6	71.6	65 20.6	1.8	73.6	65 36.5	4.2	75.7	39
40	62 52.8	−13.4	59.9	63 22.1	−11.5	61.7	63 49.7	−9.4	63.5	64 15.7	−7.3	65.3	64 39.8	−5.1	67.2	65 02.1	−2.8	69.2	65 21.9	−0.5	71.2	65 40.7	+1.9	73.3	40
41	62 39.4	15.3	57.8	63 10.6	13.4	59.5	63 40.3	11.4	61.2	64 08.4	9.4	63.0	64 34.7	7.2	64.9	64 59.3	5.1	66.8	65 21.4	2.7	68.8	65 42.6	−0.4	70.9	41
42	62 24.1	17.1	55.7	62 57.2	15.3	57.3	63 28.9	13.5	59.0	63 59.0	11.5	60.8	64 27.5	9.4	62.6	64 54.2	7.2	64.5	65 19.2	5.1	66.4	65 42.2	2.8	68.5	42
43	62 07.0	18.9	53.7	62 41.9	17.2	55.2	63 15.5	15.4	56.8	63 47.5	13.5	58.5	64 18.1	11.5	60.3	64 47.0	9.5	62.1	65 14.1	7.3	64.1	65 39.4	5.0	66.0	43
44	61 48.1	20.7	51.6	62 24.7	19.0	53.1	63 00.1	17.3	54.7	63 34.0	15.4	56.3	64 06.6	13.6	58.0	64 37.5	11.6	59.8	65 06.8	9.5	61.7	65 34.4	7.3	63.6	44

32°, 328° L.H.A. LATITUDE SAME NAME AS DECLINATION

Dec.	30° Hc	d	Z	31° Hc	d	Z	32° Hc	d	Z	33° Hc	d	Z	34° Hc	d	Z	35° Hc	d	Z	36° Hc	d	Z	37° Hc	d	Z	Dec.
0	47 15.6	+43.9	128.7	46 37.7	+44.8	129.5	45 59.2	+45.6	130.3	45 20.1	+46.3	131.1	44 40.4	+47.0	131.8	44 00.1	+47.7	132.5	43 19.3	+48.3	133.2	42 37.9	+48.9	133.9	0
1	47 59.5	43.4	127.7	47 22.5	44.1	128.5	46 44.8	45.0	129.4	46 06.4	45.8	130.2	45 27.4	46.5	130.9	44 47.8	47.2	131.7	44 07.6	47.9	132.4	43 26.8	48.6	133.1	1
2	48 42.9	42.8	126.6	48 06.7	43.7	127.5	47 29.8	44.6	128.4	46 52.2	45.4	129.2	46 13.9	46.2	130.0	45 35.0	46.9	130.8	44 55.5	47.6	131.6	44 15.4	48.2	132.3	2
3	49 25.7	42.2	125.5	48 50.4	43.1	126.5	48 14.4	44.0	127.4	47 37.6	44.8	128.3	47 00.1	45.6	129.1	46 21.9	46.4	129.9	45 43.1	47.1	130.7	45 03.6	47.9	131.5	3
4	50 07.9	41.6	124.4	49 33.5	42.6	125.4	48 58.4	43.4	126.4	48 22.4	44.3	127.3	47 45.7	45.2	128.1	47 08.3	45.7	128.9	46 30.2	46.7	129.8	45 51.5	47.4	130.6	4
5	50 49.5	+40.9	123.3	50 16.1	+41.9	124.3	49 41.8	+42.9	125.3	49 06.7	+43.8	126.2	48 30.9	+44.6	127.2	47 54.3	+45.4	128.0	47 16.9	+46.3	128.8	46 38.9	+47.0	129.7	5
6	51 30.4	40.1	122.1	50 58.0	41.2	123.2	50 24.7	42.1	124.2	49 50.5	43.2	125.2	49 15.5	44.1	126.1	48 39.7	45.0	127.1	48 03.2	45.8	128.0	47 25.9	46.6	128.8	6
7	52 10.5	39.4	120.9	51 39.2	40.5	122.0	51 06.9	41.5	123.1	50 33.7	42.5	124.1	49 59.6	43.5	125.1	49 24.7	44.4	126.1	48 49.0	45.3	127.0	48 12.5	46.1	127.9	7
8	52 49.9	38.7	119.7	52 19.7	39.8	120.8	51 48.4	40.9	121.9	51 16.2	41.9	123.0	50 43.1	42.9	124.0	50 09.1	43.9	125.0	49 34.3	44.7	126.0	48 58.6	45.6	126.9	8
9	53 28.6	37.7	118.4	52 59.5	38.9	119.6	52 29.3	40.1	120.7	51 58.1	41.2	121.8	51 26.0	42.2	122.9	50 53.0	43.2	123.9	50 19.0	44.2	124.9	49 44.2	45.1	125.9	9
10	54 06.3	+36.9	117.1	53 38.4	+38.2	118.3	53 09.4	+39.3	119.5	52 39.3	+40.5	120.6	52 08.2	+41.6	121.8	51 36.2	+42.6	122.8	51 03.2	+43.6	123.9	50 29.3	+44.5	124.9	10
11	54 43.2	36.0	115.8	54 16.6	37.2	117.0	53 48.7	38.5	118.2	53 19.8	39.7	119.4	52 49.8	40.8	120.6	52 18.8	41.9	121.7	51 46.8	42.9	122.8	51 13.8	43.9	123.8	11
12	55 19.2	34.9	114.4	54 53.8	36.3	115.7	54 27.2	37.6	116.9	53 59.5	38.8	118.2	53 30.6	40.1	119.4	53 00.7	41.1	120.5	52 29.7	42.3	121.6	51 57.7	43.3	122.7	12
13	55 54.1	34.0	113.0	55 30.1	35.4	114.3	55 04.8	36.7	115.6	54 38.3	38.0	116.8	54 10.7	39.2	118.1	53 41.8	40.5	119.3	53 12.0	41.5	120.5	52 41.0	42.6	121.6	13
14	56 28.1	32.8	111.4	56 05.5	34.3	112.8	55 41.5	35.8	114.2	55 16.3	37.1	115.5	54 49.9	38.3	116.8	54 22.3	39.6	118.0	53 53.5	40.8	119.2	53 23.6	41.9	120.4	14
15	57 00.9	+31.7	109.9	56 39.8	+33.2	111.3	56 17.3	+34.6	112.7	55 53.4	+36.1	114.1	55 28.2	+37.5	115.4	55 01.9	+38.7	116.7	54 34.3	+40.0	118.0	54 05.5	+41.2	119.2	15
16	57 32.6	30.5	108.3	57 13.0	32.1	109.8	56 51.9	33.6	111.3	56 29.5	35.1	112.7	56 05.7	36.5	114.1	55 40.6	37.8	115.4	55 14.3	39.1	116.7	54 46.7	40.4	118.0	16
17	58 03.1	29.2	106.7	57 45.1	30.8	108.2	57 25.5	32.5	109.7	57 04.6	34.0	111.3	56 42.2	35.4	112.6	56 18.4	36.9	114.0	55 53.4	38.2	115.4	55 27.1	39.5	116.7	17
18	58 32.3	27.9	105.1	58 15.9	29.7	106.6	57 58.0	31.3	108.2	57 38.6	32.8	109.7	57 17.6	34.4	111.1	56 55.3	35.9	112.6	56 31.6	37.3	114.0	56 06.6	38.6	115.3	18
19	59 00.2	26.6	103.4	58 45.6	28.2	105.0	58 29.3	30.0	106.5	58 11.4	31.7	108.1	57 52.0	33.3	109.6	57 31.2	34.7	111.1	57 08.9	36.2	112.5	56 45.2	37.6	113.9	19
20	59 26.8	+25.0	101.6	59 13.8	+26.9	103.3	58 59.3	+28.6	104.9	58 43.1	+30.3	106.5	58 25.3	+32.0	108.0	58 05.9	+33.7	109.6	57 45.1	+35.2	111.1	57 22.8	+36.7	112.5	20
21	59 51.8	23.6	99.8	59 40.7	25.5	101.5	59 27.9	27.3	103.2	59 13.4	29.1	104.8	58 57.3	30.8	106.4	58 39.6	32.4	108.0	58 20.3	34.0	109.5	57 59.5	35.6	111.0	21
22	60 15.4	22.0	98.0	60 06.2	23.9	99.7	59 55.2	25.8	101.4	59 42.5	27.7	103.1	59 28.1	29.4	104.7	59 12.0	31.2	106.4	58 54.3	32.9	107.9	58 35.1	34.4	109.5	22
23	60 37.4	20.4	96.1	60 30.1	22.4	97.8	60 21.0	24.4	99.6	60 10.2	26.2	101.3	59 57.5	28.1	103.0	59 43.2	29.8	104.7	59 27.2	31.6	106.3	59 09.5	33.3	107.9	23
24	60 57.8	18.7	94.1	60 52.5	20.7	95.9	60 45.4	22.7	97.7	60 36.4	24.7	99.5	60 25.6	26.6	101.2	60 13.0	28.5	102.9	59 58.8	30.2	104.6	59 42.8	32.0	106.3	24
25	61 16.5	+16.9	92.2	61 13.2	+19.0	94.0	61 08.1	+21.1	95.8	61 01.1	+23.1	97.6	60 52.2	+25.1	99.4	60 41.5	+27.0	101.1	60 29.0	+28.9	102.9	60 14.8	+30.6	104.6	25
26	61 33.4	15.1	90.2	61 32.2	17.3	92.0	61 29.2	19.3	93.9	61 24.2	21.4	95.7	61 17.3	23.4	97.5	61 08.5	25.4	99.3	60 57.9	27.3	101.1	60 45.4	29.3	102.8	26
27	61 48.5	13.3	88.1	61 49.5	15.5	90.0	61 48.5	17.6	91.9	61 45.6	19.7	93.7	61 40.7	21.8	95.6	61 33.9	23.9	97.4	61 25.2	25.9	99.2	61 14.7	27.7	101.0	27
28	62 01.8	11.5	86.1	62 05.0	13.6	87.9	62 06.1	15.8	89.8	62 05.3	18.0	91.7	62 02.5	20.1	93.6	61 57.8	22.1	95.5	61 51.1	24.2	97.3	61 42.4	26.3	99.2	28
29	62 13.3	9.5*	84.0	62 18.6	11.7	85.9	62 21.9	13.9	87.8	62 23.3	16.1	89.7	62 22.6	18.3	91.6	62 19.9	20.5	93.5	62 15.3	22.5	95.4	62 08.7	24.6	97.3	29
30	62 22.8	+7.5*	81.8	62 30.3	+9.7	83.7	62 35.8	+12.0	85.7	62 39.4	+14.2	87.6	62 40.9	+16.4	89.5	62 40.4	+18.6	91.5	62 37.8	+20.8	93.4	62 33.3	+22.9	95.3	30
31	62 30.3	5.5	79.7	62 40.0	7.8	81.6	62 47.8	10.0*	83.5	62 53.6	12.2	85.5	62 57.3	14.5	87.4	62 59.0	16.7	89.4	62 58.6	18.9	91.3	62 56.2	21.1	93.3	31
32	62 35.8	3.6*	77.5	62 47.8	5.8*	79.4	62 57.8	8.0*	81.4	63 05.8	10.3*	83.3	63 11.8	12.5*	85.3	63 15.7	14.8	87.3	63 17.5	17.1	89.2	63 17.3	19.3	91.2	32
33	62 39.4	1.5*	75.4	62 53.6	3.7*	77.3	63 05.8	6.0*	79.2	63 16.1	8.2*	81.1	63 24.3	10.5*	83.1	63 30.5	12.8*	85.1	63 34.6	15.1*	87.1	63 36.6	17.4*	89.1	33
34	62 40.9	-0.5*	73.2	62 57.3	1.7*	75.1	63 11.8	3.9*	77.0	63 24.3	6.2*	78.9	63 34.8	8.5*	80.9	63 43.3	10.8*	82.9	63 49.7	13.1*	84.9	63 54.0	15.4*	86.9	34
35	62 40.4	-2.6*	71.0	62 59.0	-0.4*	72.9	63 15.7	+1.8*	74.8	63 30.5	+4.1*	76.7	63 43.3	+6.4*	78.7	63 54.1	+8.7*	80.7	64 02.8	+11.0*	82.7	64 09.4	+13.3*	84.7	35
36	62 37.8	4.5*	68.8	62 58.6	2.4*	70.7	63 17.5	-0.2*	72.5	63 34.6	2.0*	74.5	63 49.7	4.3*	76.4	64 02.8	6.6*	78.4	64 13.8	8.9*	80.4	64 22.7	11.3*	82.5	36
37	62 33.3	6.6*	66.7	62 56.2	4.5*	68.5	63 17.3	2.3*	70.3	63 36.6	-0.1*	72.2	63 54.0	2.1*	74.1	64 09.4	4.4*	76.1	64 22.7	6.8*	78.2	64 34.0	9.1*	80.2	37
38	62 26.7	8.5	64.5	62 51.7	6.5*	66.3	63 15.0	4.4*	68.1	63 36.5	2.3*	70.0	63 56.1	0.0*	71.9	64 13.8	2.3*	73.8	64 29.5	4.6*	75.8	64 43.1	7.0*	77.9	38
39	62 18.2	10.5	62.4	62 45.2	8.5	64.1	63 10.6	6.5*	65.9	63 34.2	4.3*	67.7	63 56.1	-2.2*	69.6	64 16.1	0.1*	71.5	64 34.1	2.4*	73.5	64 50.1	4.7*	75.6	39
40	62 07.7	-12.3	60.3	62 36.7	-10.4	61.9	63 04.1	-8.4*	63.7	63 29.9	-6.4*	65.5	63 53.9	-4.2*	67.3	64 16.2	-2.1*	69.2	64 36.5	+0.2*	71.2	64 54.8	+2.5*	73.2	40
41	61 55.4	14.3	58.2	62 26.3	12.4	59.8	62 55.7	10.5*	61.5	63 23.5	8.5*	63.2	63 49.7	6.4*	65.1	64 14.1	4.3*	66.9	64 36.7	-2.0*	68.9	64 57.3	0.3*	70.9	41
42	61 41.1	16.1	56.1	62 13.9	14.3	57.7	62 45.2	12.4	59.3	63 15.0	10.5	61.0	63 43.3	8.5*	62.8	64 09.8	6.3*	64.6	64 34.6	4.2*	66.5	64 57.6	2.0*	68.5	42
43	61 25.0	17.8	54.1	61 59.6	16.1	55.6	62 32.8	14.4	57.2	63 04.5	12.4*	58.9	63 34.8	10.5*	60.6	64 03.5	8.5*	62.4	64 30.4	6.4*	64.2	64 55.6	4.2*	66.1	43
44	61 07.2	19.5	52.1	61 43.5	18.0	53.6	62 18.4	16.2	55.1	62 52.1	14.5	56.7	63 24.3	12.6*	58.4	63 55.0	10.6*	60.1	64 24.0	8.5*	61.9	64 51.4	6.4*	63.8	44

LATITUDE SAME NAME AS DECLINATION

N. Lat. { L.H.A. greater than 180° ...... Zn=Z ; L.H.A. less than 180° ...... Zn=360°−Z }

Dec.	30° Hc	d	Z	31° Hc	d	Z	32° Hc	d	Z	33° Hc	d	Z	34° Hc	d	Z	35° Hc	d	Z	36° Hc	d	Z	37° Hc	d	Z	Dec.
0	46 34.7	+43.4	127.6	45 57.7	+44.2	128.4	45 20.1	+45.0	129.2	44 41.9	+45.7	130.0	44 03.0	+46.5	130.7	43 23.6	+47.1	131.5	42 43.6	+47.8	132.1	42 03.1	+48.4	132.8	0
1	47 18.1	42.8	126.6	46 41.9	43.7	127.4	46 05.1	44.5	128.3	45 27.6	45.3	129.1	44 49.5	46.1	129.8	44 10.7	46.8	130.6	43 31.4	47.5	131.3	42 51.5	48.1	132.0	1
2	48 00.9	42.2	125.5	47 25.6	43.2	126.4	46 49.6	44.0	127.3	46 12.9	44.9	128.1	45 35.6	45.6	128.9	44 57.5	46.4	129.7	44 18.9	47.1	130.5	43 39.6	47.8	131.2	2
3	48 43.1	41.7	124.5	48 08.8	42.6	125.4	47 33.6	43.5	126.3	46 57.8	44.3	127.2	46 21.2	45.1	128.0	45 43.9	45.9	128.8	45 06.0	46.6	129.6	44 27.4	47.4	130.4	3
4	49 24.8	41.0	123.4	48 51.4	41.9	124.3	48 17.1	42.9	125.3	47 42.1	43.8	126.2	47 06.3	44.5	127.0	46 29.8	45.5	127.9	45 52.6	46.3	128.7	45 14.8	47.0	129.5	4
5	50 05.8	+40.3	122.2	49 33.3	+41.4	123.2	49 00.0	+42.3	124.2	48 25.9	+43.2	125.1	47 50.9	+44.2	126.1	47 15.3	+44.9	126.9	46 38.9	+45.7	127.8	46 01.8	+46.5	128.6	5
6	50 46.1	39.6	121.1	50 14.7	40.6	122.1	49 42.3	41.7	123.1	49 09.1	42.7	124.1	48 35.1	43.5	125.0	48 00.2	44.5	125.9	47 24.6	45.3	126.8	46 48.3	46.1	127.7	6
7	51 25.7	38.9	119.9	50 55.3	40.0	121.0	50 24.0	41.0	122.0	49 51.8	42.0	123.0	49 18.6	43.0	124.0	48 44.7	43.9	124.9	48 09.9	44.8	125.9	47 34.4	45.6	126.7	7
8	52 04.6	38.0	118.7	51 35.3	39.2	119.8	51 05.0	40.3	120.8	50 33.8	41.3	121.9	50 01.6	42.4	122.9	49 28.6	43.3	123.9	48 54.7	44.3	124.9	48 20.0	45.1	125.8	8
9	52 42.6	37.3	117.4	52 14.5	38.4	118.5	51 45.3	39.6	119.7	51 15.1	40.7	120.7	50 44.0	41.7	121.8	50 11.9	42.7	122.8	49 39.0	43.6	123.8	49 05.1	44.6	124.8	9
10	53 19.9	+36.3	116.1	52 52.9	+37.6	117.3	52 24.9	+38.8	118.4	51 55.8	+39.9	119.6	51 25.7	+41.0	120.7	50 54.6	+42.1	121.7	50 22.6	+43.1	122.7	49 49.7	+44.0	123.7	10
11	53 56.2	35.5	114.7	53 30.5	36.7	116.0	53 03.7	37.9	117.2	52 35.7	39.2	118.3	52 06.7	40.3	119.5	51 36.7	41.4	120.6	51 05.7	42.4	121.6	50 33.7	43.5	122.7	11
12	54 31.7	34.4	113.4	54 07.2	35.9	114.6	53 41.6	37.1	115.9	53 14.9	38.3	117.1	52 47.0	39.6	118.3	52 18.1	40.7	119.4	51 48.1	41.8	120.5	51 17.2	42.8	121.6	12
13	55 06.1	33.4	111.9	54 43.1	34.8	113.3	54 18.7	36.2	114.5	53 53.2	37.5	115.8	53 26.6	38.7	117.0	52 58.8	39.9	118.2	52 29.9	41.0	119.3	52 00.0	41.4	120.5	13
14	55 39.5	32.4	110.5	55 17.9	33.8	111.8	54 54.9	35.3	113.2	54 30.7	36.6	114.5	54 05.3	37.8	115.7	53 38.7	39.1	116.9	53 10.9	40.3	118.1	52 42.1	41.4	119.3	14
15	56 11.9	+31.3	109.0	55 51.7	+32.8	110.4	55 30.2	+34.2	111.7	55 07.3	+35.6	113.1	54 43.1	+37.0	114.4	54 17.8	+38.2	115.7	53 51.2	+39.5	116.9	53 23.5	+40.7	118.1	15
16	56 43.2	30.0	107.4	56 24.5	31.6	108.9	56 04.4	33.1	110.3	55 42.9	34.6	111.7	55 20.1	36.0	113.0	54 56.0	37.3	114.3	54 30.7	38.6	115.6	54 04.2	39.8	116.9	16
17	57 13.2	28.9	105.8	56 56.1	30.5	107.3	56 37.5	32.0	108.8	56 17.5	33.5	110.2	55 56.1	35.0	111.6	55 33.3	36.4	112.9	55 09.3	37.8	114.3	54 44.0	39.1	115.6	17
18	57 42.1	27.5	104.2	57 26.6	29.2	105.7	57 09.5	30.9	107.2	56 51.0	32.4	108.7	56 31.1	33.9	110.1	56 09.7	35.4	111.5	55 47.1	36.8	112.9	55 23.1	38.1	114.2	18
19	58 09.6	26.2	102.5	57 55.8	27.9	104.1	57 40.4	29.6	105.6	57 23.4	31.3	107.1	57 05.0	32.8	108.6	56 45.1	34.4	110.1	56 23.9	35.7	111.5	56 01.2	37.2	112.9	19
20	58 35.8	+24.8	100.8	58 23.7	+26.6	102.4	58 10.0	+28.3	104.0	57 54.7	+30.0	105.5	57 37.8	+31.7	107.1	57 19.5	+33.2	108.6	56 59.6	+34.8	110.0	56 38.4	+36.2	111.5	20
21	59 00.6	23.3	99.1	58 50.3	25.1	100.7	58 38.3	27.0	102.3	58 24.7	28.7	103.9	58 09.5	30.4	105.5	57 52.7	32.0	107.0	57 34.4	33.6	108.5	57 14.6	35.1	110.0	21
22	59 23.9	21.8	97.3	59 15.4	23.7	98.9	59 05.3	25.5	100.6	58 53.4	27.4	102.2	58 39.9	29.1	103.8	58 24.7	30.8	105.4	58 08.0	32.5	107.0	57 49.7	34.1	108.5	22
23	59 45.7	20.2	95.4	59 39.1	22.2	97.1	59 30.8	24.1	98.8	59 20.8	25.9	100.5	59 09.0	27.7	102.1	58 55.5	29.6	103.8	58 40.5	31.2	105.4	58 23.8	32.9	106.9	23
24	60 05.9	18.6	93.5	60 01.3	20.6	95.3	59 54.9	22.5	97.0	59 46.7	24.5	98.7	59 36.7	26.4	100.4	59 25.1	28.1	102.1	59 11.7	29.9	103.8	58 56.7	31.6	105.3	24
25	60 24.5	+16.9	91.6	60 21.9	+18.9	93.4	60 17.4	+21.0	95.1	60 11.2	+22.9	96.9	60 03.1	+24.8	98.6	59 53.2	+26.7	100.3	59 41.6	+28.6	102.0	59 28.3	+30.3	103.7	25
26	60 41.4	15.2	89.6	60 40.8	17.3	91.5	60 38.4	19.3	93.2	60 34.1	21.3	95.0	60 27.9	23.3	96.8	60 19.9	25.3	98.5	60 10.2	27.1	100.2	59 58.6	29.0	101.9	26
27	60 56.6	13.4	87.7	60 58.1	15.5	89.5	60 57.7	17.6	91.3	60 55.4	19.6	93.1	60 51.2	21.7	94.9	60 45.2	23.6	96.7	60 37.3	25.6	98.4	60 27.6	27.5	100.2	27
28	61 10.0	11.6	85.7	61 13.6	13.7	87.5	61 15.3	15.8	89.3	61 15.0	17.9	91.1	61 12.9	20.0	93.0	61 08.8	22.1	94.8	61 02.9	24.0	96.6	60 55.1	26.0	98.4	28
29	61 21.6	9.7	83.6	61 27.3	11.9	85.5	61 31.1	14.0	87.3	61 32.9	16.2	89.1	61 32.9	18.2	91.0	61 30.9	20.3	92.8	61 26.9	22.5	94.7	61 21.1	24.4	96.5	29
30	61 31.3	+7.9	81.6	61 39.2	+10.0	83.4	61 45.1	+12.0	85.3	61 49.1	+14.3	87.1	61 51.1	+16.5	89.0	61 51.2	+18.6	90.9	61 49.4	+20.7	92.7	61 45.5	+22.8	94.6	30
31	61 39.2	5.9	79.5	61 49.2	8.1	81.3	61 57.3	10.2	83.2	62 03.4	12.5	85.1	62 07.6	14.6	86.9	62 09.8	16.8	88.8	62 10.1	18.9	90.7	62 08.3	21.1	92.6	31
32	61 45.1	4.0	77.4	61 57.3	6.1	79.2	62 07.5	8.4	81.1	62 15.9	10.5	83.0	62 22.2	12.8	84.9	62 26.6	15.0	86.8	62 29.0	17.1	88.7	62 29.4	19.3	90.6	32
33	61 49.1	2.0	75.3	62 03.4	4.1	77.1	62 15.9	6.3	79.0	62 26.4	8.6	80.8	62 35.0	10.8	82.7	62 41.6	13.0	84.7	62 46.1	15.3	86.6	62 48.7	17.4	88.5	33
34	61 51.1	+0.1	73.2	62 07.6	2.2	75.0	62 22.2	4.4	76.8	62 35.0	6.6	78.7	62 45.8	8.8	80.6	62 54.6	11.0	82.5	63 01.4	13.3	84.5	63 06.1	15.6	86.4	34
35	61 51.2	-1.8	71.0	62 09.8	+0.3	72.8	62 26.6	+2.4	74.7	62 41.6	+4.5	76.5	62 54.6	+6.8	78.4	63 05.6	+9.1	80.4	63 14.7	+11.3	82.3	63 21.7	+13.5	84.3	35
36	61 49.4	3.9	68.9	62 10.1	-1.8	70.7	62 29.0	0.4	72.5	62 46.1	2.6	74.2	63 01.4	4.7	76.2	63 14.7	7.0	78.2	63 26.0	9.2	80.1	63 35.2	11.6	82.1	36
37	61 45.5	5.7	66.8	62 08.3	3.7	68.6	62 29.4	-1.6	70.3	62 48.7	0.5	72.2	63 06.1	2.7	74.0	63 21.7	4.9	76.0	63 35.2	7.2	77.9	63 46.8	9.5	79.9	37
38	61 39.8	7.7	64.7	62 04.6	5.7	66.4	62 27.8	3.7	68.2	62 49.2	-1.5	70.0	63 08.8	0.7	71.8	63 26.6	2.8	73.7	63 42.4	5.1	75.7	63 56.3	7.4	77.7	38
39	61 32.1	9.6	62.6	61 58.9	7.6	64.3	62 24.1	5.6	66.0	62 47.7	3.6	67.8	63 09.5	-1.5	69.6	63 29.4	0.8	71.5	63 47.5	3.0	73.4	64 03.7	5.2	75.4	39
40	61 22.5	-11.4	60.6	61 51.3	-9.6	62.2	62 18.5	-7.6	63.9	62 44.1	-5.6	65.6	63 08.0	-3.5	67.4	63 30.2	-1.4	69.3	63 50.5	+0.9	71.2	64 08.9	+3.1	73.1	40
41	61 11.1	13.2	58.5	61 41.7	11.4	60.1	62 10.9	9.5	61.7	62 38.5	7.5	63.4	63 04.5	5.5	65.2	63 28.8	3.4	67.0	63 51.4	1.3	68.9	64 12.0	1.0	70.8	41
42	60 57.9	15.1	56.5	61 30.3	13.3	58.0	62 01.4	11.5	59.6	62 31.0	9.6	61.3	62 59.0	7.6	63.0	63 25.4	5.5	64.8	63 50.1	3.4	66.6	64 13.0	1.2	68.5	42
43	60 42.8	16.7	54.5	61 17.0	15.0	56.0	61 49.9	13.3	57.5	62 21.4	11.5	59.2	62 51.4	9.5	60.8	63 19.9	7.6	62.6	63 46.7	5.5	64.4	64 11.8	3.4	66.2	43
44	60 26.1	18.5	52.6	61 02.0	16.9	54.0	61 36.6	15.2	55.5	62 09.9	13.4	57.0	62 41.9	11.6	58.7	63 12.3	9.6	60.4	63 41.2	7.6	62.1	64 08.4	5.5	63.9	44

Each cell is given as **Hc   d   Z**.

Dec.	30°	31°	32°	33°	34°	35°	36°	37°	Dec.
45	60 07.6 –20.1 50.6	60 45.1 –18.5 52.0	61 21.4 –16.9 53.5	61 56.5 –15.2 55.0	62 30.3 –13.4 56.5	63 02.7 –11.6 58.2	63 33.6 –9.7 59.9	64 02.9 –7.7 61.6	45
46	59 47.5 21.6 48.8	60 26.6 20.2 50.1	61 04.5 18.6 51.5	61 41.3 17.0 52.9	62 16.9 15.4 54.4	62 51.1 13.6 56.0	63 23.9 11.7 57.7	63 55.2 9.7 59.4	46
47	59 25.9 23.2 46.9	60 06.4 21.8 48.2	60 45.9 20.4 49.5	61 24.3 18.8 50.9	62 01.5 17.2 52.4	62 37.5 15.4 54.2	63 12.2 13.7 55.5	63 45.5 11.8 57.1	47
48	59 02.7 24.7 45.1	59 44.6 23.4 46.3	60 25.5 21.9 47.6	61 05.5 20.5 48.9	61 44.3 18.9 50.3	62 22.1 17.4 51.8	62 58.5 15.6 53.3	63 33.7 13.8 54.9	48
49	58 38.0 26.0 43.4	59 21.2 24.8 44.5	60 03.6 23.5 45.7	60 45.0 22.1 47.0	61 25.4 20.6 48.3	62 04.7 19.1 49.8	62 42.9 17.4 51.2	63 19.9 15.8 52.8	49
50	58 12.0 –27.5 41.6	58 56.4 –26.2 42.7	59 40.1 –25.0 43.9	60 22.9 –23.7 45.1	61 04.8 –22.3 46.4	61 45.6 –20.8 47.8	62 25.5 –19.3 49.2	63 04.1 –17.6 50.6	50
51	57 44.5 28.7 40.0	58 30.2 27.6 41.0	59 15.1 26.5 42.1	59 59.2 25.2 43.3	60 42.5 23.9 44.5	61 24.8 22.5 45.8	62 06.2 21.1 47.1	62 46.5 19.5 48.5	51
52	57 15.8 29.9 38.3	58 02.6 29.0 39.3	58 48.6 27.8 40.4	59 34.0 26.7 41.5	60 18.6 25.5 42.6	61 02.3 24.1 43.9	61 45.1 22.7 45.1	62 27.0 21.3 46.5	52
53	56 45.9 31.2 36.7	57 33.6 30.1 37.7	58 20.7 29.1 38.7	59 07.3 28.0 39.7	59 53.1 26.8 40.8	60 38.2 25.7 42.0	61 22.4 24.4 43.1	62 05.7 23.0 44.5	53
54	56 14.7 32.3 35.2	57 03.5 31.4 36.1	57 51.7 30.4 37.0	58 39.3 29.4 38.0	59 26.3 28.3 39.0	60 12.5 27.1 40.2	60 58.0 25.9 41.3	61 42.7 24.6 42.5	54
55	55 42.4 –33.3 33.7	56 32.1 –32.5 34.5	57 21.3 –31.6 35.4	58 09.9 –30.6 36.3	58 58.0 –29.6 37.3	59 45.4 –28.6 38.4	60 32.1 –27.4 39.5	61 18.1 –26.2 40.6	55
56	55 09.1 34.4 32.2	55 59.6 33.5 33.0	56 49.7 32.7 33.8	57 39.3 31.8 34.7	58 28.4 30.9 35.6	59 16.8 29.8 36.6	60 04.7 28.8 37.7	60 51.9 27.7 38.7	56
57	54 34.7 35.3 30.8	55 26.1 34.6 31.5	56 17.0 33.8 32.3	57 07.5 33.0 33.1	57 57.5 32.1 34.0	58 47.0 31.2 35.0	59 35.9 30.2 35.9	60 24.2 29.2 36.9	57
58	53 59.4 36.3 29.4	54 51.5 35.6 30.1	55 43.2 34.9 30.8	56 34.5 34.1 31.6	57 25.4 33.3 32.4	58 15.8 32.4 33.3	59 05.7 31.5 34.3	59 55.0 30.4 35.2	58
59	53 23.1 37.2 28.1	54 15.9 36.5 28.7	55 08.3 35.8 29.4	56 00.4 35.1 30.1	56 52.1 34.3 30.9	57 43.4 33.5 31.7	58 34.2 32.7 32.6	59 24.6 31.8 33.4	59
60	52 45.9 –38.0 26.7	53 39.4 –37.4 27.4	54 32.5 –36.7 28.0	55 25.3 –36.1 28.7	56 17.8 –35.4 29.4	57 09.9 –34.7 30.2	58 01.5 –33.8 31.0	58 52.8 –33.0 31.8	60
61	52 07.9 38.7 25.5	53 02.0 38.2 26.0	53 55.8 37.7 26.6	54 49.2 37.0 27.3	55 42.4 36.4 27.9	56 35.2 35.7 28.7	57 27.7 35.0 29.4	58 19.8 34.2 30.2	61
62	51 29.2 39.6 24.2	52 23.8 39.1 24.8	53 18.1 38.5 25.3	54 12.2 37.9 25.9	55 06.0 37.3 26.5	55 59.5 36.6 27.2	56 52.7 36.0 27.9	57 45.6 35.3 28.6	62
63	50 49.6 40.2 23.0	51 44.7 39.8 23.5	52 39.6 39.3 24.1	53 34.3 38.8 24.6	54 28.7 38.2 25.2	55 22.9 37.6 25.8	56 16.8 37.0 26.5	57 10.3 36.3 27.1	63
64	50 09.4 41.0 21.9	51 04.9 40.5 22.3	52 00.3 40.0 22.8	52 55.5 39.5 23.3	53 50.5 39.0 23.9	54 45.3 38.5 24.5	55 39.8 38.0 25.1	56 34.0 37.3 25.7	64
65	49 28.4 –41.6 20.7	50 24.4 –41.1 21.2	51 20.3 –40.7 21.6	52 16.0 –40.3 22.1	53 11.5 –39.8 22.6	54 06.8 –39.3 23.2	55 01.8 –38.8 23.7	55 56.7 –38.3 24.3	65
66	48 46.8 42.2 19.6	49 43.3 41.9 20.0	50 39.6 41.5 20.5	51 35.7 41.0 20.9	52 31.7 40.6 21.4	53 27.5 40.1 21.9	54 23.0 39.6 22.4	55 18.4 39.1 22.9	66
67	48 04.6 42.8 18.6	49 01.4 42.4 18.9	49 58.1 42.0 19.3	50 54.7 41.7 19.7	51 51.1 41.3 20.2	52 47.3 40.8 20.7	53 43.4 40.3 21.1	54 39.3 40.0 21.6	67
68	47 21.8 43.3 17.5	48 19.0 43.0 17.9	49 16.1 42.6 18.2	50 13.0 42.3 18.6	51 09.8 42.0 19.0	52 06.5 41.6 19.4	53 03.0 41.2 19.9	53 59.3 40.7 20.3	68
69	46 38.5 43.8 16.5	47 36.0 43.6 16.8	48 33.5 43.0 17.1	49 30.7 43.0 17.5	50 27.8 42.6 17.9	51 24.9 42.3 18.3	52 21.8 41.9 18.7	53 18.6 41.5 19.1	69
70	45 54.7 –44.4 15.5	46 52.4 –44.1 15.8	47 50.1 –43.5 16.1	48 47.7 –43.5 16.4	49 45.2 –43.2 16.8	50 42.6 –42.9 17.2	51 39.9 –42.6 17.5	52 37.1 –42.2 17.9	70
71	45 10.3 44.8 14.6	46 08.3 44.5 14.8	47 06.3 44.3 15.1	48 04.2 44.1 15.4	49 02.0 43.8 15.7	49 59.7 43.5 16.0	50 57.3 43.1 16.4	51 54.9 42.9 16.7	71
72	44 25.5 45.3 13.7	45 23.8 45.1 13.9	46 22.0 44.8 14.1	47 20.1 44.5 14.4	48 18.2 44.3 14.7	49 16.2 44.0 15.0	50 14.2 43.8 15.3	51 12.0 43.5 15.6	72
73	43 40.2 45.7 12.7	44 38.7 45.5 12.9	45 37.2 45.3 13.2	46 35.6 45.1 13.4	47 33.9 44.8 13.7	48 32.2 44.6 14.0	49 30.4 44.4 14.2	50 28.5 44.1 14.5	73
74	42 54.5 46.1 11.8	43 53.2 45.9 12.0	44 51.9 45.7 12.2	45 50.5 45.5 12.4	46 49.1 45.4 12.7	47 47.6 45.1 12.9	48 46.0 44.9 13.2	49 44.4 44.6 13.4	74
75	42 08.4 –46.5 11.0	43 07.3 –46.3 11.1	44 06.2 –46.1 11.3	45 05.0 –46.0 11.5	46 03.7 –45.8 11.7	47 02.5 –45.6 11.9	48 01.1 –45.4 12.2	48 59.8 –45.2 12.4	75
76	41 21.9 46.8 10.1	42 21.0 46.7 10.3	43 20.1 46.5 10.4	44 19.0 46.4 10.6	45 17.9 46.2 10.8	46 16.9 46.1 11.0	47 15.7 45.8 11.2	48 14.6 45.7 11.4	76
77	40 35.1 47.2 9.3	41 34.3 47.1 9.4	42 33.6 47.0 9.6	43 32.6 46.8 9.7	44 31.7 46.6 9.9	45 30.8 46.5 10.1	46 29.9 46.3 10.2	47 28.9 46.2 10.4	77
78	39 47.9 47.5 8.5	40 47.2 47.4 8.6	41 46.6 47.3 8.7	42 45.8 47.1 8.7	43 45.1 47.0 9.0	44 44.3 46.9 9.2	45 43.6 46.8 9.3	46 42.7 46.6 9.5	78
79	39 00.4 47.9 7.7	39 59.8 47.7 7.8	40 59.3 47.6 7.9	41 58.7 47.6 7.9	42 58.1 47.4 8.2	43 57.4 47.2 8.3	44 56.8 47.1 8.5	45 56.1 47.0 8.6	79
80	38 12.5 –48.1 6.9	39 12.1 –48.1 7.0	40 11.6 –47.8 7.1	41 11.1 –47.8 7.1	42 10.7 –47.8 7.4	43 10.2 –47.7 7.5	44 09.7 –47.6 7.6	45 09.1 –47.4 7.7	80
81	37 24.4 48.4 6.2	38 24.0 48.3 6.2	39 23.7 48.0 6.2	40 23.3 48.2 6.3	41 22.9 48.1 6.6	42 22.5 48.0 6.7	43 22.1 47.9 6.7	44 21.7 47.8 6.8	81
82	36 36.0 48.7 5.4	37 35.7 48.6 5.5	38 35.4 48.5 5.6	39 35.1 48.4 5.6	40 34.8 48.4 5.8	41 34.5 48.2 5.9	42 34.2 48.2 5.9	43 33.9 48.5 6.0	82
83	35 47.3 49.0 4.7	36 47.1 48.9 4.8	37 46.9 48.8 4.8	38 46.7 48.8 4.8	39 46.4 48.7 5.0	40 46.3 48.6 5.1	41 46.0 48.6 5.1	42 45.7 48.5 5.2	83
84	34 58.3 49.1 4.0	35 58.2 49.1 4.0	36 58.0 49.0 4.1	37 57.9 49.0 4.1	38 57.7 49.0 4.3	39 57.6 49.0 4.3	40 57.4 48.8 4.3	41 57.2 48.8 4.4	84
85	34 09.2 –49.5 3.3	35 09.1 –49.4 3.3	36 09.0 –49.4 3.4	37 08.9 –49.3 3.4	38 08.7 –49.2 3.5	39 08.6 –49.2 3.5	40 08.6 –49.2 3.6	41 08.4 –49.1 3.6	85
86	33 19.7 49.6 2.6	34 19.7 49.6 2.6	35 19.6 49.6 2.7	36 19.6 49.6 2.7	37 19.5 49.5 2.7	38 19.4 49.4 2.8	39 19.4 49.4 2.8	40 19.3 49.5 2.9	86
87	32 30.1 49.8 1.9	33 30.1 49.8 2.0	34 30.0 49.8 2.0	35 30.0 49.8 2.0	36 30.0 49.8 2.0	37 29.9 49.7 2.0	38 29.8 49.7 2.1	39 29.8 49.7 2.1	87
88	31 40.3 50.1 1.3	32 40.3 50.1 1.3	33 40.2 50.0 1.3	34 40.2 50.0 1.3	35 40.2 50.0 1.3	36 40.2 50.0 1.4	37 40.2 50.0 1.4	38 40.2 50.0 1.4	88
89	30 50.2 50.2 0.6	31 50.2 50.2 0.6	32 50.2 50.2 0.6	33 50.2 50.2 0.7	34 50.2 50.2 0.7	35 50.2 50.2 0.7	36 50.2 50.2 0.7	37 50.2 50.2 0.7	89
90	30 00.0 –50.4 0.0	31 00.0 –50.4 0.0	32 00.0 –50.4 0.0	33 00.0 –50.4 0.0	34 00.0 –50.4 0.0	35 00.0 –50.4 0.0	36 00.0 –50.4 0.0	37 00.0 –50.4 0.0	90

33°, 327° L.H.A.

LATITUDE SAME NAME AS DECLINATION

LATITUDE CONTRARY NAME TO DECLINATION — L.H.A. 33°, 327°

Dec.	30° Hc	d	Z	31° Hc	d	Z	32° Hc	d	Z	33° Hc	d	Z	34° Hc	d	Z	35° Hc	d	Z	36° Hc	d	Z	37° Hc	d	Z	Dec.
0	46 34.7	-43.9	127.6	45 57.7	-44.7	128.4	45 20.1	-45.4	129.2	44 41.9	-46.2	130.0	44 03.0	-46.9	130.7	43 23.6	-47.6	131.5	42 43.6	-48.2	132.1	42 03.1	-48.8	132.8	0
1	45 50.8	44.4	128.6	45 13.0	45.1	129.4	44 34.7	45.9	130.1	43 55.7	46.6	130.9	43 16.1	47.2	131.6	42 36.0	47.9	132.3	41 55.4	48.5	133.0	41 14.3	49.1	133.6	1
2	45 06.4	44.9	129.5	44 27.9	45.6	130.3	43 48.8	46.3	131.0	43 09.1	47.0	131.7	42 28.9	47.6	132.4	41 48.1	48.2	133.1	41 06.9	48.8	133.7	40 25.2	49.4	134.4	2
3	44 21.5	45.3	130.5	43 42.3	46.0	131.2	43 02.5	46.7	131.9	42 22.1	47.3	132.6	41 41.3	48.0	133.3	40 59.9	48.5	133.9	40 18.1	49.1	134.5	39 35.8	49.7	135.1	3
4	43 36.2	45.7	131.4	42 56.3	46.5	132.1	42 15.8	47.1	132.8	41 34.8	47.7	133.4	40 53.3	48.3	134.1	40 11.4	48.9	134.7	39 29.0	49.4	135.3	38 46.1	49.9	135.8	4
5	42 50.5	-46.2	132.3	42 09.8	-46.7	132.9	41 28.7	-47.4	133.6	40 47.1	-48.0	134.2	40 05.0	-48.6	134.8	39 22.5	-49.1	135.4	38 39.6	-49.7	136.0	37 56.2	-50.2	136.5	5
6	42 04.3	46.5	133.1	41 23.1	47.2	133.8	40 41.3	47.7	134.4	39 59.1	48.3	135.0	39 16.4	48.8	135.6	38 33.4	49.3	136.2	37 49.9	49.9	136.7	37 06.0	50.4	137.2	6
7	41 17.8	46.9	134.0	40 35.9	47.5	134.6	39 53.6	48.1	135.2	39 10.8	48.7	135.8	38 27.6	49.2	136.3	37 44.0	49.7	136.9	37 00.0	50.2	137.4	36 15.6	50.6	137.9	7
8	40 30.9	47.2	134.8	39 48.4	47.8	135.4	39 05.5	48.4	136.0	38 22.1	48.9	136.6	37 38.4	49.4	137.1	36 54.3	49.9	137.6	36 09.8	50.4	138.1	35 25.0	50.8	138.6	8
9	39 43.7	47.5	135.6	39 00.6	48.1	136.2	38 17.1	48.6	136.7	37 33.2	49.1	137.3	36 49.0	49.7	137.8	36 04.4	50.2	138.3	35 19.4	50.6	138.8	34 34.2	51.1	139.2	9
10	38 56.2	-47.9	136.4	38 12.5	-48.4	137.0	37 28.5	-49.0	137.5	36 44.1	-49.5	138.0	35 59.3	-49.9	138.5	35 14.2	-50.3	139.0	34 28.8	-50.8	139.4	33 43.1	-51.2	139.8	10
11	38 08.3	48.2	137.2	37 24.1	48.7	137.7	36 39.5	49.1	138.2	35 54.6	49.6	138.7	35 09.4	50.1	139.2	34 23.9	50.6	139.6	33 38.0	51.0	140.1	32 51.9	51.4	140.5	11
12	37 20.1	48.4	137.9	36 35.4	48.9	138.4	35 50.4	49.5	138.9	35 05.0	49.9	139.4	34 19.3	50.3	139.8	33 33.3	50.8	140.3	32 47.0	51.2	140.7	32 00.5	51.6	141.1	12
13	36 31.7	48.7	138.7	35 46.5	49.2	139.1	35 00.9	49.6	139.6	34 15.1	50.1	140.1	33 28.9	50.5	140.5	32 42.5	51.0	140.9	31 55.8	51.4	141.3	31 08.9	51.8	141.7	13
14	35 43.0	49.0	139.4	34 57.3	49.5	139.9	34 11.3	49.9	140.3	33 25.0	50.4	140.7	32 38.4	50.8	141.1	31 51.5	51.1	141.5	31 04.4	51.5	141.9	30 17.1	51.9	142.3	14
15	34 54.0	-49.2	140.1	34 07.8	-49.6	140.5	33 21.4	-50.1	141.0	32 34.6	-50.5	141.4	31 47.6	-50.9	141.8	31 00.4	-51.3	142.1	30 12.9	-51.7	142.5	29 25.2	-52.1	142.8	15
16	34 04.8	49.4	140.8	33 18.2	49.9	141.2	32 31.3	50.3	141.6	31 44.1	50.7	142.0	30 56.7	51.1	142.4	30 09.1	51.5	142.7	29 21.2	51.8	143.1	28 33.1	52.1	143.4	16
17	33 15.4	49.7	141.5	32 28.3	50.1	141.9	31 41.0	50.5	142.3	30 53.4	50.9	142.7	30 05.6	51.2	143.0	29 17.6	51.6	143.3	28 29.4	52.0	143.7	27 41.0	52.4	144.0	17
18	32 25.7	49.8	142.2	31 38.2	50.2	142.5	30 50.5	50.7	142.9	30 02.5	51.0	143.2	29 14.4	51.5	143.6	28 26.0	51.8	143.9	27 37.4	52.1	144.2	26 48.6	52.4	144.5	18
19	31 35.9	50.1	142.8	30 48.0	50.5	143.2	29 59.8	50.8	143.5	29 11.5	51.2	143.9	28 22.9	51.5	144.2	27 34.2	51.9	144.5	26 45.3	52.3	144.8	25 56.2	52.6	145.1	19
20	30 45.8	-50.2	143.4	29 57.5	-50.6	143.8	29 09.0	-51.0	144.1	28 20.3	-51.4	144.4	27 31.4	-51.7	144.8	26 42.3	-52.1	145.0	25 53.0	-52.3	145.3	25 03.6	-52.7	145.6	20
21	29 55.6	50.4	144.1	29 06.9	50.8	144.4	28 18.0	51.2	144.7	27 28.9	51.5	145.0	26 39.7	51.9	145.3	25 50.2	52.1	145.6	25 00.7	52.5	145.9	24 10.9	52.8	146.1	21
22	29 05.2	50.6	144.7	28 16.1	51.0	145.0	27 26.8	51.3	145.3	26 37.4	51.6	145.6	25 47.8	51.9	145.9	24 58.1	52.3	146.1	24 08.2	52.6	146.4	23 18.1	52.9	146.6	22
23	28 14.6	50.8	145.3	27 25.1	51.1	145.6	26 35.5	51.4	145.9	25 45.8	51.8	146.2	24 55.8	52.0	146.4	24 05.8	52.4	146.7	23 15.6	52.7	146.9	22 25.2	53.0	147.2	23
24	27 23.8	50.9	145.9	26 34.0	51.2	146.2	25 44.1	51.6	146.5	24 54.0	51.9	146.7	24 03.8	52.3	147.0	23 13.4	52.5	147.2	22 22.9	52.8	147.4	21 32.2	53.0	147.7	24
25	26 32.9	-51.1	146.5	25 42.8	-51.4	146.8	24 52.5	-51.7	147.0	24 02.1	-52.0	147.3	23 11.5	-52.3	147.5	22 20.9	-52.6	147.7	21 30.1	-52.9	148.0	20 39.2	-53.2	148.2	25
26	25 41.8	51.1	147.1	24 51.4	51.5	147.4	24 00.8	51.8	147.6	23 10.1	52.1	147.8	22 19.2	52.4	148.1	21 28.3	52.7	148.3	20 37.2	53.0	148.5	19 46.0	53.3	148.7	26
27	24 50.7	51.4	147.7	23 59.9	51.7	147.9	23 09.0	52.0	148.1	22 18.0	52.3	148.4	21 26.8	52.5	148.6	20 35.6	52.8	148.8	19 44.2	53.1	149.0	18 52.7	53.3	149.1	27
28	23 59.3	51.4	148.2	23 08.2	51.7	148.5	22 17.0	52.0	148.7	21 25.7	52.3	148.9	20 34.3	52.6	149.1	19 42.8	52.9	149.3	18 51.1	53.1	149.5	17 59.4	53.4	149.6	28
29	23 07.9	51.6	148.8	22 16.5	51.9	149.0	21 25.0	52.1	149.2	20 33.4	52.4	149.4	19 41.7	52.7	149.6	18 49.9	53.0	149.8	17 58.0	53.2	149.9	17 06.0	53.4	150.1	29
30	22 16.3	-51.7	149.4	21 24.6	-51.9	149.6	20 32.9	-52.3	149.8	19 41.0	-52.5	149.9	18 49.0	-52.8	150.1	17 56.9	-53.0	150.3	17 04.8	-53.3	150.4	16 12.6	-53.6	150.6	30
31	21 24.6	51.7	149.9	20 32.7	52.1	150.1	19 40.6	52.3	150.3	18 48.5	52.6	150.5	17 56.2	52.9	150.6	17 03.9	53.2	150.8	16 11.5	53.3	150.9	15 19.0	53.5	151.1	31
32	20 32.9	51.9	150.4	19 40.6	52.1	150.6	18 48.3	52.4	150.8	17 55.9	52.7	151.0	17 03.4	52.9	151.1	16 10.8	53.2	151.3	15 18.2	53.4	151.4	14 25.5	53.7	151.5	32
33	19 41.0	52.0	151.0	18 48.5	52.3	151.1	17 55.9	52.5	151.3	17 03.2	52.7	151.5	16 10.5	53.0	151.6	15 17.6	53.2	151.7	14 24.8	53.5	151.9	13 31.8	53.7	152.0	33
34	18 49.0	52.1	151.5	17 56.2	52.3	151.5	17 03.4	52.6	151.8	16 10.5	52.9	152.0	15 17.4	53.0	152.1	14 24.4	53.3	152.2	13 31.3	53.5	152.3	12 38.1	53.7	152.4	34
35	17 56.9	-52.1	152.0	17 03.9	-52.4	152.2	16 10.8	-52.6	152.3	15 17.6	-52.8	152.4	14 24.4	-53.1	152.6	13 31.1	-53.3	152.7	12 37.8	-53.6	152.8	11 44.4	-53.8	152.9	35
36	17 04.8	52.2	152.6	16 11.5	52.5	152.7	15 18.2	52.7	152.8	14 24.8	53.0	152.9	13 31.3	53.2	153.1	12 37.8	53.4	153.2	11 44.2	53.6	153.3	10 50.6	53.8	153.3	36
37	16 12.6	52.3	153.1	15 19.0	52.5	153.2	14 25.5	52.7	153.3	13 31.8	53.0	153.4	12 38.1	53.2	153.5	11 44.4	53.4	153.6	10 50.6	53.6	153.7	9 56.8	53.8	153.8	37
38	15 20.3	52.4	153.6	14 26.5	52.6	153.7	13 32.7	52.8	153.8	12 38.8	53.0	153.9	11 44.9	53.2	154.0	10 51.0	53.5	154.1	9 57.0	53.7	154.2	9 03.0	53.9	154.2	38
39	14 27.9	52.4	154.1	13 33.9	52.6	154.2	12 39.9	52.9	154.3	11 45.8	53.1	154.4	10 51.7	53.3	154.5	9 57.5	53.5	154.5	9 03.3	53.7	154.6	8 09.1	53.9	154.7	39
40	13 35.5	-52.5	154.6	12 41.3	-52.8	154.7	11 47.0	-53.0	154.8	10 52.7	-53.1	154.9	9 58.4	-53.4	154.9	9 04.0	-53.5	155.0	8 09.6	-53.7	155.1	7 15.2	-54.0	155.1	40
41	12 43.0	52.6	155.1	11 48.5	52.8	155.2	10 54.1	53.0	155.3	9 59.6	53.2	155.3	9 05.0	53.4	155.4	8 10.5	53.6	155.5	7 15.9	53.8	155.6	6 21.2	53.9	155.6	41
42	11 50.4	52.6	155.6	10 55.8	52.8	155.7	10 01.1	53.0	155.7	9 06.4	53.2	155.8	8 11.6	53.4	155.9	7 16.9	53.6	155.9	6 22.1	53.8	156.0	5 27.3	54.0	156.0	42
43	10 57.8	52.6	156.1	10 03.0	52.9	156.1	9 08.1	53.1	156.2	8 13.2	53.3	156.3	7 18.2	53.4	156.3	6 23.3	53.6	156.4	5 28.3	53.9	156.4	4 33.3	54.0	156.4	43
44	10 05.2	52.7	156.6	9 10.1	52.9	156.6	8 15.0	53.0	156.7	7 19.9	53.2	156.7	6 24.8	53.5	156.8	5 29.7	53.7	156.8	4 34.5	53.8	156.9	3 39.3	54.0	156.9	44

LATITUDE SAME NAME AS DECLINATION

N. Lat. { L.H.A. greater than 180°.......Zn=Z
L.H.A. less than 180°........Zn=360°−Z

Dec.	30° Hc	d	Z	31° Hc	d	Z	32° Hc	d	Z	33° Hc	d	Z	34° Hc	d	Z	35° Hc	d	Z	36° Hc	d	Z	37° Hc	d	Z	Dec.
0	45 53.2	+42.8	126.5	45 17.1	+43.7	127.4	44 40.4	+44.5	128.2	44 03.0	+45.3	128.9	43 25.0	+46.0	129.7	42 46.4	+46.7	130.4	42 07.3	+47.4	131.1	41 27.6	+48.0	131.7	0
1	46 36.0	42.3	125.5	46 00.8	43.2	126.4	45 24.9	44.0	127.2	44 48.3	44.8	128.0	44 11.0	45.6	128.8	43 33.1	46.3	129.5	42 54.7	47.0	130.2	42 15.6	47.7	130.9	1
2	47 18.3	41.7	124.5	46 44.0	42.6	125.4	46 08.9	43.4	126.2	45 33.1	44.3	127.1	44 56.6	45.1	127.9	44 19.4	45.9	128.6	43 41.7	46.6	129.4	43 03.3	47.3	130.1	2
3	48 00.0	41.1	123.4	47 26.6	42.0	124.3	46 52.3	43.0	125.2	46 17.4	43.8	126.1	45 41.7	44.6	126.9	45 05.3	45.4	127.7	44 28.3	46.2	128.5	43 50.6	46.9	129.3	3
4	48 41.1	40.5	122.3	48 08.6	41.5	123.3	47 35.3	42.4	124.2	47 01.2	43.3	125.1	46 26.3	44.2	126.0	45 50.7	45.0	126.8	45 14.5	45.7	127.6	44 37.5	46.5	128.4	4
5	49 21.6	+39.8	121.2	48 50.1	+40.8	122.2	48 17.7	+41.7	123.1	47 44.5	+42.7	124.1	47 10.5	+43.6	125.0	46 35.7	+44.5	125.8	46 00.2	+45.3	126.7	45 24.0	+46.1	127.5	5
6	50 01.4	39.0	120.0	49 30.9	40.1	121.1	48 59.4	41.2	122.1	48 27.2	42.2	123.0	47 54.1	43.0	123.9	47 20.2	43.9	124.9	46 45.5	44.8	125.7	46 10.1	45.6	126.6	6
7	50 40.4	38.4	118.9	50 11.0	39.4	119.9	49 40.6	40.5	120.9	49 09.3	41.5	121.9	48 37.1	42.5	122.9	48 04.1	43.4	123.8	47 30.3	44.3	124.8	46 55.7	45.2	125.6	7
8	51 18.8	37.5	117.6	50 50.4	38.7	118.7	50 21.1	39.8	119.8	49 50.8	40.8	120.9	49 19.6	41.9	121.8	48 47.5	42.9	122.8	48 14.6	43.8	123.8	47 40.9	44.6	124.7	8
9	51 56.3	36.7	116.4	51 29.1	37.9	117.5	51 00.9	39.0	118.6	50 31.6	40.2	119.7	50 01.5	41.2	120.7	49 30.4	42.2	121.7	48 58.4	43.2	122.7	48 25.5	44.1	123.7	9
10	52 33.0	+35.8	115.1	52 07.0	+37.1	116.3	51 39.9	+38.3	117.4	51 11.8	+39.4	118.5	50 42.7	+40.5	119.6	50 12.6	+41.6	120.6	49 41.6	+42.5	121.6	49 09.6	+43.6	122.6	10
11	53 08.8	35.0	113.8	52 44.1	36.2	115.0	52 18.2	37.5	116.1	51 51.2	38.7	117.3	51 23.2	39.8	118.4	50 54.2	40.8	119.5	50 24.1	42.0	120.5	49 53.2	42.9	121.6	11
12	53 43.8	34.0	112.4	53 20.3	35.3	113.6	52 55.7	36.6	114.9	52 29.9	38.0	116.0	52 03.0	39.0	117.2	51 35.0	40.2	118.3	51 06.1	41.2	119.4	50 36.1	42.3	120.5	12
13	54 17.8	32.9	111.0	53 55.6	34.4	112.3	53 32.3	35.7	113.5	53 07.7	37.0	114.8	52 42.0	38.3	116.0	52 15.2	39.4	117.1	51 47.3	40.6	118.3	51 18.4	41.7	119.4	13
14	54 50.7	31.9	109.6	54 30.0	33.4	110.9	54 08.0	34.7	112.1	53 44.7	36.1	113.4	53 20.3	37.3	114.7	52 54.6	38.7	115.9	52 27.9	39.8	117.1	52 00.1	40.9	118.2	14
15	55 22.6	+30.9	108.1	55 03.4	+32.3	109.4	54 42.7	+33.8	110.8	54 20.8	+35.2	112.1	53 57.6	+36.5	113.4	53 33.3	+37.7	114.6	53 07.7	+39.0	115.8	52 41.0	+40.2	117.0	15
16	55 53.5	29.6	106.6	55 35.7	31.2	108.0	55 16.5	32.7	109.3	54 56.0	34.1	110.7	54 34.1	35.6	112.0	54 11.0	36.9	113.3	53 46.7	38.2	114.5	53 21.2	39.4	115.8	16
17	56 23.1	28.5	105.0	56 06.9	30.0	106.4	55 49.2	31.6	107.8	55 30.1	33.1	109.2	55 09.7	34.5	110.6	54 47.9	36.0	111.9	54 24.9	37.3	113.2	54 00.6	38.6	114.5	17
18	56 51.6	27.2	103.4	56 36.9	28.9	104.9	56 20.8	30.5	106.3	56 03.2	32.0	107.8	55 44.2	33.5	109.2	55 23.9	34.9	110.5	55 02.2	36.3	111.9	54 39.2	37.7	113.2	18
19	57 18.8	25.9	101.8	57 05.8	27.6	103.3	56 51.3	29.2	104.8	56 35.2	30.9	106.2	56 17.7	32.5	107.7	55 58.8	34.0	109.1	55 38.5	35.4	110.5	55 16.9	36.7	111.8	19
20	57 44.7	+24.5	100.1	57 33.4	+26.3	101.6	57 20.5	+28.0	103.2	57 06.1	+29.7	104.7	56 50.2	+31.2	106.1	56 32.8	+32.8	107.6	56 13.9	+34.3	109.0	55 53.6	+35.8	110.4	20
21	58 09.2	23.1	98.4	57 59.7	24.9	99.9	57 48.5	26.7	101.5	57 35.8	28.3	103.0	57 21.4	30.1	104.6	57 05.6	31.7	106.1	56 48.2	33.3	107.5	56 29.4	34.8	109.0	21
22	58 32.3	21.6	96.6	58 24.6	23.5	98.2	58 15.2	25.3	99.8	58 04.1	27.1	101.4	57 51.5	28.8	103.0	57 37.3	30.4	104.5	57 21.5	32.1	106.0	57 04.2	33.6	107.5	22
23	58 53.9	20.1	94.8	58 48.1	22.0	96.4	58 40.5	23.8	98.1	58 31.2	25.7	99.7	58 20.3	27.5	101.3	58 07.7	29.2	102.9	57 53.6	30.8	104.4	57 37.8	32.5	106.0	23
24	59 14.0	18.6	93.0	59 10.1	20.4	94.6	59 04.3	22.4	96.3	58 56.9	24.3	98.0	58 47.8	26.0	99.6	58 36.9	27.9	101.2	58 24.4	29.6	102.8	58 10.3	31.3	104.4	24
25	59 32.6	+16.9	91.1	59 30.5	+18.9	92.8	59 26.7	+20.9	94.5	59 21.2	+22.7	96.2	59 13.8	+24.7	97.8	59 04.8	+26.5	99.5	58 54.0	+28.3	101.1	58 41.6	+30.1	102.7	25
26	59 49.5	15.2	89.2	59 49.4	17.3	90.9	59 47.6	19.2	92.6	59 43.9	21.2	94.3	59 38.5	23.1	96.0	59 31.3	25.0	97.7	59 22.3	26.9	99.4	59 11.7	28.6	101.1	26
27	60 04.7	13.5	87.3	60 06.7	15.5	89.0	60 06.8	17.6	90.7	60 05.1	19.6	92.5	60 01.6	21.6	94.2	59 56.3	23.5	95.9	59 49.2	25.4	97.6	59 40.3	27.3	99.3	27
28	60 18.2	11.8	85.3	60 22.2	13.9	87.1	60 24.4	15.9	88.8	60 24.7	17.9	90.6	60 23.2	19.9	92.3	60 19.8	22.0	94.1	60 14.6	23.9	95.8	60 07.6	25.9	97.6	28
29	60 30.0	10.0	83.3	60 36.1	12.0	85.1	60 40.3	14.1	86.9	60 42.6	16.3	88.6	60 43.1	18.3	90.4	60 41.8	20.3	92.2	60 38.5	22.4	94.0	60 33.5	24.2	95.7	29
30	60 40.0	+8.1	81.3	60 48.1	+10.3	83.1	60 54.4	+12.4	84.9	60 58.9	+14.4	86.7	61 01.4	+16.6	88.5	61 02.1	+18.6	90.3	61 00.9	+20.6	92.1	60 57.7	+22.7	93.9	30
31	60 48.1	6.3	79.3	60 58.4	8.4	81.1	61 06.8	10.5	82.8	61 13.3	12.6	84.6	61 18.0	14.7	86.5	61 20.7	16.9	88.3	61 21.5	19.0	90.1	61 20.4	21.1	92.0	31
32	60 54.4	4.5	77.2	61 06.8	6.5	79.0	61 17.3	8.6	80.8	61 25.9	10.8	82.6	61 32.7	12.9	84.6	61 37.6	15.0	86.3	61 40.5	17.2	88.1	61 41.5	19.3	90.0	32
33	60 58.9	2.5	75.2	61 13.3	4.7	76.9	61 25.9	6.8	78.7	61 36.7	8.9	80.5	61 45.6	11.1	82.4	61 52.6	13.3	84.2	61 57.7	15.4	86.1	62 00.8	17.5	88.0	33
34	61 01.4	0.7	73.1	61 18.0	2.7	74.9	61 32.7	4.9	76.7	61 45.6	7.0	78.5	61 56.7	9.2	80.5	62 05.9	11.3	82.2	62 13.1	13.5	84.0	62 18.3	15.7	85.9	34
35	61 02.1	−1.2	71.1	61 20.7	+0.8	72.8	61 37.6	+2.9	74.6	61 52.6	+5.1	76.4	62 05.9	+7.2	78.2	62 17.2	+9.4	80.1	62 26.6	+11.6	81.9	62 34.0	+13.8	83.8	35
36	61 00.9	3.2	69.0	61 21.5	−1.1	70.7	61 40.5	1.0	72.5	61 57.7	3.1	74.2	62 13.1	5.2	76.1	62 26.6	7.4*	77.9	62 38.2	9.6*	79.8	62 47.8	11.8	81.7	36
37	60 57.7	4.9	66.9	61 20.4	3.0	68.6	61 41.5	−1.0	70.3	62 00.8	1.1	72.1	62 18.3	3.3*	73.9	62 34.0	5.4*	75.8	62 47.8	7.6*	77.7	62 59.6	9.9*	79.6	37
38	60 52.8	6.9	64.9	61 17.4	4.9	66.5	61 40.5	2.9	68.2	62 01.9	1.2*	70.0	62 21.6	1.2*	71.8	62 39.4	3.4*	73.6	62 55.4	5.6*	75.5	63 09.5	7.8*	77.4	38
39	60 45.9	8.7	62.8	61 12.5	6.7	64.5	61 37.6	4.8	66.1	62 01.1	2.8*	67.9	62 22.8	−0.7	69.6	62 42.8	1.4*	71.4	63 01.0	3.6*	73.3	63 17.3	5.8*	75.2	39
40	60 37.2	−10.5	60.8	61 05.8	−8.7	62.4	61 32.8	−6.8	64.0	61 58.3	−4.8	65.7	62 22.1	−2.7	67.5	62 44.2	−0.6	69.3	63 04.6	+1.5*	71.1	63 23.1	+3.7*	73.0	40
41	60 26.7	12.8	58.8	60 57.1	10.5	60.4	61 26.0	8.6	62.0	61 53.5	6.7	63.6	62 19.4	4.8*	65.3	62 43.6	2.7*	67.1	63 06.1	−0.6*	68.9	63 26.8	1.6*	70.7	41
42	60 14.4	14.0	56.8	60 46.6	12.3	58.3	61 17.4	10.5	59.9	61 46.8	8.7	61.5	62 14.6	6.7	63.2	62 40.9	4.7*	64.9	63 05.5	2.6*	66.7	63 28.4	−0.5*	68.5	42
43	60 00.4	15.7	54.9	60 34.3	14.1	56.3	61 06.9	12.3	57.8	61 38.1	10.5	59.4	62 07.9	8.6	61.0	62 36.2	6.7	62.7	63 02.9	4.7	64.5	63 27.9	2.6*	66.3	43
44	59 44.7	17.4	53.0	60 20.2	15.7	54.4	60 54.6	14.1	55.8	61 27.6	12.3	57.3	61 59.3	10.6	58.9	62 29.5	8.6	60.6	62 58.2	6.7*	62.3	63 25.3	4.6*	64.0	44

LATITUDE SAME NAME AS DECLINATION

N. Lat. { L.H.A. greater than 180°......Zn=Z
{ L.H.A. less than 180°.........Zn=360°−Z

Dec.	30° Hc	d	Z	31° Hc	d	Z	32° Hc	d	Z	33° Hc	d	Z	34° Hc	d	Z	35° Hc	d	Z	36° Hc	d	Z	37° Hc	d	Z	Dec.
0	43 ·2	+42.3	125.5	44 36.0	+43.1	126.3	44 00.1	+44.0	127.1	43 23.6	+44.7	127.9	42 46.4	+45.5	128.6	42 08.7	+46.2	129.3	41 30.4	+46.9	130.0	40 51.6	+47.5	130.7	0
1	45 53.5	41.7	124.5	45 19.1	42.7	125.4	44 44.1	43.5	126.2	44 08.3	44.3	127.0	43 31.9	45.1	127.7	42 54.9	45.8	128.5	42 17.3	46.6	129.2	41 39.1	47.3	129.9	1
2	46 35.2	41.2	123.5	46 01.8	42.1	124.3	45 27.6	42.9	125.2	44 52.6	43.8	126.0	44 17.0	44.6	126.8	43 40.7	45.4	127.6	43 03.9	46.1	128.3	42 26.4	46.8	129.0	2
3	47 16.4	40.6	122.4	46 43.9	41.5	123.3	46 10.5	42.4	124.2	45 36.4	43.3	125.0	45 01.6	44.2	125.9	44 26.1	45.0	126.8	43 50.0	45.7	127.4	43 13.2	46.5	128.2	3
4	47 57.0	39.9	121.3	47 25.4	40.9	122.3	46 52.9	41.9	123.2	46 19.7	42.8	124.0	45 45.8	43.6	124.9	45 11.1	44.5	125.7	44 35.7	45.3	126.5	43 59.7	46.0	127.3	4
5	48 36.9	+39.3	120.2	48 06.3	+40.3	121.2	47 34.8	+41.3	122.1	47 02.5	+42.2	123.0	46 29.4	+43.2	123.9	45 55.6	+44.0	124.8	45 21.0	+44.8	125.6	44 45.7	+45.7	126.4	5
6	49 16.2	38.5	119.0	48 46.6	39.6	120.0	48 16.1	40.6	121.0	47 44.7	41.7	122.0	47 12.6	42.5	122.9	46 39.6	43.4	123.8	46 05.8	44.4	124.7	45 31.4	45.1	125.5	6
7	49 54.7	37.8	117.9	49 26.2	38.9	118.9	48 56.7	40.0	119.9	48 26.4	41.0	120.9	47 55.1	42.0	121.8	47 23.0	43.0	122.8	46 50.2	43.8	123.7	46 16.5	44.7	124.5	7
8	50 32.5	37.0	116.7	50 05.1	38.1	117.7	49 36.7	39.3	118.8	49 07.4	40.3	119.8	48 37.1	41.4	120.8	48 06.0	42.3	121.7	47 34.0	43.3	122.7	47 01.2	44.2	123.6	8
9	51 09.5	36.3	115.4	50 43.3	37.4	116.5	50 16.0	38.5	117.6	49 47.7	39.7	118.6	49 18.5	40.7	119.6	48 48.3	41.8	120.6	48 17.3	42.7	121.7	47 45.4	43.7	122.6	9
10	51 45.8	+35.3	114.1	51 20.7	+36.6	115.3	50 54.5	+37.8	116.4	50 27.4	+38.9	117.5	49 59.2	+40.0	118.5	49 30.1	+41.1	119.6	49 00.0	+42.1	120.6	48 29.0	+43.1	121.5	10
11	52 21.1	34.5	112.8	51 57.3	35.7	114.0	51 32.3	37.0	115.1	51 06.3	38.2	116.3	50 39.2	39.4	117.4	50 11.2	40.4	118.4	49 42.1	41.5	119.5	49 12.1	42.5	120.5	11
12	52 55.6	33.5	111.5	52 33.0	34.9	112.7	52 09.3	36.2	113.8	51 44.5	37.4	115.0	51 18.6	38.5	116.2	50 51.6	39.7	117.2	50 23.6	40.8	118.4	49 54.6	41.8	119.4	12
13	53 29.1	32.5	110.1	53 07.9	33.9	111.3	52 45.5	35.2	112.6	52 21.9	36.5	113.8	51 57.1	37.8	114.9	51 31.3	38.9	116.1	51 04.4	40.1	117.2	50 36.4	41.2	118.3	13
14	54 01.6	31.5	108.7	53 41.8	32.9	109.9	53 20.7	34.3	111.2	52 58.4	35.6	112.5	52 34.9	36.9	113.7	52 10.2	38.2	114.8	51 44.5	39.3	116.0	51 17.6	40.5	117.1	14
15	54 33.1	+30.5	107.2	54 14.7	+31.9	108.5	53 55.0	+33.3	109.8	53 34.0	+34.7	111.1	53 11.8	+36.1	112.4	52 48.4	+37.3	113.6	52 23.8	+38.6	114.8	51 58.1	+39.8	115.9	15
16	55 03.6	29.2	105.7	54 46.6	30.8	107.1	54 28.3	32.3	108.4	54 08.7	33.8	109.7	53 47.9	35.0	111.0	53 25.7	36.5	112.3	53 02.4	37.7	113.5	52 37.9	38.8	114.7	16
17	55 32.8	28.2	104.2	55 17.4	29.7	105.6	55 00.6	31.3	106.9	54 42.5	32.7	108.3	54 23.0	34.1	109.6	54 02.2	35.5	110.9	53 40.1	36.9	112.2	53 16.8	38.2	113.5	17
18	56 01.0	26.9	102.6	55 47.1	28.6	104.0	55 31.9	30.1	105.5	55 15.2	31.6	106.8	54 57.1	32.9	108.2	54 37.7	34.6	109.6	54 17.0	35.9	110.9	53 55.0	37.2	112.1	18
19	56 27.9	25.6	101.0	56 15.7	27.2	102.5	56 02.0	28.9	103.9	55 46.8	30.5	105.3	55 30.2	32.1	106.7	55 12.3	33.5	108.1	54 52.9	35.0	109.5	54 32.2	36.3	110.8	19
20	56 53.5	+24.3	99.3	56 42.9	+26.1	100.8	56 30.9	+27.7	102.3	56 17.3	+29.4	103.8	56 02.3	+30.9	105.2	55 45.8	+32.4	106.7	55 27.9	+33.9	108.1	55 08.6	+35.4	109.4	20
21	57 17.8	22.9	97.7	57 09.0	24.6	99.2	56 58.6	26.4	100.7	56 46.7	28.0	102.2	56 33.2	29.7	103.7	56 18.2	31.4	105.2	56 01.8	32.9	106.6	55 44.0	34.4	108.0	21
22	57 40.7	21.4	95.9	57 33.6	23.3	97.5	57 25.0	25.1	99.0	57 14.7	26.9	100.6	57 02.9	28.5	102.1	56 49.6	30.1	103.6	56 34.7	31.8	105.1	56 18.4	33.3	106.5	22
23	58 02.1	20.0	94.2	57 56.9	21.9	95.8	57 50.1	23.6	97.4	57 41.6	25.4	98.9	57 31.4	27.3	100.5	57 19.7	28.9	102.0	57 06.5	30.5	103.5	56 51.7	32.1	105.0	23
24	58 22.1	18.5	92.4	58 18.8	20.4	94.0	58 13.7	22.3	95.6	58 07.0	24.1	97.2	57 58.7	25.8	98.8	57 48.6	27.7	100.4	57 37.0	29.4	101.9	57 23.8	31.0	103.5	24
25	58 40.6	+16.9	90.6	58 39.2	+18.8	92.2	58 36.0	+20.7	93.9	58 31.1	+22.6	95.5	58 24.5	+24.5	97.1	58 16.3	+26.2	98.7	58 06.4	+28.0	100.3	57 54.8	+29.8	101.9	25
26	58 57.5	15.3	88.7	58 58.0	17.2	90.4	58 56.7	19.2	92.0	58 53.7	21.1	93.7	58 49.0	23.0	95.4	58 42.5	24.9	97.0	58 34.4	26.7	98.6	58 24.6	28.4	100.2	26
27	59 12.8	13.6	86.8	59 15.2	15.7	88.5	59 15.9	17.6	90.2	59 14.8	19.6	91.9	59 12.0	21.5	93.6	59 07.4	23.4	95.2	59 01.1	25.2	96.9	58 53.0	27.1	98.5	27
28	59 26.4	12.0	84.9	59 30.9	13.9	86.6	59 33.5	16.0	88.3	59 34.4	17.9	90.0	59 33.5	19.9	91.7	59 30.8	21.8	93.4	59 26.3	23.8	95.1	59 20.1	25.6	96.8	28
29	59 38.4	10.2	83.0	59 44.8	12.3	84.7	59 49.5	14.3	86.4	59 52.3	16.3	88.1	59 53.4	18.3	89.9	59 52.6	20.3	91.6	59 50.1	22.2	93.3	59 45.7	24.2	95.0	29
30	59 48.6	8.5	81.0	59 57.1	+10.5	82.7	60 03.8	+12.5	84.5	60 08.6	+14.6	86.2	60 11.7	+16.6	87.9	60 12.9	+18.7	89.7	60 12.3	+20.7	91.4	60 09.9	+22.6	93.2	30
31	59 57.1	6.7	79.1	60 07.6	8.7	80.8	60 16.3	10.8	82.5	60 23.2	12.9	84.2	60 28.3	14.9	86.0	60 31.6	16.9	87.8	60 33.0	19.0	89.5	60 32.5	21.1	91.3	31
32	60 03.8	4.8	77.1	60 16.3	6.9	78.8	60 27.1	9.0	80.5	60 36.1	11.0	82.3	60 43.2	13.2	84.0	60 48.5	15.3	85.8	60 52.0	17.3	87.6	60 53.6	19.3	89.4	32
33	60 08.6	3.1	75.1	60 23.2	5.1	76.8	60 36.1	7.1	78.5	60 47.1	9.3	80.3	60 56.4	11.3	82.0	61 03.8	13.4	83.8	61 09.3	15.5	85.6	61 12.9	17.6	87.4	33
34	60 11.7	+1.2	73.1	60 28.3	3.3	74.8	60 43.2	5.3	76.5	60 56.4	7.4	78.2	61 07.7	9.5	80.0	61 17.2	11.6	81.8	61 24.8	13.7	83.6	61 30.5	15.9	85.4	34
35	60 12.9	-0.6	71.1	60 31.6	+1.4	72.7	60 48.5	+3.5	74.4	61 03.8	+5.5	76.2	61 17.2	+7.6	77.9	61 28.8	+9.7	79.7	61 38.5	+11.9	81.6	61 46.4	+14.0	83.4	35
36	60 12.3	2.4	69.0	60 33.0	-0.5	70.7	60 52.0	1.6	72.4	61 09.3	3.6	74.1	61 24.8	5.7	75.9	61 38.5	7.9	77.7	61 50.4	10.0	79.5	62 00.4	12.1	81.3	36
37	60 09.9	4.2	67.0	60 32.5	2.3	68.7	60 53.6	-0.3	70.3	61 12.9	1.7	72.0	61 30.5	3.8	73.8	61 46.4	5.9	75.6	62 00.4	8.0	77.4	62 12.5	10.2	79.3	37
38	60 05.7	6.1	65.0	60 30.2	4.1	66.6	60 53.3	2.2	68.3	61 14.6	-0.1	70.0	61 34.3	1.9	71.7	61 52.3	4.0	73.6	62 08.4	6.1	75.3	62 22.7	8.3	77.1	38
39	59 59.6	7.8	63.0	60 26.1	6.0	64.6	60 51.1	4.1	66.2	61 14.5	2.1	67.9	61 36.2	-0.1	69.6	61 56.3	+2.0	71.4	62 14.5	4.2*	73.2	62 31.0	6.3*	75.0	39
40	59 51.8	-9.6	61.1	60 20.1	-7.8	62.6	60 47.0	-5.9	64.2	61 12.4	-4.0	65.8	61 36.1	-1.9	67.5	61 58.3	0.0	69.2	62 18.7	+2.1*	71.0	62 37.3	+4.3*	72.8	40
41	59 42.2	11.3	59.1	60 12.3	9.5	60.6	60 41.1	7.8	62.1	61 08.4	5.9	63.7	61 34.2	4.0	65.4	61 58.3	-1.9	67.1	62 20.8	0.2*	68.9	62 41.6	2.2*	70.7	41
42	59 30.9	13.1	57.2	60 02.8	11.4	58.6	60 33.3	9.5	60.1	61 02.5	7.7	61.7	61 30.2	5.8	63.3	61 56.4	3.9	65.0	62 21.0	-1.9*	66.7	62 43.8	0.3*	68.5	42
43	59 17.8	14.7	55.2	59 51.4	13.0	56.7	60 23.8	11.4	58.1	60 54.8	9.6	59.6	61 24.4	7.8	61.2	61 52.5	5.8	62.9	62 19.1	3.8*	64.6	62 44.1	-1.8*	66.3	43
44	59 03.1	16.3	53.4	59 38.4	14.8	54.7	60 12.4	13.1	56.1	60 45.2	11.4	57.6	61 16.6	9.6	59.2	61 46.7	7.8	60.8	62 15.3	5.9	62.4	62 42.3	3.9*	64.1	44

36°, 324° L.H.A.   LATITUDE SAME NAME AS DECLINATION

N. Lat. { L.H.A. greater than 180° ...... Zn=Z
{ L.H.A. less than 180° .... Zn=360°−Z

Dec.	30° Hc	30° d	30° Z	31° Hc	31° d	31° Z	32° Hc	32° d	32° Z	33° Hc	33° d	33° Z	34° Hc	34° d	34° Z	35° Hc	35° d	35° Z	36° Hc	36° d	36° Z	37° Hc	37° d	37° Z	Dec.
0	44 28.7	+41.7	124.5	43 54.3	+42.6	125.3	43 19.3	+43.4	126.1	42 43.6	+44.2	126.9	42 07.3	+45.0	127.6	41 30.4	+45.8	128.3	40 52.9	+46.5	129.0	40 14.9	+47.2	129.6	0
1	45 10.4	41.3	123.5	44 36.9	42.2	124.4	44 02.7	43.0	125.2	43 27.8	43.9	125.9	42 52.3	44.6	126.7	42 16.2	45.3	127.4	41 39.4	46.1	128.1	41 02.1	46.8	128.8	1
2	45 51.7	40.6	122.5	45 19.1	41.5	123.3	44 45.7	42.5	124.2	44 11.7	43.3	125.0	43 36.9	44.2	125.8	43 01.5	45.0	126.5	42 25.5	45.7	127.3	41 48.9	46.4	128.0	2
3	46 32.3	40.1	121.4	46 00.6	41.0	122.3	45 28.2	41.9	123.2	44 55.0	42.8	124.0	44 21.1	43.6	124.8	43 46.5	44.4	125.6	43 11.2	45.3	126.4	42 35.3	46.0	127.1	3
4	47 12.4	39.4	120.2	46 41.6	40.4	121.3	46 10.1	41.4	122.1	45 37.8	42.3	123.0	45 04.7	43.2	123.9	44 30.9	44.1	124.7	43 56.5	44.8	125.5	43 21.3	45.6	126.3	4
5	47 51.8	+38.7	119.2	47 22.0	+39.8	120.2	46 51.5	+40.7	121.1	46 20.1	+41.7	122.0	45 47.9	+42.6	122.9	45 15.0	+43.5	123.7	44 41.3	+44.4	124.6	44 06.9	+45.2	125.4	5
6	48 30.5	38.1	118.1	48 01.8	39.1	119.1	47 32.2	40.2	120.0	47 01.8	41.1	120.9	46 30.5	42.1	121.9	45 58.5	43.0	122.7	45 25.7	43.8	123.6	44 52.1	44.7	124.4	6
7	49 08.6	37.3	116.9	48 40.9	38.5	117.9	48 12.4	39.5	118.9	47 42.9	40.6	119.9	47 12.6	41.5	120.8	46 41.5	42.4	121.7	46 09.5	43.4	122.6	45 36.8	44.2	123.5	7
8	49 45.9	36.5	115.7	49 19.4	37.7	116.7	48 51.9	38.8	117.8	48 23.5	39.8	118.8	47 54.1	40.9	119.8	47 23.9	41.9	120.7	46 52.9	42.8	121.6	46 21.0	43.8	122.6	8
9	50 22.4	35.8	114.5	49 57.1	36.9	115.5	49 30.7	38.1	116.6	49 03.3	39.2	117.6	48 35.0	40.3	118.6	48 05.8	41.3	119.6	47 35.7	42.3	120.6	47 04.8	43.2	121.5	9
10	50 58.2	+34.9	113.2	50 34.0	+36.1	114.3	50 08.8	+37.3	115.4	49 42.5	+38.5	116.5	49 15.3	+39.6	117.5	48 47.1	+40.6	118.5	48 18.0	+41.6	119.5	47 48.0	+42.6	120.5	10
11	51 33.1	34.0	111.9	51 10.1	35.3	113.1	50 46.1	36.5	114.2	50 21.0	37.7	115.3	49 54.9	38.8	116.4	49 27.7	40.0	117.4	48 59.6	41.0	118.4	48 30.6	42.0	119.4	11
12	52 07.1	33.1	110.6	51 45.4	34.4	111.7	51 22.6	35.7	112.9	50 58.7	36.9	114.1	50 33.7	38.1	115.2	50 07.7	39.2	116.3	49 40.6	40.4	117.3	49 12.6	41.4	118.3	12
13	52 40.2	32.1	109.2	52 19.8	33.5	110.4	51 58.3	34.8	111.6	51 35.6	36.1	112.8	51 11.8	37.3	113.9	50 46.9	38.5	115.1	50 21.0	39.6	116.2	49 54.0	40.8	117.2	13
14	53 12.3	31.1	107.8	52 53.3	32.5	109.0	52 33.1	33.9	110.3	52 11.7	35.2	111.5	51 49.1	36.5	112.7	51 25.4	37.8	113.8	51 00.6	39.0	115.0	50 34.8	40.0	116.1	14
15	53 43.4	+30.0	106.4	53 25.8	+31.5	107.6	53 07.0	+32.9	108.9	52 46.9	+34.3	110.2	52 25.6	+35.7	111.4	52 03.2	+36.9	112.6	51 39.6	+38.1	113.8	51 14.8	+39.4	114.9	15
16	54 13.4	29.0	104.9	53 57.3	30.5	106.2	53 39.9	32.0	107.5	53 21.2	33.4	108.8	53 01.3	34.7	110.1	52 40.1	36.0	111.3	52 17.7	37.3	112.5	51 54.2	38.5	113.7	16
17	54 42.4	27.8	103.4	54 27.8	29.4	104.7	54 11.9	30.8	106.0	53 54.6	32.3	107.4	53 36.0	33.7	108.7	53 16.1	35.1	110.0	52 55.0	36.5	111.2	52 32.7	37.7	112.4	17
18	55 10.2	26.6	101.8	54 57.2	28.2	103.2	54 42.7	29.8	104.6	54 26.9	31.3	106.0	54 09.7	32.8	107.3	53 51.2	34.2	108.6	53 31.5	35.5	109.9	53 10.4	36.9	111.1	18
19	55 36.8	25.3	100.3	55 25.4	27.0	101.7	55 12.5	28.6	103.1	54 58.2	30.2	104.5	54 42.5	31.7	105.9	54 25.4	33.2	107.2	54 07.0	34.6	108.5	53 47.3	36.0	109.8	19
20	56 02.1	+24.1	98.6	55 52.4	+25.7	100.1	55 41.1	+27.4	101.5	55 28.4	+29.0	103.0	55 14.2	+30.6	104.4	54 58.6	+32.1	105.8	54 41.6	+33.6	107.1	54 23.3	+35.0	108.5	20
21	56 26.2	22.7	97.0	56 18.1	24.5	98.5	56 08.5	26.2	100.0	55 57.4	27.8	101.4	55 44.8	29.4	102.9	55 30.7	31.0	104.3	55 15.2	32.5	105.7	54 58.3	34.0	107.1	21
22	56 48.9	21.4	95.3	56 42.6	23.1	96.8	56 34.7	24.9	98.3	56 25.2	26.6	99.8	56 14.2	28.3	101.3	56 01.7	29.9	102.8	55 47.7	31.5	104.2	55 32.3	33.0	105.6	22
23	57 10.3	19.9	93.6	57 05.7	21.8	95.1	56 59.6	23.5	96.7	56 51.8	25.3	98.2	56 42.5	26.9	99.7	56 31.6	28.6	101.2	56 19.2	30.3	102.7	56 05.3	31.8	104.1	23
24	57 30.2	18.5	91.8	57 27.5	20.3	93.4	57 23.1	22.1	95.0	57 17.1	23.9	96.5	57 09.4	25.7	98.1	57 00.2	27.4	99.6	56 49.5	29.0	101.1	56 37.1	30.8	102.6	24
25	57 48.7	+16.9	90.1	57 47.8	+18.8	91.7	57 45.2	+20.7	93.2	57 41.0	+22.5	94.8	57 35.1	+24.3	96.4	57 27.6	+26.1	97.9	57 18.5	+27.8	99.5	57 07.9	+29.4	101.0	25
26	58 05.6	15.3	88.3	58 06.6	17.2	89.9	58 05.9	19.1	91.5	58 03.5	21.0	93.1	57 59.4	22.9	94.7	57 53.7	24.7	96.3	57 46.3	26.5	97.8	57 37.3	28.3	99.4	26
27	58 20.9	13.8	86.4	58 23.8	15.7	88.0	58 25.0	17.7	89.7	58 24.5	19.6	91.3	58 22.3	21.4	92.9	58 18.4	23.3	94.5	58 12.8	25.1	96.1	58 05.6	26.9	97.7	27
28	58 34.7	12.1	84.6	58 39.5	14.1	86.2	58 42.7	16.0	87.8	58 44.1	18.0	89.5	58 43.7	20.0	91.1	58 41.7	21.8	92.8	58 37.9	23.7	94.4	58 32.5	25.5	96.0	28
29	58 46.8	10.5	82.7	58 53.6	12.5	84.3	58 58.7	14.4	86.0	59 02.1	16.3	87.6	59 03.7	18.3	89.3	59 03.5	20.3	91.0	59 01.6	22.2	92.6	58 58.0	24.1	94.3	29
30	58 57.3	+8.7	80.8	59 06.1	+10.7	82.4	59 13.1	+12.8	84.1	59 18.4	+14.8	85.8	59 22.0	+16.7	87.4	59 23.8	+18.7	89.1	59 23.8	+20.7	90.8	59 22.1	+22.5	92.5	30
31	59 06.1	7.0	78.8	59 16.8	9.1	80.5	59 25.9	11.0	82.2	59 33.2	13.0	83.9	59 38.7	15.1	85.6	59 42.5	17.0	87.3	59 44.5	19.0	89.0	59 44.6	21.0	90.7	31
32	59 13.1	5.3	76.9	59 25.9	7.3	78.6	59 36.9	9.3	80.2	59 46.2	11.3	82.0	59 53.8	13.3	83.9	59 59.5	15.4	85.3	60 03.5	17.4	87.1	60 05.6	19.4	88.8	32
33	59 18.4	3.6	75.0	59 33.2	5.5	76.6	59 46.2	7.6	78.3	59 57.5	9.6	80.0	60 07.1	11.6	81.7	60 14.9	13.7	83.4	60 20.9	15.7	85.2	60 25.0	17.8	86.9	33
34	59 22.0	+1.8	73.0	59 38.7	3.8	74.6	59 53.8	5.7	76.3	60 07.1	7.8	78.0	60 18.7	9.9	79.7	60 28.6	11.8	81.4	60 36.6	13.9	83.2	60 42.8	16.0	85.0	34
35	59 23.8	0.0	71.0	59 42.5	+2.0	72.7	59 59.5	+4.0	74.3	60 14.9	+6.0	76.0	60 28.6	+8.0	77.7	60 40.4	+10.1	79.4	60 50.5	+12.2	81.2	60 58.8	+14.2	83.0	35
36	59 23.8	−1.7	69.1	59 44.5	0.1	70.7	60 03.5	2.1	72.3	60 20.9	4.1	74.0	60 36.6	6.2	75.7	60 50.5	8.3	77.4	61 02.7	10.3	79.2	61 13.0	12.5	81.0	36
37	59 22.1	3.5	67.1	59 44.6	−1.6	68.7	60 05.6	0.4	70.3	60 25.0	2.4	72.0	60 42.8	4.3	73.7	60 58.8	6.5	75.4	61 13.0	8.5	77.1	61 25.5	10.6	78.9	37
38	59 18.6	5.3	65.2	59 43.0	3.4	66.7	60 06.0	−1.5	68.3	60 27.4	0.4	70.0	60 47.1	2.5	71.6	61 05.2	4.5	73.3	61 21.5	6.6	75.1	61 36.1	8.6	76.9	38
39	59 13.3	7.0	63.2	59 39.6	5.2	64.7	60 04.5	3.3	66.3	60 27.8	−1.3	67.9	60 49.6	+0.6	69.6	61 09.7	2.6	71.3	61 28.1	4.7	73.0	61 44.7	6.8	74.8	39
40	59 06.3	−8.7	61.3	59 34.4	−6.9	62.8	60 01.2	−5.1	64.3	60 26.5	3.3	65.9	60 50.2	−1.3	67.5	61 12.3	+0.7	69.2	61 32.8	+2.7	70.9	61 51.5	+4.9	72.7	40
41	58 57.6	10.5	59.3	59 27.5	8.7	60.9	59 56.1	6.9	62.3	60 23.2	5.0	63.9	60 48.9	3.1	65.5	61 13.0	−1.2	67.1	61 35.5	0.9	68.8	61 56.4	2.9*	70.6	41
42	58 47.1	12.0	57.4	59 18.8	10.4	58.9	59 49.2	8.7	60.3	60 18.2	6.9	61.8	60 45.8	5.0	63.4	61 11.8	3.0	65.0	61 36.4	−1.1	66.7	61 59.3	0.9*	68.4	42
43	58 35.1	13.8	55.6	59 08.4	12.1	56.9	59 40.5	10.4	58.4	60 11.3	8.7	59.8	60 40.8	6.9	61.4	61 08.8	5.0	63.0	61 35.3	3.1	64.6	62 00.2	−1.1	66.3	43
44	58 21.3	15.3	53.7	58 56.3	13.8	55.0	59 30.1	12.1	56.4	60 02.6	10.4	57.9	60 33.9	8.7	59.4	61 03.8	6.9	60.9	61 32.2	5.0	62.5	61 59.1	3.0	64.2	44
Dec.	30°			31°			32°			33°			34°			35°			36°			37°			Dec.

LATITUDE CONTRARY NAME TO DECLINATION

Dec.	30° Hc	d	Z	31° Hc	d	Z	32° Hc	d	Z	33° Hc	d	Z	34° Hc	d	Z	35° Hc	d	Z	36° Hc	d	Z	37° Hc	d	Z	Dec.
0	43 45.6	-41.8	123.6	43 12.1	-42.7	124.7	42 37.9	-43.5	125.1	42 03.1	-44.3	125.9	41 27.6	-45.0	126.6	40 51.6	-45.7	127.3	40 14.9	-46.3	128.0	39 37.8	-47.1	128.6	0
1	43 03.8	42.3	124.6	42 29.4	43.1	125.3	41 54.4	43.8	126.0	41 18.8	44.6	126.8	40 42.6	45.3	127.5	40 05.9	46.1	128.1	39 28.6	46.8	128.8	38 50.7	47.4	129.4	1
2	42 21.5	42.8	125.5	41 46.3	43.5	126.2	41 10.6	44.3	127.0	40 34.2	45.0	127.6	39 57.3	45.8	128.3	39 19.8	46.4	129.0	38 41.8	47.0	129.6	38 03.3	47.6	130.2	2
3	41 38.7	43.2	126.5	41 02.8	44.0	127.2	40 26.3	44.8	127.8	39 49.2	45.4	128.5	39 11.5	46.0	129.2	38 33.4	46.7	129.8	37 54.8	47.4	130.4	37 15.7	48.0	131.0	3
4	40 55.5	43.6	127.4	40 18.8	44.4	128.1	39 41.5	45.0	128.7	39 03.8	45.8	129.4	38 25.5	46.5	130.0	37 46.7	47.1	130.6	37 07.4	47.7	131.2	36 27.7	48.2	131.7	4
5	40 11.9	44.1	128.3	39 34.4	44.7	128.9	38 56.5	45.5	129.6	38 18.0	46.1	130.2	37 39.0	46.7	130.8	36 59.6	47.3	131.4	36 19.7	47.9	131.9	35 39.5	48.6	132.5	5
6	39 27.8	44.5	129.2	38 49.7	45.2	129.8	38 11.0	45.8	130.4	37 31.9	46.5	131.0	36 52.3	47.1	131.6	36 12.3	47.7	132.2	35 31.8	48.2	132.7	34 50.9	48.7	133.2	6
7	38 43.3	44.8	130.0	38 04.5	45.5	130.6	37 25.2	46.1	131.2	36 45.4	46.7	131.8	36 05.2	47.3	132.3	35 24.6	47.9	132.9	34 43.6	48.5	133.4	34 02.2	49.0	133.9	7
8	37 58.5	45.2	130.9	37 19.0	45.8	131.5	36 39.1	46.5	132.0	35 58.7	47.1	132.6	35 17.9	47.6	133.1	34 36.7	48.2	133.6	33 55.1	48.7	134.1	33 13.2	49.2	134.6	8
9	37 13.3	45.5	131.7	36 33.2	46.2	132.3	35 52.6	46.7	132.8	35 11.6	47.3	133.3	34 30.3	47.9	133.8	33 48.5	48.4	134.4	33 06.4	48.9	134.8	32 24.0	49.5	135.3	9
10	36 27.8	45.9	132.5	35 47.0	46.4	133.1	35 05.9	47.1	133.6	34 24.3	47.6	134.1	33 42.4	48.2	134.6	33 00.1	48.7	135.0	32 17.5	49.2	135.5	31 34.5	49.6	135.9	10
11	35 41.9	46.1	133.3	35 00.6	46.8	133.8	34 18.8	47.3	134.3	33 36.7	47.8	134.8	32 54.2	48.3	135.3	32 11.4	48.8	135.7	31 28.3	49.3	136.2	30 44.9	49.8	136.6	11
12	34 55.8	46.5	134.1	34 13.8	47.0	134.6	33 31.5	47.6	135.1	32 48.9	48.1	135.5	32 05.9	48.6	136.0	31 22.6	49.1	136.4	30 39.0	49.6	136.8	29 55.1	50.1	137.2	12
13	34 09.3	46.7	134.9	33 26.8	47.3	135.4	32 43.9	47.8	135.8	32 00.8	48.4	136.2	31 17.3	48.8	136.7	30 33.5	49.3	137.1	29 49.4	49.8	137.5	29 05.0	50.2	137.9	13
14	33 22.6	47.0	135.6	32 39.5	47.5	136.1	31 56.1	48.0	136.5	31 12.4	48.5	136.9	30 28.5	49.1	137.3	29 44.2	49.5	137.7	28 59.6	49.9	138.1	28 14.8	50.3	138.5	14
15	32 35.6	47.3	136.4	31 52.0	47.8	136.8	31 08.1	48.3	137.2	30 23.9	48.8	137.6	29 39.4	49.2	138.0	28 54.7	49.7	138.4	28 09.7	50.1	138.7	27 24.5	50.5	139.1	15
16	31 48.3	47.5	137.1	31 04.2	48.0	137.5	30 19.8	48.5	137.9	29 35.1	48.9	138.3	28 50.2	49.4	138.7	28 05.0	49.8	139.0	27 19.6	50.3	139.4	26 34.0	50.7	139.7	16
17	31 00.8	47.8	137.8	30 16.2	48.3	138.2	29 31.3	48.7	138.6	28 46.2	49.2	139.0	28 00.8	49.6	139.3	27 15.2	50.0	139.7	26 29.3	50.4	140.0	25 43.3	50.8	140.3	17
18	30 13.0	47.9	138.5	29 27.9	48.4	138.9	28 42.6	48.9	139.3	27 57.0	49.3	139.6	27 11.2	49.7	140.0	26 25.2	50.2	140.3	25 38.9	50.5	140.6	24 52.5	51.0	140.9	18
19	29 25.1	48.2	139.2	28 39.5	48.6	139.6	27 53.7	49.1	139.9	27 07.7	49.5	140.3	26 21.5	49.9	140.6	25 35.0	50.3	140.9	24 48.4	50.8	141.2	24 01.5	51.1	141.5	19
20	28 36.9	48.4	139.9	27 50.9	48.8	140.2	27 04.6	49.2	140.6	26 18.2	49.7	140.9	25 31.5	50.0	141.2	24 44.7	50.5	141.5	23 57.6	50.8	141.8	23 10.4	51.2	142.0	20
21	27 48.5	48.6	140.6	27 02.1	49.0	140.9	26 15.4	49.4	141.2	25 28.5	49.8	141.5	24 41.5	50.3	141.8	23 54.2	50.6	142.1	23 06.8	51.0	142.3	22 19.2	51.3	142.6	21
22	26 59.9	48.7	141.2	26 13.1	49.2	141.5	25 26.0	49.6	141.8	24 38.7	50.0	142.1	23 51.2	50.3	142.4	23 03.6	50.7	142.7	22 15.8	51.1	142.9	21 27.9	51.4	143.2	22
23	26 11.2	49.0	141.9	25 23.9	49.4	142.2	24 36.4	49.7	142.5	23 48.7	50.1	142.7	23 00.9	50.5	143.0	22 12.9	50.8	143.2	21 24.8	51.2	143.5	20 36.5	51.6	143.7	23
24	25 22.2	49.0	142.5	24 34.5	49.4	142.8	23 46.7	49.9	143.1	22 58.6	50.2	143.3	22 10.4	50.6	143.6	21 22.1	51.0	143.8	20 33.6	51.3	144.0	19 44.9	51.6	144.3	24
25	24 33.2	49.3	143.2	23 45.1	49.7	143.4	22 56.8	50.0	143.7	22 08.4	50.4	143.9	21 19.8	50.7	144.2	20 31.1	51.1	144.4	19 42.3	51.4	144.6	18 53.3	51.7	144.8	25
26	23 43.9	49.4	143.8	22 55.4	49.8	144.0	22 06.8	50.2	144.3	21 18.0	50.5	144.5	20 29.1	50.9	144.7	19 40.0	51.1	145.0	18 50.9	51.5	145.1	18 01.6	51.8	145.3	26
27	22 54.5	49.5	144.4	22 05.6	49.9	144.6	21 16.6	50.2	144.9	20 27.5	50.6	145.1	19 38.2	50.9	145.3	18 48.9	51.3	145.5	17 59.4	51.6	145.7	17 09.7	51.8	145.9	27
28	22 05.0	49.7	145.0	21 15.7	50.0	145.2	20 26.4	50.4	145.5	19 36.9	50.7	145.6	18 47.3	51.0	145.9	17 57.6	51.4	146.1	17 07.8	51.7	146.2	16 17.9	52.0	146.4	28
29	21 15.3	49.8	145.6	20 25.7	50.1	145.8	19 36.0	50.5	146.0	18 46.2	50.8	146.2	17 56.3	51.1	146.4	17 06.2	51.4	146.6	16 16.1	51.7	146.7	15 25.9	52.0	146.9	29
30	20 25.5	49.9	146.2	19 35.6	50.3	146.4	18 45.5	50.6	146.6	17 55.4	50.9	146.8	17 05.2	51.2	147.0	16 14.8	51.5	147.1	15 24.4	51.9	147.3	14 33.8	52.1	147.4	30
31	19 35.6	50.1	146.8	18 45.3	50.4	147.0	17 54.9	50.7	147.2	17 04.5	51.0	147.3	16 13.9	51.3	147.5	15 23.3	51.6	147.7	14 32.5	51.9	147.8	13 41.7	52.2	147.9	31
32	18 45.5	50.1	147.4	17 54.9	50.4	147.6	17 04.2	50.7	147.7	16 13.5	51.1	147.9	15 22.6	51.4	148.0	14 31.7	51.7	148.2	13 40.6	52.0	148.4	12 49.5	52.2	148.4	32
33	17 55.4	50.3	148.0	17 04.5	50.6	148.1	16 13.5	50.9	148.3	15 22.4	51.1	148.4	14 31.2	51.4	148.6	13 40.0	51.7	148.7	12 48.7	52.0	148.8	11 57.3	52.3	148.9	33
34	17 05.1	50.4	148.5	16 13.9	50.6	148.7	15 22.6	50.9	148.8	14 31.2	51.2	149.0	13 39.8	51.5	149.1	12 48.3	51.8	149.2	11 56.7	52.1	149.3	11 05.0	52.3	149.4	34
35	16 14.8	50.4	149.1	15 23.3	50.8	149.2	14 31.7	51.1	149.4	13 40.0	51.3	149.5	12 48.3	51.6	149.6	11 56.5	51.9	149.7	11 04.6	52.1	149.9	10 12.7	52.4	149.9	35
36	15 24.4	50.6	149.7	14 32.5	50.8	149.8	13 40.6	51.1	149.9	12 48.7	51.3	150.0	11 56.7	51.6	150.2	11 04.6	51.9	150.3	10 12.5	52.2	150.3	9 20.3	52.4	150.4	36
37	14 33.8	50.6	150.2	13 41.7	50.9	150.4	12 49.5	51.1	150.5	11 57.3	51.4	150.6	11 05.0	51.7	150.7	10 12.7	52.0	150.8	9 20.3	52.2	150.9	8 27.9	52.5	150.9	37
38	13 43.2	50.6	150.8	12 50.8	50.9	150.9	11 58.4	51.2	151.0	11 05.9	51.4	151.1	10 13.3	51.7	151.2	9 20.7	52.0	151.3	8 28.1	52.3	151.3	7 35.4	52.5	151.4	38
39	12 52.6	50.8	151.3	11 59.9	51.0	151.4	11 07.2	51.3	151.5	10 14.4	51.5	151.6	9 21.6	51.8	151.7	8 28.7	52.0	151.8	7 35.9	52.3	151.8	6 42.9	52.5	151.9	39
40	12 01.8	50.8	151.9	11 08.9	51.1	152.0	10 15.9	51.3	152.1	9 22.9	51.6	152.1	8 29.8	51.8	152.2	7 36.7	52.1	152.3	6 43.6	52.3	152.3	5 50.4	52.5	152.4	40
41	11 11.0	50.8	152.4	10 17.8	51.1	152.5	9 24.6	51.4	152.6	8 31.3	51.6	152.7	7 38.0	51.9	152.7	6 44.6	52.1	152.8	5 51.3	52.4	152.8	4 57.9	52.6	152.9	41
42	10 20.2	50.9	153.0	9 26.7	51.2	153.0	8 33.2	51.4	153.1	7 39.7	51.7	153.2	6 46.1	51.9	153.2	5 52.5	52.2	153.3	4 58.9	52.4	153.3	4 05.3	52.6	153.4	42
43	9 29.3	51.0	153.5	8 35.5	51.2	153.6	7 41.8	51.5	153.6	6 48.0	51.7	153.7	5 54.2	52.0	153.7	5 00.4	52.1	153.8	4 06.6	52.4	153.8	3 12.7	52.6	153.8	43
44	8 38.3	51.0	154.0	7 44.3	51.2	154.1	6 50.3	51.4	154.2	5 56.3	51.7	154.2	5 02.3	51.9	154.3	4 08.3	52.2	154.3	3 14.2	52.4	154.3	2 20.1	52.6	154.3	44

Dec.	30° Hc	d	Z	31° Hc	d	Z	32° Hc	d	Z	33° Hc	d	Z	34° Hc	d	Z	35° Hc	d	Z	36° Hc	d	Z	37° Hc	d	Z	Dec.
0	43 02.1	-41.3	122.6	42 29.4	-42.2	123.4	41 56.0	-42.9	124.1	41 22.0	-43.7	124.9	40 47.4	-44.5	125.6	40 12.2	-45.3	126.3	39 36.4	-46.0	127.0	39 00.1	-46.7	127.6	0
1	42 20.8	41.8	123.6	41 47.2	42.6	124.4	41 13.1	43.5	125.1	40 38.3	44.2	125.8	40 02.9	44.9	126.6	39 26.9	45.6	127.1	38 50.4	46.2	127.8	38 13.4	46.9	128.4	1
2	41 39.0	42.3	124.6	41 04.6	43.1	125.3	40 29.6	43.8	126.0	39 54.1	44.6	126.7	39 18.0	45.3	127.4	38 41.3	45.9	128.0	38 04.2	46.7	128.6	37 26.5	47.3	129.2	2
3	40 56.7	42.7	125.5	40 21.5	43.4	126.2	39 45.8	44.3	126.9	39 09.5	45.1	127.5	38 32.7	45.6	128.2	37 55.4	46.3	128.8	37 17.5	46.9	129.4	36 39.2	47.5	130.0	3
4	40 14.0	43.2	126.4	39 38.1	43.9	127.1	39 01.6	44.6	127.8	38 24.6	45.3	128.4	37 47.1	46.0	129.0	37 09.1	46.7	129.6	36 30.6	47.3	130.2	35 51.7	47.9	130.7	4
5	39 30.8	-43.5	127.3	38 54.2	-44.3	128.0	38 17.0	-45.0	128.6	37 39.3	-45.7	129.2	37 01.1	-46.3	129.8	36 22.4	-46.9	130.4	35 43.3	-47.5	130.9	35 03.8	-48.1	131.5	5
6	38 47.3	44.0	128.2	38 09.9	44.7	128.9	37 32.0	45.4	129.5	36 53.6	46.0	130.0	36 14.8	46.6	130.6	35 35.5	47.2	131.2	34 55.8	47.8	131.7	34 15.7	48.3	132.2	6
7	38 03.3	44.3	129.1	37 25.2	45.0	129.7	36 46.6	45.6	130.3	36 07.6	46.3	130.8	35 28.2	46.9	131.4	34 48.3	47.5	131.9	34 08.0	48.0	132.4	33 27.4	48.6	132.9	7
8	37 19.0	44.7	130.0	36 40.2	45.4	130.5	36 01.0	46.0	131.1	35 21.3	46.5	131.6	34 41.3	47.2	132.1	34 00.8	47.7	132.6	33 20.0	48.3	133.1	32 38.8	48.8	133.6	8
9	36 34.3	45.1	130.8	35 54.8	45.7	131.3	35 15.0	46.3	131.9	34 34.8	46.9	132.4	33 54.1	47.4	132.9	33 13.1	48.0	133.4	32 31.7	48.4	133.8	31 50.0	49.1	134.3	9
10	35 49.2	-45.3	131.6	35 09.2	-46.0	132.1	34 28.7	-46.6	132.6	33 47.9	-47.2	133.1	33 06.7	-47.7	133.6	32 25.1	-48.2	134.1	31 43.2	-48.8	134.5	31 00.9	-49.2	135.0	10
11	35 03.9	45.7	132.4	34 23.2	46.3	132.9	33 42.1	46.8	133.4	33 00.7	47.4	133.9	32 19.0	48.0	134.3	31 36.9	48.5	134.8	30 54.4	48.9	135.2	30 11.7	49.5	135.6	11
12	34 18.2	46.0	133.2	33 36.9	46.5	133.7	32 55.3	47.1	134.1	32 13.3	47.6	134.6	31 31.0	48.1	135.0	30 48.4	48.7	135.5	30 05.5	49.2	135.9	29 22.2	49.6	136.3	12
13	33 32.2	46.3	134.0	32 50.4	46.9	134.4	32 08.2	47.4	134.9	31 25.7	47.9	135.3	30 42.9	48.4	135.8	29 59.7	48.9	136.2	29 16.3	49.3	136.6	28 32.6	49.8	136.9	13
14	32 45.9	46.5	134.7	32 03.5	47.0	135.2	31 20.8	47.6	135.6	30 37.8	48.1	136.0	29 54.5	48.6	136.4	29 10.8	49.0	136.8	28 27.0	49.6	137.2	27 42.8	50.0	137.6	14
15	31 59.4	-46.8	135.5	31 16.5	-47.3	135.9	30 33.2	-47.8	136.3	29 49.7	-48.3	136.7	29 05.9	-48.8	137.1	28 21.8	-49.3	137.5	27 37.4	-49.7	137.8	26 52.8	-50.1	138.2	15
16	31 12.6	47.0	136.2	30 29.2	47.6	136.6	29 45.4	48.0	137.0	29 01.4	48.6	137.4	28 17.1	49.0	137.8	27 32.5	49.4	138.1	26 47.7	49.9	138.5	26 02.7	50.3	138.8	16
17	30 25.6	47.3	136.9	29 41.6	47.8	137.3	28 57.4	48.3	137.7	28 12.8	48.7	138.1	27 28.1	49.2	138.4	26 43.1	49.6	138.8	25 57.8	50.0	139.1	25 12.4	50.5	139.4	17
18	29 38.3	47.5	137.6	28 53.8	47.9	138.0	28 09.1	48.4	138.4	27 24.1	48.9	138.7	26 38.9	49.3	139.1	25 53.5	49.8	139.4	25 07.8	50.2	139.7	24 21.9	50.5	140.0	18
19	28 50.8	47.7	138.3	28 05.9	48.2	138.7	27 20.7	48.7	139.1	26 35.2	49.0	139.4	25 49.6	49.5	139.7	25 03.7	49.9	140.0	24 17.6	50.2	140.3	23 31.4	50.7	140.6	19
20	28 03.1	-47.9	139.0	27 17.7	-48.4	139.4	26 32.0	-48.8	139.7	25 46.2	-49.3	140.0	25 00.1	-49.7	140.3	24 13.8	-50.1	140.6	23 27.3	-50.4	140.9	22 40.7	-50.9	141.2	20
21	27 15.2	48.1	139.7	26 29.3	48.5	140.0	25 43.2	49.1	140.4	24 56.9	49.4	140.7	24 10.4	49.8	140.9	23 23.7	50.2	141.2	22 36.9	50.6	141.5	21 49.8	50.9	141.7	21
22	26 27.1	48.3	140.4	25 40.8	48.8	140.7	24 54.1	49.1	141.0	24 07.5	49.5	141.3	23 20.6	49.9	141.6	22 33.5	50.3	141.8	21 46.3	50.7	142.1	20 58.9	51.1	142.3	22
23	25 38.8	48.5	141.0	24 52.0	48.8	141.3	24 05.1	49.3	141.6	23 18.0	49.7	141.9	22 30.7	50.1	142.2	21 43.2	50.4	142.4	20 55.6	50.8	142.6	20 07.8	51.1	142.9	23
24	24 50.3	48.6	141.7	24 03.2	49.1	142.0	23 15.8	49.4	142.3	22 28.3	49.8	142.5	21 40.6	50.2	142.8	20 52.8	50.6	143.0	20 04.8	50.9	143.2	19 16.7	51.3	143.4	24
25	24 01.7	-48.8	142.3	23 14.1	-49.2	142.6	22 26.4	-49.6	142.9	21 38.5	-50.0	143.1	20 50.4	-50.3	143.3	20 02.2	-50.7	143.6	19 13.9	-51.1	143.8	18 25.4	-51.4	144.0	25
26	23 12.9	48.9	143.0	22 24.9	49.3	143.2	21 36.8	49.7	143.5	20 48.5	50.1	143.7	20 00.1	50.5	143.9	19 11.5	50.8	144.2	18 22.8	51.1	144.3	17 34.0	51.4	144.5	26
27	22 24.0	49.1	143.6	21 35.6	49.5	143.8	20 47.1	49.9	144.1	19 58.4	50.2	144.3	19 09.6	50.5	144.5	18 20.7	50.8	144.7	17 31.7	51.2	144.9	16 42.6	51.6	145.1	27
28	21 34.9	49.2	144.2	20 46.1	49.6	144.5	19 57.2	49.9	144.7	19 08.2	50.3	144.9	18 19.1	50.6	145.1	17 29.9	51.0	145.3	16 40.5	51.3	145.4	15 51.0	51.6	145.6	28
29	20 45.7	49.4	144.8	19 56.5	49.7	145.1	19 07.3	50.1	145.3	18 17.9	50.4	145.4	17 28.5	50.8	145.6	16 38.9	51.1	145.8	15 49.2	51.3	146.0	14 59.4	51.6	146.1	29
30	19 56.3	-49.5	145.4	19 06.8	-49.8	145.6	18 17.2	-50.1	145.8	17 27.5	-50.5	146.0	16 37.7	-50.8	146.2	15 47.8	-51.1	146.4	14 57.8	-51.4	146.5	14 07.8	-51.8	146.6	30
31	19 06.8	49.6	146.0	18 17.0	49.9	146.2	17 27.1	50.3	146.4	16 37.0	50.6	146.6	15 46.9	50.9	146.7	14 56.7	51.2	146.9	14 06.4	51.5	147.0	13 16.0	51.8	147.2	31
32	18 17.2	49.7	146.6	17 27.1	50.1	146.8	16 36.8	50.4	146.9	15 46.4	50.6	147.1	14 56.0	50.9	147.3	14 05.5	51.3	147.4	13 14.9	51.6	147.6	12 24.2	51.9	147.6	32
33	17 27.5	49.8	147.2	16 37.0	50.1	147.4	15 46.4	50.4	147.6	14 55.8	50.8	147.7	14 05.0	51.0	147.8	13 14.2	51.4	148.0	12 23.3	51.7	148.1	11 32.3	51.9	148.2	33
34	16 37.7	49.9	147.8	15 46.9	50.2	148.0	14 56.0	50.5	148.1	14 05.0	50.8	148.2	13 14.0	51.2	148.4	12 22.8	51.4	148.5	11 31.6	51.6	148.6	10 40.4	52.0	148.7	34
35	15 47.8	-50.0	148.4	14 56.7	-50.3	148.5	14 05.5	-50.6	148.7	13 14.2	-50.9	148.8	12 22.8	-51.2	148.9	11 31.4	-51.4	149.0	10 40.0	-51.8	149.1	9 48.4	-52.0	149.2	35
36	14 57.8	50.0	149.0	14 06.4	50.4	149.1	13 14.9	50.7	149.2	12 23.3	51.0	149.3	11 31.6	51.2	149.4	10 40.0	51.6	149.5	9 48.2	51.8	149.6	8 56.4	52.0	149.7	36
37	14 07.8	50.2	149.5	13 16.0	50.4	149.7	12 24.2	50.7	149.8	11 32.3	51.0	149.9	10 40.4	51.3	150.0	9 48.4	51.6	150.1	8 56.4	51.8	150.1	8 04.3	52.1	150.2	37
38	13 17.6	50.2	150.1	12 25.6	50.5	150.2	11 33.5	50.8	150.3	10 41.3	51.0	150.4	9 49.1	51.3	150.5	8 56.9	51.7	150.5	8 04.6	51.9	150.7	7 12.3	52.1	150.7	38
39	12 27.4	50.3	150.7	11 35.0	50.5	150.8	10 42.7	50.9	150.9	9 50.2	51.1	150.9	8 57.8	51.4	151.0	8 05.2	51.6	151.1	7 12.7	51.9	151.2	6 20.1	52.1	151.2	39
40	11 37.1	-50.4	151.2	10 44.5	-50.7	151.3	9 51.8	-50.9	151.4	8 59.1	-51.2	151.5	8 06.4	-51.5	151.6	7 13.6	-51.7	151.6	6 20.8	-51.9	151.7	5 28.0	-52.2	151.7	40
41	10 46.7	50.4	151.8	9 53.8	50.7	151.9	9 00.9	51.0	151.9	8 07.9	51.2	152.0	7 14.9	51.5	152.1	6 21.9	51.7	152.1	5 28.9	52.0	152.2	4 35.8	52.2	152.2	41
42	9 56.3	50.5	152.3	9 03.1	50.7	152.4	8 09.9	51.0	152.5	7 16.7	51.2	152.5	6 23.5	51.5	152.6	5 30.2	51.7	152.6	4 36.9	52.0	152.7	3 43.6	52.2	152.7	42
43	9 05.8	50.5	152.9	8 12.4	50.8	152.9	7 18.9	51.0	153.0	6 25.5	51.3	153.1	5 32.0	51.5	153.1	4 38.5	51.8	153.1	3 44.9	52.0	153.2	2 51.4	52.3	153.2	43
44	8 15.3	50.6	153.4	7 21.6	50.8	153.5	6 27.9	51.0	153.5	5 34.2	51.3	153.6	4 40.5	51.6	153.6	3 46.7	51.8	153.7	2 52.9	52.0	153.7	1 59.1	52.2	153.7	44

42°, 318° L.H.A.

LATITUDE SAME NAME AS DECLINATION

N. Lat. { L.H.A. greater than 180° .... Zn=Z / L.H.A. less than 180° .... Zn=360°−Z

Dec.	30° Hc	30° d	30° Z	31° Hc	31° d	31° Z	32° Hc	32° d	32° Z	33° Hc	33° d	33° Z	34° Hc	34° d	34° Z	35° Hc	35° d	35° Z	36° Hc	36° d	36° Z	37° Hc	37° d	37° Z	Dec.
0	40 03.6	+38.9	119.0	39 34.1	+39.9	119.8	39 04.0	+40.7	120.5	38 33.2	+41.6	121.2	38 01.9	+42.4	121.8	37 29.9	+43.2	122.5	36 57.4	+44.0	123.1	36 24.4	+44.6	123.8	0
1	40 42.5	38.4	118.0	40 14.0	39.3	118.8	39 44.7	40.3	119.5	39 14.8	41.1	120.2	38 44.3	41.9	120.9	38 13.1	42.8	121.6	37 41.4	43.5	122.3	37 09.0	44.4	122.9	1
2	41 20.9	37.9	117.0	40 53.3	38.8	117.8	40 25.0	39.7	118.6	39 55.9	40.7	119.3	39 26.2	41.6	120.0	38 55.9	42.4	120.7	38 24.9	43.2	121.4	37 53.4	43.9	122.1	2
3	41 58.8	37.3	116.0	41 32.1	38.3	116.8	41 04.7	39.2	117.6	40 36.6	40.1	118.3	40 07.8	41.0	119.1	39 38.3	41.9	119.8	39 08.1	42.8	120.5	38 37.3	43.6	121.2	3
4	42 36.1	36.7	114.9	42 10.4	37.7	115.8	41 43.9	38.7	116.6	41 16.7	39.7	117.3	40 48.8	40.6	118.1	40 20.2	41.5	118.9	39 50.9	42.3	119.6	39 20.9	43.2	120.3	4
5	43 12.8	+36.0	113.8	42 48.1	+37.1	114.7	42 22.6	+38.2	115.5	41 56.4	+39.1	116.3	41 29.4	+40.1	117.1	41 01.7	+40.9	117.9	40 33.2	+41.9	118.7	40 04.1	+42.7	119.4	5
6	43 48.8	35.5	112.7	43 25.2	36.5	113.6	43 00.8	37.5	114.3	42 35.5	38.6	115.3	42 09.5	39.5	116.1	41 42.6	40.5	116.9	41 15.1	41.4	117.7	40 46.8	42.3	118.5	6
7	44 24.3	34.7	111.6	44 01.7	35.9	112.5	43 38.3	36.9	113.4	43 14.1	37.9	114.3	42 49.0	39.0	115.1	42 23.1	40.0	116.0	41 56.5	40.9	116.8	41 29.1	41.8	117.6	7
8	44 59.0	34.1	110.5	44 37.6	35.2	111.4	44 15.2	36.3	112.3	43 52.0	37.4	113.2	43 28.0	38.4	114.1	43 03.1	39.4	114.9	42 37.4	40.3	115.8	42 10.9	41.3	116.6	8
9	45 33.1	33.3	109.3	45 12.8	34.3	110.3	44 51.5	35.6	111.2	44 29.4	36.7	112.1	44 06.4	37.7	113.0	43 42.5	38.8	113.9	43 17.7	39.9	114.8	42 52.2	40.8	115.6	9
10	46 06.4	+32.5	108.1	45 47.2	+33.8	109.1	45 27.1	+35.0	110.1	45 06.1	+36.1	111.0	44 44.1	+37.2	111.9	44 21.3	+38.2	112.8	43 57.6	+39.2	113.7	43 33.0	+40.3	114.6	10
11	46 38.9	31.8	106.9	46 21.0	33.0	107.9	46 02.1	34.2	108.9	45 42.2	35.3	109.9	45 21.3	36.5	110.8	44 59.5	37.6	111.8	44 36.8	38.7	112.7	44 13.3	39.7	113.6	11
12	47 10.7	31.0	105.7	46 54.0	32.2	106.7	46 36.3	33.4	107.7	46 17.5	34.7	108.7	45 57.8	35.8	109.7	45 37.1	37.0	110.6	45 15.5	38.0	111.6	44 53.0	39.1	112.5	12
13	47 41.7	30.0	104.4	47 26.2	31.4	105.4	47 09.7	32.7	106.5	46 52.2	33.8	107.5	46 33.6	35.1	108.5	46 14.1	36.2	109.5	45 53.5	37.4	110.5	45 32.1	38.4	111.4	13
14	48 11.7	29.2	103.1	47 57.6	30.5	104.2	47 42.4	31.8	105.2	47 26.0	33.2	106.3	47 08.7	34.3	107.3	46 50.3	35.5	108.4	46 30.9	36.7	109.4	46 10.5	37.9	110.3	14
15	48 40.9	+28.3	101.8	48 28.1	+29.7	102.9	48 14.2	+31.0	104.0	47 59.2	+32.2	105.1	47 43.0	+33.6	106.1	47 25.8	+34.8	107.2	47 07.6	+36.0	108.2	46 48.4	+37.1	109.2	15
16	49 09.2	27.4	100.4	48 57.8	28.7	101.6	48 45.2	30.1	102.7	48 31.4	31.5	103.8	48 16.6	32.7	104.9	48 00.6	34.0	106.0	47 43.6	35.2	107.0	47 25.5	36.4	108.1	16
17	49 36.6	26.3	99.1	49 26.5	27.8	100.2	49 15.3	29.2	101.4	49 02.9	30.5	102.5	48 49.3	31.9	103.6	48 34.6	33.2	104.7	48 18.8	34.5	105.8	48 01.9	35.7	106.9	17
18	50 02.9	25.4	97.7	49 54.3	26.8	98.9	49 44.5	28.2	100.0	49 33.4	29.7	101.2	49 21.2	31.0	102.3	49 07.8	32.4	103.5	48 53.3	33.6	104.6	48 37.6	34.9	105.7	18
19	50 28.3	24.2	96.3	50 21.1	25.8	97.5	50 12.7	27.2	98.7	50 03.1	28.6	99.8	49 52.2	30.1	101.0	49 40.2	31.4	102.2	49 26.9	32.8	103.3	49 12.5	34.1	104.4	19
20	50 52.5	+23.2	94.8	50 46.9	+24.7	96.0	50 39.9	+26.2	97.3	50 31.7	+27.7	98.5	50 22.3	+29.1	99.7	50 11.6	+30.5	100.8	49 59.7	+31.9	102.0	49 46.6	+33.3	103.2	20
21	51 15.7	22.1	93.3	51 11.6	23.6	94.6	51 06.1	25.2	95.8	50 59.4	26.7	97.1	50 51.4	28.1	98.3	50 42.1	29.6	99.5	50 31.6	31.0	100.7	50 19.9	32.4	101.9	21
22	51 37.8	20.9	91.9	51 35.2	22.5	93.1	51 31.3	24.1	94.4	51 26.1	25.6	95.6	51 19.5	27.1	96.9	51 11.7	28.6	98.1	51 02.6	30.1	99.3	50 52.3	31.4	100.5	22
23	51 58.7	19.8	90.3	51 57.7	21.4	91.6	51 55.4	22.9	92.9	51 51.7	24.5	94.2	51 46.6	26.1	95.4	51 40.3	27.5	96.7	51 32.7	29.0	97.9	51 23.7	30.5	99.2	23
24	52 18.5	18.5	88.8	52 19.1	20.1	90.1	52 18.3	21.7	91.4	52 16.2	23.3	92.7	52 12.7	24.9	94.0	52 07.8	26.5	95.3	52 01.7	28.0	97.8	51 54.2	29.5	97.8	24
25	52 37.0	+17.3	87.2	52 39.2	+18.9	88.5	52 40.0	+20.6	89.9	52 39.5	+22.2	91.2	52 37.6	+23.8	92.5	52 34.3	+25.4	93.8	52 29.7	+26.9	95.1	52 23.7	+28.4	96.4	25
26	52 54.3	16.0	85.7	52 58.1	17.7	87.0	53 00.6	19.3	88.3	53 01.7	21.0	89.6	53 01.4	22.6	91.0	52 59.7	24.2	92.3	52 56.6	25.8	93.6	52 52.1	27.4	94.9	26
27	53 10.3	14.7	84.1	53 15.8	16.4	85.4	53 19.9	18.1	86.7	53 22.7	19.7	88.1	53 24.0	21.3	89.4	53 23.9	23.0	90.8	53 22.4	24.6	92.1	53 19.5	26.2	93.4	27
28	53 25.0	13.3	82.4	53 32.2	15.0	83.8	53 38.0	16.7	85.1	53 42.4	18.4	86.5	53 45.3	20.2	87.8	53 46.9	21.8	89.2	53 47.0	23.5	90.6	53 45.7	25.1	91.9	28
29	53 38.3	12.0	80.8	53 47.2	13.7	82.1	53 54.7	15.4	83.5	54 00.8	17.1	84.9	54 05.5	18.8	86.2	54 08.7	20.5	87.6	54 10.5	22.1	89.0	54 10.8	23.8	90.4	29
30	53 50.3	+10.6	79.1	54 00.9	+12.4	80.5	54 10.1	+14.1	81.9	54 17.9	+15.8	83.2	54 24.3	+17.5	84.6	54 29.2	+19.2	86.0	54 32.6	+21.0	87.4	54 34.6	+22.6	88.8	30
31	54 00.9	9.2	77.5	54 13.3	10.9	78.8	54 24.2	12.7	80.2	54 33.7	14.4	81.6	54 41.8	16.1	83.0	54 48.4	17.9	84.4	54 53.6	19.5	85.8	54 57.2	21.3	87.2	31
32	54 10.1	7.8	75.8	54 24.2	9.5	77.1	54 36.9	11.2	78.5	54 48.1	13.0	79.9	54 57.9	14.8	81.3	55 06.3	16.5	82.7	55 13.1	18.3	84.1	55 18.5	20.0	85.6	32
33	54 17.9	6.4	74.1	54 33.7	8.1	75.4	54 48.1	9.8	76.8	55 01.1	11.6	78.2	55 12.7	13.3	79.6	55 22.8	15.0	81.0	55 31.4	16.8	82.5	55 38.5	18.6	83.9	33
34	54 24.3	4.9	72.4	54 41.8	6.6	73.7	54 57.9	8.4	75.1	55 12.7	10.1	76.5	55 26.0	11.8	77.9	55 37.8	13.7	79.3	55 48.2	15.4	80.8	55 57.1	17.2	82.2	34
35	54 29.2	+3.4	70.7	54 48.4	+5.2	72.0	55 06.3	+6.8	73.4	55 22.8	+8.6	74.7	55 37.8	+10.4	76.2	55 51.5	+12.1	77.6	56 03.6	+14.0	79.0	56 14.3	+15.7	80.5	35
36	54 32.6	2.0	68.9	54 53.6	3.6	70.3	55 13.1	5.4	71.6	55 31.4	7.1	73.0	55 48.2	8.9	74.4	56 03.6	10.7	75.8	56 17.6	12.4	77.3	56 30.0	14.0	78.8	36
37	54 34.6	+0.5	67.2	54 57.2	2.2	68.5	55 18.5	3.9	69.9	55 38.5	5.6	71.2	55 57.1	7.4	72.6	56 14.3	9.1	74.1	56 30.0	11.0	75.5	56 44.3	12.7	77.0	37
38	54 35.1	−0.9	65.5	54 59.4	+0.7	66.8	55 22.4	2.4	68.1	55 44.1	4.1	69.5	56 04.5	5.8	70.9	56 23.4	7.6	72.3	56 41.0	9.4	73.7	56 57.0	11.2	75.2	38
39	54 34.2	2.5	63.8	55 00.1	−0.8	65.0	55 24.8	+0.8	66.4	55 48.2	2.5	67.7	56 10.3	4.3	69.1	56 31.0	6.1	70.5	56 50.4	7.8	71.9	57 08.2	9.7	73.4	39
40	54 31.7	−3.9	62.0	54 59.3	−2.3	63.3	55 25.6	−0.6	64.6	55 50.7	+1.0	65.9	56 14.6	+2.7	67.3	56 37.1	+4.4	68.7	56 58.2	+6.2	70.1	57 17.9	+8.0	71.6	40
41	54 27.8	5.3	60.3	54 57.0	3.8	61.6	55 25.0	2.2	62.9	55 51.7	0.5	64.1	56 17.3	1.1	65.5	56 41.5	2.9	66.9	57 04.4	4.6	68.3	57 25.9	6.4	69.7	41
42	54 22.5	6.8	58.6	54 53.2	5.3	59.8	55 22.8	3.7	61.1	55 51.2	2.1	62.4	56 18.4	−0.4	63.7	56 44.4	1.2	65.0	57 09.0	3.0	66.5	57 32.3	4.8	67.9	42
43	54 15.7	8.3	56.9	54 47.9	6.8	58.1	55 19.1	5.2	59.3	55 49.1	3.6	60.6	56 18.0	2.0	61.9	56 45.6	−0.3	63.2	57 12.0	+1.4	64.6	57 37.1	3.1	66.0	43
44	54 07.4	9.6	55.2	54 41.1	8.1	56.4	55 13.9	6.7	57.6	55 45.5	5.2	58.8	56 16.0	3.6	60.1	56 45.3	1.9	61.4	57 13.4	−0.2	62.8	57 40.2	+1.5	64.2	44

LATITUDE SAME NAME AS DECLINATION

N. Lat. { L.H.A. greater than 180°......Zn=Z ; L.H.A. less than 180°......Zn=360°−Z

Dec.	30° Hc	d	Z	31° Hc	d	Z	32° Hc	d	Z	33° Hc	d	Z	34° Hc	d	Z	35° Hc	d	Z	36° Hc	d	Z	37° Hc	d	Z	Dec.
0	39 18.0	+38.5	118.2	38 49.3	+39.4	118.9	38 19.9	+40.4	119.6	37 50.0	+41.2	120.3	37 19.4	+42.0	120.9	36 48.3	+42.8	121.6	36 16.6	+43.5	122.2	35 44.3	+44.3	122.8	0
1	39 56.5	38.0	117.2	39 28.7	38.9	117.9	39 00.3	39.8	118.7	38 31.2	40.7	119.4	38 01.4	41.6	120.0	37 31.1	42.4	120.7	37 00.1	43.2	121.4	36 28.6	44.0	122.0	1
2	40 34.5	37.4	116.2	40 07.6	38.4	116.9	39 40.1	39.3	117.7	39 11.9	40.2	118.4	38 43.0	41.1	119.1	38 13.5	41.9	119.8	37 43.3	42.8	120.5	37 12.6	43.6	121.2	2
3	41 11.9	36.9	115.2	40 46.0	37.9	115.9	40 19.4	38.9	116.7	39 52.1	39.8	117.5	39 24.1	40.7	118.2	38 55.4	41.6	118.9	38 26.1	42.4	119.6	37 56.2	43.2	120.3	3
4	41 48.8	36.3	114.1	41 23.9	37.3	114.9	40 58.3	38.3	115.7	40 31.9	39.2	116.5	40 04.8	40.2	117.2	39 37.0	41.0	118.0	39 08.5	41.9	118.7	38 39.4	42.7	119.4	4
5	42 25.1	+35.7	113.0	42 01.2	+36.8	113.9	41 36.6	+37.7	114.7	41 11.1	+38.8	115.5	40 45.0	+39.6	116.3	40 18.0	+40.7	117.0	39 50.4	+41.5	117.8	39 22.1	+42.4	118.5	5
6	43 00.8	35.0	111.9	42 38.0	36.1	112.8	42 14.3	37.2	113.6	41 49.9	38.1	114.5	41 24.6	39.1	115.3	40 58.7	40.1	116.0	40 31.9	41.1	116.8	40 04.5	41.9	117.6	6
7	43 35.8	34.4	110.8	43 14.1	35.5	111.7	42 51.5	36.5	112.6	42 28.0	37.6	113.4	42 03.8	38.6	114.2	41 38.8	39.5	115.1	41 13.0	40.5	115.9	40 46.4	41.5	116.6	7
8	44 10.2	33.7	109.7	43 49.6	34.8	110.6	43 28.0	36.0	111.5	43 05.6	37.0	112.4	42 42.4	38.0	113.2	42 18.3	39.1	114.1	41 53.5	40.0	114.9	41 27.9	40.9	115.7	8
9	44 43.9	33.0	108.5	44 24.4	34.1	109.5	44 04.0	35.2	110.4	43 42.6	36.4	111.3	43 20.4	37.5	112.2	42 57.4	38.5	113.1	42 33.5	39.5	113.9	42 08.8	40.5	114.7	9
10	45 16.9	+32.2	107.3	44 58.5	+33.5	108.3	44 39.2	+34.6	109.2	44 19.0	+35.7	110.2	43 57.9	+36.8	111.1	43 35.9	+37.8	112.0	43 13.0	+38.9	112.8	42 49.3	+39.9	113.7	10
11	45 49.1	31.5	106.1	45 32.0	32.6	107.1	45 13.8	33.9	108.1	44 54.7	35.0	109.0	44 34.7	36.1	110.0	44 13.7	37.3	110.9	43 51.9	38.3	111.8	43 29.2	39.4	112.7	11
12	46 20.6	30.6	104.9	46 04.6	31.9	105.9	45 47.7	33.1	106.9	45 29.7	34.4	107.9	45 10.8	35.5	108.8	44 51.0	36.6	109.8	44 30.2	37.7	110.7	44 08.6	38.7	111.6	12
13	46 51.2	29.9	103.7	46 36.5	31.2	104.7	46 20.8	32.4	105.7	46 04.1	33.6	106.7	45 46.3	34.8	107.7	45 27.6	35.9	108.7	45 07.9	37.1	109.6	44 47.3	38.2	110.6	13
14	47 21.1	28.9	102.4	47 07.7	30.2	103.4	46 53.2	31.5	104.5	46 37.7	32.8	105.5	46 21.1	34.0	106.5	46 03.5	35.3	107.5	45 45.0	36.4	108.5	45 25.5	37.5	109.5	14
15	47 50.0	+28.1	101.1	47 37.9	+29.4	102.2	47 24.7	+30.8	103.2	47 10.5	+32.0	104.3	46 55.1	+33.3	105.3	46 38.8	+34.5	106.3	46 21.4	+35.7	107.4	46 03.0	+36.8	108.3	15
16	48 18.1	27.1	99.8	48 07.3	28.6	100.9	47 55.5	29.8	102.0	47 42.5	31.2	103.0	47 28.4	32.5	104.1	47 13.3	33.7	105.1	46 57.1	34.9	106.2	46 39.8	36.2	107.2	16
17	48 45.2	26.2	98.4	48 35.9	27.5	99.5	48 25.3	29.0	100.7	48 13.7	30.3	101.8	48 00.9	31.6	102.8	47 47.0	32.9	103.9	47 32.0	34.2	105.0	47 16.0	35.4	106.0	17
18	49 11.4	25.2	97.0	49 03.4	26.7	98.2	48 54.3	28.0	99.3	48 44.0	29.4	100.5	48 32.5	30.8	101.6	48 19.9	32.1	102.7	48 06.2	33.4	103.8	47 51.4	34.7	104.8	18
19	49 36.6	24.1	95.7	49 30.1	25.6	96.8	49 22.3	27.1	98.0	49 13.4	28.5	99.1	49 03.3	29.9	100.3	48 52.0	31.3	101.4	48 39.6	32.6	102.5	48 26.1	33.8	103.6	19
20	50 00.7	+23.2	94.2	49 55.7	+24.6	95.4	49 49.4	+26.1	96.6	49 41.9	+27.5	97.8	49 33.2	+28.9	98.9	49 23.3	+30.3	100.1	49 12.2	+31.7	101.2	48 59.9	+33.0	102.4	20
21	50 23.9	22.0	92.8	50 20.3	23.6	94.0	50 15.5	25.0	95.2	50 09.4	26.6	96.4	50 02.1	28.0	97.6	49 53.6	29.4	98.8	49 43.9	30.8	99.9	49 32.9	32.2	101.1	21
22	50 45.9	20.9	91.3	50 43.9	22.5	92.5	50 40.5	24.0	93.8	50 36.0	25.5	95.0	50 30.1	26.9	96.2	50 23.0	28.5	97.4	50 14.7	29.8	98.6	50 05.1	31.0	99.8	22
23	51 06.8	19.7	89.8	51 06.3	21.3	91.1	51 04.5	22.9	92.3	51 01.5	24.4	93.6	50 57.1	25.9	94.8	50 51.5	27.4	96.0	50 44.5	28.9	97.2	50 36.4	30.3	98.4	23
24	51 26.5	18.6	88.3	51 27.6	20.2	89.6	51 27.4	21.8	90.8	51 25.9	23.3	92.1	51 23.0	24.9	93.3	51 18.9	26.4	94.6	51 13.4	27.9	95.8	51 06.7	29.3	97.1	24
25	51 45.1	+17.4	86.8	51 47.8	+19.0	88.1	51 49.2	+20.6	89.3	51 49.2	+22.2	90.6	51 47.9	+23.7	91.9	51 45.3	+25.3	93.1	51 41.3	+26.8	94.4	51 36.0	+28.4	95.7	25
26	52 02.5	16.1	85.2	52 06.8	17.8	86.5	52 09.8	19.3	87.8	52 11.4	21.0	89.1	52 11.6	22.6	90.4	52 10.6	24.1	91.7	52 08.1	25.8	93.0	52 04.4	27.2	94.2	26
27	52 18.6	14.9	83.7	52 24.6	16.5	85.0	52 29.1	18.2	86.3	52 32.4	19.8	87.6	52 34.2	21.5	88.9	52 34.7	23.1	90.2	52 33.9	24.6	91.5	52 31.6	26.2	92.8	27
28	52 33.5	13.6	82.1	52 41.1	15.2	83.4	52 47.3	16.9	84.7	52 52.2	18.5	86.0	52 55.7	20.1	87.3	52 57.8	21.8	88.7	52 58.5	23.4	90.0	52 57.8	25.1	91.3	28
29	52 47.1	12.2	80.5	52 56.3	13.9	81.8	53 04.2	15.6	83.1	53 10.7	17.3	84.4	53 15.8	19.0	85.8	53 19.6	20.6	87.1	53 21.9	22.3	88.4	53 22.9	23.8	89.8	29
30	52 59.3	+10.9	78.9	53 10.2	+12.6	80.2	53 19.8	+14.3	81.5	53 28.0	+16.0	82.8	53 34.8	+17.6	84.2	53 40.2	+19.3	85.5	53 44.2	+21.0	86.9	53 46.7	+22.7	88.2	30
31	53 10.2	9.6	77.2	53 22.8	11.3	78.5	53 34.1	12.9	79.9	53 44.0	14.6	81.2	53 52.4	16.4	82.6	53 59.5	18.0	83.9	54 05.2	19.7	85.3	54 09.4	21.4	86.7	31
32	53 19.8	8.2	75.6	53 34.1	9.9	76.9	53 47.0	11.6	78.2	53 58.6	13.3	79.6	54 08.8	15.0	80.9	54 17.5	16.7	82.3	54 24.9	18.4	83.7	54 30.8	20.1	85.1	32
33	53 28.0	6.8	73.9	53 44.0	8.4	75.2	53 58.6	10.2	76.5	54 11.9	11.9	77.9	54 23.8	13.6	79.3	54 34.2	15.4	80.6	54 43.3	17.0	82.0	54 50.9	18.8	83.4	33
34	53 34.8	5.4	72.2	53 52.4	7.1	73.5	54 08.8	8.7	74.9	54 23.8	10.4	76.2	54 37.4	12.2	77.6	54 49.6	13.9	79.0	55 00.3	15.7	80.4	55 09.7	17.4	81.8	34
35	53 40.2	+4.0	70.6	53 59.5	+5.7	71.9	54 17.5	+7.4	73.2	54 34.2	+9.1	74.5	54 49.6	+10.7	75.9	55 03.5	+12.5	77.3	55 16.0	+14.3	78.7	55 27.1	+16.0	80.1	35
36	53 44.2	2.5	68.9	54 05.2	4.2	70.2	54 24.9	5.9	71.5	54 43.3	7.6	72.8	55 00.3	9.4	74.2	55 16.0	11.1	75.6	55 30.3	12.8	77.0	55 43.1	14.5	78.4	36
37	53 46.7	+1.1	67.2	54 09.4	2.7	68.5	54 30.8	4.4	69.8	54 50.9	6.1	71.1	55 09.7	7.8	72.5	55 27.1	9.5	73.8	55 43.1	11.3	75.2	55 57.6	13.1	76.7	37
38	53 47.8	-0.3	65.5	54 12.1	+1.4	66.8	54 35.2	3.0	68.1	54 57.0	4.6	69.4	55 17.5	6.3	70.7	55 36.6	8.1	72.1	55 54.4	9.8	73.5	56 10.7	11.6	74.9	38
39	53 47.5	1.7	63.8	54 13.5	-0.2	65.0	54 38.2	+1.5	66.3	55 01.6	3.2	67.6	55 23.8	4.9	69.0	55 44.7	6.6	70.3	56 04.2	8.3	71.7	56 22.3	10.1	73.1	39
40	53 45.8	-3.1	62.1	54 13.3	-1.6	63.3	54 39.7	0.0	64.6	55 04.8	+1.7	65.9	55 28.7	+3.3	67.2	55 51.3	+5.0	68.6	56 12.5	+6.8	69.9	56 32.4	+8.6	71.4	40
41	53 42.7	4.6	60.4	54 11.7	3.0	61.6	54 39.7	-1.5	62.9	55 06.5	-0.1	64.1	55 32.0	1.8	65.4	55 56.3	3.5	66.8	56 19.3	5.2	68.2	56 41.0	6.9	69.6	41
42	53 38.1	6.0	58.7	54 08.7	4.5	59.9	54 38.2	2.9	61.1	55 06.6	1.3	62.4	55 33.8	-0.3	63.7	55 59.8	2.0	65.0	56 24.5	3.7	66.4	56 47.9	5.4	67.8	42
43	53 32.1	7.4	57.1	54 04.2	5.9	58.2	54 35.3	4.4	59.4	55 05.3	2.9	60.6	55 34.1	1.2	61.9	56 01.8	+0.4	63.2	56 28.2	2.1	64.6	56 53.3	3.8	65.9	43
44	53 24.7	8.8	55.4	53 58.3	7.3	56.5	54 30.9	5.9	57.7	55 02.4	4.3	58.9	55 32.9	2.8	60.1	56 02.2	-1.2	61.4	56 30.3	+0.4	62.7	56 57.1	2.2	64.1	44

44°, 316° L.H.A. LATITUDE SAME NAME AS DECLINATION

N. Lat. { L.H.A. greater than 180° ...... Zn=Z ; L.H.A. less than 180° ...... Zn=360°−Z }

Dec.	30° Hc	d	Z	31° Hc	d	Z	32° Hc	d	Z	33° Hc	d	Z	34° Hc	d	Z	35° Hc	d	Z	36° Hc	d	Z	37° Hc	d	Z	Dec.
0	38 32.0	+38.1	117.4	38 04.1	+39.0	118.1	37 35.5	+39.9	118.8	37 06.3	+40.8	119.4	36 36.6	+41.6	120.1	36 06.2	+42.4	120.7	35 35.3	+43.2	121.3	35 03.8	+44.0	121.9	0
1	39 10.1	37.6	116.4	38 43.1	38.5	117.1	38 15.4	39.5	117.8	37 47.1	40.3	118.5	37 18.2	41.1	119.2	36 48.6	42.0	119.8	36 18.5	42.8	120.5	35 47.8	43.6	121.1	1
2	39 47.7	37.0	115.4	39 21.6	38.0	116.1	38 54.9	38.9	116.8	38 27.4	39.9	117.6	37 59.3	40.8	118.3	37 30.6	41.6	118.9	37 01.3	42.4	119.6	36 31.4	43.2	120.2	2
3	40 24.7	36.5	114.3	39 59.6	37.5	115.1	39 33.8	38.5	115.9	39 07.3	39.4	116.6	38 40.1	40.3	117.3	38 12.2	41.2	118.0	37 43.7	42.0	118.7	37 14.6	42.8	119.4	3
4	41 01.2	35.9	113.3	40 37.1	36.9	114.1	40 12.3	37.9	114.9	39 46.7	38.8	115.6	39 20.4	39.8	116.4	38 53.4	40.7	117.1	38 25.7	41.6	117.8	37 57.4	42.5	118.5	4
5	41 37.1	+35.4	112.2	41 14.0	+36.4	113.0	40 50.2	+37.3	113.8	40 25.5	+38.4	114.6	40 00.2	+39.3	115.4	39 34.1	+40.2	116.1	39 07.3	+41.2	116.9	38 39.9	+42.0	117.6	5
6	42 12.5	34.9	111.1	41 50.4	35.8	112.0	41 27.5	36.8	112.8	41 03.9	37.8	113.6	40 39.5	38.8	114.4	40 14.3	39.8	115.1	39 48.5	40.6	115.9	39 21.9	41.5	116.7	6
7	42 47.1	34.1	110.0	42 26.2	35.1	110.9	42 04.3	36.1	111.7	41 41.7	37.3	112.6	41 18.3	38.2	113.4	40 54.1	39.2	114.2	40 29.1	40.2	115.0	40 03.4	41.1	115.7	7
8	43 21.2	33.3	108.9	43 01.3	34.5	109.8	42 40.3	35.6	110.7	42 19.0	36.6	111.5	41 56.5	37.7	112.4	41 33.3	38.7	113.2	41 09.3	39.7	114.0	40 44.5	40.6	114.8	8
9	43 54.5	33.8	107.8	43 35.8	33.8	108.7	43 16.1	35.0	109.6	42 55.6	36.0	110.4	42 34.2	37.1	111.3	42 12.0	38.1	112.2	41 49.0	39.1	113.0	41 25.1	40.2	113.8	9
10	44 27.2	+31.9	106.6	44 09.6	+33.1	107.5	43 51.1	+34.2	108.4	43 31.6	+35.4	109.3	43 11.3	+36.5	110.2	42 50.1	+37.6	111.1	42 28.1	+38.6	112.0	42 05.3	+39.5	112.8	10
11	44 59.1	31.2	105.4	44 42.7	32.4	106.4	44 25.3	33.6	107.3	44 07.0	34.7	108.2	43 47.8	35.8	109.1	43 27.7	36.9	110.0	43 06.7	38.0	110.9	42 44.8	39.1	111.8	11
12	45 30.3	30.4	104.2	45 15.1	31.6	105.2	44 58.9	32.8	106.1	44 41.7	34.1	107.1	44 23.6	35.2	108.0	44 04.6	36.3	108.9	43 44.7	37.4	109.8	43 23.9	38.4	110.7	12
13	46 00.7	29.5	102.9	45 46.7	30.9	104.0	45 31.7	32.1	104.9	45 15.8	33.3	105.9	44 58.8	34.5	106.9	44 40.9	35.7	107.8	44 22.1	36.7	108.8	44 02.3	37.9	109.7	13
14	46 30.2	28.8	101.7	46 17.6	30.0	102.7	46 03.8	31.3	103.7	45 49.1	32.5	104.7	45 33.3	33.8	105.7	45 16.6	34.9	106.7	44 58.8	36.1	107.7	44 40.2	37.2	108.6	14
15	46 59.0	+27.8	100.4	46 47.6	+29.2	101.5	46 35.1	+30.5	102.5	46 21.6	+31.8	103.5	46 07.1	+33.0	104.5	45 51.5	+34.2	105.6	45 34.9	+35.5	106.5	45 17.4	+36.6	107.5	15
16	47 26.8	27.0	99.1	47 16.8	28.3	100.2	47 05.6	29.7	101.2	46 53.4	30.9	102.3	46 40.1	32.2	103.3	46 25.7	33.5	104.3	46 10.4	34.7	105.4	45 54.0	35.8	106.4	16
17	47 53.8	26.0	97.8	47 45.1	27.4	98.9	47 35.3	28.7	100.0	47 24.3	30.2	101.0	47 12.3	31.4	102.1	46 59.2	32.7	103.1	46 45.1	33.9	104.2	46 29.8	35.2	105.2	17
18	48 19.8	25.0	96.4	48 12.5	26.5	97.5	48 04.0	27.9	98.6	47 54.5	29.2	99.7	47 43.7	30.6	100.8	47 31.9	31.9	101.9	47 19.0	33.2	103.0	47 05.0	34.4	104.0	18
19	48 44.8	24.1	95.1	48 39.0	25.5	96.2	48 31.9	26.9	97.3	48 23.7	28.3	98.4	48 14.3	29.7	99.5	48 03.8	31.0	100.6	47 52.2	32.3	101.7	47 39.4	33.6	102.8	19
20	49 08.9	+23.0	93.7	49 04.5	+24.5	94.8	48 58.8	+26.0	96.0	48 52.0	+27.4	97.1	48 44.0	+28.8	98.2	48 34.8	+30.2	99.4	48 24.5	+31.5	100.5	48 13.0	+32.9	101.6	20
21	49 31.9	22.0	92.2	49 29.0	23.5	93.4	49 24.8	25.0	94.6	49 19.4	26.4	95.7	49 12.8	27.8	96.9	49 05.0	29.2	98.0	48 56.0	30.6	99.2	48 45.9	31.9	100.3	21
22	49 53.9	20.9	90.8	49 52.5	22.4	91.9	49 49.8	23.9	93.2	49 45.8	25.4	94.3	49 40.6	26.9	95.5	49 34.2	28.3	96.7	49 26.6	29.7	97.9	49 17.8	31.1	99.0	22
23	50 14.8	19.8	89.3	50 14.9	21.3	90.5	50 13.7	22.8	91.7	50 11.2	24.4	92.9	50 07.5	25.9	94.1	50 02.5	27.4	95.3	49 56.3	28.8	96.5	49 48.9	30.2	97.7	23
24	50 34.6	18.6	87.9	50 36.2	20.0	89.1	50 36.5	21.8	90.3	50 35.6	23.3	91.5	50 33.4	24.8	92.7	50 29.9	26.3	93.9	50 25.1	27.8	95.2	50 19.1	29.2	96.4	24
25	50 53.2	+17.5	86.4	50 56.4	+19.1	87.6	50 58.3	+20.6	88.8	50 58.9	+22.2	90.1	50 58.2	+23.7	91.3	50 56.2	+25.2	92.5	50 52.9	+26.7	93.8	50 48.3	+28.3	95.0	25
26	51 10.7	16.3	84.8	51 15.5	17.8	86.1	51 18.9	19.5	87.3	51 21.1	21.0	88.6	51 21.9	22.6	89.8	51 21.4	24.2	91.1	51 19.6	25.7	92.3	51 16.6	27.2	93.6	26
27	51 27.0	15.0	83.3	51 33.3	16.7	84.6	51 38.4	18.3	85.8	51 42.1	19.9	87.1	51 44.5	21.5	88.3	51 45.6	23.0	89.6	51 45.3	24.6	90.9	51 43.8	26.1	92.1	27
28	51 42.0	13.8	81.7	51 50.0	15.4	83.0	51 56.7	17.0	84.3	52 02.0	18.7	85.5	52 06.0	20.3	86.8	52 08.6	21.9	88.1	52 09.9	23.5	89.4	52 09.9	25.0	90.7	28
29	51 55.8	12.6	80.2	52 05.4	14.2	81.4	52 13.7	15.8	82.7	52 20.7	17.4	84.0	52 26.3	19.0	85.3	52 30.5	20.7	86.6	52 33.4	22.3	87.9	52 34.9	23.9	89.2	29
30	52 08.4	+11.2	78.6	52 19.6	+12.9	79.8	52 29.5	+14.5	81.1	52 38.1	+16.2	82.4	52 45.3	+17.8	83.7	52 51.2	+19.5	85.0	52 55.7	+21.1	86.4	52 58.8	+22.7	87.7	30
31	52 19.6	9.9	77.0	52 32.5	11.5	78.2	52 44.0	13.2	79.5	52 54.3	14.8	80.8	53 03.1	16.6	82.1	53 10.7	18.2	83.5	53 16.8	19.9	84.8	53 21.5	21.5	86.1	31
32	52 29.5	8.6	75.4	52 44.0	10.3	76.6	52 57.2	11.9	77.9	53 09.1	13.6	79.2	53 19.7	15.2	80.5	53 28.9	16.9	81.9	53 36.7	18.5	83.2	53 43.0	20.3	84.6	32
33	52 38.1	7.2	73.7	52 54.3	8.8	75.0	53 09.1	10.6	76.3	53 22.7	12.2	77.6	53 34.9	13.9	78.9	53 45.8	15.6	80.2	53 55.2	17.3	81.6	54 03.3	19.0	83.0	33
34	52 45.3	5.9	72.1	53 03.1	7.6	73.4	53 19.7	9.2	74.6	53 34.9	10.9	75.9	53 48.8	12.6	77.3	54 01.4	14.2	78.6	54 12.5	15.9	80.0	54 22.3	17.6	81.3	34
35	52 51.2	+4.5	70.4	53 10.7	+6.1	71.7	53 28.9	+7.8	73.0	53 45.8	+9.4	74.3	54 01.4	+11.1	75.6	54 15.6	+12.8	77.0	54 28.4	+14.6	78.3	54 39.9	+16.3	79.7	35
36	52 55.7	3.1	68.8	53 16.8	4.7	70.0	53 36.7	6.3	71.3	53 55.2	8.1	72.6	54 12.5	9.8	73.9	54 28.4	11.5	75.3	54 43.0	13.2	76.6	54 56.2	14.8	78.0	36
37	52 58.8	1.8	67.1	53 21.5	3.3	68.4	53 43.0	5.0	69.6	54 03.3	6.6	70.9	54 22.3	8.3	72.2	54 39.9	10.0	73.6	54 56.2	11.7	74.9	55 11.0	13.5	76.3	37
38	53 00.6	0.3	65.5	53 24.9	1.9	66.7	53 48.0	3.6	67.9	54 09.9	5.2	69.2	54 30.6	6.8	70.5	54 49.9	8.6	71.9	55 07.9	10.3	73.2	55 24.5	12.0	74.6	38
39	53 00.9	−1.0	63.8	53 26.8	+0.6	65.0	53 51.6	2.1	66.3	54 15.1	3.8	67.5	54 37.4	5.4	68.8	54 58.5	7.1	70.2	55 18.2	8.8	71.5	55 36.5	10.5	72.9	39
40	52 59.9	−2.5	62.2	53 27.4	−0.9	63.3	53 53.7	+0.7	64.6	54 18.9	+2.3	65.8	54 42.8	+4.0	67.1	55 05.6	+5.6	68.4	55 27.0	+7.3	69.8	55 47.0	+9.1	71.1	40
41	52 57.4	3.8	60.5	53 26.5	2.3	61.7	53 54.4	−0.8	62.9	54 21.2	0.8	64.1	54 46.8	2.5	65.4	55 11.2	4.1	66.7	55 34.3	5.8	68.0	55 56.1	7.5	69.4	41
42	52 53.6	5.2	58.8	53 24.2	3.7	60.0	53 53.6	2.1	61.2	54 22.0	−0.6	62.4	54 49.3	0.9	63.6	55 15.3	2.6	64.9	55 40.1	4.3	66.3	56 03.6	6.0	67.6	42
43	52 48.4	6.5	57.2	53 20.5	5.1	58.3	53 51.5	3.6	59.5	54 21.4	2.1	60.7	54 50.2	−0.5	61.9	55 17.9	+1.1	63.2	55 44.4	2.7	64.5	56 09.6	4.4	65.8	43
44	52 41.9	7.9	55.5	53 15.4	6.5	56.6	53 47.9	5.1	57.8	54 19.3	3.5	59.0	54 49.7	2.0	60.2	55 19.0	−0.4	61.4	55 47.1	+1.2	62.7	56 14.0	2.9	64.0	44

LATITUDE SAME NAME AS DECLINATION

N. Lat. { L.H.A. greater than 180° ....Zn=Z ; L.H.A. less than 180° ....Zn=360°−Z }

Dec.	30° Hc	d	Z	31° Hc	d	Z	32° Hc	d	Z	33° Hc	d	Z	34° Hc	d	Z	35° Hc	d	Z	36° Hc	d	Z	37° Hc	d	Z	Dec.
0	36 59.0	+37.4	115.8	36 32.6	+38.3	116.4	36 05.6	+39.1	117.1	35 38.0	+40.0	117.7	35 09.8	+40.8	118.4	34 41.0	+41.6	119.0	34 11.6	+42.5	119.6	33 41.7	+43.3	120.2	0
1	37 36.4	36.8	114.8	37 10.9	37.7	115.5	36 44.7	38.7	116.2	36 18.0	39.5	116.8	35 50.6	40.4	117.5	35 22.6	41.3	118.1	34 54.1	42.1	118.7	34 25.0	42.8	119.3	1
2	38 13.2	36.3	113.8	37 48.6	37.3	114.5	37 23.4	38.2	115.2	36 57.5	39.2	115.9	36 31.0	40.0	116.6	36 03.9	40.9	117.2	35 36.2	41.7	117.8	35 07.8	42.6	118.5	2
3	38 49.5	35.7	112.8	38 25.9	36.7	113.5	38 01.6	37.7	114.2	37 36.7	38.6	114.9	37 11.0	39.6	115.6	36 44.8	40.4	116.3	36 17.9	41.3	117.0	35 50.4	42.1	117.6	3
4	39 25.2	35.2	111.7	39 02.6	36.2	112.5	38 39.3	37.2	113.2	38 15.3	38.2	114.0	37 50.6	39.1	114.7	37 25.2	40.0	115.4	36 59.2	40.9	116.1	36 32.5	41.7	116.7	4
5	40 00.4	+34.6	110.6	39 38.8	+35.7	111.5	39 16.5	+36.7	112.2	38 53.5	+37.6	113.0	38 29.7	+38.6	113.7	38 05.2	+39.6	114.4	37 40.1	+40.4	115.1	37 14.2	+41.4	115.8	5
6	40 35.0	34.0	109.6	40 14.5	35.1	110.4	39 53.2	36.1	111.2	39 31.1	37.1	112.0	39 08.3	38.1	112.7	38 44.8	39.0	113.5	38 20.5	40.0	114.2	37 55.6	40.9	114.9	6
7	41 09.0	33.4	108.5	40 49.6	34.5	109.3	40 29.3	35.5	110.2	40 08.2	36.6	110.9	39 46.4	37.6	111.7	39 23.8	38.6	112.5	39 00.5	39.5	113.2	38 36.5	40.4	114.0	7
8	41 42.4	32.8	107.4	41 24.1	33.9	108.3	41 04.8	35.0	109.1	40 44.8	36.0	109.9	40 24.0	37.0	110.7	40 02.4	38.0	111.5	39 40.0	39.0	112.3	39 16.9	40.0	113.0	8
9	42 15.2	32.0	106.3	41 57.9	33.2	107.2	41 39.8	34.3	108.0	41 20.8	35.4	108.8	41 01.0	36.5	109.7	40 40.4	37.5	110.5	40 19.0	38.5	111.3	39 56.9	39.5	112.1	9
10	42 47.2	+31.4	105.1	42 31.1	+32.5	106.0	42 14.1	+33.7	106.9	41 56.2	+34.8	107.8	41 37.5	+35.9	108.6	41 17.9	+37.0	109.4	40 57.5	+38.0	110.3	40 36.4	+38.9	111.1	10
11	43 18.6	30.6	104.0	43 03.6	31.9	104.9	42 47.8	33.0	105.8	42 31.0	34.2	106.7	42 13.4	35.2	107.5	41 54.9	36.3	108.4	41 35.5	37.4	109.2	41 15.3	38.5	110.1	11
12	43 49.2	29.9	102.8	43 35.5	31.1	103.7	43 20.8	32.3	104.6	43 05.2	33.4	105.5	42 48.6	34.6	106.4	42 31.2	35.7	107.3	42 12.9	36.8	108.2	41 53.8	37.8	109.0	12
13	44 19.1	29.1	101.6	44 06.6	30.4	102.5	43 53.1	31.6	103.5	43 38.6	32.8	104.4	43 23.2	34.0	105.3	43 06.9	35.1	106.2	42 49.7	36.2	107.1	42 31.6	37.3	108.0	13
14	44 48.2	28.3	100.4	44 37.0	29.5	101.3	44 24.7	30.8	102.3	44 11.4	32.1	103.2	43 57.2	33.3	104.2	43 42.0	34.5	105.1	43 25.9	35.6	106.0	43 08.9	36.7	106.9	14
15	45 16.5	+27.5	99.1	45 06.5	+28.7	100.1	44 55.5	+30.1	101.1	44 43.5	+31.3	102.1	44 30.5	+32.5	103.0	44 16.5	+33.7	104.0	44 01.5	+34.9	104.9	43 45.6	+36.0	105.8	15
16	45 44.0	26.7	97.8	45 35.3	28.0	98.8	45 25.6	29.2	99.9	45 14.8	30.5	100.8	45 03.0	31.8	101.8	44 50.2	33.0	102.8	44 36.4	34.2	103.8	44 21.6	35.4	104.7	16
17	46 10.7	25.7	96.5	46 03.3	27.1	97.6	45 54.8	28.5	98.6	45 45.3	29.8	99.6	45 34.8	31.0	100.6	45 23.2	32.3	101.6	45 10.6	33.5	102.6	45 57.0	34.7	103.6	17
18	46 36.4	24.8	95.2	46 30.4	26.2	96.3	46 23.3	27.5	97.3	46 15.1	28.9	98.3	46 05.8	30.2	99.4	45 55.5	31.5	100.4	45 44.1	32.8	101.4	45 31.7	34.0	102.4	18
19	47 01.2	23.9	93.9	46 56.6	25.3	95.0	46 50.8	26.7	96.0	46 44.0	28.0	97.1	46 36.0	29.4	98.1	46 27.0	30.7	99.2	46 16.9	31.9	100.2	46 05.7	33.2	101.2	19
20	47 25.1	+23.0	92.6	47 21.9	+24.4	93.6	47 17.5	+25.8	94.7	47 12.0	+27.2	95.8	47 05.4	+28.5	96.9	46 57.7	+29.8	97.9	46 48.8	+31.2	99.0	46 38.9	+32.5	100.0	20
21	47 48.1	21.9	91.2	47 46.3	23.3	92.3	47 43.3	24.8	93.4	47 39.2	26.2	94.5	47 33.9	27.6	95.6	47 27.5	29.0	96.7	47 20.0	30.3	97.7	47 11.4	31.6	98.8	21
22	48 10.0	20.9	89.8	48 09.6	22.4	90.9	48 08.1	23.8	92.0	48 05.4	25.3	93.1	48 01.5	26.7	94.3	47 56.5	28.1	95.4	47 50.3	29.5	96.5	47 43.0	30.8	97.6	22
23	48 30.9	19.9	88.4	48 32.0	21.4	89.5	48 31.9	22.9	90.6	48 30.7	24.3	91.8	48 28.2	25.7	92.9	47 56.5	27.1	94.0	48 19.8	28.5	95.2	48 13.8	29.9	96.3	23
24	48 50.8	18.8	87.0	48 53.4	20.3	88.1	48 54.8	21.8	89.2	48 55.0	23.2	90.4	48 53.9	24.8	91.5	48 51.7	26.2	92.6	48 48.3	27.6	93.8	48 43.7	29.1	95.0	24
25	49 09.6	+17.7	85.5	49 13.7	+19.1	86.7	49 16.6	+20.7	87.8	49 18.2	+22.3	89.0	49 18.7	+23.7	90.1	49 17.9	+25.2	91.3	49 15.9	+26.7	92.5	49 12.8	+28.0	93.6	25
26	49 27.3	16.6	84.0	49 32.9	18.1	85.2	49 37.3	19.6	86.4	49 40.5	21.1	87.6	49 42.4	22.7	88.7	49 43.1	24.2	89.9	49 42.6	25.7	91.1	49 40.8	27.2	92.3	26
27	49 43.9	15.4	82.6	49 51.0	17.0	83.7	49 56.9	18.6	84.9	50 01.6	20.1	86.1	50 05.1	21.6	87.3	50 07.3	23.1	88.5	50 08.3	24.6	89.7	50 08.0	26.1	90.9	27
28	49 59.3	14.2	81.1	50 08.0	15.8	82.2	50 15.5	17.4	83.4	50 21.7	18.9	84.6	50 26.7	20.5	85.8	50 30.4	22.0	87.0	50 32.9	23.5	88.3	50 34.1	25.0	89.5	28
29	50 13.5	13.1	79.5	50 23.8	14.6	80.7	50 32.9	16.2	81.9	50 40.6	17.8	83.1	50 47.2	19.3	84.4	50 52.4	20.9	85.6	50 56.4	22.5	86.8	50 59.1	24.0	88.0	29
30	50 26.6	+11.8	78.0	50 38.4	+13.5	79.2	50 49.1	+15.0	80.4	50 58.4	+16.6	81.6	51 06.5	+18.2	82.9	51 13.3	+19.8	84.1	51 18.9	+21.3	85.3	51 23.1	+22.9	86.6	30
31	50 38.4	10.7	76.5	50 51.9	12.2	77.7	51 04.1	13.7	78.9	51 15.0	15.4	80.1	51 24.7	17.0	81.3	51 33.1	18.6	82.6	51 40.2	20.2	83.8	51 46.0	21.7	85.1	31
32	50 49.1	9.3	74.9	51 04.1	10.9	76.1	51 17.8	12.6	77.3	51 30.4	14.1	78.5	51 41.7	15.7	79.8	51 51.7	17.3	81.0	52 00.4	18.9	82.3	52 07.7	20.6	83.6	32
33	50 58.4	8.1	73.4	51 15.0	9.7	74.5	51 30.4	11.3	75.8	51 44.5	12.9	77.0	51 57.4	14.5	78.2	52 09.0	16.1	79.5	52 19.3	17.7	80.8	52 28.3	19.3	82.0	33
34	51 06.5	6.8	71.8	51 24.7	8.4	73.0	51 41.7	10.0	74.2	51 57.4	11.6	75.4	52 11.9	13.2	76.6	52 25.1	14.9	77.9	52 37.0	16.5	79.2	52 47.6	18.1	80.5	34
35	51 13.3	+5.6	70.2	51 33.1	+7.1	71.4	51 51.7	+8.7	72.6	52 09.0	+10.3	73.8	52 25.1	+11.9	75.1	52 40.0	+13.5	76.3	52 53.5	+15.2	77.6	53 05.7	+16.8	78.9	35
36	51 18.9	4.2	68.6	51 40.2	5.8	69.8	52 00.4	7.3	71.0	52 19.3	9.0	72.2	52 37.0	10.6	73.4	52 53.5	12.2	74.7	53 08.7	13.8	76.0	53 22.5	15.5	77.3	36
37	51 23.1	2.9	67.0	51 46.0	4.5	68.2	52 07.7	6.1	69.4	52 28.3	7.6	70.6	52 47.6	9.3	71.8	53 05.7	10.9	73.1	53 22.5	12.6	74.4	53 38.0	14.2	75.7	37
38	51 26.0	1.7	65.4	51 50.5	3.1	66.6	52 13.8	4.7	67.7	52 35.9	6.3	68.9	52 56.9	7.9	70.2	53 16.6	9.5	71.4	53 35.1	11.1	72.7	53 52.2	12.8	74.0	38
39	51 27.7	+0.3	63.8	51 53.6	1.8	64.9	52 18.5	3.3	66.1	52 42.2	4.9	67.3	53 04.8	6.5	68.5	53 26.1	8.1	69.8	53 46.2	9.8	71.1	54 05.0	11.5	72.4	39
40	51 28.0	−1.0	62.2	51 55.4	+0.5	63.3	52 21.8	+2.0	64.5	52 47.1	+3.6	65.7	53 11.3	+5.1	66.9	53 34.2	+6.8	68.1	53 56.0	+8.4	69.4	54 16.5	+10.0	70.7	40
41	51 27.0	2.4	60.6	51 55.9	−1.0	61.7	52 23.8	0.7	62.8	52 50.7	2.2	64.0	53 16.4	3.7	65.2	53 41.0	5.3	66.4	54 04.4	6.9	67.7	54 26.5	8.6	69.0	41
42	51 24.6	3.6	59.0	51 55.1	2.2	60.1	52 24.5	−0.7	61.2	52 52.9	0.7	62.4	53 20.1	2.4	63.5	53 46.3	3.9	64.8	54 11.3	5.5	66.0	54 35.1	7.1	67.3	42
43	51 21.0	4.9	57.4	51 52.9	3.6	58.5	52 23.8	2.1	59.6	52 53.6	−0.5	60.7	53 22.5	0.9	61.9	53 50.2	2.5	63.1	54 16.8	4.1	64.3	54 42.2	5.7	65.6	43
44	51 16.1	6.3	55.8	51 49.3	4.8	56.8	52 21.7	3.4	57.9	52 53.1	2.0	59.0	53 23.4	−0.5	60.2	53 52.7	+1.0	61.4	54 20.9	2.6	62.6	54 47.9	4.2	63.9	44

LATITUDE SAME NAME AS DECLINATION

N. Lat. { L.H.A. greater than 180° ...... Zn=Z / L.H.A. less than 180° ...... Zn=360°-Z }

Dec.	30° Hc	d	Z	31° Hc	d	Z	32° Hc	d	Z	33° Hc	d	Z	34° Hc	d	Z	35° Hc	d	Z	36° Hc	d	Z	37° Hc	d	Z	Dec.
0	36 12.1	+36.9	115.7	35 46.4	+37.9	115.7	35 20.1	+38.8	116.3	34 53.3	+39.6	116.9	34 25.8	+40.5	117.5	33 57.8	+41.3	118.1	33 29.2	+42.1	118.7	33 00.1	+42.9	119.3	0
1	36 49.0	36.5	114.0	36 24.3	37.4	114.7	35 58.9	38.3	115.4	35 32.9	39.2	116.0	35 06.3	40.1	116.6	34 39.1	40.9	117.3	34 11.3	41.8	117.9	33 43.0	42.6	118.5	1
2	37 25.5	35.9	113.0	37 01.7	36.9	113.7	36 37.2	37.9	114.4	36 12.1	38.8	115.1	35 46.4	39.6	115.7	35 20.0	40.5	116.4	34 53.1	41.3	117.0	34 25.6	42.1	117.6	2
3	38 01.4	35.4	112.0	37 38.6	36.4	112.7	37 15.1	37.3	113.4	36 50.9	38.3	114.1	36 26.0	39.2	114.8	36 00.5	40.1	115.5	35 34.4	41.0	116.1	35 07.7	41.8	116.7	3
4	38 36.8	34.9	111.0	38 15.0	35.9	111.7	37 52.4	36.9	112.4	37 29.2	37.8	113.2	37 05.2	38.8	113.9	36 40.6	39.7	114.5	36 15.4	40.6	115.2	35 49.5	41.5	115.9	4
5	39 11.7	+34.3	109.9	38 50.9	+35.3	110.7	38 29.3	+36.3	111.4	38 07.0	+37.3	112.2	37 44.0	+38.3	112.9	37 20.3	+39.2	113.6	36 56.0	+40.1	114.3	36 31.0	+41.0	115.0	5
6	39 46.0	33.7	108.8	39 26.2	34.7	109.7	39 05.6	35.8	110.4	38 44.3	36.8	111.2	38 22.3	37.8	111.9	37 59.5	38.8	112.6	37 36.1	39.7	113.4	37 12.0	40.5	114.1	6
7	40 19.7	33.1	107.8	40 00.9	34.2	108.6	39 41.4	35.2	109.4	39 21.1	36.3	110.2	39 00.1	37.2	110.9	38 38.3	38.2	111.7	38 15.8	39.2	112.4	37 52.5	40.2	113.1	7
8	40 52.8	32.4	106.7	40 35.1	33.6	107.5	40 16.6	34.7	108.3	39 57.4	35.7	109.1	39 37.3	36.8	109.9	39 16.5	37.8	110.7	38 55.0	38.7	111.4	38 32.7	39.6	112.2	8
9	41 25.2	31.8	105.6	41 08.7	33.0	106.4	40 51.3	34.0	107.2	40 33.1	35.1	108.1	40 14.1	36.1	108.9	39 54.3	37.2	109.7	39 33.7	38.2	110.5	39 12.3	39.2	111.2	9
10	41 57.0	+31.1	104.4	41 41.6	+32.3	105.3	41 25.3	+33.4	106.2	41 08.2	+34.5	107.0	40 50.2	+35.6	107.8	40 31.5	+36.6	108.6	40 11.9	+37.7	109.4	39 51.5	+38.7	110.2	10
11	42 28.1	30.4	103.3	42 13.9	31.5	104.2	41 58.7	32.8	105.0	41 42.7	33.9	105.9	41 25.8	35.0	106.8	41 08.1	36.1	107.6	40 49.6	37.1	108.4	40 30.2	38.1	109.2	11
12	42 58.5	29.7	102.1	42 45.4	30.9	103.0	42 31.5	32.0	103.9	42 16.6	33.2	104.8	42 00.8	34.4	105.7	41 44.2	35.5	106.5	41 26.7	36.5	107.4	41 08.3	37.6	108.2	12
13	43 28.2	28.9	100.9	43 16.3	30.2	101.8	43 03.5	31.4	102.8	42 49.8	32.6	103.7	42 35.2	33.7	104.6	42 19.7	34.8	105.4	42 03.2	36.0	106.3	41 45.9	37.1	107.2	13
14	43 57.1	28.1	99.7	43 46.5	29.4	100.7	43 34.9	30.6	101.6	43 22.4	31.8	102.5	43 08.9	33.0	103.4	42 54.5	34.2	104.3	42 39.2	35.3	105.2	42 23.0	36.4	106.1	14
15	44 25.2	+27.3	98.5	44 15.9	+28.6	99.4	44 05.5	+29.9	100.4	43 54.2	+31.1	101.3	43 41.9	+32.3	102.3	43 28.7	+33.5	103.2	43 14.5	+34.7	104.1	42 59.4	+35.8	105.0	15
16	44 52.5	26.5	97.2	44 44.5	27.8	98.2	44 35.4	29.1	99.2	44 25.3	30.4	100.1	44 14.2	31.6	101.1	44 02.2	32.8	102.1	43 49.2	34.0	103.0	43 35.2	35.2	103.9	16
17	45 19.0	25.6	96.0	45 12.3	26.9	97.0	45 04.5	28.3	97.9	44 55.7	29.5	98.9	44 45.8	30.9	99.9	44 35.0	32.1	100.9	44 23.2	33.3	101.9	44 10.4	34.4	102.8	17
18	45 44.6	24.8	94.7	45 39.2	26.1	95.7	45 32.8	27.4	96.7	45 25.2	28.8	97.7	45 16.7	30.0	98.7	45 07.1	31.3	99.7	44 56.5	32.5	100.7	44 44.8	33.8	101.7	18
19	46 09.4	23.8	93.3	46 05.3	25.3	94.4	46 00.2	26.6	95.4	45 54.0	27.9	96.4	45 46.7	29.3	97.5	45 38.4	30.5	98.5	45 29.0	31.8	99.5	45 18.6	33.1	100.5	19
20	46 33.2	+22.9	92.0	46 30.6	+24.3	93.1	46 26.8	+25.7	94.1	46 21.9	+27.1	95.2	46 16.0	+28.4	96.2	46 08.9	+29.8	97.2	46 00.8	+31.1	98.3	45 51.7	+32.3	99.3	20
21	46 56.1	21.9	90.7	46 54.9	23.3	91.7	46 52.5	24.7	92.8	46 49.0	26.1	93.9	46 44.4	27.5	94.9	46 38.7	28.8	96.0	46 31.9	30.2	97.0	46 24.0	31.5	98.1	21
22	47 18.0	21.0	89.3	47 18.2	22.4	90.4	47 17.2	23.9	91.5	47 15.1	25.3	92.6	47 11.9	26.6	93.6	47 07.5	28.0	94.8	47 02.1	29.3	95.8	46 55.5	30.6	96.8	22
23	47 39.0	19.9	87.9	47 40.6	21.4	89.0	47 41.1	22.8	90.1	47 40.4	24.2	91.2	47 38.5	25.7	92.3	47 35.5	27.1	93.4	47 31.4	28.5	94.5	47 26.1	29.9	95.6	23
24	47 58.9	18.9	86.5	48 02.0	20.4	87.6	48 03.9	21.8	88.7	48 04.6	23.3	89.8	48 04.2	24.8	91.0	48 02.6	26.2	92.1	47 59.9	27.5	93.2	47 56.0	28.9	94.3	24
25	48 17.8	+17.8	85.1	48 22.4	+19.3	86.2	48 25.7	+20.8	87.3	48 27.9	+22.3	88.5	48 29.0	+23.7	89.6	48 28.8	+25.2	90.7	48 27.4	+26.7	91.8	48 24.9	+28.1	93.0	25
26	48 35.6	16.8	83.6	48 41.7	18.2	84.8	48 46.5	19.8	85.9	48 50.2	21.3	87.1	48 52.7	22.7	88.2	48 54.0	24.2	89.3	48 54.1	25.6	90.5	48 53.0	27.0	91.6	26
27	48 52.4	15.6	82.1	48 59.9	17.2	83.3	49 06.3	18.6	84.5	49 11.5	20.1	85.6	49 15.4	21.7	86.8	49 18.2	23.1	87.9	49 19.7	24.7	89.1	49 20.0	26.1	90.3	27
28	49 08.0	14.5	80.7	49 17.1	16.0	81.9	49 24.9	17.6	83.0	49 31.6	19.1	84.2	49 37.1	20.6	85.4	49 41.3	22.2	86.4	49 44.4	23.6	87.7	49 46.1	25.1	88.9	28
29	49 22.5	13.3	79.2	49 33.1	14.8	80.4	49 42.5	16.4	81.5	49 50.7	18.0	82.7	49 57.7	19.5	83.9	50 03.5	21.0	85.1	50 08.0	22.5	86.3	50 11.2	24.1	87.5	29
30	49 35.8	+12.1	77.7	49 47.9	+13.7	78.9	49 58.9	+15.3	80.1	50 08.7	+16.8	81.2	50 17.2	+18.3	82.4	50 24.5	+19.9	83.6	50 30.5	+21.5	84.8	50 35.3	+23.0	86.0	30
31	49 47.9	11.0	76.2	50 01.6	12.6	77.4	50 14.2	14.0	78.5	50 25.5	15.6	79.7	50 35.5	17.2	80.9	50 44.4	18.7	82.1	50 52.0	20.3	83.4	50 58.3	21.8	84.6	31
32	49 58.9	9.8	74.7	50 14.2	11.3	75.9	50 28.2	12.9	77.0	50 41.1	14.4	78.2	50 52.7	16.0	79.4	51 03.1	17.6	80.6	51 12.3	19.1	81.9	51 20.1	20.8	83.1	32
33	50 08.7	8.5	73.2	50 25.5	10.0	74.3	50 41.1	11.6	75.5	50 55.5	13.2	76.7	51 08.7	14.8	77.9	51 20.7	16.4	79.1	51 31.4	18.0	80.3	51 40.9	19.5	81.6	33
34	50 17.2	7.3	71.6	50 35.5	8.9	72.8	50 52.7	10.4	73.9	51 08.7	12.0	75.1	51 23.5	13.6	76.3	51 37.1	15.1	77.6	51 49.4	16.7	78.8	52 00.4	18.3	80.1	34
35	50 24.5	+6.0	70.1	50 44.4	+7.6	71.2	51 03.1	+9.2	72.4	51 20.7	+10.7	73.6	51 37.1	+12.3	74.8	51 52.2	+13.9	76.0	52 06.1	+15.5	77.2	52 18.7	+17.1	78.5	35
36	50 30.5	4.8	68.5	50 52.0	6.3	69.6	51 12.3	7.8	70.8	51 31.4	9.5	72.0	51 49.4	11.0	73.2	52 06.1	12.6	74.4	52 21.6	14.2	75.7	52 35.8	15.9	76.9	36
37	50 35.3	3.5	66.9	50 58.3	5.0	68.1	51 20.1	6.6	69.2	51 40.9	8.1	70.4	52 00.4	9.7	71.6	52 18.7	11.3	72.8	52 35.8	12.9	74.1	52 51.7	14.5	75.3	37
38	50 38.8	2.2	65.3	51 03.3	3.7	66.5	51 26.7	5.3	67.6	51 49.0	6.8	68.8	52 10.1	8.4	70.0	52 30.0	10.0	71.2	52 48.7	11.6	72.5	53 06.2	13.2	73.7	38
39	50 41.0	+1.0	63.8	51 07.0	2.5	64.9	51 32.0	3.9	66.0	51 55.8	5.5	67.2	52 18.5	7.1	68.4	52 40.0	8.7	69.6	53 00.3	10.3	70.8	53 19.4	11.9	72.1	39
40	50 42.0	-0.3	62.2	51 09.5	+1.1	63.3	51 35.9	+2.7	64.4	52 01.3	+4.2	65.6	52 25.6	+5.7	66.7	52 48.7	+7.3	68.0	53 10.6	+8.9	69.2	53 31.3	+10.5	70.5	40
41	50 41.7	1.6	60.6	51 10.6	-0.1	61.7	51 38.6	1.3	62.8	52 05.5	2.8	63.9	52 31.3	4.3	65.1	52 56.0	5.9	66.3	53 19.5	7.5	67.5	53 41.8	9.1	68.8	41
42	50 40.1	2.9	59.0	51 10.5	1.3	60.1	51 39.9	0.0	61.2	52 08.3	1.5	62.3	52 35.6	3.0	63.5	53 01.9	4.5	64.7	53 27.0	6.1	65.9	53 50.9	7.7	67.1	42
43	50 37.2	4.1	57.5	51 09.0	2.7	58.5	51 39.9	-1.3	59.6	52 09.8	+0.1	60.7	52 38.6	1.6	61.8	53 06.4	3.2	63.0	53 33.1	4.7	64.2	53 58.6	6.3	65.4	43
44	50 33.1	5.4	55.9	51 06.3	4.1	56.9	51 38.6	2.7	58.0	52 09.9	-1.2	59.1	52 40.2	+0.3	60.2	53 09.6	1.7	61.3	53 37.8	3.3	62.5	54 04.9	4.9	63.7	44

LATITUDE SAME NAME AS DECLINATION

N. Lat. { L.H.A. greater than 180°...... Zn=Z
{ L.H.A. less than 180°...... Zn=360°−Z

Dec.	30° Hc	d	Z	31° Hc	d	Z	32° Hc	d	Z	33° Hc	d	Z	34° Hc	d	Z	35° Hc	d	Z	36° Hc	d	Z	37° Hc	d	Z	Dec.
0	34 37.3	+36.3	113.5	34 13.1	+37.2	114.1	33 48.3	+38.1	114.7	33 22.9	+38.9	115.3	32 57.0	+39.8	115.9	32 30.5	+40.6	116.5	32 03.4	+41.5	117.1	31 35.9	+42.2	117.6	0
1	35 13.6	35.7	112.5	34 50.3	36.7	113.2	34 26.4	37.6	113.8	34 01.8	38.6	114.4	33 36.8	39.4	115.0	33 11.1	40.2	115.6	32 44.9	41.0	116.2	32 18.1	41.9	116.8	1
2	35 49.3	35.3	111.5	35 27.0	36.2	112.2	35 04.0	37.2	112.9	34 40.4	38.1	113.5	34 16.2	38.9	114.1	33 51.3	39.9	114.7	33 25.9	40.8	115.3	33 00.0	41.5	115.9	2
3	36 24.6	34.7	110.5	36 03.2	35.7	111.2	35 41.2	36.7	111.9	35 18.5	37.6	112.5	34 55.1	38.6	113.2	34 31.2	39.6	113.8	34 06.7	40.3	114.5	33 41.5	41.2	115.1	3
4	36 59.3	34.2	109.5	36 38.9	35.3	110.2	36 17.9	36.2	110.9	35 56.1	37.2	111.6	35 33.7	38.1	112.3	35 10.7	39.0	112.9	34 47.0	39.9	113.6	34 22.7	40.8	114.2	4
5	37 33.5	+33.7	108.5	37 14.2	+34.7	109.2	36 54.1	+35.7	109.9	36 33.3	+36.7	110.6	36 11.8	+37.7	111.3	35 49.7	+38.6	112.0	35 26.9	+39.5	112.6	35 03.5	+40.4	113.3	5
6	38 07.2	33.1	107.4	37 48.9	34.1	108.2	37 29.8	35.2	108.9	37 10.0	36.2	109.6	36 49.5	37.2	110.3	36 28.3	38.1	111.0	36 06.4	39.1	111.7	35 43.9	40.0	112.4	6
7	38 40.3	32.6	106.4	38 23.0	33.6	107.1	38 05.0	34.6	107.9	37 46.2	35.7	108.6	37 26.7	36.6	109.4	37 06.4	37.7	110.1	36 45.5	38.6	110.8	36 23.9	39.5	111.5	7
8	39 12.9	31.9	105.3	38 56.6	33.0	106.1	38 39.6	34.1	106.8	38 21.9	35.1	107.6	38 03.3	36.2	108.4	37 44.1	37.2	109.1	37 24.1	38.2	109.8	37 03.4	39.1	110.5	8
9	39 44.8	31.2	104.2	39 29.6	32.5	105.0	39 13.7	33.5	105.8	38 57.0	34.6	106.6	38 39.5	35.6	107.3	38 21.3	36.6	108.1	38 02.3	37.6	108.8	37 42.5	38.6	109.6	9
10	40 16.0	+30.7	103.1	40 02.1	+31.7	103.9	39 47.2	+32.9	104.7	39 31.6	+34.0	105.5	39 15.1	+35.1	106.3	38 57.9	+36.1	107.1	38 39.9	+37.1	107.8	38 21.1	+38.2	108.6	10
11	40 46.7	29.9	101.9	40 33.8	31.2	102.8	40 20.1	32.3	103.6	40 05.6	33.4	104.4	39 50.2	34.5	105.2	39 34.0	35.6	106.0	39 17.0	36.7	106.8	38 59.3	37.6	107.6	11
12	41 16.6	29.3	100.8	41 05.0	30.4	101.7	40 52.4	31.6	102.5	40 39.0	32.7	103.3	40 24.7	33.9	104.2	40 09.6	35.0	105.0	39 53.7	36.0	105.8	39 36.9	37.1	106.6	12
13	41 45.9	28.5	99.6	41 35.4	29.8	100.5	41 24.0	31.0	101.4	41 11.7	32.2	102.2	40 58.6	33.2	103.1	40 44.6	34.4	103.9	40 29.7	35.5	104.8	40 14.0	36.5	105.6	13
14	42 14.4	27.9	98.4	42 05.2	29.0	99.3	41 55.0	30.2	100.2	41 43.9	31.4	101.1	41 31.8	32.7	102.0	41 19.0	33.7	102.8	41 05.2	34.9	103.7	40 50.5	36.0	104.5	14
15	42 42.3	+27.0	97.2	42 34.2	+28.3	98.2	42 25.2	+29.6	99.1	42 15.3	+30.8	100.0	42 04.5	+31.9	100.9	41 52.7	+33.1	101.7	41 40.1	+34.2	102.6	41 26.5	+35.4	103.5	15
16	43 09.3	26.2	96.0	43 02.5	27.5	97.0	42 54.8	28.7	97.9	42 46.1	30.0	98.8	42 36.4	31.2	99.7	42 25.8	32.5	100.5	42 14.3	33.6	101.5	42 01.9	34.7	102.4	16
17	43 35.5	25.5	94.8	43 30.0	26.8	95.7	43 23.5	28.1	96.7	43 16.1	29.3	97.6	43 07.6	30.6	98.5	42 58.3	31.7	99.5	42 47.9	32.9	100.4	42 36.6	34.1	101.3	17
18	44 01.0	24.6	93.5	43 56.8	25.9	94.5	43 51.6	27.2	95.5	43 45.4	28.5	96.4	43 38.2	29.8	97.4	43 30.0	31.0	98.3	43 20.8	32.3	99.2	43 10.7	33.5	100.2	18
19	44 25.6	23.7	92.3	44 22.7	25.1	93.2	44 18.8	26.4	94.2	44 13.9	27.7	95.2	44 08.0	29.0	96.2	44 01.0	30.3	97.1	43 53.1	31.5	98.1	43 44.2	32.7	99.0	19
20	44 49.3	+22.9	91.0	44 47.8	+24.2	92.0	44 45.2	+25.6	93.0	44 41.6	+26.9	93.9	44 37.0	+28.2	94.9	44 31.3	+29.5	95.9	44 24.6	+30.8	96.9	44 16.9	+32.0	97.9	20
21	45 12.2	21.9	89.7	45 12.0	23.4	90.7	45 10.8	24.7	91.7	45 08.5	26.1	92.7	45 05.2	27.4	93.7	45 00.8	28.7	94.7	44 55.4	30.0	95.7	44 48.9	31.3	96.7	21
22	45 34.1	21.1	88.3	45 35.4	22.4	89.4	45 35.5	23.8	90.4	45 34.6	25.1	91.4	45 32.6	26.5	92.4	45 29.5	27.9	93.4	45 25.4	29.1	94.5	45 20.2	30.5	95.5	22
23	45 55.2	20.0	87.0	45 57.8	21.5	88.0	45 59.3	22.9	89.1	45 59.7	24.3	90.1	45 59.1	25.6	91.1	45 57.4	27.0	92.2	45 54.5	28.4	93.2	45 50.7	29.6	94.2	23
24	46 15.2	19.1	85.6	46 19.3	20.5	86.7	46 22.2	21.9	87.7	46 24.0	23.4	88.8	46 24.7	24.8	89.8	46 24.4	26.1	90.9	46 22.9	27.5	91.9	46 20.3	28.9	93.0	24
25	46 34.3	+18.1	84.3	46 39.8	+19.5	85.3	46 44.1	+21.0	86.4	46 47.4	+22.4	87.4	46 49.5	+23.8	88.5	46 50.5	+25.2	89.6	46 50.4	+26.6	90.6	46 49.2	+27.9	91.7	25
26	46 52.4	17.1	82.9	46 59.3	18.5	83.9	47 05.1	20.0	85.0	47 09.8	21.4	86.1	47 13.3	22.8	87.2	47 15.7	24.3	88.2	47 17.0	25.7	89.3	47 17.1	27.1	90.4	26
27	47 09.5	16.0	81.5	47 17.8	17.5	82.5	47 25.1	18.9	83.6	47 31.2	20.4	84.7	47 36.1	21.9	85.8	47 40.0	23.3	86.9	47 42.7	24.7	88.0	47 44.2	26.2	89.1	27
28	47 25.5	15.0	80.1	47 35.3	16.5	81.1	47 44.0	17.9	82.2	47 51.6	19.4	83.3	47 58.0	20.9	84.4	48 03.3	22.3	85.5	48 07.4	23.8	86.6	48 10.4	25.1	87.7	28
29	47 40.5	13.9	78.6	47 51.8	15.3	79.7	48 01.9	16.9	80.8	48 11.0	18.3	81.9	48 18.9	19.8	83.0	48 25.6	21.3	84.1	48 31.2	22.7	85.2	48 35.5	24.3	86.4	29
30	47 54.4	+12.7	77.2	48 07.1	+14.3	78.2	48 18.8	+15.7	79.3	48 29.3	+17.3	80.5	48 38.7	+18.7	81.6	48 46.9	+20.2	82.7	48 53.9	+21.7	83.8	48 59.8	+23.1	85.0	30
31	48 07.1	11.7	75.7	48 21.4	13.1	76.8	48 34.5	14.7	77.9	48 46.6	16.1	79.0	48 57.4	17.7	80.1	49 07.1	19.2	81.3	49 15.6	20.7	82.4	49 22.9	22.2	83.6	31
32	48 18.8	10.5	74.2	48 34.5	12.1	75.3	48 49.2	13.5	76.4	49 02.7	15.0	77.5	49 15.1	16.5	78.7	49 26.3	18.0	79.8	49 36.3	19.5	81.0	49 45.1	21.1	82.1	32
33	48 29.3	9.4	72.7	48 46.6	10.8	73.8	49 02.7	12.4	74.9	49 17.7	13.9	76.1	49 31.6	15.4	77.2	49 44.3	16.9	78.3	49 55.8	18.5	79.5	50 06.2	19.9	80.7	33
34	48 38.7	8.2	71.3	48 57.4	9.7	72.3	49 15.1	11.0	73.4	49 31.6	12.7	74.6	49 47.0	14.2	75.7	50 01.2	15.8	76.9	50 14.3	17.3	78.0	50 26.1	18.8	79.2	34
35	48 46.9	+7.0	69.8	49 07.1	+8.5	70.8	49 26.3	+10.0	71.9	49 44.3	+11.5	73.1	50 01.2	+13.1	74.2	50 17.0	+14.6	75.4	50 31.6	+16.1	76.5	50 44.9	+17.7	77.7	35
36	48 53.9	5.9	68.2	49 15.6	7.3	69.3	49 36.3	8.8	70.4	49 55.8	10.4	71.5	50 14.3	11.8	72.7	50 31.6	13.3	73.8	50 47.7	14.9	75.0	51 02.6	16.5	76.2	36
37	48 59.8	4.6	66.7	49 22.9	6.2	67.8	49 45.1	7.6	68.9	50 06.2	9.1	70.0	50 26.1	10.6	71.1	50 44.9	12.2	72.3	51 02.6	13.7	73.5	51 19.1	15.2	74.7	37
38	49 04.4	3.5	65.2	49 29.1	4.9	66.3	49 52.7	6.4	67.4	50 15.3	7.8	68.4	50 36.7	9.4	69.6	50 57.1	10.9	70.7	51 16.3	12.5	71.9	51 34.3	14.1	73.1	38
39	49 07.9	2.2	63.7	49 34.0	3.6	64.7	49 59.1	5.1	65.8	50 23.1	6.6	66.9	50 46.1	8.1	68.0	51 08.0	9.7	69.2	51 28.8	11.2	70.3	51 48.4	12.7	71.5	39
40	49 10.1	+1.0	62.2	49 37.6	+2.5	63.2	50 04.2	+3.9	64.3	50 29.7	+5.4	65.3	50 54.2	+6.9	66.5	51 17.7	+8.3	67.6	51 40.0	+9.9	68.8	52 01.1	+11.5	70.0	40
41	49 11.1	-0.2	60.6	49 40.1	1.1	61.6	50 08.1	2.6	62.7	50 35.1	4.1	63.8	51 01.1	5.6	64.9	51 26.0	7.1	66.0	51 49.9	8.6	67.2	52 12.6	10.1	68.4	41
42	49 10.9	1.4	59.1	49 41.3	0.0	60.1	50 10.7	1.4	61.1	50 39.2	2.8	62.2	51 06.7	4.3	63.3	51 33.1	5.8	64.4	51 58.5	7.3	65.6	52 22.7	8.9	66.7	42
43	49 09.5	2.6	57.6	49 41.3	-1.3	58.6	50 12.1	+0.2	59.6	50 42.0	1.6	60.6	51 11.0	3.0	61.7	51 38.9	4.5	62.8	52 05.8	5.9	64.0	52 31.6	7.5	65.1	43
44	49 06.9	3.8	56.0	49 40.0	2.5	57.0	50 12.3	-1.2	58.0	50 43.6	+0.2	59.0	51 14.0	1.6	60.1	51 43.4	3.1	61.2	52 11.7	4.7	62.3	52 39.1	6.1	63.5	44

Lat	30°	31°	32°	33°	34°	35°	36°	37°
45	46 56.0 −2.6	47 30.3 −1.3	48 03.9 −0.1	48 36.6 +1.2	49 08.5 +2.5	49 39.4 +4.0	50 09.5 +5.3	50 38.7 +6.7
46	46 53.4 −3.7	47 29.0 −2.5	48 03.8 −1.3	48 37.8 0.0	49 11.0 +1.4	49 43.4 +2.7	50 14.8 +4.1	50 45.4 +5.5
47	46 49.7 −4.9	47 26.5 −3.7	48 02.5 −2.4	48 37.8 −1.1	49 12.4 +0.1	49 46.1 +1.4	50 18.9 +2.8	50 50.9 +4.2
48	46 44.8 −5.9	47 22.8 −4.8	48 00.1 −3.6	48 36.7 −2.4	49 12.5 −1.1	49 47.5 +0.2	50 21.7 +1.6	50 55.1 +2.9
49	46 38.9 −7.1	47 18.0 −5.9	47 56.5 −4.7	48 34.3 −3.5	49 11.4 −2.3	49 47.7 −1.0	50 23.3 +0.2	50 58.0 +1.6
50	46 31.8 −8.1	47 12.1 −7.0	47 51.8 −5.9	48 30.8 −4.7	49 09.1 −3.5	49 46.7 −2.2	50 23.5 −0.9	50 59.6 +0.3
51	46 23.7 −9.2	47 05.1 −8.1	47 45.9 −7.0	48 26.1 −5.9	49 05.6 −4.7	49 44.5 −3.5	50 22.6 −2.3	50 59.9 −1.0
52	46 14.5 −10.3	46 57.0 −9.2	47 38.9 −8.1	48 20.2 −7.0	49 00.9 −5.9	49 41.0 −4.7	50 20.3 −3.5	50 58.9 −2.2
53	46 04.2 −11.3	46 47.8 −10.4	47 30.8 −9.3	48 13.2 −8.2	48 55.0 −7.0	49 36.3 −6.0	50 16.8 −4.8	50 56.7 −3.6
54	45 52.9 −12.4	46 37.4 −11.3	47 21.5 −10.4	48 05.0 −9.3	48 48.0 −8.3	49 30.3 −7.1	50 12.0 −6.0	50 53.1 −4.8
55	45 40.5 −13.4	46 26.1 −12.5	47 11.1 −11.5	47 55.7 −10.5	48 39.7 −9.4	49 23.2 −8.4	50 06.0 −7.2	50 48.3 −6.1
56	45 27.1 −14.3	46 13.6 −13.5	46 59.6 −12.5	47 45.2 −11.6	48 30.3 −10.6	49 14.8 −9.5	49 58.8 −8.5	50 42.2 −7.4
57	45 12.8 −15.4	46 00.1 −14.5	46 47.1 −13.6	47 33.6 −12.6	48 19.7 −11.7	49 05.3 −10.7	49 50.3 −9.7	50 34.8 −8.6
58	44 57.4 −16.4	45 45.6 −15.5	46 33.5 −14.7	47 21.0 −13.8	48 08.0 −12.8	48 54.6 −11.9	49 40.6 −10.8	50 26.2 −9.8
59	44 41.0 −17.3	45 30.1 −16.5	46 18.8 −15.6	47 07.2 −14.8	47 55.2 −14.0	48 42.7 −13.0	49 29.8 −12.1	50 16.4 −11.1
60	44 23.7 −18.2	45 13.6 −17.5	46 03.2 −16.7	46 52.4 −15.9	47 41.2 −15.0	48 29.7 −14.2	49 17.7 −13.2	50 05.3 −12.3
61	44 05.5 −19.2	44 56.1 −18.4	45 46.5 −17.7	46 36.5 −16.9	47 26.2 −16.1	48 15.5 −15.2	49 04.5 −14.4	49 53.0 −13.5
62	43 46.3 −20.1	44 37.7 −19.4	45 28.8 −18.6	46 19.6 −17.9	47 10.1 −17.1	48 00.3 −16.3	48 50.1 −15.5	49 39.5 −14.6
63	43 26.2 −20.9	44 18.3 −20.2	45 10.2 −19.6	46 01.7 −18.8	46 53.0 −18.1	47 44.0 −17.4	48 34.6 −16.6	49 24.9 −15.8
64	43 05.3 −21.8	43 58.1 −21.2	44 50.6 −20.5	45 42.9 −19.9	46 34.9 −19.2	47 26.6 −18.4	48 18.0 −17.7	49 09.1 −16.9
65	42 43.5 −22.6	43 36.9 −22.0	44 30.1 −21.4	45 23.0 −20.8	46 15.7 −20.1	47 08.2 −19.5	48 00.3 −18.7	48 52.2 −18.0
66	42 20.9 −23.4	43 14.9 −22.9	44 08.7 −22.3	45 02.2 −21.7	45 55.6 −21.1	46 48.7 −20.4	47 41.6 −19.7	48 34.2 −19.0
67	41 57.5 −24.3	42 52.0 −23.7	43 46.4 −23.2	44 40.5 −22.6	45 34.5 −22.0	46 28.3 −21.4	47 21.9 −20.8	48 15.2 −20.1
68	41 33.2 −25.0	42 28.3 −24.5	43 23.2 −24.0	44 17.9 −23.4	45 12.5 −22.8	46 06.9 −22.3	47 01.1 −21.8	47 55.1 −21.2
69	41 08.2 −25.7	42 03.8 −25.3	42 59.2 −24.8	43 54.5 −24.3	44 49.6 −23.8	45 44.6 −23.2	46 39.3 −22.7	47 33.9 −22.1
70	40 42.5 −26.5	41 38.5 −26.0	42 34.4 −25.6	43 30.2 −25.2	44 25.8 −24.6	45 21.3 −24.2	46 16.6 −23.6	47 11.8 −23.1
71	40 16.0 −27.2	41 12.5 −26.8	42 08.8 −26.4	43 05.0 −25.9	44 01.2 −25.5	44 57.1 −25.0	45 53.0 −24.6	46 48.7 −24.1
72	39 48.8 −27.9	40 45.7 −27.5	41 42.4 −27.1	42 39.1 −26.7	43 35.7 −26.3	44 32.1 −25.9	45 28.4 −25.4	46 24.6 −24.9
73	39 20.9 −28.5	40 18.2 −28.2	41 15.3 −27.8	42 12.4 −27.5	43 09.4 −27.1	44 06.2 −26.7	45 03.0 −26.3	45 59.7 −25.9
74	38 52.4 −29.2	39 50.0 −28.9	40 47.5 −28.6	41 44.9 −28.2	42 42.3 −27.9	43 39.5 −27.4	44 36.7 −27.1	45 33.8 −26.7
75	38 23.2 −29.9	39 21.1 −29.6	40 18.9 −29.2	41 16.7 −28.9	42 14.4 −28.6	43 12.1 −28.3	44 09.6 −27.9	45 07.1 −27.5
76	37 53.3 −30.4	38 51.5 −30.1	39 49.7 −29.9	40 47.8 −29.6	41 45.8 −29.3	42 43.8 −29.0	43 41.7 −28.7	44 39.6 −28.4
77	37 22.9 −31.0	38 21.4 −30.8	39 19.8 −30.5	40 18.2 −30.3	41 16.5 −30.0	42 14.8 −29.7	43 13.0 −29.4	44 11.2 −29.2
78	36 51.9 −31.6	37 50.6 −31.4	38 49.3 −31.2	39 47.9 −30.9	40 46.5 −30.7	41 45.1 −30.5	42 43.6 −30.2	43 42.1 −29.9
79	36 20.3 −32.2	37 19.2 −31.9	38 18.1 −31.7	39 17.0 −31.5	40 15.8 −31.3	41 14.6 −31.1	42 13.4 −30.9	43 12.1 −30.6
80	35 48.1 −32.7	36 47.3 −32.5	37 46.4 −32.4	38 45.5 −32.2	39 44.5 −31.9	40 43.5 −31.7	41 42.5 −31.5	42 41.5 −31.3
81	35 15.4 −33.2	36 14.8 −33.1	37 14.0 −32.9	38 13.3 −32.7	39 12.6 −32.6	40 11.8 −32.4	41 11.0 −32.2	42 10.2 −32.1
82	34 42.2 −33.7	35 41.7 −33.6	36 41.1 −33.4	37 40.6 −33.3	38 40.0 −33.2	39 39.4 −33.0	40 38.8 −32.9	41 38.1 −32.7
83	34 08.5 −34.1	35 08.1 −34.0	36 07.3 −34.0	37 07.3 −33.9	38 06.8 −33.7	39 06.4 −33.6	40 05.9 −33.4	41 05.4 −33.3
84	33 34.4 −34.7	34 34.1 −34.6	35 33.8 −34.5	36 33.4 −34.5	37 33.3 −34.2	38 32.8 −34.2	39 32.5 −34.1	40 32.1 −33.9
85	32 59.7 −35.1	33 59.5 −35.0	34 59.3 −35.0	35 59.1 −34.9	36 58.9 −34.8	37 58.6 −34.7	38 58.4 −34.6	39 58.2 −34.6
86	32 24.6 −35.5	33 24.5 −35.5	34 24.3 −35.4	35 24.2 −35.4	36 24.1 −35.3	37 23.9 −35.2	38 23.8 −35.2	39 23.6 −35.1
87	31 49.1 −36.0	32 49.0 −36.0	33 49.0 −35.9	34 48.9 −35.9	35 48.8 −35.8	36 48.7 −35.8	37 48.6 −35.7	38 48.5 −35.6
88	31 13.1 −36.4	32 13.1 −36.4	33 13.0 −36.3	34 13.0 −36.3	35 13.0 −36.2	36 12.9 −36.2	37 12.9 −36.2	38 12.9 −36.2
89	30 36.7 −36.7	31 36.7 −36.7	32 36.7 −36.7	33 36.7 −36.7	34 36.7 −36.7	35 36.7 −36.7	36 36.7 −36.7	37 36.7 −36.7
90	30 00.0 −37.1	31 00.0 −37.1	32 00.0 −37.1	33 00.0 −37.1	34 00.0 −37.2	35 00.0 −37.2	36 00.0 −37.2	37 00.0 −37.2

52°, 308° L.H.A.

LATITUDE SAME NAME AS DECLINATION

53°, 307° L.H.A.   LATITUDE SAME NAME AS DECLINATION

N. Lat. { L.H.A. greater than 180°.........Zn=Z ; L.H.A. less than 180°.........Zn=360°−Z }

Dec.	30° Hc	d	Z	31° Hc	d	Z	32° Hc	d	Z	33° Hc	d	Z	34° Hc	d	Z	35° Hc	d	Z	36° Hc	d	Z	37° Hc	d	Z	Dec.
0	31 24.7	+35.0	110.6	31 03.3	+35.9	111.2	30 41.3	+36.8	111.8	30 18.8	+37.7	112.3	29 55.7	+38.6	112.8	29 32.2	+39.4	113.4	29 08.1	+40.3	113.9	28 43.6	+41.0	114.4	0
1	31 59.7	34.5	109.7	31 39.2	35.4	110.3	31 18.1	36.4	110.8	30 56.5	37.2	111.4	30 34.3	38.1	112.0	30 11.6	39.0	112.5	29 48.4	39.8	113.0	29 24.6	40.7	113.6	1
2	32 34.2	34.0	108.7	32 14.6	35.0	109.3	31 54.5	35.9	109.9	31 33.7	36.9	110.5	31 12.4	37.8	111.1	30 50.6	38.7	111.6	30 28.2	39.6	112.2	30 05.3	40.4	112.7	2
3	33 08.2	33.6	107.7	32 49.6	34.6	108.4	32 30.4	35.6	109.0	32 10.6	36.5	109.6	31 50.2	37.4	110.2	31 29.3	38.3	110.7	31 07.8	39.1	111.3	30 45.7	40.0	111.9	3
4	33 41.8	33.1	106.7	33 24.2	34.1	107.4	33 06.0	35.0	108.0	32 47.1	36.0	108.6	32 27.6	37.0	109.2	32 07.6	37.9	109.8	31 46.9	38.8	110.4	31 25.7	39.7	111.0	4
5	34 14.9	+32.6	105.7	33 58.3	+33.6	106.4	33 41.0	+34.7	107.0	33 23.1	+35.6	107.7	33 04.6	+36.6	108.3	32 45.5	+37.5	108.8	32 25.7	+38.5	109.5	32 05.4	+39.3	110.1	5
6	34 47.5	32.1	104.7	34 31.9	33.1	105.4	34 15.7	34.1	106.1	33 58.7	35.2	106.7	33 41.2	36.1	107.3	33 23.0	37.0	107.8	33 04.2	38.0	108.5	32 44.7	38.9	109.2	6
7	35 19.6	31.6	103.7	35 05.0	32.7	104.4	34 49.8	33.7	105.1	34 33.9	34.6	105.7	34 17.3	35.7	106.4	34 00.0	36.5	106.8	33 42.2	37.5	107.6	33 23.6	38.5	108.3	7
8	35 51.2	31.0	102.6	35 37.7	32.0	103.4	35 23.5	33.1	104.1	35 08.5	34.2	104.7	34 53.0	35.1	105.4	34 36.5	36.0	105.8	34 19.7	37.2	106.8	34 02.1	38.1	107.4	8
9	36 22.2	30.4	101.6	36 09.7	31.6	102.3	35 56.6	32.6	103.0	35 42.7	33.7	103.7	35 28.1	34.7	104.4	35 12.5	35.6	104.9	34 56.9	36.7	105.8	34 40.2	37.7	106.4	9
10	36 52.6	+29.8	100.5	36 41.3	+31.1	101.2	36 29.2	+32.0	102.0	36 16.4	+33.1	102.7	36 02.8	+34.2	103.4	35 48.6	+35.2	104.1	35 33.6	+36.2	104.8	35 17.9	+37.2	105.5	10
11	37 22.4	29.3	99.4	37 12.4	30.2	100.2	37 01.2	31.5	101.0	36 49.5	32.6	101.7	36 37.0	33.7	102.4	36 23.8	34.7	103.1	36 09.8	35.7	103.8	35 55.1	36.7	104.5	11
12	37 51.7	28.6	98.3	37 42.6	29.8	99.1	37 32.7	30.9	99.8	37 22.1	32.0	100.6	37 10.7	33.1	101.4	36 58.5	34.1	102.1	36 45.5	35.2	102.8	36 31.8	36.3	103.5	12
13	38 20.3	28.0	97.2	38 12.4	29.1	98.0	38 03.6	30.3	98.8	37 54.1	31.4	99.5	37 43.8	32.5	100.3	37 32.6	33.7	101.1	37 20.7	34.7	101.8	37 08.1	35.7	102.6	13
14	38 48.3	27.3	96.1	38 41.5	28.5	96.9	38 33.9	29.7	97.7	38 25.5	30.8	98.5	38 16.3	31.9	99.2	38 06.3	33.0	100.0	37 55.4	34.2	100.8	37 43.8	35.2	101.5	14
15	39 15.6	+26.6	94.9	39 10.0	+27.8	95.7	39 03.6	+29.0	96.5	38 56.3	+30.2	97.4	38 48.2	+31.4	98.2	38 39.3	+32.5	99.0	38 29.6	+33.6	99.7	38 19.0	+34.7	100.5	15
16	39 42.2	25.9	93.8	39 37.8	27.2	94.6	39 32.6	28.4	95.4	39 26.5	29.6	96.2	39 19.6	30.7	97.1	39 11.8	31.8	97.9	39 03.2	32.9	98.7	38 53.7	34.1	99.5	16
17	40 08.1	25.2	92.6	40 05.0	26.4	93.4	40 01.0	27.6	94.3	39 56.1	28.8	95.1	39 50.3	30.0	95.9	39 43.6	31.3	96.8	39 36.1	32.4	97.6	39 27.8	33.5	98.4	17
18	40 33.3	24.5	91.4	40 31.4	25.7	92.3	40 28.6	27.0	93.1	40 24.9	28.2	94.0	40 20.3	29.4	94.8	40 14.9	30.5	95.7	40 08.5	31.8	96.5	40 01.3	32.9	97.3	18
19	40 57.8	23.7	90.2	40 57.1	25.0	91.1	40 55.6	26.2	91.9	40 53.1	27.5	92.8	40 49.7	28.7	93.7	40 45.4	30.0	94.5	40 40.3	31.1	95.4	40 34.2	32.3	96.2	19
20	41 21.5	+22.9	89.0	41 22.1	+24.2	89.9	41 21.8	+25.5	90.7	41 20.6	+26.7	91.6	41 18.4	+28.0	92.5	41 15.4	+29.2	93.4	41 11.4	+30.4	94.2	41 06.5	+31.6	95.1	20
21	41 44.4	22.1	87.7	41 46.3	23.4	88.6	41 47.3	24.7	89.5	41 47.3	26.0	90.4	41 46.4	27.2	91.3	41 44.6	28.4	92.2	41 41.8	29.7	93.1	41 38.1	30.9	94.0	21
22	42 06.5	21.3	86.5	42 09.7	22.6	87.4	42 12.0	23.9	88.3	42 13.3	25.2	89.2	42 13.6	26.5	90.1	42 13.0	27.8	91.0	42 11.5	29.0	91.9	42 09.0	30.2	92.8	22
23	42 27.8	20.5	85.2	42 32.3	21.8	86.1	42 35.9	23.1	87.1	42 38.5	24.4	88.0	42 40.1	25.7	88.9	42 40.8	27.0	89.8	42 40.5	28.3	90.7	42 39.2	29.6	91.7	23
24	42 48.3	19.5	83.9	42 54.1	20.9	84.9	42 59.0	22.2	85.8	43 02.9	23.6	86.7	43 05.8	24.9	87.7	43 07.8	26.2	88.6	43 08.8	27.4	89.5	43 08.8	28.7	90.5	24
25	43 07.8	+18.7	82.7	43 15.0	+20.1	83.6	43 21.2	+21.4	84.5	43 26.5	+22.7	85.5	43 30.7	+24.1	86.4	43 34.0	+25.4	87.4	43 36.2	+26.7	88.3	43 37.5	+28.0	89.3	25
26	43 26.5	17.8	81.4	43 35.1	19.1	82.3	43 42.6	20.6	83.2	43 49.2	21.9	84.2	43 54.8	23.3	85.1	43 59.4	24.5	86.1	44 02.9	25.9	87.1	44 05.5	27.2	88.0	26
27	43 44.3	16.9	80.0	43 54.2	18.3	80.9	44 03.2	19.6	81.9	44 11.1	21.0	82.9	44 18.1	22.2	83.9	44 23.9	23.7	84.8	44 28.8	25.0	85.8	44 32.7	26.3	86.8	27
28	44 01.2	16.0	78.7	44 12.5	17.3	79.7	44 22.8	18.7	80.6	44 32.1	20.0	81.6	44 40.3	21.5	82.6	44 47.6	22.8	83.5	44 53.8	24.0	84.5	44 59.0	25.5	85.5	28
29	44 17.2	15.0	77.4	44 29.8	16.4	78.3	44 41.5	17.7	79.3	44 52.1	19.2	80.3	45 01.8	20.5	81.2	45 10.4	21.9	82.2	45 18.0	23.2	83.2	45 24.5	24.7	84.2	29
30	44 32.2	+14.0	76.0	44 46.2	+15.4	77.0	44 59.2	+16.8	77.9	45 11.3	+18.2	78.9	45 22.3	+19.6	79.9	45 32.3	+21.0	80.9	45 41.3	+22.3	81.9	45 49.2	+23.7	82.9	30
31	44 46.2	13.0	74.6	45 01.6	14.4	75.6	45 16.0	15.9	76.6	45 29.5	17.2	77.6	45 41.9	18.6	78.6	45 53.3	20.0	79.6	46 03.6	21.4	80.6	46 12.9	22.8	81.6	31
32	44 59.2	12.1	73.3	45 16.0	13.5	74.2	45 31.9	14.8	75.2	45 46.7	16.2	76.2	46 00.5	17.6	77.2	46 13.3	19.0	78.2	46 25.0	20.5	79.2	46 35.7	21.8	80.3	32
33	45 11.3	11.0	71.9	45 29.5	12.4	72.8	45 46.7	13.8	73.8	46 02.9	15.2	74.8	46 18.1	16.7	75.8	46 32.3	18.1	76.8	46 45.5	19.4	77.9	46 57.5	20.9	78.9	33
34	45 22.3	10.0	70.5	45 41.9	11.4	71.4	46 00.5	12.8	72.4	46 18.1	14.2	73.4	46 34.8	15.6	74.4	46 50.4	17.0	75.4	47 04.9	18.4	76.4	47 18.4	19.9	77.5	34
35	45 32.3	+9.0	69.1	45 53.3	+10.3	70.0	46 13.3	+11.7	71.0	46 32.3	+13.2	72.0	46 50.4	+14.5	73.0	47 07.4	+15.9	74.0	47 23.3	+17.4	75.1	47 38.3	+18.8	76.1	35
36	45 41.3	7.9	67.7	46 03.6	9.3	68.6	46 25.0	10.7	69.6	46 45.5	12.0	70.6	47 04.9	13.5	71.6	47 23.3	15.0	72.6	47 40.7	16.4	73.7	47 57.1	17.8	74.7	36
37	45 49.2	6.8	66.3	46 12.9	8.2	67.2	46 35.7	9.6	68.2	46 57.5	11.0	69.1	47 18.4	12.4	70.2	47 38.3	13.8	71.2	47 57.1	15.2	72.2	48 14.9	16.7	73.3	37
38	45 56.0	5.8	64.8	46 21.1	7.1	65.8	46 45.3	8.5	66.7	47 08.5	9.9	67.7	47 30.8	11.3	68.7	47 52.1	12.7	69.7	48 12.3	14.2	70.8	48 31.6	15.6	71.9	38
39	46 01.8	4.7	63.4	46 28.2	6.1	64.3	46 53.8	7.4	65.3	47 18.4	8.8	66.3	47 42.1	10.2	67.3	48 04.8	11.6	68.3	48 26.5	13.0	69.3	48 47.2	14.4	70.4	39
40	46 06.5	+3.6	61.9	46 34.3	+4.9	62.9	47 01.2	+6.3	63.8	47 27.2	+7.7	64.8	47 52.3	+9.1	65.8	48 16.4	+10.5	66.8	48 39.5	+11.9	67.8	49 01.6	+13.4	68.9	40
41	46 10.1	2.5	60.5	46 39.2	3.9	61.4	47 07.5	5.2	62.4	47 34.9	6.5	63.3	48 01.4	7.9	64.4	48 26.9	9.3	65.3	48 51.4	10.8	66.4	49 15.0	12.2	67.4	41
42	46 12.6	1.4	59.1	46 43.1	2.7	60.0	47 12.7	4.0	60.9	47 41.4	5.4	61.8	48 09.3	6.8	62.8	48 36.2	8.2	63.8	49 02.2	9.6	64.9	49 27.2	11.0	65.9	42
43	46 14.0	0.4	57.6	46 45.8	1.6	58.5	47 16.7	3.0	59.4	47 46.8	4.3	60.4	48 16.1	5.6	61.3	48 44.4	7.0	62.3	49 11.8	8.3	63.4	49 38.2	9.8	64.4	43
44	46 14.4	−0.8	56.2	46 47.4	−0.5	57.0	47 19.7	1.7	57.9	47 51.1	3.1	58.9	48 21.7	4.4	59.8	48 51.4	5.8	60.8	49 20.1	7.2	61.8	49 48.0	8.6	62.9	44

55°, 305° L.H.A.

LATITUDE SAME NAME AS DECLINATION

	30°			31°			32°			33°			34°			35°			36°			37°			
	Hc	d	Z	Hc	d	Z	Hc	d	Z	Hc	d	Z	Hc	d	Z	Hc	d	Z	Hc	d	Z	Hc	d	Z	
45	44 48.8	−0.3	54.7	45 23.1	+0.9	55.6	45 56.6	+2.2	56.4	46 29.5	+3.3	57.3	47 01.5	+4.6	58.2	47 32.7	+6.0	59.1	48 03.1	+7.3	60.1	48 32.6	+8.6	61.0	45
46	44 48.5	1.4	53.3	45 24.0	−0.2	54.1	45 58.8	+1.0	55.0	46 32.8	2.3	55.8	47 06.1	3.6	56.7	47 38.7	4.8	57.6	48 10.4	6.1	58.6	48 41.2	7.5	59.5	46
47	44 47.1	2.4	51.9	45 23.8	1.3	52.7	45 59.8	−0.1	53.5	46 35.1	1.2	54.4	47 09.7	2.4	55.2	47 43.5	3.7	56.1	48 16.5	5.0	57.1	48 48.7	6.3	58.0	47
48	44 44.7	3.4	50.5	45 22.5	2.3	51.3	45 59.7	1.1	52.1	46 36.3	0.0	52.9	47 12.1	1.2	53.8	47 47.2	2.5	54.7	48 21.5	3.8	55.6	48 55.0	5.1	56.5	48
49	44 41.3	4.5	49.1	45 20.2	3.3	49.9	45 58.6	2.2	50.7	46 36.3	−1.0	51.5	47 13.2	0.2	52.3	47 49.7	1.3	53.2	48 25.3	2.6	54.1	49 00.1	3.9	55.0	49
50	44 36.8	5.5	47.7	45 16.9	4.4	48.4	45 56.4	3.3	49.2	46 35.3	2.2	50.0	47 13.5	1.0	50.8	47 51.0	0.2	51.7	48 27.9	+1.1	52.6	49 04.0	2.6	53.5	50
51	44 31.3	6.5	46.3	45 12.5	5.5	47.0	45 53.1	4.4	47.8	46 33.1	3.3	48.6	47 12.5	2.1	49.4	47 51.2	0.9	50.2	48 29.3	0.2	51.1	49 06.6	1.5	52.0	51
52	44 24.8	7.6	44.9	45 07.0	6.5	45.6	45 48.7	5.4	46.3	46 29.8	4.3	47.1	47 10.3	3.3	47.9	47 50.3	2.1	48.7	48 29.5	0.9	49.6	49 08.1	+0.3	50.4	52
53	44 17.2	8.5	43.5	45 00.5	7.5	44.2	45 43.3	6.6	44.9	46 25.5	5.5	45.7	47 07.1	4.4	46.4	47 48.2	3.3	47.2	48 28.6	2.1	48.0	49 08.4	0.9	48.9	53
54	44 08.7	9.5	42.1	44 53.0	8.6	42.8	45 36.7	7.5	43.5	46 20.0	6.5	44.2	47 02.7	5.4	45.0	47 44.9	4.4	45.7	48 26.5	3.3	46.5	49 07.5	2.2	47.4	54
55	43 59.2	10.5	40.8	44 44.4	9.6	41.4	45 29.2	8.6	42.1	46 13.5	7.6	42.8	46 57.3	6.6	43.5	47 40.5	5.5	44.3	48 23.2	4.5	45.0	49 05.3	3.4	45.8	55
56	43 48.7	11.5	39.4	44 34.8	10.5	40.0	45 20.6	9.7	40.7	46 05.9	8.7	41.3	46 50.7	7.7	42.0	47 35.0	6.7	42.8	48 18.7	5.6	43.5	49 01.9	4.5	44.3	56
57	43 37.2	12.4	38.0	44 24.3	11.6	38.6	45 10.9	10.6	39.3	45 57.2	9.8	39.9	46 43.0	8.8	40.6	47 28.3	7.8	41.3	48 13.1	6.8	42.0	48 57.4	5.8	42.8	57
58	43 24.8	13.4	36.7	44 12.7	12.5	37.3	45 00.3	11.7	37.9	45 47.4	10.8	38.5	46 34.3	9.9	39.1	47 20.5	9.0	39.8	48 06.3	7.9	40.5	48 51.8	6.9	41.3	58
59	43 11.4	14.5	35.4	44 00.2	13.5	35.9	44 48.6	12.7	36.5	45 36.6	11.8	37.1	46 24.3	10.9	37.7	47 11.5	10.0	38.4	47 58.4	9.1	39.1	48 44.7	8.1	39.8	59
60	42 57.1	15.2	34.0	43 46.7	14.5	34.6	44 35.9	−13.7	35.1	45 24.8	−12.8	35.7	46 13.4	−12.0	36.3	47 01.5	−11.1	36.9	47 49.3	−10.2	37.6	48 36.6	−9.3	38.3	60
61	42 41.9	16.2	32.7	43 32.2	15.4	33.2	44 22.2	14.6	33.7	45 12.0	13.9	34.3	46 01.4	13.1	34.9	46 50.4	12.2	35.5	47 39.1	11.4	36.1	48 27.3	10.4	36.8	61
62	42 25.7	17.0	31.4	43 16.8	16.3	31.9	44 07.6	15.6	32.4	44 58.1	14.8	32.9	45 48.3	14.0	33.5	46 38.2	13.2	34.1	47 27.7	12.4	34.7	48 16.9	11.6	35.3	62
63	42 08.7	17.9	30.1	43 00.5	17.2	30.6	43 52.0	16.5	31.1	44 43.3	15.8	31.6	45 34.3	15.1	32.1	46 25.0	14.3	32.6	47 15.3	13.5	33.2	48 05.3	12.6	33.8	63
64	41 50.8	18.7	28.8	42 43.3	18.1	29.3	43 35.5	17.4	29.7	44 27.5	16.7	30.2	45 19.2	15.2	30.7	46 10.8	15.3	31.2	47 01.8	14.5	31.8	47 52.7	13.8	32.4	64
65	41 32.1	−19.5	27.5	42 25.2	−18.9	28.0	43 18.1	−18.3	28.4	44 10.8	−17.7	28.9	45 03.2	−17.0	29.3	45 55.4	−16.4	29.8	46 47.3	−15.6	30.4	47 38.9	−14.9	30.9	65
66	41 12.6	20.4	26.3	42 06.3	19.8	26.7	42 59.8	19.2	27.1	43 53.1	18.6	27.5	44 46.2	18.0	28.0	45 39.0	17.3	28.5	46 31.7	16.7	29.0	47 24.0	15.9	29.5	66
67	40 52.2	21.2	25.0	41 46.5	20.7	25.4	42 40.6	20.1	25.8	43 34.5	19.5	26.2	44 28.3	18.9	26.6	45 21.7	18.2	27.1	46 15.0	17.6	27.6	47 08.1	17.0	28.1	67
68	40 31.0	21.9	23.8	41 25.8	21.4	24.1	42 20.5	20.9	24.5	43 15.0	20.4	24.9	44 09.3	19.8	25.3	45 03.5	19.3	25.7	45 57.4	18.6	26.2	46 51.1	18.0	26.7	68
69	40 09.1	22.8	22.6	41 04.4	22.2	22.9	41 59.6	21.8	23.3	42 54.6	21.2	23.6	43 49.5	20.7	24.0	44 44.2	20.1	24.4	45 38.8	19.6	24.8	46 33.1	18.9	25.3	69
70	39 46.3	−23.4	21.4	40 42.2	−23.1	21.7	41 37.8	−22.5	22.0	42 33.4	−22.1	22.4	43 28.8	−21.5	22.7	44 24.1	−21.1	23.1	45 19.2	−20.5	23.5	46 14.2	−20.0	23.9	70
71	39 22.9	24.2	20.2	40 19.1	23.7	20.5	41 15.3	23.3	20.8	42 11.3	22.8	21.1	43 07.3	22.5	21.4	44 03.0	21.9	21.8	44 58.7	21.5	22.1	45 54.2	20.9	22.5	71
72	38 58.7	24.9	19.0	39 55.4	24.5	19.3	40 52.0	24.1	19.6	41 48.5	23.7	19.9	42 44.8	23.2	20.2	43 41.1	22.8	20.5	44 37.2	22.3	20.8	45 33.3	21.9	21.2	72
73	38 33.8	25.6	17.8	39 30.9	25.2	18.1	40 27.9	24.9	18.3	41 24.8	24.5	18.6	42 21.6	24.1	18.9	43 18.3	23.6	19.2	44 14.9	23.2	19.5	45 11.4	22.8	19.9	73
74	38 08.2	26.2	16.7	39 05.7	25.9	16.9	40 03.0	25.5	17.2	41 00.3	25.5	17.4	41 57.5	24.8	17.7	42 54.7	24.5	18.0	43 51.7	23.6	18.2	44 48.6	23.6	18.6	74
75	37 42.0	−26.9	15.5	38 39.8	−26.6	15.8	39 37.5	−26.3	16.0	40 35.1	−25.9	16.2	41 32.7	−25.6	16.5	42 30.2	−25.2	16.7	43 27.6	−24.8	17.0	44 25.0	−24.5	17.3	75
76	37 15.1	27.6	14.4	38 13.2	27.3	14.6	39 11.2	26.9	14.8	40 09.2	26.7	15.0	41 07.1	26.3	15.3	42 05.0	26.0	15.5	43 02.8	25.7	15.7	44 00.5	25.4	16.0	76
77	36 47.6	28.2	13.3	37 45.9	27.8	13.5	38 44.3	27.6	13.7	39 42.5	27.3	13.9	40 40.8	27.1	14.1	41 39.0	26.8	14.3	42 37.1	26.5	14.5	43 35.1	26.1	14.7	77
78	36 19.4	28.7	12.2	37 18.1	28.5	12.4	38 16.8	28.3	12.5	39 15.2	28.0	12.7	40 13.7	27.7	12.9	41 12.2	27.5	13.1	42 10.6	27.3	13.3	43 09.0	27.0	13.5	78
79	35 50.7	29.3	11.1	36 49.6	29.1	11.3	37 48.4	28.9	11.4	38 47.2	28.7	11.6	39 46.0	28.5	11.7	40 44.7	28.2	11.9	41 43.4	28.0	12.1	42 42.0	27.7	12.3	79
80	35 21.4	−29.9	10.0	36 20.5	−29.7	10.2	37 19.5	−29.5	10.3	38 18.5	−29.3	10.4	39 17.5	−29.1	10.6	40 16.5	−28.9	10.7	41 15.4	−28.7	10.9	42 14.3	−28.5	11.1	80
81	34 51.5	30.4	9.0	35 50.8	30.3	9.1	36 50.0	30.1	9.2	37 48.4	29.9	9.3	38 48.4	29.6	9.5	39 47.6	29.6	9.6	40 46.7	29.3	9.7	41 45.8	29.3	9.9	81
82	34 21.1	31.0	7.9	35 20.5	30.8	8.0	36 19.3	30.5	8.1	37 19.3	30.5	8.2	38 18.7	30.4	8.4	39 18.0	30.2	8.5	40 17.4	30.1	8.6	41 16.7	29.9	8.7	82
83	33 50.1	31.4	6.9	34 49.7	31.4	7.0	35 49.2	31.2	7.1	36 48.8	31.1	7.1	37 48.3	31.0	7.2	38 47.8	30.8	7.4	39 47.3	30.7	7.5	40 46.8	30.6	7.6	83
84	33 18.7	32.0	5.9	34 18.3	31.8	5.9	35 18.0	31.7	5.9	36 17.7	31.7	6.1	37 17.3	31.5	6.2	38 17.3	31.5	6.3	39 16.6	31.5	6.4	40 16.2	31.3	6.4	84
85	32 46.7	−32.4	4.9	33 46.5	−32.4	4.9	34 46.5	−32.3	5.0	35 46.0	−32.2	5.0	36 45.8	−32.0	5.1	37 45.5	−32.0	5.2	38 45.3	−31.9	5.3	39 45.0	−31.8	5.3	85
86	32 14.3	32.9	3.9	33 14.1	32.8	3.9	34 14.0	32.8	4.0	35 13.8	32.7	4.0	36 13.7	32.6	4.1	37 13.5	32.6	4.1	38 13.4	32.5	4.2	39 13.2	32.4	4.2	86
87	31 41.4	33.4	2.9	32 41.3	33.3	2.9	33 41.2	33.3	3.0	34 41.1	33.2	3.0	35 41.0	33.1	3.0	36 41.0	33.1	3.1	37 40.9	33.1	3.1	38 40.8	33.1	3.1	87
88	31 08.0	33.8	1.9	32 08.0	33.8	1.9	33 07.9	33.7	2.0	34 07.9	33.7	2.0	35 07.9	33.6	2.0	36 07.8	33.6	2.0	37 07.8	33.6	2.1	38 07.7	33.6	2.1	88
89	30 34.2	34.2	1.0	31 34.2	34.2	1.0	32 34.2	34.2	1.0	33 34.2	34.2	1.0	34 34.2	34.2	1.0	35 34.2	34.2	1.0	36 34.2	34.2	1.0	37 34.1	34.1	1.0	89
90	30 00.0	−34.6	0.0	31 00.0	−34.6	0.0	32 00.0	−34.6	0.0	33 00.0	−34.6	0.0	34 00.0	−34.6	0.0	35 00.0	−34.7	0.0	36 00.0	−34.7	0.0	37 00.0	−34.7	0.0	90

LATITUDE CONTRARY NAME TO DECLINATION   L.H.A. 56°, 304°

Dec.	30° Hc	d	Z	31° Hc	d	Z	32° Hc	d	Z	33° Hc	d	Z	34° Hc	d	Z	35° Hc	d	Z	36° Hc	d	Z	37° Hc	d	Z	Dec.
0	28 57.9	-34.5	108.6	28 38.5	-35.4	109.2	28 18.5	-36.3	109.7	27 58.1	-37.2	110.2	27 37.1	-38.0	110.7	27 15.7	-38.8	111.2	26 53.9	-39.7	111.6	26 31.5	-40.5	112.1	0
1	28 23.4	34.8	109.6	28 03.1	35.8	110.1	27 42.2	36.6	110.6	27 20.9	37.5	111.1	26 59.1	38.3	111.5	26 36.9	39.2	112.0	26 14.2	40.0	112.5	25 51.0	40.8	112.9	1
2	27 48.6	35.3	110.5	27 27.3	36.1	111.0	27 05.6	37.0	111.5	26 43.4	37.8	111.9	26 20.8	38.7	112.4	25 57.7	39.5	112.8	25 34.2	40.3	113.3	25 10.2	41.0	113.7	2
3	27 13.3	35.5	111.4	26 51.2	36.4	111.9	26 28.6	37.3	112.3	26 05.6	38.1	112.8	25 42.1	38.9	113.2	25 18.2	39.7	113.7	24 53.9	40.5	114.1	24 29.2	41.3	114.5	3
4	26 37.8	36.0	112.3	26 14.8	36.8	112.8	25 51.3	37.6	113.2	25 27.5	38.5	113.7	25 03.2	39.3	114.1	24 38.5	40.0	114.5	24 13.4	40.8	114.9	23 47.9	41.5	115.3	4
5	26 01.8	-36.2	113.2	25 38.0	-37.1	113.6	25 13.7	-37.9	114.1	24 49.0	-38.7	114.5	24 23.9	-39.4	114.9	23 58.5	-40.3	115.3	23 32.6	-41.0	115.7	23 06.4	-41.8	116.1	5
6	25 25.6	36.5	114.1	25 00.9	37.4	114.5	24 35.8	38.2	114.9	24 10.3	39.0	115.3	23 44.5	39.8	115.7	23 18.2	40.5	116.1	22 51.6	41.3	116.5	22 24.6	42.0	116.9	6
7	24 49.1	36.9	115.0	24 23.5	37.6	115.3	23 57.6	38.4	115.8	23 31.3	39.2	116.2	23 04.7	40.0	116.6	22 37.7	40.8	116.9	22 10.3	41.4	117.3	21 42.6	42.2	117.7	7
8	24 12.2	37.1	115.8	23 45.9	38.0	116.2	23 19.2	38.8	116.6	22 52.1	39.5	117.0	22 24.7	40.3	117.4	21 56.9	40.9	117.7	21 28.9	41.7	118.1	21 00.4	42.4	118.4	8
9	23 35.1	37.5	116.7	23 07.9	38.2	117.1	22 40.4	38.9	117.4	22 12.6	39.7	117.8	21 44.4	40.4	118.2	21 16.0	41.2	118.5	20 47.2	41.9	118.8	20 18.0	42.5	119.2	9
10	22 57.6	-37.7	117.5	22 29.7	-38.5	117.9	22 01.5	-39.3	118.3	21 32.9	-40.0	118.6	21 04.0	-40.7	119.0	20 34.8	-41.4	119.3	20 05.3	-42.1	119.6	19 35.5	-42.8	119.9	10
11	22 19.9	37.9	118.4	21 51.2	38.7	118.7	21 22.2	39.4	119.1	20 52.9	40.2	119.4	20 23.3	40.9	119.8	19 53.4	41.6	120.1	19 23.2	42.3	120.4	18 52.7	43.0	120.7	11
12	21 42.0	38.2	119.2	21 12.5	38.9	119.6	20 42.8	39.7	119.9	20 12.7	40.4	120.2	19 42.4	41.1	120.5	19 11.8	41.8	120.8	18 40.9	42.5	121.1	18 09.7	43.1	121.4	12
13	21 03.8	38.5	120.0	20 33.6	39.2	120.4	20 03.1	39.9	120.7	19 32.3	40.6	121.0	19 01.3	41.3	121.3	18 30.0	42.0	121.6	17 58.4	42.6	121.9	17 26.6	43.3	122.1	13
14	20 25.3	38.7	120.9	19 54.4	39.4	121.2	19 23.2	40.1	121.5	18 51.7	40.8	121.8	18 20.0	41.5	122.1	17 48.0	42.1	122.3	17 15.8	42.8	122.6	16 43.3	43.4	122.9	14
15	19 46.6	-38.9	121.7	19 15.0	-39.6	122.0	18 43.1	-40.3	122.3	18 10.9	-41.0	122.6	17 38.5	-41.6	122.8	17 05.9	-42.3	123.1	16 33.0	-42.9	123.3	15 59.9	-43.6	123.6	15
16	19 07.7	39.1	122.5	18 35.4	39.8	122.8	18 02.8	40.5	123.1	17 29.9	41.1	123.3	16 56.9	41.9	123.6	16 23.6	42.5	123.8	15 50.1	43.1	124.1	15 16.3	43.7	124.3	16
17	18 28.6	39.3	123.3	17 55.6	40.0	123.6	17 22.3	40.7	123.8	16 48.8	41.3	124.1	16 15.0	41.9	124.3	15 41.1	42.6	124.6	15 07.0	43.2	124.8	14 32.6	43.8	125.0	17
18	17 49.3	39.5	124.1	17 15.6	40.2	124.3	16 41.6	40.8	124.6	16 07.5	41.5	124.8	15 33.1	42.1	125.1	14 58.5	42.7	125.3	14 23.7	43.3	125.5	13 48.8	43.9	125.7	18
19	17 09.8	39.6	124.9	16 35.4	40.3	125.1	16 00.8	41.0	125.4	15 26.0	41.7	125.6	14 51.0	42.3	125.8	14 15.8	42.9	126.0	13 40.4	43.5	126.2	13 04.9	44.1	126.4	19
20	16 30.2	-39.9	125.7	15 55.1	-40.5	125.9	15 19.8	-41.1	126.1	14 44.3	-41.7	126.3	14 08.7	-42.4	126.5	13 32.9	-43.0	126.7	12 56.9	-43.6	126.9	12 20.8	-44.2	127.1	20
21	15 50.3	40.0	126.4	15 14.6	40.7	126.7	14 38.7	41.3	126.9	14 02.6	41.9	127.1	13 26.3	42.5	127.3	12 49.9	43.1	127.5	12 13.3	43.7	127.6	11 36.6	44.2	127.8	21
22	15 10.3	40.2	127.2	14 33.9	40.8	127.4	13 57.4	41.5	127.6	13 20.7	42.1	127.8	12 43.8	42.6	128.0	12 06.8	43.2	128.2	11 29.6	43.7	128.3	10 52.4	44.4	128.5	22
23	14 30.1	40.3	128.0	13 53.1	40.9	128.2	13 15.9	41.5	128.4	12 38.6	42.1	128.5	12 01.2	42.8	128.7	11 23.6	43.3	128.9	10 45.9	43.9	129.0	10 08.0	44.4	129.2	23
24	13 49.8	40.5	128.7	13 12.2	41.1	128.9	12 34.4	41.7	129.1	11 56.5	42.3	129.3	11 18.4	42.8	129.4	10 40.3	43.5	129.6	10 02.0	44.0	129.7	9 23.6	44.6	129.9	24
25	13 09.3	-40.6	129.5	12 31.1	-41.2	129.7	11 52.7	-41.8	129.8	11 14.2	-42.4	130.0	10 35.6	-43.0	130.1	9 56.8	-43.5	130.3	9 18.0	-44.1	130.4	8 39.0	-44.5	130.5	25
26	12 28.7	40.7	130.3	11 49.9	41.3	130.4	11 10.9	41.9	130.4	10 31.8	42.4	130.7	9 52.6	43.0	130.9	9 13.3	43.5	131.1	8 33.9	44.1	131.2	7 54.5	44.7	131.2	26
27	11 48.0	41.0	131.0	11 08.6	41.4	131.2	10 29.0	42.0	131.3	9 49.4	42.6	131.4	9 09.6	43.1	131.6	8 29.8	43.7	131.7	7 49.8	44.2	131.8	7 09.8	44.7	131.9	27
28	11 07.0	41.0	131.8	10 27.2	41.6	131.9	9 47.0	42.1	132.0	9 06.8	42.6	132.2	8 26.5	43.2	132.3	7 46.1	43.7	132.4	7 05.6	44.2	132.5	6 25.1	44.8	132.6	28
29	10 26.0	41.0	132.5	9 45.6	41.6	132.6	9 04.9	42.1	132.6	8 24.2	42.7	132.9	7 43.3	43.2	133.0	7 02.4	43.8	133.1	6 21.4	44.3	133.1	5 40.3	44.8	133.2	29
30	9 45.2	-41.2	133.2	9 04.0	-41.7	133.4	8 22.8	-42.3	133.5	7 41.5	-42.8	133.6	7 00.1	-43.4	133.7	6 18.6	-43.8	133.8	5 37.1	-44.4	133.8	4 55.5	-44.9	133.9	30
31	9 04.0	41.2	134.0	8 22.3	41.8	134.1	7 40.5	42.3	134.2	6 58.7	42.9	134.3	6 16.7	43.3	134.4	5 34.8	43.9	134.4	4 52.7	44.4	134.5	4 10.6	44.8	134.6	31
32	8 22.8	41.4	134.7	7 40.5	41.8	134.8	6 58.2	42.4	134.9	6 15.8	42.9	135.0	5 33.4	43.5	135.1	4 50.9	44.0	135.1	4 08.3	44.4	135.2	3 25.8	45.0	135.2	32
33	7 41.5	41.4	135.4	6 58.7	42.0	135.5	6 15.8	42.4	135.5	5 32.9	43.0	135.7	4 49.9	43.4	135.8	4 06.9	43.9	135.8	3 23.9	44.5	135.9	2 40.8	44.9	135.9	33
34	7 00.1	41.5	136.2	6 16.7	41.9	136.3	5 33.4	42.5	136.3	4 49.9	43.0	136.4	4 06.5	43.5	136.4	3 23.0	44.0	136.5	2 39.5	44.5	136.5	1 55.9	44.9	136.6	34
35	6 18.6	-41.5	136.9	5 34.8	-42.1	137.0	4 50.9	-42.6	137.0	4 06.9	-43.0	137.1	3 23.0	-43.5	137.1	2 39.0	-44.0	137.2	1 55.0	-44.5	137.2	1 11.0	-45.0	137.2	35
36	5 37.1	41.6	137.6	4 52.7	42.1	137.7	4 08.3	42.5	137.7	3 23.9	43.1	137.8	2 39.5	43.6	137.8	1 55.0	44.0	137.9	1 10.5	44.5	137.9	0 26.0	-45.0	137.9	36
37	4 55.5	41.6	138.4	4 10.6	42.1	138.4	3 25.8	42.6	138.4	2 40.8	43.1	138.5	1 55.9	43.6	138.5	1 11.0	44.1	138.5	0 26.0	-44.5	138.5	0 19.0	+44.9	41.5	37
38	4 13.9	41.7	139.1	3 28.5	42.1	139.1	2 43.2	42.7	139.2	1 57.8	43.2	139.2	1 12.3	43.6	139.2	0 26.9	-44.0	139.2	0 18.5	+44.5	40.8	1 03.9	45.0	40.8	38
39	3 32.2	41.7	139.8	2 46.4	42.2	139.8	2 00.5	42.6	139.9	1 14.6	43.1	139.9	0 28.8	-43.6	139.9	0 17.1	+44.1	40.1	1 03.0	44.5	40.1	1 48.9	44.9	40.1	39
40	2 50.5	-41.7	140.5	2 04.2	-42.2	140.5	1 17.9	-42.7	140.6	0 31.5	-43.1	140.6	0 14.8	+43.6	39.4	1 01.2	+44.0	39.4	1 47.5	+44.5	39.4	2 33.8	+44.9	39.5	40
41	2 08.8	41.7	141.2	1 22.0	42.2	141.3	0 35.2	-42.7	141.3	0 11.6	+43.1	38.7	0 58.4	43.6	38.7	1 45.2	44.0	38.8	2 32.0	44.4	38.8	3 18.7	44.9	38.8	41
42	1 27.1	41.8	142.0	0 39.8	-42.2	142.0	0 07.5	+42.6	38.0	0 54.7	43.1	38.0	1 42.0	43.5	38.1	2 29.2	44.0	38.1	3 16.4	44.5	38.1	4 03.6	44.9	38.1	42
43	0 45.3	41.8	142.7	0 02.4	+42.2	37.3	0 50.1	42.7	37.3	1 37.8	43.1	37.3	2 25.5	43.6	37.4	3 13.2	44.0	37.4	4 00.9	44.4	37.4	4 48.5	44.8	37.5	43
44	0 03.5	-41.7	143.4	0 44.6	42.2	36.6	1 32.8	42.6	36.6	2 20.9	43.1	36.6	3 09.1	43.5	36.7	3 57.2	43.9	36.7	4 45.3	44.3	36.8	5 33.3	44.8	36.8	44

LATITUDE SAME NAME AS DECLINATION

58°, 302° L.H.A.

Dec.	30° Hc	d	Z	31° Hc	d	Z	32° Hc	d	Z	33° Hc	d	Z	34° Hc	d	Z	35° Hc	d	Z	36° Hc	d	Z	37° Hc	d	Z	Dec.
45	42 41.5	+1.9	54.7	43 15.9	+3.1	55.4	43 49.6	+4.2	56.2	44 22.6	+5.5	57.0	44 54.9	+6.7	57.9	45 26.4	+7.9	58.7	45 57.2	+9.2	59.6	46 27.2	+10.4	60.5	45
46	42 43.4	1.0	53.3	43 19.0	2.0	54.1	43 53.8	3.3	54.8	44 28.1	4.4	55.6	45 01.6	5.6	56.5	45 34.3	6.9	57.3	46 06.4	8.1	58.2	46 37.6	9.4	59.1	46
47	42 44.4	0.1	52.0	43 21.0	1.1	52.7	43 57.1	2.2	53.5	44 32.5	3.4	54.2	45 07.2	4.6	55.1	45 41.2	5.8	55.9	46 14.5	7.0	56.7	46 47.0	8.3	57.6	47
48	42 44.3	1.0	50.6	43 22.1	0.1	51.3	43 59.3	1.2	52.1	44 35.9	2.3	52.8	45 11.8	3.5	53.6	45 47.0	4.7	54.5	46 21.5	6.0	55.3	46 55.3	7.2	56.2	48
49	42 43.3	2.0	49.2	43 22.2	0.9	49.9	44 00.5	0.2	50.7	44 38.2	1.4	51.4	45 15.3	2.5	52.2	45 51.7	3.7	53.1	46 27.5	4.8	53.9	47 02.5	6.1	54.7	49
50	42 41.3	2.9	47.9	43 21.3	1.9	48.6	44 00.7	0.8	49.3	44 39.6	+0.3	50.0	45 17.8	+1.4	50.8	45 55.4	+2.6	51.6	46 32.3	+3.8	52.4	47 08.6	+4.9	53.3	50
51	42 38.4	3.9	46.5	43 19.4	2.9	47.2	43 59.9	1.8	47.9	44 39.9	0.8	48.6	45 19.2	0.4	49.4	45 58.0	1.5	50.2	46 36.1	2.6	51.0	47 13.5	3.9	51.8	51
52	42 34.5	4.9	45.2	43 16.5	3.8	45.8	43 58.1	2.8	46.5	44 39.1	1.8	47.2	45 19.6	0.7	48.0	45 59.5	0.4	48.7	46 38.7	1.6	49.5	47 17.4	2.7	50.3	52
53	42 29.6	5.8	43.8	43 12.7	4.9	44.4	43 55.3	3.9	45.1	44 37.3	2.8	45.8	45 18.9	1.8	46.5	45 59.9	0.7	47.3	46 40.3	0.4	48.1	47 20.1	1.6	48.9	53
54	42 23.8	6.8	42.5	43 07.8	5.8	43.1	43 51.4	4.8	43.7	44 34.5	3.8	44.4	45 17.1	2.8	45.1	45 59.2	1.7	45.8	46 40.7	0.7	46.6	47 21.7	0.4	47.4	54
55	42 17.0	7.7	41.1	43 02.0	6.7	41.7	43 46.6	5.8	42.4	44 30.7	4.9	43.0	45 14.3	3.8	43.7	45 57.5	2.9	44.4	46 40.1	1.8	45.1	47 22.1	0.7	45.9	55
56	42 09.3	8.6	39.8	42 55.3	7.8	40.4	43 40.8	6.9	41.0	44 25.8	5.8	41.6	45 10.5	4.9	42.3	45 54.6	3.9	43.0	46 38.3	2.9	43.7	47 21.4	1.8	44.4	56
57	42 00.7	9.5	38.4	42 47.5	8.7	39.0	43 33.9	7.8	39.6	44 20.0	6.9	40.2	45 05.6	6.0	40.9	45 50.7	5.0	41.5	46 35.4	4.0	42.2	47 19.6	3.0	43.0	57
58	41 51.2	10.5	37.1	42 38.8	9.6	37.7	43 26.1	8.7	38.2	44 13.1	7.9	38.8	44 59.6	7.0	39.5	45 45.7	6.1	40.1	46 31.4	5.1	40.8	47 16.6	4.1	41.5	58
59	41 40.7	11.4	35.8	42 29.2	10.6	36.3	43 17.4	9.8	36.9	44 05.2	8.9	37.5	44 52.6	8.0	38.1	45 39.7	7.1	38.7	46 26.3	6.2	39.3	47 12.5	5.2	40.0	59
60	41 29.3	12.2	34.5	42 18.6	11.4	35.0	43 07.6	10.6	35.5	43 56.3	9.9	36.1	44 44.6	9.0	36.7	45 32.6	8.2	37.3	46 20.1	7.2	37.9	47 07.3	6.4	38.5	60
61	41 17.1	13.2	33.2	42 07.2	12.4	33.7	42 57.0	11.7	34.2	43 46.4	10.8	34.7	44 35.6	10.0	35.3	45 24.4	9.2	35.8	46 12.9	8.4	36.5	47 00.9	7.4	37.1	61
62	41 03.9	13.9	31.9	41 54.8	13.3	32.3	42 45.3	12.5	32.8	43 35.6	11.8	33.3	44 25.6	11.1	33.9	45 15.2	10.2	34.4	46 04.5	9.4	34.4	46 53.5	8.6	35.6	62
63	40 50.0	14.9	30.6	41 41.5	14.2	31.0	42 32.8	13.5	31.5	43 23.8	12.8	32.0	44 14.5	12.0	32.5	45 05.0	11.3	33.0	45 55.1	10.4	33.6	46 44.9	9.6	34.2	63
64	40 35.1	15.7	29.3	41 27.3	15.0	29.7	42 19.3	14.4	30.2	43 11.0	13.7	30.7	44 02.5	13.0	31.1	44 53.7	12.2	31.7	45 44.7	11.5	32.2	46 35.3	10.7	32.7	64
65	40 19.4	16.5	28.0	41 12.3	15.9	28.4	42 04.9	15.2	28.9	42 57.3	14.6	29.3	43 49.5	13.9	29.8	44 41.5	13.2	30.3	45 33.2	12.5	30.8	46 24.6	11.8	31.3	65
66	40 02.9	17.3	26.8	40 56.4	16.8	27.2	41 49.7	16.2	27.6	42 42.7	15.5	28.0	43 35.6	14.9	28.4	44 28.3	14.3	28.9	45 20.7	13.6	29.4	46 12.8	12.8	29.9	66
67	39 45.6	18.1	25.5	40 39.6	17.5	25.9	41 33.5	17.0	26.3	42 27.2	16.4	26.7	43 20.7	15.8	27.1	44 14.0	15.1	27.5	45 07.1	14.5	28.0	46 00.0	13.9	28.5	67
68	39 27.5	18.9	24.3	40 22.1	18.4	24.6	41 16.5	18.0	25.0	42 10.8	17.3	25.4	43 04.9	16.7	25.8	43 58.9	16.1	26.2	44 52.6	15.5	26.6	45 46.1	14.8	27.1	68
69	39 08.6	19.7	23.1	40 03.7	19.2	23.4	40 58.7	18.7	23.7	41 53.5	18.1	24.1	42 48.2	17.6	24.5	43 42.8	17.1	24.9	44 37.1	16.5	25.3	45 31.3	15.9	25.7	69
70	38 48.9	20.4	21.9	39 44.5	19.9	22.2	40 40.0	19.4	22.5	41 35.4	19.0	22.8	42 30.6	18.4	23.2	43 25.7	17.9	23.5	44 20.6	17.4	23.9	45 15.4	16.8	24.3	70
71	38 28.5	21.2	20.7	39 24.6	20.7	20.9	40 20.6	20.3	21.2	41 16.4	19.8	21.5	42 12.2	19.4	21.9	43 07.8	18.9	22.2	44 03.2	18.3	22.6	44 58.6	17.8	23.0	71
72	38 07.3	21.8	19.5	39 03.9	21.5	19.7	40 00.3	21.0	20.0	40 56.6	20.6	20.3	41 52.8	20.1	20.6	42 48.9	19.7	20.9	43 44.9	19.2	21.3	44 40.8	18.8	21.6	72
73	37 45.5	22.6	18.3	38 42.4	22.2	18.5	39 39.3	21.8	18.8	40 36.0	21.4	19.1	41 32.7	21.0	19.3	42 29.2	20.5	19.6	43 25.7	20.1	20.0	44 22.0	19.6	20.3	73
74	37 22.9	23.2	17.1	38 20.2	22.9	17.3	39 17.5	22.6	17.6	40 14.6	22.1	17.8	41 11.7	21.8	18.1	42 08.7	21.4	18.4	43 05.6	21.0	18.7	44 02.4	20.6	19.0	74
75	36 59.7	23.9	16.0	37 57.3	23.5	16.2	38 54.9	23.2	16.4	39 52.5	22.9	16.6	40 49.9	22.5	16.9	41 47.3	22.2	17.1	42 44.6	21.8	17.4	43 41.8	21.4	17.7	75
76	36 35.8	24.6	14.8	37 33.8	24.3	15.0	38 31.7	24.0	15.2	39 29.6	23.7	15.4	40 27.4	23.4	15.6	41 25.1	23.0	15.9	42 22.8	22.7	16.1	43 20.4	22.3	16.4	76
77	36 11.2	25.2	13.7	37 09.5	24.9	13.8	38 07.7	24.6	14.0	39 05.9	24.4	14.2	40 04.0	24.0	14.4	41 02.1	23.7	14.6	42 00.1	23.4	14.9	42 58.1	23.1	15.1	77
78	35 46.0	25.8	12.6	36 44.6	25.6	12.7	37 43.1	25.3	12.9	38 41.5	25.0	13.1	39 40.0	24.8	13.2	40 38.4	24.6	13.4	41 36.7	24.2	13.6	42 35.0	24.1	13.9	78
79	35 20.2	26.4	11.4	36 19.0	26.2	11.5	37 17.8	26.0	11.7	38 16.5	25.8	11.9	39 15.2	25.5	12.1	40 13.8	25.2	12.2	41 12.5	25.0	12.4	42 10.9	24.7	12.6	79
80	34 53.8	27.0	10.3	35 52.8	26.8	10.5	36 51.8	26.8	10.6	37 50.7	26.3	10.7	38 49.7	26.2	10.9	39 48.6	26.0	11.1	40 47.5	25.8	11.2	41 46.3	25.5	11.4	80
81	34 26.8	27.6	9.3	35 26.0	27.4	9.4	36 25.2	27.2	9.5	37 24.4	27.1	9.6	38 23.5	26.9	9.7	39 22.6	26.6	9.9	40 21.7	26.4	10.0	41 20.8	26.3	10.2	81
82	33 59.2	28.1	8.2	34 58.6	28.0	8.3	35 58.0	27.9	8.4	36 57.3	27.6	8.5	37 56.6	27.5	8.6	38 56.0	27.4	8.7	39 55.3	27.2	8.9	40 54.5	27.0	9.0	82
83	33 31.1	28.7	7.1	34 30.6	28.5	7.2	35 30.1	28.4	7.3	36 29.7	28.3	7.4	37 29.1	28.1	7.4	38 28.6	28.0	7.6	39 28.1	27.8	7.7	40 27.5	27.6	7.8	83
84	33 02.4	29.2	6.1	34 02.1	29.1	6.1	35 01.7	28.9	6.2	36 01.4	28.9	6.3	37 01.0	28.7	6.4	38 00.6	28.6	6.5	39 00.3	28.5	6.6	39 59.9	28.4	6.6	84
85	32 33.2	29.6	5.0	33 33.0	29.6	5.1	34 32.8	29.5	5.1	35 32.5	29.4	5.2	36 32.3	29.4	5.3	37 32.0	29.2	5.4	38 31.8	29.2	5.4	39 31.5	29.1	5.5	85
86	32 03.6	30.2	4.0	33 03.4	30.1	4.0	34 03.3	30.1	4.1	35 03.1	30.0	4.1	36 02.9	29.9	4.2	37 02.8	29.9	4.3	38 02.6	29.8	4.3	39 02.4	29.7	4.4	86
87	31 33.4	30.7	3.0	32 33.3	30.6	3.0	33 33.2	30.6	3.1	34 33.1	30.5	3.1	35 33.0	30.4	3.1	36 32.9	30.4	3.2	37 32.8	30.3	3.2	38 32.7	30.3	3.3	87
88	31 02.7	31.1	2.0	32 02.7	31.1	2.0	33 02.6	31.1	2.0	34 02.6	31.1	2.0	35 02.6	31.1	2.1	36 02.5	31.0	2.1	37 02.5	31.0	2.1	38 02.4	30.9	2.2	88
89	30 31.6	31.6	1.0	31 31.6	31.6	1.0	32 31.5	31.6	1.0	33 31.5	31.5	1.0	34 31.5	31.5	1.0	35 31.5	31.5	1.0	36 31.5	31.5	1.1	37 31.5	31.5	1.1	89
90	30 00.0	-32.0	0.0	31 00.0	-32.0	0.0	32 00.0	-32.0	0.0	33 00.0	-32.0	0.0	34 00.0	-32.0	0.0	35 00.0	-32.1	0.0	36 00.0	-32.1	0.0	37 00.0	-32.1	0.0	90

244

LATITUDE SAME NAME AS DECLINATION

N. Lat. { L.H.A. greater than 180°.......Zn=Z
          L.H.A. less than 180°.........Zn=360°−Z

Dec	Hc 30°	d	Z	Hc 31°	d	Z	Hc 32°	d	Z	Hc 33°	d	Z	Hc 34°	d	Z	Hc 35°	d	Z	Hc 36°	d	Z	Hc 37°	d	Z	Dec
0	23 09.1	-32.5	104.3	22 54.1	-33.4	104.7	22 38.6	-34.3	105.1	22 22.8	-35.2	105.5	22 06.6	-36.0	105.9	21 49.9	-37.0	106.3	21 32.9	-37.8	106.7	21 15.5	-38.6	107.0	0
1	23 41.6	32.1	103.4	23 27.5	33.1	103.8	23 12.9	34.0	104.2	22 58.0	34.9	104.6	22 42.6	35.8	105.0	22 26.9	36.6	105.4	22 10.7	37.5	105.8	21 54.1	38.4	106.2	1
2	24 13.7	31.8	102.5	24 00.6	32.7	102.9	23 46.9	33.7	103.3	23 32.9	34.6	103.7	23 18.4	35.5	104.2	23 03.5	36.4	104.6	22 48.2	37.3	105.0	22 32.5	38.1	105.4	2
3	24 45.5	31.5	101.5	24 33.3	32.4	102.0	24 20.6	33.4	102.4	24 07.5	34.3	102.9	23 53.9	35.2	103.3	23 39.9	36.1	103.7	23 25.5	37.0	104.1	23 10.6	37.9	104.6	3
4	25 17.0	31.1	100.6	25 05.7	32.1	101.0	24 54.0	33.0	101.5	24 41.8	34.0	102.0	24 29.1	34.9	102.4	24 16.0	35.8	102.8	24 02.5	36.7	103.3	23 48.5	37.5	103.7	4
5	25 48.1	-30.7	99.6	25 37.8	-31.7	100.1	25 27.0	-32.7	100.6	25 15.8	-33.6	101.0	25 04.0	-34.6	101.5	24 51.8	-35.5	102.0	24 39.2	-36.4	102.4	24 26.0	-37.0	102.9	5
6	26 18.8	30.3	98.7	26 09.5	31.3	99.2	25 59.7	32.3	99.7	25 49.4	33.3	100.1	25 38.6	34.2	100.6	25 27.3	35.2	101.1	25 15.6	36.0	101.5	25 03.0	37.0	102.0	6
7	26 49.1	30.0	97.7	26 40.8	31.0	98.2	26 32.0	31.9	98.7	26 22.7	32.9	99.2	26 12.8	33.9	99.7	26 02.5	34.8	100.2	25 51.6	35.8	100.6	25 40.3	36.7	101.1	7
8	27 19.1	29.5	96.7	27 11.8	30.5	97.3	27 03.9	31.6	97.8	26 55.6	32.5	98.3	26 46.7	33.5	98.8	26 37.3	34.5	99.3	26 27.4	35.4	99.8	26 17.0	36.3	100.2	8
9	27 48.6	29.1	95.8	27 42.3	30.2	96.3	27 35.5	31.1	96.8	27 28.1	32.2	97.3	27 20.2	33.1	97.8	27 11.8	34.1	98.3	27 02.8	35.1	98.8	26 53.3	36.0	99.4	9
10	28 17.7	-28.7	94.8	28 12.5	-29.7	95.3	28 06.6	-30.8	95.8	28 00.3	-31.7	96.4	27 53.3	-32.8	96.9	27 45.9	-33.7	97.4	27 37.9	-34.7	97.9	27 29.3	-35.7	98.5	10
11	28 46.4	28.2	93.8	28 42.2	29.3	94.3	28 37.4	30.3	94.9	28 32.0	31.4	95.4	28 26.1	32.3	95.9	28 19.6	33.3	96.5	28 12.6	34.3	97.0	28 05.0	35.2	97.5	11
12	29 14.6	27.8	92.8	29 11.5	28.8	93.3	29 07.7	29.9	93.9	29 03.4	30.9	94.4	28 58.4	32.0	95.0	28 52.9	33.0	95.5	28 46.9	33.9	96.1	28 40.2	34.9	96.6	12
13	29 42.4	27.3	91.7	29 40.3	28.4	92.3	29 37.6	29.4	92.9	29 34.3	30.5	93.4	29 30.4	31.5	94.0	29 25.9	32.5	94.6	29 20.8	33.5	95.1	29 15.1	34.6	95.7	13
14	30 09.7	26.9	90.7	30 08.7	27.9	91.3	30 07.0	29.0	91.9	30 04.8	30.0	92.5	30 01.9	31.1	93.0	29 58.4	32.1	93.6	29 54.3	33.2	94.2	29 49.7	34.1	94.8	14
15	30 36.6	-26.3	89.7	30 36.6	-27.4	90.3	30 36.0	-28.5	90.9	30 34.8	-29.5	91.4	30 33.0	-30.6	92.0	30 30.5	-31.7	92.6	30 27.5	-32.6	93.2	30 23.8	-33.7	93.8	15
16	31 02.9	25.8	88.6	31 04.0	26.9	89.2	31 04.5	28.0	89.8	31 04.3	29.1	90.4	31 03.6	30.1	91.0	31 02.2	31.2	91.6	31 00.1	32.3	92.2	30 57.5	33.2	92.9	16
17	31 28.7	25.3	87.6	31 30.9	26.4	88.2	31 32.5	27.5	88.8	31 33.4	28.6	89.4	31 33.7	29.7	90.0	31 33.4	30.7	90.6	31 32.4	31.8	91.3	31 30.7	32.9	91.9	17
18	31 54.0	24.7	86.5	31 57.3	25.9	87.1	32 00.0	27.0	87.8	32 02.0	28.1	88.3	32 03.4	29.2	89.0	32 04.1	30.2	89.6	32 04.2	31.3	90.3	32 03.6	32.3	90.9	18
19	32 18.7	24.2	85.4	32 23.2	25.3	86.1	32 27.0	26.4	86.7	32 30.1	27.5	87.3	32 32.6	28.6	88.0	32 34.3	29.8	88.6	32 35.5	30.8	89.2	32 35.9	31.9	89.9	19
20	32 42.9	-23.7	84.3	32 48.5	-24.8	85.0	32 53.4	-25.9	85.6	32 57.6	-27.1	86.3	33 01.2	-28.1	86.9	33 04.1	-29.2	87.6	33 06.3	-30.3	88.2	33 07.8	-31.4	88.9	20
21	33 06.6	23.0	83.3	33 13.3	24.2	83.9	33 19.3	25.3	84.6	33 24.7	26.4	85.2	33 29.3	27.6	85.9	33 33.3	28.7	86.5	33 36.6	29.8	87.2	33 39.2	30.9	87.9	21
22	33 29.6	22.5	82.1	33 37.5	23.6	82.8	33 44.6	24.8	83.5	33 51.1	25.9	84.1	33 56.9	27.0	84.8	34 02.0	28.1	85.5	34 06.4	29.2	86.1	34 10.1	30.3	86.8	22
23	33 52.1	21.8	81.0	34 01.1	23.0	81.7	34 09.4	24.2	82.4	34 17.0	25.3	83.0	34 23.9	26.5	83.7	34 30.1	27.6	84.4	34 35.6	28.7	85.1	34 40.4	29.8	85.8	23
24	34 13.9	21.2	79.9	34 24.1	22.4	80.6	34 33.6	23.5	81.3	34 42.3	24.7	81.9	34 50.4	25.8	82.6	34 57.7	27.0	83.3	35 04.3	28.1	84.0	35 10.2	29.3	84.7	24
25	34 35.1	-20.6	78.8	34 46.5	-21.7	79.5	34 57.1	-22.9	80.1	35 07.0	-24.1	80.8	35 16.2	-25.3	81.5	35 24.7	-26.4	82.2	35 32.4	-27.6	82.9	35 39.5	-28.6	83.6	25
26	34 55.7	20.0	77.6	35 08.2	21.2	78.3	35 20.0	22.3	78.9	35 31.1	23.5	79.7	35 41.5	24.6	80.4	35 51.1	25.8	81.1	36 00.0	27.0	81.8	36 08.1	28.1	82.6	26
27	35 15.7	19.3	76.5	35 29.4	20.4	77.2	35 42.3	21.7	77.9	35 54.6	22.8	78.6	36 06.1	24.0	79.3	36 16.9	25.1	80.0	36 26.9	26.3	80.7	36 36.2	27.5	81.5	27
28	35 35.0	18.6	75.3	35 49.8	19.8	76.0	36 04.0	21.0	76.7	36 17.4	22.2	77.4	36 30.1	23.3	78.1	36 42.0	24.5	78.9	36 53.2	25.7	79.5	37 03.7	26.8	80.4	28
29	35 53.6	17.9	74.1	36 09.6	19.1	74.8	36 25.0	20.3	75.6	36 39.6	21.4	76.3	36 53.4	22.7	77.0	37 06.5	23.9	77.8	37 18.9	25.0	78.5	37 30.5	26.2	79.2	29
30	36 11.5	-17.2	73.0	36 28.7	-18.5	73.7	36 45.3	-19.6	74.4	37 01.0	-20.8	75.1	37 16.1	-22.0	75.8	37 30.4	-23.2	76.6	37 43.9	-24.4	77.3	37 56.7	-25.5	78.1	30
31	36 28.7	16.6	71.8	36 47.2	17.7	72.5	37 04.9	18.8	73.2	37 21.8	20.1	73.9	37 38.1	21.2	74.7	37 53.6	22.4	75.4	38 08.3	23.6	76.2	38 22.2	24.9	76.9	31
32	36 45.3	15.7	70.6	37 04.9	16.9	71.3	37 23.7	18.2	72.0	37 41.9	19.4	72.7	37 59.3	20.6	73.5	38 16.0	21.8	74.2	38 31.9	23.0	75.0	38 47.1	24.1	75.8	32
33	37 01.0	15.1	69.4	37 21.8	16.3	70.1	37 41.9	17.4	70.8	38 01.3	18.6	71.5	38 19.9	19.8	72.3	38 37.8	21.0	73.0	38 54.9	22.2	73.8	39 11.2	23.4	74.6	33
34	37 16.1	14.3	68.2	37 38.1	15.5	68.9	37 59.3	16.7	69.6	38 19.9	17.9	70.3	38 39.7	19.1	71.1	38 58.8	20.3	71.8	39 17.1	21.5	72.6	39 34.6	22.7	73.4	34
35	37 30.4	-13.5	66.9	37 53.6	-14.7	67.6	38 16.0	-15.9	68.4	38 37.8	-17.1	69.1	38 58.8	-18.3	69.9	39 19.1	-19.5	70.6	39 38.6	-20.7	71.4	39 57.3	-21.9	72.2	35
36	37 43.9	12.8	65.7	38 08.3	13.9	66.4	38 31.9	15.2	67.1	38 54.9	16.3	67.9	39 17.1	17.5	68.6	39 38.6	18.7	69.4	39 59.3	19.9	70.2	40 19.2	21.2	71.0	36
37	37 56.7	12.0	64.5	38 22.2	13.2	65.2	38 47.1	14.3	65.9	39 11.2	15.5	66.6	39 34.6	16.8	67.4	39 57.3	18.0	68.2	40 19.2	19.2	69.0	40 40.4	20.4	69.8	37
38	38 08.7	11.1	63.2	38 35.4	12.3	63.9	39 01.4	13.6	64.7	39 26.7	14.8	65.4	39 51.4	15.9	66.1	40 15.3	17.1	67.0	40 38.4	18.3	67.7	41 00.8	19.5	68.5	38
39	38 19.9	10.4	62.0	38 47.7	11.6	62.7	39 15.0	12.7	63.4	39 41.5	13.9	64.1	40 07.3	15.1	64.9	40 32.4	16.3	65.7	40 56.7	17.5	66.5	41 20.3	18.7	67.3	39
40	38 30.3	-9.6	60.7	38 59.3	-10.7	61.4	39 27.7	-11.9	62.1	39 55.4	-13.1	62.9	40 22.4	-14.2	63.6	40 48.7	-15.4	64.4	41 14.2	-16.7	65.2	41 39.0	-17.9	66.0	40
41	38 39.9	8.7	59.5	39 10.0	9.9	60.2	39 39.6	11.0	60.9	40 08.5	12.2	61.6	40 36.6	13.5	62.3	41 04.1	14.6	63.1	41 30.9	15.8	63.9	41 56.9	17.0	64.7	41
42	38 48.6	8.0	58.2	39 19.9	9.1	58.9	39 50.6	10.3	59.6	40 20.7	11.4	60.3	40 50.1	12.5	61.1	41 18.7	13.8	61.8	41 46.7	14.9	62.6	42 13.1	16.2	63.4	42
43	38 56.6	7.1	56.9	39 29.0	8.2	57.6	40 00.9	9.3	58.3	40 32.1	10.5	59.0	41 02.6	11.7	59.8	41 32.5	12.8	60.5	42 01.6	14.1	61.3	42 30.1	15.2	62.1	43
44	39 03.7	6.2	55.6	39 37.2	7.4	56.3	40 10.2	8.5	57.0	40 42.6	9.6	57.7	41 14.3	10.8	58.5	41 45.3	12.0	59.2	42 15.7	13.1	60.0	42 45.3	14.4	60.8	44

65°, 295° L.H.A.   LATITUDE SAME NAME AS DECLINATION

N. Lat. { L.H.A. greater than 180°.......Zn=Z
L.H.A. less than 180°.......Zn=360°-Z

Dec.	30° Hc	d	Z	31° Hc	d	Z	32° Hc	d	Z	33° Hc	d	Z	34° Hc	d	Z	35° Hc	d	Z	36° Hc	d	Z	37° Hc	d	Z	Dec.
0	21 28.1	+32.1	103.1	21 14.3	+33.0	103.5	21 00.1	+33.9	103.9	20 45.5	+34.9	104.3	20 30.6	+35.7	104.6	20 15.3	+36.5	105.0	19 59.6	+37.4	105.3	19 43.5	+38.3	105.7	0
1	22 00.2	31.8	102.2	21 47.3	32.8	102.6	21 34.0	33.7	103.0	21 20.4	34.5	103.4	21 06.3	35.4	103.8	20 51.8	36.3	104.1	20 37.0	37.2	104.5	20 21.8	38.0	104.9	1
2	22 32.0	31.5	101.3	22 20.1	32.4	101.7	22 07.7	33.3	102.1	21 54.9	34.3	102.5	21 41.7	35.2	102.9	21 28.1	36.1	103.2	21 14.2	36.9	103.7	20 59.8	37.8	104.0	2
3	23 03.5	31.1	100.4	22 52.5	32.1	100.8	22 41.0	33.1	101.2	22 29.2	33.9	101.6	22 16.9	34.8	102.0	22 04.2	35.8	102.4	21 51.1	36.6	102.8	21 37.6	37.5	103.2	3
4	23 34.6	30.8	99.4	23 24.6	31.7	99.9	23 14.1	32.7	100.3	23 03.1	33.7	100.7	22 51.7	34.6	101.1	22 40.0	35.4	101.5	22 27.7	36.4	102.0	22 15.1	37.3	102.4	4
5	24 05.4	+30.5	98.5	23 56.3	+31.5	98.9	23 46.8	+32.4	99.4	23 36.8	+33.3	99.8	23 26.3	+34.3	100.2	23 15.4	+35.2	100.7	23 04.1	+36.1	101.1	22 52.4	+37.0	101.5	5
6	24 35.9	30.1	97.6	24 27.8	31.1	98.0	24 19.2	32.0	98.5	24 10.1	33.0	98.9	24 00.6	34.0	99.3	23 50.6	34.9	99.8	23 40.2	35.8	100.2	23 29.4	36.7	100.6	6
7	25 06.0	29.8	96.6	24 58.9	30.7	97.1	24 51.2	31.8	97.5	24 43.1	32.7	98.0	24 34.6	33.6	98.4	24 25.5	34.6	98.9	24 16.0	35.5	99.3	24 06.1	36.4	99.8	7
8	25 35.8	29.3	95.6	25 29.6	30.4	96.1	25 23.0	31.3	96.6	25 15.8	32.4	97.1	25 08.2	33.3	97.5	25 00.1	34.3	98.0	24 51.5	35.2	98.5	24 42.5	36.1	98.9	8
9	26 05.1	29.0	94.7	26 00.0	30.0	95.2	25 54.3	31.0	95.6	25 48.2	31.9	96.1	25 41.5	33.0	96.6	25 34.4	33.9	97.1	25 26.7	34.9	97.6	25 18.6	35.8	98.0	9
10	26 34.1	+28.6	93.7	26 30.0	+29.5	94.2	26 25.3	+30.6	94.7	26 20.1	+31.6	95.2	26 14.5	+32.5	95.7	26 08.3	+33.5	96.2	26 01.6	+34.5	96.7	25 54.4	+35.4	97.1	10
11	27 02.7	28.1	92.7	26 59.5	29.2	93.2	26 55.9	30.2	93.7	26 51.7	31.3	94.2	26 47.0	32.3	94.7	26 41.8	33.2	95.2	26 36.1	34.1	95.7	26 29.8	35.1	96.2	11
12	27 30.8	27.7	91.7	27 28.7	28.8	92.2	27 26.1	29.8	92.8	27 23.0	30.8	93.3	27 19.3	31.8	93.8	27 15.0	32.8	94.3	27 10.2	33.8	94.8	27 04.9	34.8	95.3	12
13	27 58.5	27.3	90.7	27 57.5	28.3	91.2	27 55.9	29.4	91.8	27 53.8	30.4	92.3	27 51.1	31.5	92.8	27 47.8	32.5	93.4	27 44.0	33.5	93.9	27 39.7	34.4	94.4	13
14	28 25.8	26.8	89.7	28 25.8	27.9	90.2	28 25.3	28.9	90.8	28 24.2	30.0	91.3	28 22.5	31.0	91.9	28 20.3	32.0	92.4	28 17.5	33.0	92.9	28 14.1	34.0	93.5	14
15	28 52.6	+26.4	88.7	28 53.7	+27.5	89.2	28 54.2	+28.5	89.8	28 54.2	+29.5	90.3	28 53.5	+30.6	90.9	28 52.3	+31.6	91.4	28 50.5	+32.6	92.0	28 48.1	+33.6	92.5	15
16	29 19.0	25.9	87.7	29 21.2	26.9	88.2	29 22.7	28.1	88.8	29 23.7	29.1	89.3	29 24.1	30.1	89.9	29 23.9	31.2	90.5	29 23.1	32.2	91.0	29 21.7	33.2	91.6	16
17	29 44.9	25.4	86.7	29 48.1	26.5	87.2	29 50.8	27.5	87.8	29 52.8	28.6	88.3	29 54.2	29.7	88.9	29 55.1	30.7	89.5	29 55.3	31.8	90.1	29 54.9	32.8	90.6	17
18	30 10.3	24.9	85.6	30 14.6	26.0	86.2	30 18.3	27.1	86.7	30 21.4	28.2	87.3	30 23.9	29.3	87.9	30 25.8	30.3	88.5	30 27.1	31.3	89.1	30 27.7	32.4	89.7	18
19	30 35.2	24.4	84.5	30 40.6	25.5	85.1	30 45.4	26.6	85.7	30 49.6	27.7	86.3	30 53.2	28.7	86.9	30 56.1	29.8	87.5	30 58.4	30.9	88.1	31 00.1	31.9	88.7	19
20	30 59.6	+23.8	83.5	31 06.1	+25.0	84.1	31 12.0	+26.1	84.7	31 17.3	+27.1	85.3	31 21.9	+28.3	85.9	31 25.9	+29.3	86.5	31 29.3	+30.4	87.1	31 32.0	+31.5	87.7	20
21	31 23.4	23.4	82.4	31 31.1	24.4	83.0	31 38.1	25.5	83.6	31 44.4	26.7	84.2	31 50.2	27.7	84.8	31 55.2	28.9	85.5	31 59.7	29.9	86.1	32 03.5	30.9	86.7	21
22	31 46.8	22.7	81.3	31 55.5	23.9	81.9	32 03.6	25.0	82.5	32 11.1	26.1	83.1	32 17.9	27.2	83.8	32 24.1	28.3	84.4	32 29.6	29.4	85.1	32 34.4	30.5	85.7	22
23	32 09.5	22.2	80.2	32 19.4	23.3	80.8	32 28.6	24.5	81.5	32 37.2	25.6	82.1	32 45.1	26.7	82.7	32 52.4	27.8	83.4	32 59.0	28.9	84.0	33 04.9	30.0	84.7	23
24	32 31.7	21.7	79.1	32 42.7	22.8	79.7	32 53.1	23.9	80.4	33 02.8	25.0	81.0	33 11.8	26.2	81.7	33 20.2	27.2	82.3	33 27.9	28.3	83.0	33 34.9	29.4	83.6	24
25	32 53.4	+21.0	78.0	33 05.5	+22.2	78.6	33 17.0	+23.3	79.3	33 27.8	+24.4	79.9	33 38.0	+25.5	80.6	33 47.4	+26.7	81.2	33 56.2	+27.8	81.9	34 04.3	+28.9	82.6	25
26	33 14.4	20.4	76.9	33 27.7	21.5	77.5	33 40.3	22.7	78.2	33 52.2	23.9	78.8	34 03.5	25.0	79.5	34 14.1	26.1	80.2	34 24.0	27.2	80.8	34 33.2	28.4	81.5	26
27	33 34.8	19.8	75.8	33 49.2	21.0	76.4	34 03.0	22.1	77.1	34 16.1	23.2	77.7	34 28.5	24.4	78.4	34 40.2	25.5	79.1	34 51.2	26.7	79.8	35 01.6	27.7	80.4	27
28	33 54.6	19.2	74.6	34 10.2	20.3	75.3	34 25.1	21.5	75.9	34 39.3	22.7	76.6	34 52.9	23.8	77.3	35 05.7	25.0	78.0	35 17.9	26.0	78.7	35 29.3	27.2	79.4	28
29	34 13.8	18.5	73.5	34 30.5	19.7	74.1	34 46.6	20.8	74.8	35 02.0	22.0	75.5	35 16.7	23.1	76.2	35 30.7	24.3	76.9	35 43.9	25.5	77.6	35 56.5	26.5	78.3	29
30	34 32.3	+17.9	72.3	34 50.2	+19.1	73.0	35 07.4	+20.2	73.7	35 24.0	+21.3	74.3	35 39.8	+22.5	75.0	35 55.0	+23.6	75.7	36 09.4	+24.8	76.4	36 23.1	+25.9	77.1	30
31	34 50.2	17.2	71.2	35 09.2	18.4	71.8	35 27.6	19.5	72.5	35 45.3	20.7	73.2	36 02.3	21.9	73.9	36 18.6	23.0	74.6	36 34.2	24.1	75.3	36 49.0	25.4	76.0	31
32	35 07.4	16.6	70.0	35 27.6	17.7	70.7	35 47.1	18.9	71.3	36 06.0	20.0	72.0	36 24.2	21.1	72.7	36 41.6	22.3	73.4	36 58.3	23.5	74.2	37 14.4	24.6	74.9	32
33	35 24.0	15.8	68.8	35 45.3	17.0	69.5	36 06.0	18.2	70.2	36 26.0	19.3	70.9	36 45.3	20.5	71.6	37 03.9	21.7	72.3	37 21.8	22.9	73.0	37 39.0	24.0	73.7	33
34	35 39.8	15.2	67.6	36 02.3	16.3	68.3	36 24.2	17.4	69.0	36 45.3	18.6	69.7	37 05.8	19.8	70.4	37 25.6	20.9	71.1	37 44.7	22.1	71.8	38 03.0	23.3	72.6	34
35	35 55.0	+14.4	66.4	36 18.6	+15.6	67.1	36 41.6	+16.7	67.8	37 03.9	+17.9	68.5	37 25.6	+19.1	69.2	37 46.5	+20.3	69.9	38 06.8	+21.4	70.7	38 26.3	+22.5	71.4	35
36	36 09.4	13.7	65.2	36 34.2	14.8	65.9	36 58.3	16.1	66.6	37 21.8	17.2	67.3	37 44.7	18.3	68.0	38 06.8	19.5	68.7	38 28.2	20.6	69.5	38 48.8	21.9	70.2	36
37	36 23.1	13.0	64.0	36 49.0	14.2	64.7	37 14.4	15.2	65.4	37 39.0	16.4	66.1	38 03.0	17.6	66.8	38 26.3	18.7	67.5	38 48.8	20.0	68.3	39 10.7	21.1	69.0	37
38	36 36.1	12.2	62.8	37 03.2	13.3	63.5	37 29.6	14.5	64.2	37 55.4	15.7	64.9	38 20.6	16.8	65.6	38 45.0	18.1	66.3	39 08.8	19.1	67.1	39 31.8	20.3	67.8	38
39	36 48.3	11.5	61.6	37 16.5	12.6	62.3	37 44.1	13.8	62.9	38 11.1	14.9	63.6	38 37.4	16.0	64.4	39 03.0	17.2	65.1	39 27.9	18.4	65.8	39 52.1	19.6	66.6	39
40	36 59.8	+10.7	60.4	37 29.1	+11.9	61.0	37 57.9	+13.0	61.7	38 26.0	+14.1	62.4	38 53.4	+15.3	63.1	39 20.2	+16.5	63.9	39 46.3	+17.6	64.6	40 11.7	+18.8	65.4	40
41	37 10.5	9.9	59.1	37 41.0	11.0	59.8	38 10.9	12.1	60.5	38 40.1	13.3	61.2	39 08.7	14.5	61.9	39 36.7	15.6	62.6	40 03.9	16.8	63.3	40 30.5	17.9	64.1	41
42	37 20.4	9.2	57.9	37 52.0	10.3	58.6	38 23.0	11.4	59.2	38 53.4	12.5	59.9	39 23.2	13.6	60.6	39 52.3	14.8	61.3	40 20.7	16.0	62.1	40 48.4	17.2	62.9	42
43	37 29.6	8.4	56.7	38 02.3	9.5	57.3	38 34.4	10.6	58.0	39 05.9	11.7	58.7	39 36.8	12.9	59.4	40 07.1	14.0	60.1	40 36.7	15.1	60.8	41 05.6	16.3	61.6	43
44	37 38.0	7.6	55.4	38 11.8	8.7	56.1	38 45.0	9.8	56.7	39 17.6	10.9	57.4	39 49.7	12.0	58.1	40 21.1	13.1	58.8	40 51.8	14.3	59.5	41 21.9	15.4	60.3	44

Dec.	30°			31°			32°			33°		
45	34 15.8	+10.1	53.5	34 51.2	+11.2	54.1	35 26.2	+12.1	54.6	36 00.7	+13.1	55.2
46	34 25.9	9.4	52.3	35 02.4	10.4	52.9	35 38.3	11.5	53.4	36 13.8	12.5	54.0
47	34 35.3	8.7	51.1	35 12.8	9.7	51.7	35 49.8	10.6	52.2	36 26.3	11.7	52.8
48	34 44.0	8.0	49.9	35 22.5	8.9	50.5	36 00.4	10.0	51.0	36 38.0	10.9	51.6
49	34 52.0	7.3	48.7	35 31.4	8.3	49.2	36 10.4	9.2	49.8	36 48.9	10.2	50.4
50	34 59.3	+6.6	47.5	35 39.7	+7.4	48.0	36 19.6	+8.4	48.6	36 59.1	+9.4	49.1
51	35 05.9	5.8	46.3	35 47.1	6.8	46.8	36 28.0	7.7	47.3	37 08.5	8.6	47.9
52	35 11.7	5.1	45.1	35 53.9	6.0	45.6	36 35.7	6.9	46.1	37 17.1	7.8	46.6
53	35 16.8	4.4	43.8	35 59.9	5.2	44.3	36 42.6	6.2	44.9	37 24.9	7.1	45.4
54	35 21.2	3.6	42.6	36 05.1	4.5	43.1	36 48.8	5.3	43.6	37 32.0	6.3	44.1
55	35 24.8	+2.9	41.4	36 09.6	+3.8	41.9	36 54.1	+4.6	42.4	37 38.3	+5.4	42.9
56	35 27.7	2.1	40.2	36 13.4	2.9	40.6	36 58.7	3.8	41.1	37 43.7	4.7	41.6
57	35 29.8	1.4	38.9	36 16.3	2.2	39.4	37 02.5	3.0	39.9	37 48.4	3.8	40.4
58	35 31.2	+0.6	37.7	36 18.5	1.4	38.2	37 05.5	2.3	38.6	37 52.2	3.1	39.1
59	35 31.8	-0.1	36.5	36 19.9	+0.7	36.9	37 07.8	1.4	37.4	37 55.3	2.2	37.8
60	35 31.7	-0.8	35.3	36 20.6	-0.1	35.7	37 09.2	+0.6	36.1	37 57.5	+1.4	36.6
61	35 30.9	1.6	34.0	36 20.5	0.9	34.4	37 09.8	-0.1	34.9	37 58.9	+0.6	35.3
62	35 29.3	2.4	32.8	36 19.6	1.7	33.2	37 09.7	1.0	33.6	37 59.5	-0.2	34.0
63	35 26.9	3.1	31.6	36 17.9	2.4	32.0	37 08.7	1.7	32.4	37 59.3	1.0	32.8
64	35 23.8	3.8	30.4	36 15.5	3.2	30.7	37 07.0	2.5	31.1	37 58.3	1.9	31.5
65	35 20.0	-4.6	29.1	36 12.3	-3.9	29.5	37 04.5	-3.4	29.9	37 56.4	-2.7	30.2
66	35 15.4	5.3	27.9	36 08.4	4.7	28.2	37 01.1	4.1	28.6	37 53.7	3.5	29.0
67	35 10.1	6.0	26.7	36 03.7	5.5	27.0	36 57.0	4.9	27.4	37 50.2	4.3	27.7
68	35 04.1	6.8	25.5	35 58.2	6.2	25.8	36 52.1	5.6	26.1	37 45.9	5.1	26.4
69	34 57.3	7.5	24.3	35 52.0	7.0	24.6	36 46.5	6.5	24.9	37 40.8	5.9	25.2
70	34 49.8	-8.2	23.1	35 45.0	-7.7	23.3	36 40.0	-7.2	23.6	37 34.9	-6.7	23.9
71	34 41.6	8.9	21.8	35 37.3	8.5	22.1	36 32.8	8.0	22.4	37 28.2	7.5	22.7
72	34 32.7	9.6	20.6	35 28.8	9.2	20.9	36 24.8	8.7	21.2	37 20.7	8.2	21.4
73	34 23.1	10.3	19.4	35 19.6	9.9	19.7	36 16.1	9.5	19.9	37 12.5	9.1	20.2
74	34 12.8	11.0	18.3	35 09.7	10.6	18.5	36 06.6	10.2	18.7	37 03.4	9.8	18.9
75	34 01.8	-11.7	17.1	34 59.1	-11.3	17.3	35 56.4	-11.0	17.5	36 53.6	-10.6	17.7
76	33 50.1	12.4	15.9	34 47.8	12.0	16.1	35 45.4	11.7	16.3	36 43.0	11.4	16.5
77	33 37.7	13.0	14.7	34 35.8	12.8	14.9	35 33.7	12.4	15.1	36 31.6	12.1	15.3
78	33 24.7	13.7	13.5	34 23.0	13.4	13.7	35 21.3	13.1	13.9	36 19.5	12.8	14.0
79	33 11.0	14.3	12.4	34 09.6	14.0	12.5	35 08.2	13.8	12.7	36 06.7	13.5	12.8
80	32 56.7	-14.9	11.2	33 55.6	-14.8	11.3	34 54.4	-14.5	11.5	35 53.2	-14.3	11.6
81	32 41.8	15.6	10.1	33 40.8	15.4	10.2	34 39.9	15.2	10.3	35 38.9	15.0	10.4
82	32 26.2	16.3	8.9	33 25.4	16.0	9.0	34 24.7	15.9	9.1	35 23.9	15.7	9.2
83	32 09.9	16.8	7.8	33 09.4	16.7	7.9	34 08.8	16.5	8.0	35 08.2	16.3	8.1
84	31 53.1	17.4	6.6	32 52.7	17.3	6.7	33 52.3	17.2	6.8	34 51.9	17.1	6.9
85	31 35.7	-18.0	5.5	32 35.4	-17.9	5.6	33 35.1	-17.8	5.6	34 34.8	-17.7	5.7
86	31 17.7	18.6	4.4	32 17.5	18.5	4.4	33 17.3	18.4	4.5	34 17.1	18.3	4.6
87	30 59.1	19.1	3.3	31 59.0	19.1	3.3	32 58.9	19.0	3.4	33 58.8	19.0	3.4
88	30 40.0	19.7	2.2	31 39.9	19.7	2.2	32 39.9	19.7	2.2	33 39.8	19.6	2.3
89	30 20.3	20.3	1.1	31 20.2	20.2	1.1	32 20.2	20.2	1.1	33 20.2	20.2	1.1
90	30 00.0	-20.8	0.0	31 00.0	-20.8	0.0	32 00.0	-20.8	0.0	33 00.0	-20.8	0.0

Dec.	34°			35°			36°			37°			Dec.
45	36 34.6	+14.2	55.8	37 08.1	+15.2	56.5	37 40.9	+16.3	57.1	38 13.2	+17.4	57.8	45
46	36 48.8	13.5	54.6	37 23.3	14.5	55.2	37 57.2	15.6	55.9	38 30.6	16.6	56.5	46
47	37 02.3	12.7	53.4	37 37.8	13.7	54.0	38 12.8	14.8	54.7	38 47.2	15.8	55.3	47
48	37 15.0	11.9	52.2	37 51.5	13.0	52.8	38 27.6	13.9	53.4	39 03.0	15.1	54.1	48
49	37 26.9	11.2	50.9	38 04.5	12.2	51.5	38 41.5	13.2	52.2	39 18.1	14.2	52.8	49
50	37 38.1	+10.4	49.7	38 16.7	+11.3	50.3	38 54.7	+12.4	50.9	39 32.3	+13.4	51.6	50
51	37 48.5	9.6	48.5	38 28.0	10.6	49.1	39 07.1	11.6	49.7	39 45.7	12.6	50.3	51
52	37 58.1	8.8	47.2	38 38.6	9.8	47.8	39 18.7	10.7	48.4	39 58.3	11.7	49.0	52
53	38 06.9	8.0	46.0	38 48.4	8.9	46.5	39 29.4	9.9	47.1	40 10.0	10.9	47.7	53
54	38 14.9	7.1	44.7	38 57.3	8.1	45.3	39 39.3	9.1	45.8	40 20.9	10.0	46.4	54
55	38 22.0	+6.4	43.4	39 05.4	+7.3	44.0	39 48.4	+8.2	44.6	40 30.9	+9.2	45.2	55
56	38 28.4	5.5	42.2	39 12.7	6.4	42.7	39 56.6	7.3	43.3	40 40.1	8.2	43.8	56
57	38 33.9	4.7	40.9	39 19.1	5.6	41.4	40 03.9	6.5	42.0	40 48.3	7.4	42.5	57
58	38 38.6	3.9	39.6	39 24.7	4.7	40.1	40 10.4	5.6	40.7	40 55.7	6.5	41.2	58
59	38 42.5	3.1	38.3	39 29.4	3.9	38.8	40 16.0	4.7	39.4	41 02.2	5.6	39.9	59
60	38 45.6	+2.2	37.1	39 33.3	+3.0	37.5	40 20.7	+3.8	38.1	41 07.8	+4.6	38.6	60
61	38 47.8	1.3	35.8	39 36.3	2.1	36.2	40 24.5	3.0	36.7	41 12.4	3.8	37.3	61
62	38 49.1	+0.5	34.5	39 38.4	1.3	35.0	40 27.5	2.0	35.4	41 16.2	2.8	35.9	62
63	38 49.6	-0.3	33.2	39 39.7	+0.4	33.7	40 29.5	1.2	34.1	41 19.0	2.0	34.6	63
64	38 49.3	1.2	31.9	39 40.1	-0.5	32.4	40 30.7	+0.2	32.8	41 21.0	+1.0	33.3	64
65	38 48.1	-2.0	30.6	39 39.6	-1.3	31.1	40 30.9	-0.6	31.5	41 22.0	0.0	31.9	65
66	38 46.1	2.8	29.4	39 38.3	2.2	29.8	40 30.3	1.5	30.2	41 22.0	-0.8	30.6	66
67	38 43.3	3.7	28.1	39 36.1	3.0	28.5	40 28.8	2.5	28.9	41 21.2	1.8	29.3	67
68	38 39.6	4.5	26.8	39 33.1	4.0	27.2	40 26.3	3.3	27.5	41 19.4	2.6	28.0	68
69	38 35.1	5.4	25.5	39 29.1	4.8	25.9	40 23.0	4.2	26.2	41 16.8	3.6	26.6	69
70	38 29.7	-6.2	24.2	39 24.3	-5.6	24.6	40 18.8	-5.0	24.9	41 13.2	-4.5	25.3	70
71	38 23.5	7.0	23.0	39 18.7	6.5	23.3	40 13.8	6.0	23.6	41 08.7	5.5	24.0	71
72	38 16.5	7.8	21.7	39 12.2	7.3	22.0	40 07.8	6.8	22.3	41 03.2	6.3	22.6	72
73	38 08.7	8.6	20.4	39 04.9	8.2	20.7	40 01.0	7.7	21.0	40 56.9	7.2	21.3	73
74	38 00.1	9.4	19.2	38 56.7	9.0	19.5	39 53.3	8.6	19.7	40 49.7	8.1	20.0	74
75	37 50.7	-10.2	17.9	38 47.7	-9.8	18.2	39 44.7	-9.4	18.4	40 41.6	-9.0	18.7	75
76	37 40.5	11.0	16.7	38 37.9	10.6	16.9	39 35.3	10.3	17.2	40 32.6	9.9	17.4	76
77	37 29.5	11.8	15.5	38 27.3	11.4	15.7	39 25.0	11.0	15.9	40 22.7	10.7	16.1	77
78	37 17.7	12.5	14.2	38 15.9	12.3	14.4	39 14.0	12.0	14.6	40 12.0	11.6	14.8	78
79	37 05.2	13.3	13.0	38 03.6	13.0	13.2	39 02.0	12.7	13.3	40 00.4	12.4	13.5	79
80	36 51.9	-14.0	11.8	37 50.6	-13.7	11.9	38 49.3	-13.5	12.1	39 48.0	-13.3	12.3	80
81	36 37.9	14.8	10.6	37 36.9	14.6	10.7	38 35.8	14.3	10.8	39 34.7	14.1	11.0	81
82	36 23.1	15.5	9.3	37 22.3	15.3	9.5	38 21.5	15.1	9.6	39 20.6	14.9	9.7	82
83	36 07.6	16.2	8.2	37 07.0	16.0	8.3	38 06.4	15.9	8.4	39 05.7	15.6	8.5	83
84	35 51.4	16.9	7.0	36 51.0	16.8	7.1	37 50.5	16.6	7.1	38 50.1	16.5	7.2	84
85	35 34.5	-17.5	5.8	36 34.2	-17.4	5.9	37 33.9	-17.3	5.9	38 33.6	-17.2	6.0	85
86	35 17.0	18.3	4.6	36 16.8	18.2	4.7	37 16.6	18.1	4.7	38 16.4	18.0	4.8	86
87	34 58.7	18.9	3.4	35 58.6	18.9	3.5	36 58.5	18.8	3.5	37 58.4	18.8	3.6	87
88	34 39.8	19.6	2.3	35 39.7	19.5	2.3	36 39.7	19.5	2.3	37 39.6	19.4	2.4	88
89	34 20.2	20.2	1.1	35 20.2	20.2	1.2	36 20.2	20.2	1.2	37 20.2	20.2	1.2	89
90	34 00.0	-20.8	0.0	35 00.0	-20.8	0.0	36 00.0	-20.9	0.0	37 00.0	-20.9	0.0	90

70°, 290° L.H.A. **LATITUDE SAME NAME AS DECLINATION**

Dec.	30° Hc	d	Z	31° Hc	d	Z	32° Hc	d	Z	33° Hc	d	Z	34° Hc	d	Z	35° Hc	d	Z	36° Hc	d	Z	37° Hc	d	Z	Dec.
45	33 34.1	+10.7	53.4	34 09.6	+11.8	53.9	34 44.8	+12.7	54.5	35 19.4	+13.8	55.0	35 53.5	+14.8	55.4	36 27.4	+15.8	56.2	37 00.2	+16.9	56.8	37 32.8	+17.9	57.5	45
46	33 44.8	10.1	52.2	34 21.4	11.1	52.7	34 57.5	12.1	53.3	35 33.2	13.0	53.8	36 08.3	14.1	54.4	36 43.0	15.1	55.0	37 17.1	16.1	55.6	37 50.7	17.2	56.3	46
47	33 54.9	9.4	51.0	34 32.5	10.3	51.5	35 09.6	11.3	52.1	35 46.2	12.4	52.6	36 22.4	13.3	53.2	36 58.1	14.3	53.8	37 33.2	15.4	54.4	38 07.9	16.4	55.1	47
48	34 04.3	8.7	49.8	34 42.8	9.7	50.3	35 20.9	10.7	50.9	35 58.6	11.6	51.4	36 35.7	12.6	52.0	37 12.4	13.6	52.6	37 48.6	14.7	53.2	38 24.3	15.7	53.8	48
49	34 13.0	8.0	48.6	34 52.5	9.0	49.1	35 31.6	9.9	49.7	36 10.2	10.8	50.2	36 48.3	11.9	50.8	37 26.0	12.9	51.4	38 03.3	13.8	52.0	38 40.0	14.8	52.6	49
50	34 21.0	+7.3	47.4	35 01.5	+8.2	47.9	35 41.5	+9.1	48.5	36 21.0	+10.2	49.0	37 00.2	+11.1	49.6	37 38.9	+12.1	50.1	38 17.1	+13.1	50.7	38 54.8	+14.1	51.4	50
51	34 28.3	6.6	46.2	35 09.7	7.5	46.7	35 50.6	8.5	47.2	36 31.2	9.3	47.8	37 11.3	10.3	48.3	37 51.0	11.2	48.9	38 30.2	12.2	49.5	39 08.9	13.3	50.1	51
52	34 34.9	5.9	45.0	35 17.2	6.8	45.5	35 59.1	7.6	46.0	36 40.5	8.6	46.5	37 21.6	9.5	47.1	38 02.2	10.5	47.7	38 42.4	11.5	48.2	39 22.2	12.4	48.9	52
53	34 40.8	5.2	43.8	35 24.0	6.0	44.3	36 06.7	7.0	44.8	36 49.1	7.9	45.3	37 31.1	8.8	45.8	38 12.7	9.7	46.4	38 53.9	10.6	47.0	39 34.6	11.6	47.6	53
54	34 46.0	4.4	42.6	35 30.0	5.3	43.1	36 13.7	6.2	43.5	36 57.0	7.0	44.1	37 39.9	8.0	44.6	38 22.4	8.9	45.1	39 04.5	9.9	45.7	39 46.2	10.8	46.3	54
55	34 50.4	+3.8	41.4	35 35.3	+4.6	41.8	36 19.9	+5.4	42.3	37 04.0	+6.3	42.8	37 47.9	+7.1	43.3	38 31.3	+8.1	43.9	39 14.4	+8.9	44.4	39 57.0	+9.9	45.0	55
56	34 54.2	2.9	40.1	35 39.9	3.8	40.6	36 25.3	4.6	41.0	37 10.3	5.5	41.6	37 55.0	6.4	42.1	38 39.4	7.2	42.6	39 23.3	8.1	43.2	40 06.9	9.1	43.7	56
57	34 57.1	2.3	38.9	35 43.7	3.0	39.4	36 29.9	3.9	39.8	37 15.8	4.7	40.3	38 01.4	5.5	40.8	38 46.6	6.4	41.3	39 31.5	7.3	41.9	40 16.0	8.1	42.4	57
58	34 59.4	1.5	37.7	35 46.7	2.3	38.1	36 33.8	3.1	38.6	37 20.5	3.9	39.1	38 06.9	4.8	39.6	38 53.0	5.6	40.1	39 38.8	6.4	40.6	40 24.1	7.4	41.1	58
59	35 00.9	0.9	36.5	35 49.0	1.6	36.9	36 36.9	2.3	37.4	37 24.4	3.1	37.8	38 11.7	3.8	38.3	38 58.6	4.7	38.8	39 45.2	5.6	39.3	40 31.5	6.4	39.8	59
60	35 01.7	+0.1	35.3	35 50.6	+0.8	35.7	36 39.2	+1.5	36.1	37 27.5	+2.3	36.6	38 15.6	+3.1	37.0	39 03.3	+3.9	37.5	39 50.8	+4.7	38.0	40 37.9	+5.5	38.5	60
61	35 01.8	-0.7	34.0	35 51.4	0.0	34.4	36 40.7	0.8	34.9	37 29.8	1.6	35.3	38 18.7	2.3	35.7	39 07.2	3.1	36.2	39 55.5	3.8	36.7	40 43.4	4.7	37.2	61
62	35 01.1	-1.4	32.7	35 51.4	-0.7	33.2	36 41.5	0.0	33.6	37 31.4	+0.7	34.0	38 21.0	+1.4	34.5	39 10.3	+2.2	34.9	39 59.3	+3.1	35.4	40 48.1	+3.7	35.9	62
63	34 59.7	-2.1	31.6	35 50.7	-1.5	32.0	36 41.5	-0.8	32.4	37 32.1	-0.1	32.8	38 22.4	+0.6	33.2	39 12.5	+1.3	33.6	40 02.3	+2.1	34.1	40 51.8	+2.9	34.6	63
64	34 57.6	-2.9	30.4	35 49.2	-2.2	30.7	36 40.7	-1.6	31.1	37 32.0	-0.9	31.5	38 23.0	-0.2	31.9	39 13.8	+0.5	32.4	40 04.4	+1.2	32.8	40 54.7	+2.0	33.3	64
65	34 54.7	-3.6	29.2	35 47.0	-3.0	29.5	36 39.1	-2.3	29.9	37 31.1	-1.8	30.3	38 22.8	-1.1	30.6	39 14.3	-0.4	31.1	40 05.6	+0.3	31.5	40 56.6	+1.0	31.9	65
66	34 51.1	-4.3	27.9	35 44.0	-3.7	28.3	36 36.8	-3.2	28.6	37 29.3	-2.5	29.0	38 21.7	-1.8	29.4	39 13.9	-1.2	29.8	40 05.9	-0.6	30.2	40 57.6	+0.2	30.6	66
67	34 46.8	-5.1	26.7	35 40.3	-4.5	27.1	36 33.6	-3.9	27.4	37 26.8	-3.3	27.7	38 19.9	-2.8	28.1	39 12.7	-2.1	28.5	40 05.3	-1.4	28.9	40 57.8	-0.8	29.3	67
68	34 41.7	-5.7	25.5	35 35.8	-5.2	25.8	36 29.7	-4.6	26.1	37 23.5	-4.1	26.5	38 17.1	-3.5	26.8	39 10.6	-2.9	27.2	40 03.9	-2.3	27.6	40 57.0	-1.7	28.0	68
69	34 36.0	-6.5	24.3	35 30.6	-6.0	24.6	36 25.1	-5.5	24.9	37 19.4	-4.9	25.2	38 13.6	-4.3	25.6	39 07.7	-3.8	25.9	40 01.6	-3.2	26.3	40 55.3	-2.6	26.6	69
70	34 29.5	-7.2	23.1	35 24.6	-6.7	23.4	36 19.6	-6.2	23.7	37 14.5	-5.7	24.0	38 09.3	-5.2	24.3	39 03.9	-4.6	24.6	39 58.4	-4.1	25.0	40 52.7	-3.5	25.3	70
71	34 22.3	-7.9	21.9	35 17.9	-7.4	22.2	36 13.4	-7.0	22.4	37 08.8	-6.5	22.7	38 04.1	-6.0	23.0	38 59.3	-5.5	23.3	39 54.3	-5.0	23.7	40 49.2	-4.3	24.0	71
72	34 14.4	-8.6	20.7	35 10.5	-8.2	20.9	36 06.4	-7.7	21.2	37 02.3	-7.2	21.5	37 58.1	-6.8	21.8	38 53.8	-6.3	22.1	39 49.3	-5.8	22.4	40 44.9	-5.1	22.7	72
73	34 05.8	-9.3	19.5	35 02.3	-8.9	19.7	35 58.7	-8.4	20.0	36 55.1	-8.1	20.2	37 51.3	-7.6	20.5	38 47.5	-7.2	20.8	39 43.5	-6.6	21.1	40 39.5	-6.2	21.4	73
74	33 56.5	-10.0	18.3	34 53.4	-9.6	18.5	35 50.3	-9.2	18.8	36 47.0	-8.8	19.0	37 43.7	-8.3	19.2	38 40.3	-7.9	19.5	39 36.9	-7.6	19.8	40 33.3	-7.1	20.1	74
75	33 46.5	-10.6	17.1	34 43.8	-10.3	17.3	35 41.1	-10.0	17.5	36 38.2	-9.5	17.8	37 35.4	-9.2	17.9	38 32.4	-8.8	18.2	39 29.3	-8.3	18.5	40 26.2	-8.0	18.8	75
76	33 35.9	-11.4	15.9	34 33.5	-11.1	16.1	35 31.1	-10.6	16.3	36 28.7	-10.3	16.5	37 26.2	-10.0	16.7	38 23.6	-9.6	17.0	39 21.0	-9.3	17.2	40 18.2	-8.8	17.5	76
77	33 24.5	-12.0	14.8	34 22.5	-11.7	14.9	35 20.5	-11.4	15.1	36 18.4	-11.1	15.3	37 16.2	-10.7	15.4	38 14.0	-10.4	15.7	39 11.7	-10.0	15.9	40 09.4	-9.7	16.2	77
78	33 12.5	-12.6	13.6	34 10.8	-12.3	13.7	35 09.1	-12.1	13.9	36 07.3	-11.8	14.1	37 05.5	-11.5	14.3	38 03.6	-11.2	14.5	39 01.7	-10.9	14.7	39 59.7	-10.5	14.9	78
79	32 59.9	-13.3	12.4	33 58.5	-13.1	12.6	34 57.0	-12.8	12.7	35 55.5	-12.5	12.9	36 54.0	-12.3	13.0	37 52.4	-11.9	13.2	38 50.8	-11.7	13.4	39 49.2	-11.4	13.6	79
80	32 46.6	-13.9	11.3	33 45.4	-13.7	11.4	34 44.2	-13.4	11.5	35 43.0	-13.2	11.7	36 41.7	-12.9	11.8	37 40.5	-12.8	12.0	38 39.1	-12.4	12.1	39 37.8	-12.2	12.3	80
81	32 32.7	-14.6	10.1	33 31.7	-14.4	10.2	34 30.8	-14.2	10.3	35 29.8	-14.0	10.5	36 28.8	-13.8	10.6	37 27.7	-13.5	10.7	38 26.7	-13.1	10.9	39 25.6	-13.1	11.0	81
82	32 18.1	-15.2	9.0	33 17.3	-15.0	9.1	34 16.6	-14.8	9.2	35 15.8	-14.6	9.3	36 15.0	-14.4	9.4	37 14.2	-14.3	9.5	38 13.6	-13.8	9.6	39 12.5	-13.8	9.8	82
83	32 02.9	-15.8	7.8	33 02.3	-15.6	7.9	34 01.8	-15.5	8.0	35 01.2	-15.4	8.1	36 00.6	-15.2	8.2	36 59.9	-15.0	8.3	37 59.3	-14.7	8.4	38 58.7	-14.7	8.5	83
84	31 47.1	-16.4	6.7	32 46.7	-16.3	6.8	33 46.3	-16.2	6.8	34 45.8	-16.0	6.9	35 45.4	-15.9	7.0	36 44.9	-15.7	7.1	37 44.5	-15.6	7.2	38 44.0	-15.4	7.3	84
85	31 30.7	-17.0	5.5	32 30.4	-16.9	5.6	33 30.1	-16.8	5.7	34 29.8	-16.7	5.7	35 29.5	-16.5	5.8	36 29.2	-16.4	5.9	37 28.9	-16.3	6.0	38 28.6	-16.3	6.0	85
86	31 13.7	-17.6	4.4	32 13.5	-17.6	4.4	33 13.3	-17.4	4.5	34 13.1	-17.3	4.6	35 13.0	-17.3	4.6	36 12.8	-17.2	4.7	37 12.6	-17.1	4.8	38 12.3	-16.9	4.8	86
87	30 56.1	-18.1	3.3	31 56.0	-18.1	3.3	32 55.9	-18.1	3.4	33 55.8	-18.0	3.4	34 55.7	-17.9	3.5	35 55.6	-17.9	3.5	36 55.5	-17.8	3.5	37 55.4	-17.8	3.6	87
88	30 38.0	-18.7	2.2	31 37.9	-18.6	2.2	32 37.8	-18.7	2.2	33 37.8	-18.6	2.3	34 37.8	-18.6	2.3	35 37.7	-18.5	2.3	36 37.7	-18.5	2.4	37 37.6	-18.4	2.4	88
89	30 19.3	-19.3	1.1	31 19.3	-19.3	1.1	32 19.2	-19.2	1.1	33 19.2	-19.2	1.1	34 19.2	-19.2	1.1	35 19.2	-19.2	1.2	36 19.2	-19.2	1.2	37 19.2	-19.2	1.2	89
90	30 00.0	-19.8	0.0	31 00.0	-19.8	0.0	32 00.0	-19.8	0.0	33 00.0	-19.8	0.0	34 00.0	-19.8	0.0	35 00.0	-19.9	0.0	36 00.0	-19.9	0.0	37 00.0	-19.9	0.0	90

71°, 289° L.H.A.   **LATITUDE SAME NAME AS DECLINATION**

LATITUDE SAME NAME AS DECLINATION

N. Lat. { L.H.A. greater than 180° .... Zn=Z ; L.H.A. less than 180° .... Zn=360°−Z }

Dec.	30° Hc	d	Z	31° Hc	d	Z	32° Hc	d	Z	33° Hc	d	Z	34° Hc	d	Z	35° Hc	d	Z	36° Hc	d	Z	37° Hc	d	Z	Dec.
0	15 31.3	+31.1	99.2	15 21.6	+31.9	99.5	15 11.5	+32.9	99.8	15 01.2	+33.8	100.0	14 50.6	+34.7	100.3	14 39.8	+35.5	100.6	14 28.7	+36.3	100.8	14 17.3	+37.1	101.1	0
1	16 02.4	30.8	98.3	15 53.5	31.8	98.6	15 44.4	32.6	98.9	15 35.0	33.5	99.2	15 25.3	34.4	99.5	15 15.3	35.3	99.7	15 05.0	36.1	100.0	14 54.4	37.0	100.3	1
2	16 33.2	30.6	97.4	16 25.3	31.5	97.7	16 17.0	32.5	98.0	16 08.5	33.3	98.3	15 59.7	34.2	98.6	15 50.6	35.1	98.9	15 41.1	36.0	99.2	15 31.4	36.9	99.4	2
3	17 03.8	30.3	96.5	16 56.8	31.2	96.8	16 49.5	32.1	97.2	16 41.8	33.1	97.4	16 33.9	34.0	97.8	16 25.7	34.9	98.0	16 17.1	35.8	98.3	16 08.3	36.6	98.6	3
4	17 34.1	30.1	95.6	17 28.0	31.1	96.0	17 21.6	32.0	96.3	17 14.9	32.9	96.6	17 07.9	33.8	96.9	17 00.6	34.6	97.2	16 52.9	35.6	97.5	16 44.9	36.4	97.8	4
5	18 04.2	+29.8	94.7	17 59.1	+30.8	95.1	17 53.6	+31.7	95.4	17 47.8	+32.7	95.7	17 41.7	+33.6	96.0	17 35.2	+34.5	96.3	17 28.5	+35.3	96.6	17 21.3	+36.3	97.0	5
6	18 34.0	29.6	93.8	18 29.9	30.5	94.2	18 25.3	31.5	94.5	18 20.5	32.4	94.8	18 15.3	33.3	95.1	18 09.7	34.2	95.4	18 03.8	35.1	95.8	17 57.6	36.0	96.1	6
7	19 03.6	29.3	92.9	19 00.4	30.2	93.2	18 56.8	31.2	93.6	18 52.9	32.1	93.9	18 48.6	33.1	94.2	18 43.9	34.0	94.6	18 38.9	34.9	94.9	18 33.6	35.8	95.3	7
8	19 32.9	29.0	92.0	19 30.6	30.0	92.3	19 28.0	30.9	92.7	19 25.0	31.9	93.0	19 21.7	32.8	93.4	19 17.9	33.8	93.7	19 13.8	34.7	94.1	19 09.4	35.5	94.4	8
9	20 01.9	28.7	91.0	20 00.6	29.7	91.4	19 58.9	30.7	91.8	19 56.9	31.6	92.1	19 54.5	32.5	92.5	19 51.7	33.5	92.9	19 48.5	34.4	93.2	19 44.9	35.3	93.6	9
10	20 30.6	+28.4	90.1	20 30.3	+29.4	90.5	20 29.6	+30.4	90.9	20 28.5	+31.3	91.2	20 27.0	+32.3	91.6	20 25.2	+33.2	92.0	20 22.9	+34.1	92.3	20 20.2	+35.1	92.7	10
11	20 59.0	28.1	89.2	20 59.7	29.1	89.6	21 00.0	30.0	89.9	20 59.8	31.1	90.3	20 59.3	32.0	90.7	20 58.4	32.9	91.1	20 57.0	33.9	91.5	20 55.3	34.8	91.9	11
12	21 27.1	27.8	88.2	21 28.8	28.8	88.6	21 30.0	29.8	89.0	21 30.9	30.4	89.4	21 31.3	31.7	89.8	21 31.3	32.6	90.2	21 30.9	33.3	90.6	21 30.1	34.5	91.0	12
13	21 54.9	27.5	87.3	21 57.6	28.4	87.7	21 59.8	29.4	88.1	22 01.6	30.4	88.4	22 03.0	31.4	88.9	22 03.9	32.4	89.3	22 04.5	33.3	89.7	22 04.6	34.2	90.1	13
14	22 22.4	27.1	86.3	22 26.0	28.1	86.7	22 29.2	29.1	87.1	22 32.0	30.1	87.5	22 34.4	31.0	88.0	22 36.3	32.0	88.4	22 37.8	33.0	88.8	22 38.8	34.0	89.2	14
15	22 49.5	+26.7	85.3	22 54.1	+27.8	85.8	22 58.3	+28.8	86.2	23 02.1	+29.8	86.6	23 05.4	+30.8	87.0	23 08.3	+31.7	87.5	23 10.8	+32.6	87.9	23 12.8	+33.6	88.3	15
16	23 16.2	26.4	84.3	23 21.9	27.4	84.8	23 27.1	28.4	85.2	23 31.9	29.4	85.6	23 36.2	30.4	86.1	23 40.0	31.4	86.5	23 43.4	32.4	87.0	23 46.4	33.3	87.4	16
17	23 42.6	26.0	83.4	23 49.3	27.0	83.8	23 55.5	28.1	84.3	24 01.3	29.0	84.7	24 06.6	30.0	85.2	24 11.4	31.1	85.6	24 15.8	32.0	86.0	24 19.7	33.0	86.5	17
18	24 08.6	25.7	82.4	24 16.3	26.7	82.8	24 23.6	27.6	83.3	24 30.3	28.7	83.7	24 36.6	29.7	84.2	24 42.5	30.6	84.7	24 47.8	31.7	85.1	24 52.7	32.6	85.6	18
19	24 34.3	25.2	81.4	24 43.0	26.3	81.9	24 51.2	27.3	82.3	24 59.0	28.3	82.7	25 06.3	29.3	83.2	25 13.1	30.4	83.7	25 19.5	31.3	84.2	25 25.3	32.3	84.7	19
20	24 59.5	+24.8	80.4	25 09.3	+25.8	80.9	25 18.5	+26.9	81.3	25 27.3	+28.0	81.8	25 35.6	+29.0	82.3	25 43.5	+29.9	82.8	25 50.8	+30.9	83.2	25 57.6	+31.9	83.7	20
21	25 24.3	24.5	79.4	25 35.1	25.5	79.9	25 45.4	26.5	80.3	25 55.3	27.5	80.8	26 04.6	28.5	81.3	26 13.4	29.5	81.8	26 21.7	30.6	82.3	26 29.5	31.6	82.8	21
22	25 48.8	24.0	78.4	26 00.6	25.0	78.9	26 11.9	26.1	79.3	26 22.8	27.1	79.8	26 33.1	28.2	80.3	26 42.9	29.2	80.8	26 52.3	30.1	81.3	27 01.1	31.1	81.8	22
23	26 12.8	23.5	77.4	26 25.6	24.7	77.9	26 38.0	25.7	78.3	26 49.9	26.7	78.8	27 01.3	27.7	79.3	27 12.1	28.7	79.8	27 22.4	29.8	80.3	27 32.2	30.8	80.9	23
24	26 36.3	23.2	76.3	26 50.3	24.1	76.8	27 03.7	25.2	77.3	27 16.6	26.2	77.8	27 29.0	27.3	78.3	27 40.8	28.3	78.8	27 52.2	29.3	79.4	28 03.0	30.3	79.9	24
25	26 59.5	+22.6	75.3	27 14.4	+23.7	75.8	27 28.9	+24.8	76.3	27 42.8	+25.8	76.8	27 56.3	+26.8	77.3	28 09.1	+27.9	77.9	28 21.5	+28.9	78.4	28 33.3	+29.9	78.9	25
26	27 22.1	22.2	74.3	27 38.1	23.3	74.8	27 53.7	24.3	75.3	28 08.6	25.4	75.8	28 23.1	26.4	76.3	28 37.0	27.4	76.8	28 50.4	28.5	77.4	29 03.2	29.5	77.9	26
27	27 44.3	21.8	73.2	28 01.4	22.8	73.7	28 18.0	23.8	74.2	28 34.0	24.9	74.8	28 49.5	25.9	75.3	29 04.4	27.0	75.8	29 18.9	28.0	76.4	29 32.7	29.0	76.9	27
28	28 06.1	21.2	72.2	28 24.2	22.3	72.7	28 41.8	23.3	73.2	28 58.9	24.4	73.7	29 15.4	25.4	74.3	29 31.4	26.5	74.8	29 46.9	27.5	75.4	30 01.7	28.6	75.9	28
29	28 27.3	20.7	71.1	28 46.5	21.8	71.6	29 05.1	22.9	72.1	29 23.3	23.9	72.7	29 40.8	25.0	73.2	29 57.9	26.0	73.8	30 14.4	27.0	74.3	30 30.3	28.1	74.9	29
30	28 48.0	+20.3	70.0	29 08.3	+21.3	70.6	29 28.0	+22.3	71.1	29 47.2	+23.4	71.6	30 05.8	+24.4	72.2	30 23.9	+25.5	72.7	30 41.4	+26.6	73.3	30 58.4	+27.6	73.9	30
31	29 08.3	19.7	69.0	29 29.6	20.7	69.5	29 50.3	21.8	70.0	30 10.6	22.8	70.6	30 30.2	24.0	71.1	30 49.4	25.0	71.7	31 08.0	26.0	72.2	31 26.0	27.1	72.8	31
32	29 28.0	19.2	67.9	29 50.3	20.3	68.4	30 12.1	21.3	68.9	30 33.4	22.8	69.5	30 54.2	23.4	70.0	31 14.4	24.4	70.6	31 34.0	25.5	71.2	31 53.1	26.5	71.8	32
33	29 47.2	18.6	66.8	30 10.6	19.6	67.3	30 33.4	20.8	67.9	30 55.8	21.8	68.4	31 17.6	22.8	69.0	31 38.8	23.9	69.5	31 59.5	25.0	70.1	32 19.6	26.0	70.7	33
34	30 05.8	18.1	65.7	30 30.2	19.2	66.2	30 54.2	20.2	66.8	31 17.6	21.2	67.3	31 40.4	22.3	67.9	32 02.7	23.4	68.5	32 24.5	24.4	69.1	32 45.6	25.5	69.7	34
35	30 23.9	+17.5	64.6	30 49.4	+18.6	65.1	31 14.4	+19.6	65.7	31 38.8	+20.7	66.2	32 02.7	+21.8	66.8	32 26.1	+22.8	67.4	32 48.9	+23.8	68.0	33 11.1	+24.9	68.6	35
36	30 41.4	17.0	63.5	31 08.0	18.0	64.0	31 34.0	19.1	64.6	31 59.5	20.1	65.1	32 24.5	21.1	65.7	32 48.9	22.2	66.3	33 12.7	23.2	66.9	33 36.0	24.4	67.5	36
37	30 58.4	16.4	62.4	31 26.0	17.4	62.9	31 53.1	18.4	63.4	32 19.6	19.5	64.0	32 45.6	20.6	64.6	33 11.1	21.6	65.2	33 36.0	22.7	65.8	34 00.4	23.7	66.4	37
38	31 14.8	15.8	61.2	31 43.4	16.8	61.8	32 11.5	17.9	62.3	32 39.1	18.9	62.9	33 06.2	20.0	63.5	33 32.7	21.0	64.1	33 58.7	22.1	64.7	34 24.1	23.1	65.3	38
39	31 30.6	15.2	60.0	32 00.2	16.2	60.6	32 29.4	17.2	61.2	32 58.0	18.3	61.8	33 26.2	19.3	62.3	33 53.7	20.4	62.9	34 20.8	21.4	63.5	34 47.2	22.5	64.2	39
40	31 45.8	+14.5	59.0	32 16.4	+15.6	59.5	32 46.6	+16.7	60.1	33 16.3	+17.7	60.6	33 45.5	+18.7	61.2	34 14.1	+19.8	61.8	34 42.2	+20.8	62.4	35 09.7	+21.9	63.0	40
41	32 00.3	14.0	57.8	32 32.0	15.0	58.4	33 03.3	16.0	58.9	33 34.0	17.0	59.5	34 04.2	18.1	60.1	34 33.9	19.1	60.6	35 03.0	20.2	61.3	35 31.6	21.2	61.9	41
42	32 14.3	13.3	56.7	32 47.0	14.4	57.2	33 19.3	15.3	57.8	33 51.0	16.4	58.3	34 22.3	17.4	58.9	34 53.0	18.5	59.5	35 23.2	19.5	60.2	35 52.8	20.6	60.7	42
43	32 27.6	12.8	55.5	33 01.4	13.7	56.1	33 34.6	14.8	56.6	34 07.4	15.8	57.2	34 39.7	16.8	57.7	35 11.5	17.8	58.3	35 42.7	18.8	58.9	36 13.4	19.9	59.6	43
44	32 40.4	12.0	54.4	33 15.1	13.0	54.9	33 49.4	14.0	55.4	34 23.2	15.0	56.0	34 56.5	16.0	56.6	35 29.3	17.1	57.2	36 01.5	18.2	57.8	36 33.3	19.1	58.4	44

LATITUDE CONTRARY NAME TO DECLINATION L.H.A. 76°, 284°

Dec.	30° Hc	d	Z	31° Hc	d	Z	32° Hc	d	Z	33° Hc	d	Z	34° Hc	d	Z	35° Hc	d	Z	36° Hc	d	Z	37° Hc	d	Z	Dec.
0	12 05.6	+30.7	97.1	11 58.1	−31.7	97.3	11 50.3	−32.5	97.5	11 42.4	−33.5	97.7	11 34.2	−34.3	97.9	11 25.8	−35.2	98.1	11 17.2	−36.0	98.3	11 08.4	−36.9	98.5	0
1	11 34.9	31.0	98.0	11 26.4	31.8	98.2	11 17.8	32.7	98.4	11 08.9	33.6	98.6	10 59.9	34.5	98.8	10 50.6	35.3	99.0	10 41.2	36.2	99.2	10 31.5	37.0	99.3	1
2	11 03.9	31.0	98.9	10 54.6	32.0	99.0	10 45.1	32.9	99.2	10 35.3	33.7	99.4	10 25.4	34.6	99.6	10 15.3	35.4	99.8	10 05.0	36.3	100.0	9 54.5	37.0	100.1	2
3	10 32.9	31.2	99.7	10 22.6	32.1	99.9	10 12.2	33.0	100.1	10 01.6	33.8	100.3	9 50.8	34.7	100.4	9 39.9	35.6	100.6	9 28.7	36.3	100.8	9 17.5	37.3	101.0	3
4	10 01.7	31.4	100.6	9 50.5	32.2	100.8	9 39.2	33.1	100.9	9 27.8	34.0	101.1	9 16.1	34.8	101.3	9 04.3	35.6	101.4	8 52.4	36.5	101.6	8 40.2	37.3	101.7	4
5	9 30.3	−31.5	101.5	9 18.3	−32.4	101.6	9 06.1	−33.2	101.8	8 53.8	−34.1	101.9	8 41.3	−34.9	102.1	8 28.7	−35.8	102.2	8 15.9	−36.6	102.4	8 02.9	−37.4	102.5	5
6	8 58.8	31.6	102.3	8 45.9	32.4	102.5	8 32.9	33.3	102.6	8 19.7	34.2	102.8	8 06.4	35.0	103.0	7 52.9	35.8	103.0	7 39.3	36.7	103.2	7 25.5	37.4	103.3	6
7	8 27.2	31.7	103.2	8 13.5	32.6	103.3	7 59.6	33.5	103.5	7 45.5	34.2	103.6	7 31.4	35.2	103.7	7 17.1	36.0	103.9	7 02.6	36.9	104.0	6 48.1	37.6	104.1	7
8	7 55.5	31.8	104.0	7 40.9	32.7	104.2	7 26.1	33.5	104.3	7 11.3	34.4	104.4	6 56.2	35.2	104.5	6 41.1	36.0	104.7	6 25.9	36.9	104.8	6 10.5	37.6	104.9	8
9	7 23.7	31.9	104.9	7 08.2	32.7	105.0	6 52.6	33.5	105.1	6 36.9	34.4	105.3	6 21.0	35.2	105.3	6 05.1	36.1	105.5	5 49.0	36.8	105.6	5 32.9	37.7	105.7	9
10	6 51.8	−32.0	105.8	6 35.5	−32.9	105.9	6 19.0	−33.7	106.0	6 02.5	−34.5	106.1	5 45.8	−35.4	106.2	5 29.0	−36.1	106.3	5 12.2	−37.0	106.4	4 55.2	−37.7	106.4	10
11	6 19.8	32.1	106.6	6 02.6	32.9	106.7	5 45.3	33.8	106.8	5 27.9	34.6	106.9	5 10.4	35.4	107.0	4 52.9	36.3	107.1	4 35.2	37.0	107.2	4 17.5	37.8	107.2	11
12	5 47.7	32.1	107.5	5 29.7	33.0	107.5	5 11.5	33.8	107.6	4 53.3	34.6	107.7	4 35.0	35.5	107.8	4 16.6	36.3	107.9	3 58.2	37.0	107.9	3 39.7	37.8	108.0	12
13	5 15.6	32.3	108.3	4 56.7	33.1	108.4	4 37.7	33.9	108.5	4 18.7	34.7	108.5	3 59.5	35.5	108.6	3 40.3	36.3	108.7	3 21.2	37.1	108.7	3 01.9	37.9	108.8	13
14	4 43.3	32.3	109.1	4 23.6	33.1	109.2	4 03.8	33.9	109.3	3 44.0	34.8	109.4	3 24.1	35.6	109.4	3 04.1	36.3	109.5	2 44.1	37.1	109.6	2 24.0	37.9	109.6	14
15	4 11.0	−32.3	110.0	3 50.5	−33.2	110.1	3 29.9	−34.0	110.1	3 09.2	−34.8	110.2	2 48.5	−35.6	110.2	2 27.8	−36.4	110.3	2 07.0	−37.2	110.3	1 46.1	−37.9	110.3	15
16	3 38.7	32.4	110.8	3 17.3	33.2	110.9	2 55.9	34.0	110.9	2 34.4	34.8	111.0	2 12.9	35.6	111.0	1 51.4	36.4	111.1	1 29.8	37.1	111.1	1 08.2	37.9	111.1	16
17	3 06.3	32.4	111.7	2 44.1	33.2	111.7	2 21.9	34.1	111.8	1 59.6	34.8	111.8	1 37.3	35.6	111.8	1 15.0	36.4	111.9	0 52.7	37.2	111.9	0 30.3	−37.9	111.9	17
18	2 33.9	32.5	112.5	2 10.9	33.3	112.6	1 47.8	34.0	112.6	1 24.8	34.9	112.6	1 01.7	35.6	112.6	0 38.6	36.4	112.7	0 15.5	−37.2	112.7	0 07.6	+38.0	67.3	18
19	2 01.4	32.5	113.4	1 37.6	33.3	113.4	1 13.8	34.1	113.4	0 49.9	34.9	113.4	0 26.1	−35.7	113.4	0 02.2	−36.4	113.4	0 21.7	+37.2	66.6	0 45.6	37.9	66.6	19
20	1 28.9	−32.5	114.2	1 04.3	−33.3	114.2	0 39.7	−34.1	114.2	0 15.1	−34.9	114.2	0 09.6	+35.6	65.8	0 34.2	+36.4	65.8	0 58.9	+37.1	65.8	1 23.5	+37.9	65.8	20
21	0 56.4	32.5	115.0	0 31.0	−33.3	115.1	0 05.6	−34.1	115.1	0 19.8	+34.9	64.9	0 45.2	35.7	64.9	1 10.6	36.4	65.0	1 36.0	37.1	65.0	2 01.4	37.8	65.0	21
22	0 23.9	−32.5	115.9	0 02.3	+33.3	64.1	0 28.5	+34.1	64.1	0 54.7	34.9	64.1	1 20.9	35.6	64.1	1 47.0	36.4	64.2	2 13.1	37.2	64.2	2 39.2	37.9	64.2	22
23	0 08.6	+32.6	63.3	0 35.6	33.3	63.3	1 02.6	34.1	63.3	1 29.5	34.9	63.3	1 56.5	35.6	63.3	2 23.4	36.3	63.4	2 50.3	37.0	63.4	3 17.1	37.8	63.5	23
24	0 41.2	32.5	62.4	1 08.9	33.0	62.4	1 36.7	34.0	62.5	2 04.4	34.8	62.5	2 32.1	35.5	62.5	2 59.7	36.3	62.6	3 27.3	37.1	62.6	3 54.9	37.8	62.7	24
25	1 13.7	+32.5	61.6	1 42.2	+33.3	61.6	2 10.7	+34.0	61.6	2 39.2	+34.8	61.7	3 07.6	+35.6	61.7	3 36.0	+36.3	61.8	4 04.4	+37.0	61.8	4 32.7	+37.7	61.9	25
26	1 46.2	32.4	60.8	2 15.5	32.8	60.8	2 44.7	34.0	60.8	3 14.0	34.7	60.9	3 43.2	35.4	60.9	4 12.3	36.2	61.0	4 41.4	37.0	61.0	5 10.4	37.6	61.1	26
27	2 18.6	32.5	59.9	2 48.7	33.0	59.9	3 18.7	34.0	60.0	3 48.7	34.7	60.0	4 18.6	35.5	60.1	4 48.5	36.2	60.2	5 18.3	36.9	60.3	5 48.0	37.6	60.3	27
28	2 51.1	32.4	59.1	3 21.9	33.2	59.1	3 52.7	33.9	59.2	4 23.4	34.5	59.2	4 54.1	35.4	59.3	5 24.7	36.1	59.4	5 55.2	36.8	59.5	6 25.6	37.5	59.6	28
29	3 23.5	32.4	58.2	3 55.1	33.1	58.3	4 26.6	34.0	58.3	4 58.1	34.5	58.4	5 29.4	35.4	58.4	6 00.8	36.0	58.6	6 32.0	36.8	58.7	7 03.2	37.4	58.8	29
30	3 55.9	+32.3	57.4	4 28.2	+33.0	57.4	5 00.4	+33.8	57.5	5 32.6	+34.6	57.6	6 04.8	+35.2	57.6	6 36.8	+35.9	57.8	7 08.7	+36.7	57.8	7 40.6	+37.4	58.0	30
31	4 28.2	32.2	56.5	5 01.2	33.0	56.6	5 34.2	33.7	56.7	6 07.2	34.4	56.8	6 40.0	35.1	56.9	7 12.7	35.9	57.0	7 45.4	36.6	57.1	8 18.0	37.2	57.2	31
32	5 00.4	32.2	55.7	5 34.2	33.0	55.8	6 07.9	33.7	55.9	6 41.6	34.3	55.9	7 15.1	35.1	56.0	7 48.6	35.7	56.2	8 22.0	36.4	56.3	8 55.2	37.2	56.4	32
33	5 32.6	32.2	54.8	6 07.2	32.8	54.9	6 41.6	33.5	55.0	7 15.9	34.3	55.1	7 50.2	35.0	55.2	8 24.4	35.7	55.3	8 58.4	36.4	55.5	9 32.4	37.0	55.6	33
34	6 04.8	32.0	54.0	6 40.0	32.7	54.1	7 15.1	33.5	54.2	7 50.2	34.2	54.3	8 25.2	34.9	54.4	9 00.1	35.5	54.5	9 34.8	36.3	54.7	10 09.4	37.0	54.8	34
35	6 36.8	+31.9	53.1	7 12.7	+32.7	53.2	7 48.6	+33.4	53.3	8 24.4	+34.0	53.5	9 00.1	+34.7	53.6	9 35.6	+35.5	53.7	10 11.1	+36.1	53.9	10 46.4	+36.8	54.0	35
36	7 08.7	31.9	52.3	7 45.4	32.6	52.3	8 22.0	33.2	52.5	8 58.4	34.0	52.6	9 34.8	34.6	52.8	10 11.1	35.3	52.9	10 47.2	35.9	53.0	11 23.2	36.7	53.0	36
37	7 40.6	31.8	51.4	8 18.0	32.4	51.5	8 55.2	33.2	51.7	9 32.4	33.8	51.8	10 09.4	34.6	51.9	10 46.4	35.2	52.1	11 23.2	35.9	52.2	11 59.9	36.5	52.4	37
38	8 12.4	31.6	50.6	8 50.4	32.4	50.6	9 28.4	33.0	50.8	10 06.2	33.7	51.0	10 44.0	34.3	51.1	11 21.6	35.0	51.2	11 59.1	35.7	51.4	12 36.4	36.4	51.6	38
39	8 44.0	31.5	49.7	9 22.8	32.2	49.8	10 01.4	32.9	50.0	10 39.9	33.6	50.1	11 18.3	34.3	50.3	11 56.6	35.0	50.4	12 34.8	35.6	50.5	13 12.8	36.3	50.8	39
40	9 15.5	+31.5	48.9	9 55.0	+32.1	49.0	10 34.3	+32.7	49.1	11 13.5	+33.4	49.3	11 52.6	+34.1	49.4	12 31.6	+34.7	49.6	13 10.4	+35.4	49.8	13 49.1	+36.0	49.9	40
41	9 47.0	31.2	48.0	10 27.1	31.9	48.1	11 07.0	32.7	48.3	11 46.9	33.3	48.4	12 26.7	33.9	48.6	13 06.3	34.6	48.8	13 45.8	35.2	48.9	14 25.1	35.9	49.1	41
42	10 18.2	31.2	47.1	10 59.0	31.8	47.3	11 39.7	32.4	47.4	12 20.2	33.1	47.6	13 00.6	33.8	47.7	13 40.9	34.4	47.9	14 21.0	35.1	48.1	15 01.0	35.8	48.3	42
43	10 49.4	31.0	46.3	11 30.8	31.6	46.4	12 12.1	32.3	46.6	12 53.3	33.0	46.7	13 34.4	33.6	46.9	14 15.3	34.3	47.1	14 56.1	35.0	47.3	15 36.8	35.5	47.5	43
44	11 20.4	30.8	45.4	12 02.4	31.5	45.5	12 44.4	32.1	45.7	13 26.3	32.7	45.9	14 08.0	33.4	46.0	14 49.6	34.0	46.2	15 31.0	34.7	46.4	16 12.3	35.3	46.6	44

LATITUDE SAME NAME AS DECLINATION

Dec.	30° Hc	d	Z	31° Hc	d	Z	32° Hc	d	Z	33° Hc	d	Z	34° Hc	d	Z	35° Hc	d	Z	36° Hc	d	Z	37° Hc	d	Z	Dec.
45	11 51.2	+30.7	44.5	12 33.9	+31.3	44.7	13 16.5	+32.0	44.8	13 59.0	+32.6	44.8	14 41.4	+33.2	45.2	15 23.6	+33.9	45.4	16 05.7	+34.5	45.6	16 47.6	+35.2	45.8	45
46	12 21.9	30.5	43.8	13 05.2	31.2	43.8	13 48.5	31.8	44.0	14 31.6	32.4	44.0	15 14.6	33.1	44.3	15 57.5	33.6	44.5	16 40.2	34.3	44.7	17 22.8	34.9	44.9	46
47	12 52.4	30.3	42.8	13 36.4	30.9	42.9	14 20.3	31.5	43.1	15 04.0	32.2	43.1	15 47.7	32.8	43.4	16 31.1	33.5	43.6	17 14.5	34.1	43.9	17 57.7	34.7	44.1	47
48	13 22.7	30.2	41.9	14 07.3	30.8	42.0	14 51.8	31.4	42.2	15 36.2	32.0	42.2	16 20.5	32.6	42.6	17 04.6	33.2	42.8	17 48.6	33.8	43.0	18 32.4	34.4	43.2	48
49	13 52.9	29.9	41.0	14 38.1	30.6	41.1	15 23.2	31.2	41.3	16 08.2	31.8	41.3	16 53.1	32.4	41.7	17 37.8	33.0	41.9	18 22.4	33.6	42.1	19 06.8	34.2	42.4	49
50	14 22.8	+29.7	40.1	15 08.7	+30.3	40.3	15 54.4	+30.9	40.4	16 40.0	+31.5	40.6	17 25.5	+32.1	40.8	18 10.8	+32.7	41.0	18 56.0	+33.3	41.3	19 41.0	+34.0	41.5	50
51	14 52.5	29.6	39.2	15 39.0	30.1	39.4	16 25.3	30.7	39.5	17 11.5	31.3	39.7	17 57.6	31.9	39.9	18 43.5	32.5	40.1	19 29.3	33.1	40.4	20 15.0	33.7	40.6	51
52	15 22.1	29.3	38.3	16 09.1	29.9	38.5	16 56.0	30.5	38.6	17 42.8	31.1	38.8	18 29.5	31.7	39.0	19 16.0	32.3	39.3	20 02.4	32.9	39.5	20 48.7	33.4	39.7	52
53	15 51.4	29.1	37.4	16 39.0	29.7	37.6	17 26.5	30.3	37.7	18 13.9	30.8	37.9	19 01.2	31.4	38.1	19 48.3	32.0	38.3	20 35.3	32.5	38.6	21 22.1	33.1	38.8	53
54	16 20.5	28.8	36.5	17 08.7	29.4	36.6	17 56.8	30.0	36.8	18 44.7	30.6	37.0	19 32.6	31.1	37.2	20 20.3	31.6	37.5	21 07.8	32.3	37.7	21 55.2	32.8	37.9	54
55	16 49.3	+28.7	35.6	17 38.1	+29.2	35.7	18 26.8	+29.7	35.9	19 15.3	+30.3	36.1	20 03.7	+30.8	36.3	20 51.9	+31.4	36.6	21 40.1	+31.9	36.8	22 28.0	+32.6	37.0	55
56	17 18.0	28.3	34.6	18 07.3	28.9	34.8	18 56.5	29.4	35.0	19 45.6	30.0	35.2	20 34.5	30.6	35.4	21 23.3	31.2	35.6	22 12.0	31.7	35.9	23 00.6	32.2	36.1	56
57	17 46.3	28.1	33.7	18 36.2	28.6	33.9	19 25.9	29.2	34.1	20 15.6	29.7	34.3	21 05.1	30.2	34.5	21 54.5	30.7	34.7	22 43.7	31.3	35.0	23 32.8	31.9	35.2	57
58	18 14.4	27.8	32.8	19 04.8	28.4	33.0	19 55.1	28.9	33.2	20 45.3	29.4	33.4	21 35.3	30.0	33.6	22 25.2	30.5	33.8	23 15.0	31.1	34.0	24 04.7	31.6	34.3	58
59	18 42.2	27.6	31.8	19 33.2	28.0	32.0	20 24.0	28.5	32.2	21 14.7	29.1	32.4	22 05.3	29.6	32.6	22 55.7	30.2	32.9	23 46.1	30.6	33.1	24 36.3	31.2	33.3	59
60	19 09.8	+27.2	30.9	20 01.2	+27.8	31.1	20 52.5	+28.3	31.3	21 43.8	+28.7	31.5	22 34.9	+29.3	31.7	23 25.9	+29.8	31.9	24 16.7	+30.4	32.2	25 07.5	+30.8	32.4	60
61	19 37.0	27.0	30.0	20 29.0	27.4	30.1	21 20.8	27.9	30.3	22 12.5	28.5	30.5	23 04.2	28.9	30.8	23 55.7	29.4	31.0	24 47.1	29.9	31.2	25 38.3	30.5	31.5	61
62	20 04.0	26.7	29.0	20 56.4	27.2	29.2	21 48.8	27.6	29.4	22 41.0	28.1	29.6	23 33.1	28.6	29.8	24 25.1	29.1	30.0	25 17.0	29.6	30.3	26 08.8	30.1	30.5	62
63	20 30.7	26.3	28.1	21 23.6	26.8	28.2	22 16.4	27.3	28.4	23 09.1	27.8	28.6	24 01.7	28.2	28.8	24 54.2	28.7	29.1	25 46.6	29.2	29.3	26 38.9	29.7	29.5	63
64	20 57.0	26.0	27.1	21 50.4	26.4	27.3	22 43.7	26.9	27.5	23 36.9	27.3	27.7	24 29.9	27.9	27.9	25 22.9	28.4	28.1	26 15.8	28.8	28.3	27 08.6	29.3	28.6	64
65	21 23.0	+25.7	26.1	22 16.8	+26.2	26.3	23 10.6	+26.6	26.5	24 04.2	+27.1	26.7	24 57.8	+27.5	26.9	25 51.3	+27.9	27.1	26 44.6	+28.4	27.3	27 37.9	+28.8	27.6	65
66	21 48.7	25.3	25.2	22 43.0	25.7	25.3	23 37.2	26.1	25.5	24 31.3	26.6	25.7	25 25.3	27.1	25.9	26 19.2	27.5	26.1	27 13.0	28.0	26.3	28 06.7	28.5	26.6	66
67	22 14.0	25.0	24.2	23 08.7	25.4	24.4	24 03.4	25.8	24.5	24 57.9	26.3	24.7	25 52.4	26.6	24.9	26 46.7	27.1	25.1	27 41.0	27.6	25.3	28 35.2	28.0	25.6	67
68	22 39.0	24.7	23.2	23 34.1	25.1	23.4	24 29.2	25.4	23.5	25 24.2	25.8	23.7	26 19.0	26.3	23.9	27 13.8	26.7	24.1	28 08.6	27.1	24.3	29 03.2	27.5	24.6	68
69	23 03.7	24.2	22.2	23 59.2	24.6	22.4	24 54.6	25.1	22.5	25 50.0	25.4	22.7	26 45.3	25.8	22.9	27 40.5	26.3	23.1	28 35.7	26.6	23.3	29 30.7	27.1	23.6	69
70	23 27.9	+23.9	21.2	24 23.8	+24.3	21.4	25 19.7	+25.0	21.5	26 15.4	+25.0	21.7	27 11.1	+25.4	21.9	28 06.8	+25.8	22.1	29 02.3	+26.2	22.3	29 57.8	+26.6	22.6	70
71	23 51.8	23.5	20.2	24 48.1	23.8	20.4	25 44.3	24.2	20.5	26 40.4	24.6	20.7	27 36.5	25.0	20.9	28 32.5	25.4	21.1	29 28.5	25.7	21.3	30 24.4	26.1	21.5	71
72	24 15.3	23.0	19.2	25 11.9	23.4	19.4	26 08.5	23.7	19.5	27 05.0	24.1	19.7	28 01.5	24.4	19.9	28 57.9	24.8	20.0	29 54.2	25.2	20.2	30 50.5	25.5	20.4	72
73	24 38.3	22.7	18.2	25 35.3	23.0	18.3	26 32.2	23.4	18.5	27 29.1	23.7	18.6	28 25.9	24.0	18.8	29 22.7	24.3	19.0	30 19.4	24.8	19.2	31 16.0	25.1	19.4	73
74	25 01.0	22.2	17.2	25 58.3	22.6	17.3	26 55.6	22.8	17.5	27 52.8	23.2	17.6	28 49.9	23.6	17.8	29 47.0	23.9	17.9	30 44.1	24.2	18.1	31 41.1	24.5	18.3	74
75	25 23.2	+21.9	16.1	26 20.9	+22.1	16.3	27 18.4	+22.4	16.4	28 16.0	+22.7	16.4	29 13.5	+23.0	16.7	30 10.9	+23.3	16.9	31 08.3	+23.6	17.1	32 05.6	+24.0	17.2	75
76	25 45.1	21.3	15.1	26 43.0	21.6	15.2	27 40.8	22.0	15.4	28 38.7	22.2	15.4	29 36.5	22.5	15.7	30 34.2	22.8	15.8	31 31.9	23.1	16.0	32 29.6	23.4	16.2	76
77	26 06.4	21.0	14.1	27 04.6	21.2	14.2	28 02.8	21.4	14.3	29 00.9	21.7	14.3	29 59.0	22.0	14.6	30 57.0	22.3	14.7	31 55.0	22.6	14.9	32 53.0	22.8	15.1	77
78	26 27.4	20.4	13.0	27 25.8	20.7	13.1	28 24.2	21.0	13.3	29 22.6	21.2	13.3	30 21.0	21.4	13.5	31 19.3	21.7	13.7	32 17.6	22.0	13.8	33 15.8	22.3	14.0	78
79	26 47.8	20.0	12.0	27 46.5	20.3	12.1	28 45.2	20.4	12.2	29 43.8	20.7	12.2	30 42.4	20.9	12.4	31 41.0	21.2	12.6	32 39.6	21.3	12.7	33 38.1	21.6	12.8	79
80	27 07.8	+19.6	10.9	28 06.8	+19.7	11.0	29 05.6	+20.0	11.1	30 04.5	+20.1	11.1	31 03.3	+20.4	11.3	32 02.2	+20.5	11.5	33 00.9	+20.8	11.6	33 59.7	+21.0	11.7	80
81	27 27.4	19.0	9.8	28 26.5	19.2	9.9	29 25.6	19.4	10.0	30 24.6	19.6	10.0	31 23.7	19.8	10.2	32 22.7	20.0	10.4	33 21.7	20.2	10.5	34 20.7	20.4	10.6	81
82	27 46.4	18.5	8.8	28 45.7	18.7	8.9	29 45.0	18.8	8.9	30 44.2	19.1	8.9	31 43.5	19.2	9.1	32 42.7	19.4	9.2	33 41.9	19.6	9.3	34 41.1	19.8	9.5	82
83	28 04.9	18.1	7.7	29 04.4	18.2	7.8	30 03.8	18.4	7.9	31 03.3	18.4	7.8	32 02.7	18.6	8.0	33 02.1	18.8	8.1	34 01.5	18.9	8.2	35 00.9	19.1	8.3	83
84	28 23.0	17.5	6.6	29 22.6	17.6	6.7	30 22.2	17.7	6.8	31 21.7	17.9	6.8	32 21.3	18.0	6.9	33 20.9	18.1	7.0	34 20.4	18.3	7.1	35 20.0	18.4	7.1	84
85	28 40.5	+17.0	5.5	29 40.2	+17.1	5.6	30 39.9	+17.2	5.6	31 39.6	+17.3	5.6	32 39.3	+17.4	5.8	33 39.0	+17.5	5.8	34 38.7	+17.6	5.9	35 38.4	+17.7	6.0	85
86	28 57.5	16.4	4.4	29 57.3	16.5	4.5	30 57.1	16.6	4.5	31 56.9	16.7	4.5	32 56.7	16.8	4.6	33 56.5	16.9	4.7	34 56.3	17.0	4.7	35 56.1	17.1	4.8	86
87	29 13.9	15.9	3.3	30 13.8	16.0	3.4	31 13.7	16.0	3.4	32 13.6	16.1	3.4	33 13.5	16.2	3.5	34 13.4	16.2	3.5	35 13.3	16.3	3.6	36 13.2	16.3	3.6	87
88	29 29.8	15.4	2.2	30 29.8	15.4	2.3	31 29.7	15.5	2.3	32 29.7	15.5	2.3	33 29.7	15.5	2.3	34 29.6	15.5	2.4	35 29.6	15.5	2.4	36 29.5	15.6	2.4	88
89	29 45.2	14.8	1.1	30 45.2	14.8	1.1	31 45.2	14.8	1.1	32 45.2	14.8	1.1	33 45.2	14.8	1.2	34 45.1	14.9	1.2	35 45.1	14.9	1.2	36 45.1	14.9	1.2	89
90	30 00.0	+14.2	0.0	31 00.0	+14.2	0.0	32 00.0	+14.2	0.0	33 00.0	+14.2	0.0	34 00.0	+14.2	0.0	35 00.0	+14.2	0.0	36 00.0	+14.2	0.0	37 00.0	+14.1	0.0	90

S. Lat. { L.H.A. greater than 180°......Zn=180°−Z ; L.H.A. less than 180°......Zn=180°+Z }

LATITUDE SAME NAME AS DECLINATION

L.H.A. 104°, 256°

LATITUDE SAME NAME AS DECLINATION

N. Lat. { L.H.A. greater than 180°......Zn=Z
{ L.H.A. less than 180°.........Zn=360−Z

Dec.	30° Hc	d	Z	31° Hc	d	Z	32° Hc	d	Z	33° Hc	d	Z	34° Hc	d	Z	35° Hc	d	Z	36° Hc	d	Z	37° Hc	d	Z	Dec.
0	11 14.0	+30.5	96.6	11 07.0	+31.5	96.8	10 59.9	+32.3	97.0	10 52.5	+33.2	97.2	10 44.9	+34.1	97.4	10 37.1	+35.0	97.7	10 29.1	+35.8	97.7	10 21.0	+36.6	97.9	0
1	11 44.5	30.4	95.7	11 38.5	31.2	95.9	11 32.2	32.1	96.1	11 25.7	33.0	96.3	11 19.0	33.9	96.5	11 12.1	34.8	96.7	11 04.9	35.7	96.9	10 57.6	36.5	97.1	1
2	12 14.9	30.2	94.8	12 09.7	31.1	95.0	12 04.3	32.0	95.3	11 58.7	32.9	95.5	11 52.9	33.8	95.7	11 46.9	34.6	95.9	11 40.6	35.5	96.1	11 34.1	36.4	96.3	2
3	12 45.1	30.0	93.9	12 40.8	30.9	94.2	12 36.3	31.9	94.4	12 31.6	32.8	94.6	12 26.7	33.6	94.8	12 21.5	34.5	95.0	12 16.1	35.4	95.2	12 10.5	36.3	95.5	3
4	13 15.1	29.8	93.0	13 11.7	30.8	93.3	13 08.2	31.6	93.5	13 04.4	32.5	93.8	13 00.3	33.5	94.0	12 56.0	34.4	94.2	12 51.5	35.2	94.4	12 46.8	36.0	94.7	4
5	13 44.9	+29.6	92.2	13 42.5	+30.5	92.4	13 39.8	+31.5	92.6	13 36.9	+32.4	92.9	13 33.8	+33.3	93.1	13 30.4	+34.2	93.4	13 26.7	+35.1	93.6	13 22.8	+36.0	93.8	5
6	14 14.5	29.4	91.3	14 13.0	30.4	91.5	14 11.3	31.3	91.8	14 09.3	32.2	92.0	14 07.1	33.1	92.3	14 04.6	34.0	92.5	14 01.8	34.9	92.8	13 58.8	35.7	93.0	6
7	14 43.9	29.2	90.4	14 43.4	30.1	90.6	14 42.6	31.1	90.9	14 41.5	32.0	91.1	14 40.2	32.9	91.4	14 38.6	33.8	91.7	14 36.7	34.7	91.9	14 34.5	35.6	92.2	7
8	15 13.1	29.0	89.5	15 13.5	30.0	89.7	15 13.7	30.9	90.0	15 13.5	31.8	90.3	15 13.1	32.7	90.5	15 12.4	33.6	90.8	15 11.4	34.5	91.1	15 10.1	35.4	91.4	8
9	15 42.1	28.8	88.5	15 43.5	29.7	88.8	15 44.6	30.6	89.1	15 45.3	31.6	89.4	15 45.8	32.5	89.7	15 46.0	33.4	90.0	15 45.9	34.3	90.2	15 45.5	35.2	90.5	9
10	16 10.9	+28.5	87.6	16 13.2	+29.5	87.9	16 15.2	+30.5	88.2	16 16.9	+31.4	88.5	16 18.3	+32.3	88.8	16 19.4	+33.3	89.1	16 20.2	+34.2	89.4	16 20.7	+35.0	89.7	10
11	16 39.4	28.3	86.7	16 42.7	29.2	87.0	16 45.7	30.1	87.3	16 48.3	31.1	87.6	16 50.6	32.1	87.9	16 52.7	32.9	88.2	16 54.4	33.8	88.5	16 55.7	34.8	88.8	11
12	17 07.7	28.0	85.8	17 11.9	29.0	86.1	17 15.8	29.7	86.4	17 19.4	30.9	86.7	17 22.7	31.8	87.0	17 25.6	32.8	87.4	17 28.2	33.7	87.7	17 30.5	34.6	88.0	12
13	17 35.7	27.8	84.9	17 40.9	28.8	85.2	17 45.5	29.7	85.5	17 50.3	30.7	85.8	17 54.5	31.6	86.1	17 58.4	32.5	86.5	18 01.9	33.5	86.8	18 05.1	34.3	87.1	13
14	18 03.5	27.5	83.9	18 09.7	28.5	84.3	18 15.5	29.4	84.6	18 21.0	30.4	84.9	18 26.1	31.4	85.3	18 30.9	32.3	85.6	18 35.4	33.1	85.9	18 39.4	34.2	86.3	14
15	18 31.0	+27.2	83.0	18 38.2	+28.2	83.3	18 44.9	+29.2	83.7	18 51.4	+30.1	84.0	18 57.5	+31.0	84.4	19 03.2	+32.0	84.7	19 08.5	+33.0	85.0	19 13.6	+33.8	85.4	15
16	18 58.2	27.0	82.1	19 06.4	27.9	82.4	19 14.1	28.9	82.7	19 21.5	29.8	83.1	19 28.5	30.8	83.4	19 35.2	31.7	83.8	19 41.5	32.7	84.1	19 47.4	33.6	84.5	16
17	19 25.2	26.6	81.1	19 34.3	27.6	81.5	19 43.0	28.6	81.8	19 51.3	29.6	82.2	19 59.3	30.5	82.5	20 06.9	31.5	82.9	20 14.2	32.4	83.3	20 21.0	33.3	83.6	17
18	19 51.8	26.4	80.2	20 01.9	27.3	80.5	20 11.6	28.3	80.9	20 20.9	29.3	81.2	20 29.8	30.3	81.6	20 38.4	31.2	82.0	20 46.6	32.1	82.4	20 54.3	33.1	82.7	18
19	20 18.2	26.0	79.2	20 29.2	27.0	79.6	20 39.9	28.0	79.9	20 50.2	28.9	80.3	21 00.1	29.9	80.7	21 09.6	30.9	81.1	21 18.7	31.8	81.5	21 27.4	32.8	81.8	19
20	20 44.2	+25.7	78.2	20 56.2	+26.7	78.6	21 07.9	+27.7	79.0	21 19.1	+28.7	79.4	21 30.0	+29.6	79.8	21 40.5	+30.5	80.1	21 50.5	+31.5	80.5	22 00.2	+32.4	80.9	20
21	21 09.9	25.4	77.3	21 22.9	26.4	77.7	21 35.6	27.4	78.0	21 47.8	28.3	78.4	21 59.6	29.3	78.8	22 11.0	30.3	79.2	22 22.0	31.3	79.6	22 32.6	32.2	80.0	21
22	21 35.3	25.0	76.3	21 49.3	26.0	76.7	22 02.9	27.0	77.1	22 16.1	28.0	77.5	22 28.9	29.0	77.9	22 41.3	29.9	78.3	22 53.3	30.9	78.7	23 04.8	31.8	79.1	22
23	22 00.3	24.7	75.3	22 15.3	25.7	75.7	22 29.9	26.7	76.1	22 44.1	27.6	76.5	22 57.9	28.6	76.9	23 11.2	29.6	77.3	23 24.2	30.5	77.8	23 36.6	31.6	78.2	23
24	22 25.0	24.3	74.3	22 41.0	25.3	74.7	22 56.6	26.3	75.1	23 11.7	27.3	75.5	23 26.5	28.3	76.0	23 40.8	29.3	76.4	23 54.7	30.2	76.8	24 08.2	31.1	77.3	24
25	22 49.3	+24.0	73.4	23 06.3	+25.0	73.8	23 22.9	+25.9	74.2	23 39.0	+27.0	74.6	23 54.8	+27.9	75.0	24 10.1	+28.8	75.4	24 24.9	+29.9	75.9	24 39.3	+30.8	76.3	25
26	23 13.3	23.5	72.4	23 31.3	24.5	72.8	23 48.8	25.6	73.2	24 06.0	26.5	73.6	24 22.7	27.5	74.0	24 38.9	28.6	74.5	24 54.8	29.5	74.9	25 10.1	30.5	75.4	26
27	23 36.8	23.2	71.4	23 55.8	24.2	71.8	24 14.4	25.2	72.2	24 32.5	26.2	72.6	24 50.2	27.2	73.1	25 07.5	28.1	73.5	25 24.3	29.1	74.0	25 40.6	30.1	74.4	27
28	24 00.0	22.8	70.3	24 20.0	23.8	70.8	24 39.6	24.7	71.2	24 58.7	25.7	71.6	25 17.4	26.7	72.1	25 35.6	27.7	72.5	25 53.4	28.7	73.0	26 10.7	29.7	73.5	28
29	24 22.8	22.4	69.3	24 43.8	23.4	69.8	25 04.3	24.4	70.2	25 24.4	25.4	70.6	25 44.1	26.4	71.1	26 03.3	27.4	71.6	26 22.1	28.3	72.0	26 40.4	29.3	72.5	29
30	24 45.2	+22.0	68.3	25 07.2	+22.9	68.7	25 28.7	+24.0	69.2	25 49.8	+24.9	69.6	26 10.5	+25.9	70.1	26 30.7	+26.9	70.6	26 50.4	+27.9	71.0	27 09.7	+28.8	71.5	30
31	25 07.2	21.5	67.3	25 30.1	22.6	67.7	25 52.7	23.5	68.2	26 14.7	24.6	68.6	26 36.4	25.5	69.1	26 57.6	26.5	69.6	27 18.3	27.5	70.0	27 38.5	28.5	70.5	31
32	25 28.7	21.1	66.3	25 52.7	22.0	66.7	26 16.2	23.1	67.1	26 39.3	24.0	67.6	27 01.9	25.1	68.1	27 24.1	26.0	68.5	27 45.8	27.0	69.0	28 07.0	28.0	69.5	32
33	25 49.8	20.7	65.2	26 14.7	21.7	65.7	26 39.3	22.6	66.1	27 03.3	23.7	66.6	27 27.0	24.6	67.1	27 50.1	25.6	67.5	28 12.8	26.6	68.0	28 35.0	27.6	68.5	33
34	26 10.5	20.2	64.2	26 36.4	21.2	64.6	27 01.9	22.2	65.1	27 27.0	23.1	65.5	27 51.6	24.1	66.0	28 15.7	25.2	66.5	28 39.4	26.1	67.0	29 02.6	27.1	67.5	34
35	26 30.7	+19.7	63.1	26 57.6	+20.7	63.6	27 24.1	+21.7	64.0	27 50.1	+22.7	64.5	28 15.7	+23.7	65.0	28 40.9	+24.6	65.5	29 05.5	+25.7	66.0	29 29.7	+26.7	66.5	35
36	26 50.4	19.3	62.1	27 18.3	20.2	62.5	27 45.8	21.2	63.0	28 12.8	22.2	63.4	28 39.4	23.2	63.9	29 05.5	24.2	64.4	29 31.2	25.2	64.9	29 56.4	26.1	65.5	36
37	27 09.7	18.7	61.0	27 38.5	19.8	61.5	28 07.0	20.7	61.9	28 35.0	21.7	62.4	29 02.6	22.7	62.9	29 29.7	23.7	63.4	29 56.4	24.6	63.9	30 22.5	25.7	64.4	37
38	27 28.4	18.3	59.9	27 58.3	19.3	60.4	28 27.7	20.3	60.9	28 56.7	21.2	61.3	29 25.3	22.2	61.8	29 53.4	23.2	62.3	30 21.0	24.2	62.8	30 48.2	25.1	63.4	38
39	27 46.7	17.8	58.9	28 17.6	18.7	59.3	28 48.0	19.7	59.8	29 17.9	20.7	60.3	29 47.5	21.7	60.8	30 16.6	22.6	61.3	30 45.2	23.6	61.8	31 13.3	24.6	62.3	39
40	28 04.5	+17.3	57.8	28 36.3	+18.2	58.2	29 07.7	+19.2	58.7	29 38.6	+20.2	59.2	30 09.2	+21.1	59.7	30 39.2	+22.1	60.2	31 08.8	+23.1	60.7	31 37.9	+24.1	61.2	40
41	28 21.8	16.7	56.7	28 54.5	17.7	57.1	29 26.9	18.6	57.6	29 58.8	19.6	58.1	30 30.3	20.6	58.6	31 01.3	21.6	59.1	31 31.9	22.6	59.6	32 02.0	23.5	60.2	41
42	28 38.5	16.3	55.6	29 12.2	17.2	56.0	29 45.5	18.2	56.5	30 18.4	19.1	57.0	30 50.9	20.0	57.5	31 22.9	21.0	58.0	31 54.5	21.9	58.5	32 25.5	23.0	59.1	42
43	28 54.8	15.7	54.5	29 29.4	16.6	55.0	30 03.7	17.5	55.4	30 37.5	18.5	55.9	31 10.9	19.5	56.4	31 43.9	20.4	56.9	32 16.4	21.4	57.4	32 48.5	22.4	58.0	43
44	29 10.5	15.1	53.4	29 46.0	16.1	53.8	30 21.2	17.0	54.3	30 56.0	18.0	54.8	31 30.4	18.9	55.3	32 04.3	19.9	55.8	32 37.8	20.9	56.3	33 10.9	21.8	56.9	44

Dec.	30° Hc	30° d	30° Z	31° Hc	31° d	31° Z	32° Hc	32° d	32° Z	33° Hc	33° d	33° Z	34° Hc	34° d	34° Z	35° Hc	35° d	35° Z	36° Hc	36° d	36° Z	37° Hc	37° d	37° Z
45	29 25.6	+14.6	52.3	30 02.1	+15.5	52.7	30 38.2	+16.5	53.2	31 14.0	+17.4	53.7	31 49.3	+18.3	54.2	32 24.2	+19.3	54.7	32 58.7	+20.2	55.2	33 32.7	+21.1	55.8
46	29 40.2	14.0	51.2	30 17.6	15.0	51.6	30 54.7	15.8	52.1	31 31.4	16.7	52.6	32 07.6	17.7	53.1	32 43.5	18.6	53.6	33 18.9	19.6	54.1	33 53.8	20.6	54.6
47	29 54.2	13.5	50.0	30 32.6	14.3	50.5	31 10.5	15.3	51.0	31 48.1	16.2	51.4	32 25.3	17.1	51.9	33 02.1	18.1	52.4	33 38.5	19.0	53.0	34 14.4	19.9	53.5
48	30 07.7	12.8	48.9	30 46.9	13.8	49.4	31 25.8	14.7	49.8	32 04.3	15.6	50.3	32 42.4	16.5	50.8	33 20.2	17.4	51.3	33 57.5	18.3	51.8	34 34.3	19.3	52.4
49	30 20.5	12.3	47.8	31 00.7	13.1	48.2	31 40.5	14.0	48.7	32 19.9	14.9	49.2	32 58.9	15.9	49.6	33 37.6	16.8	50.1	34 15.8	17.7	50.7	34 53.6	18.7	51.2
50	30 32.8	+11.7	46.7	31 13.8	+12.6	47.1	31 54.5	+13.5	47.5	32 34.8	+14.4	48.0	33 14.8	+15.2	48.5	33 54.4	+16.1	49.0	34 33.5	+17.1	49.5	35 12.3	+17.9	50.0
51	30 44.5	11.1	45.5	31 26.4	11.9	45.9	32 08.0	12.8	46.4	32 49.2	13.6	46.9	33 30.0	14.6	47.3	34 10.5	15.4	47.8	34 50.6	16.3	48.3	35 30.2	17.3	48.9
52	30 55.6	10.5	44.4	31 38.3	11.4	44.8	32 20.8	12.1	45.2	33 02.8	13.1	45.7	33 44.6	13.9	46.1	34 25.9	14.8	46.7	35 06.9	15.7	47.2	35 47.5	16.6	47.7
53	31 06.1	9.9	43.2	31 49.7	10.7	43.6	32 32.9	11.6	44.1	33 15.9	12.4	44.5	33 58.5	13.2	45.0	34 40.7	14.1	45.5	35 22.6	15.0	46.0	36 04.1	15.9	46.5
54	31 16.0	9.2	42.1	32 00.4	10.0	42.5	32 44.5	10.9	42.9	33 28.3	11.7	43.4	34 11.7	12.6	43.8	34 54.8	13.4	44.3	35 37.6	14.3	44.8	36 20.0	15.1	45.3
55	31 25.2	+8.7	40.9	32 10.4	+9.5	41.3	32 55.4	+10.2	41.7	33 40.0	+11.0	42.2	34 24.3	+11.8	42.6	35 08.2	+12.8	43.1	35 51.9	+13.5	43.6	36 35.1	+14.5	44.1
56	31 33.9	8.0	39.8	32 19.9	8.7	40.2	33 05.6	9.5	40.6	33 51.0	10.4	41.0	34 36.1	11.2	41.4	35 21.0	12.0	41.9	36 05.4	12.9	42.4	36 49.6	13.7	42.9
57	31 41.9	7.3	38.6	32 28.6	8.2	39.0	33 15.1	8.9	39.4	34 01.4	9.6	39.8	34 47.3	10.5	40.3	35 33.0	11.2	40.7	36 18.3	12.1	41.2	37 03.3	12.9	41.7
58	31 49.2	6.8	37.4	32 36.8	7.4	37.8	33 24.0	8.3	38.2	34 11.0	9.0	38.6	34 57.8	9.7	39.1	35 44.2	10.6	39.5	36 30.4	11.3	40.0	37 16.2	12.2	40.5
59	31 56.0	6.0	36.3	32 44.2	6.9	36.6	33 32.3	7.5	37.0	34 20.0	8.3	37.4	35 07.5	9.1	37.8	35 54.8	9.8	38.3	36 41.7	10.6	38.7	37 28.4	11.4	39.2
60	32 02.0	+5.5	35.1	32 51.0	+6.2	35.4	33 39.8	+6.8	35.8	34 28.3	+7.6	36.2	35 16.6	+8.3	36.6	36 04.6	+9.1	37.1	36 52.3	+9.9	37.5	37 39.8	+10.6	38.0
61	32 07.5	4.7	33.9	32 57.2	5.4	34.3	33 46.6	6.2	34.6	34 35.9	6.8	35.0	35 24.9	7.6	35.4	36 13.7	8.3	35.8	37 02.2	9.0	36.3	37 50.4	9.8	36.7
62	32 12.2	4.2	32.7	33 02.6	4.8	33.1	33 52.8	5.4	33.4	34 42.7	6.2	33.8	35 32.5	6.8	34.2	36 22.0	7.5	34.6	37 11.2	8.3	35.0	38 00.2	9.1	35.5
63	32 16.4	3.4	31.5	33 07.4	4.1	31.9	33 58.2	4.8	32.2	34 48.9	5.4	32.6	35 39.3	6.1	33.0	36 29.5	6.8	33.4	37 19.5	7.5	33.8	38 09.3	8.2	34.2
64	32 19.8	2.8	30.4	33 11.5	3.4	30.7	34 03.0	4.1	31.0	34 54.3	4.7	31.4	35 45.4	5.4	31.8	36 36.3	6.1	32.1	37 27.0	6.7	32.6	38 17.5	7.4	33.0
65	32 22.6	+2.1	29.2	33 14.9	+2.8	29.5	34 07.1	+3.3	29.8	34 59.0	+4.0	30.2	35 50.8	+4.6	30.5	36 42.4	+5.2	30.9	37 33.7	+6.0	31.3	38 24.9	+6.6	31.7
66	32 24.7	1.5	28.0	33 17.7	2.0	28.3	34 10.4	2.6	28.6	35 03.0	3.2	29.0	35 55.4	3.8	29.3	36 47.6	4.5	29.7	37 39.7	5.1	30.0	38 31.5	5.8	30.4
67	32 26.2	0.8	26.8	33 19.7	1.4	27.1	34 13.0	2.0	27.4	35 06.2	2.5	27.7	35 59.2	3.1	28.1	36 52.1	3.7	28.4	37 44.8	4.3	28.8	38 37.3	4.9	29.2
68	32 27.0	0.2	25.6	33 21.1	0.6	25.9	34 15.0	1.2	26.2	35 08.7	1.8	26.5	36 02.3	2.4	26.8	36 55.8	2.9	27.2	37 49.1	3.5	27.5	38 42.2	4.1	27.9
69	32 27.2	-0.6	24.4	33 21.7	0.0	24.7	34 16.2	0.5	25.0	35 10.5	1.0	25.3	36 04.7	1.5	25.6	36 58.7	2.1	25.9	37 52.6	2.7	26.3	38 46.3	3.3	26.6
70	32 26.6	-1.1	23.3	33 21.7	-0.7	23.5	34 16.7	-0.2	23.8	35 11.5	+0.3	24.1	36 06.2	+0.9	24.4	37 00.8	+1.4	24.7	37 55.3	+1.9	25.0	38 49.6	+2.4	25.3
71	32 25.5	1.9	22.1	33 21.0	1.4	22.3	34 16.5	1.0	22.6	35 11.8	-0.4	22.8	36 07.1	0.0	23.1	37 02.2	0.5	23.4	37 57.2	1.0	23.7	38 52.0	1.6	24.0
72	32 23.6	2.5	20.9	33 19.6	2.1	21.1	34 15.5	1.6	21.4	35 11.4	1.2	21.6	36 07.1	-0.7	21.9	37 02.7	-0.2	22.2	37 58.2	0.3	22.5	38 53.6	0.8	22.8
73	32 21.1	3.2	19.7	33 17.5	2.7	19.9	34 13.9	2.4	20.2	35 10.2	1.9	20.4	36 06.4	1.5	20.6	37 02.5	1.1	20.9	37 58.5	-0.6	21.2	38 54.4	0.1	21.5
74	32 17.9	3.8	18.5	33 14.8	3.5	18.7	34 11.5	3.0	18.9	35 08.3	2.7	19.2	36 04.9	2.3	19.4	37 01.4	1.8	19.7	37 57.9	1.4	19.9	38 54.3	-1.0	20.2
75	32 14.1	-4.5	17.3	33 11.3	-4.1	17.5	34 08.5	-3.8	17.7	35 05.6	-3.4	17.9	36 02.6	-3.0	18.2	36 59.6	-2.6	18.4	37 56.5	-2.2	18.6	38 53.3	-1.8	18.9
76	32 09.6	5.2	16.2	33 07.2	4.8	16.3	34 04.7	4.5	16.5	35 02.2	4.1	16.7	35 59.6	3.7	16.9	36 57.0	3.4	17.2	37 54.3	3.0	17.4	38 51.5	2.6	17.6
77	32 04.4	5.8	15.0	33 02.4	5.5	15.2	34 00.2	5.1	15.3	34 58.1	4.9	15.5	35 55.9	4.6	15.7	36 53.6	4.2	15.9	37 51.3	3.9	16.1	38 48.9	3.5	16.3
78	31 58.6	6.4	13.8	32 56.9	6.2	14.0	33 55.1	5.8	14.1	34 53.2	5.5	14.3	35 51.3	5.5	14.5	36 49.4	4.9	14.7	37 47.4	4.6	14.9	38 45.4	4.3	15.1
79	31 52.2	7.1	12.6	32 50.7	6.8	12.8	33 49.2	6.6	12.9	34 47.7	6.3	13.1	35 46.1	6.0	13.2	36 44.5	5.8	13.4	37 42.8	5.4	13.6	38 41.1	5.1	13.8
80	31 45.1	-7.8	11.5	32 43.9	-7.5	11.6	33 42.6	-7.2	11.7	34 41.4	-7.1	11.9	35 40.1	-6.8	12.0	36 38.7	-6.5	12.2	37 37.4	-6.3	12.3	38 36.0	-6.0	12.5
81	31 37.3	8.3	10.3	32 36.4	8.2	10.4	33 35.4	8.0	10.5	34 34.3	7.7	10.7	35 33.3	7.5	10.8	36 32.2	7.3	10.9	37 31.1	7.0	11.1	38 30.0	6.8	11.2
82	31 29.0	9.0	9.1	32 28.2	8.8	9.2	33 28.2	8.6	9.4	34 26.6	8.4	9.5	35 24.9	8.0	9.6	36 24.9	8.0	9.7	37 24.1	7.9	9.8	38 23.2	7.6	10.0
83	31 20.0	9.6	8.0	32 19.4	9.4	8.1	33 18.8	9.3	8.2	34 18.2	9.1	8.3	35 17.6	9.0	8.4	36 16.9	8.8	8.5	37 16.2	8.6	8.6	38 15.6	8.5	8.7
84	31 10.4	10.2	6.8	32 10.0	10.1	6.9	33 09.5	9.9	7.0	34 09.1	9.9	7.1	35 08.6	9.7	7.2	36 08.1	9.5	7.2	37 07.6	9.3	7.3	38 07.1	9.2	7.4
85	31 00.2	-10.9	5.7	31 59.9	-10.8	5.7	32 59.6	-10.7	5.8	33 59.2	-10.5	5.9	34 58.9	-10.4	5.9	35 58.6	-10.3	6.1	36 58.3	-10.2	6.1	37 57.9	-10.0	6.2
86	30 49.3	11.4	4.5	31 49.1	11.3	4.6	32 48.9	11.2	4.6	33 48.7	11.2	4.7	34 48.5	11.1	4.8	35 48.3	11.0	4.8	36 48.1	10.9	4.9	37 47.9	10.8	4.9
87	30 37.9	12.1	3.4	31 37.8	12.0	3.4	32 37.7	12.0	3.5	33 37.5	11.8	3.6	34 37.4	11.8	3.6	35 37.3	11.7	3.6	36 37.2	11.7	3.6	37 37.1	11.6	3.7
88	30 25.8	12.6	2.3	31 25.8	12.6	2.3	32 25.7	12.5	2.3	33 25.7	12.5	2.3	34 25.6	12.4	2.4	35 25.6	12.5	2.4	36 25.5	12.4	2.4	37 25.5	12.4	2.5
89	30 13.2	13.2	1.1	31 13.2	13.2	1.1	32 13.2	13.2	1.2	33 13.2	13.2	1.2	34 13.2	13.2	1.2	35 13.1	13.1	1.2	36 13.1	13.1	1.2	37 13.1	13.1	1.2
90	30 00.0	-13.8	0.0	31 00.0	-13.8	0.0	32 00.0	-13.8	0.0	33 00.0	-13.8	0.0	34 00.0	-13.8	0.0	35 00.0	-13.8	0.0	36 00.0	-13.8	0.0	37 00.0	-13.9	0.0

LATITUDE SAME NAME AS DECLINATION

LATITUDE CONTRARY NAME TO DECLINATION   L.H.A. 77°, 283°

Dec.	30° Hc	d	Z	31° Hc	d	Z	32° Hc	d	Z	33° Hc	d	Z	34° Hc	d	Z	35° Hc	d	Z	36° Hc	d	Z	37° Hc	d	Z	Dec.
0	11 14.0	−30.6	96.6	11 07.0	−31.5	96.8	10 59.9	−32.5	97.0	10 52.5	−33.4	97.2	10 44.9	−34.2	97.4	10 37.1	−35.1	97.5	10 29.1	−35.9	97.7	10 21.0	−36.8	97.9	0
1	10 43.4	30.8	97.5	10 35.5	31.7	97.6	10 27.4	32.6	97.8	10 19.1	33.4	98.0	10 10.7	34.4	98.2	10 02.0	35.3	98.4	9 53.2	36.0	98.5	9 44.2	36.9	98.7	1
2	10 12.6	31.0	98.3	10 03.8	31.9	98.5	9 54.8	32.7	98.7	9 45.7	33.6	98.9	9 36.3	34.4	99.0	9 26.8	35.3	99.2	9 17.2	36.2	99.4	9 07.3	36.9	99.5	2
3	9 41.6	31.1	99.2	9 31.9	31.9	99.4	9 22.1	32.9	99.5	9 12.1	33.8	99.7	9 01.9	34.6	99.9	8 51.5	35.4	100.0	8 41.0	36.2	100.2	8 30.4	37.1	100.3	3
4	9 10.5	31.2	100.1	9 00.0	32.1	100.2	8 49.2	32.9	100.4	8 38.3	33.8	100.5	8 27.3	34.7	100.7	8 16.1	35.5	100.8	8 04.8	36.4	101.0	7 53.3	37.2	101.1	4
5	8 39.3	−31.3	100.9	8 27.9	−32.2	101.1	8 16.3	−33.1	101.2	8 04.5	−33.9	101.4	7 52.6	−34.8	101.5	7 40.6	−35.6	101.6	7 28.4	−36.4	101.8	7 16.1	−37.2	101.9	5
6	8 08.0	31.4	101.8	7 55.7	32.3	101.9	7 43.2	33.0	102.1	7 30.6	34.0	102.2	7 17.8	34.8	102.3	7 05.0	35.7	102.5	6 52.0	36.5	102.6	6 38.9	37.4	102.7	6
7	7 36.6	31.5	102.7	7 23.4	32.4	102.8	7 10.0	33.2	102.9	6 56.6	34.1	103.0	6 43.0	35.0	103.1	6 29.3	35.8	103.3	6 15.5	36.6	103.5	6 01.5	37.4	103.5	7
8	7 05.1	31.7	103.5	6 51.0	32.5	103.6	6 36.8	33.4	103.7	6 22.5	34.2	103.9	6 08.0	35.0	104.0	5 53.5	35.8	104.1	5 38.9	36.7	104.2	5 24.1	37.4	104.3	8
9	6 33.4	31.7	104.4	6 18.5	32.6	104.5	6 03.4	33.4	104.6	5 48.3	34.3	104.7	5 33.0	35.1	104.8	5 17.7	35.9	104.9	5 02.2	36.7	105.0	4 46.7	37.5	105.0	9
10	6 01.7	−31.8	105.2	5 45.9	−32.6	105.3	5 30.0	−33.5	105.4	5 14.0	−34.3	105.6	4 57.9	−35.1	105.6	4 41.8	−35.9	105.7	4 25.5	−36.8	105.8	4 09.2	−37.6	105.8	10
11	5 29.9	31.8	106.1	5 13.3	32.7	106.2	4 56.5	33.5	106.3	4 39.7	34.4	106.3	4 22.8	35.2	106.4	4 05.8	36.0	106.5	3 48.7	36.8	106.5	3 31.6	37.6	106.6	11
12	4 58.1	31.9	106.9	4 40.6	32.8	107.0	4 23.0	33.7	107.1	4 05.3	34.4	107.2	3 47.6	35.3	107.2	3 29.8	36.1	107.3	3 11.9	36.9	107.3	2 54.0	37.6	107.4	12
13	4 26.2	32.0	107.8	4 07.8	32.8	107.8	3 49.4	33.7	107.9	3 30.9	34.5	108.0	3 12.3	35.3	108.0	2 53.7	36.1	108.1	2 35.1	36.9	108.1	2 16.4	37.6	108.2	13
14	3 54.2	32.1	108.6	3 35.0	32.9	108.7	3 15.7	33.7	108.7	2 56.4	34.5	108.8	2 37.1	35.3	108.8	2 17.7	36.1	108.9	1 58.2	36.9	108.9	1 38.8	37.7	108.9	14
15	3 22.1	−32.0	109.5	3 02.1	−32.9	109.5	2 42.0	−33.7	109.6	2 21.9	−34.5	109.6	2 01.8	−35.4	109.7	1 41.6	−36.2	109.7	1 21.3	−36.9	109.7	1 01.1	−37.7	109.7	15
16	2 50.1	32.2	110.3	2 29.2	32.9	110.4	2 08.3	33.7	110.4	1 47.4	34.6	110.4	1 26.4	35.3	110.5	1 05.4	36.1	110.5	0 44.4	36.9	110.5	0 23.4	−37.7	110.5	16
17	2 17.9	32.1	111.2	1 56.3	33.0	111.2	1 34.6	33.8	111.2	1 12.8	34.6	111.3	0 51.1	35.4	111.3	0 29.3	36.1	111.3	0 07.5	−36.9	111.3	0 14.3	+37.6	68.7	17
18	1 45.8	32.2	112.0	1 23.3	33.0	112.0	1 00.8	33.8	112.1	0 38.2	34.5	112.1	0 15.7	35.4	112.1	0 06.9	+36.1	67.9	0 29.4	+36.9	67.9	0 51.9	37.7	67.9	18
19	1 13.6	32.2	112.9	0 50.3	33.0	112.9	0 27.0	−33.8	112.9	0 03.7	−34.6	112.9	0 19.7	+35.3	67.1	0 43.0	36.1	67.1	1 06.3	36.9	67.1	1 29.6	37.7	67.2	19
20	0 41.4	−32.2	113.7	0 17.3	−33.0	113.7	0 06.8	+33.8	66.3	0 30.9	+34.6	66.3	0 55.0	+35.4	66.3	1 19.1	+36.2	66.3	1 43.2	+36.9	66.4	2 07.3	+37.6	66.4	20
21	0 09.2	−32.1	114.5	0 15.7	+33.0	65.5	0 40.6	33.8	65.5	1 05.5	34.6	65.5	1 30.4	35.3	65.5	1 55.3	36.1	65.5	2 20.1	36.9	65.6	2 44.9	37.6	65.6	21
22	0 22.9	+32.2	64.6	0 48.7	33.0	64.6	1 14.4	33.7	64.6	1 40.1	34.5	64.7	2 05.7	35.3	64.7	2 31.4	36.1	64.7	2 57.0	36.8	64.8	3 22.5	37.6	64.8	22
23	0 55.1	32.2	63.8	1 21.7	33.0	63.8	1 48.1	33.8	63.8	2 14.6	34.5	63.8	2 41.0	35.3	63.9	3 07.4	36.0	63.9	3 33.8	36.8	64.0	4 00.1	37.5	64.0	23
24	1 27.3	32.2	62.9	1 54.6	33.0	63.0	2 21.9	33.7	63.0	2 49.1	34.5	63.0	3 16.3	35.3	63.1	3 43.5	36.0	63.1	4 10.6	36.7	63.2	4 37.6	37.5	63.3	24
25	1 59.5	+32.1	62.1	2 27.6	+32.9	62.1	2 55.6	+33.7	62.2	3 23.6	+34.4	62.2	3 51.6	+35.1	62.3	4 19.5	+35.9	62.3	4 47.3	+36.7	62.4	5 15.1	+37.4	62.5	25
26	2 31.6	32.1	61.3	3 00.5	32.8	61.3	3 29.3	33.6	61.5	3 58.0	34.4	61.4	4 26.7	35.2	61.5	4 55.4	35.9	61.5	5 24.0	36.6	61.6	5 52.5	37.3	61.7	26
27	3 03.7	32.1	60.4	3 33.3	32.9	60.4	4 02.9	33.6	60.5	4 32.4	34.4	60.6	5 01.9	35.1	60.6	5 31.3	35.8	60.7	6 00.6	36.5	60.8	6 29.8	37.3	60.9	27
28	3 35.8	32.0	59.5	4 06.2	32.7	59.6	4 36.5	33.5	59.7	5 06.8	34.2	59.7	5 37.0	35.0	59.8	6 07.1	35.7	59.9	6 37.1	36.5	60.0	7 07.1	37.2	60.1	28
29	4 07.8	32.0	58.7	4 38.9	32.6	58.8	5 10.0	33.5	58.8	5 41.0	34.2	59.0	6 12.0	34.9	59.0	6 42.8	35.7	59.0	7 13.6	36.4	59.2	7 44.3	37.1	59.3	29
30	4 39.8	+31.9	57.8	5 11.7	+32.6	57.9	5 43.5	+33.4	58.0	6 15.2	+34.2	58.1	6 46.9	+34.9	58.2	7 18.5	+35.6	58.3	7 50.0	+36.3	58.4	8 21.4	+37.0	58.5	30
31	5 11.7	31.8	57.0	5 44.3	32.6	57.1	6 16.9	33.3	57.2	6 49.4	34.0	57.3	7 21.8	34.7	57.4	7 54.1	35.5	57.5	8 26.3	36.2	57.6	8 58.4	36.9	57.7	31
32	5 43.5	31.7	56.1	6 16.9	32.4	56.2	6 50.2	33.2	56.3	7 23.4	33.9	56.4	7 56.5	34.7	56.5	8 29.6	35.3	56.7	9 02.5	36.1	56.8	9 35.3	36.8	56.9	32
33	6 15.2	31.6	55.3	6 49.4	32.3	55.4	7 23.4	33.1	55.5	7 57.3	33.9	55.5	8 31.2	34.4	55.7	9 04.9	35.3	55.8	9 38.6	35.9	56.0	10 12.1	36.6	56.1	33
34	6 46.9	31.6	54.4	7 21.8	32.3	54.5	7 56.5	33.1	54.6	8 31.2	33.7	54.8	9 05.8	34.4	54.9	9 40.2	35.2	55.0	10 14.5	35.9	55.2	10 48.7	36.6	55.3	34
35	7 18.5	+31.5	53.6	7 54.1	+32.2	53.7	8 29.6	+32.9	53.8	9 04.9	+33.7	53.9	9 40.2	+34.3	54.1	10 15.4	+35.0	54.2	10 50.4	+35.7	54.4	11 25.3	+36.4	54.5	35
36	7 50.0	31.4	52.7	8 26.3	32.1	52.8	9 02.5	32.8	53.0	9 38.6	33.5	53.0	10 14.5	34.2	53.2	10 50.4	35.0	53.4	11 26.1	35.6	53.5	12 01.7	36.1	53.7	36
37	8 21.4	31.2	51.9	8 58.4	31.9	52.0	9 35.3	32.6	52.1	10 12.1	33.3	52.2	10 48.7	34.1	52.4	11 25.3	34.7	52.6	12 01.7	35.4	52.7	12 38.0	36.1	52.9	37
38	8 52.6	31.2	51.0	9 30.3	31.7	51.1	10 07.9	32.6	51.3	10 45.4	33.3	51.4	11 22.8	33.9	51.6	12 00.0	34.6	51.7	12 37.1	35.3	51.9	13 14.1	36.0	52.1	38
39	9 23.8	31.0	50.1	10 02.2	31.7	50.3	10 40.5	32.4	50.4	11 18.7	33.1	50.6	11 56.7	33.8	50.7	12 34.6	34.5	50.9	13 12.4	35.2	51.1	13 50.1	35.8	51.2	39
40	9 54.8	+30.9	49.3	10 33.9	+31.6	49.4	11 12.9	+32.2	49.5	11 51.8	+32.9	49.7	12 30.5	+33.6	49.9	13 09.1	+34.3	50.0	13 47.6	+34.9	50.2	14 25.9	+35.6	50.4	40
41	10 25.7	30.7	48.4	11 05.5	31.4	48.5	11 45.1	32.1	48.7	12 24.7	32.8	48.8	13 04.1	33.5	49.0	13 43.4	34.1	49.2	14 22.5	34.8	49.4	15 01.5	35.4	49.6	41
42	10 56.4	30.6	47.5	11 36.9	31.3	47.7	12 17.2	32.0	47.8	12 57.5	32.6	48.0	13 37.6	33.2	48.2	14 17.5	33.9	48.4	14 57.3	34.6	48.5	15 36.9	35.3	48.8	42
43	11 27.0	30.5	46.6	12 08.2	31.1	46.8	12 49.2	31.8	47.0	13 30.1	32.4	47.1	14 10.8	33.1	47.3	14 51.4	33.8	47.5	15 31.9	34.4	47.7	16 12.2	35.1	47.9	43
44	11 57.5	30.2	45.8	12 39.3	30.9	45.9	13 21.0	31.5	46.1	14 02.5	32.2	46.3	14 43.9	32.9	46.4	15 25.2	33.5	46.6	16 06.3	34.2	46.8	16 47.3	34.8	47.1	44

#	30°	31°	32°	33°	34°	35°	36°	37°	#
45	12 27.7 +30.1	13 10.2 +30.8	13 52.5 +31.4	14 34.7 +32.1	15 16.8 +32.7	15 58.7 +33.4	16 40.5 +34.0	17 22.1 +34.6	45
46	12 57.8 30.0	13 41.0 30.5	14 23.9 31.2	15 06.8 31.8	15 49.5 32.5	16 32.1 33.1	17 14.5 33.7	17 56.7 34.4	46
47	13 27.8 29.7	14 11.5 30.1	14 55.1 31.0	15 38.6 31.7	16 22.0 32.3	17 05.2 32.9	17 48.2 33.6	18 31.1 34.2	47
48	13 57.5 29.5	14 41.9 30.1	15 26.1 30.8	16 10.3 31.4	16 54.3 32.0	17 38.1 32.7	18 21.8 33.3	19 05.3 33.9	48
49	14 27.0 29.4	15 12.0 30.0	15 56.9 30.6	16 41.7 31.2	17 26.3 31.8	18 10.8 32.4	18 55.1 33.0	19 39.2 33.7	49
50	14 56.4 +29.1	15 42.0 +29.7	16 27.5 +30.3	17 12.9 +30.9	17 58.1 +31.6	18 43.2 +32.2	19 28.1 +32.8	20 12.9 +33.4	50
51	15 25.5 28.9	16 11.7 29.5	16 57.8 30.1	17 43.8 30.7	18 29.7 31.3	19 15.4 31.9	20 00.9 32.5	20 46.3 33.1	51
52	15 54.4 28.6	16 41.2 29.3	17 27.9 29.8	18 14.5 30.5	19 01.0 31.0	19 47.3 31.6	20 33.4 32.3	21 19.4 32.8	52
53	16 23.0 28.5	17 10.5 29.0	17 57.8 29.6	18 45.0 30.1	19 32.0 30.8	20 18.9 31.4	21 05.7 31.9	21 52.2 32.6	53
54	16 51.5 28.2	17 39.5 28.7	18 27.4 29.3	19 15.1 30.0	20 02.8 30.5	20 50.3 31.0	21 37.6 31.7	22 24.8 32.2	54
55	17 19.7 +27.9	18 08.2 +28.5	18 56.7 +29.1	19 45.1 +29.6	20 33.2 +30.2	21 21.3 +30.8	22 09.3 +31.3	22 57.0 +31.9	55
56	17 47.6 27.6	18 36.7 28.3	19 25.8 28.7	20 14.7 29.3	21 03.5 29.8	21 52.1 30.5	22 40.6 31.0	23 28.9 31.6	56
57	18 15.2 27.4	19 05.0 27.9	19 54.5 28.5	20 44.0 29.0	21 33.3 29.6	22 22.6 30.1	23 11.6 30.7	24 00.5 31.3	57
58	18 42.6 27.1	19 32.9 27.6	20 23.0 28.2	21 13.0 28.8	22 02.9 29.3	22 52.7 29.8	23 42.3 30.4	24 31.8 30.9	58
59	19 09.7 26.9	20 00.5 27.4	20 51.2 27.9	21 41.8 28.3	22 32.2 28.9	23 22.5 29.5	24 12.7 30.0	25 02.7 30.5	59
60	19 36.6 +26.5	20 27.9 +27.0	21 19.1 +27.5	22 10.1 +28.1	23 01.1 +28.6	23 52.0 +29.1	24 42.7 +29.6	25 33.2 +30.2	60
61	20 03.1 26.2	20 54.9 26.7	21 46.6 27.2	22 38.2 27.7	23 29.7 28.2	24 21.1 28.7	25 12.3 29.3	26 03.4 29.8	61
62	20 29.3 25.9	21 21.6 26.4	22 13.8 26.9	23 05.9 27.4	23 57.9 27.9	24 49.8 28.4	25 41.6 28.8	26 33.2 29.4	62
63	20 55.2 25.6	21 48.0 26.0	22 40.7 26.5	23 33.3 27.0	24 25.8 27.5	25 18.2 28.0	26 10.4 28.5	27 02.6 29.0	63
64	21 20.8 25.2	22 14.0 25.7	23 07.2 26.2	24 00.3 26.6	24 53.3 27.1	25 46.2 27.5	26 38.9 28.1	27 31.6 28.5	64
65	21 46.0 +24.9	22 39.7 +25.4	23 33.4 +25.8	24 26.9 +26.3	25 20.4 +26.7	26 13.7 +27.2	27 07.0 +27.6	28 00.1 +28.2	65
66	22 10.9 24.5	23 05.1 24.9	23 59.2 25.4	24 53.2 25.8	25 47.1 26.3	26 40.9 26.8	27 34.6 27.3	28 28.3 27.6	66
67	22 35.4 24.2	23 30.0 24.6	24 24.6 25.0	25 19.0 25.5	26 13.4 25.9	27 07.7 26.3	28 01.9 26.7	28 55.9 27.3	67
68	22 59.6 23.8	23 54.6 24.2	24 49.6 24.6	25 44.5 25.0	26 39.3 25.4	27 34.0 25.9	28 28.6 26.4	29 23.2 26.7	68
69	23 23.4 23.4	24 18.8 23.8	25 14.2 24.2	26 09.5 24.6	27 04.7 25.1	27 59.9 25.4	28 55.0 25.8	29 49.9 26.3	69
70	23 46.8 +23.0	24 42.6 +23.4	25 38.4 +23.8	26 34.1 +24.2	27 29.8 +24.5	28 25.3 +25.0	29 20.8 +25.4	30 16.2 +25.8	70
71	24 09.8 22.6	25 06.0 23.0	26 02.2 23.3	26 58.3 23.7	27 54.3 24.1	28 50.3 24.5	29 46.2 24.8	30 42.0 25.2	71
72	24 32.4 22.2	25 29.0 22.5	26 25.5 22.9	27 22.0 23.3	28 18.4 23.6	29 14.8 24.0	30 11.0 24.4	31 07.2 24.8	72
73	24 54.6 21.8	25 51.5 22.2	26 48.4 22.5	27 45.3 22.8	28 42.0 23.2	29 38.8 23.4	30 35.4 23.9	31 32.0 24.2	73
74	25 16.4 21.3	26 13.7 21.6	27 10.9 22.0	28 08.1 22.3	29 05.2 22.6	30 02.2 23.0	30 59.3 23.3	31 56.2 23.7	74
75	25 37.7 +21.0	26 35.3 +21.2	27 32.9 +21.5	28 30.4 +21.8	29 27.8 +22.1	30 25.2 +22.5	31 22.6 +22.7	32 19.9 +23.1	75
76	25 58.7 20.4	26 56.5 20.8	27 54.4 21.0	28 52.2 21.3	29 49.9 21.7	30 47.7 21.9	31 45.3 22.3	32 43.0 22.5	76
77	26 19.1 20.0	27 17.3 20.2	28 15.4 20.5	29 13.5 20.8	30 11.6 21.0	31 09.6 21.3	32 07.6 21.6	33 05.5 21.9	77
78	26 39.1 19.6	27 37.5 19.8	28 35.9 20.1	29 34.3 20.3	30 32.6 20.6	31 30.9 20.8	32 29.2 21.1	33 27.4 21.4	78
79	26 58.7 19.0	27 57.3 19.3	28 56.0 19.5	29 54.6 19.7	30 53.2 20.0	31 51.7 20.3	32 50.3 20.4	33 48.8 20.7	79
80	27 17.7 +18.6	28 16.6 +18.8	29 15.5 +19.0	30 14.3 +19.2	31 13.2 +19.4	32 12.0 +19.6	33 10.7 +19.9	34 09.5 +20.1	80
81	27 36.3 18.1	28 35.4 18.2	29 34.5 18.4	30 33.5 18.7	31 32.6 18.8	32 31.6 19.0	33 30.6 19.2	34 30.6 19.4	81
82	27 54.4 17.5	28 53.6 17.8	29 52.9 17.9	30 52.2 18.0	31 51.4 18.2	32 50.6 18.4	33 49.8 18.6	34 49.0 18.8	82
83	28 11.9 17.1	29 11.4 17.2	30 10.8 17.2	31 10.2 17.5	32 09.6 17.7	33 09.0 17.9	34 08.4 18.0	35 07.8 18.1	83
84	28 29.0 16.5	29 28.6 16.6	30 28.2 16.7	31 27.7 16.9	32 27.3 17.0	33 26.9 17.1	34 26.4 17.3	35 25.9 17.5	84
85	28 45.5 +16.0	29 45.2 +16.1	30 44.9 +16.2	31 44.6 +16.3	32 44.3 +16.4	33 44.0 +16.5	34 43.7 +16.6	35 43.4 +16.7	85
86	29 01.5 15.5	30 01.3 15.6	31 01.1 15.7	32 00.9 15.7	33 00.7 15.8	34 00.5 15.9	35 00.3 16.0	36 00.1 16.1	86
87	29 17.0 14.9	30 17.0 14.9	31 16.8 15.1	32 16.6 15.1	33 16.3 15.2	34 16.4 15.3	35 16.3 15.3	36 16.3 15.3	87
88	29 31.9 14.3	30 31.8 14.4	31 31.8 14.4	32 31.7 14.5	33 31.7 14.5	34 31.6 14.6	35 31.6 14.5	36 31.5 14.6	88
89	29 46.2 13.8	30 46.2 13.8	31 46.2 13.8	32 46.2 13.8	33 46.2 13.8	34 46.2 13.8	35 46.1 13.9	36 46.1 13.9	89
90	30 00.0 +13.2	31 00.0 +13.2	32 00.0 +13.2	33 00.0 +13.2	34 00.0 +13.1	35 00.0 +13.1	36 00.0 +13.1	37 00.0 +13.1	90

L.H.A. 103°, 257°

LATITUDE SAME NAME AS DECLINATION

S. Lat. { L.H.A. greater than 180°......Zn=180°−Z
{ L.H.A. less than 180°.........Zn=180°+Z

255

N. Lat. { L.H.A. greater than 180°...... Zn=Z ; L.H.A. less than 180°...... Zn=360°-Z }

Dec.	30° Hc	d	Z	31° Hc	d	Z	32° Hc	d	Z	33° Hc	d	Z	34° Hc	d	Z	35° Hc	d	Z	36° Hc	d	Z	37° Hc	d	Z	Dec.
0	10 22.4	+30.4	96.1	10 15.9	+31.4	96.2	10 09.3	+32.3	96.4	10 02.5	+33.1	96.6	9 55.5	+34.0	96.8	9 48.4	+34.8	97.0	9 41.0	+35.7	97.1	9 33.5	+36.5	97.3	0
1	10 52.8	30.3	95.2	10 47.3	31.2	95.4	10 41.6	32.1	95.6	10 35.6	33.0	95.8	10 29.5	33.9	95.9	10 23.2	34.8	96.1	10 16.7	35.6	96.3	10 10.0	36.5	96.5	1
2	11 23.1	30.1	94.3	11 18.5	31.0	94.5	11 13.7	31.9	94.7	11 08.6	32.9	94.9	11 03.4	33.7	95.1	10 58.0	34.6	95.3	10 52.3	35.5	95.4	10 46.5	36.3	95.7	2
3	11 53.2	30.0	93.4	11 49.5	30.9	93.6	11 45.6	31.8	93.8	11 41.5	32.7	93.9	11 37.1	33.6	94.1	11 32.6	34.4	94.5	11 27.8	35.3	94.5	11 22.8	36.2	94.9	3
4	12 23.2	29.7	92.5	12 20.4	30.7	92.8	12 17.4	31.6	93.0	12 14.2	32.5	93.2	12 10.7	33.4	93.4	12 07.0	34.3	93.6	12 03.1	35.2	93.8	11 59.0	36.0	94.1	4
5	12 52.9	+29.6	91.7	12 51.1	+30.5	91.9	12 49.0	+31.5	92.1	12 46.7	+32.3	92.3	12 44.1	+33.3	92.6	12 41.3	+34.2	92.8	12 38.3	+35.0	92.9	12 35.0	+35.9	93.2	5
6	13 22.5	29.5	90.8	13 21.6	30.4	91.0	13 20.5	31.2	91.2	13 19.0	32.2	91.5	13 17.4	33.1	91.7	13 15.5	34.0	91.9	13 13.3	34.9	92.2	13 10.9	35.7	92.4	6
7	13 52.0	29.2	89.9	13 52.0	30.1	90.1	13 51.7	31.1	90.3	13 51.2	32.0	90.6	13 50.5	32.9	90.8	13 49.5	33.8	91.1	13 48.2	34.7	91.3	13 46.6	35.6	91.6	7
8	14 21.2	29.0	89.0	14 22.1	30.0	89.2	14 22.8	30.9	89.5	14 23.2	31.8	89.7	14 23.4	32.7	90.0	14 23.3	33.6	90.2	14 22.9	34.5	90.5	14 22.2	35.4	90.8	8
9	14 50.2	28.8	88.1	14 52.1	29.7	88.3	14 53.7	30.7	88.6	14 55.0	31.6	88.9	14 56.1	32.5	89.1	14 56.9	33.4	89.4	14 57.4	34.3	89.7	14 57.6	35.2	89.9	9
10	15 19.0	+28.5	87.1	15 21.8	+29.5	87.4	15 24.4	+30.4	87.7	15 26.6	+31.4	88.0	15 28.6	+32.3	88.2	15 30.3	+33.2	88.5	15 31.7	+34.1	88.8	15 32.8	+35.0	89.1	10
11	15 47.5	28.4	86.2	15 51.3	29.3	86.5	15 54.8	30.3	86.8	15 58.0	31.2	87.1	16 00.9	32.1	87.4	16 03.5	33.1	87.7	16 05.8	34.0	87.9	16 07.8	34.8	88.2	11
12	16 15.9	28.1	85.3	16 20.6	29.1	85.6	16 25.1	30.0	85.9	16 29.2	30.9	86.2	16 33.0	31.9	86.5	16 36.6	32.8	86.8	16 39.8	33.7	87.1	16 42.6	34.7	87.4	12
13	16 44.0	27.9	84.4	16 49.7	28.8	84.7	16 55.1	29.8	85.0	17 00.2	30.7	85.3	17 04.9	31.7	85.6	17 09.4	32.5	85.9	17 13.5	33.5	86.2	17 17.3	34.3	86.5	13
14	17 11.9	27.6	83.5	17 18.5	28.6	83.8	17 24.9	29.5	84.1	17 30.9	30.5	84.4	17 36.6	31.4	84.7	17 41.9	32.4	85.0	17 47.0	33.2	85.4	17 51.6	34.2	85.7	14
15	17 39.5	+27.3	82.5	17 47.1	+28.3	82.9	17 54.4	+29.3	83.2	18 01.4	+30.2	83.5	18 08.0	+31.1	83.8	18 14.3	+32.1	84.1	18 20.2	+33.0	84.5	18 25.8	+33.9	84.8	15
16	18 06.8	27.1	81.6	18 15.4	28.0	81.9	18 23.7	29.0	82.3	18 31.6	29.9	82.6	18 39.1	30.9	82.9	18 46.4	31.8	83.3	18 53.2	32.8	83.6	18 59.7	33.7	83.9	16
17	18 33.9	26.8	80.7	18 43.4	27.8	81.0	18 52.7	28.7	81.3	19 01.5	29.7	81.7	19 10.0	30.7	82.0	19 18.2	31.6	82.4	19 26.0	32.5	82.7	19 33.4	33.4	83.1	17
18	19 00.7	26.5	79.7	19 11.2	27.5	80.1	19 21.4	28.4	80.4	19 31.2	29.4	80.8	19 40.7	30.3	81.1	19 49.8	31.3	81.5	19 58.5	32.2	81.8	20 06.8	33.2	82.2	18
19	19 27.2	26.2	78.8	19 38.7	27.2	79.1	19 49.8	28.2	79.5	20 00.6	29.1	79.8	20 11.0	30.1	80.2	20 21.1	31.0	80.6	20 30.7	32.0	80.9	20 40.0	32.9	81.3	19
20	19 53.4	+25.9	77.8	20 05.9	+26.8	78.2	20 18.0	+27.8	78.5	20 29.7	+28.8	78.9	20 41.1	+29.8	79.3	20 52.1	+30.7	79.6	21 02.7	+31.6	80.0	21 12.9	+32.6	80.4	20
21	20 19.3	25.5	76.9	20 32.7	26.6	77.2	20 45.8	27.6	77.6	20 58.5	28.5	78.0	21 10.9	29.4	78.3	21 22.8	30.4	78.7	21 34.3	31.4	79.1	21 45.5	32.3	79.5	21
22	20 44.8	25.3	75.9	20 59.3	26.2	76.3	21 13.4	27.2	76.6	21 27.0	28.2	77.0	21 40.3	29.2	77.4	21 53.2	30.1	77.8	22 05.7	31.1	78.2	22 17.8	32.0	78.6	22
23	21 10.1	24.9	74.9	21 25.5	25.9	75.3	21 40.6	26.8	75.7	21 55.2	27.9	76.1	22 09.5	28.8	76.5	22 23.3	29.8	76.9	22 36.8	30.7	77.3	22 49.8	31.7	77.7	23
24	21 35.0	24.6	73.9	21 51.4	25.6	74.3	22 07.4	26.6	74.7	22 23.1	27.5	75.1	22 38.3	28.5	75.5	22 53.1	29.4	75.9	23 07.5	30.4	76.3	23 21.5	31.3	76.7	24
25	21 59.6	+24.2	73.0	22 17.0	+25.2	73.3	22 34.0	+26.2	73.7	22 50.6	+27.1	74.1	23 06.8	+28.1	74.6	23 22.5	+29.1	75.0	23 37.9	+30.1	75.4	23 52.8	+31.0	75.8	25
26	22 23.8	23.9	72.0	22 42.2	24.8	72.4	23 00.2	25.8	72.8	23 17.7	26.8	73.2	23 34.9	27.8	73.6	23 51.6	28.8	74.1	24 08.0	29.7	74.4	24 23.8	30.7	74.9	26
27	22 47.7	23.5	71.0	23 07.0	24.5	71.4	23 26.0	25.4	71.8	23 44.5	26.5	72.2	24 02.7	27.4	72.6	24 20.4	28.4	73.1	24 37.7	29.3	73.5	24 54.5	30.3	73.9	27
28	23 11.2	23.1	70.0	23 31.5	24.1	70.4	23 51.4	25.1	70.8	24 11.0	26.0	71.2	24 30.1	27.0	71.6	24 48.8	28.0	72.1	25 07.0	29.0	72.5	25 24.8	29.9	73.0	28
29	23 34.3	22.7	69.0	23 55.6	23.7	69.4	24 16.5	24.7	69.8	24 37.0	25.7	70.2	24 57.1	26.7	70.7	25 16.8	27.6	71.1	25 36.0	28.6	71.6	25 54.7	29.6	72.0	29
30	23 57.0	+22.3	68.0	24 19.3	+23.3	68.4	24 41.2	+24.2	68.8	25 02.7	+25.3	69.2	25 23.8	+26.3	69.7	25 44.4	+27.2	70.1	26 04.6	+28.1	70.6	26 24.3	+29.1	71.0	30
31	24 19.3	21.9	66.9	24 42.6	22.9	67.4	25 05.5	23.9	67.8	25 28.0	24.8	68.2	25 50.0	25.8	68.7	26 11.6	26.8	69.1	26 32.7	27.8	69.6	26 53.4	28.8	70.1	31
32	24 41.2	21.5	65.9	25 05.5	22.5	66.3	25 29.4	23.4	66.8	25 52.8	24.4	67.2	26 15.8	25.4	67.7	26 38.4	26.4	68.1	27 00.5	27.4	68.6	27 22.2	28.3	69.1	32
33	25 02.7	21.1	64.9	25 28.0	22.0	65.3	25 52.8	23.0	65.8	26 17.2	24.0	66.2	26 41.2	25.0	66.7	27 04.8	25.9	67.1	27 27.9	26.9	67.6	27 50.5	27.9	68.1	33
34	25 23.8	20.6	63.9	25 50.0	21.6	64.3	26 15.8	22.6	64.7	26 41.2	23.6	65.2	27 06.2	24.5	65.6	27 30.7	25.5	66.1	27 54.8	26.5	66.6	28 18.4	27.4	67.1	34
35	25 44.4	+20.2	62.8	26 11.6	+21.1	63.2	26 38.4	+22.1	63.7	27 04.8	+23.1	64.1	27 30.7	+24.1	64.6	27 56.2	+25.1	65.1	28 21.3	+26.0	65.6	28 45.8	+27.0	66.1	35
36	26 04.6	19.7	61.8	26 32.7	20.7	62.2	27 00.5	21.7	62.6	27 27.9	22.6	63.1	27 54.8	23.6	63.6	28 21.3	24.5	64.1	28 47.3	25.5	64.5	29 12.8	26.6	65.0	36
37	26 24.3	19.2	60.7	26 53.4	20.2	61.2	27 22.2	21.2	61.6	27 50.5	22.2	62.1	28 18.4	23.1	62.5	28 45.8	24.1	63.0	29 12.8	25.1	63.5	29 39.4	26.0	64.0	37
38	26 43.5	18.8	59.7	27 13.6	19.8	60.1	27 43.4	20.7	60.5	28 12.7	21.6	61.0	28 41.5	22.7	61.5	29 09.9	23.6	62.0	29 37.9	24.6	62.5	30 05.4	25.5	63.0	38
39	27 02.3	18.3	58.6	27 33.4	19.2	59.0	28 04.1	20.2	59.5	28 34.3	21.2	60.0	29 04.2	22.1	60.4	29 33.5	23.1	60.9	30 02.5	24.0	61.4	30 30.9	25.1	61.9	39
40	27 20.6	+17.8	57.5	27 52.6	+18.8	58.0	28 24.3	+19.7	58.4	28 55.5	+20.7	58.9	29 26.3	+21.6	59.4	29 56.6	+22.6	59.9	30 26.5	+23.6	60.4	30 56.0	+24.5	60.9	40
41	27 38.4	17.3	56.4	28 11.4	18.2	56.9	28 44.0	19.2	57.3	29 16.2	20.1	57.8	29 47.9	21.1	58.3	30 19.2	22.1	58.8	30 50.1	23.0	59.3	31 20.5	24.0	59.8	41
42	27 55.7	16.8	55.4	28 29.6	17.8	55.8	29 03.2	18.6	56.3	29 36.3	19.6	56.7	30 09.0	20.6	57.2	30 41.3	21.5	57.7	31 13.1	22.5	58.2	31 44.5	23.4	58.7	42
43	28 12.5	16.3	54.3	28 47.4	17.2	54.7	29 21.8	18.2	55.2	29 55.9	19.1	55.6	30 29.6	20.0	56.1	31 02.8	21.0	56.6	31 35.6	21.9	57.1	32 07.9	22.9	57.6	43
44	28 28.8	15.7	53.2	29 04.6	16.6	53.6	29 40.0	17.6	54.1	30 15.0	18.5	54.5	30 49.6	19.4	55.0	31 23.8	20.4	55.5	31 57.5	21.4	56.0	32 30.8	22.3	56.6	44

84°, 276° L.H.A.   LATITUDE SAME NAME AS DECLINATION

Dec.	30° Hc	d	Z	31° Hc	d	Z	32° Hc	d	Z	33° Hc	d	Z	34° Hc	d	Z	35° Hc	d	Z	36° Hc	d	Z	37° Hc	d	Z	Dec.
0	5 11.9	+30.1	93.0	5 08.4	+31.0	93.1	5 05.1	+31.9	93.2	5 01.8	+32.7	93.3	4 58.3	+33.6	93.4	4 54.7	+34.5	93.4	4 51.1	+35.3	93.5	4 47.3	+36.2	93.6	0
1	5 41.7	30.0	92.1	5 39.4	30.9	92.2	5 37.0	31.8	92.3	5 34.5	32.7	92.4	5 31.9	33.6	92.5	5 29.2	34.3	92.6	5 26.4	35.3	92.7	5 23.5	36.2	92.8	1
2	6 11.7	29.9	91.3	6 10.3	30.9	91.4	6 08.8	31.8	91.5	6 07.2	32.6	91.6	6 05.5	33.5	91.7	6 03.7	34.3	91.8	6 01.7	35.3	91.9	5 59.7	36.0	92.0	2
3	6 41.6	29.9	90.4	6 41.2	30.7	90.5	6 40.6	31.6	90.6	6 39.8	32.6	90.7	6 39.0	33.4	90.9	6 38.0	34.3	91.0	6 37.0	35.1	91.1	6 35.7	36.0	91.2	3
4	7 11.5	29.7	89.5	7 11.9	30.7	89.6	7 12.2	31.6	89.8	7 12.4	32.4	89.9	7 12.4	33.3	90.0	7 12.3	34.2	90.1	7 12.1	35.1	90.3	7 11.7	35.9	90.4	4
5	7 41.2	+29.6	88.6	7 42.6	+30.5	88.8	7 43.8	+31.4	88.9	7 44.8	+32.4	89.1	7 45.7	+33.3	89.2	7 46.5	+34.1	89.3	7 47.2	+34.9	89.5	7 47.6	+35.9	89.6	5
6	8 10.8	29.5	87.8	8 13.1	30.4	87.9	8 15.2	31.3	88.1	8 17.2	32.2	88.3	8 19.0	33.1	88.3	8 20.6	34.0	88.5	8 22.1	34.9	88.7	8 23.5	35.7	88.8	6
7	8 40.3	29.4	86.9	8 43.5	30.3	87.0	8 46.5	31.3	87.2	8 49.4	32.1	87.3	8 52.1	33.0	87.5	8 54.6	33.9	87.7	8 57.0	34.7	87.8	8 59.2	35.6	88.0	7
8	9 09.7	29.3	86.0	9 13.8	30.2	86.2	9 17.8	31.0	86.3	9 21.5	32.0	86.5	9 25.1	32.9	86.7	9 28.5	33.8	86.8	9 31.7	34.7	87.0	9 34.8	35.5	87.2	8
9	9 39.0	29.1	85.1	9 44.0	30.1	85.3	9 48.8	31.0	85.5	9 53.5	31.9	85.6	9 58.0	32.7	85.8	10 02.3	33.6	86.0	10 06.4	34.5	86.2	10 10.3	35.4	86.3	9
10	10 08.1	+29.0	84.2	10 14.1	+29.9	84.4	10 19.8	+30.8	84.6	10 25.4	+31.7	84.8	10 30.7	+32.6	85.0	10 35.9	+33.5	85.1	10 40.9	+34.4	85.3	10 45.7	+35.2	85.5	10
11	10 37.1	28.8	83.3	10 44.0	29.7	83.5	10 50.6	30.7	83.7	10 57.1	31.6	83.9	11 03.3	32.5	84.1	11 09.4	33.4	84.3	11 15.3	34.1	84.5	11 20.9	35.1	84.7	11
12	11 05.9	28.7	82.4	11 13.7	29.6	82.6	11 21.3	30.5	82.8	11 28.7	31.4	83.0	11 35.8	32.3	83.2	11 42.8	33.2	83.5	11 49.5	34.1	83.7	11 56.0	35.0	83.9	12
13	11 34.6	28.5	81.6	11 43.3	29.4	81.8	11 51.8	30.4	82.0	12 00.1	31.2	82.2	12 08.1	32.2	82.4	12 16.0	33.0	82.6	12 23.6	33.9	82.8	12 31.0	34.8	83.0	13
14	12 03.1	28.3	80.7	12 12.7	29.3	80.9	12 22.2	30.1	81.1	12 31.3	31.1	81.3	12 40.3	32.0	81.5	12 49.0	32.9	81.7	12 57.5	33.8	82.0	13 05.8	34.6	82.2	14
15	12 31.4	+28.2	79.8	12 42.0	+29.1	80.0	12 52.3	+30.0	80.2	13 02.4	+30.9	80.4	13 12.3	+31.8	80.7	13 21.9	+32.7	80.9	13 31.3	+33.6	81.1	13 40.4	+34.5	81.4	15
16	12 59.6	28.0	78.8	13 11.1	28.9	79.1	13 22.3	29.8	79.3	13 33.3	30.8	79.5	13 44.1	31.6	79.8	13 54.6	32.6	80.0	14 04.9	33.4	80.3	14 14.9	34.3	80.5	16
17	13 27.6	27.7	77.9	13 40.0	28.7	78.2	13 52.1	29.7	78.4	14 04.1	30.5	78.7	14 15.7	31.5	78.9	14 27.2	32.3	79.2	14 38.3	33.2	79.4	14 49.2	34.1	79.7	17
18	13 55.3	27.6	77.0	14 08.7	28.5	77.3	14 21.8	29.4	77.5	14 34.6	30.3	77.8	14 47.2	31.2	78.0	14 59.5	32.1	78.3	15 11.5	33.1	78.6	15 23.3	33.9	78.8	18
19	14 22.9	27.3	76.1	14 37.2	28.2	76.4	14 51.2	29.2	76.6	15 04.9	30.2	76.9	15 18.4	31.1	77.1	15 31.6	32.0	77.4	15 44.6	32.8	77.7	15 57.2	33.7	78.0	19
20	14 50.2	+27.2	75.2	15 05.4	+28.1	75.4	15 20.4	+29.0	75.6	15 35.1	+29.9	76.0	15 49.5	+30.8	76.3	16 03.6	+31.7	76.5	16 17.4	+32.6	76.8	16 30.9	+33.5	77.1	20
21	15 17.4	26.9	74.3	15 33.5	27.8	74.5	15 49.4	28.7	74.8	16 05.0	29.6	75.1	16 20.3	30.5	75.4	16 35.3	31.5	75.6	16 50.0	32.4	75.9	17 04.4	33.3	76.2	21
22	15 44.3	26.6	73.3	16 01.3	27.4	73.6	16 18.1	28.5	73.9	16 34.6	29.5	74.2	16 50.8	30.4	74.5	17 06.8	31.2	74.8	17 22.4	32.1	75.1	17 37.7	33.1	75.4	22
23	16 10.9	26.3	72.4	16 28.9	27.4	72.7	16 46.6	28.3	73.0	17 04.1	29.2	73.3	17 21.2	30.1	73.6	17 38.0	31.0	73.9	17 54.5	32.0	74.2	18 10.8	32.8	74.5	23
24	16 37.4	26.1	71.5	16 56.3	27.1	71.8	17 14.9	28.0	72.0	17 33.3	28.9	72.3	17 51.3	29.9	72.7	18 09.0	30.8	73.0	18 26.5	31.6	73.3	18 43.6	32.5	73.6	24
25	17 03.5	+25.9	70.5	17 23.4	+26.8	70.8	17 42.9	+27.8	71.1	18 02.2	+28.7	71.4	18 21.2	+29.5	71.7	18 39.8	+30.5	72.1	18 58.1	+31.4	72.4	19 16.1	+32.3	72.7	25
26	17 29.4	25.7	69.6	17 50.2	26.6	69.9	18 10.7	27.5	70.2	18 30.9	28.4	70.5	18 50.7	29.4	70.8	19 10.3	30.2	71.1	19 29.5	31.1	71.5	19 48.4	32.0	71.8	26
27	17 55.1	25.3	68.6	18 16.8	26.3	68.9	18 38.2	27.2	69.3	18 59.3	28.1	69.6	19 20.1	29.0	69.9	19 40.5	30.0	70.2	20 00.6	30.9	70.6	20 20.4	31.8	70.9	27
28	18 20.4	25.1	67.7	18 43.1	26.0	68.0	19 05.4	26.9	68.3	19 27.4	27.8	68.6	19 49.1	28.8	69.0	20 10.5	29.6	69.3	20 31.5	30.6	69.7	20 52.2	31.4	70.0	28
29	18 45.5	24.8	66.7	19 09.1	25.7	67.0	19 32.3	26.6	67.4	19 55.2	27.6	67.7	20 17.9	28.4	68.0	20 40.1	29.4	68.4	21 02.1	30.2	68.7	21 23.6	31.2	69.1	29
30	19 10.3	+24.5	65.8	19 34.8	+25.4	66.1	19 58.9	+26.3	66.4	20 22.8	+27.2	66.8	20 46.3	+28.1	67.1	21 09.5	+29.0	67.4	21 32.3	+30.0	67.8	21 54.8	+30.9	68.2	30
31	19 34.8	24.1	64.8	20 00.2	25.0	65.1	20 25.2	26.0	65.5	20 50.0	26.9	65.8	21 14.4	27.9	66.1	21 38.5	28.8	66.5	22 02.3	29.6	66.9	22 25.7	30.5	67.3	31
32	19 58.9	23.9	63.8	20 25.2	24.8	64.2	20 51.2	25.7	64.5	21 16.9	26.6	64.8	21 42.3	27.5	65.2	22 07.3	28.4	65.6	22 31.9	29.3	65.9	22 56.2	30.2	66.3	32
33	20 22.8	23.5	62.8	20 50.0	24.4	63.2	21 16.9	25.4	63.5	21 43.5	26.3	63.9	22 09.8	27.1	64.2	22 35.7	28.0	64.6	23 01.2	29.0	65.0	23 26.4	29.8	65.4	33
34	20 46.3	23.2	61.9	21 14.4	24.1	62.2	21 42.3	25.0	62.5	22 09.8	25.9	62.9	22 36.9	26.8	63.3	23 03.7	27.7	63.7	23 30.2	28.6	64.0	23 56.2	29.6	64.4	34
35	21 09.5	+22.8	60.9	21 38.5	+23.8	61.2	22 07.3	+24.6	61.6	22 35.7	+25.5	61.9	23 03.7	+26.5	62.3	23 31.4	+27.4	62.7	23 58.8	+28.2	63.1	24 25.8	+29.1	63.5	35
36	21 32.3	22.5	59.9	22 02.3	23.4	60.2	22 31.9	24.3	60.6	23 01.2	25.2	61.0	23 30.2	26.0	61.3	23 58.8	27.0	61.7	24 27.0	27.9	62.1	24 54.9	28.8	62.5	36
37	21 54.8	22.1	58.9	22 25.7	23.0	59.2	22 56.2	23.9	59.6	23 26.4	24.8	60.0	23 56.2	25.7	60.3	24 25.8	26.6	60.7	24 54.9	27.5	61.1	25 23.7	28.4	61.5	37
38	22 16.9	21.8	57.9	22 48.7	22.6	58.2	23 20.1	23.5	58.6	23 51.2	24.4	59.0	24 21.9	25.4	59.4	24 52.4	26.2	59.7	25 22.4	27.1	60.2	25 52.1	28.0	60.6	38
39	22 38.7	21.3	56.9	23 11.3	22.3	57.2	23 43.6	23.2	57.6	24 15.6	24.0	58.0	24 47.3	24.9	58.4	25 18.6	25.8	58.8	25 49.5	26.7	59.2	26 20.1	27.6	59.6	39
40	23 00.0	+21.0	55.9	23 33.6	+21.8	56.2	24 06.8	+22.7	56.6	24 39.6	+23.6	57.0	25 12.2	+24.5	57.4	25 44.4	+25.4	57.8	26 16.2	+26.3	58.2	26 47.7	+27.1	58.6	40
41	23 21.0	20.6	54.8	23 55.4	21.5	55.2	24 29.5	22.3	55.6	25 03.3	23.2	55.9	25 36.7	24.1	56.3	26 09.8	24.9	56.7	26 42.5	25.8	57.2	27 14.8	26.8	57.6	41
42	23 41.6	20.2	53.8	24 16.9	21.0	54.2	24 51.8	21.9	54.5	25 26.5	22.7	54.9	26 00.8	23.6	55.3	26 34.7	24.6	55.7	27 08.3	25.4	56.2	27 41.6	26.3	56.6	42
43	24 01.8	19.7	52.8	24 37.9	20.6	53.2	25 13.7	21.5	53.5	25 49.2	22.4	53.9	26 24.4	23.2	54.3	26 59.3	24.1	54.7	27 33.7	25.0	55.1	28 07.9	25.8	55.6	43
44	24 21.5	19.4	51.7	24 58.5	20.2	52.1	25 35.2	21.1	52.5	26 11.6	21.9	52.9	26 47.6	22.8	53.3	27 23.4	23.6	53.7	27 58.7	24.5	54.1	28 33.7	25.4	54.5	44

85°, 275° L.H.A.   LATITUDE SAME NAME AS DECLINATION

N. Lat. { L.H.A. greater than 180° ..... Zn=Z
L.H.A. less than 180° ..... Zn=360°−Z

Dec.	30° Hc	d	Z	31° Hc	d	Z	32° Hc	d	Z	33° Hc	d	Z	34° Hc	d	Z	35° Hc	d	Z	36° Hc	d	Z	37° Hc	d	Z	Dec.
0	4 19.7	+30.1	92.5	4 17.1	+30.9	92.6	4 14.3	+31.9	92.7	4 11.5	+32.7	92.7	4 08.6	+33.6	92.8	4 05.6	+34.5	92.9	4 02.6	+35.3	92.9	3 59.5	+36.2	93.0	0
1	4 49.8	30.0	91.6	4 48.0	30.9	91.7	4 46.2	31.8	91.8	4 44.2	32.7	91.9	4 42.2	33.6	92.0	4 40.1	34.4	92.1	4 37.9	35.3	92.1	4 35.7	36.1	92.2	1
2	5 19.8	29.9	90.8	5 18.9	30.8	90.9	5 18.0	31.7	91.0	5 16.9	32.6	91.0	5 15.8	33.5	91.1	5 14.5	34.4	91.2	5 13.2	35.2	91.3	5 11.8	36.0	91.4	2
3	5 49.7	29.8	89.9	5 49.7	30.8	90.0	5 49.7	31.6	90.1	5 49.5	32.6	90.2	5 49.3	33.4	90.3	5 48.9	34.3	90.4	5 48.4	35.2	90.5	5 47.8	36.0	90.6	3
4	6 19.5	29.8	89.0	6 20.5	30.6	89.1	6 21.3	31.6	89.2	6 22.1	32.4	89.4	6 22.7	33.3	89.5	6 23.2	34.2	89.5	6 23.6	35.0	89.7	6 23.8	35.9	89.8	4
5	6 49.3	+29.6	88.1	6 51.1	+30.6	88.3	6 52.9	+31.5	88.4	6 54.5	+32.4	88.5	6 56.0	+33.3	88.6	6 57.4	+34.1	88.8	6 58.6	+35.0	88.9	6 59.7	+35.9	89.0	5
6	7 18.9	29.6	87.3	7 21.7	30.5	87.4	7 24.4	31.3	87.5	7 26.9	32.2	87.7	7 29.3	33.1	87.8	7 31.5	34.0	87.9	7 33.6	34.9	88.1	7 35.6	35.7	88.2	6
7	7 48.5	29.4	86.4	7 52.2	30.3	86.5	7 55.7	31.3	86.7	7 59.1	32.2	86.8	8 02.4	33.0	87.0	8 05.5	33.9	87.1	8 08.5	34.8	87.2	8 11.3	35.7	87.4	7
8	8 17.9	29.3	85.5	8 22.5	30.3	85.7	8 27.0	31.1	85.8	8 31.3	32.0	86.0	8 35.4	33.0	86.1	8 39.4	33.9	86.3	8 43.3	34.7	86.4	8 47.0	35.5	86.6	8
9	8 47.2	29.2	84.6	8 52.8	30.1	84.8	8 58.1	31.1	84.9	9 03.3	32.0	85.1	9 08.4	32.8	85.3	9 13.3	33.7	85.4	9 18.0	34.5	85.6	9 22.5	35.4	85.7	9
10	9 16.4	+29.1	83.7	9 22.9	+30.0	83.9	9 29.2	+30.9	84.1	9 35.3	+31.8	84.2	9 41.2	+32.7	84.4	9 47.0	+33.5	84.6	9 52.5	+34.5	84.8	9 57.9	+35.3	84.9	10
11	9 45.5	28.9	82.9	9 52.9	29.8	83.0	10 00.1	30.7	83.2	10 07.1	31.6	83.4	10 13.9	32.6	83.6	10 20.5	33.4	83.7	10 27.0	34.3	83.9	10 33.2	35.2	84.1	11
12	10 14.4	28.8	82.0	10 22.7	29.7	82.2	10 30.8	30.7	82.3	10 38.7	31.6	82.5	10 46.5	32.4	82.7	10 54.0	33.3	82.9	11 01.3	34.2	83.1	11 08.4	35.1	83.3	12
13	10 43.2	28.7	81.1	10 52.4	29.6	81.3	11 01.5	30.4	81.5	11 10.3	31.3	81.7	11 18.9	32.2	81.9	11 27.3	33.1	82.0	11 35.5	34.0	82.3	11 43.5	35.0	82.5	13
14	11 11.9	28.4	80.2	11 22.0	29.4	80.4	11 31.9	30.3	80.6	11 41.6	31.3	80.8	11 51.1	32.2	81.0	12 00.4	33.0	81.2	12 09.5	33.9	81.4	12 18.4	34.7	81.6	14
15	11 40.3	+28.4	79.3	11 51.4	+29.2	79.5	12 02.2	+30.2	79.7	12 12.9	+31.0	79.9	12 23.3	+31.9	80.1	12 33.4	+32.9	80.3	12 43.4	+33.7	80.6	12 53.1	+34.6	80.8	15
16	12 08.7	28.1	78.4	12 20.6	29.1	78.6	12 32.4	29.9	78.8	12 43.9	30.9	79.0	12 55.2	31.8	79.3	13 06.3	32.6	79.5	13 17.1	33.5	79.7	13 27.7	34.4	79.9	16
17	12 36.8	27.9	77.5	12 49.7	28.9	77.7	13 02.3	29.8	77.9	13 14.8	30.7	78.2	13 27.0	31.6	78.4	13 38.9	32.5	78.6	13 50.6	33.4	78.9	14 02.1	34.3	79.1	17
18	13 04.7	27.8	76.6	13 18.6	28.6	76.8	13 32.1	29.6	77.0	13 45.5	30.5	77.3	13 58.6	31.4	77.5	14 11.4	32.3	77.8	14 24.0	33.2	78.0	14 36.4	34.0	78.3	18
19	13 32.5	27.6	75.7	13 47.2	28.5	75.9	14 01.7	29.4	76.1	14 16.0	30.3	76.4	14 30.0	31.2	76.6	14 43.7	32.1	76.9	14 57.2	33.0	77.1	15 10.4	33.9	77.4	19
20	14 00.1	+27.3	74.7	14 15.7	+28.3	75.0	14 31.1	+29.2	75.2	14 46.3	+30.1	75.5	15 01.2	+31.0	75.7	15 15.8	+31.9	76.1	15 30.2	+32.8	76.3	15 44.3	+33.7	76.6	20
21	14 27.4	27.1	73.8	14 44.0	28.1	74.1	15 00.3	29.0	74.3	15 16.4	29.9	74.6	15 32.2	30.8	74.9	15 47.7	31.7	75.1	16 03.0	32.6	75.4	16 18.0	33.4	75.7	21
22	14 54.5	27.0	72.9	15 12.1	27.8	73.2	15 29.3	28.8	73.4	15 46.3	29.5	73.7	16 03.0	30.6	74.0	16 19.4	31.5	74.2	16 35.6	32.3	74.5	16 51.4	33.2	74.8	22
23	15 21.5	26.6	72.0	15 39.9	27.4	72.2	15 58.1	28.5	72.5	16 15.9	29.5	72.8	16 33.6	30.3	73.1	16 50.9	31.2	73.4	17 07.9	32.1	73.7	17 24.6	33.1	74.0	23
24	15 48.1	26.5	71.1	16 07.5	27.4	71.3	16 26.6	28.3	71.6	16 45.4	29.2	71.9	17 03.9	30.1	72.2	17 22.1	31.0	72.5	17 40.0	31.9	72.8	17 57.7	32.7	73.1	24
25	16 14.6	+26.2	70.1	16 34.9	+27.1	70.4	16 54.9	+28.0	70.7	17 14.6	+28.9	71.0	17 34.0	+29.8	71.3	17 53.1	+30.8	71.6	18 11.9	+31.7	71.9	18 30.4	+32.6	72.2	25
26	16 40.8	25.9	69.2	17 02.0	26.9	69.5	17 22.9	27.8	69.8	17 43.5	28.7	70.1	18 03.8	29.6	70.4	18 23.9	30.4	70.7	18 43.6	31.3	71.0	19 03.0	32.2	71.3	26
27	17 06.7	25.7	68.2	17 28.9	26.6	68.5	17 50.7	27.5	68.8	18 12.2	28.4	69.1	18 33.4	29.3	69.4	18 54.3	30.3	69.8	19 14.9	31.2	70.1	19 35.2	32.0	70.4	27
28	17 32.4	25.4	67.3	17 55.5	26.3	67.6	18 18.2	27.2	67.9	18 40.6	28.2	68.2	19 02.7	29.1	68.5	19 24.6	29.9	68.8	19 46.1	30.8	69.2	20 07.2	31.7	69.5	28
29	17 57.8	25.2	66.3	18 21.8	26.0	66.6	18 45.4	27.0	66.9	19 08.8	27.8	67.3	19 31.8	28.8	67.6	19 54.5	29.7	67.9	20 16.9	30.5	68.3	20 38.9	31.5	68.6	29
30	18 23.0	+24.8	65.4	18 47.8	+25.8	65.7	19 12.4	+26.6	66.0	19 36.6	+27.6	66.3	20 00.6	+28.4	66.7	20 24.2	+29.3	67.0	20 47.4	+30.3	67.3	21 10.4	+31.1	67.7	30
31	18 47.8	24.6	64.4	19 13.6	25.4	64.7	19 39.0	26.4	65.1	20 04.2	27.3	65.4	20 29.0	28.2	65.7	20 53.5	29.1	66.1	21 17.7	30.0	66.4	21 41.5	30.9	66.8	31
32	19 12.4	24.2	63.5	19 39.0	25.2	63.8	20 05.4	25.7	64.1	20 31.5	26.9	64.4	20 57.2	27.8	64.8	21 22.6	28.7	65.1	21 47.7	29.6	65.5	22 12.4	30.5	65.9	32
33	19 36.6	24.0	62.5	20 04.2	24.8	62.8	20 31.1	25.4	63.1	20 58.4	26.6	63.4	21 25.0	27.6	63.8	21 51.3	28.5	64.2	22 17.3	29.3	64.5	22 42.9	30.2	64.9	33
34	20 00.6	23.6	61.5	20 29.0	24.5	61.8	20 57.2	25.4	62.2	21 25.0	26.3	62.5	21 52.6	27.2	62.9	22 19.8	28.0	63.2	22 46.6	29.0	63.6	23 13.1	29.9	64.0	34
35	20 24.2	+23.2	60.5	20 53.5	+24.2	60.9	21 22.6	+25.1	61.2	21 51.3	+26.0	61.5	22 19.8	+26.8	61.9	22 47.8	+27.8	62.3	23 15.6	+28.6	62.7	23 43.0	+29.5	63.0	35
36	20 47.4	23.0	59.5	21 17.7	23.8	59.9	21 47.7	24.7	60.1	22 17.3	25.6	60.6	22 46.6	26.5	60.9	23 15.6	27.4	61.3	23 44.2	28.3	61.7	24 12.5	29.1	62.1	36
37	21 10.4	22.6	58.6	21 41.5	23.5	58.9	22 12.4	24.3	59.2	22 42.9	25.3	59.6	23 13.1	26.1	60.0	23 43.0	27.0	60.3	24 12.5	27.9	60.7	24 41.6	28.8	61.1	37
38	21 33.0	22.2	57.6	22 05.0	23.1	57.9	22 36.7	24.0	58.3	23 08.2	24.8	58.6	23 39.2	25.8	59.0	24 10.0	26.6	59.4	24 40.4	27.5	59.8	25 10.4	28.4	60.2	38
39	21 55.2	21.9	56.6	22 28.1	22.8	56.9	23 00.7	23.7	57.3	23 33.0	24.5	57.6	24 05.0	25.4	58.0	24 36.6	26.3	58.4	25 07.9	27.1	58.8	25 38.8	28.0	59.2	39
40	22 17.1	+21.5	55.6	22 50.9	+22.4	55.9	23 24.4	+23.2	56.3	23 57.5	+24.1	56.6	24 30.4	+25.0	57.0	25 02.9	+25.8	57.4	25 35.0	+26.8	57.8	26 06.8	+27.7	58.2	40
41	22 38.6	21.1	54.6	23 13.3	21.9	54.9	23 47.6	22.9	55.3	24 21.6	23.8	55.6	24 55.4	24.5	56.0	25 28.7	25.5	56.4	26 01.8	26.3	56.8	26 34.5	27.2	57.2	41
42	22 59.7	20.8	53.5	23 35.2	21.6	53.9	24 10.5	22.4	54.3	24 45.4	23.3	54.6	25 19.9	24.2	55.0	25 54.2	25.0	55.4	26 28.1	25.9	55.8	27 01.7	26.7	56.2	42
43	23 20.5	20.3	52.5	23 56.8	21.6	52.9	24 32.9	22.0	53.2	25 08.7	22.9	53.6	25 44.1	23.9	54.0	26 19.2	24.6	54.4	26 54.0	25.5	54.8	27 28.4	26.4	55.2	43
44	23 40.8	19.9	51.5	24 18.0	20.8	51.8	24 54.9	21.6	52.2	25 31.6	22.4	52.6	26 07.9	23.3	53.0	26 43.8	24.2	53.4	27 19.5	25.0	53.8	27 54.8	25.8	54.2	44

	30°			31°			32°			33°			34°			35°			36°			37°			
45	23 20.7	+20.1	50.2	23 59.0	+20.9	50.5	24 37.0	+21.7	50.9	25 14.7	+22.6	51.2	25 52.1	+23.4	51.6	26 29.2	+24.2	52.0	27 05.9	+25.2	52.4	27 42.4	+25.9	52.8	45
46	23 40.8	19.7	49.2	24 19.9	20.5	49.5	24 58.7	21.4	49.9	25 37.3	22.1	50.2	26 15.5	23.0	50.6	26 53.4	23.9	51.0	27 31.1	24.6	51.4	28 08.3	25.5	51.8	46
47	24 00.5	19.3	48.5	24 40.4	20.1	48.5	25 20.1	20.9	48.8	25 59.4	21.7	49.2	26 38.5	22.6	49.6	27 17.3	23.3	50.0	27 55.7	24.2	50.4	28 33.8	25.0	50.8	47
48	24 19.8	18.9	47.1	25 00.5	19.7	47.4	25 41.0	20.4	47.8	26 21.1	21.3	48.2	27 01.0	22.1	48.5	27 40.6	22.9	48.9	28 19.9	23.7	49.3	28 58.8	24.6	49.7	48
49	24 38.7	18.4	46.1	25 20.2	19.2	46.4	26 01.4	20.0	46.7	26 42.4	20.8	47.1	27 23.1	21.6	47.5	28 03.5	22.4	47.9	28 43.6	23.2	48.3	29 23.4	24.0	48.7	49
50	24 57.1	+18.0	45.0	25 39.4	+18.8	45.3	26 21.4	+19.6	45.7	27 03.2	+20.3	46.1	27 44.7	+21.1	46.4	28 25.9	+21.9	46.8	29 06.8	+22.8	47.2	29 47.4	+23.6	47.6	50
51	25 15.1	17.5	44.0	25 58.2	18.3	44.3	26 41.0	19.0	44.6	27 23.5	19.9	45.0	28 05.8	20.7	45.4	28 47.8	21.5	45.8	29 29.6	22.2	46.2	30 11.0	23.0	46.6	51
52	25 32.6	17.1	42.9	26 16.5	17.8	43.2	27 00.0	18.6	43.6	27 43.4	19.3	43.9	28 26.5	20.1	44.3	29 09.3	20.9	44.7	29 51.8	21.7	45.1	30 34.0	22.5	45.5	52
53	25 49.7	16.6	41.8	26 34.3	17.3	42.2	27 18.6	18.1	42.5	28 02.7	18.9	42.9	28 46.6	19.6	43.2	29 30.2	20.4	43.6	30 13.5	21.1	44.0	30 56.5	21.9	44.4	53
54	26 06.3	16.1	40.8	26 51.6	16.9	41.1	27 36.7	17.6	41.4	28 21.6	18.3	41.8	29 06.2	19.1	42.2	29 50.6	19.8	42.5	30 34.6	20.7	42.9	31 18.4	21.4	43.3	54
55	26 22.4	+15.7	39.7	27 08.5	+16.4	40.0	27 54.3	+17.1	40.4	28 39.9	+17.9	40.7	29 25.3	+18.6	41.1	30 10.4	+19.3	41.4	30 55.3	+20.0	41.8	31 39.8	+20.9	42.2	55
56	26 38.1	15.1	38.6	27 24.9	15.8	38.9	28 11.4	16.6	39.3	28 57.8	17.3	39.6	29 43.9	18.0	40.0	30 29.7	18.8	40.3	31 15.3	19.5	40.7	32 00.7	20.2	41.1	56
57	26 53.2	14.7	37.5	27 40.7	15.4	37.8	28 28.0	16.0	38.2	29 15.1	16.7	38.5	30 01.9	17.5	38.9	30 48.5	18.2	39.2	31 34.8	18.9	39.6	32 20.9	19.7	40.0	57
58	27 07.9	14.2	36.4	27 56.1	14.8	36.8	28 44.0	15.6	37.1	29 31.8	16.2	37.4	30 19.4	16.9	37.8	31 06.7	17.6	38.1	31 53.7	18.4	38.5	32 40.6	19.0	38.9	58
59	27 22.1	13.6	35.3	28 10.9	14.3	35.7	28 59.6	14.9	36.0	29 48.0	15.7	36.3	30 36.3	16.3	36.7	31 24.3	17.0	37.0	32 12.1	17.7	37.4	32 59.6	18.5	37.8	59
60	27 35.7	+13.1	34.2	28 25.2	+13.8	34.6	29 14.5	+14.4	34.9	30 03.7	+15.0	35.2	30 52.6	+15.7	35.5	31 41.3	+16.4	35.9	32 29.8	+17.1	36.3	33 18.1	+17.8	36.6	60
61	27 48.8	12.6	33.1	28 39.0	13.2	33.4	29 28.9	13.9	33.8	30 18.7	14.5	34.1	31 08.3	15.2	34.4	31 57.7	15.9	34.8	32 46.9	16.5	35.1	33 35.9	17.2	35.5	61
62	28 01.4	12.1	32.0	28 52.2	12.7	32.3	29 42.8	13.3	32.6	30 33.3	13.9	32.9	31 23.5	14.6	33.3	32 13.6	15.2	33.6	33 03.4	15.9	34.0	33 53.1	16.5	34.3	62
63	28 13.5	11.5	30.9	29 04.9	12.1	31.2	29 56.1	12.7	31.5	30 47.2	13.3	31.8	31 38.1	13.9	32.1	32 28.8	14.6	32.5	33 19.3	15.3	32.8	34 09.6	15.9	33.2	63
64	28 25.0	11.0	29.8	29 17.0	11.5	30.1	30 08.8	12.2	30.4	31 00.5	12.7	30.7	31 52.0	13.4	31.0	32 43.4	13.9	31.3	33 34.5	14.6	31.7	34 25.5	15.2	32.0	64
65	28 36.0	+10.4	28.7	29 28.5	+11.0	29.0	30 21.0	+11.5	29.2	31 13.2	+12.2	29.5	32 05.4	+12.7	29.8	32 57.3	+13.3	30.2	33 49.1	+13.9	30.5	34 40.7	+14.6	30.8	65
66	28 46.4	9.9	27.6	29 39.5	10.4	27.8	30 32.5	11.0	28.1	31 25.4	11.5	28.4	32 18.1	12.0	28.7	33 10.6	12.7	29.0	34 03.0	13.3	29.3	34 55.3	13.8	29.7	66
67	28 56.3	9.3	26.4	29 49.9	9.8	26.7	30 43.5	10.3	27.0	31 36.9	10.9	27.2	32 30.1	11.5	27.5	33 23.3	12.0	27.8	34 16.3	12.5	28.1	35 09.1	13.1	28.5	67
68	29 05.6	8.7	25.3	29 59.7	9.3	25.6	30 53.8	9.7	25.8	31 47.8	10.2	26.1	32 41.6	10.8	26.4	33 35.3	11.3	26.7	34 28.8	11.9	27.0	35 22.2	12.5	27.3	68
69	29 14.3	8.1	24.2	30 09.0	8.6	24.5	31 03.5	9.2	24.7	31 58.0	9.6	24.9	32 52.4	10.1	25.2	33 46.6	10.6	25.5	34 40.7	11.2	25.8	35 34.7	11.7	26.1	69
70	29 22.4	+7.6	23.0	30 17.6	+8.0	23.3	31 12.7	+8.5	23.5	32 07.6	+8.9	23.8	33 02.5	+9.5	24.0	33 57.2	+10.0	24.3	34 51.9	+10.4	24.6	35 46.4	+11.0	24.9	70
71	29 30.0	7.0	21.9	30 25.6	7.5	22.1	31 21.2	7.9	22.4	32 16.6	8.4	22.6	33 12.0	8.8	22.8	34 07.2	9.3	23.1	35 02.3	9.8	23.4	35 57.4	10.2	23.7	71
72	29 37.0	6.4	20.8	30 33.1	6.8	21.0	31 29.1	7.2	21.2	32 25.0	7.6	21.4	33 20.8	8.1	21.7	34 16.5	8.6	21.9	35 12.1	9.0	22.2	36 07.6	9.5	22.4	72
73	29 43.4	5.8	19.6	30 39.9	6.2	19.8	31 36.3	6.6	20.0	32 32.6	7.1	20.2	33 28.9	7.4	20.5	34 25.1	7.8	20.7	35 21.1	8.3	21.0	36 17.1	8.8	21.2	73
74	29 49.2	5.2	18.5	30 46.1	5.6	18.7	31 42.9	6.0	18.9	32 39.7	6.3	19.1	33 36.3	6.8	19.3	34 32.9	7.2	19.5	35 29.4	7.6	19.7	36 25.9	8.0	20.0	74
75	29 54.4	+4.7	17.3	30 51.7	+5.0	17.5	31 48.9	+5.3	17.7	32 46.0	+5.7	17.9	33 43.1	+6.0	18.1	34 40.1	+6.4	18.3	35 37.0	+6.9	18.5	36 33.9	+7.2	18.8	75
76	29 59.1	4.0	16.2	30 56.7	4.3	16.3	31 54.2	4.7	16.5	32 51.7	5.0	16.7	33 49.1	5.4	16.9	34 46.5	5.8	17.1	35 43.9	6.0	17.3	36 41.1	6.5	17.5	76
77	30 03.1	3.4	15.0	31 01.0	3.7	15.2	31 58.9	4.0	15.3	32 56.7	4.4	15.5	33 54.5	4.7	15.7	34 52.3	5.0	15.9	35 49.9	5.4	16.1	36 47.6	5.7	16.3	77
78	30 06.5	2.8	13.9	31 04.7	3.1	14.0	32 02.9	3.4	14.2	33 01.1	3.6	14.3	33 59.2	4.0	14.5	34 57.3	4.2	14.7	35 55.3	4.6	14.8	36 53.3	4.9	15.0	78
79	30 09.3	2.2	12.7	31 07.8	2.5	12.8	32 06.3	2.7	13.0	33 04.7	3.0	13.1	34 03.2	3.2	13.3	35 01.5	3.6	13.4	35 59.9	3.8	13.6	36 58.2	4.1	13.8	79
80	30 11.5	+1.6	11.6	31 10.3	+1.8	11.7	32 09.0	+2.1	11.8	33 07.7	+2.3	11.9	34 06.4	+2.6	12.1	35 05.1	+2.8	12.2	36 03.7	+3.1	12.4	37 02.3	+3.3	12.5	80
81	30 13.1	1.0	10.4	31 12.1	1.2	10.5	32 11.1	1.4	10.6	33 10.0	1.7	10.7	34 09.0	1.8	10.9	35 07.9	2.1	11.0	36 06.8	2.3	11.1	37 05.6	2.6	11.3	81
82	30 14.1	0.3	9.2	31 13.3	0.5	9.3	32 12.5	0.7	9.4	33 11.7	0.9	9.5	34 10.8	1.2	9.7	35 10.0	1.3	9.8	36 09.1	1.5	9.9	37 08.2	1.7	10.0	82
83	30 14.4	-0.2	8.1	31 13.8	0.0	8.2	32 13.2	0.1	8.3	33 12.6	0.3	8.4	34 12.0	0.4	8.4	35 11.3	0.6	8.6	36 10.6	0.8	8.7	37 09.9	1.0	8.8	83
84	30 14.2	0.8	6.9	31 13.8	-0.7	7.0	32 13.3	-0.6	7.1	33 12.9	-0.5	7.2	34 12.4	-0.3	7.2	35 11.9	-0.1	7.3	36 11.4	0.0	7.4	37 10.9	-0.2	7.5	84
85	30 13.4	-1.5	5.8	31 13.1	-1.4	5.8	32 12.7	-1.2	5.9	33 12.4	-1.1	6.0	34 12.1	-1.0	6.0	35 11.8	-0.9	6.1	36 11.4	-0.7	6.2	37 11.1	-0.7	6.3	85
86	30 11.9	2.1	4.6	31 11.7	2.0	4.6	32 11.5	1.9	4.7	33 11.3	1.8	4.8	34 11.1	1.7	4.8	35 10.9	1.6	4.9	36 10.7	1.6	4.9	37 10.4	1.4	5.0	86
87	30 09.8	2.6	3.5	31 09.7	2.6	3.5	32 09.6	2.5	3.5	33 09.5	2.5	3.6	34 09.4	2.4	3.6	35 09.3	2.4	3.7	36 09.1	2.2	3.7	37 09.0	2.2	3.8	87
88	30 07.2	3.3	2.3	31 07.1	3.2	2.3	32 07.1	3.2	2.4	33 07.0	3.2	2.4	34 07.0	3.2	2.4	35 06.9	3.1	2.4	36 06.9	3.1	2.5	37 06.8	3.0	2.5	88
89	30 03.9	3.9	1.2	31 03.9	3.9	1.2	32 03.9	3.9	1.2	33 03.8	3.9	1.2	34 03.8	3.8	1.2	35 03.8	3.8	1.2	36 03.8	3.8	1.2	37 03.8	3.8	1.3	89
90	30 00.0	-4.5	0.0	31 00.0	-4.5	0.0	32 00.0	-4.5	0.0	33 00.0	-4.5	0.0	34 00.0	-4.5	0.0	35 00.0	-4.5	0.0	36 00.0	-4.6	0.0	37 00.0	-4.6	0.0	90

N. Lat. { L.H.A. greater than 180°......Zn=Z ; L.H.A. less than 180°......Zn=360°–Z }

Dec.	30° Hc	d	Z	31° Hc	d	Z	32° Hc	d	Z	33° Hc	d	Z	34° Hc	d	Z	35° Hc	d	Z	36° Hc	d	Z	37° Hc	d	Z	Dec.
0	0 00.0	+30.0	90.0	0 00.0	+30.9	90.0	0 00.0	+31.8	90.0	0 00.0	+32.7	90.0	0 00.0	+33.6	90.0	0 00.0	+34.4	90.0	0 00.0	+35.3	90.0	0 00.0	+36.1	90.0	0
1	0 30.0	30.0	89.1	0 30.9	30.9	89.1	0 31.8	31.8	89.2	0 32.7	32.6	89.2	0 33.6	33.5	89.2	0 34.4	34.4	89.2	0 35.3	35.2	89.2	0 36.1	36.1	89.2	1
2	1 00.0	30.0	88.3	1 01.8	30.9	88.3	1 03.6	31.8	88.3	1 05.3	32.7	88.3	1 07.1	33.5	88.3	1 08.8	34.4	88.4	1 10.5	35.3	88.4	1 12.2	36.1	88.4	2
3	1 30.0	29.9	87.4	1 32.7	30.8	87.4	1 35.4	31.7	87.5	1 38.0	32.6	87.5	1 40.6	33.5	87.5	1 43.2	34.3	87.5	1 45.8	35.2	87.6	1 48.3	36.1	87.6	3
4	1 59.9	30.0	86.5	2 03.5	30.9	86.6	2 07.1	31.7	86.6	2 10.6	32.6	86.6	2 14.1	33.5	86.7	2 17.6	34.3	86.7	2 21.0	35.2	86.8	2 24.4	36.0	86.8	4
5	2 29.9	+29.9	85.7	2 34.4	+30.8	85.7	2 38.8	+31.7	85.8	2 43.2	+32.6	85.8	2 47.6	+33.5	85.9	2 51.9	+34.3	85.9	2 56.2	+35.1	86.0	3 00.4	+36.0	86.0	5
6	2 59.8	29.8	84.8	3 05.2	30.7	84.9	3 10.5	31.6	84.9	3 15.8	32.5	84.9	3 21.1	33.4	85.0	3 26.2	34.3	85.1	3 31.3	35.2	85.1	3 36.4	36.0	85.2	6
7	3 29.6	29.8	83.9	3 35.9	30.7	84.0	3 42.1	31.6	84.0	3 48.3	32.5	84.1	3 54.5	33.3	84.2	4 00.5	34.2	84.2	4 06.5	35.0	84.4	4 12.4	35.9	84.4	7
8	3 59.4	29.8	83.1	4 06.6	30.7	83.1	4 13.8	31.5	83.2	4 20.8	32.5	83.2	4 27.8	33.3	83.4	4 34.7	34.2	83.4	4 41.5	35.0	83.5	4 48.3	35.8	83.6	8
9	4 29.2	29.7	82.2	4 37.3	30.6	82.3	4 45.3	31.5	82.3	4 53.3	32.3	82.4	5 01.1	33.2	82.5	5 08.9	34.1	82.6	5 16.5	35.0	82.7	5 24.1	35.8	82.8	9
10	4 58.9	+29.6	81.3	5 07.9	+30.5	81.4	5 16.8	+31.4	81.5	5 25.6	+32.3	81.6	5 34.3	+33.2	81.7	5 43.0	+34.0	81.7	5 51.5	+34.9	81.9	5 59.9	+35.7	82.0	10
11	5 28.5	29.5	80.4	5 38.4	30.4	80.5	5 48.2	31.3	80.6	5 57.9	32.2	80.7	6 07.5	33.1	80.8	6 17.0	33.9	80.9	6 26.4	34.8	81.1	6 35.6	35.6	81.2	11
12	5 58.0	29.5	79.6	6 08.8	30.4	79.7	6 19.5	31.3	79.8	6 30.1	32.1	79.9	6 40.6	33.0	80.0	6 50.9	33.9	80.1	7 01.2	34.7	80.2	7 11.3	35.5	80.4	12
13	6 27.5	29.4	78.7	6 39.2	30.3	78.8	6 50.8	31.1	78.9	7 02.2	32.1	79.0	7 13.6	32.9	79.2	7 24.8	33.8	79.2	7 35.9	34.6	79.4	7 46.8	35.5	79.6	13
14	6 56.9	29.2	77.8	7 09.5	30.1	77.9	7 21.9	31.1	78.1	7 34.3	31.9	78.2	7 46.5	32.8	78.3	7 58.6	33.6	78.5	8 10.5	34.5	78.6	8 22.3	35.4	78.7	14
15	7 26.1	+29.2	76.9	7 39.6	+30.1	77.1	7 53.0	+30.9	77.2	8 06.2	+31.8	77.3	8 19.3	+32.7	77.5	8 32.2	+33.6	77.6	8 45.0	+34.4	77.8	8 57.7	+35.2	77.9	15
16	7 55.3	29.1	76.1	8 09.7	29.9	76.2	8 23.9	30.9	76.3	8 38.0	31.8	76.5	8 52.0	32.6	76.6	9 05.8	33.4	76.8	9 19.4	34.3	76.9	9 32.9	35.1	77.1	16
17	8 24.4	28.9	75.2	8 39.6	29.8	75.3	8 54.8	30.7	75.5	9 09.8	31.5	75.6	9 24.6	32.4	75.8	9 39.2	33.4	75.9	9 53.7	34.2	76.1	10 08.0	35.1	76.3	17
18	8 53.3	28.8	74.3	9 09.5	29.7	74.4	9 25.5	30.6	74.6	9 41.3	31.5	74.8	9 57.0	32.4	74.9	10 12.6	33.1	75.1	10 27.9	34.0	75.3	10 43.1	34.8	75.5	18
19	9 22.1	28.7	73.4	9 39.1	29.6	73.6	9 56.1	30.4	73.7	10 12.8	31.3	73.9	10 29.4	32.2	74.1	10 45.7	33.1	74.2	11 01.9	33.9	74.4	11 17.9	34.8	74.6	19
20	9 50.8	+28.5	72.5	10 08.7	+29.5	72.7	10 26.5	+30.3	72.8	10 44.1	+31.2	73.0	11 01.6	+32.0	73.2	11 18.8	+32.9	73.4	11 35.8	+33.8	73.6	11 52.7	+34.6	73.8	20
21	10 19.3	28.4	71.6	10 38.2	29.3	71.8	10 56.8	30.2	72.0	11 15.3	31.0	72.2	11 33.6	31.9	72.3	11 51.7	32.8	72.5	12 09.6	33.6	72.7	12 27.3	34.4	73.0	21
22	10 47.7	28.3	70.7	11 07.5	29.1	70.9	11 27.0	30.0	71.1	11 46.3	30.9	71.3	12 05.5	31.7	71.5	12 24.5	32.5	71.7	12 43.2	33.4	71.9	13 01.7	34.3	72.1	22
23	11 16.0	28.0	69.8	11 36.6	28.8	70.0	11 57.0	29.8	70.2	12 17.2	30.7	70.4	12 37.2	31.6	70.6	12 57.0	32.5	70.8	13 16.6	33.3	71.0	13 36.0	34.1	71.3	23
24	11 44.0	27.9	68.9	12 05.5	28.8	69.1	12 26.8	29.7	69.3	12 47.9	30.5	69.5	13 08.8	31.4	69.7	13 29.5	32.2	70.0	13 49.9	33.1	70.2	14 10.1	34.0	70.4	24
25	12 11.9	+27.8	68.0	12 34.3	+28.6	68.2	12 56.5	+29.5	68.4	13 18.4	+30.4	68.6	13 40.2	+31.2	68.9	14 01.7	+32.1	69.1	14 23.0	+32.9	69.3	14 44.1	+33.7	69.6	25
26	12 39.7	27.5	67.1	13 02.9	28.4	67.3	13 26.0	29.2	67.5	13 48.8	30.1	67.8	14 11.4	31.0	68.0	14 33.8	31.9	68.2	14 55.9	32.7	68.5	15 17.8	33.6	68.7	26
27	13 07.2	27.4	66.2	13 31.3	28.3	66.4	13 55.2	29.1	66.6	14 18.9	30.0	66.9	14 42.4	30.8	67.1	15 05.6	31.7	67.3	15 28.6	32.5	67.6	15 51.4	33.3	67.9	27
28	13 34.6	27.1	65.3	13 59.6	28.0	65.5	14 24.3	28.9	65.7	14 48.9	29.7	66.0	15 13.2	30.6	66.2	15 37.3	31.4	66.5	16 01.1	32.3	66.7	16 24.7	33.1	67.0	28
29	14 01.7	27.0	64.4	14 27.6	27.8	64.6	14 53.2	28.7	64.8	15 18.6	29.5	65.1	15 43.8	30.4	65.3	16 08.7	31.2	65.6	16 33.4	32.1	65.8	16 57.8	32.9	66.1	29
30	14 28.7	+26.7	63.4	14 55.4	+27.6	63.7	15 21.9	+28.4	63.9	15 48.1	+29.3	64.2	16 14.2	+30.1	64.4	16 39.9	+31.0	64.7	17 05.5	+31.8	65.0	17 30.7	+32.7	65.2	30
31	14 55.4	26.5	62.5	15 23.0	27.3	62.7	15 50.3	28.2	63.0	16 17.4	29.1	63.3	16 44.3	29.9	63.5	17 10.9	30.8	63.8	17 37.3	31.6	64.1	18 03.4	32.4	64.4	31
32	15 21.9	26.2	61.6	15 50.3	27.1	61.8	16 18.5	28.0	62.1	16 46.5	28.8	62.4	17 14.2	29.7	62.6	17 41.7	30.5	62.9	18 08.9	31.4	63.2	18 35.8	32.2	63.5	32
33	15 48.1	26.1	60.6	16 17.4	26.9	60.9	16 46.5	27.7	61.1	17 15.3	28.6	61.4	17 43.9	29.4	61.6	18 12.2	30.3	62.0	18 40.3	31.0	62.3	19 08.0	31.9	62.6	33
34	16 14.2	25.7	59.7	16 44.3	26.6	60.0	17 14.2	27.5	60.2	17 43.9	28.3	60.5	18 13.3	29.2	60.8	18 42.5	29.9	61.1	19 11.3	30.9	61.4	19 39.9	31.7	61.7	34
35	16 39.9	+25.6	58.8	17 10.9	+26.4	59.0	17 41.7	+27.2	59.3	18 12.2	+28.1	59.6	18 42.5	+28.8	59.9	19 12.4	+29.8	60.2	19 42.2	+30.5	60.5	20 11.6	+31.4	60.8	35
36	17 05.5	25.2	57.8	17 37.3	26.1	58.1	18 08.9	26.9	58.3	18 40.3	27.7	58.6	19 11.3	28.6	58.9	19 42.2	29.4	59.2	20 12.7	30.3	59.6	20 43.0	31.1	59.9	36
37	17 30.7	25.0	56.9	18 03.4	25.8	57.1	18 35.8	26.7	57.4	19 08.0	27.5	57.7	19 39.9	28.3	58.0	20 11.6	29.1	58.3	20 43.0	29.9	58.6	21 14.1	30.7	59.0	37
38	17 55.7	24.7	55.9	18 29.2	25.6	56.2	19 02.5	26.3	56.5	19 35.5	27.2	56.8	20 08.2	28.1	57.1	20 40.7	28.9	57.4	21 12.9	29.7	57.7	21 44.8	30.5	58.0	38
39	18 20.4	24.4	55.0	18 54.8	25.2	55.2	19 28.8	26.1	55.5	20 02.7	26.9	55.8	20 36.3	27.7	56.1	21 09.6	28.5	56.4	21 42.6	29.3	56.8	22 15.3	30.2	57.1	39
40	18 44.8	+24.2	54.0	19 20.0	+24.9	54.3	19 54.9	+25.7	54.6	20 29.6	+26.5	54.9	21 04.0	+27.3	55.2	21 38.1	+28.2	55.5	22 11.9	+29.0	55.8	22 45.5	+29.8	56.2	40
41	19 09.0	23.8	53.0	19 44.9	24.6	53.3	20 20.6	25.5	53.6	20 56.1	26.3	53.9	21 31.3	27.1	54.2	22 06.3	27.8	54.5	22 40.9	28.7	54.9	23 15.3	29.5	55.2	41
42	19 32.8	23.5	52.1	20 09.5	24.3	52.3	20 46.1	25.1	52.6	21 22.4	25.9	52.9	21 58.4	26.7	53.2	22 34.1	27.6	53.6	23 09.6	28.3	53.9	23 44.8	29.1	54.3	42
43	19 56.3	23.1	51.1	20 33.8	24.0	51.4	21 11.2	24.8	51.7	21 48.3	25.5	52.0	22 25.1	26.4	52.3	23 01.7	27.1	52.6	23 37.9	28.0	53.0	24 13.9	28.8	53.3	43
44	20 19.4	22.9	50.1	20 57.8	23.7	50.4	21 36.0	24.4	50.7	22 13.8	25.3	51.0	22 51.5	26.0	51.3	23 28.8	26.8	51.7	24 05.9	27.6	52.0	24 42.7	28.4	52.4	44

LATITUDE CONTRARY NAME TO DECLINATION

Dec.	38° Hc	d	Z	39° Hc	d	Z	40° Hc	d	Z	41° Hc	d	Z	42° Hc	d	Z	43° Hc	d	Z	44° Hc	d	Z	45° Hc	d	Z	Dec.
0	51 59.3	-60.0	178.4	50 59.4	-60.0	178.4	49 59.4	-60.0	178.4	48 59.4	-60.0	178.5	47 59.4	-60.0	178.5	46 59.4	-60.0	178.5	45 59.5	-60.0	178.6	44 59.5	-60.0	178.6	0
1	50 59.3	59.9	178.4	49 59.4	60.0	178.4	48 59.4	60.0	178.4	47 59.4	60.0	178.5	46 59.4	60.0	178.5	45 59.4	59.9	178.6	44 59.5	60.0	178.6	43 59.5	60.0	178.6	1
2	49 59.4	60.0	178.5	48 59.4	60.0	178.5	47 59.4	60.0	178.5	46 59.4	60.0	178.5	45 59.4	60.0	178.6	44 59.5	60.0	178.6	43 59.5	60.0	178.6	42 59.5	60.0	178.6	2
3	48 59.4	60.0	178.5	47 59.4	60.0	178.5	46 59.4	60.0	178.5	45 59.4	60.0	178.6	44 59.4	59.9	178.6	43 59.5	60.0	178.6	42 59.5	60.0	178.6	41 59.5	60.0	178.7	3
4	47 59.4	60.0	178.5	46 59.4	60.0	178.5	45 59.4	60.0	178.6	44 59.4	59.9	178.6	43 59.5	60.0	178.6	42 59.5	60.0	178.7	41 59.5	60.0	178.7	40 59.5	60.0	178.7	4
5	46 59.4	-60.0	178.6	45 59.4	-60.0	178.6	44 59.4	-60.0	178.6	43 59.5	-60.0	178.6	42 59.5	-60.0	178.7	41 59.5	-60.0	178.7	40 59.5	-60.0	178.7	39 59.5	-60.0	178.7	5
6	45 59.4	60.0	178.6	44 59.4	60.0	178.6	43 59.4	59.9	178.6	42 59.5	60.0	178.6	41 59.5	60.0	178.7	40 59.5	60.0	178.7	39 59.5	60.0	178.7	38 59.5	60.0	178.7	6
7	44 59.4	60.0	178.6	43 59.4	60.0	178.6	42 59.5	60.0	178.6	41 59.5	60.0	178.7	40 59.5	60.0	178.7	39 59.5	60.0	178.7	38 59.5	60.0	178.7	37 59.5	60.0	178.7	7
8	43 59.4	59.9	178.6	42 59.4	59.9	178.6	41 59.5	60.0	178.7	40 59.5	60.0	178.7	39 59.5	60.0	178.7	38 59.5	60.0	178.7	37 59.5	60.0	178.8	36 59.5	60.0	178.8	8
9	42 59.4	60.0	178.7	41 59.5	60.0	178.7	40 59.5	60.0	178.7	39 59.5	60.0	178.7	38 59.5	60.0	178.8	37 59.5	60.0	178.8	36 59.5	60.0	178.8	35 59.5	60.0	178.8	9
10	41 59.5	-60.0	178.7	40 59.5	-60.0	178.7	39 59.5	-60.0	178.7	38 59.5	-60.0	178.7	37 59.5	-60.0	178.8	36 59.5	-60.0	178.8	35 59.5	-60.0	178.8	34 59.5	-60.0	178.8	10
11	40 59.5	60.0	178.7	39 59.5	60.0	178.7	38 59.5	60.0	178.7	37 59.5	60.0	178.8	36 59.5	60.0	178.8	35 59.5	60.0	178.8	34 59.5	59.9	178.8	33 59.6	60.0	178.8	11
12	39 59.5	60.0	178.7	38 59.5	60.0	178.7	37 59.5	60.0	178.8	36 59.5	60.0	178.8	35 59.5	60.0	178.8	34 59.5	60.0	178.8	33 59.6	60.0	178.8	32 59.6	60.0	178.8	12
13	38 59.5	60.0	178.8	37 59.5	60.0	178.8	36 59.5	60.0	178.8	35 59.5	60.0	178.8	34 59.5	60.0	178.8	33 59.5	60.0	178.8	32 59.6	60.0	178.9	31 59.6	60.0	178.9	13
14	37 59.5	60.0	178.8	36 59.5	60.0	178.8	35 59.5	60.0	178.8	34 59.5	60.0	178.8	33 59.5	59.9	178.9	32 59.5	59.9	178.9	31 59.6	60.0	178.9	30 59.6	60.0	178.9	14
15	36 59.5	-60.0	178.8	35 59.5	-60.0	178.8	34 59.5	-60.0	178.8	33 59.5	-60.0	178.8	32 59.6	-60.0	178.8	31 59.6	-60.0	178.9	30 59.6	-60.0	178.9	29 59.6	-60.0	178.9	15
16	35 59.5	60.0	178.8	34 59.5	60.0	178.8	33 59.5	60.0	178.8	32 59.5	59.9	178.9	31 59.6	60.0	178.9	30 59.6	60.0	178.9	29 59.6	60.0	178.9	28 59.6	60.0	178.9	16
17	34 59.5	60.0	178.8	33 59.5	60.0	178.9	32 59.5	59.9	178.9	31 59.6	60.0	178.9	30 59.6	60.0	178.9	29 59.6	60.0	178.9	28 59.6	60.0	178.9	27 59.6	60.0	178.9	17
18	33 59.5	60.0	178.9	32 59.5	60.0	178.9	31 59.6	60.0	178.9	30 59.6	60.0	178.9	29 59.6	60.0	178.9	28 59.6	60.0	178.9	27 59.6	59.9	178.9	26 59.6	60.0	178.9	18
19	32 59.5	59.9	178.9	31 59.5	59.9	178.9	30 59.6	60.0	178.9	29 59.6	60.0	178.9	28 59.6	60.0	178.9	27 59.6	60.0	179.0	26 59.6	60.0	179.0	25 59.6	60.0	178.9	19
20	31 59.5	-60.0	178.9	30 59.6	-60.0	178.9	29 59.6	-60.0	178.9	28 59.6	-60.0	178.9	27 59.6	-60.0	178.9	26 59.6	-60.0	178.9	25 59.6	-60.0	179.0	24 59.6	-60.0	179.0	20
21	30 59.6	60.0	178.9	29 59.6	60.0	178.9	28 59.6	60.0	178.9	27 59.6	60.0	178.9	26 59.6	60.0	179.0	25 59.6	60.0	179.0	24 59.6	60.0	179.0	23 59.6	60.0	179.0	21
22	29 59.6	60.0	178.9	28 59.6	60.0	178.9	27 59.6	60.0	178.9	26 59.6	60.0	179.0	25 59.6	60.0	179.0	24 59.6	60.0	179.0	23 59.6	60.0	179.0	22 59.6	60.0	179.0	22
23	28 59.6	60.0	179.0	27 59.6	60.0	179.0	26 59.6	60.0	179.0	25 59.6	60.0	179.0	24 59.6	60.0	179.0	23 59.6	60.0	179.0	22 59.6	60.0	179.0	21 59.6	60.0	179.0	23
24	27 59.6	60.0	179.0	26 59.6	60.0	179.0	25 59.6	60.0	179.0	24 59.6	60.0	179.0	23 59.6	60.0	179.0	22 59.6	60.0	179.0	21 59.6	60.0	179.0	20 59.6	60.0	179.0	24
25	26 59.6	-60.0	179.0	25 59.6	-60.0	179.0	24 59.6	-60.0	179.0	23 59.6	-60.0	179.0	22 59.6	-60.0	179.0	21 59.6	-60.0	179.1	20 59.6	-60.0	179.1	19 59.6	-60.0	179.0	25
26	25 59.6	60.0	179.0	24 59.6	60.0	179.0	23 59.6	60.0	179.0	22 59.6	60.0	179.0	21 59.6	60.0	179.1	20 59.6	60.0	179.1	19 59.6	60.0	179.1	18 59.6	60.0	179.1	26
27	24 59.6	60.0	179.0	23 59.6	60.0	179.0	22 59.6	60.0	179.0	21 59.6	60.0	179.1	20 59.6	60.0	179.1	19 59.6	60.0	179.1	18 59.7	60.0	179.1	17 59.7	60.0	179.1	27
28	23 59.6	60.0	179.1	22 59.6	60.0	179.1	21 59.6	60.0	179.1	20 59.6	60.0	179.1	19 59.6	60.0	179.1	18 59.6	60.0	179.1	17 59.7	59.9	179.1	16 59.7	60.0	179.1	28
29	22 59.6	60.0	179.1	21 59.6	60.0	179.1	20 59.6	60.0	179.1	19 59.6	60.0	179.1	18 59.6	60.0	179.1	17 59.6	60.0	179.1	16 59.7	60.0	179.1	15 59.7	60.0	179.1	29
30	21 59.6	-60.0	179.1	20 59.6	-60.0	179.1	19 59.6	-60.0	179.1	18 59.6	-60.0	179.1	17 59.6	-59.9	179.1	16 59.7	-60.0	179.1	15 59.7	-60.0	179.1	14 59.7	-60.0	179.1	30
31	20 59.6	60.0	179.1	19 59.6	60.0	179.1	18 59.6	60.0	179.1	17 59.6	60.0	179.1	16 59.7	60.0	179.1	15 59.7	60.0	179.2	14 59.7	60.0	179.1	13 59.7	60.0	179.1	31
32	19 59.6	60.0	179.1	18 59.6	60.0	179.1	17 59.6	60.0	179.1	16 59.6	59.9	179.1	15 59.7	60.0	179.2	14 59.7	60.0	179.2	13 59.7	60.0	179.2	12 59.7	60.0	179.1	32
33	18 59.6	60.0	179.1	17 59.6	60.0	179.1	16 59.6	59.9	179.1	15 59.7	60.0	179.2	14 59.7	60.0	179.2	13 59.7	60.0	179.2	12 59.7	60.0	179.2	11 59.7	60.0	179.2	33
34	17 59.6	60.0	179.1	16 59.6	59.9	179.1	15 59.7	60.0	179.1	14 59.7	60.0	179.2	13 59.7	60.0	179.2	12 59.7	60.0	179.2	11 59.7	60.0	179.2	10 59.7	60.0	179.2	34
35	16 59.6	-59.9	179.1	15 59.7	-60.0	179.1	14 59.7	-60.0	179.2	13 59.7	-60.0	179.2	12 59.7	-60.0	179.2	11 59.7	-60.0	179.2	10 59.7	-60.0	179.2	9 59.7	-60.0	179.2	35
36	15 59.7	60.0	179.2	14 59.7	60.0	179.2	13 59.7	60.0	179.2	12 59.7	60.0	179.2	11 59.7	60.0	179.2	10 59.7	60.0	179.2	9 59.7	60.0	179.2	8 59.7	59.9	179.2	36
37	14 59.7	60.0	179.2	13 59.7	60.0	179.2	12 59.7	60.0	179.2	11 59.7	60.0	179.2	10 59.7	60.0	179.2	9 59.7	60.0	179.2	8 59.7	60.0	179.2	7 59.7	60.0	179.2	37
38	13 59.7	60.0	179.2	12 59.7	60.0	179.2	11 59.7	60.0	179.2	10 59.7	60.0	179.2	9 59.7	60.0	179.2	8 59.7	60.0	179.2	7 59.7	60.0	179.2	6 59.7	60.0	179.2	38
39	12 59.7	60.0	179.2	11 59.7	60.0	179.2	10 59.7	60.0	179.2	9 59.7	60.0	179.2	8 59.7	60.0	179.2	7 59.7	60.0	179.2	6 59.7	60.0	179.2	5 59.7	60.0	179.2	39
40	11 59.7	-60.0	179.2	10 59.7	-60.0	179.2	9 59.7	-60.0	179.2	8 59.7	-60.0	179.2	7 59.7	-60.0	179.2	6 59.7	-60.0	179.2	5 59.7	-60.0	179.2	4 59.7	-60.0	179.2	40
41	10 59.7	60.0	179.2	9 59.7	60.0	179.2	8 59.7	60.0	179.2	7 59.7	60.0	179.3	6 59.7	60.0	179.3	5 59.7	60.0	179.3	4 59.7	60.0	179.3	3 59.7	60.0	179.3	41
42	9 59.7	60.0	179.2	8 59.7	60.0	179.2	7 59.7	60.0	179.3	6 59.7	60.0	179.3	5 59.7	60.0	179.3	4 59.7	60.0	179.3	3 59.7	60.0	179.3	2 59.7	60.0	179.3	42
43	8 59.7	60.0	179.3	7 59.7	60.0	179.3	6 59.7	60.0	179.3	5 59.7	60.0	179.3	4 59.7	60.0	179.3	3 59.7	60.0	179.3	2 59.7	60.0	179.3	1 59.7	60.0	179.3	43
44	7 59.7	60.0	179.3	6 59.7	60.0	179.3	5 59.7	60.0	179.3	4 59.7	60.0	179.3	3 59.7	60.0	179.3	2 59.7	60.0	179.3	1 59.7	60.0	179.3	0 59.7	60.0	179.3	44

LATITUDE CONTRARY NAME TO DECLINATION

Dec.	38° Hc	d	Z	39° Hc	d	Z	40° Hc	d	Z	41° Hc	d	Z	42° Hc	d	Z	43° Hc	d	Z	44° Hc	d	Z	45° Hc	d	Z	Dec.
0	51 57.3	-59.9	176.8	50 57.4	-59.9	176.8	49 57.5	-59.9	176.9	48 57.6	-60.0	177.0	47 57.7	-60.0	177.0	46 57.8	-60.0	177.1	45 57.8	-59.9	177.1	44 57.9	-60.0	177.2	0
1	50 57.4	60.0	176.8	49 57.5	60.0	176.9	48 57.6	60.0	177.0	47 57.6	59.9	177.0	46 57.7	59.9	177.1	45 57.8	60.0	177.1	44 57.8	60.0	177.2	43 57.9	59.9	177.2	1
2	49 57.4	59.9	176.9	48 57.5	59.9	176.9	47 57.6	59.9	177.0	46 57.7	60.0	177.1	45 57.8	60.0	177.1	44 57.8	59.9	177.2	43 57.9	60.0	177.2	42 57.9	60.0	177.3	2
3	48 57.5	60.0	177.0	47 57.6	60.0	177.0	46 57.7	60.0	177.1	45 57.7	59.9	177.1	44 57.8	60.0	177.2	43 57.9	60.0	177.2	42 57.9	59.9	177.3	41 58.0	60.0	177.3	3
4	47 57.5	59.9	177.0	46 57.6	59.9	177.1	45 57.7	60.0	177.1	44 57.8	60.0	177.2	43 57.8	59.9	177.2	42 57.9	60.0	177.3	41 58.0	60.0	177.3	40 58.0	59.9	177.4	4
5	46 57.6	-60.0	177.1	45 57.7	-60.0	177.1	44 57.8	-59.9	177.2	43 57.8	-59.9	177.2	42 57.9	-60.0	177.3	41 58.0	-60.0	177.3	40 58.0	-59.9	177.4	39 58.1	-60.0	177.4	5
6	45 57.6	59.9	177.1	44 57.7	59.9	177.2	43 57.8	60.0	177.2	42 57.9	60.0	177.3	41 57.9	60.0	177.3	40 58.0	60.0	177.4	39 58.0	60.0	177.4	38 58.1	60.0	177.4	6
7	44 57.7	60.0	177.2	43 57.8	60.0	177.2	42 57.8	60.0	177.3	41 57.9	59.9	177.3	40 58.0	59.9	177.4	39 58.0	59.9	177.4	38 58.1	60.0	177.4	37 58.1	59.9	177.5	7
8	43 57.7	60.0	177.2	42 57.8	60.0	177.3	41 57.9	59.9	177.3	40 57.9	60.0	177.4	39 58.0	60.0	177.4	38 58.1	60.0	177.4	37 58.1	60.0	177.5	36 58.2	60.0	177.5	8
9	42 57.8	60.0	177.3	41 57.8	59.9	177.3	40 57.9	60.0	177.4	39 58.0	60.0	177.4	38 58.0	60.0	177.4	37 58.1	60.0	177.5	36 58.1	59.9	177.5	35 58.2	60.0	177.6	9
10	41 57.8	-59.9	177.4	40 57.9	-60.0	177.4	39 57.9	-59.9	177.4	38 58.0	-60.0	177.5	37 58.1	-60.0	177.5	36 58.1	-60.0	177.5	35 58.2	-60.0	177.6	34 58.2	-60.0	177.6	10
11	40 57.9	59.9	177.4	39 57.9	59.9	177.4	38 58.0	60.0	177.5	37 58.0	59.9	177.5	36 58.1	60.0	177.5	35 58.1	59.9	177.6	34 58.2	60.0	177.6	33 58.3	59.9	177.6	11
12	39 57.9	60.0	177.4	38 58.0	60.0	177.5	37 58.0	60.0	177.5	36 58.1	60.0	177.6	35 58.1	59.9	177.6	34 58.2	60.0	177.6	33 58.2	59.9	177.6	32 58.3	60.0	177.7	12
13	38 57.9	60.0	177.5	37 58.0	60.0	177.5	36 58.1	59.9	177.6	35 58.1	60.0	177.6	34 58.1	60.0	177.6	33 58.2	60.0	177.6	32 58.3	60.0	177.7	31 58.3	60.0	177.7	13
14	37 58.0	59.9	177.5	36 58.0	60.0	177.6	35 58.1	60.0	177.6	34 58.1	59.9	177.6	33 58.2	60.0	177.7	32 58.2	59.9	177.7	31 58.3	60.0	177.7	30 58.3	60.0	177.7	14
15	36 58.0	-60.0	177.6	35 58.1	-60.0	177.6	34 58.1	-60.0	177.6	33 58.2	-60.0	177.7	32 58.2	-60.0	177.7	31 58.3	-60.0	177.7	30 58.3	-60.0	177.7	29 58.3	-59.9	177.8	15
16	35 58.0	59.9	177.7	34 58.1	60.0	177.7	33 58.1	59.9	177.7	32 58.2	60.0	177.7	31 58.2	59.9	177.7	30 58.3	60.0	177.8	29 58.3	59.9	177.8	28 58.4	60.0	177.8	16
17	34 58.1	60.0	177.7	33 58.1	59.9	177.7	32 58.2	60.0	177.7	31 58.2	59.9	177.7	30 58.3	60.0	177.8	29 58.3	60.0	177.8	28 58.4	60.0	177.8	27 58.4	60.0	177.8	17
18	33 58.1	60.0	177.7	32 58.2	60.0	177.7	31 58.2	60.0	177.7	30 58.2	60.0	177.8	29 58.3	60.0	177.8	28 58.3	60.0	177.8	27 58.4	60.0	177.8	26 58.4	60.0	177.9	18
19	32 58.1	59.9	177.8	31 58.2	60.0	177.8	30 58.2	59.9	177.8	29 58.3	60.0	177.8	28 58.3	59.9	177.8	27 58.4	59.9	177.9	26 58.4	60.0	177.9	25 58.4	59.9	177.9	19
20	31 58.2	-60.0	177.8	30 58.2	-60.0	177.8	29 58.3	-60.0	177.8	28 58.3	-60.0	177.9	27 58.3	-60.0	177.9	26 58.4	-60.0	177.9	25 58.4	-59.9	177.9	24 58.5	-60.0	177.9	20
21	30 58.2	59.9	177.9	29 58.2	59.9	177.9	28 58.3	60.0	177.9	27 58.3	59.9	177.9	26 58.4	60.0	177.9	25 58.4	59.9	177.9	24 58.5	60.0	177.9	23 58.5	60.0	178.0	21
22	29 58.2	60.0	177.9	28 58.3	60.0	177.9	27 58.3	60.0	177.9	26 58.4	60.0	177.9	25 58.4	59.9	177.9	24 58.4	60.0	178.0	23 58.5	60.0	178.0	22 58.5	60.0	178.0	22
23	28 58.3	60.0	177.9	27 58.3	60.0	177.9	26 58.3	59.9	177.9	25 58.4	60.0	178.0	24 58.4	60.0	178.0	23 58.5	60.0	178.0	22 58.5	60.0	178.0	21 58.5	60.0	178.0	23
24	27 58.3	59.9	177.9	26 58.3	59.9	178.0	25 58.4	60.0	178.0	24 58.4	59.9	178.0	23 58.4	60.0	178.0	22 58.5	60.0	178.0	21 58.5	59.9	178.0	20 58.5	59.9	178.0	24
25	26 58.3	-59.9	178.0	25 58.4	-60.0	178.0	24 58.4	-60.0	178.0	23 58.4	-60.0	178.0	22 58.5	-60.0	178.0	21 58.5	-60.0	178.1	20 58.5	-60.0	178.1	19 58.6	-60.0	178.1	25
26	25 58.4	60.0	178.0	24 58.4	60.0	178.0	23 58.4	60.0	178.0	22 58.5	60.0	178.1	21 58.5	60.0	178.1	20 58.5	59.9	178.1	19 58.6	60.0	178.1	18 58.6	60.0	178.1	26
27	24 58.4	60.0	178.0	23 58.4	60.0	178.1	22 58.4	60.0	178.1	21 58.5	60.0	178.1	20 58.5	60.0	178.1	19 58.6	60.0	178.1	18 58.6	60.0	178.1	17 58.6	60.0	178.1	27
28	23 58.4	60.0	178.1	22 58.4	59.9	178.1	21 58.5	60.0	178.1	20 58.5	60.0	178.1	19 58.5	59.9	178.1	18 58.6	60.0	178.1	17 58.6	60.0	178.1	16 58.6	60.0	178.2	28
29	22 58.4	59.9	178.1	21 58.5	60.0	178.1	20 58.5	60.0	178.1	19 58.5	59.9	178.1	18 58.6	60.0	178.2	17 58.6	60.0	178.2	16 58.6	59.9	178.2	15 58.7	59.9	178.2	29
30	21 58.5	-59.9	178.1	20 58.5	-60.0	178.1	19 58.5	-60.0	178.2	18 58.6	-60.0	178.2	17 58.6	-60.0	178.2	16 58.6	-59.9	178.2	15 58.6	-60.0	178.2	14 58.7	-60.0	178.3	30
31	20 58.5	60.0	178.2	19 58.5	60.0	178.2	18 58.5	59.9	178.2	17 58.6	60.0	178.2	16 58.6	60.0	178.2	15 58.6	60.0	178.2	14 58.7	60.0	178.2	13 58.7	60.0	178.3	31
32	19 58.5	60.0	178.2	18 58.5	60.0	178.2	17 58.6	60.0	178.2	16 58.6	60.0	178.2	15 58.6	59.9	178.3	14 58.7	60.0	178.3	13 58.7	60.0	178.3	12 58.7	60.0	178.3	32
33	18 58.5	60.0	178.2	17 58.6	59.9	178.2	16 58.6	60.0	178.3	15 58.6	60.0	178.3	14 58.6	60.0	178.3	13 58.7	60.0	178.3	12 58.7	60.0	178.3	11 58.7	60.0	178.3	33
34	17 58.6	59.9	178.3	16 58.6	60.0	178.3	15 58.6	60.0	178.3	14 58.6	59.9	178.3	13 58.7	60.0	178.3	12 58.7	59.9	178.3	11 58.7	59.9	178.3	10 58.7	59.9	178.3	34
35	16 58.6	-60.0	178.3	15 58.6	-60.0	178.3	14 58.6	-60.0	178.3	13 58.7	-60.0	178.3	12 58.7	-60.0	178.3	11 58.7	-60.0	178.3	10 58.7	-60.0	178.3	9 58.8	-60.0	178.3	35
36	15 58.6	60.0	178.3	14 58.6	59.9	178.3	13 58.7	59.9	178.3	12 58.7	60.0	178.4	11 58.7	59.9	178.4	10 58.7	59.9	178.4	9 58.8	60.0	178.4	8 58.8	60.0	178.4	36
37	14 58.6	60.0	178.4	13 58.7	60.0	178.4	12 58.7	60.0	178.4	11 58.7	60.0	178.4	10 58.7	60.0	178.4	9 58.8	60.0	178.4	8 58.8	60.0	178.4	7 58.8	60.0	178.4	37
38	13 58.7	60.0	178.4	12 58.7	60.0	178.4	11 58.7	60.0	178.4	10 58.7	59.9	178.4	9 58.8	59.9	178.4	8 58.8	60.0	178.4	7 58.8	60.0	178.4	6 58.8	60.0	178.4	38
39	12 58.7	60.0	178.4	11 58.7	59.9	178.4	10 58.7	59.9	178.4	9 58.8	60.0	178.4	8 58.8	60.0	178.4	7 58.8	60.0	178.4	6 58.8	59.9	178.4	5 58.8	59.9	178.4	39
40	11 58.7	-60.0	178.4	10 58.7	-59.9	178.4	9 58.8	-60.0	178.5	8 58.8	-60.0	178.5	7 58.8	-60.0	178.5	6 58.8	-60.0	178.5	5 58.8	-60.0	178.5	4 58.9	-60.0	178.5	40
41	10 58.7	59.9	178.5	9 58.8	60.0	178.5	8 58.8	60.0	178.5	7 58.8	59.9	178.5	6 58.8	60.0	178.5	5 58.8	59.9	178.5	4 58.9	60.0	178.5	3 58.9	60.0	178.5	41
42	9 58.8	60.0	178.5	8 58.8	60.0	178.5	7 58.8	60.0	178.5	6 58.8	60.0	178.5	5 58.8	59.9	178.5	4 58.9	60.0	178.5	3 58.9	60.0	178.5	2 58.9	60.0	178.5	42
43	8 58.8	60.0	178.5	7 58.8	60.0	178.5	6 58.8	60.0	178.5	5 58.8	60.0	178.5	4 58.9	60.0	178.5	3 58.9	60.0	178.5	2 58.9	60.0	178.5	1 58.9	59.9	178.5	43
44	7 58.8	60.0	178.5	6 58.8	60.0	178.6	5 58.8	59.9	178.6	4 58.9	60.0	178.6	3 58.9	60.0	178.6	2 58.9	60.0	178.6	1 58.9	59.9	178.6	0 58.9	-59.9	178.6	44

5°, 355° L.H.A.　　LATITUDE SAME NAME AS DECLINATION

N. Lat. { L.H.A. greater than 180°......Zn=Z ; L.H.A. less than 180°.........Zn=360°−Z }

Dec.	38° Hc	d	Z	39° Hc	d	Z	40° Hc	d	Z	41° Hc	d	Z	42° Hc	d	Z	43° Hc	d	Z	44° Hc	d	Z	45° Hc	d	Z	Dec.
0	51 43.3	+59.6	171.9	50 43.9	+59.6	172.1	49 44.5	+59.6	172.2	48 45.0	+59.7	172.4	47 45.5	+59.7	172.6	46 46.0	+59.7	172.7	45 46.5	+59.7	172.8	44 46.9	+59.8	172.9	0
1	52 42.9	59.6	171.7	51 43.5	59.6	171.9	50 44.1	59.7	172.1	49 44.7	59.7	172.2	48 45.2	59.7	172.4	47 45.7	59.8	172.6	46 46.2	59.8	172.7	45 46.7	59.8	172.8	1
2	53 42.5	59.6	171.5	52 43.2	59.6	171.7	51 43.8	59.6	171.9	50 44.4	59.6	172.1	49 44.9	59.7	172.3	48 45.5	59.7	172.5	47 46.0	59.7	172.6	46 46.5	59.8	172.8	2
3	54 42.1	59.6	171.3	53 42.8	59.6	171.5	52 43.4	59.6	171.7	51 44.0	59.7	171.9	50 44.6	59.7	172.1	49 45.2	59.7	172.3	48 45.7	59.7	172.4	47 46.2	59.8	172.6	3
4	55 41.7	59.5	171.1	54 42.4	59.5	171.3	53 43.1	59.6	171.5	52 43.7	59.5	171.7	51 44.3	59.7	171.9	50 45.0	59.7	172.1	49 45.4	59.7	172.3	48 46.0	59.7	172.4	4
5	56 41.2	+59.5	170.9	55 42.0	+59.5	171.1	54 42.7	+59.5	171.4	53 43.3	+59.6	171.6	52 44.0	+59.6	171.8	51 44.6	+59.7	171.9	50 45.1	+59.7	172.1	49 45.7	+59.7	172.3	5
6	57 40.7	59.5	170.7	56 41.5	59.5	170.9	55 42.2	59.6	171.2	54 42.9	59.6	171.4	53 43.6	59.6	171.6	52 44.2	59.6	171.8	51 44.8	59.7	172.0	50 45.4	59.7	172.1	6
7	58 40.2	59.5	170.4	57 41.0	59.5	170.7	56 41.8	59.6	170.9	55 42.5	59.6	171.2	54 43.2	59.6	171.4	53 43.9	59.6	171.6	52 44.5	59.6	171.8	51 45.1	59.7	172.0	7
8	59 39.7	59.4	170.2	58 40.5	59.5	170.4	57 41.4	59.5	170.7	56 42.1	59.5	171.0	55 42.8	59.6	171.2	54 43.5	59.7	171.4	53 44.2	59.7	171.6	52 44.8	59.7	171.8	8
9	60 39.1	59.4	169.9	59 40.0	59.5	170.2	58 40.9	59.5	170.5	57 41.7	59.5	170.7	56 42.4	59.6	171.0	55 43.2	59.6	171.2	54 43.9	59.6	171.4	53 44.5	59.7	171.6	9
10	61 38.5	+59.4	169.6	60 39.5	+59.4	169.9	59 40.4	+59.4	170.2	58 41.2	+59.5	170.5	57 42.0	+59.6	170.8	56 42.8	+59.5	171.0	55 43.5	+59.6	171.2	54 44.2	+59.6	171.5	10
11	62 37.9	59.3	169.3	61 38.9	59.3	169.6	60 39.8	59.4	169.9	59 40.7	59.5	170.2	58 41.6	59.5	170.6	57 42.3	59.6	170.8	56 43.1	59.6	171.0	55 43.8	59.6	171.3	11
12	63 37.2	59.2	168.9	62 38.2	59.4	169.3	61 39.2	59.4	169.7	60 40.2	59.4	169.9	59 41.1	59.5	170.3	58 41.9	59.5	170.6	57 42.7	59.6	170.8	56 43.4	59.7	171.1	12
13	64 36.4	59.3	168.6	63 37.6	59.2	169.0	62 38.6	59.3	169.4	61 39.6	59.4	169.6	60 40.6	59.4	170.0	59 41.4	59.5	170.3	58 42.3	59.5	170.6	57 43.1	59.6	170.9	13
14	65 35.6	59.1	168.2	64 36.8	59.2	168.6	63 38.0	59.3	169.0	62 39.0	59.4	169.4	61 40.0	59.4	169.7	60 40.9	59.5	170.1	59 41.8	59.5	170.4	58 42.6	59.6	170.6	14
15	66 34.7	+59.1	167.8	65 36.0	+59.2	168.2	64 37.3	+59.2	168.7	63 38.4	+59.3	169.1	62 39.4	+59.4	169.4	61 40.4	+59.5	169.8	60 41.3	+59.5	170.1	59 42.2	+59.5	170.4	15
16	67 33.8	59.0	167.3	66 35.2	59.1	167.8	65 36.5	59.2	168.3	64 37.7	59.3	168.7	63 38.8	59.4	169.1	62 39.9	59.4	169.5	61 40.8	59.5	169.8	60 41.7	59.6	170.1	16
17	68 32.8	58.9	166.8	67 34.3	59.0	167.4	66 35.7	59.1	167.9	65 37.0	59.2	168.4	64 38.2	59.2	168.7	63 39.3	59.3	169.2	62 40.3	59.4	169.5	61 41.3	59.4	169.9	17
18	69 31.7	58.7	166.3	68 33.3	58.9	166.9	67 34.8	59.0	167.4	66 36.2	59.1	168.0	65 37.4	59.3	168.4	64 38.6	59.4	168.8	63 39.7	59.4	169.2	62 40.7	59.5	169.6	18
19	70 30.4	58.7	165.7	69 32.2	58.8	166.4	68 33.8	59.0	167.0	67 35.3	59.1	167.5	66 36.7	59.1	168.0	65 37.9	59.3	168.5	64 39.1	59.3	168.9	63 40.2	59.4	169.3	19
20	71 29.1	+58.5	165.1	70 31.0	+58.7	165.8	69 32.8	+58.8	166.4	68 34.4	+58.9	167.0	67 35.8	+59.1	167.6	66 37.2	+59.2	168.1	65 38.4	+59.3	168.5	64 39.6	+59.3	169.0	20
21	72 27.6	58.3	164.3	71 29.7	58.6	165.1	70 31.6	58.7	165.9	69 33.3	58.9	166.5	68 34.9	59.0	167.2	67 36.4	59.1	167.7	66 37.7	59.2	168.2	65 38.9	59.3	168.6	21
22	73 25.9	58.1	163.5	72 28.2	58.4	164.4	71 30.3	58.6	165.2	70 32.2	58.8	166.0	69 33.9	58.9	166.6	68 35.5	59.0	167.2	67 36.9	59.1	167.7	66 38.2	59.3	168.2	22
23	74 24.0	57.9	162.6	73 26.6	58.3	163.6	72 28.9	58.4	164.5	71 31.0	58.6	165.3	70 32.8	58.8	166.1	69 34.5	59.0	166.7	68 36.0	59.1	167.3	67 37.5	59.1	167.8	23
24	75 21.9	57.6	161.6	74 24.8	57.9	162.8	73 27.3	58.3	163.8	72 29.6	58.5	164.7	71 31.6	58.7	165.4	70 33.5	58.8	166.1	69 35.1	59.0	166.8	68 36.6	59.1	167.4	24
25	76 19.5	+57.2	160.5	75 22.7	+57.7	161.8	74 25.6	+57.9	162.9	73 28.1	+58.2	163.9	72 30.3	+58.5	164.8	71 32.3	+58.7	165.6	70 34.1	+58.9	166.3	69 35.7	+59.0	166.9	25
26	77 16.7	56.8	159.2	76 20.4	57.3	160.7	75 23.5	57.8	161.9	74 26.3	58.1	163.0	73 28.8	58.3	164.0	72 31.0	58.5	164.9	71 33.0	58.7	165.7	70 34.7	58.9	166.4	26
27	78 13.5	56.1	157.6	77 17.7	56.8	159.3	76 21.3	57.3	160.8	75 24.4	57.8	162.0	74 27.1	58.1	163.2	73 29.5	58.4	164.1	72 31.7	58.6	165.0	71 33.6	58.8	165.8	27
28	79 09.7	55.4	155.8	78 14.5	56.3	157.8	77 18.6	56.9	159.5	76 22.2	57.4	160.9	75 25.2	57.9	162.2	74 27.9	58.2	163.3	73 30.3	58.4	164.3	72 32.4	58.7	165.1	28
29	80 05.1	54.5	153.7	79 10.8	55.6	156.0	78 15.5	56.4	158.0	77 19.6	57.0	159.7	76 23.1	57.5	161.1	75 26.1	57.9	162.4	74 28.7	58.3	163.4	73 31.1	58.5	164.4	29
30	80 59.6	+53.2	151.2	80 06.4	+54.6	153.9	79 11.9	+55.7	156.2	78 16.6	+56.5	158.2	77 20.6	+57.1	159.9	76 24.0	+57.6	161.3	75 27.0	+57.9	162.5	74 29.6	+58.2	163.6	30
31	81 52.8	51.5*	148.1	81 01.0	53.4	151.4	80 07.6	54.8	154.2	79 13.1	55.8	156.5	78 17.7	56.5	158.2	77 21.6	57.2	160.2	76 24.9	57.7	161.5	75 27.8	58.1	162.7	31
32	82 44.3	49.0*	144.2	81 54.4	51.6*	148.3	81 02.4	53.5	151.7	80 08.9	54.9	154.4	79 14.2	56.0	156.7	78 18.8	56.6	158.6	77 22.6	57.2	160.2	76 25.9	57.7	161.6	32
33	83 33.3	45.5*	139.4	82 46.0	49.2*	144.5	81 55.9	51.8*	148.6	81 03.8	53.7	151.9	80 10.2	55.0	154.7	79 15.4	56.1	156.9	78 19.8	56.8	158.8	77 23.6	57.3	160.4	33
34	84 18.8	40.4*	133.2	83 35.2	45.8*	139.7	82 47.7	49.5*	144.8	81 57.5	52.0*	148.9	81 05.2	53.9	152.2	80 11.5	55.1	154.9	79 16.6	56.2	157.1	78 23.6	56.9	159.0	34
35	84 59.2	+32.9*	125.2	84 21.0	+40.7*	133.5	83 37.2	+46.0*	140.0	82 49.5	+49.7*	145.1	81 59.1	+52.2*	149.2	81 06.6	+54.1	152.5	80 12.8	+55.3	155.2	79 17.8	+56.3	157.4	35
36	85 32.1	22.5*	115.1	85 01.7	33.2*	125.6	84 24.3	41.0*	133.9	83 39.2	46.3*	140.4	82 51.3	49.9*	145.5	82 00.7	52.4	149.5	81 08.1	54.2	152.8	80 14.1	55.5	155.4	36
37	85 54.6	9.0*	102.6	85 34.9	22.8*	115.6	85 04.2	33.6*	125.6	84 25.5	41.4*	134.2	83 41.2	46.4*	140.7	82 53.1	50.2*	149.8	82 02.3	52.6	149.8	81 09.6	54.3	153.1	37
38	86 03.6	-5.9*	88.5	85 57.7	9.2*	102.8	85 37.8	23.1*	115.6	85 06.9	33.9*	126.3	84 27.8	41.7*	134.6	83 43.3	46.9*	141.1	82 54.9	50.4*	146.2	82 03.9	52.9	150.2	38
39	85 57.7	19.9*	74.1	86 06.0	6.0*	88.4	86 00.9	9.3*	102.8	85 40.8	23.4*	115.9	85 09.5	34.3*	126.3	84 30.2	42.0*	141.5	83 45.3	47.3*	141.5	82 56.8	50.6	146.5	39
40	85 37.8	-30.9*	61.2	86 00.9	-20.1*	73.9	86 10.2	-6.0*	88.4	86 04.2	+9.4*	103.1	85 43.8	+23.7*	115.9	85 12.2	+34.7*	127.0	84 32.6	+42.3*	135.4	83 47.4	+47.6*	141.9	40
41	85 06.9	39.1*	50.6	85 40.8	31.3*	60.8	86 04.2	20.4*	73.6	86 13.6	6.1*	88.4	86 07.5	9.6*	103.3	85 46.9	24.0*	116.6	85 14.9	35.1*	127.4	84 35.0	42.7*	135.8	41
42	84 27.8	44.5*	42.2	85 09.5	39.3*	50.1	85 45.8	31.6*	60.5	86 07.5	20.8*	73.4	86 17.1	6.2*	88.4	86 10.9	9.7*	103.5	85 50.0	24.3*	117.0	85 17.7	35.4*	127.9	42
43	83 43.3	48.4*	35.7	84 30.2	45.2*	42.2	85 12.2	39.6*	49.7	85 46.9	32.0*	60.1	86 10.9	20.9*	73.4	86 14.3	6.3*	88.3	86 14.3	9.9*	103.7	85 53.1	24.7*	117.3	43
44	82 54.9	51.0*	30.6	83 45.3	48.5*	35.2	84 32.6	45.2*	41.2	85 14.9	39.9*	49.2	85 50.0	32.3*	59.6	86 14.3	21.2*	72.9	86 24.2	-6.4*	88.3	86 17.8	+10.1*	103.9	44

6°, 354° L.H.A.   LATITUDE SAME NAME AS DECLINATION

N. Lat. { L.H.A. greater than 180° ...... Zn=Z
          L.H.A. less than 180° .... Zn=360°−Z }

Dec.	38° Hc	38° d	38° Z	39° Hc	39° d	39° Z	40° Hc	40° d	40° Z	41° Hc	41° d	41° Z	42° Hc	42° d	42° Z	43° Hc	43° d	43° Z	44° Hc	44° d	44° Z	45° Hc	45° d	45° Z	Dec.
0	51 36.0	+59.5	170.3	50 36.8	+59.5	170.3	49 37.6	+59.6	170.7	48 38.4	+59.6	170.9	47 39.2	+59.5	171.1	46 39.9	+59.6	171.2	45 40.6	+59.6	171.4	44 41.2	+59.7	171.5	0
1	52 35.5	59.4	170.1	51 36.3	59.5	170.1	50 37.2	59.5	170.5	49 38.0	59.5	170.7	48 38.7	59.6	170.9	47 39.5	59.6	171.1	46 40.2	59.7	171.2	45 40.9	59.6	171.4	1
2	53 34.9	59.4	169.9	52 35.8	59.5	170.1	51 36.7	59.5	170.3	50 37.5	59.5	170.5	49 38.3	59.6	170.7	48 39.1	59.6	170.9	47 39.8	59.7	171.1	46 40.5	59.7	171.2	2
3	54 34.3	59.4	169.6	53 35.3	59.4	169.9	52 36.2	59.5	170.1	51 37.0	59.5	170.3	50 37.9	59.6	170.5	49 38.7	59.6	170.7	48 39.4	59.6	170.9	47 40.2	59.6	171.1	3
4	55 33.7	59.3	169.4	54 34.7	59.4	169.6	53 35.6	59.5	169.9	52 36.5	59.5	170.1	51 37.4	59.5	170.3	50 38.3	59.5	170.5	49 39.1	59.5	170.7	48 39.8	59.6	170.9	4
5	56 33.0	+59.3	169.1	55 34.1	+59.3	169.4	54 35.1	+59.4	169.6	53 36.0	+59.5	169.9	52 36.9	+59.5	170.1	51 37.8	+59.5	170.3	50 38.6	+59.6	170.5	49 39.4	+59.6	170.7	5
6	57 32.3	59.3	168.8	56 33.4	59.4	169.1	55 34.5	59.3	169.4	54 35.5	59.4	169.7	53 36.4	59.5	169.9	52 37.3	59.5	170.1	51 38.2	59.5	170.4	50 39.0	59.6	170.6	6
7	58 31.6	59.2	168.5	57 32.8	59.3	168.9	56 33.9	59.3	169.1	55 34.9	59.4	169.4	54 35.9	59.4	169.7	53 36.8	59.5	169.9	52 37.7	59.5	170.2	51 38.6	59.6	170.4	7
8	59 30.8	59.2	168.2	58 32.0	59.3	168.6	57 33.2	59.3	168.9	56 34.3	59.4	169.2	55 35.3	59.4	169.4	54 36.3	59.5	169.7	53 37.3	59.5	170.0	52 38.2	59.5	170.2	8
9	60 30.0	59.1	167.9	59 31.3	59.2	168.3	58 32.5	59.3	168.6	57 33.7	59.3	168.9	56 34.8	59.3	169.2	55 35.8	59.4	169.5	54 36.8	59.4	169.7	53 37.7	59.5	170.0	9
10	61 29.1	+59.1	167.5	60 30.5	+59.1	167.9	59 31.8	+59.2	168.3	58 33.0	+59.3	168.6	57 34.1	+59.4	168.8	56 35.2	+59.4	169.2	55 36.3	+59.4	169.5	54 37.2	+59.5	169.8	10
11	62 28.2	59.0	167.2	61 29.6	59.1	167.6	60 31.0	59.2	168.0	59 32.3	59.2	168.3	58 33.5	59.3	168.7	57 34.6	59.3	169.0	56 35.7	59.4	169.3	55 36.7	59.4	169.5	11
12	63 27.2	58.9	166.9	62 28.7	59.1	167.2	61 30.2	59.1	167.6	60 31.5	59.2	168.0	59 32.8	59.3	168.4	58 34.0	59.3	168.7	57 35.1	59.4	169.0	56 36.2	59.5	169.3	12
13	64 26.1	58.9	166.3	63 27.8	58.9	166.8	62 29.3	59.1	167.2	61 30.7	59.1	167.7	60 32.1	59.2	168.1	59 33.3	59.3	168.4	58 34.5	59.3	168.7	57 35.7	59.4	169.0	13
14	65 25.0	58.8	165.9	64 26.7	58.9	166.4	63 28.4	59.0	166.9	62 29.9	59.1	167.3	61 31.3	59.2	167.7	60 32.6	59.2	168.1	59 33.9	59.3	168.5	58 35.1	59.3	168.8	14
15	66 23.8	+58.6	165.4	65 25.6	+58.8	165.9	64 27.4	+58.9	166.5	63 29.0	+59.0	166.9	62 30.5	+59.1	167.4	61 31.9	+59.2	167.8	60 33.2	+59.3	168.1	59 34.4	+59.4	168.5	15
16	67 22.4	58.6	164.9	66 24.4	58.7	165.5	65 26.3	58.8	166.0	64 28.0	58.9	166.5	63 29.3	59.1	167.0	62 31.5	59.1	167.4	61 32.5	59.2	167.8	60 33.8	59.3	168.2	16
17	68 21.0	58.4	164.3	67 23.1	58.6	164.9	66 25.1	58.7	165.5	65 26.9	58.9	166.1	64 28.6	59.0	166.6	63 30.2	59.1	167.1	62 31.7	59.2	167.5	61 33.1	59.2	167.9	17
18	69 19.4	58.3	163.6	68 21.7	58.5	164.4	67 23.8	58.7	165.0	66 25.8	58.8	165.6	65 27.5	58.8	166.2	64 29.3	59.0	166.7	63 30.9	59.1	167.1	62 32.3	59.2	167.6	18
19	70 17.7	58.3	163.0	69 20.2	58.5	163.7	68 22.5	58.5	164.4	67 24.6	58.7	165.1	66 26.5	58.8	165.7	65 28.3	58.9	166.2	64 30.0	59.0	166.7	63 31.5	59.2	167.2	19
20	71 15.7	+57.9	162.2	70 18.5	+58.1	163.1	69 21.0	+58.3	163.8	68 23.2	+58.6	164.5	67 25.3	+58.7	165.2	66 27.2	+58.9	165.8	65 29.0	+59.0	166.3	64 30.7	+59.0	166.8	20
21	72 13.6	57.7	161.4	71 16.6	58.0	162.3	70 19.3	58.2	163.2	69 21.8	58.4	163.9	68 24.0	58.6	164.6	67 26.1	58.7	165.3	66 28.0	58.9	165.9	65 29.7	59.0	166.4	21
22	73 11.3	57.3	160.4	72 14.6	57.7	161.5	71 17.5	58.0	162.4	70 20.2	58.2	163.3	69 22.6	58.5	164.0	68 24.8	58.7	164.7	67 26.9	58.8	165.4	66 28.7	58.9	165.9	22
23	74 08.6	57.1	159.4	73 12.3	57.4	160.5	72 15.5	57.8	161.6	71 18.4	58.0	162.5	70 21.1	58.3	163.4	69 23.5	58.5	164.1	68 25.7	58.8	164.8	67 27.7	58.8	165.5	23
24	75 05.7	56.6	158.2	74 09.7	57.1	159.5	73 13.3	57.5	160.7	72 16.5	57.8	161.7	71 19.4	58.1	162.7	70 22.0	58.3	163.5	69 24.3	58.6	164.2	68 26.5	58.7	164.9	24
25	76 02.3	+56.1	156.9	75 06.8	+56.7	158.4	74 10.8	+57.2	159.7	73 14.3	+57.6	160.8	72 17.5	+57.9	161.9	71 20.3	+58.2	162.8	70 22.9	+58.4	163.6	69 25.2	+58.6	164.4	25
26	76 58.4	55.6	155.4	76 03.5	56.3	157.0	75 08.0	56.8	158.5	73 11.9	57.3	159.8	73 15.4	57.6	161.0	72 18.5	57.9	162.0	71 21.3	58.3	162.9	70 23.8	58.6	163.7	26
27	77 54.0	54.7	153.6	76 59.8	55.6	155.5	76 04.8	56.3	157.2	75 09.2	56.8	158.7	74 13.0	57.4	160.0	73 16.4	57.8	161.1	72 19.5	58.0	162.1	71 22.2	58.3	163.0	27
28	78 48.7	53.8	151.6	77 55.4	54.9	153.8	77 01.1	55.8	155.7	76 06.0	56.5	157.4	75 10.4	56.9	158.9	74 14.2	57.4	160.1	73 17.5	57.8	161.3	72 20.5	58.1	162.3	28
29	79 42.5	52.6	149.2	78 50.3	53.9	151.8	77 56.9	55.0	154.0	77 02.5	55.5	155.9	76 07.3	56.6	157.6	75 11.6	57.0	159.0	74 15.3	57.5	160.3	73 18.6	57.9	161.4	29
30	80 35.1	+51.0	146.4	79 44.2	+52.8	149.5	78 51.9	+54.1	152.0	77 58.3	+55.2	154.3	77 03.9	+55.9	156.1	76 08.6	+56.7	157.8	75 12.8	+57.2	159.2	74 16.5	+57.5	160.5	30
31	81 26.1	48.8	143.0	80 37.0	51.1	146.7	79 46.0	52.9	149.7	78 53.5	54.2	152.3	77 59.8	55.3	154.5	77 05.3	56.1	156.4	76 10.0	56.7	158.0	75 14.0	57.3	159.4	31
32	81 14.9	45.9	138.9	81 28.1	49.1	143.3	80 38.9	51.4	146.9	79 47.7	53.1	150.0	78 55.1	54.4	152.5	78 01.4	55.4	154.7	77 06.7	56.1	156.6	76 11.3	56.8	158.2	32
33	83 00.8	42.0	133.9	82 17.2	46.2	139.2	81 30.3	49.2	143.6	80 40.8	51.6	146.9	79 49.5	53.3	150.2	78 56.8	54.5	152.8	78 02.9	55.5	155.0	77 08.1	56.3	156.8	33
34	83 42.8	36.5	127.7	83 03.4	42.2	134.2	82 19.5	46.5	139.5	81 32.4	49.5	143.9	80 42.8	51.8	147.5	79 51.3	53.5	150.5	78 58.4	54.8	153.1	78 04.4	55.7	155.2	34
35	84 19.3	+29.2	120.1	83 45.6	+36.9	128.0	83 06.0	+42.6	134.5	82 21.9	+46.8	139.9	81 34.6	+49.7	144.2	80 44.8	+52.0	147.8	79 53.2	+53.6	150.8	79 00.1	+54.9	153.3	35
36	84 48.5	19.7	110.8	84 22.5	29.6	120.4	83 48.6	37.2	128.4	83 08.7	42.9	134.9	82 24.3	46.9	140.2	81 36.8	50.0	144.6	80 46.8	52.1	148.1	79 55.0	53.8	151.1	36
37	85 08.2	+8.2	100.0	84 52.1	19.9	111.1	84 25.8	29.9	120.7	83 51.6	37.5	128.7	83 11.4	43.2	135.3	82 26.8	47.3	140.6	81 39.0	50.3	144.9	80 48.8	52.4	148.5	37
38	85 16.4	−4.4	88.2	85 12.0	+8.3	100.1	84 55.7	29.9	120.7	84 29.1	30.2	121.0	83 54.6	37.9	129.1	83 14.1	43.6	135.6	82 29.3	47.6	140.9	81 41.2	50.6	145.3	38
39	85 12.0	16.3	76.1	85 20.3	−4.4	88.1	85 15.9	+8.4	100.3	84 59.3	20.7	111.3	84 32.5	30.6	121.5	83 57.7	38.2	129.5	83 16.9	43.9	136.0	82 31.8	47.9	141.3	39
40	84 55.7	−26.6	64.9	85 15.9	−16.6	75.9	85 24.3	−4.5	88.1	85 19.8	+8.6	100.4	85 03.1	+20.7	111.8	84 35.9	+31.0	121.7	84 00.8	+38.6	129.9	83 19.7	+44.2	136.4	40
41	84 29.1	34.5	55.2	84 59.3	26.8	64.6	85 19.8	16.7	75.7	85 28.4	−4.6	88.0	85 23.8	+8.7	100.5	85 06.9	21.0	112.1	84 39.4	31.4	122.1	84 03.9	39.1	130.3	41
42	83 54.6	40.5	47.1	84 32.5	34.8	54.8	85 03.1	27.2	64.3	85 23.8	16.9	75.5	85 32.5	−4.6	88.0	85 27.9	+8.9	100.7	85 10.8	21.3	112.4	84 43.0	31.7	122.5	42
43	83 14.1	44.8	40.5	83 57.7	40.8	46.6	84 35.9	35.1	54.3	85 06.9	27.5	63.9	85 27.9	17.1	75.2	85 36.8	−4.7	88.0	85 32.1	+9.0	100.9	85 14.7	21.7	112.8	43
44	82 29.3	48.1	35.1	83 16.9	45.1	40.0	84 00.8	41.1	46.1	84 39.4	35.5	53.9	85 10.8	27.8	63.5	85 32.1	17.4	75.0	85 41.1	−4.7	87.9	85 36.4	+9.1	101.0	44

LATITUDE SAME NAME AS DECLINATION

N. Lat. { L.H.A. greater than 180° .... Zn=Z ; L.H.A. less than 180° .... Zn=360°−Z

Dec.	38° Hc	d	Z	39° Hc	d	Z	40° Hc	d	Z	41° Hc	d	Z	42° Hc	d	Z	43° Hc	d	Z	44° Hc	d	Z	45° Hc	d	Z	Dec.
0	51 27.4	+59.3	168.7	50 28.5	+59.4	169.0	49 29.6	+59.4	169.2	48 30.7	+59.4	169.6	47 31.7	+59.4	169.7	46 32.6	+59.5	169.8	45 33.6	+59.5	170.0	44 34.5	+59.5	170.1	0
1	52 26.7	59.2	168.5	51 27.9	59.2	168.7	50 29.0	59.3	169.0	49 30.1	59.4	169.4	48 31.1	59.4	169.5	47 32.1	59.5	169.6	46 33.1	59.5	169.8	45 34.0	59.6	170.0	1
2	53 25.9	59.2	168.2	52 27.1	59.3	168.5	51 28.3	59.3	168.8	50 29.5	59.3	169.2	49 30.5	59.4	169.3	48 31.6	59.4	169.4	47 32.6	59.5	169.6	46 33.6	59.5	169.8	2
3	54 25.1	59.2	167.9	53 26.4	59.3	168.2	52 27.6	59.3	168.5	51 28.8	59.3	169.0	50 29.9	59.4	169.1	49 31.0	59.5	169.2	48 32.1	59.5	169.4	47 33.1	59.5	169.6	3
4	55 24.3	59.1	167.6	54 25.6	59.2	167.9	53 26.9	59.2	168.2	52 28.1	59.3	168.7	51 29.3	59.4	168.9	50 30.5	59.3	169.0	49 31.5	59.5	169.2	48 32.6	59.5	169.4	4
5	56 23.4	+59.0	167.3	55 24.8	+59.1	167.7	54 26.1	+59.2	168.0	53 27.4	+59.3	168.4	52 28.7	+59.3	168.6	51 29.8	+59.4	168.8	50 31.0	+59.4	169.0	49 32.1	+59.4	169.2	5
6	57 22.4	59.0	167.0	56 23.9	59.1	167.3	55 25.3	59.1	167.7	54 26.7	59.2	168.2	53 28.0	59.2	168.4	52 29.2	59.4	168.6	51 30.4	59.4	168.8	50 31.5	59.4	169.0	6
7	58 21.4	59.0	166.7	57 23.0	59.1	167.0	56 24.5	59.1	167.4	55 25.9	59.2	167.9	54 27.3	59.2	168.1	53 28.6	59.3	168.3	52 29.8	59.3	168.5	51 30.9	59.5	168.8	7
8	59 20.4	58.9	166.3	58 22.1	58.9	166.7	57 23.6	59.0	167.1	56 25.1	59.2	167.6	55 26.5	59.2	167.9	54 27.9	59.4	168.1	53 29.1	59.4	168.3	52 30.4	59.4	168.6	8
9	60 19.3	58.8	165.9	59 21.0	59.0	166.3	58 22.7	59.0	166.7	57 24.3	59.0	167.3	56 25.7	59.2	167.5	55 27.1	59.3	167.7	54 28.5	59.3	168.0	53 29.7	59.4	168.3	9
10	61 18.1	+58.8	165.5	60 20.0	+58.8	166.0	59 21.7	+59.0	166.4	58 23.3	+59.1	167.0	57 24.9	+59.1	167.3	56 26.4	+59.2	167.5	55 27.8	+59.2	167.8	54 29.1	+59.3	168.1	10
11	62 16.9	58.6	165.1	61 18.8	58.8	165.6	60 20.7	58.8	166.0	59 22.4	58.9	166.6	58 24.0	59.1	166.9	57 25.6	59.1	167.2	56 27.0	59.2	167.5	55 28.4	59.3	167.8	11
12	63 15.5	58.6	164.6	62 17.6	58.7	165.1	61 19.5	58.9	165.6	60 21.3	59.0	166.2	59 23.1	59.0	166.5	58 24.7	59.1	166.8	57 26.2	59.2	167.1	56 27.7	59.2	167.5	12
13	64 14.1	58.5	164.1	63 16.3	58.6	164.7	62 18.4	58.7	165.2	61 20.3	58.8	165.8	60 22.1	59.0	166.2	59 23.8	59.1	166.5	58 25.4	59.1	166.9	57 26.9	59.2	167.3	13
14	65 12.6	58.3	163.6	64 14.9	58.5	164.2	63 17.1	58.6	164.7	62 19.1	58.8	165.3	61 21.1	58.8	165.8	60 22.9	58.9	166.2	59 24.5	59.1	166.5	58 26.1	59.2	166.9	14
15	66 10.9	+58.2	163.1	65 13.4	+58.4	163.7	64 15.7	+58.6	164.3	63 17.9	+58.7	164.8	62 19.9	+58.8	165.3	61 21.8	+59.0	165.8	60 23.6	+59.0	166.2	59 25.3	+59.1	166.6	15
16	67 09.1	58.1	162.4	66 11.8	58.3	163.1	65 14.3	58.4	163.8	64 16.6	58.6	164.3	63 18.7	58.8	164.9	62 20.8	58.8	165.4	61 22.6	59.0	165.8	60 24.4	59.1	166.3	16
17	68 07.2	57.9	161.8	67 10.1	58.1	162.5	66 12.7	58.3	163.2	65 15.2	58.5	163.8	64 17.5	58.6	164.4	63 19.6	58.8	165.0	62 21.6	58.9	165.4	61 23.5	58.9	165.9	17
18	69 05.1	57.6	161.1	68 08.2	57.9	161.9	67 11.0	58.2	162.6	66 13.7	58.3	163.2	65 16.1	58.5	163.9	64 18.4	58.6	164.5	63 20.5	58.8	165.0	62 22.4	59.0	165.5	18
19	70 02.7	57.5	160.3	69 06.1	57.8	161.2	68 09.2	58.0	162.0	67 12.0	58.2	162.6	66 14.6	58.4	163.3	65 17.0	58.6	164.0	64 19.3	58.7	164.5	63 21.4	58.8	165.1	19
20	71 00.2	+57.2	159.4	70 03.9	+57.5	160.4	69 07.2	+57.8	161.3	68 10.2	+58.1	162.1	67 13.0	+58.3	162.8	66 15.6	+58.5	163.5	65 18.0	+58.6	164.1	64 20.2	+58.8	164.7	20
21	71 57.4	56.9	158.4	71 01.4	57.2	159.5	70 05.0	57.6	160.5	69 08.3	57.8	161.4	68 11.3	58.1	162.2	67 14.1	58.3	162.9	66 16.6	58.5	163.6	65 19.0	58.6	164.2	21
22	72 54.3	56.5	157.4	71 58.6	57.0	158.6	71 02.6	57.3	159.6	70 06.1	57.7	160.6	69 09.4	57.9	161.5	68 12.4	58.1	162.3	67 15.1	58.4	163.0	66 17.6	58.6	163.7	22
23	73 50.8	56.1	156.2	72 55.6	56.6	157.5	71 59.9	57.1	158.7	71 03.8	57.4	159.8	70 07.3	57.8	160.7	69 10.5	58.0	161.6	68 13.5	58.2	162.4	67 16.2	58.4	163.1	23
24	74 46.9	55.5	154.9	73 52.2	56.2	156.4	72 57.0	56.6	157.7	72 01.2	57.1	158.7	71 05.1	57.4	159.8	70 08.5	57.8	160.9	69 11.7	58.1	161.6	68 14.6	58.3	162.5	24
25	75 42.4	+55.0	153.4	74 48.4	+55.7	155.1	73 53.6	+56.3	156.5	72 58.3	+56.8	157.8	72 02.5	+57.2	159.0	71 06.3	+57.6	160.1	70 09.8	+57.8	161.0	69 12.9	+58.1	161.9	25
26	76 37.4	54.2	151.7	75 44.1	55.0	153.6	74 49.9	55.8	155.3	73 55.1	56.4	156.7	72 59.7	56.9	158.0	72 03.9	57.3	159.2	71 07.6	57.6	160.2	70 11.0	57.9	161.1	26
27	77 31.6	53.2	149.8	76 39.1	54.3	151.9	75 45.7	55.2	153.8	74 51.5	55.9	155.4	73 56.6	56.5	156.8	73 01.2	56.9	158.2	72 05.2	57.4	159.3	71 08.9	57.7	160.4	27
28	78 24.8	52.1	147.6	77 33.4	53.4	150.0	76 40.9	54.5	152.2	75 47.4	55.3	154.0	74 53.1	56.0	155.6	73 58.1	56.6	157.1	73 02.6	57.1	158.3	72 06.6	57.5	159.5	28
29	79 16.9	50.5	145.0	78 26.8	52.3	147.8	77 35.4	53.5	150.3	76 42.7	54.6	152.4	75 49.1	55.5	154.1	74 54.7	56.2	155.8	73 59.7	56.7	157.2	73 04.1	57.1	158.5	29
30	80 07.4	+48.7	142.0	79 19.1	+50.8	145.3	78 28.9	+52.5	148.1	77 37.3	+53.8	150.5	76 44.6	+54.7	152.5	75 50.9	+55.5	154.4	74 56.4	+56.2	156.0	74 01.2	+56.8	157.5	30
31	80 56.1	46.3	138.5	80 09.9	48.9	142.3	79 21.4	51.0	145.6	78 31.1	52.6	148.3	77 39.3	53.9	150.6	76 46.4	54.9	152.8	75 52.6	55.7	154.7	74 58.0	56.4	156.2	31
32	81 42.4	43.0	134.2	80 58.8	46.5	138.8	80 12.4	49.1	142.6	79 23.7	51.2	145.8	78 33.2	52.8	148.4	77 41.3	54.1	151.0	76 48.3	55.1	153.0	75 54.4	55.8	154.9	32
33	82 25.4	38.8	129.2	81 45.3	43.3	134.5	81 01.5	46.8	139.1	80 14.9	49.4	142.9	79 26.0	51.4	145.9	78 35.4	53.0	148.9	77 43.4	54.2	151.1	76 50.2	55.2	153.3	33
34	83 04.2	33.3	123.1	82 28.6	39.2	129.5	81 48.3	43.6	134.9	81 04.3	47.0	139.4	80 17.4	49.7	142.9	79 28.4	51.6	146.4	78 37.6	53.2	149.1	77 45.4	54.4	151.5	34
35	83 37.5	+26.4	115.9	83 07.8	+33.6	123.4	82 31.9	+39.5	129.8	81 51.3	+44.0	135.2	81 07.1	+47.3	139.2	80 20.0	+49.9	143.2	79 30.8	+51.8	146.7	78 39.8	+53.4	149.5	35
36	84 03.9	17.6	107.6	83 41.4	26.7	116.3	83 11.4	34.0	123.8	82 35.3	39.8	130.2	81 54.4	44.3	135.2	81 09.9	47.6	140.1	80 22.6	50.2	143.9	79 33.2	52.1	147.1	36
37	84 21.5	+7.6	98.1	84 08.1	17.9	107.7	83 45.4	27.0	116.5	83 15.1	34.4	124.1	82 38.7	40.1	130.0	81 57.5	44.6	135.9	81 12.8	47.9	140.4	80 25.3	50.4	144.2	37
38	84 29.1	−3.1	87.8	84 26.0	+7.7	98.2	84 12.4	18.1	108.0	83 49.5	27.2	116.8	83 18.8	34.8	123.9	82 42.1	40.5	130.9	82 00.7	44.9	136.3	81 15.7	48.2	140.8	38
39	84 26.0	−13.6	77.5	84 33.7	−3.2	87.8	84 30.5	+7.8	98.2	84 16.7	18.4	108.2	83 53.6	27.6	116.5	83 22.6	35.2	124.8	82 45.6	40.9	131.3	82 03.9	45.3	136.7	39
40	84 12.4	−22.9	67.6	84 30.5	−13.8	77.3	84 38.3	−3.2	87.7	84 35.1	+8.0	98.4	84 21.2	+18.7	107.9	83 57.8	+27.9	117.4	83 26.5	+35.5	125.2	82 49.2	+41.2	131.7	40
41	83 49.5	30.7	58.8	84 16.7	23.1	67.3	84 35.1	13.9	77.1	84 43.1	−3.2	87.7	84 39.9	8.1	98.2	84 25.7	19.0	108.7	84 02.0	28.4	117.8	83 30.4	35.9	125.6	41
42	83 18.8	36.7	51.1	83 53.6	31.0	58.6	84 21.2	23.4	67.0	84 39.9	14.2	76.9	84 48.0	−3.3	87.7	84 44.7	8.2	98.5	84 30.4	19.2	108.9	84 06.3	28.8	118.1	42
43	82 42.1	41.4	44.6	83 22.6	37.0	50.6	83 57.8	31.3	57.9	84 25.7	23.7	66.7	84 44.7	14.3	77.2	84 52.9	−3.3	87.6	84 49.6	8.4	98.7	84 35.1	19.5	109.2	43
44	82 00.7	45.0	39.1	82 45.6	41.7	44.1	83 26.5	37.3	50.1	84 02.0	31.6	57.5	84 30.4	24.1	67.0	84 49.6	14.5	76.5	84 58.0	−3.4	87.6	84 54.6	8.5	98.9	44

LATITUDE SAME NAME AS DECLINATION

N. Lat. { L.H.A. greater than 180° ..... Zn=Z
L.H.A. less than 180° ..... Zn=360°−Z

Dec.	38° Hc	d	Z	39° Hc	d	Z	40° Hc	d	Z	41° Hc	d	Z	42° Hc	d	Z	43° Hc	d	Z	44° Hc	d	Z	45° Hc	d	Z	Dec.
0	51 17.5	+59.1	167.1	50 19.0	+59.1	167.4	49 20.4	+59.2	167.7	48 21.8	+59.2	167.9	47 23.1	+59.2	168.1	46 24.3	+59.4	168.2	45 25.5	+59.4	168.6	44 26.7	+59.4	168.8	0
1	52 16.6	59.0	166.9	51 18.1	59.1	167.1	50 19.6	59.1	167.4	49 21.0	59.2	167.7	48 22.3	59.3	167.9	47 23.7	59.3	168.1	46 24.9	59.4	168.4	45 26.1	59.4	168.6	1
2	53 15.6	58.9	166.6	52 17.2	59.0	166.9	51 18.7	59.1	167.1	50 20.2	59.2	167.4	49 21.6	59.2	167.7	48 23.0	59.2	167.9	47 24.3	59.3	168.1	46 25.5	59.4	168.4	2
3	54 14.5	58.9	166.2	53 16.2	59.0	166.6	52 17.8	59.1	166.9	51 19.4	59.1	167.2	50 20.8	59.2	167.4	49 22.2	59.3	167.7	48 23.6	59.3	167.9	47 24.9	59.4	168.1	3
4	55 13.4	58.9	165.9	54 15.2	58.9	166.3	53 16.9	59.0	166.6	52 18.5	59.1	166.9	51 20.0	59.2	167.2	50 21.5	59.2	167.4	49 22.9	59.3	167.7	48 24.2	59.4	167.9	4
5	56 12.3	+58.8	165.6	55 14.1	+58.9	165.9	54 15.9	+59.0	166.3	53 17.6	+59.0	166.6	52 19.2	+59.1	166.9	51 20.7	+59.2	167.2	50 22.2	+59.2	167.4	49 23.6	+59.3	167.7	5
6	57 11.1	58.7	165.2	56 13.0	58.8	165.6	55 14.9	58.9	166.0	54 16.6	59.0	166.3	53 18.3	59.1	166.6	52 19.9	59.1	166.9	51 21.4	59.2	167.2	50 22.9	59.3	167.5	6
7	58 09.8	58.7	164.8	57 11.8	58.8	165.2	56 13.8	58.8	165.6	55 15.6	58.9	166.0	54 17.4	59.0	166.3	53 19.0	59.1	166.6	52 20.6	59.2	166.9	51 22.1	59.3	167.2	7
8	59 08.5	58.5	164.4	58 10.6	58.7	164.8	57 12.6	58.7	165.2	56 14.6	58.9	165.6	55 16.4	59.0	166.0	54 18.1	59.0	166.3	53 19.8	59.1	166.7	52 21.4	59.3	167.0	8
9	60 07.0	58.5	164.0	59 09.3	58.5	164.4	58 11.4	58.7	164.9	57 13.4	58.7	165.3	56 15.4	58.9	165.7	55 17.2	59.0	166.0	54 18.9	59.1	166.4	53 20.6	59.2	166.7	9
10	61 05.5	+58.4	163.5	60 07.9	+58.5	164.0	59 10.1	+58.7	164.5	58 12.3	+58.7	164.9	57 14.3	+58.8	165.3	56 16.2	+58.9	165.7	55 18.0	+59.0	166.1	54 19.7	+59.1	166.4	10
11	62 03.9	58.3	163.0	61 06.4	58.4	163.6	60 08.8	58.4	164.1	59 11.0	58.6	164.5	58 13.1	58.8	165.0	57 15.1	58.9	165.4	56 17.0	59.0	165.8	55 18.8	59.1	166.1	11
12	63 02.2	58.1	162.5	62 04.8	58.2	163.1	61 07.4	58.4	163.6	60 09.7	58.6	164.1	59 12.0	58.6	164.6	58 14.0	58.8	165.0	57 16.0	59.0	165.5	56 17.9	59.0	165.8	12
13	64 00.3	58.0	162.0	63 03.0	58.2	162.6	62 05.8	58.2	163.2	61 08.3	58.5	163.7	60 10.7	58.6	164.2	59 12.9	58.7	164.6	58 15.0	58.8	165.1	57 16.9	59.0	165.5	13
14	64 58.3	57.9	161.4	64 01.4	58.0	162.0	63 04.2	58.1	162.7	62 06.8	58.3	163.2	61 09.3	58.5	163.7	60 11.6	58.7	164.2	59 13.8	58.8	164.7	58 15.9	58.9	165.1	14
15	65 56.2	+57.7	160.7	64 59.4	+58.0	161.5	64 02.5	+58.1	162.2	63 05.3	+58.3	162.7	62 07.9	+58.4	163.3	61 10.3	+58.6	163.8	60 12.6	+58.8	164.3	59 14.8	+58.9	164.8	15
16	66 53.9	57.5	160.1	65 57.4	57.7	160.8	65 00.6	58.0	161.5	64 03.6	58.1	162.2	63 06.3	58.3	162.8	62 08.9	58.5	163.3	61 11.4	58.6	163.9	60 13.7	58.7	164.4	16
17	67 51.4	57.3	159.3	66 55.1	57.6	160.2	65 58.6	57.8	160.9	65 01.7	58.1	161.6	64 04.7	58.2	162.3	63 07.4	58.4	162.9	62 10.0	58.6	163.4	61 12.4	58.7	164.0	17
18	68 48.7	57.1	158.5	67 52.7	57.4	159.4	66 56.4	57.6	160.2	65 59.8	57.9	161.0	65 02.9	58.1	161.7	64 05.8	58.3	162.4	63 08.6	58.4	163.0	62 11.1	58.6	163.5	18
19	69 45.8	56.7	157.6	68 50.1	57.1	158.6	67 54.0	57.5	159.5	66 57.7	57.7	160.4	66 01.0	58.0	161.1	65 04.1	58.2	161.8	64 07.0	58.4	162.5	63 09.7	58.5	163.1	19
20	70 42.5	+56.4	156.7	69 47.2	+56.8	157.8	68 51.5	+57.2	158.7	67 55.4	+57.5	159.6	66 59.0	+57.7	160.5	66 02.3	+58.0	161.2	65 05.4	+58.2	161.9	64 08.2	+58.4	162.6	20
21	71 38.9	56.1	155.6	70 44.0	56.5	156.8	69 48.7	56.9	157.9	68 52.9	57.2	158.9	67 56.7	57.6	159.8	67 00.3	57.8	160.6	66 03.6	58.1	161.3	65 06.6	58.3	162.0	21
22	72 35.0	55.6	154.5	71 40.5	56.1	155.8	70 45.6	56.6	156.9	69 50.1	57.1	158.0	68 54.3	57.3	159.0	67 58.1	57.7	159.9	67 01.7	57.9	160.6	66 04.9	58.1	161.4	22
23	73 30.6	55.0	153.2	72 36.7	55.7	154.6	71 42.2	56.2	155.9	70 47.2	56.7	157.1	69 51.7	57.1	158.2	68 55.8	57.4	159.1	67 59.6	57.7	160.0	67 03.0	58.0	160.8	23
24	74 25.6	54.5	151.7	73 32.4	55.2	153.3	72 38.4	55.8	154.8	71 43.9	56.3	156.1	70 48.8	56.8	157.2	69 53.2	57.2	158.3	68 57.3	57.5	159.3	68 01.0	57.8	160.1	24
25	75 20.1	+53.6	150.1	74 27.6	+54.5	151.9	73 34.2	+55.4	153.5	72 40.2	+55.9	154.9	71 45.6	+56.4	156.2	70 50.4	+56.9	157.4	69 54.8	+57.3	158.5	68 58.8	+57.6	159.4	25
26	76 13.7	52.8	148.3	75 22.1	53.9	150.3	74 29.5	54.8	152.1	73 36.1	55.5	153.7	72 42.0	56.0	155.1	71 47.3	56.5	156.5	70 52.1	56.9	157.6	69 56.4	57.3	158.6	26
27	77 06.5	51.7	146.2	76 16.0	52.9	148.5	75 24.3	53.9	150.5	74 31.6	54.8	152.3	73 38.0	55.6	153.9	72 43.8	56.2	155.3	71 49.0	56.7	156.6	70 53.7	57.1	157.7	27
28	77 58.2	50.3	143.9	77 08.9	51.8	146.5	76 18.2	52.9	148.6	75 26.4	54.1	150.7	74 33.6	54.9	152.5	73 40.0	55.7	154.1	72 45.7	56.3	155.6	71 50.8	56.8	156.8	28
29	78 48.5	48.6	141.2	78 00.7	50.6	144.1	77 11.3	52.1	146.7	76 20.5	53.3	149.0	75 28.6	54.3	151.0	74 35.7	55.1	152.7	73 42.0	55.8	154.3	72 47.6	56.4	155.7	29
30	79 37.1	+46.4	138.0	78 51.3	+48.8	141.4	78 03.4	+50.7	144.4	77 13.8	+52.3	147.0	76 22.9	+53.4	149.2	75 30.8	+54.5	151.2	74 37.8	+55.3	153.0	73 44.0	+55.9	154.5	30
31	80 23.5	43.8	134.4	79 40.1	46.7	138.1	78 54.1	49.1	141.1	78 06.1	50.9	144.7	77 16.3	52.5	147.2	76 25.3	53.6	149.5	75 33.1	54.6	151.4	74 39.9	55.4	153.2	31
32	81 07.3	40.4	130.1	80 26.8	44.1	134.7	79 43.2	47.0	138.6	78 57.0	49.3	142.0	78 08.8	51.1	144.9	77 18.9	52.6	147.5	76 27.7	53.8	149.7	75 35.3	54.8	151.7	32
33	81 47.7	36.1	125.1	81 10.9	40.7	130.4	80 30.2	44.3	135.0	79 46.3	47.3	138.6	78 59.9	49.6	142.3	78 11.5	51.4	145.2	77 21.5	52.8	147.8	76 30.1	54.0	150.0	33
34	82 23.8	30.6	119.3	81 51.6	36.4	125.4	81 14.5	41.1	130.7	80 33.6	44.7	135.0	79 49.5	47.5	139.2	79 02.9	49.8	142.6	78 14.3	51.6	145.5	77 24.1	53.0	148.1	34
35	82 54.4	+24.1	112.6	82 28.0	+31.0	119.6	81 55.6	+36.7	125.7	81 18.3	+41.3	131.1	80 37.0	+45.0	135.6	79 52.7	+47.9	139.6	79 05.9	+50.1	142.9	78 17.1	+51.9	145.8	35
36	83 18.5	16.1	104.9	82 59.0	24.3	112.8	82 32.3	31.4	119.9	81 59.6	37.1	126.1	81 22.0	41.7	131.4	80 40.6	45.3	136.0	79 56.0	48.1	139.9	79 09.0	50.3	143.3	36
37	83 34.6	7.3	96.5	83 23.3	16.4	105.1	83 03.7	24.6	113.1	82 36.7	31.7	120.0	82 03.7	37.5	126.4	81 25.9	42.0	131.8	80 44.1	45.7	136.3	79 59.3	48.4	140.3	37
38	83 41.9	-2.2	87.5	83 39.7	7.4	96.6	83 28.3	16.6	105.3	83 08.4	25.0	113.3	82 41.2	32.1	120.5	82 07.9	37.9	126.8	81 29.8	42.4	132.5	80 47.7	46.0	136.7	38
39	83 39.7	11.4	78.4	83 47.1	-2.2	87.5	83 44.9	7.5	96.6	83 33.4	16.8	105.5	83 13.3	25.3	113.6	82 45.8	32.4	120.8	82 12.2	38.2	127.1	81 33.7	42.8	132.5	39
40	83 28.3	-19.9	69.7	83 44.9	-11.5	78.3	83 52.4	-2.2	87.4	83 50.2	+7.7	96.7	83 38.6	+17.1	105.7	83 18.2	+25.6	113.9	82 50.4	+32.8	121.2	82 16.5	+38.6	127.5	40
41	83 08.4	27.2	61.6	83 33.4	20.1	69.4	83 50.2	11.6	78.1	83 57.9	-2.2	87.4	83 55.7	7.7	96.8	83 43.8	17.4	105.9	83 23.2	26.0	114.2	82 55.1	33.2	121.6	41
42	82 41.2	33.3	54.3	83 13.3	27.0	61.2	83 38.6	20.4	69.1	83 55.7	11.9	77.9	84 03.4	-2.2	87.3	84 01.2	7.9	96.9	83 49.2	17.6	106.1	83 28.3	26.3	114.5	42
43	82 07.9	38.1	48.0	82 45.8	33.6	53.9	83 18.2	27.8	60.8	83 43.8	20.6	68.8	84 01.2	12.0	77.7	84 09.1	-2.3	87.3	84 06.8	8.1	97.0	83 54.6	18.0	106.4	43
44	81 29.8	42.1	42.6	82 12.2	38.5	47.6	82 50.4	33.9	53.4	83 23.2	28.1	60.4	83 49.2	20.9	68.4	84 06.8	12.2	77.5	84 14.9	-2.3	87.2	84 12.6	8.1	97.1	44

9°, 351° L.H.A.   LATITUDE SAME NAME AS DECLINATION

Dec.	38° Hc	d	Z	39° Hc	d	Z	40° Hc	d	Z	41° Hc	d	Z	42° Hc	d	Z	43° Hc	d	Z	44° Hc	d	Z	45° Hc	d	Z	Dec.
0	51 06.4	+58.8	165.6	50 08.2	+58.9	165.9	49 10.0	+59.0	166.2	48 11.7	+59.0	166.4	47 13.3	+59.1	166.7	46 14.9	+59.2	166.9	45 16.5	+59.2	167.2	44 17.9	+59.3	167.4	0
1	52 05.2	58.7	165.3	51 07.1	58.8	165.6	50 09.0	58.9	165.9	49 10.7	59.0	166.2	48 12.4	59.1	166.4	47 14.1	59.1	166.7	46 15.7	59.2	166.9	45 17.2	59.2	167.2	1
2	53 03.9	58.7	164.9	52 05.9	58.8	165.3	51 07.9	58.8	165.6	50 09.7	59.0	165.9	49 11.5	59.0	166.2	48 13.2	59.1	166.4	47 14.9	59.1	166.7	46 16.4	59.3	166.9	2
3	54 02.6	58.6	164.6	53 04.7	58.8	164.9	52 06.7	58.8	165.3	51 08.7	58.9	165.6	50 10.5	59.0	165.9	49 12.3	59.1	166.2	48 14.0	59.1	166.4	47 15.7	59.1	166.7	3
4	55 01.2	58.6	164.2	54 03.5	58.6	164.6	53 05.6	58.7	164.9	52 07.6	58.8	165.3	51 09.5	58.9	165.6	50 11.4	59.0	165.9	49 13.1	59.1	166.2	48 14.8	59.2	166.4	4
5	55 59.8	+58.5	163.8	55 02.1	+58.6	164.2	54 04.3	+58.7	164.6	53 06.4	+58.8	165.0	52 08.4	+58.9	165.3	51 10.4	+58.9	165.6	50 12.2	+59.1	165.9	49 14.0	+59.1	166.2	5
6	56 58.3	58.4	163.4	56 00.7	58.5	163.8	55 03.0	58.4	164.3	54 05.2	58.8	164.6	53 07.3	58.8	165.0	52 09.3	58.9	165.3	51 11.3	59.0	165.6	50 13.1	59.0	165.9	6
7	57 56.7	58.3	163.0	56 59.2	58.5	163.4	56 01.7	58.5	163.9	55 04.0	58.7	164.3	54 06.2	58.8	164.6	53 08.3	58.8	165.0	52 10.3	58.9	165.3	51 12.2	59.0	165.7	7
8	58 55.0	58.2	162.5	57 57.7	58.3	163.0	57 00.2	58.4	163.4	56 02.7	58.6	163.9	55 04.9	58.7	164.3	54 07.1	58.7	164.7	53 09.2	58.9	165.0	52 11.2	59.0	165.4	8
9	59 53.2	58.1	162.1	58 56.0	58.2	162.6	57 58.6	58.3	162.9	57 01.3	58.5	163.5	56 03.7	58.6	163.9	55 06.0	58.7	164.3	54 08.1	58.7	164.7	53 10.2	59.0	165.1	9
10	60 51.3	+58.0	161.6	59 54.3	+58.2	162.1	58 57.1	+58.3	162.6	57 59.8	+58.4	163.1	57 02.3	+58.6	163.6	56 04.7	+58.7	164.0	55 07.0	+58.7	164.4	54 09.2	+58.8	164.7	10
11	61 49.3	57.9	161.0	60 52.5	58.0	161.6	59 55.4	58.2	162.2	58 58.2	58.4	162.7	58 00.9	58.5	163.1	57 03.4	58.6	163.6	56 05.8	58.6	164.0	55 08.0	58.9	164.4	11
12	62 47.2	57.7	160.5	61 50.5	57.9	161.1	60 53.6	58.1	161.7	59 56.6	58.3	162.2	58 59.4	58.4	162.7	58 02.0	58.4	163.2	57 04.5	58.5	163.6	56 06.9	58.7	164.1	12
13	63 44.9	57.5	159.9	62 48.4	57.8	160.5	61 51.7	58.0	161.1	60 54.9	58.1	161.7	59 57.8	58.3	162.3	59 00.4	58.4	162.8	58 03.2	58.5	163.3	57 05.7	58.7	163.7	13
14	64 42.4	57.3	159.2	63 46.2	57.6	159.9	62 49.7	57.8	160.6	61 53.0	58.0	161.2	60 56.1	58.2	161.8	59 59.0	58.3	162.3	59 01.8	58.3	162.8	58 04.4	58.6	163.3	14
15	65 39.7	+57.2	158.5	64 43.8	+57.4	159.3	63 47.5	+57.7	160.0	62 51.0	+57.9	160.7	61 54.3	+58.1	161.3	60 57.4	+58.2	161.9	60 00.1	+58.3	162.4	59 03.0	+58.6	162.9	15
16	66 36.9	56.9	157.7	65 41.2	57.2	158.6	64 45.2	57.5	159.4	63 48.9	57.7	160.1	62 52.4	57.9	160.7	61 55.6	58.1	161.4	60 58.7	58.1	161.9	60 01.6	58.4	162.5	16
17	67 33.8	56.7	156.9	66 38.4	57.0	157.8	65 42.7	57.3	158.7	64 46.6	57.6	159.4	63 50.3	57.8	160.2	62 53.8	58.0	160.8	61 57.0	58.1	161.5	61 00.0	58.4	162.0	17
18	68 30.5	56.3	156.0	67 35.4	56.7	157.0	66 40.0	57.1	157.9	65 44.2	57.4	158.8	64 48.1	57.7	159.5	63 51.8	57.9	160.2	62 55.2	57.9	160.9	61 58.4	58.2	161.5	18
19	69 26.8	56.0	155.1	68 32.1	56.5	156.2	67 37.1	56.8	157.1	66 41.6	57.1	158.0	65 45.8	57.4	158.8	64 49.7	57.7	159.7	63 53.3	57.7	160.4	62 56.6	58.2	161.0	19
20	70 22.8	+55.6	154.0	69 28.6	+56.1	155.3	68 33.9	+56.5	156.3	67 38.7	+56.9	157.3	66 43.2	+57.3	158.2	65 47.4	+57.5	159.0	64 51.2	+57.8	159.8	63 54.8	+58.0	160.5	20
21	71 18.4	55.1	152.9	70 24.7	55.7	154.2	69 30.4	56.2	155.3	68 35.6	56.7	156.4	67 40.5	56.9	157.4	66 44.9	57.3	158.3	65 49.0	57.6	159.1	64 52.8	57.8	159.9	21
22	72 13.5	54.7	151.6	71 20.4	55.3	153.0	70 26.6	55.8	154.3	69 32.3	56.3	155.5	68 37.4	56.6	156.6	67 42.2	57.1	157.5	66 46.6	57.4	158.5	65 50.6	57.5	159.2	22
23	73 08.2	53.9	150.2	72 15.7	54.7	151.8	71 22.4	55.4	153.2	70 28.6	55.9	154.5	69 34.2	56.4	155.6	68 39.3	56.8	156.7	67 44.0	57.2	157.7	66 48.3	57.5	158.6	23
24	74 02.1	53.3	148.7	73 10.4	54.1	150.4	72 17.8	54.9	152.0	71 24.5	55.5	153.4	70 30.6	56.0	154.6	69 36.1	56.5	155.8	68 41.2	56.9	156.8	67 45.8	57.3	157.8	24
25	74 55.4	+52.4	147.0	74 04.5	+53.4	148.9	73 12.7	+54.3	150.6	72 20.0	+55.0	152.1	71 26.6	+55.7	153.5	70 32.6	+56.2	154.8	69 38.1	+56.6	156.0	68 43.1	+57.0	157.0	25
26	75 47.8	51.3	145.2	74 57.9	52.6	147.2	74 07.0	53.5	149.1	73 15.0	54.5	150.8	72 22.3	55.1	152.3	71 28.8	55.7	153.7	70 34.7	56.3	155.0	69 40.1	56.7	156.1	26
27	76 39.1	50.0	142.9	75 50.5	51.5	145.3	75 00.5	52.8	147.4	74 09.5	53.7	149.3	73 17.4	54.6	151.0	72 24.5	55.3	152.5	71 31.0	55.9	153.9	70 36.8	56.4	155.2	27
28	77 29.1	48.6	140.4	76 42.0	50.3	143.1	75 53.3	51.7	145.5	75 03.2	52.9	147.6	74 12.0	53.8	149.5	73 19.8	54.8	151.1	72 26.9	55.4	152.7	71 33.2	56.0	154.1	28
29	78 17.7	46.6	137.6	77 32.3	48.7	140.7	76 45.0	50.5	143.5	75 56.0	51.9	145.7	75 05.9	53.1	147.9	74 14.6	54.0	149.7	73 22.3	54.8	151.4	72 29.2	55.3	153.0	29
30	79 04.3	+44.4	134.4	78 21.0	+47.0	137.9	77 35.5	+49.0	140.9	76 48.0	+50.7	143.6	75 59.0	+52.1	146.0	75 08.6	+53.3	148.1	74 17.2	+54.2	150.0	73 24.8	+55.0	151.7	30
31	79 48.7	41.5	130.7	79 08.0	44.6	134.7	78 24.5	47.2	138.1	77 38.7	49.3	141.2	76 51.1	50.9	143.9	76 01.9	52.3	146.3	75 11.4	53.5	148.4	74 19.8	54.4	150.2	31
32	80 30.2	38.0	126.5	79 52.6	41.8	131.0	79 11.7	44.9	135.0	78 28.0	47.5	138.4	77 42.0	49.6	141.5	76 54.2	51.2	144.2	76 04.9	52.5	146.5	75 14.2	53.7	148.6	32
33	81 08.2	33.7	121.6	80 34.4	38.4	126.8	79 56.6	42.2	131.3	79 15.5	45.2	135.3	78 31.6	47.7	138.7	77 45.4	49.8	141.8	76 57.4	51.4	144.5	76 07.9	52.7	146.8	33
34	81 41.9	28.4	116.1	81 12.8	34.0	121.9	80 38.8	38.6	127.1	80 00.7	42.5	131.6	79 19.3	45.5	135.6	78 35.2	48.0	139.1	77 48.8	50.0	142.1	77 00.6	51.7	144.8	34
35	82 10.3	+22.3	109.8	81 46.8	+28.8	116.3	81 17.4	+34.4	122.2	80 43.2	+39.0	127.4	80 04.8	+42.8	131.9	79 23.2	+45.9	135.9	78 38.8	+48.3	139.4	77 52.3	+50.2	142.4	35
36	82 32.6	15.0	102.8	82 15.6	22.5	110.0	81 51.8	29.1	116.6	81 22.2	34.7	122.5	80 47.6	39.4	127.7	80 09.1	43.1	132.3	79 27.1	46.2	136.3	78 42.5	48.6	139.7	36
37	82 47.6	+7.0	95.2	82 38.1	15.2	102.9	82 20.9	22.8	110.2	81 56.9	29.5	116.6	81 27.0	35.1	122.8	80 52.2	39.7	128.1	80 13.3	43.5	132.6	79 31.1	46.5	136.6	37
38	82 54.6	−1.3	87.2	82 53.3	+7.2	95.3	82 43.7	15.5	103.1	82 26.4	23.1	110.5	82 02.1	29.9	116.9	81 31.9	35.5	123.2	80 56.8	40.1	128.4	80 17.6	43.9	133.0	38
39	82 53.3	9.6	79.1	83 00.5	−1.3	87.2	82 59.2	+7.3	95.3	82 49.5	15.7	103.2	82 32.0	23.4	110.7	82 07.4	30.2	117.5	81 36.9	35.9	123.5	81 01.5	40.5	128.8	39
40	82 43.7	−17.3	71.2	82 59.2	9.7	79.0	83 06.5	−1.3	87.1	83 05.2	+7.4	95.4	82 55.4	+15.9	103.4	82 37.6	+23.8	111.0	82 12.8	+30.6	117.8	81 42.0	+36.3	123.9	40
41	82 26.4	24.3	63.8	82 49.5	17.5	71.0	83 05.2	9.8	78.8	83 12.6	−1.3	87.0	83 11.3	7.6	95.4	83 01.4	16.2	103.8	82 43.4	24.1	111.2	82 18.3	30.9	118.2	41
42	82 02.1	30.2	57.0	82 32.0	24.6	63.4	82 55.4	17.8	70.7	83 11.3	9.8	78.6	83 18.9	−1.3	87.0	83 17.6	7.7	95.5	83 07.5	16.4	103.8	82 49.2	24.5	111.5	42
43	81 31.9	35.1	51.0	82 07.4	30.5	56.6	82 37.6	24.8	63.1	83 01.4	18.0	70.4	83 17.6	10.1	78.4	83 25.3	−1.4	86.9	83 23.9	7.8	95.6	83 13.7	16.7	104.0	43
44	80 56.8	39.2	45.7	81 36.9	35.4	50.5	82 12.8	30.8	56.2	82 43.4	25.1	62.7	83 07.5	18.3	70.1	83 23.9	10.2	78.2	83 31.7	−1.3	86.9	83 30.4	8.0	95.7	44

N. Lat { L.H.A. greater than 180°......Zn=Z
L.H.A. less than 180°......Zn=360°−Z

Dec.	38° Hc	d	Z	39° Hc	d	Z	40° Hc	d	Z	41° Hc	d	Z	42° Hc	d	Z	43° Hc	d	Z	44° Hc	d	Z	45° Hc	d	Z	Dec.
0	50 54.0	+58.5	164.0	49 56.2	+58.7	164.3	48 58.4	+58.7	164.7	48 00.5	+58.8	165.0	47 02.5	+58.9	165.2	46 04.5	+58.9	165.5	45 06.3	+59.1	165.8	44 08.2	+59.1	166.0	0
1	51 52.5	58.5	163.7	50 54.9	58.5	164.0	49 57.1	58.7	164.4	48 59.3	58.8	164.7	48 01.4	58.9	165.0	47 03.4	59.0	165.2	46 05.4	59.0	165.5	45 07.3	59.0	165.8	1
2	52 51.0	58.4	163.3	51 53.4	58.6	163.7	50 55.8	58.6	164.0	49 58.1	58.7	164.4	49 00.3	58.8	164.7	48 02.4	58.8	165.0	47 04.4	58.9	165.2	46 06.3	59.0	165.5	2
3	53 49.4	58.3	162.9	52 52.0	58.4	163.3	51 54.4	58.6	163.7	50 56.8	58.7	164.0	49 59.1	58.7	164.4	49 01.3	58.8	164.7	48 03.3	58.9	165.0	47 05.4	59.0	165.2	3
4	54 47.7	58.2	162.5	53 50.4	58.4	162.9	52 53.0	58.5	163.3	51 55.5	58.6	163.7	50 57.8	58.7	164.0	50 00.1	58.7	164.4	49 02.3	58.8	164.7	48 04.4	58.9	165.0	4
5	55 45.9	+58.2	162.1	54 48.8	+58.3	162.5	53 51.5	+58.4	163.0	52 54.1	+58.5	163.3	51 56.5	+58.5	163.7	50 58.9	+58.7	164.1	50 01.1	+58.9	164.4	49 03.3	+58.9	164.7	5
6	56 44.1	58.0	161.6	55 47.1	58.2	162.1	54 49.9	58.3	162.6	53 52.6	58.5	163.0	52 55.2	58.5	163.4	51 57.6	58.7	163.7	51 00.0	58.8	164.1	50 02.2	58.9	164.4	6
7	57 42.1	58.0	161.2	56 45.3	58.1	161.7	55 48.2	58.3	162.1	54 51.1	58.3	162.6	53 53.7	58.6	163.0	52 56.3	58.6	163.4	51 58.8	58.8	163.8	51 01.1	58.8	164.1	7
8	58 40.1	57.8	160.7	57 43.4	58.1	161.2	56 46.5	58.1	161.7	55 49.4	58.3	162.2	54 52.3	58.3	162.6	53 54.9	58.6	163.0	52 57.5	58.6	163.4	51 59.9	58.8	163.8	8
9	59 37.9	57.7	160.2	58 41.4	57.9	160.7	57 44.6	58.1	161.3	56 47.7	58.3	161.7	55 50.7	58.3	162.2	54 53.5	58.5	162.6	53 56.1	58.7	163.1	52 58.7	58.7	163.5	9
10	60 35.6	+57.6	159.6	59 39.3	+57.7	160.2	58 42.7	+57.9	160.8	57 46.0	+58.1	161.3	56 49.0	+58.3	161.8	55 52.0	+58.4	162.3	54 54.8	+58.5	162.7	53 57.4	+58.6	163.1	10
11	61 33.2	57.3	159.0	60 37.0	57.5	159.7	59 40.6	57.9	160.3	58 44.1	58.0	160.8	57 47.3	58.2	161.4	56 50.4	58.3	161.8	55 53.3	58.4	162.3	54 56.0	58.6	162.7	11
12	62 30.5	57.3	158.4	61 34.6	57.5	159.1	60 38.5	57.6	159.7	59 42.1	57.8	160.3	58 45.5	58.0	160.9	57 48.7	58.2	161.4	56 51.7	58.4	161.9	55 54.6	58.5	162.4	12
13	63 27.8	57.0	157.8	62 32.1	57.3	158.5	61 36.1	57.6	159.2	60 39.9	57.8	159.8	59 43.5	58.0	160.4	58 46.9	58.1	160.9	57 50.1	58.3	161.5	56 53.1	58.5	162.0	13
14	64 24.8	56.8	157.0	63 29.4	57.1	157.8	62 33.7	57.3	158.6	61 37.6	57.6	159.2	60 41.5	57.9	159.9	59 45.0	58.0	160.5	58 48.4	58.3	161.0	57 51.6	58.5	161.5	14
15	65 21.6	+56.5	156.3	64 26.5	+56.8	157.1	63 31.0	+57.2	157.9	62 35.3	+57.4	158.6	61 39.3	+57.6	159.3	60 43.0	+57.9	159.9	59 46.6	+58.0	160.5	58 49.9	+58.2	161.1	15
16	66 18.1	56.3	155.5	65 23.3	56.7	156.4	64 28.2	57.0	157.2	63 32.7	57.3	158.0	62 36.9	57.5	158.7	61 40.9	57.7	159.4	60 44.6	58.0	160.0	59 48.1	58.2	160.6	16
17	67 14.4	55.9	154.6	66 20.0	56.3	155.6	65 25.2	56.7	156.6	64 30.0	57.0	157.3	63 34.4	57.4	158.1	62 38.6	57.6	158.8	61 42.6	57.8	159.5	60 46.3	58.0	160.1	17
18	68 10.3	55.6	153.6	67 16.3	56.1	154.7	66 21.9	56.4	155.7	65 27.0	56.8	156.6	64 31.8	57.1	157.4	63 36.2	57.4	158.2	62 40.4	57.6	158.9	61 44.3	57.8	159.6	18
19	69 05.9	55.2	152.6	68 12.4	55.7	153.8	67 18.3	56.2	154.8	66 23.8	56.6	155.8	65 28.9	56.9	156.7	64 33.6	57.3	157.5	63 38.0	57.5	158.3	62 42.1	57.8	159.0	19
20	70 01.1	+54.8	151.5	69 08.1	+55.3	152.7	68 14.5	+55.8	153.9	67 20.4	+56.3	154.9	66 25.8	+56.7	155.9	65 30.9	+57.0	156.8	64 35.5	+57.3	157.6	63 39.9	+57.6	158.4	20
21	70 55.9	54.2	150.4	70 03.4	54.9	151.6	69 10.3	55.5	152.9	68 16.7	55.9	154.0	67 22.5	56.4	155.1	66 27.9	56.7	156.0	65 32.8	57.1	156.9	64 37.5	57.3	157.8	21
22	71 50.1	53.6	149.2	70 58.3	54.4	150.4	70 05.8	55.0	151.8	69 12.6	55.6	153.0	68 18.9	56.0	154.2	67 24.6	56.5	155.2	66 29.9	56.9	156.2	65 34.8	57.2	157.1	22
23	72 43.7	52.8	147.8	71 52.7	53.7	149.1	71 00.8	54.5	150.6	70 08.2	55.1	151.9	69 14.9	55.7	153.2	68 21.1	56.2	154.3	67 26.8	56.6	155.4	66 32.0	57.0	156.3	23
24	73 36.5	52.1	145.8	72 46.4	53.0	147.6	71 55.3	53.9	149.3	71 03.3	54.6	150.6	70 10.6	55.3	152.1	69 17.3	55.8	153.4	68 23.4	56.3	154.6	67 29.0	56.7	155.5	24
25	74 28.6	+51.0	144.0	73 39.4	+52.2	146.0	72 49.2	+53.2	147.8	71 57.9	+54.1	149.4	71 05.9	+54.7	150.9	70 13.1	+55.4	152.3	69 19.7	+55.9	153.5	68 25.7	+56.4	154.7	25
26	75 19.6	49.9	142.0	74 31.6	51.3	144.2	73 42.4	52.4	146.2	72 52.0	53.4	148.0	72 00.6	54.3	149.6	71 08.5	54.9	151.1	70 15.6	55.5	152.5	69 22.1	56.0	153.7	26
27	76 09.5	48.5	139.7	75 22.9	50.1	142.2	74 34.8	51.4	144.4	73 45.4	52.6	146.4	72 54.9	53.5	148.2	72 03.4	54.4	149.9	71 11.1	55.1	151.3	70 18.1	55.7	152.7	27
28	76 58.0	46.8	137.2	76 13.0	48.7	139.9	75 26.2	50.3	142.4	74 38.0	51.6	144.7	73 48.4	52.8	146.6	72 57.8	53.7	148.4	72 06.2	54.5	150.1	71 13.8	55.2	151.5	28
29	77 44.8	44.8	134.3	77 01.7	47.1	137.4	76 16.5	49.0	140.2	75 29.6	50.6	142.7	74 41.2	51.9	144.9	73 51.5	53.0	146.9	73 00.7	53.9	148.7	72 09.0	54.7	150.3	29
30	78 29.6	+42.3	131.1	77 48.8	+45.1	134.6	77 05.5	+47.3	137.7	76 20.2	+49.2	140.5	75 33.1	+50.7	142.9	74 44.5	+52.1	145.2	73 54.6	+53.2	147.1	73 03.7	+54.1	148.9	30
31	79 11.9	39.5	127.4	78 33.9	42.6	131.3	77 52.8	45.4	134.8	77 09.4	47.6	138.0	76 23.8	49.5	140.7	75 36.6	51.0	143.2	74 47.8	52.3	145.4	73 57.8	53.4	147.4	31
32	79 51.4	35.9	123.3	79 16.5	39.8	127.7	78 38.2	43.0	131.6	77 57.0	45.7	135.1	77 13.3	47.9	138.3	76 27.6	49.7	141.0	75 40.1	51.3	143.5	74 51.2	52.5	145.7	32
33	80 27.3	31.6	118.6	79 56.3	36.2	123.5	79 21.2	40.1	127.7	78 42.7	43.3	131.7	78 01.2	46.0	135.4	77 17.3	48.2	138.6	76 31.4	49.9	141.3	75 43.7	51.5	143.8	33
34	80 58.9	26.6	113.3	80 32.5	32.0	118.8	80 01.3	36.6	123.8	79 26.0	40.4	128.3	78 47.2	43.6	132.2	78 05.5	46.3	135.8	77 21.3	48.5	138.9	76 35.2	50.2	141.6	34
35	81 25.5	+20.8	107.4	81 04.5	+26.9	113.5	80 37.9	+32.3	119.1	80 06.4	+36.9	124.1	79 30.8	+40.8	128.6	78 51.8	+43.9	132.6	78 09.8	+46.6	136.1	77 25.4	+48.8	139.2	35
36	81 46.3	14.2	101.0	81 31.4	21.1	107.6	81 10.2	27.3	113.8	80 43.3	32.7	119.4	80 11.6	37.3	124.4	79 35.7	41.2	128.9	78 56.4	44.3	132.9	78 14.2	46.9	136.4	36
37	82 00.5	6.9	94.1	81 52.5	14.4	101.1	81 37.5	21.3	107.8	81 16.0	27.6	114.0	80 48.9	33.1	119.7	80 16.9	37.7	124.8	79 40.7	41.5	129.2	79 01.1	44.7	133.3	37
38	82 07.4	−0.5	86.9	82 06.9	7.0	94.1	81 58.8	14.6	101.2	81 43.6	21.7	108.0	81 22.0	27.9	114.3	80 54.6	33.4	120.0	80 22.2	38.1	125.1	79 45.8	41.9	129.7	38
39	82 06.9	8.1	79.6	82 13.9	−0.5	86.8	82 13.4	7.2	94.2	82 05.3	14.8	101.4	81 49.9	22.0	108.2	81 28.0	28.3	114.6	81 00.3	33.8	120.3	80 27.7	38.4	125.5	39
40	81 58.8	15.2	72.5	82 13.4	8.1	79.4	82 20.6	−0.5	86.6	82 20.1	+7.3	94.2	82 11.9	+15.0	101.5	81 56.3	+22.3	108.5	81 34.1	+28.7	114.9	81 06.1	−34.3	120.7	40
41	81 43.6	21.6	65.6	82 05.3	15.4	72.2	82 20.1	8.2	79.3	82 27.4	−0.6	86.7	82 26.9	7.5	94.3	82 18.6	15.5	101.7	82 02.8	22.6	108.7	81 40.4	29.0	115.2	41
42	81 22.0	27.4	59.3	81 49.9	21.9	65.3	82 11.9	15.6	71.9	82 26.9	8.3	79.1	82 34.4	−0.5	86.6	82 33.9	7.5	94.3	82 25.4	15.5	101.8	82 09.4	23.0	109.0	42
43	80 54.6	32.4	53.5	81 28.0	27.7	58.9	81 56.3	22.2	64.9	82 18.5	15.8	71.6	82 33.9	8.5	78.9	82 41.4	−0.5	86.6	82 40.9	7.8	94.4	82 32.4	15.7	102.0	43
44	80 22.2	36.4	48.3	81 00.3	32.6	53.0	81 34.1	28.0	58.4	82 02.8	22.4	64.5	82 25.4	16.0	71.3	82 40.9	8.5	78.7	82 48.7	−0.6	86.5	82 48.1	+7.9	94.5	44

Zn=Z
Zn=360°−Z

11°, 349° L.H.A. LATITUDE SAME NAME AS DECLINATION

N. Lat. { L.H.A. greater than 180°......Zn=Z
L.H.A. less than 180°.........Zn=360°−Z }

Zn=Z
Zn=360°−Z

Dec.	38° Hc	d	Z	39° Hc	d	Z	40° Hc	d	Z	41° Hc	d	Z	42° Hc	d	Z	43° Hc	d	Z	44° Hc	d	Z	45° Hc	d	Z	Dec.
0	50 40.3	+58.3	162.5	49 43.1	+58.3	162.8	48 45.7	+58.5	163.2	47 48.2	+58.6	163.5	46 50.6	+58.7	163.8	45 53.0	+58.7	164.1	44 55.2	+58.9	164.4	43 57.4	+58.9	164.6	0
1	51 38.6	+58.2	162.1	50 41.4	+58.3	162.5	49 44.2	+58.4	162.8	48 46.8	+58.5	163.2	47 49.3	+58.6	163.5	46 51.7	+58.7	163.8	45 54.1	+58.8	164.1	44 56.3	+58.9	164.4	1
2	52 36.8	+58.0	161.7	51 39.7	+58.2	162.1	50 42.6	+58.3	162.5	49 45.3	+58.5	162.8	48 47.9	+58.6	163.2	47 50.4	+58.7	163.5	46 52.9	+58.7	163.8	45 55.2	+58.8	164.1	2
3	53 34.8	+58.0	161.3	52 37.9	+58.0	161.7	51 40.9	+58.3	162.1	50 43.8	+58.4	162.5	49 46.5	+58.5	162.8	48 49.1	+58.6	163.2	47 51.6	+58.7	163.5	46 54.0	+58.8	163.8	3
4	54 32.8	+57.9	160.8	53 36.1	+58.0	161.3	52 39.2	+58.2	161.7	51 42.1	+58.3	162.1	50 45.0	+58.4	162.5	49 47.7	+58.6	162.9	48 50.3	+58.7	163.2	47 52.8	+58.8	163.5	4
5	55 30.7	+57.8	160.4	54 34.1	+58.0	160.9	53 37.4	+58.1	161.3	52 40.5	+58.3	161.7	51 43.4	+58.4	162.1	50 46.3	+58.5	162.5	49 49.0	+58.6	162.9	48 51.6	+58.7	163.2	5
6	56 28.5	+57.7	159.9	55 32.1	+57.8	160.4	54 35.5	+58.0	160.9	53 38.7	+58.2	161.3	52 41.8	+58.3	161.8	51 44.8	+58.4	162.2	50 47.6	+58.5	162.5	49 50.3	+58.6	162.9	6
7	57 26.2	+57.7	159.4	56 29.9	+57.8	159.9	55 33.5	+57.9	160.4	54 36.9	+58.0	160.9	53 40.1	+58.1	161.4	52 43.2	+58.3	161.8	51 46.1	+58.5	162.2	50 48.9	+58.6	162.6	7
8	58 23.7	+57.5	158.9	57 27.7	+57.5	159.4	56 31.4	+57.8	159.9	55 34.9	+58.0	160.4	54 38.2	+58.1	160.9	53 41.5	+58.3	161.4	52 44.6	+58.3	161.8	51 47.5	+58.5	162.2	8
9	59 21.2	+57.2	158.3	58 25.3	+57.5	158.9	57 29.2	+57.7	159.5	56 32.9	+57.9	160.0	55 36.4	+58.1	160.5	54 39.8	+58.2	161.0	53 43.0	+58.1	161.4	52 46.0	+58.5	161.9	9
10	60 18.4	+57.1	157.7	59 22.8	+57.3	158.4	58 26.9	+57.5	159.0	57 30.8	+57.7	159.6	56 34.5	+57.9	160.1	55 38.0	+58.1	160.6	54 41.3	+58.3	161.0	53 44.5	+58.4	161.5	10
11	61 15.5	+56.9	157.1	60 20.1	+57.1	157.7	59 24.4	+57.3	158.4	58 28.5	+57.6	159.0	57 32.4	+57.8	159.6	56 36.1	+58.0	160.1	55 39.6	+58.1	160.6	54 42.9	+58.3	161.1	11
12	62 12.4	+56.7	156.4	61 17.2	+57.0	157.1	60 21.8	+57.3	157.8	59 26.1	+57.5	158.5	58 30.2	+57.7	159.1	57 34.1	+57.9	159.6	56 37.7	+58.0	160.2	55 41.2	+58.2	160.7	12
13	63 09.1	+56.4	155.7	62 14.2	+56.8	156.5	61 19.1	+57.0	157.2	60 23.6	+57.3	157.9	59 27.9	+57.6	158.5	58 31.9	+57.8	159.1	57 35.8	+57.9	159.7	56 39.4	+58.1	160.2	13
14	64 05.5	+56.2	154.9	63 11.0	+56.5	155.8	62 16.1	+56.9	156.6	61 20.9	+57.2	157.3	60 25.4	+57.4	158.0	59 29.7	+57.6	158.6	58 33.7	+57.8	159.2	57 37.5	+58.0	159.8	14
15	65 01.7	+55.9	154.1	64 07.5	+56.3	155.0	63 13.0	+56.6	155.9	62 18.0	+56.9	156.7	61 22.8	+57.2	157.4	60 27.3	+57.5	158.1	59 31.5	+57.7	158.7	58 35.5	+57.9	159.3	15
16	65 57.6	+55.6	153.2	65 03.8	+56.1	154.2	64 09.6	+56.4	155.1	63 15.0	+56.8	155.9	62 20.0	+57.1	156.7	61 24.8	+57.3	157.5	60 29.2	+57.6	158.1	59 33.4	+57.8	158.8	16
17	66 53.2	+55.3	152.3	65 59.9	+55.7	153.3	65 06.0	+56.1	154.3	64 11.7	+56.5	155.2	63 17.1	+56.8	156.1	62 22.1	+57.1	156.8	61 26.8	+57.4	157.6	60 31.2	+57.6	158.2	17
18	67 48.5	+54.8	151.3	66 55.6	+55.3	152.4	66 02.1	+55.9	153.5	65 08.2	+56.3	154.4	64 13.9	+56.6	155.3	63 19.2	+56.9	156.2	62 24.2	+57.2	156.9	61 28.8	+57.5	157.6	18
19	68 43.3	+54.4	150.2	67 50.9	+55.0	151.4	66 58.0	+55.4	152.5	66 04.5	+55.9	153.6	65 10.5	+56.3	154.6	64 16.1	+56.7	155.4	63 21.4	+57.0	156.3	62 26.3	+57.3	157.1	19
20	69 37.7	+53.8	149.0	68 45.9	+54.5	150.3	67 53.4	+55.1	151.6	67 00.4	+55.6	152.7	66 06.8	+56.1	153.7	65 12.8	+56.5	154.7	64 18.4	+56.8	155.6	63 23.6	+57.1	156.4	20
21	70 31.5	+53.2	147.7	69 40.4	+54.0	149.1	68 48.5	+54.7	150.5	67 56.0	+55.2	151.7	67 02.9	+55.7	152.8	66 09.3	+56.1	153.9	65 15.2	+56.5	154.8	64 20.7	+56.9	155.7	21
22	71 24.7	+52.6	146.3	70 34.4	+53.4	147.9	69 43.2	+54.1	149.3	68 51.2	+54.8	150.6	67 58.6	+55.4	151.8	67 05.4	+55.9	153.0	66 11.7	+56.3	154.0	65 17.6	+56.7	155.0	22
23	72 17.3	+51.7	144.7	71 27.8	+52.7	146.5	70 37.3	+53.6	148.0	69 46.0	+54.3	149.4	68 54.0	+54.9	150.8	68 01.3	+55.5	152.0	67 08.0	+56.0	153.1	66 14.3	+56.4	154.2	23
24	73 09.0	+50.8	143.0	72 20.5	+51.9	144.9	71 30.9	+52.9	146.6	70 40.3	+53.7	148.1	69 48.9	+54.4	149.5	68 56.8	+55.0	151.0	68 04.0	+55.6	152.2	67 10.7	+56.1	153.3	24
25	73 59.8	+49.8	141.1	73 12.4	+51.0	143.2	72 23.8	+52.1	145.1	71 34.0	+53.0	146.8	70 43.3	+53.9	148.4	69 51.8	+54.6	149.9	68 59.6	+55.3	151.2	68 06.8	+55.7	152.4	25
26	74 49.6	+48.4	139.1	74 03.4	+50.0	141.4	73 15.9	+51.2	143.4	72 27.1	+52.3	145.2	71 37.2	+53.3	147.0	70 46.4	+54.1	148.6	69 54.8	+54.8	150.0	69 02.5	+55.4	151.3	26
27	75 38.0	+46.9	136.8	74 53.4	+48.7	139.3	74 07.1	+50.2	141.6	73 19.4	+51.4	143.6	72 30.5	+52.5	145.6	71 40.5	+53.4	147.3	70 49.6	+54.3	148.8	69 57.9	+54.9	150.2	27
28	76 25.2	+45.2	134.2	75 42.1	+47.2	137.0	74 57.3	+48.9	139.5	74 10.9	+50.3	141.7	73 23.0	+51.7	143.9	72 33.9	+52.6	145.8	71 43.9	+53.7	147.5	70 52.8	+54.4	149.0	28
29	77 10.1	+43.0	131.3	76 29.3	+45.4	134.4	75 46.2	+47.5	137.2	75 01.3	+49.1	139.7	74 14.7	+50.6	142.1	73 26.7	+51.8	144.1	72 37.5	+52.9	146.0	71 47.2	+53.8	147.7	29
30	77 53.1	+40.6	128.1	77 14.7	+43.3	131.5	76 33.7	+45.7	134.7	75 50.4	+47.8	137.4	75 05.3	+49.4	140.0	74 18.5	+50.9	142.3	73 30.4	+52.1	144.4	72 41.0	+53.1	146.3	30
31	78 33.7	+37.5	124.4	77 58.0	+40.9	128.1	77 19.4	+43.7	131.8	76 38.2	+46.0	134.7	75 54.7	+48.0	137.5	75 09.4	+49.7	140.3	74 22.5	+51.1	142.6	73 34.1	+52.3	144.7	31
32	79 11.2	+34.0	120.4	78 38.9	+37.9	124.7	78 03.1	+41.1	128.6	77 24.2	+44.0	131.9	76 42.7	+46.4	135.2	75 59.1	+48.3	138.1	75 13.6	+49.9	140.6	74 26.4	+51.4	142.9	32
33	79 45.2	+29.9	115.9	79 16.8	+34.3	120.7	78 44.2	+38.3	125.0	78 08.2	+41.5	128.7	77 29.1	+44.3	132.4	76 47.4	+46.6	135.6	76 03.5	+48.6	138.4	75 17.8	+50.2	140.9	33
34	80 15.1	+25.1	110.9	79 51.1	+30.3	116.1	79 22.5	+34.7	120.9	78 49.7	+38.6	124.9	78 13.4	+41.8	128.9	77 34.0	+44.6	132.7	76 52.1	+46.9	135.9	76 08.0	+48.9	138.7	34
35	80 40.2	+19.6	105.4	80 21.4	+25.4	111.1	79 57.2	+30.6	116.4	79 28.3	+35.1	121.0	78 55.2	+39.0	125.6	78 18.6	+42.3	129.5	77 39.0	+45.0	133.0	76 56.9	+47.2	136.2	35
36	80 59.8	+13.5	99.5	80 46.8	+19.8	105.6	80 27.8	+25.7	111.3	80 03.4	+30.9	116.4	79 34.2	+35.4	121.5	79 00.9	+39.3	125.9	78 24.0	+42.6	129.9	77 44.1	+45.3	133.4	36
37	81 13.3	+6.9	93.2	81 06.6	+13.7	99.6	80 53.5	+20.1	105.7	80 34.3	+26.0	111.3	80 09.6	+31.3	116.8	79 40.2	+35.8	121.8	79 06.6	+39.7	126.2	78 29.4	+43.0	130.2	37
38	81 20.2	+0.1	86.6	81 20.3	+7.1	93.2	81 13.6	+13.9	99.7	81 00.3	+20.5	105.8	80 40.9	+26.4	111.8	80 16.0	+31.7	117.2	79 46.3	+36.2	122.1	79 12.4	+40.1	126.6	38
39	81 20.3	−6.7	80.0	81 27.4	+0.1	86.5	81 27.5	+7.2	93.2	81 20.8	+14.1	99.7	81 07.3	+20.7	106.1	80 47.7	+26.7	112.0	80 22.5	+32.1	117.5	79 52.5	+36.6	122.5	39
40	81 13.6	−13.3	73.4	81 27.5	−6.7	79.8	81 34.7	+0.2	86.5	81 34.9	+7.3	93.2	81 28.0	+14.4	99.9	81 14.4	+21.1	106.3	80 54.6	+27.1	112.3	80 29.1	+32.5	117.8	40
41	81 00.3	−19.4	67.1	81 20.8	−13.5	73.1	81 34.9	−6.9	79.6	81 42.4	+0.2	86.4	81 42.4	+7.5	93.2	81 35.5	+14.6	100.0	81 21.7	+21.3	106.5	81 01.6	+27.4	112.3	41
42	80 40.9	−24.9	61.1	81 07.3	−19.6	66.7	81 28.0	−13.6	72.9	81 42.6	−6.9	79.6	81 49.9	+0.2	86.3	81 50.1	+7.6	93.3	81 43.0	+14.9	100.2	81 29.0	+21.7	106.8	42
43	80 16.0	−29.7	55.6	80 47.7	−25.2	60.7	81 14.4	−19.8	66.4	81 35.5	−13.8	72.9	81 50.1	−7.1	79.3	81 57.7	+0.2	86.2	81 57.9	+7.7	93.3	81 50.7	+15.1	100.3	43
44	79 46.3	−33.9	50.6	80 22.5	−30.0	55.2	80 54.6	−25.5	60.3	81 21.7	−20.1	66.3	81 43.0	−14.0	72.3	81 57.9	−7.2	79.1	82 05.6	+0.2	86.2	82 05.8	+7.9	93.4	44

269

12°, 348° L.H.A.   LATITUDE SAME NAME AS DECLINATION

Dec.	38° Hc	d	Z	39° Hc	d	Z	40° Hc	d	Z	41° Hc	d	Z	42° Hc	d	Z	43° Hc	d	Z	44° Hc	d	Z	45° Hc	d	Z	Dec.
0	50 25.5	+57.9	161.0	49 28.7	+58.1	161.3	48 31.8	+58.2	161.7	47 34.8	+58.3	162.0	46 37.7	+58.4	162.4	45 40.4	+58.6	162.7	44 43.1	+58.7	163.0	43 45.7	+58.7	163.3	0
1	51 23.4	57.9	160.5	50 26.8	58.0	160.9	49 30.0	58.1	161.3	48 33.1	58.3	161.7	47 36.1	58.4	162.0	46 39.0	58.4	162.4	45 41.7	58.6	162.7	44 44.4	58.7	163.0	1
2	52 21.3	57.8	160.1	51 24.8	57.9	160.5	50 28.1	58.1	160.9	49 31.4	58.1	161.3	48 34.5	58.3	161.7	47 37.4	58.5	162.0	46 40.3	58.5	162.4	45 43.1	58.6	162.7	2
3	53 19.0	57.7	159.7	52 22.7	57.7	160.1	51 26.2	58.0	160.5	50 29.5	58.0	161.0	49 32.8	58.2	161.3	48 35.9	58.3	161.7	47 38.8	58.4	162.0	46 41.7	58.5	162.4	3
4	54 16.7	57.5	159.2	53 20.5	57.7	159.7	52 24.2	57.8	160.1	51 27.7	58.0	160.6	50 31.0	58.2	161.0	49 34.2	58.3	161.3	48 37.3	58.4	161.7	47 40.3	58.5	162.1	4
5	55 14.2	+57.4	158.7	54 18.2	+57.6	159.2	53 22.0	+57.8	159.7	52 25.7	+57.9	160.1	51 29.2	+58.1	160.6	50 32.5	+58.2	161.0	49 35.7	+58.4	161.4	48 38.8	+58.5	161.7	5
6	56 11.6	57.3	158.2	55 15.8	57.5	158.7	54 19.8	57.7	159.2	53 23.6	57.8	159.7	52 27.3	57.9	160.2	51 30.7	58.2	160.6	50 34.1	58.2	161.0	49 37.3	58.4	161.4	6
7	57 08.9	57.1	157.6	56 13.3	57.3	158.2	55 17.5	57.5	158.8	54 21.4	57.8	159.3	53 25.2	57.9	159.7	52 28.9	58.0	160.2	51 32.3	58.2	160.6	50 35.7	58.3	161.0	7
8	58 06.0	57.0	157.1	57 10.6	57.2	157.7	56 15.0	57.4	158.3	55 19.2	57.6	158.8	54 23.1	57.8	159.3	53 26.9	58.0	159.8	52 30.5	58.2	160.2	51 34.0	58.3	160.7	8
9	59 03.0	56.8	156.5	58 07.8	57.1	157.1	57 12.4	57.3	157.7	56 16.8	57.5	158.3	55 20.9	57.5	158.8	54 24.9	57.9	159.3	53 28.7	57.9	159.8	52 32.3	58.2	160.3	9
10	59 59.8	+56.5	155.8	59 04.9	+56.8	156.5	58 09.7	+57.1	157.2	57 14.3	+57.3	157.8	56 18.6	+57.6	158.3	55 22.8	+57.7	158.9	54 26.7	+57.9	159.4	53 30.5	+58.0	159.9	10
11	60 56.3	56.4	155.2	60 01.7	56.7	155.9	59 06.8	56.9	156.6	58 11.6	57.2	157.2	57 16.2	57.4	157.8	56 20.5	57.7	158.4	55 24.6	57.9	158.9	54 28.5	58.0	159.4	11
12	61 52.7	56.1	154.5	60 58.4	56.5	155.2	60 03.8	56.7	156.0	59 08.8	57.1	156.6	58 13.6	57.3	157.3	57 18.2	57.5	157.9	56 22.5	57.6	158.5	55 26.5	57.9	159.0	12
13	62 48.8	55.9	153.7	61 54.9	56.2	154.5	61 00.5	56.6	155.3	60 05.9	56.8	156.0	59 10.9	57.1	156.7	58 15.7	57.3	157.3	57 20.2	57.6	158.0	56 24.4	57.8	158.5	13
14	63 44.7	55.6	152.9	62 51.1	56.0	153.8	61 57.1	56.3	154.6	61 02.7	56.7	155.4	60 08.0	57.0	156.1	59 13.0	57.2	156.8	58 17.8	57.4	157.4	57 22.2	57.7	158.0	14
15	64 40.3	+55.3	152.0	63 47.1	+55.7	153.0	62 53.4	+56.1	153.9	61 59.4	+56.4	154.7	61 05.0	+56.7	155.5	60 10.2	+57.1	156.2	59 15.2	+57.3	156.9	58 19.9	+57.5	157.5	15
16	65 35.6	54.9	151.1	64 42.8	55.4	152.1	63 49.5	55.8	153.2	62 55.8	56.2	153.9	62 01.7	56.6	154.8	61 07.3	56.8	155.5	60 12.5	57.1	156.3	59 17.4	57.4	157.0	16
17	66 30.5	54.4	150.1	65 38.2	55.0	151.2	64 45.3	55.5	152.2	63 52.0	55.9	153.2	62 58.3	56.3	154.1	62 04.1	56.7	154.9	61 09.6	57.0	155.7	60 14.8	57.2	156.4	17
18	67 24.9	54.1	149.0	66 33.2	54.6	150.2	65 40.8	55.2	151.3	64 47.9	55.7	152.3	63 54.6	56.0	153.3	63 00.8	56.4	154.2	62 06.6	56.7	155.0	61 12.0	57.1	155.8	18
19	68 19.0	53.5	147.9	67 27.8	54.2	149.1	66 36.0	54.7	150.3	65 43.6	55.2	151.4	64 50.6	55.8	152.5	63 57.2	56.1	153.4	63 03.3	56.5	154.3	62 09.1	56.8	155.1	19
20	69 12.5	+52.9	146.6	68 22.0	+53.6	148.0	67 30.7	+54.4	149.3	66 38.8	+54.9	150.5	65 46.4	+55.4	151.6	64 53.3	+55.9	152.6	63 59.8	+56.3	153.5	63 05.9	+56.7	154.4	20
21	70 05.4	52.2	145.3	69 15.6	53.1	146.8	68 25.1	53.8	148.2	67 33.7	54.5	149.4	66 41.8	55.0	150.6	65 49.2	55.5	151.7	64 56.1	56.0	152.7	64 02.6	56.3	153.7	21
22	70 57.6	51.5	143.8	70 08.7	52.5	145.4	69 18.9	53.3	146.9	68 28.2	54.0	148.3	67 36.8	54.6	149.6	66 44.7	55.2	150.8	65 52.1	55.7	151.9	64 58.9	56.2	152.9	22
23	71 49.1	50.6	142.2	71 01.2	51.6	144.0	70 12.2	52.6	145.6	69 22.2	53.4	147.1	68 31.4	54.2	148.5	67 39.9	54.8	149.8	66 47.8	55.3	150.9	65 55.1	55.8	152.0	23
24	72 39.7	49.6	140.4	71 52.8	50.9	142.4	71 04.8	51.8	144.1	70 15.6	52.8	145.8	69 25.6	53.6	147.3	68 34.7	54.3	148.7	67 43.1	54.9	149.9	66 50.9	55.4	151.1	24
25	73 29.3	+48.4	138.5	72 43.7	+49.8	140.6	71 56.6	+51.1	142.6	71 08.4	+52.1	144.3	70 19.2	+53.0	146.0	69 29.0	+53.8	147.5	68 38.0	+54.5	148.9	67 46.3	+55.1	150.1	25
26	74 17.7	47.1	136.3	73 33.5	48.6	138.7	72 47.7	50.0	140.8	72 00.5	51.3	142.8	71 12.2	52.3	144.6	70 22.8	53.2	146.3	69 32.5	54.0	147.7	68 41.4	54.7	149.1	26
27	75 04.8	45.4	134.0	74 22.1	47.3	136.6	73 37.7	48.9	138.9	72 51.8	50.2	141.0	72 04.5	51.4	143.0	71 16.0	52.5	144.8	70 26.5	53.3	146.4	69 36.1	54.1	147.9	27
28	75 50.2	43.6	131.4	75 09.4	45.8	134.2	74 26.6	47.6	136.8	73 42.0	49.2	139.1	72 55.9	50.5	141.3	72 08.5	51.7	143.2	71 19.8	52.7	145.0	70 30.2	53.6	146.6	28
29	76 33.8	41.4	128.5	75 55.2	43.8	131.6	75 14.2	46.0	134.5	74 31.2	47.8	137.1	73 46.4	49.4	139.4	73 00.2	50.7	141.5	72 12.5	51.9	143.5	71 23.8	52.9	145.2	29
30	77 15.2	+38.8	125.3	76 39.0	+41.8	128.8	76 00.2	+44.2	131.9	75 19.0	+46.4	134.7	74 35.8	+48.2	137.3	73 50.9	+49.7	139.7	73 04.4	+51.0	141.8	72 16.7	+52.1	143.7	30
31	77 54.0	35.9	121.8	77 20.8	39.1	125.6	76 44.4	42.0	129.0	76 05.4	44.5	132.2	75 24.0	46.6	135.0	74 40.6	48.4	137.6	73 55.4	50.0	139.9	73 08.8	51.3	142.1	31
32	78 29.9	32.4*	117.8	77 59.9	36.2*	122.1	77 26.4	39.6*	125.8	76 49.9	42.3*	129.3	76 10.6	44.8	132.4	75 29.0	46.9	135.3	74 45.4	48.7	137.9	74 00.1	50.2	140.2	32
33	79 02.3	28.3*	113.5	78 36.1	32.8*	118.1	78 06.0	36.5*	122.3	77 32.2	39.9*	126.1	76 55.4	42.7*	129.6	76 15.9	45.2	132.7	75 34.1	47.2	135.6	74 50.3	48.9	138.2	33
34	79 30.6	23.8*	108.8	78 58.9	28.7*	113.7	78 42.5	33.1*	118.3	78 12.1	36.9*	122.5	77 38.1	40.3*	126.4	77 01.1	43.0*	129.9	76 21.3	45.5	133.1	75 39.2	47.6	135.9	34
35	79 54.4	+18.6*	103.6	79 37.6	+24.0*	109.0	79 15.6	+29.0*	114.0	78 49.0	+33.4*	118.6	78 18.4	+37.2*	122.8	77 44.1	+40.6*	126.7	77 06.8	+43.4*	130.2	76 26.8	+45.8	133.4	35
36	80 13.0	13.0*	98.1	80 01.6	18.9*	103.8	79 44.6	24.4*	109.1	79 22.4	29.4*	114.2	78 55.6	33.8*	118.9	78 24.7	37.7*	123.1	77 50.2	41.0*	127.4	77 12.6	43.8*	130.6	36
37	80 26.0	7.0*	92.3	80 20.5	13.3*	98.2	80 09.0	19.2*	103.9	79 51.8	24.8*	109.3	79 29.4	29.8*	114.4	79 02.4	34.2*	119.2	78 31.2	38.0*	123.5	77 56.4	41.3*	127.4	37
38	80 33.0	0.8*	86.3	80 33.8	7.1*	92.3	80 28.2	13.4*	98.3	80 16.6	19.4*	104.1	79 59.2	25.1*	109.6	79 36.6	30.1*	114.7	79 09.2	34.6*	119.5	78 37.7	38.5*	123.8	38
39	80 33.8	-5.6	80.2	80 40.9	0.7*	86.2	80 41.6	7.3*	92.3	80 36.0	13.7	98.3	80 24.3	19.7*	104.2	80 06.7	25.4*	109.8	79 43.8	30.5*	115.0	79 16.2	35.0*	119.8	39
40	80 28.2	-11.6	74.2	80 41.6	-5.6	80.0	80 48.9	+0.8*	86.1	80 49.7	+7.3	92.3	80 44.0	+13.9*	98.5	80 32.1	+20.1*	104.4	80 14.3	+25.8*	110.1	79 51.2	+30.9*	115.3	40
41	80 16.6	17.4	68.3	80 36.0	11.7	73.9	80 49.7	-5.7	79.9	80 57.0	0.9	86.1	80 57.9	7.5*	92.3	80 52.2	14.0	98.6	80 40.1	20.4*	104.6	80 22.1	26.1*	110.3	41
42	79 59.2	22.6	62.7	80 24.3	17.6	68.0	80 44.0	11.9*	73.6	80 57.9	5.7*	79.7	81 05.4	0.8*	86.0	81 06.2	7.7	92.4	81 00.5	14.3*	98.7	80 48.2	20.7*	104.8	42
43	79 36.6	27.4	57.5	80 06.7	22.9	62.3	80 32.1	17.8*	67.6	80 52.2	12.1*	73.4	81 06.2	5.7*	79.5	81 13.9	0.9*	85.9	81 14.8	7.7*	92.4	81 08.9	14.6*	98.8	43
44	79 09.2	31.5*	52.6	79 43.8	27.6	57.0	80 14.3	23.1*	61.9	80 40.1	18.0*	67.3	81 00.5	12.3*	73.1	81 14.8	5.9*	79.3	81 22.5	1.0*	85.8	81 23.5	7.8*	92.4	44

13°, 347° L.H.A. LATITUDE SAME NAME AS DECLINATION

Latitudes 38°–41°

Dec.	38° Hc	d	Z	39° Hc	d	Z	40° Hc	d	Z	41° Hc	d	Z	Dec.
0	50 09.5	+57.6	159.4	49 13.2	+57.8	159.7	48 16.8	+57.9	160.2	47 20.3	+58.0	160.6	0
1	51 07.1	57.5	159.0	50 11.0	57.7	159.4	49 14.7	57.9	159.8	48 18.3	58.0	160.2	1
2	52 04.6	57.4	158.5	51 08.7	57.5	159.0	50 12.6	57.7	159.4	49 16.3	57.9	159.8	2
3	53 02.0	57.3	158.1	52 06.2	57.5	158.5	51 10.3	57.6	159.0	50 14.2	57.9	159.4	3
4	53 59.3	57.1	157.6	53 03.7	57.3	158.1	52 07.9	57.6	158.6	51 12.0	57.7	159.0	4
5	54 56.4	+57.0	157.0	54 01.0	+57.3	157.6	53 05.5	+57.4	158.1	52 09.7	+57.6	158.5	5
6	55 53.4	56.8	156.5	54 58.3	56.8	157.1	54 02.9	57.3	157.6	53 07.3	57.5	158.1	6
7	56 50.2	56.7	155.9	55 55.3	57.0	156.5	55 00.2	57.1	157.1	54 04.8	57.4	157.6	7
8	57 46.9	56.5	155.3	56 52.3	56.7	155.9	55 57.3	57.1	156.6	55 02.2	57.2	157.1	8
9	58 43.4	56.3	154.7	57 49.0	56.6	155.3	56 54.4	56.8	156.0	55 59.4	57.1	156.6	9
10	59 39.7	+56.1	154.0	58 45.6	+56.4	154.7	57 51.2	+56.7	155.6	56 56.5	+57.0	156.0	10
11	60 35.8	55.8	153.3	59 42.0	56.2	154.0	58 47.9	56.5	154.8	57 53.5	56.7	155.5	11
12	61 31.6	55.6	152.5	60 38.2	55.9	153.3	59 44.4	56.2	154.1	58 50.2	56.6	154.8	12
13	62 27.2	55.2	151.7	61 34.1	55.7	152.6	60 40.6	56.1	153.4	59 46.8	56.4	154.1	13
14	63 22.4	55.0	150.9	62 29.8	55.4	151.8	61 36.7	55.8	152.7	60 43.2	56.1	153.4	14
15	64 17.4	+54.5	149.9	63 25.2	+55.0	150.9	62 32.5	+55.5	151.9	61 39.3	+55.9	152.8	15
16	65 11.9	54.2	149.0	64 20.2	54.7	150.0	63 28.0	55.2	151.0	62 35.2	55.7	152.0	16
17	66 06.1	53.7	147.9	65 14.9	54.4	149.1	64 23.2	54.8	150.2	63 30.9	55.0	151.2	17
18	66 59.8	53.2	146.8	66 09.3	53.8	148.0	65 18.0	54.5	149.2	64 26.2	55.0	150.3	18
19	67 53.0	52.7	145.6	67 03.1	53.4	146.9	66 12.5	54.0	148.2	65 21.2	54.6	149.3	19
20	68 45.7	+52.0	144.3	67 56.5	+52.8	145.7	67 06.5	+53.5	147.1	66 15.8	+54.2	148.3	20
21	69 37.7	51.2	142.9	68 49.3	52.2	144.5	68 00.0	53.0	145.9	67 10.0	53.7	147.2	21
22	70 28.9	50.4	141.4	69 41.5	51.4	143.1	68 53.0	52.4	144.6	68 03.7	53.1	146.1	22
23	71 19.3	49.5	139.7	70 32.9	50.7	141.6	69 45.4	51.7	143.2	68 56.8	52.6	144.8	23
24	72 08.8	48.4	137.9	71 23.6	49.7	139.9	70 37.1	50.8	141.7	69 49.4	51.9	143.4	24
25	72 57.2	+47.1	135.9	72 13.3	+48.6	138.1	71 27.9	+50.0	140.1	70 41.3	+51.0	141.9	25
26	73 44.3	45.7	133.8	73 01.9	47.4	136.1	72 17.9	48.8	138.3	71 32.3	50.2	140.3	26
27	74 30.0	44.0	131.4	73 49.3	46.0	134.0	73 06.7	47.7	136.4	72 22.5	49.2	138.5	27
28	75 14.0	42.1	128.8	74 35.3	44.3	131.6	73 54.4	46.3	134.2	73 11.7	47.9	136.6	28
29	75 56.1	39.9	125.9	75 19.6	42.4	129.0	74 40.7	44.6	131.9	73 59.6	46.6	134.5	29
30	76 36.0	+37.3	122.8	76 02.0	+40.2	126.2	75 25.3	+42.7	129.3	74 46.2	+44.9	132.1	30
31	77 13.3	34.3	119.3	76 42.2	37.7	123.0	76 08.0	40.6	126.4	75 31.1	43.0	129.6	31
32	77 47.6	31.0	115.5	77 19.9	34.7	119.6	76 48.6	38.0	123.3	76 14.2	40.9	126.7	32
33	78 18.6	27.0	111.4	77 54.6	31.2	115.8	77 26.6	35.0	119.8	76 55.1	38.3	123.5	33
34	78 45.6	22.7	106.9	78 25.8	27.4	111.6	78 01.6	31.6	116.0	77 33.4	35.4	120.1	34
35	79 08.3	+17.9	102.1	78 53.2	+23.0	107.1	78 33.2	+27.8	111.8	78 08.8	+32.0	116.2	35
36	79 26.2	12.6	96.9	79 16.2	18.1	102.2	79 01.0	23.3	107.2	78 40.8	28.1	112.0	36
37	79 38.8	7.1	91.5	79 34.3	12.9	97.0	79 24.3	18.4	102.3	79 08.9	23.6	107.4	37
38	79 45.9	+1.3	86.0	79 47.2	7.1	91.5	79 42.7	13.0	97.0	79 32.5	18.7	102.4	38
39	79 47.2	−4.5	80.4	79 54.3	+1.4	85.9	79 55.7	7.3	91.5	79 51.2	13.2	97.1	39
40	79 42.7	−10.2	74.7	79 55.7	−4.5	80.2	80 03.0	+1.4	85.8	80 04.4	+7.5	91.5	40
41	79 32.5	15.6	69.3	79 51.2	10.3	74.5	80 04.4	−4.6	80.0	80 11.9	+1.4	85.7	41
42	79 16.9	20.6	64.0	79 40.9	15.8	69.0	79 59.8	10.3	74.3	80 13.3	−4.6	79.8	42
43	78 56.3	25.1	59.0	79 25.1	20.8	63.6	79 49.5	16.0	68.6	80 08.7	10.7	74.0	43
44	78 31.2	29.3	54.4	79 04.3	25.4	58.6	79 33.5	21.1	63.2	79 58.2	16.2	68.3	44

Latitudes 42°–45°

Dec.	42° Hc	d	Z	43° Hc	d	Z	44° Hc	d	Z	45° Hc	d	Z	Dec.
0	46 23.6	+58.2	161.0	45 26.9	+58.3	161.3	44 30.0	+58.4	161.6	43 33.0	+58.5	161.9	0
1	47 21.8	58.1	160.6	46 25.2	58.2	161.0	45 28.4	58.3	161.3	44 31.5	58.5	161.6	1
2	48 19.9	58.1	160.2	47 23.4	58.2	160.6	46 26.7	58.3	161.0	45 30.0	58.4	161.3	2
3	49 18.0	57.9	159.8	48 21.6	58.0	160.2	47 25.0	58.2	160.6	46 28.4	58.3	161.0	3
4	50 15.9	57.9	159.4	49 19.6	58.1	159.9	48 23.2	58.2	160.3	47 26.7	58.3	160.6	4
5	51 13.8	+57.7	159.0	50 17.7	+57.9	159.5	49 21.4	+58.1	159.9	48 25.0	+58.2	160.3	5
6	52 11.5	57.6	158.6	51 15.6	57.8	159.1	50 19.5	58.0	159.5	49 23.2	58.2	159.9	6
7	53 09.2	57.6	158.1	52 13.4	57.8	158.6	51 17.5	57.9	159.1	50 21.4	58.0	159.5	7
8	54 06.8	57.4	157.7	53 11.2	57.6	158.2	52 15.4	57.8	158.7	51 19.4	58.0	159.1	8
9	55 04.2	57.4	157.2	54 08.8	57.6	157.7	53 13.2	57.7	158.2	52 17.4	57.9	158.7	9
10	56 01.6	+57.1	156.6	55 06.4	+57.4	157.2	54 10.9	+57.6	157.8	53 15.3	+57.8	158.3	10
11	56 58.7	57.1	156.1	56 03.8	57.1	156.7	55 08.5	57.5	157.3	54 13.1	57.7	157.8	11
12	57 55.8	56.8	155.5	57 01.0	57.1	156.2	56 06.0	57.4	156.8	55 10.8	57.5	157.3	12
13	58 52.6	56.7	154.9	57 58.1	57.0	155.6	57 03.4	57.2	156.2	56 08.3	57.5	156.8	13
14	59 49.3	56.5	154.3	58 55.1	56.8	155.0	58 00.6	57.0	155.7	57 05.8	57.3	156.3	14
15	60 45.8	+56.3	153.6	59 51.9	+56.6	154.4	58 57.6	+56.9	155.1	58 03.1	+57.1	155.8	15
16	61 42.1	56.0	152.9	60 48.5	56.3	153.7	59 54.5	56.7	154.5	59 00.2	57.0	155.2	16
17	62 38.1	55.7	152.1	61 44.8	56.2	153.0	60 51.2	56.5	153.8	59 57.2	56.8	154.6	17
18	63 33.8	55.5	151.3	62 41.0	55.9	152.2	61 47.7	56.2	153.1	60 54.0	56.6	153.9	18
19	64 29.3	55.1	150.4	63 36.9	55.5	151.4	62 43.9	56.0	152.3	61 50.6	56.4	153.2	19
20	65 24.4	+54.8	149.5	64 32.4	+55.3	150.5	63 39.9	+55.8	151.5	62 47.0	+56.1	152.5	20
21	66 19.2	54.3	148.5	65 27.7	54.9	149.6	64 35.7	55.4	150.7	63 43.1	55.8	151.7	21
22	67 13.5	53.9	147.4	66 22.6	54.5	148.6	65 31.1	55.0	149.8	64 38.9	55.6	150.8	22
23	68 07.4	53.3	146.2	67 17.1	54.1	147.6	66 26.1	54.7	148.8	65 34.5	55.2	149.9	23
24	69 00.7	52.8	145.0	68 11.2	53.5	146.4	67 20.8	54.2	147.8	66 29.7	54.8	149.0	24
25	69 53.5	+52.1	143.6	69 04.7	+52.9	145.2	68 15.0	+53.7	146.6	67 24.5	+54.4	147.9	25
26	70 45.6	51.3	142.0	69 57.6	52.3	143.8	69 08.7	53.2	145.4	68 18.9	53.9	146.8	26
27	71 36.9	50.4	140.5	70 49.9	51.6	142.4	70 01.9	52.5	144.1	69 12.8	53.4	145.6	27
28	72 27.3	49.4	138.8	71 41.5	50.6	140.8	70 54.4	51.7	142.6	70 06.2	52.7	144.3	28
29	73 16.7	48.2	136.9	72 32.1	49.7	139.0	71 46.1	50.9	141.0	70 58.9	52.0	142.9	29
30	74 04.9	+46.8	134.7	73 21.8	+48.5	137.1	72 37.0	+49.9	139.3	71 50.9	+51.1	141.3	30
31	74 51.7	45.3	132.4	74 10.3	47.1	135.0	73 26.9	48.8	137.4	72 42.0	50.2	139.6	31
32	75 37.0	43.4	129.8	74 57.4	45.6	132.7	74 15.7	47.5	135.3	73 32.2	49.1	137.7	32
33	76 20.4	41.2	126.7	75 43.0	43.7	130.1	75 03.2	45.9	133.0	74 21.3	47.7	135.6	33
34	77 01.6	38.8	123.8	76 26.7	41.6	127.3	75 49.1	44.1	130.4	75 09.0	46.3	133.3	34
35	77 40.4	+35.7	120.3	77 08.3	+39.1	124.1	76 33.2	+42.0	127.6	75 55.3	+44.4	130.8	35
36	78 16.1	32.4	116.5	77 47.4	36.2	120.6	77 15.2	39.4	124.4	76 39.7	42.4	127.9	36
37	78 48.5	28.4	112.8	78 23.6	32.8	116.8	77 54.6	36.4	120.9	77 22.1	39.8	124.8	37
38	79 16.9	24.0	107.6	78 56.3	28.8	112.5	78 31.0	33.1	117.0	78 01.9	37.0	121.3	38
39	79 40.9	18.9	102.6	79 25.1	24.4	107.8	79 04.3	29.2	112.8	78 38.9	33.5	117.4	39
40	79 59.8	+13.5	97.2	79 49.5	+19.2	102.7	79 33.5	+24.7	108.0	79 12.4	+29.6	113.0	40
41	80 13.3	7.6	91.5	80 08.7	13.7	97.3	79 58.2	19.5	102.9	79 42.0	25.0	108.3	41
42	80 20.9	+1.5	85.6	80 22.4	7.7	91.5	80 17.7	13.9	97.4	80 07.0	19.9	103.1	42
43	80 22.4	−4.7	79.7	80 30.1	+1.5	85.6	80 31.6	7.9	91.5	80 26.9	14.2	97.5	43
44	80 17.7	10.7	73.7	80 31.6	−4.7	79.5	80 39.5	+1.6	85.5	80 41.1	+7.9	91.6	44

14°, 346° L.H.A.

LATITUDE SAME NAME AS DECLINATION

N. Lat. { L.H.A. greater than 180°......Zn=Z
L.H.A. less than 180°.........Zn=360°−Z }

Dec.	38° Hc	d	Z	39° Hc	d	Z	40° Hc	d	Z	41° Hc	d	Z	42° Hc	d	Z	43° Hc	d	Z	44° Hc	d	Z	45° Hc	d	Z	Dec.
0	49 52.3	+57.3	158.0	48 56.6	+57.4	158.4	48 00.7	+57.7	158.8	47 04.7	+57.8	159.2	46 08.6	+57.9	159.6	45 12.3	+58.0	159.9	44 15.9	+58.1	160.3	43 19.3	+58.3	160.6	0
1	50 49.6	57.1	157.5	49 54.0	57.4	157.9	48 58.4	57.5	158.4	48 02.5	57.7	158.8	47 06.5	57.8	159.2	46 10.3	58.0	159.6	45 14.0	58.1	159.9	44 17.6	58.3	160.2	1
2	51 46.7	57.0	157.0	50 51.4	57.2	157.5	49 55.9	57.4	157.9	49 00.2	57.5	158.4	48 04.3	57.8	158.8	47 08.3	57.9	159.2	46 12.1	58.1	159.6	45 15.9	58.1	159.9	2
3	52 43.7	56.9	156.5	51 48.6	57.1	157.0	50 53.3	57.3	157.5	49 57.7	57.5	157.9	49 02.1	57.6	158.4	48 06.2	57.8	158.8	47 10.2	57.9	159.2	46 14.0	58.1	159.6	3
4	53 40.6	56.7	156.0	52 45.7	57.0	156.5	51 50.6	57.1	157.0	50 55.2	57.4	157.5	49 59.7	57.6	158.0	49 04.0	57.7	158.4	48 08.1	57.9	158.8	47 12.1	58.1	159.2	4
5	54 37.3	+56.6	155.4	53 42.7	+56.8	156.0	52 47.7	+57.1	156.5	51 52.6	+57.3	157.0	50 57.3	+57.4	157.5	50 01.7	+57.7	158.0	49 06.0	+57.8	158.4	48 10.2	+57.9	158.8	5
6	55 33.9	56.4	154.8	54 39.5	56.6	155.4	53 44.8	56.9	156.0	52 49.9	57.1	156.5	51 54.7	57.4	157.1	50 59.4	57.5	157.5	50 03.8	57.7	158.0	49 08.1	57.9	158.4	6
7	56 30.3	56.2	154.2	55 36.1	56.5	154.8	54 41.7	56.7	155.5	53 47.0	57.0	156.0	52 52.1	57.2	156.6	51 56.9	57.4	157.1	51 01.5	57.6	157.6	50 06.0	57.8	158.0	7
8	57 26.5	56.0	153.6	56 32.6	56.3	154.2	55 38.4	56.6	154.9	54 44.0	56.8	155.5	53 49.3	57.0	156.1	52 54.3	57.3	156.6	51 59.1	57.5	157.1	51 03.8	57.8	157.6	8
9	58 22.5	55.8	152.9	57 28.9	56.1	153.6	56 35.0	56.4	154.3	55 40.8	56.7	154.9	54 46.3	57.0	155.6	53 51.6	57.0	156.1	52 56.6	57.5	156.6	52 01.5	57.5	157.2	9
10	59 18.3	+55.5	152.2	58 25.0	+55.9	152.9	57 31.4	+56.3	153.7	56 37.5	+56.5	154.3	55 43.3	+56.8	155.0	54 48.8	+57.0	155.6	53 54.0	+57.3	156.1	52 59.0	+57.5	156.7	10
11	60 13.8	55.3	151.4	59 20.9	55.7	152.2	58 27.7	55.9	153.0	57 34.0	56.3	153.7	56 40.1	56.6	154.4	55 45.8	56.9	155.0	54 51.3	57.1	155.6	53 56.5	57.4	156.2	11
12	61 09.1	55.0	150.6	60 16.6	55.5	151.5	59 23.6	55.8	152.3	58 30.3	56.1	153.1	57 36.7	56.4	153.8	56 42.7	56.7	154.5	55 48.4	57.0	155.1	54 53.9	57.2	155.7	12
13	62 04.1	54.6	149.8	61 12.0	55.1	150.7	60 19.4	55.5	151.6	59 26.4	55.9	152.4	58 33.1	56.2	153.1	57 39.4	56.5	153.9	56 45.4	56.8	154.5	55 51.1	57.0	155.2	13
14	62 58.7	54.3	148.9	62 07.1	54.7	149.9	61 14.9	55.2	150.8	60 22.3	55.7	151.7	59 29.3	56.0	152.5	58 35.9	56.4	153.2	57 42.2	56.6	153.9	56 48.1	57.0	154.6	14
15	63 53.0	+53.8	147.9	63 01.8	+54.4	149.0	62 10.1	+54.9	150.0	61 18.0	+55.3	150.9	60 25.3	+55.8	151.7	59 32.3	+56.1	152.6	58 38.8	+56.5	153.3	57 45.1	+56.7	154.0	15
16	64 46.8	53.5	146.9	63 56.2	54.1	148.0	63 05.0	54.6	149.1	62 13.3	55.1	150.1	61 21.1	55.5	151.0	60 28.4	55.9	151.8	59 35.3	56.2	152.7	58 41.8	56.6	153.4	16
17	65 40.3	52.9	145.8	64 50.3	53.6	147.0	63 59.6	54.2	148.2	63 08.4	54.7	149.2	62 16.6	55.1	150.2	61 24.3	55.6	151.1	60 31.5	56.0	152.0	59 38.4	56.3	152.8	17
18	66 33.2	52.4	144.7	65 43.9	53.1	146.0	64 53.8	53.7	147.2	64 03.1	54.3	148.3	63 11.7	54.9	149.3	62 19.9	55.3	150.3	61 27.5	55.8	151.2	60 34.7	56.1	152.1	18
19	67 25.6	51.7	143.4	66 37.0	52.5	144.8	65 47.5	53.3	146.1	64 57.4	54.0	147.3	64 06.6	54.5	148.3	63 15.2	55.0	149.5	62 23.3	55.4	150.4	61 30.8	55.9	151.3	19
20	68 17.3	+51.1	142.1	67 29.5	+52.0	143.6	66 40.8	+52.8	145.0	65 51.3	+53.5	146.2	65 01.1	+54.1	147.4	64 10.2	+54.6	148.5	63 18.7	+55.2	149.6	62 26.7	+55.6	150.6	20
21	69 08.4	50.3	140.6	68 21.5	51.2	142.2	67 33.6	52.1	143.7	66 44.8	52.9	145.1	65 55.2	53.6	146.4	65 04.8	54.3	147.6	64 13.9	54.8	148.7	63 22.3	55.3	149.7	21
22	69 58.7	49.3	139.1	69 12.7	50.5	140.8	68 25.7	51.5	142.4	67 37.7	52.3	143.9	66 48.8	53.1	145.3	65 59.1	53.8	146.6	65 08.7	54.4	147.7	64 17.6	55.0	148.9	22
23	70 48.0	48.4	137.4	70 03.2	49.6	139.2	69 17.2	50.7	141.0	68 30.0	51.7	142.6	67 41.9	52.5	144.1	66 52.9	53.3	145.4	66 03.1	54.0	146.6	65 12.6	54.6	147.9	23
24	71 36.4	47.2	135.5	70 52.8	48.6	137.6	70 07.9	49.8	139.4	69 21.7	50.9	141.2	68 34.4	51.9	142.8	67 46.2	52.7	144.3	66 57.1	53.5	145.6	66 07.2	54.1	146.9	24
25	72 23.6	+45.9	133.5	71 41.4	+47.5	135.7	70 57.7	+48.9	137.8	70 12.6	+50.1	139.6	69 26.3	+51.2	141.4	68 38.9	+52.1	143.0	67 50.6	+52.9	144.5	67 01.3	+53.7	145.8	25
26	73 09.5	44.4	131.4	72 28.9	46.2	133.7	71 46.6	47.7	136.0	71 02.7	49.1	138.0	70 17.5	50.3	139.9	69 31.0	51.4	141.6	68 43.5	52.3	143.2	67 55.0	53.2	144.7	26
27	73 53.9	42.7	129.0	73 15.1	44.7	131.6	72 34.3	46.5	134.0	71 51.8	48.1	136.2	71 07.8	49.4	138.2	70 22.4	50.6	140.1	69 35.8	51.7	141.8	68 48.2	52.5	143.4	27
28	74 36.6	40.7	126.4	73 59.8	43.0	129.2	73 20.8	45.0	131.8	72 39.9	46.7	134.2	71 57.2	48.3	136.4	71 13.0	49.7	138.4	70 27.5	50.8	140.3	69 40.7	51.9	142.0	28
29	75 17.3	38.5	123.6	74 42.8	41.0	126.6	74 05.8	43.3	129.4	73 26.6	45.3	132.1	72 45.5	47.1	134.5	72 02.7	48.5	136.7	71 18.3	49.9	138.7	70 32.6	51.0	140.6	29
30	75 55.8	+35.9	120.5	75 23.8	+38.8	123.8	74 49.1	+41.4	126.9	74 11.9	+43.7	129.7	73 32.6	+45.6	132.3	72 51.2	+47.4	134.7	72 08.2	+48.9	136.9	71 23.6	+50.2	139.0	30
31	76 31.7	32.9	117.1	76 02.6	36.3	120.7	75 30.5	39.1	124.0	74 55.6	41.7	127.1	74 18.2	43.9	130.0	73 38.6	45.9	132.6	72 57.1	47.6	135.0	72 13.8	49.2	137.2	31
32	77 04.6	29.7	113.5	76 38.9	33.3	117.3	76 09.6	36.6	120.9	75 37.3	39.5	124.3	75 02.1	42.1	127.4	74 24.5	44.3	130.2	73 44.7	46.3	132.9	73 03.0	47.9	135.3	32
33	77 34.3	25.9	109.5	77 12.2	30.0	113.6	76 46.2	33.7	117.6	76 16.8	37.0	121.2	75 44.2	39.9	124.6	75 08.8	42.5	127.7	74 31.0	44.6	130.5	73 50.9	46.6	133.2	33
34	78 00.2	21.8	105.2	77 42.2	26.2	109.7	77 19.9	30.4	113.9	76 53.8	34.0	117.8	76 24.1	37.3	121.5	75 51.3	40.2	124.8	75 15.6	42.8	128.0	74 37.5	45.0	130.8	34
35	78 22.0	+17.2	100.7	78 08.4	+22.1	105.4	77 50.3	+26.6	109.8	77 27.8	+30.7	114.1	77 01.4	+34.5	118.0	76 31.5	+37.7	121.7	75 58.4	+40.7	125.1	75 22.5	+43.2	128.3	35
36	78 39.2	12.3	95.9	78 30.5	17.5	100.8	78 16.9	22.3	105.5	77 58.5	27.0	110.0	77 35.9	31.0	114.3	77 09.2	34.8	118.3	76 39.1	38.1	122.0	76 05.7	41.0	125.5	36
37	78 51.5	7.2	90.8	78 48.0	12.5	95.9	78 39.2	17.8	100.9	78 25.5	22.7	105.7	78 06.9	27.3	110.3	77 44.0	31.5	114.6	77 17.2	35.2	118.6	76 46.7	38.5	122.4	37
38	78 58.7	1.8	85.7	79 00.5	7.3	90.8	78 57.0	12.7	95.9	78 48.2	18.0	101.0	78 34.2	23.1	105.8	78 15.5	27.7	110.5	77 52.4	31.8	114.8	77 25.2	35.6	118.9	38
39	79 00.5	−3.5	80.4	79 07.8	1.9	85.7	79 09.7	7.5	90.8	79 06.2	12.9	96.0	78 57.3	18.3	101.1	78 43.2	23.3	106.0	78 24.2	28.1	110.7	78 00.8	32.3	115.1	39
40	78 57.0	−8.8	75.2	79 09.7	−3.5	80.3	79 17.2	+1.9	85.5	79 19.1	+7.6	90.8	79 15.6	+13.1	96.1	79 06.5	+18.6	101.2	78 52.3	+23.7	106.2	78 33.1	+28.4	111.0	40
41	78 48.2	14.0	70.1	79 06.2	8.9	75.0	79 19.1	−3.5	80.1	79 26.7	2.0	85.4	79 28.7	7.8	90.8	79 25.1	13.4	96.1	79 16.0	18.9	101.4	79 01.5	24.7	106.4	41
42	78 34.2	18.7	65.1	78 57.3	14.1	69.8	79 15.6	9.1	74.7	79 28.7	−3.6	79.9	79 36.5	2.0	85.3	79 38.5	7.9	90.8	79 34.9	13.6	96.2	79 25.6	19.2	101.5	42
43	78 15.5	23.1	60.4	78 43.2	19.0	64.8	79 06.5	14.2	69.5	79 25.1	9.1	74.5	79 38.5	−3.6	79.8	79 46.4	2.1	85.2	79 48.5	8.0	90.8	79 44.8	13.8	96.3	43
44	77 52.4	27.2	55.9	78 24.2	23.4	60.0	78 52.3	19.2	64.4	79 16.0	14.5	69.1	79 34.9	9.3	74.2	79 48.5	−3.7	79.6	79 56.5	2.1	85.1	79 58.6	8.2	90.8	44

16°, 344° L.H.A.   LATITUDE SAME NAME AS DECLINATION

Dec.	38° Hc	d	Z	39° Hc	d	Z	40° Hc	d	Z	41° Hc	d	Z	42° Hc	d	Z	43° Hc	d	Z	44° Hc	d	Z	45° Hc	d	Z	Dec.
0	49 14.6	+56.5	155.0	48 20.1	+56.7	155.5	47 25.4	+56.9	156.0	46 30.5	+57.1	156.4	45 35.4	+57.4	156.8	44 40.2	+57.5	157.2	43 44.8	+57.7	157.6	42 49.3	+57.8	157.9	0
1	50 11.1	56.4	154.5	49 16.8	56.6	155.0	48 22.3	56.9	155.5	47 27.6	57.1	155.9	46 32.8	57.2	156.4	45 37.7	57.4	156.8	44 42.5	57.5	157.2	43 47.1	57.7	157.6	1
2	51 07.5	56.2	154.0	50 13.4	56.5	154.5	49 19.2	56.7	155.0	48 24.7	56.9	155.5	47 30.0	57.1	155.9	46 35.1	57.3	156.4	45 40.0	57.4	156.8	44 44.8	57.6	157.2	2
3	52 03.7	56.0	153.4	51 09.9	56.3	154.0	50 15.9	56.5	154.5	49 21.6	56.8	155.0	48 27.1	57.0	155.5	47 32.4	57.2	155.9	46 37.5	57.3	156.4	45 42.5	57.4	156.8	3
4	52 59.7	55.9	152.8	52 06.2	56.2	153.4	51 12.4	56.4	154.0	50 18.4	56.6	154.5	49 24.1	56.9	155.0	48 29.6	57.1	155.5	47 34.9	57.3	155.9	46 40.1	57.4	156.4	4
5	53 55.6	+55.6	152.2	53 02.4	+55.9	152.8	52 08.8	+56.3	153.4	51 15.0	+56.6	154.0	50 21.0	+56.8	154.5	49 26.7	+57.0	155.0	48 32.2	+57.2	155.5	47 37.5	+57.3	156.0	5
6	54 51.2	55.5	151.6	53 58.3	55.8	152.2	53 05.1	56.1	152.8	52 11.6	56.3	153.4	51 17.8	56.6	154.0	50 23.7	56.9	154.5	49 29.4	57.1	155.0	48 34.9	57.3	155.5	6
7	55 46.7	55.2	150.9	54 54.1	55.6	151.6	54 01.2	55.9	152.2	53 07.9	56.2	152.9	52 14.4	56.4	153.5	51 20.6	56.7	154.0	50 26.5	57.0	154.6	49 32.2	57.2	155.1	7
8	56 41.9	55.0	150.2	55 49.7	55.3	150.9	54 57.1	55.7	151.6	54 04.1	56.0	152.3	53 10.8	56.3	152.9	52 17.3	56.6	153.5	51 23.5	56.8	154.1	50 29.4	57.0	154.6	8
9	57 36.9	54.7	149.4	56 45.0	55.1	150.2	55 52.8	55.4	151.0	55 00.1	55.8	151.7	54 07.1	56.2	152.3	53 13.9	56.4	152.9	52 20.3	56.7	153.5	51 26.4	57.0	154.1	9
10	58 31.6	+54.4	148.7	57 40.1	+54.9	149.5	56 48.2	+55.3	150.3	55 55.9	+55.6	151.0	55 03.3	+55.9	151.7	54 10.3	+56.2	152.4	53 17.0	+56.5	153.0	52 23.4	+56.7	153.6	10
11	59 26.0	54.1	147.9	58 35.0	54.5	148.7	57 43.5	54.9	149.6	56 51.5	55.4	150.3	55 59.2	55.7	151.1	55 06.5	56.1	151.8	54 13.5	56.3	152.4	53 20.1	56.7	153.1	11
12	60 20.1	53.7	147.0	59 29.5	54.3	147.9	58 38.4	54.7	148.8	57 46.9	55.1	149.6	56 54.9	55.5	150.4	56 02.6	55.8	151.1	55 09.8	56.1	151.8	54 16.8	56.5	152.5	12
13	61 13.8	53.4	146.1	60 23.8	53.8	147.1	59 33.1	54.4	148.0	58 42.0	54.9	148.8	57 50.4	55.3	149.7	56 58.4	55.7	150.5	56 06.0	56.0	151.2	55 13.3	56.3	151.9	13
14	62 07.2	52.9	145.1	61 17.6	53.6	146.2	60 27.5	54.1	147.2	59 36.9	54.5	148.1	58 45.7	55.0	149.0	57 54.1	55.3	149.8	57 02.0	55.8	150.6	56 09.6	56.1	151.3	14
15	63 00.1	+52.4	144.1	62 11.2	+53.0	145.2	61 21.6	+53.6	146.3	60 31.4	+54.2	147.2	59 40.7	+54.7	148.2	58 49.4	+55.2	149.0	57 57.8	+55.5	149.9	57 05.7	+55.9	150.7	15
16	63 52.5	52.0	143.0	63 04.2	52.7	144.2	62 15.2	53.3	145.3	61 25.6	53.8	146.4	60 35.4	54.4	147.4	59 44.6	54.8	148.3	58 53.3	55.3	149.2	58 01.6	55.6	150.0	16
17	64 44.5	51.3	141.8	63 56.9	52.1	143.1	63 08.5	52.8	144.3	62 19.4	53.5	145.4	61 29.7	54.0	146.5	60 39.4	54.5	147.5	59 48.6	55.0	148.4	58 57.2	55.5	149.3	17
18	65 35.8	50.7	140.6	64 49.0	51.5	142.0	64 01.3	52.3	143.2	63 12.9	53.0	144.4	62 23.7	53.6	145.5	61 33.9	54.2	146.6	60 43.6	54.7	147.6	59 52.7	55.1	148.5	18
19	66 26.5	50.0	139.3	65 40.5	51.0	140.7	64 53.6	51.8	142.1	64 05.9	52.5	143.4	63 17.3	53.2	144.6	62 28.1	53.8	145.7	61 38.3	54.3	146.7	60 47.8	54.9	147.7	19
20	67 16.5	+49.2	137.9	66 31.5	+50.2	139.4	65 45.4	+51.1	140.9	64 58.4	+51.9	142.2	64 10.5	+52.7	143.5	63 21.9	+53.4	144.7	62 32.6	+54.0	145.8	61 42.7	+54.5	146.9	20
21	68 05.7	48.3	136.4	67 21.7	49.4	138.0	66 36.5	50.5	139.6	65 50.3	51.4	141.0	65 03.2	52.2	142.4	64 15.3	52.9	143.7	63 26.6	53.5	144.9	62 37.2	54.1	146.0	21
22	68 54.0	47.4	134.8	68 11.1	48.6	136.5	67 27.0	49.7	138.2	66 41.7	50.7	139.8	65 55.4	51.6	141.2	65 08.2	52.4	142.6	64 20.1	53.1	143.8	63 31.3	53.8	145.0	22
23	69 41.4	46.2	133.0	68 59.7	47.6	134.9	68 16.7	48.8	136.7	67 32.4	49.9	138.4	66 47.0	50.9	139.9	66 00.6	51.8	141.4	65 13.2	52.6	142.7	64 25.1	53.3	144.0	23
24	70 27.6	45.0	131.2	69 47.3	46.5	133.2	69 05.5	47.9	135.1	68 22.3	49.1	136.9	67 37.9	50.2	138.6	66 52.4	51.1	140.1	66 05.8	52.1	141.6	65 18.4	52.8	142.9	24
25	71 12.6	+43.6	129.1	70 33.8	+45.3	131.4	69 53.4	+46.8	133.4	69 11.4	+48.2	135.3	68 28.1	+49.3	137.1	67 43.5	+50.5	138.8	66 57.9	+51.4	140.3	66 11.2	+52.3	141.8	25
26	71 56.2	42.0	127.0	71 19.1	43.9	129.3	70 40.2	45.5	131.6	69 59.6	47.0	133.6	69 17.4	48.5	135.5	68 34.0	49.6	137.3	67 49.3	50.7	139.0	67 03.5	51.6	140.5	26
27	72 38.2	40.2	124.6	72 03.0	42.3	127.2	71 25.7	44.2	129.5	70 46.6	45.9	131.8	70 05.9	47.3	133.8	69 23.6	48.7	135.7	68 40.0	49.9	137.5	67 55.1	51.0	139.2	27
28	73 18.4	38.2	122.1	72 45.3	40.6	124.8	72 09.9	42.7	127.4	71 32.5	44.5	129.8	70 53.2	46.2	132.0	70 12.3	47.7	134.1	69 29.9	48.9	136.0	68 46.1	50.1	137.8	28
29	73 56.6	36.0	119.4	73 25.9	38.5	122.3	72 52.6	40.9	125.0	72 17.0	43.0	127.6	71 39.4	44.9	130.0	71 00.0	46.5	132.2	70 18.8	48.0	134.3	69 36.2	49.3	136.2	29
30	74 32.6	+33.5	116.4	74 04.4	+36.4	119.5	73 33.5	+38.9	122.5	73 00.0	+41.3	125.3	72 24.3	+43.3	127.8	71 46.5	+45.2	130.2	71 06.8	+46.9	132.5	70 25.5	+48.3	134.6	30
31	75 06.1	30.6	113.2	74 40.8	33.8	116.6	74 12.4	36.7	119.8	73 41.3	39.3	122.7	73 07.6	41.6	125.5	72 31.7	43.7	128.1	71 53.7	45.5	130.5	71 13.8	47.1	132.8	31
32	75 36.7	27.5	109.8	75 14.6	31.0	113.4	74 49.1	34.2	116.8	74 20.6	37.0	120.0	73 49.2	39.7	123.0	73 15.4	41.9	125.8	72 39.2	44.0	128.4	72 00.9	45.9	130.8	32
33	76 04.2	24.1	106.2	75 45.6	27.9	110.0	75 23.3	31.4	113.6	74 57.6	34.6	117.0	74 28.9	37.4	120.2	73 57.3	40.1	123.2	73 23.2	42.4	126.0	72 46.8	44.4	128.7	33
34	76 28.3	20.4	102.3	76 13.5	24.4	106.3	75 54.7	28.2	110.2	75 32.2	31.7	113.8	75 06.3	35.0	117.2	74 37.4	37.8	120.5	74 05.6	40.4	123.5	73 31.2	42.7	126.3	34
35	76 48.7	+16.3	98.3	76 37.9	+20.6	102.4	76 22.9	+24.8	106.5	76 03.9	+28.6	110.3	75 41.3	+32.1	114.0	75 15.2	+35.3	117.5	74 46.0	+38.2	120.8	74 13.9	+40.8	123.8	35
36	77 05.0	12.0	94.0	76 58.5	16.6	98.3	76 47.7	20.9	102.5	76 32.5	25.1	106.6	76 13.4	29.0	110.5	75 50.5	32.5	114.3	75 24.7	35.7	117.8	74 54.7	38.7	121.1	36
37	77 17.0	7.4	89.6	77 15.1	12.2	94.0	77 08.6	16.8	98.4	76 57.6	21.3	102.7	76 42.4	25.4	106.8	76 23.0	29.4	110.8	75 59.9	33.0	114.5	75 33.4	36.1	118.1	37
38	77 24.4	+2.7	85.1	77 27.3	7.6	89.5	77 25.4	12.4	94.0	77 18.9	17.1	98.5	77 07.8	21.6	102.8	76 52.4	25.8	107.0	76 32.9	29.7	111.0	76 09.5	33.3	114.8	38
39	77 27.3	-1.9	80.5	77 34.9	+2.9	84.9	77 37.8	7.8	89.5	77 36.0	12.6	94.0	77 29.4	17.3	98.5	77 18.2	21.9	102.9	77 02.6	26.2	107.2	76 42.8	30.2	111.2	39
40	77 25.4	6.5	75.9	77 37.8	-1.8	80.3	77 45.6	+3.0	84.8	77 48.6	+7.9	89.5	77 46.7	+12.9	94.1	77 40.1	+17.6	98.6	77 28.8	+22.2	103.1	77 13.0	+26.5	107.4	40
41	77 18.9	11.1	71.3	77 36.0	6.6	75.6	77 48.6	-1.9	80.1	77 56.5	3.1	84.7	77 59.6	8.0	89.4	77 57.7	13.1	94.1	77 51.0	17.9	98.8	77 39.5	22.6	103.3	41
42	77 07.8	15.4	66.9	77 29.4	11.2	71.0	77 46.7	6.6	75.2	77 59.6	-1.9	79.9	78 07.6	3.2	84.6	78 10.8	8.2	89.4	78 08.9	13.3	94.2	78 02.1	18.2	98.9	42
43	76 52.4	19.5	62.6	77 18.2	15.6	66.5	77 40.1	11.3	70.7	77 57.7	6.7	75.1	78 10.8	-1.9	79.8	78 19.0	3.2	84.5	78 22.2	8.3	89.4	78 20.3	13.5	94.2	43
44	76 32.9	23.4	58.5	77 02.6	19.8	62.1	77 28.8	15.8	66.1	77 51.0	11.5	70.4	78 08.9	6.8	74.9	78 22.2	-1.9	79.6	78 30.5	3.3	84.4	78 33.8	8.5	89.3	44

LATITUDE SAME NAME AS DECLINATION

N. Lat. { L.H.A. greater than 180°......Zn=Z
{ L.H.A. less than 180°.........Zn=360°−Z

Dec.	38° Hc	d	Z	39° Hc	d	Z	40° Hc	d	Z	41° Hc	d	Z	42° Hc	d	Z	43° Hc	d	Z	44° Hc	d	Z	45° Hc	d	Z	Dec.
0	48 54.1	+56.1	153.6	48 00.2	+56.4	154.1	47 06.1	+56.6	154.6	46 11.9	+56.8	155.0	45 17.4	+57.0	155.4	44 22.7	+57.2	155.9	43 27.9	+57.4	156.2	42 32.9	+57.5	156.6	0
1	49 50.2	56.0	153.0	48 56.6	56.2	153.6	48 02.7	56.5	154.1	47 08.7	56.7	154.5	46 14.4	56.9	155.0	45 19.9	57.1	155.4	44 25.3	57.3	155.8	43 30.4	57.5	156.2	1
2	50 46.2	55.7	152.5	49 52.8	56.1	153.0	48 59.2	56.3	153.6	48 05.4	56.5	154.1	47 11.3	56.8	154.5	46 17.0	57.0	155.0	45 22.6	57.2	155.4	44 27.9	57.4	155.8	2
3	51 41.9	55.7	151.9	50 48.9	55.9	152.5	49 55.5	56.2	153.0	49 01.9	56.5	153.6	48 08.1	56.7	154.1	47 14.0	56.9	154.5	46 19.8	57.1	155.0	45 25.3	57.3	155.4	3
4	52 37.6	55.4	151.3	51 44.8	55.7	151.9	50 51.7	56.0	152.5	49 58.4	56.2	153.0	49 04.8	56.5	153.6	48 10.9	56.8	154.1	47 16.9	56.9	154.5	46 22.6	57.2	155.0	4
5	53 33.0	+55.2	150.6	52 40.5	+55.5	151.3	51 47.7	+55.9	151.9	50 54.6	+56.2	152.5	50 01.3	+56.4	153.0	49 07.7	+56.6	153.6	48 13.8	+56.9	154.1	47 19.8	+57.1	154.5	5
6	54 28.2	54.9	150.0	53 36.0	55.4	150.7	52 43.6	55.5	151.3	51 50.8	55.9	151.9	50 57.7	56.2	152.5	50 04.3	56.5	153.1	49 10.7	56.6	153.6	48 16.9	56.9	154.1	6
7	55 23.1	54.7	149.3	54 31.4	55.0	150.0	53 39.2	55.5	150.7	52 46.7	55.8	151.3	51 53.9	56.1	151.9	51 00.8	56.4	152.5	50 07.5	56.6	153.1	49 13.8	56.9	153.6	7
8	56 17.8	54.5	148.5	55 26.4	54.9	149.3	54 34.7	55.0	150.0	53 42.5	55.6	150.7	52 50.0	55.9	151.3	51 57.2	56.0	151.9	51 04.1	56.4	152.5	50 10.7	56.7	153.1	8
9	57 12.3	54.1	147.8	56 21.3	54.6	148.6	55 29.9	55.0	149.3	54 38.1	55.3	150.1	53 45.9	55.7	150.8	52 53.4	56.0	151.4	52 00.5	56.3	152.0	51 07.4	56.6	152.6	9
10	58 06.4	+53.9	147.0	57 15.9	+54.3	147.8	56 24.9	+54.7	148.6	55 33.4	+55.2	149.4	54 41.6	+55.5	150.1	53 49.4	+55.8	150.8	52 56.8	+56.2	151.5	52 04.0	+56.4	152.1	10
11	59 00.3	53.4	146.1	58 10.2	54.0	147.0	57 19.6	54.4	147.9	56 28.6	54.8	148.7	55 37.1	55.3	149.5	54 45.2	55.6	150.2	53 53.0	55.8	150.9	53 00.4	56.3	151.5	11
12	59 53.7	53.1	145.2	59 04.2	53.6	146.2	58 14.0	54.2	147.1	57 23.4	54.6	147.9	56 32.4	55.0	148.7	55 40.8	55.4	149.5	54 48.9	55.8	150.2	53 56.7	56.1	150.9	12
13	60 46.8	52.7	144.3	59 57.8	53.3	145.3	59 08.2	53.8	146.3	58 18.0	54.0	147.2	57 27.4	54.7	148.0	56 36.2	55.2	148.8	55 44.7	55.5	149.6	54 52.8	55.9	150.3	13
14	61 39.5	52.3	143.3	60 51.1	52.8	144.4	60 02.0	53.4	145.4	59 12.3	54.0	146.3	58 22.1	54.5	147.3	57 31.4	54.9	148.1	56 40.2	55.4	148.9	55 48.7	55.6	149.7	14
15	62 31.8	+51.7	142.3	61 43.9	+52.5	143.4	60 55.4	+53.1	144.5	60 06.3	+53.6	145.5	59 16.6	+54.1	146.5	58 26.3	+54.6	147.3	57 35.6	+54.6	148.2	56 44.4	+55.5	149.0	15
16	63 23.5	51.1	141.1	62 36.4	51.9	142.4	61 48.5	52.6	143.5	60 59.9	53.2	144.6	60 10.7	53.8	145.6	59 20.9	54.3	146.5	58 30.6	54.8	147.4	57 39.8	55.2	148.3	16
17	64 14.6	50.6	140.0	63 28.3	51.3	141.1	62 41.1	52.1	142.5	61 53.1	52.8	143.6	61 04.5	53.4	144.7	60 15.2	54.0	145.7	59 25.4	54.5	146.7	58 35.0	54.9	147.6	17
18	65 05.2	49.9	138.7	64 19.6	50.8	140.1	63 33.2	51.0	141.4	62 45.9	52.4	142.6	61 57.9	53.0	143.7	61 09.2	53.6	144.8	60 19.9	54.1	145.8	59 29.9	54.7	146.8	18
19	65 55.1	49.1	137.4	65 10.4	50.1	138.8	64 24.8	51.0	140.2	63 38.3	51.8	141.5	62 50.9	52.5	142.7	62 02.8	53.2	143.9	61 14.0	53.8	144.9	60 24.6	54.3	146.0	19
20	66 44.2	+48.3	135.9	66 00.5	+49.4	137.5	65 15.8	+50.3	139.0	64 30.1	+51.2	140.3	63 43.4	+52.0	141.6	62 56.0	+52.7	142.9	62 07.8	+53.4	144.0	61 18.9	+54.0	145.1	20
21	67 32.5	47.4	134.4	66 49.9	48.6	136.1	66 06.1	49.7	137.6	65 21.3	50.6	139.1	64 35.4	51.5	140.5	63 48.7	52.2	141.8	63 01.2	52.9	143.0	62 12.9	53.6	144.2	21
22	68 19.9	46.4	132.8	67 38.5	47.6	134.6	66 55.8	48.8	136.2	66 11.9	49.8	137.8	65 26.9	50.8	139.3	64 40.9	51.7	140.7	63 54.1	52.4	142.0	63 06.5	53.1	143.2	22
23	69 06.3	45.2	131.0	68 26.1	46.7	132.9	67 44.6	47.9	134.7	67 01.7	49.1	136.4	66 17.7	50.1	138.0	65 32.6	51.1	139.5	64 46.5	52.0	140.8	63 59.6	52.7	142.1	23
24	69 51.5	43.9	129.1	69 12.8	45.5	131.2	68 32.5	46.9	133.1	67 50.8	48.2	134.9	67 07.8	49.4	136.6	66 23.7	50.3	138.2	65 38.5	51.3	139.6	64 52.3	52.1	141.0	24
25	70 35.4	+42.5	127.1	69 58.3	+44.2	129.3	69 19.4	+45.8	131.4	68 39.0	+47.2	133.3	67 57.2	+48.4	135.1	67 14.0	+49.7	136.8	66 29.8	+50.6	138.4	65 44.4	+51.5	139.8	25
26	71 17.9	40.9	125.0	70 42.5	42.8	127.3	70 05.2	44.6	129.5	69 26.2	46.1	131.6	68 45.6	47.6	133.5	68 03.7	48.7	135.3	67 20.4	49.9	137.0	66 35.9	50.9	138.6	26
27	71 58.8	39.1	122.6	71 25.3	41.3	125.1	70 49.8	43.1	127.5	70 12.3	44.9	129.7	69 33.2	46.4	131.8	68 52.4	47.8	133.7	68 10.3	49.0	135.5	67 26.8	50.2	137.2	27
28	72 37.9	37.1	120.1	72 06.6	39.4	122.8	71 32.9	41.6	125.3	70 57.2	43.5	127.7	70 19.6	44.8	129.9	69 40.2	46.8	132.0	68 59.3	48.1	133.9	68 17.0	49.3	135.8	28
29	73 15.0	34.9	117.5	72 46.0	37.5	120.3	72 14.5	39.8	123.0	71 40.7	41.9	125.6	71 04.8	43.8	127.8	70 27.0	45.5	130.2	69 47.4	47.1	132.2	69 06.3	48.4	134.2	29
30	73 49.9	+32.4	114.6	73 23.5	+35.2	117.6	72 54.3	+37.8	120.5	72 22.6	+40.2	123.2	71 48.6	+42.3	125.8	71 12.5	+44.2	128.2	70 34.5	+45.8	130.4	69 54.7	+47.4	132.5	30
31	74 22.3	29.7	111.5	73 58.7	32.8	114.8	73 32.1	35.7	117.8	73 02.8	38.2	120.7	72 30.9	40.5	123.5	71 56.7	42.6	126.0	71 20.3	44.6	128.4	70 42.1	46.2	130.7	31
32	74 52.0	26.7	108.2	74 31.5	30.1	111.7	74 07.8	33.1	114.9	73 41.0	36.0	118.1	73 11.4	38.6	121.0	72 39.3	40.9	123.7	72 04.9	43.0	126.3	71 28.3	44.9	128.7	32
33	75 18.7	23.3	104.8	75 01.6	27.0	108.4	74 40.9	30.4	111.8	74 17.0	33.5	115.2	73 50.0	36.4	118.3	73 20.2	39.0	121.2	72 47.9	41.3	124.0	72 13.2	43.4	126.6	33
34	75 42.0	19.8	101.1	75 28.6	23.6	104.8	75 11.3	27.4	108.5	74 50.5	30.8	112.0	74 26.4	33.9	115.4	73 59.2	36.7	118.5	73 29.2	39.3	121.2	72 56.6	41.6	124.3	34
35	76 01.8	+16.0	97.2	75 52.2	+20.1	101.2	75 38.7	+24.0	105.0	75 21.3	+27.3	108.7	75 00.3	+31.1	112.2	74 35.9	+34.3	115.6	74 08.5	+37.2	118.8	73 38.2	+39.8	121.8	35
36	76 17.8	11.9	93.2	76 12.3	16.2	97.2	76 02.7	20.4	101.2	75 49.0	24.3	105.1	75 31.4	28.1	108.9	75 10.2	31.6	112.5	74 45.7	34.7	115.9	74 18.0	37.6	119.1	36
37	76 29.7	7.7	89.0	76 28.5	12.2	93.2	76 23.1	16.4	97.3	76 13.3	20.4	101.3	75 59.5	24.7	105.3	75 41.8	28.4	109.1	75 20.4	31.9	112.7	74 55.6	35.1	116.1	37
38	76 37.4	3.3	84.7	76 40.7	7.8	89.0	76 39.5	12.4	93.2	76 34.0	16.8	97.4	76 24.2	21.0	101.5	76 10.2	25.1	105.4	75 52.3	28.9	109.3	75 30.7	32.4	112.9	38
39	76 40.7	−1.2	80.4	76 48.5	+3.4	84.6	76 51.9	7.9	88.9	76 50.8	12.5	93.2	76 45.2	17.0	97.4	76 35.3	21.3	101.6	76 21.2	25.4	105.6	76 03.1	29.2	109.5	39
40	76 39.5	−5.5	76.1	76 51.9	−1.1	80.2	76 59.8	+3.5	84.5	77 03.3	+8.1	88.8	77 02.2	+12.8	93.2	76 56.6	+17.3	97.5	76 46.6	+21.7	101.7	76 32.3	+25.8	105.8	40
41	76 34.0	9.8	71.8	76 50.8	5.6	75.9	77 03.3	−1.1	80.1	77 11.4	3.6	84.4	77 15.0	8.2	88.8	77 13.9	13.0	93.3	77 08.3	17.5	97.6	76 58.1	22.0	101.9	41
42	76 24.2	14.0	67.6	76 45.2	9.9	71.5	77 02.2	5.6	75.6	77 15.0	−1.1	79.9	77 23.2	3.7	84.3	77 26.9	8.4	88.8	77 25.8	13.2	93.3	77 20.1	17.9	97.7	42
43	76 10.2	17.9	63.5	76 35.3	14.1	67.2	76 56.6	10.0	71.2	77 13.9	5.6	75.4	77 26.9	−1.1	79.7	77 35.3	3.7	84.2	77 39.0	8.6	88.7	77 38.0	13.4	93.3	43
44	75 52.3	21.6	59.5	76 21.2	18.1	63.0	76 46.6	14.3	66.8	77 08.3	10.2	70.9	77 25.8	5.7	75.1	77 39.0	−1.0	79.5	77 47.6	3.8	84.1	77 51.4	8.7	88.7	44

19°, 341° L.H.A.   LATITUDE SAME NAME AS DECLINATION

N. Lat. { L.H.A. greater than 180° ...... Zn=Z
         L.H.A. less than 180° ...... Zn=360°−Z }

Dec.	38° Hc	d	Z	39° Hc	d	Z	40° Hc	d	Z	41° Hc	d	Z	42° Hc	d	Z	43° Hc	d	Z	44° Hc	d	Z	45° Hc	d	Z	Dec.
0	48 10.0	+55.2	150.8	47 17.4	+55.6	151.3	46 24.7	+55.8	151.8	45 31.7	+56.1	152.3	44 38.4	+56.4	152.8	43 45.0	+56.6	153.2	42 51.3	+56.8	153.6	41 57.5	+57.0	154.0	0
1	49 05.2	55.2	150.2	48 13.0	55.5	150.8	47 20.5	55.5	151.3	46 27.8	56.0	151.8	45 34.8	56.2	152.3	44 41.6	56.4	152.8	43 48.1	56.7	153.2	42 54.5	56.9	153.6	1
2	50 00.4	54.9	149.6	49 08.5	55.2	150.2	48 16.3	55.5	150.7	47 23.8	55.8	151.3	46 31.0	56.1	151.8	45 38.0	56.4	152.3	44 44.8	56.6	152.7	43 51.4	56.8	153.2	2
3	50 55.3	54.7	149.0	50 03.7	55.0	149.6	49 11.8	55.4	150.2	48 19.6	55.7	150.7	47 27.1	56.0	151.3	46 34.4	56.2	151.8	45 41.4	56.5	152.3	44 48.2	56.7	152.7	3
4	51 50.0	54.4	148.3	50 58.7	54.9	148.9	50 07.2	55.1	149.6	49 15.3	55.5	150.2	48 23.1	55.8	150.7	47 30.6	56.1	151.3	46 37.9	56.4	151.8	45 44.9	56.6	152.3	4
5	52 44.4	+54.3	147.6	51 53.6	+54.6	148.3	51 02.3	+55.0	148.9	50 10.8	+55.3	149.6	49 18.9	+55.6	150.2	48 26.7	+55.9	150.7	47 34.2	+56.2	151.3	46 41.5	+56.4	151.8	5
6	53 38.7	53.9	146.9	52 48.2	54.4	147.6	51 57.3	54.8	148.3	51 06.1	55.1	149.0	50 14.5	55.5	149.6	49 22.6	55.8	150.2	48 30.4	56.1	150.7	47 37.9	56.3	151.3	6
7	54 32.6	53.7	146.1	53 42.6	54.1	146.9	52 52.1	54.5	147.6	52 01.2	54.9	148.3	51 10.0	55.2	149.0	50 18.4	55.6	149.6	49 26.5	55.9	150.2	48 34.2	56.2	150.8	7
8	55 26.3	53.3	145.4	54 36.7	53.8	146.2	53 46.6	54.3	146.9	52 56.1	54.7	147.7	52 05.2	55.1	148.4	51 14.0	55.4	149.0	50 22.4	55.7	149.6	49 30.4	56.0	150.2	8
9	56 19.6	53.0	144.6	55 30.5	53.5	145.4	54 40.9	53.9	146.2	53 50.8	54.4	147.0	53 00.3	54.8	147.7	52 09.4	55.1	148.4	51 18.1	55.5	149.0	50 26.4	55.9	149.7	9
10	57 12.6	+52.7	143.7	56 24.0	+53.2	144.6	55 34.8	+53.7	145.4	54 45.2	+54.1	146.2	53 55.1	+54.6	147.0	53 04.5	+55.0	147.7	52 13.6	+55.4	148.4	51 22.3	+55.7	149.1	10
11	58 05.3	52.3	142.8	57 17.2	52.8	143.8	56 28.5	53.4	144.6	55 39.3	53.9	145.5	54 49.7	54.3	146.3	53 59.5	54.8	147.1	53 09.0	55.1	147.8	52 18.0	55.5	148.5	11
12	58 57.6	51.8	141.9	58 10.0	52.5	142.9	57 21.9	53.0	143.8	56 33.2	53.6	144.7	55 44.0	54.0	145.6	54 54.3	54.4	146.4	54 04.1	54.9	147.1	53 13.5	55.3	147.9	12
13	59 49.4	51.3	140.9	59 02.5	52.0	141.9	58 14.9	52.7	143.0	57 26.8	53.2	143.9	56 38.0	53.7	144.8	55 48.7	54.2	145.7	54 59.0	54.6	146.4	54 08.8	55.0	147.2	13
14	60 40.7	50.9	139.8	59 54.5	51.6	140.9	59 07.6	52.2	142.0	58 20.0	52.8	143.0	57 31.7	53.4	144.0	56 42.9	53.9	144.9	55 53.6	54.3	145.7	55 03.8	54.8	146.5	14
15	61 31.6	+50.3	138.7	60 46.1	+51.0	139.9	59 59.8	+51.8	141.0	59 12.8	+52.4	142.1	58 25.1	+53.1	143.1	57 36.8	+53.6	144.0	56 48.0	+54.1	144.9	55 58.6	+54.6	145.8	15
16	62 21.9	49.6	137.6	61 37.1	50.5	138.8	60 51.6	51.2	140.0	60 05.2	52.0	141.1	59 18.2	52.6	142.2	58 30.4	53.2	143.2	57 42.1	53.8	144.1	56 53.2	54.2	145.0	16
17	63 11.5	49.0	136.3	62 27.6	50.0	137.7	61 42.8	50.8	138.8	60 57.2	51.5	140.1	60 10.8	52.2	141.2	59 23.6	52.9	142.3	58 35.9	53.4	143.2	57 47.4	54.0	144.3	17
18	64 00.5	48.3	135.0	63 17.6	49.2	136.5	62 33.6	50.1	137.8	61 48.7	51.0	139.0	61 03.0	51.7	140.2	60 16.5	52.4	141.4	59 29.3	53.0	142.4	58 41.4	53.6	143.4	18
19	64 48.8	47.4	133.7	64 06.8	48.5	135.2	63 23.7	49.5	136.6	62 39.7	50.4	137.9	61 54.7	51.2	139.2	61 08.9	51.9	140.4	60 22.3	52.6	141.5	59 35.0	53.3	142.6	19
20	65 36.2	+46.6	132.2	64 55.3	+47.7	133.8	64 13.2	+48.8	135.3	63 30.1	+49.7	136.7	62 45.9	+50.6	138.0	62 00.8	+51.5	139.3	61 14.9	+52.2	140.5	60 28.3	+52.8	141.6	20
21	66 22.8	45.6	130.7	65 43.0	46.9	132.3	65 02.0	48.0	134.0	64 19.8	49.1	135.4	63 36.5	49.9	136.9	62 52.3	50.9	138.2	62 07.1	51.7	139.5	61 21.1	52.4	140.7	21
22	67 08.4	44.5	129.0	66 29.9	45.9	130.8	65 50.0	47.1	132.5	65 08.9	48.2	134.1	64 26.6	49.3	135.6	63 43.2	50.2	137.0	62 58.8	51.1	138.4	62 13.5	51.9	139.6	22
23	67 52.9	43.3	127.3	67 15.8	44.8	129.2	66 37.1	46.2	131.0	65 57.1	47.5	132.7	65 15.9	48.5	134.3	64 33.4	49.6	135.8	63 49.9	50.6	137.2	63 05.4	51.4	138.5	23
24	68 36.2	42.0	125.4	68 00.6	43.6	127.4	67 23.3	45.1	129.3	66 44.6	46.5	131.1	66 04.4	47.8	132.8	65 23.0	48.9	134.4	64 40.5	49.8	135.9	63 56.8	50.8	137.4	24
25	69 18.2	+40.5	123.4	68 44.2	+42.3	125.5	68 08.4	+44.0	127.6	67 31.1	+45.4	129.5	66 52.2	+46.7	131.1	66 11.9	+48.0	133.0	65 30.3	+49.2	134.6	64 47.6	+50.1	136.1	25
26	69 58.7	38.9	121.3	69 26.5	40.9	123.6	68 52.4	42.6	125.7	68 16.5	44.3	127.8	67 38.9	45.8	129.7	66 59.9	47.1	131.5	66 19.5	48.3	133.2	65 37.7	49.5	134.8	26
27	70 37.6	37.1	119.0	70 07.4	39.2	121.4	69 35.0	41.2	123.7	69 00.8	42.9	126.0	68 24.7	44.6	128.0	67 47.0	46.1	129.9	67 07.8	47.4	131.9	66 27.2	48.6	133.4	27
28	71 14.7	35.1	116.6	70 46.6	37.5	119.2	70 16.2	39.6	121.6	69 43.7	41.6	123.9	69 09.3	43.3	126.1	68 33.1	44.9	128.2	67 55.2	46.4	130.1	67 15.8	47.7	131.9	28
29	71 49.8	33.0	114.1	71 24.1	35.5	116.8	70 55.8	37.9	119.4	70 25.3	40.0	121.8	69 52.6	42.0	124.1	69 18.0	43.7	126.3	68 41.6	45.3	128.4	68 03.5	46.8	130.4	29
30	72 22.8	+30.7	111.3	71 59.6	+33.4	114.2	71 33.7	+35.9	116.9	71 05.3	+38.2	119.6	70 34.6	+40.3	122.0	70 01.7	+42.3	124.4	69 26.9	+44.0	126.6	68 50.3	+45.6	128.6	30
31	72 53.5	28.0	108.5	72 33.0	30.9	111.5	72 09.6	33.7	114.4	71 43.5	36.3	117.1	71 14.9	38.6	119.8	70 44.0	40.7	122.2	70 10.9	42.7	124.6	69 35.9	44.4	126.8	31
32	73 21.5	25.2	105.4	73 03.9	28.4	108.9	72 43.3	31.4	111.6	72 19.8	34.1	114.6	71 53.5	36.7	117.3	71 24.7	39.0	120.0	70 53.6	41.1	122.5	70 20.3	43.1	124.9	32
33	73 46.7	22.2	102.2	73 32.3	25.6	105.5	73 14.7	28.7	108.6	72 53.9	31.7	111.6	72 30.2	34.5	114.7	72 03.7	37.1	117.6	71 34.7	39.4	120.2	71 03.4	41.5	122.7	33
34	74 08.9	18.9	98.8	73 57.9	22.5	102.3	73 43.4	25.9	105.6	73 25.6	29.2	108.9	73 04.7	32.1	112.0	72 40.8	34.9	115.0	72 14.1	37.5	117.8	71 44.9	39.8	120.5	34
35	74 27.8	+15.5	95.3	74 20.4	+19.2	98.9	74 09.3	+22.9	102.4	73 54.8	+26.2	105.8	73 36.8	+29.5	109.0	73 15.7	+32.5	112.2	72 51.6	+35.3	115.2	72 24.7	+37.9	118.0	35
36	74 43.3	11.9	91.7	74 39.6	15.8	95.3	74 32.2	19.5	98.9	74 21.0	23.2	102.5	74 06.3	26.7	105.9	73 48.2	29.9	109.2	73 26.9	32.9	112.4	73 02.6	35.7	115.4	36
37	74 55.2	8.0	87.9	74 55.4	12.0	91.7	74 51.7	16.0	95.4	74 44.2	19.8	99.0	74 33.0	23.5	102.6	74 18.1	27.0	106.1	73 59.8	30.3	109.4	73 38.3	33.3	112.6	37
38	75 03.2	4.2	84.1	75 07.4	8.3	87.9	75 07.7	12.3	91.6	75 04.0	16.3	95.4	74 56.5	20.1	99.1	74 45.1	23.9	102.7	74 30.1	27.4	106.2	74 11.6	30.7	109.6	38
39	75 07.4	0.3	80.2	75 15.7	4.3	84.1	75 20.0	8.4	87.8	75 20.3	12.5	91.6	75 16.6	16.5	95.4	75 09.0	20.4	99.2	74 57.5	24.2	102.9	74 42.3	27.8	106.4	39
40	75 07.7	−3.7	76.3	75 20.0	+0.3	80.2	75 28.4	+4.4	83.9	75 32.8	+8.5	87.7	75 33.1	+12.7	91.6	75 29.4	+16.8	95.5	75 21.7	+20.8	99.3	75 10.1	+24.6	103.0	40
41	75 04.0	7.5	72.5	75 20.3	−3.7	76.1	75 32.8	0.3	79.9	75 41.3	4.5	83.7	75 45.8	8.8	87.7	75 46.2	13.0	91.6	75 42.5	17.1	95.5	75 34.7	21.1	99.4	41
42	74 56.5	11.4	68.6	75 16.6	7.6	72.5	75 33.1	−3.7	75.9	75 45.8	0.4	79.7	75 54.6	4.6	83.6	75 59.2	8.8	87.6	75 59.6	13.1	91.6	75 55.8	17.4	95.6	42
43	74 45.1	15.0	64.9	75 09.0	11.5	68.3	75 29.4	7.7	71.9	75 46.2	−3.7	75.6	75 59.2	0.4	79.5	76 08.0	4.7	83.5	76 12.7	9.1	87.5	76 13.2	13.4	91.6	43
44	74 30.1	18.5	61.2	74 57.5	15.2	64.5	75 21.7	11.6	67.9	75 42.5	7.8	71.6	75 59.6	−3.8	75.4	76 12.7	0.5	79.3	76 21.8	4.8	83.4	76 26.6	9.2	87.5	44

22°, 338° L.H.A.

LATITUDE SAME NAME AS DECLINATION

N. Lat. { L.H.A. greater than 180° .... Zn=Z
{ L.H.A. less than 180° .... Zn=360°−Z

Dec.	38° Hc	d	Z	39° Hc	d	Z	40° Hc	d	Z	41° Hc	d	Z	42° Hc	d	Z	43° Hc	d	Z	44° Hc	d	Z	45° Hc	d	Z	Dec.
0	46 56.4	+54.0	146.7	46 06.0	+54.4	147.3	45 15.4	+54.7	147.8	44 24.4	+55.1	148.4	43 33.2	+55.3	148.9	42 41.7	+55.5	149.4	41 50.0	+55.8	149.8	40 58.0	+56.1	150.3	0
1	47 50.4	53.7	146.1	47 00.4	54.1	146.7	46 10.1	54.5	147.3	45 19.5	54.8	147.8	44 28.5	55.2	148.3	43 37.3	55.5	148.8	42 45.8	55.8	149.3	41 54.1	56.0	149.8	1
2	48 44.1	53.6	145.4	47 54.5	54.0	146.0	47 04.6	54.3	146.7	46 14.3	54.7	147.2	45 23.7	55.0	147.8	44 32.8	55.3	148.3	43 41.6	55.6	148.8	42 50.1	55.9	149.3	2
3	49 37.7	53.2	144.7	48 48.5	53.5	145.4	47 58.9	54.1	146.0	47 09.0	54.4	146.6	46 18.7	54.8	147.2	45 28.1	55.1	147.8	44 37.2	55.5	148.3	43 46.0	55.8	148.8	3
4	50 30.9	53.0	144.0	49 42.2	53.4	144.7	48 53.0	53.9	145.4	48 03.4	54.3	146.0	47 13.5	54.6	146.6	46 23.2	55.0	147.2	45 32.7	55.3	147.8	44 41.8	55.6	148.3	4
5	51 23.9	+52.7	143.3	50 35.6	+53.2	144.0	49 46.9	+53.6	144.7	48 57.7	+54.0	145.4	48 08.1	+54.5	146.0	47 18.2	+54.8	146.6	46 28.0	+55.1	147.2	45 37.4	+55.4	147.8	5
6	52 16.6	52.4	142.5	51 28.8	52.9	143.3	50 40.5	53.4	144.0	49 51.7	53.8	144.7	49 02.6	54.2	145.4	48 13.0	54.6	146.0	47 23.1	54.9	146.6	46 32.8	55.3	147.2	6
7	53 09.0	52.1	141.7	52 21.7	52.6	142.5	51 33.9	53.0	143.3	50 45.5	53.6	144.0	49 56.8	54.0	144.7	49 07.6	54.4	145.4	48 18.0	54.8	146.0	47 28.1	55.1	146.6	7
8	54 01.1	51.7	140.8	53 14.3	52.2	141.7	52 26.9	52.8	142.5	51 39.1	53.3	143.3	50 50.8	53.7	144.0	50 02.0	54.1	144.7	49 12.8	54.6	145.4	48 23.2	54.8	146.0	8
9	54 52.8	51.3	140.0	54 06.5	51.9	140.9	53 19.7	52.5	141.7	52 32.4	52.9	142.5	51 44.5	53.4	143.3	50 56.1	53.9	144.0	50 07.4	54.3	144.8	49 18.1	54.6	145.4	9
10	55 44.1	+50.9	139.1	54 58.4	+51.5	140.0	54 12.2	+52.1	140.9	53 25.3	+52.7	141.8	52 37.9	+53.2	142.6	51 50.0	+53.7	143.3	51 01.7	+54.1	144.1	50 12.9	+54.5	144.8	10
11	56 35.0	50.4	138.1	55 49.9	51.1	139.1	55 04.3	51.7	140.0	54 18.0	52.3	140.9	53 31.1	52.9	141.8	52 43.7	53.4	142.6	51 55.8	53.8	143.4	51 07.4	54.3	144.1	11
12	57 25.4	49.9	137.1	56 41.0	50.7	138.2	55 56.0	51.3	139.1	55 10.3	51.9	140.1	54 24.0	52.5	141.0	53 37.1	53.0	141.8	52 49.6	53.6	142.7	52 01.7	54.0	143.4	12
13	58 15.3	49.4	136.1	57 31.7	50.2	137.2	56 47.3	50.9	138.2	56 02.2	51.6	139.2	55 16.5	52.2	140.2	54 30.1	52.8	141.1	53 43.2	53.2	141.9	52 55.7	53.7	142.7	13
14	59 04.7	48.8	135.0	58 21.9	49.6	136.1	57 38.2	50.4	137.2	56 53.8	51.1	138.3	56 08.7	51.7	139.3	55 22.9	52.3	140.2	54 36.4	53.0	141.1	53 49.4	53.5	142.0	14
15	59 53.5	+48.2	133.8	59 11.5	+49.1	135.0	58 28.6	+49.9	136.2	57 44.9	+50.6	137.3	57 00.4	+51.4	138.4	56 15.2	+52.0	139.4	55 29.4	+52.6	140.3	54 42.9	+53.2	141.2	15
16	60 41.7	47.5	132.6	60 00.6	48.4	133.9	59 18.5	49.3	135.1	58 35.5	50.2	136.3	57 51.8	50.9	137.4	57 07.2	51.6	138.4	56 22.0	52.2	139.4	55 36.1	52.8	140.4	16
17	61 29.2	46.8	131.4	60 49.0	47.8	132.7	60 07.8	48.8	134.0	59 25.7	49.6	135.2	58 42.7	50.4	136.4	57 58.8	51.2	137.5	57 14.2	51.8	138.5	56 28.9	52.5	139.6	17
18	62 16.0	46.0	130.0	61 36.8	47.1	131.5	60 56.6	48.0	132.8	60 15.3	49.0	134.1	59 33.1	49.8	135.3	58 50.0	50.6	136.5	58 06.0	51.4	137.6	57 21.4	52.0	138.6	18
19	63 02.0	45.1	128.6	62 23.9	46.2	130.1	61 44.6	47.4	131.6	61 04.3	48.3	132.9	60 22.9	49.3	134.2	59 40.6	50.1	135.4	58 57.4	50.9	136.6	58 13.4	51.7	137.7	19
20	63 47.1	+44.1	127.2	63 10.1	+45.5	128.7	62 32.0	+46.5	130.3	61 52.6	+47.7	131.7	61 12.2	+48.6	133.0	60 30.7	+49.6	134.3	59 48.3	+50.4	135.6	59 05.1	+51.1	136.8	20
21	64 31.2	43.1	125.6	63 55.6	44.4	127.3	63 18.5	45.8	128.9	62 40.3	46.9	130.4	62 00.8	48.0	131.8	61 20.3	48.9	133.2	60 38.7	49.9	134.5	59 56.2	50.7	135.7	21
22	65 14.3	42.0	124.0	64 40.0	43.5	125.7	64 04.3	44.8	127.4	63 27.2	46.0	129.0	62 48.8	47.2	130.5	62 09.2	48.3	132.0	61 28.6	49.2	133.3	60 46.9	50.1	134.6	22
23	65 56.3	40.8	122.2	65 23.5	42.3	124.1	64 49.1	43.7	125.9	64 13.2	45.1	127.5	63 36.0	46.3	129.1	62 57.5	47.5	130.7	62 17.8	48.5	132.1	61 37.0	49.5	133.5	23
24	66 37.1	39.4	120.4	66 05.8	41.1	122.4	65 32.8	42.7	124.2	64 58.3	44.1	126.0	64 22.3	45.5	127.7	63 45.0	46.6	129.3	63 06.3	47.8	130.8	62 26.5	48.9	132.3	24
25	67 16.5	+37.9	118.5	66 46.9	+39.8	120.6	66 15.5	+41.5	122.5	65 42.4	+43.1	124.4	65 07.8	+44.4	126.2	64 31.6	+45.8	127.9	63 54.1	+47.1	129.5	63 15.4	+48.1	131.0	25
26	67 54.4	36.4	116.5	67 26.7	38.3	118.6	66 57.0	40.1	120.7	66 25.5	41.8	122.7	65 52.2	43.4	124.6	65 17.4	44.9	126.3	64 41.2	46.1	128.1	64 03.5	47.3	129.7	26
27	68 30.8	34.6	114.3	68 05.0	36.7	116.6	67 37.1	38.7	118.8	67 07.3	40.5	120.8	66 35.6	42.2	122.8	66 02.3	43.7	124.7	65 27.3	45.2	126.5	64 50.8	46.5	128.3	27
28	69 05.4	32.8	112.1	68 41.7	35.0	114.4	68 15.8	37.1	116.7	67 47.8	39.1	118.9	67 17.8	40.9	121.0	66 46.0	42.6	123.0	66 12.5	44.1	124.9	65 37.3	45.5	126.7	28
29	69 38.2	30.7	109.7	69 16.7	33.2	112.2	68 52.9	35.4	114.6	68 26.9	37.5	116.9	67 58.7	39.5	119.1	67 28.6	41.2	121.2	66 56.6	42.9	123.2	66 22.8	44.5	125.1	29
30	70 08.9	+28.5	107.2	69 49.9	+31.1	109.8	69 28.3	+33.5	112.3	69 04.4	+35.7	114.7	68 38.2	+37.8	117.1	68 09.8	+39.9	119.3	67 39.5	+41.7	121.4	67 07.3	+43.3	123.4	30
31	70 37.4	26.2	104.6	70 21.0	28.9	107.3	70 01.8	31.5	109.9	69 40.1	34.0	112.5	69 16.0	36.2	114.9	68 49.7	38.3	117.2	68 21.2	40.2	119.5	67 50.6	42.1	121.6	31
32	71 03.6	23.7	101.8	70 49.9	26.5	104.6	70 33.3	29.3	107.4	70 14.1	31.8	110.0	69 52.2	34.3	112.6	69 28.0	36.6	115.1	69 01.4	38.7	117.4	68 32.7	40.7	119.7	32
33	71 27.3	20.9	99.0	71 16.4	24.0	101.9	71 02.6	26.9	104.7	70 45.9	29.7	107.5	70 26.5	32.3	110.2	70 04.6	34.7	112.8	69 40.1	37.0	115.3	69 13.4	39.1	117.7	33
34	71 48.2	18.2	96.0	71 40.4	21.3	99.0	71 29.5	24.3	101.9	71 15.6	27.3	104.8	70 58.8	30.1	107.6	70 39.3	32.7	110.4	70 17.1	35.1	113.0	69 52.5	37.4	115.5	34
35	72 06.4	+15.1*	92.9	72 01.7	+18.4*	96.0	71 53.8	+21.7	99.0	71 42.9	+24.7	102.0	71 28.9	+27.6	105.0	71 12.0	+30.4	107.8	70 52.2	+33.1	110.5	70 29.9	+35.5	113.2	35
36	72 21.5	12.0*	89.7	72 20.1	15.4*	92.9	72 15.5	18.7*	96.0	72 07.6	21.9*	99.1	71 56.5	25.1*	102.1	71 42.4	28.0*	105.1	71 25.3	30.9*	108.0	71 05.4	33.6*	110.7	36
37	72 33.5	8.8*	86.5	72 35.5	12.2*	89.7	72 34.2	15.6*	92.9	72 29.5	19.0*	96.0	72 21.6	22.3*	99.2	72 10.4	25.5*	102.2	71 56.2	28.4*	105.2	71 39.0	31.2*	108.1	37
38	72 42.3	5.4*	83.2	72 47.7	9.0*	86.4	72 49.8	12.5*	89.6	72 48.5	16.0*	92.8	72 43.9	19.3*	96.1	72 35.9	22.6*	99.2	72 24.6	25.8*	102.4	72 10.2	28.9*	105.4	38
39	72 47.7	2.1*	79.8	72 56.7	5.6*	83.0	73 02.3	9.1*	86.3	73 04.5	12.6*	89.6	73 03.2	16.2*	92.8	72 58.5	19.6*	96.1	72 50.4	23.0*	99.3	72 39.1	26.2*	102.5	39
40	72 49.8	−1.3*	76.4	73 02.3	+2.2*	79.6	73 11.4	+5.7*	82.9	73 17.1	+9.3*	86.2	73 19.4	+12.9*	89.5	73 18.1	+16.5*	92.9	73 13.4	+20.0*	96.2	73 05.3	+23.3*	99.4	40
41	72 48.5	4.6*	73.0	73 04.5	1.3*	76.2	73 17.1	2.3*	79.4	73 26.4	5.9*	82.7	73 32.3	9.5*	86.1	73 34.6	13.1*	89.5	73 33.4	16.7*	92.9	73 28.6	20.3*	96.2	41
42	72 43.9	8.0*	69.7	73 03.2	4.7*	72.8	73 19.4	1.3*	75.9	73 32.3	2.3*	79.2	73 41.8	5.9*	82.6	73 47.7	9.7*	86.0	73 50.1	13.4*	89.6	73 48.9	17.0*	92.9	42
43	72 35.9	11.3*	66.4	72 58.5	8.1*	69.3	73 18.1	4.7*	72.5	73 34.6	1.2*	75.7	73 47.7	2.4*	79.0	73 57.4	6.1*	82.4	74 03.5	9.8*	85.9	74 05.9	13.6*	89.4	43
44	72 24.6	14.4*	63.1	72 50.4	11.3*	66.0	73 13.4	8.1*	69.0	73 33.4	4.8*	72.2	73 50.1	1.2*	75.4	74 03.5	2.4*	78.8	74 13.3	6.2*	82.3	74 19.5	10.0*	85.8	44

LATITUDE SAME NAME AS DECLINATION

N. Lat. { L.H.A. greater than 180°...... Zn=Z / L.H.A. less than 180°...... Zn=360°−Z

Dec.	38° Hc	d	Z	39° Hc	d	Z	40° Hc	d	Z	41° Hc	d	Z	42° Hc	d	Z	43° Hc	d	Z	44° Hc	d	Z	45° Hc	d	Z	Dec.
0	44 35.7	+51.7	140.4	43 49.4	+52.2	141.0	43 02.6	+52.7	141.6	42 15.4	+53.1	142.2	41 27.8	+53.5	142.7	40 39.9	+53.9	143.2	39 51.7	+54.2	143.7	39 03.2	+54.5	144.2	0
1	45 27.6	51.5	139.7	44 41.6	52.0	140.3	43 55.3	52.4	140.9	43 08.5	52.8	141.5	42 21.3	53.3	142.1	41 33.8	53.7	142.7	40 45.9	54.1	143.2	39 57.7	54.4	143.7	1
2	46 19.1	51.1	138.9	45 33.6	51.7	139.6	44 47.7	52.2	140.3	44 01.3	52.7	140.9	43 14.6	53.1	141.5	42 27.5	53.4	142.1	41 40.0	53.8	142.6	40 52.1	54.3	143.1	2
3	47 10.2	50.9	138.2	46 25.3	51.4	138.9	45 39.9	51.9	139.6	44 54.0	52.4	140.2	44 07.7	52.8	140.8	43 20.9	53.3	141.4	42 33.8	53.7	142.0	41 46.4	54.0	142.6	3
4	48 01.1	50.5	137.4	47 16.7	51.1	138.1	46 31.8	51.6	138.9	45 46.4	52.1	139.5	45 00.5	52.6	140.1	44 14.2	53.1	140.8	43 27.5	53.5	141.4	42 40.4	53.9	142.0	4
5	48 51.6	+50.2	136.6	48 07.8	+50.7	137.3	47 23.4	+51.3	138.1	46 38.5	+51.8	138.8	45 53.1	+52.4	139.5	45 07.3	+52.8	140.1	44 21.0	+53.3	140.8	43 34.3	+53.7	141.4	5
6	49 41.8	49.8	135.7	48 58.5	50.5	136.5	48 14.7	51.0	137.3	47 30.3	51.6	138.1	46 45.5	52.0	138.8	46 00.1	52.6	139.5	45 14.3	53.0	140.1	44 28.0	53.5	140.8	6
7	50 31.6	49.4	134.9	49 49.0	50.0	135.7	49 05.7	50.7	136.5	48 21.9	51.2	137.3	47 37.5	51.8	138.0	46 52.7	52.3	138.8	46 07.3	52.8	139.5	45 21.5	53.3	140.1	7
8	51 21.0	48.9	134.0	50 39.0	49.7	134.8	49 56.4	50.3	135.7	49 13.1	51.0	136.5	48 29.3	51.5	137.3	47 45.0	52.0	138.0	47 00.1	52.6	138.8	46 14.8	53.0	139.5	8
9	52 09.9	48.6	133.0	51 28.7	49.2	133.9	50 46.7	49.9	134.8	50 04.1	50.5	135.7	49 20.8	51.2	136.5	48 37.0	51.7	137.3	47 52.7	52.2	138.0	47 07.8	52.8	138.8	9
10	52 58.5	+48.0	132.1	52 17.9	+48.8	133.0	51 36.6	+49.5	134.0	50 54.6	+50.2	134.8	50 12.0	+50.8	135.7	49 28.7	+51.5	136.5	48 44.9	+52.0	137.3	48 00.6	+52.5	138.1	10
11	53 46.5	47.5	131.1	53 06.7	48.3	132.1	52 26.1	49.0	133.1	51 44.8	49.8	134.0	51 02.8	50.4	134.9	50 20.2	51.0	135.7	49 36.9	51.7	136.5	48 53.1	52.2	137.3	11
12	54 34.0	46.9	130.0	53 55.0	47.7	131.1	53 15.1	48.6	132.1	52 34.6	49.3	133.1	51 53.2	50.1	134.0	51 11.2	50.7	134.9	50 28.6	51.3	135.8	49 45.3	51.9	136.6	12
13	55 20.9	46.3	128.9	54 42.7	47.3	130.0	54 03.7	48.1	131.1	53 23.9	48.9	132.1	52 43.3	49.6	133.1	52 01.9	50.3	134.0	51 19.9	51.0	134.9	50 37.2	51.6	135.8	13
14	56 07.2	45.7	127.8	55 30.0	46.6	128.9	54 51.8	47.5	130.1	54 12.8	48.3	131.1	53 32.9	49.1	132.1	52 52.2	49.9	133.1	52 10.9	50.5	134.1	51 28.8	51.2	135.0	14
15	56 52.9	+45.0	126.6	56 16.6	+46.0	127.8	55 39.3	+47.0	129.0	55 01.1	+47.9	130.1	54 22.0	+48.7	131.2	53 42.1	+49.5	132.2	53 01.4	+50.2	133.2	52 20.0	+50.9	134.1	15
16	57 37.9	44.3	125.4	57 02.6	45.3	126.7	56 26.3	46.3	127.9	55 49.0	47.2	129.0	55 10.7	48.1	130.2	54 31.6	48.9	131.2	53 51.6	49.8	132.3	53 10.9	50.4	133.3	16
17	58 22.2	43.4	124.1	57 47.9	44.6	125.4	57 12.6	45.6	126.7	56 36.2	46.7	127.9	55 58.8	47.6	129.1	55 20.5	48.5	130.2	54 41.4	49.2	131.3	54 01.3	50.1	132.4	17
18	59 05.6	42.6	122.8	58 32.5	43.8	124.2	57 58.2	45.0	125.5	57 22.9	45.9	126.8	56 46.4	47.0	128.0	56 09.0	47.9	129.2	55 30.6	48.8	130.3	54 51.4	49.5	131.4	18
19	59 48.2	41.7	121.4	59 16.3	43.0	122.8	58 43.2	44.1	124.2	58 08.8	45.3	125.6	57 33.4	46.3	126.9	56 56.9	47.3	128.1	56 19.4	48.2	129.3	55 40.9	49.1	130.4	19
20	60 29.9	+40.8	120.0	59 59.3	+42.1	121.5	59 27.3	+43.4	122.9	58 54.1	+44.5	124.3	58 19.7	+45.6	125.7	57 44.2	+46.6	126.9	57 07.6	+47.6	128.1	56 30.0	+48.5	129.4	20
21	61 10.7	39.7	118.5	60 41.4	41.1	120.0	60 10.7	42.4	121.5	59 38.6	43.8	123.0	59 05.3	44.9	124.4	58 30.8	46.0	125.8	57 55.2	47.0	127.1	57 18.5	48.0	128.3	21
22	61 50.4	38.5	116.9	61 22.5	40.0	118.5	60 53.1	41.5	120.1	60 22.3	42.8	121.6	59 50.2	44.0	123.1	59 16.8	45.2	124.5	58 42.2	46.3	125.9	58 06.5	47.3	127.2	22
23	62 28.9	37.4	115.2	62 02.5	39.0	117.0	61 34.6	40.4	118.6	61 05.1	41.8	120.1	60 34.2	43.2	121.7	60 02.0	44.4	123.2	59 28.5	45.6	124.6	58 53.8	46.7	126.0	23
24	63 06.3	36.0	113.5	62 41.5	37.7	115.3	62 15.0	39.3	117.0	61 46.9	40.9	118.7	61 17.4	42.2	120.3	60 46.4	43.6	121.7	60 14.1	44.8	123.3	59 40.5	45.9	124.8	24
25	63 42.3	+34.7	111.7	63 19.2	+36.5	113.6	62 54.3	+38.1	115.4	62 27.8	+39.7	117.1	61 59.6	+41.2	118.8	61 30.0	+42.6	120.4	60 58.9	+43.9	122.0	60 26.4	+45.2	123.5	25
26	64 17.0	33.2	109.9	63 55.7	35.0	111.8	63 32.4	36.9	113.7	63 07.5	38.5	115.5	62 40.8	40.1	117.2	62 12.6	41.6	118.9	61 42.8	43.0	120.6	61 11.6	44.3	122.1	26
27	64 50.2	31.7	107.9	64 30.7	33.6	109.9	64 09.3	35.5	111.9	63 46.0	37.3	113.7	63 20.9	39.0	115.6	62 54.2	40.5	117.4	62 25.8	42.0	119.1	61 55.9	43.4	120.7	27
28	65 21.8	30.0	105.9	65 04.3	32.0	108.0	64 44.8	34.0	110.0	64 23.3	35.8	112.0	63 59.9	37.6	113.9	63 34.7	39.3	115.7	63 07.8	40.9	117.5	62 39.3	42.4	119.2	28
29	65 51.8	28.1	103.8	65 36.3	30.4	106.0	65 18.8	32.4	108.1	64 59.1	34.5	110.1	64 37.5	36.3	112.1	64 14.0	38.1	114.0	63 48.7	39.8	115.9	63 21.7	41.3	117.7	29
30	66 19.9	+26.3	101.6	66 06.7	+28.6	103.9	65 51.2	+30.7	106.0	65 33.6	+32.8	108.1	65 13.8	+34.9	110.2	64 52.1	+36.7	112.2	64 28.5	+38.5	114.2	64 03.0	+40.2	116.0	30
31	66 46.2	24.2*	99.4	66 35.2	26.6	101.7	66 21.9	28.9	103.9	66 06.4	31.1	106.1	65 48.7	33.2	108.2	65 28.8	35.3	110.3	65 07.0	37.1	112.4	64 43.2	38.9	114.3	31
32	67 10.4	22.1*	97.1	67 01.8	24.6*	99.4	66 50.8	27.1*	101.7	66 37.5	29.3	104.0	66 21.9	31.5	106.2	66 04.1	33.6	108.4	65 44.1	35.7	110.5	65 22.1	37.6	112.5	32
33	67 32.5	20.0*	94.6	67 26.4	22.5*	97.0	67 17.9	24.9*	99.4	67 06.8	27.4	101.8	66 53.4	29.8	104.0	66 37.7	32.0	106.2	66 19.8	34.1	108.5	65 59.7	36.1	110.6	33
34	67 52.5	17.5*	92.1	67 48.9	20.3*	94.6	67 42.8	22.9*	97.0	67 34.2	25.4*	99.4	67 23.2	27.8*	101.8	67 09.7	30.1	104.1	66 53.9	32.4	106.4	66 35.8	34.5	108.6	34
35	68 10.0	+15.2*	89.6	68 09.2	+17.8*	92.1	68 05.7	+20.5*	94.6	67 59.6	+23.2*	97.0	67 51.0	+25.7*	99.5	67 39.8	+28.2	101.9	67 26.3	+30.5	104.2	67 10.3	+32.9	106.6	35
36	68 25.2	12.7*	87.0	68 27.0	15.5*	89.5	68 26.2	18.2*	92.0	68 22.8	20.9*	94.6	68 16.7	23.6*	97.1	68 08.0	26.2*	99.5	67 56.8	28.6	102.0	67 43.2	30.9	104.4	36
37	68 37.9	10.1*	84.3	68 42.5	12.9*	86.9	68 44.4	15.8*	89.4	68 43.7	18.6*	92.0	68 40.3	21.2*	94.6	68 34.2	23.9*	97.1	68 25.4	26.6*	99.6	68 14.1	29.1*	102.1	37
38	68 48.0	7.4*	81.6	68 55.4	10.3*	84.2	69 00.2	13.1*	86.8	69 02.2	16.0*	89.4	69 01.5	18.8*	92.0	68 58.1	21.6*	94.6	68 52.0	24.2*	97.1	68 43.2	26.9*	99.7	38
39	68 55.4	4.8*	78.8	69 05.7	7.6*	81.4	69 13.3	10.5*	84.0	69 18.2	13.4*	86.6	69 20.3	16.3*	89.3	69 19.7	19.1*	91.9	69 16.2	22.0*	94.6	69 10.1	24.7*	97.2	39
40	69 00.2	+2.0*	76.1	69 13.3	+4.9*	78.6	69 23.8	+7.8*	81.2	69 31.6	+10.7*	83.9	69 36.6	+13.6*	86.5	69 38.8	+16.6*	89.3	69 38.2	+19.4*	91.9	69 34.8	+22.2*	94.6	40
41	69 02.2	−0.7*	73.3	69 18.2	2.1*	75.8	69 31.6	5.0*	78.4	69 42.3	7.9*	81.0	69 50.2	10.9*	83.7	69 55.4	13.9*	86.5	69 57.6	16.9*	89.2	69 57.0	19.8*	91.9	41
42	69 01.5	3.4*	70.5	69 20.3	−0.6*	73.0	69 36.6	2.2*	75.5	69 50.2	5.2*	78.2	70 01.1	8.2*	80.9	70 09.3	11.1*	83.6	70 14.5	14.1*	86.4	70 16.8	17.2*	89.2	42
43	68 58.1	6.1*	67.7	69 19.7	3.5*	70.1	69 38.8	−0.6*	72.7	69 55.4	2.2*	75.3	70 09.3	5.2*	78.0	70 20.4	8.2*	80.7	70 28.6	11.3*	83.5	70 34.0	14.3*	86.3	43
44	68 52.0	8.8*	64.9	69 16.2	6.1*	67.3	69 38.2	3.4*	69.8	69 57.6	−0.6*	72.4	70 14.5	2.3*	75.0	70 28.6	5.4*	77.7	70 39.9	8.4*	80.5	70 48.3	11.5*	83.4	44

L.H.A. greater than 180°...... Zn=Z
L.H.A. less than 180°...... Zn=360°−Z

Dec.	38° Hc	d	Z	39° Hc	d	Z	40° Hc	d	Z	41° Hc	d	Z	42° Hc	d	Z	43° Hc	d	Z	44° Hc	d	Z	45° Hc	d	Z	Dec.
0	36 29.6	-46.1	125.3	35 54.6	-46.7	125.9	35 19.2	-47.4	126.5	34 43.3	-48.0	127.0	34 06.9	-48.6	127.6	33 30.1	-49.2	128.1	32 52.8	-49.7	128.6	32 15.2	-50.3	129.1	0
1	35 43.5	46.5	126.1	35 07.9	47.1	126.7	34 31.8	47.7	127.2	33 55.3	48.3	127.8	33 18.3	48.9	128.3	32 40.9	49.4	128.8	32 03.1	49.9	129.3	31 24.9	50.4	129.8	1
2	35 57.0	46.7	126.9	34 20.8	47.3	127.4	33 44.1	47.9	128.0	33 07.0	48.5	128.5	32 29.4	49.0	129.0	31 51.5	49.6	129.5	31 13.2	50.2	129.9	30 34.5	50.7	130.4	2
3	34 10.3	46.9	127.6	33 33.5	47.6	128.2	32 56.2	48.2	128.7	32 18.5	48.8	129.2	31 40.4	49.3	129.7	31 01.9	49.8	130.1	30 23.0	50.3	130.6	29 43.8	50.8	131.0	3
4	33 23.4	47.3	128.4	32 45.9	47.8	128.9	32 08.0	48.4	129.4	31 29.7	48.9	129.9	30 51.1	49.5	130.3	30 12.1	50.0	130.8	29 32.7	50.5	131.2	28 53.0	50.9	131.6	4
5	32 36.1	-47.5	129.1	31 58.1	-48.1	129.6	31 19.6	-48.6	130.1	30 40.8	-49.2	130.5	30 01.6	-49.7	131.0	29 22.1	-50.2	131.4	28 42.2	-50.6	131.8	28 02.1	-51.2	132.2	5
6	31 48.6	47.7	129.8	31 10.0	48.3	130.3	30 31.0	48.9	130.8	29 51.6	49.3	131.2	29 11.9	49.8	131.6	28 31.9	50.3	132.0	27 51.6	50.8	132.4	27 10.9	51.2	132.8	6
7	31 00.9	48.0	130.6	30 21.7	48.5	131.0	29 42.1	49.0	131.5	29 02.3	49.6	131.9	28 22.1	50.1	132.3	27 41.6	50.5	132.7	27 00.8	50.8	133.0	26 19.7	51.4	133.4	7
8	30 12.9	48.2	131.3	29 33.2	48.7	131.7	28 53.1	49.2	132.1	28 12.7	49.7	132.5	27 32.0	50.2	132.9	26 51.1	50.7	133.3	26 09.8	51.1	133.6	25 28.3	51.6	134.0	8
9	29 24.7	48.4	131.9	28 44.5	48.9	132.4	28 03.9	49.4	132.7	27 23.0	49.9	133.1	26 41.8	50.3	133.5	26 00.4	50.8	133.9	25 18.7	51.2	134.2	24 36.7	51.6	134.5	9
10	28 36.3	-48.6	132.6	27 55.6	-49.1	133.0	27 14.5	-49.6	133.4	26 33.1	-50.0	133.8	25 51.5	-50.5	134.1	25 09.6	-50.9	134.5	24 27.5	-51.4	134.8	23 45.1	-51.8	135.1	10
11	27 47.7	48.7	133.3	27 06.5	49.3	133.7	26 24.9	49.7	134.0	25 43.1	50.2	134.4	25 01.0	50.7	134.7	24 18.7	51.1	135.1	23 36.1	51.5	135.3	22 53.3	51.9	135.6	11
12	26 59.0	49.0	133.9	26 17.2	49.4	134.3	25 35.2	49.9	134.6	24 52.9	50.4	135.0	24 10.3	50.7	135.3	23 27.6	51.3	135.6	22 44.6	51.6	135.9	22 01.4	52.0	136.2	12
13	26 10.0	49.1	134.6	25 27.8	49.6	134.9	24 45.3	50.1	135.3	24 02.5	50.5	135.6	23 19.6	50.9	135.9	22 36.4	51.3	136.2	21 53.0	51.7	136.5	21 09.4	52.1	136.7	13
14	25 20.9	49.3	135.2	24 38.2	49.8	135.5	23 55.2	50.2	135.9	23 12.0	50.6	136.2	22 28.7	51.1	136.5	21 45.1	51.5	136.7	21 01.3	51.8	137.0	20 17.3	52.2	137.3	14
15	24 31.6	-49.5	135.8	23 48.4	-49.9	136.2	23 05.0	-50.3	136.5	22 21.4	-50.7	136.7	21 37.6	-51.1	137.0	20 53.6	-51.5	137.3	20 09.5	-52.0	137.5	19 25.1	-52.3	137.8	15
16	23 42.1	49.7	136.5	22 58.5	50.0	136.8	22 14.7	50.4	137.1	21 30.7	50.9	137.3	20 46.5	51.3	137.6	20 02.1	51.6	137.8	19 17.5	52.0	138.1	18 32.8	52.3	138.3	16
17	22 52.5	49.8	137.1	22 08.5	50.2	137.4	21 24.3	50.6	137.7	20 39.8	50.9	137.9	19 55.2	51.3	138.1	19 10.5	51.8	138.4	18 25.5	52.1	138.6	17 40.5	52.5	138.8	17
18	22 02.8	49.9	137.7	21 18.3	50.2	138.0	20 33.7	50.7	138.2	19 48.9	51.1	138.5	19 03.9	51.5	138.7	18 18.7	51.8	138.9	17 33.4	52.1	139.1	16 48.0	52.5	139.3	18
19	21 12.9	50.0	138.3	20 28.1	50.4	138.5	19 43.0	50.8	138.8	18 57.8	51.2	139.0	18 12.4	51.5	139.2	17 26.9	51.9	139.4	16 41.3	52.3	139.6	15 55.5	52.6	139.8	19
20	20 22.9	-50.1	138.9	19 37.7	-50.5	139.1	18 52.2	-50.9	139.3	18 06.6	-51.3	139.6	17 20.9	-51.6	139.8	16 35.0	-52.0	140.0	15 49.0	-52.2	140.2	15 02.9	-52.7	140.3	20
21	19 32.8	50.2	139.5	18 47.2	50.6	139.7	18 01.3	50.9	139.9	17 15.4	51.4	140.1	16 29.3	51.7	140.3	15 43.0	52.0	140.5	14 56.7	52.4	140.7	14 10.2	52.7	140.8	21
22	18 42.6	50.3	140.0	17 56.6	50.7	140.3	17 10.4	51.1	140.5	16 24.0	51.4	140.6	15 37.6	51.8	140.8	14 51.0	52.2	141.0	14 04.3	52.4	141.2	13 17.5	52.8	141.3	22
23	17 52.3	50.4	140.6	17 05.9	50.8	140.8	16 19.3	51.2	141.0	15 32.6	51.5	141.2	14 45.8	51.9	141.4	13 58.9	52.2	141.5	13 11.9	52.5	141.7	12 24.7	52.8	141.8	23
24	17 01.9	50.6	141.2	16 15.1	50.9	141.4	15 28.1	51.2	141.5	14 41.1	51.6	141.7	13 53.9	51.9	141.9	13 06.7	52.3	142.0	12 19.4	52.6	142.2	11 31.9	52.8	142.3	24
25	16 11.3	-50.6	141.7	15 24.2	-51.0	141.9	14 36.9	-51.3	142.1	13 49.5	-51.6	142.2	13 02.0	-52.0	142.4	12 14.4	-52.3	142.5	11 26.8	-52.6	142.7	10 39.1	-53.0	142.8	25
26	15 20.7	50.6	142.3	14 33.2	51.0	142.5	13 45.6	51.4	142.6	12 57.9	51.7	142.8	12 10.0	52.0	142.9	11 22.1	52.3	143.1	10 34.2	52.7	143.2	9 46.1	52.9	143.2	26
27	14 30.1	50.8	142.9	13 42.2	51.1	143.0	12 54.2	51.4	143.2	12 06.1	51.7	143.3	11 18.0	52.1	143.4	10 29.8	52.4	143.5	9 41.5	52.7	143.6	8 53.2	53.0	143.7	27
28	13 39.3	50.9	143.4	12 51.1	51.2	143.5	12 02.8	51.5	143.7	11 14.4	51.8	143.8	10 25.9	52.1	143.9	9 37.4	52.4	144.0	8 48.8	52.7	144.1	8 00.2	53.0	144.2	28
29	12 48.4	50.9	144.0	11 59.9	51.2	144.1	11 11.3	51.6	144.2	10 22.6	51.9	144.3	9 33.8	52.2	144.4	8 45.0	52.5	144.5	7 56.1	52.8	144.6	7 07.2	53.1	144.7	29
30	11 57.5	-50.9	144.5	11 08.7	-51.3	144.6	10 19.7	-51.6	144.7	9 30.7	-51.9	144.8	8 41.6	-52.3	144.9	7 52.5	-52.5	145.0	7 03.3	-52.8	145.1	6 14.1	-53.1	145.1	30
31	11 06.6	51.1	145.0	10 17.4	51.4	145.1	9 28.1	51.6	145.2	8 38.8	52.0	145.3	7 49.4	52.2	145.4	7 00.0	52.5	145.5	6 10.5	52.8	145.6	5 21.0	53.1	145.6	31
32	10 15.5	51.0	145.6	9 26.0	51.4	145.7	8 36.5	51.7	145.8	7 46.8	52.0	145.8	6 57.2	52.3	145.9	6 07.5	52.6	146.0	5 17.7	52.8	146.0	4 27.9	53.1	146.1	32
33	9 24.5	51.2	146.1	8 34.6	51.4	146.2	7 44.8	51.8	146.2	6 54.8	52.0	146.3	6 04.9	52.3	146.4	5 14.9	52.6	146.5	4 24.9	52.9	146.5	3 34.8	53.1	146.5	33
34	8 33.3	51.1	146.6	7 43.2	51.5	146.7	6 53.0	51.7	146.8	6 02.8	52.0	146.8	5 12.6	52.4	146.9	4 22.3	52.6	146.9	3 32.0	52.9	147.0	2 41.7	53.2	147.0	34
35	7 42.2	-51.2	147.2	6 51.7	-51.5	147.2	6 01.3	-51.8	147.3	5 10.8	-52.1	147.3	4 20.2	-52.3	147.4	3 29.7	-52.6	147.4	2 39.1	-52.9	147.5	1 48.5	-53.1	147.5	35
36	6 51.0	51.3	147.7	6 00.2	51.5	147.7	5 09.5	51.8	147.9	4 18.7	52.1	147.9	3 27.9	52.4	147.9	2 37.1	52.7	147.9	1 46.2	52.9	147.9	0 55.4	53.2	147.9	36
37	5 59.7	51.3	148.2	5 08.7	51.5	148.3	4 17.7	51.9	148.3	3 26.6	52.1	148.3	2 35.5	52.3	148.4	1 44.4	52.6	148.4	0 53.3	52.9	148.4	0 02.2	-53.1	148.4	37
38	5 08.5	51.3	148.7	4 17.2	51.6	148.8	3 25.8	51.9	148.8	2 34.5	52.1	148.8	1 43.2	52.4	148.9	0 51.8	+52.6	148.9	0 00.4	-52.8	148.9	0 50.9	+53.2	31.1	38
39	4 17.2	51.4	149.3	3 25.6	51.6	149.3	2 34.0	51.9	149.3	1 42.4	52.1	149.3	0 50.8	+52.4	149.3	0 00.8	+52.7	30.7	0 52.4	+52.9	30.7	1 44.1	53.1	30.7	39
40	3 25.8	-51.3	149.8	2 34.0	-51.6	149.8	1 42.1	-51.8	149.8	0 50.3	-52.1	149.8	0 01.6	+52.4	30.2	0 53.5	+52.6	30.2	1 45.3	+52.9	30.2	2 37.2	+53.1	30.2	40
41	2 34.5	51.3	150.3	1 42.4	51.6	150.3	0 50.3	-51.9	150.3	0 01.9	+52.1	29.7	0 54.0	52.4	29.7	1 46.1	52.6	29.7	2 38.2	52.9	29.7	3 30.3	53.2	29.7	41
42	1 43.2	51.4	150.8	0 50.8	-51.6	150.8	0 01.6	+51.9	29.2	0 54.0	52.1	29.2	1 46.4	52.3	29.2	2 38.7	52.7	29.2	3 31.1	52.9	29.2	4 23.5	53.0	29.3	42
43	0 51.8	51.4	151.3	0 00.8	+51.6	28.7	0 53.5	51.9	28.7	1 46.1	52.1	28.7	2 38.7	52.4	28.7	3 31.4	52.6	28.7	4 24.0	52.8	28.8	5 16.6	53.0	28.8	43
44	0 00.4	-51.3	151.8	0 52.4	51.7	28.2	1 45.3	51.9	28.2	2 38.2	52.1	28.2	3 31.1	52.4	28.2	4 24.0	52.6	28.3	5 16.8	52.8	28.3	6 09.6	53.1	28.3	44

53°, 307° L.H.A.

LATITUDE SAME NAME AS DECLINATION

	38°	39°	40°	41°	42°	43°	44°	45°	
45	50 24.9 +8.8 62.4	50 52.2 +10.2 63.5	51 18.4 +11.7 64.6	51 43.6 +13.2 65.7	52 07.7 +14.7 66.9	52 30.7 +16.2 68.1	52 52.4 +17.8 69.3	53 13.0 +19.3 70.6	45
46	50 33.7 7.5 60.8	51 02.4 9.0 61.9	51 30.1 10.5 63.0	51 56.8 11.9 64.2	52 22.4 13.4 65.3	52 46.9 14.9 66.5	53 10.2 16.5 67.7	53 32.3 18.1 69.0	46
47	50 41.2 6.3 59.3	51 11.4 7.7 60.3	51 40.6 9.1 61.4	52 08.7 10.6 62.6	52 35.8 12.1 63.7	53 01.8 13.7 64.9	53 26.7 15.2 66.1	53 50.4 16.7 67.4	47
48	50 47.5 5.0 57.7	51 19.1 6.4 58.8	51 49.7 7.9 59.8	52 19.3 9.3 61.0	52 47.9 10.8 62.1	53 15.5 12.3 63.3	53 41.9 13.8 64.5	54 07.1 15.4 65.7	48
49	50 52.5 3.7 56.1	51 25.5 5.1 57.2	51 57.6 6.5 58.2	52 28.6 8.0 59.3	52 58.7 9.5 60.5	53 27.8 10.9 61.7	53 55.7 12.4 62.9	54 22.5 14.0 64.1	49
50	50 56.2 +2.5 54.6	51 30.6 +3.8 55.6	52 04.1 +5.2 56.6	52 36.6 +6.6 57.7	53 08.2 +8.0 58.8	53 38.7 +9.5 60.0	54 08.1 +11.1 61.2	54 36.5 +12.6 62.4	50
51	50 58.7 +1.1 53.0	51 34.4 2.5 54.0	52 09.3 3.8 55.0	52 43.2 5.3 56.1	53 16.2 6.7 57.2	53 48.2 8.2 58.3	54 19.2 9.7 59.5	54 49.1 11.2 60.7	51
52	50 59.8 −0.1 51.4	51 36.9 +1.2 52.4	52 13.1 2.5 53.4	52 48.5 3.8 54.4	53 22.9 5.3 55.5	53 56.4 6.7 56.6	54 28.9 8.2 57.8	55 00.3 9.7 59.0	52
53	50 59.7 1.4 49.8	51 38.1 −0.2 50.7	52 15.6 +1.2 51.7	52 52.3 2.5 52.8	53 28.2 3.9 53.8	54 03.1 5.3 55.0	54 37.1 6.7 56.1	55 10.0 8.3 57.3	53
54	50 58.3 2.7 48.2	51 37.9 1.5 49.1	52 16.8 −0.2 50.1	52 54.8 +1.2 51.1	53 32.1 2.5 52.2	54 08.4 3.9 53.3	54 43.8 5.3 54.4	55 18.3 6.8 55.6	54
55	50 55.6 −4.0 46.6	51 36.4 −2.8 47.5	52 16.6 −1.6 48.5	52 55.7 −0.3 49.5	53 34.6 +1.0 50.5	54 12.3 +2.4 51.6	54 49.1 +3.9 52.7	55 25.1 +5.2 53.8	55
56	50 51.5 5.2 45.0	51 33.6 4.1 45.9	52 15.0 2.9 46.8	52 55.0 1.7 47.8	53 35.6 −0.4 48.8	54 14.7 +1.0 49.8	54 53.0 2.3 50.9	55 30.3 3.8 52.1	56
57	50 46.3 6.6 43.5	51 29.5 5.4 44.3	52 12.1 4.2 45.2	52 54.0 3.0 46.1	53 35.2 1.7 47.1	54 15.7 −0.5 48.1	54 55.3 +0.9 49.2	55 34.1 2.2 50.3	57
58	50 39.7 7.8 41.9	51 24.1 6.7 42.7	52 07.9 5.6 43.6	52 51.0 4.4 44.5	53 33.5 3.2 45.4	54 15.2 2.0 46.4	54 56.2 −0.7 47.4	55 36.3 +0.7 48.5	58
59	50 31.9 9.1 40.3	51 17.4 8.0 41.1	52 02.3 6.9 42.0	52 46.6 5.8 42.8	53 30.3 4.7 43.8	54 13.2 3.4 44.7	54 55.5 2.1 45.7	55 37.0 −0.8 46.8	59
60	50 22.8 −10.3 38.8	51 09.4 −9.3 39.5	51 55.4 −8.3 40.4	52 40.8 −7.1 41.2	53 25.6 −6.0 42.1	54 09.8 −4.8 43.0	54 53.4 −3.6 44.0	55 36.2 −2.4 45.0	60
61	50 12.5 11.5 37.2	51 00.1 10.6 38.0	51 47.1 9.5 38.7	52 33.7 8.5 39.6	53 19.6 7.4 40.4	54 05.0 6.3 41.3	54 49.8 5.1 42.2	55 33.8 3.8 43.2	61
62	50 01.0 12.7 35.7	50 49.5 11.7 36.4	51 37.6 10.8 37.2	52 25.2 9.8 37.9	53 12.2 8.7 38.8	53 58.7 7.6 39.6	54 44.7 6.6 40.5	55 30.0 5.4 41.4	62
63	49 48.3 13.9 34.2	50 37.8 13.0 34.9	51 26.8 12.1 35.6	52 15.4 11.2 36.3	53 03.5 10.2 37.1	53 51.1 9.1 37.9	54 38.1 8.0 38.8	55 24.6 6.9 39.7	63
64	49 34.4 15.0 32.7	50 24.8 14.2 33.3	51 14.7 13.3 33.6	52 04.2 12.4 34.7	52 53.3 11.4 35.5	53 42.0 10.5 36.3	54 30.1 9.5 37.1	55 17.7 8.4 37.9	64
65	49 19.4 −16.2 31.2	50 10.6 −15.4 31.8	51 01.4 −14.6 32.5	51 51.8 −13.7 33.1	52 41.9 −12.8 33.8	53 31.5 −11.9 34.6	54 20.6 −10.8 35.4	55 09.3 −9.9 36.2	65
66	49 03.2 17.3 29.7	49 55.2 16.6 30.3	50 46.8 15.7 30.9	51 38.1 14.9 31.6	52 29.1 14.1 32.2	53 19.6 13.2 32.9	54 09.8 12.3 33.7	54 59.4 11.3 34.5	66
67	48 45.9 18.3 28.3	49 38.6 17.6 28.8	50 31.1 17.0 29.4	51 23.2 16.2 30.0	52 15.0 15.4 30.6	53 06.4 14.5 31.3	53 57.5 13.6 32.0	54 48.1 12.7 32.8	67
68	48 27.6 19.5 26.8	49 21.0 18.8 27.4	50 14.1 18.0 27.9	51 07.0 17.3 28.5	51 59.6 16.6 29.1	52 51.9 15.8 29.7	53 43.9 15.0 30.4	54 35.4 14.1 31.1	68
69	48 08.1 20.5 25.4	49 02.2 19.9 25.9	49 56.1 19.2 26.4	50 49.7 18.5 26.9	51 43.0 17.8 27.5	52 36.1 17.1 28.1	53 28.9 16.3 28.7	54 21.3 15.5 29.4	69
70	47 47.6 −21.5 24.0	48 42.3 −20.9 24.5	49 36.9 −20.3 24.9	50 31.2 −19.7 25.4	51 25.2 −19.0 26.0	52 19.0 −18.3 26.5	53 12.6 −17.6 27.1	54 05.8 −16.8 27.8	70
71	47 26.1 22.5 22.6	48 21.4 21.9 23.1	49 16.6 21.4 23.5	50 11.5 20.8 24.0	51 06.2 20.2 24.5	52 00.7 19.5 25.0	52 55.0 18.9 25.5	53 49.0 18.2 26.1	71
72	47 03.6 23.4 21.2	47 59.5 22.9 21.6	48 55.2 22.4 22.1	49 50.7 21.9 22.5	50 46.0 21.3 23.0	51 41.2 20.7 23.5	52 36.1 20.1 24.0	53 30.8 19.4 24.5	72
73	46 40.2 24.4 19.9	47 36.6 24.0 20.3	48 32.8 23.5 20.7	49 28.8 22.9 21.1	50 24.7 22.3 21.5	51 20.5 21.9 21.9	52 16.0 21.2 22.4	53 11.4 20.7 22.9	73
74	46 15.8 25.3 18.6	47 12.6 24.8 18.9	48 09.3 24.4 19.3	49 05.9 23.9 19.6	50 02.4 23.5 20.0	50 58.6 22.9 20.5	51 54.8 22.4 20.9	52 50.7 21.8 21.4	74
75	45 50.5 −26.1 17.3	46 47.8 −25.8 17.6	47 44.9 −25.3 17.9	48 42.0 −25.0 18.3	49 38.9 −24.5 18.5	50 35.7 −24.0 19.0	51 32.4 −23.6 19.4	52 28.9 −23.1 19.8	75
76	45 24.4 27.0 16.0	46 22.0 26.6 16.3	47 19.6 26.3 16.6	48 17.0 25.9 16.9	49 14.4 25.5 17.2	50 11.7 25.1 17.6	51 08.8 24.6 17.9	52 05.8 24.3 18.3	76
77	44 57.4 27.9 14.7	45 55.4 27.6 15.0	46 53.3 27.2 15.2	47 51.1 26.8 15.5	48 48.9 26.5 15.8	49 46.6 26.1 16.2	50 44.2 25.7 16.5	51 41.6 25.2 16.8	77
78	44 29.5 28.6 13.5	45 27.8 28.3 13.7	46 26.1 28.1 13.9	47 24.3 27.7 14.2	48 22.4 27.4 14.5	49 20.5 27.1 14.8	50 18.5 26.8 15.1	51 16.4 26.4 15.4	78
79	44 00.9 29.5 12.2	44 59.5 29.2 12.4	45 58.0 28.9 12.7	46 56.6 28.7 12.9	47 55.0 28.3 13.1	48 53.4 28.0 13.4	49 51.7 27.7 13.7	50 50.0 27.4 14.0	79
80	43 31.4 −30.1 11.0	44 30.3 −29.9 11.2	45 29.1 −29.7 11.4	46 27.9 −29.4 11.6	47 26.7 −29.2 11.8	48 25.4 −28.9 12.1	49 24.0 −28.6 12.3	50 22.6 −28.3 12.6	80
81	43 01.3 30.9 9.8	44 00.4 30.4 9.9	44 59.4 30.4 10.2	45 58.5 30.3 10.4	46 57.5 30.1 10.5	47 56.5 29.9 10.7	48 55.4 29.6 11.0	49 54.3 29.4 11.2	81
82	42 30.4 31.6 8.7	43 29.7 31.4 8.8	44 29.0 31.0 9.0	45 28.2 31.0 9.1	46 27.4 30.8 9.3	47 26.6 30.6 9.5	48 25.8 30.5 9.6	49 24.9 30.2 9.8	82
83	41 58.8 32.3 7.5	42 58.3 32.2 7.6	43 57.7 32.0 7.8	44 57.2 31.9 7.9	45 56.6 31.7 8.0	46 56.0 31.5 8.2	47 55.3 31.3 8.4	48 54.7 31.1 8.5	83
84	41 26.5 32.9 6.4	42 26.1 32.8 6.5	43 25.7 32.6 6.6	44 25.3 32.5 6.7	45 24.9 32.4 6.8	46 24.5 32.3 7.0	47 24.0 32.1 7.1	48 23.6 32.0 7.2	84
85	40 53.6 −33.6 5.3	41 53.3 −33.4 5.4	42 53.1 −33.4 5.5	43 52.8 −33.3 5.5	44 52.5 −33.1 5.7	45 51.9 −32.9 5.7	46 51.9 −32.9 5.8	47 51.6 −32.8 6.0	85
86	40 20.0 34.1 4.2	41 19.9 34.1 4.3	42 19.7 34.0 4.3	43 19.5 33.9 4.4	44 19.4 33.9 4.5	45 19.2 33.8 4.6	46 19.0 33.7 4.6	47 18.8 33.6 4.7	86
87	39 45.9 34.8 3.1	40 45.8 34.7 3.2	41 45.7 34.6 3.2	42 45.6 34.6 3.3	43 45.5 34.5 3.3	44 45.4 34.5 3.4	45 45.3 34.4 3.4	46 45.2 34.4 3.5	87
88	39 11.1 35.1 2.1	40 11.1 35.3 2.1	41 11.1 35.3 2.1	42 11.0 35.2 2.2	43 11.0 35.2 2.2	44 10.9 35.1 2.3	45 10.9 35.1 2.3	46 10.8 35.0 2.3	88
89	38 35.8 35.8 1.0	39 35.8 35.8 1.0	40 35.8 35.8 1.1	41 35.8 35.8 1.1	42 35.8 35.8 1.1	43 35.8 35.8 1.1	44 35.8 35.8 1.1	45 35.8 35.8 1.1	89
90	38 00.0 −36.4 0.0	39 00.0 −36.4 0.0	40 00.0 −36.4 0.0	41 00.0 −36.4 0.0	42 00.0 −36.4 0.0	43 00.0 −36.4 0.0	44 00.0 −36.4 0.0	45 00.0 −36.4 0.0	90

LATITUDE SAME NAME AS DECLINATION

N. Lat. { L.H.A. greater than 180° ...... Zn=Z
{ L.H.A. less than 180° .... Zn=360°−Z

Dec.	38° Hc	d	Z	39° Hc	d	Z	40° Hc	d	Z	41° Hc	d	Z	42° Hc	d	Z	43° Hc	d	Z	44° Hc	d	Z	45° Hc	d	Z	Dec.
0	27 35.6	+41.5	114.1	27 10.8	+42.3	114.6	26 45.7	+43.0	115.0	26 20.1	+43.8	115.5	25 54.0	+44.5	115.9	25 27.6	+45.2	116.4	25 00.8	+45.8	116.8	24 33.5	+46.6	117.2	0
1	28 17.1	41.2	113.3	27 53.1	42.1	113.8	27 28.7	42.8	114.3	27 03.9	43.5	114.7	26 38.5	44.3	115.2	26 12.8	45.1	115.6	25 46.6	45.7	116.1	25 20.1	46.3	116.5	1
2	28 58.3	41.0	112.5	28 35.2	41.7	113.0	28 11.5	42.5	113.5	27 47.4	43.3	113.9	27 22.8	44.1	114.4	26 57.8	44.7	114.9	26 32.3	45.5	115.3	26 06.4	46.2	115.8	2
3	29 39.3	40.8	111.6	29 16.9	41.4	112.1	28 54.0	42.3	112.7	28 30.7	43.0	113.2	28 06.9	43.7	113.7	27 42.5	44.6	114.1	27 17.8	45.2	114.6	26 52.6	45.9	115.1	3
4	30 19.9	40.3	110.8	29 58.3	41.2	111.3	29 36.3	41.9	111.8	29 13.7	42.7	112.4	28 50.6	43.5	112.9	28 27.1	44.2	113.4	28 03.0	45.0	113.9	27 38.5	45.7	114.4	4
5	31 00.2	+39.9	109.9	30 39.5	+40.7	110.5	30 18.2	+41.6	111.0	29 56.4	+42.4	111.6	29 34.1	+43.2	112.1	29 11.3	+44.0	112.6	28 48.0	+44.7	113.1	28 24.2	+45.5	113.6	5
6	31 40.1	39.6	109.0	31 20.2	40.5	109.6	30 59.8	41.3	110.2	30 38.8	42.2	110.7	30 17.3	42.9	111.3	29 55.3	43.7	111.8	29 32.7	44.5	112.4	29 09.7	45.2	112.9	6
7	32 19.7	39.1	108.1	32 00.7	40.0	108.7	31 41.1	40.9	109.3	31 21.0	41.7	109.9	31 00.2	42.7	110.5	30 39.0	43.4	111.0	30 17.2	44.2	111.6	29 54.9	44.9	112.1	7
8	32 58.8	38.8	107.2	32 40.7	39.8	107.9	32 22.0	40.6	108.5	32 02.7	41.5	109.1	31 42.9	42.2	109.6	31 22.4	43.1	110.2	31 01.4	43.9	110.8	30 39.8	44.7	111.4	8
9	33 37.6	38.4	106.3	33 20.5	39.3	107.0	33 02.6	40.2	107.6	32 44.2	41.1	108.2	32 25.1	42.0	108.8	32 05.5	42.8	109.4	31 45.3	43.6	110.0	31 24.5	44.3	110.6	9
10	34 16.0	+38.0	105.4	33 59.8	+38.9	106.1	33 42.8	+39.9	106.7	33 25.3	+40.7	107.3	33 07.1	+41.6	108.0	32 48.3	+42.4	108.6	32 28.9	+43.2	109.2	32 08.8	+44.1	109.8	10
11	34 54.0	37.5	104.5	34 38.7	38.5	105.1	34 22.7	39.4	105.8	34 06.0	40.3	106.5	33 48.7	41.2	107.1	33 30.7	42.1	107.7	33 12.1	43.0	108.4	32 52.9	43.8	109.0	11
12	35 31.5	37.1	103.5	35 17.2	38.0	104.2	35 02.1	39.0	104.9	34 46.3	40.0	105.6	34 29.9	40.9	106.2	34 12.8	41.8	106.9	33 55.1	42.6	107.5	33 36.7	43.4	108.2	12
13	36 08.6	36.6	102.6	35 55.2	37.6	103.2	35 41.1	38.5	104.0	35 26.3	39.5	104.6	35 10.8	40.4	105.3	34 54.6	41.3	106.0	34 37.7	42.2	106.7	34 20.1	43.1	107.3	13
14	36 45.2	36.1	101.6	36 32.8	37.1	102.3	36 19.6	38.2	103.0	36 05.8	39.1	103.7	35 51.2	40.0	104.4	35 35.9	41.0	105.1	35 19.9	41.9	105.8	35 03.2	42.8	106.5	14
15	37 21.3	+35.5	100.6	37 09.9	+36.6	101.3	36 57.8	+37.6	102.0	36 44.9	+38.6	102.8	36 31.2	+39.6	103.5	36 16.9	+40.5	104.2	36 01.8	+41.4	104.9	35 46.0	+42.3	105.6	15
16	37 56.8	35.1	99.5	37 46.5	36.1	100.3	37 35.4	37.1	101.1	37 23.5	38.1	101.8	37 10.8	39.2	102.6	36 57.4	40.1	103.3	36 43.2	41.1	104.0	36 28.3	42.0	104.7	16
17	38 31.9	34.5	98.5	38 22.6	35.6	99.3	38 12.5	36.6	100.1	38 01.6	37.7	100.8	37 50.0	38.6	101.6	37 37.5	39.7	102.4	37 24.3	40.6	103.1	37 10.3	41.6	103.8	17
18	39 06.4	33.9	97.5	38 58.2	35.0	98.3	38 49.1	36.1	99.1	38 39.3	37.1	99.8	38 28.6	38.2	100.6	38 17.2	39.2	101.4	38 04.9	40.2	102.2	37 51.9	41.1	102.9	18
19	39 40.3	33.3	96.4	39 33.2	34.4	97.2	39 25.2	35.6	98.0	39 16.4	36.7	98.8	39 06.8	37.7	99.6	38 56.4	38.7	100.4	38 45.1	39.7	101.2	38 33.0	40.7	102.0	19
20	40 13.6	+32.7	95.3	40 07.6	+33.9	96.1	40 00.8	+34.9	97.0	39 53.1	+36.0	97.8	39 44.5	+37.1	98.6	39 35.1	+38.1	99.5	39 24.8	+39.2	100.3	39 13.7	+40.2	101.1	20
21	40 46.3	32.1	94.2	40 41.5	33.2	95.1	40 35.7	34.4	95.9	40 29.1	35.5	96.8	40 21.6	36.6	97.6	40 13.2	37.7	98.4	40 04.0	38.7	99.3	39 53.9	39.7	100.1	21
22	41 18.4	31.4	93.1	41 14.7	32.6	94.0	41 10.1	33.8	94.8	41 04.6	34.9	95.7	40 58.2	36.0	96.6	40 50.9	37.1	97.4	40 42.7	38.2	98.3	40 33.6	39.2	99.1	22
23	41 49.8	30.7	91.9	41 47.3	31.9	92.8	41 43.9	33.1	93.7	41 39.5	34.3	94.6	41 34.2	35.4	95.5	41 28.0	36.5	96.4	41 20.9	37.6	97.3	41 12.8	38.7	98.1	23
24	42 20.5	30.0	90.8	42 19.2	31.2	91.7	42 17.0	32.4	92.6	42 13.8	33.6	93.5	42 09.6	34.8	94.4	42 04.5	35.9	95.3	41 58.5	37.0	96.2	41 51.5	38.2	97.1	24
25	42 50.5	+29.3	89.6	42 50.4	+30.5	90.5	42 49.4	+31.7	91.5	42 47.4	+32.9	92.4	42 44.4	+34.1	93.3	42 40.4	+35.3	94.2	42 35.5	+36.5	95.1	42 29.7	+37.5	96.1	25
26	43 19.8	28.5	88.4	43 20.9	29.8	89.4	43 21.1	31.0	90.3	43 20.3	32.3	91.2	43 18.5	33.5	92.2	43 15.7	34.7	93.1	43 12.0	35.8	94.1	43 07.2	37.0	95.0	26
27	43 48.3	27.7	87.2	43 50.7	29.0	88.2	43 52.1	30.3	89.1	43 52.6	31.5	90.1	43 52.0	32.7	91.0	43 50.4	34.0	92.0	43 47.8	35.2	93.0	43 44.2	36.3	93.9	27
28	44 16.0	26.9	86.0	44 19.7	28.2	86.9	44 22.4	29.5	87.9	44 24.1	30.8	88.9	44 24.7	32.1	89.9	44 24.4	33.2	90.8	44 23.0	34.4	91.8	44 20.5	35.7	92.8	28
29	44 42.9	26.1	84.7	44 47.9	27.4	85.7	44 51.9	28.7	86.7	44 54.9	30.0	87.7	44 56.8	31.3	88.7	44 57.6	32.6	89.7	44 57.4	33.8	90.7	44 56.2	35.0	91.7	29
30	45 09.0	+25.2	83.4	45 15.3	+26.6	84.4	45 20.6	+27.9	85.4	45 24.9	+29.2	86.5	45 28.1	+30.4	87.5	45 30.2	+31.7	88.5	45 31.2	+33.1	89.5	45 31.2	+34.3	90.5	30
31	45 34.2	24.4	82.1	45 41.9	25.7	83.2	45 48.5	27.1	84.2	45 54.1	28.3	85.2	45 58.5	29.7	86.2	46 01.9	31.0	87.3	46 04.3	32.2	88.3	46 05.5	33.5	89.3	31
32	45 58.6	23.4	80.8	46 07.6	24.8	81.9	46 15.6	26.1	82.9	46 22.4	27.5	83.9	46 28.2	28.9	85.0	46 32.9	30.2	86.0	46 36.5	31.5	87.1	46 39.0	32.8	88.1	32
33	46 22.0	22.5	79.5	46 32.4	23.9	80.5	46 41.7	25.3	81.6	46 49.9	26.7	82.6	46 57.1	28.0	83.7	47 03.1	29.3	84.8	47 08.0	30.7	85.8	47 11.8	32.0	86.9	33
34	46 44.5	21.5	78.2	46 56.3	22.9	79.2	47 07.0	24.3	80.3	47 16.6	25.7	81.3	47 25.1	27.0	82.4	47 32.4	28.5	83.5	47 38.7	29.8	84.6	47 43.8	31.1	85.7	34
35	47 06.0	+20.5	76.8	47 19.2	+21.9	77.8	47 31.3	+23.3	78.9	47 42.3	+24.7	80.0	47 52.1	+26.2	81.1	48 00.9	+27.5	82.2	48 08.5	+28.9	83.3	48 14.9	+30.3	84.4	35
36	47 26.5	19.6	75.4	47 41.1	21.0	76.5	47 54.6	22.4	77.5	48 07.0	23.8	78.6	48 18.3	25.2	79.7	48 28.4	26.6	80.8	48 37.4	28.0	82.0	48 45.2	29.4	83.1	36
37	47 46.1	18.5	74.0	48 02.1	19.9	75.1	48 17.0	21.3	76.2	48 30.8	22.8	77.2	48 43.5	24.2	78.4	48 55.0	25.6	79.5	49 05.4	27.0	80.6	49 14.6	28.4	81.8	37
38	48 04.6	17.4	72.6	48 22.0	18.8	73.7	48 38.3	20.3	74.7	48 53.6	21.7	75.8	49 07.7	23.1	77.0	49 20.6	24.6	78.1	49 32.4	26.0	79.2	49 43.0	27.5	80.4	38
39	48 22.0	16.3	71.1	48 40.8	17.8	72.2	48 58.6	19.2	73.3	49 15.3	20.7	74.4	49 30.8	22.1	75.5	49 45.2	23.6	76.7	49 58.4	25.1	77.8	50 10.5	26.4	79.0	39
40	48 38.3	+15.3	69.7	48 58.6	+16.7	70.8	49 17.8	+18.2	71.9	49 36.0	+19.5	73.0	49 52.9	+21.1	74.1	50 08.8	+22.5	75.3	50 23.5	+23.9	76.4	50 36.9	+25.5	77.6	40
41	48 53.6	14.1	68.2	49 15.3	15.5	69.3	49 36.0	16.9	70.4	49 55.5	18.5	71.5	50 14.0	19.9	72.7	50 31.3	21.4	73.8	50 47.4	22.9	75.0	51 02.4	24.3	76.2	41
42	49 07.7	12.9	66.7	49 30.8	14.4	67.8	49 52.9	15.9	68.9	50 14.0	17.3	70.0	50 33.9	18.8	71.2	50 52.7	20.3	72.3	51 10.3	21.8	73.5	51 26.7	23.3	74.7	42
43	49 20.6	11.8	65.3	49 45.2	13.2	66.3	50 08.8	14.7	67.4	50 31.3	16.1	68.5	50 52.7	17.6	69.7	51 13.0	19.1	70.8	51 32.1	20.6	72.0	51 50.0	22.1	73.2	43
44	49 32.4	10.6	63.7	49 58.4	12.1	64.8	50 23.5	13.4	65.9	50 47.4	15.0	67.0	51 10.3	16.4	68.2	51 32.1	17.9	69.3	51 52.7	19.4	70.5	52 12.1	20.9	71.7	44

LATITUDE SAME NAME AS DECLINATION

N. Lat. { L.H.A. greater than 180°......Zn=Z
L.H.A. less than 180°......Zn=360°-Z

Dec.	38° Hc	d	Z	39° Hc	d	Z	40° Hc	d	Z	41° Hc	d	Z	42° Hc	d	Z	43° Hc	d	Z	44° Hc	d	Z	45° Hc	d	Z	Dec.
0	26 52.3	+41.2	113.3	26 28.3	+42.0	113.8	26 03.7	+42.8	114.2	25 39.0	+43.6	114.7	25 13.8	+44.3	115.1	24 48.1	+45.0	115.5	24 22.1	+45.6	115.9	23 55.6	+46.4	116.3	0
1	27 33.5	41.0	112.5	27 10.3	41.8	113.0	26 46.7	42.5	113.4	26 22.6	43.3	113.9	25 58.1	44.0	114.3	25 33.1	44.8	114.8	25 07.7	45.3	115.2	24 42.0	46.1	115.6	1
2	28 14.5	40.7	111.7	27 52.1	41.5	112.2	27 29.2	42.3	112.7	27 05.9	43.0	113.1	26 42.1	43.8	113.6	26 17.9	44.5	114.1	25 53.2	45.2	114.5	25 28.1	45.9	114.9	2
3	28 55.2	40.4	110.8	28 33.6	41.2	111.4	28 11.5	42.0	111.9	27 48.9	42.8	112.3	27 25.9	43.5	112.8	27 02.4	44.2	113.3	26 38.4	44.8	113.8	26 14.0	45.7	114.2	3
4	29 35.6	40.0	110.0	29 14.8	40.9	110.5	28 53.5	41.7	111.0	28 31.7	42.4	111.6	28 09.4	43.3	112.1	27 46.6	44.1	112.5	27 23.4	44.8	113.0	26 59.7	45.5	113.5	4
5	30 15.6	+39.7	109.1	29 55.7	+40.5	109.7	29 35.2	+41.4	110.2	29 14.2	+42.2	110.7	28 52.7	+43.0	111.3	28 30.7	+43.7	111.8	28 08.2	+44.5	112.3	27 45.2	+45.2	112.8	5
6	30 55.3	39.3	108.3	30 36.2	40.2	108.8	30 16.6	41.0	109.4	29 56.4	41.9	109.9	29 35.7	42.7	110.5	29 14.4	43.5	111.0	28 52.7	44.2	111.5	28 30.4	45.0	112.0	6
7	31 34.6	39.0	107.4	31 16.4	39.9	108.0	30 57.6	40.7	108.5	30 38.3	41.5	109.1	30 18.4	42.4	109.7	29 57.9	43.2	110.2	29 36.9	43.9	110.7	29 15.4	44.8	111.3	7
8	32 13.6	38.6	106.5	31 56.3	39.5	107.1	31 38.3	40.4	107.7	31 19.8	41.3	108.3	31 00.8	42.0	108.8	30 41.1	42.9	109.4	30 20.9	43.7	110.0	30 00.2	44.4	110.5	8
9	32 52.2	38.2	105.6	32 35.8	39.1	106.2	32 18.7	40.0	106.8	32 01.1	40.9	107.4	31 42.8	41.8	108.0	31 24.0	42.6	108.6	31 04.6	43.4	109.2	30 44.6	44.2	109.7	9
10	33 30.4	+37.7	104.7	33 14.9	+38.7	105.3	32 58.7	+39.7	105.9	32 42.0	+40.5	106.5	32 24.6	+41.4	107.1	32 06.6	+42.2	107.8	31 48.0	+43.1	108.3	31 28.8	+43.9	108.9	10
11	34 08.1	37.4	103.7	33 53.6	38.3	104.4	33 38.4	39.2	105.0	33 22.5	40.1	105.7	33 06.0	41.0	106.3	32 48.8	41.9	106.9	32 31.1	42.7	107.5	32 12.7	43.6	108.1	11
12	34 45.5	36.9	102.8	34 31.9	37.8	103.4	34 17.6	38.8	104.1	34 02.6	39.8	104.8	33 47.0	40.7	105.4	33 30.7	41.6	106.1	33 13.8	42.4	106.7	32 56.3	43.2	107.3	12
13	35 22.4	36.4	101.8	35 09.7	37.5	102.5	34 56.4	38.4	103.2	34 42.4	39.3	103.9	34 27.7	40.2	104.5	34 12.3	41.2	105.2	33 56.2	42.1	105.8	33 39.5	43.0	106.5	13
14	35 58.8	35.9	100.8	35 47.2	36.9	101.5	35 34.8	37.9	102.2	35 21.7	38.9	102.9	35 07.9	39.9	103.6	34 53.5	40.7	104.3	34 38.3	41.7	105.0	34 22.5	42.5	105.6	14
15	36 34.7	+35.5	99.8	36 24.1	+36.5	100.5	36 12.7	+37.5	101.3	36 00.6	+38.5	102.0	35 47.8	+39.4	102.7	35 34.2	+40.4	103.4	35 20.0	+41.3	104.1	35 05.0	+42.2	104.8	15
16	37 10.2	34.9	98.8	37 00.6	35.9	99.6	36 50.2	37.0	100.3	36 39.1	38.0	101.0	36 27.2	38.6	101.8	36 14.6	40.0	102.4	36 01.3	40.9	103.2	35 47.2	41.8	103.9	16
17	37 45.1	34.4	97.8	37 36.5	35.3	98.6	37 27.2	36.5	99.3	37 17.1	37.5	100.1	37 06.2	38.6	100.8	36 54.6	39.5	101.6	36 42.2	40.4	102.3	36 29.0	41.4	103.0	17
18	38 19.5	33.8	96.8	38 12.0	34.9	97.5	38 03.7	36.0	98.3	37 54.6	37.1	99.1	37 44.8	38.0	99.9	37 34.1	39.0	100.6	37 22.6	40.1	101.4	37 10.4	41.0	102.1	18
19	38 53.3	33.2	95.7	38 46.9	34.3	96.5	38 39.7	35.4	97.3	38 31.7	36.5	98.1	38 22.8	37.6	98.9	38 13.1	38.6	99.7	38 02.7	39.6	100.4	37 51.4	40.6	101.2	19
20	39 26.5	+32.6	94.6	39 21.2	+33.8	95.4	39 15.1	+34.9	96.3	39 08.2	+35.9	97.1	39 00.4	+37.0	97.9	38 51.7	+38.1	98.7	38 42.3	+39.1	99.5	38 32.0	+40.1	100.3	20
21	39 59.1	32.1	93.5	39 55.0	33.2	94.4	39 50.0	34.3	95.2	39 44.1	35.4	96.0	39 37.4	36.5	96.9	39 29.8	37.5	97.7	39 21.4	38.5	98.5	39 12.1	39.6	99.3	21
22	40 31.2	31.3	92.4	40 28.2	32.5	93.3	40 24.3	33.7	94.1	40 19.5	34.8	95.0	40 13.9	35.9	95.8	40 07.3	37.1	96.7	39 59.9	38.1	97.5	39 51.7	39.1	98.3	22
23	41 02.5	30.7	91.3	41 00.7	31.9	92.2	40 58.0	33.0	93.0	40 54.3	34.2	93.9	40 49.8	35.3	94.8	40 44.4	36.4	95.6	40 38.0	37.6	96.5	40 30.8	38.6	97.3	23
24	41 33.2	30.0	90.2	41 32.6	31.2	91.0	41 31.0	32.4	91.9	41 28.5	33.6	92.8	41 25.1	34.8	93.7	41 20.8	35.9	94.6	41 15.6	36.9	95.5	41 09.4	38.1	96.3	24
25	42 03.2	+29.3	89.0	42 03.8	+30.5	89.9	42 03.4	+31.8	90.8	42 02.1	+32.9	91.7	41 59.9	+34.1	92.6	41 56.7	+35.2	93.5	41 52.5	+36.4	94.4	41 47.5	+37.5	95.3	25
26	42 32.5	28.6	87.8	42 34.3	29.8	88.7	42 35.2	31.0	89.7	42 35.0	32.3	90.6	42 34.0	33.4	91.5	42 31.9	34.6	92.4	42 28.9	35.8	93.3	42 25.0	36.9	94.2	26
27	43 01.1	27.8	86.6	43 04.1	29.1	87.6	43 06.2	30.3	88.5	43 07.3	31.5	89.4	43 07.4	32.8	90.4	43 06.5	34.0	91.3	43 04.7	35.1	92.2	43 01.9	36.2	93.2	27
28	43 28.9	27.0	85.4	43 33.2	28.3	86.4	43 36.5	29.6	87.3	43 38.8	30.8	88.3	43 40.2	32.0	89.2	43 40.5	33.3	90.2	43 39.8	34.5	91.1	43 38.1	35.7	92.1	28
29	43 55.9	26.2	84.2	44 01.5	27.5	85.1	44 06.1	28.7	86.1	44 09.6	30.1	87.1	44 12.2	31.3	88.0	44 13.8	32.5	89.0	44 14.3	33.8	90.0	44 13.8	34.9	91.0	29
30	44 22.1	+25.3	82.9	44 29.0	+26.6	83.9	44 34.8	+28.0	84.9	44 39.7	+29.3	85.9	44 43.5	+30.6	86.8	44 46.3	+31.8	87.8	44 48.1	+33.0	88.8	44 48.8	+34.3	89.8	30
31	44 47.4	24.5	81.6	44 55.6	25.9	82.6	45 02.8	27.2	83.6	45 09.0	28.4	84.6	45 14.1	29.7	85.6	45 18.1	31.1	86.6	45 21.1	32.3	87.6	45 23.1	33.5	88.7	31
32	45 11.9	23.6	80.4	45 21.5	24.9	81.3	45 30.0	26.3	82.4	45 37.4	27.7	83.4	45 43.8	28.9	84.4	45 49.2	30.2	85.4	45 53.4	31.6	86.4	45 56.6	32.9	87.5	32
33	45 35.5	22.7	79.0	45 46.4	24.1	80.0	45 56.3	25.4	81.1	46 05.1	26.7	82.1	46 12.7	28.1	83.1	46 19.4	29.5	84.2	46 25.0	30.7	85.2	46 29.5	32.0	86.3	33
34	45 58.2	21.8	77.7	46 10.5	23.1	78.7	46 21.7	24.5	79.8	46 31.8	25.9	80.8	46 40.9	27.2	81.8	46 48.9	28.5	82.9	46 55.7	29.9	84.0	47 01.5	31.2	85.0	34
35	46 20.0	+20.8	76.4	46 33.6	+22.2	77.4	46 46.2	+23.6	78.4	46 57.7	+25.0	79.5	47 08.1	+26.3	80.5	47 17.4	+27.7	81.6	47 25.6	+29.1	82.7	47 32.7	+30.4	83.8	35
36	46 40.8	19.9	75.0	46 55.8	21.3	75.9	47 09.8	22.6	77.1	47 22.7	24.0	78.1	47 34.4	25.4	79.1	47 45.1	26.8	80.3	47 54.7	28.1	81.4	48 03.1	29.5	82.5	36
37	47 00.7	18.8	73.6	47 17.1	20.2	74.7	47 32.4	21.6	75.7	47 46.7	23.0	76.8	47 59.8	24.5	77.9	48 11.9	25.8	79.0	48 22.8	27.2	80.1	48 32.6	28.6	81.2	37
38	47 19.5	17.8	72.2	47 37.3	19.2	73.3	47 54.0	20.6	74.3	48 09.7	22.0	75.4	48 24.3	23.4	76.5	48 37.7	24.9	77.6	48 50.0	26.3	78.7	49 01.2	27.7	79.8	38
39	47 37.3	16.7	70.8	47 56.5	18.1	71.9	48 14.6	19.6	72.9	48 31.7	21.0	74.0	48 47.7	22.4	75.1	49 02.6	23.9	76.2	49 16.3	25.3	77.3	49 28.9	26.6	78.5	39
40	47 54.0	+15.7	69.4	48 14.6	+17.1	70.4	48 34.2	+18.5	71.5	48 52.7	+19.9	72.6	49 10.1	+21.4	73.7	49 26.4	+22.8	74.8	49 41.6	+24.2	75.9	49 55.5	+25.7	77.1	40
41	48 09.7	14.6	67.9	48 31.7	16.0	69.0	48 52.7	17.4	70.1	49 12.6	18.9	71.1	49 31.5	20.3	72.3	49 49.2	21.7	73.4	50 05.8	23.2	74.5	50 21.2	24.7	75.7	41
42	48 24.3	13.4	66.5	48 47.7	14.9	67.5	49 10.1	16.3	68.6	49 31.5	17.7	69.7	49 51.8	19.1	70.8	50 10.9	20.7	71.9	50 29.0	22.1	73.1	50 45.9	23.5	74.2	42
43	48 37.7	12.3	65.0	49 02.6	13.7	66.1	49 26.4	15.2	67.1	49 49.2	16.6	68.2	50 10.9	18.1	69.3	50 31.6	19.5	70.5	50 51.1	21.0	71.6	51 09.4	22.5	72.8	43
44	48 50.0	11.2	63.5	49 16.3	12.6	64.6	49 41.6	13.9	65.6	50 05.8	15.4	66.7	50 29.0	16.9	67.8	50 51.1	18.3	69.0	51 12.1	19.8	70.1	51 31.9	21.3	71.3	44

LATITUDE SAME NAME AS DECLINATION

N. Lat. { L.H.A. greater than 180°......Zn=Z ; L.H.A. less than 180°......Zn=360°-Z }

Dec.	38° Hc	d	Z	39° Hc	d	Z	40° Hc	d	Z	41° Hc	d	Z	42° Hc	d	Z	43° Hc	d	Z	44° Hc	d	Z	45° Hc	d	Z	Dec.
0	25 24.9	+40.8	111.8	25 02.4	+41.6	112.2	24 39.5	+42.4	112.7	24 16.2	+43.1	113.1	23 52.5	+43.8	113.5	23 28.4	+44.5	113.9	23 03.9	+45.2	114.3	22 39.1	+45.8	114.7	0
1	26 05.7	40.5	111.0	25 44.0	41.3	111.4	25 21.9	42.0	111.9	24 59.3	42.8	112.3	24 36.3	43.6	112.7	24 12.9	44.3	113.2	23 49.1	45.0	113.6	23 24.9	45.7	114.0	1
2	26 46.2	40.2	110.2	26 25.3	41.0	110.6	26 03.9	41.8	111.1	25 42.1	42.6	111.5	25 19.9	43.3	112.0	24 57.2	44.1	112.4	24 34.1	44.8	112.8	24 10.6	45.5	113.3	2
3	27 26.4	39.9	109.3	27 06.3	40.7	109.8	26 45.7	41.6	110.3	26 24.7	42.3	110.8	26 03.2	43.1	111.2	25 41.3	43.8	111.7	25 18.9	44.6	112.1	24 56.1	45.3	112.5	3
4	28 06.3	39.6	108.5	27 47.0	40.4	109.0	27 27.3	41.2	109.5	27 07.0	42.1	110.0	26 46.3	42.8	110.4	26 25.1	43.6	110.9	26 03.5	44.3	111.4	25 41.4	45.1	111.8	4
5	28 45.9	+39.2	107.6	28 27.4	+40.1	108.1	28 08.5	+40.9	108.7	27 49.1	+41.7	109.2	27 29.1	+42.6	109.6	27 08.7	+43.4	110.1	26 47.8	+44.1	110.6	26 26.5	+44.8	111.1	5
6	29 25.1	38.9	106.8	29 07.5	39.8	107.3	28 49.4	40.7	107.8	28 30.8	41.5	108.3	28 11.7	42.3	108.8	27 52.1	43.0	109.4	27 31.9	43.9	109.8	27 11.3	44.6	110.3	6
7	30 04.0	38.6	105.9	29 47.3	39.5	106.4	29 30.1	40.3	107.0	29 12.3	41.2	107.5	28 54.0	42.0	108.0	28 35.1	42.8	108.6	28 15.8	43.6	109.1	27 55.9	44.4	109.6	7
8	30 42.6	38.2	105.0	30 26.8	39.1	105.6	30 10.4	40.0	106.1	29 53.5	40.8	106.7	29 36.0	41.6	107.2	29 17.9	42.5	107.8	28 59.4	43.3	108.3	28 40.3	44.0	108.8	8
9	31 20.8	37.8	104.1	31 05.9	38.7	104.7	30 50.4	39.6	105.3	30 34.3	40.5	105.8	30 17.6	41.4	106.4	30 00.4	42.2	107.0	29 42.7	43.0	107.5	29 24.3	43.9	108.0	9
10	31 58.6	+37.4	103.2	31 44.6	+38.3	103.8	31 30.0	+39.3	104.4	31 14.8	+40.2	105.0	30 59.0	+41.0	105.6	30 42.6	+41.9	106.2	30 25.7	+42.7	106.7	30 08.2	+43.5	107.3	10
11	32 36.0	37.0	102.3	32 22.9	38.0	102.9	32 09.3	38.8	103.5	31 55.0	39.7	104.1	31 40.0	40.7	104.7	31 24.5	41.6	105.3	31 08.4	42.4	105.9	30 51.7	43.2	106.5	11
12	33 13.0	36.6	101.3	33 00.9	37.5	102.0	32 48.1	38.5	102.6	32 34.7	39.5	103.2	32 20.7	40.4	103.8	32 06.1	41.2	104.4	31 50.8	42.1	105.0	31 34.9	42.9	105.6	12
13	33 49.6	36.1	100.4	33 38.4	37.2	101.0	33 26.6	38.1	101.7	33 14.2	39.0	102.3	33 01.0	40.0	103.0	32 47.3	40.8	103.6	32 32.9	41.7	104.2	32 17.8	42.6	104.8	13
14	34 25.7	35.7	99.4	34 15.6	36.6	100.1	34 04.7	37.7	100.7	33 53.2	38.6	101.4	33 41.0	39.5	102.1	33 28.1	40.5	102.7	33 14.6	41.4	103.3	33 00.4	42.3	104.0	14
15	35 01.4	+35.2	98.4	34 52.2	+36.2	99.1	34 42.4	+37.2	99.8	34 31.8	+38.2	100.5	34 20.5	+39.2	101.2	34 08.6	+40.1	101.8	33 56.0	+41.0	102.5	33 42.7	+41.9	103.1	15
16	35 36.6	34.7	97.4	35 28.4	35.8	98.1	35 19.6	36.7	98.8	35 10.0	37.7	99.5	34 59.7	38.7	100.2	34 48.7	39.7	100.9	34 37.0	40.6	101.6	34 24.6	41.5	102.3	16
17	36 11.3	34.1	96.4	36 04.2	35.2	97.1	35 56.3	36.3	97.9	35 47.7	37.3	98.6	35 38.4	38.3	99.3	35 28.4	39.2	100.0	35 17.6	40.2	100.7	35 06.1	41.1	101.4	17
18	36 45.4	33.7	95.4	36 39.4	34.7	96.1	36 32.6	35.8	96.9	36 25.0	36.8	97.6	36 16.7	37.8	98.3	36 07.6	38.8	99.1	35 57.8	39.8	99.8	35 47.2	40.8	100.5	18
19	37 19.1	33.1	94.4	37 14.1	34.1	95.1	37 08.4	35.2	95.9	37 01.8	36.4	96.6	36 54.5	37.4	97.4	36 46.4	38.4	98.1	36 37.6	39.3	98.9	36 28.0	40.3	99.6	19
20	37 52.2	+32.5	93.3	37 48.3	+33.6	94.1	37 43.6	+34.8	94.9	37 38.2	+35.7	95.6	37 31.9	+36.8	96.4	37 24.8	+37.9	97.2	37 16.9	+38.9	97.9	37 08.3	+39.9	98.7	20
21	38 24.7	31.9	92.2	38 21.9	33.1	93.0	38 18.4	34.1	93.8	38 13.9	35.3	94.6	38 08.7	36.3	95.4	38 02.7	37.4	96.2	37 55.8	38.4	97.0	37 48.2	39.4	97.7	21
22	38 56.6	31.4	91.2	38 55.0	32.5	92.0	38 52.5	33.6	92.8	38 49.2	34.7	93.6	38 45.0	35.8	94.4	38 40.1	36.8	95.2	38 34.2	37.9	96.0	38 27.6	38.9	96.8	22
23	39 28.0	30.7	90.1	39 27.5	31.8	90.9	39 26.1	33.0	91.7	39 23.9	34.1	92.5	39 20.8	35.3	93.4	39 16.9	36.3	94.2	39 12.1	37.4	95.0	39 06.5	38.5	95.8	23
24	39 58.7	30.0	88.9	39 59.3	31.3	89.8	39 59.1	32.4	90.6	39 58.0	33.6	91.5	39 56.1	34.6	92.3	39 53.2	35.8	93.1	39 49.5	36.9	94.0	39 45.0	37.9	94.8	24
25	40 28.7	+29.4	87.8	40 30.6	+30.5	88.7	40 31.5	+31.8	89.5	40 31.6	+32.9	90.4	40 30.7	+34.1	91.2	40 29.0	+35.2	92.1	40 26.4	+36.3	92.9	40 22.9	+37.4	93.8	25
26	40 58.1	28.0	86.7	41 01.0	29.9	87.5	41 03.3	31.0	88.4	41 04.5	32.2	89.3	41 04.8	33.4	90.1	41 04.2	34.6	91.0	41 02.7	35.7	91.9	41 00.3	36.8	92.7	26
27	41 26.7	28.0	85.5	41 31.0	29.2	86.4	41 34.3	30.4	87.3	41 36.7	31.6	88.1	41 38.2	32.8	89.0	41 38.8	33.9	89.9	41 38.4	35.1	90.8	41 37.1	36.2	91.7	27
28	41 54.7	27.2	84.3	42 00.2	28.4	85.2	42 04.7	29.7	86.1	42 08.3	30.9	87.0	42 11.0	32.1	87.9	42 12.7	33.3	88.8	42 13.5	34.5	89.7	42 13.3	35.6	90.6	28
29	42 21.9	26.7	83.1	42 28.6	27.7	84.0	42 34.4	29.0	84.9	42 39.2	30.2	85.8	42 43.1	31.4	86.8	42 46.0	32.7	87.7	42 48.0	33.8	88.6	42 48.9	35.0	89.5	29
30	42 48.3	+25.7	81.9	42 56.3	+27.0	82.8	43 03.4	+28.2	83.7	43 09.4	+29.5	84.7	43 14.5	+30.7	85.6	43 18.7	+31.9	86.5	43 21.8	+33.1	87.5	43 23.9	+34.4	88.4	30
31	43 14.0	24.8	80.6	43 23.3	26.1	81.6	43 31.6	27.4	82.5	43 38.9	28.7	83.5	43 45.2	30.0	84.4	43 50.6	31.2	85.4	43 54.9	32.5	86.3	43 58.3	33.6	87.3	31
32	43 38.8	24.1	79.4	43 49.4	25.3	80.3	43 59.0	26.6	81.3	44 07.6	27.9	82.2	44 15.2	29.2	83.2	44 21.8	30.4	84.2	44 27.4	31.7	85.2	44 31.9	33.0	86.1	32
33	44 02.9	23.1	78.1	44 14.7	24.5	79.1	44 25.6	25.8	80.0	44 35.5	27.1	81.0	44 44.4	28.3	82.0	44 52.2	29.7	83.0	44 59.1	30.9	84.0	45 04.9	32.1	85.0	33
34	44 26.0	22.3	76.8	44 39.2	23.6	77.8	44 51.4	24.9	78.8	45 02.6	26.2	79.7	45 12.7	27.6	80.7	45 21.9	28.8	81.7	45 30.0	30.1	82.7	45 37.0	31.5	83.8	34
35	44 48.3	+21.4	75.5	45 02.8	+22.7	76.5	45 16.3	+24.0	77.5	45 28.8	+25.4	78.5	45 40.3	+26.7	79.5	45 50.7	+28.1	80.5	46 00.1	+29.4	81.5	46 08.5	+30.6	82.5	35
36	45 09.7	20.4	74.2	45 25.5	21.8	75.2	45 40.3	23.2	76.2	45 54.2	24.5	77.2	46 07.0	25.8	78.2	46 18.8	27.1	79.2	46 29.5	28.4	80.2	46 39.1	29.8	81.3	36
37	45 30.1	19.5	72.9	45 47.3	20.9	73.8	46 03.5	22.2	74.8	46 18.7	23.5	75.9	46 32.8	24.9	76.9	46 45.9	26.3	77.9	46 57.9	27.6	79.0	47 08.9	28.9	80.0	37
38	45 49.6	18.6	71.5	46 08.2	19.8	72.5	46 25.7	21.2	73.5	46 42.2	22.6	74.5	46 57.7	24.0	75.5	47 12.2	25.3	76.6	47 25.5	26.7	77.6	47 37.8	28.1	78.7	38
39	46 08.2	17.5	70.1	46 28.0	18.9	71.1	46 46.9	20.3	72.1	47 04.8	21.7	73.2	47 21.7	23.0	74.2	47 37.5	24.4	75.3	47 52.2	25.8	76.3	48 05.9	27.1	77.4	39
40	46 25.7	+16.5	68.8	46 46.9	+17.9	69.8	47 07.2	+19.3	70.8	47 26.5	+20.6	71.8	47 44.7	+22.0	72.8	48 01.9	+23.4	73.9	48 18.0	+24.8	75.0	48 33.0	+26.2	76.1	40
41	46 42.2	15.5	67.4	47 04.8	16.9	68.4	47 26.5	18.2	69.4	47 47.1	19.6	70.4	48 06.7	21.0	71.4	48 25.3	22.4	72.5	48 42.8	23.8	73.6	48 59.2	25.2	74.7	41
42	46 57.7	14.5	66.0	47 21.7	15.8	66.9	47 44.7	17.2	68.0	48 06.7	18.6	69.0	48 27.7	20.0	70.0	48 47.7	21.4	71.1	49 06.6	22.8	72.2	49 24.4	24.2	73.3	42
43	47 12.2	13.3	64.5	47 37.5	14.7	65.5	48 01.9	16.1	66.5	48 25.3	17.5	67.6	48 47.7	18.9	68.6	49 09.1	20.3	69.7	49 29.4	21.7	70.8	49 48.6	23.1	71.9	43
44	47 25.5	12.3	63.1	47 52.2	13.7	64.1	48 18.0	15.0	65.1	48 42.8	16.4	66.1	49 06.6	17.8	67.2	49 29.4	19.2	68.2	49 51.1	20.6	69.3	50 11.7	22.1	70.5	44

58°, 302° L.H.A. LATITUDE SAME NAME AS DECLINATION

Lat	38° Hc	d	Z	39° Hc	d	Z	40° Hc	d	Z	41° Hc	d	Z	42° Hc	d	Z	43° Hc	d	Z	44° Hc	d	Z	45° Hc	d	Z	Lat
45	46 56.3	+11.7	61.4	47 24.5	+13.1	62.4	47 51.9	+14.4	63.4	48 18.3	+15.8	64.4	48 43.8	+17.2	65.4	49 08.3	+18.5	66.4	49 31.8	+19.9	67.5	49 54.2	+21.4	68.6	45
46	47 08.0	10.7	60.0	47 37.6	12.0	60.9	48 06.3	13.3	61.9	48 34.1	14.7	62.9	49 01.0	16.0	63.9	49 26.8	17.5	65.0	49 51.7	18.8	66.0	50 15.6	20.2	67.1	46
47	47 18.7	9.6	58.5	47 49.6	10.9	59.5	48 19.6	12.3	60.4	48 48.8	13.5	61.4	49 17.0	14.9	62.5	49 44.3	16.3	63.5	50 10.5	17.7	64.6	50 35.8	19.1	65.7	47
48	47 28.3	8.5	57.1	48 00.5	9.7	58.0	48 31.9	11.0	59.0	49 02.3	12.4	60.0	49 31.9	13.8	61.0	50 00.6	15.1	62.0	50 28.2	16.6	63.1	50 54.9	17.9	64.2	48
49	47 36.8	7.3	55.6	48 10.2	8.7	56.5	48 42.9	9.9	57.5	49 14.7	11.3	58.5	49 45.7	12.6	59.5	50 15.7	13.9	60.5	50 44.8	15.3	61.6	51 12.8	16.8	62.6	49
50	47 44.1	+6.2	54.1	48 18.9	+7.4	55.1	48 52.8	+8.8	56.0	49 26.0	+10.0	57.0	49 58.3	+11.3	57.9	50 29.6	+12.8	59.0	51 00.1	+14.1	60.0	51 29.6	+15.5	61.1	50
51	47 50.3	5.0	52.7	48 26.3	6.3	53.6	49 01.6	7.5	54.5	49 36.0	8.9	55.4	50 09.6	10.2	56.4	50 42.4	11.5	57.4	51 14.2	12.9	58.6	51 45.1	14.3	59.6	51
52	47 55.3	3.9	51.2	48 32.6	5.1	52.1	49 09.1	6.4	53.0	49 44.9	7.6	53.9	50 19.8	8.9	54.9	50 53.9	10.3	55.9	51 27.1	11.6	56.9	51 59.4	13.0	58.0	52
53	47 59.2	2.8	49.7	48 37.7	3.9	50.6	49 15.5	5.1	51.4	49 52.5	6.4	52.4	50 28.7	7.7	53.3	51 04.2	9.0	54.3	51 38.7	10.4	55.3	52 12.4	11.7	56.4	53
54	48 02.0	1.6	48.2	48 41.6	2.8	49.0	49 20.6	4.0	49.8	49 58.9	5.2	50.8	50 36.4	6.5	51.8	51 13.2	7.7	52.7	51 49.1	9.0	53.7	52 24.1	10.4	54.8	54
55	48 03.6	+0.4	46.7	48 44.4	+1.5	47.5	49 24.6	+2.7	48.4	50 04.1	+3.9	49.3	50 42.9	+5.1	50.2	51 20.9	+6.4	51.1	51 58.1	+7.8	52.1	52 34.5	+9.1	53.2	55
56	48 04.0	-0.8	45.2	48 45.9	0.4	46.0	49 27.3	1.5	46.8	50 08.0	2.7	47.7	50 48.0	3.9	48.6	51 27.3	5.1	49.6	52 05.9	6.4	50.5	52 43.6	7.7	51.5	56
57	48 03.2	1.9	43.7	48 46.3	-0.8	44.5	49 28.8	0.3	45.3	50 10.7	1.4	46.2	50 51.9	2.6	47.0	51 32.4	3.9	48.0	52 12.3	5.0	48.9	52 51.3	6.4	49.9	57
58	48 01.3	3.1	42.2	48 45.5	2.1	43.0	49 29.1	-1.0	43.8	50 12.1	0.2	44.6	50 54.5	1.3	45.5	51 36.3	2.5	46.4	52 17.3	3.8	47.3	52 57.7	4.9	48.3	58
59	47 58.2	4.2	40.7	48 43.4	3.2	41.5	49 28.1	2.1	42.2	50 12.3	-1.1	43.0	50 55.8	0.1	43.9	51 38.8	1.2	44.7	52 21.1	2.3	45.6	53 02.6	3.6	46.6	59
60	47 54.0	-5.4	39.2	48 40.2	-4.4	39.9	49 26.0	-3.4	40.7	50 11.2	-2.4	41.5	50 55.9	-1.3	42.3	51 40.0	-0.2	43.1	52 23.4	+1.0	44.0	53 06.2	+2.2	44.9	60
61	47 48.6	6.6	37.7	48 35.8	5.6	38.4	49 22.6	4.6	39.1	50 08.8	3.6	39.9	50 54.6	2.6	40.7	51 39.8	1.5	41.5	52 24.4	0.3	42.4	53 08.4	0.9	43.3	61
62	47 42.0	7.6	36.3	48 30.2	6.7	36.9	49 18.0	5.9	37.6	50 05.2	4.8	38.4	50 52.0	3.8	39.1	51 38.3	2.7	39.9	52 24.1	1.7	40.7	53 09.3	0.6	41.6	62
63	47 34.4	8.8	34.8	48 23.5	8.0	35.4	49 12.1	7.0	36.1	50 00.4	6.1	36.8	50 48.2	5.1	37.5	51 35.6	4.2	38.3	52 22.4	3.1	39.1	53 08.7	2.0	39.9	63
64	47 25.6	9.9	33.3	48 15.5	9.0	33.9	49 05.1	8.2	34.6	49 54.3	7.3	35.3	50 43.1	6.4	36.0	51 31.4	5.4	36.7	52 19.3	4.4	37.5	53 06.7	3.4	38.3	64
65	47 15.7	-11.0	31.9	48 06.5	-10.2	32.5	48 56.9	-9.4	33.1	49 47.0	-8.5	33.7	50 36.7	-7.6	34.4	51 26.0	-6.7	35.1	52 14.9	-5.7	35.8	53 03.3	-4.7	36.6	65
66	47 04.7	12.1	30.4	47 56.3	11.4	31.0	48 47.5	10.5	31.6	49 38.5	9.7	32.2	50 29.1	8.9	32.8	51 19.3	8.0	33.5	52 09.2	7.1	34.2	52 58.6	6.2	34.9	66
67	46 52.6	13.2	29.0	47 44.9	12.5	29.5	48 37.0	11.7	30.1	49 28.8	11.0	30.7	50 20.2	10.1	31.3	51 11.3	9.3	31.9	52 02.1	8.4	32.6	52 52.4	7.5	33.3	67
68	46 39.4	14.2	27.6	47 32.5	13.5	28.1	48 25.3	12.8	28.6	49 17.8	12.0	29.2	50 10.1	11.3	29.7	51 02.0	10.5	30.3	51 53.7	9.8	31.0	52 44.9	8.8	31.7	68
69	46 25.2	15.2	26.2	47 19.0	14.6	26.6	48 12.5	13.9	27.1	49 05.8	13.3	27.7	49 58.8	12.6	28.2	50 51.5	11.8	28.8	51 43.9	11.0	29.4	52 36.1	10.2	30.0	69
70	46 10.0	-16.3	24.8	47 04.4	-15.7	25.2	47 58.6	-15.1	25.7	48 52.5	-14.4	26.2	49 46.2	-13.7	26.7	50 39.7	-13.0	27.2	51 32.9	-12.2	27.8	52 25.9	-11.5	28.4	70
71	45 53.7	17.2	23.4	46 48.7	16.7	23.8	47 43.5	16.1	24.2	48 38.1	15.5	24.7	49 32.5	14.8	25.2	50 26.7	14.2	25.7	51 20.7	13.5	26.2	52 14.4	12.8	26.8	71
72	45 36.5	18.3	22.0	46 32.0	17.7	22.4	47 27.4	17.1	22.8	48 22.6	16.5	23.2	49 17.7	16.0	23.7	50 12.5	15.4	24.2	51 07.2	14.8	24.7	52 01.6	14.1	25.2	72
73	45 18.2	19.1	20.6	46 14.3	18.7	21.0	47 10.3	18.2	21.4	48 06.1	17.7	21.8	49 01.7	17.1	22.2	49 57.1	16.5	22.7	50 52.4	15.9	23.1	51 47.5	15.3	23.6	73
74	44 59.1	20.2	19.2	45 55.6	19.6	19.6	46 52.1	19.2	20.0	47 48.4	18.7	20.4	48 44.6	18.2	20.8	49 40.6	17.2	21.2	50 36.5	17.2	21.6	51 32.2	16.6	22.1	74
75	44 38.9	-21.0	18.0	45 36.0	-20.7	18.3	46 32.9	-20.2	18.6	47 29.7	-19.8	19.0	48 26.4	-19.3	19.3	49 22.9	-18.8	19.6	50 19.3	-18.2	20.1	51 15.6	-17.7	20.5	75
76	44 17.9	21.9	16.7	45 15.3	21.5	16.9	46 12.7	21.2	17.2	47 09.9	20.7	17.6	48 07.1	20.3	17.9	49 04.1	19.8	18.2	50 01.1	19.4	18.6	50 57.9	19.0	19.0	76
77	43 56.0	22.8	15.4	44 53.8	22.4	15.6	45 51.5	22.0	15.9	46 49.2	21.7	16.2	47 46.8	21.3	16.5	48 44.3	20.9	16.8	49 41.7	20.5	17.2	50 38.9	20.0	17.5	77
78	43 33.2	23.6	14.1	44 31.4	23.4	14.3	45 29.5	23.0	14.6	46 27.5	22.5	14.8	47 25.5	22.3	15.1	48 23.4	22.0	15.4	49 21.2	21.6	15.7	50 18.9	21.2	16.0	78
79	43 09.6	24.5	12.8	44 08.0	24.1	13.0	45 06.5	23.9	13.3	46 04.8	23.6	13.5	47 03.2	23.3	13.7	48 01.4	22.9	14.0	48 59.6	22.6	14.3	49 57.7	22.3	14.6	79
80	42 45.1	-25.3	11.6	43 43.9	-25.1	11.8	44 42.6	-24.8	12.0	45 41.2	-24.4	12.2	46 39.9	-24.0	12.4	47 38.5	-24.0	12.6	48 37.0	-23.7	12.9	49 35.4	-23.3	13.1	80
81	42 19.8	26.0	10.5	43 18.8	25.8	10.5	44 17.8	25.6	10.7	45 16.8	25.4	10.9	46 15.7	25.2	11.1	47 14.5	24.8	11.3	48 13.3	24.6	11.5	49 12.1	24.3	11.7	81
82	41 53.8	26.8	9.1	42 53.0	26.6	9.3	43 52.2	26.4	9.4	44 51.4	26.2	9.6	45 50.5	26.0	9.8	46 49.7	25.8	9.9	47 48.7	25.5	10.1	48 47.8	25.3	10.3	82
83	41 27.0	27.6	7.9	42 26.4	27.4	8.1	43 25.8	27.2	8.2	44 25.2	27.1	8.3	45 24.5	26.8	8.5	46 23.9	26.7	8.6	47 23.2	26.5	8.8	48 22.5	26.3	9.0	83
84	40 59.4	28.2	6.7	41 59.0	28.2	6.8	42 58.6	28.0	7.0	43 58.1	27.7	7.1	44 57.7	27.7	7.3	45 57.2	27.5	7.3	46 56.7	27.4	7.5	47 56.2	27.2	7.6	84
85	40 31.2	-28.9	5.6	41 30.9	-28.8	5.7	42 30.6	-28.7	5.8	43 30.3	-28.6	5.8	44 30.0	-28.5	5.9	45 29.7	-28.4	6.1	46 29.3	-28.2	6.2	47 29.0	-28.1	6.3	85
86	40 02.3	29.7	4.4	41 02.1	29.6	4.5	42 01.9	29.5	4.6	43 01.7	29.4	4.6	44 01.5	29.3	4.7	45 01.3	29.2	4.8	46 01.1	29.1	4.9	47 00.9	29.0	5.0	86
87	39 32.6	30.2	3.3	40 32.5	30.2	3.3	41 32.4	30.1	3.4	42 32.3	30.0	3.4	43 32.2	30.0	3.5	44 32.1	29.9	3.6	45 32.0	29.9	3.6	46 31.9	29.9	3.7	87
88	39 02.4	30.9	2.2	40 02.3	30.8	2.2	41 02.3	30.8	2.2	42 02.3	30.8	2.2	43 02.2	30.7	2.3	44 02.2	30.8	2.4	45 02.1	30.7	2.4	46 02.0	30.8	2.4	88
89	38 31.5	31.5	1.1	39 31.5	31.5	1.1	40 31.5	31.5	1.1	41 31.5	31.5	1.1	42 31.5	31.5	1.2	43 31.4	31.4	1.2	44 31.4	31.4	1.2	45 31.4	31.4	1.2	89
90	38 00.0	-32.1	0.0	39 00.0	-32.1	0.0	40 00.0	-32.1	0.0	41 00.0	-32.1	0.0	42 00.0	-32.1	0.0	43 00.0	-32.1	0.0	44 00.0	-32.2	0.0	45 00.0	-32.2	0.0	90

LATITUDE CONTRARY NAME TO DECLINATION   L.H.A. 60°, 300°

Dec.	38° Hc	d	Z	39° Hc	d	Z	40° Hc	d	Z	41° Hc	d	Z	42° Hc	d	Z	43° Hc	d	Z	44° Hc	d	Z	45° Hc	d	Z	Dec.
0	23 12.2	-40.3	109.6	22 51.9	-41.1	110.0	22 31.3	-41.9	110.4	22 10.2	-42.6	110.7	21 48.8	-43.4	111.1	21 27.0	-44.1	111.5	21 04.8	-44.8	111.9	20 42.3	-45.5	112.2	0
1	22 31.9	40.5	110.4	22 10.8	41.3	110.8	21 49.4	42.1	111.1	21 27.6	42.8	111.5	21 05.4	43.5	111.9	20 42.9	44.2	112.2	20 20.0	44.9	112.6	19 56.8	45.6	112.9	1
2	21 51.4	40.8	111.2	21 29.5	41.5	111.5	21 07.3	42.3	111.9	20 44.8	43.0	112.3	20 21.9	43.7	112.6	19 58.7	44.5	112.9	19 35.1	45.1	113.3	19 11.2	45.7	113.6	2
3	21 10.6	41.0	112.0	20 48.0	41.8	112.3	20 25.0	42.4	112.7	20 01.8	43.2	113.0	19 38.2	43.9	113.3	19 14.2	44.5	113.7	18 50.0	45.2	114.0	18 25.5	45.9	114.3	3
4	20 29.6	41.2	112.7	20 06.2	41.9	113.1	19 42.6	42.7	113.4	19 18.6	43.4	113.7	18 54.3	44.1	114.1	18 29.7	44.8	114.4	18 04.8	45.4	114.7	17 39.6	46.0	115.0	4
5	19 48.4	-41.4	113.5	19 24.3	-42.1	113.8	18 59.9	-42.8	114.2	18 35.2	-43.5	114.5	18 10.2	-44.2	114.8	17 44.9	-44.9	115.1	17 19.4	-45.6	115.3	16 53.6	-46.2	115.6	5
6	19 07.0	41.6	114.3	18 42.2	42.3	114.6	18 17.1	43.0	114.9	17 51.7	43.7	115.2	17 26.0	44.4	115.5	17 00.0	45.0	115.8	16 33.8	45.6	116.0	16 07.4	46.3	116.3	6
7	18 25.4	41.8	115.0	17 59.9	42.5	115.3	17 34.1	43.2	115.6	17 08.0	43.9	115.9	16 41.6	44.5	116.2	16 15.0	45.1	116.4	15 48.2	45.8	116.7	15 21.1	46.4	117.0	7
8	17 43.6	41.9	115.8	17 17.4	42.6	116.1	16 50.9	43.3	116.4	16 24.1	44.0	116.6	15 57.1	44.6	116.9	15 29.9	45.3	117.1	15 02.4	45.9	117.4	14 34.7	46.5	117.6	8
9	17 01.7	42.1	116.5	16 34.8	42.8	116.8	16 07.6	43.5	117.1	15 40.1	44.1	117.3	15 12.5	44.8	117.6	14 44.6	45.4	117.8	14 16.5	46.0	118.0	13 48.2	46.6	118.3	9
10	16 19.6	-42.3	117.3	15 52.0	-43.0	117.5	15 24.1	-43.6	117.8	14 56.0	-44.2	118.0	14 27.7	-44.9	118.3	13 59.2	-45.5	118.5	13 30.5	-46.1	118.7	13 01.6	-46.7	118.9	10
11	15 37.3	42.4	118.0	15 09.0	43.1	118.3	14 40.5	43.9	118.5	14 11.8	44.4	118.7	13 42.8	45.0	119.0	13 13.7	45.6	119.1	12 44.4	46.3	119.4	12 14.9	46.9	119.6	11
12	14 54.9	42.5	118.8	14 25.9	43.2	119.0	13 56.8	43.9	119.2	13 27.4	44.5	119.4	12 57.8	45.1	119.6	12 28.1	45.7	119.8	11 58.1	46.3	120.0	11 28.0	46.8	120.2	12
13	14 12.4	42.7	119.5	13 42.7	43.3	119.7	13 12.9	44.0	119.9	12 42.9	44.6	120.1	12 12.7	45.2	120.3	11 42.4	45.8	120.5	11 11.8	46.4	120.7	10 41.2	47.0	120.8	13
14	13 29.7	42.8	120.2	12 59.4	43.4	120.4	12 28.9	44.0	120.6	11 58.3	44.7	120.8	11 27.5	45.3	121.0	10 56.6	45.9	121.1	10 25.4	46.4	121.3	9 54.2	47.0	121.5	14
15	12 46.9	-42.9	120.9	12 16.0	-43.6	121.1	11 44.9	-44.2	121.3	11 13.6	-44.8	121.5	10 42.2	-45.4	121.6	10 10.7	-46.0	121.8	9 39.0	-46.6	121.9	9 07.2	-47.1	122.1	15
16	12 04.0	43.1	121.6	11 32.4	43.6	121.8	11 00.7	44.3	122.0	10 28.8	44.8	122.2	9 56.8	45.4	122.3	9 24.7	46.0	122.5	8 52.4	46.6	122.6	8 20.1	47.2	122.7	16
17	11 20.9	43.1	122.4	10 48.8	43.8	122.5	10 16.4	44.4	122.7	9 44.0	45.0	122.8	9 11.4	45.6	123.0	8 38.7	46.1	123.1	8 05.8	46.7	123.2	7 32.9	47.2	123.3	17
18	10 37.8	43.2	123.1	10 05.0	43.8	123.2	9 32.1	44.5	123.4	8 59.0	45.0	123.5	8 25.8	45.6	123.6	7 52.6	46.2	123.7	7 19.2	46.7	123.9	6 45.7	47.3	124.0	18
19	9 54.6	43.4	123.8	9 21.2	43.9	123.9	8 47.6	44.5	124.0	8 14.0	45.1	124.2	7 40.2	45.6	124.3	7 06.4	46.2	124.4	6 32.5	46.8	124.5	5 58.4	47.2	124.6	19
20	9 11.3	-43.4	124.5	8 37.3	-44.0	124.6	8 03.1	-44.5	124.7	7 28.9	-45.1	124.8	6 54.6	-45.7	124.9	6 20.2	-46.3	125.0	5 45.7	-46.8	125.1	5 11.2	-47.4	125.2	20
21	8 27.9	43.5	125.2	7 53.3	44.1	125.3	7 18.6	44.7	125.4	6 43.8	45.2	125.5	6 08.9	45.8	125.6	5 33.9	46.3	125.7	4 58.9	46.8	125.8	4 23.8	47.4	125.8	21
22	7 44.4	43.6	125.9	7 09.2	44.1	126.0	6 33.9	44.7	126.1	5 58.6	45.3	126.2	5 23.1	45.8	126.2	4 47.6	46.3	126.3	4 12.1	46.9	126.4	3 36.5	47.4	126.4	22
23	7 00.9	43.6	126.6	6 25.1	44.2	126.7	5 49.2	44.7	126.7	5 13.3	45.3	126.8	4 37.3	45.8	126.9	4 01.3	46.4	127.0	3 25.2	46.9	127.0	2 49.1	47.4	127.0	23
24	6 17.3	43.7	127.3	5 40.9	44.2	127.3	5 04.5	44.8	127.4	4 28.0	45.3	127.5	3 51.5	45.9	127.5	3 14.9	46.4	127.6	2 38.3	46.9	127.6	2 01.7	47.5	127.7	24
25	5 33.6	-43.7	127.9	4 56.7	-44.2	128.0	4 19.7	-44.8	128.1	3 42.7	-45.3	128.1	3 05.6	-45.9	128.2	2 28.5	-46.4	128.2	1 51.4	-46.9	128.3	1 14.2	-47.4	128.3	25
26	4 49.9	43.7	128.6	4 12.5	44.3	128.7	3 34.9	44.8	128.7	2 57.4	45.4	128.8	2 19.7	45.9	128.8	1 42.1	46.4	128.9	1 04.5	47.0	128.9	0 26.8	-47.4	128.9	26
27	4 06.2	43.8	129.3	3 28.2	44.3	129.4	2 50.1	44.9	129.4	2 12.0	45.4	129.4	1 33.8	45.9	129.5	0 55.7	46.4	129.5	0 17.5	-46.9	129.5	0 20.6	+47.5	50.5	27
28	3 22.4	43.8	130.0	2 43.8	44.3	130.0	2 05.2	44.9	130.1	1 26.6	45.4	130.1	0 47.9	45.9	130.1	0 09.3	-46.5	130.1	0 29.4	+46.9	49.9	1 08.1	47.4	49.9	28
29	2 38.6	43.8	130.7	1 59.5	44.4	130.7	1 20.3	44.8	130.7	0 41.2	-45.4	130.8	0 02.0	-45.9	130.8	0 37.2	+46.4	49.2	1 16.3	47.0	49.3	1 55.5	47.4	49.3	29
30	1 54.8	-43.8	131.4	1 15.1	-44.3	131.4	0 35.5	-44.9	131.4	0 04.2	+45.4	48.6	0 43.9	+45.9	48.6	1 23.6	+46.4	48.6	2 03.3	+46.9	48.6	2 42.9	+47.4	48.7	30
31	1 11.0	43.9	132.1	0 30.8	-44.4	132.1	0 09.4	+44.9	47.9	0 49.6	45.4	47.9	1 29.8	45.9	48.0	2 10.0	46.4	48.0	2 50.2	46.9	48.0	3 30.3	47.3	48.0	31
32	0 27.1	-43.9	132.7	0 13.6	+44.4	47.3	0 54.3	44.9	47.3	1 35.0	45.4	47.3	2 15.7	45.9	47.3	2 56.4	46.4	47.3	3 37.1	46.8	47.4	4 17.7	47.3	47.4	32
33	0 16.8	+43.8	46.6	0 58.0	44.4	46.6	1 39.2	44.9	46.6	2 20.4	45.4	46.6	3 01.6	45.9	46.7	3 42.8	46.3	46.7	4 23.9	46.8	46.8	5 05.0	47.3	46.8	33
34	1 00.6	43.8	45.9	1 42.4	44.3	45.9	2 24.1	44.8	45.9	3 05.8	45.4	46.0	3 47.5	45.8	46.0	4 29.1	46.4	46.1	5 10.7	46.8	46.1	5 52.3	47.3	46.2	34
35	1 44.4	+43.9	45.2	2 26.7	+44.3	45.2	3 08.9	+44.9	45.3	3 51.2	+45.3	45.3	4 33.3	+45.8	45.4	5 15.5	+46.2	45.4	5 57.5	+46.8	45.5	6 39.6	+47.2	45.6	35
36	2 28.3	43.8	44.5	3 11.0	44.3	44.6	3 53.8	44.8	44.6	4 36.5	45.3	44.7	5 19.1	45.8	44.7	6 01.7	46.3	44.8	6 44.3	46.7	44.9	7 26.8	47.1	45.0	36
37	3 12.1	43.8	43.8	3 55.3	44.3	43.9	4 38.6	44.7	43.9	5 21.8	45.2	44.0	6 04.9	45.7	44.1	6 48.0	46.1	44.1	7 31.0	46.6	44.2	8 13.9	47.1	44.3	37
38	3 55.9	43.7	43.2	4 39.6	44.2	43.2	5 23.3	44.7	43.3	6 07.0	45.2	43.3	6 50.6	45.7	43.4	7 34.1	46.2	43.5	8 17.6	46.6	43.6	9 01.0	47.1	43.7	38
39	4 39.6	43.7	42.5	5 23.9	44.1	42.5	6 08.0	44.7	42.6	6 52.2	45.1	42.7	7 36.3	45.6	42.8	8 20.3	46.0	42.9	9 04.2	46.5	42.9	9 48.1	47.0	43.1	39
40	5 23.3	+43.7	41.8	6 08.0	+44.1	41.9	6 52.7	+44.6	42.0	7 37.3	+45.1	42.0	8 21.9	+45.5	42.1	9 06.3	+46.0	42.2	9 50.7	+46.5	42.3	10 35.1	+46.9	42.4	40
41	6 07.0	43.6	41.1	6 52.2	44.1	41.2	7 37.3	44.6	41.3	8 22.4	45.0	41.3	9 07.4	45.5	41.5	9 52.3	46.0	41.6	10 37.2	46.4	41.7	11 22.0	46.8	41.8	41
42	6 50.6	43.5	40.4	7 36.3	44.0	40.5	8 21.9	44.4	40.6	9 07.4	44.9	40.7	9 52.9	45.4	40.8	10 38.3	45.8	40.9	11 23.6	46.2	41.0	12 08.8	46.7	41.2	42
43	7 34.1	43.5	39.7	8 20.3	43.9	39.8	9 06.3	44.4	39.9	9 52.3	44.9	40.0	10 38.3	45.3	40.1	11 24.1	45.7	40.2	12 09.8	46.2	40.4	12 55.5	46.6	40.5	43
44	8 17.6	43.4	39.0	9 04.2	43.9	39.1	9 50.7	44.4	39.2	10 37.2	44.8	39.3	11 23.6	45.2	39.5	12 09.8	45.7	39.6	12 56.0	46.1	39.7	13 42.1	46.6	39.9	44

Dec.	38° Hc d Z	39° Hc d Z	40° Hc d Z	41° Hc d Z	42° Hc d Z	43° Hc d Z	44° Hc d Z	45° Hc d Z	Dec.
45	43 29.8 +14.6 60.3	43 59.1 +15.9 61.1	44 27.7 +17.1 62.0	44 55.5 +18.3 62.9	45 22.5 +19.5 63.8	45 48.6 +20.8 64.7	46 13.8 +22.1 65.6	46 38.1 +23.4 66.6	45
46	43 44.4 13.7 58.9	44 15.0 14.8 59.8	44 44.8 16.1 60.6	45 13.8 17.4 61.5	45 42.0 18.6 62.4	46 09.4 19.9 63.3	46 35.9 21.1 64.3	47 01.5 22.4 65.2	46
47	43 58.1 12.7 57.6	44 29.8 14.0 58.4	45 00.9 15.1 59.3	45 31.2 16.3 60.1	46 00.6 17.6 61.0	46 29.3 18.8 62.0	46 57.0 20.2 62.9	47 23.9 21.5 63.9	47
48	44 10.8 11.7 56.2	44 43.8 12.9 57.1	45 16.0 14.1 57.9	45 47.5 15.4 58.8	46 18.2 16.6 59.7	46 48.1 17.9 60.6	47 17.2 19.1 61.5	47 45.4 20.4 62.5	48
49	44 22.5 10.7 54.9	44 56.7 11.9 55.7	45 30.1 13.2 56.5	46 02.9 14.3 57.4	46 34.8 15.6 58.3	47 06.0 16.8 59.2	47 36.3 18.1 60.1	48 05.8 19.4 61.1	49
50	44 33.2 9.8 53.5	45 08.6 +10.9 54.3	45 43.3 +12.1 55.1	46 17.2 +13.3 56.0	46 50.4 +14.5 56.9	47 22.8 +15.8 57.8	47 54.4 +17.1 58.7	48 25.2 +18.3 59.7	50
51	44 43.0 8.7 52.1	45 19.5 9.9 52.9	45 54.4 11.0 53.7	46 30.5 12.3 54.6	47 04.9 13.5 55.4	47 38.6 14.7 56.3	48 11.5 15.9 57.3	48 43.5 17.2 58.2	51
52	44 51.7 7.7 50.7	45 29.4 8.8 51.5	46 06.4 10.0 52.3	46 42.8 11.2 53.1	47 18.4 12.4 54.0	47 53.3 13.6 54.9	48 27.4 14.9 55.8	49 00.7 16.1 56.8	52
53	44 59.4 6.7 49.3	45 38.2 7.8 50.1	46 16.4 9.0 50.9	46 54.0 10.0 51.7	47 30.8 11.3 52.6	48 06.9 12.5 53.4	48 42.3 13.7 54.3	49 16.8 15.0 55.3	53
54	45 06.1 5.6 47.9	45 46.0 6.8 48.7	46 25.4 7.8 49.4	47 04.0 9.0 50.3	47 42.1 10.1 51.1	48 19.4 11.4 52.0	48 56.0 12.6 52.9	49 31.8 13.9 53.8	54
55	45 11.7 +4.6 46.5	45 52.8 +5.6 47.2	46 33.2 +6.8 48.0	47 13.0 +7.9 48.8	47 52.2 +9.1 49.6	48 30.8 +10.2 50.5	49 08.6 +11.4 51.4	49 45.7 +12.6 52.3	55
56	45 16.3 3.6 45.1	45 58.4 4.6 45.8	46 40.0 5.6 46.6	47 20.9 6.8 47.3	48 01.3 7.9 48.2	48 41.0 9.0 49.0	49 20.0 10.3 49.9	49 58.3 11.5 50.8	56
57	45 19.9 2.4 43.7	46 03.0 3.5 44.4	46 45.6 4.6 45.1	47 27.7 5.7 45.9	48 09.2 6.7 46.7	48 50.0 7.9 47.5	49 30.3 9.0 48.4	50 09.8 10.2 49.2	57
58	45 22.3 1.5 42.2	46 06.5 2.5 42.9	46 50.2 3.5 43.6	47 33.4 4.5 44.4	48 15.9 5.6 45.2	48 57.9 6.7 46.0	49 39.3 7.8 46.8	50 20.0 9.0 47.7	58
59	45 23.8 +0.3 40.8	46 09.0 +1.3 41.5	46 53.7 +2.3 42.2	47 37.9 +3.3 42.9	48 21.5 +4.4 43.7	49 04.6 +5.5 44.5	49 47.1 +6.7 45.3	50 29.0 +7.8 46.2	59
60	45 24.1 −0.7 39.4	46 10.3 +0.2 40.0	46 56.0 +1.2 40.7	47 41.2 +2.2 41.4	48 25.9 +3.3 42.2	49 10.1 +4.3 43.0	49 53.8 +5.4 43.8	50 36.8 +6.5 44.6	60
61	45 23.4 1.7 38.0	46 10.5 0.8 38.6	46 57.2 +0.1 39.3	47 43.4 +1.1 40.0	48 29.2 +2.1 40.7	49 14.4 +3.1 41.4	49 59.2 +4.1 42.3	50 43.3 +5.3 43.0	61
62	45 21.7 2.9 36.5	46 09.7 1.9 37.2	46 57.3 −1.0 37.8	47 44.5 −0.1 38.5	48 31.3 +0.8 39.2	49 17.5 +1.9 39.9	50 03.3 +2.9 40.7	50 48.6 +3.9 41.5	62
63	45 18.8 3.8 35.1	46 07.8 3.1 35.7	46 56.3 2.2 36.3	47 44.4 1.2 36.9	48 32.1 0.3 37.7	49 19.4 +0.7 38.4	50 06.2 +1.7 39.1	50 52.5 +2.7 39.9	63
64	45 15.0 5.0 33.7	46 04.7 4.1 34.3	46 54.1 3.2 34.9	47 43.2 2.3 35.5	48 31.8 1.5 36.1	49 20.1 −0.4 36.8	50 07.9 +0.4 37.5	50 55.2 +1.4 38.3	64
65	45 10.0 −5.9 32.3	46 00.6 −5.2 32.8	46 50.9 −4.4 33.4	47 40.8 −3.6 34.0	48 30.3 −2.6 34.6	49 19.5 −1.8 35.3	50 08.3 −0.9 36.0	50 56.6 −0.1 36.7	65
66	45 04.1 7.0 30.9	45 55.4 6.2 31.4	46 46.5 5.5 31.9	47 37.2 4.7 32.5	48 27.7 3.9 33.1	49 17.7 3.0 33.8	50 07.4 2.1 34.4	50 56.7 1.1 35.1	66
67	44 57.1 8.1 29.5	45 49.2 7.3 30.0	46 41.0 6.6 30.5	47 32.6 5.8 31.0	48 23.8 5.0 31.6	49 14.7 4.2 32.2	50 05.3 3.2 32.9	50 55.6 2.4 33.5	67
68	44 49.0 9.0 28.1	45 41.9 8.4 28.5	46 34.4 7.6 29.0	47 26.8 7.0 29.6	48 18.8 6.2 30.1	49 10.5 5.4 30.7	50 02.0 4.6 31.3	50 53.1 3.8 31.9	68
69	44 40.0 10.1 26.7	45 33.5 9.4 27.1	46 26.8 8.8 27.6	47 19.8 8.0 28.1	48 12.6 7.3 28.6	49 05.1 6.6 29.2	49 57.4 5.9 29.8	50 49.3 5.0 30.4	69
70	44 29.9 −11.1 25.3	45 24.1 −10.5 25.7	46 18.0 −9.8 26.2	47 11.8 −9.2 26.6	48 05.3 −8.5 27.1	48 58.5 −7.8 27.7	49 51.5 −7.0 28.2	50 44.3 −6.3 28.8	70
71	44 18.8 11.9 23.9	45 13.6 11.5 24.3	46 08.2 10.9 24.7	47 02.6 10.3 25.2	47 56.8 9.7 25.7	48 50.7 8.9 26.2	49 44.5 8.3 26.7	50 38.0 7.6 27.2	71
72	44 06.8 13.0 22.6	45 02.1 12.4 22.9	45 57.3 11.9 23.3	46 52.3 11.3 23.8	47 47.1 10.7 24.2	48 41.8 10.1 24.7	49 36.2 9.5 25.1	50 30.4 8.8 25.7	72
73	43 53.8 14.0 21.2	44 49.7 13.5 21.5	45 45.7 13.0 21.9	46 41.0 12.4 22.3	47 36.4 11.9 22.7	48 31.7 11.3 23.1	49 26.7 10.7 23.6	50 21.6 10.1 24.1	73
74	43 39.8 14.9 19.8	44 36.2 14.5 20.2	45 32.4 13.9 20.5	46 28.6 13.5 20.9	47 24.5 12.9 21.3	48 20.4 12.4 21.7	49 16.0 11.8 22.1	50 11.5 11.2 22.6	74
75	43 24.9 −15.9 18.5	44 21.7 −15.4 18.8	45 18.5 −15.0 19.1	46 15.1 −14.5 19.5	47 11.6 −14.0 19.8	48 08.0 −13.5 20.2	49 04.2 −13.0 20.6	50 00.3 −12.5 21.0	75
76	43 09.0 16.7 17.2	44 06.3 16.3 17.5	45 03.5 15.9 17.8	46 00.6 15.5 18.1	46 57.6 15.1 18.4	47 54.5 14.7 18.8	48 51.2 14.1 19.1	49 47.8 13.6 19.5	76
77	42 52.3 17.6 15.9	43 50.0 17.3 16.1	44 47.6 16.9 16.4	45 45.1 16.5 16.7	46 42.5 16.1 17.0	47 39.8 15.6 17.3	48 37.1 15.3 17.6	49 34.2 14.8 17.9	77
78	42 34.7 18.6 14.6	43 32.7 18.2 14.8	44 30.7 17.9 15.1	45 28.6 17.5 15.3	46 26.4 17.1 15.6	47 24.2 16.8 15.9	48 21.8 16.3 16.2	49 19.4 15.9 16.5	78
79	42 16.1 19.3 13.3	43 14.5 19.1 13.5	44 12.8 18.7 13.7	45 11.1 18.5 14.0	46 09.3 18.1 14.2	47 07.4 17.8 14.5	48 05.5 17.5 14.7	49 03.5 17.1 15.0	79
80	41 56.8 −20.2 12.0	42 55.4 −19.9 12.2	43 54.1 −19.7 12.4	44 52.6 −19.4 12.6	45 51.2 −19.1 12.8	46 49.6 −18.8 13.1	47 48.0 −18.4 13.3	48 46.4 −18.1 13.6	80
81	41 36.6 21.1 10.7	42 35.5 20.8 10.9	43 34.4 20.6 11.1	44 33.2 20.3 11.3	45 32.1 20.1 11.5	46 30.8 19.7 11.7	47 29.6 19.5 11.9	48 28.3 19.3 12.1	81
82	41 15.5 21.8 9.5	42 14.7 21.6 9.6	43 13.8 21.6 9.8	44 12.9 21.2 9.8	45 12.0 21.0 10.1	46 11.1 20.8 10.3	47 10.1 20.5 10.5	48 09.0 20.2 10.7	82
83	40 53.7 22.6 8.3	41 53.1 22.3 8.4	42 52.4 22.3 8.5	43 51.7 22.1 8.7	44 51.0 21.9 8.8	45 50.3 21.7 9.1	46 49.6 21.5 9.3	47 48.8 21.3 9.3	83
84	40 31.1 23.4 7.0	41 30.6 23.2 7.1	42 30.1 23.1 7.3	43 29.6 22.9 7.4	44 29.1 22.7 7.5	45 28.6 22.6 7.6	46 28.1 22.5 7.8	47 27.5 22.2 7.9	84
85	40 07.7 −24.1 5.8	41 07.4 −24.0 5.9	42 07.0 −23.8 6.0	43 06.7 −23.8 6.1	44 06.4 −23.7 6.1	45 06.0 −23.5 6.3	46 05.6 −23.3 6.4	47 05.3 −23.3 6.5	85
86	39 43.6 24.9 4.6	40 43.4 24.8 4.7	41 43.2 24.7 4.8	42 42.9 24.7 4.9	43 42.7 24.5 4.9	44 42.5 24.4 5.1	45 42.3 24.4 5.1	46 17.9 24.1 5.2	86
87	39 18.7 25.5 3.5	40 18.6 25.5 3.5	41 18.5 25.4 3.6	42 18.4 25.4 3.7	43 18.2 25.2 3.7	44 18.1 25.2 3.7	45 18.0 25.2 3.8	45 52.8 25.1 3.9	87
88	38 53.2 26.3 2.3	39 53.1 26.2 2.3	40 53.1 26.2 2.4	41 53.0 26.1 2.4	42 53.0 26.1 2.4	43 52.9 26.1 2.5	44 52.8 26.0 2.5	45 26.8 26.0 2.6	88
89	38 26.9 26.9 1.1	39 26.9 26.9 1.2	40 26.9 26.9 1.2	41 26.9 26.9 1.2	42 26.9 26.9 1.2	43 26.8 26.8 1.2	44 26.8 26.8 1.2	45 26.8 26.8 1.3	89
90	38 00.0 −27.6 0.0	39 00.0 −27.6 0.0	40 00.0 −27.6 0.0	41 00.0 −27.6 0.0	42 00.0 −27.6 0.0	43 00.0 −27.6 0.0	44 00.0 −27.6 0.0	45 00.0 −27.7 0.0	90

63°, 297° L.H.A.　　　　　LATITUDE SAME NAME AS DECLINATION

L.H.A.	38°	39°	40°	41°	42°	43°	44°	45°	
45	42 48.8 +15.1 60.0	43 18.4 +16.3 60.9	43 47.2 +17.6 61.7	44 15.3 +18.8 62.5	44 42.5 +20.1 63.4	45 09.0 +21.2 64.3	45 34.5 +22.6 65.2	45 59.2 +23.8 66.2	45
46	43 03.9 14.3 58.7	43 34.7 15.5 59.5	44 04.8 16.6 60.4	44 34.1 17.8 61.2	45 02.6 19.1 62.1	45 30.2 20.4 63.0	45 57.1 21.6 63.9	46 23.9 22.9 64.8	46
47	43 18.2 13.3 57.4	43 50.2 14.5 58.2	44 21.4 15.7 59.0	44 51.9 16.9 59.9	45 21.7 18.1 60.7	45 50.6 19.4 61.6	46 18.7 20.6 62.6	46 45.9 21.9 63.5	47
48	43 31.5 12.4 56.0	44 04.7 13.5 56.8	44 37.1 14.8 57.7	45 08.8 16.0 58.5	45 39.8 17.2 59.4	46 10.0 18.4 60.3	46 39.3 19.7 61.2	47 07.8 20.9 62.1	48
49	43 43.9 11.4 54.7	44 18.2 12.6 55.5	44 51.9 13.7 56.3	45 24.8 14.9 57.1	45 57.0 16.1 58.0	46 28.4 17.4 58.9	46 59.0 18.6 59.8	47 28.7 19.9 60.7	49
50	43 55.3 +10.4 53.3	44 30.8 +11.6 54.1	45 05.6 +12.8 54.9	45 39.7 +14.0 55.8	46 13.1 +15.2 56.6	46 45.8 +16.2 57.5	47 17.6 +17.6 58.4	47 48.6 +18.9 59.3	50
51	44 05.7 9.5 52.0	44 42.4 10.5 52.7	45 18.4 11.7 53.5	45 53.7 12.9 54.4	46 28.3 14.1 55.2	47 02.1 15.3 56.1	47 35.2 16.6 57.0	48 07.5 17.8 57.9	51
52	44 15.2 8.4 50.6	44 52.9 9.6 51.3	45 30.1 10.7 52.1	46 06.6 11.9 53.0	46 42.4 13.0 53.8	47 17.4 14.3 54.7	47 51.8 15.4 55.6	48 25.3 16.7 56.5	52
53	44 23.6 7.4 49.2	45 02.5 8.6 50.0	45 40.8 9.7 50.7	46 18.5 10.8 51.5	46 55.4 12.0 52.4	47 31.7 13.2 53.2	48 07.2 14.4 54.1	48 42.0 15.6 55.0	53
54	44 31.0 6.5 47.8	45 11.1 7.5 48.6	45 50.5 8.6 49.3	46 29.3 9.7 50.1	47 07.4 10.9 50.9	47 44.9 12.1 51.8	48 21.6 13.3 52.7	48 57.6 14.5 53.6	54
55	44 37.5 +5.4 46.4	45 18.6 +6.4 47.1	45 59.1 +7.5 47.9	46 39.0 +8.7 48.7	47 18.3 +9.8 49.5	47 57.0 +10.9 50.3	48 34.9 +12.1 51.2	49 12.1 +13.4 52.1	55
56	44 42.9 4.3 45.0	45 25.0 5.4 45.7	46 06.6 6.5 46.5	46 47.7 7.5 47.2	47 28.1 8.7 48.0	48 07.9 9.8 48.9	48 47.0 11.0 49.7	49 25.5 12.2 50.6	56
57	44 47.2 3.4 43.6	45 30.4 4.4 44.3	46 13.1 5.4 45.0	46 55.2 6.5 45.8	47 36.8 7.5 46.6	48 17.7 8.7 47.4	48 58.0 9.9 48.2	49 37.7 11.0 49.1	57
58	44 50.6 2.3 42.2	45 34.8 3.3 42.9	46 18.5 4.3 43.6	47 01.7 5.3 44.3	47 44.3 6.5 45.1	48 26.4 7.5 45.9	49 07.9 8.6 46.7	49 48.7 9.8 47.6	58
59	44 52.9 1.2 40.8	45 38.1 2.2 41.5	46 22.8 3.2 42.1	47 07.0 4.3 42.9	47 50.8 5.3 43.6	48 33.9 6.4 44.4	49 16.5 7.4 45.2	49 58.5 8.5 46.0	59
60	44 54.1 +0.2 39.4	45 40.3 +1.1 40.0	46 26.0 +2.1 40.7	47 11.3 +3.1 41.4	47 56.1 +4.1 42.1	48 40.3 +5.1 42.9	49 23.9 +6.3 43.7	50 07.0 +7.4 44.5	60
61	44 54.3 -0.8 38.0	45 41.4 0.1 38.6	46 28.1 1.0 39.2	47 14.4 1.9 39.9	48 00.1 3.0 40.6	48 45.4 4.0 41.4	49 30.2 5.0 42.1	50 14.4 6.1 42.9	61
62	44 53.5 1.9 36.6	45 41.5 -1.0 37.2	46 29.1 -0.1 38.5	47 16.3 0.9 38.5	48 03.1 1.8 39.1	48 49.4 2.8 39.9	49 35.2 3.8 40.6	50 20.5 4.8 41.4	62
63	44 51.6 2.9 35.1	45 40.5 2.0 35.7	46 29.0 1.1 37.8	47 17.2 -0.3 37.0	48 04.9 +0.6 37.6	48 52.2 1.6 38.3	49 39.0 2.6 39.1	50 25.3 3.6 39.8	63
64	44 48.7 3.9 33.7	45 38.5 3.2 34.3	46 27.9 2.3 36.3	47 16.9 1.4 35.5	48 05.5 -0.5 36.1	48 53.8 0.4 36.8	49 41.6 1.3 37.5	50 28.9 2.4 38.3	64
65	44 44.8 -5.0 32.3	45 35.3 -4.2 32.9	46 25.6 -3.4 33.4	47 15.5 -2.6 34.0	48 05.0 -1.7 34.7	48 54.2 -0.9 35.3	49 42.9 -0.1 36.0	50 31.3 +1.0 36.7	65
66	44 39.8 6.0 30.9	45 31.1 5.2 31.4	46 22.2 4.5 31.9	47 12.9 3.7 32.6	48 03.3 2.9 33.2	48 53.3 2.0 33.8	49 43.0 1.1 34.4	50 32.3 0.2 35.1	66
67	44 33.8 7.0 29.5	45 25.9 6.4 30.0	46 17.7 5.6 30.5	47 09.2 4.8 31.1	48 00.4 4.0 31.7	48 51.3 3.2 32.3	49 41.9 2.4 32.9	50 32.1 1.5 33.5	67
68	44 26.8 8.1 28.1	45 19.5 7.3 28.6	46 12.1 6.7 29.1	47 04.4 5.9 29.6	47 56.4 5.2 30.2	48 48.1 4.3 30.7	49 39.5 3.6 31.3	50 30.6 2.8 32.0	68
69	44 18.7 9.0 26.8	45 12.2 8.4 27.2	46 05.4 7.7 27.7	46 58.5 7.1 28.2	47 51.2 6.3 28.7	48 43.7 5.6 29.2	49 35.9 4.8 29.8	50 27.8 4.0 30.4	69
70	44 09.7 -10.1 25.4	45 03.8 -9.4 25.8	45 57.7 -8.8 26.2	46 51.4 -8.1 26.7	47 44.9 -7.5 27.2	48 38.1 -6.7 27.7	49 31.1 -6.0 28.3	50 23.8 -5.3 28.8	70
71	43 59.6 11.0 24.0	44 54.4 10.5 24.4	45 48.9 9.8 24.8	46 43.3 9.2 25.3	47 37.4 8.6 25.7	48 31.3 7.8 26.2	49 25.1 7.3 26.7	50 18.5 6.5 27.3	71
72	43 48.6 11.9 22.6	44 43.9 11.4 23.0	45 39.1 10.9 23.4	46 34.1 10.4 23.8	47 28.8 9.7 24.2	48 23.3 9.0 24.7	49 17.8 8.4 25.2	50 12.0 7.8 25.7	72
73	43 36.7 13.0 21.3	44 32.5 12.4 21.6	45 28.2 11.9 22.0	46 23.7 11.3 22.4	47 19.1 10.8 22.8	48 14.3 10.2 23.2	49 09.4 9.6 23.7	50 04.2 9.0 24.2	73
74	43 23.7 13.9 19.9	44 20.1 13.4 20.3	45 16.3 12.9 20.6	46 12.4 12.4 21.0	47 08.3 11.9 21.4	48 04.1 11.3 21.8	48 59.8 10.8 22.2	49 55.2 10.2 22.6	74
75	43 09.8 -14.8 18.6	44 06.7 -14.4 18.9	45 03.4 -13.9 19.2	46 00.0 -13.5 19.6	46 56.4 -12.9 19.9	47 52.8 -12.5 20.3	48 49.0 -12.0 20.7	49 45.0 -11.4 21.1	75
76	42 55.0 15.7 17.3	43 52.3 15.3 17.6	44 49.5 14.9 17.9	45 46.5 14.5 18.1	46 43.5 14.1 18.5	47 40.3 13.5 18.8	48 37.0 13.0 19.2	49 33.6 12.5 19.6	76
77	42 39.3 16.6 16.0	43 37.0 16.3 16.2	44 34.6 15.9 16.5	45 32.0 15.4 16.8	46 29.4 15.0 17.1	47 26.8 14.7 17.4	48 24.0 14.2 17.7	49 21.1 13.8 18.1	77
78	42 22.7 17.5 14.7	43 20.7 17.1 14.9	44 18.7 16.8 15.1	45 16.6 16.5 15.4	46 14.4 16.1 15.7	47 12.1 15.7 15.9	48 09.8 15.3 16.3	49 07.3 14.9 16.6	78
79	42 05.2 18.3 13.4	43 03.6 18.1 13.6	44 01.9 17.7 13.8	45 00.1 17.4 14.0	45 58.3 17.1 14.3	46 56.4 16.7 14.5	47 54.5 16.4 14.8	48 52.4 16.0 15.1	79
80	41 46.9 -19.2 12.1	42 45.5 -18.9 12.3	43 44.2 -18.7 12.5	44 42.7 -18.3 12.7	45 41.2 -18.0 12.9	46 39.7 -17.8 13.1	47 38.1 -17.5 13.4	48 36.4 -17.1 13.7	80
81	41 27.7 20.0 10.8	42 26.6 19.8 11.0	43 25.5 19.5 11.2	44 24.4 19.3 11.4	45 23.2 19.1 11.5	46 21.9 18.7 11.8	47 20.6 18.4 12.0	48 19.3 18.2 12.2	81
82	41 07.7 20.8 9.6	42 06.8 20.4 9.7	43 06.0 20.4 9.9	44 05.1 20.2 10.0	45 04.1 19.9 10.2	46 03.2 19.8 10.4	47 02.2 19.5 10.6	48 01.1 19.2 10.8	82
83	40 46.9 21.6 8.3	41 46.2 21.4 8.4	42 45.6 21.3 8.6	43 44.9 21.1 8.7	44 44.2 20.9 8.9	45 43.4 20.6 9.0	46 42.7 20.5 9.2	47 41.9 20.2 9.4	83
84	40 25.3 22.4 7.1	41 24.8 22.3 7.2	42 24.3 22.1 7.3	43 23.8 21.9 7.4	44 23.3 21.8 7.6	45 22.8 21.6 7.7	46 22.2 21.4 7.8	47 21.7 21.3 8.0	84
85	40 02.9 -23.2 5.9	41 02.5 -23.0 6.0	42 02.2 -22.9 6.1	43 01.9 -22.8 6.2	44 01.5 -22.6 6.3	45 01.2 -22.6 6.4	46 00.8 -22.4 6.5	47 00.4 -22.2 6.6	85
86	39 39.7 23.9 4.7	40 39.5 23.8 4.7	41 39.3 23.7 4.8	42 39.1 23.6 4.9	43 38.9 23.4 5.0	44 38.6 23.3 5.0	45 38.4 23.3 5.1	46 38.2 23.2 5.2	86
87	39 15.8 24.5 3.5	40 15.7 24.5 3.5	41 15.6 24.4 3.6	42 15.5 24.4 3.6	43 15.4 24.3 3.7	44 15.3 24.3 3.8	45 15.1 24.2 3.8	46 15.0 24.1 3.9	87
88	38 51.3 25.3 2.3	39 51.2 25.2 2.3	40 51.2 25.3 2.3	41 51.1 25.2 2.4	42 51.1 25.2 2.5	43 51.0 25.1 2.5	44 50.9 25.0 2.5	45 50.9 25.0 2.6	88
89	38 26.0 26.0 1.1	39 26.0 26.0 1.2	40 25.9 25.9 1.2	41 25.9 25.9 1.2	42 25.9 25.9 1.2	43 25.9 25.9 1.2	44 25.9 25.9 1.3	45 25.9 25.9 1.3	89
90	38 00.0 -26.6 0.0	39 00.0 -26.6 0.0	40 00.0 -26.7 0.0	41 00.0 -26.7 0.0	42 00.0 -26.7 0.0	43 00.0 -26.7 0.0	44 00.0 -26.7 0.0	45 00.0 -26.7 0.0	90

64°, 296° L.H.A.

LATITUDE SAME NAME AS DECLINATION

65°, 295° L.H.A. LATITUDE SAME NAME AS DECLINATION

Dec.	38° Hc	d	Z	39° Hc	d	Z	40° Hc	d	Z	41° Hc	d	Z	42° Hc	d	Z	43° Hc	d	Z	44° Hc	d	Z	45° Hc	d	Z	Dec.
0	19 27.2	+39.0	106.0	19 10.4	+39.9	106.4	18 53.4	+40.6	106.7	18 36.0	+41.4	107.0	18 18.3	+42.2	107.3	18 00.2	+43.0	107.6	17 41.9	+43.7	107.9	17 23.3	+44.3	108.2	0
1	20 06.2	38.9	105.7	19 50.3	39.7	105.6	19 34.0	40.5	105.9	19 17.4	41.3	106.2	19 00.5	42.0	106.6	18 43.2	42.8	106.9	18 25.6	43.5	107.2	18 07.6	44.3	107.5	1
2	20 45.1	38.6	104.4	20 30.0	39.4	104.8	20 14.5	40.2	105.1	19 58.7	41.0	105.5	19 42.5	41.8	105.8	19 26.0	42.5	106.2	19 09.1	43.3	106.5	18 51.9	44.0	106.8	2
3	21 23.7	38.4	103.6	21 09.4	39.2	104.0	20 54.7	40.1	104.3	20 39.7	40.8	104.7	20 24.3	41.6	105.1	20 08.5	42.4	105.4	19 52.4	43.2	105.8	19 35.9	43.9	106.1	3
4	22 02.1	38.1	102.8	21 48.6	39.0	103.1	21 34.8	39.8	103.5	21 20.5	40.7	103.9	21 05.9	41.4	104.3	20 50.9	42.2	104.7	20 35.6	42.9	105.0	20 19.8	43.7	105.4	4
5	22 40.2	+37.8	101.9	22 27.6	+38.7	102.3	22 14.6	+39.5	102.7	22 01.2	+40.3	103.1	21 47.3	+41.2	103.5	21 33.1	+42.0	103.9	21 18.5	+42.8	104.3	21 03.5	+43.6	104.7	5
6	23 18.0	37.6	101.1	23 06.3	38.5	101.5	22 54.1	39.1	101.9	22 41.5	40.2	102.3	22 28.5	41.0	102.7	22 15.1	41.8	103.1	22 01.3	42.5	103.5	21 47.1	43.3	103.9	6
7	23 55.6	37.3	100.2	23 44.8	38.1	100.7	23 33.2	39.1	101.1	23 21.7	39.9	101.5	23 09.5	40.7	101.9	22 56.9	41.5	102.3	22 43.8	42.4	102.8	22 30.4	43.1	103.2	7
8	24 32.9	37.0	99.4	24 22.9	37.9	99.8	24 12.5	38.8	100.3	24 01.6	39.6	100.7	23 50.2	40.5	101.1	23 38.4	41.3	101.6	23 26.2	42.1	102.0	23 13.5	42.9	102.4	8
9	25 09.9	36.7	98.5	25 00.8	37.6	99.0	24 51.3	38.4	99.4	24 41.2	39.4	99.9	24 30.7	40.2	100.3	24 19.7	41.0	100.8	24 08.3	41.8	101.2	23 56.4	42.6	101.6	9
10	25 46.6	+36.4	97.6	25 38.4	+37.3	98.1	25 29.7	+38.2	98.6	25 20.6	+39.0	99.0	25 10.9	+39.9	99.5	25 00.7	+40.8	100.0	24 50.1	+41.6	100.4	24 39.0	+42.5	100.9	10
11	26 23.0	36.1	96.7	26 15.7	37.0	97.2	26 07.9	37.9	97.7	25 59.6	38.8	98.2	25 50.8	39.7	98.7	25 41.5	40.5	99.2	25 31.7	41.4	99.6	25 21.5	42.1	100.1	11
12	26 59.1	35.7	95.8	26 52.7	36.7	96.3	26 45.8	37.6	96.8	26 38.4	38.5	97.3	26 30.5	39.3	97.8	26 22.0	40.3	98.3	26 13.1	41.1	98.8	26 03.6	42.0	99.3	12
13	27 34.8	35.4	94.9	27 29.4	36.3	95.5	27 23.4	37.2	96.0	27 16.9	38.1	96.5	27 09.8	39.1	97.0	27 02.3	39.9	97.5	26 54.2	40.8	98.0	26 45.6	41.6	98.5	13
14	28 10.2	34.9	94.0	28 05.7	35.9	94.6	28 00.6	36.9	95.1	27 55.0	37.8	95.6	27 48.9	38.7	96.1	27 42.2	39.6	96.7	27 35.0	40.5	97.2	27 27.2	41.4	97.7	14
15	28 45.1	+34.6	93.1	28 41.6	+35.6	93.6	28 37.5	+36.5	94.2	28 32.8	+37.5	94.7	28 27.6	+38.4	95.3	28 21.8	+39.3	95.8	28 15.5	+40.2	96.3	28 08.6	+41.0	96.9	15
16	29 19.7	34.3	92.2	29 17.2	35.2	92.7	29 14.0	36.2	93.3	29 10.3	37.1	93.8	29 06.0	38.1	94.4	29 01.1	39.0	95.0	28 55.7	39.8	95.5	28 49.6	40.8	96.1	16
17	29 54.0	33.8	91.2	29 52.4	34.8	91.8	29 50.2	35.8	92.3	29 47.4	36.8	92.9	29 44.1	37.6	93.5	29 40.1	38.6	94.1	29 35.5	39.6	94.6	29 30.4	40.4	95.2	17
18	30 27.8	33.3	90.3	30 27.2	34.4	90.9	30 26.0	35.4	91.4	30 24.2	36.3	92.0	30 21.7	37.4	92.6	30 18.7	38.3	93.2	30 15.1	39.1	93.8	30 10.8	40.1	94.4	18
19	31 01.1	33.0	89.3	31 01.6	33.9	89.9	31 01.4	34.9	90.5	31 00.5	36.0	91.1	30 59.1	36.9	91.7	30 57.0	37.8	92.3	30 54.2	38.9	92.9	30 50.9	39.7	93.5	19
20	31 34.1	+32.5	88.3	31 35.5	+33.5	88.9	31 36.3	+34.6	89.5	31 36.5	+35.5	90.2	31 36.0	+36.5	90.8	31 34.8	+37.5	91.4	31 33.1	+38.4	92.0	31 30.6	+39.4	92.6	20
21	32 06.6	32.0	87.3	32 09.0	33.1	88.0	32 10.9	34.1	88.6	32 12.0	35.1	89.2	32 12.5	36.1	89.8	32 12.3	37.1	90.5	32 11.5	38.1	91.1	32 10.0	39.0	91.7	21
22	32 38.6	31.5	86.3	32 42.1	32.6	87.0	32 45.0	33.6	87.6	32 47.1	34.7	88.3	32 48.6	35.7	88.9	32 49.4	36.7	89.5	32 49.6	37.6	90.2	32 49.0	38.7	90.8	22
23	33 10.1	31.1	85.3	33 14.7	32.1	86.0	33 18.6	33.1	86.6	33 21.8	34.2	87.3	33 24.3	35.2	87.9	33 26.1	36.2	88.6	33 27.2	37.3	89.2	33 27.7	38.2	89.9	23
24	33 41.2	30.5	84.3	33 46.8	31.6	85.0	33 51.7	32.7	85.6	33 56.0	33.7	86.3	33 59.5	34.8	87.0	34 02.3	35.8	87.6	34 04.5	36.7	88.3	34 05.9	37.7	89.0	24
25	34 11.7	+30.0	83.3	34 18.4	+31.1	83.9	34 24.4	+32.2	84.6	34 29.7	+33.2	85.3	34 34.3	+34.2	86.0	34 38.1	+35.3	86.7	34 41.2	+36.4	87.4	34 43.6	+37.4	88.0	25
26	34 41.7	29.5	82.2	34 49.5	30.5	82.9	34 56.6	31.6	83.6	35 02.9	32.7	84.3	35 08.5	33.8	85.0	35 13.4	34.8	85.7	35 17.6	35.8	86.4	35 21.0	36.9	87.1	26
27	35 11.2	28.9	81.1	35 20.0	30.0	81.8	35 28.2	31.1	82.5	35 35.6	32.2	83.3	35 42.3	33.3	84.0	35 48.2	34.4	84.7	35 53.4	35.4	85.4	35 57.9	36.4	86.1	27
28	35 40.1	28.3	80.1	35 50.0	29.5	80.8	35 59.3	30.5	81.5	36 07.8	31.6	82.2	36 15.6	32.7	82.9	36 22.6	33.8	83.7	36 28.8	34.9	84.4	36 34.3	35.9	85.1	28
29	36 08.4	27.7	79.0	36 19.5	28.8	79.7	36 29.8	30.0	80.4	36 39.4	31.1	81.2	36 48.3	32.1	81.9	36 56.4	33.2	82.6	37 03.7	34.3	83.4	37 10.2	35.4	84.1	29
30	36 36.1	+27.1	77.9	36 48.3	+28.2	78.6	36 59.8	+29.3	79.3	37 10.5	+30.5	80.1	37 20.4	+31.6	80.8	37 29.6	+32.7	81.6	37 38.0	+33.8	82.3	37 45.6	+34.9	83.1	30
31	37 03.2	26.4	76.8	37 16.5	27.6	77.5	37 29.1	28.8	78.2	37 41.0	29.9	79.0	37 52.0	31.0	79.8	38 02.3	32.1	80.5	38 11.8	33.2	81.3	38 20.5	34.3	82.1	31
32	37 29.6	25.8	75.6	37 44.1	27.0	76.4	37 57.9	28.1	77.1	38 10.9	29.2	77.9	38 23.0	30.4	78.7	38 34.4	31.5	79.5	38 45.0	32.6	80.2	38 54.8	33.7	81.0	32
33	37 55.4	25.2	74.5	38 11.1	26.3	75.2	38 26.0	27.4	76.0	38 40.1	28.6	76.8	38 53.4	29.8	77.6	39 05.9	30.9	78.4	39 17.6	32.1	79.1	39 28.5	33.2	80.0	33
34	38 20.6	24.4	73.3	38 37.4	25.6	74.1	38 53.4	26.8	74.9	39 08.7	28.0	75.7	39 23.2	29.1	76.4	39 36.8	30.3	77.2	39 49.7	31.4	78.1	40 01.7	32.5	78.9	34
35	38 45.0	+23.8	72.2	39 03.0	+24.9	72.9	39 20.2	+26.1	73.7	39 36.7	+27.2	74.5	39 52.3	+28.4	75.3	40 07.1	+29.6	76.1	40 21.1	+30.7	76.9	40 34.2	+31.9	77.8	35
36	39 08.8	23.0	71.0	39 27.9	24.2	71.8	39 46.3	25.4	72.6	40 03.9	26.6	73.3	40 20.7	27.7	74.2	40 36.7	28.9	74.9	40 51.8	30.1	75.8	41 06.1	31.2	76.7	36
37	39 31.8	22.3	69.8	39 52.1	23.5	70.6	40 11.7	24.7	71.4	40 30.5	25.8	72.2	40 48.4	27.1	73.0	41 05.6	28.2	73.8	41 21.9	29.3	74.7	41 37.3	30.5	75.5	37
38	39 54.1	21.5	68.6	40 15.6	22.7	69.4	40 36.4	23.9	70.2	40 56.3	25.1	71.0	41 15.5	26.2	71.8	41 33.8	27.4	72.6	41 51.2	28.7	73.5	42 07.8	29.9	74.4	38
39	40 15.6	20.8	67.4	40 38.3	22.0	68.2	41 00.3	23.1	69.0	41 21.4	24.3	69.8	41 41.7	25.6	70.6	42 01.2	26.8	71.5	42 19.9	27.9	72.3	42 37.7	29.1	73.2	39
40	40 36.4	+19.9	66.1	41 00.3	+21.1	66.9	41 23.4	+22.3	67.7	41 45.7	+23.6	68.6	42 07.3	+24.7	69.4	42 28.0	+25.9	70.2	42 47.8	+27.2	71.1	43 06.8	+28.3	72.0	40
41	40 56.3	19.2	64.9	41 21.4	20.3	65.7	41 45.7	21.6	66.5	42 09.3	22.7	67.3	42 32.0	23.9	68.2	42 53.9	25.1	69.0	43 15.0	26.3	69.9	43 35.1	27.6	70.8	41
42	41 15.5	18.3	63.6	41 41.7	19.5	64.4	42 07.3	20.7	65.2	42 32.0	21.9	66.1	42 55.9	23.1	66.9	43 19.0	24.4	67.8	43 41.3	25.6	68.7	44 02.7	26.8	69.6	42
43	41 33.8	17.4	62.4	42 01.2	18.7	63.2	42 28.0	19.8	64.0	42 53.9	21.1	64.8	43 19.0	22.3	65.6	43 43.4	23.5	66.5	44 06.9	24.7	67.4	44 29.5	25.9	68.3	43
44	41 51.2	16.6	61.1	42 19.9	17.8	61.9	42 47.8	19.0	62.7	43 15.0	20.1	63.5	43 41.3	21.4	64.4	44 06.9	22.6	65.2	44 31.6	23.8	66.1	44 55.4	25.1	67.0	44

287

66°, 294° L.H.A.　　LATITUDE SAME NAME AS DECLINATION

N. Lat. {L.H.A. greater than 180° ...... Zn=Z ; L.H.A. less than 180° ...... Zn=360°−Z}

Dec.	38° Hc	38° d	38° Z	39° Hc	39° d	39° Z	40° Hc	40° d	40° Z	41° Hc	41° d	41° Z	42° Hc	42° d	42° Z	43° Hc	43° d	43° Z	44° Hc	44° d	44° Z	45° Hc	45° d	45° Z	Dec.
0	18 41.6	+38.9	105.3	18 25.6	+39.7	105.7	18 09.3	+40.5	106.0	17 52.6	+41.3	106.3	17 35.6	+42.1	106.6	17 18.3	+42.8	106.9	17 00.8	+43.5	107.2	16 42.9	+44.2	107.5	0
1	19 20.5	38.7	104.5	19 05.3	39.5	104.9	18 49.8	40.3	105.2	18 33.9	41.1	105.5	18 17.7	41.8	105.8	18 01.1	42.6	106.2	17 44.3	43.3	106.5	17 27.1	44.1	106.8	1
2	19 59.2	38.5	103.7	19 44.8	39.3	104.1	19 30.1	40.0	104.4	19 15.0	40.8	104.7	18 59.5	41.7	105.1	18 43.7	42.5	105.4	18 27.6	43.0	105.7	18 11.2	43.9	106.1	2
3	20 37.7	38.2	102.9	20 24.1	39.0	103.3	20 10.1	39.9	103.6	19 55.8	40.7	104.0	19 41.2	41.5	104.3	19 26.2	42.1	104.7	19 10.8	43.0	105.0	18 55.1	43.7	105.3	3
4	21 15.9	38.0	102.1	21 03.1	38.9	102.4	20 50.0	39.7	102.8	20 36.5	40.5	103.2	20 22.7	41.2	103.6	20 08.4	42.1	103.9	19 53.8	42.8	104.3	19 38.8	43.6	104.6	4
5	21 53.9	+37.7	101.2	21 42.0	+38.6	101.6	21 29.7	+39.4	102.0	21 17.0	+40.2	102.4	21 03.9	+41.1	102.8	20 50.5	+41.8	103.1	20 36.6	+42.7	103.5	20 22.4	+43.4	103.9	5
6	22 31.6	37.5	100.4	22 20.6	38.3	100.8	22 09.1	39.2	101.2	21 57.2	40.1	101.6	21 45.0	40.8	102.0	21 32.3	41.6	102.4	21 19.3	42.4	102.8	21 05.8	43.2	103.1	6
7	23 09.1	37.1	99.6	22 58.9	38.0	100.0	22 48.3	38.9	100.4	22 37.3	39.7	100.8	22 25.8	40.6	101.2	22 13.9	41.5	101.6	22 01.7	42.2	102.0	21 49.0	43.0	102.4	7
8	23 46.2	36.9	98.7	23 36.9	37.8	99.1	23 27.2	38.7	99.6	23 17.0	39.5	100.0	23 06.4	40.4	100.4	22 55.4	41.1	100.8	22 43.9	42.0	101.2	22 32.0	42.8	101.6	8
9	24 23.1	36.6	97.8	24 14.7	37.5	98.3	24 05.9	38.4	98.7	23 56.5	39.3	99.2	23 46.8	40.1	99.6	23 36.5	41.0	100.0	23 25.9	41.7	100.5	23 14.8	42.5	100.9	9
10	24 59.7	+36.3	97.0	24 52.2	+37.2	97.4	24 44.3	+38.1	97.9	24 35.8	+39.0	98.3	24 26.9	+39.8	98.8	24 17.5	+40.7	99.2	24 07.6	+41.5	99.7	23 57.3	+42.3	100.1	10
11	25 36.0	36.0	96.1	25 29.4	36.9	96.6	25 22.4	37.8	97.0	25 14.8	38.7	97.5	25 06.7	39.6	98.0	24 58.2	40.4	98.4	24 49.1	41.3	98.9	24 39.6	42.1	99.3	11
12	26 12.0	35.7	95.2	26 06.3	36.6	95.7	26 00.2	37.5	96.2	25 53.5	38.4	96.6	25 46.3	39.2	97.1	25 38.6	40.1	97.6	25 30.4	41.0	98.1	25 21.7	41.9	98.5	12
13	26 47.7	35.3	94.3	26 42.9	36.3	94.8	26 37.7	37.1	95.3	26 31.9	38.0	95.8	26 25.5	39.0	96.3	26 18.7	39.9	96.7	26 11.4	40.7	97.3	26 03.6	41.5	97.8	13
14	27 23.0	34.9	93.4	27 19.2	35.9	93.9	27 14.8	36.9	94.4	27 09.9	37.8	94.9	27 04.5	38.7	95.4	26 58.6	39.5	95.9	26 52.1	40.4	96.4	26 45.1	41.3	96.9	14
15	27 57.9	+34.6	92.5	27 55.1	+35.5	93.0	27 51.7	+36.4	93.5	27 47.7	+37.4	94.0	27 43.2	+38.3	94.6	27 38.1	+39.3	95.1	27 32.5	+40.2	95.6	27 26.4	+41.0	96.1	15
16	28 32.5	34.2	91.6	28 30.6	35.2	92.1	28 28.1	36.2	92.6	28 25.1	37.1	93.1	28 21.5	38.0	93.7	28 17.4	38.9	94.2	28 12.7	39.8	94.8	28 07.4	40.7	95.3	16
17	29 06.7	33.8	90.6	29 05.8	34.8	91.2	29 04.3	35.7	91.7	29 02.2	36.7	92.3	28 59.5	37.6	92.8	28 56.3	38.6	93.4	28 52.5	39.5	93.9	28 48.1	40.4	94.5	17
18	29 40.5	33.4	89.6	29 40.6	34.3	90.2	29 40.0	35.4	90.8	29 38.9	36.3	91.4	29 37.2	37.3	91.9	29 34.9	38.2	92.5	29 32.0	39.1	93.1	29 28.5	40.0	93.6	18
19	30 13.9	32.9	88.7	30 14.9	34.0	89.3	30 15.4	35.0	89.9	30 15.2	36.0	90.4	30 14.5	36.9	91.0	30 13.1	37.9	91.6	30 11.1	38.8	92.2	30 08.5	39.8	92.8	19
20	30 46.8	+32.6	87.7	30 48.9	+33.6	88.3	30 50.4	+34.5	88.9	30 51.2	+35.5	89.5	30 51.4	+36.5	90.1	30 51.0	+37.5	90.7	30 49.9	+38.5	91.3	30 48.3	+39.3	91.9	20
21	31 19.4	32.0	86.7	31 22.5	33.1	87.3	31 24.9	34.1	88.0	31 26.7	35.2	88.6	31 27.9	36.1	89.2	31 28.5	37.1	89.8	31 28.4	38.0	90.4	31 27.6	39.0	91.0	21
22	31 51.4	31.6	85.7	31 55.6	32.6	86.4	31 59.0	33.7	87.0	32 01.9	34.7	87.6	32 04.0	35.7	88.2	32 05.6	36.6	88.9	32 06.4	37.7	89.5	32 06.6	38.6	90.1	22
23	32 23.0	31.2	84.7	32 28.2	32.2	85.4	32 32.7	33.2	86.0	32 36.6	34.2	86.6	32 39.7	35.3	87.3	32 42.2	36.3	87.9	32 44.1	37.2	88.6	32 45.2	38.3	89.2	23
24	32 54.2	30.6	83.7	33 00.4	31.7	84.4	33 05.9	32.8	85.0	33 10.8	33.8	85.7	33 15.0	34.8	86.3	33 18.5	35.8	87.0	33 21.3	36.8	87.6	33 23.5	37.8	88.3	24
25	33 24.8	+30.1	82.7	33 32.1	+31.2	83.4	33 38.7	+32.2	84.0	33 44.6	+33.3	84.7	33 49.8	+34.3	85.3	33 54.3	+35.4	86.0	33 58.1	+36.4	86.7	34 01.3	+37.3	87.4	25
26	33 54.9	29.6	81.7	34 03.3	30.6	82.3	34 10.9	31.8	82.9	34 17.9	32.8	83.7	34 24.1	33.9	84.4	34 29.7	34.9	85.0	34 34.5	35.9	85.7	34 38.6	36.9	86.4	26
27	34 24.5	29.0	80.6	34 33.9	30.2	81.3	34 42.7	31.2	81.9	34 50.7	32.3	82.7	34 58.0	33.3	83.4	35 04.6	34.4	84.0	35 10.4	35.5	84.7	35 15.6	36.4	85.5	27
28	34 53.5	28.5	79.5	35 04.1	29.5	80.2	35 13.9	30.6	80.9	35 23.0	31.7	81.6	35 31.3	32.9	82.3	35 39.0	33.9	83.0	35 45.9	34.9	83.8	35 52.0	36.0	84.5	28
29	35 22.0	27.9	78.5	35 33.6	29.0	79.2	35 44.5	30.2	79.8	35 54.7	31.2	80.6	36 04.2	32.3	81.3	36 12.9	33.3	82.0	36 20.8	34.5	82.8	36 28.0	35.5	83.5	29
30	35 49.9	+27.3	77.4	36 02.6	+28.5	78.1	36 14.7	+29.5	78.8	36 25.9	+30.7	79.5	36 36.5	+31.7	80.3	36 46.2	+32.9	81.0	36 55.3	+33.9	81.7	37 03.5	+35.0	82.5	30
31	36 17.2	26.7	76.3	36 31.1	27.8	77.0	36 44.2	28.9	77.7	36 56.6	30.0	78.5	37 08.2	31.2	79.2	37 19.1	32.2	79.9	37 29.2	33.3	80.7	37 38.5	34.4	81.5	31
32	36 43.9	26.0	75.2	36 58.9	27.2	75.9	37 13.1	28.3	76.6	37 26.6	29.5	77.4	37 39.4	30.5	78.1	37 51.3	31.7	78.9	38 02.5	32.8	79.6	38 12.9	33.9	80.4	32
33	37 09.9	25.4	74.0	37 26.1	26.5	74.8	37 41.4	27.7	75.5	37 56.1	28.8	76.3	38 09.9	30.0	77.0	38 23.0	31.1	77.8	38 35.3	32.2	78.6	38 46.8	33.3	79.4	33
34	37 35.3	24.8	72.9	37 52.6	25.9	73.6	38 09.1	27.1	74.4	38 24.9	28.2	75.2	38 39.9	29.3	75.9	38 54.1	30.4	76.7	39 07.5	31.6	77.5	39 20.1	32.7	78.3	34
35	38 00.1	+24.0	71.7	38 18.5	+25.2	72.5	38 36.2	+26.3	73.3	38 53.1	+27.5	74.0	39 09.2	+28.7	74.8	39 24.5	+29.8	75.6	39 39.1	+30.9	76.4	39 52.8	+32.0	77.2	35
36	38 24.1	23.4	70.6	38 43.7	24.5	71.3	39 02.5	25.7	72.1	39 20.6	26.8	72.9	39 37.9	28.0	73.7	39 54.3	29.2	74.5	40 10.0	30.3	75.3	40 24.8	31.5	76.1	36
37	38 47.5	22.6	69.4	39 08.2	23.8	70.2	39 28.2	25.0	70.9	39 47.4	26.2	71.7	40 05.9	27.3	72.5	40 23.5	28.4	73.3	40 40.3	29.6	74.1	40 56.3	30.7	75.0	37
38	39 10.1	21.9	68.2	39 32.0	23.1	69.0	39 53.2	24.2	69.7	40 13.6	25.4	70.5	40 33.2	26.5	71.3	40 51.9	27.7	72.2	41 09.9	28.9	73.0	41 27.0	30.1	73.8	38
39	39 32.0	21.2	67.0	39 55.1	22.3	67.8	40 17.4	23.5	68.6	40 39.0	24.6	69.3	40 59.7	25.9	70.2	41 19.7	27.0	71.0	41 38.8	28.2	71.8	41 57.1	29.4	72.7	39
40	39 53.2	+20.4	65.8	40 17.4	+21.6	66.6	40 40.9	+22.7	67.3	41 03.6	+23.9	68.1	41 25.6	+25.1	69.0	41 46.7	+26.3	69.8	42 07.0	+27.5	70.6	42 26.5	+28.6	71.5	40
41	40 13.6	19.6	64.6	40 39.0	20.7	65.3	41 03.6	22.0	66.1	41 27.5	23.2	66.9	41 50.7	24.3	67.7	42 13.0	25.5	68.6	42 34.5	26.7	69.4	42 55.1	27.9	70.3	41
42	40 33.2	18.7	63.3	40 59.7	20.0	64.1	41 25.6	21.1	64.9	41 50.7	22.3	65.6	42 15.0	23.5	66.5	42 38.5	24.7	67.4	43 01.2	25.9	68.2	43 23.0	27.1	69.1	42
43	40 51.9	18.0	62.1	41 19.7	19.1	62.8	41 46.7	20.3	63.6	42 13.0	21.5	64.4	42 38.5	22.7	65.3	43 03.2	23.9	66.1	43 27.1	25.1	67.0	43 50.1	26.3	67.9	43
44	41 09.9	17.1	60.8	41 38.8	18.3	61.6	42 07.0	19.5	62.4	42 34.5	20.6	63.2	43 01.2	21.8	64.0	43 27.1	23.0	64.9	43 52.2	24.2	65.7	44 16.4	25.5	66.6	44

69°, 291° L.H.A.   LATITUDE SAME NAME AS DECLINATION

N. Lat { L.H.A. greater than 180°......Zn=Z
         L.H.A. less than 180°......Zn=360°−Z

Dec.	38° Hc	38° d	38° Z	39° Hc	39° d	39° Z	40° Hc	40° d	40° Z	41° Hc	41° d	41° Z	42° Hc	42° d	42° Z	43° Hc	43° d	43° Z	44° Hc	44° d	44° Z	45° Hc	45° d	45° Z	Dec.
0	16 24.2	+38.4	103.3	16 10.3	+39.2	103.6	15 56.0	+40.0	103.9	15 41.5	+40.8	104.1	15 26.7	+41.6	104.4	15 11.7	+42.3	104.7	14 56.3	+43.1	104.9	14 40.7	+43.8	105.2	0
1	17 02.6	38.2	102.5	16 49.5	39.0	102.8	16 36.0	39.9	103.1	16 22.3	40.7	103.4	16 08.3	41.4	103.7	15 54.0	42.1	103.9	15 39.4	42.9	104.2	15 24.5	43.7	104.5	1
2	17 40.8	38.1	101.7	17 28.5	38.9	102.0	17 15.9	39.7	102.3	17 03.0	40.4	102.6	16 49.7	41.3	102.9	16 36.2	42.0	103.2	16 22.3	42.8	103.5	16 08.2	43.5	103.8	2
3	18 18.9	37.8	100.9	18 07.4	38.6	101.2	17 55.6	39.4	101.5	17 43.4	40.3	101.8	17 31.0	41.0	102.1	17 18.2	41.8	102.4	17 05.1	42.6	102.7	16 51.7	43.4	103.0	3
4	18 56.7	37.6	100.1	18 46.0	38.5	100.4	18 35.0	39.3	100.7	18 23.7	40.1	101.1	18 12.0	40.9	101.4	18 00.0	41.7	101.7	17 47.7	42.5	102.0	17 35.1	43.2	102.3	4
5	19 34.3	+37.4	99.2	19 24.5	+38.2	99.6	19 14.3	+39.1	99.9	19 03.8	+39.9	100.3	18 52.9	+40.7	100.6	18 41.7	+41.5	100.9	18 30.2	+42.2	101.3	18 18.3	+43.0	101.6	5
6	20 11.7	37.1	98.4	20 02.7	38.0	98.8	19 53.4	38.8	99.1	19 43.7	39.7	99.5	19 33.6	40.5	99.8	19 23.2	41.3	100.1	19 12.4	42.1	100.5	19 01.3	42.9	100.9	6
7	20 48.8	36.9	97.6	20 40.7	37.8	97.9	20 32.2	38.7	98.3	20 23.4	39.4	98.7	20 14.1	40.3	99.0	20 04.5	41.1	99.4	19 54.5	41.9	99.8	19 44.2	42.6	100.1	7
8	21 25.7	36.6	96.7	21 18.5	37.5	97.1	21 10.9	38.3	97.5	21 02.8	39.3	97.9	20 54.4	40.1	98.2	20 45.6	40.9	98.6	20 36.4	41.7	99.0	20 26.8	42.5	99.4	8
9	22 02.3	36.4	95.9	21 56.0	37.2	96.3	21 49.2	38.2	96.7	21 42.1	39.0	97.1	21 34.5	39.8	97.5	21 26.5	40.7	97.8	21 18.1	41.5	98.2	21 09.3	42.3	98.6	9
10	22 38.7	+36.1	95.0	22 33.2	+37.0	95.4	22 27.4	+37.8	95.8	22 21.1	+38.7	96.2	22 14.3	+39.6	96.6	22 07.2	+40.4	97.0	21 59.6	+41.3	97.5	21 51.6	+42.1	97.9	10
11	23 14.8	35.8	94.1	23 10.2	36.7	94.6	23 05.2	37.6	95.0	22 59.8	38.5	95.4	22 53.9	39.4	95.8	22 47.6	40.2	96.3	22 40.9	41.0	96.7	22 33.7	41.8	97.1	11
12	23 50.6	35.5	93.3	23 46.9	36.5	93.7	23 42.8	37.4	94.1	23 38.3	38.2	94.6	23 33.3	39.0	95.0	23 27.8	39.9	95.4	23 21.9	40.8	95.9	23 15.5	41.6	96.3	12
13	24 26.1	35.2	92.4	24 23.4	36.1	92.8	24 20.2	37.0	93.3	24 16.5	37.9	93.7	24 12.3	38.9	94.2	24 07.7	39.7	94.6	24 02.7	40.5	95.1	23 57.1	41.4	95.5	13
14	25 01.3	34.8	91.5	24 59.5	35.8	91.9	24 57.2	36.7	92.4	24 54.4	37.6	92.9	24 51.2	38.5	93.3	24 47.4	39.4	93.8	24 43.2	40.3	94.3	24 38.5	41.1	94.7	14
15	25 36.1	+34.6	90.6	25 35.3	+35.5	91.1	25 33.9	+36.1	91.5	25 32.0	+37.4	92.0	25 29.7	+38.2	92.5	25 26.8	+39.1	93.0	25 23.5	+40.0	93.4	25 19.6	+40.9	93.9	15
16	26 10.7	34.2	89.7	26 10.8	35.1	90.2	26 10.0	36.4	90.7	26 09.4	37.0	91.1	26 07.9	37.9	91.6	26 05.9	38.9	92.1	26 03.5	39.7	92.6	26 00.5	40.5	93.1	16
17	26 44.9	33.8	88.8	26 45.9	34.8	89.3	26 46.4	35.7	89.8	26 46.4	36.7	90.3	26 45.8	37.6	90.8	26 44.8	38.5	91.3	26 43.2	39.4	91.8	26 41.0	40.3	92.3	17
18	27 18.7	33.4	87.8	27 20.7	34.4	88.3	27 22.1	35.4	88.9	27 23.1	36.3	89.4	27 23.4	37.3	89.9	27 23.3	38.2	90.4	27 22.6	39.1	90.9	27 21.3	40.0	91.5	18
19	27 52.1	33.1	86.9	27 55.1	34.1	87.4	27 57.5	35.1	88.0	27 59.4	36.0	88.5	28 00.7	37.0	89.0	28 01.5	37.8	89.5	28 01.7	38.8	90.1	28 01.3	39.7	90.6	19
20	28 25.2	+32.7	85.9	28 29.2	+33.6	86.5	28 32.6	+34.6	87.0	28 35.4	+35.6	87.6	28 37.7	+36.5	88.1	28 39.3	+37.6	88.7	28 40.5	+38.4	89.2	28 41.0	+39.3	89.8	20
21	28 57.9	32.3	85.0	29 02.8	33.3	85.5	29 07.2	34.3	86.1	29 11.0	35.3	86.7	29 14.2	36.2	87.2	29 16.9	37.1	87.8	29 18.9	38.1	88.3	29 20.3	39.1	88.9	21
22	29 30.2	31.8	84.0	29 36.1	32.9	84.6	29 41.5	33.8	85.2	29 46.3	34.8	85.7	29 50.4	35.9	86.3	29 54.0	36.8	86.9	29 57.0	37.7	87.4	29 59.4	38.6	88.0	22
23	30 02.0	31.4	83.0	30 09.0	32.4	83.6	30 15.3	33.5	84.3	30 21.1	34.4	84.8	30 26.3	35.4	85.4	30 30.8	36.4	86.0	30 34.7	37.4	86.5	30 38.0	38.3	87.1	23
24	30 33.4	31.0	82.1	30 41.4	32.0	82.6	30 48.8	33.0	83.2	30 55.5	34.0	83.8	31 01.7	35.0	84.4	31 07.2	36.0	85.0	31 12.1	36.9	85.6	31 16.3	37.9	86.2	24
25	31 04.4	+30.5	81.1	31 13.4	+31.5	81.7	31 21.8	+32.5	82.3	31 29.5	+33.6	82.9	31 36.7	+34.6	83.5	31 43.2	+35.5	84.1	31 49.0	+36.6	84.7	31 54.2	+37.6	85.3	25
26	31 34.9	30.0	80.1	31 44.9	31.1	80.7	31 54.3	32.1	81.3	32 03.1	33.1	81.9	32 11.3	34.1	82.5	32 18.7	35.2	83.1	32 25.6	36.1	83.8	32 31.8	37.1	84.4	26
27	32 04.9	29.5	79.0	32 16.0	30.5	79.7	32 26.4	31.6	80.3	32 36.2	32.7	80.9	32 45.4	33.7	81.5	32 53.9	34.7	82.2	33 01.7	35.7	82.8	33 08.9	36.7	83.5	27
28	32 34.4	29.0	78.0	32 46.5	30.1	78.6	32 58.0	30.9	79.3	33 08.9	32.2	79.9	33 19.1	33.2	80.6	33 28.6	34.1	81.2	33 37.4	35.3	81.9	33 45.6	36.2	82.5	28
29	33 03.4	28.5	77.0	33 16.6	29.6	77.6	33 28.9	30.6	78.2	33 41.1	31.6	78.9	33 52.3	32.6	79.6	34 02.8	33.8	80.2	34 12.7	34.7	80.9	34 21.8	35.8	81.6	29
30	33 31.9	+27.9	75.9	33 46.2	+29.0	76.6	33 59.8	+30.1	77.2	34 12.7	+31.2	77.9	34 25.0	+32.2	78.5	34 36.6	+33.2	79.2	34 47.4	+34.3	79.9	34 57.6	+35.3	80.6	30
31	33 59.8	27.4	74.8	34 15.2	28.4	75.5	34 29.9	29.5	76.2	34 43.9	30.6	76.8	34 57.2	31.7	77.5	35 09.8	32.8	78.2	35 21.7	33.8	78.9	35 32.9	34.9	79.6	31
32	34 27.2	26.8	73.8	34 43.6	28.0	74.4	34 59.4	29.0	75.1	35 14.5	30.1	75.7	35 28.9	31.1	76.5	35 42.6	32.2	77.2	35 55.5	33.3	77.9	36 07.8	34.3	78.6	32
33	34 54.0	26.3	72.7	35 11.6	27.3	73.4	35 28.4	28.4	74.0	35 44.6	29.5	74.7	36 00.0	30.6	75.4	36 14.8	31.6	76.1	36 28.8	32.7	76.8	36 42.1	33.8	77.6	33
34	35 20.3	25.6	71.6	35 38.9	26.7	72.3	35 56.8	27.8	72.9	36 14.1	28.9	73.6	36 30.6	30.0	74.4	36 46.4	31.1	75.1	37 01.5	32.2	75.8	37 15.9	33.2	76.5	34
35	35 45.9	+25.0	70.5	36 05.6	+26.1	71.2	36 24.6	+27.2	71.9	36 43.0	+28.3	72.6	37 00.6	+29.4	73.3	37 17.5	+30.5	74.0	37 33.7	+31.6	74.7	37 49.1	+32.7	75.5	35
36	36 10.9	24.3	69.3	36 31.7	25.5	70.0	36 51.8	26.6	70.7	37 11.3	27.7	71.5	37 30.0	28.8	72.2	37 48.0	29.9	72.9	38 05.3	30.9	73.7	38 21.8	32.0	74.4	36
37	36 35.2	23.8	68.2	36 57.2	24.8	68.9	37 18.4	26.0	69.6	37 39.0	27.0	70.3	37 58.8	28.2	71.1	38 17.9	29.3	71.8	38 36.2	30.4	72.6	38 53.8	31.5	73.3	37
38	36 59.0	23.0	67.1	37 22.0	24.2	67.8	37 44.4	25.2	68.5	38 06.0	26.4	69.2	38 27.0	27.5	69.9	38 47.2	28.6	70.7	39 06.6	29.7	71.5	39 25.3	30.8	72.2	38
39	37 22.0	22.4	65.9	37 46.2	23.4	66.6	38 09.6	24.6	67.3	38 32.4	25.7	68.1	38 54.5	26.8	68.8	39 15.8	27.9	69.5	39 36.3	29.1	70.3	39 56.1	30.2	71.1	39
40	37 44.4	+21.6	64.7	38 09.6	+22.8	65.4	38 34.2	+23.9	66.2	38 58.1	+25.0	66.9	39 21.3	+26.1	67.7	39 43.7	+27.3	68.4	40 05.4	+28.4	69.2	40 26.3	+29.6	70.0	40
41	38 06.0	21.0	63.6	38 32.4	22.1	64.3	38 58.1	23.2	65.0	39 23.1	24.3	65.7	39 47.4	25.5	66.5	40 11.0	26.6	67.3	40 33.8	27.7	68.0	40 55.9	28.8	68.8	41
42	38 27.0	20.2	62.4	38 54.5	21.3	63.1	39 21.3	22.4	63.8	39 47.4	23.6	64.5	40 12.9	24.7	65.3	40 37.6	25.8	66.1	41 01.5	27.0	66.9	41 24.7	28.1	67.7	42
43	38 47.2	19.4	61.2	39 15.8	20.5	61.9	39 43.7	21.7	62.6	40 11.0	22.8	63.3	40 37.6	24.0	64.1	41 03.4	25.1	64.9	41 28.5	26.2	65.7	41 52.8	27.4	66.5	43
44	39 06.6	18.7	59.9	39 36.3	19.8	60.7	40 05.4	20.9	61.4	40 33.8	22.1	62.1	41 01.5	23.2	62.9	41 28.5	24.3	63.7	41 54.7	25.5	64.5	42 20.2	26.6	65.3	44

Dec.	38° Hc	d	Z	39° Hc	d	Z	40° Hc	d	Z	41° Hc	d	Z	42° Hc	d	Z	43° Hc	d	Z	44° Hc	d	Z	45° Hc	d	Z	Dec.
0	16 24.2	−38.6	103.3	16 10.3	−39.4	103.6	15 56.0	−40.2	103.9	15 41.5	−41.0	104.1	15 26.7	−41.7	104.4	15 11.7	−42.5	104.7	14 56.3	−43.2	104.9	14 40.7	−43.9	105.2	0
1	15 45.6	38.8	104.1	15 30.9	39.6	104.4	15 15.8	40.3	104.6	15 00.5	41.1	104.9	14 45.0	41.9	105.1	14 29.2	42.6	105.4	14 13.1	43.5	105.6	13 56.8	44.0	105.9	1
2	15 06.8	38.9	104.9	14 51.3	39.7	105.1	14 35.5	40.5	105.4	14 19.4	41.2	105.6	14 03.1	42.0	105.9	13 46.6	42.8	106.1	13 29.8	43.5	106.4	13 12.8	44.2	106.6	2
3	14 27.9	39.1	105.7	14 11.6	39.9	105.9	13 55.0	40.6	106.2	13 38.2	41.4	106.4	13 21.1	42.1	106.6	13 03.8	42.8	106.8	12 46.3	43.7	107.1	12 28.6	44.2	107.3	3
4	13 48.8	39.2	106.5	13 31.7	40.0	106.7	13 14.4	40.8	106.9	12 56.8	41.5	107.1	12 39.0	42.2	107.4	12 21.0	43.0	107.6	12 02.8	43.7	107.8	11 44.4	44.4	108.0	4
5	13 09.6	−39.4	107.2	12 51.7	−40.2	107.5	12 33.6	−40.9	107.7	12 15.3	−41.7	107.9	11 56.8	−42.4	108.1	11 38.0	−43.0	108.3	11 19.1	−43.8	108.5	11 00.0	−44.4	108.7	5
6	12 30.2	39.5	108.0	12 11.5	40.3	108.2	11 52.7	41.0	108.4	11 33.6	41.7	108.6	11 14.4	42.5	108.8	10 55.0	43.2	109.0	10 35.3	43.8	109.2	10 15.6	44.6	109.3	6
7	11 50.7	39.6	108.8	11 31.3	40.4	109.0	11 11.7	41.1	109.2	10 51.9	41.9	109.4	10 31.9	42.5	109.5	10 11.8	43.3	109.7	9 51.5	44.0	109.9	9 31.0	44.6	110.0	7
8	11 11.1	39.8	109.5	10 50.9	40.5	109.7	10 30.6	41.3	109.9	10 10.0	41.9	110.1	9 49.4	42.7	110.2	9 28.5	43.3	110.4	9 07.5	44.0	110.6	8 46.4	44.7	110.7	8
9	10 31.3	39.8	110.3	10 10.4	40.6	110.5	9 49.3	41.3	110.6	9 28.1	42.0	110.8	9 06.7	42.7	111.0	8 45.2	43.4	111.1	8 23.5	44.1	111.2	8 01.7	44.7	111.4	9
10	9 51.5	−40.0	111.1	9 29.8	−40.7	111.2	9 08.0	−41.4	111.4	8 46.1	−42.1	111.5	8 24.0	−42.8	111.7	8 01.8	−43.5	111.8	7 39.4	−44.1	111.9	7 17.0	−44.8	112.0	10
11	9 11.5	40.1	111.8	8 49.1	40.8	112.0	8 26.6	41.5	112.1	8 04.0	42.2	112.2	7 41.2	42.9	112.4	7 18.3	43.6	112.5	6 55.3	44.2	112.6	6 32.2	44.9	112.7	11
12	8 31.4	40.1	112.6	8 08.3	40.8	112.7	7 45.1	41.6	112.8	7 21.8	42.3	113.0	6 58.3	42.9	113.1	6 34.7	43.6	113.2	6 11.1	44.3	113.3	5 47.3	44.9	113.4	12
13	7 51.3	40.2	113.3	7 27.5	41.0	113.4	7 03.5	41.6	113.6	6 39.5	42.3	113.7	6 15.4	43.0	113.8	5 51.1	43.6	113.9	5 26.8	44.3	114.0	5 02.4	45.0	114.1	13
14	7 11.1	40.3	114.1	6 46.5	40.9	114.2	6 21.9	41.7	114.3	5 57.2	42.4	114.4	5 32.4	43.1	114.5	5 07.5	43.7	114.6	4 42.5	44.4	114.6	4 17.4	45.0	114.7	14
15	6 30.8	−40.4	114.8	6 05.6	−41.1	114.9	5 40.2	−41.7	115.0	5 14.8	−42.4	115.1	4 49.3	−43.1	115.2	4 23.8	−43.8	115.3	3 58.1	−44.4	115.3	3 32.4	−45.0	115.4	15
16	5 50.4	40.4	115.6	5 24.5	41.1	115.7	4 58.5	41.8	115.7	4 32.4	42.5	115.8	4 06.2	43.1	115.9	3 40.0	43.8	116.0	3 13.7	44.4	116.0	2 47.4	45.0	116.0	16
17	5 10.0	40.5	116.3	4 43.4	41.2	116.4	4 16.7	41.8	116.5	3 49.9	42.5	116.5	3 23.1	43.1	116.6	2 56.2	43.8	116.6	2 29.3	44.4	116.7	2 02.4	45.1	116.7	17
18	4 29.5	40.5	117.0	4 02.2	41.2	117.1	3 34.9	41.9	117.2	3 07.4	42.5	117.2	2 40.0	43.2	117.3	2 12.4	43.8	117.3	1 44.9	44.4	117.3	1 17.3	45.1	117.4	18
19	3 49.0	40.5	117.8	3 21.0	41.2	117.8	2 53.0	41.9	117.9	2 24.9	42.6	117.9	1 56.8	43.2	118.0	1 28.6	43.8	118.0	1 00.5	44.5	118.0	0 32.3	−45.1	118.0	19
20	3 08.5	−40.6	118.5	2 39.8	−41.3	118.6	2 11.1	−41.9	118.6	1 42.3	−42.5	118.6	1 13.6	−43.2	118.7	0 44.8	−43.8	118.7	0 16.0	−44.5	118.7	0 12.8	+45.1	61.3	20
21	2 27.9	40.6	119.3	1 58.5	41.2	119.3	1 29.2	42.0	119.3	0 59.8	42.6	119.3	0 30.4	−43.2	119.4	0 01.0	−43.9	119.4	0 28.5	+44.4	60.0	0 57.9	45.0	60.7	21
22	1 47.3	40.6	120.0	1 17.3	41.3	120.0	0 47.2	41.9	120.0	0 17.2	−42.6	120.0	0 12.8	+43.2	60.0	0 42.9	+43.8	60.0	1 12.9	44.5	59.3	1 42.9	45.1	60.0	22
23	1 06.7	40.7	120.7	0 36.0	−41.3	120.7	0 05.3	−41.9	120.7	0 25.4	+42.5	59.2	0 56.0	43.2	59.3	1 26.7	43.8	59.3	1 57.4	44.4	58.6	2 28.0	45.0	59.3	23
24	0 26.0	−40.6	121.5	0 05.3	+41.3	58.5	0 36.6	+42.0	58.5	1 07.9	42.6	58.5	1 39.2	43.2	58.6	2 10.5	43.8	58.6	2 41.8	44.4	58.0	3 13.0	45.0	58.7	24
25	0 14.6	+40.6	57.8	0 46.6	+41.3	57.8	1 18.6	+41.9	57.8	1 50.5	+42.6	57.8	2 22.4	+43.2	57.9	2 54.3	+43.8	57.9	3 26.2	+44.4	57.3	3 58.0	+45.0	58.0	25
26	0 55.2	40.7	57.1	1 27.9	41.2	57.1	2 00.5	41.9	57.1	2 33.1	42.5	57.1	3 05.6	43.1	57.2	3 38.1	43.7	57.2	4 10.6	44.3	56.6	4 43.0	44.9	57.3	26
27	1 35.9	40.6	56.3	2 09.1	41.3	56.3	2 42.4	41.8	56.4	3 15.6	42.5	56.4	3 48.7	43.1	56.5	4 21.8	43.7	56.5	4 54.9	44.3	55.9	5 27.9	44.9	56.7	27
28	2 16.5	40.6	55.6	2 50.4	41.2	55.6	3 24.2	41.9	55.7	3 58.1	42.4	55.6	4 31.8	43.1	55.8	5 05.5	43.7	55.8	5 39.2	44.3	55.2	6 12.8	44.8	56.0	28
29	2 57.1	40.5	54.8	3 31.6	41.2	54.9	4 06.1	41.8	54.9	4 40.5	42.4	55.0	5 14.9	43.0	55.1	5 49.2	43.6	55.2	6 23.5	44.2	54.6	6 57.6	44.8	55.3	29
30	3 37.6	+40.6	54.1	4 12.8	+41.1	54.2	4 47.9	+41.8	54.2	5 22.9	+42.4	54.3	5 57.9	+43.0	54.4	6 32.8	+43.6	54.5	7 07.7	+44.1	53.9	7 42.4	+44.7	54.7	30
31	4 18.2	40.4	53.4	4 53.9	41.1	53.4	5 29.7	41.7	53.5	6 05.3	42.3	53.6	6 40.9	42.9	53.7	7 16.4	43.5	53.8	7 51.8	44.1	53.2	8 27.1	44.7	54.0	31
32	4 58.6	40.5	52.6	5 35.0	41.0	52.7	6 11.4	41.6	52.8	6 47.6	42.3	52.9	7 23.8	42.8	53.0	7 59.9	43.4	53.1	8 35.9	44.0	52.5	9 11.8	44.5	53.3	32
33	5 39.1	40.4	51.9	6 16.1	41.0	52.0	6 53.0	41.6	52.0	7 29.9	42.2	52.2	8 06.6	42.8	52.3	8 43.3	43.3	52.4	9 19.9	43.9	51.8	9 56.3	44.5	52.6	33
34	6 19.5	40.3	51.1	6 57.1	40.9	51.2	7 34.6	41.5	51.3	8 12.0	42.1	51.4	8 49.4	42.7	51.6	9 26.6	43.3	51.7	10 03.8	43.8	51.1	10 40.8	44.4	52.0	34
35	6 59.8	+40.2	50.4	7 38.0	+40.8	50.5	8 16.1	+41.4	50.6	8 54.1	+42.1	50.7	9 32.1	+42.6	50.8	10 09.9	+43.2	51.0	10 47.6	+43.8	50.4	11 25.2	+44.3	51.3	35
36	7 40.0	40.2	49.6	8 18.8	40.8	49.8	8 57.5	41.4	49.9	9 36.2	41.9	50.0	10 14.7	42.5	50.1	10 53.1	43.0	50.3	11 31.4	43.6	49.7	12 09.5	44.2	50.6	36
37	8 20.2	40.1	48.9	8 59.6	40.6	49.0	9 38.9	41.2	49.1	10 18.1	41.8	49.3	10 57.2	42.4	49.4	11 36.1	43.0	49.6	12 15.0	43.5	49.0	12 53.7	44.1	49.9	37
38	9 00.3	39.9	48.1	9 40.2	40.6	48.3	10 20.1	41.1	48.4	10 59.9	41.7	48.5	11 39.6	42.3	48.7	12 19.1	42.9	48.9	12 58.5	43.4	48.3	13 37.8	44.0	49.2	38
39	9 40.2	39.9	47.4	10 20.8	40.5	47.5	11 01.3	41.0	47.7	11 41.6	41.6	47.8	12 21.9	42.1	48.0	13 02.0	42.7	48.1	13 41.9	43.2	47.6	14 21.8	43.8	48.5	39
40	10 20.1	+39.8	46.6	11 01.3	+40.3	46.8	11 42.3	+40.9	46.9	12 23.2	+41.5	47.1	13 04.0	+42.1	47.2	13 44.7	+42.6	47.4	14 25.2	+43.2	46.9	15 05.6	+43.7	47.8	40
41	10 59.9	39.7	45.9	11 41.6	40.3	46.0	12 23.2	40.8	46.2	13 04.7	41.4	46.3	13 46.1	41.9	46.5	14 27.3	42.5	46.7	15 08.4	43.0	46.2	15 49.3	43.6	47.1	41
42	11 39.6	39.5	45.1	12 21.9	40.1	45.3	13 04.0	40.7	45.4	13 46.1	41.2	45.6	14 28.0	41.8	45.8	15 09.8	42.3	46.0	15 51.4	42.9	45.4	16 32.9	43.5	46.4	42
43	12 19.1	39.4	44.3	13 02.0	39.9	44.5	13 44.7	40.5	44.7	14 27.3	41.2	44.8	15 09.8	41.6	45.0	15 52.1	42.2	45.2	16 34.3	42.7	44.7	17 16.4	43.2	45.6	43
44	12 58.5	39.3	43.6	13 41.9	39.9	43.7	14 25.2	40.4	43.9	15 08.4	40.9	44.1	15 51.4	41.5	44.3	16 34.3	42.1	44.5	17 17.1	42.5	44.0	17 59.6	43.1	44.9	44

	38°	39°	40°	41°	42°	43°	44°	45°	
45	13 37.8 +39.1 42.8	14 21.8 +39.7 43.0	15 05.6 +40.3 43.1	15 49.3 +40.8 43.3	16 32.9 +41.3 43.5	17 16.4 +41.8 43.7	17 59.6 +42.4 44.0	18 42.7 +43.0 44.2	45
46	14 16.9 39.0 42.0	15 01.5 39.5 42.2	15 45.9 40.0 42.4	16 30.1 40.6 42.4	17 14.2 41.2 42.8	17 58.2 41.7 43.0	18 42.0 42.3 43.2	19 25.7 42.7 43.4	46
47	14 55.9 38.8 41.2	15 41.0 39.3 41.4	16 25.9 39.9 41.6	17 10.7 40.5 41.6	17 55.4 41.0 41.8	18 39.9 41.5 42.2	19 24.3 42.0 42.5	20 08.4 42.6 42.7	47
48	15 34.7 38.7 40.4	16 20.3 39.2 40.6	17 05.8 39.7 40.8	17 51.2 40.3 40.8	18 36.4 40.7 41.2	19 21.4 41.3 41.5	20 06.3 41.8 41.7	20 51.0 42.4 41.9	48
49	16 13.4 38.4 39.6	16 59.5 39.0 39.8	17 45.5 39.6 40.0	18 31.4 40.1 40.0	19 17.1 40.6 40.5	20 02.7 41.1 40.7	20 48.1 41.7 40.9	21 33.4 42.1 41.2	49
50	16 51.8 +38.3 38.8	17 38.5 +38.8 39.0	18 25.1 +39.3 39.2	19 11.5 +39.8 39.2	19 57.7 +40.4 39.7	20 43.8 +40.9 39.9	21 29.8 +41.4 40.2	22 15.5 +42.0 40.4	50
51	17 30.1 38.1 38.0	18 17.3 38.6 38.1	19 04.4 39.1 38.4	19 51.3 39.7 38.4	20 38.1 40.2 38.9	21 24.7 40.7 39.1	22 11.2 41.2 39.4	22 57.5 41.7 39.6	51
52	18 08.2 37.9 37.2	18 55.9 38.4 37.4	19 43.5 38.9 37.6	20 31.0 39.4 37.6	21 18.3 39.9 38.1	22 05.4 40.4 38.3	22 52.4 40.9 38.6	23 39.2 41.5 38.9	52
53	18 46.1 37.6 36.4	19 34.3 38.2 36.6	20 22.4 38.7 36.8	21 10.4 39.2 36.8	21 58.2 39.7 37.3	22 45.8 40.2 37.5	23 33.3 40.7 37.8	24 20.7 41.2 38.1	53
54	19 23.7 37.5 35.6	20 12.5 37.9 35.8	21 01.1 38.4 36.0	21 49.6 38.9 36.0	22 37.9 39.4 36.5	23 26.0 40.0 36.7	24 14.0 40.5 37.0	25 01.9 40.9 37.3	54
55	20 01.2 +37.2 34.7	20 50.4 +37.7 35.0	21 39.5 +38.2 35.2	22 28.5 +38.7 35.2	23 17.3 +39.2 35.7	24 06.0 +39.7 35.9	24 54.5 +40.2 36.2	25 42.8 +40.7 36.5	55
56	20 38.4 36.9 33.9	21 28.1 37.5 34.1	22 17.7 38.0 34.3	23 07.2 38.4 34.3	23 56.5 38.9 34.8	24 45.7 39.4 35.1	25 34.7 39.9 35.4	26 23.5 40.5 35.6	56
57	21 15.3 36.8 33.1	22 05.6 37.2 33.1	22 55.7 37.6 33.5	23 45.6 38.2 33.5	24 35.4 38.7 34.0	25 25.1 39.1 34.3	26 14.6 39.6 34.5	27 04.0 40.1 34.8	57
58	21 52.1 36.4 32.2	22 42.8 36.9 32.4	23 33.3 37.4 32.7	24 23.8 37.9 32.7	25 14.1 38.3 33.2	26 04.2 38.9 33.4	26 54.2 39.4 33.7	27 44.1 39.8 34.0	58
59	22 28.5 36.2 31.4	23 19.7 36.6 31.6	24 10.7 37.1 31.8	25 01.7 37.5 31.8	25 52.4 38.1 32.3	26 43.1 38.5 32.6	27 33.6 39.0 32.8	28 23.9 39.5 33.1	59
60	23 04.7 +35.8 30.5	23 56.3 +36.3 30.7	24 47.8 +36.8 30.9	25 39.2 +37.3 30.9	26 30.5 +37.7 31.4	27 21.6 +38.2 31.7	28 12.6 +38.7 32.0	29 03.4 +39.1 32.3	60
61	23 40.5 35.6 29.6	24 32.6 36.1 29.8	25 24.6 36.5 30.1	26 16.5 36.9 30.1	27 08.2 37.4 30.3	27 59.8 38.3 30.8	28 51.3 38.3 31.1	29 42.5 38.9 31.4	61
62	24 16.1 35.3 28.7	25 08.7 35.7 29.0	26 01.1 36.2 29.2	26 53.4 36.7 29.2	27 45.6 37.1 29.7	28 37.7 37.5 30.0	29 29.6 38.0 30.2	30 21.4 38.4 30.5	62
63	24 51.4 35.0 27.8	25 44.4 35.4 28.1	26 37.3 35.8 28.3	27 30.1 36.2 28.3	28 22.7 36.7 28.8	29 15.2 37.2 29.1	30 07.6 37.6 29.3	30 59.8 38.1 29.6	63
64	25 26.4 34.6 26.9	26 19.8 35.1 27.2	27 13.1 35.5 27.4	28 06.3 36.0 27.4	28 59.4 36.4 27.9	29 52.4 36.7 28.2	30 45.2 37.3 28.4	31 37.9 37.7 28.7	64
65	26 01.0 +34.3 26.0	26 54.9 +34.7 26.3	27 48.6 +35.1 26.5	28 42.3 +35.5 26.5	29 35.8 +36.0 27.0	30 29.2 +36.4 27.2	31 22.5 +36.8 27.5	32 15.6 +37.3 27.8	65
66	26 35.3 33.9 25.1	27 29.6 34.3 25.3	28 23.7 34.8 25.6	29 17.8 35.2 25.6	30 11.8 35.5 26.1	31 05.6 36.0 26.3	31 59.3 36.5 26.6	32 52.9 36.9 26.9	66
67	27 09.2 33.7 24.2	28 03.9 34.0 24.2	28 58.5 34.3 24.6	29 53.0 34.7 24.6	30 47.3 35.2 25.1	31 41.6 35.6 25.4	32 35.8 36.0 25.7	33 29.8 36.6 25.9	67
68	27 42.8 33.2 23.3	28 37.9 33.5 23.5	29 32.8 34.0 23.7	30 27.7 34.4 23.7	31 22.5 34.8 24.2	32 17.2 35.2 24.4	33 11.8 35.5 24.7	34 06.2 36.0 25.0	68
69	28 16.0 32.8 22.3	29 11.4 33.2 22.5	30 06.8 33.5 22.8	31 02.1 33.9 22.8	31 57.3 34.3 23.2	32 52.4 34.7 23.5	33 47.3 35.2 23.7	34 42.2 35.5 24.0	69
70	28 48.8 +32.3 21.4	29 44.6 +32.7 21.6	30 40.3 +33.2 21.8	31 36.0 +33.5 21.8	32 31.6 +33.9 22.3	33 27.1 +34.2 22.5	34 22.5 +34.6 22.8	35 17.7 +35.1 23.0	70
71	29 21.1 32.0 20.4	30 17.3 32.4 20.6	31 13.5 32.6 20.8	32 09.5 33.0 20.8	33 05.5 33.4 21.3	34 01.3 33.8 21.5	34 57.1 34.1 21.8	35 52.8 34.5 22.0	71
72	29 53.1 31.5 19.4	30 49.7 31.8 19.6	31 46.1 32.2 19.8	32 42.5 32.6 19.8	33 38.9 32.9 20.3	34 35.1 33.3 20.5	35 31.2 33.7 20.8	36 27.3 34.0 21.0	72
73	30 24.6 31.1 18.5	31 21.5 31.4 18.6	32 18.3 31.8 18.8	33 15.1 32.1 18.8	34 11.8 32.4 19.3	35 08.4 32.7 19.5	36 04.9 33.1 19.7	37 01.3 33.5 20.0	73
74	30 55.7 30.7 17.5	31 52.9 31.0 17.5	32 50.1 31.2 17.8	33 47.2 31.5 17.8	34 44.2 31.9 18.3	35 41.1 32.6 18.5	36 38.0 32.6 18.7	37 34.8 32.9 18.9	74
75	31 26.4 +30.1 16.5	32 23.9 +30.4 16.6	33 21.3 +30.8 16.8	34 18.7 +31.1 16.8	35 16.1 +31.3 17.2	36 13.4 +31.6 17.4	37 10.6 +32.0 17.7	38 07.7 +32.3 17.9	75
76	31 56.5 29.7 15.4	32 54.3 29.9 15.6	33 52.1 30.2 15.8	34 49.8 30.5 15.8	35 47.4 30.9 16.2	36 45.0 31.2 16.4	37 42.6 31.4 16.6	38 40.0 31.8 16.8	76
77	32 26.2 29.4 14.4	33 24.2 29.4 14.4	34 22.3 29.7 14.7	35 20.3 30.0 14.7	36 18.3 30.2 15.1	37 16.2 30.5 15.3	38 14.0 30.8 15.5	39 11.8 31.1 15.7	77
78	32 55.3 28.6 13.4	33 53.7 28.8 13.5	34 52.0 29.1 13.7	35 50.3 29.3 13.7	36 48.5 29.6 14.0	37 46.7 29.9 14.2	38 44.8 30.2 14.4	39 42.9 30.5 14.6	78
79	33 23.9 28.1 12.3	34 22.5 28.4 12.3	35 21.1 28.6 12.6	36 19.6 28.8 12.6	37 18.1 29.1 12.9	38 16.6 29.3 13.1	39 15.0 29.6 13.3	40 13.4 29.8 13.5	79
80	33 52.0 +27.6 11.3	34 50.9 +27.7 11.4	35 49.7 +27.9 11.5	36 48.4 +28.2 11.5	37 47.2 +28.4 11.8	38 45.9 +28.6 12.0	39 44.6 +28.8 12.2	40 43.2 +29.1 12.4	80
81	34 19.6 27.0 10.2	35 18.6 27.2 10.3	36 17.6 27.4 10.4	37 16.6 27.4 10.4	38 15.6 27.8 10.7	39 14.5 28.0 10.9	40 13.4 28.2 11.0	41 12.3 28.4 11.2	81
82	34 46.6 26.3 9.1	35 45.8 26.6 9.2	36 45.0 26.7 9.3	37 44.2 26.9 9.3	38 43.4 27.1 9.6	39 42.5 27.3 9.7	40 41.6 27.5 9.9	41 40.7 27.7 10.0	82
83	35 12.9 25.8 8.0	36 12.4 25.9 8.1	37 11.7 26.1 8.2	38 11.1 26.3 8.3	39 10.5 26.4 8.4	40 09.8 26.6 8.6	41 09.1 26.8 8.7	42 08.4 27.0 8.8	83
84	35 38.7 25.2 6.9	36 38.3 25.3 7.0	37 37.8 25.5 7.1	38 37.4 25.5 7.1	39 36.9 25.7 7.3	40 36.4 25.9 7.4	41 35.9 26.0 7.5	42 35.4 26.2 7.6	84
85	36 03.9 +24.6 5.8	37 03.6 +24.7 5.9	38 03.3 +24.8 5.9	39 03.0 +24.8 6.0	40 02.6 +25.0 6.1	41 02.3 +25.1 6.2	42 01.9 +25.3 6.4	43 01.6 +25.3 6.4	85
86	36 28.5 23.9 4.6	37 28.3 23.9 4.7	38 28.1 24.0 4.8	39 27.8 24.2 4.8	40 27.6 24.3 4.9	41 27.4 24.4 5.0	42 27.2 24.4 5.1	43 26.9 24.6 5.1	86
87	36 52.4 23.2 3.5	37 52.2 23.3 3.5	38 52.1 23.4 3.6	39 52.0 23.4 3.6	40 51.9 23.5 3.7	41 51.6 23.5 3.8	42 51.6 23.7 3.9	43 51.5 23.7 3.9	87
88	37 15.6 22.5 2.3	38 15.5 22.6 2.4	39 15.5 22.6 2.4	40 15.4 22.7 2.4	41 15.4 22.7 2.5	42 15.3 22.8 2.5	43 15.3 22.8 2.6	44 15.2 22.8 2.6	88
89	37 38.1 21.9 1.2	38 38.1 21.9 1.2	39 38.1 21.9 1.2	40 38.1 21.9 1.2	41 38.1 21.9 1.2	42 38.1 21.9 1.2	43 38.1 21.9 1.3	44 38.0 22.0 1.3	89
90	38 00.0 +21.1 0.0	39 00.0 +21.1 0.0	40 00.0 +21.1 0.0	41 00.0 +21.1 0.0	42 00.0 +21.1 0.0	43 00.0 +21.1 0.0	44 00.0 +21.1 0.0	45 00.0 +21.0 0.0	90
	38°	39°	40°	41°	42°	43°	44°	45°	

LATITUDE SAME NAME AS DECLINATION

N. Lat. { L.H.A. greater than 180°......Zn=Z
{ L.H.A. less than 180°.........Zn=360°−Z

Dec.	38° Hc	d	Z	39° Hc	d	Z	40° Hc	d	Z	41° Hc	d	Z	42° Hc	d	Z	43° Hc	d	Z	44° Hc	d	Z	45° Hc	d	Z	Dec.
0	15 38.1	+38.3	102.6	15 24.9	+39.1	102.9	15 11.3	+39.9	103.2	14 57.5	+40.7	103.4	14 43.5	+41.4	103.7	14 29.1	+42.2	103.9	14 14.6	+42.9	104.2	13 59.7	+43.7	104.4	0
1	16 16.4	38.1	101.8	16 04.0	38.9	102.1	15 51.2	39.7	102.4	15 38.2	40.5	102.7	15 24.9	41.3	102.9	15 11.3	42.1	103.2	14 57.5	42.8	103.5	14 43.4	43.5	103.7	1
2	16 54.5	37.9	101.0	16 42.9	38.7	101.3	16 30.9	39.6	101.6	16 18.7	40.4	101.9	16 06.2	41.1	102.2	15 53.4	41.9	102.5	15 40.3	42.6	102.7	15 26.9	43.4	103.0	2
3	17 32.4	37.7	100.2	17 21.6	38.5	100.5	17 10.5	39.3	100.8	16 59.1	40.1	101.1	16 47.3	41.0	101.4	16 35.3	41.7	101.7	16 22.9	42.5	102.0	16 10.3	43.3	102.3	3
4	18 10.1	37.5	99.4	18 00.1	38.4	99.7	17 49.8	39.2	100.0	17 39.2	40.0	100.3	17 28.3	40.8	100.7	17 17.0	41.6	101.0	17 05.4	42.4	101.3	16 53.6	43.1	101.6	4
5	18 47.6	+37.2	98.6	18 38.5	+38.1	98.9	18 29.0	+39.0	99.2	18 19.2	+39.8	99.6	18 09.1	+40.6	99.9	17 58.6	+41.4	100.2	17 47.8	+42.2	100.5	17 36.7	+42.9	100.8	5
6	19 24.8	37.1	97.7	19 16.6	37.9	98.1	19 08.0	38.7	98.4	18 59.0	39.6	98.8	18 49.7	40.4	99.1	18 40.0	41.2	99.4	18 30.0	41.9	99.8	18 19.6	42.8	100.1	6
7	20 01.9	36.8	96.9	19 54.5	37.7	97.3	19 46.7	38.5	97.6	19 38.6	39.3	98.0	19 30.1	40.2	98.3	19 21.2	41.0	98.6	19 11.9	41.9	99.0	19 02.4	42.5	99.4	7
8	20 38.7	36.6	96.1	20 32.2	37.4	96.4	20 25.2	38.3	96.8	20 17.9	39.2	97.2	20 10.3	39.9	97.5	20 02.2	40.8	97.9	19 53.8	41.6	98.3	19 44.9	42.4	98.6	8
9	21 15.3	36.3	95.2	21 09.6	37.2	95.6	21 03.5	38.1	96.0	20 57.1	38.9	96.4	20 50.2	39.8	96.7	20 43.0	40.6	97.1	20 35.4	41.4	97.5	20 27.3	42.2	97.9	9
10	21 51.6	+36.0	94.4	21 46.8	+36.9	94.8	21 41.6	+37.8	95.2	21 36.0	+38.7	95.5	21 30.0	+39.5	95.9	21 23.6	+40.4	96.3	21 16.8	+41.2	96.7	21 09.5	+42.0	97.1	10
11	22 27.6	35.8	93.5	22 23.7	36.7	93.9	22 19.4	37.6	94.3	22 14.7	38.4	94.7	22 09.5	39.3	95.1	22 04.0	40.1	95.5	21 58.0	40.9	95.9	21 51.5	41.8	96.3	11
12	23 03.4	35.4	92.6	23 00.4	36.4	93.0	22 57.0	37.3	93.5	22 53.1	38.2	93.9	22 48.8	39.1	94.3	22 44.1	39.9	94.7	22 38.9	40.8	95.1	22 33.3	41.6	95.6	12
13	23 38.8	35.2	91.7	23 36.8	36.1	92.2	23 34.3	37.0	92.6	23 31.3	37.9	93.1	23 27.9	38.7	93.5	23 24.0	39.6	93.9	23 19.7	40.4	94.4	23 14.9	41.3	94.8	13
14	24 14.0	34.9	90.9	24 12.9	35.7	91.3	24 11.3	36.7	91.8	24 09.2	37.6	92.2	24 06.6	38.5	92.7	24 03.6	39.4	93.1	24 00.1	40.3	93.5	23 56.2	41.1	94.0	14
15	24 48.9	+34.5	90.0	24 48.6	+35.5	90.4	24 48.0	+36.4	90.9	24 46.8	+37.3	91.4	24 45.1	+38.2	91.8	24 43.0	+39.1	92.3	24 40.4	+39.9	92.7	24 37.3	+40.8	93.2	15
16	25 23.4	34.2	89.1	25 24.1	35.2	89.5	25 24.4	36.0	90.0	25 24.1	37.0	90.5	25 23.3	38.0	91.0	25 22.1	38.8	91.4	25 20.3	39.7	91.9	25 18.1	40.5	92.4	16
17	25 57.6	33.8	88.2	25 59.3	34.8	88.6	26 00.4	35.8	89.1	26 01.1	36.7	89.6	26 01.3	37.6	90.1	26 00.9	38.5	90.6	26 00.0	39.4	91.1	25 58.6	40.3	91.6	17
18	26 31.4	33.5	87.2	26 34.1	34.5	87.7	26 36.2	35.4	88.2	26 37.8	36.4	88.7	26 38.9	37.2	89.2	26 39.4	38.2	89.7	26 39.4	39.1	90.2	26 38.9	40.0	90.7	18
19	27 04.9	33.2	86.3	27 08.6	34.1	86.8	27 11.6	35.1	87.3	27 14.2	36.0	87.8	27 16.1	37.0	88.4	27 17.6	37.9	88.9	27 18.5	38.8	89.4	27 18.9	39.7	89.9	19
20	27 38.1	+32.7	85.4	27 42.7	+33.7	85.9	27 46.7	+34.7	86.4	27 50.2	+35.6	86.9	27 53.1	+36.6	87.5	27 55.5	+37.5	88.0	27 57.3	+38.5	88.5	27 58.6	+39.3	89.1	20
21	28 10.8	32.4	84.4	28 16.4	33.3	84.9	28 21.4	34.3	85.5	28 25.8	35.3	86.0	28 29.7	36.3	86.6	28 33.0	37.2	87.1	28 35.8	38.1	87.7	28 37.9	39.1	88.2	21
22	28 43.2	31.9	83.5	28 49.7	33.0	84.0	28 55.7	33.9	84.5	29 01.1	34.9	85.1	29 06.0	35.8	85.7	29 10.2	36.8	86.2	29 13.9	37.8	86.8	29 17.0	38.7	87.3	22
23	29 15.1	31.5	82.5	29 22.7	32.5	83.0	29 29.6	33.6	83.6	29 36.0	34.5	84.2	29 41.8	35.5	84.7	29 47.0	36.5	85.3	29 51.7	37.4	85.9	29 55.7	38.3	86.4	23
24	29 46.6	31.1	81.5	29 55.2	32.1	82.1	30 03.2	33.1	82.6	30 10.5	34.1	83.2	30 17.3	35.1	83.8	30 23.5	36.1	84.4	30 29.1	37.0	85.0	30 34.0	38.0	85.6	24
25	30 17.7	+30.6	80.5	30 27.3	+31.6	81.1	30 36.3	+32.6	81.7	30 44.6	+33.7	82.3	30 52.4	+34.7	82.9	30 59.6	+35.6	83.5	31 06.1	+36.6	84.1	31 12.0	+37.6	84.7	25
26	30 48.3	30.2	79.5	30 58.9	31.2	80.1	31 08.9	32.3	80.7	31 18.3	33.3	81.3	31 27.1	34.2	81.9	31 35.2	35.3	82.5	31 42.7	36.2	83.1	31 49.6	37.2	83.7	26
27	31 18.5	29.7	78.5	31 30.1	30.8	79.1	31 41.2	31.7	79.7	31 51.6	32.7	80.3	32 01.3	33.8	80.9	32 10.5	34.8	81.6	32 18.9	35.8	82.2	32 26.8	36.7	82.8	27
28	31 48.2	29.2	77.5	32 00.9	30.2	78.1	32 12.9	31.3	78.7	32 24.3	32.4	79.3	32 35.1	33.4	80.0	32 45.3	34.3	80.6	32 54.7	35.4	81.2	33 03.5	36.4	81.9	28
29	32 17.4	28.7	76.5	32 31.1	29.8	77.1	32 44.2	30.8	77.7	32 56.7	31.8	78.3	33 08.5	32.8	79.0	33 19.6	33.9	79.6	33 30.1	34.9	80.3	33 39.9	35.9	80.9	29
30	32 46.1	+28.1	75.4	33 00.9	+29.2	76.0	33 15.0	+30.3	76.7	33 28.5	+31.3	77.3	33 41.3	+32.4	78.0	33 53.5	+33.4	78.6	34 05.0	+34.4	79.3	34 15.8	+35.4	80.0	30
31	33 14.2	27.7	74.4	33 30.1	28.7	75.0	33 45.3	29.7	75.6	33 59.8	30.8	76.3	34 13.7	31.9	77.0	34 26.9	32.9	77.6	34 39.4	34.0	78.3	34 51.2	35.0	79.0	31
32	33 41.9	27.0	73.3	33 58.8	28.1	73.9	34 15.0	29.3	74.6	34 30.6	30.3	75.3	34 45.6	31.3	75.9	34 59.8	32.4	76.6	35 13.4	33.4	77.3	35 26.2	34.5	78.0	32
33	34 08.9	26.6	72.2	34 26.9	27.6	72.9	34 44.3	28.6	73.5	35 00.9	29.8	74.2	35 16.9	30.8	74.9	35 32.2	31.9	75.6	35 46.8	32.9	76.3	36 00.7	33.9	77.0	33
34	34 35.5	25.9	71.1	34 54.5	27.0	71.8	35 12.9	28.1	72.5	35 30.7	29.1	73.1	35 47.7	30.3	73.8	36 04.1	31.3	74.5	36 19.7	32.4	75.2	36 34.6	33.5	76.0	34
35	35 01.4	+25.3	70.0	35 21.5	+26.4	70.7	35 41.0	+27.5	71.4	35 59.8	+28.6	72.1	36 18.0	+29.6	72.8	36 35.4	+30.7	73.5	36 52.1	+31.8	74.2	37 08.1	+32.8	74.9	35
36	35 26.7	24.7	68.9	35 47.9	25.8	69.6	36 08.5	26.9	70.3	36 28.4	28.0	71.0	36 47.6	29.1	71.7	37 06.1	30.2	72.4	37 23.9	31.2	73.1	37 40.9	32.3	73.9	36
37	35 51.4	24.1	67.8	36 13.7	25.2	68.5	36 35.4	26.3	69.2	36 56.4	27.3	69.9	37 16.7	28.4	70.6	37 36.3	29.5	71.3	37 55.1	30.7	72.0	38 13.2	31.8	72.8	37
38	36 15.5	23.4	66.7	36 38.9	24.5	67.4	37 01.7	25.6	68.1	37 23.7	26.8	68.8	37 45.1	27.8	69.5	38 05.8	28.9	70.2	38 25.8	30.0	71.0	38 45.0	31.1	71.7	38
39	36 38.9	22.8	65.5	37 03.4	23.8	66.2	37 27.3	24.9	66.9	37 50.5	26.0	67.6	38 12.9	27.2	68.4	38 34.7	28.3	69.0	38 55.8	29.3	69.8	39 16.1	30.4	70.6	39
40	37 01.7	+22.0	64.4	37 27.3	+23.2	65.1	37 52.2	+24.3	65.8	38 16.5	+25.4	66.5	38 40.1	+26.5	67.2	39 03.0	+27.6	68.0	39 25.1	+28.8	68.7	39 46.5	+29.9	69.5	40
41	37 23.7	21.4	63.2	37 50.5	22.4	63.9	38 16.5	23.6	64.6	38 41.9	24.7	65.3	39 06.6	25.8	66.1	39 30.6	26.9	66.8	39 53.9	28.0	67.6	40 16.4	29.1	68.4	41
42	37 45.1	20.7	62.0	38 12.9	21.8	62.7	38 40.1	22.9	63.4	39 06.6	24.0	64.2	39 32.4	25.1	64.9	39 57.5	26.2	65.7	40 21.9	27.3	66.4	40 45.5	28.5	67.2	42
43	38 05.8	20.0	60.8	38 34.7	21.0	61.5	39 03.0	22.1	62.2	39 30.6	23.3	63.0	39 57.5	24.4	63.7	40 23.7	25.5	64.5	40 49.2	26.6	65.2	41 14.0	27.7	66.0	43
44	38 25.8	19.2	59.6	38 55.8	20.3	60.3	39 25.1	21.4	61.0	39 53.9	22.5	61.8	40 21.9	23.6	62.5	40 49.2	24.8	63.3	41 15.8	25.9	64.1	41 41.7	27.0	64.9	44

LATITUDE SAME NAME AS DECLINATION

N. Lat. { L.H.A. greater than 180° ...... Zn=Z
{ L.H.A. less than 180° ...... Zn=360°-Z

Dec.	38° Hc	d	Z	39° Hc	d	Z	40° Hc	d	Z	41° Hc	d	Z	42° Hc	d	Z	43° Hc	d	Z	44° Hc	d	Z	45° Hc	d	Z	Dec.
0	13 19.2	+37.9	100.7	13 08.0	+38.7	100.9	12 56.5	+39.5	101.1	12 44.9	+40.2	101.3	12 32.9	+41.1	101.6	12 20.8	+41.8	101.8	12 08.4	+42.6	102.0	11 55.9	+43.3	102.2	0
1	13 57.1	37.7	99.9	13 46.7	38.5	100.1	13 36.0	39.4	100.3	13 25.1	40.0	100.6	13 14.0	40.9	100.8	13 02.6	41.7	101.0	12 51.0	42.5	101.3	12 39.2	43.2	101.5	1
2	14 34.8	37.6	99.1	14 25.2	38.4	99.3	14 15.4	39.2	99.6	14 05.3	40.0	99.8	13 54.9	40.8	100.1	13 44.3	41.6	100.3	13 33.5	42.3	100.5	13 22.4	43.1	100.8	2
3	15 12.4	37.4	98.3	15 03.6	38.3	98.5	14 54.6	39.1	98.8	14 45.3	39.9	99.0	14 35.7	40.7	99.3	14 25.9	41.4	99.6	14 15.8	42.2	99.8	14 05.5	42.9	100.1	3
4	15 49.8	37.2	97.4	15 41.9	38.0	97.7	15 33.7	38.8	98.1	15 25.2	39.7	98.1	15 16.4	40.5	98.5	15 07.3	41.3	98.8	14 58.0	42.1	99.1	14 48.4	42.8	99.3	4
5	16 27.0	+37.0	96.6	16 19.9	+37.9	96.9	16 12.5	+38.7	97.2	16 04.9	+39.5	97.5	15 56.9	+40.3	97.8	15 48.6	+41.1	98.1	15 40.1	+41.9	98.3	15 31.2	+42.7	98.6	5
6	17 04.0	36.8	95.8	16 57.8	37.6	96.1	16 51.2	38.5	96.4	16 44.4	39.3	96.7	16 37.2	40.2	97.0	16 29.7	41.0	97.3	16 22.0	41.7	97.6	16 13.9	42.5	97.9	6
7	17 40.8	36.6	95.0	17 35.4	37.5	95.3	17 29.7	38.4	95.6	17 23.7	39.2	95.9	17 17.4	40.0	96.2	17 10.7	40.8	96.5	17 03.7	41.6	96.8	16 56.4	42.4	97.1	7
8	18 17.4	36.4	94.1	18 12.9	37.3	94.5	18 08.1	38.1	94.8	18 02.9	38.9	95.1	17 57.4	39.7	95.4	17 51.5	40.6	95.8	17 45.3	41.4	96.1	17 38.8	42.2	96.4	8
9	18 53.8	36.2	93.3	18 50.2	37.0	93.6	18 46.2	37.9	94.0	18 41.8	38.8	94.3	18 37.1	39.6	94.7	18 32.1	40.4	95.0	18 26.7	41.2	95.3	18 21.0	42.0	95.7	9
10	19 30.0	+35.9	92.5	19 27.2	+36.8	92.8	19 24.1	+37.7	93.2	19 20.6	+38.5	93.5	19 16.7	+39.4	93.9	19 12.5	+40.2	94.2	19 07.9	+41.0	94.6	19 03.0	+41.8	94.9	10
11	20 05.9	35.7	91.6	20 04.0	36.6	92.0	20 01.8	37.4	92.3	19 59.1	38.3	92.7	19 56.1	39.2	93.1	19 52.7	39.9	93.4	19 48.9	40.9	93.8	19 44.8	41.6	94.1	11
12	20 41.6	35.4	90.7	20 40.6	36.3	91.1	20 39.2	37.2	91.5	20 37.4	38.1	91.9	20 35.3	38.9	92.3	20 32.7	39.8	92.6	20 29.8	40.6	93.0	20 26.4	41.5	93.4	12
13	21 17.0	35.2	89.9	21 16.9	36.1	90.3	21 16.4	37.0	90.7	21 15.5	37.9	91.1	21 14.2	38.7	91.4	21 12.5	39.6	91.8	21 10.4	40.4	92.2	21 07.9	41.2	92.6	13
14	21 52.2	34.8	89.0	21 53.0	35.8	89.4	21 53.4	36.7	89.8	21 53.4	37.5	90.2	21 52.9	38.5	90.6	21 52.1	39.3	91.0	21 50.8	40.2	91.4	21 49.1	41.0	91.8	14
15	22 27.0	+34.6	88.1	22 28.8	+35.5	88.5	22 30.1	+36.4	89.0	22 30.9	+37.4	89.4	22 31.4	+38.2	89.8	22 31.4	+39.1	90.2	22 31.0	+39.9	90.6	22 30.1	+40.7	91.0	15
16	23 01.6	34.3	87.2	23 04.3	35.2	87.7	23 06.5	36.1	88.1	23 08.3	37.0	88.5	23 09.6	37.9	89.0	23 10.5	38.8	89.4	23 10.9	39.6	89.8	23 10.8	40.6	90.2	16
17	23 35.9	34.0	86.4	23 39.5	34.9	86.8	23 42.6	35.9	87.2	23 45.3	36.8	87.7	23 47.5	37.7	88.1	23 49.3	38.5	88.5	23 50.5	39.5	89.0	23 51.4	40.4	89.4	17
18	24 09.9	33.7	85.5	24 14.4	34.6	85.9	24 18.5	35.5	86.4	24 22.1	36.4	86.8	24 25.2	37.3	87.3	24 27.8	38.3	87.7	24 30.0	39.1	88.2	24 31.6	40.0	88.6	18
19	24 43.6	33.3	84.5	24 49.0	34.3	85.0	24 54.0	35.2	85.5	24 58.5	36.2	85.9	25 02.5	37.1	86.4	25 06.1	37.9	86.9	25 09.1	38.9	87.3	25 11.6	39.8	87.8	19
20	25 16.9	+33.0	83.6	25 23.3	+34.0	84.1	25 29.2	+34.9	84.6	25 34.7	+35.8	85.0	25 39.6	+36.7	85.5	25 44.0	+37.7	86.0	25 48.0	+38.5	86.5	25 51.4	+39.4	87.0	20
21	25 49.9	32.6	82.7	25 57.3	33.5	83.2	26 04.1	34.6	83.7	26 10.5	35.5	84.2	26 16.3	36.5	84.6	26 21.7	37.3	85.1	26 26.5	38.3	85.6	26 30.8	39.2	86.1	21
22	26 22.5	32.3	81.8	26 30.8	33.3	82.3	26 38.7	34.2	82.8	26 46.0	35.1	83.3	26 52.8	36.1	83.8	26 59.0	37.0	84.3	27 04.8	37.9	84.8	27 10.0	38.8	85.3	22
23	26 54.8	31.9	80.8	27 04.1	32.8	81.3	27 12.9	33.8	81.8	27 21.1	34.8	82.3	27 28.9	35.7	82.9	27 36.0	36.7	83.4	27 42.7	37.6	83.9	27 48.8	38.5	84.4	23
24	27 26.7	31.4	79.9	27 36.9	32.5	80.4	27 46.7	33.5	80.9	27 55.9	34.4	81.4	28 04.6	35.4	82.0	28 12.7	36.3	82.5	28 20.3	37.2	83.0	28 27.3	38.2	83.6	24
25	27 58.1	+31.1	78.9	28 09.4	+32.1	79.4	28 20.2	+33.0	80.0	28 30.3	+34.1	80.5	28 40.0	+35.0	81.0	28 49.0	+36.0	81.6	28 57.5	+36.9	82.1	29 05.5	+37.8	82.7	25
26	28 29.2	30.7	77.9	28 41.5	31.7	78.5	28 53.2	32.7	79.0	29 04.4	33.6	79.6	29 15.0	34.6	80.1	29 25.0	35.6	80.7	29 34.4	36.6	81.2	29 43.3	37.5	81.8	26
27	28 59.9	30.2	77.0	29 13.2	31.2	77.5	29 25.9	32.2	78.1	29 38.0	33.2	78.6	29 49.6	34.1	79.2	30 00.6	35.1	79.7	30 11.0	36.1	80.3	30 20.8	37.1	80.9	27
28	29 30.1	29.8	76.0	29 44.4	30.8	76.5	29 58.1	31.8	77.1	30 11.2	32.8	77.6	30 23.8	33.8	78.2	30 35.7	34.8	78.8	30 47.1	35.7	79.4	30 57.9	36.7	80.0	28
29	29 59.9	29.4	75.0	30 15.2	30.4	75.5	30 29.9	31.4	76.1	30 44.0	32.4	76.7	30 57.6	33.3	77.3	31 10.5	34.4	77.8	31 22.8	35.4	78.4	31 34.6	36.3	79.0	29
30	30 29.3	+28.8	74.0	30 45.6	+29.9	74.5	31 01.3	+30.9	75.1	31 16.4	+31.9	75.7	31 30.9	+32.9	76.3	31 44.9	+33.9	76.9	31 58.2	+34.9	77.5	32 10.9	+35.8	78.1	30
31	30 58.1	28.4	72.9	31 15.5	29.4	73.5	31 32.2	30.4	74.1	31 48.3	31.5	74.7	32 03.8	32.5	75.3	32 18.8	33.4	75.9	32 33.1	34.4	76.5	32 46.7	35.5	77.2	31
32	31 26.5	27.9	71.9	31 44.9	28.9	72.5	32 02.6	29.9	73.1	32 19.8	30.9	73.7	32 36.3	32.0	74.3	32 52.2	33.0	74.9	33 07.5	34.0	75.6	33 22.2	34.9	76.2	32
33	31 54.4	27.4	70.9	32 13.8	28.4	71.5	32 32.5	29.5	72.1	32 50.7	30.5	72.7	33 08.3	31.5	73.3	33 25.2	32.5	73.9	33 41.5	33.5	74.6	33 57.1	34.6	75.2	33
34	32 21.8	26.8	69.8	32 42.2	27.8	70.4	33 02.0	28.9	71.1	33 21.2	29.9	71.6	33 39.8	30.9	72.3	33 57.7	32.0	72.9	34 15.0	33.0	73.6	34 31.7	34.0	74.2	34
35	32 48.6	+26.3	68.8	33 10.0	+27.4	69.4	33 30.9	+28.4	70.0	33 51.1	+29.4	70.6	34 10.7	+30.5	71.2	34 29.7	+31.5	71.9	34 48.0	+32.5	72.6	35 05.7	+33.5	73.2	35
36	33 14.9	25.7	67.7	33 37.4	26.8	68.3	33 59.3	27.8	68.9	34 20.5	28.9	69.6	34 41.2	29.9	70.2	35 01.2	30.9	70.9	35 20.5	32.0	71.5	35 39.2	33.0	72.2	36
37	33 40.6	25.2	66.6	34 04.2	26.2	67.2	34 27.1	27.3	67.8	34 49.4	28.3	68.5	35 11.1	29.3	69.1	35 32.1	30.4	69.8	35 52.5	31.4	70.5	36 12.2	32.5	71.2	37
38	34 05.8	24.6	65.5	34 30.4	25.6	66.1	34 54.4	26.6	66.8	35 17.7	27.7	67.4	35 40.4	28.8	68.1	36 02.5	29.8	68.7	36 23.9	30.9	69.4	36 44.7	31.9	70.1	38
39	34 30.4	24.0	64.4	34 56.0	25.0	65.0	35 21.0	26.1	65.7	35 45.4	27.2	66.3	36 09.2	28.2	67.0	36 32.3	29.3	67.7	36 54.8	30.3	68.4	37 16.6	31.3	69.1	39
40	34 54.4	+23.3	63.3	35 21.0	+24.4	63.9	35 47.1	+25.5	64.6	36 12.6	+26.5	65.2	36 37.4	+27.6	65.9	37 01.6	+28.6	66.5	37 25.1	+29.7	67.3	37 47.9	+30.8	68.0	40
41	35 17.7	22.7	62.2	35 45.4	23.8	62.8	36 12.6	24.8	63.4	36 39.1	25.9	64.1	37 05.0	26.9	64.8	37 30.2	28.0	65.5	37 54.8	29.0	66.2	38 18.7	30.1	66.9	41
42	35 40.4	22.1	61.0	36 09.2	23.1	61.7	36 37.4	24.2	62.3	37 05.0	25.2	63.0	37 31.9	26.3	63.7	37 58.2	27.4	64.4	38 23.8	28.5	65.1	38 48.8	29.5	65.8	42
43	36 02.5	21.4	59.9	36 32.3	22.5	60.5	37 01.6	23.5	61.2	37 30.2	24.6	61.8	37 58.2	25.7	62.5	38 25.6	26.7	63.2	38 52.3	27.7	63.9	39 18.3	28.8	64.7	43
44	36 23.9	20.8	58.7	36 54.8	21.8	59.4	37 25.1	22.8	60.0	37 54.8	23.9	60.7	38 23.8	25.0	61.4	38 52.3	26.0	62.1	39 20.0	27.1	62.8	39 47.1	28.2	63.5	44

Dec.	38° Hc	d	Z	39° Hc	d	Z	40° Hc	d	Z	41° Hc	d	Z	42° Hc	d	Z	43° Hc	d	Z	44° Hc	d	Z	45° Hc	d	Z	Dec.
0	10 12.6	−37.6	98.1	10 04.1	−38.4	98.3	9 55.4	−39.2	98.4	9 46.5	−40.0	98.6	9 37.4	−40.8	98.8	9 28.2	−41.6	98.9	9 18.7	−42.2	99.1	9 09.2	−43.1	99.3	0
1	9 35.0	37.7	98.9	9 25.7	38.5	99.0	9 16.2	39.3	99.2	9 06.5	40.1	99.4	8 56.6	40.8	99.5	8 46.6	41.6	99.7	8 36.5	42.4	99.8	8 26.1	43.0	100.0	1
2	8 57.3	37.8	99.7	8 47.2	38.6	99.8	8 36.9	39.4	100.0	8 26.4	40.2	100.1	8 15.8	41.0	100.3	8 05.0	41.7	100.4	7 54.1	42.4	100.5	7 43.1	43.2	100.7	2
3	8 19.5	37.8	100.5	8 08.6	38.7	100.6	7 57.5	39.4	100.7	7 46.2	40.2	100.9	7 34.8	41.0	101.0	7 23.3	41.7	101.1	7 11.7	42.5	101.3	6 59.9	43.2	101.4	3
4	7 41.7	38.0	101.2	7 29.9	38.8	101.4	7 18.0	39.6	101.5	7 06.0	40.3	101.6	6 53.8	41.0	101.7	6 41.6	41.9	101.9	6 29.2	42.6	102.0	6 16.7	43.3	102.1	4
5	7 03.7	−38.1	102.0	6 51.1	−38.8	102.1	6 38.4	−39.6	102.3	6 25.7	−40.4	102.4	6 12.8	−41.2	102.5	5 59.7	−41.8	102.6	5 46.6	−42.6	102.7	5 33.4	−43.3	102.8	5
6	6 25.6	38.1	102.8	6 12.3	38.9	102.8	5 58.8	39.7	103.0	5 45.3	40.5	103.1	5 31.6	41.2	103.2	5 17.9	42.0	103.3	5 04.0	42.6	103.4	4 50.1	43.4	103.5	6
7	5 47.5	38.2	103.6	5 33.4	39.0	103.7	5 19.1	39.7	103.8	5 04.8	40.5	103.9	4 50.4	41.2	103.9	4 35.9	41.9	104.0	4 21.4	42.7	104.1	4 06.7	43.4	104.2	7
8	5 09.3	38.2	104.3	4 54.4	39.0	104.4	4 39.4	39.8	104.5	4 24.3	40.6	104.6	4 09.2	41.3	104.7	3 54.0	42.1	104.7	3 38.7	42.8	104.8	3 23.3	43.4	104.9	8
9	4 31.1	38.3	105.1	4 15.4	39.1	105.2	3 59.6	39.8	105.3	3 43.8	40.6	105.3	3 27.9	41.3	105.4	3 11.9	42.0	105.4	2 55.9	42.7	105.5	2 39.9	43.5	105.5	9
10	3 52.8	−38.3	105.9	3 36.3	−39.1	106.0	3 19.8	−39.9	106.0	3 03.2	−40.6	106.1	2 46.6	−41.4	106.1	2 29.9	−42.1	106.2	2 13.2	−42.8	106.2	1 56.4	−43.4	106.2	10
11	3 14.5	38.4	106.7	2 57.2	39.1	106.7	2 39.9	39.9	106.8	2 22.6	40.6	106.8	2 05.2	41.3	106.8	1 47.8	42.0	106.9	1 30.4	42.8	106.9	1 13.0	43.5	106.9	11
12	2 36.1	38.4	107.5	2 18.1	39.2	107.5	2 00.0	39.9	107.5	1 42.0	40.7	107.5	1 23.9	41.4	107.5	1 05.8	42.1	107.6	0 47.6	42.8	107.6	0 29.5	−43.5	107.6	12
13	1 57.7	38.4	108.2	1 38.9	39.1	108.2	1 20.1	39.9	108.3	1 01.3	40.6	108.3	0 42.5	41.4	108.3	0 23.7	−42.1	108.3	0 04.8	−42.8	108.3	0 14.0	+43.5	71.7	13
14	1 19.3	38.5	109.0	0 59.8	39.2	109.0	0 40.2	39.9	109.0	0 20.7	40.7	109.0	0 01.1	−41.4	109.0	0 18.4	+42.1	71.0	0 38.0	+42.8	71.0	0 57.5	43.5	71.0	14
15	0 40.8	−38.4	109.7	0 20.6	−39.2	109.7	0 00.3	−39.9	109.8	0 20.0	+40.6	69.5	0 40.3	+41.3	70.3	1 00.5	+42.1	70.3	1 20.8	+42.7	70.3	1 41.0	+43.4	70.3	15
16	0 02.4	−38.4	110.5	0 18.6	+39.2	69.5	0 39.6	+40.0	69.5	1 00.6	40.6	68.8	1 21.6	41.3	69.5	1 42.6	42.1	69.6	2 03.5	42.8	69.6	2 24.4	43.5	69.6	16
17	0 36.0	+38.5	68.7	0 57.8	39.2	68.7	1 19.6	39.9	68.8	1 41.3	40.6	68.0	2 03.0	41.3	68.8	2 24.7	42.0	68.8	2 46.3	42.7	68.9	3 07.9	43.4	68.9	17
18	1 14.5	38.4	68.0	1 37.0	39.1	68.0	1 59.5	39.9	68.0	2 21.9	40.6	68.0	2 44.3	41.3	68.1	3 06.7	42.0	68.1	3 29.0	42.7	68.2	3 51.3	43.4	68.2	18
19	1 52.9	38.4	67.2	2 16.1	39.2	67.2	2 39.4	39.8	67.3	3 02.5	40.6	67.3	3 25.6	41.3	67.4	3 48.7	42.0	67.4	4 11.7	42.7	67.5	4 34.7	43.3	67.6	19
20	2 31.3	+38.4	66.4	2 55.3	+39.1	66.5	3 19.2	+39.8	66.5	3 43.1	+40.5	66.6	4 06.9	+41.3	66.6	4 30.7	+41.9	66.7	4 54.4	+42.6	66.8	5 18.0	+43.3	66.9	20
21	3 09.7	38.3	65.6	3 34.4	39.0	65.7	3 59.0	39.8	65.8	4 23.6	40.5	65.8	4 48.2	41.2	65.9	5 12.6	41.9	66.0	5 37.0	42.6	66.1	6 01.3	43.2	66.2	21
22	3 48.0	38.3	64.9	4 13.4	39.1	64.9	4 38.8	39.6	65.0	5 04.1	40.5	65.0	5 29.4	41.1	65.2	5 54.5	41.8	65.3	6 19.6	42.5	65.4	6 44.5	43.2	65.5	22
23	4 26.3	38.2	64.1	4 52.5	38.9	64.2	5 18.6	39.6	64.3	5 44.6	40.4	64.3	6 10.5	41.1	64.4	6 36.3	41.8	64.5	7 02.1	42.4	64.7	7 27.7	43.1	64.8	23
24	5 04.5	38.2	63.3	5 31.4	38.9	63.4	5 58.2	39.7	63.5	6 25.0	40.3	63.6	6 51.6	41.0	63.7	7 18.1	41.7	63.8	7 44.5	42.4	63.9	8 10.8	43.1	64.1	24
25	5 42.7	+38.2	62.6	6 10.3	+38.9	62.7	6 37.9	+39.5	62.8	7 05.3	+40.2	62.9	7 32.6	+40.9	62.9	7 59.8	+41.6	63.1	8 26.9	+42.3	63.2	8 53.9	+42.9	63.4	25
26	6 20.9	38.0	61.8	6 49.2	38.8	61.9	7 17.4	39.5	62.0	7 45.5	40.2	62.1	8 13.5	40.9	62.2	8 41.4	41.6	62.4	9 09.2	42.3	62.5	9 36.8	42.9	62.7	26
27	6 58.9	38.0	61.0	7 28.0	38.7	61.1	7 56.9	39.4	61.2	8 25.7	40.1	61.4	8 54.4	40.8	61.5	9 23.0	41.4	61.6	9 51.4	42.1	61.8	10 19.7	42.8	61.9	27
28	7 36.9	37.9	60.2	8 06.7	38.6	60.3	8 36.3	39.3	60.5	9 05.8	40.0	60.6	9 35.2	40.7	60.8	10 04.4	41.4	60.9	10 33.5	42.1	61.1	11 02.5	42.7	61.2	28
29	8 14.8	37.8	59.4	8 45.3	38.5	59.6	9 15.6	39.2	59.7	9 45.8	39.9	59.9	10 15.9	40.5	60.0	10 45.8	41.2	60.2	11 15.6	41.9	60.3	11 45.2	42.5	60.5	29
30	8 52.6	+37.7	58.7	9 23.8	+38.4	58.8	9 54.8	+39.1	58.9	10 25.7	+39.8	59.1	10 56.4	+40.5	59.3	11 27.0	+41.2	59.4	11 57.5	+41.8	59.6	12 27.7	+42.5	59.8	30
31	9 30.3	37.6	57.9	10 02.2	38.3	58.0	10 33.9	39.0	58.2	11 05.5	39.6	58.3	11 36.9	40.3	58.5	12 08.2	41.0	58.7	12 39.3	41.7	58.9	13 10.2	42.3	59.1	31
32	10 07.9	37.5	57.1	10 40.5	38.2	57.2	11 12.9	38.9	57.4	11 45.1	39.6	57.6	12 17.2	40.3	57.7	12 49.2	40.9	57.9	13 21.0	41.5	58.1	13 52.5	42.2	58.3	32
33	10 45.4	37.4	56.3	11 18.7	38.0	56.4	11 51.8	38.7	56.6	12 24.7	39.4	56.8	12 57.5	40.1	57.0	13 30.1	40.7	57.2	14 02.5	41.4	57.4	14 34.7	42.1	57.6	33
34	11 22.8	37.2	55.5	11 56.7	37.9	55.7	12 30.5	38.6	55.8	13 04.1	39.3	56.0	13 37.6	39.9	56.2	14 10.8	40.6	56.4	14 43.9	41.3	56.6	15 16.8	41.9	56.9	34
35	12 00.0	+37.1	54.7	12 34.6	+37.8	54.9	13 09.1	+38.5	55.1	13 43.4	+39.1	55.2	14 17.5	+39.8	55.5	14 51.4	+40.5	55.7	15 25.2	+41.1	55.9	15 58.7	+41.8	56.1	35
36	12 37.1	37.0	53.9	13 12.4	37.7	54.1	13 47.6	38.3	54.3	14 22.5	39.0	54.5	14 57.3	39.6	54.7	15 31.9	40.3	54.9	16 06.3	41.0	55.1	16 40.5	41.6	55.4	36
37	13 14.1	36.8	53.1	13 50.1	37.4	53.3	14 25.9	38.1	53.5	15 01.5	38.8	53.7	15 36.9	39.5	53.9	16 12.2	40.1	54.1	16 47.3	40.7	54.4	17 22.1	41.4	54.6	37
38	13 50.9	36.6	52.3	14 27.5	37.4	52.5	15 04.0	38.0	52.7	15 40.3	38.7	52.9	16 16.4	39.3	53.1	16 52.3	39.8	53.4	17 28.0	40.5	53.6	18 03.5	41.3	53.9	38
39	14 27.5	36.5	51.4	15 04.9	37.1	51.7	15 42.0	37.8	51.9	16 19.0	38.4	52.1	16 55.7	39.1	52.3	17 32.3	39.8	52.6	18 08.6	40.5	52.8	18 44.8	41.1	53.1	39
40	15 04.0	+36.3	50.6	15 42.0	+37.0	50.8	16 19.8	+37.6	51.1	16 57.4	+38.3	51.3	17 34.8	+39.0	51.5	18 12.1	+39.5	51.8	18 49.1	+40.2	52.1	19 25.9	+40.8	52.3	40
41	15 40.3	36.1	49.8	16 19.0	36.7	50.0	16 57.4	37.4	50.2	17 35.7	38.1	50.5	18 13.8	38.7	50.7	18 51.6	39.4	51.0	19 29.3	40.0	51.3	20 06.7	40.7	51.5	41
42	16 16.4	35.9	49.0	16 55.7	36.6	49.2	17 34.8	37.4	49.4	18 13.8	37.8	49.7	18 52.5	38.5	49.9	19 31.0	39.2	50.2	20 09.3	39.8	50.5	20 47.4	40.2	50.8	42
43	16 52.3	35.7	48.1	17 32.3	36.3	48.4	18 12.1	37.0	48.6	18 51.6	37.7	48.9	19 31.0	38.3	49.1	20 10.2	38.9	49.4	20 49.1	39.6	49.7	21 27.8	40.0	50.0	43
44	17 28.0	35.5	47.3	18 08.6	36.2	47.5	18 49.1	36.8	47.8	19 29.3	37.4	48.0	20 09.3	38.1	48.3	20 49.1	38.7	48.6	21 28.7	39.3	48.9	22 08.0	40.0	49.2	44

	38° Hc	d	Z	39° Hc	d	Z	40° Hc	d	Z	41° Hc	d	Z	42° Hc	d	Z	43° Hc	d	Z	44° Hc	d	Z	45° Hc	d	Z	
45	18 03.5	+35.3	46.4	18 44.8	+35.9	46.7	19 25.6	+36.5	46.9	20 06.7	+37.2	47.2	20 47.4	+37.8	47.5	21 27.8	+38.5	47.8	22 08.0	+39.2	48.1	22 48.0	+39.8	48.4	45
46	18 38.8	35.0	45.6	19 20.7	35.7	45.8	20 02.4	36.3	46.1	20 43.9	37.0	46.4	21 25.2	37.6	46.6	22 06.3	38.2	46.9	22 47.2	38.8	47.2	23 27.8	39.5	47.5	46
47	19 13.8	34.8	44.7	19 56.4	35.4	45.0	20 38.7	36.1	45.2	21 20.9	36.7	45.5	22 02.8	37.3	45.8	22 44.5	38.0	46.1	23 26.0	38.6	46.4	24 07.3	39.2	46.7	47
48	19 48.6	34.6	43.9	20 31.8	35.2	44.1	21 14.8	35.8	44.4	21 57.6	36.4	44.7	22 40.1	37.1	45.0	23 22.5	37.7	45.3	24 04.6	38.3	45.6	24 46.5	38.9	45.9	48
49	20 23.2	34.3	43.0	21 07.0	34.9	43.3	21 50.6	35.5	43.5	22 34.0	36.1	43.8	23 17.2	36.7	43.9	24 00.2	37.3	44.1	24 42.9	38.0	44.7	25 25.4	38.7	45.1	49
50	20 57.5	+34.0	42.1	21 41.9	+34.6	42.4	22 26.1	+35.3	42.7	23 10.1	+35.9	42.7	23 53.9	+36.5	42.9	24 37.5	+37.2	43.5	25 20.9	+37.7	43.9	26 04.1	+38.3	44.2	50
51	21 31.5	33.7	41.2	22 16.5	34.4	41.5	23 01.4	34.9	41.8	23 46.0	35.6	42.1	24 30.4	36.2	42.1	25 14.7	36.7	42.7	25 58.6	37.5	43.0	26 42.4	38.0	43.3	51
52	22 05.2	33.5	40.3	22 50.9	34.0	40.6	23 36.3	34.7	40.9	24 21.6	35.2	41.1	25 06.6	35.9	41.2	25 51.4	36.2	41.8	26 36.1	37.0	42.1	27 20.4	37.7	42.5	52
53	22 38.7	33.1	39.4	23 24.9	33.7	39.7	24 11.0	34.3	40.0	24 56.8	35.0	40.3	25 42.5	35.5	40.3	26 27.6	36.2	40.9	27 13.1	36.8	41.3	27 58.1	37.4	41.6	53
54	23 11.8	32.8	38.5	23 58.6	33.5	38.8	24 45.3	34.0	39.1	25 31.8	34.6	39.4	26 18.0	35.2	39.4	27 04.1	35.8	40.0	27 49.9	36.4	40.4	28 35.5	37.0	40.7	54
55	23 44.6	+32.5	37.6	24 32.1	+33.0	37.9	25 19.3	+33.7	38.2	26 06.4	+34.2	38.5	26 53.2	+34.9	38.5	27 39.9	+35.4	39.1	28 26.3	+36.1	39.5	29 12.5	+36.7	39.8	55
56	24 17.1	32.2	36.7	25 05.1	32.8	37.0	25 53.0	33.3	37.3	26 40.6	33.9	37.5	27 28.1	34.5	37.6	28 15.3	35.1	38.2	29 02.4	35.6	38.6	29 49.2	36.2	38.9	56
57	24 49.3	31.8	35.8	25 37.9	32.4	36.1	26 26.3	33.0	36.3	27 14.5	33.6	36.6	28 02.6	34.1	36.6	28 50.4	34.7	37.3	29 38.0	35.3	37.6	30 25.4	35.9	38.0	57
58	25 21.1	31.5	34.8	26 10.3	32.0	35.1	26 59.3	32.5	35.4	27 48.1	33.1	35.7	28 36.7	33.7	35.7	29 25.1	34.3	36.4	30 13.3	34.9	36.7	31 01.3	35.5	37.1	58
59	25 52.6	31.1	33.9	26 42.3	31.6	34.2	27 31.8	32.2	34.5	28 21.2	32.8	34.8	29 10.4	33.3	34.8	29 59.4	33.9	35.4	30 48.2	34.6	35.8	31 36.8	35.1	36.1	59
60	26 23.7	+30.7	32.9	27 13.9	+31.3	33.2	28 04.0	+31.8	33.5	28 54.0	+32.3	33.8	29 43.7	+33.0	33.8	30 33.3	+33.5	34.5	31 22.7	+34.0	34.8	32 11.9	+34.6	35.2	60
61	26 54.4	30.3	32.0	27 45.2	30.8	32.3	28 35.8	31.4	32.5	29 26.3	32.0	32.8	30 16.7	32.4	32.8	31 06.8	33.0	33.5	31 56.7	33.6	33.8	32 46.5	34.1	34.2	61
62	27 24.7	29.9	31.0	28 16.0	30.5	31.3	29 07.2	31.0	31.6	29 58.3	31.5	31.9	30 49.1	32.1	31.9	31 39.8	32.6	32.5	32 30.3	33.2	32.8	33 20.6	33.7	33.2	62
63	27 54.6	29.5	30.0	28 46.5	30.0	30.3	29 38.2	30.5	30.6	30 29.8	31.0	30.9	31 21.2	31.5	30.9	32 12.4	32.1	31.5	33 03.5	32.6	31.9	33 54.3	33.2	32.2	63
64	28 24.1	29.0	29.1	29 16.5	29.5	29.3	30 08.7	30.1	29.6	31 00.8	30.6	29.9	31 52.7	31.1	29.9	32 44.5	31.6	30.5	33 36.1	32.2	30.9	34 27.5	32.7	31.2	64
65	28 53.1	+28.7	28.1	29 46.0	+29.1	28.3	30 38.8	+29.6	28.6	31 31.4	+30.1	28.9	32 23.8	+30.7	28.9	33 16.1	+31.2	29.5	34 08.3	+31.6	29.8	35 00.2	+32.2	30.2	65
66	29 21.8	28.1	27.0	30 15.1	28.7	27.3	31 08.4	29.1	27.6	32 01.5	29.6	27.9	32 54.5	30.1	27.9	33 47.3	30.6	28.5	34 39.9	31.2	28.8	35 32.4	31.7	29.1	66
67	29 49.9	27.7	26.0	30 43.8	28.1	26.3	31 37.5	28.6	26.6	32 31.1	29.1	26.8	33 24.6	29.6	26.8	34 17.9	30.1	27.4	35 11.1	30.6	27.8	36 04.1	31.1	28.1	67
68	30 17.6	27.2	25.0	31 11.9	27.7	25.3	32 06.1	28.1	25.5	33 00.2	28.6	25.8	33 54.2	29.0	25.8	34 48.0	29.5	26.4	35 41.7	30.0	26.7	36 35.2	30.5	27.0	68
69	30 44.8	26.7	24.0	31 39.6	27.1	24.2	32 34.2	27.6	24.5	33 28.8	28.0	24.7	34 23.2	28.5	24.7	35 17.5	29.0	25.3	36 11.7	29.4	25.6	37 05.7	29.9	26.0	69
70	31 11.5	+26.2	22.9	32 06.7	+26.6	23.2	33 01.8	+27.1	23.4	33 56.8	+27.5	23.7	34 51.7	+28.0	23.7	35 46.5	+28.4	24.3	36 41.1	+28.9	24.6	37 35.6	+29.4	24.9	70
71	31 37.7	25.7	21.9	32 33.3	26.1	22.1	33 28.9	26.5	22.4	34 24.3	26.9	22.6	35 19.7	27.3	22.6	36 14.9	27.8	23.2	37 10.0	28.2	23.5	38 05.0	28.6	23.8	71
72	32 03.4	25.1	20.8	32 59.4	25.5	21.0	33 55.4	25.9	21.3	34 51.2	26.4	21.5	35 47.0	26.8	21.5	36 42.7	27.1	22.1	37 38.2	27.6	22.3	38 33.6	28.1	22.6	72
73	32 28.5	24.6	19.7	33 24.9	25.0	20.0	34 21.3	25.3	20.2	35 17.6	25.7	20.4	36 13.8	26.1	20.4	37 09.8	26.6	20.9	38 05.8	27.0	21.2	39 01.7	27.4	21.5	73
74	32 53.1	24.0	18.7	33 49.9	24.4	18.9	34 46.6	24.8	19.1	35 43.3	25.1	19.3	36 39.9	25.5	19.3	37 36.4	25.9	19.8	38 32.8	26.3	20.1	39 29.1	26.7	20.4	74
75	33 17.1	+23.4	17.6	34 14.3	+23.7	17.6	35 11.4	+24.1	18.0	36 08.4	+24.5	18.2	37 05.4	+24.8	18.2	38 02.3	+25.2	18.7	38 59.1	+25.6	18.9	39 55.8	+26.0	19.2	75
76	33 40.5	22.9	16.5	34 38.0	23.2	16.6	35 35.5	23.5	16.9	36 32.9	23.8	17.1	37 30.2	24.2	17.1	38 27.5	24.5	17.5	39 24.7	24.8	17.8	40 21.8	25.2	18.0	76
77	34 03.4	22.2	15.3	35 01.2	22.5	15.5	35 59.0	22.8	15.7	36 56.7	23.2	15.9	37 54.4	23.5	15.9	38 52.0	23.8	16.4	39 49.5	24.2	16.6	40 47.0	24.5	16.8	77
78	34 25.6	21.6	14.2	35 23.7	21.9	14.4	36 21.8	22.2	14.6	37 19.9	22.5	14.8	38 17.9	22.8	14.8	39 15.8	23.1	15.2	40 13.7	23.4	15.4	41 11.5	23.8	15.6	78
79	34 47.2	21.0	13.1	35 45.6	21.3	13.2	36 44.0	21.5	13.4	37 42.4	21.7	13.6	38 40.7	22.0	13.6	39 38.9	22.4	14.0	40 37.1	22.7	14.2	41 35.3	22.9	14.4	79
80	35 08.2	+20.3	11.9	36 06.9	+20.5	12.1	37 05.5	+20.8	12.2	38 04.1	+21.1	12.4	39 02.7	+21.3	12.6	40 01.3	+21.6	12.8	40 59.8	+21.8	13.0	41 58.2	+22.1	13.2	80
81	35 28.5	19.7	10.8	36 27.4	19.9	10.9	37 26.3	20.1	11.1	38 25.2	20.3	11.2	39 24.0	20.6	11.4	40 22.9	20.8	11.5	41 21.6	21.1	11.7	42 20.3	21.4	11.9	81
82	35 48.2	19.0	9.6	36 47.3	19.2	9.7	37 46.4	19.4	9.9	38 45.5	19.6	10.0	39 44.6	19.8	10.2	40 43.7	20.0	10.3	41 42.7	20.2	10.5	42 41.7	20.4	10.6	82
83	36 07.2	18.3	8.5	37 06.5	18.5	8.6	38 05.8	18.7	8.7	39 05.1	18.8	8.8	40 04.4	19.0	8.9	41 03.7	19.2	9.1	42 02.9	19.4	9.2	43 02.1	19.6	9.3	83
84	36 25.5	17.5	7.3	37 25.0	17.7	7.4	38 24.5	17.9	7.5	39 23.9	18.1	7.6	40 23.4	18.2	7.7	41 22.9	18.3	7.8	42 22.3	18.5	7.9	43 21.7	18.7	8.1	84
85	36 43.0	+16.9	6.1	37 42.7	+17.0	6.2	38 42.4	+17.1	6.2	39 42.0	+17.2	6.3	40 41.6	+17.4	6.3	41 41.2	+17.6	6.5	42 40.8	+17.7	6.6	43 40.4	+17.8	6.7	85
86	36 59.9	16.2	4.9	37 59.7	16.2	4.9	38 59.5	16.3	5.0	39 59.2	16.5	5.1	40 59.0	16.6	5.1	41 58.8	16.6	5.2	42 58.5	16.8	5.3	43 58.2	16.9	5.4	86
87	37 16.1	15.4	3.7	38 15.9	15.5	3.7	39 15.8	15.6	3.8	40 15.7	15.6	3.8	41 15.6	15.7	3.8	42 15.4	15.8	4.0	43 15.3	15.8	4.0	44 15.1	15.9	4.1	87
88	37 31.5	14.6	2.5	38 31.4	14.7	2.5	39 31.4	14.7	2.5	40 31.3	14.8	2.6	41 31.2	14.9	2.6	42 31.2	14.8	2.6	43 31.1	14.9	2.7	44 31.0	15.0	2.7	88
89	37 46.1	13.9	1.2	38 46.1	13.9	1.2	39 46.1	13.9	1.3	40 46.1	13.9	1.3	41 46.1	13.9	1.3	42 46.0	14.0	1.3	43 46.0	14.0	1.3	44 46.0	14.0	1.4	89
90	38 00.0	+13.1	0.0	39 00.0	+13.1	0.0	40 00.0	+13.1	0.0	41 00.0	+13.1	0.0	42 00.0	+13.0	0.0	43 00.0	+13.0	0.0	44 00.0	+13.0	0.0	45 00.0	+13.0	0.0	90

S. Lat. { L.H.A. greater than 180°......Zn=180°−Z
{ L.H.A. less than 180°.........Zn=180°+Z

LATITUDE SAME NAME AS DECLINATION

L.H.A. 103°, 257°

79°, 281° L.H.A.

LATITUDE SAME NAME AS DECLINATION

N. Lat. $\begin{cases} \text{L.H.A. greater than } 180° \ldots\ldots \text{Zn=Z} \\ \text{L.H.A. less than } 180° \ldots\ldots \text{Zn=360°−Z} \end{cases}$

Dec.	38° Hc	38° d	38° Z	39° Hc	39° d	39° Z	40° Hc	40° d	40° Z	41° Hc	41° d	41° Z	42° Hc	42° d	42° Z	43° Hc	43° d	43° Z	44° Hc	44° d	44° Z	45° Hc	45° d	45° Z	Dec.
0	8 38.9	+37.3	96.8	8 31.7	+38.1	97.0	8 24.3	+38.9	97.1	8 16.8	+39.7	97.3	8 09.1	+40.5	97.4	8 01.3	+41.3	97.6	7 53.3	+42.1	97.7	7 45.2	+42.8	97.8	0
1	9 16.2	37.2	96.0	9 09.8	38.0	96.2	9 03.2	38.9	96.4	8 56.5	39.7	96.5	8 49.6	40.5	96.7	8 42.6	41.2	96.8	8 35.4	41.9	97.0	8 28.0	42.7	97.1	1
2	9 53.4	37.1	95.2	9 47.8	37.9	95.4	9 42.1	38.7	95.6	9 36.2	39.5	95.7	9 30.1	40.3	95.9	9 23.8	41.1	96.1	9 17.3	41.9	96.2	9 10.7	42.7	96.4	2
3	10 30.5	37.0	94.4	10 25.7	37.9	94.6	10 20.8	38.6	94.8	10 15.7	39.4	95.0	10 10.4	40.2	95.2	10 04.9	41.0	95.3	9 59.2	41.8	95.5	9 53.4	42.5	95.7	3
4	11 07.5	36.8	93.6	11 03.6	37.6	93.8	10 59.4	38.6	94.0	10 55.1	39.4	94.2	10 50.6	40.1	94.4	10 45.9	40.9	94.6	10 41.0	41.7	94.8	10 35.9	42.4	95.0	4
5	11 44.3	+36.7	92.8	11 41.2	+37.6	93.0	11 38.0	+38.3	93.2	11 34.5	+39.1	93.4	11 30.7	+40.0	93.7	11 26.8	+40.8	93.9	11 22.7	+41.5	94.1	11 18.3	+42.3	94.3	5
6	12 21.0	36.6	92.0	12 18.8	37.4	92.2	12 16.3	38.3	92.5	12 13.6	39.1	92.7	12 10.7	39.9	92.9	12 07.6	40.7	93.1	12 04.2	41.5	93.3	12 00.6	42.3	93.5	6
7	12 57.6	36.4	91.2	12 56.2	37.3	91.4	12 54.6	38.1	91.7	12 52.7	38.9	91.9	12 50.6	39.7	92.2	12 48.3	40.5	92.4	12 45.7	41.3	92.6	12 42.9	42.1	92.8	7
8	13 34.0	36.3	90.4	13 33.5	37.1	90.6	13 32.7	37.9	90.9	13 31.6	38.8	91.1	13 30.3	39.6	91.4	13 28.8	40.4	91.6	13 27.0	41.2	91.8	13 25.0	41.9	92.1	8
9	14 10.3	36.1	89.6	14 10.6	36.9	89.8	14 10.6	37.8	90.1	14 10.4	38.7	90.3	14 09.9	39.5	90.6	14 09.2	40.3	90.8	14 08.2	41.1	91.1	14 06.9	41.9	91.3	9
10	14 46.4	+35.9	88.7	14 47.5	+36.8	89.0	14 48.4	+37.7	89.3	14 49.1	+38.4	89.5	14 49.4	+39.3	89.8	14 49.5	+40.1	90.0	14 49.3	+40.9	90.3	14 48.8	+41.7	90.6	10
11	15 22.3	35.7	87.9	15 24.3	36.6	88.2	15 26.1	37.4	88.5	15 27.5	38.3	88.7	15 28.7	39.1	89.0	15 29.6	39.9	89.3	15 30.2	40.6	89.6	15 30.5	41.5	89.9	11
12	15 58.0	35.5	87.1	16 00.9	36.4	87.4	16 03.5	37.3	87.7	16 05.8	38.1	87.9	16 07.8	39.0	88.2	16 09.5	39.8	88.5	16 10.9	40.6	88.8	16 12.0	41.4	89.1	12
13	16 33.5	35.4	86.2	16 37.3	36.2	86.5	16 40.8	37.0	86.9	16 43.9	37.9	87.1	16 46.8	38.7	87.4	16 49.3	39.6	87.7	16 51.5	40.3	88.0	16 53.4	41.2	88.3	13
14	17 08.9	35.1	85.4	17 13.5	36.0	85.7	17 17.8	36.9	86.0	17 21.8	37.8	86.3	17 25.5	38.6	86.6	17 28.9	39.4	87.0	17 31.9	40.2	87.3	17 34.6	41.0	87.6	14
15	17 44.0	+34.9	84.5	17 49.5	+35.8	84.9	17 54.7	+36.7	85.2	17 59.6	+37.5	85.5	18 04.1	+38.4	85.8	18 08.3	+39.2	86.2	18 12.1	+40.1	86.5	18 15.6	+40.9	86.8	15
16	18 18.9	34.6	83.7	18 25.3	35.6	84.0	18 31.4	36.4	84.4	18 37.1	37.3	84.7	18 42.5	38.1	85.0	18 47.5	39.0	85.4	18 52.2	39.8	85.7	18 56.5	40.6	86.0	16
17	18 53.5	34.5	82.8	19 00.9	35.3	83.2	19 07.8	36.2	83.5	19 14.4	37.1	83.9	19 20.6	38.0	84.2	19 26.5	38.8	84.6	19 32.0	39.6	84.9	19 37.1	40.5	85.3	17
18	19 28.0	34.1	82.0	19 36.2	35.1	82.3	19 44.0	36.0	82.7	19 51.5	36.8	83.0	19 58.6	37.7	83.4	20 05.3	38.6	83.8	20 11.6	39.5	84.1	20 17.6	40.2	84.5	18
19	20 02.1	34.0	81.1	20 11.3	34.8	81.5	20 20.0	35.7	81.8	20 28.3	36.6	82.2	20 36.3	37.5	82.6	20 43.9	38.3	83.0	20 51.1	39.1	83.3	20 57.8	40.1	83.7	19
20	20 36.1	+33.6	80.2	20 46.1	+34.6	80.6	20 55.7	+35.5	81.0	21 04.9	+36.4	81.3	21 13.8	+37.2	81.7	21 22.2	+38.1	82.1	21 30.2	+39.0	82.5	21 37.9	+39.8	82.9	20
21	21 09.7	33.4	79.3	21 20.6	34.3	79.7	21 31.2	35.1	80.1	21 41.3	36.1	80.5	21 51.0	37.0	80.9	22 00.3	37.8	81.3	22 09.2	38.7	81.7	22 17.7	39.5	82.1	21
22	21 43.1	33.1	78.4	21 54.9	34.0	78.8	22 06.3	35.0	79.2	22 17.4	35.8	79.6	22 28.0	36.7	80.0	22 38.1	37.6	80.4	22 47.9	38.4	80.9	22 57.2	39.3	81.3	22
23	22 16.2	32.8	77.5	22 28.9	33.7	77.9	22 41.3	34.6	78.3	22 53.2	35.5	78.8	23 04.7	36.4	79.2	23 15.7	37.3	79.6	23 26.3	38.2	80.0	23 36.5	39.0	80.4	23
24	22 49.0	32.4	76.6	23 02.6	33.4	77.0	23 15.9	34.3	77.5	23 28.7	35.2	77.9	23 41.1	36.1	78.3	23 53.0	37.0	78.7	24 04.5	37.9	79.2	24 15.5	38.8	79.6	24
25	23 21.4	+32.2	75.7	23 36.0	+33.1	76.1	23 50.2	+34.0	76.6	24 03.9	+34.9	77.0	24 17.2	+35.8	77.4	24 30.0	+36.7	77.9	24 42.4	+37.6	78.3	24 54.3	+38.5	78.8	25
26	23 53.6	31.8	74.8	24 09.1	32.8	75.2	24 24.2	33.7	75.7	24 38.8	34.6	76.1	24 53.0	35.5	76.5	25 06.7	36.4	77.0	25 20.0	37.3	77.5	25 32.8	38.2	78.0	26
27	24 25.4	31.5	73.9	24 41.9	32.4	74.3	24 57.9	33.3	74.7	25 13.4	34.3	75.2	25 28.5	35.2	75.6	25 43.1	36.1	76.1	25 57.3	37.0	76.6	26 11.0	37.8	77.1	27
28	24 56.9	31.1	72.9	25 14.3	32.0	73.4	25 31.2	33.0	73.8	25 47.7	33.9	74.3	26 03.7	34.8	74.8	26 19.2	35.8	75.2	26 34.3	36.6	75.7	26 48.8	37.6	76.2	28
29	25 28.0	30.8	72.0	25 46.3	31.7	72.4	26 04.2	32.6	72.9	26 21.6	33.6	73.4	26 38.5	34.5	73.9	26 55.0	35.4	74.3	27 10.9	36.4	74.8	27 26.4	37.2	75.3	29
30	25 58.8	+30.3	71.0	26 18.0	+31.4	71.5	26 36.8	+32.3	72.0	26 55.2	+33.2	72.4	27 13.0	+34.2	72.9	27 30.4	+35.1	73.4	27 47.3	+35.9	74.0	28 03.6	+36.9	74.4	30
31	26 29.1	30.0	70.1	26 49.4	30.9	70.5	27 09.1	31.9	71.0	27 28.4	32.8	71.5	27 47.2	33.7	72.0	28 05.5	34.6	72.5	28 23.2	35.6	73.0	28 40.5	36.5	73.5	31
32	26 59.1	29.6	69.1	27 20.3	30.5	69.6	27 41.0	31.5	70.1	28 01.2	32.4	70.6	28 20.9	33.4	71.1	28 40.1	34.3	71.6	28 58.8	35.3	72.1	29 17.0	36.1	72.6	32
33	27 28.7	29.2	68.1	27 50.8	30.2	68.6	28 12.5	31.1	69.1	28 33.6	32.1	69.6	28 54.3	33.0	70.1	29 14.4	33.9	70.6	29 34.1	34.8	71.2	29 53.1	35.8	71.7	33
34	27 57.9	28.7	67.1	28 21.0	29.7	67.6	28 43.6	30.6	68.1	29 05.7	31.6	68.6	29 27.3	32.5	69.2	29 48.3	33.5	69.7	30 08.9	34.4	70.2	30 28.9	35.4	70.8	34
35	28 26.6	+28.3	66.1	28 50.7	+29.2	66.6	29 14.2	+30.2	67.1	29 37.3	+31.1	67.7	29 59.8	+32.1	68.2	30 21.8	+33.1	68.7	30 43.3	+34.0	69.3	31 04.3	+34.9	69.8	35
36	28 54.9	27.9	65.1	29 19.9	28.8	65.6	29 44.4	29.8	66.2	30 08.4	30.8	66.7	30 31.9	31.7	67.2	30 54.9	32.6	67.8	31 17.3	33.6	68.3	31 39.2	34.5	68.9	36
37	29 22.8	27.4	64.1	29 48.7	28.4	64.6	30 14.2	29.3	65.2	30 39.2	30.2	65.7	31 03.6	31.2	66.2	31 27.5	32.2	66.8	31 50.9	33.1	67.4	32 13.7	34.1	67.9	37
38	29 50.2	26.9	63.1	30 17.1	27.9	63.6	30 43.5	28.8	64.1	31 09.4	29.8	64.7	31 34.8	30.8	65.2	31 59.7	31.7	65.8	32 24.0	32.7	66.4	32 47.8	33.6	67.0	38
39	30 17.1	26.4	62.1	30 45.0	27.3	62.6	31 12.3	28.4	63.1	31 39.2	29.3	63.7	32 05.6	30.2	64.2	32 31.4	31.2	64.8	32 56.7	32.2	65.4	33 21.4	33.1	66.0	39
40	30 43.5	+25.9	61.0	31 12.3	+26.9	61.5	31 40.7	+27.8	62.1	32 08.5	+28.8	62.7	32 35.8	+29.8	63.2	33 02.6	+30.8	63.8	33 28.9	+31.7	64.4	33 54.5	+32.7	65.0	40
41	31 09.4	25.4	60.0	31 39.2	26.4	60.5	32 08.5	27.3	61.0	32 37.3	28.3	61.6	33 05.6	29.2	62.2	33 33.4	30.2	62.7	34 00.6	31.1	63.3	34 27.2	32.1	64.0	41
42	31 34.8	24.9	58.9	32 05.6	25.8	59.4	32 35.8	26.8	60.0	33 05.6	27.8	60.5	33 34.8	28.8	61.1	34 03.6	29.6	61.7	34 31.7	30.7	62.3	34 59.3	31.6	62.9	42
43	31 59.7	24.3	57.8	32 31.4	25.3	58.4	33 02.6	26.3	58.9	33 33.4	27.2	59.5	34 03.6	28.1	60.1	34 33.2	29.2	60.7	35 02.4	30.1	61.3	35 30.9	31.1	61.9	43
44	32 24.0	23.8	56.8	32 56.7	24.7	57.3	33 28.9	25.6	57.8	34 00.6	26.6	58.4	34 31.7	27.6	59.0	35 02.4	28.5	59.6	35 32.5	29.5	60.2	36 02.0	30.5	60.8	44

80°, 280° L.H.A.   LATITUDE SAME NAME AS DECLINATION

N. Lat. { L.H.A. greater than 180°......Zn=Z
L.H.A. less than 180°......Zn=360°−Z

Dec.	38° Hc	38° d	38° Z	39° Hc	39° d	39° Z	40° Hc	40° d	40° Z	41° Hc	41° d	41° Z	42° Hc	42° d	42° Z	43° Hc	43° d	43° Z	44° Hc	44° d	44° Z	45° Hc	45° d	45° Z	Dec.
0	7 51.9	+37.2	96.2	7 45.3	+38.1	96.3	7 38.7	+38.8	96.5	7 31.8	+39.7	96.6	7 24.9	+40.4	96.7	7 17.8	+41.2	96.9	7 10.5	+42.0	97.0	7 03.2	+42.7	97.1	0
1	8 29.1	37.2	95.4	8 23.4	38.0	95.6	8 17.5	38.8	95.7	8 11.5	39.6	95.8	8 05.3	40.4	96.0	7 59.0	41.1	96.1	7 52.5	41.9	96.3	7 45.9	42.6	96.4	1
2	9 06.3	37.0	94.6	9 01.4	37.9	94.8	8 56.3	38.7	94.9	8 51.1	39.5	95.1	8 45.7	40.3	95.2	8 40.1	41.1	95.4	8 34.4	41.8	95.5	8 28.5	42.6	95.7	2
3	9 43.3	37.0	93.8	9 39.3	37.7	94.0	9 35.0	38.6	94.2	9 30.6	39.4	94.3	9 26.0	40.1	94.5	9 21.2	40.9	94.6	9 16.2	41.8	94.8	9 11.1	42.5	95.0	3
4	10 20.3	36.8	93.0	10 17.0	37.7	93.2	10 13.6	38.5	93.4	10 10.0	39.2	93.6	10 06.1	40.1	93.7	10 02.1	40.9	93.9	9 58.0	41.6	94.1	9 53.6	42.4	94.3	4
5	10 57.1	+36.7	92.2	10 54.7	+37.5	92.4	10 52.1	+38.3	92.6	10 49.2	+39.2	92.8	10 46.2	+40.0	93.0	10 43.0	+40.8	93.2	10 39.6	+41.5	93.4	10 36.0	+42.3	93.5	5
6	11 33.8	36.5	91.4	11 32.2	37.4	91.6	11 30.4	38.2	91.8	11 28.4	39.0	92.0	11 26.2	39.8	92.2	11 23.8	40.6	92.4	11 21.1	41.3	92.6	11 18.3	42.2	92.8	6
7	12 10.3	36.4	90.6	12 09.6	37.2	90.8	12 08.6	38.1	91.0	12 07.4	39.0	91.2	12 06.0	39.8	91.5	12 04.4	40.5	91.7	12 02.6	41.3	91.9	12 00.5	42.1	92.1	7
8	12 46.8	36.3	89.8	12 46.8	37.2	90.0	12 46.7	38.0	90.2	12 46.4	38.7	90.5	12 45.8	39.6	90.7	12 44.9	40.4	90.9	12 43.9	41.1	91.1	12 42.6	41.9	91.4	8
9	13 23.0	36.1	89.0	13 24.0	36.9	89.2	13 24.7	37.8	89.4	13 25.1	38.7	89.7	13 25.4	39.4	89.9	13 25.3	40.3	90.2	13 25.0	41.1	90.4	13 24.5	41.8	90.6	9
10	13 59.1	+35.9	88.1	14 00.9	+36.8	88.4	14 02.5	+37.6	88.6	14 03.8	+38.4	88.9	14 04.8	+39.3	89.1	14 05.6	+40.1	89.4	14 06.1	+40.9	89.6	14 06.3	+41.7	89.9	10
11	14 35.0	35.8	87.3	14 37.7	36.6	87.6	14 40.1	37.5	87.8	14 42.2	38.4	88.1	14 44.1	39.2	88.4	14 45.7	39.9	88.6	14 47.0	40.8	88.9	14 48.0	41.6	89.1	11
12	15 10.8	35.6	86.5	15 14.3	36.5	86.8	15 17.6	37.3	87.0	15 20.6	38.1	87.3	15 23.3	38.9	87.6	15 25.6	39.8	87.8	15 27.8	40.6	88.1	15 29.6	41.4	88.4	12
13	15 46.4	35.4	85.6	15 50.8	36.2	85.9	15 54.9	37.1	86.2	15 58.7	38.0	86.5	16 02.2	38.8	86.8	16 05.4	39.7	87.1	16 08.4	40.4	87.4	16 11.0	41.2	87.6	13
14	16 21.8	35.1	84.8	16 27.0	36.1	85.1	16 32.0	36.9	85.4	16 36.7	37.8	85.7	16 41.0	38.6	86.0	16 45.1	39.4	86.3	16 48.8	40.3	86.6	16 52.2	41.1	86.9	14
15	16 56.9	+35.0	84.0	17 03.1	+35.8	84.3	17 08.9	+36.8	84.6	17 14.5	+37.5	84.9	17 19.6	+38.5	85.2	17 24.5	+39.3	85.5	17 29.1	+40.1	85.8	17 33.3	+40.9	86.1	15
16	17 31.9	34.8	83.1	17 38.9	35.7	83.4	17 45.7	36.5	83.7	17 52.0	37.4	84.1	17 58.1	38.2	84.4	18 03.8	39.0	84.7	18 09.1	39.9	85.0	18 14.2	40.7	85.4	16
17	18 06.7	34.5	82.3	18 14.6	35.4	82.6	18 22.2	36.3	82.9	18 29.4	37.2	83.2	18 36.3	38.0	83.6	18 42.8	38.9	83.9	18 49.0	39.7	84.2	18 54.9	40.5	84.6	17
18	18 41.2	34.3	81.4	18 50.0	35.2	81.7	18 58.5	36.0	82.1	19 06.6	36.9	82.4	19 14.3	37.8	82.8	19 21.7	38.7	83.1	19 28.7	39.5	83.4	19 35.4	40.3	83.8	18
19	19 15.5	34.0	80.5	19 25.2	34.9	80.9	19 34.5	35.8	81.2	19 43.5	36.7	81.6	19 52.1	37.6	81.9	20 00.4	38.4	82.3	20 08.2	39.3	82.6	20 15.7	40.1	83.0	19
20	19 49.5	+33.8	79.6	20 00.1	+34.7	80.0	20 10.3	+35.6	80.4	20 20.2	+36.5	80.7	20 29.7	+37.3	81.1	20 38.8	+38.2	81.5	20 47.5	+39.0	81.8	20 55.8	+39.9	82.2	20
21	20 23.3	33.5	78.8	20 34.8	34.4	79.1	20 45.9	35.3	79.5	20 56.7	36.2	79.9	21 07.0	37.1	80.3	21 17.0	37.9	80.6	21 26.5	38.8	81.0	21 35.7	39.6	81.4	21
22	20 56.8	33.3	77.9	21 09.2	34.2	78.2	21 21.2	35.1	78.6	21 32.9	35.9	79.0	21 44.1	36.8	79.4	21 54.9	37.7	79.8	22 05.3	38.6	80.2	22 15.3	39.4	80.6	22
23	21 30.1	32.9	77.0	21 43.4	33.8	77.4	21 56.3	34.8	77.8	22 08.8	35.7	78.2	22 20.9	36.6	78.6	22 32.6	37.4	79.0	22 43.9	38.3	79.4	22 54.7	39.2	79.8	23
24	22 03.0	32.7	76.1	22 17.2	33.6	76.5	22 31.1	34.4	76.9	22 44.5	35.3	77.3	22 57.5	36.2	77.7	23 10.0	37.2	78.1	23 22.2	38.0	78.5	23 33.9	38.8	79.0	24
25	22 35.7	+32.3	75.2	22 50.8	+33.3	75.6	23 05.5	+34.2	76.0	23 19.8	+35.1	76.4	23 33.7	+36.0	76.8	23 47.2	+36.8	77.3	24 00.2	+37.7	77.7	24 12.7	+38.6	78.1	25
26	23 08.0	32.0	74.3	23 24.1	32.9	74.7	23 39.7	33.9	75.1	23 54.9	34.8	75.5	24 09.7	35.7	76.0	24 24.0	36.6	76.4	24 37.9	37.5	76.8	24 51.3	38.4	77.3	26
27	23 40.0	31.7	73.3	23 57.0	32.7	73.8	24 13.6	33.5	74.2	24 29.7	34.5	74.6	24 45.4	35.3	75.1	25 00.6	36.3	75.5	25 15.4	37.1	76.0	25 29.7	38.0	76.4	27
28	24 11.7	31.4	72.4	24 29.7	32.2	72.8	24 47.1	33.2	73.3	25 04.2	34.1	73.7	25 20.7	35.1	74.2	25 36.9	35.9	74.6	25 52.5	36.8	75.1	26 07.7	37.7	75.6	28
29	24 43.1	31.0	71.5	25 01.9	32.0	71.9	25 20.3	32.9	72.4	25 38.3	33.8	72.8	25 55.8	34.7	73.3	26 12.8	35.6	73.8	26 29.3	36.6	74.2	26 45.4	37.4	74.7	29
30	25 14.1	+30.7	70.5	25 33.9	+31.6	71.0	25 53.2	+32.5	71.4	26 12.1	+33.4	71.9	26 30.5	+34.3	72.4	26 48.4	+35.3	72.9	27 05.9	+36.1	73.3	27 22.8	+37.1	73.8	30
31	25 44.8	30.2	69.6	26 05.5	31.2	70.0	26 25.7	32.2	70.5	26 45.5	33.1	71.0	27 04.8	34.0	71.5	27 23.7	34.9	71.9	27 42.0	35.8	72.4	27 59.9	36.7	72.9	31
32	26 15.0	29.9	68.6	26 36.7	30.8	69.1	26 57.9	31.7	69.6	27 18.6	32.7	70.0	27 38.8	33.6	70.5	27 58.6	34.5	71.0	28 17.8	35.5	71.5	28 36.6	36.3	72.0	32
33	26 44.9	29.5	67.7	27 07.5	30.0	68.1	27 29.6	31.4	68.6	27 51.3	32.3	69.1	28 12.4	33.3	69.6	28 33.1	34.2	70.1	28 53.3	35.0	70.6	29 12.9	36.0	71.1	33
34	27 14.4	29.2	66.7	27 37.9	30.0	67.1	28 01.0	30.9	67.6	28 23.6	31.9	68.1	28 45.7	32.8	68.6	29 07.3	33.7	69.2	29 28.3	34.7	69.7	29 48.9	35.6	70.2	34
35	27 43.5	+28.6	65.7	28 07.9	+29.6	66.2	28 31.9	+30.6	66.7	28 55.5	+31.4	67.2	29 18.5	+32.4	67.7	29 41.0	+33.4	68.2	30 03.0	+34.3	68.7	30 24.5	+35.2	69.3	35
36	28 12.1	28.2	64.7	28 37.5	29.2	65.2	29 02.5	30.1	65.7	29 26.9	31.1	66.2	29 50.9	32.0	66.7	30 14.4	32.9	67.3	30 37.3	33.8	67.8	30 59.7	34.8	68.3	36
37	28 40.3	27.8	63.7	29 06.7	28.7	64.2	29 32.6	29.6	64.7	29 58.0	30.6	65.2	30 22.9	31.5	65.7	30 47.3	32.5	66.3	31 11.1	33.5	66.8	31 34.5	34.3	67.4	37
38	29 08.1	27.3	62.7	29 35.4	28.3	63.2	30 02.2	29.2	63.7	30 28.6	30.1	64.2	30 54.4	31.1	64.7	31 19.8	32.0	65.3	31 44.6	32.9	65.9	32 08.8	33.9	66.4	38
39	29 35.4	26.8	61.7	30 03.7	27.7	62.2	30 31.4	28.8	62.7	30 58.7	29.7	63.2	31 25.5	30.6	63.8	31 51.8	31.5	64.3	32 17.5	32.5	64.9	32 42.7	33.5	65.5	39
40	30 02.2	+26.4	60.6	30 31.4	+27.3	61.1	31 00.2	+28.2	61.7	31 28.4	+29.2	62.2	31 56.1	+30.2	62.7	32 23.3	+31.1	63.3	32 50.0	+32.1	63.9	33 16.2	+32.9	64.5	40
41	30 28.6	25.8	59.6	30 58.7	26.8	60.1	31 28.4	27.7	60.7	31 57.6	28.7	61.2	32 26.3	29.6	61.7	32 54.4	30.6	62.3	33 22.1	31.5	62.9	33 49.1	32.5	63.5	41
42	30 54.4	25.4	58.5	31 25.5	26.3	59.1	31 56.1	27.2	59.6	32 26.3	28.1	60.1	32 55.9	29.1	60.7	33 25.0	30.1	61.3	33 53.6	31.0	61.8	34 21.6	32.0	62.4	42
43	31 19.8	24.8	57.5	31 51.8	25.7	58.0	32 23.3	26.7	58.5	32 54.4	27.7	59.1	33 25.0	28.6	59.6	33 55.1	29.5	60.2	34 24.6	30.5	60.8	34 53.6	31.4	61.4	43
44	31 44.6	24.2	56.4	32 17.5	25.2	56.9	32 50.0	26.2	57.5	33 22.1	27.0	58.0	33 53.6	28.0	58.6	34 24.6	29.0	59.2	34 55.1	29.9	59.8	35 25.0	30.9	60.4	44

84°, 276° L.H.A.   LATITUDE SAME NAME AS DECLINATION

Dec.	38° Hc	d	Z	39° Hc	d	Z	40° Hc	d	Z	41° Hc	d	Z	42° Hc	d	Z	43° Hc	d	Z	44° Hc	d	Z	45° Hc	d	Z	Dec.
0	4 43.5	+37.0	93.7	4 39.6	+37.8	93.8	4 35.6	+38.6	93.9	4 31.5	+39.4	93.9	4 27.3	+40.3	94.0	4 23.1	+41.0	94.1	4 18.7	+41.8	94.2	4 14.3	+42.5	94.3	0
1	5 20.5	37.0	92.9	5 17.4	37.8	93.0	5 14.2	38.6	93.1	5 10.9	39.5	93.2	5 07.6	40.2	93.3	5 04.1	40.9	93.4	5 00.5	41.7	93.5	4 56.8	42.5	93.5	1
2	5 57.5	36.9	92.1	5 55.2	37.8	92.2	5 52.8	38.6	92.3	5 50.4	39.3	92.4	5 47.8	40.1	92.5	5 45.0	41.0	92.6	5 42.2	41.7	92.7	5 39.3	42.5	92.8	2
3	6 34.4	36.8	91.3	6 33.0	37.6	91.4	6 31.4	38.5	91.6	6 29.7	39.3	91.7	6 27.9	40.1	91.8	6 26.0	40.8	91.9	6 23.9	41.6	92.0	6 21.8	42.3	92.1	3
4	7 11.2	36.8	90.5	7 10.6	37.6	90.7	7 09.9	38.4	90.8	7 09.0	39.2	90.9	7 08.0	40.0	91.0	7 06.8	40.8	91.2	7 05.5	41.6	91.3	7 04.1	42.3	91.4	4
5	7 48.0	+36.7	89.7	7 48.2	+37.5	89.9	7 48.3	+38.3	90.0	7 48.2	+39.1	90.1	7 48.0	+39.9	90.3	7 47.6	+40.7	90.4	7 47.1	+41.4	90.6	7 46.4	+42.2	90.7	5
6	8 24.7	36.5	88.9	8 25.7	37.4	89.1	8 26.6	38.2	89.2	8 27.3	39.0	89.4	8 27.9	39.8	89.5	8 28.3	40.6	89.7	8 28.5	41.4	89.8	8 28.6	42.2	90.0	6
7	9 01.2	36.5	88.1	9 03.1	37.3	88.3	9 04.8	38.1	88.5	9 06.3	39.0	88.6	9 07.7	39.7	88.8	9 08.9	40.5	88.9	9 09.9	41.3	89.1	9 10.8	42.1	89.3	7
8	9 37.7	36.3	87.3	9 40.4	37.3	87.5	9 42.9	38.0	87.7	9 45.3	38.8	87.8	9 47.4	39.7	88.0	9 49.4	40.5	88.2	9 51.2	41.2	88.3	9 52.9	41.9	88.5	8
9	10 14.0	36.3	86.5	10 17.6	37.0	86.7	10 20.9	37.9	86.9	10 24.1	38.7	87.1	10 27.1	39.5	87.3	10 29.9	40.3	87.4	10 32.4	41.1	87.6	10 34.8	41.9	87.8	9
10	10 50.3	+36.1	85.7	10 54.6	+37.0	85.9	10 58.8	+37.8	86.1	11 02.8	+38.6	86.3	11 06.6	+39.4	86.5	11 10.2	+40.2	86.7	11 13.5	+41.0	86.9	11 16.7	+41.8	87.1	10
11	11 26.4	35.9	84.9	11 31.6	36.8	85.1	11 36.6	37.7	85.3	11 41.4	38.5	85.5	11 46.0	39.3	85.7	11 50.4	40.1	85.9	11 54.5	40.9	86.1	11 58.5	41.6	86.3	11
12	12 02.3	35.8	84.1	12 08.4	36.7	84.3	12 14.3	37.5	84.5	12 19.9	38.3	84.7	12 25.3	39.1	84.9	12 30.5	39.9	85.2	12 35.4	40.8	85.4	12 40.1	41.5	85.6	12
13	12 38.1	35.7	83.3	12 45.1	36.5	83.5	12 51.8	37.3	83.7	12 58.2	38.2	83.9	13 04.4	39.1	84.2	13 10.4	39.8	84.4	13 16.2	40.6	84.6	13 21.6	41.4	84.9	13
14	13 13.8	35.5	82.4	13 21.6	36.5	82.7	13 29.1	37.2	82.9	13 36.4	38.1	83.1	13 43.5	38.8	83.4	13 50.2	39.7	83.6	13 56.8	40.4	83.9	14 03.0	41.3	84.1	14
15	13 49.3	+35.4	81.6	13 58.0	+36.2	81.8	14 06.3	+37.1	82.1	14 14.5	+37.8	82.3	14 22.3	+38.7	82.6	14 29.9	+39.5	82.9	14 37.2	+40.4	83.1	14 44.3	+41.1	83.4	15
16	14 24.7	35.1	80.8	14 34.2	36.0	81.0	14 43.4	36.9	81.3	14 52.3	37.8	81.5	15 01.0	38.6	81.8	15 09.4	39.4	82.1	15 17.6	40.1	82.3	15 25.4	41.0	82.6	16
17	14 59.8	35.0	79.9	15 10.2	35.8	80.2	15 20.3	36.7	80.5	15 30.1	37.5	80.7	15 39.6	38.3	81.0	15 48.8	39.0	81.3	15 57.7	40.0	81.6	16 06.4	40.8	81.9	17
18	15 34.8	34.8	79.1	15 46.0	35.7	79.4	15 57.0	36.5	79.6	16 07.6	37.4	79.8	16 17.9	38.2	80.2	16 28.0	39.0	80.5	16 37.7	39.9	80.8	16 47.2	40.6	81.1	18
19	16 09.6	34.6	78.2	16 21.7	35.4	78.5	16 33.5	36.3	78.8	16 45.0	37.1	79.1	16 56.1	38.0	79.4	17 07.0	38.8	79.7	17 17.6	39.6	80.0	17 27.8	40.5	80.3	19
20	16 44.2	+34.4	77.4	16 57.1	+35.3	77.7	17 09.8	+36.1	78.0	17 22.1	+37.0	78.3	17 34.1	+37.8	78.6	17 45.8	+38.7	78.9	17 57.2	+39.5	79.2	18 08.3	+40.2	79.5	20
21	17 18.6	34.1	76.5	17 32.4	35.0	76.8	17 45.9	35.9	77.1	17 59.1	36.7	77.5	18 11.9	37.6	77.8	18 24.5	38.4	78.1	18 36.7	39.2	78.4	18 48.5	40.1	78.8	21
22	17 52.7	33.9	75.7	18 07.4	34.8	76.0	18 21.8	35.6	76.3	18 35.8	36.5	76.6	18 49.5	37.4	77.0	19 02.9	38.2	77.3	19 15.9	39.0	77.6	19 28.6	39.8	78.0	22
23	18 26.6	33.7	74.8	18 42.2	34.6	75.1	18 57.4	35.5	75.5	19 12.3	36.3	75.8	19 26.9	37.1	76.1	19 41.1	37.9	76.5	19 54.9	38.9	76.8	20 08.4	39.7	77.2	23
24	19 00.3	33.5	73.9	19 16.8	34.3	74.3	19 32.9	35.2	74.6	19 48.6	36.1	74.9	20 04.0	36.9	75.3	20 19.1	37.7	75.7	20 33.8	38.6	76.0	20 48.1	39.4	76.4	24
25	19 33.8	+33.2	73.1	19 51.1	+34.1	73.4	20 08.1	+34.9	73.7	20 24.7	+35.8	74.1	20 40.9	+36.7	74.5	20 56.8	+37.6	74.8	21 12.4	+38.3	75.2	21 27.5	+39.2	75.6	25
26	20 07.0	32.9	72.2	20 25.2	33.8	72.5	20 43.0	34.7	72.9	21 00.5	35.5	73.2	21 17.6	36.4	73.6	21 34.4	37.2	74.0	21 50.7	38.1	74.4	22 06.7	38.9	74.8	26
27	20 39.9	32.6	71.3	20 59.0	33.5	71.6	21 17.7	34.4	72.0	21 36.0	35.3	72.4	21 54.0	36.2	72.8	22 11.6	37.0	73.1	22 28.8	37.9	73.5	22 45.6	38.7	73.9	27
28	21 12.5	32.4	70.4	21 32.5	33.2	70.7	21 52.1	34.1	71.1	22 11.3	35.0	71.5	22 30.2	35.8	71.9	22 48.6	36.7	72.3	23 06.7	37.5	72.7	23 24.3	38.4	73.1	28
29	21 44.9	32.0	69.5	22 05.7	33.0	69.8	22 26.2	33.8	70.2	22 46.3	34.7	70.6	23 06.0	35.6	71.0	23 25.3	36.5	71.4	23 44.2	37.3	71.8	24 02.7	38.2	72.3	29
30	22 16.9	+31.8	68.6	22 38.7	+32.6	68.9	23 00.0	+33.6	69.3	23 21.0	+34.4	69.7	23 41.6	+35.3	70.1	24 01.8	+36.1	70.6	24 21.5	+37.0	71.0	24 40.9	+37.8	71.4	30
31	22 48.7	31.4	67.6	23 11.3	32.3	68.0	23 33.6	33.2	68.4	23 55.4	34.1	68.8	24 16.9	34.9	69.3	24 37.9	35.8	69.7	24 58.5	36.7	70.1	25 18.7	37.6	70.6	31
32	23 20.1	31.1	66.7	23 43.6	32.0	67.1	24 06.8	32.8	67.5	24 29.5	33.8	67.9	24 51.8	34.7	68.4	25 13.7	35.5	68.8	25 35.2	36.4	69.2	25 56.3	37.2	69.7	32
33	23 51.2	30.7	65.8	24 15.6	31.7	66.2	24 39.6	32.6	66.6	25 03.3	33.4	67.0	25 26.5	34.3	67.5	25 49.2	35.2	67.9	26 11.6	36.0	68.4	26 33.5	36.9	68.8	33
34	24 21.9	30.5	64.8	24 47.3	31.3	65.3	25 12.2	32.2	65.6	25 36.7	33.1	66.1	26 00.8	33.9	66.6	26 24.4	34.9	67.0	26 47.6	35.8	67.5	27 10.4	36.6	67.9	34
35	24 52.4	+30.0	63.9	25 18.6	+30.9	64.3	25 44.4	+31.8	64.7	26 09.8	+32.7	65.2	26 34.7	+33.6	65.6	26 59.3	+34.4	66.1	27 23.4	+35.3	66.6	27 47.0	+36.2	67.0	35
36	25 22.4	29.7	62.9	25 49.5	30.6	63.4	26 16.2	31.5	63.8	26 42.5	32.3	64.2	27 08.3	33.3	64.7	27 33.7	34.2	65.2	27 58.7	35.0	65.7	28 23.2	35.9	66.1	36
37	25 52.1	29.3	62.0	26 20.1	30.1	62.4	26 47.7	31.0	62.8	27 14.8	32.0	63.3	27 41.6	32.8	63.8	28 07.9	33.7	64.2	28 33.7	34.6	64.7	28 59.1	35.5	65.2	37
38	26 21.4	28.8	61.0	26 50.2	29.8	61.4	27 18.7	30.7	61.9	27 46.8	31.6	62.3	28 14.4	32.6	62.8	28 41.6	33.3	63.3	29 08.3	34.2	63.8	29 34.6	35.1	64.3	38
39	26 50.2	28.5	60.0	27 20.0	29.4	60.5	27 49.4	30.3	60.9	28 18.4	31.1	61.4	28 46.9	32.0	61.9	29 14.9	33.0	62.4	29 42.5	33.9	62.9	30 09.7	34.7	63.4	39
40	27 18.7	+28.1	59.0	27 49.4	+29.0	59.5	28 19.7	+29.8	59.9	28 49.5	+30.7	60.4	29 18.9	+31.6	60.9	29 47.9	+32.5	61.4	30 16.4	+33.4	61.9	30 44.4	+34.3	62.4	40
41	27 46.8	27.6	58.0	28 18.4	28.5	58.5	28 49.5	29.5	59.0	29 20.2	30.3	59.4	29 50.5	31.2	59.9	30 20.4	32.1	60.4	30 49.8	32.9	60.9	31 18.7	33.8	61.5	41
42	28 14.4	27.2	57.0	28 46.9	28.0	57.5	29 18.9	29.0	58.0	29 50.5	29.9	58.4	30 21.7	30.8	59.0	30 52.5	31.6	59.4	31 22.7	32.6	60.0	31 52.5	33.4	60.5	42
43	28 41.6	26.7	56.0	29 14.9	27.6	56.5	29 47.9	28.5	56.9	30 20.4	29.4	57.4	30 52.5	30.2	58.0	31 24.1	31.2	58.4	31 55.3	32.0	59.0	32 25.9	33.0	59.5	43
44	29 08.3	26.3	55.0	29 42.5	27.2	55.5	30 16.4	28.0	55.9	30 49.8	28.9	56.4	31 22.7	29.8	56.9	31 55.3	30.6	57.4	32 27.3	31.6	58.0	32 58.9	32.4	58.5	44

85°, 275° L.H.A.   LATITUDE SAME NAME AS DECLINATION

N. Lat. { L.H.A. greater than 180°......Zn=Z
L.H.A. less than 180°.........Zn=360°−Z

Dec.	38° Hc	d	Z	39° Hc	d	Z	40° Hc	d	Z	41° Hc	d	Z	42° Hc	d	Z	43° Hc	d	Z	44° Hc	d	Z	45° Hc	d	Z	Dec.
0	3 56.3	+37.0	93.1	3 53.0	+37.8	93.2	3 49.7	+38.6	93.2	3 46.3	+39.4	93.3	3 42.8	+40.2	93.4	3 39.3	+41.0	93.4	3 35.7	+41.7	93.5	3 32.0	+42.5	93.5	0
1	4 33.3	36.9	92.3	4 30.8	37.8	92.4	4 28.3	38.6	92.5	4 25.7	39.4	92.5	4 23.0	40.2	92.6	4 20.3	40.9	92.7	4 17.4	41.7	92.8	4 14.5	42.4	92.8	1
2	5 10.2	36.9	91.5	5 08.6	37.7	91.6	5 06.9	38.5	91.7	5 05.1	39.3	91.8	5 03.2	40.1	91.9	5 01.2	40.9	91.9	4 59.1	41.7	92.0	4 56.9	42.4	92.1	2
3	5 47.1	36.9	90.7	5 46.3	37.7	90.8	5 45.4	38.5	90.9	5 44.4	39.3	91.0	5 43.3	40.1	91.1	5 42.1	40.8	91.2	5 40.8	41.6	91.3	5 39.3	42.4	91.4	3
4	6 24.0	36.7	89.9	6 24.0	37.6	90.0	6 23.9	38.4	90.1	6 23.7	39.2	90.3	6 23.4	40.0	90.4	6 22.9	40.8	90.4	6 22.4	41.5	90.6	6 21.7	42.3	90.7	4
5	7 00.7	+36.7	89.1	7 01.6	+37.5	89.2	7 02.3	+38.3	89.4	7 02.9	+39.1	89.5	7 03.4	+39.9	89.6	7 03.7	+40.7	89.7	7 03.9	+41.5	89.9	7 04.0	+42.2	90.0	5
6	7 37.4	36.6	88.3	7 39.1	37.4	88.5	7 40.6	38.3	88.6	7 42.0	39.1	88.7	7 43.3	39.8	88.9	7 44.4	40.6	89.0	7 45.4	41.4	89.1	7 46.2	42.2	89.3	6
7	8 14.0	36.5	87.5	8 16.5	37.3	87.7	8 18.9	38.1	87.8	8 21.1	38.9	88.0	8 23.1	39.8	88.1	8 25.0	40.6	88.2	8 26.8	41.3	88.4	8 28.4	42.1	88.6	7
8	8 50.5	36.4	86.7	8 53.8	37.2	86.9	8 57.0	38.1	87.0	9 00.0	38.9	87.2	9 02.9	39.6	87.3	9 05.6	40.4	87.5	9 08.1	41.2	87.7	9 10.5	42.0	87.8	8
9	9 26.9	36.2	85.9	9 31.0	37.2	86.1	9 35.1	37.9	86.2	9 38.9	38.7	86.4	9 42.5	39.6	86.6	9 46.0	40.4	86.8	9 49.3	41.2	86.9	9 52.5	41.9	87.1	9
10	10 03.1	+36.2	85.1	10 08.2	+37.0	85.3	10 13.0	+37.8	85.5	10 17.6	+38.7	85.6	10 22.1	+39.5	85.8	10 26.4	+40.2	86.0	10 30.5	+41.0	86.2	10 34.4	+41.8	86.4	10
11	10 39.3	36.0	84.3	10 45.2	36.8	84.5	10 50.8	37.7	84.7	10 56.3	38.5	84.9	11 01.6	39.3	85.1	11 06.6	40.0	85.3	11 11.5	40.9	85.4	11 16.2	41.6	85.6	11
12	11 15.3	35.9	83.5	11 22.0	36.8	83.7	11 28.5	37.6	83.9	11 34.8	38.4	84.1	11 40.9	39.2	84.3	11 46.8	40.0	84.5	11 52.4	40.8	84.7	11 57.8	41.6	84.9	12
13	11 51.2	35.8	82.7	11 58.8	36.6	82.9	12 06.1	37.5	83.1	12 13.2	38.3	83.3	12 20.1	39.1	83.5	12 26.8	39.7	83.7	12 33.2	40.7	84.0	12 39.4	41.5	84.2	13
14	12 27.0	35.6	81.8	12 35.4	36.4	82.1	12 43.6	37.2	82.3	12 51.5	38.1	82.5	12 59.2	38.9	82.7	13 06.7	39.7	83.0	13 13.9	40.5	83.2	13 20.9	41.3	83.4	14
15	13 02.6	+35.4	81.0	13 11.8	+36.3	81.2	13 20.8	+37.2	81.5	13 29.6	+38.0	81.7	13 38.1	+38.8	82.0	13 46.4	+39.6	82.2	13 54.4	+40.4	82.4	14 02.2	+41.2	82.7	15
16	13 38.0	35.3	80.2	13 48.1	36.2	80.4	13 58.0	36.9	80.7	14 07.6	37.8	80.9	14 16.9	38.7	81.2	14 26.0	39.5	81.4	14 34.8	40.3	81.7	14 43.4	41.0	81.9	16
17	14 13.3	35.1	79.4	14 24.3	35.9	79.6	14 35.0	36.8	79.9	14 45.4	37.7	80.1	14 55.6	38.4	80.4	15 05.5	39.3	80.6	15 15.1	40.1	80.9	15 24.4	40.9	81.2	17
18	14 48.4	35.0	78.5	15 00.2	35.8	78.8	15 11.8	36.6	79.0	15 23.1	37.4	79.3	15 34.0	38.3	79.6	15 44.8	39.1	79.9	15 55.2	39.9	80.1	16 05.3	40.7	80.4	18
19	15 23.4	34.7	77.7	15 36.0	35.6	77.9	15 48.4	36.5	78.2	16 00.5	37.3	78.5	16 12.3	38.2	78.8	16 23.9	38.9	79.1	16 35.1	39.8	79.4	16 46.0	40.6	79.7	19
20	15 58.1	+34.5	76.8	16 11.6	+35.4	77.1	16 24.9	+36.2	77.4	16 37.8	+37.1	77.7	16 50.5	+37.9	78.0	17 02.8	+38.8	78.3	17 14.9	+39.5	78.6	17 26.6	+40.4	78.9	20
21	16 32.6	34.4	76.0	16 47.0	35.2	76.3	17 01.1	36.1	76.6	17 14.9	36.9	76.9	17 28.4	37.7	77.2	17 41.6	38.5	77.5	17 54.4	39.4	77.8	18 07.0	40.1	78.1	21
22	17 07.0	34.1	75.1	17 22.2	35.0	75.4	17 37.2	35.8	75.7	17 51.8	36.7	76.0	18 06.1	37.6	76.3	18 20.1	38.4	76.7	18 33.8	39.2	77.0	18 47.1	40.0	77.3	22
23	17 41.1	33.9	74.3	17 57.2	34.8	74.6	18 13.0	35.6	74.9	18 28.5	36.5	75.2	18 43.7	37.3	75.5	18 58.5	38.1	75.9	19 13.0	38.9	76.2	19 27.1	39.8	76.5	23
24	18 15.0	33.6	73.4	18 32.0	34.5	73.7	18 48.6	35.4	74.0	19 05.0	36.2	74.4	19 21.0	37.1	74.7	19 36.6	38.0	75.0	19 51.9	38.8	75.4	20 06.9	39.6	75.7	24
25	18 48.6	+33.4	72.5	19 06.5	+34.3	72.8	19 24.0	+35.1	73.2	19 41.2	+36.0	73.5	19 58.1	+36.8	73.9	20 14.6	+37.6	74.2	20 30.7	+38.5	74.6	20 46.5	+39.3	74.9	25
26	19 22.0	33.2	71.6	19 40.8	34.0	72.0	19 59.1	34.9	72.3	20 17.2	35.7	72.7	20 34.9	36.6	73.0	20 52.2	37.5	73.4	21 09.2	38.3	73.8	21 25.8	39.1	74.1	26
27	19 55.2	32.9	70.8	20 14.8	33.7	71.1	20 34.0	34.7	71.4	20 52.9	35.5	71.8	21 11.5	36.3	72.2	21 29.7	37.2	72.5	21 47.5	38.0	72.9	22 04.9	38.9	73.3	27
28	20 28.1	32.6	69.9	20 48.5	33.5	70.2	21 08.7	34.3	70.6	21 28.4	35.3	70.9	21 47.8	36.1	71.3	22 06.9	36.9	71.7	22 25.5	37.8	72.1	22 43.8	38.6	72.5	28
29	21 00.7	32.3	69.0	21 22.0	33.2	69.3	21 43.0	34.1	69.7	22 03.7	34.9	70.1	22 23.9	35.8	70.5	22 43.8	36.7	70.8	23 03.3	37.5	71.2	23 22.4	38.3	71.7	29
30	21 33.0	+32.0	68.1	21 55.2	+32.9	68.4	22 17.1	+33.8	68.8	22 38.6	+34.7	69.2	22 59.7	+35.5	69.6	23 20.5	+36.3	70.0	23 40.8	+37.2	70.4	24 00.7	+38.1	70.8	30
31	22 05.0	31.7	67.1	22 28.1	32.6	67.5	22 50.9	33.5	67.9	23 13.3	34.3	68.3	23 35.2	35.3	68.7	23 56.8	36.1	69.1	24 18.0	36.9	69.5	24 38.8	37.7	70.0	31
32	22 36.7	31.5	66.2	23 00.7	32.3	66.6	23 24.4	33.2	67.0	23 47.6	34.0	67.4	24 10.5	34.9	67.8	24 32.9	35.8	68.2	24 54.9	36.7	68.7	25 16.5	37.5	69.1	32
33	23 08.2	31.0	65.3	23 33.0	32.0	65.7	23 57.5	32.9	66.1	24 21.6	33.8	66.5	24 45.4	34.5	66.9	25 08.7	35.4	67.3	25 31.6	36.3	67.8	25 54.0	37.2	68.2	33
34	23 39.2	30.8	64.4	24 05.0	31.6	64.8	24 30.4	32.5	65.2	24 55.4	33.3	65.6	25 19.9	34.3	66.0	25 44.1	35.1	66.4	26 07.9	35.9	66.9	26 31.2	36.8	67.4	34
35	24 10.0	+30.4	63.4	24 36.6	+31.3	63.8	25 02.9	+32.1	64.3	25 28.7	+33.1	64.7	25 54.2	+33.9	65.1	26 19.2	+34.8	65.6	26 43.8	+35.7	66.0	27 08.0	+36.5	66.5	35
36	24 40.4	30.0	62.5	25 07.9	30.9	62.9	25 35.0	31.8	63.3	26 01.8	32.7	63.8	26 28.1	33.6	64.2	26 54.0	34.4	64.7	27 19.5	35.3	65.1	27 44.5	36.1	65.6	36
37	25 10.4	29.7	61.5	25 38.8	30.6	62.0	26 06.8	31.5	62.4	26 34.5	32.3	62.8	27 01.7	33.1	63.2	27 28.4	34.1	63.7	27 54.8	34.9	64.2	28 20.6	35.8	64.7	37
38	25 40.1	29.3	60.6	26 09.4	30.2	61.0	26 38.3	31.0	61.4	27 06.8	31.9	61.9	27 34.8	32.8	62.3	28 02.5	33.7	62.8	28 29.7	34.5	63.3	28 56.4	35.4	63.8	38
39	26 09.4	28.9	59.6	26 39.6	29.7	60.0	27 09.3	30.7	60.4	27 38.7	31.5	60.9	28 07.6	32.4	61.4	28 36.2	33.2	61.9	29 04.2	34.2	62.3	29 31.8	35.1	62.8	39
40	26 38.3	+28.5	58.6	27 09.3	+29.4	59.1	27 40.0	+30.2	59.5	28 10.2	+31.1	60.0	28 40.0	+32.0	60.4	29 09.4	+32.9	61.0	29 38.4	+33.7	61.4	30 06.9	+34.6	61.9	40
41	27 06.8	28.0	57.6	27 38.7	28.9	58.1	28 10.2	29.8	58.5	28 41.3	30.7	59.0	29 12.0	31.6	59.5	29 42.3	32.5	60.0	30 12.1	33.4	60.4	30 41.5	34.2	61.0	41
42	27 34.8	27.7	56.6	28 07.6	28.6	57.1	28 40.0	29.4	57.5	29 12.0	30.3	58.0	29 43.6	31.2	58.5	30 14.8	32.0	59.0	30 45.5	32.9	59.5	31 15.7	33.8	60.0	42
43	28 02.5	27.2	55.6	28 36.2	28.0	56.1	29 09.4	29.0	56.5	29 42.3	29.8	57.0	30 14.8	30.7	57.5	30 46.8	31.6	58.0	31 18.4	32.4	58.5	31 49.5	33.3	59.0	43
44	28 29.7	26.7	54.6	29 04.2	27.6	55.1	29 38.4	28.5	55.5	30 12.1	29.4	56.0	30 45.5	30.2	56.5	31 18.4	31.1	57.0	31 50.8	32.0	57.5	32 22.8	32.9	58.1	44

INTERPOLATION TABLE

Left Table — Altitude Difference (d)

Dec. Inc.	Tens 10'	20'	30'	40'	50'	Decimals	Units 0'	1'	2'	3'	4'	5'	6'	7'	8'	9'
0.0	0.0	0.0	0.0	0.0	0.0	.0	0.0	0.0	0.0	0.0	0.0	0.0	0.0	0.0	0.0	0.0
0.1	0.0	0.0	0.0	0.1	0.1	.1	0.0	0.0	0.0	0.0	0.0	0.0	0.0	0.0	0.0	0.0
0.2	0.0	0.0	0.1	0.1	0.2	.2	0.0	0.0	0.0	0.0	0.0	0.0	0.0	0.0	0.0	0.0
0.3	0.0	0.1	0.1	0.2	0.3	.3	0.0	0.0	0.0	0.0	0.0	0.0	0.0	0.0	0.0	0.0
0.4	0.1	0.1	0.2	0.3	0.3	.4	0.0	0.0	0.0	0.0	0.0	0.0	0.0	0.0	0.1	0.1
0.5	0.1	0.2	0.3	0.3	0.4	.5	0.0	0.0	0.0	0.0	0.0	0.0	0.0	0.0	0.0	0.0
0.6	0.1	0.2	0.3	0.4	0.5	.6	0.0	0.0	0.0	0.0	0.0	0.0	0.1	0.1	0.1	0.1
0.7	0.1	0.3	0.4	0.5	0.6	.7	0.0	0.0	0.0	0.0	0.0	0.0	0.1	0.1	0.1	0.1
0.8	0.1	0.3	0.4	0.6	0.7	.8	0.0	0.0	0.0	0.0	0.0	0.0	0.1	0.1	0.1	0.1
0.9	0.2	0.3	0.5	0.6	0.8	.9	0.0	0.0	0.0	0.0	0.0	0.0	0.1	0.1	0.1	0.1
1.0	0.1	0.3	0.5	0.6	0.8	.0	0.0	0.0	0.0	0.0	0.0	0.1	0.1	0.1	0.1	0.1
1.1	0.2	0.3	0.5	0.7	0.9	.1	0.0	0.0	0.0	0.0	0.0	0.1	0.1	0.1	0.1	0.1
1.2	0.2	0.4	0.6	0.8	1.0	.2	0.0	0.0	0.0	0.0	0.1	0.1	0.1	0.1	0.1	0.1
1.3	0.2	0.4	0.6	0.9	1.1	.3	0.0	0.0	0.0	0.0	0.1	0.1	0.1	0.1	0.1	0.1
1.4	0.2	0.5	0.7	0.9	1.2	.4	0.0	0.0	0.0	0.0	0.1	0.1	0.1	0.1	0.1	0.1
1.5	0.3	0.5	0.8	1.0	1.3	.5	0.0	0.0	0.1	0.1	0.1	0.1	0.1	0.1	0.1	0.1
1.6	0.3	0.5	0.8	1.1	1.3	.6	0.0	0.0	0.1	0.1	0.1	0.1	0.1	0.2	0.2	0.2
1.7	0.3	0.6	0.9	1.2	1.4	.7	0.0	0.0	0.1	0.1	0.1	0.1	0.1	0.2	0.2	0.2
1.8	0.3	0.6	0.9	1.2	1.5	.8	0.0	0.0	0.1	0.1	0.1	0.1	0.1	0.2	0.2	0.2
1.9	0.4	0.7	1.0	1.3	1.6	.9	0.0	0.0	0.1	0.1	0.1	0.1	0.1	0.2	0.2	0.2
2.0	0.3	0.6	1.0	1.3	1.6	.0	0.0	0.0	0.1	0.1	0.2	0.2	0.2	0.2	0.3	0.3
2.1	0.3	0.7	1.0	1.4	1.7	.1	0.0	0.0	0.1	0.1	0.2	0.2	0.2	0.3	0.3	0.4
2.2	0.3	0.7	1.1	1.4	1.8	.2	0.0	0.1	0.1	0.1	0.2	0.2	0.3	0.3	0.3	0.4
2.3	0.4	0.8	1.1	1.5	1.9	.3	0.0	0.1	0.1	0.2	0.2	0.2	0.3	0.3	0.3	0.4
2.4	0.4	0.8	1.2	1.6	2.0	.4	0.0	0.1	0.1	0.2	0.2	0.2	0.3	0.3	0.3	0.4
2.5	0.4	0.8	1.3	1.7	2.1	.5	0.0	0.1	0.1	0.2	0.2	0.2	0.3	0.3	0.4	0.4
2.6	0.4	0.9	1.3	1.7	2.2	.6	0.0	0.1	0.1	0.2	0.2	0.3	0.3	0.3	0.4	0.4
2.7	0.5	0.9	1.4	1.8	2.3	.7	0.0	0.1	0.1	0.2	0.2	0.3	0.3	0.3	0.4	0.4
2.8	0.5	1.0	1.4	1.9	2.4	.8	0.0	0.1	0.1	0.2	0.2	0.3	0.3	0.4	0.4	0.5
2.9	0.5	1.0	1.5	2.0	2.5	.9	0.0	0.1	0.2	0.2	0.2	0.3	0.3	0.4	0.4	0.5
3.0	0.5	1.0	1.5	2.0	2.5	.0	0.0	0.1	0.1	0.2	0.2	0.3	0.3	0.4	0.4	0.5
3.1	0.5	1.0	1.5	2.0	2.6	.1	0.0	0.1	0.1	0.2	0.2	0.3	0.4	0.4	0.5	0.5
3.2	0.5	1.0	1.6	2.1	2.6	.2	0.0	0.1	0.2	0.2	0.3	0.3	0.4	0.4	0.5	0.5
3.3	0.5	1.1	1.6	2.2	2.7	.3	0.1	0.1	0.2	0.2	0.3	0.3	0.4	0.4	0.5	0.5
3.4	0.6	1.1	1.7	2.3	2.8	.4	0.1	0.1	0.2	0.2	0.3	0.3	0.4	0.4	0.5	0.5
3.5	0.6	1.2	1.8	2.3	2.9	.5	0.0	0.1	0.2	0.2	0.3	0.3	0.4	0.4	0.5	0.6
3.6	0.6	1.2	1.8	2.4	3.0	.6	0.0	0.1	0.2	0.2	0.3	0.3	0.4	0.5	0.5	0.6
3.7	0.6	1.3	1.9	2.5	3.1	.7	0.0	0.1	0.2	0.2	0.3	0.3	0.4	0.5	0.5	0.6
3.8	0.7	1.3	1.9	2.6	3.2	.8	0.0	0.1	0.2	0.3	0.3	0.3	0.4	0.5	0.6	0.6
3.9	0.7	1.3	2.0	2.6	3.3	.9	0.1	0.1	0.2	0.3	0.3	0.3	0.4	0.5	0.6	0.6

Double Second Diff. and Corr. (left):
- 0.0 0.0 / 48.2
- 16.2 0.1 / 48.6 0.1
- 8.2 0.1 / 24.6 / 41.0 0.2
- 5.0 0.1 / 15.0 0.2 / 25.0 / 35.1 0.3
- 3.6 0.1 / 10.9 0.2 / 18.2 / 25.5 0.4 / 32.8 / 40.1 0.5

Right Table — Altitude Difference (d)

Dec. Inc.	Tens 10'	20'	30'	40'	50'	Decimals	Units 0'	1'	2'	3'	4'	5'	6'	7'	8'	9'
8.0	1.3	2.6	4.0	5.3	6.6	.0	0.0	0.0	0.3	0.4	0.6	0.6	0.8	0.9	1.1	1.3
8.1	1.3	2.7	4.0	5.4	6.7	.1	0.0	0.2	0.3	0.4	0.6	0.7	0.8	0.9	1.1	1.3
8.2	1.3	2.7	4.1	5.4	6.8	.2	0.0	0.2	0.3	0.5	0.6	0.7	0.9	1.0	1.2	1.3
8.3	1.4	2.8	4.1	5.5	6.9	.3	0.0	0.2	0.3	0.5	0.6	0.8	0.9	1.0	1.2	1.3
8.4	1.4	2.8	4.2	5.6	7.0	.4	0.1	0.2	0.3	0.5	0.6	0.8	0.9	1.0	1.2	1.3
8.5	1.4	2.8	4.3	5.7	7.1	.5	0.1	0.2	0.4	0.5	0.6	0.8	0.9	1.1	1.2	1.3
8.6	1.4	2.9	4.3	5.7	7.2	.6	0.1	0.2	0.4	0.5	0.7	0.8	0.9	1.1	1.2	1.4
8.7	1.5	2.9	4.4	5.8	7.3	.7	0.1	0.3	0.4	0.5	0.7	0.8	1.0	1.1	1.2	1.4
8.8	1.5	3.0	4.4	5.9	7.4	.8	0.1	0.3	0.4	0.5	0.7	0.8	1.0	1.1	1.3	1.4
8.9	1.5	3.0	4.5	6.0	7.5	.9	0.2	0.3	0.4	0.6	0.7	0.8	1.0	1.1	1.3	1.4
9.0	1.5	3.0	4.5	6.0	7.5	.0	0.1	0.2	0.3	0.5	0.6	0.8	0.9	1.1	1.2	1.4
9.1	1.5	3.0	4.5	6.0	7.6	.1	0.0	0.2	0.3	0.5	0.7	0.8	1.0	1.1	1.3	1.4
9.2	1.5	3.1	4.6	6.1	7.6	.2	0.0	0.2	0.4	0.5	0.7	0.8	1.0	1.1	1.3	1.5
9.3	1.6	3.1	4.6	6.2	7.7	.3	0.1	0.2	0.4	0.5	0.7	0.9	1.0	1.2	1.3	1.5
9.4	1.6	3.1	4.7	6.3	7.8	.4	0.1	0.2	0.4	0.5	0.7	0.9	1.0	1.2	1.4	1.5
9.5	1.6	3.2	4.8	6.3	7.9	.5	0.1	0.3	0.4	0.6	0.7	0.9	1.0	1.2	1.4	1.5
9.6	1.6	3.2	4.8	6.4	8.0	.6	0.1	0.3	0.4	0.6	0.7	0.9	1.1	1.2	1.4	1.5
9.7	1.6	3.3	4.9	6.5	8.1	.7	0.1	0.3	0.4	0.6	0.8	0.9	1.1	1.3	1.4	1.6
9.8	1.7	3.3	4.9	6.6	8.2	.8	0.1	0.3	0.5	0.6	0.8	0.9	1.1	1.3	1.4	1.6
9.9	1.7	3.3	5.0	6.6	8.3	.9	0.1	0.3	0.5	0.6	0.8	0.9	1.1	1.3	1.4	1.6
10.0	1.6	3.3	5.0	6.6	8.3	.0	0.1	0.2	0.3	0.5	0.7	0.9	1.0	1.2	1.4	1.6
10.1	1.7	3.3	5.0	6.7	8.4	.1	0.1	0.2	0.4	0.5	0.7	0.9	1.1	1.2	1.4	1.6
10.2	1.7	3.4	5.1	6.8	8.5	.2	0.1	0.2	0.4	0.6	0.7	0.9	1.1	1.3	1.4	1.6
10.3	1.7	3.4	5.1	6.9	8.6	.3	0.1	0.2	0.4	0.6	0.8	0.9	1.1	1.3	1.5	1.6
10.4	1.7	3.5	5.2	6.9	8.7	.4	0.1	0.2	0.4	0.6	0.8	0.9	1.1	1.3	1.5	1.6
10.5	1.8	3.5	5.3	7.0	8.8	.5	0.1	0.3	0.4	0.6	0.8	1.0	1.1	1.3	1.5	1.7
10.6	1.8	3.5	5.3	7.1	8.8	.6	0.1	0.3	0.5	0.6	0.8	1.0	1.2	1.3	1.5	1.7
10.7	1.8	3.6	5.4	7.2	8.9	.7	0.1	0.3	0.5	0.7	0.8	1.0	1.2	1.4	1.5	1.7
10.8	1.8	3.6	5.4	7.2	9.0	.8	0.1	0.3	0.5	0.7	0.9	1.0	1.2	1.4	1.6	1.7
10.9	1.9	3.7	5.5	7.3	9.1	.9	0.2	0.3	0.5	0.7	0.9	1.0	1.2	1.4	1.6	1.7
11.0	1.8	3.6	5.5	7.3	9.1	.0	0.0	0.2	0.4	0.6	0.8	1.0	1.2	1.3	1.5	1.7
11.1	1.8	3.7	5.5	7.4	9.2	.1	0.0	0.2	0.4	0.6	0.8	1.0	1.2	1.4	1.6	1.7
11.2	1.8	3.7	5.6	7.4	9.3	.2	0.0	0.2	0.4	0.6	0.8	1.0	1.2	1.4	1.6	1.8
11.3	1.9	3.8	5.6	7.5	9.4	.3	0.1	0.3	0.5	0.7	0.9	1.1	1.2	1.4	1.6	1.8
11.4	1.9	3.8	5.7	7.6	9.5	.4	0.2	0.3	0.5	0.7	0.9	1.1	1.2	1.4	1.6	1.8
11.5	1.9	3.8	5.8	7.7	9.6	.5	0.1	0.3	0.5	0.7	0.9	1.1	1.2	1.4	1.6	1.8
11.6	1.9	3.9	5.8	7.7	9.7	.6	0.1	0.3	0.5	0.7	0.9	1.1	1.3	1.5	1.7	1.8
11.7	2.0	3.9	5.9	7.8	9.8	.7	0.1	0.3	0.5	0.7	0.9	1.1	1.3	1.5	1.7	1.9
11.8	2.0	4.0	5.9	7.9	9.9	.8	0.1	0.3	0.5	0.7	0.9	1.1	1.3	1.5	1.7	1.9
11.9	2.0	4.0	6.0	8.0	10.0	.9	0.2	0.4	0.6	0.7	0.9	1.1	1.3	1.5	1.7	1.9

Double Second Diff. and Corr. (right):
- 1.6 0.1 / 4.8 0.2 / 8.0 0.3 / 11.2 0.4 / 14.5 0.5 / 17.7 0.6 / 20.9 0.7 / 24.1 0.8 / 27.3 0.9 / 30.5 1.0 / 33.7 / 36.9 1.1
- 1.4 0.1 / 4.2 0.2 / 7.1 0.3 / 9.9 0.4 / 12.7 0.5 / 15.5 0.6 / 18.4 0.7 / 21.2 0.8 / 24.0 0.9 / 26.8 1.0 / 29.7 1.1 / 32.5 / 35.3 1.2
- 1.3 0.1 / 3.8 0.2 / 6.3 0.3 / 8.9 0.4 / 11.4 0.5 / 14.0 0.6 / 16.5 0.7 / 19.0 0.8 / 21.6 0.9 / 24.1

Interpolation / Correction Table

Altitudes 12.0–15.9

Alt	10′	20′	30′	40′	50′
12.0	2.0	4.0	6.0	8.0	10.0
12.1	2.0	4.0	6.0	8.0	10.1
12.2	2.0	4.0	6.1	8.1	10.1
12.3	2.0	4.1	6.1	8.2	10.2
12.4	2.1	4.1	6.2	8.3	10.3
12.5	2.1	4.2	6.3	8.3	10.4
12.6	2.1	4.2	6.3	8.4	10.5
12.7	2.1	4.3	6.4	8.5	10.6
12.8	2.2	4.3	6.4	8.6	10.7
12.9	2.2	4.3	6.5	8.6	10.8
13.0	2.1	4.3	6.5	8.6	10.8
13.1	2.2	4.3	6.5	8.7	10.9
13.2	2.2	4.4	6.6	8.8	11.0
13.3	2.2	4.4	6.6	8.9	11.1
13.4	2.2	4.5	6.7	8.9	11.2
13.5	2.3	4.5	6.8	9.0	11.3
13.6	2.3	4.5	6.8	9.1	11.3
13.7	2.3	4.6	6.9	9.2	11.4
13.8	2.3	4.6	6.9	9.2	11.5
13.9	2.4	4.7	7.0	9.3	11.6
14.0	2.3	4.6	7.0	9.3	11.6
14.1	2.3	4.7	7.0	9.4	11.7
14.2	2.3	4.7	7.1	9.4	11.8
14.3	2.4	4.8	7.1	9.5	11.9
14.4	2.4	4.8	7.2	9.6	12.0
14.5	2.4	4.8	7.3	9.7	12.1
14.6	2.4	4.9	7.3	9.7	12.2
14.7	2.5	4.9	7.4	9.8	12.3
14.8	2.5	5.0	7.4	9.9	12.4
14.9	2.5	5.0	7.5	10.0	12.5
15.0	2.5	5.0	7.5	10.0	12.5
15.1	2.5	5.0	7.5	10.1	12.6
15.2	2.5	5.0	7.6	10.1	12.6
15.3	2.5	5.1	7.6	10.2	12.7
15.4	2.6	5.1	7.7	10.3	12.8
15.5	2.6	5.2	7.8	10.3	12.9
15.6	2.6	5.2	7.8	10.4	13.0
15.7	2.6	5.3	7.9	10.5	13.1
15.8	2.7	5.3	7.9	10.6	13.2
15.9	2.7	5.3	8.0	10.6	13.3

Tenths correction (columns 0′–9′):

	0′	1′	2′	3′	4′	5′	6′	7′	8′	9′
.0	0.0	0.0	0.2	0.4	0.6	0.8	1.0	1.2	1.5	1.7
.1	0.0	0.0	0.2	0.4	0.6	0.9	1.1	1.3	1.5	1.7
.2	0.0	0.0	0.2	0.5	0.7	0.9	1.1	1.3	1.5	1.7
.3	0.1	0.1	0.3	0.5	0.7	0.9	1.1	1.3	1.5	1.7
.4	0.1	0.1	0.3	0.5	0.7	1.0	1.2	1.4	1.6	1.7
.5	0.1	0.1	0.3	0.5	0.7	0.9	1.1	1.4	1.6	1.8
.6	0.1	0.1	0.3	0.5	0.7	0.9	1.1	1.4	1.6	1.8
.7	0.1	0.2	0.4	0.6	0.8	1.0	1.2	1.4	1.6	1.8
.8	0.2	0.2	0.4	0.6	0.8	1.0	1.2	1.5	1.7	1.9
.9	0.2	0.2	0.4	0.6	0.8	1.0	1.2	1.5	1.7	1.9

Double-Second-Difference (arg / corr):
1.0/26.7, 1.1/29.2, 1.2/31.7, 1.3/34.3; 0.1/1.2, 0.2/3.5, 0.3/5.8, 0.4/8.1, 0.5/10.5, 0.6/12.8, 0.7/15.1, 0.8/17.4, 0.9/19.8, 1.0/22.1, 1.1/24.4, 1.2/26.7, 1.3/29.1, 1.4/31.4, 1.5/33.7, –/36.0; 0.1/1.1, 0.2/3.2, 0.3/5.3, 0.4/7.5, 0.5/9.6, 0.6/11.7, 0.7/13.9, 0.8/16.0, 0.9/18.1, 1.0/20.3, 1.1/22.4, 1.2/24.5, 1.3/26.7, 1.4/28.8, 1.5/30.9, 1.6/33.1, /35.2

Altitudes 4.0–7.9

Alt	10′	20′	30′	40′	50′
4.0	0.6	1.3	2.0	2.6	3.3
4.1	0.7	1.3	2.0	2.7	3.4
4.2	0.7	1.4	2.1	2.8	3.5
4.3	0.7	1.4	2.1	2.9	3.6
4.4	0.7	1.5	2.2	2.9	3.7
4.5	0.8	1.5	2.3	3.0	3.8
4.6	0.8	1.5	2.3	3.1	3.8
4.7	0.8	1.6	2.4	3.2	3.9
4.8	0.8	1.6	2.4	3.2	4.0
4.9	0.9	1.7	2.5	3.3	4.1
5.0	0.8	1.6	2.5	3.3	4.1
5.1	0.8	1.7	2.5	3.4	4.2
5.2	0.8	1.7	2.6	3.4	4.3
5.3	0.9	1.8	2.6	3.5	4.4
5.4	0.9	1.8	2.7	3.6	4.5
5.5	0.9	1.8	2.8	3.7	4.6
5.6	0.9	1.9	2.8	3.7	4.7
5.7	1.0	1.9	2.9	3.8	4.8
5.8	1.0	2.0	2.9	3.9	4.9
5.9	1.0	2.0	3.0	4.0	5.0
6.0	1.0	2.0	3.0	4.0	5.0
6.1	1.0	2.0	3.0	4.0	5.1
6.2	1.0	2.0	3.1	4.1	5.1
6.3	1.0	2.1	3.1	4.2	5.2
6.4	1.1	2.1	3.2	4.3	5.3
6.5	1.1	2.2	3.3	4.3	5.4
6.6	1.1	2.2	3.3	4.4	5.5
6.7	1.1	2.3	3.4	4.5	5.6
6.8	1.2	2.3	3.4	4.6	5.7
6.9	1.2	2.3	3.5	4.6	5.8
7.0	1.1	2.3	3.5	4.6	5.8
7.1	1.2	2.3	3.5	4.7	5.9
7.2	1.2	2.4	3.6	4.8	6.0
7.3	1.2	2.4	3.6	4.9	6.1
7.4	1.2	2.5	3.7	4.9	6.2
7.5	1.3	2.5	3.8	5.0	6.3
7.6	1.3	2.5	3.8	5.1	6.3
7.7	1.3	2.6	3.9	5.2	6.4
7.8	1.3	2.6	3.9	5.2	6.5
7.9	1.4	2.7	4.0	5.3	6.6

Tenths correction (columns 0′–9′):

	0′	1′	2′	3′	4′	5′	6′	7′	8′	9′
.0	0.0	0.0	0.1	0.2	0.3	0.4	0.5	0.6	0.6	0.7
.1	0.0	0.0	0.1	0.2	0.3	0.4	0.5	0.6	0.6	0.7
.2	0.0	0.0	0.2	0.2	0.3	0.4	0.5	0.6	0.7	0.7
.3	0.0	0.1	0.2	0.3	0.4	0.4	0.5	0.6	0.7	0.7
.4	0.0	0.1	0.2	0.3	0.4	0.5	0.6	0.6	0.7	0.7
.5	0.0	0.1	0.2	0.3	0.4	0.5	0.6	0.7	0.8	0.9
.6	0.0	0.1	0.2	0.3	0.4	0.5	0.6	0.7	0.8	0.9
.7	0.1	0.2	0.3	0.4	0.5	0.6	0.7	0.8	0.9	1.0
.8	0.1	0.2	0.3	0.4	0.5	0.6	0.7	0.8	0.9	1.0
.9	0.1	0.2	0.3	0.4	0.5	0.6	0.7	0.8	0.9	1.0

Double-Second-Difference (arg / corr):
0.1/2.9, 0.2/8.6, 0.3/14.4, 0.4/20.2, 0.5/25.9, 0.6/31.7, 0.7/37.5; 0.1/2.4, 0.2/7.2, 0.3/12.0, 0.4/16.8, 0.5/21.6, 0.6/26.4, 0.7/31.2, 0.8/36.0; 0.1/2.1, 0.2/6.2, 0.3/10.4, 0.4/14.5, 0.5/18.6, 0.6/22.8, 0.7/26.9, 0.8/31.1, 0.9/35.2; 0.1/1.8, 0.2/5.5, 0.3/9.1, 0.4/12.8, 0.5/16.5, 0.6/20.1, 0.7/23.8, 0.8/27.4, 0.9/31.1, /34.7

The Double-Second-Difference correction (Corr.) is always to be added to the tabulated altitude.

INTERPOLATION TABLE

Altitude Difference (d) — Dec. Inc. 16.0–19.9

Tens

Dec. Inc.	10'	20'	30'	40'	50'
16.0	2.6	5.3	8.0	10.6	13.3
16.1	2.7	5.3	8.0	10.7	13.4
16.2	2.7	5.4	8.1	10.8	13.5
16.3	2.7	5.4	8.1	10.9	13.6
16.4	2.7	5.5	8.2	10.9	13.7
16.5	2.8	5.5	8.3	11.0	13.8
16.6	2.8	5.5	8.3	11.1	13.8
16.7	2.8	5.6	8.4	11.2	13.9
16.8	2.8	5.6	8.4	11.2	14.0
16.9	2.9	5.7	8.5	11.3	14.1
17.0	2.8	5.6	8.5	11.3	14.1
17.1	2.8	5.7	8.5	11.4	14.2
17.2	2.8	5.7	8.6	11.4	14.3
17.3	2.9	5.8	8.6	11.5	14.4
17.4	2.9	5.8	8.7	11.6	14.5
17.5	2.9	5.8	8.8	11.7	14.6
17.6	2.9	5.9	8.8	11.7	14.7
17.7	3.0	5.9	8.9	11.8	14.8
17.8	3.0	6.0	8.9	11.9	14.9
17.9	3.0	6.0	9.0	12.0	15.0
18.0	3.0	6.0	9.0	12.0	15.0
18.1	3.0	6.0	9.0	12.1	15.1
18.2	3.0	6.1	9.1	12.1	15.2
18.3	3.0	6.1	9.1	12.2	15.2
18.4	3.1	6.1	9.2	12.3	15.3
18.5	3.1	6.2	9.3	12.3	15.4
18.6	3.1	6.2	9.3	12.4	15.5
18.7	3.1	6.2	9.4	12.5	15.6
18.8	3.2	6.3	9.4	12.6	15.7
18.9	3.2	6.3	9.5	12.6	15.8
19.0	3.1	6.3	9.5	12.6	15.8
19.1	3.2	6.3	9.5	12.7	15.9
19.2	3.2	6.4	9.6	12.8	16.0
19.3	3.2	6.4	9.6	12.9	16.1
19.4	3.2	6.5	9.7	12.9	16.2
19.5	3.3	6.5	9.8	13.0	16.3
19.6	3.3	6.5	9.8	13.1	16.3
19.7	3.3	6.6	9.9	13.2	16.4
19.8	3.3	6.6	9.9	13.2	16.5
19.9	3.4	6.7	10.0	13.3	16.6

Decimals / Units

Decimals	0'	1'	2'	3'	4'	5'	6'	7'	8'	9'
.0	0.0	0.3	0.5	0.8	1.1	1.4	1.6	1.9	2.2	2.5
.1	0.0	0.3	0.6	0.9	1.1	1.4	1.7	2.0	2.2	2.5
.2	0.1	0.3	0.6	0.9	1.2	1.4	1.7	2.0	2.3	2.5
.3	0.1	0.4	0.6	0.9	1.2	1.5	1.7	2.0	2.3	2.6
.4	0.1	0.4	0.7	0.9	1.2	1.5	1.8	2.0	2.3	2.6
.5	0.1	0.4	0.7	1.0	1.2	1.5	1.8	2.1	2.3	2.6
.6	0.2	0.4	0.7	1.0	1.3	1.5	1.8	2.1	2.4	2.6
.7	0.2	0.5	0.7	1.0	1.3	1.6	1.8	2.1	2.4	2.7
.8	0.2	0.5	0.8	1.0	1.3	1.6	1.9	2.1	2.4	2.7
.9	0.2	0.5	0.8	1.1	1.3	1.6	1.9	2.2	2.4	2.7
.0	0.0	0.3	0.6	0.9	1.2	1.5	1.7	2.0	2.3	2.6
.1	0.1	0.3	0.6	0.9	1.2	1.5	1.8	2.1	2.4	2.7
.2	0.1	0.3	0.6	1.0	1.2	1.5	1.8	2.1	2.4	2.7
.3	0.1	0.4	0.7	1.0	1.3	1.5	1.8	2.1	2.4	2.7
.4	0.1	0.4	0.7	1.0	1.3	1.6	1.9	2.2	2.4	2.7
.5	0.1	0.4	0.7	1.0	1.3	1.6	1.9	2.2	2.5	2.8
.6	0.2	0.5	0.8	1.1	1.3	1.6	1.9	2.2	2.5	2.8
.7	0.2	0.5	0.8	1.1	1.4	1.7	2.0	2.2	2.5	2.8
.8	0.2	0.5	0.8	1.1	1.4	1.7	2.0	2.3	2.6	2.9
.9	0.3	0.6	0.8	1.1	1.4	1.7	2.0	2.3	2.6	2.9
.0	0.0	0.3	0.6	0.9	1.2	1.5	1.8	2.1	2.4	2.7
.1	0.0	0.3	0.6	1.0	1.3	1.6	1.9	2.2	2.5	2.8
.2	0.1	0.4	0.7	1.0	1.3	1.6	1.9	2.2	2.5	2.8
.3	0.1	0.4	0.7	1.0	1.3	1.6	1.9	2.2	2.5	2.8
.4	0.1	0.4	0.7	1.1	1.4	1.7	2.0	2.3	2.6	2.9
.5	0.2	0.5	0.8	1.1	1.4	1.7	2.0	2.3	2.6	2.9
.6	0.2	0.5	0.8	1.1	1.4	1.7	2.0	2.3	2.7	3.0
.7	0.2	0.5	0.8	1.2	1.4	1.7	2.1	2.4	2.7	3.0
.8	0.2	0.6	0.9	1.2	1.5	1.8	2.1	2.4	2.7	3.0
.9	0.3	0.6	0.9	1.2	1.5	1.8	2.1	2.4	2.8	3.1
.0	0.0	0.3	0.6	1.0	1.3	1.6	1.9	2.3	2.6	2.9
.1	0.0	0.4	0.7	1.0	1.3	1.7	2.0	2.3	2.6	3.0
.2	0.1	0.4	0.7	1.1	1.4	1.7	2.0	2.4	2.7	3.0
.3	0.1	0.4	0.7	1.1	1.4	1.8	2.1	2.4	2.7	3.1
.4	0.1	0.5	0.8	1.1	1.4	1.8	2.1	2.4	2.8	3.1
.5	0.2	0.5	0.8	1.1	1.5	1.8	2.1	2.4	2.8	3.1
.6	0.2	0.5	0.8	1.2	1.5	1.8	2.1	2.5	2.8	3.1
.7	0.2	0.5	0.9	1.2	1.5	1.9	2.2	2.5	2.8	3.2
.8	0.3	0.6	0.9	1.2	1.6	1.9	2.2	2.5	2.9	3.2
.9	0.3	0.6	0.9	1.3	1.6	1.9	2.2	2.6	2.9	3.2

Double Second Diff. and Corr. (16.0–19.9)

Diff.	Corr.
1.0	0.1
3.0	0.2
4.9	0.3
6.9	0.4
8.9	0.5
10.8	0.6
12.8	0.7
14.8	0.8
16.7	0.9
18.7	1.0
20.7	1.1
22.7	1.2
24.6	1.3
26.6	1.4
28.6	1.5
30.5	1.6
32.5	1.7
34.5	
0.9	0.1
2.8	0.2
4.6	0.3
6.5	0.4
8.3	0.5
10.2	0.6
12.0	0.7
13.9	0.8
15.7	0.9
17.6	1.0
19.4	1.1
21.3	1.2
23.1	1.3
25.0	1.4
26.8	1.5
28.7	1.6
30.5	1.7
32.3	1.8
34.2	

Altitude Difference (d) — Dec. Inc. 24.0–27.9

Tens

Dec. Inc.	10'	20'	30'	40'	50'
24.0	4.0	8.0	12.0	16.0	20.0
24.1	4.0	8.0	12.0	16.0	20.1
24.2	4.0	8.0	12.1	16.1	20.1
24.3	4.0	8.1	12.1	16.2	20.2
24.4	4.1	8.1	12.2	16.3	20.3
24.5	4.1	8.2	12.3	16.3	20.4
24.6	4.1	8.2	12.3	16.4	20.5
24.7	4.1	8.3	12.4	16.5	20.6
24.8	4.2	8.3	12.4	16.6	20.7
24.9	4.2	8.3	12.5	16.6	20.8
25.0	4.1	8.3	12.5	16.6	20.8
25.1	4.2	8.3	12.5	16.7	20.9
25.2	4.2	8.4	12.6	16.8	21.0
25.3	4.2	8.4	12.6	16.9	21.1
25.4	4.2	8.5	12.7	16.9	21.2
25.5	4.3	8.5	12.8	17.0	21.3
25.6	4.3	8.5	12.8	17.1	21.3
25.7	4.3	8.6	12.9	17.2	21.4
25.8	4.3	8.6	12.9	17.2	21.5
25.9	4.4	8.7	13.0	17.3	21.6
26.0	4.3	8.6	13.0	17.3	21.6
26.1	4.3	8.7	13.0	17.4	21.7
26.2	4.3	8.7	13.1	17.4	21.8
26.3	4.4	8.8	13.1	17.5	21.9
26.4	4.4	8.8	13.2	17.6	22.0
26.5	4.4	8.8	13.3	17.7	22.1
26.6	4.4	8.9	13.3	17.7	22.2
26.7	4.5	8.9	13.4	17.8	22.3
26.8	4.5	9.0	13.4	17.9	22.4
26.9	4.5	9.0	13.5	17.9	22.5
27.0	4.5	9.0	13.5	18.0	22.5
27.1	4.5	9.0	13.5	18.0	22.6
27.2	4.5	9.1	13.6	18.1	92.6
27.3	4.6	9.1	13.6	18.2	22.7
27.4	4.6	9.1	13.7	18.3	22.8
27.5	4.6	9.2	13.8	18.3	22.9
27.6	4.6	9.2	13.8	18.4	23.0
27.7	4.6	9.2	13.9	18.5	23.1
27.8	4.7	9.3	13.9	18.6	23.2
27.9	4.7	9.3	14.0	18.6	23.3

Decimals / Units

Decimals	0'	1'	2'	3'	4'	5'	6'	7'	8'	9'
.0	0.0	0.4	0.8	1.2	1.6	2.0	2.4	2.9	3.3	3.7
.1	0.0	0.4	0.9	1.3	1.7	2.1	2.5	2.9	3.3	3.7
.2	0.1	0.5	0.9	1.3	1.7	2.1	2.5	2.9	3.3	3.8
.3	0.1	0.5	0.9	1.3	1.8	2.2	2.6	3.0	3.4	3.8
.4	0.2	0.6	1.0	1.4	1.8	2.2	2.6	3.0	3.4	3.8
.5	0.2	0.6	1.0	1.4	1.8	2.2	2.7	3.1	3.5	3.9
.6	0.2	0.6	1.1	1.5	1.9	2.3	2.7	3.1	3.5	3.9
.7	0.3	0.7	1.1	1.5	1.9	2.3	2.7	3.1	3.6	4.0
.8	0.3	0.7	1.1	1.6	2.0	2.4	2.8	3.2	3.6	4.0
.9	0.4	0.8	1.2	1.6	2.0	2.4	2.8	3.2	3.6	4.0
.0	0.0	0.4	0.8	1.3	1.7	2.1	2.5	3.0	3.4	3.8
.1	0.1	0.5	0.9	1.3	1.7	2.2	2.6	3.0	3.4	3.9
.2	0.1	0.5	0.9	1.4	1.8	2.2	2.6	3.1	3.5	3.9
.3	0.1	0.6	1.0	1.4	1.8	2.3	2.7	3.1	3.5	4.0
.4	0.2	0.6	1.0	1.5	1.9	2.3	2.7	3.1	3.6	4.0
.5	0.2	0.6	1.1	1.5	1.9	2.3	2.8	3.2	3.6	4.0
.6	0.3	0.7	1.1	1.5	2.0	2.4	2.8	3.2	3.7	4.1
.7	0.3	0.7	1.1	1.6	2.0	2.4	2.8	3.3	3.7	4.1
.8	0.3	0.8	1.2	1.6	2.0	2.5	2.9	3.3	3.7	4.2
.9	0.4	0.8	1.2	1.7	2.1	2.5	2.9	3.4	3.8	4.2
.0	0.0	0.4	0.9	1.3	1.8	2.2	2.6	3.1	3.5	4.0
.1	0.0	0.5	0.9	1.4	1.8	2.3	2.7	3.1	3.6	4.0
.2	0.1	0.5	1.0	1.4	1.9	2.3	2.7	3.2	3.6	4.1
.3	0.1	0.6	1.0	1.5	1.9	2.3	2.8	3.2	3.7	4.1
.4	0.2	0.6	1.1	1.5	2.0	2.4	2.8	3.3	3.7	4.2
.5	0.2	0.7	1.1	1.5	2.0	2.4	2.9	3.3	3.8	4.2
.6	0.3	0.7	1.2	1.6	2.1	2.5	2.9	3.4	3.8	4.2
.7	0.3	0.7	1.2	1.6	2.1	2.5	3.0	3.4	3.8	4.3
.8	0.4	0.8	1.2	1.7	2.1	2.6	3.0	3.4	3.9	4.3
.9	0.4	0.9	1.3	1.7	2.2	2.6	3.0	3.5	3.9	4.4
.0	0.0	0.5	0.9	1.4	1.8	2.3	2.7	3.2	3.6	4.1
.1	0.0	0.5	1.0	1.4	1.9	2.3	2.8	3.2	3.7	4.1
.2	0.1	0.6	1.0	1.5	1.9	2.4	2.8	3.3	3.7	4.2
.3	0.1	0.6	1.1	1.5	2.0	2.4	2.9	3.3	3.8	4.2
.4	0.2	0.6	1.1	1.6	2.0	2.5	2.9	3.4	3.8	4.3
.5	0.2	0.7	1.1	1.6	2.1	2.5	3.0	3.4	3.9	4.4
.6	0.3	0.7	1.2	1.6	2.1	2.6	3.0	3.5	3.9	4.4
.7	0.3	0.8	1.2	1.7	2.1	2.6	3.1	3.5	4.0	4.4
.8	0.4	0.8	1.3	1.7	2.2	2.7	3.1	3.6	4.0	4.5
.9	0.4	0.9	1.3	1.8	2.2	2.7	3.2	3.6	4.1	4.5

Double Second Diff. and Corr. (24.0–27.9)

Diff.	Corr.
0.8	0.1
2.5	0.2
4.1	0.3
5.8	0.4
7.4	0.5
9.1	0.6
10.7	0.7
12.3	0.8
14.0	0.9
15.6	1.0
17.3	1.1
18.9	1.2
20.6	1.3
22.2	1.4
23.9	1.5
25.5	1.6
27.2	1.7
28.8	1.8
30.4	1.9
32.1	2.0
33.7	2.0
35.4	2.1
0.8	0.1
2.4	0.2
4.0	0.3
5.7	0.4
7.3	0.5
8.9	0.6
10.5	0.7
12.1	0.8
13.7	0.9
15.4	1.0
17.0	1.1
18.6	1.2
20.2	1.3
21.8	1.4
23.4	1.5
25.1	1.6
26.7	1.7
28.3	1.8
29.9	1.9
31.5	2.0
33.1	2.0
34.7	2.1

Upper table (28.0 – 31.9)

Alt	10'	20'	30'	40'	50'	dec	0'	1'	2'	3'	4'	5'	6'	7'	8'	9'
28.0	4.6	9.3	14.0	18.6	23.3	.0	0.0	0.5	0.9	1.4	1.9	2.4	2.8	3.3	3.8	4.3
28.1	4.7	9.3	14.0	18.7	23.4	.1	0.0	0.5	1.0	1.4	1.9	2.4	2.9	3.3	3.8	4.3
28.2	4.7	9.4	14.1	18.8	23.5	.2	0.1	0.6	1.0	1.5	2.0	2.5	2.9	3.4	3.9	4.4
28.3	4.7	9.4	14.1	18.9	23.6	.3	0.1	0.6	1.1	1.6	2.0	2.5	3.0	3.5	3.9	4.4
28.4	4.7	9.5	14.2	18.9	23.7	.4	0.2	0.7	1.1	1.6	2.1	2.6	3.0	3.5	4.0	4.5
28.5	4.8	9.5	14.3	19.0	23.8	.5	0.2	0.7	1.2	1.7	2.1	2.6	3.1	3.6	4.0	4.5
28.6	4.8	9.5	14.3	19.1	23.8	.6	0.3	0.8	1.2	1.7	2.2	2.7	3.1	3.6	4.1	4.6
28.7	4.8	9.6	14.4	19.2	23.9	.7	0.3	0.8	1.3	1.8	2.2	2.7	3.2	3.7	4.1	4.6
28.8	4.8	9.6	14.4	19.2	24.0	.8	0.4	0.9	1.3	1.8	2.3	2.8	3.2	3.7	4.2	4.7
28.9	4.9	9.7	14.5	19.3	24.1	.9	0.4	0.9	1.4	1.9	2.3	2.8	3.3	3.8	4.2	4.7
29.0	4.8	9.6	14.5	19.3	24.1	.0	0.0	0.5	1.0	1.5	2.0	2.5	2.9	3.4	3.9	4.4
29.1	4.8	9.7	14.5	19.4	24.2	.1	0.0	0.5	1.0	1.5	2.0	2.5	3.0	3.4	3.9	4.4
29.2	4.8	9.7	14.6	19.4	24.3	.2	0.1	0.6	1.1	1.6	2.1	2.6	3.0	3.5	4.0	4.5
29.3	4.9	9.8	14.6	19.5	24.4	.3	0.1	0.6	1.1	1.6	2.1	2.6	3.1	3.6	4.1	4.6
29.4	4.9	9.8	14.7	19.6	24.5	.4	0.2	0.7	1.2	1.7	2.2	2.7	3.1	3.6	4.1	4.6
29.5	4.9	9.8	14.8	19.7	24.6	.5	0.2	0.7	1.2	1.7	2.3	2.7	3.2	3.7	4.2	4.7
29.6	4.9	9.9	14.8	19.7	24.7	.6	0.3	0.8	1.3	1.8	2.3	2.8	3.2	3.7	4.3	4.8
29.7	5.0	9.9	14.9	19.8	24.8	.7	0.3	0.8	1.3	1.8	2.4	2.8	3.3	3.8	4.3	4.8
29.8	5.0	10.0	14.9	19.9	24.9	.8	0.4	0.9	1.4	1.9	2.4	2.9	3.3	3.8	4.4	4.9
29.9	5.0	10.0	15.0	20.0	25.0	.9	0.4	0.9	1.4	1.9	2.4	2.9	3.4	3.9	4.4	4.9
30.0	5.0	10.0	15.0	20.0	25.0	.0	0.0	0.5	1.0	1.5	2.0	2.5	3.0	3.6	4.1	4.6
30.1	5.0	10.0	15.0	20.0	25.1	.1	0.0	0.6	1.1	1.6	2.1	2.6	3.1	3.6	4.3	4.8
30.2	5.0	10.0	15.1	20.1	25.1	.2	0.1	0.6	1.1	1.6	2.2	2.7	3.2	3.7	4.3	4.8
30.3	5.0	10.1	15.1	20.2	25.2	.3	0.2	0.7	1.2	1.7	2.2	2.7	3.2	3.7	4.3	4.8
30.4	5.1	10.1	15.2	20.3	25.3	.4	0.2	0.7	1.2	1.7	2.3	2.8	3.3	3.8	4.3	4.8
30.5	5.1	10.2	15.3	20.3	25.4	.5	0.3	0.8	1.3	1.8	2.3	2.8	3.3	3.8	4.4	4.9
30.6	5.1	10.2	15.4	20.4	25.5	.6	0.3	0.8	1.3	1.8	2.4	2.9	3.4	3.9	4.4	4.9
30.7	5.1	10.3	15.4	20.5	25.6	.7	0.4	0.9	1.4	1.9	2.4	2.9	3.4	3.9	4.4	4.9
30.8	5.1	10.3	15.5	20.6	25.7	.8	0.4	0.9	1.4	1.9	2.5	3.0	3.5	4.0	4.5	5.0
30.9	5.2	10.3	15.5	20.6	25.8	.9	0.5	1.0	1.5	2.0	2.5	3.0	3.5	4.0	4.5	5.0
31.0	5.1	10.3	15.5	20.6	25.8	.0	0.0	0.5	1.1	1.6	2.1	2.6	3.1	3.7	4.2	4.7
31.1	5.2	10.3	15.5	20.7	25.9	.1	0.1	0.6	1.1	1.6	2.2	2.7	3.2	3.7	4.3	4.8
31.2	5.2	10.4	15.6	20.8	26.0	.2	0.1	0.6	1.2	1.7	2.2	2.8	3.3	3.8	4.3	4.8
31.3	5.2	10.4	15.6	20.9	26.1	.3	0.2	0.7	1.2	1.7	2.3	2.8	3.3	3.8	4.4	4.9
31.4	5.2	10.5	15.7	20.9	26.2	.4	0.2	0.7	1.3	1.8	2.3	2.9	3.4	3.9	4.4	4.9
31.5	5.3	10.5	15.8	21.0	26.3	.5	0.3	0.8	1.3	1.8	2.4	2.9	3.4	3.9	4.5	5.0
31.6	5.3	10.5	15.8	21.1	26.3	.6	0.3	0.8	1.4	1.9	2.4	3.0	3.5	4.0	4.5	5.0
31.7	5.3	10.6	15.9	21.2	26.4	.7	0.4	0.9	1.4	1.9	2.5	3.0	3.5	4.0	4.6	5.1
31.8	5.3	10.6	15.9	21.2	26.5	.8	0.4	0.9	1.5	2.0	2.5	3.1	3.6	4.1	4.6	5.1
31.9	5.4	10.7	16.0	21.3	26.6	.9	0.5	1.0	1.5	2.0	2.6	3.1	3.6	4.1	4.7	5.2

v or d correction (upper table): 0.8→0.1, 2.4→0.2, 4.0→0.3, 5.6→0.4, 7.2→0.5, 8.8→0.6, 10.4→0.7, 12.0→0.8, 13.6→0.9, 15.2→1.0, 16.8→1.1, 18.4→1.2, 20.0→1.3, 21.6→1.4, 23.2→1.5, 24.8→1.6, 26.4→1.7, 28.0→1.8, 29.6→1.9, 31.2→2.0, 32.8→2.1, 34.4

Lower table (20.0 – 23.9)

Alt	10'	20'	30'	40'	50'	dec	0'	1'	2'	3'	4'	5'	6'	7'	8'	9'
20.0	3.3	6.6	10.0	13.3	16.6	.0	0.0	0.3	0.7	1.0	1.4	1.7	2.0	2.4	2.7	3.1
20.1	3.3	6.7	10.0	13.4	16.7	.1	0.0	0.4	0.7	1.1	1.4	1.8	2.1	2.4	2.8	3.1
20.2	3.3	6.7	10.1	13.4	16.8	.2	0.1	0.4	0.8	1.1	1.4	1.8	2.1	2.5	2.8	3.1
20.3	3.4	6.8	10.1	13.5	16.9	.3	0.1	0.5	0.8	1.2	1.5	1.8	2.2	2.5	2.8	3.2
20.4	3.4	6.8	10.2	13.6	17.0	.4	0.1	0.5	0.8	1.2	1.5	1.9	2.2	2.5	2.9	3.2
20.5	3.4	6.8	10.3	13.7	17.1	.5	0.2	0.5	0.9	1.2	1.6	1.9	2.2	2.6	2.9	3.2
20.6	3.4	6.9	10.3	13.7	17.2	.6	0.2	0.5	0.9	1.2	1.6	1.9	2.3	2.6	2.9	3.3
20.7	3.5	6.9	10.4	13.8	17.3	.7	0.2	0.6	0.9	1.3	1.6	2.0	2.3	2.6	3.0	3.3
20.8	3.5	7.0	10.4	13.9	17.4	.8	0.3	0.6	1.0	1.3	1.7	2.0	2.4	2.7	3.0	3.4
20.9	3.5	7.0	10.5	14.0	17.5	.9	0.3	0.6	1.0	1.3	1.7	2.0	2.4	2.7	3.0	3.4
21.0	3.5	7.0	10.5	14.0	17.5	.0	0.0	0.4	0.7	1.1	1.4	1.8	2.1	2.5	2.9	3.2
21.1	3.5	7.0	10.6	14.1	17.6	.1	0.0	0.4	0.8	1.1	1.5	1.8	2.2	2.5	2.9	3.2
21.2	3.5	7.1	10.6	14.1	17.7	.2	0.1	0.4	0.8	1.2	1.5	1.9	2.2	2.6	2.9	3.3
21.3	3.6	7.1	10.7	14.2	17.7	.3	0.1	0.5	0.9	1.2	1.6	1.9	2.3	2.6	3.0	3.3
21.4	3.6	7.1	10.7	14.3	17.8	.4	0.1	0.5	0.9	1.3	1.6	1.9	2.3	2.7	3.0	3.4
21.5	3.6	7.2	10.8	14.3	17.9	.5	0.2	0.5	0.9	1.3	1.6	2.0	2.3	2.7	3.1	3.4
21.6	3.6	7.2	10.8	14.4	18.0	.6	0.2	0.6	0.9	1.3	1.7	2.0	2.4	2.7	3.1	3.4
21.7	3.6	7.3	10.9	14.5	18.1	.7	0.2	0.6	1.0	1.3	1.7	2.0	2.4	2.8	3.1	3.5
21.8	3.7	7.3	10.9	14.6	18.2	.8	0.3	0.6	1.0	1.4	1.7	2.1	2.4	2.8	3.2	3.5
21.9	3.7	7.3	11.0	14.6	18.3	.9	0.3	0.7	1.0	1.4	1.8	2.1	2.5	2.8	3.2	3.5
22.0	3.6	7.3	11.0	14.6	18.3	.0	0.0	0.4	0.7	1.1	1.5	1.9	2.2	2.6	3.0	3.4
22.1	3.7	7.3	11.0	14.7	18.4	.1	0.1	0.4	0.8	1.2	1.5	1.9	2.3	2.6	3.0	3.4
22.2	3.7	7.4	11.1	14.8	18.5	.2	0.1	0.4	0.8	1.2	1.6	1.9	2.3	2.7	3.1	3.4
22.3	3.7	7.4	11.1	14.8	18.6	.3	0.1	0.5	0.9	1.2	1.6	2.0	2.4	2.7	3.1	3.5
22.4	3.7	7.5	11.2	14.9	18.7	.4	0.1	0.5	0.9	1.3	1.6	2.0	2.4	2.8	3.1	3.5
22.5	3.8	7.5	11.3	15.0	18.8	.5	0.2	0.5	0.9	1.3	1.7	2.1	2.4	2.8	3.2	3.6
22.6	3.8	7.5	11.3	15.1	18.8	.6	0.2	0.6	1.0	1.3	1.7	2.1	2.5	2.8	3.2	3.6
22.7	3.8	7.6	11.4	15.2	18.9	.7	0.2	0.6	1.0	1.4	1.8	2.1	2.5	2.9	3.3	3.6
22.8	3.8	7.6	11.4	15.2	19.0	.8	0.3	0.6	1.0	1.4	1.8	2.2	2.5	2.9	3.3	3.7
22.9	3.9	7.7	11.5	15.3	19.1	.9	0.3	0.7	1.1	1.5	1.8	2.2	2.6	3.0	3.3	3.7
23.0	3.8	7.6	11.5	15.3	19.1	.0	0.0	0.4	0.8	1.2	1.6	2.0	2.3	2.7	3.1	3.5
23.1	3.8	7.7	11.5	15.4	19.2	.1	0.1	0.4	0.8	1.2	1.6	2.0	2.4	2.8	3.2	3.6
23.2	3.8	7.7	11.6	15.4	19.3	.2	0.1	0.5	0.8	1.2	1.6	2.0	2.4	2.8	3.2	3.6
23.3	3.9	7.8	11.6	15.5	19.4	.3	0.1	0.5	0.9	1.3	1.7	2.1	2.5	2.9	3.3	3.6
23.4	3.9	7.8	11.7	15.6	19.5	.4	0.1	0.5	0.9	1.3	1.7	2.1	2.5	2.9	3.3	3.7
23.5	3.9	7.8	11.8	15.7	19.6	.5	0.2	0.6	1.0	1.4	1.8	2.2	2.5	2.9	3.3	3.7
23.6	3.9	7.9	11.8	15.7	19.7	.6	0.2	0.6	1.0	1.4	1.8	2.2	2.6	3.0	3.4	3.8
23.7	3.9	7.9	11.9	15.8	19.7	.7	0.3	0.7	1.1	1.4	1.8	2.2	2.6	3.0	3.4	3.8
23.8	4.0	8.0	11.9	15.9	19.9	.8	0.3	0.7	1.1	1.5	1.9	2.3	2.7	3.1	3.4	3.8
23.9	4.0	8.0	12.0	16.0	20.0	.9	0.4	0.7	1.1	1.5	1.9	2.3	2.7	3.1	3.5	3.9

v or d correction (lower table): 0.9→0.1, 2.6→0.2, 4.4→0.3, 6.2→0.4, 7.9→0.5, 9.7→0.6, 11.4→0.7, 13.2→0.8, 14.9→0.9, 16.7→1.0, 18.5→1.1, 20.2→1.2, 22.0→1.3, 23.7→1.4, 25.5→1.5, 27.3→1.6, 29.0→1.7, 30.8→1.8, 32.5→1.9, 34.3

The Double-Second-Difference correction (Corr.) is always to be added to the tabulated altitude.

ALTITUDE CORRECTION TABLES 10°–90°—SUN, STARS, PLANETS

SUN

OCT.–MAR. App. Alt.	Lower Limb	Upper Limb	APR.–SEPT. App. Alt.	Lower Limb	Upper Limb
9 34	+10.8	−22.7	9 39	+10.6	−22.4
9 45	+10.9	−22.6	9 51	+10.7	−22.3
9 56	+11.0	−22.5	10 03	+10.8	−22.2
10 08	+11.1	−22.4	10 15	+10.9	−22.1
10 21	+11.2	−22.3	10 27	+11.0	−22.0
10 34	+11.3	−22.2	10 40	+11.1	−21.9
10 47	+11.4	−22.1	10 54	+11.2	−21.8
11 01	+11.5	−22.0	11 08	+11.3	−21.7
11 15	+11.6	−21.9	11 23	+11.4	−21.6
11 30	+11.7	−21.8	11 38	+11.5	−21.5
11 46	+11.8	−21.7	11 54	+11.6	−21.4
12 02	+11.9	−21.6	12 10	+11.7	−21.3
12 19	+12.0	−21.5	12 28	+11.8	−21.2
12 37	+12.1	−21.4	12 46	+11.9	−21.1
12 55	+12.2	−21.3	13 05	+12.0	−21.0
13 14	+12.3	−21.2	13 24	+12.1	−20.9
13 35	+12.4	−21.1	13 45	+12.2	−20.8
13 56	+12.5	−21.0	14 07	+12.3	−20.7
14 18	+12.6	−20.9	14 30	+12.4	−20.6
14 42	+12.7	−20.8	14 54	+12.5	−20.5
15 06	+12.8	−20.7	15 19	+12.6	−20.4
15 32	+12.9	−20.6	15 46	+12.7	−20.3
15 59	+13.0	−20.5	16 14	+12.8	−20.2
16 28	+13.1	−20.4	16 44	+12.9	−20.1
16 59	+13.2	−20.3	17 15	+13.0	−20.0
17 32	+13.3	−20.2	17 48	+13.1	−19.9
18 06	+13.4	−20.1	18 24	+13.2	−19.8
18 42	+13.5	−20.0	19 01	+13.3	−19.7
19 21	+13.6	−19.9	19 42	+13.4	−19.6
20 03	+13.7	−19.8	20 25	+13.5	−19.5
20 48	+13.8	−19.7	21 11	+13.6	−19.4
21 35	+13.9	−19.6	22 00	+13.7	−19.3
22 26	+14.0	−19.5	22 54	+13.8	−19.2
23 22	+14.1	−19.4	23 51	+13.9	−19.1
24 21	+14.2	−19.3	24 53	+14.0	−19.0
25 26	+14.3	−19.2	26 00	+14.1	−18.9
26 36	+14.4	−19.1	27 13	+14.2	−18.8
27 52	+14.5	−19.0	28 33	+14.3	−18.7
29 15	+14.6	−18.9	30 00	+14.4	−18.6
30 46	+14.7	−18.8	31 35	+14.5	−18.5
32 26	+14.8	−18.7	33 20	+14.6	−18.4
34 17	+14.9	−18.6	35 17	+14.7	−18.3
36 20	+15.0	−18.5	37 26	+14.8	−18.2
38 36	+15.1	−18.4	39 50	+14.9	−18.1
41 08	+15.2	−18.3	42 31	+15.0	−18.0
43 59	+15.3	−18.2	45 31	+15.1	−17.9
47 10	+15.4	−18.1	48 55	+15.2	−17.8
50 46	+15.5	−18.0	52 44	+15.3	−17.7
54 49	+15.6	−17.9	57 02	+15.4	−17.6
59 23	+15.7	−17.8	61 51	+15.5	−17.5
64 30	+15.8	−17.7	67 17	+15.6	−17.4
70 12	+15.9	−17.6	73 16	+15.7	−17.3
76 26	+16.0	−17.5	79 43	+15.8	−17.2
83 05	+16.1	−17.4	86 32	+15.9	−17.1
90 00			90 00		

STARS AND PLANETS

App. Alt.	Corrn	App. Alt.	Additional Corrn
9 56	−5.3		**1968**
10 08	−5.2		
10 20	−5.1		**VENUS**
10 33	−5.0		Jan. 1–Dec. 14
10 46	−4.9		
11 00	−4.8	0°	
11 14	−4.7	42	+0.1
11 29	−4.6		
11 45	−4.5		Dec. 15–Dec. 31
12 01	−4.4		
12 18	−4.3	0°	
12 35	−4.2	47	+0.2
12 54	−4.1		
13 13	−4.0		
13 33	−3.9		
13 54	−3.8		
14 16	−3.7		
14 40	−3.6		
15 04	−3.5		
15 30	−3.4		
15 57	−3.3		
16 26	−3.2		
16 56	−3.1		
17 28	−3.0		
18 02	−2.9		
18 38	−2.8		**MARS**
19 17	−2.7		Jan. 1–Dec. 31
19 58	−2.6		
20 42	−2.5	0°	
21 28	−2.4	60	+0.1
22 19	−2.3		
23 13	−2.2		
24 11	−2.1		
25 14	−2.0		
26 22	−1.9		
27 36	−1.8		
28 56	−1.7		
30 24	−1.6		
32 00	−1.5		
33 45	−1.4		
35 40	−1.3		
37 48	−1.2		
40 08	−1.1		
42 44	−1.0		
45 36	−0.9		
48 47	−0.8		
52 18	−0.7		
56 11	−0.6		
60 28	−0.5		
65 08	−0.4		
70 11	−0.3		
75 34	−0.2		
81 13	−0.1		
87 03	0.0		
90 00			

DIP

Ht. of Eye (ft.)	Corrn	Ht. of Eye (ft.)	Corrn
1.1	−1.1	44	−6.5
1.4	−1.2	45	−6.6
1.6	−1.3	47	−6.7
1.9	−1.4	48	−6.8
2.2	−1.5	49	−6.9
2.5	−1.6	51	−7.0
2.8	−1.7	52	−7.1
3.2	−1.8	54	−7.2
3.6	−1.9	55	−7.3
4.0	−2.0	57	−7.4
4.4	−2.1	58	−7.5
4.9	−2.2	60	−7.6
5.3	−2.3	62	−7.7
5.8	−2.4	63	−7.8
6.3	−2.5	65	−7.9
6.9	−2.6	67	−8.0
7.4	−2.7	68	−8.1
8.0	−2.8	70	−8.2
8.6	−2.9	72	−8.3
9.2	−3.0	74	−8.4
9.8	−3.1	75	−8.5
10.5	−3.2	77	−8.6
11.2	−3.3	79	−8.7
11.9	−3.4	81	−8.8
12.6	−3.5	83	−8.9
13.3	−3.6	85	−9.0
14.1	−3.7	87	−9.1
14.9	−3.8	88	−9.2
15.7	−3.9	90	−9.3
16.5	−4.0	92	−9.4
17.4	−4.1	94	−9.5
18.3	−4.2	96	−9.6
19.1	−4.3	98	−9.7
20.1	−4.4	101	−9.8
21.0	−4.5	103	−9.9
22.0	−4.6	105	−10.0
22.9	−4.7	107	−10.1
23.9	−4.8	109	−10.2
24.9	−4.9	111	−10.3
26.0	−5.0	113	−10.4
27.1	−5.1	116	−10.5
28.1	−5.2	118	−10.6
29.2	−5.3	120	−10.7
30.4	−5.4	122	−10.8
31.5	−5.5	125	−10.9
32.7	−5.6	127	−11.0
33.9	−5.7	129	−11.1
35.1	−5.8	132	−11.2
36.3	−5.9	134	−11.3
37.6	−6.0	136	−11.4
38.9	−6.1	139	−11.5
40.1	−6.2	141	−11.6
41.5	−6.3	144	−11.7
42.8	−6.4	146	−11.8
44.2		149	

App. Alt. = Apparent altitude = Sextant altitude corrected for index error and dip.

ALTITUDE CORRECTION TABLES 0°–10°—SUN, STARS, PLANETS

App. Alt.	OCT.–MAR. SUN APR.–SEPT.				STARS PLANETS	App. Alt.	OCT.–MAR. SUN APR.–SEPT.				STARS PLANETS
	Lower Limb	Upper Limb	Lower Limb	Upper Limb			Lower Limb	Upper Limb	Lower Limb	Upper Limb	
° ′	′	′	′	′	′	° ′	′	′	′	′	′
0 00	−18·2	−51·7	−18·4	−51·4	−34·5	3 30	+ 3·3	−30·2	+ 3·1	−29·9	−13·0
03	17·5	51·0	17·8	50·8	33·8	35	3·6	29·9	3·3	29·7	12·7
06	16·9	50·4	17·1	50·1	33·2	40	3·8	29·7	3·5	29·5	12·5
09	16·3	49·8	16·5	49·5	32·6	45	4·0	29·5	3·7	29·3	12·3
12	15·7	49·2	15·9	48·9	32·0	50	4·2	29·3	3·9	29·1	12·1
15	15·1	48·6	15·3	48·3	31·4	3 55	4·4	29·1	4·1	28·9	11·9
0 18	−14·5	−48·0	−14·8	−47·8	−30·8	4 00	+ 4·5	−29·0	+ 4·3	−28·7	−11·8
21	14·0	47·5	14·2	47·2	30·3	05	4·7	28·8	4·5	28·5	11·6
24	13·5	47·0	13·7	46·7	29·8	10	4·9	28·6	4·6	28·4	11·4
27	12·9	46·4	13·2	46·2	29·2	15	5·1	28·4	4·8	28·2	11·2
30	12·4	45·9	12·7	45·7	28·7	20	5·2	28·3	5·0	28·0	11·1
33	11·9	45·4	12·2	45·2	28·2	25	5·4	28·1	5·1	27·9	10·9
0 36	−11·5	−45·0	−11·7	−44·7	−27·8	4 30	+ 5·6	−27·9	+ 5·3	−27·7	−10·7
39	11·0	44·5	11·2	44·2	27·3	35	5·7	27·8	5·5	27·5	10·6
42	10·5	44·0	10·8	43·8	26·8	40	5·9	27·6	5·6	27·4	10·4
45	10·1	43·6	10·3	43·3	26·4	45	6·0	27·5	5·8	27·2	10·3
48	9·6	43·1	9·9	42·9	25·9	50	6·2	27·3	5·9	27·1	10·1
51	9·2	42·7	9·5	42·5	25·5	4 55	6·3	27·2	6·0	27·0	10·0
0 54	− 8·8	−42·3	− 9·1	−42·1	−25·1	5 00	+ 6·4	−27·1	+ 6·2	−26·8	− 9·9
0 57	8·4	41·9	8·7	41·7	24·7	05	6·6	26·9	6·3	26·7	9·7
1 00	8·0	41·5	8·3	41·3	24·3	10	6·7	26·8	6·4	26·6	9·6
03	7·7	41·2	7·9	40·9	24·0	15	6·8	26·7	6·6	26·4	9·5
06	7·3	40·8	7·5	40·5	23·6	20	6·9	26·6	6·7	26·3	9·4
09	6·9	40·4	7·2	40·2	23·2	25	7·1	26·4	6·8	26·2	9·2
1 12	− 6·6	−40·1	− 6·8	−39·8	−22·9	5 30	+ 7·2	−26·3	+ 6·9	−26·1	− 9·1
15	6·2	39·7	6·5	39·5	22·5	35	7·3	26·2	7·0	26·0	9·0
18	5·9	39·4	6·2	39·2	22·2	40	7·4	26·1	7·2	25·8	8·9
21	5·6	39·1	5·8	38·8	21·9	45	7·5	26·0	7·3	25·7	8·8
24	5·3	38·8	5·5	38·5	21·6	50	7·6	25·9	7·4	25·6	8·7
27	4·9	38·4	5·2	38·2	21·2	5 55	7·7	25·8	7·5	25·5	8·6
1 30	− 4·6	−38·1	− 4·9	−37·9	−20·9	6 00	+ 7·8	−25·7	+ 7·6	−25·4	− 8·5
35	4·2	37·7	4·4	37·4	20·5	10	8·0	25·5	7·8	25·2	8·3
40	3·7	37·2	4·0	37·0	20·0	20	8·2	25·3	8·0	25·0	8·1
45	3·2	36·7	3·5	36·5	19·5	30	8·4	25·1	8·1	24·9	7·9
50	2·8	36·3	3·1	36·1	19·1	40	8·6	24·9	8·3	24·7	7·7
1 55	2·4	35·9	2·6	35·6	18·7	6 50	8·7	24·8	8·5	24·5	7·6
2 00	− 2·0	−35·5	− 2·2	−35·2	−18·3	7 00	+ 8·9	−24·6	+ 8·6	−24·4	− 7·4
05	1·6	35·1	1·8	34·8	17·9	10	9·1	24·4	8·8	24·2	7·2
10	1·2	34·7	1·5	34·5	17·5	20	9·2	24·3	9·0	24·0	7·1
15	0·9	34·4	1·1	34·1	17·2	30	9·3	24·2	9·1	23·9	7·0
20	0·5	34·0	0·8	33·8	16·8	40	9·5	24·0	9·2	23·8	6·8
25	− 0·2	33·7	0·4	33·4	16·5	7 50	9·6	23·9	9·4	23·6	6·7
2 30	+ 0·2	−33·3	− 0·1	−33·1	−16·1	8 00	+ 9·7	−23·8	+ 9·5	−23·5	− 6·6
35	0·5	33·0	+ 0·2	32·8	15·8	10	9·9	23·6	9·6	23·4	6·4
40	0·8	32·7	0·5	32·5	15·5	20	10·0	23·5	9·7	23·3	6·3
45	1·1	32·4	0·8	32·2	15·2	30	10·1	23·4	9·8	23·2	6·2
50	1·4	32·1	1·1	31·9	14·9	40	10·2	23·3	10·0	23·0	6·1
2 55	1·6	31·9	1·4	31·6	14·7	8 50	10·3	23·2	10·1	22·9	6·0
3 00	+ 1·9	−31·6	+ 1·7	−31·3	−14·4	9 00	+10·4	−23·1	+10·2	−22·8	− 5·9
05	2·2	31·3	1·9	31·1	14·1	10	10·5	23·0	10·3	22·7	5·8
10	2·4	31·1	2·1	30·9	13·9	20	10·6	22·9	10·4	22·6	5·7
15	2·6	30·9	2·4	30·6	13·7	30	10·7	22·8	10·5	22·5	5·6
20	2·9	30·6	2·6	30·4	13·4	40	10·8	22·7	10·6	22·4	5·5
25	3·1	30·4	2·9	30·1	13·2	9 50	10·9	22·6	10·6	22·4	5·4
3 30	+ 3·3	−30·2	+ 3·1	−29·9	−13·0	10 00	+11·0	−22·5	+10·7	−22·3	− 5·3

Additional corrections for temperature and pressure are given on the following page.

For bubble sextant observations ignore dip and use the star corrections for Sun, planets, and stars.

App. Alt.	A	B	C	D	E	F	G	H	J	K	L	M	N	App. Alt.
0 00	−6.9	−5.7	−4.6	−3.4	−2.3	−1.1	0.0	+1.1	+2.3	+3.4	+4.6	+5.7	+6.9	0 00
0 30	5.2	4.4	3.5	2.6	1.7	0.9	0.0	0.9	1.7	2.6	3.5	4.4	5.2	0 30
1 00	4.3	3.5	2.8	2.1	1.4	0.7	0.0	0.7	1.4	2.1	2.8	3.5	4.3	1 00
1 30	3.5	2.9	2.4	1.8	1.2	0.6	0.0	0.6	1.2	1.8	2.4	2.9	3.5	1 30
2 00	3.0	2.5	2.0	1.5	1.0	0.5	0.0	0.5	1.0	1.5	2.0	2.5	3.0	2 00
2 30	−2.5	−2.1	1.6	−1.2	−0.8	−0.4	0.0	+0.4	+0.8	+1.2	+1.6	+2.1	+2.5	2 30
3 00	2.2	1.8	1.5	1.1	0.7	0.4	0.0	0.4	0.7	1.1	1.5	1.8	2.2	3 00
3 30	2.0	1.6	1.3	1.0	0.7	0.3	0.0	0.3	0.7	1.0	1.3	1.6	2.0	3 30
4 00	1.8	1.5	1.2	0.9	0.6	0.3	0.0	0.3	0.6	0.9	1.2	1.5	1.8	4 00
4 30	1.6	1.4	1.1	0.8	0.5	0.3	0.0	0.3	0.5	0.8	1.1	1.4	1.6	4 30
5 00	−1.5	−1.3	−1.0	−0.8	−0.5	−0.2	0.0	+0.2	+0.5	+0.8	+1.0	+1.3	+1.5	5 00
6	1.3	1.1	0.9	0.6	0.4	0.2	0.0	0.2	0.4	0.6	0.9	1.1	1.3	6
7	1.1	0.9	0.7	0.6	0.4	0.2	0.0	0.2	0.4	0.6	0.7	0.9	1.1	7
8	1.0	0.8	0.7	0.5	0.3	0.2	0.0	0.2	0.3	0.5	0.7	0.8	1.0	8
9	0.9	0.7	0.6	0.4	0.3	0.1	0.0	0.1	0.3	0.4	0.6	0.7	0.9	9
10 00	−0.8	−0.7	−0.5	−0.4	−0.3	−0.1	0.0	+0.1	+0.3	+0.4	+0.5	+0.7	+0.8	10 00
12	0.7	0.6	0.5	0.3	0.2	0.1	0.0	0.1	0.2	0.3	0.5	0.6	0.7	12
14	0.6	0.5	0.4	0.3	0.2	0.1	0.0	0.1	0.2	0.3	0.4	0.5	0.6	14
16	0.5	0.4	0.3	0.3	0.2	0.1	0.0	0.1	0.2	0.3	0.3	0.4	0.5	16
18	0.4	0.4	0.3	0.2	0.2	0.1	0.0	0.1	0.2	0.2	0.3	0.4	0.4	18
20 00	−0.4	−0.3	−0.3	−0.2	−0.1	−0.1	0.0	+0.1	+0.1	+0.2	+0.3	+0.3	+0.4	20 00
25	0.3	0.3	0.2	0.2	0.1	−0.1	0.0	+0.1	0.1	0.2	0.2	0.3	0.3	25
30	0.3	0.2	0.2	0.1	0.1	0.0	0.0	0.0	0.1	0.1	0.2	0.2	0.3	30
35	0.2	0.2	0.1	0.1	0.1	0.0	0.0	0.0	0.1	0.1	0.1	0.2	0.2	35
40	0.2	0.1	0.1	0.1	−0.1	0.0	0.0	0.0	+0.1	0.1	0.1	0.1	0.2	40
50 00	−0.1	−0.1	−0.1	−0.1	0.0	0.0	0.0	0.0	0.0	+0.1	+0.1	+0.1	+0.1	50 00

The graph is entered with arguments temperature and pressure to find a zone letter; using as arguments this zone letter and apparent altitude (sextant altitude corrected for dip), a correction is taken from the table. This correction is to be applied to the sextant altitude in addition to the corrections for standard conditions. (for the Sun, planets and stars from the inside front cover and for the Moon from the inside back cover).

1968 APRIL 12, 13, 14 (FRI., SAT., SUN.)

G.M.T.	ARIES G.H.A.	VENUS −3.3 G.H.A.	Dec.	MARS +1.6 G.H.A.	Dec.	JUPITER −1.9 G.H.A.	Dec.	SATURN +0.9 G.H.A.	Dec.	STARS Name	S.H.A.	Dec.
d h	° ′	° ′	° ′	° ′	° ′	° ′	° ′	° ′	° ′		° ′	° ′
12 00	200 15.3	196 09.6 N	0 07.1	161 43.4 N15	12.5	51 36.1 N13	59.7	184 26.6 N	4 19.6	Acamar	315 44.5	S 40 25.9
01	215 17.8	211 09.2	08.3	176 44.1	13.1	66 38.6	59.8	199 28.8	19.7	Achernar	335 52.4	S 57 23.9
02	230 20.3	226 08.9	09.5	191 44.8	13.7	81 41.2	59.8	214 31.0	19.8	Acrux	173 47.4	S 62 55.5
03	245 22.7	241 08.5 ··	10.7	206 45.4 ··	14.3	96 43.7 ··	59.8	229 33.1 ··	20.0	Adhara	255 39.5	S 28 55.8
04	260 25.2	256 08.1	11.9	221 46.1	14.9	111 46.2	59.8	244 35.3	20.1	Aldebaran	291 28.9	N 16 26.9
05	275 27.7	271 07.8	13.1	236 46.8	15.5	126 48.8	59.8	259 37.5	20.2			
06	290 30.1	286 07.4 N	0 14.3	251 47.5 N15	16.1	141 51.3 N13	59.9	274 39.7 N	4 20.3	Alioth	166 49.7	N 56 07.9
07	305 32.6	301 07.1	15.6	266 48.2	16.7	156 53.9	59.9	289 41.8	20.4	Alkaid	153 25.1	N 49 28.1
08	320 35.1	316 06.7	16.8	281 48.9	17.3	171 56.4	59.9	304 44.0	20.6	Al Na'ir	28 26.6	S 47 06.9
F 09	335 37.5	331 06.3 ··	18.0	296 49.6 ··	17.8	186 58.9 ··	59.9	319 46.2 ··	20.7	Alnilam	276 21.2	S 1 13.2
R 10	350 40.0	346 06.0	19.2	311 50.2	18.4	202 01.5 13	59.9	334 48.4	20.8	Alphard	218 29.5	S 8 31.3
I 11	5 42.4	1 05.6	20.4	326 50.9	19.0	217 04.0 14	00.0	349 50.5	20.9			
D 12	20 44.9	16 05.2 N	0 21.6	341 51.6 N15	19.6	232 06.5 N14	00.0	4 52.7 N	4 21.0	Alphecca	126 39.6	N 26 49.0
A 13	35 47.4	31 04.9	22.9	356 52.3	20.2	247 09.1	00.0	19 54.9	21.1	Alpheratz	358 19.4	N 28 54.7
Y 14	50 49.8	46 04.5	24.1	11 53.0	20.8	262 11.6	00.0	34 57.0	21.3	Altair	62 41.6	N 8 46.7
15	65 52.3	61 04.2 ··	25.3	26 53.7 ··	21.4	277 14.2 ··	00.0	49 59.2 ··	21.4	Ankaa	353 49.5	S 42 28.7
16	80 54.8	76 03.8	26.5	41 54.4	22.0	292 16.7	00.1	65 01.4	21.5	Antares	113 08.0	S 26 21.9
17	95 57.2	91 03.4	27.7	56 55.0	22.5	307 19.2	00.1	80 03.6	21.6			
18	110 59.7	106 03.1 N	0 28.9	71 55.7 N15	23.1	322 21.8 N14	00.1	95 05.7 N	4 21.7	Arcturus	146 26.5	N 19 20.6
19	126 02.2	121 02.7	30.1	86 56.4	23.7	337 24.3	00.1	110 07.9	21.9	Atria	108 40.3	S 68 58.3
20	141 04.6	136 02.4	31.4	101 57.1	24.3	352 26.8	00.1	125 10.1	22.0	Avior	234 32.1	S 59 24.6
21	156 07.1	151 02.0 ··	32.6	116 57.8 ··	24.9	7 29.4 ··	00.2	140 12.3 ··	22.1	Bellatrix	279 08.9	N 6 19.4
22	171 09.5	166 01.6	33.8	131 58.5	25.5	22 31.9	00.2	155 14.4	22.2	Betelgeuse	271 38.4	N 7 24.2
23	186 12.0	181 01.3	35.0	146 59.1	26.1	37 34.4	00.2	170 16.6	22.3			
13 00	201 14.5	196 00.9 N	0 36.2	161 59.8 N15	26.6	52 37.0 N14	00.2	185 18.8 N	4 22.5	Canopus	264 11.5	S 52 40.8
01	216 16.9	211 00.5	37.4	177 00.5	27.2	67 39.5	00.2	200 21.0	22.6	Capella	281 25.3	N 45 58.3
02	231 19.4	226 00.2	38.7	192 01.2	27.8	82 42.0	00.3	215 23.1	22.7	Deneb	49 55.0	N 45 09.5
03	246 21.9	240 59.8 ··	39.9	207 01.9 ··	28.4	97 44.6 ··	00.3	230 25.3 ··	22.8	Denebola	183 08.1	N 14 44.9
04	261 24.3	255 59.5	41.1	222 02.6	29.0	112 47.1	00.3	245 27.5	22.9	Diphda	349 30.4	S 18 09.7
05	276 26.8	270 59.1	42.3	237 03.3	29.6	127 49.6	00.3	260 29.6	23.0			
06	291 29.3	285 58.7 N	0 43.5	252 03.9 N15	30.1	142 52.2 N14	00.3	275 31.8 N	4 23.2	Dubhe	194 32.6	N 61 55.5
07	306 31.7	300 58.4	44.7	267 04.6	30.7	157 54.7	00.3	290 34.0	23.3	Elnath	278 56.0	N 28 35.1
S 08	321 34.2	315 58.0	46.0	282 05.3	31.3	172 57.2	00.4	305 36.2	23.4	Eltanin	91 01.8	N 51 29.1
A 09	336 36.7	330 57.6 ··	47.2	297 06.0 ··	31.9	187 59.8 ··	00.4	320 38.3 ··	23.5	Enif	34 20.9	N 9 43.4
T 10	351 39.1	345 57.3	48.4	312 06.7	32.5	203 02.3	00.4	335 40.5	23.6	Fomalhaut	16 01.8	S 29 47.5
U 11	6 41.6	0 56.9	49.6	327 07.4	33.1	218 04.8	00.4	350 42.7	23.8			
R 12	21 44.0	15 56.6 N	0 50.8	342 08.0 N15	33.6	233 07.3 N14	00.4	5 44.9 N	4 23.9	Gacrux	172 38.9	S 56 56.3
D 13	36 46.5	30 56.2	52.0	357 08.7	34.2	248 09.9	00.4	20 47.0	24.0	Gienah	176 27.3	S 17 22.1
A 14	51 49.0	45 55.8	53.2	12 09.4	34.8	263 12.4	00.5	35 49.2	24.1	Hadar	149 36.2	S 60 13.3
Y 15	66 51.4	60 55.5 ··	54.5	27 10.1 ··	35.4	278 14.9 ··	00.5	50 51.4 ··	24.2	Hamal	328 39.8	N 23 18.7
16	81 53.9	75 55.1	55.7	42 10.8	36.0	293 17.5	00.5	65 53.6	24.3	Kaus Aust.	84 29.0	S 34 24.2
17	96 56.4	90 54.7	56.9	57 11.5	36.5	308 20.0	00.5	80 55.7	24.5			
18	111 58.8	105 54.4 N	0 58.1	72 12.1 N15	37.1	323 22.5 N14	00.5	95 57.9 N	4 24.6	Kochab	137 16.8	N 74 16.9
19	127 01.3	120 54.0	0 59.3	87 12.8	37.7	338 25.0	00.5	111 00.1	24.7	Markab	14 12.7	N 15 01.8
20	142 03.8	135 53.7	1 00.5	102 13.5	38.3	353 27.6	00.6	126 02.3	24.8	Menkar	314 51.1	N 3 57.9
21	157 06.2	150 53.3 ··	01.8	117 14.2 ··	38.9	8 30.1 ··	00.6	141 04.4 ··	24.9	Menkent	148 47.7	S 36 13.0
22	172 08.7	165 52.9	03.0	132 14.9	39.4	23 32.6	00.6	156 06.6	25.1	Miaplacidus	221 47.0	S 69 35.3
23	187 11.1	180 52.6	04.2	147 15.6	40.0	38 35.2	00.6	171 08.8	25.2			
14 00	202 13.6	195 52.2 N	1 05.4	162 16.2 N15	40.6	53 37.7 N14	00.6	186 10.9 N	4 25.3	Mirfak	309 30.0	N 49 45.1
01	217 16.1	210 51.8	06.6	177 16.9	41.2	68 40.2	00.7	201 13.1	25.4	Nunki	76 40.5	S 26 20.4
02	232 18.5	225 51.5	07.8	192 17.6	41.7	83 42.7	00.7	216 15.3	25.5	Peacock	54 12.9	S 56 50.2
03	247 21.0	240 51.1 ··	09.1	207 18.3 ··	42.3	98 45.3 ··	00.7	231 17.5 ··	25.7	Pollux	244 09.4	N 28 06.4
04	262 23.5	255 50.8	10.3	222 19.0	42.9	113 47.8	00.7	246 19.6	25.8	Procyon	245 35.5	N 5 18.5
05	277 25.9	270 50.4	11.5	237 19.6	43.5	128 50.3	00.7	261 21.8	25.9			
06	292 28.4	285 50.0 N	1 12.7	252 20.3 N15	44.1	143 52.8 N14	00.7	276 24.0 N	4 26.0	Rasalhague	96 38.0	N 12 34.6
07	307 30.9	300 49.7	13.9	267 21.0	44.6	158 55.4	00.7	291 26.2	26.1	Regulus	208 19.6	N 12 07.4
08	322 33.3	315 49.3	15.1	282 21.7	45.2	173 57.9	00.7	306 28.3	26.2	Rigel	281 45.1	S 8 14.2
S 09	337 35.8	330 49.0 ··	16.4	297 22.4 ··	45.8	189 00.4 ··	00.8	321 30.5 ··	26.4	Rigil Kent.	140 38.1	S 60 42.3
U 10	352 38.2	345 48.6	17.6	312 23.1	46.4	204 02.9	00.8	336 32.7	26.5	Sabik	102 51.6	S 15 41.4
N 11	7 40.7	0 48.2	18.8	327 23.7	46.9	219 05.4	00.8	351 34.9	26.6			
D 12	22 43.2	15 47.9 N	1 20.0	342 24.4 N15	47.5	234 08.0 N14	00.8	6 37.0 N	4 26.7	Schedar	350 20.5	N 56 21.7
A 13	37 45.6	30 47.5	21.2	357 25.1	48.1	249 10.5	00.8	21 39.2	26.8	Shaula	97 08.2	S 37 05.0
Y 14	52 48.1	45 47.1	22.4	12 25.8	48.6	264 13.0	00.8	36 41.4	27.0	Sirius	259 04.0	S 16 40.4
15	67 50.6	60 46.8 ··	23.6	27 26.5 ··	49.2	279 15.5 ··	00.8	51 43.6 ··	27.1	Spica	159 07.0	S 10 59.9
16	82 53.0	75 46.4	24.9	42 27.2	49.8	294 18.1	00.9	66 45.7	27.2	Suhail	223 17.6	S 43 18.4
17	97 55.5	90 46.1	26.1	57 27.8	50.4	309 20.6	00.9	81 47.9	27.3			
18	112 58.0	105 45.7 N	1 27.3	72 28.5 N15	50.9	324 23.1 N14	00.9	96 50.1 N	4 27.4	Vega	81 02.0	N 38 44.8
19	128 00.4	120 45.3	28.5	87 29.2	51.5	339 25.6	00.9	111 52.2	27.6	Zuben'ubi	137 43.0	S 15 54.8
20	143 02.9	135 45.0	29.7	102 29.9	52.1	354 28.1	00.9	126 54.4	27.7			
21	158 05.4	150 44.6 ··	30.9	117 30.5 ··	52.7	9 30.6 ··	00.9	141 56.6 ··	27.8		S.H.A.	Mer. Pass.
22	173 07.8	165 44.2	32.2	132 31.2	53.2	24 33.2	00.9	156 58.8	27.9		° ′	h m
23	188 10.3	180 43.9	33.4	147 31.9	53.8	39 35.7	00.9	172 00.9	28.0	Venus	354 46.4	10 56
Mer. Pass. 10 33.3		v −0.4	d 1.2	v 0.7	d 0.6	v 2.5	d 0.0	v 2.2	d 0.1	Mars	320 45.3	13 11
										Jupiter	211 22.5	20 26
										Saturn	344 04.3	11 37

1968 APRIL 12, 13, 14 (FRI., SAT., SUN.)

G.M.T.	SUN G.H.A.	Dec.	MOON G.H.A.	v	Dec.	d	H.P.
12 00	179 46.8	N 8 37.6	14 45.0	11.0	S 1 03.5	17.6	60.3
01	194 46.9	38.5	29 15.0	11.0	1 21.1	17.6	60.3
02	209 47.1	39.4	43 45.0	11.0	1 38.7	17.6	60.4
03	224 47.3	.. 40.4	58 15.0	10.9	1 56.3	17.6	60.4
04	239 47.4	41.3	72 44.9	10.9	2 13.9	17.6	60.4
05	254 47.6	42.2	87 14.8	10.9	2 31.5	17.6	60.4
06	269 47.8	N 8 43.1	101 44.7	10.8	S 2 49.1	17.6	60.5
07	284 47.9	44.0	116 14.5	10.8	3 06.7	17.6	60.5
F 08	299 48.1	44.9	130 44.3	10.7	3 24.3	17.6	60.5
R 09	314 48.3	.. 45.8	145 14.0	10.7	3 41.9	17.6	60.5
I 10	329 48.4	46.7	159 43.7	10.6	3 59.5	17.6	60.6
D 11	344 48.6	47.7	174 13.3	10.6	4 17.1	17.6	60.6
A 12	359 48.7	N 8 48.6	188 42.8	10.6	S 4 34.7	17.5	60.6
Y 13	14 48.9	49.5	203 12.4	10.4	4 52.2	17.6	60.6
14	29 49.1	50.4	217 41.8	10.4	5 09.8	17.5	60.6
15	44 49.2	.. 51.3	232 11.2	10.4	5 27.3	17.5	60.7
16	59 49.4	52.2	246 40.6	10.3	5 44.8	17.5	60.7
17	74 49.6	53.1	261 09.9	10.2	6 02.3	17.5	60.7
18	89 49.7	N 8 54.0	275 39.1	10.2	S 6 19.8	17.4	60.7
19	104 49.9	54.9	290 08.3	10.1	6 37.2	17.5	60.7
20	119 50.0	55.8	304 37.4	10.1	6 54.7	17.4	60.8
21	134 50.2	.. 56.7	319 06.5	10.0	7 12.1	17.3	60.8
22	149 50.4	57.7	333 35.5	9.9	7 29.4	17.4	60.8
23	164 50.5	58.6	348 04.4	9.9	7 46.8	17.3	60.8
13 00	179 50.7	N 8 59.5	2 33.3	9.8	S 8 04.1	17.2	60.8
01	194 50.8	9 00.4	17 02.1	9.7	8 21.3	17.2	60.9
02	209 51.0	01.3	31 30.8	9.7	8 38.5	17.2	60.9
03	224 51.2	.. 02.2	45 59.5	9.6	8 55.7	17.2	60.9
04	239 51.3	03.1	60 28.1	9.5	9 12.9	17.1	60.9
05	254 51.5	04.0	74 56.6	9.5	9 30.0	17.0	60.9
06	269 51.7	N 9 04.9	89 25.1	9.3	S 9 47.0	17.0	60.9
S 07	284 51.8	05.8	103 53.4	9.3	10 04.0	17.0	60.9
A 08	299 52.0	06.7	118 21.7	9.3	10 21.0	16.9	61.0
T 09	314 52.1	.. 07.6	132 50.0	9.1	10 37.9	16.8	61.0
U 10	329 52.3	08.5	147 18.1	9.1	10 54.7	16.8	61.0
R 11	344 52.5	09.4	161 46.2	9.0	11 11.5	16.7	61.0
D 12	359 52.6	N 9 10.3	176 14.2	8.9	S 11 28.2	16.7	61.0
A 13	14 52.8	11.2	190 42.1	8.9	11 44.9	16.6	61.0
Y 14	29 52.9	12.1	205 10.0	8.7	12 01.5	16.5	61.0
15	44 53.1	.. 13.0	219 37.7	8.7	12 18.0	16.5	61.0
16	59 53.3	13.9	234 05.4	8.6	12 34.5	16.4	61.0
17	74 53.4	14.9	248 33.0	8.5	12 50.9	16.3	61.0
18	89 53.6	N 9 15.8	263 00.5	8.4	S 13 07.2	16.2	61.1
19	104 53.7	16.7	277 27.9	8.4	13 23.4	16.2	61.1
20	119 53.9	17.6	291 55.3	8.2	13 39.6	16.1	61.1
21	134 54.0	.. 18.5	306 22.5	8.2	13 55.7	16.0	61.1
22	149 54.2	19.4	320 49.7	8.1	14 11.7	15.9	61.1
23	164 54.4	20.3	335 16.8	8.0	14 27.6	15.8	61.1
14 00	179 54.5	N 9 21.2	349 43.8	7.9	S 14 43.4	15.8	61.1
01	194 54.7	22.1	4 10.7	7.8	14 59.2	15.6	61.1
02	209 54.8	23.0	18 37.5	7.7	15 14.8	15.6	61.1
03	224 55.0	.. 23.9	33 04.2	7.6	15 30.4	15.4	61.1
04	239 55.2	24.8	47 30.8	7.6	15 45.8	15.4	61.1
05	254 55.3	25.7	61 57.4	7.4	16 01.2	15.3	61.1
06	269 55.5	N 9 26.6	76 23.8	7.4	S 16 16.5	15.1	61.1
07	284 55.6	27.5	90 50.2	7.2	16 31.6	15.1	61.1
08	299 55.8	28.4	105 16.4	7.2	16 46.7	14.9	61.1
S 09	314 55.9	.. 29.3	119 42.6	7.1	17 01.6	14.9	61.1
U 10	329 56.1	30.2	134 08.7	7.0	17 16.5	14.7	61.1
N 11	344 56.2	31.1	148 34.7	6.9	17 31.2	14.6	61.1
D 12	359 56.4	N 9 32.0	163 00.6	6.8	S 17 45.8	14.5	61.1
A 13	14 56.6	32.8	177 26.4	6.7	18 00.3	14.4	61.1
Y 14	29 56.7	33.7	191 52.1	6.6	18 14.7	14.3	61.1
15	44 56.9	.. 34.6	206 17.7	6.5	18 29.0	14.1	61.1
16	59 57.0	35.5	220 43.2	6.4	18 43.1	14.0	61.1
17	74 57.2	36.4	235 08.6	6.3	18 57.1	13.9	61.1
18	89 57.3	N 9 37.3	249 33.9	6.2	S 19 11.0	13.8	61.1
19	104 57.5	38.2	263 59.1	6.1	19 24.8	13.6	61.1
20	119 57.6	39.1	278 24.2	6.1	19 38.4	13.5	61.0
21	134 57.8	.. 40.0	292 49.3	5.9	19 51.9	13.4	61.0
22	149 58.0	40.9	307 14.2	5.9	20 05.3	13.2	61.0
23	164 58.1	41.8	321 39.1	5.7	20 18.5	13.1	61.0
	S.D. 16.0	d 0.9	S.D. 16.5		16.6		16.6

Moonrise

Lat.	Twilight Naut.	Civil	Sun-rise	12	13	14	15
N 72	////	02 16	03 51	19 06	22 06	■	■
N 70	////	02 48	04 06	18 56	21 33	■	■
68	01 11	03 11	04 18	18 47	21 09	24 15	00 15
66	01 57	03 28	04 28	18 40	20 51	23 24	
64	02 26	03 42	04 36	18 34	20 37	22 53	25 46
62	02 47	03 54	04 43	18 29	20 25	22 30	24 46
60	03 04	04 04	04 49	18 25	20 15	22 11	24 13
N 58	03 18	04 12	04 55	18 21	20 06	21 56	23 48
56	03 30	04 20	05 00	18 18	19 58	21 43	23 27
54	03 40	04 26	05 04	18 15	19 51	21 32	23 12
52	03 48	04 32	05 08	18 12	19 45	21 22	22 58
50	03 56	04 38	05 11	18 09	19 40	21 13	22 46
45	04 12	04 49	05 19	18 04	19 28	20 54	22 21
N 40	04 24	04 57	05 25	18 00	19 18	20 39	22 01
35	04 34	05 05	05 31	17 56	19 10	20 27	21 44
30	04 42	05 11	05 35	17 53	19 03	20 16	21 30
20	04 55	05 21	05 44	17 47	18 50	19 57	21 06
N 10	05 05	05 29	05 51	17 42	18 40	19 41	20 45
0	05 12	05 36	05 57	17 37	18 30	19 26	20 26
S 10	05 18	05 42	06 04	17 33	18 20	19 11	20 07
20	05 22	05 48	06 10	17 28	18 10	18 55	19 46
30	05 26	05 54	06 18	17 23	17 58	18 37	19 23
35	05 27	05 57	06 22	17 20	17 51	18 27	19 09
40	05 28	06 00	06 27	17 16	17 43	18 15	18 54
45	05 29	06 03	06 33	17 12	17 35	18 01	18 35
S 50	05 29	06 06	06 39	17 08	17 24	17 45	18 12
52	05 29	06 08	06 42	17 05	17 19	17 37	18 01
54	05 29	06 10	06 46	17 03	17 14	17 28	17 49
56	05 28	06 12	06 49	17 00	17 08	17 19	17 35
58	05 28	06 13	06 53	16 58	17 02	17 08	17 19
S 60	05 27	06 15	06 58	16 54	16 54	16 55	16 59

Moonset

Lat.	Sun-set	Twilight Civil	Naut.	12	13	14	15
N 72	20 14	21 52	////	04 38	03 56	02 49	■
N 70	19 58	21 18	////	04 42	04 10	03 25	■
68	19 46	20 54	23 03	04 44	04 21	03 50	02 44
66	19 36	20 36	22 10	04 47	04 30	04 10	03 36
64	19 27	20 21	21 40	04 49	04 38	04 26	04 09
62	19 20	20 09	21 17	04 51	04 45	04 40	04 33
60	19 13	19 59	21 00	04 52	04 51	04 51	04 53
N 58	19 08	19 50	20 46	04 54	04 57	05 01	05 09
56	19 03	19 43	20 34	04 55	05 01	05 10	05 23
54	18 58	19 36	20 23	04 56	05 06	05 18	05 35
52	18 54	19 30	20 14	04 57	05 10	05 25	05 45
50	18 51	19 25	20 06	04 58	05 13	05 31	05 55
45	18 43	19 13	19 50	05 00	05 21	05 41	06 15
N 40	18 36	19 05	19 38	05 02	05 28	05 57	06 31
35	18 31	18 57	19 28	05 03	05 33	06 06	06 45
30	18 26	18 50	19 19	05 05	05 38	06 15	06 57
20	18 18	18 40	19 06	05 07	05 47	06 30	07 18
N 10	18 10	18 32	18 57	05 09	05 54	06 43	07 37
0	18 04	18 25	18 49	05 11	06 02	06 56	07 54
S 10	17 57	18 19	18 43	05 13	06 09	07 08	08 11
20	17 51	18 13	18 38	05 15	06 17	07 22	08 29
30	17 43	18 07	18 35	05 17	06 26	07 37	08 51
35	17 38	18 04	18 33	05 18	06 31	07 46	09 03
40	17 33	18 01	18 32	05 20	06 37	07 56	09 18
45	17 28	17 57	18 31	05 21	06 43	08 08	09 35
S 50	17 21	17 54	18 31	05 23	06 52	08 23	09 57
52	17 18	17 52	18 31	05 24	06 56	08 30	10 07
54	17 14	17 50	18 31	05 25	07 00	08 38	10 19
56	17 11	17 48	18 32	05 26	07 04	08 47	10 32
58	17 07	17 47	18 32	05 28	07 10	08 57	10 48
S 60	17 02	17 44	18 32	05 29	07 16	09 08	11 07

Day	SUN Eqn. of Time 00h	12h	Mer. Pass.	MOON Mer. Pass. Upper	Lower	Age	Phase
	m s	m s	h m	h m	h m	d	
12	00 53	00 45	12 01	23 49	11 24	15	◯
13	00 38	00 30	12 00	24 43	12 16	16	
14	00 22	00 15	12 00	00 43	13 11	17	

G.M.T.	ARIES G.H.A.	VENUS −3.3 G.H.A.	Dec.	MARS +1.6 G.H.A.	Dec.	JUPITER −1.9 G.H.A.	Dec.	SATURN +0.9 G.H.A.	Dec.	STARS Name	S.H.A.	Dec.
15 00	203 12.8	195 43.5 N 1	34.6	162 32.6 N15	54.4	54 38.2 N14	01.0	187 03.1 N 4	28.1	Acamar	315 44.5	S 40 25.9
01	218 15.2	210 43.2	35.8	177 33.3	54.9	69 40.7	01.0	202 05.3	28.3	Achernar	335 52.4	S 57 23.8
02	233 17.7	225 42.8	37.0	192 33.9	55.5	84 43.2	01.0	217 07.5	28.4	Acrux	173 47.4	S 62 55.6
03	248 20.1	240 42.4 ··	38.2	207 34.6 ··	56.1	99 45.8 ··	01.0	232 09.6 ··	28.5	Adhara	255 39.5	S 28 55.8
04	263 22.6	255 42.1	39.5	222 35.3	56.7	114 48.3	01.0	247 11.8	28.6	Aldebaran	291 28.9	N 16 26.9
05	278 25.1	270 41.7	40.7	237 36.0	57.2	129 50.8	01.0	262 14.0	28.7			
06	293 27.5	285 41.3 N 1	41.9	252 36.7 N15	57.8	144 53.3 N14	01.0	277 16.2 N 4	28.9	Alioth	166 49.8	N 56 07.9
07	308 30.0	300 41.0	43.1	267 37.3	58.4	159 55.8	01.0	292 18.3	29.0	Alkaid	153 25.0	N 49 28.2
08	323 32.5	315 40.6	44.3	282 38.0	58.9	174 58.3	01.1	307 20.5	29.1	Al Na'ir	28 26.6	S 47 06.9
M 09	338 34.9	330 40.3 ··	45.5	297 38.7 15	59.5	190 00.9 ··	01.1	322 22.7 ··	29.2	Alnilam	276 21.2	S 1 13.2
O 10	353 37.4	345 39.9	46.7	312 39.4 16	00.1	205 03.4	01.1	337 24.8	29.3	Alphard	218 29.6	S 8 31.3
N 11	8 39.9	0 39.5	48.0	327 40.1	00.6	220 05.9	01.1	352 27.0	29.4			
D 12	23 42.3	15 39.2 N 1	49.2	342 40.7 N16	01.2	235 08.4 N14	01.1	7 29.2 N 4	29.6	Alphecca	126 39.6	N 26 49.0
A 13	38 44.8	30 38.8	50.4	357 41.4	01.8	250 10.9	01.1	22 31.4	29.7	Alpheratz	358 19.3	N 28 54.7
Y 14	53 47.2	45 38.4	51.6	12 42.1	02.3	265 13.4	01.1	37 33.5	29.8	Altair	62 41.6	N 8 46.7
15	68 49.7	60 38.1 ··	52.8	27 42.8 ··	02.9	280 15.9 ··	01.1	52 35.7 ··	29.9	Ankaa	353 49.5	S 42 28.7
16	83 52.2	75 37.7	54.0	42 43.5	03.5	295 18.5	01.2	67 37.9	30.0	Antares	113 08.0	S 26 21.9
17	98 54.6	90 37.3	55.2	57 44.1	04.0	310 21.0	01.2	82 40.1	30.1			
18	113 57.1	105 37.0 N 1	56.5	72 44.8 N16	04.6	325 23.5 N14	01.2	97 42.2 N 4	30.3	Arcturus	146 26.5	N 19 20.6
19	128 59.6	120 36.6	57.7	87 45.5	05.2	340 26.0	01.2	112 44.4	30.4	Atria	108 40.3	S 68 58.3
20	144 02.0	135 36.3 1	58.9	102 46.2	05.7	355 28.5	01.2	127 46.6	30.5	Avior	234 32.1	S 59 24.6
21	159 04.5	150 35.9 2	00.1	117 46.9 ··	06.3	10 31.0 ··	01.2	142 48.8 ··	30.6	Bellatrix	279 08.9	N 6 19.4
22	174 07.0	165 35.5	01.3	132 47.5	06.9	25 33.5	01.2	157 50.9	30.7	Betelgeuse	271 38.4	N 7 24.2
23	189 09.4	180 35.2	02.5	147 48.2	07.4	40 36.0	01.2	172 53.1	30.9			
16 00	204 11.9	195 34.8 N 2	03.8	162 48.9 N16	08.0	55 38.6 N14	01.2	187 55.3 N 4	31.0	Canopus	264 11.5	S 52 40.8
01	219 14.4	210 34.4	05.0	177 49.6	08.6	70 41.1	01.3	202 57.5	31.1	Capella	281 25.3	N 45 58.3
02	234 16.8	225 34.1	06.2	192 50.2	09.1	85 43.6	01.3	217 59.6	31.2	Deneb	49 55.0	N 45 09.5
03	249 19.3	240 33.7 ··	07.4	207 50.9 ··	09.7	100 46.1 ··	01.3	233 01.8 ··	31.3	Denebola	183 08.1	N 14 44.9
04	264 21.7	255 33.4	08.6	222 51.6	10.3	115 48.6	01.3	248 04.0	31.4	Diphda	349 30.4	S 18 09.7
05	279 24.2	270 33.0	09.8	237 52.3	10.8	130 51.1	01.3	263 06.1	31.6			
06	294 26.7	285 32.6 N 2	11.0	252 53.0 N16	11.4	145 53.6 N14	01.3	278 08.3 N 4	31.7	Dubhe	194 32.6	N 61 55.6
07	309 29.1	300 32.3	12.3	267 53.6	12.0	160 56.1	01.3	293 10.5	31.8	Elnath	278 56.1	N 28 35.1
T 08	324 31.6	315 31.9	13.5	282 54.3	12.5	175 58.6	01.3	308 12.7	31.9	Eltanin	91 01.8	N 51 29.1
U 09	339 34.1	330 31.5 ··	14.7	297 55.0 ··	13.1	191 01.1 ··	01.3	323 14.8 ··	32.0	Enif	34 20.8	N 9 43.5
E 10	354 36.5	345 31.2	15.9	312 55.7	13.6	206 03.7	01.3	338 17.0	32.1	Fomalhaut	16 01.8	S 29 47.5
S 11	9 39.0	0 30.8	17.1	327 56.3	14.2	221 06.2	01.4	353 19.2	32.3			
D 12	24 41.5	15 30.4 N 2	18.3	342 57.0 N16	14.8	236 08.7 N14	01.4	8 21.4 N 4	32.4	Gacrux	172 38.9	S 56 56.3
A 13	39 43.9	30 30.1	19.5	357 57.7	15.3	251 11.2	01.4	23 23.5	32.5	Gienah	176 27.3	S 17 22.1
Y 14	54 46.4	45 29.7	20.8	12 58.4	15.9	266 13.7	01.4	38 25.7	32.6	Hadar	149 36.2	S 60 13.3
15	69 48.9	60 29.3 ··	22.0	27 59.1 ··	16.4	281 16.2 ··	01.4	53 27.9 ··	32.7	Hamal	328 39.8	N 23 18.7
16	84 51.3	75 29.0	23.2	42 59.7	17.0	296 18.7	01.4	68 30.1	32.9	Kaus Aust.	84 29.0	S 34 24.2
17	99 53.8	90 28.6	24.4	58 00.4	17.6	311 21.2	01.4	83 32.2	33.0			
18	114 56.2	105 28.2 N 2	25.6	73 01.1 N16	18.1	326 23.7 N14	01.4	98 34.4 N 4	33.1	Kochab	137 16.8	N 74 16.9
19	129 58.7	120 27.9	26.8	88 01.8	18.7	341 26.2	01.4	113 36.6	33.2	Markab	14 12.7	N 15 01.8
20	145 01.2	135 27.5	28.0	103 02.4	19.2	356 28.7	01.4	128 38.8	33.3	Menkar	314 51.1	N 3 58.0
21	160 03.6	150 27.2 ··	29.3	118 03.1 ··	19.8	11 31.2 ··	01.4	143 40.9 ··	33.4	Menkent	148 47.7	S 36 13.0
22	175 06.1	165 26.8	30.5	133 03.8	20.4	26 33.7	01.4	158 43.1	33.6	Miaplacidus	221 47.1	S 69 35.3
23	190 08.6	180 26.4	31.7	148 04.5	20.9	41 36.2	01.5	173 45.3	33.7			
17 00	205 11.0	195 26.1 N 2	32.9	163 05.1 N16	21.5	56 38.7 N14	01.5	188 47.5 N 4	33.8	Mirfak	309 30.0	N 49 45.1
01	220 13.5	210 25.7	34.1	178 05.8	22.0	71 41.2	01.5	203 49.6	33.9	Nunki	76 40.5	S 26 20.4
02	235 16.0	225 25.3	35.3	193 06.5	22.6	86 43.7	01.5	218 51.8	34.0	Peacock	54 12.9	S 56 50.2
03	250 18.4	240 25.0 ··	36.5	208 07.2 ··	23.2	101 46.2 ··	01.5	233 54.0 ··	34.1	Pollux	244 09.4	N 28 06.4
04	265 20.9	255 24.6	37.8	223 07.8	23.7	116 48.7	01.5	248 56.2	34.3	Procyon	245 35.5	N 5 18.5
05	280 23.4	270 24.2	39.0	238 08.5	24.3	131 51.3	01.5	263 58.3	34.4			
06	295 25.8	285 23.9 N 2	40.2	253 09.2 N16	24.8	146 53.8 N14	01.5	279 00.5 N 4	34.5	Rasalhague	96 38.0	N 12 34.6
W 07	310 28.3	300 23.5	41.4	268 09.9	25.4	161 56.3	01.5	294 02.7	34.6	Regulus	208 19.6	N 12 07.4
E 08	325 30.7	315 23.1	42.6	283 10.5	25.9	176 58.8	01.5	309 04.9	34.7	Rigel	281 45.1	S 8 14.2
D 09	340 33.2	330 22.8 ··	43.8	298 11.2 ··	26.5	192 01.3 ··	01.5	324 07.0 ··	34.8	Rigil Kent.	140 38.1	S 60 42.3
N 10	355 35.7	345 22.4	45.0	313 11.9	27.0	207 03.8	01.5	339 09.2	35.0	Sabik	102 51.5	S 15 41.4
E 11	10 38.1	0 22.0	46.2	328 12.6	27.6	222 06.3	01.5	354 11.4	35.1			
S 12	25 40.6	15 21.7 N 2	47.5	343 13.2 N16	28.2	237 08.8 N14	01.5	9 13.6 N 4	35.2	Schedar	350 20.4	N 56 21.7
D 13	40 43.1	30 21.3	48.7	358 13.9	28.7	252 11.3	01.6	24 15.7	35.3	Shaula	97 08.1	S 37 05.0
A 14	55 45.5	45 20.9	49.9	13 14.6	29.3	267 13.8	01.6	39 17.9	35.4	Sirius	259 04.0	S 16 40.4
Y 15	70 48.0	60 20.6 ··	51.1	28 15.3 ··	29.8	282 16.3 ··	01.6	54 20.1 ··	35.6	Spica	159 07.0	S 10 59.9
16	85 50.5	75 20.2	52.3	43 15.9	30.4	297 18.8	01.6	69 22.3	35.7	Suhail	223 17.6	S 43 18.4
17	100 52.9	90 19.8	53.5	58 16.6	30.9	312 21.3	01.6	84 24.4	35.8			
18	115 55.4	105 19.5 N 2	54.7	73 17.3 N16	31.5	327 23.8 N14	01.6	99 26.6 N 4	35.9	Vega	81 02.0	N 38 44.8
19	130 57.9	120 19.1	55.9	88 18.0	32.0	342 26.2	01.6	114 28.8	36.0	Zuben'ubi	137 43.0	S 15 54.8
20	146 00.3	135 18.7	57.2	103 18.6	32.6	357 28.7	01.6	129 31.0	36.1			
21	161 02.8	150 18.4 ··	58.4	118 19.3 ··	33.1	12 31.2 ··	01.6	144 33.1 ··	36.3		S.H.A.	Mer. Pass.
22	176 05.2	165 18.0 2	59.6	133 20.0	33.7	27 33.7	01.6	159 35.3	36.4	Venus	351 22.9	10 58
23	191 07.7	180 17.6 3	00.8	148 20.7	34.2	42 36.2	01.6	174 37.5	36.5	Mars	318 37.0	13 08
Mer. Pass. 10 21.5		v −0.4 d 1.2		v 0.7 d 0.6		v 2.5 d 0.0		v 2.2 d 0.1		Jupiter	211 26.7	20 14
										Saturn	343 43.4	11 27

G.M.T.	SUN G.H.A.	Dec.	MOON G.H.A.	v	Dec.	d	H.P.
	° ′	° ′	° ′	′	° ′	′	′
15 00	179 58·3 N 9 42·7		336 03·8	5·7	S 20 31·6	13·0	61·0
01	194 58·4	43·6	350 28·5	5·5	20 44·6	12·8	61·0
02	209 58·6	44·5	4 53·0	5·5	20 57·4	12·7	61·0
03	224 58·7 ··	45·4	19 17·5	5·4	21 10·1	12·5	61·0
04	239 58·9	46·3	33 41·9	5·2	21 22·6	12·4	61·0
05	254 59·0	47·2	48 06·1	5·2	21 35·0	12·2	61·0
06	269 59·2 N 9 48·1		62 30·3	5·1	S 21 47·2	12·0	61·0
07	284 59·3	49·0	76 54·4	5·0	21 59·2	12·0	60·9
08	299 59·5	49·8	91 18·4	5·0	22 11·2	11·7	60·9
M 09	314 59·6 ··	50·7	105 42·4	4·8	22 22·9	11·6	60·9
O 10	329 59·8	51·6	120 06·2	4·7	22 34·5	11·4	60·9
N 11	344 59·9	52·5	134 29·9	4·7	22 45·9	11·3	60·9
D 12	0 00·1 N 9 53·4		148 53·6	4·6	S 22 57·2	11·1	60·9
A 13	15 00·3	54·3	163 17·2	4·5	23 08·3	11·0	60·9
Y 14	30 00·4	55·2	177 40·7	4·4	23 19·3	10·8	60·9
15	45 00·6 ··	56·1	192 04·1	4·3	23 30·1	10·6	60·8
16	60 00·7	57·0	206 27·4	4·2	23 40·7	10·4	60·8
17	75 00·9	57·9	220 50·6	4·2	23 51·1	10·3	60·8
18	90 01·0 N 9 58·8		235 13·8	4·0	S 24 01·4	10·1	60·8
19	105 01·2 9 59·6		249 36·8	4·1	24 11·5	9·9	60·8
20	120 01·3 10 00·5		263 59·9	3·9	24 21·4	9·7	60·7
21	135 01·5 ·· 01·4		278 22·8	3·8	24 31·1	9·6	60·7
22	150 01·6 02·3		292 45·6	3·8	24 40·7	9·3	60·7
23	165 01·8 03·2		307 08·4	3·7	24 50·0	9·2	60·7
16 00	180 01·9 N10 04·1		321 31·1	3·7	S 24 59·2	9·1	60·7
01	195 02·1 05·0		335 53·8	3·5	25 08·3	8·8	60·7
02	210 02·2 05·9		350 16·3	3·5	25 17·1	8·6	60·6
03	225 02·4 ·· 06·7		4 38·8	3·5	25 25·7	8·5	60·6
04	240 02·5 07·6		19 01·3	3·5	25 34·2	8·3	60·6
05	255 02·7 08·5		33 23·6	3·4	25 42·5	8·0	60·6
06	270 02·8 N10 09·4		47 46·0	3·2	S 25 50·5	7·9	60·5
07	285 03·0 10·3		62 08·2	3·2	25 58·4	7·7	60·5
T 08	300 03·1 11·2		76 30·4	3·2	26 06·1	7·5	60·5
U 09	315 03·3 ·· 12·1		90 52·6	3·1	26 13·6	7·4	60·5
E 10	330 03·4 12·9		105 14·7	3·0	26 21·0	7·1	60·5
S 11	345 03·6 13·8		119 36·7	3·0	26 28·1	6·9	60·4
D 12	0 03·7 N10 14·7		133 58·7	3·0	S 26 35·0	6·7	60·4
A 13	15 03·9 15·6		148 20·7	2·9	26 41·7	6·5	60·4
Y 14	30 04·0 16·5		162 42·6	2·9	26 48·2	6·4	60·4
15	45 04·2 ·· 17·4		177 04·5	2·8	26 54·6	6·1	60·3
16	60 04·3 18·2		191 26·3	2·8	27 00·7	5·9	60·3
17	75 04·5 19·1		205 48·1	2·8	27 06·6	5·8	60·3
18	90 04·6 N10 20·0		220 09·9	2·7	S 27 12·4	5·5	60·3
19	105 04·7 20·9		234 31·6	2·7	27 17·9	5·3	60·2
20	120 04·9 21·8		248 53·3	2·7	27 23·2	5·1	60·2
21	135 05·0 ·· 22·7		263 15·0	2·7	27 28·3	4·9	60·2
22	150 05·2 23·5		277 36·6	2·7	27 33·2	4·8	60·1
23	165 05·3 24·4		291 58·3	2·6	27 38·0	4·5	60·1
17 00	180 05·5 N10 25·3		306 19·9	2·6	S 27 42·5	4·3	60·1
01	195 05·6 26·2		320 41·5	2·6	27 46·8	4·1	60·1
02	210 05·8 27·1		335 03·1	2·6	27 50·9	3·9	60·0
03	225 05·9 ·· 27·9		349 24·7	2·6	27 54·8	3·7	60·0
04	240 06·1 28·8		3 46·3	2·6	27 58·5	3·5	60·0
05	255 06·2 29·7		18 07·9	2·5	28 02·0	3·2	59·9
06	270 06·4 N10 30·6		32 29·4	2·6	S 28 05·2	3·1	59·9
07	285 06·5 31·5		46 51·0	2·6	28 08·3	2·9	59·9
W 08	300 06·6 32·3		61 12·6	2·6	28 11·2	2·7	59·9
E 09	315 06·8 ·· 33·2		75 34·2	2·6	28 13·9	2·4	59·8
D 10	330 06·9 34·1		89 55·8	2·6	28 16·3	2·3	59·8
N 11	345 07·1 35·0		104 17·4	2·6	28 18·6	2·0	59·8
E 12	0 07·2 N10 35·8		118 39·0	2·7	S 28 20·6	1·9	59·7
S 13	15 07·4 36·7		133 00·7	2·7	28 22·5	1·6	59·7
D 14	30 07·5 37·6		147 22·4	2·7	28 24·1	1·5	59·7
A 15	45 07·7 ·· 38·5		161 44·1	2·7	28 25·6	1·2	59·7
Y 16	60 07·8 39·3		176 05·8	2·7	28 26·8	1·0	59·6
17	75 07·9 40·2		190 27·5	2·8	28 27·8	0·9	59·6
18	90 08·1 N10 41·1		204 49·3	2·9	S 28 28·7	0·6	59·6
19	105 08·2 42·0		219 11·2	2·8	28 29·3	0·4	59·5
20	120 08·4 42·8		233 33·0	2·9	28 29·7	0·2	59·5
21	135 08·5 ·· 43·7		247 54·9	3·0	28 29·9	0·0	59·5
22	150 08·7 44·6		262 16·9	3·0	28 29·9	0·1	59·4
23	165 08·8 45·5		276 38·9	3·0	28 29·8	0·4	59·4
	S.D. 16·0 d 0·9		S.D. 16·6		16·5		16·3

Lat.	Twilight Naut.	Civil	Sun- rise	Moonrise 15	16	17	18
°	h m	h m	h m	h m	h m	h m	h m
N 72	////	01 48	03 33	■	■	■	■
N 70	////	02 27	03 51	■	■	■	■
68	////	02 54	04 05	00 15	■	■	■
66	01 33	03 14	04 16	■	■	■	■
64	02 08	03 30	04 26	25 46	01 46	■	■
62	02 33	03 43	04 34	24 46	00 46	■	■
60	02 52	03 54	04 40	24 13	00 13	02 09	03 28
N 58	03 07	04 04	04 47	23 48	25 32	01 32	02 46
56	03 20	04 12	04 52	23 28	25 05	01 05	02 18
54	03 31	04 19	04 57	23 12	24 44	00 44	01 56
52	03 41	04 25	05 01	22 58	24 27	00 27	01 37
50	03 49	04 31	05 05	22 46	24 12	00 12	01 22
45	04 06	04 43	05 14	22 21	23 42	24 51	00 51
N 40	04 19	04 53	05 21	22 01	23 18	24 26	00 26
35	04 30	05 01	05 27	21 44	22 59	24 06	00 06
30	04 39	05 08	05 32	21 30	22 43	23 49	24 47
20	04 53	05 19	05 41	21 06	22 15	23 21	24 20
N 10	05 03	05 28	05 49	20 45	21 51	22 56	23 57
0	05 11	05 35	05 56	20 26	21 29	22 33	23 35
S 10	05 18	05 42	06 04	20 07	21 07	22 10	23 13
20	05 23	05 49	06 11	19 46	20 44	21 45	22 49
30	05 27	05 55	06 20	19 23	20 16	21 17	22 22
35	05 29	05 59	06 24	19 09	20 00	21 00	22 06
40	05 31	06 03	06 30	18 54	19 42	20 40	21 47
45	05 32	06 06	06 36	18 35	19 19	20 16	21 24
S 50	05 33	06 11	06 44	18 12	18 51	19 45	20 55
52	05 34	06 13	06 47	18 01	18 37	19 30	20 40
54	05 34	06 15	06 51	17 49	18 22	19 12	20 23
56	05 34	06 17	06 55	17 35	18 03	18 51	20 03
58	05 34	06 20	07 00	17 19	17 40	18 23	19 38
S 60	05 34	06 22	07 05	16 59	17 10	17 44	19 04

Lat.	Sun- set	Twilight Civil	Naut.	Moonset 15	16	17	18
°	h m	h m	h m	h m	h m	h m	h m
N 72	20 30	22 21	////	■	■	■	■
N 70	20 12	21 38	////	■	■	■	■
68	19 58	21 09	////	02 44	■	■	■
66	19 46	20 49	22 35	03 36	■	■	■
64	19 36	20 32	21 56	04 09	03 23	■	■
62	19 28	20 19	21 30	04 33	04 23	■	■
60	19 21	20 08	21 11	04 53	04 58	05 15	06 10
N 58	19 14	19 58	20 55	05 09	05 23	05 53	06 52
56	19 09	19 50	20 42	05 23	05 43	06 19	07 21
54	19 04	19 42	20 30	05 35	06 00	06 41	07 42
52	18 59	19 36	20 21	05 45	06 14	06 58	08 00
50	18 55	19 30	20 12	05 55	06 26	07 13	08 15
45	18 47	19 18	19 55	06 15	06 53	07 44	08 47
N 40	18 39	19 08	19 41	06 31	07 14	08 08	09 11
35	18 33	18 59	19 31	06 45	07 32	08 27	09 30
30	18 28	18 52	19 22	06 57	07 47	08 44	09 47
20	18 19	18 41	19 08	07 18	08 13	09 12	10 16
N 10	18 11	18 32	18 57	07 37	08 35	09 37	10 40
0	18 03	18 24	18 48	07 54	08 56	10 00	11 03
S 10	17 56	18 17	18 42	08 11	09 16	10 22	11 26
20	17 48	18 11	18 36	08 29	09 39	10 47	11 50
30	17 40	18 04	18 32	08 51	10 05	11 15	12 18
35	17 35	18 00	18 30	09 03	10 20	11 32	12 34
40	17 29	17 56	18 28	09 18	10 38	11 52	12 54
45	17 23	17 52	18 27	09 35	11 00	12 15	13 17
S 50	17 15	17 48	18 25	09 57	11 27	12 46	13 47
52	17 11	17 46	18 25	10 07	11 41	13 01	14 02
54	17 08	17 44	18 25	10 19	11 56	13 19	14 19
56	17 03	17 41	18 24	10 32	12 15	13 41	14 39
58	16 59	17 39	18 24	10 48	12 37	14 08	15 04
S 60	16 53	17 36	18 24	11 07	13 06	14 47	15 39

Day	SUN Eqn. of Time 00h	12h	Mer. Pass.	MOON Mer. Pass. Upper	Lower	Age	Phase
	m s	m s	h m	h m	h m	d	
15	00 07	00 00	12 00	01 40	14 10	18	◯
16	00 07	00 15	12 00	02 41	15 12	19	
17	00 22	00 29	12 00	03 44	16 16	20	

G.M.T.	ARIES G.H.A.	VENUS −3.3 G.H.A.	Dec.	MARS +1.7 G.H.A.	Dec.	JUPITER −1.8 G.H.A.	Dec.	SATURN +0.9 G.H.A.	Dec.	STARS Name	S.H.A.	Dec.
d h	° '	° '	° '	° '	° '	° '	° '	° '	° '		° '	° '
18 00	206 10.2	195 17.3 N 3	02.0	163 21.3 N16	34.8	57 38.7 N14	01.6	189 39.7 N 4	36.6	Acamar	315 44.5	S 40 25.9
01	221 12.6	210 16.9	03.2	178 22.0	35.3	72 41.2	01.6	204 41.8	36.7	Achernar	335 52.4	S 57 23.8
02	236 15.1	225 16.5	04.4	193 22.7	35.9	87 43.7	01.6	219 44.0	36.8	Acrux	173 47.4	S 62 55.6
03	251 17.6	240 16.2 ··	05.6	208 23.4 ··	36.4	102 46.2 ··	01.6	234 46.2 ··	37.0	Adhara	255 39.5	S 28 55.8
04	266 20.0	255 15.8	06.8	223 24.0	37.0	117 48.7	01.6	249 48.4	37.1	Aldebaran	291 28.9	N 16 26.9
05	281 22.5	270 15.4	08.1	238 24.7	37.5	132 51.2	01.6	264 50.5	37.2			
T 06	296 25.0	285 15.1 N 3	09.3	253 25.4 N16	38.1	147 53.7 N14	01.6	279 52.7 N 4	37.3	Alioth	166 49.7	N 56 07.9
H 07	311 27.4	300 14.7	10.5	268 26.1	38.6	162 56.2	01.6	294 54.9	37.4	Alkaid	153 25.0	N 49 28.2
U 08	326 29.9	315 14.3	11.7	283 26.7	39.2	177 58.7	01.6	309 57.1	37.5	Al Na'ir	28 26.6	S 47 06.9
R 09	341 32.4	330 14.0 ··	12.9	298 27.4 ··	39.7	193 01.2 ··	01.7	324 59.2 ··	37.7	Alnilam	276 21.3	S 1 13.2
S 10	356 34.8	345 13.6	14.1	313 28.1	40.3	208 03.7	01.7	340 01.4	37.8	Alphard	218 29.6	S 8 31.3
D 11	11 37.3	0 13.3	15.3	328 28.8	40.8	223 06.2	01.7	355 03.6	37.9			
A 12	26 39.7	15 12.9 N 3	16.5	343 29.4 N16	41.4	238 08.7 N14	01.7	10 05.8 N 4	38.0	Alphecca	126 39.6	N 26 49.0
Y 13	41 42.2	30 12.5	17.7	358 30.1	41.9	253 11.2	01.7	25 07.9	38.1	Alpheratz	358 19.3	N 28 54.7
14	56 44.7	45 12.1	19.0	13 30.8	42.5	268 13.6	01.7	40 10.1	38.2	Altair	62 41.5	N 8 46.7
15	71 47.1	60 11.8 ··	20.2	28 31.4 ··	43.0	283 16.1 ··	01.7	55 12.3 ··	38.4	Ankaa	353 49.5	S 42 28.7
16	86 49.6	75 11.4	21.4	43 32.1	43.6	298 18.6	01.7	70 14.5	38.5	Antares	113 08.0	S 26 21.9
17	101 52.1	90 11.0	22.6	58 32.8	44.1	313 21.1	01.7	85 16.6	38.6			
18	116 54.5	105 10.7 N 3	23.8	73 33.5 N16	44.7	328 23.6 N14	01.7	100 18.8 N 4	38.7	Arcturus	146 26.5	N 19 20.7
19	131 57.0	120 10.3	25.0	88 34.1	45.2	343 26.1	01.7	115 21.0	38.8	Atria	108 40.3	S 68 58.3
20	146 59.5	135 09.9	26.2	103 34.8	45.8	358 28.6	01.7	130 23.2	38.9	Avior	234 32.2	S 59 24.6
21	162 01.9	150 09.6 ··	27.4	118 35.5 ··	46.3	13 31.1 ··	01.7	145 25.3 ··	39.1	Bellatrix	279 08.9	N 6 19.4
22	177 04.4	165 09.2	28.6	133 36.1	46.9	28 33.6	01.7	160 27.5	39.2	Betelgeuse	271 38.5	N 7 24.2
23	192 06.9	180 08.8	29.8	148 36.8	47.4	43 36.1	01.7	175 29.7	39.3			
19 00	207 09.3	195 08.4 N 3	31.1	163 37.5 N16	47.9	58 38.5 N14	01.7	190 31.9 N 4	39.4	Canopus	264 11.6	S 52 40.8
01	222 11.8	210 08.1	32.3	178 38.2	48.5	73 41.0	01.7	205 34.0	39.5	Capella	281 25.3	N 45 58.3
02	237 14.2	225 07.7	33.5	193 38.8	49.0	88 43.5	01.7	220 36.2	39.6	Deneb	49 55.0	N 45 09.5
03	252 16.7	240 07.3 ··	34.7	208 39.5 ··	49.6	103 46.0 ··	01.7	235 38.4 ··	39.8	Denebola	183 08.1	N 14 44.9
04	267 19.2	255 07.0	35.9	223 40.2	50.1	118 48.5	01.7	250 40.6	39.9	Diphda	349 30.3	S 18 09.7
05	282 21.6	270 06.6	37.1	238 40.9	50.7	133 51.0	01.7	265 42.7	40.0			
F 06	297 24.1	285 06.2 N 3	38.3	253 41.5 N16	51.2	148 53.5 N14	01.7	280 44.9 N 4	40.1	Dubhe	194 32.6	N 61 55.6
R 07	312 26.6	300 05.9	39.5	268 42.2	51.7	163 56.0	01.7	295 47.1	40.2	Elnath	278 56.1	N 28 35.1
I 08	327 29.0	315 05.5	40.7	283 42.9	52.3	178 58.4	01.7	310 49.3	40.3	Eltanin	91 01.7	N 51 29.1
D 09	342 31.5	330 05.1 ··	41.9	298 43.5 ··	52.8	194 00.9 ··	01.7	325 51.4 ··	40.5	Enif	34 20.8	N 9 43.5
A 10	357 34.0	345 04.7	43.1	313 44.2	53.4	209 03.4	01.7	340 53.6	40.6	Fomalhaut	16 01.7	S 29 47.5
Y 11	12 36.4	0 04.4	44.3	328 44.9	53.9	224 05.9	01.7	355 55.8	40.7			
12	27 38.9	15 04.0 N 3	45.6	343 45.6 N16	54.5	239 08.4 N14	01.7	10 58.0 N 4	40.8	Gacrux	172 38.9	S 56 56.3
13	42 41.3	30 03.6	46.8	358 46.2	55.0	254 10.9	01.7	26 00.1	40.9	Gienah	176 27.3	S 17 22.1
14	57 43.8	45 03.3	48.0	13 46.9	55.5	269 13.3	01.7	41 02.3	41.0	Hadar	149 36.2	S 60 13.4
15	72 46.3	60 02.9 ··	49.2	28 47.6 ··	56.1	284 15.8 ··	01.7	56 04.5 ··	41.2	Hamal	328 39.8	N 23 18.7
16	87 48.7	75 02.5	50.4	43 48.2	56.6	299 18.3	01.7	71 06.7	41.3	Kaus Aust.	84 28.9	S 34 24.2
17	102 51.2	90 02.2	51.6	58 48.9	57.2	314 20.8	01.7	86 08.8	41.4			
18	117 53.7	105 01.8 N 3	52.8	73 49.6 N16	57.7	329 23.3 N14	01.7	101 11.0 N 4	41.5	Kochab	137 16.8	N 74 16.9
19	132 56.1	120 01.4	54.0	88 50.2	58.2	344 25.8	01.7	116 13.2	41.6	Markab	14 12.7	N 15 01.8
20	147 58.6	135 01.0	55.2	103 50.9	58.8	359 28.2	01.7	131 15.4	41.7	Menkar	314 51.1	N 3 58.0
21	163 01.1	150 00.7 ··	56.4	118 51.6 ··	59.3	14 30.7 ··	01.7	146 17.5 ··	41.8	Menkent	148 47.7	S 36 13.0
22	178 03.5	165 00.3	57.6	133 52.3 16	59.9	29 33.2	01.7	161 19.7	42.0	Miaplacidus	221 47.1	S 69 35.4
23	193 06.0	179 59.9 3	58.8	148 52.9 17	00.4	44 35.7	01.7	176 21.9	42.1			
20 00	208 08.5	194 59.6 N 4	00.0	163 53.6 N17	00.9	59 38.2 N14	01.7	191 24.1 N 4	42.2	Mirfak	309 30.0	N 49 45.1
01	223 10.9	209 59.2	01.2	178 54.3	01.5	74 40.7	01.7	206 26.2	42.3	Nunki	76 40.5	S 26 20.4
02	238 13.4	224 58.8	02.5	193 54.9	02.0	89 43.1	01.7	221 28.4	42.4	Peacock	54 12.8	S 56 50.2
03	253 15.8	239 58.4 ··	03.7	208 55.6 ··	02.5	104 45.6 ··	01.7	236 30.6 ··	42.5	Pollux	244 09.5	N 28 06.4
04	268 18.3	254 58.1	04.9	223 56.3	03.1	119 48.1	01.7	251 32.8	42.7	Procyon	245 35.5	N 5 18.5
05	283 20.8	269 57.7	06.1	238 57.0	03.6	134 50.6	01.7	266 34.9	42.8			
S 06	298 23.2	284 57.3 N 4	07.3	253 57.6 N17	04.2	149 53.1 N14	01.7	281 37.1 N 4	42.9	Rasalhague	96 38.0	N 12 34.6
A 07	313 25.7	299 56.9	08.5	268 58.3	04.7	164 55.5	01.7	296 39.3	43.0	Regulus	208 19.6	N 12 07.4
T 08	328 28.2	314 56.6	09.7	283 59.0	05.2	179 58.0	01.7	311 41.5	43.1	Rigel	281 45.1	S 8 14.2
U 09	343 30.6	329 56.2 ··	10.9	298 59.6 ··	05.8	195 00.5 ··	01.7	326 43.7 ··	43.2	Rigil Kent.	140 38.1	S 60 42.3
R 10	358 33.1	344 55.8	12.1	314 00.3	06.3	210 03.0	01.7	341 45.8	43.4	Sabik	102 51.5	S 15 41.4
D 11	13 35.6	359 55.5	13.3	329 01.0	06.8	225 05.4	01.7	356 48.0	43.5			
A 12	28 38.0	14 55.1 N 4	14.5	344 01.6 N17	07.4	240 07.9 N14	01.7	11 50.2 N 4	43.6	Schedar	350 20.4	N 56 21.6
Y 13	43 40.5	29 54.7	15.7	359 02.3	07.9	255 10.4	01.7	26 52.4	43.7	Shaula	97 08.1	S 37 05.0
14	58 43.0	44 54.3	16.9	14 03.0	08.4	270 12.9	01.7	41 54.5	43.8	Sirius	259 04.0	S 16 40.3
15	73 45.4	59 54.0 ··	18.1	29 03.6 ··	09.0	285 15.4 ··	01.7	56 56.7 ··	43.9	Spica	159 07.0	S 10 59.9
16	88 47.9	74 53.6	19.3	44 04.3	09.5	300 17.8	01.7	71 58.9	44.1	Suhail	223 17.6	S 43 18.4
17	103 50.3	89 53.2	20.5	59 05.0	10.0	315 20.3	01.7	87 01.1	44.2			
18	118 52.8	104 52.8 N 4	21.7	74 05.6 N17	10.6	330 22.8 N14	01.7	102 03.2 N 4	44.3	Vega	81 02.0	N 38 44.8
19	133 55.3	119 52.5	22.9	89 06.3	11.1	345 25.3	01.7	117 05.4	44.4	Zuben'ubi	137 43.0	S 15 54.8
20	148 57.7	134 52.1	24.1	104 07.0	11.6	0 27.7	01.7	132 07.6	44.5		S.H.A.	Mer. Pass.
21	164 00.2	149 51.7 ··	25.4	119 07.6 ··	12.2	15 30.2 ··	01.7	147 09.8 ··	44.6		° '	h m
22	179 02.7	164 51.3	26.6	134 08.3	12.7	30 32.7	01.7	162 11.9	44.8	Venus	347 59.1	11 00
23	194 05.1	179 51.0	27.8	149 09.0	13.2	45 35.2	01.7	177 14.1	44.9	Mars	316 28.2	13 05
Mer. Pass.	10 09.7	v −0.4	d 1.2	v 0.7	d 0.5	v 2.5	d 0.0	v 2.2	d 0.1	Jupiter	211 29.2	20 02
										Saturn	343 22.6	11 16

1968 APRIL 18, 19, 20 (THURS., FRI., SAT.)

G.M.T.	SUN G.H.A.	Dec.	MOON G.H.A.	v	Dec.	d	H.P.
18 00	180 08.9	N10 46.3	291 00.9	3.1	S28 29.4	0.6	59.4
01	195 09.1	47.2	305 23.0	3.2	28 28.8	0.8	59.3
02	210 09.2	48.1	319 45.2	3.2	28 28.0	0.9	59.3
03	225 09.4 ..	49.0	334 07.4	3.3	28 27.1	1.2	59.3
04	240 09.5	49.8	348 29.7	3.3	28 25.9	1.4	59.2
05	255 09.6	50.7	2 52.0	3.4	28 24.5	1.5	59.2
06	270 09.8	N10 51.6	17 14.4	3.5	S28 23.0	1.8	59.2
T 07	285 09.9	52.5	31 36.9	3.5	28 21.2	1.9	59.1
H 08	300 10.1	53.3	45 59.4	3.6	28 19.3	2.1	59.1
U 09	315 10.2 ..	54.2	60 22.0	3.7	28 17.2	2.3	59.1
R 10	330 10.3	55.1	74 44.7	3.7	28 14.9	2.6	59.0
S 11	345 10.5	55.9	89 07.4	3.9	28 12.3	2.7	59.0
D 12	0 10.6	N10 56.8	103 30.3	3.9	S28 09.6	3.0	59.0
A 13	15 10.8	57.7	117 53.2	4.0	28 06.8	3.1	58.9
Y 14	30 10.9	58.5	132 16.2	4.1	28 03.7	3.3	58.9
15	45 11.0	10 59.4	146 39.3	4.2	28 00.4	3.4	58.9
16	60 11.2	11 00.3	161 02.5	4.2	27 57.0	3.6	58.8
17	75 11.3	01.1	175 25.7	4.4	27 53.4	3.8	58.8
18	90 11.5	N11 02.0	189 49.1	4.4	S27 49.6	4.0	58.8
19	105 11.6	02.9	204 12.5	4.6	27 45.6	4.1	58.7
20	120 11.7	03.7	218 36.1	4.6	27 41.5	4.4	58.7
21	135 11.9 ..	04.6	232 59.7	4.7	27 37.1	4.5	58.7
22	150 12.0	05.5	247 23.4	4.9	27 32.6	4.6	58.6
23	165 12.2	06.3	261 47.3	4.9	27 28.0	4.9	58.6
19 00	180 12.3	N11 07.2	276 11.2	5.0	S27 23.1	5.0	58.6
01	195 12.4	08.1	290 35.2	5.2	27 18.1	5.2	58.5
02	210 12.6	08.9	304 59.4	5.2	27 12.9	5.3	58.5
03	225 12.7 ..	09.8	319 23.6	5.4	27 07.6	5.6	58.5
04	240 12.8	10.7	333 48.0	5.4	27 02.0	5.7	58.4
05	255 13.0	11.5	348 12.4	5.6	26 56.3	5.8	58.4
06	270 13.1	N11 12.4	2 37.0	5.7	S26 50.5	6.0	58.4
07	285 13.3	13.3	17 01.7	5.8	26 44.5	6.2	58.3
F 08	300 13.4	14.1	31 26.5	5.9	26 38.3	6.3	58.3
R 09	315 13.5 ..	15.0	45 51.4	6.0	26 32.0	6.5	58.3
I 10	330 13.7	15.9	60 16.4	6.1	26 25.5	6.6	58.2
11	345 13.8	16.7	74 41.5	6.3	26 18.9	6.8	58.2
D 12	0 13.9	N11 17.6	89 06.8	6.4	S26 12.1	6.9	58.2
A 13	15 14.1	18.4	103 32.2	6.4	26 05.2	7.1	58.1
Y 14	30 14.2	19.3	117 57.6	6.6	25 58.1	7.3	58.1
15	45 14.3 ..	20.2	132 23.2	6.8	25 50.8	7.3	58.1
16	60 14.5	21.0	146 49.0	6.8	25 43.5	7.6	58.0
17	75 14.6	21.9	161 14.8	7.0	25 35.9	7.6	58.0
18	90 14.7	N11 22.7	175 40.8	7.0	S25 28.3	7.8	58.0
19	105 14.9	23.6	190 06.8	7.2	25 20.5	8.0	57.9
20	120 15.0	24.5	204 33.0	7.4	25 12.5	8.1	57.9
21	135 15.2 ..	25.3	218 59.4	7.4	25 04.4	8.2	57.9
22	150 15.3	26.2	233 25.8	7.6	24 56.2	8.3	57.8
23	165 15.4	27.0	247 52.4	7.6	24 47.9	8.5	57.8
20 00	180 15.6	N11 27.9	262 19.0	7.8	S24 39.4	8.7	57.8
01	195 15.7	28.8	276 45.8	8.0	24 30.7	8.7	57.7
02	210 15.8	29.6	291 12.8	8.0	24 22.0	8.9	57.7
03	225 15.9 ..	30.5	305 39.8	8.2	24 13.1	9.0	57.7
04	240 16.1	31.3	320 07.0	8.3	24 04.1	9.1	57.6
05	255 16.2	32.2	334 34.3	8.4	23 55.0	9.3	57.6
06	270 16.3	N11 33.0	349 01.7	8.5	S23 45.7	9.3	57.6
S 07	285 16.5	33.9	3 29.2	8.7	23 36.4	9.5	57.5
A 08	300 16.6	34.8	17 56.9	8.8	23 26.9	9.6	57.5
T 09	315 16.7 ..	35.6	32 24.7	8.9	23 17.3	9.8	57.5
U 10	330 16.9	36.5	46 52.6	9.0	23 07.5	9.8	57.4
R 11	345 17.0	37.3	61 20.6	9.2	22 57.7	10.0	57.4
D 12	0 17.1	N11 38.2	75 48.8	9.2	S22 47.7	10.0	57.4
A 13	15 17.3	39.0	90 17.0	9.4	22 37.7	10.2	57.3
Y 14	30 17.4	39.9	104 45.4	9.5	22 27.5	10.3	57.3
15	45 17.5 ..	40.7	119 13.9	9.7	22 17.2	10.4	57.3
16	60 17.7	41.6	133 42.6	9.7	22 06.8	10.5	57.2
17	75 17.8	42.4	148 11.3	9.9	21 56.3	10.5	57.2
18	90 17.9	N11 43.3	162 40.2	10.0	S21 45.8	10.7	57.2
19	105 18.0	44.1	177 09.2	10.1	21 35.1	10.8	57.2
20	120 18.2	45.0	191 38.3	10.2	21 24.3	10.9	57.1
21	135 18.3 ..	45.8	206 07.5	10.3	21 13.4	11.0	57.1
22	150 18.4	46.7	220 36.8	10.5	21 02.4	11.1	57.1
23	165 18.6	47.6	235 06.3	10.6	20 51.3	11.2	57.0
	S.D. 15.9	d 0.9	S.D. 16.1		15.8		15.6

Moonrise

Lat.	Twilight Naut.	Civil	Sun-rise	Moonrise 18	19	20	21
N 72	////	01 12	03 15	■	■	■	
N 70	////	02 05	03 36	■	■	■	06 42
68	////	02 37	03 52	■	■	■	05 43
66	01 02	03 00	04 05	■	■	06 17	05 08
64	01 49	03 18	04 15	■	■	05 06	04 43
62	02 18	03 32	04 24	■	04 44	04 30	04 23
60	02 39	03 44	04 32	03 28	03 56	04 04	04 06
N 58	02 57	03 55	04 39	02 46	03 25	03 43	03 53
56	03 11	04 04	04 45	02 18	03 02	03 26	03 41
54	03 22	04 11	04 50	01 56	02 43	03 12	03 30
52	03 33	04 18	04 55	01 37	02 27	02 59	03 21
50	03 42	04 25	04 59	01 22	02 13	02 48	03 12
45	04 00	04 38	05 09	00 51	01 44	02 24	02 54
N 40	04 14	04 48	05 16	00 26	01 22	02 05	02 39
35	04 26	04 57	05 23	00 06	01 03	01 50	02 27
30	04 35	05 04	05 29	24 47	00 47	01 36	02 16
20	04 50	05 16	05 39	24 20	00 20	01 12	01 57
N 10	05 01	05 26	05 48	23 57	24 52	00 52	01 41
0	05 10	05 35	05 56	23 35	24 33	00 33	01 25
S 10	05 18	05 42	06 04	23 13	24 13	00 13	01 09
20	05 24	05 50	06 12	22 49	23 53	24 53	00 53
30	05 29	05 57	06 21	22 22	23 29	24 33	00 33
35	05 31	06 01	06 27	22 06	23 14	24 22	00 22
40	05 34	06 05	06 33	21 47	22 58	24 09	00 09
45	05 36	06 10	06 40	21 24	22 38	23 53	25 06
S 50	05 38	06 15	06 48	20 55	22 13	23 34	24 53
52	05 38	06 18	06 52	20 40	22 01	23 25	24 47
54	05 39	06 20	06 57	20 23	21 48	23 15	24 40
56	05 40	06 23	07 01	20 03	21 32	23 03	24 32
58	05 40	06 26	07 06	19 38	21 13	22 50	24 23
S 60	05 41	06 29	07 12	19 04	20 49	22 34	24 13

Moonset

Lat.	Sun-set	Twilight Civil	Naut.	Moonset 18	19	20	21
N 72	20 47	23 01	////	■	■	■	■
N 70	20 26	22 00	////	■	■	■	08 52
68	20 10	21 26	////	■	■	■	09 50
66	19 56	21 02	23 09	■	■	07 28	10 23
64	19 45	20 43	22 15	■	■	08 38	10 47
62	19 36	20 28	21 44	■	07 02	09 13	11 06
60	19 28	20 16	21 22	06 10	07 50	09 39	11 22
N 58	19 21	20 06	21 04	06 52	08 20	09 58	11 35
56	19 15	19 56	20 50	07 20	08 43	10 15	11 46
54	19 09	19 48	20 38	07 42	09 02	10 29	11 56
52	19 05	19 41	20 27	08 00	09 17	10 41	12 04
50	19 00	19 35	20 18	08 16	09 31	10 52	12 12
45	18 50	19 22	20 00	08 47	09 59	11 14	12 29
N 40	18 42	19 11	19 45	09 11	10 20	11 32	12 42
35	18 36	19 02	19 33	09 30	10 38	11 47	12 53
30	18 30	18 54	19 24	09 47	10 54	12 00	13 03
20	18 20	18 42	19 09	10 16	11 20	12 22	13 20
N 10	18 11	18 32	18 57	10 40	11 42	12 41	13 35
0	18 02	18 24	18 48	11 03	12 03	12 58	13 48
S 10	17 54	18 16	18 40	11 26	12 24	13 16	14 02
20	17 46	18 08	18 34	11 50	12 46	13 34	14 16
30	17 36	18 01	18 29	12 18	13 11	13 55	14 32
35	17 31	17 57	18 26	12 34	13 26	14 08	14 42
40	17 25	17 52	18 24	12 54	13 43	14 22	14 52
45	17 18	17 47	18 22	13 17	14 04	14 39	15 05
S 50	17 09	17 42	18 20	13 47	14 30	14 59	15 20
52	17 05	17 40	18 19	14 02	14 42	15 09	15 27
54	17 01	17 37	18 18	14 19	14 56	15 20	15 35
56	16 56	17 34	18 18	14 39	15 13	15 32	15 43
58	16 51	17 31	18 17	15 04	15 32	15 46	15 53
S 60	16 45	17 28	18 16	15 39	15 57	16 03	16 04

SUN / MOON

Day	SUN Eqn. of Time 00h	12h	Mer. Pass.	MOON Mer. Pass. Upper	Lower	Age	Phase
	m s	m s	h m	h m	h m	d	
18	00 35	00 42	11 59	04 48	17 19	21	
19	00 49	00 55	11 59	05 49	18 18	22	
20	01 02	01 08	11 59	06 46	19 12	23	

1968 APRIL 21, 22, 23 (SUN., MON., TUES.)

G.M.T.	ARIES G.H.A.	VENUS −3.3 G.H.A.	Dec.	MARS +1.7 G.H.A.	Dec.	JUPITER −1.8 G.H.A.	Dec.	SATURN +0.9 G.H.A.	Dec.	STARS Name	S.H.A.	Dec.
21 00	209 07.6	194 50.6 N 4	29.0	164 09.6 N17	13.8	60 37.6 N14	01.7	192 16.3 N 4	45.0	Acamar	315 44.5	S 40 25.9
01	224 10.1	209 50.2	30.2	179 10.3	14.3	75 40.1	01.7	207 18.5	45.1	Achernar	335 52.4	S 57 23.8
02	239 12.5	224 49.8	31.4	194 11.0	14.8	90 42.6	01.7	222 20.7	45.2	Acrux	173 47.4	S 62 55.6
03	254 15.0	239 49.5 ..	32.6	209 11.6 ..	15.4	105 45.1 ..	01.7	237 22.8 ..	45.3	Adhara	255 39.5	S 28 55.8
04	269 17.5	254 49.1	33.8	224 12.3	15.9	120 47.5	01.7	252 25.0	45.4	Aldebaran	291 28.9	N 16 26.9
05	284 19.9	269 48.7	35.0	239 13.0	16.4	135 50.0	01.7	267 27.2	45.6			
S 06	299 22.4	284 48.3 N 4	36.2	254 13.6 N17	16.9	150 52.5 N14	01.7	282 29.4 N 4	45.7	Alioth	166 49.8	N 56 07.9
U 07	314 24.8	299 48.0	37.4	269 14.3	17.5	165 54.9	01.7	297 31.5	45.8	Alkaid	153 25.0	N 49 28.2
N 08	329 27.3	314 47.6	38.6	284 15.0	18.0	180 57.4	01.7	312 33.7	45.9	Al Na'ir	28 26.6	S 47 06.9
D 09	344 29.8	329 47.2 ..	39.8	299 15.6 ..	18.5	195 59.9 ..	01.7	327 35.9 ..	46.0	Alnilam	276 21.3	S 1 13.2
A 10	359 32.2	344 46.8	41.0	314 16.3	19.1	211 02.4	01.7	342 38.1	46.1	Alphard	218 29.6	S 8 31.3
Y 11	14 34.7	359 46.5	42.2	329 17.0	19.6	226 04.8	01.7	357 40.2	46.3			
12	29 37.2	14 46.1 N 4	43.4	344 17.6 N17	20.1	241 07.3 N14	01.6	12 42.4 N 4	46.4	Alphecca	126 39.5	N 26 49.0
13	44 39.6	29 45.7	44.6	359 18.3	20.6	256 09.8	01.6	27 44.6	46.5	Alpheratz	358 19.3	N 28 54.7
14	59 42.1	44 45.3	45.8	14 19.0	21.2	271 12.2	01.6	42 46.8	46.6	Altair	62 41.5	N 8 46.7
15	74 44.6	59 45.0 ..	47.0	29 19.6 ..	21.7	286 14.7 ..	01.6	57 48.9 ..	46.7	Ankaa	353 49.5	S 42 28.7
16	89 47.0	74 44.6	48.2	44 20.3	22.2	301 17.2	01.6	72 51.1	46.8	Antares	113 07.9	S 26 21.9
17	104 49.5	89 44.2	49.4	59 21.0	22.7	316 19.6	01.6	87 53.3	46.9			
18	119 51.9	104 43.8 N 4	50.6	74 21.6 N17	23.3	331 22.1 N14	01.6	102 55.5 N 4	47.1	Arcturus	146 26.5	N 19 20.7
19	134 54.4	119 43.4	51.8	89 22.3	23.8	346 24.6	01.6	117 57.7	47.2	Atria	108 40.2	S 68 58.3
20	149 56.9	134 43.1	53.0	104 23.0	24.3	1 27.0	01.6	132 59.8	47.3	Avior	234 32.2	S 59 24.6
21	164 59.3	149 42.7 ..	54.2	119 23.6 ..	24.8	16 29.5 ..	01.6	148 02.0 ..	47.4	Bellatrix	279 08.9	N 6 19.4
22	180 01.8	164 42.3	55.4	134 24.3	25.4	31 32.0	01.6	163 04.2	47.5	Betelgeuse	271 38.5	N 7 24.2
23	195 04.3	179 41.9	56.6	149 25.0	25.9	46 34.4	01.6	178 06.4	47.6			
22 00	210 06.7	194 41.6 N 4	57.8	164 25.6 N17	26.4	61 36.9 N14	01.6	193 08.5 N 4	47.8	Canopus	264 11.6	S 52 40.8
01	225 09.2	209 41.2 4	59.0	179 26.3	26.9	76 39.4	01.6	208 10.7	47.9	Capella	281 25.3	N 45 58.3
02	240 11.7	224 40.8 5	00.2	194 27.0	27.5	91 41.8	01.6	223 12.9	48.0	Deneb	49 54.9	N 45 09.5
03	255 14.1	239 40.5 ..	01.4	209 27.6 ..	28.0	106 44.3 ..	01.6	238 15.1 ..	48.1	Denebola	183 08.1	N 14 44.9
04	270 16.6	254 40.0	02.6	224 28.3	28.5	121 46.8	01.6	253 17.2	48.2	Diphda	349 30.3	S 18 09.7
05	285 19.0	269 39.7	03.8	239 29.0	29.0	136 49.2	01.6	268 19.4	48.3			
M 06	300 21.5	284 39.3 N 5	05.0	254 29.6 N17	29.6	151 51.7 N14	01.6	283 21.6 N 4	48.4	Dubhe	194 32.6	N 61 55.6
O 07	315 24.0	299 38.9	06.2	269 30.3	30.1	166 54.2	01.5	298 23.8	48.6	Elnath	278 56.1	N 28 35.1
N 08	330 26.4	314 38.5	07.4	284 31.0	30.6	181 56.6	01.5	313 26.0	48.7	Eltanin	91 01.7	N 51 29.1
D 09	345 28.9	329 38.2 ..	08.6	299 31.6 ..	31.1	196 59.1 ..	01.5	328 28.1 ..	48.8	Enif	34 20.8	N 9 43.5
A 10	0 31.4	344 37.8	09.8	314 32.3	31.6	212 01.5	01.5	343 30.3	48.9	Fomalhaut	16 01.7	S 29 47.5
Y 11	15 33.8	359 37.4	11.0	329 33.0	32.2	227 04.0	01.5	358 32.5	49.0			
12	30 36.3	14 37.0 N 5	12.2	344 33.6 N17	32.7	242 06.5 N14	01.5	13 34.7 N 4	49.1	Gacrux	172 38.9	S 56 56.3
13	45 38.8	29 36.6	13.4	359 34.3	33.2	257 08.9	01.5	28 36.8	49.2	Gienah	176 27.3	S 17 22.1
14	60 41.2	44 36.3	14.6	14 34.9	33.7	272 11.4	01.5	43 39.0	49.4	Hadar	149 36.2	S 60 13.4
15	75 43.7	59 35.9 ..	15.8	29 35.6 ..	34.2	287 13.9 ..	01.5	58 41.2 ..	49.5	Hamal	328 39.8	N 23 18.7
16	90 46.2	74 35.5	17.0	44 36.3	34.8	302 16.3	01.5	73 43.4	49.6	Kaus Aust.	84 28.9	S 34 24.2
17	105 48.6	89 35.1	18.2	59 36.9	35.3	317 18.8	01.5	88 45.5	49.7			
18	120 51.1	104 34.7 N 5	19.4	74 37.6 N17	35.8	332 21.2 N14	01.5	103 47.7 N 4	49.8	Kochab	137 16.8	N 74 17.0
19	135 53.5	119 34.3	20.6	89 38.3	36.3	347 23.7	01.5	118 49.9	49.9	Markab	14 12.6	N 15 01.8
20	150 56.0	134 34.0	21.8	104 38.9	36.8	2 26.2	01.5	133 52.1	50.1	Menkar	314 51.1	N 3 58.0
21	165 58.5	149 33.6 ..	23.0	119 39.6 ..	37.4	17 28.6 ..	01.4	148 54.3 ..	50.2	Menkent	148 47.7	S 36 13.0
22	181 00.9	164 33.2	24.2	134 40.3	37.9	32 31.1	01.4	163 56.4	50.3	Miaplacidus	221 47.2	S 69 35.4
23	196 03.4	179 32.8	25.3	149 40.9	38.4	47 33.5	01.4	178 58.6	50.4			
23 00	211 05.9	194 32.4 N 5	26.5	164 41.6 N17	38.9	62 36.0 N14	01.4	194 00.8 N 4	50.5	Mirfak	309 30.0	N 49 45.1
01	226 08.3	209 32.1	27.7	179 42.2	39.4	77 38.5	01.4	209 03.0	50.6	Nunki	76 40.5	S 26 20.4
02	241 10.8	224 31.7	28.9	194 42.9	39.9	92 40.9	01.4	224 05.1	50.7	Peacock	54 12.8	S 56 50.2
03	256 13.3	239 31.3 ..	30.1	209 43.6 ..	40.5	107 43.4 ..	01.4	239 07.3 ..	50.9	Pollux	244 09.5	N 28 06.4
04	271 15.7	254 30.9	31.3	224 44.2	41.0	122 45.8	01.4	254 09.5	51.0	Procyon	245 35.5	N 5 18.5
05	286 18.2	269 30.5	32.5	239 44.9	41.5	137 48.3	01.4	269 11.7	51.1			
T 06	301 20.7	284 30.1 N 5	33.7	254 45.6 N17	42.0	152 50.7 N14	01.4	284 13.9 N 4	51.2	Rasalhague	96 37.9	N 12 34.6
U 07	316 23.1	299 29.8	34.9	269 46.2	42.5	167 53.2	01.4	299 16.0	51.3	Regulus	208 19.6	N 12 07.4
E 08	331 25.6	314 29.4	36.1	284 46.9	43.0	182 55.7	01.4	314 18.2	51.4	Rigel	281 45.1	S 8 14.2
S 09	346 28.0	329 29.0 ..	37.3	299 47.6 ..	43.5	197 58.1 ..	01.3	329 20.4 ..	51.5	Rigil Kent.	140 38.0	S 60 42.3
D 10	1 30.5	344 28.6	38.5	314 48.2	44.1	213 00.6	01.3	344 22.6	51.7	Sabik	102 51.5	S 15 41.4
A 11	16 33.0	359 28.2	39.7	329 48.9	44.6	228 03.0	01.3	359 24.7	51.8			
Y 12	31 35.4	14 27.8 N 5	40.9	344 49.5 N17	45.1	243 05.5 N14	01.3	14 26.9 N 4	51.9	Schedar	350 20.4	N 56 21.6
13	46 37.9	29 27.5	42.1	359 50.2	45.6	258 07.9	01.3	29 29.1	52.0	Shaula	97 08.1	S 37 05.0
14	61 40.4	44 27.1	43.3	14 50.9	46.1	273 10.4	01.3	44 31.3	52.1	Sirius	259 04.0	S 16 40.3
15	76 42.8	59 26.7 ..	44.5	29 51.5 ..	46.6	288 12.8 ..	01.3	59 33.5 ..	52.2	Spica	159 07.0	S 10 59.9
16	91 45.3	74 26.3	45.6	44 52.2	47.1	303 15.3	01.3	74 35.6	52.3	Suhail	223 17.7	S 43 18.4
17	106 47.8	89 25.9	46.8	59 52.8	47.6	318 17.7	01.3	89 37.8	52.5			
18	121 50.2	104 25.5 N 5	48.0	74 53.5 N17	48.2	333 20.2 N14	01.3	104 40.0 N 4	52.6	Vega	81 01.9	N 38 44.8
19	136 52.7	119 25.1	49.2	89 54.2	48.7	348 22.6	01.2	119 42.2	52.7	Zuben'ubi	137 43.0	S 15 54.8
20	151 55.2	134 24.8	50.4	104 54.8	49.2	3 25.1	01.2	134 44.3	52.8			
21	166 57.6	149 24.4 ..	51.6	119 55.5 ..	49.7	18 27.6 ..	01.2	149 46.5 ..	52.9		S.H.A.	Mer. Pass.
22	182 00.1	164 24.0	52.8	134 56.2	50.2	33 30.0	01.2	164 48.7	53.0	Venus	344 34.9	11 02
23	197 02.5	179 23.6	54.0	149 56.8	50.7	48 32.5	01.2	179 50.9	53.1	Mars	314 18.9	13 02
										Jupiter	211 30.2	19 50
Mer. Pass. 9 57.9	v −0.4 d 1.2	v 0.7 d 0.5		v 2.5 d 0.0		v 2.2 d 0.1				Saturn	343 01.8	11 06

314

G.M.T.	SUN G.H.A.	SUN Dec.	MOON G.H.A.	v	MOON Dec.	d	H.P.
	° '	° '	° '	'	° '	'	'
21 00	180 18·7	N 11 48·4	249 35·9	10·6	S 20 40·1	11·3	57·0
01	195 18·8	49·3	264 05·5	10·8	20 28·8	11·3	57·0
02	210 18·9	50·1	278 35·3	10·9	20 17·5	11·5	56·9
03	225 19·1 ··	51·0	293 05·2	11·1	20 06·0	11·5	56·9
04	240 19·2	51·8	307 35·3	11·1	19 54·5	11·6	56·9
05	255 19·3	52·6	322 05·4	11·2	19 42·9	11·7	56·9
06	270 19·5	N 11 53·5	336 35·6	11·4	S 19 31·2	11·8	56·8
07	285 19·6	54·3	351 06·0	11·5	19 19·4	11·9	56·8
08	300 19·7	55·2	5 36·5	11·5	19 07·5	12·0	56·8
S 09	315 19·8 ··	56·0	20 07·0	11·7	18 55·5	12·0	56·7
U 10	330 20·0	56·9	34 37·7	11·8	18 43·5	12·1	56·7
N 11	345 20·1	57·7	49 08·5	11·9	18 31·4	12·2	56·7
D 12	0 20·2	N 11 58·6	63 39·4	12·0	S 18 19·2	12·2	56·7
A 13	15 20·3	11 59·4	78 10·4	12·1	18 07·0	12·4	56·6
Y 14	30 20·5	12 00·3	92 41·5	12·2	17 54·6	12·4	56·6
15	45 20·6 ··	01·1	107 12·7	12·3	17 42·2	12·5	56·6
16	60 20·7	02·0	121 44·0	12·4	17 29·7	12·5	56·5
17	75 20·9	02·8	136 15·4	12·5	17 17·2	12·6	56·5
18	90 21·0	N 12 03·7	150 46·9	12·6	S 17 04·6	12·7	56·5
19	105 21·1	04·5	165 18·5	12·7	16 51·9	12·7	56·5
20	120 21·2	05·3	179 50·2	12·8	16 39·2	12·8	56·4
21	135 21·4 ··	06·2	194 22·0	12·8	16 26·4	12·9	56·4
22	150 21·5	07·0	208 53·8	13·0	16 13·5	12·9	56·4
23	165 21·6	07·9	223 25·8	13·1	16 00·6	13·0	56·3
22 00	180 21·7	N 12 08·7	237 57·9	13·2	S 15 47·6	13·1	56·3
01	195 21·9	09·6	252 30·1	13·2	15 34·5	13·1	56·3
02	210 22·0	10·4	267 02·3	13·4	15 21·4	13·2	56·3
03	225 22·1 ··	11·2	281 34·7	13·4	15 08·2	13·2	56·2
04	240 22·2	12·1	296 07·1	13·5	14 55·0	13·2	56·2
05	255 22·3	12·9	310 39·6	13·6	14 41·8	13·4	56·2
06	270 22·5	N 12 13·8	325 12·2	13·7	S 14 28·4	13·3	56·2
07	285 22·6	14·6	339 44·9	13·8	14 15·1	13·5	56·1
08	300 22·7	15·4	354 17·7	13·9	14 01·6	13·4	56·1
M 09	315 22·8 ··	16·3	8 50·6	13·9	13 48·2	13·6	56·1
O 10	330 23·0	17·1	23 23·5	14·0	13 34·6	13·5	56·1
N 11	345 23·1	18·0	37 56·5	14·1	13 21·1	13·6	56·0
D 12	0 23·2	N 12 18·8	52 29·6	14·2	S 13 07·5	13·7	56·0
A 13	15 23·3	19·6	67 02·8	14·3	12 53·8	13·7	56·0
Y 14	30 23·4	20·5	81 36·1	14·3	12 40·1	13·7	56·0
15	45 23·6 ··	21·3	96 09·4	14·4	12 26·4	13·8	55·9
16	60 23·7	22·2	110 42·8	14·5	12 12·6	13·8	55·9
17	75 23·8	23·0	125 16·3	14·6	11 58·8	13·9	55·9
18	90 23·9	N 12 23·8	139 49·9	14·6	S 11 44·9	13·9	55·9
19	105 24·0	24·7	154 23·5	14·7	11 31·0	13·9	55·8
20	120 24·2	25·5	168 57·2	14·7	11 17·1	14·0	55·8
21	135 24·3 ··	26·3	183 30·9	14·9	11 03·1	14·0	55·8
22	150 24·4	27·2	198 04·8	14·9	10 49·1	14·0	55·8
23	165 24·5	28·0	212 38·7	14·9	10 35·1	14·1	55·7
23 00	180 24·6	N 12 28·8	227 12·6	15·0	S 10 21·0	14·1	55·7
01	195 24·7	29·7	241 46·6	15·1	10 06·9	14·1	55·7
02	210 24·9	30·5	256 20·7	15·2	9 52·8	14·2	55·7
03	225 25·0 ··	31·3	270 54·9	15·2	9 38·6	14·2	55·7
04	240 25·1	32·2	285 29·1	15·3	9 24·4	14·2	55·6
05	255 25·2	33·0	300 03·4	15·3	9 10·2	14·2	55·6
06	270 25·3	N 12 33·8	314 37·7	15·4	S 8 56·0	14·3	55·6
07	285 25·5	34·7	329 12·1	15·4	8 41·7	14·3	55·6
T 08	300 25·6	35·5	343 46·5	15·5	8 27·4	14·3	55·5
U 09	315 25·7 ··	36·3	358 21·0	15·5	8 13·1	14·3	55·5
E 10	330 25·8	37·2	12 55·5	15·6	7 58·8	14·4	55·5
S 11	345 25·9	38·0	27 30·1	15·7	7 44·4	14·4	55·5
D 12	0 26·0	N 12 38·8	42 04·8	15·7	S 7 30·0	14·4	55·5
A 13	15 26·2	39·6	56 39·5	15·7	7 15·6	14·4	55·4
Y 14	30 26·3	40·5	71 14·2	15·8	7 01·2	14·4	55·4
15	45 26·4 ··	41·3	85 49·0	15·9	6 46·8	14·5	55·4
16	60 26·5	42·1	100 23·9	15·8	6 32·3	14·4	55·4
17	75 26·6	43·0	114 58·7	16·0	6 17·9	14·5	55·4
18	90 26·7	N 12 43·8	129 33·7	15·9	S 6 03·4	14·5	55·3
19	105 26·9	44·6	144 08·6	16·0	5 48·9	14·5	55·3
20	120 27·0	45·4	158 43·6	16·1	5 34·4	14·5	55·3
21	135 27·1 ··	46·3	173 18·7	16·1	5 19·9	14·6	55·3
22	150 27·2	47·1	187 53·8	16·1	5 05·3	14·5	55·3
23	165 27·3	47·9	202 28·9	16·2	4 50·8	14·5	55·2
	S.D. 15·9	d 0·8	S.D. 15·4		15·3		15·1

Lat.	Twilight Naut.	Twilight Civil	Sun-rise	Moonrise 21	Moonrise 22	Moonrise 23	Moonrise 24
°	h m	h m	h m	h m	h m	h m	h m
N 72	////	////	02 57	■■	05 53	05 01	04 24
N 70	////	01 39	03 20	06 42	05 23	04 47	04 19
68	////	02 19	03 38	05 43	05 01	04 36	04 15
66	////	02 45	03 53	05 08	04 43	04 26	04 12
64	01 27	03 05	04 05	04 43	04 29	04 18	04 09
62	02 02	03 21	04 15	04 23	04 17	04 12	04 07
60	02 26	03 35	04 23	04 06	04 07	04 06	04 04
N 58	02 45	03 46	04 31	03 53	03 57	04 01	04 02
56	03 01	03 55	04 37	03 41	03 49	03 56	04 01
54	03 14	04 04	04 43	03 30	03 42	03 51	03 59
52	03 25	04 11	04 48	03 21	03 36	03 48	03 58
50	03 34	04 18	04 53	03 12	03 30	03 44	03 56
45	03 54	04 32	05 04	02 54	03 17	03 37	03 53
N 40	04 09	04 44	05 12	02 39	03 07	03 30	03 51
35	04 21	04 53	05 19	02 27	02 58	03 25	03 49
30	04 32	05 01	05 26	02 16	02 50	03 20	03 47
20	04 48	05 14	05 37	01 57	02 36	03 11	03 44
N 10	05 00	05 25	05 46	01 41	02 24	03 04	03 41
0	05 09	05 34	05 55	01 25	02 13	02 57	03 38
S 10	05 18	05 42	06 04	01 09	02 01	02 50	03 35
20	05 25	05 50	06 13	00 53	01 49	02 42	03 33
30	05 31	05 59	06 23	00 33	01 35	02 33	03 29
35	05 34	06 03	06 29	00 22	01 27	02 28	03 27
40	05 36	06 08	06 36	00 09	01 17	02 23	03 25
45	05 39	06 14	06 44	25 06	01 06	02 16	03 23
S 50	05 42	06 20	06 53	24 53	00 53	02 08	03 20
52	05 43	06 22	06 57	24 47	00 47	02 04	03 18
54	05 44	06 25	07 02	24 40	00 40	02 00	03 17
56	05 45	06 28	07 07	24 32	00 32	01 55	03 15
58	05 46	06 32	07 13	24 23	00 23	01 50	03 13
S 60	05 47	06 36	07 19	24 13	00 13	01 44	03 11

Lat.	Sun-set	Twilight Civil	Twilight Naut.	Moonset 21	Moonset 22	Moonset 23	Moonset 24
°	h m	h m	h m	h m	h m	h m	h m
N 72	21 05	////	////	■■	11 20	13 43	15 47
N 70	20 40	22 26	////	08 52	11 48	13 54	15 48
68	20 22	21 44	////	09 50	12 08	14 03	15 49
66	20 07	21 16	////	10 23	12 24	14 10	15 50
64	19 55	20 55	22 38	10 47	12 37	14 17	15 51
62	19 44	20 38	22 00	11 06	12 48	14 22	15 51
60	19 35	20 25	21 34	11 22	12 57	14 26	15 52
N 58	19 28	20 13	21 14	11 35	13 05	14 30	15 52
56	19 21	20 03	20 59	11 46	13 12	14 34	15 53
54	19 15	19 54	20 45	11 56	13 18	14 37	15 53
52	19 10	19 47	20 34	12 04	13 24	14 40	15 53
50	19 05	19 40	20 24	12 12	13 29	14 43	15 54
45	18 54	19 26	20 04	12 29	13 40	14 48	15 54
N 40	18 45	19 14	19 49	12 42	13 49	14 53	15 55
35	18 38	19 05	19 36	12 53	13 57	14 57	15 55
30	18 32	18 56	19 26	13 03	14 03	15 00	15 56
20	18 21	18 43	19 10	13 20	14 15	15 07	15 56
N 10	18 11	18 32	18 57	13 35	14 25	15 12	15 57
0	18 02	18 23	18 48	13 48	14 34	15 17	15 57
S 10	17 53	18 15	18 39	14 02	14 43	15 22	15 58
20	17 44	18 06	18 32	14 16	14 53	15 27	15 59
30	17 33	17 58	18 26	14 32	15 04	15 33	15 59
35	17 27	17 53	18 23	14 42	15 11	15 36	15 59
40	17 21	17 48	18 20	14 52	15 18	15 40	16 00
45	17 13	17 43	18 17	15 05	15 26	15 44	16 00
S 50	17 03	17 37	18 14	15 20	15 36	15 49	16 01
52	16 59	17 34	18 13	15 27	15 41	15 51	16 01
54	16 54	17 31	18 12	15 35	15 46	15 54	16 01
56	16 49	17 28	18 11	15 43	15 51	15 57	16 01
58	16 43	17 24	18 10	15 53	15 58	16 00	16 02
S 60	16 36	17 20	18 09	16 04	16 04	16 03	16 02

Day	SUN Eqn. of Time 00h	SUN Eqn. of Time 12h	SUN Mer. Pass.	MOON Mer. Pass. Upper	MOON Mer. Pass. Lower	Age	Phase
	m s	m s	h m	h m	h m	d	
21	01 15	01 21	11 59	07 37	20 01	24	
22	01 27	01 33	11 58	08 24	20 46	25	◖
23	01 38	01 44	11 58	09 07	21 28	26	

Mag.	Name and No.		S.H.A.						Declination						
			JAN.	FEB.	MAR.	APR.	MAY	JUNE		JAN.	FEB.	MAR.	APR.	MAY	JUNE
3·1	γ Ursæ Minoris †	129	48·8	48·2	47·7	47·3	47·3	47·4	N.71	56·5	56·4	56·5	56·6	56·7	56·9
3·1	γ Trianguli Aust.	131	02·3	01·7	01·2	00·8	00·6	00·6	S.68	33·6	33·6	33·7	33·9	34·0	34·1
2·7	β Libræ	131	11·0	10·8	10·6	10·4	10·3	10·3	S. 9	16·0	16·1	16·2	16·2	16·2	16·2
2·8	β Lupi	135	53·9	53·6	53·3	53·1	53·0	53·0	S.43	00·3	00·4	00·5	00·6	00·7	00·7
2·2	β Ursæ Minoris 40	137	18·3	17·7	17·2	16·8	16·8	17·0	N.74	16·8	16·8	16·8	16·9	17·1	17·2
2·9	α Libræ 39	137	43·7	43·4	43·2	43·0	43·0	42·9	S.15	54·6	54·7	54·8	54·8	54·8	54·8
2·6	ε Bootis	139	06·3	06·0	05·8	05·7	05·6	05·6	N.27	12·3	12·2	12·2	12·2	12·3	12·4
2·9	α Lupi	140	03·4	03·1	02·8	02·6	02·5	02·5	S.47	15·0	15·1	15·2	15·3	15·4	15·5
0·1	α Centauri 38	140	39·1	38·7	38·3	38·1	38·0	38·1	S.60	42·0	42·0	42·2	42·3	42·4	42·5
2·6	η Centauri	141	38·3	38·0	37·7	37·6	37·5	37·5	S.42	01·0	01·1	01·2	01·3	01·4	01·5
3·0	γ Bootis	142	18·2	18·0	17·7	17·6	17·5	17·6	N.38	26·6	26·5	26·5	26·6	26·7	26·8
0·2	α Bootis 37	146	27·1	26·8	26·6	26·5	26·5	26·5	N.19	20·7	20·6	20·6	20·7	20·7	20·8
2·3	θ Centauri 36	148	48·3	48·1	47·8	47·7	47·6	47·7	S.36	12·7	12·8	12·9	13·0	13·1	13·2
0·9	β Centauri 35	149	37·2	36·7	36·4	36·2	36·2	36·2	S.60	13·0	13·1	13·2	13·3	13·5	13·6
3·1	ζ Centauri	151	37·2	36·9	36·7	36·5	36·5	36·5	S.47	07·8	07·9	08·0	08·1	08·2	08·3
2·8	η Bootis	151	42·7	42·4	42·2	42·1	42·1	42·1	N.18	33·3	33·2	33·2	33·2	33·3	33·4
1·9	η Ursæ Majoris 34	153	25·7	25·4	25·2	25·1	25·1	25·2	N.49	28·0	28·0	28·1	28·2	28·3	28·4
2·6	ε Centauri †	155	32·5	32·2	31·9	31·8	31·8	31·8	S.53	18·1	18·2	18·3	18·4	18·6	18·6
1·2	α Virginis 33	159	07·5	07·3	07·1	07·0	07·0	07·0	S.10	59·7	59·8	59·9	59·9	59·9	59·9
2·2	ζ Ursæ Majoris	159	20·2	19·9	19·7	19·6	19·6	19·7	N.55	05·2	05·2	05·3	05·4	05·5	05·6
2·9	ι Centauri	160	18·3	18·0	17·8	17·7	17·7	17·7	S.36	32·5	32·6	32·7	32·9	32·9	33·0
3·0	ε Virginis	164	51·2	51·0	50·9	50·8	50·8	50·8	N.11	07·7	07·6	07·6	07·6	07·7	07·7
2·9	α Canum Venat.	166	21·9	21·6	21·5	21·4	21·4	21·5	N.38	29·2	29·2	29·2	29·3	29·4	29·5
1·7	ε Ursæ Majoris 32	166	50·4	50·0	49·8	49·8	49·8	50·0	N.56	07·7	07·7	07·8	07·9	08·0	08·1
1·5	β Crucis	168	32·6	32·2	32·0	32·0	32·0	32·2	S.59	30·6	30·7	30·9	31·0	31·2	31·3
2·9	γ Virginis	169	59·5	59·2	59·1	59·1	59·1	59·1	S. 1	16·5	16·6	16·6	16·6	16·6	16·6
2·4	γ Centauri	170	04·0	03·7	03·5	03·5	03·5	03·6	S.48	46·8	47·0	47·1	47·3	47·4	47·4
2·9	α Muscæ	171	11·3	10·9	10·7	10·6	10·7	11·0	S.68	57·3	57·4	57·6	57·8	57·9	58·0
2·8	β Corvi	171	49·5	49·3	49·1	49·1	49·1	49·2	S.23	13·1	13·2	13·3	13·4	13·5	13·5
1·6	γ Crucis 31	172	39·4	39·1	38·9	38·9	39·0	39·1	S.56	55·8	56·0	56·1	56·3	56·4	56·5
1·1	α Crucis 30	173	48·0	47·6	47·4	47·4	47·5	47·7	S.62	55·1	55·2	55·4	55·5	55·7	55·8
2·8	γ Corvi 29	176	27·6	27·4	27·3	27·3	27·3	27·4	S.17	21·8	21·9	22·0	22·1	22·1	22·1
2·9	δ Centauri	178	19·6	19·4	19·3	19·2	19·3	19·4	S.50	32·4	32·6	32·8	32·9	33·0	33·0
2·5	γ Ursæ Majoris	181	57·3	57·0	56·9	56·9	57·0	57·2	N.53	52·1	52·2	52·3	52·4	52·5	52·5
2·2	β Leonis 28	183	08·4	08·3	08·2	08·1	08·2	08·3	N.14	45·0	44·9	44·9	44·9	45·0	45·0
2·6	δ Leonis	191	53·7	53·5	53·4	53·4	53·5	53·6	N.20	41·9	41·8	41·9	41·9	41·9	42·0
3·2	ψ Ursæ Majoris	193	01·6	01·4	01·3	01·3	01·4	01·6	N.44	40·2	40·2	40·3	40·4	40·5	40·5
2·0	α Ursæ Majoris 27	194	32·9	32·6	32·5	32·6	32·8	33·0	N.61	55·3	55·3	55·4	55·6	55·6	55·7
2·4	β Ursæ Majoris	195	00·7	00·4	00·3	00·4	00·6	00·8	N.56	33·1	33·1	33·2	33·4	33·4	33·4
2·8	μ Velorum*	198	39·0	38·9	38·8	38·9	39·0	39·2	S.49	14·8	15·0	15·2	15·3	15·4	15·4
3·0	θ Carinæ* †	199	32·6	32·4	32·4	32·6	32·8	33·1	S.64	13·3	13·5	13·7	13·8	13·9	14·0
2·3	γ Leonis	205	26·6	26·5	26·4	26·5	26·6	26·6	N.20	00·2	00·2	00·2	00·2	00·3	00·3
1·3	α Leonis 26	208	19·7	19·6	19·6	19·6	19·7	19·8	N.12	07·5	07·4	07·4	07·4	07·4	07·5
3·1	ε Leonis	213	59·2	59·0	59·0	59·1	59·1	59·3	N.23	55·3	55·3	55·3	55·4	55·4	55·5
3·0	N Velorum	217	26·0	25·9	26·0	26·1	26·4	26·6	S.56	53·3	53·5	53·7	53·8	53·8	53·8
2·2	α Hydræ 25	218	29·6	29·5	29·5	29·6	29·7	29·7	S. 8	31·1	31·2	31·2	31·3	31·2	31·2
2·6	κ Velorum*	219	42·9	42·8	42·9	43·1	43·3	43·5	S.54	52·2	52·4	52·5	52·7	52·7	52·7
2·2	ι Carinæ*	220	56·1	56·1	56·2	56·4	56·7	56·9	S.59	08·3	08·4	08·6	08·7	08·7	08·7
1·8	β Carinæ* 24	221	46·6	46·5	46·7	47·1	47·5	47·9	S.69	34·9	35·1	35·2	35·4	35·4	35·4
2·2	λ Velorum* 23	223	17·5	17·4	17·5	17·6	17·8	17·9	S.43	18·0	18·2	18·3	18·4	18·4	18·3
3·1	ι Ursæ Majoris	225	44·1	44·0	44·1	44·2	44·4	44·5	N.48	10·1	10·2	10·3	10·3	10·3	10·3
2·0	δ Velorum*	229	02·3	02·3	02·4	02·6	02·9	03·1	S.54	35·3	35·4	35·6	35·7	35·7	35·6
1·7	ε Carinæ* 22	234	31·7	31·7	31·9	32·1	32·4	32·6	S.59	24·2	24·4	24·5	24·6	24·6	24·5
1·9	γ Velorum*	237	51·5	51·5	51·6	51·8	52·0	52·1	S.47	14·4	14·5	14·7	14·7	14·7	14·6
2·9	ρ Puppis*	238	27·0	27·0	27·1	27·2	27·3	27·4	S.24	12·6	12·7	12·8	12·8	12·8	12·7
2·3	ζ Puppis*	239	22·8	22·8	22·9	23·1	23·2	23·3	S.39	54·6	54·8	54·9	54·9	54·9	54·8
1·2	β Geminorum 21	244	09·3	09·3	09·3	09·5	09·6	09·6	N.28	06·4	06·4	06·4	06·4	06·4	06·4
0·5	α Canis Minoris 20	245	35·3	35·3	35·4	35·5	35·6	35·6	N. 5	18·6	18·5	18·5	18·5	18·5	18·6

* Formerly Argus   † Not suitable for use with H.O. 214 (H.D. 486)

Mag.	Name and No.		S.H.A. JULY	AUG.	SEPT.	OCT.	NOV.	DEC.	Declination JULY	AUG.	SEPT.	OCT.	NOV.	DEC.
3·1	γ Ursæ Minoris †	129	47·8	48·3	48·8	49·1	49·3	49·2	N. 71 56·9	57·0	56·9	56·8	56·6	56·4
3·1	γ Trianguli Aust.	131	00·8	01·1	01·4	01·6	01·6	01·3	S. 68 34·2	34·3	34·2	34·1	34·0	33·9
2·7	β Libræ	131	10·3	10·4	10·5	10·5	10·5	10·3	S. 9 16·2	16·1	16·1	16·1	16·2	16·2
2·8	β Lupi	135	53·1	53·2	53·3	53·4	53·3	53·1	S. 43 00·8	00·8	00·7	00·7	00·6	00·6
2·2	Kochab 40	137	17·5	18·1	18·6	19·0	19·1	18·9	N. 74 17·3	17·3	17·2	17·0	16·8	16·7
2·9	Zubenelgenubi 39	137	43·0	43·1	43·2	43·2	43·1	43·0	S. 15 54·8	54·8	54·8	54·8	54·8	54·8
2·6	ε Bootis	139	05·7	05·8	05·9	06·0	05·9	05·8	N. 27 12·5	12·5	12·5	12·4	12·2	12·1
2·9	α Lupi	140	02·6	02·8	02·9	03·0	02·9	02·7	S. 47 15·5	15·5	15·5	15·4	15·3	15·3
0·1	Rigil Kent. 38	140	38·2	38·5	38·7	38·8	38·7	38·4	S. 60 42·6	42·6	42·5	42·4	42·3	42·3
2·6	η Centauri	141	37·5	37·7	37·8	37·8	37·8	37·5	S. 42 01·5	01·5	01·4	01·4	01·3	01·3
3·0	γ Bootis	142	17·7	17·8	18·0	18·0	18·0	17·8	N. 38 26·9	26·9	26·8	26·7	26·5	26·4
0·2	Arcturus 37	146	26·6	26·7	26·7	26·8	26·7	26·5	N. 19 20·8	20·8	20·8	20·7	20·6	20·5
2·3	Menkent 36	148	47·7	47·9	47·9	48·0	47·9	47·6	S. 36 13·2	13·1	13·1	13·0	13·0	13·0
0·9	Hadar 35	149	36·4	36·6	36·8	36·9	36·7	36·4	S. 60 13·6	13·6	13·5	13·4	13·3	13·3
3·1	ζ Centauri	151	36·6	36·8	36·9	36·9	36·8	36·5	S. 47 08·3	08·3	08·2	08·1	08·1	08·0
2·8	η Bootis	151	42·2	42·3	42·4	42·4	42·3	42·1	N. 18 33·4	33·4	33·4	33·3	33·2	33·0
1·9	Alkaid 34	153	25·3	25·5	25·6	25·7	25·6	25·4	N. 49 28·4	28·4	28·3	28·1	28·0	27·8
2·6	ε Centauri †	155	32·0	32·2	32·3	32·3	32·3	32·2	S. 53 18·7	18·6	18·6	18·5	18·4	18·4
1·2	Spica 33	159	07·1	07·2	07·2	07·2	07·1	06·9	S. 10 59·9	59·9	59·8	59·8	59·9	60·0
2·2	Mizar	159	19·9	20·1	20·3	20·3	20·2	19·9	N. 55 05·6	05·5	05·5	05·3	05·1	05·0
2·9	ι Centauri	160	17·8	18·0	18·0	18·0	17·9	17·6	S. 36 33·0	32·9	32·9	32·8	32·8	32·8
3·0	ε Virginis	164	50·9	51·0	51·0	51·0	50·9	50·7	N. 11 07·8	07·8	07·7	07·7	07·6	07·5
2·9	Cor Caroli	166	21·6	21·8	21·8	21·8	21·6	21·4	N. 38 29·5	29·5	29·4	29·2	29·1	28·9
1·7	Alioth 32	166	50·2	50·4	50·5	50·5	50·3	50·0	N. 56 08·1	08·0	07·9	07·8	07·6	07·4
1·5	Mimosa	168	32·4	32·6	32·7	32·6	32·4	32·0	S. 59 31·3	31·2	31·1	31·0	30·9	30·9
2·9	γ Virginis	169	59·2	59·2	59·3	59·2	59·1	58·9	S. 1 16·6	16·6	16·6	16·6	16·7	16·8
2·4	Muhlifain	170	03·8	03·9	04·0	03·9	03·7	03·4	S. 48 47·4	47·4	47·3	47·2	47·1	47·1
2·9	α Muscæ	171	11·3	11·6	11·8	11·7	11·4	10·9	S. 68 58·0	58·0	57·8	57·7	57·6	57·6
2·8	β Corvi	171	49·2	49·3	49·3	49·3	49·1	48·9	S. 23 13·5	13·4	13·4	13·3	13·3	13·4
1·6	Gacrux 31	172	39·3	39·5	39·5	39·5	39·3	38·9	S. 56 56·5	56·4	56·3	56·2	56·1	56·1
1·1	Acrux 30	173	47·9	48·2	48·3	48·2	47·9	47·5	S. 62 55·8	55·7	55·6	55·4	55·4	55·4
2·8	Gienah 29	176	27·4	27·5	27·5	27·4	27·3	27·0	S. 17 22·1	22·0	22·0	22·0	22·0	22·1
2·9	δ Centauri	178	19·6	19·7	19·8	19·7	19·5	19·1	S. 50 33·0	32·9	32·8	32·7	32·7	32·7
2·5	Phecda	181	57·4	57·5	57·5	57·4	57·2	56·8	N. 53 52·5	52·4	52·3	52·1	51·9	51·8
2·2	Denebola 28	183	08·3	08·4	08·3	08·3	08·1	07·8	N. 14 45·0	45·0	45·0	44·9	44·8	44·7
2·6	δ Leonis	191	53·6	53·7	53·6	53·5	53·3	53·1	N. 20 42·0	42·0	41·9	41·8	41·7	41·6
3·2	ψ Ursæ Majoris	193	01·7	01·7	01·7	01·5	01·3	01·0	N. 44 40·5	40·4	40·2	40·1	40·0	39·9
2·0	Dubhe 27	194	33·2	33·3	33·3	33·1	32·7	32·3	N. 61 55·6	55·5	55·3	55·1	55·0	54·9
2·4	Merak	195	00·9	01·0	00·9	00·7	00·4	00·1	N. 56 33·4	33·3	33·1	33·0	32·8	32·7
2·8	μ Velorum*	198	39·4	39·4	39·4	39·2	39·0	38·6	S. 49 15·3	15·2	15·1	15·0	15·0	15·0
3·0	θ Carinæ* †	199	33·4	33·5	33·5	33·3	32·9	32·5	S. 64 13·9	13·8	13·6	13·5	13·5	13·5
2·3	Algeiba	205	26·7	26·7	26·6	26·4	26·2	25·9	N. 19 60·3	60·3	60·2	60·1	60·0	59·9
1·3	Regulus 26	208	19·8	19·8	19·7	19·5	19·3	19·1	N. 12 07·5	07·5	07·5	07·4	07·3	07·2
3·1	ε Leonis	213	59·3	59·2	59·1	58·9	58·7	58·4	N. 23 55·4	55·4	55·3	55·2	55·1	55·1
3·0	N Velorum	217	26·8	26·8	26·7	26·4	26·1	25·7	S. 56 53·7	53·6	53·4	53·4	53·4	53·5
2·2	Alphard 25	218	29·8	29·7	29·6	29·4	29·2	29·0	S. 8 31·2	31·1	31·1	31·1	31·1	31·2
2·6	κ Velorum*	219	43·6	43·6	43·5	43·2	42·9	42·6	S. 54 52·5	52·4	52·3	52·2	52·2	52·3
2·2	ι Carinæ*	220	57·1	57·1	56·9	56·6	56·3	55·9	S. 59 08·6	08·4	08·3	08·2	08·2	08·3
1·8	Miaplacidus 24	221	48·2	48·2	48·1	47·7	47·2	46·7	S. 69 35·2	35·1	35·0	34·9	34·9	35·0
2·2	Suhail 23	223	18·0	18·0	17·8	17·6	17·3	17·1	S. 43 18·2	18·1	18·0	17·9	18·0	18·1
3·1	ι Ursæ Majoris	225	44·5	44·4	44·2	43·9	43·6	43·2	N. 48 10·2	10·1	10·0	09·9	09·9	09·8
2·0	δ Velorum*	229	03·2	03·1	03·0	02·7	02·4	02·1	S. 54 35·5	35·3	35·2	35·2	35·2	35·3
1·7	Avior 22	234	32·7	32·7	32·5	32·2	31·8	31·5	S. 59 24·4	24·2	24·1	24·1	24·1	24·2
1·9	γ Velorum*	237	52·2	52·1	51·9	51·6	51·4	51·1	S. 47 14·5	14·3	14·2	14·2	14·2	14·4
2·9	ρ Puppis*	238	27·4	27·3	27·1	26·9	26·7	26·5	S. 24 12·6	12·5	12·4	12·4	12·5	12·6
2·3	ζ Puppis*	239	23·4	23·3	23·1	22·9	22·6	22·4	S. 39 54·7	54·6	54·5	54·4	54·5	54·6
1·2	Pollux 21	244	09·5	09·4	09·2	08·9	08·7	08·4	N. 28 06·4	06·4	06·3	06·3	06·3	06·2
0·5	Procyon 20	245	35·5	35·4	35·2	35·0	34·8	34·6	N. 5 18·6	18·6	18·6	18·6	18·6	18·5

* Formerly Argus † Not suitable for use with H.O. 214 (H.D. 486)

POLARIS (POLE STAR) TABLES, 1968
FOR DETERMINING LATITUDE FROM SEXTANT ALTITUDE AND FOR AZIMUTH

L.H.A. ARIES	120°–129°	130°–139°	140°–149°	150°–159°	160°–169°	170°–179°	180°–189°	190°–199°	200°–209°	210°–219°	220°–229°	230°–239°
	a_0	a_0	a_0	a_0	a_0	a_0	a_0	a_0	a_0	a_0	a_0	a_0
°	° ′	° ′	° ′	° ′	° ′	° ′	° ′	° ′	° ′	° ′	° ′	° ′
0	0 59·0	1 08·1	1 17·0	1 25·2	1 32·7	1 39·2	1 44·4	1 48·3	1 50·7	1 51·5	1 50·8	1 48·5
1	0 59·9	09·0	17·8	26·0	33·4	39·7	44·9	48·6	50·8	51·5	50·6	48·2
2	1 00·8	09·9	18·7	26·8	34·1	40·3	45·3	48·9	51·0	51·5	50·4	47·8
3	01·7	10·8	19·5	27·6	34·8	40·9	45·7	49·2	51·1	51·4	50·2	47·5
4	02·7	11·7	20·4	28·3	35·4	41·4	46·1	49·4	51·2	51·4	50·0	47·1
5	1 03·6	1 12·6	1 21·2	1 29·1	1 36·1	1 41·9	1 46·5	1 49·7	1 51·3	1 51·3	1 49·8	1 46·8
6	04·5	13·5	22·0	29·8	36·7	42·5	46·9	49·9	51·4	51·2	49·6	46·4
7	05·4	14·4	22·8	30·6	37·3	43·0	47·3	50·1	51·4	51·1	49·3	46·0
8	06·3	15·2	23·6	31·3	38·0	43·5	47·6	50·3	51·5	51·0	49·1	45·6
9	07·2	16·1	24·4	32·0	38·6	43·9	48·0	50·5	51·5	50·9	48·8	45·2
10	1 08·1	1 17·0	1 25·2	1 32·7	1 39·2	1 44·4	1 48·3	1 50·7	1 51·5	1 50·8	1 48·5	1 44·7

Lat.	a_1	a_1	a_1	a_1	a_1	a_1	a_1	a_1	a_1	a_1	a_1	a_1
°	′	′	′	′	′	′	′	′	′	′	′	′
0	0·1	0·2	0·2	0·3	0·4	0·4	0·5	0·6	0·6	0·6	0·6	0·5
10	·2	·2	·3	·3	·4	·5	·5	·6	·6	·6	·6	·5
20	·3	·3	·3	·4	·4	·5	·5	·6	·6	·6	·6	·5
30	·4	·4	·4	·4	·5	·5	·6	·6	·6	·6	·6	·6
40	0·5	0·5	0·5	0·5	0·5	0·6	0·6	0·6	0·6	0·6	0·6	0·6
45	·5	·5	·5	·5	·6	·6	·6	·6	·6	·6	·6	·6
50	·6	·6	·6	·6	·6	·6	·6	·6	·6	·6	·6	·6
55	·7	·7	·7	·7	·6	·6	·6	·6	·6	·6	·6	·6
60	·8	·8	·8	·7	·7	·7	·6	·6	·6	·6	·6	·6
62	0·9	0·9	0·8	0·8	0·7	0·7	0·7	0·6	0·6	0·6	0·6	0·6
64	0·9	0·9	0·9	·8	·8	·7	·7	·6	·6	·6	·6	·7
66	1·0	1·0	1·0	0·9	·8	·7	·7	·6	·6	·6	·6	·7
68	1·1	1·1	1·0	1·0	0·9	0·8	0·7	0·6	0·6	0·6	0·6	0·7

Month	a_2	a_2	a_2	a_2	a_2	a_2	a_2	a_2	a_2	a_2	a_2	a_2
	′	′	′	′	′	′	′	′	′	′	′	′
Jan.	0·6	0·6	0·6	0·6	0·6	0·5	0·5	0·5	0·5	0·5	0·5	0·5
Feb.	·8	·7	·7	·7	·7	·6	·6	·6	·6	·5	·5	·5
Mar.	·9	·9	0·9	0·8	·8	·8	·8	·7	·7	·6	·6	·5
Apr.	0·9	0·9	1·0	1·0	0·9	0·9	0·9	0·9	0·8	0·7	0·7	0·6
May	·9	·9	1·0	1·0	1·0	1·0	1·0	1·0	0·9	0·9	·8	·8
June	·8	·8	0·9	0·9	1·0	1·0	1·0	1·0	1·0	1·0	0·9	0·9
July	0·6	0·7	0·8	0·8	0·9	0·9	1·0	1·0	1·0	1·0	1·0	1·0
Aug.	·4	·5	·6	·6	·7	·8	0·8	0·9	0·9	1·0	1·0	1·0
Sept.	·3	·4	·4	·5	·5	·6	·7	·7	·8	0·8	0·9	0·9
Oct.	0·2	0·2	0·3	0·3	0·3	0·4	0·5	0·5	0·6	0·7	0·7	0·8
Nov.	·2	·2	·2	·2	·2	·3	·3	·3	·4	·5	·5	·6
Dec.	0·3	0·2	0·2	0·2	0·2	0·2	0·2	0·2	0·3	0·3	0·4	0·5

Lat.	AZIMUTH											
°	°	°	°	°	°	°	°	°	°	°	°	°
0	359·1	359·2	359·2	359·3	359·4	359·5	359·6	359·8	359·9	0·1	0·2	0·4
20	359·1	359·1	359·1	359·2	359·3	359·5	359·6	359·7	359·9	0·1	0·2	0·4
40	358·9	358·9	359·0	359·1	359·2	359·3	359·5	359·7	359·9	0·1	0·3	0·5
50	358·6	358·7	358·8	358·9	359·0	359·2	359·4	359·6	359·9	0·1	0·3	0·6
55	358·5	358·5	358·6	358·8	358·9	359·1	359·4	359·6	359·9	0·1	0·4	0·6
60	358·2	358·3	358·4	358·6	358·8	359·0	359·3	359·5	359·8	0·1	0·4	0·7
65	357·9	358·0	358·1	358·3	358·6	358·8	359·1	359·5	359·8	0·2	0·5	0·8

ILLUSTRATION

On 1968 January 22 at G.M.T. 22ʰ 17ᵐ 50ˢ in longitude W. 55° 19′ the corrected apparent altitude of *Polaris* was 49° 31′·6.

From the daily pages :	° ′
G.H.A. Aries (22ʰ)	91 19·3
Increment (17ᵐ 50ˢ)	4 28·2
Longitude (west)	−55 19
L.H.A. Aries	40 29

	° ′
Corr. App. Alt.	49 31·6
a_0 (argument 40° 29′)	0 06·9
a_1 (lat. 50° approx.)	0·6
a_2 (January)	0·7
Sum − 1° = Lat. =	48 39·8

POLARIS (POLE STAR) TABLES, 1968

FOR DETERMINING LATITUDE FROM SEXTANT ALTITUDE AND FOR AZIMUTH

L.H.A. ARIES	240°–249°	250°–259°	260°–269°	270°–279°	280°–289°	290°–299°	300°–309°	310°–319°	320°–329°	330°–339°	340°–349°	350°–359°
°	a_0	a_0	a_0	a_0	a_0	a_0	a_0	a_0	a_0	a_0	a_0	a_0
0	1 44·7	1 39·6	1 33·2	1 25·8	1 17·5	1 08·7	0 59·6	0 50·4	0 41·5	0 33·1	0 25·4	0 18·8
1	44·3	39·0	32·5	25·0	16·7	07·8	58·7	49·5	40·6	32·3	24·7	18·2
2	43·8	38·4	31·8	24·2	15·8	06·9	57·7	48·6	39·8	31·5	24·0	17·6
3	43·3	37·8	31·1	23·4	14·9	06·0	56·8	47·7	38·9	30·7	23·3	17·1
4	42·8	37·1	30·3	22·6	14·1	05·1	55·9	46·8	38·1	29·9	22·7	16·5
5	1 42·3	1 36·5	1 29·6	1 21·7	1 13·2	1 04·2	0 55·0	0 45·9	0 37·2	0 29·1	0 22·0	0 16·0
6	41·8	35·9	28·8	20·9	12·3	03·3	54·1	45·0	36·4	28·4	21·3	15·4
7	41·2	35·2	28·1	20·1	11·4	02·3	53·2	44·1	35·5	27·6	20·7	14·9
8	40·7	34·5	27·3	19·2	10·5	01·4	52·2	43·3	34·7	26·9	20·1	14·4
9	40·1	33·9	26·5	18·4	09·6	1 00·5	51·3	42·4	33·9	26·2	19·4	13·9
10	1 39·6	1 33·2	1 25·8	1 17·5	1 08·7	0 59·6	0 50·4	0 41·5	0 33·1	0 25·4	0 18·8	0 13·4

Lat.	a_1	a_1	a_1	a_1	a_1	a_1	a_1	a_1	a_1	a_1	a_1	a_1
°												
0	0·4	0·4	0·3	0·2	0·2	0·1	0·1	0·2	0·2	0·3	0·4	0·4
10	·5	·4	·3	·3	·2	·2	·2	·2	·3	·3	·4	·5
20	·5	·4	·4	·3	·3	·3	·3	·3	·3	·4	·4	·5
30	·5	·5	·4	·4	·4	·4	·4	·4	·4	·4	·5	·5
40	0·6	0·5	0·5	0·5	0·5	0·5	0·5	0·5	0·5	0·5	0·5	0·6
45	·6	·6	·5	·5	·5	·5	·5	·5	·5	·5	·6	·6
50	·6	·6	·6	·6	·6	·6	·6	·6	·6	·6	·6	·6
55	·6	·6	·7	·7	·7	·7	·7	·7	·7	·7	·6	·6
60	·7	·7	·7	·8	·8	·8	·8	·8	·8	·7	·7	·7
62	0·7	0·7	0·8	0·8	0·9	0·9	0·9	0·9	0·8	0·8	0·7	0·7
64	·7	·8	·8	·9	0·9	0·9	0·9	0·9	0·9	·8	·8	·7
66	·7	·8	·9	0·9	1·0	1·0	1·0	1·0	1·0	0·9	·8	·7
68	0·8	0·9	0·9	1·0	1·1	1·1	1·1	1·1	1·0	1·0	0·9	0·8

Month	a_2	a_2	a_2	a_2	a_2	a_2	a_2	a_2	a_2	a_2	a_2	a_2
Jan.	0·5	0·6	0·6	0·6	0·6	0·6	0·6	0·6	0·6	0·6	0·6	0·7
Feb.	·5	·5	·4	·4	·4	·4	·4	·5	·5	·5	·5	·6
Mar.	·5	·4	·4	·4	·4	·3	·3	·3	·3	·4	·4	·4
Apr.	0·6	0·5	0·4	0·4	0·4	0·3	0·3	0·3	0·2	0·2	0·3	0·3
May	·7	·6	·6	·5	·4	·4	·3	·3	·2	·2	·2	·2
June	·8	·8	·7	·6	·6	·5	·4	·4	·3	·3	·2	·2
July	0·9	0·9	0·8	0·8	0·7	0·7	0·6	0·5	0·4	0·4	0·3	0·3
Aug.	1·0	1·0	0·9	0·9	0·9	·8	·8	·7	·6	·6	·5	·4
Sept.	1·0	1·0	1·0	1·0	1·0	0·9	0·9	0·8	·8	·7	·7	·6
Oct.	0·8	0·9	0·9	1·0	1·0	1·0	1·0	1·0	0·9	0·9	0·9	0·8
Nov.	·7	·8	·8	0·9	0·9	1·0	1·0	1·0	1·0	1·0	1·0	0·9
Dec.	0·5	0·6	0·7	0·8	0·8	0·9	0·9	1·0	1·0	1·0	1·0	1·0

Lat.	AZIMUTH											
°	°	°	°	°	°	°	°	°	°	°	°	°
0	0·5	0·6	0·7	0·8	0·8	0·9	0·9	0·8	0·8	0·7	0·6	0·5
20	0·5	0·7	0·8	0·8	0·9	0·9	0·9	0·9	0·9	0·8	0·7	0·5
40	0·6	0·8	0·9	1·0	1·1	1·1	1·1	1·1	1·0	0·9	0·8	0·7
50	0·8	1·0	1·1	1·2	1·3	1·4	1·4	1·3	1·2	1·1	1·0	0·8
55	0·9	1·1	1·2	1·4	1·5	1·5	1·5	1·5	1·4	1·3	1·1	0·9
60	1·0	1·2	1·4	1·6	1·7	1·8	1·8	1·7	1·6	1·5	1·3	1·0
65	1·1	1·4	1·7	1·9	2·0	2·1	2·1	2·0	1·9	1·7	1·5	1·2

Latitude = Apparent altitude (Corrected for refraction) $- 1° + a_0 + a_1 + a_2$

The table is entered with L.H.A. Aries to determine the column to be used; each column refers to a range of 10°. a_0 is taken, with mental interpolation, from the upper table with the units of L.H.A. Aries in degrees as argument; a_1, a_2 are taken, without interpolation, from the second and third tables with arguments latitude and month respectively. a_0, a_1, a_2 are always positive. The final table gives the azimuth of *Polaris*.

CONVERSION OF ARC TO TIME

0°–59°		60°–119°		120°–179°		180°–239°		240°–299°		300°–359°		′	0′·00	0′·25	0′·50	0′·75
°	h m	°	h m	°	h m	°	h m	°	h m	°	h m	′	m s	m s	m s	m s
0	0 00	60	4 00	120	8 00	180	12 00	240	16 00	300	20 00	0	0 00	0 01	0 02	0 03
1	0 04	61	4 04	121	8 04	181	12 04	241	16 04	301	20 04	1	0 04	0 05	0 06	0 07
2	0 08	62	4 08	122	8 08	182	12 08	242	16 08	302	20 08	2	0 08	0 09	0 10	0 11
3	0 12	63	4 12	123	8 12	183	12 12	243	16 12	303	20 12	3	0 12	0 13	0 14	0 15
4	0 16	64	4 16	124	8 16	184	12 16	244	16 16	304	20 16	4	0 16	0 17	0 18	0 19
5	0 20	65	4 20	125	8 20	185	12 20	245	16 20	305	20 20	5	0 20	0 21	0 22	0 23
6	0 24	66	4 24	126	8 24	186	12 24	246	16 24	306	20 24	6	0 24	0 25	0 26	0 27
7	0 28	67	4 28	127	8 28	187	12 28	247	16 28	307	20 28	7	0 28	0 29	0 30	0 31
8	0 32	68	4 32	128	8 32	188	12 32	248	16 32	308	20 32	8	0 32	0 33	0 34	0 35
9	0 36	69	4 36	129	8 36	189	12 36	249	16 36	309	20 36	9	0 36	0 37	0 38	0 39
10	0 40	70	4 40	130	8 40	190	12 40	250	16 40	310	20 40	10	0 40	0 41	0 42	0 43
11	0 44	71	4 44	131	8 44	191	12 44	251	16 44	311	20 44	11	0 44	0 45	0 46	0 47
12	0 48	72	4 48	132	8 48	192	12 48	252	16 48	312	20 48	12	0 48	0 49	0 50	0 51
13	0 52	73	4 52	133	8 52	193	12 52	253	16 52	313	20 52	13	0 52	0 53	0 54	0 55
14	0 56	74	4 56	134	8 56	194	12 56	254	16 56	314	20 56	14	0 56	0 57	0 58	0 59
15	1 00	75	5 00	135	9 00	195	13 00	255	17 00	315	21 00	15	1 00	1 01	1 02	1 03
16	1 04	76	5 04	136	9 04	196	13 04	256	17 04	316	21 04	16	1 04	1 05	1 06	1 07
17	1 08	77	5 08	137	9 08	197	13 08	257	17 08	317	21 08	17	1 08	1 09	1 10	1 11
18	1 12	78	5 12	138	9 12	198	13 12	258	17 12	318	21 12	18	1 12	1 13	1 14	1 15
19	1 16	79	5 16	139	9 16	199	13 16	259	17 16	319	21 16	19	1 16	1 17	1 18	1 19
20	1 20	80	5 20	140	9 20	200	13 20	260	17 20	320	21 20	20	1 20	1 21	1 22	1 23
21	1 24	81	5 24	141	9 24	201	13 24	261	17 24	321	21 24	21	1 24	1 25	1 26	1 27
22	1 28	82	5 28	142	9 28	202	13 28	262	17 28	322	21 28	22	1 28	1 29	1 30	1 31
23	1 32	83	5 32	143	9 32	203	13 32	263	17 32	323	21 32	23	1 32	1 33	1 34	1 35
24	1 36	84	5 36	144	9 36	204	13 36	264	17 36	324	21 36	24	1 36	1 37	1 38	1 39
25	1 40	85	5 40	145	9 40	205	13 40	265	17 40	325	21 40	25	1 40	1 41	1 42	1 43
26	1 44	86	5 44	146	9 44	206	13 44	266	17 44	326	21 44	26	1 44	1 45	1 46	1 47
27	1 48	87	5 48	147	9 48	207	13 48	267	17 48	327	21 48	27	1 48	1 49	1 50	1 51
28	1 52	88	5 52	148	9 52	208	13 52	268	17 52	328	21 52	28	1 52	1 53	1 54	1 55
29	1 56	89	5 56	149	9 56	209	13 56	269	17 56	329	21 56	29	1 56	1 57	1 58	1 59
30	2 00	90	6 00	150	10 00	210	14 00	270	18 00	330	22 00	30	2 00	2 01	2 02	2 03
31	2 04	91	6 04	151	10 04	211	14 04	271	18 04	331	22 04	31	2 04	2 05	2 06	2 07
32	2 08	92	6 08	152	10 08	212	14 08	272	18 08	332	22 08	32	2 08	2 09	2 10	2 11
33	2 12	93	6 12	153	10 12	213	14 12	273	18 12	333	22 12	33	2 12	2 13	2 14	2 15
34	2 16	94	6 16	154	10 16	214	14 16	274	18 16	334	22 16	34	2 16	2 17	2 18	2 19
35	2 20	95	6 20	155	10 20	215	14 20	275	18 20	335	22 20	35	2 20	2 21	2 22	2 23
36	2 24	96	6 24	156	10 24	216	14 24	276	18 24	336	22 24	36	2 24	2 25	2 26	2 27
37	2 28	97	6 28	157	10 28	217	14 28	277	18 28	337	22 28	37	2 28	2 29	2 30	2 31
38	2 32	98	6 32	158	10 32	218	14 32	278	18 32	338	22 32	38	2 32	2 33	2 34	2 35
39	2 36	99	6 36	159	10 36	219	14 36	279	18 36	339	22 36	39	2 36	2 37	2 38	2 39
40	2 40	100	6 40	160	10 40	220	14 40	280	18 40	340	22 40	40	2 40	2 41	2 42	2 43
41	2 44	101	6 44	161	10 44	221	14 44	281	18 44	341	22 44	41	2 44	2 45	2 46	2 47
42	2 48	102	6 48	162	10 48	222	14 48	282	18 48	342	22 48	42	2 48	2 49	2 50	2 51
43	2 52	103	6 52	163	10 52	223	14 52	283	18 52	343	22 52	43	2 52	2 53	2 54	2 55
44	2 56	104	6 56	164	10 56	224	14 56	284	18 56	344	22 56	44	2 56	2 57	2 58	2 59
45	3 00	105	7 00	165	11 00	225	15 00	285	19 00	345	23 00	45	3 00	3 01	3 02	3 03
46	3 04	106	7 04	166	11 04	226	15 04	286	19 04	346	23 04	46	3 04	3 05	3 06	3 07
47	3 08	107	7 08	167	11 08	227	15 08	287	19 08	347	23 08	47	3 08	3 09	3 10	3 11
48	3 12	108	7 12	168	11 12	228	15 12	288	19 12	348	23 12	48	3 12	3 13	3 14	3 15
49	3 16	109	7 16	169	11 16	229	15 16	289	19 16	349	23 16	49	3 16	3 17	3 18	3 19
50	3 20	110	7 20	170	11 20	230	15 20	290	19 20	350	23 20	50	3 20	3 21	3 22	3 23
51	3 24	111	7 24	171	11 24	231	15 24	291	19 24	351	23 24	51	3 24	3 25	3 26	3 27
52	3 28	112	7 28	172	11 28	232	15 28	292	19 28	352	23 28	52	3 28	3 29	3 30	3 31
53	3 32	113	7 32	173	11 32	233	15 32	293	19 32	353	23 32	53	3 32	3 33	3 34	3 35
54	3 36	114	7 36	174	11 36	234	15 36	294	19 36	354	23 36	54	3 36	3 37	3 38	3 39
55	3 40	115	7 40	175	11 40	235	15 40	295	19 40	355	23 40	55	3 40	3 41	3 42	3 43
56	3 44	116	7 44	176	11 44	236	15 44	296	19 44	356	23 44	56	3 44	3 45	3 46	3 47
57	3 48	117	7 48	177	11 48	237	15 48	297	19 48	357	23 48	57	3 48	3 49	3 50	3 51
58	3 52	118	7 52	178	11 52	238	15 52	298	19 52	358	23 52	58	3 52	3 53	3 54	3 55
59	3 56	119	7 56	179	11 56	239	15 56	299	19 56	359	23 56	59	3 56	3 57	3 58	3 59

The above table is for converting expressions in arc to their equivalent in time ; its main use in this Almanac is for the conversion of longitude for application to L.M.T. (*added* if *west*, *subtracted* if *east*) to give G.M.T. or vice versa, particularly in the case of sunrise, sunset, etc.

0^m	SUN PLANETS	ARIES	MOON	v or Corr^n d		v or Corr^n d		v or Corr^n d	
s	° ′	° ′	° ′	′	′	′	′	′	′
00	0 00·0	0 00·0	0 00·0	0·0	0·0	6·0	0·1	12·0	0·1
01	0 00·3	0 00·3	0 00·2	0·1	0·0	6·1	0·1	12·1	0·1
02	0 00·5	0 00·5	0 00·5	0·2	0·0	6·2	0·1	12·2	0·1
03	0 00·8	0 00·8	0 00·7	0·3	0·0	6·3	0·1	12·3	0·1
04	0 01·0	0 01·0	0 01·0	0·4	0·0	6·4	0·1	12·4	0·1
05	0 01·3	0 01·3	0 01·2	0·5	0·0	6·5	0·1	12·5	0·1
06	0 01·5	0 01·5	0 01·4	0·6	0·0	6·6	0·1	12·6	0·1
07	0 01·8	0 01·8	0 01·7	0·7	0·0	6·7	0·1	12·7	0·1
08	0 02·0	0 02·0	0 01·9	0·8	0·0	6·8	0·1	12·8	0·1
09	0 02·3	0 02·3	0 02·1	0·9	0·0	6·9	0·1	12·9	0·1
10	0 02·5	0 02·5	0 02·4	1·0	0·0	7·0	0·1	13·0	0·1
11	0 02·8	0 02·8	0 02·6	1·1	0·0	7·1	0·1	13·1	0·1
12	0 03·0	0 03·0	0 02·9	1·2	0·0	7·2	0·1	13·2	0·1
13	0 03·3	0 03·3	0 03·1	1·3	0·0	7·3	0·1	13·3	0·1
14	0 03·5	0 03·5	0 03·3	1·4	0·0	7·4	0·1	13·4	0·1
15	0 03·8	0 03·8	0 03·6	1·5	0·0	7·5	0·1	13·5	0·1
16	0 04·0	0 04·0	0 03·8	1·6	0·0	7·6	0·1	13·6	0·1
17	0 04·3	0 04·3	0 04·1	1·7	0·0	7·7	0·1	13·7	0·1
18	0 04·5	0 04·5	0 04·3	1·8	0·0	7·8	0·1	13·8	0·1
19	0 04·8	0 04·8	0 04·5	1·9	0·0	7·9	0·1	13·9	0·1
20	0 05·0	0 05·0	0 04·8	2·0	0·0	8·0	0·1	14·0	0·1
21	0 05·3	0 05·3	0 05·0	2·1	0·0	8·1	0·1	14·1	0·1
22	0 05·5	0 05·5	0 05·2	2·2	0·0	8·2	0·1	14·2	0·1
23	0 05·8	0 05·8	0 05·5	2·3	0·0	8·3	0·1	14·3	0·1
24	0 06·0	0 06·0	0 05·7	2·4	0·0	8·4	0·1	14·4	0·1
25	0 06·3	0 06·3	0 06·0	2·5	0·0	8·5	0·1	14·5	0·1
26	0 06·5	0 06·5	0 06·2	2·6	0·0	8·6	0·1	14·6	0·1
27	0 06·8	0 06·8	0 06·4	2·7	0·0	8·7	0·1	14·7	0·1
28	0 07·0	0 07·0	0 06·7	2·8	0·0	8·8	0·1	14·8	0·1
29	0 07·3	0 07·3	0 06·9	2·9	0·0	8·9	0·1	14·9	0·1
30	0 07·5	0 07·5	0 07·2	3·0	0·0	9·0	0·1	15·0	0·1
31	0 07·8	0 07·8	0 07·4	3·1	0·0	9·1	0·1	15·1	0·1
32	0 08·0	0 08·0	0 07·6	3·2	0·0	9·2	0·1	15·2	0·1
33	0 08·3	0 08·3	0 07·9	3·3	0·0	9·3	0·1	15·3	0·1
34	0 08·5	0 08·5	0 08·1	3·4	0·0	9·4	0·1	15·4	0·1
35	0 08·8	0 08·8	0 08·4	3·5	0·0	9·5	0·1	15·5	0·1
36	0 09·0	0 09·0	0 08·6	3·6	0·0	9·6	0·1	15·6	0·1
37	0 09·3	0 09·3	0 08·8	3·7	0·0	9·7	0·1	15·7	0·1
38	0 09·5	0 09·5	0 09·1	3·8	0·0	9·8	0·1	15·8	0·1
39	0 09·8	0 09·8	0 09·3	3·9	0·0	9·9	0·1	15·9	0·1
40	0 10·0	0 10·0	0 09·5	4·0	0·0	10·0	0·1	16·0	0·1
41	0 10·3	0 10·3	0 09·8	4·1	0·0	10·1	0·1	16·1	0·1
42	0 10·5	0 10·5	0 10·0	4·2	0·0	10·2	0·1	16·2	0·1
43	0 10·8	0 10·8	0 10·3	4·3	0·0	10·3	0·1	16·3	0·1
44	0 11·0	0 11·0	0 10·5	4·4	0·0	10·4	0·1	16·4	0·1
45	0 11·3	0 11·3	0 10·7	4·5	0·0	10·5	0·1	16·5	0·1
46	0 11·5	0 11·5	0 11·0	4·6	0·0	10·6	0·1	16·6	0·1
47	0 11·8	0 11·8	0 11·2	4·7	0·0	10·7	0·1	16·7	0·1
48	0 12·0	0 12·0	0 11·5	4·8	0·0	10·8	0·1	16·8	0·1
49	0 12·3	0 12·3	0 11·7	4·9	0·0	10·9	0·1	16·9	0·1
50	0 12·5	0 12·5	0 11·9	5·0	0·0	11·0	0·1	17·0	0·1
51	0 12·8	0 12·8	0 12·2	5·1	0·0	11·1	0·1	17·1	0·1
52	0 13·0	0 13·0	0 12·4	5·2	0·0	11·2	0·1	17·2	0·1
53	0 13·3	0 13·3	0 12·6	5·3	0·0	11·3	0·1	17·3	0·1
54	0 13·5	0 13·5	0 12·9	5·4	0·0	11·4	0·1	17·4	0·1
55	0 13·8	0 13·8	0 13·1	5·5	0·0	11·5	0·1	17·5	0·1
56	0 14·0	0 14·0	0 13·4	5·6	0·0	11·6	0·1	17·6	0·1
57	0 14·3	0 14·3	0 13·6	5·7	0·0	11·7	0·1	17·7	0·1
58	0 14·5	0 14·5	0 13·8	5·8	0·0	11·8	0·1	17·8	0·1
59	0 14·8	0 14·8	0 14·1	5·9	0·0	11·9	0·1	17·9	0·1
60	0 15·0	0 15·0	0 14·3	6·0	0·1	12·0	0·1	18·0	0·2

1^m	SUN PLANETS	ARIES	MOON	v or Corr^n d		v or Corr^n d		v or Corr^n d	
s	° ′	° ′	° ′	′	′	′	′	′	′
00	0 15·0	0 15·0	0 14·3	0·0	0·0	6·0	0·2	12·0	0·3
01	0 15·3	0 15·3	0 14·6	0·1	0·0	6·1	0·2	12·1	0·3
02	0 15·5	0 15·5	0 14·8	0·2	0·0	6·2	0·2	12·2	0·3
03	0 15·8	0 15·8	0 15·0	0·3	0·0	6·3	0·2	12·3	0·3
04	0 16·0	0 16·0	0 15·3	0·4	0·0	6·4	0·2	12·4	0·3
05	0 16·3	0 16·3	0 15·5	0·5	0·0	6·5	0·2	12·5	0·3
06	0 16·5	0 16·5	0 15·7	0·6	0·0	6·6	0·2	12·6	0·3
07	0 16·8	0 16·8	0 16·0	0·7	0·0	6·7	0·2	12·7	0·3
08	0 17·0	0 17·0	0 16·2	0·8	0·0	6·8	0·2	12·8	0·3
09	0 17·3	0 17·3	0 16·5	0·9	0·0	6·9	0·2	12·9	0·3
10	0 17·5	0 17·5	0 16·7	1·0	0·0	7·0	0·2	13·0	0·3
11	0 17·8	0 17·8	0 16·9	1·1	0·0	7·1	0·2	13·1	0·3
12	0 18·0	0 18·0	0 17·2	1·2	0·0	7·2	0·2	13·2	0·3
13	0 18·3	0 18·3	0 17·4	1·3	0·0	7·3	0·2	13·3	0·3
14	0 18·5	0 18·6	0 17·7	1·4	0·0	7·4	0·2	13·4	0·3
15	0 18·8	0 18·8	0 17·9	1·5	0·0	7·5	0·2	13·5	0·3
16	0 19·0	0 19·1	0 18·1	1·6	0·0	7·6	0·2	13·6	0·3
17	0 19·3	0 19·3	0 18·4	1·7	0·0	7·7	0·2	13·7	0·3
18	0 19·5	0 19·6	0 18·6	1·8	0·0	7·8	0·2	13·8	0·3
19	0 19·8	0 19·8	0 18·9	1·9	0·0	7·9	0·2	13·9	0·3
20	0 20·0	0 20·1	0 19·1	2·0	0·1	8·0	0·2	14·0	0·4
21	0 20·3	0 20·3	0 19·3	2·1	0·1	8·1	0·2	14·1	0·4
22	0 20·5	0 20·6	0 19·6	2·2	0·1	8·2	0·2	14·2	0·4
23	0 20·8	0 20·8	0 19·8	2·3	0·1	8·3	0·2	14·3	0·4
24	0 21·0	0 21·1	0 20·0	2·4	0·1	8·4	0·2	14·4	0·4
25	0 21·3	0 21·3	0 20·3	2·5	0·1	8·5	0·2	14·5	0·4
26	0 21·5	0 21·6	0 20·5	2·6	0·1	8·6	0·2	14·6	0·4
27	0 21·8	0 21·8	0 20·8	2·7	0·1	8·7	0·2	14·7	0·4
28	0 22·0	0 22·1	0 21·0	2·8	0·1	8·8	0·2	14·8	0·4
29	0 22·3	0 22·3	0 21·2	2·9	0·1	8·9	0·2	14·9	0·4
30	0 22·5	0 22·6	0 21·5	3·0	0·1	9·0	0·2	15·0	0·4
31	0 22·8	0 22·8	0 21·7	3·1	0·1	9·1	0·2	15·1	0·4
32	0 23·0	0 23·1	0 22·0	3·2	0·1	9·2	0·2	15·2	0·4
33	0 23·3	0 23·3	0 22·2	3·3	0·1	9·3	0·2	15·3	0·4
34	0 23·5	0 23·6	0 22·4	3·4	0·1	9·4	0·2	15·4	0·4
35	0 23·8	0 23·8	0 22·7	3·5	0·1	9·5	0·2	15·5	0·4
36	0 24·0	0 24·1	0 22·9	3·6	0·1	9·6	0·2	15·6	0·4
37	0 24·3	0 24·3	0 23·1	3·7	0·1	9·7	0·2	15·7	0·4
38	0 24·5	0 24·6	0 23·4	3·8	0·1	9·8	0·2	15·8	0·4
39	0 24·8	0 24·8	0 23·6	3·9	0·1	9·9	0·2	15·9	0·4
40	0 25·0	0 25·1	0 23·9	4·0	0·1	10·0	0·3	16·0	0·4
41	0 25·3	0 25·3	0 24·1	4·1	0·1	10·1	0·3	16·1	0·4
42	0 25·5	0 25·6	0 24·3	4·2	0·1	10·2	0·3	16·2	0·4
43	0 25·8	0 25·8	0 24·6	4·3	0·1	10·3	0·3	16·3	0·4
44	0 26·0	0 26·1	0 24·8	4·4	0·1	10·4	0·3	16·4	0·4
45	0 26·3	0 26·3	0 25·1	4·5	0·1	10·5	0·3	16·5	0·4
46	0 26·5	0 26·6	0 25·3	4·6	0·1	10·6	0·3	16·6	0·4
47	0 26·8	0 26·8	0 25·5	4·7	0·1	10·7	0·3	16·7	0·4
48	0 27·0	0 27·1	0 25·8	4·8	0·1	10·8	0·3	16·8	0·4
49	0 27·3	0 27·3	0 26·0	4·9	0·1	10·9	0·3	16·9	0·4
50	0 27·5	0 27·6	0 26·2	5·0	0·1	11·0	0·3	17·0	0·4
51	0 27·8	0 27·8	0 26·5	5·1	0·1	11·1	0·3	17·1	0·4
52	0 28·0	0 28·1	0 26·7	5·2	0·1	11·2	0·3	17·2	0·4
53	0 28·3	0 28·3	0 27·0	5·3	0·1	11·3	0·3	17·3	0·4
54	0 28·5	0 28·6	0 27·2	5·4	0·1	11·4	0·3	17·4	0·4
55	0 28·8	0 28·8	0 27·4	5·5	0·1	11·5	0·3	17·5	0·4
56	0 29·0	0 29·1	0 27·7	5·6	0·1	11·6	0·3	17·6	0·4
57	0 29·3	0 29·3	0 27·9	5·7	0·1	11·7	0·3	17·7	0·4
58	0 29·5	0 29·6	0 28·2	5·8	0·1	11·8	0·3	17·8	0·4
59	0 29·8	0 29·8	0 28·4	5·9	0·1	11·9	0·3	17·9	0·4
60	0 30·0	0 30·1	0 28·6	6·0	0·2	12·0	0·3	18·0	0·5

$\overset{m}{6}$	SUN PLANETS	ARIES	MOON	v or Corrⁿ d		v or Corrⁿ d		v or Corrⁿ d		$\overset{m}{7}$	SUN PLANETS	ARIES	MOON	v or Corrⁿ d		v or Corrⁿ d		v or Corrⁿ d	
s	° ′	° ′	° ′	′	′	′	′	′	′	s	° ′	° ′	° ′	′	′	′	′	′	′
00	1 30·0	1 30·2	1 25·9	0·0	0·0	6·0	0·7	12·0	1·3	00	1 45·0	1 45·3	1 40·2	0·0	0·0	6·0	0·8	12·0	1·5
01	1 30·3	1 30·5	1 26·1	0·1	0·0	6·1	0·7	12·1	1·3	01	1 45·3	1 45·5	1 40·5	0·1	0·0	6·1	0·8	12·1	1·5
02	1 30·5	1 30·7	1 26·4	0·2	0·0	6·2	0·7	12·2	1·3	02	1 45·5	1 45·8	1 40·7	0·2	0·0	6·2	0·8	12·2	1·5
03	1 30·8	1 31·0	1 26·6	0·3	0·0	6·3	0·7	12·3	1·3	03	1 45·8	1 46·0	1 40·9	0·3	0·0	6·3	0·8	12·3	1·5
04	1 31·0	1 31·2	1 26·9	0·4	0·0	6·4	0·7	12·4	1·3	04	1 46·0	1 46·3	1 41·2	0·4	0·1	6·4	0·8	12·4	1·6
05	1 31·3	1 31·5	1 27·1	0·5	0·1	6·5	0·7	12·5	1·4	05	1 46·3	1 46·5	1 41·4	0·5	0·1	6·5	0·8	12·5	1·6
06	1 31·5	1 31·8	1 27·3	0·6	0·1	6·6	0·7	12·6	1·4	06	1 46·5	1 46·8	1 41·6	0·6	0·1	6·6	0·8	12·6	1·6
07	1 31·8	1 32·0	1 27·6	0·7	0·1	6·7	0·7	12·7	1·4	07	1 46·8	1 47·0	1 41·9	0·7	0·1	6·7	0·8	12·7	1·6
08	1 32·0	1 32·3	1 27·8	0·8	0·1	6·8	0·7	12·8	1·4	08	1 47·0	1 47·3	1 42·1	0·8	0·1	6·8	0·9	12·8	1·6
09	1 32·3	1 32·5	1 28·0	0·9	0·1	6·9	0·7	12·9	1·4	09	1 47·3	1 47·5	1 42·4	0·9	0·1	6·9	0·9	12·9	1·6
10	1 32·5	1 32·8	1 28·3	1·0	0·1	7·0	0·8	13·0	1·4	10	1 47·5	1 47·8	1 42·6	1·0	0·1	7·0	0·9	13·0	1·6
11	1 32·8	1 33·0	1 28·5	1·1	0·1	7·1	0·8	13·1	1·4	11	1 47·8	1 48·0	1 42·8	1·1	0·1	7·1	0·9	13·1	1·6
12	1 33·0	1 33·3	1 28·8	1·2	0·1	7·2	0·8	13·2	1·4	12	1 48·0	1 48·3	1 43·1	1·2	0·2	7·2	0·9	13·2	1·7
13	1 33·3	1 33·5	1 29·0	1·3	0·1	7·3	0·8	13·3	1·4	13	1 48·3	1 48·5	1 43·3	1·3	0·2	7·3	0·9	13·3	1·7
14	1 33·5	1 33·8	1 29·2	1·4	0·2	7·4	0·8	13·4	1·5	14	1 48·5	1 48·8	1 43·6	1·4	0·2	7·4	0·9	13·4	1·7
15	1 33·8	1 34·0	1 29·5	1·5	0·2	7·5	0·8	13·5	1·5	15	1 48·8	1 49·0	1 43·8	1·5	0·2	7·5	0·9	13·5	1·7
16	1 34·0	1 34·3	1 29·7	1·6	0·2	7·6	0·8	13·6	1·5	16	1 49·0	1 49·3	1 44·0	1·6	0·2	7·6	1·0	13·6	1·7
17	1 34·3	1 34·5	1 30·0	1·7	0·2	7·7	0·8	13·7	1·5	17	1 49·3	1 49·5	1 44·3	1·7	0·2	7·7	1·0	13·7	1·7
18	1 34·5	1 34·8	1 30·2	1·8	0·2	7·8	0·8	13·8	1·5	18	1 49·5	1 49·8	1 44·5	1·8	0·2	7·8	1·0	13·8	1·7
19	1 34·8	1 35·0	1 30·4	1·9	0·2	7·9	0·9	13·9	1·5	19	1 49·8	1 50·1	1 44·8	1·9	0·2	7·9	1·0	13·9	1·7
20	1 35·0	1 35·3	1 30·7	2·0	0·2	8·0	0·9	14·0	1·5	20	1 50·0	1 50·3	1 45·0	2·0	0·3	8·0	1·0	14·0	1·8
21	1 35·3	1 35·5	1 30·9	2·1	0·2	8·1	0·9	14·1	1·5	21	1 50·3	1 50·6	1 45·2	2·1	0·3	8·1	1·0	14·1	1·8
22	1 35·5	1 35·8	1 31·1	2·2	0·2	8·2	0·9	14·2	1·5	22	1 50·5	1 50·8	1 45·5	2·2	0·3	8·2	1·0	14·2	1·8
23	1 35·8	1 36·0	1 31·4	2·3	0·2	8·3	0·9	14·3	1·5	23	1 51·0	1 51·1	1 45·7	2·3	0·3	8·3	1·0	14·3	1·8
24	1 36·0	1 36·3	1 31·6	2·4	0·3	8·4	0·9	14·4	1·6	24	1 51·0	1 51·3	1 45·9	2·4	0·3	8·4	1·1	14·4	1·8
25	1 36·3	1 36·5	1 31·9	2·5	0·3	8·5	0·9	14·5	1·6	25	1 51·3	1 51·6	1 46·2	2·5	0·3	8·5	1·1	14·5	1·8
26	1 36·5	1 36·8	1 32·1	2·6	0·3	8·6	0·9	14·6	1·6	26	1 51·5	1 51·8	1 46·4	2·6	0·3	8·6	1·1	14·6	1·8
27	1 36·8	1 37·0	1 32·3	2·7	0·3	8·7	0·9	14·7	1·6	27	1 51·8	1 52·1	1 46·7	2·7	0·3	8·7	1·1	14·7	1·8
28	1 37·0	1 37·3	1 32·6	2·8	0·3	8·8	1·0	14·8	1·6	28	1 52·0	1 52·3	1 46·9	2·8	0·4	8·8	1·1	14·8	1·9
29	1 37·3	1 37·5	1 32·8	2·9	0·3	8·9	1·0	14·9	1·6	29	1 52·3	1 52·6	1 47·1	2·9	0·4	8·9	1·1	14·9	1·9
30	1 37·5	1 37·8	1 33·1	3·0	0·3	9·0	1·0	15·0	1·6	30	1 52·5	1 52·8	1 47·4	3·0	0·4	9·0	1·1	15·0	1·9
31	1 37·8	1 38·0	1 33·3	3·1	0·3	9·1	1·0	15·1	1·6	31	1 52·8	1 53·1	1 47·6	3·1	0·4	9·1	1·1	15·1	1·9
32	1 38·0	1 38·3	1 33·5	3·2	0·3	9·2	1·0	15·2	1·6	32	1 53·0	1 53·3	1 47·9	3·2	0·4	9·2	1·2	15·2	1·9
33	1 38·3	1 38·5	1 33·8	3·3	0·4	9·3	1·0	15·3	1·7	33	1 53·3	1 53·6	1 48·1	3·3	0·4	9·3	1·2	15·3	1·9
34	1 38·5	1 38·8	1 34·0	3·4	0·4	9·4	1·0	15·4	1·7	34	1 53·5	1 53·8	1 48·3	3·4	0·4	9·4	1·2	15·4	1·9
35	1 38·8	1 39·0	1 34·3	3·5	0·4	9·5	1·0	15·5	1·7	35	1 53·8	1 54·1	1 48·6	3·5	0·4	9·5	1·2	15·5	1·9
36	1 39·0	1 39·3	1 34·5	3·6	0·4	9·6	1·0	15·6	1·7	36	1 54·0	1 54·3	1 48·8	3·6	0·5	9·6	1·2	15·6	2·0
37	1 39·3	1 39·5	1 34·7	3·7	0·4	9·7	1·1	15·7	1·7	37	1 54·3	1 54·6	1 49·0	3·7	0·5	9·7	1·2	15·7	2·0
38	1 39·5	1 39·8	1 35·0	3·8	0·4	9·8	1·1	15·8	1·7	38	1 54·5	1 54·8	1 49·3	3·8	0·5	9·8	1·2	15·8	2·0
39	1 39·8	1 40·0	1 35·2	3·9	0·4	9·9	1·1	15·9	1·7	39	1 54·8	1 55·1	1 49·5	3·9	0·5	9·9	1·2	15·9	2·0
40	1 40·0	1 40·3	1 35·4	4·0	0·4	10·0	1·1	16·0	1·7	40	1 55·0	1 55·3	1 49·8	4·0	0·5	10·0	1·3	16·0	2·0
41	1 40·3	1 40·5	1 35·7	4·1	0·4	10·1	1·1	16·1	1·7	41	1 55·3	1 55·6	1 50·0	4·1	0·5	10·1	1·3	16·1	2·0
42	1 40·5	1 40·8	1 35·9	4·2	0·5	10·2	1·1	16·2	1·8	42	1 55·5	1 55·8	1 50·2	4·2	0·5	10·2	1·3	16·2	2·0
43	1 40·8	1 41·0	1 36·2	4·3	0·5	10·3	1·1	16·3	1·8	43	1 55·8	1 56·1	1 50·5	4·3	0·5	10·3	1·3	16·3	2·0
44	1 41·0	1 41·3	1 36·4	4·4	0·5	10·4	1·1	16·4	1·8	44	1 56·0	1 56·3	1 50·7	4·4	0·6	10·4	1·3	16·4	2·1
45	1 41·3	1 41·5	1 36·6	4·5	0·5	10·5	1·1	16·5	1·8	45	1 56·3	1 56·6	1 51·0	4·5	0·6	10·5	1·3	16·5	2·1
46	1 41·5	1 41·8	1 36·9	4·6	0·5	10·6	1·1	16·6	1·8	46	1 56·5	1 56·8	1 51·2	4·6	0·6	10·6	1·3	16·6	2·1
47	1 41·8	1 42·0	1 37·1	4·7	0·5	10·7	1·2	16·7	1·8	47	1 56·8	1 57·1	1 51·4	4·7	0·6	10·7	1·3	16·7	2·1
48	1 42·0	1 42·3	1 37·4	4·8	0·5	10·8	1·2	16·8	1·8	48	1 57·0	1 57·3	1 51·7	4·8	0·6	10·8	1·4	16·8	2·1
49	1 42·3	1 42·5	1 37·6	4·9	0·5	10·9	1·2	16·9	1·8	49	1 57·3	1 57·6	1 51·9	4·9	0·6	10·9	1·4	16·9	2·1
50	1 42·5	1 42·8	1 37·8	5·0	0·5	11·0	1·2	17·0	1·8	50	1 57·5	1 57·8	1 52·1	5·0	0·6	11·0	1·4	17·0	2·1
51	1 42·8	1 43·0	1 38·1	5·1	0·6	11·1	1·2	17·1	1·9	51	1 57·8	1 58·1	1 52·4	5·1	0·6	11·1	1·4	17·1	2·1
52	1 43·0	1 43·3	1 38·3	5·2	0·6	11·2	1·2	17·2	1·9	52	1 58·0	1 58·3	1 52·6	5·2	0·7	11·2	1·4	17·2	2·2
53	1 43·3	1 43·5	1 38·5	5·3	0·6	11·3	1·2	17·3	1·9	53	1 58·3	1 58·6	1 52·9	5·3	0·7	11·3	1·4	17·3	2·2
54	1 43·5	1 43·8	1 38·8	5·4	0·6	11·4	1·2	17·4	1·9	54	1 58·5	1 58·8	1 53·1	5·4	0·7	11·4	1·4	17·4	2·2
55	1 43·8	1 44·0	1 39·0	5·5	0·6	11·5	1·2	17·5	1·9	55	1 58·8	1 59·1	1 53·3	5·5	0·7	11·5	1·4	17·5	2·2
56	1 44·0	1 44·3	1 39·3	5·6	0·6	11·6	1·3	17·6	1·9	56	1 59·0	1 59·3	1 53·6	5·6	0·7	11·6	1·5	17·6	2·2
57	1 44·3	1 44·5	1 39·5	5·7	0·6	11·7	1·3	17·7	1·9	57	1 59·3	1 59·6	1 53·8	5·7	0·7	11·7	1·5	17·7	2·2
58	1 44·5	1 44·8	1 39·7	5·8	0·6	11·8	1·3	17·8	1·9	58	1 59·5	1 59·8	1 54·1	5·8	0·7	11·8	1·5	17·8	2·2
59	1 44·8	1 45·0	1 40·0	5·9	0·6	11·9	1·3	17·9	1·9	59	1 59·8	2 00·1	1 54·3	5·9	0·7	11·9	1·5	17·9	2·2
60	1 45·0	1 45·3	1 40·2	6·0	0·7	12·0	1·3	18·0	2·0	60	2 00·0	2 00·3	1 54·5	6·0	0·8	12·0	1·5	18·0	2·3

10^m	SUN PLANETS	ARIES	MOON	v or Corr^n d		v or Corr^n d		v or Corr^n d	
s	° ′	° ′	° ′	′	′	′	′	′	′
00	2 30·0	2 30·4	2 23·2	0·0	0·0	6·0	1·1	12·0	2·1
01	2 30·3	2 30·7	2 23·4	0·1	0·0	6·1	1·1	12·1	2·1
02	2 30·5	2 30·9	2 23·6	0·2	0·0	6·2	1·1	12·2	2·1
03	2 30·8	2 31·2	2 23·9	0·3	0·1	6·3	1·1	12·3	2·2
04	2 31·0	2 31·4	2 24·1	0·4	0·1	6·4	1·1	12·4	2·2
05	2 31·3	2 31·7	2 24·4	0·5	0·1	6·5	1·1	12·5	2·2
06	2 31·5	2 31·9	2 24·6	0·6	0·1	6·6	1·2	12·6	2·2
07	2 31·8	2 32·2	2 24·8	0·7	0·1	6·7	1·2	12·7	2·2
08	2 32·0	2 32·4	2 25·1	0·8	0·1	6·8	1·2	12·8	2·2
09	2 32·3	2 32·7	2 25·3	0·9	0·2	6·9	1·2	12·9	2·3
10	2 32·5	2 32·9	2 25·6	1·0	0·2	7·0	1·2	13·0	2·3
11	2 32·8	2 33·2	2 25·8	1·1	0·2	7·1	1·2	13·1	2·3
12	2 33·0	2 33·4	2 26·0	1·2	0·2	7·2	1·3	13·2	2·3
13	2 33·3	2 33·7	2 26·3	1·3	0·2	7·3	1·3	13·3	2·3
14	2 33·5	2 33·9	2 26·5	1·4	0·2	7·4	1·3	13·4	2·3
15	2 33·8	2 34·2	2 26·7	1·5	0·3	7·5	1·3	13·5	2·4
16	2 34·0	2 34·4	2 27·0	1·6	0·3	7·6	1·3	13·6	2·4
17	2 34·3	2 34·7	2 27·2	1·7	0·3	7·7	1·3	13·7	2·4
18	2 34·5	2 34·9	2 27·5	1·8	0·3	7·8	1·4	13·8	2·4
19	2 34·8	2 35·2	2 27·7	1·9	0·3	7·9	1·4	13·9	2·4
20	2 35·0	2 35·4	2 27·9	2·0	0·4	8·0	1·4	14·0	2·5
21	2 35·3	2 35·7	2 28·2	2·1	0·4	8·1	1·4	14·1	2·5
22	2 35·5	2 35·9	2 28·4	2·2	0·4	8·2	1·4	14·2	2·5
23	2 35·8	2 36·2	2 28·7	2·3	0·4	8·3	1·5	14·3	2·5
24	2 36·0	2 36·4	2 28·9	2·4	0·4	8·4	1·5	14·4	2·5
25	2 36·3	2 36·7	2 29·1	2·5	0·4	8·5	1·5	14·5	2·5
26	2 36·5	2 36·9	2 29·4	2·6	0·5	8·6	1·5	14·6	2·6
27	2 36·8	2 37·2	2 29·6	2·7	0·5	8·7	1·5	14·7	2·6
28	2 37·0	2 37·4	2 29·8	2·8	0·5	8·8	1·5	14·8	2·6
29	2 37·3	2 37·7	2 30·1	2·9	0·5	8·9	1·6	14·9	2·6
30	2 37·5	2 37·9	2 30·3	3·0	0·5	9·0	1·6	15·0	2·6
31	2 37·8	2 38·2	2 30·6	3·1	0·5	9·1	1·6	15·1	2·6
32	2 38·0	2 38·4	2 30·8	3·2	0·6	9·2	1·6	15·2	2·7
33	2 38·3	2 38·7	2 31·0	3·3	0·6	9·3	1·6	15·3	2·7
34	2 38·5	2 38·9	2 31·3	3·4	0·6	9·4	1·6	15·4	2·7
35	2 38·8	2 39·2	2 31·5	3·5	0·6	9·5	1·7	15·5	2·7
36	2 39·0	2 39·4	2 31·8	3·6	0·6	9·6	1·7	15·6	2·7
37	2 39·3	2 39·7	2 32·0	3·7	0·6	9·7	1·7	15·7	2·7
38	2 39·5	2 39·9	2 32·2	3·8	0·7	9·8	1·7	15·8	2·8
39	2 39·8	2 40·2	2 32·5	3·9	0·7	9·9	1·7	15·9	2·8
40	2 40·0	2 40·4	2 32·7	4·0	0·7	10·0	1·8	16·0	2·8
41	2 40·3	2 40·7	2 32·9	4·1	0·7	10·1	1·8	16·1	2·8
42	2 40·5	2 40·9	2 33·2	4·2	0·7	10·2	1·8	16·2	2·8
43	2 40·8	2 41·2	2 33·4	4·3	0·8	10·3	1·8	16·3	2·9
44	2 41·0	2 41·4	2 33·7	4·4	0·8	10·4	1·8	16·4	2·9
45	2 41·3	2 41·7	2 33·9	4·5	0·8	10·5	1·8	16·5	2·9
46	2 41·5	2 41·9	2 34·1	4·6	0·8	10·6	1·9	16·6	2·9
47	2 41·8	2 42·2	2 34·4	4·7	0·8	10·7	1·9	16·7	2·9
48	2 42·0	2 42·4	2 34·6	4·8	0·8	10·8	1·9	16·8	2·9
49	2 42·3	2 42·7	2 34·9	4·9	0·9	10·9	1·9	16·9	3·0
50	2 42·5	2 42·9	2 35·1	5·0	0·9	11·0	1·9	17·0	3·0
51	2 42·8	2 43·2	2 35·3	5·1	0·9	11·1	1·9	17·1	3·0
52	2 43·0	2 43·4	2 35·6	5·2	0·9	11·2	2·0	17·2	3·0
53	2 43·3	2 43·7	2 35·8	5·3	0·9	11·3	2·0	17·3	3·0
54	2 43·5	2 43·9	2 36·1	5·4	0·9	11·4	2·0	17·4	3·0
55	2 43·8	2 44·2	2 36·3	5·5	1·0	11·5	2·0	17·5	3·1
56	2 44·0	2 44·4	2 36·5	5·6	1·0	11·6	2·0	17·6	3·1
57	2 44·3	2 44·7	2 36·8	5·7	1·0	11·7	2·0	17·7	3·1
58	2 44·5	2 45·0	2 37·0	5·8	1·0	11·8	2·1	17·8	3·1
59	2 44·8	2 45·2	2 37·2	5·9	1·0	11·9	2·1	17·9	3·1
60	2 45·0	2 45·5	2 37·5	6·0	1·1	12·0	2·1	18·0	3·2

11^m	SUN PLANETS	ARIES	MOON	v or Corr^n d		v or Corr^n d		v or Corr^n d	
s	° ′	° ′	° ′	′	′	′	′	′	′
00	2 45·0	2 45·5	2 37·5	0·0	0·0	6·0	1·2	12·0	2·3
01	2 45·3	2 45·7	2 37·7	0·1	0·0	6·1	1·2	12·1	2·3
02	2 45·5	2 46·0	2 38·0	0·2	0·0	6·2	1·2	12·2	2·3
03	2 45·8	2 46·2	2 38·2	0·3	0·1	6·3	1·2	12·3	2·4
04	2 46·0	2 46·5	2 38·4	0·4	0·1	6·4	1·2	12·4	2·4
05	2 46·3	2 46·7	2 38·7	0·5	0·1	6·5	1·2	12·5	2·4
06	2 46·5	2 47·0	2 38·9	0·6	0·1	6·6	1·3	12·6	2·4
07	2 46·8	2 47·2	2 39·2	0·7	0·1	6·7	1·3	12·7	2·4
08	2 47·0	2 47·5	2 39·4	0·8	0·2	6·8	1·3	12·8	2·5
09	2 47·3	2 47·7	2 39·6	0·9	0·2	6·9	1·3	12·9	2·5
10	2 47·5	2 48·0	2 39·9	1·0	0·2	7·0	1·3	13·0	2·5
11	2 47·8	2 48·2	2 40·1	1·1	0·2	7·1	1·4	13·1	2·5
12	2 48·0	2 48·5	2 40·3	1·2	0·2	7·2	1·4	13·2	2·5
13	2 48·3	2 48·7	2 40·6	1·3	0·2	7·3	1·4	13·3	2·5
14	2 48·5	2 49·0	2 40·8	1·4	0·3	7·4	1·4	13·4	2·6
15	2 48·8	2 49·2	2 41·1	1·5	0·3	7·5	1·4	13·5	2·6
16	2 49·0	2 49·5	2 41·3	1·6	0·3	7·6	1·5	13·6	2·6
17	2 49·3	2 49·7	2 41·5	1·7	0·3	7·7	1·5	13·7	2·6
18	2 49·5	2 50·0	2 41·8	1·8	0·3	7·8	1·5	13·8	2·6
19	2 49·8	2 50·2	2 42·0	1·9	0·4	7·9	1·5	13·9	2·7
20	2 50·0	2 50·5	2 42·3	2·0	0·4	8·0	1·5	14·0	2·7
21	2 50·3	2 50·7	2 42·5	2·1	0·4	8·1	1·6	14·1	2·7
22	2 50·5	2 51·0	2 42·7	2·2	0·4	8·2	1·6	14·2	2·7
23	2 50·8	2 51·2	2 43·0	2·3	0·4	8·3	1·6	14·3	2·7
24	2 51·0	2 51·5	2 43·2	2·4	0·5	8·4	1·6	14·4	2·8
25	2 51·3	2 51·7	2 43·4	2·5	0·5	8·5	1·6	14·5	2·8
26	2 51·5	2 52·0	2 43·7	2·6	0·5	8·6	1·6	14·6	2·8
27	2 51·8	2 52·2	2 43·9	2·7	0·5	8·7	1·7	14·7	2·8
28	2 52·0	2 52·5	2 44·2	2·8	0·5	8·8	1·7	14·8	2·8
29	2 52·3	2 52·7	2 44·4	2·9	0·6	8·9	1·7	14·9	2·9
30	2 52·5	2 53·0	2 44·6	3·0	0·6	9·0	1·7	15·0	2·9
31	2 52·8	2 53·2	2 44·9	3·1	0·6	9·1	1·7	15·1	2·9
32	2 53·0	2 53·5	2 45·1	3·2	0·6	9·2	1·8	15·2	2·9
33	2 53·3	2 53·7	2 45·4	3·3	0·6	9·3	1·8	15·3	2·9
34	2 53·5	2 54·0	2 45·6	3·4	0·7	9·4	1·8	15·4	3·0
35	2 53·8	2 54·2	2 45·8	3·5	0·7	9·5	1·8	15·5	3·0
36	2 54·0	2 54·5	2 46·1	3·6	0·7	9·6	1·8	15·6	3·0
37	2 54·3	2 54·7	2 46·3	3·7	0·7	9·7	1·9	15·7	3·0
38	2 54·5	2 55·0	2 46·6	3·8	0·7	9·8	1·9	15·8	3·0
39	2 54·8	2 55·2	2 46·8	3·9	0·7	9·9	1·9	15·9	3·0
40	2 55·0	2 55·5	2 47·0	4·0	0·8	10·0	1·9	16·0	3·1
41	2 55·3	2 55·7	2 47·3	4·1	0·8	10·1	1·9	16·1	3·1
42	2 55·5	2 56·0	2 47·5	4·2	0·8	10·2	2·0	16·2	3·1
43	2 55·8	2 56·2	2 47·7	4·3	0·8	10·3	2·0	16·3	3·1
44	2 56·0	2 56·5	2 48·0	4·4	0·8	10·4	2·0	16·4	3·1
45	2 56·3	2 56·7	2 48·2	4·5	0·9	10·5	2·0	16·5	3·2
46	2 56·5	2 57·0	2 48·5	4·6	0·9	10·6	2·0	16·6	3·2
47	2 56·8	2 57·2	2 48·7	4·7	0·9	10·7	2·1	16·7	3·2
48	2 57·0	2 57·5	2 48·9	4·8	0·9	10·8	2·1	16·8	3·2
49	2 57·3	2 57·7	2 49·2	4·9	0·9	10·9	2·1	16·9	3·2
50	2 57·5	2 58·0	2 49·4	5·0	1·0	11·0	2·1	17·0	3·3
51	2 57·8	2 58·2	2 49·7	5·1	1·0	11·1	2·1	17·1	3·3
52	2 58·0	2 58·5	2 49·9	5·2	1·0	11·2	2·1	17·2	3·3
53	2 58·3	2 58·7	2 50·1	5·3	1·0	11·3	2·2	17·3	3·3
54	2 58·5	2 59·0	2 50·4	5·4	1·0	11·4	2·2	17·4	3·3
55	2 58·8	2 59·2	2 50·6	5·5	1·1	11·5	2·2	17·5	3·4
56	2 59·0	2 59·5	2 50·8	5·6	1·1	11·6	2·2	17·6	3·4
57	2 59·3	2 59·7	2 51·1	5·7	1·1	11·7	2·2	17·7	3·4
58	2 59·5	3 00·0	2 51·3	5·8	1·1	11·8	2·3	17·8	3·4
59	2 59·8	3 00·2	2 51·6	5·9	1·1	11·9	2·3	17·9	3·4
60	3 00·0	3 00·5	2 51·8	6·0	1·2	12·0	2·3	18·0	3·5

12ᵐ

12ᵐ s	SUN PLANETS ° ′	ARIES ° ′	MOON ° ′	v or Corrⁿ d ′ ′	v or Corrⁿ d ′ ′	v or Corrⁿ d ′ ′
00	3 00·0	3 00·5	2 51·8	0·0 0·0	6·0 1·3	12·0 2·5
01	3 00·3	3 00·7	2 52·0	0·1 0·0	6·1 1·3	12·1 2·5
02	3 00·5	3 01·0	2 52·3	0·2 0·0	6·2 1·3	12·2 2·5
03	3 00·8	3 01·2	2 52·5	0·3 0·1	6·3 1·3	12·3 2·6
04	3 01·0	3 01·5	2 52·8	0·4 0·1	6·4 1·3	12·4 2·6
05	3 01·3	3 01·7	2 53·0	0·5 0·1	6·5 1·4	12·5 2·6
06	3 01·5	3 02·0	2 53·2	0·6 0·1	6·6 1·4	12·6 2·6
07	3 01·8	3 02·2	2 53·5	0·7 0·1	6·7 1·4	12·7 2·6
08	3 02·0	3 02·5	2 53·7	0·8 0·2	6·8 1·4	12·8 2·7
09	3 02·3	3 02·7	2 53·9	0·9 0·2	6·9 1·4	12·9 2·7
10	3 02·5	3 03·0	2 54·2	1·0 0·2	7·0 1·5	13·0 2·7
11	3 02·8	3 03·3	2 54·4	1·1 0·2	7·1 1·5	13·1 2·7
12	3 03·0	3 03·5	2 54·7	1·2 0·3	7·2 1·5	13·2 2·8
13	3 03·3	3 03·8	2 54·9	1·3 0·3	7·3 1·5	13·3 2·8
14	3 03·5	3 04·0	2 55·1	1·4 0·3	7·4 1·5	13·4 2·8
15	3 03·8	3 04·3	2 55·4	1·5 0·3	7·5 1·6	13·5 2·8
16	3 04·0	3 04·5	2 55·6	1·6 0·3	7·6 1·6	13·6 2·8
17	3 04·3	3 04·8	2 55·9	1·7 0·4	7·7 1·6	13·7 2·9
18	3 04·5	3 05·0	2 56·1	1·8 0·4	7·8 1·6	13·8 2·9
19	3 04·8	3 05·3	2 56·3	1·9 0·4	7·9 1·6	13·9 2·9
20	3 05·0	3 05·5	2 56·6	2·0 0·4	8·0 1·7	14·0 2·9
21	3 05·3	3 05·8	2 56·8	2·1 0·4	8·1 1·7	14·1 2·9
22	3 05·5	3 06·0	2 57·0	2·2 0·5	8·2 1·7	14·2 3·0
23	3 05·8	3 06·3	2 57·3	2·3 0·5	8·3 1·7	14·3 3·0
24	3 06·0	3 06·5	2 57·5	2·4 0·5	8·4 1·8	14·4 3·0
25	3 06·3	3 06·8	2 57·8	2·5 0·5	8·5 1·8	14·5 3·0
26	3 06·5	3 07·0	2 58·0	2·6 0·5	8·6 1·8	14·6 3·0
27	3 06·8	3 07·3	2 58·2	2·7 0·6	8·7 1·8	14·7 3·1
28	3 07·0	3 07·5	2 58·5	2·8 0·6	8·8 1·8	14·8 3·1
29	3 07·3	3 07·8	2 58·7	2·9 0·6	8·9 1·9	14·9 3·1
30	3 07·5	3 08·0	2 59·0	3·0 0·6	9·0 1·9	15·0 3·1
31	3 07·8	3 08·3	2 59·2	3·1 0·6	9·1 1·9	15·1 3·1
32	3 08·0	3 08·5	2 59·4	3·2 0·7	9·2 1·9	15·2 3·2
33	3 08·3	3 08·8	2 59·7	3·3 0·7	9·3 1·9	15·3 3·2
34	3 08·5	3 09·0	2 59·9	3·4 0·7	9·4 2·0	15·4 3·2
35	3 08·8	3 09·3	3 00·2	3·5 0·7	9·5 2·0	15·5 3·2
36	3 09·0	3 09·5	3 00·4	3·6 0·8	9·6 2·0	15·6 3·3
37	3 09·3	3 09·8	3 00·6	3·7 0·8	9·7 2·0	15·7 3·3
38	3 09·5	3 10·0	3 00·9	3·8 0·8	9·8 2·0	15·8 3·3
39	3 09·8	3 10·3	3 01·1	3·9 0·8	9·9 2·1	15·9 3·3
40	3 10·0	3 10·5	3 01·3	4·0 0·8	10·0 2·1	16·0 3·3
41	3 10·3	3 10·8	3 01·6	4·1 0·9	10·1 2·1	16·1 3·4
42	3 10·5	3 11·0	3 01·8	4·2 0·9	10·2 2·1	16·2 3·4
43	3 10·8	3 11·3	3 02·1	4·3 0·9	10·3 2·1	16·3 3·4
44	3 11·0	3 11·5	3 02·3	4·4 0·9	10·4 2·2	16·4 3·4
45	3 11·3	3 11·8	3 02·5	4·5 0·9	10·5 2·2	16·5 3·4
46	3 11·5	3 12·0	3 02·8	4·6 1·0	10·6 2·2	16·6 3·5
47	3 11·8	3 12·3	3 03·0	4·7 1·0	10·7 2·2	16·7 3·5
48	3 12·0	3 12·5	3 03·3	4·8 1·0	10·8 2·3	16·8 3·5
49	3 12·3	3 12·8	3 03·5	4·9 1·0	10·9 2·3	16·9 3·5
50	3 12·5	3 13·0	3 03·7	5·0 1·0	11·0 2·3	17·0 3·5
51	3 12·8	3 13·3	3 04·0	5·1 1·1	11·1 2·3	17·1 3·6
52	3 13·0	3 13·5	3 04·2	5·2 1·1	11·2 2·3	17·2 3·6
53	3 13·3	3 13·8	3 04·4	5·3 1·1	11·3 2·4	17·3 3·6
54	3 13·5	3 14·0	3 04·7	5·4 1·1	11·4 2·4	17·4 3·6
55	3 13·8	3 14·3	3 04·9	5·5 1·1	11·5 2·4	17·5 3·6
56	3 14·0	3 14·5	3 05·2	5·6 1·2	11·6 2·4	17·6 3·7
57	3 14·3	3 14·8	3 05·4	5·7 1·2	11·7 2·4	17·7 3·7
58	3 14·5	3 15·0	3 05·6	5·8 1·2	11·8 2·5	17·8 3·7
59	3 14·8	3 15·3	3 05·9	5·9 1·2	11·9 2·5	17·9 3·7
60	3 15·0	3 15·5	3 06·1	6·0 1·3	12·0 2·5	18·0 3·8

13ᵐ

13ᵐ s	SUN PLANETS ° ′	ARIES ° ′	MOON ° ′	v or Corrⁿ d ′ ′	v or Corrⁿ d ′ ′	v or Corrⁿ d ′ ′
00	3 15·0	3 15·5	3 06·1	0·0 0·0	6·0 1·4	12·0 2·7
01	3 15·3	3 15·8	3 06·4	0·1 0·0	6·1 1·4	12·1 2·7
02	3 15·5	3 16·0	3 06·6	0·2 0·0	6·2 1·4	12·2 2·7
03	3 15·8	3 16·3	3 06·8	0·3 0·1	6·3 1·4	12·3 2·8
04	3 16·0	3 16·5	3 07·1	0·4 0·1	6·4 1·4	12·4 2·8
05	3 16·3	3 16·8	3 07·3	0·5 0·1	6·5 1·5	12·5 2·8
06	3 16·5	3 17·0	3 07·5	0·6 0·1	6·6 1·5	12·6 2·8
07	3 16·8	3 17·3	3 07·8	0·7 0·2	6·7 1·5	12·7 2·9
08	3 17·0	3 17·5	3 08·0	0·8 0·2	6·8 1·5	12·8 2·9
09	3 17·3	3 17·8	3 08·3	0·9 0·2	6·9 1·6	12·9 2·9
10	3 17·5	3 18·0	3 08·5	1·0 0·2	7·0 1·6	13·0 2·9
11	3 17·8	3 18·3	3 08·7	1·1 0·2	7·1 1·6	13·1 2·9
12	3 18·0	3 18·5	3 09·0	1·2 0·3	7·2 1·6	13·2 3·0
13	3 18·3	3 18·8	3 09·2	1·3 0·3	7·3 1·6	13·3 3·0
14	3 18·5	3 19·0	3 09·5	1·4 0·3	7·4 1·7	13·4 3·0
15	3 18·8	3 19·3	3 09·7	1·5 0·3	7·5 1·7	13·5 3·0
16	3 19·0	3 19·5	3 09·9	1·6 0·4	7·6 1·7	13·6 3·1
17	3 19·3	3 19·8	3 10·2	1·7 0·4	7·7 1·7	13·7 3·1
18	3 19·5	3 20·0	3 10·4	1·8 0·4	7·8 1·8	13·8 3·1
19	3 19·8	3 20·3	3 10·7	1·9 0·4	7·9 1·8	13·9 3·1
20	3 20·0	3 20·5	3 10·9	2·0 0·5	8·0 1·8	14·0 3·2
21	3 20·3	3 20·8	3 11·1	2·1 0·5	8·1 1·8	14·1 3·2
22	3 20·5	3 21·0	3 11·4	2·2 0·5	8·2 1·8	14·2 3·2
23	3 20·8	3 21·3	3 11·6	2·3 0·5	8·3 1·9	14·3 3·2
24	3 21·0	3 21·6	3 11·8	2·4 0·5	8·4 1·9	14·4 3·2
25	3 21·3	3 21·8	3 12·1	2·5 0·6	8·5 1·9	14·5 3·3
26	3 21·5	3 22·1	3 12·3	2·6 0·6	8·6 1·9	14·6 3·3
27	3 21·8	3 22·3	3 12·6	2·7 0·6	8·7 2·0	14·7 3·3
28	3 22·0	3 22·6	3 12·8	2·8 0·6	8·8 2·0	14·8 3·3
29	3 22·3	3 22·8	3 13·0	2·9 0·7	8·9 2·0	14·9 3·4
30	3 22·5	3 23·1	3 13·3	3·0 0·7	9·0 2·0	15·0 3·4
31	3 22·8	3 23·3	3 13·5	3·1 0·7	9·1 2·0	15·1 3·4
32	3 23·0	3 23·6	3 13·8	3·2 0·7	9·2 2·1	15·2 3·4
33	3 23·3	3 23·8	3 14·0	3·3 0·7	9·3 2·1	15·3 3·4
34	3 23·5	3 24·1	3 14·2	3·4 0·8	9·4 2·1	15·4 3·5
35	3 23·8	3 24·3	3 14·5	3·5 0·8	9·5 2·1	15·5 3·5
36	3 24·0	3 24·6	3 14·7	3·6 0·8	9·6 2·2	15·6 3·5
37	3 24·3	3 24·8	3 14·9	3·7 0·8	9·7 2·2	15·7 3·5
38	3 24·5	3 25·1	3 15·2	3·8 0·9	9·8 2·2	15·8 3·6
39	3 24·8	3 25·3	3 15·4	3·9 0·9	9·9 2·2	15·9 3·6
40	3 25·0	3 25·6	3 15·7	4·0 0·9	10·0 2·3	16·0 3·6
41	3 25·3	3 25·8	3 15·9	4·1 0·9	10·1 2·3	16·1 3·6
42	3 25·5	3 26·1	3 16·1	4·2 0·9	10·2 2·3	16·2 3·6
43	3 25·8	3 26·3	3 16·4	4·3 1·0	10·3 2·3	16·3 3·7
44	3 26·0	3 26·6	3 16·6	4·4 1·0	.10·4 2·3	16·4 3·7
45	3 26·3	3 26·8	3 16·9	4·5 1·0	10·5 2·4	16·5 3·7
46	3 26·5	3 27·1	3 17·1	4·6 1·0	10·6 2·4	16·6 3·7
47	3 26·8	3 27·3	3 17·3	4·7 1·1	10·7 2·4	16·7 3·8
48	3 27·0	3 27·6	3 17·6	4·8 1·1	10·8 2·4	16·8 3·8
49	3 27·3	3 27·8	3 17·8	4·9 1·1	10·9 2·5	16·9 3·8
50	3 27·5	3 28·1	3 18·0	5·0 1·1	11·0 2·5	17·0 3·8
51	3 27·8	3 28·3	3 18·3	5·1 1·1	11·1 2·5	17·1 3·8
52	3 28·0	3 28·6	3 18·5	5·2 1·2	11·2 2·5	17·2 3·9
53	3 28·3	3 28·8	3 18·8	5·3 1·2	11·3 2·5	17·3 3·9
54	3 28·5	3 29·1	3 19·0	5·4 1·2	11·4 2·6	17·4 3·9
55	3 28·8	3 29·3	3 19·2	5·5 1·2	11·5 2·6	17·5 3·9
56	3 29·0	3 29·6	3 19·5	5·6 1·3	11·6 2·6	17·6 4·0
57	3 29·3	3 29·8	3 19·7	5·7 1·3	11·7 2·6	17·7 4·0
58	3 29·5	3 30·1	3 20·0	5·8 1·3	11·8 2·7	17·8 4·0
59	3 29·8	3 30·3	3 20·2	5·9 1·3	11·9 2·7	17·9 4·0
60	3 30·0	3 30·6	3 20·4	6·0 1·4	12·0 2·7	18·0 4·1

14m

14 s	SUN PLANETS	ARIES	MOON	v or Corrn d	v or Corrn d	v or Corrn d
	° '	° '	° '	' '	' '	' '
00	3 30·0	3 30·6	3 20·4	0·0 0·0	6·0 1·5	12·0 2·9
01	3 30·3	3 30·8	3 20·7	0·1 0·0	6·1 1·5	12·1 2·9
02	3 30·5	3 31·1	3 20·9	0·2 0·0	6·2 1·5	12·2 2·9
03	3 30·8	3 31·3	3 21·1	0·3 0·1	6·3 1·5	12·3 3·0
04	3 31·0	3 31·6	3 21·4	0·4 0·1	6·4 1·5	12·4 3·0
05	3 31·3	3 31·8	3 21·6	0·5 0·1	6·5 1·6	12·5 3·0
06	3 31·5	3 32·1	3 21·9	0·6 0·1	6·6 1·6	12·6 3·0
07	3 31·8	3 32·3	3 22·1	0·7 0·2	6·7 1·6	12·7 3·1
08	3 32·0	3 32·6	3 22·3	0·8 0·2	6·8 1·6	12·8 3·1
09	3 32·3	3 32·8	3 22·6	0·9 0·2	6·9 1·7	12·9 3·1
10	3 32·5	3 33·1	3 22·8	1·0 0·2	7·0 1·7	13·0 3·1
11	3 32·8	3 33·3	3 23·1	1·1 0·3	7·1 1·7	13·1 3·2
12	3 33·0	3 33·6	3 23·3	1·2 0·3	7·2 1·7	13·2 3·2
13	3 33·3	3 33·8	3 23·6	1·3 0·3	7·3 1·8	13·3 3·2
14	3 33·5	3 34·1	3 23·8	1·4 0·3	7·4 1·8	13·4 3·2
15	3 33·8	3 34·3	3 24·0	1·5 0·4	7·5 1·8	13·5 3·3
16	3 34·0	3 34·6	3 24·3	1·6 0·4	7·6 1·8	13·6 3·3
17	3 34·3	3 34·8	3 24·5	1·7 0·4	7·7 1·9	13·7 3·3
18	3 34·5	3 35·1	3 24·7	1·8 0·4	7·8 1·9	13·8 3·3
19	3 34·8	3 35·3	3 25·0	1·9 0·5	7·9 1·9	13·9 3·4
20	3 35·0	3 35·6	3 25·2	2·0 0·5	8·0 1·9	14·0 3·4
21	3 35·3	3 35·8	3 25·4	2·1 0·5	8·1 2·0	14·1 3·4
22	3 35·5	3 36·1	3 25·7	2·2 0·5	8·2 2·0	14·2 3·4
23	3 35·8	3 36·3	3 25·9	2·3 0·6	8·3 2·0	14·3 3·5
24	3 36·0	3 36·6	3 26·2	2·4 0·6	8·4 2·0	14·4 3·5
25	3 36·3	3 36·8	3 26·4	2·5 0·6	8·5 2·1	14·5 3·5
26	3 36·5	3 37·1	3 26·6	2·6 0·6	8·6 2·1	14·6 3·5
27	3 36·8	3 37·3	3 26·9	2·7 0·7	8·7 2·1	14·7 3·6
28	3 37·0	3 37·6	3 27·1	2·8 0·7	8·8 2·1	14·8 3·6
29	3 37·3	3 37·8	3 27·4	2·9 0·7	8·9 2·2	14·9 3·6
30	3 37·5	3 38·1	3 27·6	3·0 0·7	9·0 2·2	15·0 3·6
31	3 37·8	3 38·3	3 27·8	3·1 0·7	9·1 2·2	15·1 3·6
32	3 38·0	3 38·6	3 28·1	3·2 0·8	9·2 2·2	15·2 3·7
33	3 38·3	3 38·8	3 28·3	3·3 0·8	9·3 2·2	15·3 3·7
34	3 38·5	3 39·1	3 28·5	3·4 0·8	9·4 2·3	15·4 3·7
35	3 38·8	3 39·3	3 28·8	3·5 0·8	9·5 2·3	15·5 3·7
36	3 39·0	3 39·6	3 29·0	3·6 0·9	9·6 2·3	15·6 3·8
37	3 39·3	3 39·9	3 29·3	3·7 0·9	9·7 2·3	15·7 3·8
38	3 39·5	3 40·1	3 29·5	3·8 0·9	9·8 2·4	15·8 3·8
39	3 39·8	3 40·4	3 29·7	3·9 0·9	9·9 2·4	15·9 3·8
40	3 40·0	3 40·6	3 30·0	4·0 1·0	10·0 2·4	16·0 3·9
41	3 40·3	3 40·9	3 30·2	4·1 1·0	10·1 2·4	16·1 3·9
42	3 40·5	3 41·1	3 30·5	4·2 1·0	10·2 2·5	16·2 3·9
43	3 40·8	3 41·4	3 30·7	4·3 1·0	10·3 2·5	16·3 3·9
44	3 41·0	3 41·6	3 30·9	4·4 1·1	10·4 2·5	16·4 4·0
45	3 41·3	3 41·9	3 31·2	4·5 1·1	10·5 2·5	16·5 4·0
46	3 41·5	3 42·1	3 31·4	4·6 1·1	10·6 2·6	16·6 4·0
47	3 41·8	3 42·4	3 31·6	4·7 1·1	10·7 2·6	16·7 4·0
48	3 42·0	3 42·6	3 31·9	4·8 1·2	10·8 2·6	16·8 4·1
49	3 42·3	3 42·9	3 32·1	4·9 1·2*	10·9 2·6	16·9 4·1
50	3 42·5	3 43·1	3 32·4	5·0 1·2	11·0 2·7	17·0 4·1
51	3 42·8	3 43·4	3 32·6	5·1 1·2	11·1 2·7	17·1 4·1
52	3 43·0	3 43·6	3 32·8	5·2 1·3	11·2 2·7	17·2 4·2
53	3 43·3	3 43·9	3 33·1	5·3 1·3	11·3 2·7	17·3 4·2
54	3 43·5	3 44·1	3 33·3	5·4 1·3	11·4 2·8	17·4 4·2
55	3 43·8	3 44·4	3 33·6	5·5 1·3	11·5 2·8	17·5 4·2
56	3 44·0	3 44·6	3 33·8	5·6 1·4	11·6 2·8	17·6 4·3
57	3 44·3	3 44·9	3 34·0	5·7 1·4	11·7 2·8	17·7 4·3
58	3 44·5	3 45·1	3 34·3	5·8 1·4	11·8 2·9	17·8 4·3
59	3 44·8	3 45·4	3 34·5	5·9 1·4	11·9 2·9	17·9 4·3
60	3 45·0	3 45·6	3 34·8	6·0 1·5	12·0 2·9	18·0 4·4

15m

15 s	SUN PLANETS	ARIES	MOON	v or Corrn d	v or Corrn d	v or Corrn d
	° '	° '	° '	' '	' '	' '
00	3 45·0	3 45·6	3 34·8	0·0 0·0	6·0 1·6	12·0 3·1
01	3 45·3	3 45·9	3 35·0	0·1 0·0	6·1 1·6	12·1 3·1
02	3 45·5	3 46·1	3 35·2	0·2 0·1	6·2 1·6	12·2 3·2
03	3 45·8	3 46·4	3 35·5	0·3 0·1	6·3 1·6	12·3 3·2
04	3 46·0	3 46·6	3 35·7	0·4 0·1	6·4 1·7	12·4 3·2
05	3 46·3	3 46·9	3 35·9	0·5 0·1	6·5 1·7	12·5 3·2
06	3 46·5	3 47·1	3 36·2	0·6 0·2	6·6 1·7	12·6 3·3
07	3 46·8	3 47·4	3 36·4	0·7 0·2	6·7 1·7	12·7 3·3
08	3 47·0	3 47·6	3 36·7	0·8 0·2	6·8 1·8	12·8 3·3
09	3 47·3	3 47·9	3 36·9	0·9 0·2	6·9 1·8	12·9 3·3
10	3 47·5	3 48·1	3 37·1	1·0 0·3	7·0 1·8	13·0 3·4
11	3 47·8	3 48·4	3 37·4	1·1 0·3	7·1 1·8	13·1 3·4
12	3 48·0	3 48·6	3 37·6	1·2 0·3	7·2 1·9	13·2 3·4
13	3 48·3	3 48·9	3 37·9	1·3 0·3	7·3 1·9	13·3 3·4
14	3 48·5	3 49·1	3 38·1	1·4 0·4	7·4 1·9	13·4 3·5
15	3 48·8	3 49·4	3 38·3	1·5 0·4	7·5 1·9	13·5 3·5
16	3 49·0	3 49·6	3 38·6	1·6 0·4	7·6 2·0	13·6 3·5
17	3 49·3	3 49·9	3 38·8	1·7 0·4	7·7 2·0	13·7 3·5
18	3 49·5	3 50·1	3 39·0	1·8 0·5	7·8 2·0	13·8 3·6
19	3 49·8	3 50·4	3 39·3	1·9 0·5	7·9 2·0	13·9 3·6
20	3 50·0	3 50·6	3 39·5	2·0 0·5	8·0 2·1	14·0 3·6
21	3 50·3	3 50·9	3 39·8	2·1 0·5	8·1 2·1	14·1 3·6
22	3 50·5	3 51·1	3 40·0	2·2 0·6	8·2 2·1	14·2 3·7
23	3 50·8	3 51·4	3 40·2	2·3 0·6	8·3 2·1	14·3 3·7
24	3 51·0	3 51·6	3 40·5	2·4 0·6	8·4 2·2	14·4 3·7
25	3 51·3	3 51·9	3 40·7	2·5 0·6	8·5 2·2	14·5 3·7
26	3 51·5	3 52·1	3 41·0	2·6 0·7	8·6 2·2	14·6 3·8
27	3 51·8	3 52·4	3 41·2	2·7 0·7	8·7 2·2	14·7 3·8
28	3 52·0	3 52·6	3 41·4	2·8 0·7	8·8 2·3	14·8 3·8
29	3 52·3	3 52·9	3 41·7	2·9 0·7	8·9 2·3	14·9 3·8
30	3 52·5	3 53·1	3 41·9	3·0 0·8	9·0 2·3	15·0 3·9
31	3 52·8	3 53·4	3 42·1	3·1 0·8	9·1 2·4	15·1 3·9
32	3 53·0	3 53·6	3 42·4	3·2 0·8	9·2 2·4	15·2 3·9
33	3 53·3	3 53·9	3 42·6	3·3 0·9	9·3 2·4	15·3 4·0
34	3 53·5	3 54·1	3 42·9	3·4 0·9	9·4 2·4	15·4 4·0
35	3 53·8	3 54·4	3 43·1	3·5 0·9	9·5 2·5	15·5 4·0
36	3 54·0	3 54·6	3 43·3	3·6 0·9	9·6 2·5	15·6 4·0
37	3 54·3	3 54·9	3 43·6	3·7 1·0	9·7 2·5	15·7 4·1
38	3 54·5	3 55·1	3 43·8	3·8 1·0	9·8 2·5	15·8 4·1
39	3 54·8	3 55·4	3 44·1	3·9 1·0	9·9 2·6	15·9 4·1
40	3 55·0	3 55·6	3 44·3	4·0 1·0	10·0 2·6	16·0 4·1
41	3 55·3	3 55·9	3 44·5	4·1 1·1	10·1 2·6	16·1 4·2
42	3 55·5	3 56·1	3 44·8	4·2 1·1	10·2 2·6	16·2 4·2
43	3 55·8	3 56·4	3 45·0	4·3 1·1	10·3 2·7	16·3 4·2
44	3 56·0	3 56·6	3 45·2	4·4 1·1	10·4 2·7	16·4 4·2
45	3 56·3	3 56·9	3 45·5	4·5 1·2	10·5 2·7	16·5 4·3
46	3 56·5	3 57·1	3 45·7	4·6 1·2	10·6 2·7	16·6 4·3
47	3 56·8	3 57·4	3 46·0	4·7 1·2	10·7 2·8	16·7 4·3
48	3 57·0	3 57·6	3 46·2	4·8 1·2	10·8 2·8	16·8 4·3
49	3 57·3	3 57·9	3 46·4	4·9 1·3	10·9 2·8	16·9 4·4
50	3 57·5	3 58·2	3 46·7	5·0 1·3	11·0 2·8	17·0 4·4
51	3 57·8	3 58·4	3 46·9	5·1 1·3	11·1 2·9	17·1 4·4
52	3 58·0	3 58·7	3 47·2	5·2 1·3	11·2 2·9	17·2 4·4
53	3 58·3	3 58·9	3 47·4	5·3 1·4	11·3 2·9	17·3 4·5
54	3 58·5	3 59·2	3 47·6	5·4 1·4	11·4 2·9	17·4 4·5
55	3 58·8	3 59·4	3 47·9	5·5 1·4	11·5 3·0	17·5 4·5
56	3 59·0	3 59·7	3 48·1	5·6 1·4	11·6 3·0	17·6 4·5
57	3 59·3	3 59·9	3 48·4	5·7 1·5	11·7 3·0	17·7 4·6
58	3 59·5	4 00·2	3 48·6	5·8 1·5	11·8 3·0	17·8 4·6
59	3 59·8	4 00·4	3 48·8	5·9 1·5	11·9 3·1	17·9 4·6
60	4 00·0	4 00·7	3 49·1	6·0 1·6	12·0 3·1	18·0 4·7

16ᵐ

16ᵐ (s)	SUN PLANETS	ARIES	MOON	v or Corrⁿ d	v or Corrⁿ d	v or Corrⁿ d
	° ′	° ′	° ′	′ ′	′ ′	′ ′
00	4 00·0	4 00·7	3 49·1	0·0 0·0	6·0 1·7	12·0 3·3
01	4 00·3	4 00·9	3 49·3	0·1 0·0	6·1 1·7	12·1 3·3
02	4 00·5	4 01·2	3 49·5	0·2 0·1	6·2 1·7	12·2 3·4
03	4 00·8	4 01·4	3 49·8	0·3 0·1	6·3 1·7	12·3 3·4
04	4 01·0	4 01·7	3 50·0	0·4 0·1	6·4 1·8	12·4 3·4
05	4 01·3	4 01·9	3 50·3	0·5 0·1	6·5 1·8	12·5 3·4
06	4 01·5	4 02·2	3 50·5	0·6 0·2	6·6 1·8	12·6 3·5
07	4 01·8	4 02·4	3 50·7	0·7 0·2	6·7 1·8	12·7 3·5
08	4 02·0	4 02·7	3 51·0	0·8 0·2	6·8 1·9	12·8 3·5
09	4 02·3	4 02·9	3 51·2	0·9 0·2	6·9 1·9	12·9 3·5
10	4 02·5	4 03·2	3 51·5	1·0 0·3	7·0 1·9	13·0 3·6
11	4 02·8	4 03·4	3 51·7	1·1 0·3	7·1 2·0	13·1 3·6
12	4 03·0	4 03·7	3 51·9	1·2 0·3	7·2 2·0	13·2 3·6
13	4 03·3	4 03·9	3 52·2	1·3 0·4	7·3 2·0	13·3 3·7
14	4 03·5	4 04·2	3 52·4	1·4 0·4	7·4 2·0	13·4 3·7
15	4 03·8	4 04·4	3 52·6	1·5 0·4	7·5 2·1	13·5 3·7
16	4 04·0	4 04·7	3 52·9	1·6 0·4	7·6 2·1	13·6 3·7
17	4 04·3	4 04·9	3 53·1	1·7 0·5	7·7 2·1	13·7 3·8
18	4 04·5	4 05·2	3 53·4	1·8 0·5	7·8 2·1	13·8 3·8
19	4 04·8	4 05·4	3 53·6	1·9 0·5	7·9 2·2	13·9 3·8
20	4 05·0	4 05·7	3 53·8	2·0 0·6	8·0 2·2	14·0 3·9
21	4 05·3	4 05·9	3 54·1	2·1 0·6	8·1 2·2	14·1 3·9
22	4 05·5	4 06·2	3 54·3	2·2 0·6	8·2 2·3	14·2 3·9
23	4 05·8	4 06·4	3 54·6	2·3 0·6	8·3 2·3	14·3 3·9
24	4 06·0	4 06·7	3 54·8	2·4 0·7	8·4 2·3	14·4 4·0
25	4 06·3	4 06·9	3 55·0	2·5 0·7	8·5 2·3	14·5 4·0
26	4 06·5	4 07·2	3 55·3	2·6 0·7	8·6 2·4	14·6 4·0
27	4 06·8	4 07·4	3 55·5	2·7 0·7	8·7 2·4	14·7 4·0
28	4 07·0	4 07·7	3 55·7	2·8 0·8	8·8 2·4	14·8 4·1
29	4 07·3	4 07·9	3 56·0	2·9 0·8	8·9 2·4	14·9 4·1
30	4 07·5	4 08·2	3 56·2	3·0 0·8	9·0 2·5	15·0 4·1
31	4 07·8	4 08·4	3 56·5	3·1 0·9	9·1 2·5	15·1 4·2
32	4 08·0	4 08·7	3 56·7	3·2 0·9	9·2 2·5	15·2 4·2
33	4 08·3	4 08·9	3 56·9	3·3 0·9	9·3 2·6	15·3 4·2
34	4 08·5	4 09·2	3 57·2	3·4 0·9	9·4 2·6	15·4 4·2
35	4 08·8	4 09·4	3 57·4	3·5 1·0	9·5 2·6	15·5 4·3
36	4 09·0	4 09·7	3 57·7	3·6 1·0	9·6 2·6	15·6 4·3
37	4 09·3	4 09·9	3 57·9	3·7 1·0	9·7 2·7	15·7 4·3
38	4 09·5	4 10·2	3 58·1	3·8 1·0	9·8 2·7	15·8 4·3
39	4 09·8	4 10·4	3 58·4	3·9 1·1	9·9 2·7	15·9 4·4
40	4 10·0	4 10·7	3 58·6	4·0 1·1	10·0 2·8	16·0 4·4
41	4 10·3	4 10·9	3 58·8	4·1 1·1	10·1 2·8	16·1 4·4
42	4 10·5	4 11·2	3 59·1	4·2 1·2	10·2 2·8	16·2 4·5
43	4 10·8	4 11·4	3 59·3	4·3 1·2	10·3 2·8	16·3 4·5
44	4 11·0	4 11·7	3 59·6	4·4 1·2	10·4 2·9	16·4 4·5
45	4 11·3	4 11·9	3 59·8	4·5 1·2	10·5 2·9	16·5 4·5
46	4 11·5	4 12·2	4 00·0	4·6 1·3	10·6 2·9	16·6 4·6
47	4 11·8	4 12·4	4 00·3	4·7 1·3	10·7 2·9	16·7 4·6
48	4 12·0	4 12·7	4 00·5	4·8 1·3	10·8 3·0	16·8 4·6
49	4 12·3	4 12·9	4 00·8	4·9 1·3	10·9 3·0	16·9 4·6
50	4 12·5	4 13·2	4 01·0	5·0 1·4	11·0 3·0	17·0 4·7
51	4 12·8	4 13·4	4 01·2	5·1 1·4	11·1 3·1	17·1 4·7
52	4 13·0	4 13·7	4 01·5	5·2 1·4	11·2 3·1	17·2 4·7
53	4 13·3	4 13·9	4 01·7	5·3 1·5	11·3 3·1	17·3 4·8
54	4 13·5	4 14·2	4 02·0	5·4 1·5	11·4 3·1	17·4 4·8
55	4 13·8	4 14·4	4 02·2	5·5 1·5	11·5 3·2	17·5 4·8
56	4 14·0	4 14·7	4 02·4	5·6 1·5	11·6 3·2	17·6 4·8
57	4 14·3	4 14·9	4 02·7	5·7 1·6	11·7 3·2	17·7 4·9
58	4 14·5	4 15·2	4 02·9	5·8 1·6	11·8 3·2	17·8 4·9
59	4 14·8	4 15·4	4 03·1	5·9 1·6	11·9 3·3	17·9 4·9
60	4 15·0	4 15·7	4 03·4	6·0 1·7	12·0 3·3	18·0 5·0

17ᵐ

17ᵐ (s)	SUN PLANETS	ARIES	MOON	v or Corrⁿ d	v or Corrⁿ d	v or Corrⁿ d
	° ′	° ′	° ′	′ ′	′ ′	′ ′
00	4 15·0	4 15·7	4 03·4	0·0 0·0	6·0 1·8	12·0 3·5
01	4 15·3	4 15·9	4 03·6	0·1 0·0	6·1 1·8	12·1 3·5
02	4 15·5	4 16·2	4 03·9	0·2 0·1	6·2 1·8	12·2 3·6
03	4 15·8	4 16·5	4 04·1	0·3 0·1	6·3 1·8	12·3 3·6
04	4 16·0	4 16·7	4 04·3	0·4 0·1	6·4 1·9	12·4 3·6
05	4 16·3	4 17·0	4 04·6	0·5 0·1	6·5 1·9	12·5 3·6
06	4 16·5	4 17·2	4 04·8	0·6 0·2	6·6 1·9	12·6 3·7
07	4 16·8	4 17·5	4 05·1	0·7 0·2	6·7 2·0	12·7 3·7
08	4 17·0	4 17·7	4 05·3	0·8 0·2	6·8 2·0	12·8 3·7
09	4 17·3	4 18·0	4 05·5	0·9 0·3	6·9 2·0	12·9 3·8
10	4 17·5	4 18·2	4 05·8	1·0 0·3	7·0 2·0	13·0 3·8
11	4 17·8	4 18·5	4 06·0	1·1 0·3	7·1 2·1	13·1 3·8
12	4 18·0	4 18·7	4 06·2	1·2 0·4	7·2 2·1	13·2 3·9
13	4 18·3	4 19·0	4 06·5	1·3 0·4	7·3 2·1	13·3 3·9
14	4 18·5	4 19·2	4 06·7	1·4 0·4	7·4 2·2	13·4 3·9
15	4 18·8	4 19·5	4 07·0	1·5 0·4	7·5 2·2	13·5 3·9
16	4 19·0	4 19·7	4 07·2	1·6 0·5	7·6 2·2	13·6 4·0
17	4 19·3	4 20·0	4 07·4	1·7 0·5	7·7 2·2	13·7 4·0
18	4 19·5	4 20·2	4 07·7	1·8 0·5	7·8 2·3	13·8 4·0
19	4 19·8	4 20·5	4 07·9	1·9 0·6	7·9 2·3	13·9 4·1
20	4 20·0	4 20·7	4 08·2	2·0 0·6	8·0 2·3	14·0 4·1
21	4 20·3	4 21·0	4 08·4	2·1 0·6	8·1 2·4	14·1 4·1
22	4 20·5	4 21·2	4 08·6	2·2 0·6	8·2 2·4	14·2 4·1
23	4 20·8	4 21·5	4 08·9	2·3 0·7	8·3 2·4	14·3 4·2
24	4 21·0	4 21·7	4 09·1	2·4 0·7	8·4 2·5	14·4 4·2
25	4 21·3	4 22·0	4 09·3	2·5 0·7	8·5 2·5	14·5 4·2
26	4 21·5	4 22·2	4 09·6	2·6 0·8	8·6 2·5	14·6 4·3
27	4 21·8	4 22·5	4 09·8	2·7 0·8	8·7 2·5	14·7 4·3
28	4 22·0	4 22·7	4 10·1	2·8 0·8	8·8 2·6	14·8 4·3
29	4 22·3	4 23·0	4 10·3	2·9 0·8	8·9 2·6	14·9 4·3
30	4 22·5	4 23·2	4 10·5	3·0 0·9	9·0 2·6	15·0 4·4
31	4 22·8	4 23·5	4 10·8	3·1 0·9	9·1 2·7	15·1 4·4
32	4 23·0	4 23·7	4 11·0	3·2 0·9	9·2 2·7	15·2 4·4
33	4 23·3	4 24·0	4 11·3	3·3 1·0	9·3 2·7	15·3 4·5
34	4 23·5	4 24·2	4 11·5	3·4 1·0	9·4 2·7	15·4 4·5
35	4 23·8	4 24·5	4 11·7	3·5 1·0	9·5 2·8	15·5 4·5
36	4 24·0	4 24·7	4 12·0	3·6 1·1	9·6 2·8	15·6 4·6
37	4 24·3	4 25·0	4 12·2	3·7 1·1	9·7 2·8	15·7 4·6
38	4 24·5	4 25·2	4 12·5	3·8 1·1	9·8 2·9	15·8 4·6
39	4 24·8	4 25·5	4 12·7	3·9 1·1	9·9 2·9	15·9 4·6
40	4 25·0	4 25·7	4 12·9	4·0 1·2	10·0 2·9	16·0 4·7
41	4 25·3	4 26·0	4 13·2	4·1 1·2	10·1 2·9	16·1 4·7
42	4 25·5	4 26·2	4 13·4	4·2 1·2	10·2 3·0	16·2 4·7
43	4 25·8	4 26·5	4 13·6	4·3 1·3	10·3 3·0	16·3 4·8
44	4 26·0	4 26·7	4 13·9	4·4 1·3	10·4 3·0	16·4 4·8
45	4 26·3	4 27·0	4 14·1	4·5 1·3	10·5 3·1	16·5 4·8
46	4 26·5	4 27·2	4 14·4	4·6 1·3	10·6 3·1	16·6 4·8
47	4 26·8	4 27·5	4 14·6	4·7 1·4	10·7 3·1	16·7 4·9
48	4 27·0	4 27·7	4 14·8	4·8 1·4	10·8 3·2	16·8 4·9
49	4 27·3	4 28·0	4 15·1	4·9 1·4	10·9 3·2	16·9 4·9
50	4 27·5	4 28·2	4 15·3	5·0 1·5	11·0 3·2	17·0 5·0
51	4 27·8	4 28·5	4 15·6	5·1 1·5	11·1 3·2	17·1 5·0
52	4 28·0	4 28·7	4 15·8	5·2 1·5	11·2 3·3	17·2 5·0
53	4 28·3	4 29·0	4 16·0	5·3 1·5	11·3 3·3	17·3 5·0
54	4 28·5	4 29·2	4 16·3	5·4 1·6	11·4 3·3	17·4 5·1
55	4 28·8	4 29·5	4 16·5	5·5 1·6	11·5 3·4	17·5 5·1
56	4 29·0	4 29·7	4 16·7	5·6 1·6	11·6 3·4	17·6 5·1
57	4 29·3	4 30·0	4 17·0	5·7 1·7	11·7 3·4	17·7 5·2
58	4 29·5	4 30·2	4 17·2	5·8 1·7	11·8 3·4	17·8 5·2
59	4 29·8	4 30·5	4 17·5	5·9 1·7	11·9 3·5	17·9 5·2
60	4 30·0	4 30·7	4 17·7	6·0 1·8	12·0 3·5	18·0 5·3

20^m

20^m	SUN PLANETS	ARIES	MOON	v or Corr^n d		v or Corr^n d		v or Corr^n d	
s	° ′	° ′	° ′	′	′	′	′	′	′
00	5 00·0	5 00·8	4 46·3	0·0	0·0	6·0	2·1	12·0	4·1
01	5 00·3	5 01·1	4 46·6	0·1	0·0	6·1	2·1	12·1	4·1
02	5 00·5	5 01·3	4 46·8	0·2	0·1	6·2	2·1	12·2	4·2
03	5 00·8	5 01·6	4 47·0	0·3	0·1	6·3	2·2	12·3	4·2
04	5 01·0	5 01·8	4 47·3	0·4	0·1	6·4	2·2	12·4	4·2
05	5 01·3	5 02·1	4 47·5	0·5	0·2	6·5	2·2	12·5	4·3
06	5 01·5	5 02·3	4 47·8	0·6	0·2	6·6	2·3	12·6	4·3
07	5 01·8	5 02·6	4 48·0	0·7	0·2	6·7	2·3	12·7	4·3
08	5 02·0	5 02·8	4 48·2	0·8	0·3	6·8	2·3	12·8	4·4
09	5 02·3	5 03·1	4 48·5	0·9	0·3	6·9	2·4	12·9	4·4
10	5 02·5	5 03·3	4 48·7	1·0	0·3	7·0	2·4	13·0	4·4
11	5 02·8	5 03·6	4 49·0	1·1	0·4	7·1	2·4	13·1	4·5
12	5 03·0	5 03·8	4 49·2	1·2	0·4	7·2	2·5	13·2	4·5
13	5 03·3	5 04·1	4 49·4	1·3	0·4	7·3	2·5	13·3	4·5
14	5 03·5	5 04·3	4 49·7	1·4	0·5	7·4	2·5	13·4	4·6
15	5 03·8	5 04·6	4 49·9	1·5	0·5	7·5	2·6	13·5	4·6
16	5 04·0	5 04·8	4 50·2	1·6	0·5	7·6	2·6	13·6	4·6
17	5 04·3	5 05·1	4 50·4	1·7	0·6	7·7	2·6	13·7	4·7
18	5 04·5	5 05·3	4 50·6	1·8	0·6	7·8	2·7	13·8	4·7
19	5 04·8	5 05·6	4 50·9	1·9	0·6	7·9	2·7	13·9	4·7
20	5 05·0	5 05·8	4 51·1	2·0	0·7	8·0	2·7	14·0	4·8
21	5 05·3	5 06·1	4 51·3	2·1	0·7	8·1	2·8	14·1	4·8
22	5 05·5	5 06·3	4 51·6	2·2	0·8	8·2	2·8	14·2	4·9
23	5 05·8	5 06·6	4 51·8	2·3	0·8	8·3	2·8	14·3	4·9
24	5 06·0	5 06·8	4 52·1	2·4	0·8	8·4	2·9	14·4	4·9
25	5 06·3	5 07·1	4 52·3	2·5	0·9	8·5	2·9	14·5	5·0
26	5 06·5	5 07·3	4 52·5	2·6	0·9	8·6	2·9	14·6	5·0
27	5 06·8	5 07·6	4 52·8	2·7	0·9	8·7	3·0	14·7	5·0
28	5 07·0	5 07·8	4 53·0	2·8	1·0	8·8	3·0	14·8	5·1
29	5 07·3	5 08·1	4 53·3	2·9	1·0	8·9	3·0	14·9	5·1
30	5 07·5	5 08·3	4 53·5	3·0	1·0	9·0	3·1	15·0	5·1
31	5 07·8	5 08·6	4 53·7	3·1	1·1	9·1	3·1	15·1	5·2
32	5 08·0	5 08·8	4 54·0	3·2	1·1	9·2	3·1	15·2	5·2
33	5 08·3	5 09·1	4 54·2	3·3	1·1	9·3	3·2	15·3	5·2
34	5 08·5	5 09·3	4 54·4	3·4	1·2	9·4	3·2	15·4	5·3
35	5 08·8	5 09·6	4 54·7	3·5	1·2	9·5	3·2	15·5	5·3
36	5 09·0	5 09·8	4 54·9	3·6	1·2	9·6	3·3	15·6	5·3
37	5 09·3	5 10·1	4 55·2	3·7	1·3	9·7	3·3	15·7	5·4
38	5 09·5	5 10·3	4 55·4	3·8	1·3	9·8	3·3	15·8	5·4
39	5 09·8	5 10·6	4 55·6	3·9	1·3	9·9	3·4	15·9	5·4
40	5 10·0	5 10·8	4 55·9	4·0	1·4	10·0	3·4	16·0	5·5
41	5 10·3	5 11·1	4 56·1	4·1	1·4	10·1	3·5	16·1	5·5
42	5 10·5	5 11·4	4 56·4	4·2	1·4	10·2	3·5	16·2	5·5
43	5 10·8	5 11·6	4 56·6	4·3	1·5	10·3	3·5	16·3	5·6
44	5 11·0	5 11·9	4 56·8	4·4	1·5	10·4	3·6	16·4	5·6
45	5 11·3	5 12·1	4 57·1	4·5	1·5	10·5	3·6	16·5	5·6
46	5 11·5	5 12·4	4 57·3	4·6	1·6	10·6	3·6	16·6	5·7
47	5 11·8	5 12·6	4 57·5	4·7	1·6	10·7	3·7	16·7	5·7
48	5 12·0	5 12·9	4 57·8	4·8	1·6	10·8	3·7	16·8	5·7
49	5 12·3	5 13·1	4 58·0	4·9	1·7	10·9	3·7	16·9	5·8
50	5 12·5	5 13·4	4 58·3	5·0	1·7	11·0	3·8	17·0	5·8
51	5 12·8	5 13·6	4 58·5	5·1	1·7	11·1	3·8	17·1	5·8
52	5 13·0	5 13·9	4 58·7	5·2	1·8	11·2	3·8	17·2	5·9
53	5 13·3	5 14·1	4 59·0	5·3	1·8	11·3	3·9	17·3	5·9
54	5 13·5	5 14·4	4 59·2	5·4	1·8	11·4	3·9	17·4	5·9
55	5 13·8	5 14·6	4 59·5	5·5	1·9	11·5	3·9	17·5	6·0
56	5 14·0	5 14·9	4 59·7	5·6	1·9	11·6	4·0	17·6	6·0
57	5 14·3	5 15·1	4 59·9	5·7	1·9	11·7	4·0	17·7	6·0
58	5 14·5	5 15·4	5 00·2	5·8	2·0	11·8	4·0	17·8	6·1
59	5 14·8	5 15·6	5 00·4	5·9	2·0	11·9	4·1	17·9	6·1
60	5 15·0	5 15·9	5 00·7	6·0	2·1	12·0	4·1	18·0	6·2

21^m

21^m	SUN PLANETS	ARIES	MOON	v or Corr^n d		v or Corr^n d		v or Corr^n d	
s	° ′	° ′	° ′	′	′	′	′	′	′
00	5 15·0	5 15·9	5 00·7	0·0	0·0	6·0	2·2	12·0	4·3
01	5 15·3	5 16·1	5 00·9	0·1	0·0	6·1	2·2	12·1	4·3
02	5 15·5	5 16·4	5 01·1	0·2	0·1	6·2	2·2	12·2	4·4
03	5 15·8	5 16·6	5 01·4	0·3	0·1	6·3	2·3	12·3	4·4
04	5 16·0	5 16·9	5 01·6	0·4	0·1	6·4	2·3	12·4	4·4
05	5 16·3	5 17·1	5 01·8	0·5	0·2	6·5	2·3	12·5	4·5
06	5 16·5	5 17·4	5 02·1	0·6	0·2	6·6	2·4	12·6	4·5
07	5 16·8	5 17·6	5 02·3	0·7	0·3	6·7	2·4	12·7	4·6
08	5 17·0	5 17·9	5 02·6	0·8	0·3	6·8	2·4	12·8	4·6
09	5 17·3	5 18·1	5 02·8	0·9	0·3	6·9	2·5	12·9	4·6
10	5 17·5	5 18·4	5 03·0	1·0	0·4	7·0	2·5	13·0	4·7
11	5 17·8	5 18·6	5 03·3	1·1	0·4	7·1	2·5	13·1	4·7
12	5 18·0	5 18·9	5 03·5	1·2	0·4	7·2	2·6	13·2	4·7
13	5 18·3	5 19·1	5 03·8	1·3	0·5	7·3	2·6	13·3	4·8
14	5 18·5	5 19·4	5 04·0	1·4	0·5	7·4	2·7	13·4	4·8
15	5 18·8	5 19·6	5 04·2	1·5	0·5	7·5	2·7	13·5	4·8
16	5 19·0	5 19·9	5 04·5	1·6	0·6	7·6	2·7	13·6	4·9
17	5 19·3	5 20·1	5 04·7	1·7	0·6	7·7	2·8	13·7	4·9
18	5 19·5	5 20·4	5 04·9	1·8	0·6	7·8	2·8	13·8	4·9
19	5 19·8	5 20·6	5 05·2	1·9	0·7	7·9	2·8	13·9	5·0
20	5 20·0	5 20·9	5 05·4	2·0	0·7	8·0	2·9	14·0	5·0
21	5 20·3	5 21·1	5 05·7	2·1	0·8	8·1	2·9	14·1	5·1
22	5 20·5	5 21·4	5 05·9	2·2	0·8	8·2	2·9	14·2	5·1
23	5 20·8	5 21·6	5 06·1	2·3	0·8	8·3	3·0	14·3	5·1
24	5 21·0	5 21·9	5 06·4	2·4	0·9	8·4	3·0	14·4	5·2
25	5 21·3	5 22·1	5 06·6	2·5	0·9	8·5	3·0	14·5	5·2
26	5 21·5	5 22·4	5 06·9	2·6	0·9	8·6	3·1	14·6	5·2
27	5 21·8	5 22·6	5 07·1	2·7	1·0	8·7	3·1	14·7	5·3
28	5 22·0	5 22·9	5 07·3	2·8	1·0	8·8	3·2	14·8	5·3
29	5 22·3	5 23·1	5 07·6	2·9	1·0	8·9	3·2	14·9	5·3
30	5 22·5	5 23·4	5 07·8	3·0	1·1	9·0	3·2	15·0	5·4
31	5 22·8	5 23·6	5 08·0	3·1	1·1	9·1	3·3	15·1	5·4
32	5 23·0	5 23·9	5 08·3	3·2	1·1	9·2	3·3	15·2	5·4
33	5 23·3	5 24·1	5 08·5	3·3	1·2	9·3	3·3	15·3	5·5
34	5 23·5	5 24·4	5 08·8	3·4	1·2	9·4	3·4	15·4	5·5
35	5 23·8	5 24·6	5 09·0	3·5	1·3	9·5	3·4	15·5	5·6
36	5 24·0	5 24·9	5 09·2	3·6	1·3	9·6	3·4	15·6	5·6
37	5 24·3	5 25·1	5 09·5	3·7	1·3	9·7	3·5	15·7	5·6
38	5 24·5	5 25·4	5 09·7	3·8	1·4	9·8	3·5	15·8	5·7
39	5 24·8	5 25·6	5 10·0	3·9	1·4	9·9	3·5	15·9	5·7
40	5 25·0	5 25·9	5 10·2	4·0	1·4	10·0	3·6	16·0	5·7
41	5 25·3	5 26·1	5 10·4	4·1	1·5	10·1	3·6	16·1	5·8
42	5 25·5	5 26·4	5 10·7	4·2	1·5	10·2	3·7	16·2	5·8
43	5 25·8	5 26·6	5 10·9	4·3	1·5	10·3	3·7′	16·3	5·8
44	5 26·0	5 26·9	5 11·1	4·4	1·6	10·4	3·7	16·4	5·9
45	5 26·3	5 27·1	5 11·4	4·5	1·6	10·5	3·8	16·5	5·9
46	5 26·5	5 27·4	5 11·6	4·6	1·6	10·6	3·8	16·6	5·9
47	5 26·8	5 27·6	5 11·9	4·7	1·7	10·7	3·8	16·7	6·0
48	5 27·0	5 27·9	5 12·1	4·8	1·7	10·8	3·9	16·8	6·0
49	5 27·3	5 28·1	5 12·3	4·9	1·8	10·9	3·9	16·9	6·1
50	5 27·5	5 28·4	5 12·6	5·0	1·8	11·0	3·9	17·0	6·1
51	5 27·8	5 28·6	5 12·8	5·1	1·8	11·1	4·0	17·1	6·1
52	5 28·0	5 28·9	5 13·1	5·2	1·9	11·2	4·0	17·2	6·2
53	5 28·3	5 29·1	5 13·3	5·3	1·9	11·3	4·0	17·3	6·2
54	5 28·5	5 29·4	5 13·5	5·4	1·9	11·4	4·1	17·4	6·2
55	5 28·8	5 29·7	5 13·8	5·5	2·0	11·5	4·1	17·5	6·3
56	5 29·0	5 29·9	5 14·0	5·6	2·0	11·6	4·2	17·6	6·3
57	5 29·3	5 30·2	5 14·3	5·7	2·1	11·7	4·2	17·7	6·3
58	5 29·5	5 30·4	5 14·5	5·8	2·1	11·8	4·2	17·8	6·4
59	5 29·8	5 30·7	5 14·7	5·9	2·1	11·9	4·3	17·9	6·4
60	5 30·0	5 30·9	5 15·0	6·0	2·2	12·0	4·3	18·0	6·5

24ᵐ

24ᵐ s	SUN PLANETS ° '	ARIES ° '	MOON ° '	v or d Corrⁿ		v or d Corrⁿ		v or d Corrⁿ	
00	6 00·0	6 01·0	5 43·6	0·0	0·0	6·0	2·5	12·0	4·9
01	6 00·3	6 01·2	5 43·8	0·1	0·0	6·1	2·5	12·1	4·9
02	6 00·5	6 01·5	5 44·1	0·2	0·1	6·2	2·5	12·2	5·0
03	6 00·8	6 01·7	5 44·3	0·3	0·1	6·3	2·6	12·3	5·0
04	6 01·0	6 02·0	5 44·6	0·4	0·2	6·4	2·6	12·4	5·1
05	6 01·3	6 02·2	5 44·8	0·5	0·2	6·5	2·7	12·5	5·1
06	6 01·5	6 02·5	5 45·0	0·6	0·2	6·6	2·7	12·6	5·1
07	6 01·8	6 02·7	5 45·3	0·7	0·3	6·7	2·7	12·7	5·2
08	6 02·0	6 03·0	5 45·5	0·8	0·3	6·8	2·8	12·8	5·2
09	6 02·3	6 03·2	5 45·7	0·9	0·4	6·9	2·8	12·9	5·3
10	6 02·5	6 03·5	5 46·0	1·0	0·4	7·0	2·9	13·0	5·3
11	6 02·8	6 03·7	5 46·2	1·1	0·4	7·1	2·9	13·1	5·3
12	6 03·0	6 04·0	5 46·5	1·2	0·5	7·2	2·9	13·2	5·4
13	6 03·3	6 04·2	5 46·7	1·3	0·5	7·3	3·0	13·3	5·4
14	6 03·5	6 04·5	5 46·9	1·4	0·6	7·4	3·0	13·4	5·5
15	6 03·8	6 04·7	5 47·2	1·5	0·6	7·5	3·1	13·5	5·5
16	6 04·0	6 05·0	5 47·4	1·6	0·7	7·6	3·1	13·6	5·6
17	6 04·3	6 05·2	5 47·7	1·7	0·7	7·7	3·1	13·7	5·6
18	6 04·5	6 05·5	5 47·9	1·8	0·7	7·8	3·2	13·8	5·6
19	6 04·8	6 05·7	5 48·1	1·9	0·8	7·9	3·2	13·9	5·7
20	6 05·0	6 06·0	5 48·4	2·0	0·8	8·0	3·3	14·0	5·7
21	6 05·3	6 06·3	5 48·6	2·1	0·9	8·1	3·3	14·1	5·8
22	6 05·5	6 06·5	5 48·8	2·2	0·9	8·2	3·3	14·2	5·8
23	6 05·8	6 06·8	5 49·1	2·3	0·9	8·3	3·4	14·3	5·8
24	6 06·0	6 07·0	5 49·3	2·4	1·0	8·4	3·4	14·4	5·9
25	6 06·3	6 07·3	5 49·6	2·5	1·0	8·5	3·5	14·5	5·9
26	6 06·5	6 07·5	5 49·8	2·6	1·1	8·6	3·5	14·6	6·0
27	6 06·8	6 07·8	5 50·0	2·7	1·1	8·7	3·6	14·7	6·0
28	6 07·0	6 08·0	5 50·3	2·8	1·1	8·8	3·6	14·8	6·0
29	6 07·3	6 08·3	5 50·5	2·9	1·2	8·9	3·6	14·9	6·1
30	6 07·5	6 08·5	5 50·8	3·0	1·2	9·0	3·7	15·0	6·1
31	6 07·8	6 08·8	5 51·0	3·1	1·3	9·1	3·7	15·1	6·2
32	6 08·0	6 09·0	5 51·2	3·2	1·3	9·2	3·8	15·2	6·2
33	6 08·3	6 09·3	5 51·5	3·3	1·3	9·3	3·8	15·3	6·2
34	6 08·5	6 09·5	5 51·7	3·4	1·4	9·4	3·8	15·4	6·3
35	6 08·8	6 09·8	5 52·0	3·5	1·4	9·5	3·9	15·5	6·3
36	6 09·0	6 10·0	5 52·2	3·6	1·5	9·6	3·9	15·6	6·4
37	6 09·3	6 10·3	5 52·4	3·7	1·5	9·7	4·0	15·7	6·4
38	6 09·5	6 10·5	5 52·7	3·8	1·6	9·8	4·0	15·8	6·5
39	6 09·8	6 10·8	5 52·9	3·9	1·6	9·9	4·0	15·9	6·5
40	6 10·0	6 11·0	5 53·1	4·0	1·6	10·0	4·1	16·0	6·5
41	6 10·3	6 11·3	5 53·4	4·1	1·7	10·1	4·1	16·1	6·6
42	6 10·5	6 11·5	5 53·6	4·2	1·7	10·2	4·2	16·2	6·6
43	6 10·8	6 11·8	5 53·9	4·3	1·8	10·3	4·2	16·3	6·7
44	6 11·0	6 12·0	5 54·1	4·4	1·8	10·4	4·2	16·4	6·7
45	6 11·3	6 12·3	5 54·3	4·5	1·8	10·5	4·3	16·5	6·7
46	6 11·5	6 12·5	5 54·6	4·6	1·9	10·6	4·3	16·6	6·8
47	6 11·8	6 12·8	5 54·8	4·7	1·9	10·7	4·4	16·7	6·8
48	6 12·0	6 13·0	5 55·1	4·8	2·0	10·8	4·4	16·8	6·9
49	6 12·3	6 13·3	5 55·3	4·9	2·0	10·9	4·5	16·9	6·9
50	6 12·5	6 13·5	5 55·5	5·0	2·0	11·0	4·5	17·0	6·9
51	6 12·8	6 13·8	5 55·8	5·1	2·1	11·1	4·5	17·1	7·0
52	6 13·0	6 14·0	5 56·0	5·2	2·1	11·2	4·6	17·2	7·0
53	6 13·3	6 14·3	5 56·2	5·3	2·2	11·3	4·6	17·3	7·1
54	6 13·5	6 14·5	5 56·5	5·4	2·2	11·4	4·7	17·4	7·1
55	6 13·8	6 14·8	5 56·7	5·5	2·2	11·5	4·7	17·5	7·1
56	6 14·0	6 15·0	5 57·0	5·6	2·3	11·6	4·7	17·6	7·2
57	6 14·3	6 15·3	5 57·2	5·7	2·3	11·7	4·8	17·7	7·2
58	6 14·5	6 15·5	5 57·4	5·8	2·4	11·8	4·8	17·8	7·3
59	6 14·8	6 15·8	5 57·7	5·9	2·4	11·9	4·9	17·9	7·3
60	6 15·0	6 16·0	5 57·9	6·0	2·5	12·0	4·9	18·0	7·4

25ᵐ

25ᵐ s	SUN PLANETS ° '	ARIES ° '	MOON ° '	v or d Corrⁿ		v or d Corrⁿ		v or d Corrⁿ	
00	6 15·0	6 16·0	5 57·9	0·0	0·0	6·0	2·6	12·0	5·1
01	6 15·3	6 16·3	5 58·2	0·1	0·0	6·1	2·6	12·1	5·1
02	6 15·5	6 16·5	5 58·4	0·2	0·1	6·2	2·6	12·2	5·2
03	6 15·8	6 16·8	5 58·6	0·3	0·1	6·3	2·7	12·3	5·2
04	6 16·0	6 17·0	5 58·9	0·4	0·2	6·4	2·7	12·4	5·2
05	6 16·3	6 17·3	5 59·1	0·5	0·2	6·5	2·8	12·5	5·3
06	6 16·5	6 17·5	5 59·3	0·6	0·3	6·6	2·8	12·6	5·4
07	6 16·8	6 17·8	5 59·6	0·7	0·3	6·7	2·8	12·7	5·4
08	6 17·0	6 18·0	5 59·8	0·8	0·3	6·8	2·9	12·8	5·4
09	6 17·3	6 18·3	6 00·1	0·9	0·4	6·9	2·9	12·9	5·5
10	6 17·5	6 18·5	6 00·3	1·0	0·4	7·0	3·0	13·0	5·5
11	6 17·8	6 18·8	6 00·5	1·1	0·5	7·1	3·0	13·1	5·6
12	6 18·0	6 19·0	6 00·8	1·2	0·5	7·2	3·1	13·2	5·6
13	6 18·3	6 19·3	6 01·0	1·3	0·6	7·3	3·1	13·3	5·7
14	6 18·5	6 19·5	6 01·3	1·4	0·6	7·4	3·1	13·4	5·7
15	6 18·8	6 19·8	6 01·5	1·5	0·6	7·5	3·2	13·5	5·7
16	6 19·0	6 20·0	6 01·7	1·6	0·7	7·6	3·2	13·6	5·8
17	6 19·3	6 20·3	6 02·0	1·7	0·7	7·7	3·3	13·7	5·8
18	6 19·5	6 20·5	6 02·2	1·8	0·8	7·8	3·3	13·8	5·9
19	6 19·8	6 20·8	6 02·5	1·9	0·8	7·9	3·4	13·9	5·9
20	6 20·0	6 21·0	6 02·7	2·0	0·9	8·0	3·4	14·0	6·0
21	6 20·3	6 21·3	6 02·9	2·1	0·9	8·1	3·4	14·1	6·0
22	6 20·5	6 21·5	6 03·2	2·2	0·9	8·2	3·5	14·2	6·0
23	6 20·8	6 21·8	6 03·4	2·3	1·0	8·3	3·5	14·3	6·1
24	6 21·0	6 22·0	6 03·6	2·4	1·0	8·4	3·6	14·4	6·1
25	6 21·3	6 22·3	6 03·9	2·5	1·1	8·5	3·6	14·5	6·2
26	6 21·5	6 22·5	6 04·1	2·6	1·1	8·6	3·7	14·6	6·2
27	6 21·8	6 22·8	6 04·4	2·7	1·1	8·7	3·7	14·7	6·2
28	6 22·0	6 23·0	6 04·6	2·8	1·2	8·8	3·7	14·8	6·3
29	6 22·3	6 23·3	6 04·8	2·9	1·2	8·9	3·8	14·9	6·3
30	6 22·5	6 23·5	6 05·1	3·0	1·3	9·0	3·8	15·0	6·4
31	6 22·8	6 23·8	6 05·3	3·1	1·3	9·1	3·9	15·1	6·4
32	6 23·0	6 24·0	6 05·6	3·2	1·4	9·2	3·9	15·2	6·5
33	6 23·3	6 24·3	6 05·8	3·3	1·4	9·3	4·0	15·3	6·5
34	6 23·5	6 24·5	6 06·0	3·4	1·4	9·4	4·0	15·4	6·5
35	6 23·8	6 24·8	6 06·3	3·5	1·5	9·5	4·0	15·5	6·6
36	6 24·0	6 25·1	6 06·5	3·6	1·5	9·6	4·1	15·6	6·6
37	6 24·3	6 25·3	6 06·7	3·7	1·6	9·7	4·1	15·7	6·7
38	6 24·5	6 25·6	6 07·0	3·8	1·6	9·8	4·2	15·8	6·7
39	6 24·8	6 25·8	6 07·2	3·9	1·7	9·9	4·2	15·9	6·8
40	6 25·0	6 26·1	6 07·5	4·0	1·7	10·0	4·3	16·0	6·8
41	6 25·3	6 26·3	6 07·7	4·1	1·7	10·1	4·3	16·1	6·8
42	6 25·5	6 26·6	6 07·9	4·2	1·8	10·2	4·3	16·2	6·9
43	6 25·8	6 26·8	6 08·2	4·3	1·8	10·3	4·4	16·3	6·9
44	6 26·0	6 27·1	6 08·4	4·4	1·9	10·4	4·4	16·4	7·0
45	6 26·3	6 27·3	6 08·7	4·5	1·9	10·5	4·5	16·5	7·0
46	6 26·5	6 27·6	6 08·9	4·6	2·0	10·6	4·5	16·6	7·0
47	6 26·8	6 27·8	6 09·1	4·7	2·0	10·7	4·5	16·7	7·1
48	6 27·0	6 28·1	6 09·4	4·8	2·0	10·8	4·6	16·8	7·1
49	6 27·3	6 28·3	6 09·6	4·9	2·1	10·9	4·6	16·9	7·2
50	6 27·5	6 28·6	6 09·8	5·0	2·1	11·0	4·7	17·0	7·2
51	6 27·8	6 28·8	6 10·1	5·1	2·2	11·1	4·7	17·1	7·3
52	6 28·0	6 29·1	6 10·3	5·2	2·2	11·2	4·8	17·2	7·3
53	6 28·3	6 29·3	6 10·6	5·3	2·3	11·3	4·8	17·3	7·4
54	6 28·5	6 29·6	6 10·8	5·4	2·3	11·4	4·8	17·4	7·4
55	6 28·8	6 29·8	6 11·0	5·5	2·3	11·5	4·9	17·5	7·4
56	6 29·0	6 30·1	6 11·3	5·6	2·4	11·6	4·9	17·6	7·5
57	6 29·3	6 30·3	6 11·5	5·7	2·4	11·7	5·0	17·7	7·5
58	6 29·5	6 30·6	6 11·8	5·8	2·5	11·8	5·0	17·8	7·6
59	6 29·8	6 30·8	6 12·0	5·9	2·5	11·9	5·1	17·9	7·6
60	6 30·0	6 31·1	6 12·2	6·0	2·6	12·0	5·1	18·0	7·7

26^m

26^m	SUN PLANETS	ARIES	MOON	v or Corr^n d		v or Corr^n d		v or Corr^n d	
s	° ′	° ′	° ′	′	′	′	′	′	′
00	6 30.0	6 31.1	6 12.2	0.0	0.0	6.0	2.7	12.0	5.3
01	6 30.3	6 31.3	6 12.5	0.1	0.0	6.1	2.7	12.1	5.3
02	6 30.5	6 31.6	6 12.7	0.2	0.1	6.2	2.7	12.2	5.4
03	6 30.8	6 31.8	6 12.9	0.3	0.1	6.3	2.8	12.3	5.4
04	6 31.0	6 32.1	6 13.2	0.4	0.2	6.4	2.8	12.4	5.5
05	6 31.3	6 32.3	6 13.4	0.5	0.2	6.5	2.9	12.5	5.5
06	6 31.5	6 32.6	6 13.7	0.6	0.3	6.6	2.9	12.6	5.6
07	6 31.8	6 32.8	6 13.9	0.7	0.3	6.7	3.0	12.7	5.6
08	6 32.0	6 33.1	6 14.1	0.8	0.4	6.8	3.0	12.8	5.7
09	6 32.3	6 33.3	6 14.4	0.9	0.4	6.9	3.0	12.9	5.7
10	6 32.5	6 33.6	6 14.6	1.0	0.4	7.0	3.1	13.0	5.7
11	6 32.8	6 33.8	6 14.9	1.1	0.5	7.1	3.1	13.1	5.8
12	6 33.0	6 34.1	6 15.1	1.2	0.5	7.2	3.2	13.2	5.8
13	6 33.3	6 34.3	6 15.3	1.3	0.6	7.3	3.2	13.3	5.9
14	6 33.5	6 34.6	6 15.6	1.4	0.6	7.4	3.3	13.4	5.9
15	6 33.8	6 34.8	6 15.8	1.5	0.7	7.5	3.3	13.5	6.0
16	6 34.0	6 35.1	6 16.1	1.6	0.7	7.6	3.4	13.6	6.0
17	6 34.3	6 35.3	6 16.3	1.7	0.8	7.7	3.4	13.7	6.1
18	6 34.5	6 35.6	6 16.5	1.8	0.8	7.8	3.4	13.8	6.1
19	6 34.8	6 35.8	6 16.8	1.9	0.8	7.9	3.5	13.9	6.1
20	6 35.0	6 36.1	6 17.0	2.0	0.9	8.0	3.5	14.0	6.2
21	6 35.3	6 36.3	6 17.2	2.1	0.9	8.1	3.6	14.1	6.2
22	6 35.5	6 36.6	6 17.5	2.2	1.0	8.2	3.6	14.2	6.3
23	6 35.8	6 36.8	6 17.7	2.3	1.0	8.3	3.7	14.3	6.3
24	6 36.0	6 37.1	6 18.0	2.4	1.1	8.4	3.7	14.4	6.4
25	6 36.3	6 37.3	6 18.2	2.5	1.1	8.5	3.8	14.5	6.4
26	6 36.5	6 37.6	6 18.4	2.6	1.1	8.6	3.8	14.6	6.4
27	6 36.8	6 37.8	6 18.7	2.7	1.2	8.7	3.8	14.7	6.5
28	6 37.0	6 38.1	6 18.9	2.8	1.2	8.8	3.9	14.8	6.5
29	6 37.3	6 38.3	6 19.2	2.9	1.3	8.9	3.9	14.9	6.6
30	6 37.5	6 38.6	6 19.4	3.0	1.3	9.0	4.0	15.0	6.6
31	6 37.8	6 38.8	6 19.6	3.1	1.4	9.1	4.0	15.1	6.7
32	6 38.0	6 39.1	6 19.9	3.2	1.4	9.2	4.1	15.2	6.7
33	6 38.3	6 39.3	6 20.1	3.3	1.5	9.3	4.1	15.3	6.8
34	6 38.5	6 39.6	6 20.3	3.4	1.5	9.4	4.2	15.4	6.8
35	6 38.8	6 39.8	6 20.6	3.5	1.5	9.5	4.2	15.5	6.8
36	6 39.0	6 40.1	6 20.8	3.6	1.6	9.6	4.2	15.6	6.9
37	6 39.3	6 40.3	6 21.1	3.7	1.6	9.7	4.3	15.7	6.9
38	6 39.5	6 40.6	6 21.3	3.8	1.7	9.8	4.3	15.8	7.0
39	6 39.8	6 40.8	6 21.5	3.9	1.7	9.9	4.4	15.9	7.0
40	6 40.0	6 41.1	6 21.8	4.0	1.8	10.0	4.4	16.0	7.1
41	6 40.3	6 41.3	6 22.0	4.1	1.8	10.1	4.5	16.1	7.1
42	6 40.5	6 41.6	6 22.3	4.2	1.9	10.2	4.5	16.2	7.2
43	6 40.8	6 41.8	6 22.5	4.3	1.9	10.3	4.5	16.3	7.2
44	6 41.0	6 42.1	6 22.7	4.4	1.9	10.4	4.6	16.4	7.2
45	6 41.3	6 42.3	6 23.0	4.5	2.0	10.5	4.6	16.5	7.3
46	6 41.5	6 42.6	6 23.2	4.6	2.0	10.6	4.7	16.6	7.3
47	6 41.8	6 42.8	6 23.4	4.7	2.1	10.7	4.7	16.7	7.4
48	6 42.0	6 43.1	6 23.7	4.8	2.1	10.8	4.8	16.8	7.4
49	6 42.3	6 43.4	6 23.9	4.9	2.2	10.9	4.8	16.9	7.5
50	6 42.5	6 43.6	6 24.2	5.0	2.2	11.0	4.9	17.0	7.5
51	6 42.8	6 43.9	6 24.4	5.1	2.3	11.1	4.9	17.1	7.6
52	6 43.0	6 44.1	6 24.6	5.2	2.3	11.2	4.9	17.2	7.6
53	6 43.3	6 44.4	6 24.9	5.3	2.3	11.3	5.0	17.3	7.6
54	6 43.5	6 44.6	6 25.1	5.4	2.4	11.4	5.0	17.4	7.7
55	6 43.8	6 44.9	6 25.4	5.5	2.4	11.5	5.1	17.5	7.7
56	6 44.0	6 45.1	6 25.6	5.6	2.5	11.6	5.1	17.6	7.8
57	6 44.3	6 45.4	6 25.8	5.7	2.5	11.7	5.2	17.7	7.8
58	6 44.5	6 45.6	6 26.1	5.8	2.6	11.8	5.2	17.8	7.9
59	6 44.8	6 45.9	6 26.3	5.9	2.6	11.9	5.3	17.9	7.9
60	6 45.0	6 46.1	6 26.6	6.0	2.7	12.0	5.3	18.0	8.0

27^m

27^m	SUN PLANETS	ARIES	MOON	v or Corr^n d		v or Corr^n d		v or Corr^n d	
s	° ′	° ′	° ′	′	′	′	′	′	′
00	6 45.0	6 46.1	6 26.6	0.0	0.0	6.0	2.8	12.0	5.5
01	6 45.3	6 46.4	6 26.8	0.1	0.0	6.1	2.8	12.1	5.5
02	6 45.5	6 46.6	6 27.0	0.2	0.1	6.2	2.8	12.2	5.6
03	6 45.8	6 46.9	6 27.3	0.3	0.1	6.3	2.9	12.3	5.6
04	6 46.0	6 47.1	6 27.5	0.4	0.2	6.4	2.9	12.4	5.7
05	6 46.3	6 47.4	6 27.7	0.5	0.2	6.5	3.0	12.5	5.7
06	6 46.5	6 47.6	6 28.0	0.6	0.3	6.6	3.0	12.6	5.8
07	6 46.8	6 47.9	6 28.2	0.7	0.3	6.7	3.1	12.7	5.8
08	6 47.0	6 48.1	6 28.5	0.8	0.4	6.8	3.1	12.8	5.9
09	6 47.3	6 48.4	6 28.7	0.9	0.4	6.9	3.2	12.9	5.9
10	6 47.5	6 48.6	6 28.9	1.0	0.5	7.0	3.2	13.0	6.0
11	6 47.8	6 48.9	6 29.2	1.1	0.5	7.1	3.3	13.1	6.0
12	6 48.0	6 49.1	6 29.4	1.2	0.6	7.2	3.3	13.2	6.1
13	6 48.3	6 49.4	6 29.7	1.3	0.6	7.3	3.3	13.3	6.1
14	6 48.5	6 49.6	6 29.9	1.4	0.6	7.4	3.4	13.4	6.1
15	6 48.8	6 49.9	6 30.1	1.5	0.7	7.5	3.4	13.5	6.2
16	6 49.0	6 50.1	6 30.4	1.6	0.7	7.6	3.5	13.6	6.2
17	6 49.3	6 50.4	6 30.6	1.7	0.8	7.7	3.5	13.7	6.3
18	6 49.5	6 50.6	6 30.8	1.8	0.8	7.8	3.6	13.8	6.3
19	6 49.8	6 50.9	6 31.1	1.9	0.9	7.9	3.6	13.9	6.4
20	6 50.0	6 51.1	6 31.3	2.0	0.9	8.0	3.7	14.0	6.4
21	6 50.3	6 51.4	6 31.6	2.1	1.0	8.1	3.7	14.1	6.5
22	6 50.5	6 51.6	6 31.8	2.2	1.0	8.2	3.8	14.2	6.5
23	6 50.8	6 51.9	6 32.0	2.3	1.1	8.3	3.8	14.3	6.6
24	6 51.0	6 52.1	6 32.3	2.4	1.1	8.4	3.9	14.4	6.6
25	6 51.3	6 52.4	6 32.5	2.5	1.1	8.5	3.9	14.5	6.6
26	6 51.5	6 52.6	6 32.8	2.6	1.2	8.6	3.9	14.6	6.7
27	6 51.8	6 52.9	6 33.0	2.7	1.2	8.7	4.0	14.7	6.7
28	6 52.0	6 53.1	6 33.2	2.8	1.3	8.8	4.0	14.8	6.8
29	6 52.3	6 53.4	6 33.5	2.9	1.3	8.9	4.1	14.9	6.8
30	6 52.5	6 53.6	6 33.7	3.0	1.4	9.0	4.1	15.0	6.9
31	6 52.8	6 53.9	6 33.9	3.1	1.4	9.1	4.2	15.1	6.9
32	6 53.0	6 54.1	6 34.2	3.2	1.5	9.2	4.2	15.2	7.0
33	6 53.3	6 54.4	6 34.4	3.3	1.5	9.3	4.3	15.3	7.0
34	6 53.5	6 54.6	6 34.7	3.4	1.6	9.4	4.3	15.4	7.1
35	6 53.8	6 54.9	6 34.9	3.5	1.6	9.5	4.4	15.5	7.1
36	6 54.0	6 55.1	6 35.1	3.6	1.7	9.6	4.4	15.6	7.2
37	6 54.3	6 55.4	6 35.4	3.7	1.7	9.7	4.4	15.7	7.2
38	6 54.5	6 55.6	6 35.6	3.8	1.7	9.8	4.5	15.8	7.2
39	6 54.8	6 55.9	6 35.9	3.9	1.8	9.9	4.5	15.9	7.3
40	6 55.0	6 56.1	6 36.1	4.0	1.8	10.0	4.6	16.0	7.3
41	6 55.3	6 56.4	6 36.3	4.1	1.9	10.1	4.6	16.1	7.4
42	6 55.5	6 56.6	6 36.6	4.2	1.9	10.2	4.7	16.2	7.4
43	6 55.8	6 56.9	6 36.8	4.3	2.0	10.3	4.7	16.3	7.5
44	6 56.0	6 57.1	6 37.0	4.4	2.0	10.4	4.8	16.4	7.5
45	6 56.3	6 57.4	6 37.3	4.5	2.1	10.5	4.8	16.5	7.6
46	6 56.5	6 57.6	6 37.5	4.6	2.1	10.6	4.9	16.6	7.6
47	6 56.8	6 57.9	6 37.8	4.7	2.2	10.7	4.9	16.7	7.7
48	6 57.0	6 58.1	6 38.0	4.8	2.2	10.8	5.0	16.8	7.7
49	6 57.3	6 58.4	6 38.2	4.9	2.2	10.9	5.0	16.9	7.7
50	6 57.5	6 58.6	6 38.5	5.0	2.3	11.0	5.0	17.0	7.8
51	6 57.8	6 58.9	6 38.7	5.1	2.3	11.1	5.1	17.1	7.8
52	6 58.0	6 59.1	6 39.0	5.2	2.4	11.2	5.1	17.2	7.9
53	6 58.3	6 59.4	6 39.2	5.3	2.4	11.3	5.2	17.3	7.9
54	6 58.5	6 59.6	6 39.4	5.4	2.5	11.4	5.2	17.4	8.0
55	6 58.8	6 59.9	6 39.7	5.5	2.5	11.5	5.3	17.5	8.0
56	6 59.0	7 00.1	6 39.9	5.6	2.6	11.6	5.3	17.6	8.1
57	6 59.3	7 00.4	6 40.2	5.7	2.6	11.7	5.4	17.7	8.1
58	6 59.5	7 00.6	6 40.4	5.8	2.7	11.8	5.4	17.8	8.2
59	6 59.8	7 00.9	6 40.6	5.9	2.7	11.9	5.5	17.9	8.2
60	7 00.0	7 01.1	6 40.9	6.0	2.8	12.0	5.5	18.0	8.3

28ᵐ	SUN PLANETS	ARIES	MOON	v or Corrⁿ d	v or Corrⁿ d	v or Corrⁿ d
s	° ′	° ′	° ′	′ ′	′ ′	′ ′
00	7 00·0	7 01·1	6 40·9	0·0 0·0	6·0 2·9	12·0 5·7
01	7 00·3	7 01·4	6 41·1	0·1 0·0	6·1 2·9	12·1 5·7
02	7 00·5	7 01·7	6 41·3	0·2 0·1	6·2 2·9	12·2 5·8
03	7 00·8	7 01·9	6 41·6	0·3 0·1	6·3 3·0	12·3 5·8
04	7 01·0	7 02·2	6 41·8	0·4 0·2	6·4 3·0	12·4 5·9
05	7 01·3	7 02·4	6 42·1	0·5 0·2	6·5 3·1	12·5 5·9
06	7 01·5	7 02·7	6 42·3	0·6 0·3	6·6 3·1	12·6 6·0
07	7 01·8	7 02·9	6 42·5	0·7 0·3	6·7 3·2	12·7 6·0
08	7 02·0	7 03·2	6 42·8	0·8 0·4	6·8 3·2	12·8 6·1
09	7 02·3	7 03·4	6 43·0	0·9 0·4	6·9 3·3	12·9 6·1
10	7 02·5	7 03·7	6 43·3	1·0 0·5	7·0 3·3	13·0 6·2
11	7 02·8	7 03·9	6 43·5	1·1 0·5	7·1 3·4	13·1 6·2
12	7 03·0	7 04·2	6 43·7	1·2 0·6	7·2 3·4	13·2 6·3
13	7 03·3	7 04·4	6 44·0	1·3 0·6	7·3 3·5	13·3 6·3
14	7 03·5	7 04·7	6 44·2	1·4 0·7	7·4 3·5	13·4 6·4
15	7 03·8	7 04·9	6 44·4	1·5 0·7	7·5 3·6	13·5 6·4
16	7 04·0	7 05·2	6 44·7	1·6 0·8	7·6 3·6	13·6 6·5
17	7 04·3	7 05·4	6 44·9	1·7 0·8	7·7 3·7	13·7 6·5
18	7 04·5	7 05·7	6 45·2	1·8 0·9	7·8 3·7	13·8 6·6
19	7 04·8	7 05·9	6 45·4	1·9 0·9	7·9 3·8	13·9 6·6
20	7 05·0	7 06·2	6 45·6	2·0 1·0	8·0 3·8	14·0 6·7
21	7 05·3	7 06·4	6 45·9	2·1 1·0	8·1 3·8	14·1 6·7
22	7 05·5	7 06·7	6 46·1	2·2 1·0	8·2 3·9	14·2 6·7
23	7 05·8	7 06·9	6 46·4	2·3 1·1	8·3 3·9	14·3 6·8
24	7 06·0	7 07·2	6 46·6	2·4 1·1	8·4 4·0	14·4 6·8
25	7 06·3	7 07·4	6 46·8	2·5 1·2	8·5 4·0	14·5 6·9
26	7 06·5	7 07·7	6 47·1	2·6 1·2	8·6 4·1	14·6 6·9
27	7 06·8	7 07·9	6 47·3	2·7 1·3	8·7 4·1	14·7 7·0
28	7 07·0	7 08·2	6 47·5	2·8 1·3	8·8 4·2	14·8 7·0
29	7 07·3	7 08·4	6 47·8	2·9 1·4	8·9 4·2	14·9 7·1
30	7 07·5	7 08·7	6 48·0	3·0 1·4	9·0 4·3	15·0 7·1
31	7 07·8	7 08·9	6 48·3	3·1 1·5	9·1 4·3	15·1 7·2
32	7 08·0	7 09·2	6 48·5	3·2 1·5	9·2 4·4	15·2 7·2
33	7 08·3	7 09·4	6 48·7	3·3 1·6	9·3 4·4	15·3 7·3
34	7 08·5	7 09·7	6 49·0	3·4 1·6	9·4 4·5	15·4 7·3
35	7 08·8	7 09·9	6 49·2	3·5 1·7	9·5 4·5	15·5 7·4
36	7 09·0	7 10·2	6 49·5	3·6 1·7	9·6 4·6	15·6 7·4
37	7 09·3	7 10·4	6 49·7	3·7 1·8	9·7 4·6	15·7 7·5
38	7 09·5	7 10·7	6 49·9	3·8 1·8	9·8 4·7	15·8 7·5
39	7 09·8	7 10·9	6 50·2	3·9 1·9	9·9 4·7	15·9 7·6
40	7 10·0	7 11·2	6 50·4	4·0 1·9	10·0 4·8	16·0 7·6
41	7 10·3	7 11·4	6 50·6	4·1 1·9	10·1 4·8	16·1 7·6
42	7 10·5	7 11·7	6 50·9	4·2 2·0	10·2 4·8	16·2 7·7
43	7 10·8	7 11·9	6 51·1	4·3 2·0	10·3 4·9	16·3 7·7
44	7 11·0	7 12·2	6 51·4	4·4 2·1	10·4 4·9	16·4 7·8
45	7 11·3	7 12·4	6 51·6	4·5 2·1	10·5 5·0	16·5 7·8
46	7 11·5	7 12·7	6 51·8	4·6 2·2	10·6 5·0	16·6 7·9
47	7 11·8	7 12·9	6 52·1	4·7 2·2	10·7 5·1	16·7 7·9
48	7 12·0	7 13·2	6 52·3	4·8 2·3	10·8 5·1	16·8 8·0
49	7 12·3	7 13·4	6 52·6	4·9 2·3	10·9 5·2	16·9 8·0
50	7 12·5	7 13·7	6 52·8	5·0 2·4	11·0 5·2	17·0 8·1
51	7 12·8	7 13·9	6 53·0	5·1 2·4	11·1 5·3	17·1 8·1
52	7 13·0	7 14·2	6 53·3	5·2 2·5	11·2 5·3	17·2 8·2
53	7 13·3	7 14·4	6 53·5	5·3 2·5	11·3 5·4	17·3 8·2
54	7 13·5	7 14·7	6 53·8	5·4 2·6	11·4 5·4	17·4 8·3
55	7 13·8	7 14·9	6 54·0	5·5 2·6	11·5 5·5	17·5 8·3
56	7 14·0	7 15·2	6 54·2	5·6 2·7	11·6 5·5	17·6 8·4
57	7 14·3	7 15·4	6 54·5	5·7 2·7	11·7 5·6	17·7 8·4
58	7 14·5	7 15·7	6 54·7	5·8 2·8	11·8 5·6	17·8 8·5
59	7 14·8	7 15·9	6 54·9	5·9 2·8	11·9 5·7	17·9 8·5
60	7 15·0	7 16·2	6 55·2	6·0 2·9	12·0 5·7	18·0 8·6

29ᵐ	SUN PLANETS	ARIES	MOON	v or Corrⁿ d	v or Corrⁿ d	v or Corrⁿ d
s	° ′	° ′	° ′	′ ′	′ ′	′ ′
00	7 15·0	7 16·2	6 55·2	0·0 0·0	6·0 3·0	12·0 5·9
01	7 15·3	7 16·4	6 55·4	0·1 0·0	6·1 3·0	12·1 5·9
02	7 15·5	7 16·7	6 55·7	0·2 0·1	6·2 3·0	12·2 6·0
03	7 15·8	7 16·9	6 55·9	0·3 0·1	6·3 3·1	12·3 6·0
04	7 16·0	7 17·2	6 56·1	0·4 0·2	6·4 3·1	12·4 6·1
05	7 16·3	7 17·4	6 56·4	0·5 0·2	6·5 3·2	12·5 6·1
06	7 16·5	7 17·7	6 56·6	0·6 0·3	6·6 3·2	12·6 6·2
07	7 16·8	7 17·9	6 56·9	0·7 0·3	6·7 3·3	12·7 6·2
08	7 17·0	7 18·2	6 57·1	0·8 0·4	6·8 3·3	12·8 6·3
09	7 17·3	7 18·4	6 57·3	0·9 0·4	6·9 3·4	12·9 6·3
10	7 17·5	7 18·7	6 57·6	1·0 0·5	7·0 3·4	13·0 6·4
11	7 17·8	7 18·9	6 57·8	1·1 0·5	7·1 3·5	13·1 6·4
12	7 18·0	7 19·2	6 58·0	1·2 0·6	7·2 3·5	13·2 6·5
13	7 18·3	7 19·4	6 58·3	1·3 0·6	7·3 3·6	13·3 6·5
14	7 18·5	7 19·7	6 58·5	1·4 0·7	7·4 3·6	13·4 6·6
15	7 18·8	7 20·0	6 58·8	1·5 0·7	7·5 3·7	13·5 6·6
16	7 19·0	7 20·2	6 59·0	1·6 0·8	7·6 3·7	13·6 6·7
17	7 19·3	7 20·5	6 59·2	1·7 0·8	7·7 3·8	13·7 6·7
18	7 19·5	7 20·7	6 59·5	1·8 0·9	7·8 3·8	13·8 6·8
19	7 19·8	7 21·0	6 59·7	1·9 0·9	7·9 3·9	13·9 6·8
20	7 20·0	7 21·2	7 00·0	2·0 1·0	8·0 3·9	14·0 6·9
21	7 20·3	7 21·5	7 00·2	2·1 1·0	8·1 4·0	14·1 6·9
22	7 20·5	7 21·7	7 00·4	2·2 1·1	8·2 4·0	14·2 7·0
23	7 20·8	7 22·0	7 00·7	2·3 1·1	8·3 4·1	14·3 7·0
24	7 21·0	7 22·2	7 00·9	2·4 1·2	8·4 4·1	14·4 7·1
25	7 21·3	7 22·5	7 01·1	2·5 1·2	8·5 4·2	14·5 7·1
26	7 21·5	7 22·7	7 01·4	2·6 1·3	8·6 4·2	14·6 7·2
27	7 21·8	7 23·0	7 01·6	2·7 1·3	8·7 4·3	14·7 7·2
28	7 22·0	7 23·2	7 01·9	2·8 1·4	8·8 4·3	14·8 7·3
29	7 22·3	7 23·5	7 02·1	2·9 1·4	8·9 4·4	14·9 7·3
30	7 22·5	7 23·7	7 02·3	3·0 1·5	9·0 4·4	15·0 7·4
31	7 22·8	7 24·0	7 02·6	3·1 1·5	9·1 4·5	15·1 7·4
32	7 23·0	7 24·2	7 02·8	3·2 1·6	9·2 4·5	15·2 7·5
33	7 23·3	7 24·5	7 03·1	3·3 1·6	9·3 4·6	15·3 7·5
34	7 23·5	7 24·7	7 03·3	3·4 1·7	9·4 4·6	15·4 7·6
35	7 23·8	7 25·0	7 03·5	3·5 1·7	9·5 4·7	15·5 7·6
36	7 24·0	7 25·2	7 03·8	3·6 1·8	9·6 4·7	15·6 7·7
37	7 24·3	7 25·5	7 04·0	3·7 1·8	9·7 4·8	15·7 7·7
38	7 24·5	7 25·7	7 04·3	3·8 1·9	9·8 4·8	15·8 7·8
39	7 24·8	7 26·0	7 04·5	3·9 1·9	9·9 4·9	15·9 7·8
40	7 25·0	7 26·2	7 04·7	4·0 2·0	10·0 4·9	16·0 7·9
41	7 25·3	7 26·5	7 05·0	4·1 2·0	10·1 5·0	16·1 7·9
42	7 25·5	7 26·7	7 05·2	4·2 2·1	10·2 5·0	16·2 8·0
43	7 25·8	7 27·0	7 05·4	4·3 2·1	10·3 5·1	16·3 8·0
44	7 26·0	7 27·2	7 05·7	4·4 2·2	10·4 5·1	16 4 8·1
45	7 26·3	7 27·5	7 05·9	4·5 2·2	10·5 5·2	16·5 8·1
46	7 26·5	7 27·7	7 06·2	4·6 2·3	10·6 5·2	16·6 8·2
47	7 26·8	7 28·0	7 06·4	4·7 2·3	10·7 5·3	16·7 8·2
48	7 27·0	7 28·2	7 06·6	4·8 2·4	10·8 5·3	16·8 8·3
49	7 27·3	7 28·5	7 06·9	4·9 2·4	10·9 5·4	16·9 8·3
50	7 27·5	7 28·7	7 07·1	5·0 2·5	11·0 5·4	17·0 8·4
51	7 27·8	7 29·0	7 07·4	5·1 2·5	11·1 5·5	17·1 8·4
52	7 28·0	7 29·2	7 07·6	5·2 2·6	11·2 5·5	17·2 8·5
53	7 28·3	7 29·5	7 07·8	5·3 2·6	11·3 5·6	17·3 8·5
54	7 28·5	7 29·7	7 08·1	5·4 2·7	11·4 5·6	17·4 8·6
55	7 28·8	7 30·0	7 08·3	5·5 2·7	11·5 5·7	17·5 8·6
56	7 29·0	7 30·2	7 08·5	5·6 2·8	11·6 5·7	17·6 8·7
57	7 29·3	7 30·5	7 08·8	5·7 2·8	11·7 5·8	17·7 8·7
58	7 29·5	7 30·7	7 09·0	5·8 2·9	11·8 5·8	17·8 8·8
59	7 29·8	7 31·0	7 09·3	5·9 2·9	11·9 5·9	17·9 8·8
60	7 30·0	7 31·2	7 09·5	6·0 3·0	12·0 5·9	18·0 8·9

330

34ᵐ	SUN PLANETS	ARIES	MOON	v or Corrⁿ d		v or Corrⁿ d		v or Corrⁿ d	
s	° ′	° ′	° ′	′	′	′	′	′	′
00	8 30·0	8 31·4	8 06·8	0·0	0·0	6·0	3·5	12·0	6·9
01	8 30·3	8 31·6	8 07·0	0·1	0·1	6·1	3·5	12·1	7·0
02	8 30·5	8 31·9	8 07·2	0·2	0·1	6·2	3·6	12·2	7·0
03	8 30·8	8 32·1	8 07·5	0·3	0·2	6·3	3·6	12·3	7·1
04	8 31·0	8 32·4	8 07·7	0·4	0·2	6·4	3·7	12·4	7·1
05	8 31·3	8 32·6	8 08·0	0·5	0·3	6·5	3·7	12·5	7·2
06	8 31·5	8 32·9	8 08·2	0·6	0·3	6·6	3·8	12·6	7·2
07	8 31·8	8 33·1	8 08·4	0·7	0·4	6·7	3·9	12·7	7·3
08	8 32·0	8 33·4	8 08·7	0·8	0·5	6·8	3·9	12·8	7·4
09	8 32·3	8 33·7	8 08·9	0·9	0·5	6·9	4·0	12·9	7·4
10	8 32·5	8 33·9	8 09·2	1·0	0·6	7·0	4·0	13·0	7·5
11	8 32·8	8 34·2	8 09·4	1·1	0·6	7·1	4·1	13·1	7·5
12	8 33·0	8 34·4	8 09·6	1·2	0·7	7·2	4·1	13·2	7·6
13	8 33·3	8 34·7	8 09·9	1·3	0·7	7·3	4·2	13·3	7·6
14	8 33·5	8 34·9	8 10·1	1·4	0·8	7·4	4·3	13·4	7·7
15	8 33·8	8 35·2	8 10·3	1·5	0·9	7·5	4·3	13·5	7·8
16	8 34·0	8 35·4	8 10·6	1·6	0·9	7·6	4·4	13·6	7·8
17	8 34·3	8 35·7	8 10·8	1·7	1·0	7·7	4·4	13·7	7·9
18	8 34·5	8 35·9	8 11·1	1·8	1·0	7·8	4·5	13·8	7·9
19	8 34·8	8 36·2	8 11·3	1·9	1·1	7·9	4·5	13·9	8·0
20	8 35·0	8 36·4	8 11·5	2·0	1·2	8·0	4·6	14·0	8·1
21	8 35·3	8 36·7	8 11·8	2·1	1·2	8·1	4·7	14·1	8·1
22	8 35·5	8 36·9	8 12·0	2·2	1·3	8·2	4·7	14·2	8·2
23	8 35·8	8 37·2	8 12·3	2·3	1·3	8·3	4·8	14·3	8·2
24	8 36·0	8 37·4	8 12·5	2·4	1·4	8·4	4·8	14·4	8·3
25	8 36·3	8 37·7	8 12·7	2·5	1·4	8·5	4·9	14·5	8·3
26	8 36·5	8 37·9	8 13·0	2·6	1·5	8·6	4·9	14·6	8·4
27	8 36·8	8 38·2	8 13·2	2·7	1·6	8·7	5·0	14·7	8·5
28	8 37·0	8 38·4	8 13·4	2·8	1·6	8·8	5·1	14·8	8·5
29	8 37·3	8 38·7	8 13·7	2·9	1·7	8·9	5·1	14·9	8·6
30	8 37·5	8 38·9	8 13·9	3·0	1·7	9·0	5·2	15·0	8·6
31	8 37·8	8 39·2	8 14·2	3·1	1·8	9·1	5·2	15·1	8·7
32	8 38·0	8 39·4	8 14·4	3·2	1·8	9·2	5·3	15·2	8·7
33	8 38·3	8 39·7	8 14·6	3·3	1·9	9·3	5·3	15·3	8·8
34	8 38·5	8 39·9	8 14·9	3·4	2·0	9·4	5·4	15·4	8·9
35	8 38·8	8 40·2	8 15·1	3·5	2·0	9·5	5·5	15·5	8·9
36	8 39·0	8 40·4	8 15·4	3·6	2·1	9·6	5·5	15·6	9·0
37	8 39·3	8 40·7	8 15·6	3·7	2·1	9·7	5·6	15·7	9·0
38	8 39·5	8 40·9	8 15·8	3·8	2·2	9·8	5·6	15·8	9·1
39	8 39·8	8 41·2	8 16·1	3·9	2·2	9·9	5·7	15·9	9·1
40	8 40·0	8 41·4	8 16·3	4·0	2·3	10·0	5·8	16·0	9·2
41	8 40·3	8 41·7	8 16·5	4·1	2·4	10·1	5·8	16·1	9 3
42	8 40·5	8 41·9	8 16·8	4·2	2·4	10·2	5·9	16·2	9·3
43	8 40·8	8 42·2	8 17·0	4·3	2·5	10·3	5·9	16·3	9·4
44	8 41·0	8 42·4	8 17·3	4·4	2·5	10·4	6·0	16·4	9·4
45	8 41·3	8 42·7	8 17·5	4·5	2·6	10·5	6·0	16·5	9·5
46	8 41·5	8 42·9	8 17·7	4·6	2·6	10·6	6·1	16·6	9·5
47	8 41·8	8 43·2	8 18·0	4·7	2·7	10·7	6·2	16·7	9·6
48	8 42·0	8 43·4	8 18·2	4·8	2·8	10·8	6·2	16·8	9·7
49	8 42·3	8 43·7	8 18·5	4·9	2·8	10·9	6·3	16·9	9·7
50	8 42·5	8 43·9	8 18·7	5·0	2·9	11·0	6·3	17·0	9·8
51	8 42·8	8 44·2	8 18·9	5·1	2·9	11·1	6·4	17·1	9·8
52	8 43·0	8 44·4	8 19·2	5·2	3·0	11·2	6·4	17·2	9·9
53	8 43·3	8 44·7	8 19·4	5·3	3·0	11·3	6·5	17·3	9·9
54	8 43·5	8 44·9	8 19·7	5·4	3·1	11·4	6·6	17·4	10·0
55	8 43·8	8 45·2	8 19·9	5·5	3·2	11·5	6·6	17·5	10·1
56	8 44·0	8 45·4	8 20·1	5·6	3·2	11·6	6·7	17·6	10·1
57	8 44·3	8 45·7	8 20·4	5·7	3·3	11·7	6·7	17·7	10·2
58	8 44·5	8 45·9	8 20·6	5·8	3·3	11·8	6·8	17·8	10·2
59	8 44·8	8 46·2	8 20·8	5·9	3·4	11·9	6·8	17·9	10·3
60	8 45·0	8 46·4	8 21·1	6·0	3·5	12·0	6·9	18·0	10·4

35ᵐ	SUN PLANETS	ARIES	MOON	v or Corrⁿ d		v or Corrⁿ d		v or Corrⁿ d	
s	° ′	° ′	° ′	′	′	′	′	′	′
00	8 45·0	8 46·4	8 21·1	0·0	0·0	6·0	3·6	12·0	7·1
01	8 45·3	8 46·7	8 21·3	0·1	0·1	6·1	3·6	12·1	7·2
02	8 45·5	8 46·9	8 21·6	0·2	0·1	6·2	3·7	12·2	7·2
03	8 45·8	8 47·2	8 21·8	0·3	0·2	6·3	3·7	12·3	7·3
04	8 46·0	8 47·4	8 22·0	0·4	0·2	6·4	3·8	12·4	7·3
05	8 46·3	8 47·7	8 22·3	0·5	0·3	6·5	3·8	12·5	7·4
06	8 46·5	8 47·9	8 22·5	0·6	0·4	6·6	3·9	12·6	7·5
07	8 46·8	8 48·2	8 22·8	0·7	0·4	6·7	4·0	12·7	7·5
08	8 47·0	8 48·4	8 23·0	0·8	0·5	6·8	4·0	12·8	7·6
09	8 47·3	8 48·7	8 23·2	0·9	0·5	6·9	4·1	12·9	7·6
10	8 47·5	8 48·9	8 23·5	1·0	0·6	7·0	4·1	13·0	7·7
11	8 47·8	8 49·2	8 23·7	1·1	0·7	7·1	4·2	13·1	7·8
12	8 48·0	8 49·4	8 23·9	1·2	0·7	7·2	4·3	13·2	7·8
13	8 48·3	8 49·7	8 24·2	1·3	0·8	7·3	4·3	13·3	7·9
14	8 48·5	8 49·9	8 24·4	1·4	0·8	7·4	4·4	13·4	7·9
15	8 48·8	8 50·2	8 24·7	1·5	0·9	7·5	4·4	13·5	8·0
16	8 49·0	8 50·4	8 24·9	1·6	0·9	7·6	4·5	13·6	8·0
17	8 49·3	8 50·7	8 25·1	1·7	1·0	7·7	4·6	13·7	8·1
18	8 49·5	8 50·9	8 25·4	1·8	1·1	7·8	4·6	13·8	8·2
19	8 49·8	8 51·2	8 25·6	1·9	1·1	7·9	4·7	13·9	8·2
20	8 50·0	8 51·5	8 25·9	2·0	1·2	8·0	4·7	14·0	8·3
21	8 50·3	8 51·7	8 26·1	2·1	1·2	8·1	4·8	14·1	8·3
22	8 50·5	8 52·0	8 26·3	2·2	1·3	8·2	4·8	14·2	8·4
23	8 50·8	8 52·2	8 26·6	2·3	1·4	8·3	4·9	14·3	8·5
24	8 51·0	8 52·5	8 26·8	2·4	1·4	8·4	5·0	14·4	8·5
25	8 51·3	8 52·7	8 27·0	2·5	1·5	8·5	5·0	14·5	8·6
26	8 51·5	8 53·0	8 27·3	2·6	1·5	8·6	5·1	14·6	8·6
27	8 51·8	8 53·2	8 27·5	2·7	1·6	8·7	5·1	14·7	8·7
28	8 52·0	8 53·5	8 27·8	2·8	1·7	8·8	5·2	14·8	8·8
29	8 52·3	8 53·7	8 28·0	2·9	1·7	8·9	5·3	14·9	8·8
30	8 52·5	8 54·0	8 28·2	3·0	1·8	9·0	5·3	15·0	8·9
31	8 52·8	8 54·2	8 28·5	3·1	1·8	9·1	5·4	15·1	8·9
32	8 53·0	8 54·5	8 28·7	3·2	1·9	9·2	5·4	15·2	9·0
33	8 53·3	8 54·7	8 29·0	3·3	2·0	9·3	5·5	15·3	9·1
34	8 53·5	8 55·0	8 29·2	3·4	2·0	9·4	5·6	15·4	9·1
35	8 53·8	8 55·2	8 29·4	3·5	2·1	9·5	5·6	15·5	9·2
36	8 54·0	8 55·5	8 29·7	3·6	2·1	9·6	5·7	15·6	9·2
37	8 54·3	8 55·7	8 29·9	3·7	2·2	9·7	5·7	15·7	9·3
38	8 54·5	8 56·0	8 30·2	3·8	2·2	9·8	5·8	15·8	9·3
39	8 54·8	8 56·2	8 30·4	3·9	2·3	9·9	5·9	15·9	9·4
40	8 55·0	8 56·5	8 30·6	4·0	2·4	10·0	5·9	16·0	9·5
41	8 55·3	8 56·7	8 30·9	4·1	2·4	10·1	6·0	16·1	9·5
42	8 55·5	8 57·0	8 31·1	4·2	2·5	10·2	6·0	16·2	9·6
43	8 55·8	8 57·2	8 31·3	4·3	2·5	10·3	6·1	16·3	9·6
44	8 56·0	8 57·5	8 31·6	4·4	2·6	10·4	6·2	16·4	9·7
45	8 56·3	8 57·7	8 31·8	4·5	2·7	10·5	6·2	16·5	9·8
46	8 56·5	8 58·0	8 32·1	4·6	2·7	10·6	6·3	16·6	9·8
47	8 56·8	8 58·2	8 32·3	4·7	2·8	10·7	6·3	16·7	9·9
48	8 57·0	8 58·5	8 32·5	4·8	2·8	10·8	6·4	16·8	9·9
49	8 57·3	8 58·7	8 32·8	4·9	2·9	10·9	6·4	16·9	10·0
50	8 57·5	8 59·0	8 33·0	5·0	3·0	11·0	6·5	17·0	10·1
51	8 57·8	8 59·2	8 33·3	5·1	3·0	11·1	6·6	17·1	10·1
52	8 58·0	8 59·5	8 33·5	5·2	3·1	11·2	6·6	17·2	10·2
53	8 58·3	8 59·7	8 33·7	5·3	3·1	11·3	6·7	17·3	10·2
54	8 58·5	9 00·0	8 34·0	5·4	3·2	11·4	6·7	17·4	10·3
55	8 58·8	9 00·2	8 34·2	5·5	3·3	11·5	6·8	17·5	10·4
56	8 59·0	9 00·5	8 34·4	5·6	3·3	11·6	6·9	17·6	10·4
57	8 59·3	9 00·7	8 34·7	5·7	3·4	11·7	6·9	17·7	10·5
58	8 59·5	9 01·0	8 34·9	5·8	3·4	11·8	7·0	17·8	10·5
59	8 59·8	9 01·2	8 35·2	5·9	3·5	11·9	7·0	17·9	10·6
60	9 00·0	9 01·5	8 35·4	6·0	3·6	12·0	7·1	18·0	10·7

36ᵐ

36ᵐ s	SUN PLANETS	ARIES	MOON	v or Corrⁿ d	v or Corrⁿ d	v or Corrⁿ d
00	9 00·0	9 01·5	8 35·4	0·0 0·0	6·0 3·7	12·0 7·3
01	9 00·3	9 01·7	8 35·6	0·1 0·1	6·1 3·7	12·1 7·4
02	9 00·5	9 02·0	8 35·9	0·2 0·1	6·2 3·8	12·2 7·4
03	9 00·8	9 02·2	8 36·1	0·3 0·2	6·3 3·8	12·3 7·5
04	9 01·0	9 02·5	8 36·4	0·4 0·2	6·4 3·9	12·4 7·5
05	9 01·3	9 02·7	8 36·6	0·5 0·3	6·5 4·0	12·5 7·6
06	9 01·5	9 03·0	8 36·8	0·6 0·4	6·6 4·0	12·6 7·7
07	9 01·8	9 03·2	8 37·1	0·7 0·4	6·7 4·1	12·7 7·7
08	9 02·0	9 03·5	8 37·3	0·8 0·5	6·8 4·1	12·8 7·8
09	9 02·3	9 03·7	8 37·5	0·9 0·5	6·9 4·2	12·9 7·8
10	9 02·5	9 04·0	8 37·8	1·0 0·6	7·0 4·3	13·0 7·9
11	9 02·8	9 04·2	8 38·0	1·1 0·7	7·1 4·3	13·1 8·0
12	9 03·0	9 04·5	8 38·3	1·2 0·7	7·2 4·4	13·2 8·0
13	9 03·3	9 04·7	8 38·5	1·3 0·8	7·3 4·4	13·3 8·1
14	9 03·5	9 05·0	8 38·7	1·4 0·9	7·4 4·5	13·4 8·2
15	9 03·8	9 05·2	8 39·0	1·5 0·9	7·5 4·6	13·5 8·2
16	9 04·0	9 05·5	8 39·2	1·6 1·0	7·6 4·6	13·6 8·3
17	9 04·3	9 05·7	8 39·5	1·7 1·0	7·7 4·7	13·7 8·3
18	9 04·5	9 06·0	8 39·7	1·8 1·1	7·8 4·7	13·8 8·4
19	9 04·8	9 06·2	8 39·9	1·9 1·2	7·9 4·8	13·9 8·5
20	9 05·0	9 06·5	8 40·2	2·0 1·2	8·0 4·9	14·0 8·5
21	9 05·3	9 06·7	8 40·4	2·1 1·3	8·1 4·9	14·1 8·6
22	9 05·5	9 07·0	8 40·6	2·2 1·3	8·2 5·0	14·2 8·6
23	9 05·8	9 07·2	8 40·9	2·3 1·4	8·3 5·0	14·3 8·7
24	9 06·0	9 07·5	8 41·1	2·4 1·5	8·4 5·1	14·4 8·8
25	9 06·3	9 07·7	8 41·4	2·5 1·5	8·5 5·2	14·5 8·8
26	9 06·5	9 08·0	8 41·6	2·6 1·6	8·6 5·2	14·6 8·9
27	9 06·8	9 08·2	8 41·8	2·7 1·6	8·7 5·3	14·7 8·9
28	9 07·0	9 08·5	8 42·1	2·8 1·7	8·8 5·4	14·8 9·0
29	9 07·3	9 08·7	8 42·3	2·9 1·8	8·9 5·4	14·9 9·1
30	9 07·5	9 09·0	8 42·6	3·0 1·8	9·0 5·5	15·0 9·1
31	9 07·8	9 09·2	8 42·8	3·1 1·9	9·1 5·5	15·1 9·2
32	9 08·0	9 09·5	8 43·0	3·2 1·9	9·2 5·6	15·2 9·2
33	9 08·3	9 09·8	8 43·3	3·3 2·0	9·3 5·7	15·3 9·3
34	9 08·5	9 10·0	8 43·5	3·4 2·1	9·4 5·7	15·4 9·4
35	9 08·8	9 10·3	8 43·8	3·5 2·1	9·5 5·8	15·5 9·4
36	9 09·0	9 10·5	8 44·0	3·6 2·2	9·6 5·8	15·6 9·5
37	9 09·3	9 10·8	8 44·2	3·7 2·3	9·7 5·9	15·7 9·6
38	9 09·5	9 11·0	8 44·5	3·8 2·3	9·8 6·0	15·8 9·6
39	9 09·8	9 11·3	8 44·7	3·9 2·4	9·9 6·0	15·9 9·7
40	9 10·0	9 11·5	8 44·9	4·0 2·4	10·0 6·1	16·0 9·7
41	9 10·3	9 11·8	8 45·2	4·1 2·5	10·1 6·1	16·1 9·8
42	9 10·5	9 12·0	8 45·4	4·2 2·6	10·2 6·2	16·2 9·9
43	9 10·8	9 12·3	8 45·7	4·3 2·6	10·3 6·3	16·3 9·9
44	9 11·0	9 12·5	8 45·9	4·4 2·7	10·4 6·3	16·4 10·0
45	9 11·3	9 12·8	8 46·1	4·5 2·7	10·5 6·4	16·5 10·0
46	9 11·5	9 13·0	8 46·4	4·6 2·8	10·6 6·4	16·6 10·1
47	9 11·8	9 13·3	8 46·6	4·7 2·9	10·7 6·5	16·7 10·2
48	9 12·0	9 13·5	8 46·9	4·8 2·9	10·8 6·6	16·8 10·2
49	9 12·3	9 13·8	8 47·1	4·9 3·0	10·9 6·6	16·9 10·3
50	9 12·5	9 14·0	8 47·3	5·0 3·0	11·0 6·7	17·0 10·3
51	9 12·8	9 14·3	8 47·6	5·1 3·1	11·1 6·8	17·1 10·4
52	9 13·0	9 14·5	8 47·8	5·2 3·2	11·2 6·8	17·2 10·5
53	9 13·3	9 14·8	8 48·0	5·3 3·2	11·3 6·9	17·3 10·5
54	9 13·5	9 15·0	8 48·3	5·4 3·3	11·4 6·9	17·4 10·6
55	9 13·8	9 15·3	8 48·5	5·5 3·3	11·5 7·0	17·5 10·6
56	9 14·0	9 15·5	8 48·8	5·6 3·4	11·6 7·1	17·6 10·7
57	9 14·3	9 15·8	8 49·0	5·7 3·5	11·7 7·1	17·7 10·8
58	9 14·5	9 16·0	8 49·2	5·8 3·5	11·8 7·2	17·8 10·8
59	9 14·8	9 16·3	8 49·5	5·9 3·6	11·9 7·2	17·9 10·9
60	9 15·0	9 16·5	8 49·7	6·0 3·7	12·0 7·3	18·0 11·0

37ᵐ

37ᵐ s	SUN PLANETS	ARIES	MOON	v or Corrⁿ d	v or Corrⁿ d	v or Corrⁿ d
00	9 15·0	9 16·5	8 49·7	0·0 0·0	6·0 3·8	12·0 7·5
01	9 15·3	9 16·8	8 50·0	0·1 0·1	6·1 3·8	12·1 7·6
02	9 15·5	9 17·0	8 50·2	0·2 0·1	6·2 3·9	12·2 7·6
03	9 15·8	9 17·3	8 50·4	0·3 0·2	6·3 3·9	12·3 7·7
04	9 16·0	9 17·5	8 50·7	0·4 0·3	6·4 4·0	12·4 7·8
05	9 16·3	9 17·8	8 50·9	0·5 0·3	6·5 4·1	12·5 7·8
06	9 16·5	9 18·0	8 51·1	0·6 0·4	6·6 4·1	12·6 7·9
07	9 16·8	9 18·3	8 51·4	0·7 0·4	6·7 4·2	12·7 7·9
08	9 17·0	9 18·5	8 51·6	0·8 0·5	6·8 4·3	12·8 8·0
09	9 17·3	9 18·8	8 51·9	0·9 0·6	6·9 4·3	12·9 8·1
10	9 17·5	9 19·0	8 52·1	1·0 0·6	7·0 4·4	13·0 8·1
11	9 17·8	9 19·3	8 52·3	1·1 0·7	7·1 4·4	13·1 8·2
12	9 18·0	9 19·5	8 52·6	1·2 0·8	7·2 4·5	13·2 8·3
13	9 18·3	9 19·8	8 52·8	1·3 0·8	7·3 4·6	13·3 8·3
14	9 18·5	9 20·0	8 53·1	1·4 0·9	7·4 4·6	13·4 8·4
15	9 18·8	9 20·3	8 53·3	1·5 0·9	7·5 4·7	13·5 8·4
16	9 19·0	9 20·5	8 53·5	1·6 1·0	7·6 4·8	13·6 8·5
17	9 19·3	9 20·8	8 53·8	1·7 1·1	7·7 4·8	13·7 8·6
18	9 19·5	9 21·0	8 54·0	1·8 1·1	7·8 4·9	13·8 8·6
19	9 19·8	9 21·3	8 54·3	1·9 1·2	7·9 4·9	13·9 8·7
20	9 20·0	9 21·5	8 54·5	2·0 1·3	8·0 5·0	14·0 8·8
21	9 20·3	9 21·8	8 54·7	2·1 1·3	8·1 5·1	14·1 8·8
22	9 20·5	9 22·0	8 55·0	2·2 1·4	8·2 5·1	14·2 8·9
23	9 20·8	9 22·3	8 55·2	2·3 1·4	8·3 5·2	14·3 8·9
24	9 21·0	9 22·5	8 55·4	2·4 1·5	8·4 5·3	14·4 9·0
25	9 21·3	9 22·8	8 55·7	2·5 1·6	8·5 5·3	14·5 9·1
26	9 21·5	9 23·0	8 55·9	2·6 1·6	8·6 5·4	14·6 9·1
27	9 21·8	9 23·3	8 56·2	2·7 1·7	8·7 5·4	14·7 9·2
28	9 22·0	9 23·5	8 56·4	2·8 1·8	8·8 5·5	14·8 9·3
29	9 22·3	9 23·8	8 56·6	2·9 1·8	8·9 5·6	14·9 9·3
30	9 22·5	9 24·0	8 56·9	3·0 1·9	9·0 5·6	15·0 9·4
31	9 22·8	9 24·3	8 57·1	3·1 1·9	9·1 5·7	15·1 9·4
32	9 23·0	9 24·5	8 57·4	3·2 2·0	9·2 5·8	15·2 9·5
33	9 23·3	9 24·8	8 57·6	3·3 2·1	9·3 5·8	15·3 9·6
34	9 23·5	9 25·0	8 57·8	3·4 2·1	9·4 5·9	15·4 9·6
35	9 23·8	9 25·3	8 58·1	3·5 2·2	9·5 5·9	15·5 9·7
36	9 24·0	9 25·5	8 58·3	3·6 2·3	9·6 6·0	15·6 9·8
37	9 24·3	9 25·8	8 58·5	3·7 2·3	9·7 6·1	15·7 9·8
38	9 24·5	9 26·0	8 58·8	3·8 2·4	9·8 6·1	15·8 9·9
39	9 24·8	9 26·3	8 59·0	3·9 2·4	9·9 6·2	15·9 9·9
40	9 25·0	9 26·5	8 59·3	4·0 2·5	10·0 6·3	16·0 10·0
41	9 25·3	9 26·8	8 59·5	4·1 2·6	10·1 6·3	16·1 10·1
42	9 25·5	9 27·0	8 59·7	4·2 2·6	10·2 6·4	16·2 10·1
43	9 25·8	9 27·3	9 00·0	4·3 2·7	10·3 6·4	16·3 10·2
44	9 26·0	9 27·5	9 00·2	4·4 2·8	10·4 6·5	16·4 10·3
45	9 26·3	9 27·8	9 00·5	4·5 2·8	10·5 6·6	16·5 10·3
46	9 26·5	9 28·1	9 00·7	4·6 2·9	10·6 6·6	16·6 10·4
47	9 26·8	9 28·3	9 00·9	4·7 2·9	10·7 6·7	16·7 10·4
48	9 27·0	9 28·6	9 01·2	4·8 3·0	10·8 6·8	16·8 10·5
49	9 27·3	9 28·8	9 01·4	4·9 3·1	10·9 6·8	16·9 10·6
50	9 27·5	9 29·1	9 01·6	5·0 3·1	11·0 6·9	17·0 10·6
51	9 27·8	9 29·3	9 01·9	5·1 3·2	11·1 6·9	17·1 10·7
52	9 28·0	9 29·6	9 02·1	5·2 3·3	11·2 7·0	17·2 10·8
53	9 28·3	9 29·8	9 02·4	5·3 3·3	11·3 7·1	17·3 10·8
54	9 28·5	9 30·1	9 02·6	5·4 3·4	11·4 7·1	17·4 10·9
55	9 28·8	9 30·3	9 02·8	5·5 3·4	11·5 7·2	17·5 10·9
56	9 29·0	9 30·6	9 03·1	5·6 3·5	11·6 7·3	17·6 11·0
57	9 29·3	9 30·8	9 03·3	5·7 3·6	11·7 7·3	17·7 11·1
58	9 29·5	9 31·1	9 03·6	5·8 3·6	11·8 7·4	17·8 11·1
59	9 29·8	9 31·3	9 03·8	5·9 3·7	11·9 7·4	17·9 11·2
60	9 30·0	9 31·6	9 04·0	6·0 3·8	12·0 7·5	18·0 11·3

38m

s	SUN PLANETS	ARIES	MOON	v or Corrn d		v or Corrn d		v or Corrn d	
00	9 30·0	9 31·6	9 04·0	0·0	0·0	6·0	3·9	12·0	7·7
01	9 30·3	9 31·8	9 04·3	0·1	0·1	6·1	3·9	12·1	7·8
02	9 30·5	9 32·1	9 04·5	0·2	0·1	6·2	4·0	12·2	7·8
03	9 30·8	9 32·3	9 04·7	0·3	0·2	6·3	4·0	12·3	7·9
04	9 31·0	9 32·6	9 05·0	0·4	0·3	6·4	4·1	12·4	8·0
05	9 31·3	9 32·8	9 05·2	0·5	0·3	6·5	4·2	12·5	8·0
06	9 31·5	9 33·1	9 05·5	0·6	0·4	6·6	4·2	12·6	8·1
07	9 31·8	9 33·3	9 05·7	0·7	0·4	6·7	4·3	12·7	8·1
08	9 32·0	9 33·6	9 05·9	0·8	0·5	6·8	4·4	12·8	8·2
09	9 32·3	9 33·8	9 06·2	0·9	0·6	6·9	4·4	12·9	8·3
10	9 32·5	9 34·1	9 06·4	1·0	0·6	7·0	4·5	13·0	8·3
11	9 32·8	9 34·3	9 06·7	1·1	0·7	7·1	4·6	13·1	8·4
12	9 33·0	9 34·6	9 06·9	1·2	0·8	7·2	4·6	13·2	8·5
13	9 33·3	9 34·8	9 07·1	1·3	0·8	7·3	4·7	13·3	8·5
14	9 33·5	9 35·1	9 07·4	1·4	0·9	7·4	4·7	13·4	8·6
15	9 33·8	9 35·3	9 07·6	1·5	1·0	7·5	4·8	13·5	8·7
16	9 34·0	9 35·6	9 07·9	1·6	1·0	7·6	4·9	13·6	8·7
17	9 34·3	9 35·8	9 08·1	1·7	1·1	7·7	4·9	13·7	8·8
18	9 34·5	9 36·1	9 08·3	1·8	1·2	7·8	5·0	13·8	8·9
19	9 34·8	9 36·3	9 08·6	1·9	1·2	7·9	5·1	13·9	8·9
20	9 35·0	9 36·6	9 08·8	2·0	1·3	8·0	5·1	14·0	9·0
21	9 35·3	9 36·8	9 09·0	2·1	1·3	8·1	5·2	14·1	9·0
22	9 35·5	9 37·1	9 09·3	2·2	1·4	8·2	5·3	14·2	9·1
23	9 35·8	9 37·3	9 09·5	2·3	1·5	8·3	5·3	14·3	9·2
24	9 36·0	9 37·6	9 09·8	2·4	1·5	8·4	5·4	14·4	9·2
25	9 36·3	9 37·8	9 10·0	2·5	1·6	8·5	5·5	14·5	9·3
26	9 36·5	9 38·1	9 10·2	2·6	1·7	8·6	5·5	14·6	9·4
27	9 36·8	9 38·3	9 10·5	2·7	1·7	8·7	5·6	14·7	9·4
28	9 37·0	9 38·6	9 10·7	2·8	1·8	8·8	5·6	14·8	9·5
29	9 37·3	9 38·8	9 11·0	2·9	1·9	8·9	5·7	14·9	9·6
30	9 37·5	9 39·1	9 11·2	3·0	1·9	9·0	5·8	15·0	9·6
31	9 37·8	9 39·3	9 11·4	3·1	2·0	9·1	5·8	15·1	9·7
32	9 38·0	9 39·6	9 11·7	3·2	2·1	9·2	5·9	15·2	9·8
33	9 38·3	9 39·8	9 11·9	3·3	2·1	9·3	6·0	15·3	9·8
34	9 38·5	9 40·1	9 12·1	3·4	2·2	9·4	6·0	15·4	9·9
35	9 38·8	9 40·3	9 12·4	3·5	2·2	9·5	6·1	15·5	9·9
36	9 39·0	9 40·6	9 12·6	3·6	2·3	9·6	6·2	15·6	10·0
37	9 39·3	9 40·8	9 12·9	3·7	2·4	9·7	6·2	15·7	10·1
38	9 39·5	9 41·1	9 13·1	3·8	2·4	9·8	6·3	15·8	10·1
39	9 39·8	9 41·3	9 13·3	3·9	2·5	9·9	6·4	15·9	10·2
40	9 40·0	9 41·6	9 13·6	4·0	2·6	10·0	6·4	16·0	10·3
41	9 40·3	9 41·8	9 13·8	4·1	2·6	10·1	6·5	16·1	10·3
42	9 40·5	9 42·1	9 14·1	4·2	2·7	10·2	6·5	16·2	10·4
43	9 40·8	9 42·3	9 14·3	4·3	2·8	10·3	6·6	16·3	10·5
44	9 41·0	9 42·6	9 14·5	4·4	2·8	10·4	6·7	16·4	10·5
45	9 41·3	9 42·8	9 14·8	4·5	2·9	10·5	6·7	16·5	10·6
46	9 41·5	9 43·1	9 15·0	4·6	3·0	10·6	6·8	16·6	10·7
47	9 41·8	9 43·3	9 15·2	4·7	3·0	10·7	6·9	16·7	10·7
48	9 42·0	9 43·6	9 15·5	4·8	3·1	10·8	6·9	16·8	10·8
49	9 42·3	9 43·8	9 15·7	4·9	3·1	10·9	7·0	16·9	10·8
50	9 42·5	9 44·1	9 16·0	5·0	3·2	11·0	7·1	17·0	10·9
51	9 42·8	9 44·3	9 16·2	5·1	3·3	11·1	7·1	17·1	11·0
52	9 43·0	9 44·6	9 16·4	5·2	3·3	11·2	7·2	17·2	11·0
53	9 43·3	9 44·8	9 16·7	5·3	3·4	11·3	7·3	17·3	11·1
54	9 43·5	9 45·1	9 16·9	5·4	3·5	11·4	7·3	17·4	11·2
55	9 43·8	9 45·3	9 17·2	5·5	3·5	11·5	7·4	17·5	11·2
56	9 44·0	9 45·6	9 17·4	5·6	3·6	11·6	7·4	17·6	11·3
57	9 44·3	9 45·8	9 17·6	5·7	3·7	11·7	7·5	17·7	11·4
58	9 44·5	9 46·1	9 17·9	5·8	3·7	11·8	7·6	17·8	11·4
59	9 44·8	9 46·4	9 18·1	5·9	3·8	11·9	7·6	17·9	11·5
60	9 45·0	9 46·6	9 18·4	6·0	3·9	12·0	7·7	18·0	11·6

39m

s	SUN PLANETS	ARIES	MOON	v or Corrn d		v or Corrn d		v or Corrn d	
00	9 45·0	9 46·6	9 18·4	0·0	0·0	6·0	4·0	12·0	7·9
01	9 45·3	9 46·9	9 18·6	0·1	0·1	6·1	4·0	12·1	8·0
02	9 45·5	9 47·1	9 18·8	0·2	0·1	6·2	4·1	12·2	8·0
03	9 45·8	9 47·4	9 19·1	0·3	0·2	6·3	4·1	12·3	8·1
04	9 46·0	9 47·6	9 19·3	0·4	0·3	6·4	4·2	12·4	8·2
05	9 46·3	9 47·9	9 19·5	0·5	0·3	6·5	4·3	12·5	8·2
06	9 46·5	9 48·1	9 19·8	0·6	0·4	6·6	4·3	12·6	8·3
07	9 46·8	9 48·4	9 20·0	0·7	0·5	6·7	4·4	12·7	8·4
08	9 47·0	9 48·6	9 20·3	0·8	0·5	6·8	4·5	12·8	8·4
09	9 47·3	9 48·9	9 20·5	0·9	0·6	6·9	4·5	12·9	8·5
10	9 47·5	9 49·1	9 20·7	1·0	0·7	7·0	4·6	13·0	8·6
11	9 47·8	9 49·4	9 21·0	1·1	0·7	7·1	4·7	13·1	8·6
12	9 48·0	9 49·6	9 21·2	1·2	0·8	7·2	4·7	13·2	8·7
13	9 48·3	9 49·9	9 21·5	1·3	0·9	7·3	4·8	13·3	8·8
14	9 48·5	9 50·1	9 21·7	1·4	0·9	7·4	4·9	13·4	8·8
15	9 48·8	9 50·4	9 21·9	1·5	1·0	7·5	4·9	13·5	8·9
16	9 49·0	9 50·6	9 22·2	1·6	1·1	7·6	5·0	13·6	9·0
17	9 49·3	9 50·9	9 22·4	1·7	1·1	7·7	5·1	13·7	9·0
18	9 49·5	9 51·1	9 22·6	1·8	1·2	7·8	5·1	13·8	9·1
19	9 49·8	9 51·4	9 22·9	1·9	1·3	7·9	5·2	13·9	9·2
20	9 50·0	9 51·6	9 23·1	2·0	1·3	8·0	5·3	14·0	9·2
21	9 50·3	9 51·9	9 23·4	2·1	1·4	8·1	5·3	14·1	9·3
22	9 50·5	9 52·1	9 23·6	2·2	1·4	8·2	5·4	14·2	9·3
23	9 50·8	9 52·4	9 23·8	2·3	1·5	8·3	5·5	14·3	9·4
24	9 51·0	9 52·6	9 24·1	2·4	1·6	8·4	5·5	14·4	9·5
25	9 51·3	9 52·9	9 24·3	2·5	1·6	8·5	5·6	14·5	9·5
26	9 51·5	9 53·1	9 24·6	2·6	1·7	8·6	5·7	14·6	9·6
27	9 51·8	9 53·4	9 24·8	2·7	1·8	8·7	5·7	14·7	9·7
28	9 52·0	9 53·6	9 25·0	2·8	1·8	8·8	5·8	14·8	9·7
29	9 52·3	9 53·9	9 25·3	2·9	1·9	8·9	5·9	14·9	9·8
30	9 52·5	9 54·1	9 25·5	3·0	2·0	9·0	5·9	15·0	9·9
31	9 52·8	9 54·4	9 25·7	3·1	2·0	9·1	6·0	15·1	9·9
32	9 53·0	9 54·6	9 26·0	3·2	2·1	9·2	6·1	15·2	10·0
33	9 53·3	9 54·9	9 26·2	3·3	2·2	9·3	6·1	15·3	10·1
34	9 53·5	9 55·1	9 26·5	3·4	2·2	9·4	6·2	15·4	10·1
35	9 53·8	9 55·4	9 26·7	3·5	2·3	9·5	6·3	15·5	10·2
36	9 54·0	9 55·6	9 26·9	3·6	2·4	9·6	6·3	15·6	10·3
37	9 54·3	9 55·9	9 27·2	3·7	2·4	9·7	6·4	15·7	10·3
38	9 54·5	9 56·1	9 27·4	3·8	2·5	9·8	6·5	15·8	10·4
39	9 54·8	9 56·4	9 27·7	3·9	2·6	9·9	6·5	15·9	10·5
40	9 55·0	9 56·6	9 27·9	4·0	2·6	10·0	6·6	16·0	10·5
41	9 55·3	9 56·9	9 28·1	4·1	2·7	10·1	6·6	16·1	10·6
42	9 55·5	9 57·1	9 28·4	4·2	2·8	10·2	6·7	16·2	10·7
43	9 55·8	9 57·4	9 28·6	4·3	2·8	10·3	6·8	16·3	10·7
44	9 56·0	9 57·6	9 28·8	4·4	2·9	10·4	6·8	16·4	10·8
45	9 56·3	9 57·9	9 29·1	4·5	3·0	10·5	6·9	16·5	10·9
46	9 56·5	9 58·1	9 29·3	4·6	3·0	10·6	7·0	16·6	10·9
47	9 56·8	9 58·4	9 29·6	4·7	3·1	10·7	7·0	16·7	11·0
48	9 57·0	9 58·6	9 29·8	4·8	3·2	10·8	7·1	16·8	11·1
49	9 57·3	9 58·9	9 30·0	4·9	3·2	10·9	7·2	16·9	11·1
50	9 57·5	9 59·1	9 30·3	5·0	3·3	11·0	7·2	17·0	11·2
51	9 57·8	9 59·4	9 30·5	5·1	3·4	11·1	7·3	17·1	11·3
52	9 58·0	9 59·6	9 30·8	5·2	3·4	11·2	7·4	17·2	11·3
53	9 58·3	9 59·9	9 31·0	5·3	3·5	11·3	7·4	17·3	11·4
54	9 58·5	10 00·1	9 31·2	5·4	3·6	11·4	7·5	17·4	11·5
55	9 58·8	10 00·4	9 31·5	5·5	3·6	11·5	7·6	17·5	11·5
56	9 59·0	10 00·6	9 31·7	5·6	3·7	11·6	7·6	17·6	11·6
57	9 59·3	10 00·9	9 32·0	5·7	3·8	11·7	7·7	17·7	11·7
58	9 59·5	10 01·1	9 32·2	5·8	3·8	11·8	7·8	17·8	11·7
59	9 59·8	10 01·4	9 32·4	5·9	3·9	11·9	7·8	17·9	11·8
60	10 00·0	10 01·6	9 32·7	6·0	4·0	12·0	7·9	18·0	11·9

42ᵐ

42ᵐ s	SUN PLANETS ° '	ARIES ° '	MOON ° '	v or d '	Corrⁿ '	v or d '	Corrⁿ '	v or d '	Corrⁿ '
00	10 30·0	10 31·7	10 01·3	0·0	0·0	6·0	4·3	12·0	8·5
01	10 30·3	10 32·0	10 01·5	0·1	0·1	6·1	4·3	12·1	8·6
02	10 30·5	10 32·2	10 01·8	0·2	0·1	6·2	4·4	12·2	8·6
03	10 30·8	10 32·5	10 02·0	0·3	0·2	6·3	4·5	12·3	8·7
04	10 31·0	10 32·7	10 02·3	0·4	0·3	6·4	4·5	12·4	8·8
05	10 31·3	10 33·0	10 02·5	0·5	0·4	6·5	4·6	12·5	8·9
06	10 31·5	10 33·2	10 02·7	0·6	0·4	6·6	4·7	12·6	8·9
07	10 31·8	10 33·5	10 03·0	0·7	0·5	6·7	4·7	12·7	9·0
08	10 32·0	10 33·7	10 03·2	0·8	0·6	6·8	4·8	12·8	9·1
09	10 32·3	10 34·0	10 03·4	0·9	0·6	6·9	4·9	12·9	9·1
10	10 32·5	10 34·2	10 03·7	1·0	0·7	7·0	5·0	13·0	9·2
11	10 32·8	10 34·5	10 03·9	1·1	0·8	7·1	5·0	13·1	9·3
12	10 33·0	10 34·7	10 04·2	1·2	0·9	7·2	5·1	13·2	9·4
13	10 33·3	10 35·0	10 04·4	1·3	0·9	7·3	5·2	13·3	9·4
14	10 33·5	10 35·2	10 04·6	1·4	1·0	7·4	5·2	13·4	9·5
15	10 33·8	10 35·5	10 04·9	1·5	1·1	7·5	5·3	13·5	9·6
16	10 34·0	10 35·7	10 05·1	1·6	1·1	7·6	5·4	13·6	9·6
17	10 34·3	10 36·0	10 05·4	1·7	1·2	7·7	5·5	13·7	9·7
18	10 34·5	10 36·2	10 05·6	1·8	1·3	7·8	5·5	13·8	9·8
19	10 34·8	10 36·5	10 05·8	1·9	1·3	7·9	5·6	13·9	9·8
20	10 35·0	10 36·7	10 06·1	2·0	1·4	8·0	5·7	14·0	9·9
21	10 35·3	10 37·0	10 06·3	2·1	1·5	8·1	5·7	14·1	10·0
22	10 35·5	10 37·2	10 06·5	2·2	1·6	8·2	5·8	14·2	10·1
23	10 35·8	10 37·5	10 06·8	2·3	1·6	8·3	5·9	14·3	10·1
24	10 36·0	10 37·7	10 07·0	2·4	1·7	8·4	6·0	14·4	10·2
25	10 36·3	10 38·0	10 07·3	2·5	1·8	8·5	6·0	14·5	10·3
26	10 36·5	10 38·2	10 07·5	2·6	1·8	8·6	6·1	14·6	10·3
27	10 36·8	10 38·5	10 07·7	2·7	1·9	8·7	6·2	14·7	10·4
28	10 37·0	10 38·7	10 08·0	2·8	2·0	8·8	6·2	14·8	10·5
29	10 37·3	10 39·0	10 08·2	2·9	2·1	8·9	6·3	14·9	10·6
30	10 37·5	10 39·2	10 08·5	3·0	2·1	9·0	6·4	15·0	10·6
31	10 37·8	10 39·5	10 08·7	3·1	2·2	9·1	6·4	15·1	10·7
32	10 38·0	10 39·7	10 08·9	3·2	2·3	9·2	6·5	15·2	10·8
33	10 38·3	10 40·0	10 09·2	3·3	2·3	9·3	6·6	15·3	10·8
34	10 38·5	10 40·2	10 09·4	3·4	2·4	9·4	6·7	15·4	10·9
35	10 38·8	10 40·5	10 09·7	3·5	2·5	9·5	6·7	15·5	11·0
36	10 39·0	10 40·7	10 09·9	3·6	2·6	9·6	6·8	15·6	11·1
37	10 39·3	10 41·0	10 10·1	3·7	2·6	9·7	6·9	15·7	11·1
38	10 39·5	10 41·3	10 10·4	3·8	2·7	9·8	6·9	15·8	11·2
39	10 39·8	10 41·5	10 10·6	3·9	2·8	9·9	7·0	15·9	11·3
40	10 40·0	10 41·8	10 10·8	4·0	2·8	10·0	7·1	16·0	11·3
41	10 40·3	10 42·0	10 11·1	4·1	2·9	10·1	7·2	16·1	11·4
42	10 40·5	10 42·3	10 11·3	4·2	3·0	10·2	7·2	16·2	11·5
43	10 40·8	10 42·5	10 11·6	4·3	3·0	10·3	7·3	16·3	11·5
44	10 41·0	10 42·8	10 11·8	4·4	3·1	10·4	7·4	16·4	11·6
45	10 41·3	10 43·0	10 12·0	4·5	3·2	10·5	7·4	16·5	11·7
46	10 41·5	10 43·3	10 12·3	4·6	3·3	10·6	7·5	16·6	11·8
47	10 41·8	10 43·5	10 12·5	4·7	3·3	10·7	7·6	16·7	11·8
48	10 42·0	10 43·8	10 12·8	4·8	3·4	10·8	7·7	16·8	11·9
49	10 42·3	10 44·0	10 13·0	4·9	3·5	10·9	7·7	16·9	12·0
50	10 42·5	10 44·3	10 13·2	5·0	3·5	11·0	7·8	17·0	12·0
51	10 42·8	10 44·5	10 13·5	5·1	3·6	11·1	7·9	17·1	12·1
52	10 43·0	10 44·8	10 13·7	5·2	3·7	11·2	7·9	17·2	12·2
53	10 43·3	10 45·0	10 13·9	5·3	3·8	11·3	8·0	17·3	12·3
54	10 43·5	10 45·3	10 14·2	5·4	3·8	11·4	8·1	17·4	12·3
55	10 43·8	10 45·5	10 14·4	5·5	3·9	11·5	8·1	17·5	12·4
56	10 44·0	10 45·8	10 14·7	5·6	4·0	11·6	8·2	17·6	12·5
57	10 44·3	10 46·0	10 14·9	5·7	4·0	11·7	8·3	17·7	12·5
58	10 44·5	10 46·3	10 15·1	5·8	4·1	11·8	8·4	17·8	12·6
59	10 44·8	10 46·5	10 15·4	5·9	4·2	11·9	8·4	17·9	12·7
60	10 45·0	10 46·8	10 15·6	6·0	4·3	12·0	8·5	18·0	12·8

43ᵐ

43ᵐ s	SUN PLANETS ° '	ARIES ° '	MOON ° '	v or d '	Corrⁿ '	v or d '	Corrⁿ '	v or d '	Corrⁿ '
00	10 45·0	10 46·8	10 15·6	0·0	0·0	6·0	4·4	12·0	8·7
01	10 45·3	10 47·0	10 15·9	0·1	0·1	6·1	4·4	12·1	8·8
02	10 45·5	10 47·3	10 16·1	0·2	0·1	6·2	4·5	12·2	8·8
03	10 45·8	10 47·5	10 16·3	0·3	0·2	6·3	4·6	12·3	8·9
04	10 46·0	10 47·8	10 16·6	0·4	0·3	6·4	4·6	12·4	9·0
05	10 46·3	10 48·0	10 16·8	0·5	0·4	6·5	4·7	12·5	9·1
06	10 46·5	10 48·3	10 17·0	0·6	0·4	6·6	4·8	12·6	9·1
07	10 46·8	10 48·5	10 17·3	0·7	0·5	6·7	4·9	12·7	9·2
08	10 47·0	10 48·8	10 17·5	0·8	0·6	6·8	4·9	12·8	9·3
09	10 47·3	10 49·0	10 17·8	0·9	0·7	6·9	5·0	12·9	9·4
10	10 47·5	10 49·3	10 18·0	1·0	0·7	7·0	5·1	13·0	9·4
11	10 47·8	10 49·5	10 18·2	1·1	0·8	7·1	5·1	13·1	9·5
12	10 48·0	10 49·8	10 18·5	1·2	0·9	7·2	5·2	13·2	9·6
13	10 48·3	10 50·0	10 18·7	1·3	0·9	7·3	5·3	13·3	9·6
14	10 48·5	10 50·3	10 19·0	1·4	1·0	7·4	5·4	13·4	9·7
15	10 48·8	10 50·5	10 19·2	1·5	1·1	7·5	5·4	13·5	9·8
16	10 49·0	10 50·8	10 19·4	1·6	1·2	7·6	5·5	13·6	9·9
17	10 49·3	10 51·0	10 19·7	1·7	1·2	7·7	5·6	13·7	9·9
18	10 49·5	10 51·3	10 19·9	1·8	1·3	7·8	5·7	13·8	10·0
19	10 49·8	10 51·5	10 20·2	1·9	1·4	7·9	5·7	13·9	10·1
20	10 50·0	10 51·8	10 20·4	2·0	1·5	8·0	5·8	14·0	10·2
21	10 50·3	10 52·0	10 20·6	2·1	1·5	8·1	5·9	14·1	10·2
22	10 50·5	10 52·3	10 20·9	2·2	1·6	8·2	5·9	14·2	10·3
23	10 50·8	10 52·5	10 21·1	2·3	1·7	8·3	6·0	14·3	10·4
24	10 51·0	10 52·8	10 21·3	2·4	1·7	8·4	6·1	14·4	10·4
25	10 51·3	10 53·0	10 21·6	2·5	1·8	8·5	6·2	14·5	10·5
26	10 51·5	10 53·3	10 21·8	2·6	1·9	8·6	6·2	14·6	10·6
27	10 51·8	10 53·5	10 22·1	2·7	2·0	8·7	6·3	14·7	10·7
28	10 52·0	10 53·8	10 22·3	2·8	2·0	8·8	6·4	14·8	10·7
29	10 52·3	10 54·0	10 22·5	2·9	2·1	8·9	6·5	14·9	10·8
30	10 52·5	10 54·3	10 22·8	3·0	2·2	9·0	6·5	15·0	10·9
31	10 52·8	10 54·5	10 23·0	3·1	2·2	9·1	6·6	15·1	10·9
32	10 53·0	10 54·8	10 23·3	3·2	2·3	9·2	6·7	15·2	11·0
33	10 53·3	10 55·0	10 23·5	3·3	2·4	9·3	6·7	15·3	11·1
34	10 53·5	10 55·3	10 23·7	3·4	2·5	9·4	6·8	15·4	11·2
35	10 53·8	10 55·5	10 24·0	3·5	2·5	9·5	6·9	15·5	11·2
36	10 54·0	10 55·8	10 24·2	3·6	2·6	9·6	7·0	15·6	11·3
37	10 54·3	10 56·0	10 24·4	3·7	2·7	9·7	7·0	15·7	11·4
38	10 54·5	10 56·3	10 24·7	3·8	2·8	9·8	7·1	15·8	11·5
39	10 54·8	10 56·5	10 24·9	3·9	2·8	9·9	7·2	15·9	11·5
40	10 55·0	10 56·8	10 25·2	4·0	2·9	10·0	7·3	16·0	11·6
41	10 55·3	10 57·0	10 25·4	4·1	3·0	10·1	7·3	16·1	11·7
42	10 55·5	10 57·3	10 25·6	4·2	3·0	10·2	7·4	16·2	11·7
43	10 55·8	10 57·5	10 25·9	4·3	3·1	10·3	7·5	16·3	11·8
44	10 56·0	10 57·8	10 26·1	4·4	3·2	10·4	7·5	16·4	11·9
45	10 56·3	10 58·0	10 26·4	4·5	3·3	10·5	7·6	16·5	12·0
46	10 56·5	10 58·3	10 26·6	4·6	3·3	10·6	7·7	16·6	12·0
47	10 56·8	10 58·5	10 26·8	4·7	3·4	10·7	7·8	16·7	12·1
48	10 57·0	10 58·8	10 27·1	4·8	3·5	10·8	7·8	16·8	12·2
49	10 57·3	10 59·0	10 27·3	4·9	3·6	10·9	7·9	16·9	12·3
50	10 57·5	10 59·3	10 27·5	5·0	3·6	11·0	8·0	17·0	12·3
51	10 57·8	10 59·6	10 27·8	5·1	3·7	11·1	8·0	17·1	12·4
52	10 58·0	10 59·8	10 28·0	5·2	3·8	11·2	8·1	17·2	12·5
53	10 58·3	11 00·1	10 28·3	5·3	3·8	11·3	8·2	17·3	12·5
54	10 58·5	11 00·3	10 28·5	5·4	3·9	11·4	8·3	17·4	12·6
55	10 58·8	11 00·6	10 28·7	5·5	4·0	11·5	8·3	17·5	12·7
56	10 59·0	11 00·8	10 29·0	5·6	4·1	11·6	8·4	17·6	12·8
57	10 59·3	11 01·1	10 29·2	5·7	4·1	11·7	8·5	17·7	12·8
58	10 59·5	11 01·3	10 29·5	5·8	4·2	11·8	8·6	17·8	12·9
59	10 59·8	11 01·6	10 29·7	5·9	4·3	11·9	8·6	17·9	13·0
60	11 00·0	11 01·8	10 29·9	6·0	4·4	12·0	8·7	18·0	13·1

44ᵐ

44ᵐ	SUN PLANETS	ARIES	MOON	v or Corrⁿ d	v or Corrⁿ d	v or Corrⁿ d
s	° ′	° ′	° ′	′ ′	′ ′	′ ′
00	11 00.0	11 01.8	10 29.9	0.0 0.0	6.0 4.5	12.0 8.9
01	11 00.3	11 02.1	10 30.2	0.1 0.1	6.1 4.5	12.1 9.0
02	11 00.5	11 02.3	10 30.4	0.2 0.1	6.2 4.6	12.2 9.0
03	11 00.8	11 02.6	10 30.6	0.3 0.2	6.3 4.7	12.3 9.1
04	11 01.0	11 02.8	10 30.9	0.4 0.3	6.4 4.7	12.4 9.2
05	11 01.3	11 03.1	10 31.1	0.5 0.4	6.5 4.8	12.5 9.3
06	11 01.5	11 03.3	10 31.4	0.6 0.4	6.6 4.9	12.6 9.3
07	11 01.8	11 03.6	10 31.6	0.7 0.5	6.7 5.0	12.7 9.4
08	11 02.0	11 03.8	10 31.8	0.8 0.6	6.8 5.0	12.8 9.5
09	11 02.3	11 04.1	10 32.1	0.9 0.7	6.9 5.1	12.9 9.6
10	11 02.5	11 04.3	10 32.3	1.0 0.7	7.0 5.2	13.0 9.6
11	11 02.8	11 04.6	10 32.6	1.1 0.8	7.1 5.3	13.1 9.7
12	11 03.0	11 04.8	10 32.8	1.2 0.9	7.2 5.3	13.2 9.8
13	11 03.3	11 05.1	10 33.0	1.3 1.0	7.3 5.4	13.3 9.9
14	11 03.5	11 05.3	10 33.3	1.4 1.0	7.4 5.5	13.4 9.9
15	11 03.8	11 05.6	10 33.5	1.5 1.1	7.5 5.6	13.5 10.0
16	11 04.0	11 05.8	10 33.8	1.6 1.2	7.6 5.6	13.6 10.1
17	11 04.3	11 06.1	10 34.0	1.7 1.3	7.7 5.7	13.7 10.2
18	11 04.5	11 06.3	10 34.2	1.8 1.3	7.8 5.8	13.8 10.2
19	11 04.8	11 06.6	10 34.5	1.9 1.4	7.9 5.9	13.9 10.3
20	11 05.0	11 06.8	10 34.7	2.0 1.5	8.0 5.9	14.0 10.4
21	11 05.3	11 07.1	10 34.9	2.1 1.6	8.1 6.0	14.1 10.5
22	11 05.5	11 07.3	10 35.2	2.2 1.6	8.2 6.1	14.2 10.5
23	11 05.8	11 07.6	10 35.4	2.3 1.7	8.3 6.2	14.3 10.6
24	11 06.0	11 07.8	10 35.7	2.4 1.8	8.4 6.2	14.4 10.7
25	11 06.3	11 08.1	10 35.9	2.5 1.9	8.5 6.3	14.5 10.8
26	11 06.5	11 08.3	10 36.1	2.6 1.9	8.6 6.4	14.6 10.8
27	11 06.8	11 08.6	10 36.4	2.7 2.0	8.7 6.5	14.7 10.9
28	11 07.0	11 08.8	10 36.6	2.8 2.1	8.8 6.5	14.8 11.0
29	11 07.3	11 09.1	10 36.9	2.9 2.2	8.9 6.6	14.9 11.1
30	11 07.5	11 09.3	10 37.1	3.0 2.2	9.0 6.7	15.0 11.1
31	11 07.8	11 09.6	10 37.3	3.1 2.3	9.1 6.7	15.1 11.2
32	11 08.0	11 09.8	10 37.6	3.2 2.4	9.2 6.8	15.2 11.3
33	11 08.3	11 10.1	10 37.8	3.3 2.4	9.3 6.9	15.3 11.3
34	11 08.5	11 10.3	10 38.0	3.4 2.5	9.4 7.0	15.4 11.4
35	11 08.8	11 10.6	10 38.3	3.5 2.6	9.5 7.0	15.5 11.5
36	11 09.0	11 10.8	10 38.5	3.6 2.7	9.6 7.1	15.6 11.6
37	11 09.3	11 11.1	10 38.8	3.7 2.7	9.7 7.2	15.7 11.6
38	11 09.5	11 11.3	10 39.0	3.8 2.8	9.8 7.3	15.8 11.7
39	11 09.8	11 11.6	10 39.2	3.9 2.9	9.9 7.3	15.9 11.8
40	11 10.0	11 11.8	10 39.5	4.0 3.0	10.0 7.4	16.0 11.9
41	11 10.3	11 12.1	10 39.7	4.1 3.0	10.1 7.5	16.1 11.9
42	11 10.5	11 12.3	10 40.0	4.2 3.1	10.2 7.6	16.2 12.0
43	11 10.8	11 12.6	10 40.2	4.3 3.2	10.3 7.6	16.3 12.1
44	11 11.0	11 12.8	10 40.4	4.4 3.3	10.4 7.7	16.4 12.2
45	11 11.3	11 13.1	10 40.7	4.5 3.3	10.5 7.8	16.5 12.2
46	11 11.5	11 13.3	10 40.9	4.6 3.4	10.6 7.9	16.6 12.3
47	11 11.8	11 13.6	10 41.1	4.7 3.5	10.7 7.9	16.7 12.4
48	11 12.0	11 13.8	10 41.4	4.8 3.6	10.8 8.0	16.8 12.5
49	11 12.3	11 14.1	10 41.6	4.9 3.6	10.9 8.1	16.9 12.5
50	11 12.5	11 14.3	10 41.9	5.0 3.7	11.0 8.2	17.0 12.6
51	11 12.8	11 14.6	10 42.1	5.1 3.8	11.1 8.2	17.1 12.7
52	11 13.0	11 14.8	10 42.3	5.2 3.9	11.2 8.3	17.2 12.8
53	11 13.3	11 15.1	10 42.6	5.3 3.9	11.3 8.4	17.3 12.8
54	11 13.5	11 15.3	10 42.8	5.4 4.0	11.4 8.5	17.4 12.9
55	11 13.8	11 15.6	10 43.1	5.5 4.1	11.5 8.5	17.5 13.0
56	11 14.0	11 15.8	10 43.3	5.6 4.2	11.6 8.6	17.6 13.1
57	11 14.3	11 16.1	10 43.5	5.7 4.2	11.7 8.7	17.7 13.1
58	11 14.5	11 16.3	10 43.8	5.8 4.3	11.8 8.8	17.8 13.2
59	11 14.8	11 16.6	10 44.0	5.9 4.4	11.9 8.8	17.9 13.3
60	11 15.0	11 16.8	10 44.3	6.0 4.5	12.0 8.9	18.0 13.4

45ᵐ

45ᵐ	SUN PLANETS	ARIES	MOON	v or Corrⁿ d	v or Corrⁿ d	v or Corrⁿ d
s	° ′	° ′	° ′	′ ′	′ ′	′ ′
00	11 15.0	11 16.8	10 44.3	0.0 0.0	6.0 4.6	12.0 9.1
01	11 15.3	11 17.1	10 44.5	0.1 0.1	6.1 4.6	12.1 9.2
02	11 15.5	11 17.3	10 44.7	0.2 0.2	6.2 4.7	12.2 9.3
03	11 15.8	11 17.6	10 45.0	0.3 0.2	6.3 4.8	12.3 9.3
04	11 16.0	11 17.9	10 45.2	0.4 0.3	6.4 4.9	12.4 9.4
05	11 16.3	11 18.1	10 45.4	0.5 0.4	6.5 4.9	12.5 9.5
06	11 16.5	11 18.4	10 45.7	0.6 0.5	6.6 5.0	12.6 9.6
07	11 16.8	11 18.6	10 45.9	0.7 0.5	6.7 5.1	12.7 9.6
08	11 17.0	11 18.9	10 46.2	0.8 0.6	6.8 5.2	12.8 9.7
09	11 17.3	11 19.1	10 46.4	0.9 0.7	6.9 5.2	12.9 9.8
10	11 17.5	11 19.4	10 46.6	1.0 0.8	7.0 5.3	13.0 9.9
11	11 17.8	11 19.6	10 46.9	1.1 0.8	7.1 5.4	13.1 9.9
12	11 18.0	11 19.9	10 47.1	1.2 0.9	7.2 5.5	13.2 10.0
13	11 18.3	11 20.1	10 47.4	1.3 1.0	7.3 5.5	13.3 10.1
14	11 18.5	11 20.4	10 47.6	1.4 1.1	7.4 5.6	13.4 10.2
15	11 18.8	11 20.6	10 47.8	1.5 1.1	7.5 5.7	13.5 10.2
16	11 19.0	11 20.9	10 48.1	1.6 1.2	7.6 5.8	13.6 10.3
17	11 19.3	11 21.1	10 48.3	1.7 1.3	7.7 5.8	13.7 10.4
18	11 19.5	11 21.4	10 48.5	1.8 1.4	7.8 5.9	13.8 10.5
19	11 19.8	11 21.6	10 48.8	1.9 1.4	7.9 6.0	13.9 10.5
20	11 20.0	11 21.9	10 49.0	2.0 1.5	8.0 6.1	14.0 10.6
21	11 20.3	11 22.1	10 49.3	2.1 1.6	8.1 6.1	14.1 10.7
22	11 20.5	11 22.4	10 49.5	2.2 1.7	8.2 6.2	14.2 10.8
23	11 20.8	11 22.6	10 49.7	2.3 1.7	8.3 6.3	14.3 10.8
24	11 21.0	11 22.9	10 50.0	2.4 1.8	8.4 6.4	14.4 10.9
25	11 21.3	11 23.1	10 50.2	2.5 1.9	8.5 6.4	14.5 11.0
26	11 21.5	11 23.4	10 50.5	2.6 2.0	8.6 6.5	14.6 11.1
27	11 21.8	11 23.6	10 50.7	2.7 2.0	8.7 6.6	14.7 11.1
28	11 22.0	11 23.9	10 51.0	2.8 2.1	8.8 6.7	14.8 11.2
29	11 22.3	11 24.1	10 51.2	2.9 2.2	8.9 6.7	14.9 11.3
30	11 22.5	11 24.4	10 51.4	3.0 2.3	9.0 6.8	15.0 11.4
31	11 22.8	11 24.6	10 51.6	3.1 2.4	9.1 6.9	15.1 11.5
32	11 23.0	11 24.9	10 51.9	3.2 2.4	9.2 7.0	15.2 11.5
33	11 23.3	11 25.1	10 52.1	3.3 2.5	9.3 7.1	15.3 11.6
34	11 23.5	11 25.4	10 52.4	3.4 2.6	9.4 7.1	15.4 11.7
35	11 23.8	11 25.6	10 52.6	3.5 2.7	9.5 7.2	15.5 11.8
36	11 24.0	11 25.9	10 52.8	3.6 2.7	9.6 7.3	15.6 11.8
37	11 24.3	11 26.1	10 53.1	3.7 2.8	9.7 7.4	15.7 11.9
38	11 24.5	11 26.4	10 53.3	3.8 2.9	9.8 7.4	15.8 12.0
39	11 24.8	11 26.6	10 53.6	3.9 3.0	9.9 7.5	15.9 12.1
40	11 25.0	11 26.9	10 53.8	4.0 3.0	10.0 7.6	16.0 12.1
41	11 25.3	11 27.1	10 54.0	4.1 3.1	10.1 7.7	16.1 12.2
42	11 25.5	11 27.4	10 54.3	4.2 3.2	10.2 7.7	16.2 12.3
43	11 25.8	11 27.6	10 54.5	4.3 3.3	10.3 7.8	16.3 12.4
44	11 26.0	11 27.9	10 54.7	4.4 3.3	10.4 7.9	16.4 12.4
45	11 26.3	11 28.1	10 55.0	4.5 3.4	10.5 8.0	16.5 12.5
46	11 26.5	11 28.4	10 55.2	4.6 3.5	10.6 8.0	16.6 12.6
47	11 26.8	11 28.6	10 55.5	4.7 3.6	10.7 8.1	16.7 12.7
48	11 27.0	11 28.9	10 55.7	4.8 3.6	10.8 8.2	16.8 12.7
49	11 27.3	11 29.1	10 55.9	4.9 3.7	10.9 8.3	16.9 12.8
50	11 27.5	11 29.4	10 56.2	5.0 3.8	11.0 8.3	17.0 12.9
51	11 27.8	11 29.6	10 56.4	5.1 3.9	11.1 8.4	17.1 13.0
52	11 28.0	11 29.9	10 56.7	5.2 3.9	11.2 8.5	17.2 13.0
53	11 28.3	11 30.1	10 56.9	5.3 4.0	11.3 8.6	17.3 13.1
54	11 28.5	11 30.4	10 57.1	5.4 4.1	11.4 8.6	17.4 13.2
55	11 28.8	11 30.6	10 57.4	5.5 4.2	11.5 8.7	17.5 13.3
56	11 29.0	11 30.9	10 57.6	5.6 4.2	11.6 8.8	17.6 13.3
57	11 29.3	11 31.1	10 57.9	5.7 4.3	11.7 8.9	17.7 13.4
58	11 29.5	11 31.4	10 58.1	5.8 4.4	11.8 8.9	17.8 13.5
59	11 29.8	11 31.6	10 58.3	5.9 4.5	11.9 9.0	17.9 13.6
60	11 30.0	11 31.9	10 58.6	6.0 4.6	12.0 9.1	18.0 13.7

46ᵐ	SUN PLANETS	ARIES	MOON	v or d	Corrⁿ	v or d	Corrⁿ	v or d	Corrⁿ
s	° ′	° ′	° ′	′	′	′	′	′	′
00	11 30·0	11 31·9	10 58·6	0·0	0·0	6·0	4·7	12·0	9·3
01	11 30·3	11 32·1	10 58·8	0·1	0·1	6·1	4·7	12·1	9·4
02	11 30·5	11 32·4	10 59·0	0·2	0·2	6·2	4·8	12·2	9·5
03	11 30·8	11 32·6	10 59·3	0·3	0·2	6·3	4·9	12·3	9·5
04	11 31·0	11 32·9	10 59·5	0·4	0·3	6·4	5·0	12·4	9·6
05	11 31·3	11 33·1	10 59·8	0·5	0·4	6·5	5·0	12·5	9·7
06	11 31·5	11 33·4	11 00·0	0·6	0·5	6·6	5·1	12·6	9·8
07	11 31·8	11 33·6	11 00·2	0·7	0·5	6·7	5·2	12·7	9·8
08	11 32·0	11 33·9	11 00·5	0·8	0·6	6·8	5·3	12·8	9·9
09	11 32·3	11 34·1	11 00·7	0·9	0·7	6·9	5·3	12·9	10·0
10	11 32·5	11 34·4	11 01·0	1·0	0·8	7·0	5·4	13·0	10·1
11	11 32·8	11 34·6	11 01·2	1·1	0·9	7·1	5·5	13·1	10·2
12	11 33·0	11 34·9	11 01·4	1·2	0·9	7·2	5·6	13·2	10·2
13	11 33·3	11 35·1	11 01·7	1·3	1·0	7·3	5·7	13·3	10·3
14	11 33·5	11 35·4	11 01·9	1·4	1·1	7·4	5·7	13·4	10·4
15	11 33·8	11 35·6	11 02·1	1·5	1·2	7·5	5·8	13·5	10·5
16	11 34·0	11 35·9	11 02·4	1·6	1·2	7·6	5·9	13·6	10·5
17	11 34·3	11 36·2	11 02·6	1·7	1·3	7·7	6·0	13·7	10·6
18	11 34·5	11 36·4	11 02·9	1·8	1·4	7·8	6·0	13·8	10·7
19	11 34·8	11 36·7	11 03·1	1·9	1·5	7·9	6·1	13·9	10·8
20	11 35·0	11 36·9	11 03·3	2·0	1·6	8·0	6·2	14·0	10·9
21	11 35·3	11 37·2	11 03·6	2·1	1·6	8·1	6·3	14·1	10·9
22	11 35·5	11 37·4	11 03·8	2·2	1·7	8·2	6·4	14·2	11·0
23	11 35·8	11 37·7	11 04·1	2·3	1·8	8·3	6·4	14·3	11·1
24	11 36·0	11 37·9	11 04·3	2·4	1·9	8·4	6·5	14·4	11·2
25	11 36·3	11 38·2	11 04·5	2·5	1·9	8·5	6·6	14·5	11·2
26	11 36·5	11 38·4	11 04·8	2·6	2·0	8·6	6·7	14·6	11·3
27	11 36·8	11 38·7	11 05·0	2·7	2·1	8·7	6·7	14·7	11·4
28	11 37·0	11 38·9	11 05·2	2·8	2·2	8·8	6·8	14·8	11·5
29	11 37·3	11 39·2	11 05·5	2·9	2·2	8·9	6·9	14·9	11·5
30	11 37·5	11 39·4	11 05·7	3·0	2·3	9·0	7·0	15·0	11·6
31	11 37·8	11 39·7	11 06·0	3·1	2·4	9·1	7·1	15·1	11·7
32	11 38·0	11 39·9	11 06·2	3·2	2·5	9·2	7·1	15·2	11·8
33	11 38·3	11 40·2	11 06·4	3·3	2·6	9·3	7·2	15·3	11·9
34	11 38·5	11 40·4	11 06·7	3·4	2·6	9·4	7·3	15·4	11·9
35	11 38·8	11 40·7	11 06·9	3·5	2·7	9·5	7·4	15·5	12·0
36	11 39·0	11 40·9	11 07·2	3·6	2·8	9·6	7·4	15·6	12·1
37	11 39·3	11 41·2	11 07·4	3·7	2·9	9·7	7·5	15·7	12·2
38	11 39·5	11 41·4	11 07·6	3·8	2·9	9·8	7·6	15·8	12·2
39	11 39·8	11 41·7	11 07·9	3·9	3·0	9·9	7·7	15·9	12·3
40	11 40·0	11 41·9	11 08·1	4·0	3·1	10·0	7·8	16·0	12·4
41	11 40·3	11 42·2	11 08·3	4·1	3·2	10·1	7·8	16·1	12·5
42	11 40·5	11 42·4	11 08·6	4·2	3·3	10·2	7·9	16·2	12·6
43	11 40·8	11 42·7	11 08·8	4·3	3·3	10·3	8·0	16·3	12·6
44	11 41·0	11 42·9	11 09·1	4·4	3·4	10·4	8·1	16·4	12·7
45	11 41·3	11 43·2	11 09·3	4·5	3·5	10·5	8·1	16·5	12·8
46	11 41·5	11 43·4	11 09·5	4·6	3·6	10·6	8·2	16·6	12·9
47	11 41·8	11 43·7	11 09·8	4·7	3·6	10·7	8·3	16·7	12·9
48	11 42·0	11 43·9	11 10·0	4·8	3·7	10·8	8·4	16·8	13·0
49	11 42·3	11 44·2	11 10·3	4·9	3·8	10·9	8·4	16·9	13·1
50	11 42·5	11 44·4	11 10·5	5·0	3·9	11·0	8·5	17·0	13·2
51	11 42·8	11 44·7	11 10·7	5·1	4·0	11·1	8·6	17·1	13·3
52	11 43·0	11 44·9	11 11·0	5·2	4·0	11·2	8·7	17·2	13·3
53	11 43·3	11 45·2	11 11·2	5·3	4·1	11·3	8·8	17·3	13·4
54	11 43·5	11 45·4	11 11·5	5·4	4·2	11·4	8·8	17·4	13·5
55	11 43·8	11 45·7	11 11·7	5·5	4·3	11·5	8·9	17·5	13·6
56	11 44·0	11 45·9	11 11·9	5·6	4·3	11·6	9·0	17·6	13·6
57	11 44·3	11 46·2	11 12·2	5·7	4·4	11·7	9·1	17·7	13·7
58	11 44·5	11 46·4	11 12·4	5·8	4·5	11·8	9·1	17·8	13·8
59	11 44·8	11 46·7	11 12·6	5·9	4·6	11·9	9·2	17·9	13·9
60	11 45·0	11 46·9	11 12·9	6·0	4·7	12·0	9·3	18·0	14·0

47ᵐ	SUN PLANETS	ARIES	MOON	v or d	Corrⁿ	v or d	Corrⁿ	v or d	Corrⁿ
s	° ′	° ′	° ′	′	′	′	′	′	′
00	11 45·0	11 46·9	11 12·9	0·0	0·0	6·0	4·8	12·0	9·5
01	11 45·3	11 47·2	11 13·1	0·1	0·1	6·1	4·8	12·1	9·6
02	11 45·5	11 47·4	11 13·4	0·2	0·2	6·2	4·9	12·2	9·7
03	11 45·8	11 47·7	11 13·6	0·3	0·2	6·3	5·0	12·3	9·7
04	11 46·0	11 47·9	11 13·8	0·4	0·3	6·4	5·1	12·4	9·8
05	11 46·3	11 48·2	11 14·1	0·5	0·4	6·5	5·1	12·5	9·9
06	11 46·5	11 48·4	11 14·3	0·6	0·5	6·6	5·2	12·6	10·0
07	11 46·8	11 48·7	11 14·6	0·7	0·6	6·7	5·3	12·7	10·1
08	11 47·0	11 48·9	11 14·8	0·8	0·6	6·8	5·4	12·8	10·1
09	11 47·3	11 49·2	11 15·0	0·9	0·7	6·9	5·5	12·9	10·2
10	11 47·5	11 49·4	11 15·3	1·0	0·8	7·0	5·5	13·0	10·3
11	11 47·8	11 49·7	11 15·5	1·1	0·9	7·1	5·6	13·1	10·4
12	11 48·0	11 49·9	11 15·7	1·2	1·0	7·2	5·7	13·2	10·5
13	11 48·3	11 50·2	11 16·0	1·3	1·0	7·3	5·8	13·3	10·5
14	11 48·5	11 50·4	11 16·2	1·4	1·1	7·4	5·9	13·4	10·6
15	11 48·8	11 50·7	11 16·5	1·5	1·2	7·5	5·9	13·5	10·7
16	11 49·0	11 50·9	11 16·7	1·6	1·3	7·6	6·0	13·6	10·8
17	11 49·3	11 51·2	11 16·9	1·7	1·3	7·7	6·1	13·7	10·8
18	11 49·5	11 51·4	11 17·2	1·8	1·4	7·8	6·2	13·8	10·9
19	11 49·8	11 51·7	11 17·4	1·9	1·5	7·9	6·3	13·9	11·0
20	11 50·0	11 51·9	11 17·7	2·0	1·6	8·0	6·3	14·0	11·1
21	11 50·3	11 52·2	11 17·9	2·1	1·7	8·1	6·4	14·1	11·2
22	11 50·5	11 52·4	11 18·1	2·2	1·7	8·2	6·5	14·2	11·2
23	11 50·8	11 52·7	11 18·4	2·3	1·8	8·3	6·6	14·3	11·3
24	11 51·0	11 52·9	11 18·6	2·4	1·9	8·4	6·7	14·4	11·4
25	11 51·3	11 53·2	11 18·8	2·5	2·0	8·5	6·7	14·5	11·5
26	11 51·5	11 53·4	11 19·1	2·6	2·1	8·6	6·8	14·6	11·6
27	11 51·8	11 53·7	11 19·3	2·7	2·1	8·7	6·9	14·7	11·6
28	11 52·0	11 53·9	11 19·6	2·8	2·2	8·8	7·0	14·8	11·7
29	11 52·3	11 54·2	11 19·8	2·9	2·3	8·9	7·0	14·9	11·8
30	11 52·5	11 54·5	11 20·0	3·0	2·4	9·0	7·1	15·0	11·9
31	11 52·8	11 54·7	11 20·3	3·1	2·5	9·1	7·2	15·1	12·0
32	11 53·0	11 55·0	11 20·5	3·2	2·5	9·2	7·3	15·2	12·0
33	11 53·3	11 55·2	11 20·8	3·3	2·6	9·3	7·4	15·3	12·1
34	11 53·5	11 55·5	11 21·0	3·4	2·7	9·4	7·4	15·4	12·2
35	11 53·8	11 55·7	11 21·2	3·5	2·8	9·5	7·5	15·5	12·3
36	11 54·0	11 56·0	11 21·5	3·6	2·9	9·6	7·6	15·6	12·4
37	11 54·3	11 56·2	11 21·7	3·7	2·9	9·7	7·7	15·7	12·4
38	11 54·5	11 56·5	11 22·0	3·8	3·0	9·8	7·8	15·8	12·5
39	11 54·8	11 56·7	11 22·2	3·9	3·1	9·9	7·8	15·9	12·6
40	11 55·0	11 57·0	11 22·4	4·0	3·2	10·0	7·9	16·0	12·7
41	11 55·3	11 57·2	11 22·7	4·1	3·2	10·1	8·0	16·1	12·7
42	11 55·5	11 57·5	11 22·9	4·2	3·3	10·2	8·1	16·2	12·8
43	11 55·8	11 57·7	11 23·1	4·3	3·4	10·3	8·2	16·3	12·9
44	11 56·0	11 58·0	11 23·4	4·4	3·5	10·4	8·2	16·4	13·0
45	11 56·3	11 58·2	11 23·6	4·5	3·6	10·5	8·3	16·5	13·1
46	11 56·5	11 58·5	11 23·9	4·6	3·6	10·6	8·4	16·6	13·1
47	11 56·8	11 58·7	11 24·1	4·7	3·7	10·7	8·5	16·7	13·2
48	11 57·0	11 59·0	11 24·3	4·8	3·8	10·8	8·6	16·8	13·3
49	11 57·3	11 59·2	11 24·6	4·9	3·9	10·9	8·6	16·9	13·4
50	11 57·5	11 59·5	11 24·8	5·0	4·0	11·0	8·7	17·0	13·5
51	11 57·8	11 59·7	11 25·1	5·1	4·0	11·1	8·8	17·1	13·5
52	11 58·0	12 00·0	11 25·3	5·2	4·1	11·2	8·9	17·2	13·6
53	11 58·3	12 00·2	11 25·5	5·3	4·2	11·3	8·9	17·3	13·7
54	11 58·5	12 00·5	11 25·8	5·4	4·3	11·4	9·0	17·4	13·8
55	11 58·8	12 00·7	11 26·0	5·5	4·4	11·5	9·1	17·5	13·9
56	11 59·0	12 01·0	11 26·2	5·6	4·4	11·6	9·2	17·6	13·9
57	11 59·3	12 01·2	11 26·5	5·7	4·5	11·7	9·3	17·7	14·0
58	11 59·5	12 01·5	11 26·7	5·8	4·6	11·8	9·3	17·8	14·1
59	11 59·8	12 01·7	11 27·0	5·9	4·7	11·9	9·4	17·9	14·2
60	12 00·0	12 02·0	11 27·2	6·0	4·8	12·0	9·5	18·0	14·3

48ᵐ

48ᵐ s	SUN PLANETS	ARIES	MOON	v or d	Corrⁿ	v or d	Corrⁿ	v or d	Corrⁿ
00	12 00·0	12 02·0	11 27·2	0·0	0·0	6·0	4·9	12·0	9·7
01	12 00·3	12 02·2	11 27·4	0·1	0·1	6·1	4·9	12·1	9·8
02	12 00·5	12 02·5	11 27·7	0·2	0·2	6·2	5·0	12·2	9·9
03	12 00·8	12 02·7	11 27·9	0·3	0·2	6·3	5·1	12·3	9·9
04	12 01·0	12 03·0	11 28·2	0·4	0·3	6·4	5·2	12·4	10·0
05	12 01·3	12 03·2	11 28·4	0·5	0·4	6·5	5·3	12·5	10·1
06	12 01·5	12 03·5	11 28·6	0·6	0·5	6·6	5·3	12·6	10·2
07	12 01·8	12 03·7	11 28·9	0·7	0·6	6·7	5·4	12·7	10·3
08	12 02·0	12 04·0	11 29·1	0·8	0·6	6·8	5·5	12·8	10·3
09	12 02·3	12 04·2	11 29·3	0·9	0·7	6·9	5·6	12·9	10·4
10	12 02·5	12 04·5	11 29·6	1·0	0·8	7·0	5·7	13·0	10·5
11	12 02·8	12 04·7	11 29·8	1·1	0·9	7·1	5·7	13·1	10·6
12	12 03·0	12 05·0	11 30·1	1·2	1·0	7·2	5·8	13·2	10·7
13	12 03·3	12 05·2	11 30·3	1·3	1·1	7·3	5·9	13·3	10·8
14	12 03·5	12 05·5	11 30·5	1·4	1·1	7·4	6·0	13·4	10·8
15	12 03·8	12 05·7	11 30·8	1·5	1·2	7·5	6·1	13·5	10·9
16	12 04·0	12 06·0	11 31·0	1·6	1·3	7·6	6·1	13·6	11·0
17	12 04·3	12 06·2	11 31·3	1·7	1·4	7·7	6·2	13·7	11·1
18	12 04·5	12 06·5	11 31·5	1·8	1·5	7·8	6·3	13·8	11·2
19	12 04·8	12 06·7	11 31·7	1·9	1·5	7·9	6·4	13·9	11·2
20	12 05·0	12 07·0	11 32·0	2·0	1·6	8·0	6·5	14·0	11·3
21	12 05·3	12 07·2	11 32·2	2·1	1·7	8·1	6·5	14·1	11·4
22	12 05·5	12 07·5	11 32·4	2·2	1·8	8·2	6·6	14·2	11·5
23	12 05·8	12 07·7	11 32·7	2·3	1·9	8·3	6·7	14·3	11·6
24	12 06·0	12 08·0	11 32·9	2·4	1·9	8·4	6·8	14·4	11·6
25	12 06·3	12 08·2	11 33·2	2·5	2·0	8·5	6·9	14·5	11·7
26	12 06·5	12 08·5	11 33·4	2·6	2·1	8·6	7·0	14·6	11·8
27	12 06·8	12 08·7	11 33·6	2·7	2·2	8·7	7·0	14·7	11·9
28	12 07·0	12 09·0	11 33·9	2·8	2·3	8·8	7·1	14·8	12·0
29	12 07·3	12 09·2	11 34·1	2·9	2·3	8·9	7·2	14·9	12·0
30	12 07·5	12 09·5	11 34·4	3·0	2·4	9·0	7·3	15·0	12·1
31	12 07·8	12 09·7	11 34·6	3·1	2·5	9·1	7·4	15·1	12·2
32	12 08·0	12 10·0	11 34·8	3·2	2·6	9·2	7·4	15·2	12·3
33	12 08·3	12 10·2	11 35·1	3·3	2·7	9·3	7·5	15·3	12·4
34	12 08·5	12 10·5	11 35·3	3·4	2·7	9·4	7·6	15·4	12·4
35	12 08·8	12 10·7	11 35·6	3·5	2·8	9·5	7·7	15·5	12·5
36	12 09·0	12 11·0	11 35·8	3·6	2·9	9·6	7·8	15·6	12·6
37	12 09·3	12 11·2	11 36·0	3·7	3·0	9·7	7·8	15·7	12·7
38	12 09·5	12 11·5	11 36·3	3·8	3·1	9·8	7·9	15·8	12·8
39	12 09·8	12 11·7	11 36·5	3·9	3·2	9·9	8·0	15·9	12·9
40	12 10·0	12 12·0	11 36·7	4·0	3·2	10·0	8·1	16·0	12·9
41	12 10·3	12 12·2	11 37·0	4·1	3·3	10·1	8·2	16·1	13·0
42	12 10·5	12 12·5	11 37·2	4·2	3·4	10·2	8·2	16·2	13·1
43	12 10·8	12 12·8	11 37·5	4·3	3·5	10·3	8·3	16·3	13·2
44	12 11·0	12 13·0	11 37·7	4·4	3·6	10·4	8·4	16·4	13·3
45	12 11·3	12 13·3	11 37·9	4·5	3·6	10·5	8·5	16·5	13·3
46	12 11·5	12 13·5	11 38·2	4·6	3·7	10·6	8·6	16·6	13·4
47	12 11·8	12 13·8	11 38·4	4·7	3·8	10·7	8·6	16·7	13·5
48	12 12·0	12 14·0	11 38·7	4·8	3·9	10·8	8·7	16·8	13·6
49	12 12·3	12 14·3	11 38·9	4·9	4·0	10·9	8·8	16·9	13·7
50	12 12·5	12 14·5	11 39·1	5·0	4·0	11·0	8·9	17·0	13·7
51	12 12·8	12 14·8	11 39·4	5·1	4·1	11·1	9·0	17·1	13·8
52	12 13·0	12 15·0	11 39·6	5·2	4·2	11·2	9·1	17·2	13·9
53	12 13·3	12 15·3	11 39·8	5·3	4·3	11·3	9·1	17·3	14·0
54	12 13·5	12 15·5	11 40·1	5·4	4·4	11·4	9·2	17·4	14·1
55	12 13·8	12 15·8	11 40·3	5·5	4·4	11·5	9·3	17·5	14·1
56	12 14·0	12 16·0	11 40·6	5·6	4·5	11·6	9·4	17·6	14·2
57	12 14·3	12 16·3	11 40·8	5·7	4·6	11·7	9·5	17·7	14·3
58	12 14·5	12 16·5	11 41·0	5·8	4·7	11·8	9·5	17·8	14·4
59	12 14·8	12 16·8	11 41·3	5·9	4·8	11·9	9·6	17·9	14·5
60	12 15·0	12 17·0	11 41·5	6·0	4·9	12·0	9·7	18·0	14·6

49ᵐ

49ᵐ s	SUN PLANETS	ARIES	MOON	v or d	Corrⁿ	v or d	Corrⁿ	v or d	Corrⁿ
00	12 15·0	12 17·0	11 41·5	0·0	0·0	6·0	5·0	12·0	9·9
01	12 15·3	12 17·3	11 41·8	0·1	0·1	6·1	5·0	12·1	10·0
02	12 15·5	12 17·5	11 42·0	0·2	0·2	6·2	5·1	12·2	10·1
03	12 15·8	12 17·8	11 42·2	0·3	0·2	6·3	5·2	12·3	10·1
04	12 16·0	12 18·0	11 42·5	0·4	0·3	6·4	5·3	12·4	10·2
05	12 16·3	12 18·3	11 42·7	0·5	0·4	6·5	5·4	12·5	10·3
06	12 16·5	12 18·5	11 42·9	0·6	0·5	6·6	5·4	12·6	10·5
07	12 16·8	12 18·8	11 43·2	0·7	0·6	6·7	5·5	12·7	10·5
08	12 17·0	12 19·0	11 43·4	0·8	0·7	6·8	5·6	12·8	10·6
09	12 17·3	12 19·3	11 43·7	0·9	0·7	6·9	5·7	12·9	10·6
10	12 17·5	12 19·5	11 43·9	1·0	0·8	7·0	5·8	13·0	10·7
11	12 17·8	12 19·8	11 44·1	1·1	0·9	7·1	5·9	13·1	10·8
12	12 18·0	12 20·0	11 44·4	1·2	1·0	7·2	5·9	13·2	10·9
13	12 18·3	12 20·3	11 44·6	1·3	1·1	7·3	6·0	13·3	11·0
14	12 18·5	12 20·5	11 44·9	1·4	1·2	7·4	6·1	13·4	11·1
15	12 18·8	12 20·8	11 45·1	1·5	1·2	7·5	6·2	13·5	11·1
16	12 19·0	12 21·0	11 45·3	1·6	1·3	7·6	6·3	13·6	11·2
17	12 19·3	12 21·3	11 45·6	1·7	1·4	7·7	6·4	13·7	11·3
18	12 19·5	12 21·5	11 45·8	1·8	1·5	7·8	6·4	13·8	11·4
19	12 19·8	12 21·8	11 46·1	1·9	1·6	7·9	6·5	13·9	11·5
20	12 20·0	12 22·0	11 46·3	2·0	1·7	8·0	6·6	14·0	11·6
21	12 20·3	12 22·3	11 46·5	2·1	1·7	8·1	6·7	14·1	11·6
22	12 20·5	12 22·5	11 46·8	2·2	1·8	8·2	6·8	14·2	11·7
23	12 20·8	12 22·8	11 47·0	2·3	1·9	8·3	6·8	14·3	11·8
24	12 21·0	12 23·0	11 47·2	2·4	2·0	8·4	6·9	14·4	11·9
25	12 21·3	12 23·3	11 47·5	2·5	2·1	8·5	7·0	14·5	12·0
26	12 21·5	12 23·5	11 47·7	2·6	2·1	8·6	7·1	14·6	12·0
27	12 21·8	12 23·8	11 48·0	2·7	2·2	8·7	7·2	14·7	12·1
28	12 22·0	12 24·0	11 48·2	2·8	2·3	8·8	7·3	14·8	12·2
29	12 22·3	12 24·3	11 48·4	2·9	2·4	8·9	7·3	14·9	12·3
30	12 22·5	12 24·5	11 48·7	3·0	2·5	9·0	7·4	15·0	12·4
31	12 22·8	12 24·8	11 48·9	3·1	2·6	9·1	7·5	15·1	12·5
32	12 23·0	12 25·0	11 49·2	3·2	2·6	9·2	7·6	15·2	12·5
33	12 23·3	12 25·3	11 49·4	3·3	2·7	9·3	7·7	15·3	12·6
34	12 23·5	12 25·5	11 49·6	3·4	2·8	9·4	7·8	15·4	12·7
35	12 23·8	12 25·8	11 49·9	3·5	2·9	9·5	7·8	15·5	12·8
36	12 24·0	12 26·0	11 50·1	3·6	3·0	9·6	7·9	15·6	12·9
37	12 24·3	12 26·3	11 50·3	3·7	3·1	9·7	8·0	15·7	13·0
38	12 24·5	12 26·5	11 50·6	3·8	3·1	9·8	8·1	15·8	13·0
39	12 24·8	12 26·8	11 50·8	3·9	3·2	9·9	8·2	15·9	13·1
40	12 25·0	12 27·0	11 51·1	4·0	3·3	10·0	8·3	16·0	13·2
41	12 25·3	12 27·3	11 51·3	4·1	3·4	10·1	8·3	16·1	13·3
42	12 25·5	12 27·5	11 51·5	4·2	3·5	10·2	8·4	16·2	13·4
43	12 25·8	12 27·8	11 51·8	4·3	3·5	10·3	8·5	16·3	13·4
44	12 26·0	12 28·0	11 52·0	4·4	3·6	10·4	8·6	16·4	13·5
45	12 26·3	12 28·3	11 52·3	4·5	3·7	10·5	8·7	16·5	13·6
46	12 26·5	12 28·5	11 52·5	4·6	3·8	10·6	8·7	16·6	13·7
47	12 26·8	12 28·8	11 52·7	4·7	3·9	10·7	8·8	16·7	13·8
48	12 27·0	12 29·0	11 53·0	4·8	4·0	10·8	8·9	16·8	13·9
49	12 27·3	12 29·3	11 53·2	4·9	4·0	10·9	9·0	16·9	13·9
50	12 27·5	12 29·5	11 53·4	5·0	4·1	11·0	9·1	17·0	14·0
51	12 27·8	12 29·8	11 53·7	5·1	4·2	11·1	9·2	17·1	14·1
52	12 28·0	12 30·0	11 53·9	5·2	4·3	11·2	9·2	17·2	14·2
53	12 28·3	12 30·3	11 54·2	5·3	4·4	11·3	9·3	17·3	14·3
54	12 28·5	12 30·5	11 54·4	5·4	4·5	11·4	9·4	17·4	14·4
55	12 28·8	12 30·8	11 54·6	5·5	4·5	11·5	9·5	17·5	14·4
56	12 29·0	12 31·1	11 54·9	5·6	4·6	11·6	9·6	17·6	14·5
57	12 29·3	12 31·3	11 55·1	5·7	4·7	11·7	9·7	17·7	14·6
58	12 29·5	12 31·6	11 55·3	5·8	4·8	11·8	9·7	17·8	14·7
59	12 29·8	12 31·8	11 55·6	5·9	4·9	11·9	9·8	17·9	14·8
60	12 30·0	12 32·1	11 55·8	6·0	5·0	12·0	9·9	18·0	14·9

50ᵐ

50ᵐ s	SUN PLANETS ° ′	ARIES ° ′	MOON ° ′	v or d Corrⁿ ′ ′	v or d Corrⁿ ′ ′	v or d Corrⁿ ′ ′
00	12 30·0	12 32·1	11 55·8	0·0 0·0	6·0 5·1	12·0 10·1
01	12 30·3	12 32·3	11 56·1	0·1 0·1	6·1 5·1	12·1 10·2
02	12 30·5	12 32·6	11 56·3	0·2 0·2	6·2 5·2	12·2 10·3
03	12 30·8	12 32·8	11 56·5	0·3 0·3	6·3 5·3	12·3 10·4
04	12 31·0	12 33·1	11 56·8	0·4 0·3	6·4 5·4	12·4 10·4
05	12 31·3	12 33·3	11 57·0	0·5 0·4	6·5 5·5	12·5 10·5
06	12 31·5	12 33·6	11 57·3	0·6 0·5	6·6 5·6	12·6 10·6
07	12 31·8	12 33·8	11 57·5	0·7 0·6	6·7 5·6	12·7 10·7
08	12 32·0	12 34·1	11 57·7	0·8 0·7	6·8 5·7	12·8 10·8
09	12 32·3	12 34·3	11 58·0	0·9 0·8	6·9 5·8	12·9 10·9
10	12 32·5	12 34·6	11 58·2	1·0 0·8	7·0 5·9	13·0 10·9
11	12 32·8	12 34·8	11 58·5	1·1 0·9	7·1 6·0	13·1 11·0
12	12 33·0	12 35·1	11 58·7	1·2 1·0	7·2 6·1	13·2 11·1
13	12 33·3	12 35·3	11 59·0	1·3 1·1	7·3 6·1	13·3 11·2
14	12 33·5	12 35·6	11 59·2	1·4 1·2	7·4 6·2	13·4 11·3
15	12 33·8	12 35·8	11 59·4	1·5 1·3	7·5 6·3	13·5 11·4
16	12 34·0	12 36·1	11 59·7	1·6 1·3	7·6 6·4	13·6 11·4
17	12 34·3	12 36·3	11 59·9	1·7 1·4	7·7 6·5	13·7 11·5
18	12 34·5	12 36·6	12 00·1	1·8 1·5	7·8 6·6	13·8 11·6
19	12 34·8	12 36·8	12 00·4	1·9 1·6	7·9 6·6	13·9 11·7
20	12 35·0	12 37·1	12 00·6	2·0 1·7	8·0 6·7	14·0 11·8
21	12 35·3	12 37·3	12 00·8	2·1 1·8	8·1 6·8	14·1 11·9
22	12 35·5	12 37·6	12 01·1	2·2 1·9	8·2 6·9	14·2 12·0
23	12 35·8	12 37·8	12 01·3	2·3 1·9	8·3 7·0	14·3 12·0
24	12 36·0	12 38·1	12 01·6	2·4 2·0	8·4 7·1	14·4 12·1
25	12 36·3	12 38·3	12 01·8	2·5 2·1	8·5 7·2	14·5 12·2
26	12 36·5	12 38·6	12 02·0	2·6 2·2	8·6 7·2	14·6 12·3
27	12 36·8	12 38·8	12 02·3	2·7 2·3	8·7 7·3	14·7 12·4
28	12 37·0	12 39·1	12 02·5	2·8 2·4	8·8 7·4	14·8 12·5
29	12 37·3	12 39·3	12 02·8	2·9 2·4	8·9 7·5	14·9 12·5
30	12 37·5	12 39·6	12 03·0	3·0 2·5	9·0 7·6	15·0 12·6
31	12 37·8	12 39·8	12 03·2	3·1 2·6	9·1 7·7	15·1 12·7
32	12 38·0	12 40·1	12 03·5	3·2 2·7	9·2 7·7	15·2 12·8
33	12 38·3	12 40·3	12 03·7	3·3 2·8	9·3 7·8	15·3 12·9
34	12 38·5	12 40·6	12 03·9	3·4 2·9	9·4 7·9	15·4 13·0
35	12 38·8	12 40·8	12 04·2	3·5 2·9	9·5 8·0	15·5 13·0
36	12 39·0	12 41·1	12 04·4	3·6 3·0	9·6 8·1	15·6 13·1
37	12 39·3	12 41·3	12 04·7	3·7 3·1	9·7 8·2	15·7 13·2
38	12 39·5	12 41·6	12 04·9	3·8 3·2	9·8 8·2	15·8 13·3
39	12 39·8	12 41·8	12 05·1	3·9 3·3	9·9 8·3	15·9 13·4
40	12 40·0	12 42·1	12 05·4	4·0 3·4	10·0 8·4	16·0 13·5
41	12 40·3	12 42·3	12 05·6	4·1 3·5	10·1 8·5	16·1 13·6
42	12 40·5	12 42·6	12 05·9	4·2 3·5	10·2 8·6	16·2 13·6
43	12 40·8	12 42·8	12 06·1	4·3 3·6	10·3 8·7	16·3 13·7
44	12 41·0	12 43·1	12 06·3	4·4 3·7	10·4 8·8	16·4 13·8
45	12 41·3	12 43·3	12 06·6	4·5 3·8	10·5 8·8	16·5 13·9
46	12 41·5	12 43·6	12 06·8	4·6 3·9	10·6 8·9	16·6 14·0
47	12 41·8	12 43·8	12 07·0	4·7 4·0	10·7 9·0	16·7 14·1
48	12 42·0	12 44·1	12 07·3	4·8 4·0	10·8 9·1	16·8 14·1
49	12 42·3	12 44·3	12 07·5	4·9 4·1	10·9 9·2	16·9 14·2
50	12 42·5	12 44·6	12 07·8	5·0 4·2	11·0 9·3	17·0 14·3
51	12 42·8	12 44·8	12 08·0	5·1 4·3	11·1 9·3	17·1 14·4
52	12 43·0	12 45·1	12 08·2	5·2 4·4	11·2 9·4	17·2 14·5
53	12 43·3	12 45·3	12 08·5	5·3 4·5	11·3 9·5	17·3 14·6
54	12 43·5	12 45·6	12 08·7	5·4 4·5	11·4 9·6	17·4 14·6
55	12 43·8	12 45·8	12 09·0	5·5 4·6	11·5 9·7	17·5 14·7
56	12 44·0	12 46·1	12 09·2	5·6 4·7	11·6 9·8	17·6 14·8
57	12 44·3	12 46·3	12 09·4	5·7 4·8	11·7 9·8	17·7 14·9
58	12 44·5	12 46·6	12 09·7	5·8 4·9	11·8 9·9	17·8 15·0
59	12 44·8	12 46·8	12 09·9	5·9 5·0	11·9 10·0	17·9 15·1
60	12 45·0	12 47·1	12 10·2	6·0 5·1	12·0 10·1	18·0 15·2

51ᵐ

51ᵐ s	SUN PLANETS ° ′	ARIES ° ′	MOON ° ′	v or d Corrⁿ ′ ′	v or d Corrⁿ ′ ′	v or d Corrⁿ ′ ′
00	12 45·0	12 47·1	12 10·2	0·0 0·0	6·0 5·2	12·0 10·3
01	12 45·3	12 47·3	12 10·4	0·1 0·1	6·1 5·2	12·1 10·4
02	12 45·5	12 47·6	12 10·6	0·2 0·2	6·2 5·3	12·2 10·5
03	12 45·8	12 47·8	12 10·9	0·3 0·3	6·3 5·4	12·3 10·6
04	12 46·0	12 48·1	12 11·1	0·4 0·3	6·4 5·5	12·4 10·6
05	12 46·3	12 48·3	12 11·3	0·5 0·4	6·5 5·6	12·5 10·7
06	12 46·5	12 48·6	12 11·6	0·6 0·5	6·6 5·7	12·6 10·8
07	12 46·8	12 48·8	12 11·8	0·7 0·6	6·7 5·8	12·7 10·9
08	12 47·0	12 49·1	12 12·1	0·8 0·7	6·8 5·8	12·8 11·0
09	12 47·3	12 49·4	12 12·3	0·9 0·8	6·9 5·9	12·9 11·1
10	12 47·5	12 49·6	12 12·5	1·0 0·9	7·0 6·0	13·0 11·2
11	12 47·8	12 49·9	12 12·8	1·1 0·9	7·1 6·1	13·1 11·2
12	12 48·0	12 50·1	12 13·0	1·2 1·0	7·2 6·2	13·2 11·3
13	12 48·3	12 50·4	12 13·3	1·3 1·1	7·3 6·3	13·3 11·4
14	12 48·5	12 50·6	12 13·5	1·4 1·2	7·4 6·3	13·4 11·5
15	12 48·8	12 50·9	12 13·7	1·5 1·3	7·5 6·4	13·5 11·6
16	12 49·0	12 51·1	12 14·0	1·6 1·4	7·6 6·5	13·6 11·7
17	12 49·3	12 51·4	12 14·2	1·7 1·5	7·7 6·6	13·7 11·8
18	12 49·5	12 51·6	12 14·4	1·8 1·5	7·8 6·7	13·8 11·8
19	12 49·8	12 51·9	12 14·7	1·9 1·6	7·9 6·8	13·9 11·9
20	12 50·0	12 52·1	12 14·9	2·0 1·7	8·0 6·9	14·0 12·0
21	12 50·3	12 52·4	12 15·2	2·1 1·8	8·1 7·0	14·1 12·1
22	12 50·5	12 52·6	12 15·4	2·2 1·9	8·2 7·0	14·2 12·2
23	12 50·8	12 52·9	12 15·6	2·3 2·0	8·3 7·1	14·3 12·3
24	12 51·0	12 53·1	12 15·9	2·4 2·1	8·4 7·2	14·4 12·4
25	12 51·3	12 53·4	12 16·1	2·5 2·1	8·5 7·3	14·5 12·4
26	12 51·5	12 53·6	12 16·4	2·6 2·2	8·6 7·4	14·6 12·5
27	12 51·8	12 53·9	12 16·6	2·7 2·3	8·7 7·5	14·7 12·6
28	12 52·0	12 54·1	12 16·8	2·8 2·4	8·8 7·6	14·8 12·7
29	12 52·3	12 54·4	12 17·1	2·9 2·5	8·9 7·6	14·9 12·8
30	12 52·5	12 54·6	12 17·3	3·0 2·6	9·0 7·7	15·0 12·9
31	12 52·8	12 54·9	12 17·5	3·1 2·7	9·1 7·8	15·1 13·0
32	12 53·0	12 55·1	12 17·8	3·2 2·7	9·2 7·9	15·2 13·0
33	12 53·3	12 55·4	12 18·0	3·3 2·8	9·3 8·0	15·3 13·1
34	12 53·5	12 55·6	12 18·3	3·4 2·9	9·4 8·1	15·4 13·2
35	12 53·8	12 55·9	12 18·5	3·5 3·0	9·5 8·2	15·5 13·3
36	12 54·0	12 56·1	12 18·7	3·6 3·1	9·6 8·2	15·6 13·4
37	12 54·3	12 56·4	12 19·0	3·7 3·2	9·7 8·3	15·7 13·5
38	12 54·5	12 56·6	12 19·2	3·8 3·3	9·8 8·4	15·8 13·6
39	12 54·8	12 56·9	12 19·5	3·9 3·3	9·9 8·5	15·9 13·6
40	12 55·0	12 57·1	12 19·7	4·0 3·4	10·0 8·6	16·0 13·7
41	12 55·3	12 57·4	12 19·9	4·1 3·5	10·1 8·7	16·1 13·8
42	12 55·5	12 57·6	12 20·2	4·2 3·6	10·2 8·8	16·2 13·9
43	12 55·8	12 57·9	12 20·4	4·3 3·7	10·3 8·8	16·3 14·0
44	12 56·0	12 58·1	12 20·6	4·4 3·8	10·4 8·9	16·4 14·1
45	12 56·3	12 58·4	12 20·9	4·5 3·9	10·5 9·0	16·5 14·2
46	12 56·5	12 58·6	12 21·1	4·6 3·9	10·6 9·1	16·6 14·2
47	12 56·8	12 58·9	12 21·4	4·7 4·0	10·7 9·2	16·7 14·3
48	12 57·0	12 59·1	12 21·6	4·8 4·1	10·8 9·3	16·8 14·4
49	12 57·3	12 59·4	12 21·8	4·9 4·2	10·9 9·4	16·9 14·5
50	12 57·5	12 59·6	12 22·1	5·0 4·3	11·0 9·4	17·0 14·6
51	12 57·8	12 59·9	12 22·3	5·1 4·4	11·1 9·5	17·1 14·7
52	12 58·0	13 00·1	12 22·6	5·2 4·5	11·2 9·6	17·2 14·8
53	12 58·3	13 00·4	12 22·8	5·3 4·5	11·3 9·7	17·3 14·8
54	12 58·5	13 00·6	12 23·0	5·4 4·6	11·4 9·8	17·4 14·9
55	12 58·8	13 00·9	12 23·3	5·5 4·7	11·5 9·9	17·5 15·0
56	12 59·0	13 01·1	12 23·5	5·6 4·8	11·6 10·0	17·6 15·1
57	12 59·3	13 01·4	12 23·8	5·7 4·9	11·7 10·0	17·7 15·2
58	12 59·5	13 01·6	12 24·0	5·8 5·0	11·8 10·1	17·8 15·3
59	12 59·8	13 01·9	12 24·2	5·9 5·1	11·9 10·2	17·9 15·4
60	13 00·0	13 02·1	12 24·5	6·0 5·2	12·0 10·3	18·0 15·5

52ᵐ

52ᵐ s	SUN PLANETS ° ′	ARIES ° ′	MOON ° ′	v or d ′	Corrⁿ ′	v or d ′	Corrⁿ ′	v or d ′	Corrⁿ ′
00	13 00·0	13 02·1	12 24·5	0·0	0·0	6·0	5·3	12·0	10·5
01	13 00·3	13 02·4	12 24·7	0·1	0·1	6·1	5·3	12·1	10·6
02	13 00·5	13 02·6	12 24·9	0·2	0·2	6·2	5·4	12·2	10·7
03	13 00·8	13 02·9	12 25·2	0·3	0·3	6·3	5·5	12·3	10·8
04	13 01·0	13 03·1	12 25·4	0·4	0·4	6·4	5·6	12·4	10·9
05	13 01·3	13 03·4	12 25·7	0·5	0·4	6·5	5·7	12·5	10·9
06	13 01·5	13 03·6	12 25·9	0·6	0·5	6·6	5·8	12·6	11·0
07	13 01·8	13 03·9	12 26·1	0·7	0·6	6·7	5·9	12·7	11·1
08	13 02·0	13 04·1	12 26·4	0·8	0·7	6·8	6·0	12·8	11·2
09	13 02·3	13 04·4	12 26·6	0·9	0·8	6·9	6·0	12·9	11·3
10	13 02·5	13 04·6	12 26·9	1·0	0·9	7·0	6·1	13·0	11·4
11	13 02·8	13 04·9	12 27·1	1·1	1·0	7·1	6·2	13·1	11·5
12	13 03·0	13 05·1	12 27·3	1·2	1·1	7·2	6·3	13·2	11·6
13	13 03·3	13 05·4	12 27·6	1·3	1·1	7·3	6·4	13·3	11·6
14	13 03·5	13 05·6	12 27·8	1·4	1·2	7·4	6·5	13·4	11·7
15	13 03·8	13 05·9	12 28·0	1·5	1·3	7·5	6·6	13·5	11·8
16	13 04·0	13 06·1	12 28·3	1·6	1·4	7·6	6·7	13·6	11·9
17	13 04·3	13 06·4	12 28·5	1·7	1·5	7·7	6·7	13·7	12·0
18	13 04·5	13 06·6	12 28·8	1·8	1·6	7·8	6·8	13·8	12·1
19	13 04·8	13 06·9	12 29·0	1·9	1·7	7·9	6·9	13·9	12·2
20	13 05·0	13 07·1	12 29·2	2·0	1·8	8·0	7·0	14·0	12·3
21	13 05·3	13 07·4	12 29·5	2·1	1·8	8·1	7·1	14·1	12·3
22	13 05·5	13 07·7	12 29·7	2·2	1·9	8·2	7·2	14·2	12·4
23	13 05·8	13 07·9	12 30·0	2·3	2·0	8·3	7·3	14·3	12·5
24	13 06·0	13 08·2	12 30·2	2·4	2·1	8·4	7·4	14·4	12·6
25	13 06·3	13 08·4	12 30·4	2·5	2·2	8·5	7·4	14·5	12·7
26	13 06·5	13 08·7	12 30·7	2·6	2·3	8·6	7·5	14·6	12·8
27	13 06·8	13 08·9	12 30·9	2·7	2·4	8·7	7·6	14·7	12·9
28	13 07·0	13 09·2	12 31·1	2·8	2·5	8·8	7·7	14·8	13·0
29	13 07·3	13 09·4	12 31·4	2·9	2·5	8·9	7·8	14·9	13·0
30	13 07·5	13 09·7	12 31·6	3·0	2·6	9·0	7·9	15·0	13·1
31	13 07·8	13 09·9	12 31·9	3·1	2·7	9·1	8·0	15·1	13·2
32	13 08·0	13 10·2	12 32·1	3·2	2·8	9·2	8·1	15·2	13·3
33	13 08·3	13 10·4	12 32·3	3·3	2·9	9·3	8·1	15·3	13·4
34	13 08·5	13 10·7	12 32·6	3·4	3·0	9·4	8·2	15·4	13·5
35	13 08·8	13 10·9	12 32·8	3·5	3·1	9·5	8·3	15·5	13·6
36	13 09·0	13 11·2	12 33·1	3·6	3·2	9·6	8·4	15·6	13·7
37	13 09·3	13 11·4	12 33·3	3·7	3·2	9·7	8·5	15·7	13·7
38	13 09·5	13 11·7	12 33·5	3·8	3·3	9·8	8·6	15·8	13·8
39	13 09·8	13 11·9	12 33·8	3·9	3·4	9·9	8·7	15·9	13·9
40	13 10·0	13 12·2	12 34·0	4·0	3·5	10·0	8·8	16·0	14·0
41	13 10·3	13 12·4	12 34·2	4·1	3·6	10·1	8·8	16·1	14·1
42	13 10·5	13 12·7	12 34·5	4·2	3·7	10·2	8·9	16·2	14·2
43	13 10·8	13 12·9	12 34·7	4·3	3·8	10·3	9·0	16·3	14·3
44	13 11·0	13 13·2	12 35·0	4·4	3·9	10·4	9·1	16·4	14·4
45	13 11·3	13 13·4	12 35·2	4·5	3·9	10·5	9·2	16·5	14·4
46	13 11·5	13 13·7	12 35·4	4·6	4·0	10·6	9·3	16·6	14·5
47	13 11·8	13 13·9	12 35·7	4·7	4·1	10·7	9·4	16·7	14·6
48	13 12·0	13 14·2	12 35·9	4·8	4·2	10·8	9·5	16·8	14·7
49	13 12·3	13 14·4	12 36·2	4·9	4·3	10·9	9·5	16·9	14·8
50	13 12·5	13 14·7	12 36·4	5·0	4·4	11·0	9·6	17·0	14·9
51	13 12·8	13 14·9	12 36·6	5·1	4·5	11·1	9·7	17·1	15·0
52	13 13·0	13 15·2	12 36·9	5·2	4·6	11·2	9·8	17·2	15·1
53	13 13·3	13 15·4	12 37·1	5·3	4·6	11·3	9·9	17·3	15·1
54	13 13·5	13 15·7	12 37·4	5·4	4·7	11·4	10·0	17·4	15·2
55	13 13·8	13 15·9	12 37·6	5·5	4·8	11·5	10·1	17·5	15·3
56	13 14·0	13 16·2	12 37·8	5·6	4·9	11·6	10·2	17·6	15·4
57	13 14·3	13 16·4	12 38·1	5·7	5·0	11·7	10·2	17·7	15·5
58	13 14·5	13 16·7	12 38·3	5·8	5·1	11·8	10·3	17·8	15·6
59	13 14·8	13 16·9	12 38·5	5·9	5·2	11·9	10·4	17·9	15·7
60	13 15·0	13 17·2	12 38·8	6·0	5·3	12·0	10·5	18·0	15·8

53ᵐ

53ᵐ s	SUN PLANETS ° ′	ARIES ° ′	MOON ° ′	v or d ′	Corrⁿ ′	v or d ′	Corrⁿ ′	v or d ′	Corrⁿ ′
00	13 15·0	13 17·2	12 38·8	0·0	0·0	6·0	5·4	12·0	10·7
01	13 15·3	13 17·4	12 39·0	0·1	0·1	6·1	5·4	12·1	10·8
02	13 15·5	13 17·7	12 39·3	0·2	0·2	6·2	5·5	12·2	10·9
03	13 15·8	13 17·9	12 39·5	0·3	0·3	6·3	5·6	12·3	11·0
04	13 16·0	13 18·2	12 39·7	0·4	0·4	6·4	5·7	12·4	11·1
05	13 16·3	13 18·4	12 40·0	0·5	0·4	6·5	5·8	12·5	11·1
06	13 16·5	13 18·7	12 40·2	0·6	0·5	6·6	5·9	12·6	11·2
07	13 16·8	13 18·9	12 40·5	0·7	0·6	6·7	6·0	12·7	11·3
08	13 17·0	13 19·2	12 40·7	0·8	0·7	6·8	6·1	12·8	11·4
09	13 17·3	13 19·4	12 40·9	0·9	0·8	6·9	6·2	12·9	11·5
10	13 17·5	13 19·7	12 41·2	1·0	0·9	7·0	6·2	13·0	11·6
11	13 17·8	13 19·9	12 41·4	1·1	1·0	7·1	6·3	13·1	11·7
12	13 18·0	13 20·2	12 41·6	1·2	1·1	7·2	6·4	13·2	11·8
13	13 18·3	13 20·4	12 41·9	1·3	1·2	7·3	6·5	13·3	11·9
14	13 18·5	13 20·7	12 42·1	1·4	1·2	7·4	6·6	13·4	11·9
15	13 18·8	13 20·9	12 42·4	1·5	1·3	7·5	6·7	13·5	12·0
16	13 19·0	13 21·2	12 42·6	1·6	1·4	7·6	6·8	13·6	12·1
17	13 19·3	13 21·4	12 42·8	1·7	1·5	7·7	6·9	13·7	12·2
18	13 19·5	13 21·7	12 43·1	1·8	1·6	7·8	7·0	13·8	12·3
19	13 19·8	13 21·9	12 43·3	1·9	1·7	7·9	7·0	13·9	12·4
20	13 20·0	13 22·2	12 43·6	2·0	1·8	8·0	7·1	14·0	12·5
21	13 20·3	13 22·4	12 43·8	2·1	1·9	8·1	7·2	14·1	12·6
22	13 20·5	13 22·7	12 44·0	2·2	2·0	8·2	7·3	14·2	12·7
23	13 20·8	13 22·9	12 44·3	2·3	2·1	8·3	7·4	14·3	12·8
24	13 21·0	13 23·2	12 44·5	2·4	2·1	8·4	7·5	14·4	12·8
25	13 21·3	13 23·4	12 44·7	2·5	2·2	8·5	7·6	14·5	12·9
26	13 21·5	13 23·7	12 45·0	2·6	2·3	8·6	7·7	14·6	13·0
27	13 21·8	13 23·9	12 45·2	2·7	2·4	8·7	7·8	14·7	13·1
28	13 22·0	13 24·2	12 45·5	2·8	2·5	8·8	7·8	14·8	13·2
29	13 22·3	13 24·4	12 45·7	2·9	2·6	8·9	7·9	14·9	13·3
30	13 22·5	13 24·7	12 45·9	3·0	2·7	9·0	8·0	15·0	13·4
31	13 22·8	13 24·9	12 46·2	3·1	2·8	9·1	8·1	15·1	13·5
32	13 23·0	13 25·2	12 46·4	3·2	2·9	9·2	8·2	15·2	13·6
33	13 23·3	13 25·4	12 46·7	3·3	2·9	9·3	8·3	15·3	13·6
34	13 23·5	13 25·7	12 46·9	3·4	3·0	9·4	8·4	15·4	13·7
35	13 23·8	13 26·0	12 47·1	3·5	3·1	9·5	8·5	15·5	13·8
36	13 24·0	13 26·2	12 47·4	3·6	3·2	9·6	8·6	15·6	13·9
37	13 24·3	13 26·5	12 47·6	3·7	3·3	9·7	8·6	15·7	14·0
38	13 24·5	13 26·7	12 47·9	3·8	3·4	9·8	8·7	15·8	14·1
39	13 24·8	13 27·0	12 48·1	3·9	3·5	9·9	8·8	15·9	14·2
40	13 25·0	13 27·2	12 48·3	4·0	3·6	10·0	8·9	16·0	14·3
41	13 25·3	13 27·5	12 48·6	4·1	3·7	10·1	9·0	16·1	14·4
42	13 25·5	13 27·7	12 48·8	4·2	3·7	10·2	9·1	16·2	14·4
43	13 25·8	13 28·0	12 49·0	4·3	3·8	10·3	9·2	16·3	14·5
44	13 26·0	13 28·2	12 49·3	4·4	3·9	10·4	9·3	16·4	14·6
45	13 26·3	13 28·5	12 49·5	4·5	4·0	10·5	9·4	16·5	14·7
46	13 26·5	13 28·7	12 49·8	4·6	4·1	10·6	9·5	16·6	14·8
47	13 26·8	13 29·0	12 50·0	4·7	4·2	10·7	9·5	16·7	14·9
48	13 27·0	13 29·2	12 50·2	4·8	4·3	10·8	9·6	16·8	15·0
49	13 27·3	13 29·5	12 50·5	4·9	4·4	10·9	9·7	16·9	15·1
50	13 27·5	13 29·7	12 50·7	5·0	4·5	11·0	9·8	17·0	15·2
51	13 27·8	13 30·0	12 51·0	5·1	4·5	11·1	9·9	17·1	15·2
52	13 28·0	13 30·2	12 51·2	5·2	4·6	11·2	10·0	17·2	15·3
53	13 28·3	13 30·5	12 51·4	5·3	4·7	11·3	10·1	17·3	15·4
54	13 28·5	13 30·7	12 51·7	5·4	4·8	11·4	10·2	17·4	15·5
55	13 28·8	13 31·0	12 51·9	5·5	4·9	11·5	10·3	17·5	15·6
56	13 29·0	13 31·2	12 52·1	5·6	5·0	11·6	10·3	17·6	15·7
57	13 29·3	13 31·5	12 52·4	5·7	5·1	11·7	10·4	17·7	15·8
58	13 29·5	13 31·7	12 52·6	5·8	5·2	11·8	10·5	17·8	15·9
59	13 29·8	13 32·0	12 52·9	5·9	5·3	11·9	10·6	17·9	16·0
60	13 30·0	13 32·2	12 53·1	6·0	5·4	12·0	10·7	18·0	16·1

54ᵐ	SUN PLANETS	ARIES	MOON	v or Corrⁿ d		v or Corrⁿ d		v or Corrⁿ d	
s	° ′	° ′	° ′	′	′	′	′	′	′
00	13 30.0	13 32.2	12 53.1	0.0	0.0	6.0	5.5	12.0	10.9
01	13 30.3	13 32.5	12 53.3	0.1	0.1	6.1	5.5	12.1	11.0
02	13 30.5	13 32.7	12 53.6	0.2	0.2	6.2	5.6	12.2	11.1
03	13 30.8	13 33.0	12 53.8	0.3	0.3	6.3	5.7	12.3	11.2
04	13 31.0	13 33.2	12 54.1	0.4	0.4	6.4	5.8	12.4	11.3
05	13 31.3	13 33.5	12 54.3	0.5	0.5	6.5	5.9	12.5	11.4
06	13 31.5	13 33.7	12 54.5	0.6	0.5	6.6	6.0	12.6	11.4
07	13 31.8	13 34.0	12 54.8	0.7	0.6	6.7	6.1	12.7	11.5
08	13 32.0	13 34.2	12 55.0	0.8	0.7	6.8	6.2	12.8	11.6
09	13 32.3	13 34.5	12 55.2	0.9	0.8	6.9	6.3	12.9	11.7
10	13 32.5	13 34.7	12 55.5	1.0	0.9	7.0	6.4	13.0	11.8
11	13 32.8	13 35.0	12 55.7	1.1	1.0	7.1	6.4	13.1	11.9
12	13 33.0	13 35.2	12 56.0	1.2	1.1	7.2	6.5	13.2	12.0
13	13 33.3	13 35.5	12 56.2	1.3	1.2	7.3	6.6	13.3	12.1
14	13 33.5	13 35.7	12 56.4	1.4	1.3	7.4	6.7	13.4	12.2
15	13 33.8	13 36.0	12 56.7	1.5	1.4	7.5	6.8	13.5	12.3
16	13 34.0	13 36.2	12 56.9	1.6	1.5	7.6	6.9	13.6	12.4
17	13 34.3	13 36.5	12 57.2	1.7	1.5	7.7	7.0	13.7	12.4
18	13 34.5	13 36.7	12 57.4	1.8	1.6	7.8	7.1	13.8	12.5
19	13 34.8	13 37.0	12 57.6	1.9	1.7	7.9	7.2	13.9	12.6
20	13 35.0	13 37.2	12 57.9	2.0	1.8	8.0	7.3	14.0	12.7
21	13 35.3	13 37.5	12 58.1	2.1	1.9	8.1	7.4	14.1	12.8
22	13 35.5	13 37.7	12 58.3	2.2	2.0	8.2	7.4	14.2	12.9
23	13 35.8	13 38.0	12 58.6	2.3	2.1	8.3	7.5	14.3	13.0
24	13 36.0	13 38.2	12 58.8	2.4	2.2	8.4	7.6	14.4	13.1
25	13 36.3	13 38.5	12 59.1	2.5	2.3	8.5	7.7	14.5	13.2
26	13 36.5	13 38.7	12 59.3	2.6	2.4	8.6	7.8	14.6	13.3
27	13 36.8	13 39.0	12 59.5	2.7	2.5	8.7	7.9	14.7	13.4
28	13 37.0	13 39.2	12 59.8	2.8	2.5	8.8	8.0	14.8	13.4
29	13 37.3	13 39.5	13 00.0	2.9	2.6	8.9	8.1	14.9	13.5
30	13 37.5	13 39.7	13 00.3	3.0	2.7	9.0	8.2	15.0	13.6
31	13 37.8	13 40.0	13 00.5	3.1	2.8	9.1	8.3	15.1	13.7
32	13 38.0	13 40.2	13 00.7	3.2	2.9	9.2	8.4	15.2	13.8
33	13 38.3	13 40.5	13 01.0	3.3	3.0	9.3	8.4	15.3	13.9
34	13 38.5	13 40.7	13 01.2	3.4	3.1	9.4	8.5	15.4	14.0
35	13 38.8	13 41.0	13 01.5	3.5	3.2	9.5	8.6	15.5	14.1
36	13 39.0	13 41.2	13 01.7	3.6	3.3	9.6	8.7	15.6	14.2
37	13 39.3	13 41.5	13 01.9	3.7	3.4	9.7	8.8	15.7	14.3
38	13 39.5	13 41.7	13 02.2	3.8	3.5	9.8	8.9	15.8	14.4
39	13 39.8	13 42.0	13 02.4	3.9	3.5	9.9	9.0	15.9	14.4
40	13 40.0	13 42.2	13 02.6	4.0	3.6	10.0	9.1	16.0	14.5
41	13 40.3	13 42.5	13 02.9	4.1	3.7	10.1	9.2	16.1	14.6
42	13 40.5	13 42.7	13 03.1	4.2	3.8	10.2	9.3	16.2	14.7
43	13 40.8	13 43.0	13 03.4	4.3	3.9	10.3	9.4	16.3	14.8
44	13 41.0	13 43.2	13 03.6	4.4	4.0	10.4	9.4	16.4	14.9
45	13 41.3	13 43.5	13 03.8	4.5	4.1	10.5	9.5	16.5	15.0
46	13 41.5	13 43.7	13 04.1	4.6	4.2	10.6	9.6	16.6	15.1
47	13 41.8	13 44.0	13 04.3	4.7	4.3	10.7	9.7	16.7	15.2
48	13 42.0	13 44.3	13 04.6	4.8	4.4	10.8	9.8	16.8	15.3
49	13 42.3	13 44.5	13 04.8	4.9	4.5	10.9	9.9	16.9	15.4
50	13 42.5	13 44.8	13 05.0	5.0	4.5	11.0	10.0	17.0	15.4
51	13 42.8	13 45.0	13 05.3	5.1	4.6	11.1	10.1	17.1	15.5
52	13 43.0	13 45.3	13 05.5	5.2	4.7	11.2	10.2	17.2	15.6
53	13 43.3	13 45.5	13 05.7	5.3	4.8	11.3	10.3	17.3	15.7
54	13 43.5	13 45.8	13 06.0	5.4	4.9	11.4	10.4	17.4	15.8
55	13 43.8	13 46.0	13 06.2	5.5	5.0	11.5	10.4	17.5	15.9
56	13 44.0	13 46.3	13 06.5	5.6	5.1	11.6	10.5	17.6	16.0
57	13 44.3	13 46.5	13 06.7	5.7	5.2	11.7	10.6	17.7	16.1
58	13 44.5	13 46.8	13 06.9	5.8	5.3	11.8	10.7	17.8	16.2
59	13 44.8	13 47.0	13 07.2	5.9	5.4	11.9	10.8	17.9	16.3
60	13 45.0	13 47.3	13 07.4	6.0	5.5	12.0	10.9	18.0	16.4

55ᵐ	SUN PLANETS	ARIES	MOON	v or Corrⁿ d		v or Corrⁿ d		v or Corrⁿ d	
s	° ′	° ′	° ′	′	′	′	′	′	′
00	13 45.0	13 47.3	13 07.4	0.0	0.0	6.0	5.6	12.0	11.1
01	13 45.3	13 47.5	13 07.7	0.1	0.1	6.1	5.6	12.1	11.2
02	13 45.5	13 47.8	13 07.9	0.2	0.2	6.2	5.7	12.2	11.3
03	13 45.8	13 48.0	13 08.1	0.3	0.3	6.3	5.8	12.3	11.4
04	13 46.0	13 48.3	13 08.4	0.4	0.4	6.4	5.9	12.4	11.5
05	13 46.3	13 48.5	13 08.6	0.5	0.5	6.5	6.0	12.5	11.6
06	13 46.5	13 48.8	13 08.8	0.6	0.6	6.6	6.1	12.6	11.7
07	13 46.8	13 49.0	13 09.1	0.7	0.6	6.7	6.2	12.7	11.7
08	13 47.0	13 49.3	13 09.3	0.8	0.7	6.8	6.3	12.8	11.8
09	13 47.3	13 49.5	13 09.6	0.9	0.8	6.9	6.4	12.9	11.9
10	13 47.5	13 49.8	13 09.8	1.0	0.9	7.0	6.5	13.0	12.0
11	13 47.8	13 50.0	13 10.0	1.1	1.0	7.1	6.6	13.1	12.1
12	13 48.0	13 50.3	13 10.3	1.2	1.1	7.2	6.7	13.2	12.2
13	13 48.3	13 50.5	13 10.5	1.3	1.2	7.3	6.8	13.3	12.3
14	13 48.5	13 50.8	13 10.8	1.4	1.3	7.4	6.8	13.4	12.4
15	13 48.8	13 51.0	13 11.0	1.5	1.4	7.5	6.9	13.5	12.5
16	13 49.0	13 51.3	13 11.2	1.6	1.5	7.6	7.0	13.6	12.6
17	13 49.3	13 51.5	13 11.5	1.7	1.6	7.7	7.1	13.7	12.7
18	13 49.5	13 51.8	13 11.7	1.8	1.7	7.8	7.2	13.8	12.8
19	13 49.8	13 52.0	13 12.0	1.9	1.8	7.9	7.3	13.9	12.9
20	13 50.0	13 52.3	13 12.2	2.0	1.9	8.0	7.4	14.0	13.0
21	13 50.3	13 52.5	13 12.4	2.1	1.9	8.1	7.5	14.1	13.0
22	13 50.5	13 52.8	13 12.7	2.2	2.0	8.2	7.6	14.2	13.1
23	13 50.8	13 53.0	13 12.9	2.3	2.1	8.3	7.7	14.3	13.2
24	13 51.0	13 53.3	13 13.1	2.4	2.2	8.4	7.8	14.4	13.3
25	13 51.3	13 53.5	13 13.4	2.5	2.3	8.5	7.9	14.5	13.4
26	13 51.5	13 53.8	13 13.6	2.6	2.4	8.6	8.0	14.6	13.5
27	13 51.8	13 54.0	13 13.9	2.7	2.5	8.7	8.0	14.7	13.6
28	13 52.0	13 54.3	13 14.1	2.8	2.6	8.8	8.1	14.8	13.7
29	13 52.3	13 54.5	13 14.3	2.9	2.7	8.9	8.2	14.9	13.8
30	13 52.5	13 54.8	13 14.6	3.0	2.8	9.0	8.3	15.0	13.9
31	13 52.8	13 55.0	13 14.8	3.1	2.9	9.1	8.4	15.1	14.0
32	13 53.0	13 55.3	13 15.1	3.2	3.0	9.2	8.5	15.2	14.1
33	13 53.3	13 55.5	13 15.3	3.3	3.1	9.3	8.6	15.3	14.2
34	13 53.5	13 55.8	13 15.5	3.4	3.1	9.4	8.7	15.4	14.2
35	13 53.8	13 56.0	13 15.8	3.5	3.2	9.5	8.8	15.5	14.3
36	13 54.0	13 56.3	13 16.0	3.6	3.3	9.6	8.9	15.6	14.4
37	13 54.3	13 56.5	13 16.2	3.7	3.4	9.7	9.0	15.7	14.5
38	13 54.5	13 56.8	13 16.5	3.8	3.5	9.8	9.1	15.8	14.6
39	13 54.8	13 57.0	13 16.7	3.9	3.6	9.9	9.1	15.9	14.7
40	13 55.0	13 57.3	13 17.0	4.0	3.7	10.0	9.3	16.0	14.8
41	13 55.3	13 57.5	13 17.2	4.1	3.8	10.1	9.3	16.1	14.9
42	13 55.5	13 57.8	13 17.4	4.2	3.9	10.2	9.4	16.2	15.0
43	13 55.8	13 58.0	13 17.7	4.3	4.0	10.3	9.5	16.3	15.1
44	13 56.0	13 58.3	13 17.9	4.4	4.1	10.4	9.6	16.4	15.2
45	13 56.3	13 58.5	13 18.2	4.5	4.2	10.5	9.7	16.5	15.3
46	13 56.5	13 58.8	13 18.4	4.6	4.3	10.6	9.8	16.6	15.4
47	13 56.8	13 59.0	13 18.6	4.7	4.3	10.7	9.9	16.7	15.4
48	13 57.0	13 59.3	13 18.9	4.8	4.4	10.8	10.0	16.8	15.5
49	13 57.3	13 59.5	13 19.1	4.9	4.5	10.9	10.1	16.9	15.6
50	13 57.5	13 59.8	13 19.3	5.0	4.6	11.0	10.2	17.0	15.7
51	13 57.8	14 00.0	13 19.6	5.1	4.7	11.1	10.3	17.1	15.8
52	13 58.0	14 00.3	13 19.8	5.2	4.8	11.2	10.4	17.2	15.9
53	13 58.3	14 00.5	13 20.1	5.3	4.9	11.3	10.5	17.3	16.0
54	13 58.5	14 00.8	13 20.3	5.4	5.0	11.4	10.5	17.4	16.1
55	13 58.8	14 01.0	13 20.5	5.5	5.1	11.5	10.6	17.5	16.2
56	13 59.0	14 01.3	13 20.8	5.6	5.2	11.6	10.7	17.6	16.3
57	13 59.3	14 01.5	13 21.0	5.7	5.3	11.7	10.8	17.7	16.4
58	13 59.5	14 01.8	13 21.3	5.8	5.4	11.8	10.9	17.8	16.5
59	13 59.8	14 02.0	13 21.5	5.9	5.5	11.9	11.0	17.9	16.6
60	14 00.0	14 02.3	13 21.7	6.0	5.6	12.0	11.1	18.0	16.7

58ᵐ

58ᵐ s	SUN PLANETS ° '	ARIES ° '	MOON ° '	v or d '	Corrn '	v or d '	Corrn '	v or d '	Corrn '
00	14 30·0	14 32·4	13 50·4	0·0	0·0	6·0	5·9	12·0	11·7
01	14 30·3	14 32·6	13 50·6	0·1	0·1	6·1	5·9	12·1	11·8
02	14 30·5	14 32·9	13 50·8	0·2	0·2	6·2	6·0	12·2	11·9
03	14 30·8	14 33·1	13 51·1	0·3	0·3	6·3	6·1	12·3	12·0
04	14 31·0	14 33·4	13 51·3	0·4	0·4	6·4	6·2	12·4	12·1
05	14 31·3	14 33·6	13 51·6	0·5	0·5	6·5	6·3	12·5	12·2
06	14 31·5	14 33·9	13 51·8	0·6	0·6	6·6	6·4	12·6	12·3
07	14 31·8	14 34·1	13 52·0	0·7	0·7	6·7	6·5	12·7	12·4
08	14 32·0	14 34·4	13 52·3	0·8	0·8	6·8	6·6	12·8	12·5
09	14 32·3	14 34·6	13 52·5	0·9	0·9	6·9	6·7	12·9	12·6
10	14 32·5	14 34·9	13 52·8	1·0	1·0	7·0	6·8	13·0	12·7
11	14 32·8	14 35·1	13 53·0	1·1	1·1	7·1	6·9	13·1	12·8
12	14 33·0	14 35·4	13 53·2	1·2	1·2	7·2	7·0	13·2	12·9
13	14 33·3	14 35·6	13 53·5	1·3	1·3	7·3	7·1	13·3	13·0
14	14 33·5	14 35·9	13 53·7	1·4	1·4	7·4	7·2	13·4	13·1
15	14 33·8	14 36·1	13 53·9	1·5	1·5	7·5	7·3	13·5	13·2
16	14 34·0	14 36·4	13 54·2	1·6	1·6	7·6	7·4	13·6	13·3
17	14 34·3	14 36·6	13 54·4	1·7	1·7	7·7	7·5	13·7	13·4
18	14 34·5	14 36·9	13 54·7	1·8	1·8	7·8	7·6	13·8	13·5
19	14 34·8	14 37·1	13 54·9	1·9	1·9	7·9	7·7	13·9	13·6
20	14 35·0	14 37·4	13 55·1	2·0	2·0	8·0	7·8	14·0	13·7
21	14 35·3	14 37·6	13 55·4	2·1	2·0	8·1	7·9	14·1	13·7
22	14 35·5	14 37·9	13 55·6	2·2	2·1	8·2	8·0	14·2	13·8
23	14 35·8	14 38·1	13 55·9	2·3	2·2	8·3	8·1	14·3	13·9
24	14 36·0	14 38·4	13 56·1	2·4	2·3	8·4	8·2	14·4	14·0
25	14 36·3	14 38·6	13 56·3	2·5	2·4	8·5	8·3	14·5	14·1
26	14 36·5	14 38·9	13 56·6	2·6	2·5	8·6	8·4	14·6	14·2
27	14 36·8	14 39·2	13 56·8	2·7	2·6	8·7	8·5	14·7	14·3
28	14 37·0	14 39·4	13 57·0	2·8	2·7	8·8	8·6	14·8	14·4
29	14 37·3	14 39·7	13 57·3	2·9	2·8	8·9	8·7	14·9	14·5
30	14 37·5	14 39·9	13 57·5	3·0	2·9	9·0	8·8	15·0	14·6
31	14 37·8	14 40·2	13 57·8	3·1	3·0	9·1	8·9	15·1	14·7
32	14 38·0	14 40·4	13 58·0	3·2	3·1	9·2	9·0	15·2	14·8
33	14 38·3	14 40·7	13 58·3	3·3	3·2	9·3	9·1	15·3	14·9
34	14 38·5	14 40·9	13 58·5	3·4	3·3	9·4	9·2	15·4	15·0
35	14 38·8	14 41·2	13 58·7	3·5	3·4	9·5	9·3	15·5	15·1
36	14 39·0	14 41·4	13 59·0	3·6	3·5	9·6	9·4	15·6	15·2
37	14 39·3	14 41·7	13 59·2	3·7	3·6	9·7	9·5	15·7	15·3
38	14 39·5	14 41·9	13 59·4	3·8	3·7	9·8	9·6	15·8	15·4
39	14 39·8	14 42·2	13 59·7	3·9	3·8	9·9	9·7	15·9	15·5
40	14 40·0	14 42·4	13 59·9	4·0	3·9	10·0	9·8	16·0	15·6
41	14 40·3	14 42·7	14 00·1	4·1	4·0	10·1	9·8	16·1	15·7
42	14 40·5	14 42·9	14 00·4	4·2	4·1	10·2	9·9	16·2	15·8
43	14 40·8	14 43·2	14 00·6	4·3	4·2	10·3	10·0	16·3	15·9
44	14 41·0	14 43·4	14 00·9	4·4	4·3	10·4	10·1	16·4	16·0
45	14 41·3	14 43·7	14 01·1	4·5	4·4	10·5	10·2	16·5	16·1
46	14 41·5	14 43·9	14 01·3	4·6	4·5	10·6	10·3	16·6	16·2
47	14 41·8	14 44·2	14 01·6	4·7	4·6	10·7	10·4	16·7	16·3
48	14 42·0	14 44·4	14 01·8	4·8	4·7	10·8	10·5	16·8	16·4
49	14 42·3	14 44·7	14 02·1	4·9	4·8	10·9	10·6	16·9	16·5
50	14 42·5	14 44·9	14 02·3	5·0	4·9	11·0	10·7	17·0	16·6
51	14 42·8	14 45·2	14 02·5	5·1	5·0	11·1	10·8	17·1	16·7
52	14 43·0	14 45·4	14 02·8	5·2	5·1	11·2	10·9	17·2	16·8
53	14 43·3	14 45·7	14 03·0	5·3	5·2	11·3	11·0	17·3	16·9
54	14 43·5	14 45·9	14 03·3	5·4	5·3	11·4	11·1	17·4	17·0
55	14 43·8	14 46·2	14 03·5	5·5	5·4	11·5	11·2	17·5	17·1
56	14 44·0	14 46·4	14 03·7	5·6	5·5	11·6	11·3	17·6	17·2
57	14 44·3	14 46·7	14 04·0	5·7	5·6	11·7	11·4	17·7	17·3
58	14 44·5	14 46·9	14 04·2	5·8	5·7	11·8	11·5	17·8	17·4
59	14 44·8	14 47·2	14 04·4	5·9	5·8	11·9	11·6	17·9	17·5
60	14 45·0	14 47·4	14 04·7	6·0	5·9	12·0	11·7	18·0	17·6

59ᵐ

59ᵐ s	SUN PLANETS ° '	ARIES ° '	MOON ° '	v or d '	Corrn '	v or d '	Corrn '	v or d '	Corrn '
00	14 45·0	14 47·4	14 04·7	0·0	0·0	6·0	6·0	12·0	11·9
01	14 45·3	14 47·7	14 04·9	0·1	0·1	6·1	6·0	12·1	12·0
02	14 45·5	14 47·9	14 05·2	0·2	0·2	6·2	6·1	12·2	12·1
03	14 45·8	14 48·2	14 05·4	0·3	0·3	6·3	6·2	12·3	12·2
04	14 46·0	14 48·4	14 05·6	0·4	0·4	6·4	6·3	12·4	12·3
05	14 46·3	14 48·7	14 05·9	0·5	0·5	6·5	6·4	12·5	12·4
06	14 46·5	14 48·9	14 06·1	0·6	0·6	6·6	6·5	12·6	12·5
07	14 46·8	14 49·2	14 06·4	0·7	0·7	6·7	6·6	12·7	12·6
08	14 47·0	14 49·4	14 06·6	0·8	0·8	6·8	6·7	12·8	12·7
09	14 47·3	14 49·7	14 06·8	0·9	0·9	6·9	6·8	12·9	12·8
10	14 47·5	14 49·9	14 07·1	1·0	1·0	7·0	6·9	13·0	12·9
11	14 47·8	14 50·2	14 07·3	1·1	1·1	7·1	7·0	13·1	13·0
12	14 48·0	14 50·4	14 07·5	1·2	1·2	7·2	7·1	13·2	13·1
13	14 48·3	14 50·7	14 07·8	1·3	1·3	7·3	7·2	13·3	13·2
14	14 48·5	14 50·9	14 08·0	1·4	1·4	7·4	7·3	13·4	13·3
15	14 48·8	14 51·2	14 08·3	1·5	1·5	7·5	7·4	13·5	13·4
16	14 49·0	14 51·4	14 08·5	1·6	1·6	7·6	7·5	13·6	13·5
17	14 49·3	14 51·7	14 08·7	1·7	1·7	7·7	7·6	13·7	13·6
18	14 49·5	14 51·9	14 09·0	1·8	1·8	7·8	7·7	13·8	13·7
19	14 49·8	14 52·2	14 09·2	1·9	1·9	7·9	7·8	13·9	13·8
20	14 50·0	14 52·4	14 09·5	2·0	2·0	8·0	7·9	14·0	13·9
21	14 50·3	14 52·7	14 09·7	2·1	2·1	8·1	8·0	14·1	14·0
22	14 50·5	14 52·9	14 09·9	2·2	2·2	8·2	8·1	14·2	14·1
23	14 50·8	14 53·2	14 10·2	2·3	2·3	8·3	8·2	14·3	14·2
24	14 51·0	14 53·4	14 10·4	2·4	2·4	8·4	8·3	14·4	14·3
25	14 51·3	14 53·7	14 10·6	2·5	2·5	8·5	8·4	14·5	14·4
26	14 51·5	14 53·9	14 10·9	2·6	2·6	8·6	8·5	14·6	14·5
27	14 51·8	14 54·2	14 11·1	2·7	2·7	8·7	8·6	14·7	14·6
28	14 52·0	14 54·4	14 11·4	2·8	2·8	8·8	8·7	14·8	14·7
29	14 52·3	14 54·7	14 11·6	2·9	2·9	8·9	8·8	14·9	14·8
30	14 52·5	14 54·9	14 11·8	3·0	3·0	9·0	8·9	15·0	14·9
31	14 52·8	14 55·2	14 12·1	3·1	3·1	9·1	9·0	15·1	15·0
32	14 53·0	14 55·4	14 12·3	3·2	3·2	9·2	9·1	15·2	15·1
33	14 53·3	14 55·7	14 12·6	3·3	3·3	9·3	9·2	15·3	15·2
34	14 53·5	14 55·9	14 12·8	3·4	3·4	9·4	9·3	15·4	15·3
35	14 53·8	14 56·2	14 13·0	3·5	3·5	9·5	9·4	15·5	15·4
36	14 54·0	14 56·4	14 13·3	3·6	3·6	9·6	9·5	15·6	15·5
37	14 54·3	14 56·7	14 13·5	3·7	3·7	9·7	9·6	15·7	15·6
38	14 54·5	14 56·9	14 13·8	3·8	3·8	9·8	9·7	15·8	15·7
39	14 54·8	14 57·2	14 14·0	3·9	3·9	9·9	9·8	15·9	15·8
40	14 55·0	14 57·5	14 14·2	4·0	4·0	10·0	9·9	16·0	15·9
41	14 55·3	14 57·7	14 14·5	4·1	4·1	10·1	10·0	16·1	16·0
42	14 55·5	14 58·0	14 14·7	4·2	4·2	10·2	10·1	16·2	16·1
43	14 55·8	14 58·2	14 14·9	4·3	4·3	10·3	10·2	16·3	16·2
44	14 56·0	14 58·5	14 15·2	4·4	4·4	10·4	10·3	16·4	16·3
45	14 56·3	14 58·7	14 15·4	4·5	4·5	10·5	10·4	16·5	16·4
46	14 56·5	14 59·0	14 15·7	4·6	4·6	10·6	10·5	16·6	16·5
47	14 56·8	14 59·2	14 15·9	4·7	4·7	10·7	10·6	16·7	16·6
48	14 57·0	14 59·5	14 16·1	4·8	4·8	10·8	10·7	16·8	16·7
49	14 57·3	14 59·7	14 16·4	4·9	4·9	10·9	10·8	16·9	16·8
50	14 57·5	15 00·0	14 16·6	5·0	5·0	11·0	10·9	17·0	16·9
51	14 57·8	15 00·2	14 16·9	5·1	5·1	11·1	11·0	17·1	17·0
52	14 58·0	15 00·5	14 17·1	5·2	5·2	11·2	11·1	17·2	17·1
53	14 58·3	15 00·7	14 17·3	5·3	5·3	11·3	11·2	17·3	17·2
54	14 58·5	15 01·0	14 17·6	5·4	5·4	11·4	11·3	17·4	17·3
55	14 58·8	15 01·2	14 17·8	5·5	5·5	11·5	11·4	17·5	17·4
56	14 59·0	15 01·5	14 18·0	5·6	5·6	11·6	11·5	17·6	17·5
57	14 59·3	15 01·7	14 18·3	5·7	5·7	11·7	11·6	17·7	17·6
58	14 59·5	15 02·0	14 18·5	5·8	5·8	11·8	11·7	17·8	17·7
59	14 59·8	15 02·2	14 18·8	5·9	5·9	11·9	11·8	17·9	17·8
60	15 00·0	15 02·5	14 19·0	6·0	6·0	12·0	11·9	18·0	17·9

TABLE I—FOR LATITUDE

Tabular Interval 10°	Tabular Interval 5°	Tabular Interval 2°	Difference between the times for consecutive latitudes 5m	10m	15m	20m	25m	30m	35m	40m	45m	50m	55m	60m	1h 05m	1h 10m	1h 15m	1h 20m
0 30	0 15	0 06	0	0	1	1	1	1	1	2	2	2	2	2	0 02	0 02	0 02	0 02
1 00	0 30	0 12	0	1	1	2	2	3	3	3	4	4	4	5	05	05	05	05
1 30	0 45	0 18	1	1	2	3	3	4	4	5	5	6	7	7	07	07	07	07
2 00	1 00	0 24	1	2	3	4	5	5	6	7	7	8	9	10	10	10	10	10
2 30	1 15	0 30	1	2	4	5	6	7	8	9	9	10	11	12	12	13	13	13
3 00	1 30	0 36	1	3	4	6	7	8	9	10	11	12	13	14	0 15	0 15	0 16	0 16
3 30	1 45	0 42	2	3	5	7	8	10	11	12	13	14	16	17	18	18	19	19
4 00	2 00	0 48	2	4	6	8	9	11	13	14	15	16	18	19	20	21	22	22
4 30	2 15	0 54	2	4	7	9	11	13	15	16	18	19	21	22	23	24	25	26
5 00	2 30	1 00	2	5	7	10	12	14	16	18	20	22	23	25	26	27	28	29
5 30	2 45	1 06	3	5	8	11	13	16	18	20	22	24	26	28	0 29	0 30	0 31	0 32
6 00	3 00	1 12	3	6	9	12	14	17	20	22	24	26	29	31	32	33	34	36
6 30	3 15	1 18	3	6	10	13	16	19	22	24	26	29	31	34	36	37	38	40
7 00	3 30	1 24	3	7	10	14	17	20	23	26	29	31	34	37	39	41	42	44
7 30	3 45	1 30	4	7	11	15	18	22	25	28	31	34	37	40	43	44	46	48
8 00	4 00	1 36	4	8	12	16	20	23	27	30	34	37	41	44	0 47	0 48	0 51	0 53
8 30	4 15	1 42	4	8	13	17	21	25	29	33	36	40	44	48	0 51	0 53	0 56	0 58
9 00	4 30	1 48	4	9	13	18	22	27	31	35	39	43	47	52	0 55	0 58	1 01	1 04
9 30	4 45	1 54	5	9	14	19	24	28	33	38	45	47	51	56	1 00	1 04	1 08	1 12
10 00	5 00	2 00	5	10	15	20	25	30	35	40	45	50	55	60	1 05	1 10	1 15	1 20

Table I is for interpolating the L.M.T. of sunrise, twilight, moonrise, etc., for latitude. It is to be entered, in the appropriate column on the left, with the difference between true latitude and the nearest tabular latitude which is *less* than the true latitude; and with the argument at the top which is the nearest value of the difference between the times for the tabular latitude and the next higher one; the correction so obtained is applied to the time for the tabular latitude; the sign of the correction can be seen by inspection. It is to be noted that the interpolation is not linear, so that when using this table it is essential to take out the tabular phenomenon for the latitude *less* than the true latitude.

TABLE II—FOR LONGITUDE

Long. East or West	Difference between the times for given date and preceding date (for east longitude) or for given date and following date (for west longitude) 10m	20m	30m	40m	50m	60m	1h+ 10m	20m	30m	1h+ 40m	50m	60m	2h 10m	2h 20m	2h 30m	2h 40m	2h 50m	3h 00m
0	0	0	0	0	0	0	0	0	0	0	0	0	0 00	0 00	0 00	0 00	0 00	0 00
10	0	1	1	1	1	2	2	2	2	3	3	3	04	04	04	04	05	05
20	1	1	2	2	3	3	4	4	5	6	6	7	07	08	08	09	09	10
30	1	2	2	3	4	5	6	7	7	8	9	10	11	12	12	13	14	15
40	1	2	3	4	6	7	8	9	10	11	12	13	14	16	17	18	19	20
50	1	3	4	6	7	8	10	11	12	14	15	17	0 18	0 19	0 21	0 22	0 24	0 25
60	2	3	5	7	8	10	12	13	15	17	18	20	22	23	25	27	28	30
70	2	4	6	8	10	12	14	16	17	19	21	23	25	27	29	31	33	35
80	2	4	7	9	11	13	16	18	20	22	24	27	29	31	33	36	38	40
90	2	5	7	10	12	15	17	20	22	25	27	30	32	35	37	40	42	45
100	3	6	8	11	14	17	19	22	25	28	31	33	0 36	0 39	0 42	0 44	0 47	0 50
110	3	6	9	12	15	18	21	24	27	31	34	37	40	43	46	49	0 52	0 55
120	3	7	10	13	17	20	23	27	30	33	37	40	43	47	50	53	0 57	1 00
130	4	7	11	14	18	22	25	29	32	36	40	43	47	51	54	0 58	1 01	1 05
140	4	8	12	16	19	23	27	31	35	39	43	47	51	54	0 58	1 02	1 06	1 10
150	4	8	13	17	21	25	29	33	38	42	46	50	0 54	0 58	1 03	1 07	1 11	1 15
160	4	9	13	18	22	27	31	36	40	44	49	53	0 58	1 02	1 07	1 11	1 16	1 20
170	5	9	14	19	24	28	33	38	42	47	52	57	1 01	1 06	1 11	1 16	1 20	1 25
180	5	10	15	20	25	30	35	40	45	50	55	60	1 05	1 10	1 15	1 20	1 25	1 30

Table II is for interpolating the L.M.T. of moonrise, moonset and the Moon's meridian passage for longitude. It is entered with longitude and with the difference between the times for the given date and for the preceding date (in east longitudes) or following date (in west longitudes). The correction is normally *added* for west longitudes and *subtracted* for east longitudes, but if, as occasionally happens, the times become earlier each day instead of later, the signs of the corrections must be reversed.

App. Alt.	0°–4° Corrⁿ	5°–9° Corrⁿ	10°–14° Corrⁿ	15°–19° Corrⁿ	20°–24° Corrⁿ	25°–29° Corrⁿ	30°–34° Corrⁿ	App. Alt.
00	0 33·8	5 58·2	10 62·1	15 62·8	20 62·2	25 60·8	30 58·9	00
10	35·9	58·5	62·2	62·8	62·1	60·8	58·8	10
20	37·8	58·7	62·2	62·8	62·1	60·7	58·8	20
30	39·6	58·9	62·3	62·8	62·1	60·7	58·7	30
40	41·2	59·1	62·3	62·8	62·0	60·6	58·6	40
50	42·6	59·3	62·4	62·7	62·0	60·6	58·5	50
00	1 44·0	6 59·5	11 62·4	16 62·7	21 62·0	26 60·5	31 58·5	00
10	45·2	59·7	62·4	62·7	61·9	60·4	58·4	10
20	46·3	59·9	62·5	62·7	61·9	60·4	58·3	20
30	47·3	60·0	62·5	62·7	61·9	60·3	58·2	30
40	48·3	60·2	62·5	62·7	61·8	60·3	58·2	40
50	49·2	60·3	62·6	62·7	61·8	60·2	58·1	50
00	2 50·0	7 60·5	12 62·6	17 62·7	22 61·7	27 60·1	32 58·0	00
10	50·8	60·6	62·6	62·6	61·7	60·1	57·9	10
20	51·4	60·7	62·6	62·6	61·6	60·0	57·8	20
30	52·1	60·9	62·7	62·6	61·6	59·9	57·8	30
40	52·7	61·0	62·7	62·6	61·5	59·9	57·7	40
50	53·3	61·1	62·7	62·6	61·5	59·8	57·6	50
00	3 53·8	8 61·2	13 62·7	18 62·5	23 61·5	28 59·7	33 57·5	00
10	54·3	61·3	62·7	62·5	61·4	59·7	57·4	10
20	54·8	61·4	62·7	62·5	61·4	59·6	57·4	20
30	55·2	61·5	62·8	62·5	61·3	59·6	57·3	30
40	55·6	61·6	62·8	62·4	61·3	59·5	57·2	40
50	56·0	61·6	62·8	62·4	61·2	59·4	57·1	50
00	4 56·4	9 61·7	14 62·8	19 62·4	24 61·2	29 59·3	34 57·0	00
10	56·7	61·8	62·8	62·3	61·1	59·3	56·9	10
20	57·1	61·9	62·8	62·3	61·1	59·2	56·9	20
30	57·4	61·9	62·8	62·3	61·0	59·1	56·8	30
40	57·7	62·0	62·8	62·2	60·9	59·1	56·7	40
50	57·9	62·1	62·8	62·2	60·9	59·0	56·6	50

H.P.	L	U	L	U	L	U	L	U	L	U	L	U	L	U	H.P.
54·0	0·3	0·9	0·3	0·9	0·4	1·0	0·5	1·1	0·6	1·2	0·7	1·3	0·9	1·5	54·0
54·3	0·7	1·1	0·7	1·2	0·7	1·2	0·8	1·3	0·9	1·4	1·1	1·5	1·2	1·7	54·3
54·6	1·1	1·4	1·1	1·4	1·1	1·4	1·2	1·5	1·3	1·6	1·4	1·7	1·5	1·8	54·6
54·9	1·4	1·6	1·5	1·6	1·5	1·6	1·6	1·7	1·6	1·8	1·8	1·9	1·9	2·0	54·9
55·2	1·8	1·8	1·8	1·8	1·9	1·9	1·9	1·9	2·0	2·0	2·1	2·1	2·2	2·2	55·2
55·5	2·2	2·0	2·2	2·0	2·3	2·1	2·3	2·1	2·4	2·2	2·4	2·3	2·5	2·4	55·5
55·8	2·6	2·2	2·6	2·2	2·6	2·3	2·7	2·3	2·7	2·4	2·8	2·4	2·9	2·5	55·8
56·1	3·0	2·4	3·0	2·5	3·0	2·5	3·0	2·5	3·1	2·6	3·1	2·6	3·2	2·7	56·1
56·4	3·4	2·7	3·4	2·7	3·4	2·7	3·4	2·7	3·4	2·8	3·5	2·8	3·5	2·9	56·4
56·7	3·7	2·9	3·7	2·9	3·8	2·9	3·8	2·9	3·8	3·0	3·8	3·0	3·9	3·0	56·7
57·0	4·1	3·1	4·1	3·1	4·1	3·1	4·1	3·1	4·2	3·1	4·2	3·2	4·2	3·2	57·0
57·3	4·5	3·3	4·5	3·3	4·5	3·3	4·5	3·3	4·5	3·3	4·5	3·4	4·6	3·4	57·3
57·6	4·9	3·5	4·9	3·5	4·9	3·5	4·9	3·5	4·9	3·5	4·9	3·5	4·9	3·6	57·6
57·9	5·3	3·8	5·3	3·8	5·2	3·8	5·2	3·7	5·2	3·7	5·2	3·7	5·2	3·7	57·9
58·2	5·6	4·0	5·6	4·0	5·6	4·0	5·6	4·0	5·6	3·9	5·6	3·9	5·6	3·9	58·2
58·5	6·0	4·2	6·0	4·2	6·0	4·2	6·0	4·2	6·0	4·1	5·9	4·1	5·9	4·1	58·5
58·8	6·4	4·4	6·4	4·4	6·4	4·4	6·3	4·4	6·3	4·3	6·3	4·3	6·2	4·2	58·8
59·1	6·8	4·6	6·8	4·6	6·7	4·6	6·7	4·6	6·7	4·5	6·6	4·5	6·6	4·4	59·1
59·4	7·2	4·8	7·1	4·8	7·1	4·8	7·1	4·8	7·0	4·7	7·0	4·7	6·9	4·6	59·4
59·7	7·5	5·1	7·5	5·0	7·5	5·0	7·5	5·0	7·4	4·9	7·3	4·8	7·2	4·7	59·7
60·0	7·9	5·3	7·9	5·3	7·9	5·2	7·8	5·2	7·8	5·1	7·7	5·0	7·6	4·9	60·0
60·3	8·3	5·5	8·3	5·5	8·2	5·4	8·2	5·4	8·1	5·3	8·0	5·2	7·9	5·1	60·3
60·6	8·7	5·7	8·7	5·7	8·6	5·7	8·6	5·6	8·5	5·5	8·4	5·4	8·2	5·3	60·6
60·9	9·1	5·9	9·0	5·9	9·0	5·9	8·9	5·8	8·8	5·7	8·7	5·6	8·5	5·4	60·9
61·2	9·5	6·2	9·4	6·1	9·4	6·1	9·3	6·0	9·2	5·9	9·1	5·8	8·9	5·6	61·2
61·5	9·8	6·4	9·8	6·3	9·7	6·3	9·7	6·2	9·5	6·1	9·4	5·9	9·2	5·8	61·5

DIP

Ht. of Eye	Corrⁿ	Ht. of Eye	Corrⁿ	Ht. of Eye	Corrⁿ
ft.		ft.		ft.	
4·0	−2·0	24	−4·9	63	−7·8
4·4	−2·1	26	−5·0	65	−7·9
4·9	−2·2	27	−5·1	67	−8·0
5·3	−2·3	28	−5·2	68	−8·1
5·8	−2·4	29	−5·3	70	−8·2
6·3	−2·5	30	−5·4	72	−8·3
6·9	−2·6	31	−5·5	74	−8·4
7·4	−2·7	32	−5·6	75	−8·5
8·0	−2·8	33	−5·7	77	−8·6
8·6	−2·9	35	−5·8	79	−8·7
9·2	−3·0	36	−5·9	81	−8·8
9·8	−3·1	37	−6·0	83	−8·9
10·5	−3·2	38	−6·1	85	−9·0
11·2	−3·3	40	−6·2	87	−9·1
11·9	−3·4	41	−6·3	88	−9·2
12·6	−3·5	42	−6·4	90	−9·3
13·3	−3·6	44	−6·5	92	−9·4
14·1	−3·7	45	−6·6	94	−9·5
14·9	−3·8	46	−6·7	96	−9·6
15·7	−3·9	48	−6·8	98	−9·7
16·5	−4·0	49	−6·9	101	−9·8
17·4	−4·1	51	−7·0	103	−9·9
18·3	−4·2	52	−7·1	105	−10·0
19·1	−4·3	54	−7·2	107	−10·1
20·1	−4·4	55	−7·3	109	−10·2
21·0	−4·5	57	−7·4	111	−10·3
22·0	−4·6	58	−7·5	113	−10·4
22·9	−4·7	60	−7·6	116	−10·5
23·9	−4·8	62	−7·7	118	−10·6
24·9		63		120	

MOON CORRECTION TABLE

The correction is in two parts; the first correction is taken from the upper part of the table with argument apparent altitude, and the second from the lower part, with argument H.P., in the same column as that from which the first correction was taken. Separate corrections are given in the lower part for lower (L) and upper (U) limbs. All corrections are to be **added** to apparent altitude, *but 30′ is to be subtracted from the altitude of the upper limb.*

For corrections for pressure and temperature see page A4.

For bubble sextant observations ignore dip, take the mean of upper and lower limb corrections and subtract 15′ from the altitude.

App. Alt. = Apparent altitude = Sextant altitude corrected for index error and dip.